INTERNATIONAL MANAGEMENT

Managing Across Borders and Cultures
TEXT AND CASES
Eighth Edition

HELEN DERESKY
Professor Emerita, State University of New York–Plattsburgh

Boston   Columbus   Indianapolis   New York   San Francisco   Upper Saddle River

Amsterdam   Cape Town   Dubai   London   Madrid   Milan   Munich   Paris   Montréal   Toronto

Delhi   Mexico City   São Paulo   Sydney   Hong Kong   Seoul   Singapore   Taipei   Tokyo

Editor in Chief: Stephanie Wall
Senior Acquisitions Editor: Kris Ellis-Levy
Editorial Project Manager: Sarah Holle
Editorial Assistant: Bernard Ollila IV
Director of Marketing: Maggie Moylan
Senior Marketing Manager: Erin Gardner
Senior Managing Editor: Judy Leale
Senior Production Project Manager: Ann Pulido
Operations Specialist: Cathleen Petersen
Creative Art Director: Blair Brown

Art Director: Steve Frim
Interior and Cover Designer: Blackhorse Designs
Media Project Manager, Editorial: Denise Vaughn
Media Project Manager, Production: Lisa Rinaldi
Composition/Full-Service Project Management: Emily Bush,
   S4Carlisle Publishing Services
Printer/Binder: Courier/Kendallville
Cover Printer: Lehigh-Phoenix Color/Hagerstown
Text Font: Times LT Std 10/12

Credits and acknowledgments borrowed from other sources and reproduced, with permission, in this textbook appear on the appropriate page within text.

Microsoft® and Windows® are registered trademarks of the Microsoft Corporation in the U.S.A. and other countries. Screen shots and icons reprinted with permission from the Microsoft Corporation. This book is not sponsored or endorsed by or affiliated with the Microsoft Corporation.

Many of the designations by manufacturers and sellers to distinguish their products are claimed as trademarks. Where those designations appear in this book, and the publisher was aware of a trademark claim, the designations have been printed in initial caps or all caps.

Library of Congress Cataloging-in-Publication Data
Deresky, Helen.
  International management : managing across borders and cultures : text and cases / Helen Deresky. — 8th ed.
    p. cm.
Includes bibliographical references and index.
ISBN-13: 978-0-13-306212-0
ISBN-10: 0-13-306212-0
1. International business enterprises—Management.   2. International business
enterprises—Management—Case studies.   3. Industrial management.
I. Title.
HD62.4.D47 2014
658'.049—dc23
                        2012027789

10 9 8 7 6 5 4

ISBN 10:   0-13-306212-0
ISBN 13: 978-0-13-306212-0

*To my husband, John, and my children, John, Mark, and Lara,
for their love and support*

Brief Contents

Contents

Preface

EIGHTH EDITION CHANGES

- **Comprehensive cases: 11 of the 12 comprehensive cases are new and current; one is a popular one from the seventh edition.** The case selection provides increased coverage of emerging markets and high-technology companies. A range of topics and geographic locations is included, as well as an interactive Ethics Role Playing Case.

- **Integrative Section: There are two new comprehensive cases in the Integrative section that are exciting because they cover topics from throughout the book: Mahindra and Mahindra, an "emerging" giant, and the Volkswagen-Suzuki breakup. In addition, the popular Integrative Term Project has been retained.**

- **A new feature box called "Under the Lens"** has been added—one or two in each chapter. This feature gives an in-depth look at important aspects of the chapter subjects, including, for example, "Doing Business in Brazil," "How Feng Shui Affects Business," "Negotiations and Decisions to Save the Eurozone System," and "How SMEs Can Internationalize."

- **Maps added throughout.**

- **Chapter-Opening Profiles: Nine of the 11 Opening Profiles are new, keeping two favorites. Examples are "The Globalization of Risk," and "The Impact of Social Media on Global Business."**

- **Chapter-Ending Cases: There are eight new chapter-ending cases, keeping three favorites.** Examples are "Apple's IPhone – Not 'Made in America,'" and "Facebook's Continued Negotiations in China."

- All of the "Comparative Management in Focus" sections have been revised and updated. These provide in-depth comparative applications of chapter topics in a broad range of specific countries or regions.

- All of the "Management in Action" boxes have been replaced or updated.

- New coverage of the global economic crisis and its effects on strategy has been added throughout the eighth edition.

- Updated coverage of developments in globalization and its growing nationalist backlash.

- **Expanded and updated coverage of management issues regarding emerging market economies—in particular China, India, Brazil, and Russia.**

- Expanded section on strategies for emerging markets.

- **Added and expanded sections on small businesses and strategies for SMEs.**

- **Expanded sections on "born global" companies and on strategy models.**

- NEW research data added on expatriate assignments and relocation.

The eighth edition of *International Management: Managing Across Borders and Cultures* **prepares students and practicing managers** for careers in a dynamic global environment wherein they will be responsible for effective strategic, organizational, and interpersonal management. While managing within international and cross-cultural contexts has been the focus of this text since the first edition, the eighth edition portrays the burgeoning level, scope, and complexity of international business facing managers in the twenty-first century. The eighth edition explores how recent developments and trends within a hypercompetitive global arena present managers with challenging situations; it guides the reader as to what actions to take, and how to develop the skills necessary to design and implement global strategies, to conduct effective cross-national interactions, and to manage daily operations in foreign subsidiaries. Companies of all sizes wishing to operate overseas are faced with varied and dynamic environments in which they must accurately assess the political, legal, technological, competitive, and cultural factors that shape their strategies and operations. The fate of overseas operations depends greatly on the international manager's cultural skills and sensitivity, as well as the ability to carry out the company's strategy within the context of the host country's business practices.

In the eighth edition, cross-cultural management and competitive strategy are evaluated in the context of global changes—including the rapidly growing influence of technology, e-business, and social media on business strategy and operations, including "born globals"; the "Eurozone crisis"; the increasing trade among the Americas; and the emerging markets and rapidly growing economies in Asia—that require new management applications. In the eighth edition we have added focus on how rapidly developing economies, in particular the "BRICS," present the manager with challenging strategic decisions in an increasingly "flat world," as posited by Thomas Friedman. In addition, the eighth edition includes increased emphasis on small- and medium-sized businesses and their strategies. Throughout, the text emphasizes how the variable of culture interacts with other national and international factors to affect managerial processes and behaviors. Concerns about corporate social responsibility (CSR), sustainability, and ethics while operating in global locations are addressed at length.

This textbook is designed for undergraduate and graduate students majoring in international business or general management. Graduate students might be asked to focus more heavily on the comprehensive cases that conclude each part of the book and to complete the term project in greater detail. It is assumed, though not essential, that most students using *International Management: Managing Across Borders and Cultures,* Eighth Edition, will have taken a basic principles of management course. Although this text is primarily intended for business students, it is also useful for practicing managers and for students majoring in other areas, such as political science or international relations, who would benefit from a background in international management.

EIGHTH EDITION FEATURES

- **Streamlined text** in eleven chapters, with particular focus on global strategic positioning, entry strategies and alliances, effective cross-cultural understanding and management, and developing and retaining an effective global management cadre. The eighth edition has been revised to reflect current research, current events, and global developments, and includes company examples from the popular press. The following section summarizes specific features and changes:

NEW COMPREHENSIVE CASES IN EIGHTH EDITION

1. **An Ethics Role-Playing Case: Stockholders versus Stakeholders (Global/Sri Lanka)**
2. **BlackBerry in International Markets (Global/Middle East)**
3. **Google's Orkut in Brazil: What's So Social About it? (Brazil)**
4. **MTV Networks: The Arabian Challenge (Saudi Arabia)**
5. **Alibaba in 2011: Competing in China and Beyond**
6. **Carrefour's Misadventure in Russia**
7. **Walmart's Expansion in Africa**
8. **Evaluating the Chrysler-Fiat Auto Alliance in 2012 (Italy/U.S./Global)**
9. **Foreign Investment in Chinese Banking Sector: HR Challenges (China)**
10. **Indra Nooyi: A Transcultural Leader (India/Global)**
11. **Mahindra and Mahindra (B): An Emerging Global Giant? (India Global)**
12. **After the Breakup: The Troubled Alliance Between Volkswagen and Suzuki (Germany/Japan)**

COVERAGE AND FEATURES BY PART AND CHAPTER

PART 1: The Global Manager's Environment
Chapter 1: Assessing the Environment: Political, Economic, Legal, Technological

New opening profile: "The Globalization of Risk".

Updated Comparative Management in Focus (CMF): "China Helps Prop Up the Global Economy.

Updated Management in Action (MA): "Intel Brings Changes to Vietnam's Economy and Culture"

New Box Feature—Under the Lens: Information Technology

New End Case: "Apple's iPhone—Not "Made in America"

Chapter 1 has been revised and updated to reflect developments and events in global business. In Chapter 1 we introduce trends and developments facing international managers, and then expand those topics in the context of the subsequent chapters. For example, we discuss developments in globalization and its growing nationalist backlash that resulted, in particular, from the global economic crisis and the Eurozone problems. We discuss the effects on global business of the rapidly growing economies of China and India and other emerging economies such as Brazil, Russia, and those in Africa; the globalization of human capital; the escalating role of Information Technology and social media; and the global spread of e-business. In addition, we have added material and focus on small and medium-sized companies here and throughout the book. We follow these trends and their effects on the role of the international manager throughout the book.

Chapter 2: Managing Interdependence—Social Responsibility, Ethics, Sustainability

New Opening Profile: McDonald's CSR Experience in China: Interview with Bob Langert, VP for Corporate Social Responsibility

New Under the Lens: Shareholders Pressure Wal-Mart for Transparency about How Its Suppliers Treat Workers

Revised CMF: Doing Business in China—CSR and the Human Rights Challenge

New Under the Lens: BP's Sustainability Systems Under Fire

New MA: TerraCycle—Social Entrepreneurship Goes Global

End Case: Nike's CSR challenge

Chapter 2, as indicated by the new title, takes a long-term view of the company's global stakeholders and its strategy. It includes an expanded section on Sustainability Strategies, including a new model. The chapter is updated throughout, with new examples, and has a new section on Ethics in Uses of Technology.

PART 2: The Cultural Context of Global Management
Chapter 3: Understanding the Role of Culture

Opening Profile: Adjusting Business to Saudi Arabian Culture

New Under the Lens: Religion and the Workplace

MA: Updated "India's IT Industry Brings Cultural Changes"

CMF: Expanded Profiles in Culture: Japan, Germany, Latin America.

New Under the Lens: Doing Business in Brazil—Language, Customs, Culture, and Etiquette

End Case: Australia and New Zealand: Doing Business with Indonesia

Chapter 3 examines the pervasive effect of culture on the manager's role. It includes a new section, "Consequence or Cause"; expanded coverage of culture's effects on management; and increased emphasis on CQ (cultural quotient). In particular, this chapter presents ways for managers to anticipate, understand, and therefore adjust to working with people in other countries; those ways include understanding the variables of culture through research and how to develop a descriptive basis for a cultural profile. Several countries are represented, including an in-depth look at Brazil.

Chapter 4: Communicating Across Cultures

New Opening Profile: The Impact of Social Media on Global Business

New Under the Lens: Communicating in India—Language, Culture, Customs, and Etiquette

New Under the Lens: How Feng Shui Affects Business

MA: Oriental Poker Face: Eastern Deception or Western Inscrutability?

CMF: Communicating with Arabs

New Under the Lens: Google's "Street View" makes Friends in Japan but Clashes with European Culture

New End Case: Miscommunications with a Brazilian Auto Parts Manufacturer.

Chapter 4 links culture and communication in its various forms and focuses on how that affects business transactions and how managers should act in other cultural settings. In particular, the section on Non-verbal Communication has been expanded in the eighth edition, along with the addition of three illustrative "Lens" sections.

Chapter 5: Cross-cultural Negotiation and Decision Making

New Opening Profile: Shiseido and Bare Escentuals—Cultural Conflicts in Negotiations

MA: Cultural Misunderstanding—The Danone-Wahaha Joint Venture in China Splits After Years of Legal Dispute

Revised and Expanded CMF—Negotiating with the Chinese

New Under the Lens: Negotiations and Decisions to Save the Eurozone System

CMF: Decision Making in Japanese Companies

New End Case: Facebook's Continued Negotiations in China.

Chapter 5 continues the link among the variables of culture, communication, negotiation, and decision making—they are all intertwined. New examples, features, and cases are introduced to explain and illustrate the effects on the manager's role.

PART 3: Formulating and Implementing Strategy for International and Global Operations

Chapter 6: Formulating Strategy

Opening Profile: Global Companies Take Advantage of Opportunities in South Africa

MA: Updated and revised: Global Economic Downturn Causes Mexico's Cemex to Retrench

New Under the Lens: India Says No to Foreign Ownership of Supermarkets

CMF: Expanded and Updated: Strategic Planning for Emerging Markets

New End Case: Search Engines in Global Business

Chapter 6 explains the reasons that firms choose to take their business abroad, and the various means for them to do so. The steps in developing those strategies, for firms of all sizes, are examined, along with the explanatory models and the pros and cons of those options. The eighth edition expands on e-business and "born globals," and includes an expanded, revised section on strategic planning for emerging markets, including an extensive discussion of a study of 247 executives by Deloitte Review regarding their strategies in emerging markets. Discussion of cultural distance relative to strategic planning has been added. Throughout, there are new features and updated examples.

Chapter 7: Implementing Strategy: Strategic Alliances; Small Businesses; Emerging Economy Firms

New Opening Profile: From BP to Exxon: Beware the Alliance with the Bear!

New Under the Lens: Dancing with Gorillas: How SMEs Can Internationalize Through Relationships with Foreign Multinationals

CMF: revised and updated: Joint Ventures in the Russian Federation

New Under the Lens: Breaking Down Barriers for Small Business Exports

New Under the Lens: Global Supply Chain Risks—The Japanese Disaster

MA: Mittal's Marriage to Arcelor Breaks the Marwari Rules

New End Case: The Nokia-Microsoft Alliance in the Global Smartphone Industry (Circa 2011)

Chapter 7, as indicated by the new title and the new features above, includes new sections regarding implementing strategies for small businesses and for emerging economy firms, as well as expanded coverage of implementing alliances. The revised CMF on JVs in the Russian Federation, as well as the feature on the global effects of the Japanese disaster in 2011, provide further updates on issues facing managers.

Chapter 8: Organization Structure and Control Systems

New Opening Profile: Kraft's Post-Merger Integration and Reorganization

Updated Under the Lens: Samsung Electronics Reorganizes to Fight Downturn

Updated MA: Procter & Gamble's "Think Globally–Act Locally" Structure—10 Years of Success

CMF: Changing Organizational Structures of Emerging Market Companies

New Under the Lens: FIFA—Restructuring for Governance Oversight of Ethics

New End Case: HSBC's Global Reorganization and Corporate Performance in 2012

Chapter 8 further examines how to effectively implement strategy by setting up appropriate structural and control systems. The eighth edition gives updated text and new features and cases to explain why and how the way the firm organizes must change to reflect strategic change, which in turn responds to competitive and other environmental factors affecting the industry and the firm. Issues of monitoring, controlling, and evaluating the firm's ongoing performance is discussed.

PART 4: Global Human Resources Management

Chapter 9: Staffing, Training, and Compensation for Global Operations

Opening Profile: Staffing Company Operations in Emerging Markets

New Under the Lens: Tata's Staffing Challenges in the United States

MA: Updated: Success! Starbucks' Java Style Helps to Recruit, Train, and Retain Local Managers in Beijing

CMF: IHRM practices in various countries

End Case: Kelly's Assignment in Japan

Chapter 9 continues strategy implementation by focusing on the IHRM issues of preparing and placing managers in overseas locations, as well as hiring, training, and compensating local managers. The eighth edition includes updated research information, in particular regarding the "war for talent" around the world, and new coverage of the staffing option called "inpatriates."

Chapter 10: Developing a Global Management Cadre

Opening Profile: The Expat Life

New Lens: Expatriates' Careers Add to Knowledge Transfer

MA: Updated: The Role of Women in International Management

New Under the Lens: Vietnam—The Union Role in Achieving Manufacturing Sustainability and Global Competitiveness

CMF: Updated: Labor Relations in Germany

New End Case: Expatriate Management in AstraZeneca.

Chapter 10 focuses on ways to maximize the long-term value to the firm of its expatriates, maximize the opportunities of its women in management, and effectively manage its knowledge transfer and the global management teams and virtual teams. In addition, this chapter brings new focus to understanding the role of organized labor around the world and its impact on strategy and HRM. New survey results regarding expatriate retention and the roles of their families are examined, as well as a new feature examining the role of expatriates' careers in knowledge transfer to the firm.

Chapter 11: Motivating and Leading

Opening Profile: The EU Business Leader—Myth or Reality?

CMF Updated: Motivation in Mexico

NEW Under the Lens: Global Leaders from India

MA: Leadership in a Digital World

NEW End Case: The Olympus Debacle—Western Leader Clashes with Japan's Corporate Leadership Style

Chapter 11 of the eighth edition has been updated with new examples and research, and a new feature on Global Leaders from India, as well as a new end case. The chapter focuses on both classical and modern research on motivation and leadership in the global arena; specific attention is paid to "Global Mindset" characteristics and behaviors that are typical of successful "cross-cultural" leaders. Finally, an integrative model is presented which illustrates the complexities of the leader's role in various contextual, stakeholder, and cross-border environments.

Additional Eighth Edition Features:

- **Experiential Exercises** at the end of each chapter, challenging students on topics such as ethics in decision making, cross-cultural negotiations, and strategic planning.

- **Integrative Section** – Two new cases (Cases 11 and 12) incorporating a range of topics and locations covered in the text. These cases challenge students to consider the relationships among the topics and steps in this text and to use a systems approach to problem solving for the global manager's role, as well as illustrating the complexity of that role.

- **Integrative Term Project** outlined at the end of the text and providing a vehicle for research and application of the course content.

SUPPLEMENTS PACKAGE

All of the following supplements can be downloaded from our Instructor Resource Center. Request your user name and password from your Pearson Sales Representative. www.pearsonhighered.com/irc

If you ever need assistance, our dedicated technical support team is ready to help with the media supplements that accompany this text. Visit **http://247pearsoned.custhelp.com** for answers to frequently asked questions and user support.

Instructor's Manual: The Instructor's Manual has been completely revised. For each chapter, the Instructor's Manual provides a comprehensive lecture outline with references to slides in the PowerPoint package, chapter discussion questions and answers, as well as additional Teaching Resources, a list of related Web sites, and additional Experiential Exercises for selected chapters.

Test Item File: The Test Item File consists of a selection of multiple choice, true/false, and essay questions. Each question is followed by a rating of easy, moderate, or difficult, and a classification of either application or recall to help you build a well-balanced test.

PowerPoints: A fully revised, comprehensive package of slides, which outline each chapter and include exhibits from the text. The PowerPoint package is designed to aid the educator and supplement in-class lectures.

TestGen software: Containing all of the questions in the printed Test Item File, TestGen is a comprehensive suite of tools for testing and assessment.

Video Library: Videos illustrating the most important subject topics are available on DVD for in classroom use by instructors, includes videos mapped to Pearson textbooks.

COMPANION WEB SITE

The companion Web site for this text, located at http://www.pearsonhighered.com/deresky provides valuable resources for both students and professors, including an interactive student study guide.

ACKNOWLEDGMENTS

The author would like to acknowledge, with thanks, the individuals who made this text possible. For the eighth edition, these people include Bruce Rosenthal who updated the Instructor's Manual and PowerPoints; the test Bank supplement was authored by experts with extensive experience in assessment and test creation. Each question has been carefully reviewed and edited to ensure accuracy and appropriateness.

The author would also like to thank the following reviewers:

Gary Falcone, Rider University Lawrenceville, NJ
William Wardrope, University of Central Oklahoma, Edmond, OK
Eric Rodriguez, Everest College, Los Angeles, CA
Paul Melendez, University of Arizona, Tucson, AZ
Kathy Wood, University of Tennessee, Knoxville, TN
Daniel Zisk, James Madison University, Harrisonburg, VA
Dinah Payne, University of New Orleans, New Orleans, LA
Marion White, James Madison University, Harrisonburg, VA
Gary Tucker, Northwestern Oklahoma State University, Alva, OK
David Turnspeed, University of South Alabama, Mobile, AL
Lauren Migenes, University of Central Florida, Orlando, FL
Steven Jenner, California State University, Dominguez Hills, CA
Arthur De George, University of Central Florida, Orlando, FL

—*Helen Deresky*

The Global Manager's Environment

CHAPTER 1

Assessing the Environment
Political, Economic, Legal, Technological

OUTLINE

OBJECTIVES

1. To understand the global business environment and how it affects the strategic and operational decisions which managers must make.

2. To critically assess the developments, advantages, and disadvantages of globalization.

3. To review the role of technology in international business.

4. To develop an appreciation for the ways in which political, economic, legal and technological factors and changes impact the opportunities that companies face.

5. To discuss the complexities of the international manager's job.

OPENING PROFILE: THE GLOBALIZATION OF RISK[1]

Firms' risk analysts were certainly scratching their heads going into 2012 after the confluence of events in 2011 caused such a global ripple effect of business risk. The World Economic Forum Global Risks 2012 Report (based on 469 social experts and industry leaders) highlighted the world's interconnected and rapidly developing socio-economic risks. The report points out that severe income disparity and chronic fiscal imbalances would be the top two risks facing business leaders and policy makers for 2012 and the next decade; it also raises the concern that those macro risks will reverse the gains of globalization. Contributing largely to those escalating risks, the global debt crisis continued unabated; in Europe, in particular, problems in major debtor countries such as Greece, Italy, and Ireland threatened to break up the eurozone and implode the euro. Leaders in stronger countries such as Germany and France struggled to put together a rescue plan. As the global recession, started in 2008, continued to eat away at business profits and people's jobs, homes, and lifestyles, the observation quoted below is still relevant.

> *A perilous global crisis of confidence has revealed both the scale and the limitations of globalization.*[2]

People around the world made their fears known as they sought redress for their various situations. Most surprising were the massive "Arab Spring" protests, which spread like wildfire through social media and Internet technology. Their long-term effects are not yet known. Following those, the protest movement spread in the West and was known in the United States as the "Occupy" movement, in which people were protesting what they perceived as "Wall Street" excesses and income inequality.

It is clear that the global credit crunch has hit consumers and businesses alike as uncertainty about the future cripples spending and investment, and has a ripple effect around the world. Firms are reluctant to expand their business in troubled countries, consumers are reluctant to spend, and so the global economy retracts. Even the rapidly developing emerging economies are adversely affected by the reduced demand from developed economies.

Add to this the political uncertainty of leadership changes around the world, such as in China, and increasing tensions with Iran, and you have a cauldron of political, economic, and financial risks.

In 2011 it also became apparent to risk analysts that there are natural disasters that can cripple business activities in far-flung countries from where the disaster occurs, and these cannot be anticipated, although back-up plans can be put in place. This realization came after the Japanese 9.0 magnitude earthquake killing 20,000 people. The resulting tsunami and problems in the nuclear reactors was devastating to Japan's people and economy. Supply chains around the world were disrupted from the shutdown of manufacturing plants and infrastructure in Japan; this disaster and the devastating flooding in Thailand in November 2011 highlighted the need for resilient business models in response to crises of unforeseen magnitude. "The question now is, has the quest for lowest-cost production and hyper-lean supply chains overridden and exposed vulnerability to significant business risk?"[3]

Clearly, globalization has compounded the types and level of business risks to which firms are exposed and the speed with which they might be impacted. Managers around the world must be attuned to what types of situations make their firms vulnerable and plan accordingly. Carlos Ghosn, the CEO of Nissan, told an audience in New York:

> *There's going to be another crisis. We don't know what kind of crisis, where it is going to hit us, and when it is going to hit us, but every time there is a crisis we are going to learn from it.*

> FORTUNE,
> December 26, 2011.[4]

Half of the global growth now comes from emerging markets.

ROBERT ZOELLICK, PRESIDENT, WORLD BANK,
SEPTEMBER 19, 2011.[5]

As evidenced in the opening profile, managers in the twenty-first century are being challenged to operate in an increasingly complex, interdependent, networked, and changing global environment. In a globalized economy, developments such as those described in the opening profile can have repercussions around the world almost instantaneously. Clearly, those involved in international and global business have to adjust their strategies and management styles to those kinds of global developments as well as to those regions of the world in which they want to operate, whether directly or through some form of alliance.

Typical challenges that managers face involve politics, cultural differences, global competition, terrorism, and technology. In addition, the opportunities and risks of the global marketplace increasingly bring with them the societal obligations of operating in a global community. An example is the dilemma faced by Western drug manufacturers of how to fulfill their responsibilities to stockholders, acquire capital for research and development (R&D), and protect their patents while also being good global citizens by responding to the cry for free or low-cost drugs for AIDS in poor countries. Managers in those companies are struggling to find ways to balance their social responsibilities, their images, and their competitive strategies.

To compete aggressively, firms must make considerable investments overseas—not only capital investment but also investment in well-trained managers with the skills essential to working effectively in a multicultural environment. In any foreign environment, managers need to handle a set of dynamic and fast-changing variables, including the all-pervasive variable of culture that affects every facet of daily life. Added to that "behavioral software" are the challenges of the burgeoning use of technological software and the borderless Internet, which are rapidly changing the dynamics of competition and operations.

International management, then, is the process of developing strategies, designing and operating systems, and working with people around the world to ensure sustained competitive advantage. Those management functions are shaped by the prevailing conditions and ongoing developments in the world, as outlined in the following sections.

THE GLOBAL BUSINESS ENVIRONMENT

Following is a summary of some of the global situations and trends that managers need to monitor and incorporate in their strategic and operational planning.

Globalization

The World Trade Organization (WTO) warned in September 2011 that the expansion in global trade had slowed sharply, and that "the slowdown in trade was concentrated in the advanced economies, particularly Europe, suggesting that it was related to the sovereign debt crisis in the eurozone."[6] Clearly, the financial linkages around the world are just one phenomenon of globalization. Business competitiveness has now evolved to a level of sophistication commonly called **globalization**—global competition characterized by networks of international linkages that bind countries, institutions, and people in an interdependent global economy. Economic integration results from the lessening of trade barriers and the increased flow of goods and services, capital, labor, and technology around the world. The invisible hand of global competition is being propelled by the phenomenon of an increasingly borderless world, by technological advancements, and by the rise of emerging markets such as China and India—a process that Thomas Friedman refers to as "leveling the playing field" among countries—or, the "flattening of the world."[7]

Emerging economies now produce as much trade, capital, and knowledge flow as do developed economies.[8] Sirkin et al. use the term "globality," stating that business these days is all about "competing with everyone from everywhere for everything."[9] On a more strategic level, Ghemawat argues, rather, that the business world is in a state of "semi-globalization"—that various metrics show that only 10 to 25 percent of economic activity is truly global. He bases this conviction on his analysis that "most types of economic activity that can be conducted either within or across borders are still quite localized by country."[10] Ghemawat poses that we are in an "unevenly globalized world" and that business opportunities and threats depend on the individual perspective of country, company, and industry.[11] He observes that, as emerging market countries have gained in wealth and power and increasingly call their own shots, there is a reverse trend of globalization taking place— evolving fragmentation—which he says is, ironically, a ripple effect of globalization.[12] Examples of such localization trends are the activities of firms such as Alibaba, Infosys, Carrefour, General Motors, and Pizza Hut that now focus on tailoring their products to emerging-market consumers.

GLOBAL TRENDS

The rapid development of globalization is attributable to many factors, including the burgeoning use of technology and its accompanying uses in international business; political developments that enable cross-border trade agreements; and global competition for the growing numbers of consumers around the world. From studies by Bisson et al. and others, we can also identify five key global trends that provide both challenges and opportunities for companies to incorporate into their strategic planning:[13]

- The changing balance of growth toward emerging markets compared with developed ones, along with the growing number of middle-class consumers in those areas.
- The need for increased productivity and consumption in developed countries in order to stimulate their economies.
- The increasing global interconnectivity—technologically and otherwise, as previously discussed, and in particular the phenomenon of an "electronically flattened earth" that gives rise to increased opportunity and fast-developing competition.
- The increasing gap between demand and supply of natural resources, in particular to supply developing economies, along with the push for environmental protection.
- The challenge facing governments to develop policies for economic growth and financial stability.[14]

Globality and Emerging Markets

Nestlé said on July 11, 2011 that it had agreed to pay $1.7 billion for a 60 percent stake in a big Chinese confectioner, in one of the biggest deals ever by a foreign company in China.[15]

It is clear that globalization—in the broader sense—has led to the narrowing of differences in regional output growth rates, driven largely by increases led by China, India, Brazil and Russia (often called the BRICs, which together accounted for over 18 percent of global gross domestic product (GDP) as of 2011[16]). There is no doubt that the global economic turmoil has curtailed investment, and company executives remained wary of investment in 2012. However, global trade is increasingly including those developing nations judged to have significant growth potential, with investments from developed economies to emerging economies of over $1,000 billion a year as of 2011.[17] Exhibit 1-1 shows the 2012 results from research by the A. T. Kearney Company of the Foreign Direct Investment (FDI) intentions and preferences of the leaders of top companies in 17 industry sectors spanning six continents; the companies participating in the survey account for over $2 trillion in global revenue. The exhibit shows the top 25 countries in which those executives have confidence for their investment opportunities. Their results show that China, India, and Brazil continue to rank at the top of the FDI Confidence Index, along with the United States (although the U.S. rank dropped two places since 2010, burdened by debt and financial instability).[18] In fact over half of global FDI inflows were from emerging markets for the first time in history, and now comprise more than half of the Index's top 25 countries. South Africa, which was unranked in 2010, rebounded to 11th place. Russia fell from 9th place in 2007 to 12th in 2012. Overall, it is clear that the phenomenon of such rapidly developing economies, says Fareed Zakaria, is something much broader than the much-ballyhooed rise of China or even Asia. Rather, he says:

It is the rise of the rest—the rest of the world.[19]

"The rest," he says, include countries such as Brazil, Mexico, South Korea, Taiwan, India, China, and Russia. He states that, as traditional industries in the United States continue to decline, "the rest" are picking up those opportunities. Even so, the United States remains dominant in many "new age" industries such as nanotechnology and biotechnology. It is clear, also, that as emerging markets continue to grow their countries' economies, they will provide growth markets for the products and services of developed economies.

Evidence of the growing number of companies from emerging markets can be seen in the Fortune 500 rankings of the world's biggest firms. The Global 500 is increasingly global. While the U.S. still dominates the list, with 133 companies, that number is down from 185 a decade ago. China continues to move up the list, with 61 companies—versus just 12 in 2001—while many companies from India, Russia, Brazil, and other growth economies are moving up in the rankings. Examples of "emerging giants" are, from China, Huwei Technologies, Lenovo Group, and Baosteel; those from India include Infosys Technologies, Tata Group, and Bharti Airtel;

MAP 1.1 Emerging Economies

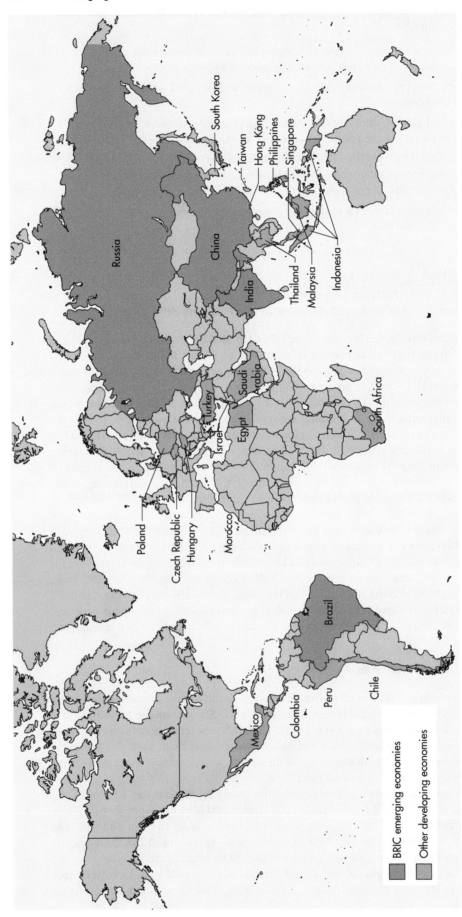

South Korea

Taiwan
Hong Kong
Philippines
Singapore

Russia

China

India

Thailand
Malaysia
Indonesia

Saudi Arabia

Turkey
Israel
Egypt

South Africa

Poland
Czech Republic
Hungary
Morocco

Brazil

Mexico

Colombia
Peru
Chile

BRIC emerging economies

Other developing economies

EXHIBIT 1-1   **2012 Foreign Direct Investment Confidence Index Top 25 Targets for FDI**   The main types of FDI are acquisition of a subsidiary or production facility, joint ventures, licensing, and investing in new facilities or expansion of existing facilities.

Ranking   Values calculated on a 0 to 3 scale

2007	2010	2012		Value
1	1	1	China	1.87
2	3	2	India	1.73
6	4	3	Brazil	1.60
3	2	4	United States	1.52
10	5	5	Germany	1.52
11	7	6	Australia	1.52
7	24	7	Singapore	1.47
4	10	8	United Kingdom	1.47
21	19	9	Indonesia	1.45
16	20	10	Malaysia	1.41
18	–	11	South Africa	1.40
9	18	12	Russia	1.39
20	23	13	Turkey	1.39
12	12	14	Vietnam	1.38
8	11	15	United Arab Emirates	1.38
–	–	16	Thailand	1.37
13	13	17	France	1.37
–	–	18	Taiwan	1.36
24	–	19	South Korea	1.35
14	9	20	Canada	1.34
15	–	21	Japan	1.31
–	–	22	Switzerland	1.30
22	6	23	Poland	1.30
–	–	24	Spain	1.29
–	–	25	The Netherlands	1.27

Low confidence   High confidence

■ Maintained ranking   ⊞ Moved up   ⊟ Moved down

from Brazil they include Embraer and Votorantim Group; from Mexico, Group Bimbo; Gazprom from Russia, and Bumi Resources from Indonesia—to name a few.

> *Simply put: If you're doing business with the biggest companies in the world, you're not just spending time in New York, London, and Hong Kong.*[20]

FORTUNE,
JULY 25, 2011.

Further evidence that "globalization" is no longer just another word for "Americanization" is the increase in the number of emerging-market companies acquiring established large businesses and brands from the so-called "developed" countries. For example, in 2008 the Budweiser brand, America's favorite beer, was bought by InBev, a Belgian-Brazilian conglomerate, and also in 2008, "several of America's leading financial institutions avoided bankruptcy only by going cap in hand to the sovereign-wealth funds (state-owned investment funds) of various Arab kingdoms and the Chinese government."[21] Clearly, companies in emerging markets are providing many tangible business opportunities for investment and alliances around the world, as well as establishing themselves as competitors to reckon with.

Backlash against Globalization

As we consider the many facets of globalization and how they intertwine, we observe how economic power and shifting opinions and ideals about politics and religion, for example, result in an increasing backlash against globalization and a rekindling of nationalism. Globalization has been propelled by capitalism and open markets, most notably by Western companies. Now "economic power is shifting fast to the emerging nations of the south. China and India are replacing the U.S. as the engines of world economic growth."[22]

The rising nationalist tendencies are evident as emerging and developing nations—wielding their economic power in attempted takeovers and inroads around the world—encounter protectionism. There is hostility to takeovers such as the Indian company Mittal Steel's bid for Europe's largest steel company, Arcelor. In particular, as the demand on energy resources burgeons with heightened industrial activity in China, we see increased protectionism of those resources around the world as Russia, Venezuela, and Bolivia have privatized their energy resources.

The backlash against globalization comes from those who feel that it benefits advanced industrial nations at the expense of many other countries and the people within them who are not sharing in those benefits. Joseph Stiglitz, a Nobel Laureate, for example, argues that such an economic system has been pressed upon many developing countries at the expense of their sovereignty, their well-being, and their environment. Critics point to the growing numbers of people around the world living in poverty.[23] Recently, globalization has also become increasingly unpopular with many in the United States as growth in emerging markets raises prices for energy and commodities; as their jobs are being lost overseas, driving down wages; and as the weak dollar makes companies in the United States vulnerable to foreign buyers.[24]

While the debate about the effects of globalization continues, it is clear that economic globalization will be advanced by corporations looking to maximize their profits with global efficiencies, by politicians and leaders wishing to advance their countries' economies, and by technological and transportation advances that make their production and supply networks more efficient. However, pressure by parties against those trends, as well as the resurgence in nationalism and protectionism, may serve to pull back those advances to a more regional scope in some areas, or limit them to bilateral pacts.[25]

In addition, while competition to provide the best and cheapest products to consumers exerts pressure on corporations to maximize efficiencies around the world, there is also increasing pressure and publicity for them to consider the social responsibility of their activities (discussed further in Chapter 2).

Effects of Institutions on Global Trade[26]

Two major groups of institutions (supranational and national) play a differing role in globalization. Supranational institutions such as the World Trade Organization (WTO) and the International Labor Organization (ILO) promote the convergence of how international activities should be conducted. For example, the WTO promotes the lowering of tariffs and a common set of trade rules among its member countries. Similarly, the ILO promotes common standards of how workers should be treated. While many supranational institutions frequently promote rules or laws favorable to foreign firms (e.g., requiring intellectual property rights protections in China), others have been criticized for infringing on national sovereignty (e.g., challenges to certain environmental laws in the United States).

National institutions, in contrast, play a role in creating favorable conditions for domestic firms and may make it more difficult for foreign firms to compete in those countries. For example, the stringent drug testing rules required by the U.S. Food and Drug Administration (FDA) and the anti-dumping rules enforced by the U.S. Department of Commerce's International Trade Administration (ITA) act as entry barriers for foreign firms (see Chapter 6 for a more detailed discussion of these entry barriers).

Some supranational institutions represent the interests of a smaller group of countries. For example, the European Commission acts in the interest of the 27 EU members as a whole rather than the interest of individual member countries. The European Commission is the executive arm of the EU and is responsible for implementing the decisions of the European Parliament and the European Council. Of relevance to international business, the European Commission speaks for the EU at the World Trade Organization, and is responsible for negotiating trade agreements on behalf of the EU.[27]

Effects of Globalization on Corporations

In returning to our discussion at the corporate level, we can see that almost all firms around the world are affected to some extent by globalization. Firms from any country now compete with companies at home and abroad, and domestic competitors are competing on price by outsourcing or offshoring resources and services anywhere in the world. Often it is difficult to tell which competing products or services are of domestic or foreign origin. Examples abound—for example, do you really drive an American car?

> *Look at your vehicle identification number (VIN): If it starts with 1 it is made in America, 2, Canada, 3, Mexico, 4, anywhere else in the world. The only cars allowed to park in a UAW plant are those with VIN numbers beginning with 1 and 2.*[28]

Hondas are made in Ohio; Buicks are made in Germany. In contrast, Japan's Toyota Sienna model is far more American, with 90 percent local components being assembled in Indiana.[29] This didn't happen overnight. Toyota has been investing in North America for 20 years in plants, suppliers, and dealerships, as well as design, testing, and research centers. Toyota became the largest auto manufacturer in the world in sales in 2009. In fact, on June 1, 2009, General Motors filed for Chapter 11 bankruptcy, pushed into a temporary partial nationalization by the U.S. government in order to save the company in a drastically downsized form.[30]

Clearly, competition has no borders, with most global companies producing and selling more of their global brands and services abroad than domestically. Cisco Systems gets 55 percent of its revenues from overseas and CEO John Chambers predicted that 70 percent of the firm's growth will come from overseas.[31] Avon, for example, estimates it employs 5 million sales representatives globally; Nestlé has 50 percent of its sales outside of its home market; Coca-Cola has 80 percent; and Procter & Gamble has 65 percent. The Tata Group, a conglomerate originating in India, has operations in 85 countries and has made a number of acquisitions of large firms around the world.

Investment by global companies around the world means that this aspect of globalization benefits developing economies—through the transfer of financial, technological, and managerial resources, as well as through the development of local allies that later become self-sufficient and have other operations. Global companies are becoming less tied to specific locations, and their operations and allies are spread around the world as they source and coordinate resources and activities in the most suitable areas and as technology facilitates faster and more flexible interactions and greater efficiencies. In fact, as noted in discussions in the 2012 World Economic Forum: "it is that the world's largest companies are moving beyond governments and countries that they perceive to be inept and anemic. They are operating in a space that is increasingly supranational—disconnected from local concerns and the problems of their home markets."[32]

It is essential, therefore, for managers to look beyond their domestic market. If they do not, they will be even further behind the majority of managers who have already recognized that they must have a global vision for their firms, beginning with preparing themselves with the skills and tools of managing in a global environment. Companies that desire to remain globally competitive and to expand their operations to other countries will have to develop a cadre of top management with experience operating abroad and an understanding of what it takes to do business in other countries and to work with people of other cultures. Many large firms around the world are getting to the stage of evolution known as the stateless multinational, where work is sourced wherever it is most efficient; the result of this stage of development is that

> *for business leaders, building a firm that is seamlessly integrated across time zones and cultures presents daunting obstacles.*[33]

Already it is clear that top managers are locating anywhere in the world where the firm has operations or is looking for opportunities, rather than trying to run the show from a headquarters building in the home country. Jeff Immelt, for example, who is Chairman and CEO of General Electric (GE), calls himself a "globalist." GE is clearly a global company—half of GE's 300,000 employees are overseas, and 60 percent of its revenues come from overseas. "Petropolis," for example, GE's company town plant in Brazil, has 8,000 employees and is growing at a rate of 35 percent a year, compared to one percent in the United States. When Leslie Stahl, in an interview on October 9, 2011 for the CBS program *60 Minutes*, pressured Mr. Immelt about GE's many jobs overseas that could be in the United States, he responded that those plants order components from GE's U.S. plants, and he defended the company's global strategy as being responsible to the shareholders and responsible to grow the company's revenues.

SMALL AND MEDIUM-SIZED ENTERPRISES (SMEs)

SMEs are also affected by, and in turn affect, globalization. They play a vital role in contributing to their national economies—through employment, new job creation, development of new products and services, and international operations, typically exporting. The vast majority (about 98 percent) of businesses in developed economies are small and medium-sized enterprises, which are typically referred to as those companies having fewer than 500 employees. Small businesses are rapidly discovering foreign markets. Although many small businesses are affected by globalism only to the extent that they face competing products from abroad, an increasing number of entrepreneurs are being approached by potential offshore customers, thanks to the burgeoning number of trade shows, federal and state export initiatives, and the growing use of Web sites that ease making contact and placing orders online.[34]

There has never been a better time for SMEs to go global; the Internet is as valid a tool for small companies to find customers and suppliers around the world as it is for large companies. By using the Internet, email, and web-conferencing, small companies can inexpensively contact customers and set up their global businesses. One example of a very small start-up that went global quickly is that of Groupon Inc., a local e-commerce marketplace that connects merchants to consumers by offering goods and services at a discount through on-line coupons. The idea was conceived by Groupon's CEO Andrew Mason and rapidly caught on. Groupon has quickly become one of the success stories of the new generation of Internet start-ups. As of September 30, 2011, the Company featured deals from over 190,000 merchants worldwide across over 190 categories of goods and services. Mason employs people in a number of countries to tailor their approach locally to the local commerce markets worldwide in the leisure, recreation, food-service, and retail sectors.[35]

Regional Trading Blocs

Much of today's world trade takes place within three regional free-trade blocs (Western Europe, Asia, and the Americas). These trade blocs are continually expanding their borders to include neighboring countries, either directly or with separate agreements.

THE EUROPEAN UNION The European Union (EU) comprises a 27-nation unified "borderless" market of approximately 500 million people, as shown in Map 1.2. Countries around the world trade with the EU countries. The United States, for example, had a two-way trade of $560 billion and a $3 trillion two-way investment relationship as of 2011. Although trade continued to grow in 2010 despite the 2008 global financial crisis, the EU GDP growth was only at 1.8 percent that year and economic problems in some member states continuing into 2012 were adversely affecting the EU as a whole, resulting in global financial repercussions. Many were questioning the stability of the euro, as discussed in the Financial Times:

> The future of the eurozone, and the capacity of the 17-nation currency union to recover from the debt crisis among its peripheral members, depends on the performance of the German economy more than on any other in Europe.[36]

The importance of Germany to the eurozone is clear, but it is also a two-way street. "Germany's prosperity is inextricably linked with the success and survival of the single currency, with more than 38 percent of German exports going to its eurozone partners, and almost 58 percent to the 27 members of the European Union."[37] The strength of the German manufacturing model is evidenced by the fact that, while Germany has about a quarter of the population of the United States, and a quarter of the U.S. GDP (Gross Domestic Product), it exports more than the United States.[38] Germans were concerned, however, that their economic strength would be diluted by the need to help prop up weaker economies in the eurozone, such as Greece.

In spite of those problems, the World Economic Forum's 2012–2013 Global Competitiveness Index (GCI) shows that six out of the top ten countries are in Europe (see Table 1–1). Interestingly, the United States had slipped to seventh from second place in 2010. The GCI is based on twelve pillars of competitiveness that provide attractive conditions and incentives for both local and foreign companies to do business there.[39] However, the elimination of internal tariffs and customs, as well as financial and commercial barriers has not eliminated national pride. Although most people in Europe are thought of simply as Europeans, they still think of

MAP 1.2 **European Union**

EU members using the euro
EU members using own national currency
Countries not members of the EU
Cities over 1 million
Capitals over 1 million

themselves first as British, French, Danish, Italian, etc., and are wary of giving too much power to centralized institutions or of giving up their national culture. The continuing enlargement of the EU to include many less prosperous countries has also promoted divisions among the "older" members.[40] In addition, continuing eurozone problems in 2012 prompted skepticism of any further enlargement.

Global managers face two major tasks. One is strategic: how firms outside of Europe can deal with the implications of the EU and of what some have called a "Fortress Europe"—that is, a market giving preference to insiders. While firms must have a pan-European business strategy, they must realize that suitable market entry strategies must be considered on a country-by-country basis.

While the European Union continues to move in the direction of a Single Market, the reality today is that U.S. exporters in some sectors continue to face barriers to entry in the EU market. In the world of the Internet and e-commerce, some of these barriers are still pronounced.[41]

TABLE 1–1   2012–2013 Global Competitiveness Index (7 is highest score)

Rank	Country	Score
1	Switzerland	5.72
2	Singapore	5.67
3	Finland	5.55
4	Sweden	5.53
5	Netherlands	5.50
6	Germany	5.81
7	U.S.	5.47
8	U.K.	5.45
9	Hong Kong	5.41
10	Japan	5.40

Source: Based on selected data from www.worldeconomicforum.org, September 7, 2012.

The other task is cultural: How to deal effectively with multiple sets of national cultures, traditions, and customs within Europe, such as differing attitudes about how much time should be spent on work versus leisure activities.

ASIA

It would be difficult to overstate the power of the fundamental drivers of Asian growth. First, Asian economies have been enjoying a remarkable period of "productivity catch-up," adopting modern technologies, industrial practices, and ways of organizing—in some cases leapfrogging Western competitors.[42]

Manufacturing accounts for approximately 30 percent of GDP in Asia's emerging markets, helping to fuel the demand for materials and supplies from the developed world, and lending hope for a quick global economic recovery.[43] Japan and the Four Tigers—Singapore, Hong Kong, Taiwan, and South Korea have provided most of the capital and expertise for Asia's developing countries. Now the focus is on China's role in driving closer integration in the region through its rapidly growing exports. Japan continues to negotiate trade agreements with its neighbors; China is negotiating with the entire thirteen-member Association of Southeast Asian Nations (ASEAN), while ASEAN is negotiating for earlier development of its own free trade area, ASEAN Free Trade Area (AFTA).

The Chinese market offers big opportunities for foreign investment, but you must learn to tolerate ambiguity and find a godfather to look after your political connections.[44]

China has enjoyed success as an export powerhouse, a status built on its strengths of low costs and a constant flow of capital. Its growth phenomenon is further discussed in the accompanying feature "Comparative Management in Focus—China Helps Prop Up the Global Economy."

 COMPARATIVE MANAGEMENT IN FOCUS

China Helps Prop Up the Global Economy

Headline GDP numbers won't tell the real story, even if that number is 8% or 9%. The growth rate in many cities is well above that, in the range of 15% to 20%, and that is what matters for the global system.[45]

If I say I want to open a campus in China . . . they'll say, "What do you need?"

JOHN CHAMBERS, CISCO SYSTEMS CHAIRMAN AND CEO,

April 2012.[46]

Indeed, in spite of some recent pullback, there is no doubt that the rise in China's GDP has helped prop up the global system. While China's growth rate in 2011 was 8.9 percent, down from

9.1 percent in 2010, it was "hardly a sign of a 'hard' landing."[47] U.S. exports to China rose 542 percent to $103.9 billion in 2011 from $16.2 billion in 2000, making it the third-largest U.S. export market.[48] China is the second-largest trading partner with the United States, after Canada, and it is the world's second largest recipient of FDI after the United States—investment largely coming from MNCs (Multinational Corporations). China's gross domestic product (GDP) growth rate—over 9 percent a year for thirty years—has been the fastest in the world.[49] Its economy has doubled every eight years for thirty years and the income of its people has increased sevenfold. With most of the world in an economic downturn, China has continued to grow because of its aggressive approach to the slowdown by committing $586 billion—9 percent of GDP—to infrastructure projects, and because its banking system remained relatively unscathed compared with others around the world. Indeed, China surpassed Germany in 2009 as the world's largest exporter.[50] Continuing its aggressive long-term approach, China stepped up to the plate to take advantage of the economic downturn by going on a major shopping spree, investing in energy and other natural resources that could give it an economic advantage it has never had before. Examples were lending the Brazilian oil giant Petrobras $10 billion in exchange for a long-term commitment to send oil to China, and similar deals with Russia and Venezuela.[51]

In March 2012, however, Chinese Premier Wen Jiabao raised eyebrows when he announced the government is targeting only 7.5% growth for 2012. This announcement signaled that Beijing is willing to tolerate slower growth in the name of better growth. Indeed, many welcomed such a goal, hoping that China will be able to contribute to global "rebalancing" by shifting away from export- and investment-dependence and toward domestic consumption. However, it also signaled more government intervention rather than a market-based approach.[52] In addition, the announcement of China's new leadership, set for November 2012, was being anxiously awaited.

Nevertheless, China has become a battleground for companies wanting a piece of the action in this rapidly growing economy. In fact, over 400 of the *Fortune* Global 500 companies are operating there. China's rapid rise—and the burgeoning opportunities for foreign businesses—is partly attributable to its membership in the WTO and its actions taken for structural reforms and the opening of many of its industries to foreign investment. However, foreign companies are increasingly protesting the protectionism that the Chinese government uses by taking advantage of its original WTO membership, which gave concessions to a then-categorized less-developed economy. China is now a hybrid/market-driven economy—driven by competition, capital, and entrepreneurship.

In addition to the large companies that continue to earn considerable returns on their investments in and exports to China, SMEs are also active and gaining ground in this complex country; but all companies are advised to do their homework first, as advised by the Foreign Commercial Service (FCS):

> *FCS counsels American companies that to be a success in China, they must thoroughly investigate the market, take heed of product standards, pre-qualify potential business partners and craft contracts that assure payment and minimize misunderstandings between the parties.*[53]

What accounts for China's rapid rise? China's recent exports in a single day have been more than it exported in all of 1978. With its 1.3 billion people, China benefits greatly from its large and rapidly growing foreign and domestic market size, which provides significant economies of scale. Innovation is becoming another competitive advantage, with rising company spending on R&D coupled with strong university-industry research collaboration, and an increasing rate of patenting. In addition, China has the world's largest foreign-exchange reserves—U.S. $3.2 trillion in 2011, although at a slowing trend in 2012 because of its narrowing trade surplus.[54] Not to be overlooked is the fact that the Chinese government often subsidizes and supports its manufacturing base.

China's vast population of low-wage workers and massive consumer market potential has attracted offshoring of manufacturing from companies around the world. In fact there are 49,000 U.S. companies alone operating in China. It is this low-cost manufacturing base that has contributed greatly to its exports and growth, as a major factor in China's uniqueness, making it the world's largest manufacturer, second-largest consumer, largest saver, and probably the second-largest military spender. China has the world's largest shipped goods port capacity. For these reasons, China would seem well positioned to expand globally as long as global demand for its products and manufacturing continues. However, in 2012, some firms were noting that their Chinese labor costs were increasing, energy and shipping costs were rising, and the Chinese currency was appreciating—making it less advantageous to manufacture there than in the past.[55] In fact, in April 2012, the Boston Consulting Group reported on the results of their survey of companies with over $1 billion sales, which indicated that "more than a third of large manufacturers are considering reshoring from China to the U.S.," citing labor costs and product quality as primary considerations.[56]

(Continued)

In all, China is still a developing country, with considerable differences between urban and rural areas making for quite varied markets. The great diversity is indicated by China's eight major languages, several dialects, and several other minority languages. Mandarin is the main language in the north; Cantonese in the south, in particular in Hong Kong. Each language reflects its own history and culture, and therefore markets and economies. Generally speaking, it is clear that China is aggressively opening its doors. However, the fact remains that, in virtually all industrial sectors, state firms play a significant or dominant role. Sixteen state-owned enterprises (SOEs) make up about half of GDP. In addition, central, regional, and local political influences create unpredictability for businesses, as do the arbitrary legal systems, suspect data, and underdeveloped infrastructure.[57] The FCS cautions investors to beware of the following factors:

- China's legal and regulatory system is arbitrary. Protection of intellectual property rights is critical.
- In spite of its progress toward a market economy, China still leans toward protecting its local firms, especially the state-owned ones, from imports, and promotes their exports.
- Political goals and agendas often take precedence over commercially-based decisions.
- Discrepancies of business practices make it difficult for SMEs with limited budgets to get started. The FCS advises those firms to start with fostering a sales network through regional agents or distributors who can assist in keeping track of policy and regulation updates and have local contacts.[58]

How to negotiate with the Chinese is the subject of a further feature in Chapter 5. Presented here are ten basic tips for doing business in China, published by Mia Doucet in CanadExport:

TEN TIPS FOR DOING BUSINESS IN CHINA

When doing business in China, the ability to navigate cross-cultural issues is just as important as the goods and services you bring to the marketplace. This is true whether your company is just now considering the China market, recently gained its first sale or maintains an in-country presence.

Tip #1: Never underestimate the importance of existing connections. You need to be dealing with a Chinese person of influence. If that person feels you are trustworthy enough, and if they can get their network of contacts to trust you, there is a chance you will succeed. Asians want to do business with people they trust. But there is no real trust unless a person is in their circle. At first, they don't know if you will be a good partner. Show respect by keeping some distance. Focus on building the relationship before talking business. Do not go for big profit on your first contract.

Tip #2: To protect your intellectual property, use the same due diligence you would in the West.

Tip #3: Never pressure your Asian colleagues for a decision. To speed up the decision process, slow down. Start from the beginning and work through to a solution in a logical, step-by-step fashion. Then stand your ground.

Tip #4: The negotiation process will be anything but smooth. Your best strategy is a walk away mentality. You have to go in trying not to make the deal. Explain your position in clear, concise words. State your terms clearly. Respectfully. Then be prepared to walk away if your terms are not met.

Tip #5: Respect face. Never argue or voice a difference of opinion with anyone—even a member of your own team. Never make the other person wrong. Never say "no" directly, as that is considered rude and arrogant.

Tip #6: Account for the fact that most Asians understand less spoken English than we think they do. The easiest thing in the world is for a Chinese to say yes. Their smiles and nods have more to do with saving face than getting your meaning. Talk in short sentences. Listen more than you speak. Pause between sentences. Find four or five easy ways to say the same thing. Never ask a question that can be answered with a simple yes. Avoid all slang. Skip humour altogether.

Tip #7: Manage the way you present written information. Document everything in writing and in precise detail. Present your ideas in stages. Write clearly, using plain English text. In order to appeal to Asian visual bias, use sketches, charts, and diagrams.

Tip #8: Prepare for every interaction. Do not count on your ability to wing it. A lack of preparedness can cause loss of face and trust. Do not give or expect to receive partial answers from your Chinese colleagues, as that is considered offensive.

Tip #9: Make sure your facts are 100% accurate in every detail, or you will lose credibility. Do not present an idea or theory that has not been fully researched, proven, or studied beforehand. If you make a mistake, you are not to be trusted.

Tip #10: Everyone on your team needs to know how to avoid costly gaffes.

Most of us are not by nature sensitive to the differences in culture—we have to be taught. Time-honoured passive resistance could bring your company to its knees. It makes sense to teach people the cross-cultural factors that have a direct impact on your profits.

Source: Mia Doucet, author of the award-winning book *China in Motion*, prepared these tips for *CanadExport*, "Ten Tips for Doing Business in China," February 5, 2009. Used with permission of CanadExport, Foreign Affairs and International Trade Canada, September 15, 2011.

India: the 2011 GDP growth for India was 7.4 percent (down from 9.9 percent in 2010). Clearly there is much opportunity for foreign businesses in India, with its one-billion-plus population and a great potential for continued growth. Total bilateral trade with the U.S. for 2010 was $48.8 billion.[59] However, in early 2012, a proposed raft of new taxes led a group of 250,000 global companies to warn that India would "lose significant ground as a destination for international investment" if it adopted the tax changes.[60] With its slow pace of reform, as well as continuing corruption cases, India is losing opportunities to other emerging markets which are more investor friendly. Nevertheless, India ranked second on the A.T. Kearney FDI Confidence Index as shown in Exhibit 1-1.

While China is known as the world's factory, India has become known as the world's services supplier, providing highly skilled and educated workers to foreign companies. India is the world's leader for outsourced back-office services, and increasingly for high-tech services, with outsourcing firms such as Infosys becoming global giants themselves. India is the fastest-growing free-market democracy, yet its biggest hindrance to growth, in particular for the manufacturing sector, remains its poor infrastructure, with both local and foreign companies experiencing traffic gridlocks and power outages. However, much of India's growth has been in technology industries that have not been affected by poor roads, compared with China's manufacturing-based growth. Nevertheless, with growth second only to China, optimism abounds in India about the country's prospects. The expanding middle class of almost 300 million is fuelling demand-led growth. Increasing deregulation is allowing whole sectors to be competitive. Here, too, there is considerable diversity in markets, incomes, and economies; there are fifteen major languages and over 1,600 dialects. Yet India's rise is largely fueled by family firms that often maintain pyramid structures and grow vertically out of convenience because of problems with red-tape, erratic supply chains, and infrastructure:

> *Adaptable, ingenious and combustible, the family firm remains the backbone of India's private sector, not an anachronism. . . . The oldest, such as Aditya Birla, Tata and Bajaj, stretch back over three or more generations and are wily survivors.*[61]

Even so, approximately 40 percent of the profits of India's 100 biggest listed firms come from state-controlled firms; an estimated two-thirds of production from India's finance, energy, and natural resources firms is state controlled, despite India's moves toward further privatization.[62]

A common comparison between China and India notes that China's economy grows because of its government, while India's economy grows in spite of it. However, with its one billion people, many are still mired in poverty. Per capita GDP is below $1,000, although the poverty rate is half that of twenty years ago. While India's large upcoming youth bulge—compared with China—will bring a wave of workers for the economy, it will also bring many more mouths to feed. (India has the largest working-age population in the world, with about one-third under age 25, and one-third under age 15, while China is experiencing the results of its one-child policy.)

In many areas in India the economic transformation is startling, with growth fed by firms like the Tata Group—a global conglomerate producing everything from cars and steel to software and consulting systems. In August 2008, India joined a free-trade agreement with the ten fast-growing countries in the Association of South-East Asian Nations (ASEAN)—making it clear that a regional deal was preferable to a compromise to protect its farmers by saying "no" to the multilateral trading system in the Doha trade talks.[63] Further discussion of doing business in India is included in Chapter 4.

In **South Asia**, an agreement was signed to form the South Asia Association of Regional Cooperation (SAARC), a free trade pact among seven South Asian nations: Bangladesh, Bhutan, India, the Maldives, Nepal, Pakistan, and Sri Lanka, effective January 1, 2006. The agreement was to lower tariffs to 25 percent within three to five years, and to eliminate them within seven years. The member nations comprise 1.5 billion people, with an estimated one-third of them living in poverty. Officials in those countries hope to follow the success of the other Asian regional bloc, the ASEAN.

Australia—although not regarded as part of Southeast Asia, but rather of the region called Oceania, which also includes New Zealand and neighboring islands in the Pacific Ocean—did sign an ASEAN friendship treaty with Southeast Asia. Australia is one of the richest countries in the world, with the mining industry responsible for attracting about a third of its investment inflows. Over 50 percent of her exports go to East Asia, with more transported through the region to markets around the world Australia ranks 6th in the 2012 FDI Confidence Index shown in Exhibit 1-1—actually with the same score as the United States and Germany.

THE AMERICAS **NAFTA**: The goal of the North American Free Trade Agreement (NAFTA) between the United States, Canada, and Mexico was to bring faster growth, more jobs, better working conditions, and a cleaner environment for all as a result of increased exports and trade. This trading bloc—"one America"—has 421 million consumers. The Canada-United States trade is the largest bilateral flow between two countries. In addition, the vast majority—around 84 percent—of both Canadian and Mexican exports goes to the United States. Mexico is the United States' 3rd largest trade partner (after Canada and China) and 2nd largest export market for U.S. products. From Mexico's perspective, the country's exports have exploded under NAFTA; U.S-Mexico bilateral trade increased from $88 billion in 1993, the year prior to the implementation of NAFTA, to $383 billion (estimated) in 2010, an increase of 335 percent.[64] However, Mexico's dependence on the United States for its exports—NAFTA's greatest success—was shown to be a liability in the global economic downturn as Mexico felt the full brunt of declining consumption in the United States. The auto industry, for example, which has flourished under NAFTA, ground to a virtual standstill early in 2009. Mexican auto exports fell more than 50 percent in the first two months of 2009 compared with 2008, and production dropped almost 45 percent. However, in 2011 and 2012, Mexico's growth rate picked up from increasing exports to the U.S. and was on track at around 4 percent growth.[65] Nevertheless Mexico fell off the 2012 FDI Confidence Index; indeed Canada fell from 9th place in 2010 to 20th in 2012, clearly suffering the impact of a decline in the U.S. economy.[66]

Mexican trade policy is among the most open in the world, and the country has become an important exporting and importing power. While the Mexican economic cycles are very dependent on the American economy, she has signed 12 trade agreements with 43 nations, putting 90 percent of its trade under free trade regulations.[67]

Recently, considerable violence among drug gangs, especially in border areas, has created insecurity for businesspeople. In addition, competition from China for offshored jobs from foreign firms has put downward pressure on opportunities for Mexico, as manufacturing facilities and some service facilities migrate from Mexico to China in a race for the lowest cost operations.[68]

MERCOSUR is the fourth largest trading bloc after the EU, NAFTA, and ASEAN. Established in 1991, it comprises the original parties—Brazil, Argentina, Paraguay, and Uruguay; Venezuela is an applicant country awaiting ratification. This regional trading bloc comprises 250 million people and accounts for 75 percent of South America's GDP.

Brazil

Foreign companies are turning to Brazil not just for the size of its booming domestic market, but also as a platform to its Spanish-speaking neighbors. Fiat's factory in Brazil, for example, is the second biggest in the world.[69]

The Federal Republic of Brazil is Latin America's biggest economy and is the fifth largest country in the world in terms of land mass and population, with about 193 million people. According to the U.S. Department of Commerce, Brazil is the 7th largest economy in the world. Bolstered by demand from China and elsewhere for its raw materials, by strong domestic demand, and by a growing middle class, Brazil's economy grew by 7.3 percent in 2010, and ranked 3rd in the 2012 FDI Confidence Index (see Exhibit 1-1).

While most of the developed world has been mired in debt and stunted growth prospects, Brazil's economy is stable and growth prospects are bright. Yet poor infrastructure remains an obstacle (less than 10 percent of roads are paved), and drastic inequality among Brazil's people hampers domestic growth. However, there will be considerable investment and export opportunities as Brazil spends billions in infrastructure development while it prepares for the World Cup in 2014 and the Olympics in 2016. Further discussion regarding doing business in Brazil is included in Chapter 3.

CAFTA: Modeled after the NAFTA agreement, the goal of the U.S.-Central America Free Trade Agreement (**CAFTA**) was to promote trade liberalization between the United States and five Central American countries: Costa Rica, El Salvador, Guatemala, Honduras, and Nicaragua. In 2004, the Dominican Republic joined the negotiations, and the agreement was renamed DR-CAFTA. Since then, U.S. exports to those countries have grown considerably because of the phase-out of most tariffs. CAFTA is considered to be a stepping-stone to the larger Free Trade Area of the Americas (FTAA) that would encompass 34 economies, but which has met with considerable resistance.[70]

Other recent agreements include three trade agreements between the United States and South Korea, Colombia and Panama, all passed on October 12, 2011, bringing to 20 the total number of free trade agreements with the United States.[71]

Other Regions in the World

Sweeping political, economic, and social changes around the world present new challenges to global managers. The move toward privatization has had an enormous influence on the world economy. Economic freedom is a critical factor in the relative wealth of nations.

One of the most striking changes today is that most nations have suddenly begun to develop decentralized, free-market systems in order to manage a global economy of intense competition, the complexity of high-tech industrialization, and an awakening hunger for freedom.

THE RUSSIAN FEDERATION

Coca-Cola Co. and Coca-Cola Hellenic Bottling Company SA, plan to invest $3 billion in Russia over the next five years as part of an ongoing push into emerging markets.

AP IN *NEW YORK TIMES*,
SEPTEMBER 26, 2011.[72]

Foreign investment in Russia, as well as its consumers' climbing confidence and affluence, bode well for the economy. GDP growth for 2011 was about 4.3 percent. Membership in the WTO in 2011 promised additional trade liberalization. Until recently, Russia has been regarded as more politically stable. New land, legal, and labor codes have encouraged foreign firms to take advantage of opportunities in that immense area, in particular the vast natural resources and the well-educated population of 145 million. Moscow, in particular, is teeming with new construction sites, high-end cars, and new restaurants. Export opportunities abound in Russia, with a growing middle class and vast infrastructure needs. However, corruption and government interference persist, along with excessive regulations, lack of the rule of law, and infrastructure problems. The protests of the people in 2011 and 2012 indicated considerable unrest about political procedures that resulted in the return of President Putin. Further discussion of the business environment in Russia is in Chapter 7.

THE MIDDLE EAST

"You start to differentiate in a post-Arab spring world and you look at the different markets that were affected," says Mustafa Abdel-Wadood, chief executive at Abraaj.[73]

FINANCIAL TIMES U.K.,
SEPTEMBER 22, 2011.

The changing geopolitical landscape due to the revolutions across the region, which toppled leaders in Tunisia and Egypt and ousted the regime of Colonel Muammer Gaddafi in Libya, have made investors wary, but looking for opportunities. Egypt, where the political landscape has been redrawn in recent months, is beginning to attract interest from Gulf, Western, and Asian international investors. "I think the main theme when considering whether to enter these markets is the potential for long-term growth that will ultimately lead to a more positive outcome."[74]

According to *The Arab World Competitiveness Report* by the World Economic Forum, the United Arab Emirates is the most competitive economy in the Arab world among the countries at the third and most advanced stage of development. It is followed by Qatar and Kuwait. Among countries at the second stage of development, Tunisia and Oman are the best performing Arab economies while Egypt is the regional best performer in the third group of countries. The Forum predicted there will be prosperity with challenges for the Middle East:

> Oil and gas revenues provide unique investment opportunities, but the region's greatest challenges are likely to be in managing expectations, lowering trade and investment barriers and educating the next generation to handle the wealth that is now being produced. Education is the biggest challenge.[75]

DEVELOPING ECONOMIES

Developing Economies are characterized by change that has come about more slowly as they struggle with low gross national product (GNP) and low per capita income, as well as the burdens of large, relatively unskilled populations and high international debt. Their economic situation and the often-unacceptable level of government intervention discourage the foreign investment they need. Many countries in Central and South America, the Middle East, and Africa desperately hope to attract foreign investment to stimulate economic growth.

THE AFRICAN UNION (AU)

The AU comprises the 53 African countries and was formed from the original Organization of African Unity (OAU) primarily to deal with political issues. According to the International Monetary Fund (IMF), as of 2012, seven of the world's ten fastest growing economies are in Africa. However, there continue to be many major problems in the region. Unfortunately, Africa has received little interest from most of the world's investors, although it receives increasing investment from companies in South Africa, which has the region's biggest economy. On the bright side, however, trade between China and Africa has risen from $10 billion in 2000 to well over $100 billion today. In fact, China's appetite for commodities has led to a $12 billion FDI in 2011.[76] At a growth rate of over 5.2 percent in 2011, more than double that predicted for the U.S. or Europe, prospects for Africa are improving. For example, Coca-Cola's chief executive has targeted the African continent as one of the company's top investment priorities.[77]

South Africa: The South African economy has been growing continuously since 1998, amid a more stable political environment since the defeat of apartheid. This is the longest economic upswing in the country's history although unemployment remains very high.[78] South Africa is a country of 48.7 million people that is rich in diverse cultures, people, and natural resources. "Enjoying remarkable macroeconomic stability and a pro-business environment, South Africa is a logical and attractive choice for U.S. companies to enter the African continent."[79]

The rapid growth of consumer demand, along with increasing tourism and foreign business investment, has made the country's outlook very positive. Foreign investment is encouraged through the Strategic Industrial Project, which provides approved companies with substantial tax reductions as well as other incentives. These incentives, along with more political stability, encouraged the return of most of the foreign companies that had left during the apartheid era. In addition, companies in South Africa no doubt realize that they have a competitive edge on the African continent that they do not have in more developed parts of the world.[80] There is further discussion of the business climate in South Africa in the Chapter 6 opening profile.

For firms willing to take the economic and political risks, developing economies offer considerable potential for international business. Assessing the risk-return trade-offs and keeping up with political developments in these developing countries are two of the many demands on international managers. Among proactive managers taking advantage of such opportunities are those at Intel—a corporation that epitomizes the ways in which "globalization" is affecting less-developed countries (LDCs) and developing economies such as Vietnam, as discussed in the accompanying Management Focus.

The Globalization of Information Technology

Of all the developments propelling global business today, the one that is transforming the international manager's agenda more than any other is the rapid advance in information technology (IT). The explosive growth of IT is both a cause and an effect of globalism. The role of IT in international management is discussed under a later heading "The Technological Environment."

MANAGEMENT IN ACTION
Intel Brings Changes to Vietnam's Economy and Culture[81]

Intel Plant Put Vietnam on High-Tech Map
Intel CEO Paul Otellini, Bloomberg News—October 29, 2010[82]

The United States opened trade relations with Vietnam in 2000, opening the way for that country's expansion. Although Vietnam is a communist country, its rapid growth can be attributed to its entrepreneurial traditions and those aspects of globalization that attract corporations such as Intel to take advantage of new markets and lower costs of production. While the debate continues about whether globalization brings overall positive or negative effects to less developed countries, the inevitable march of trade and investment has led Daniel Altman to believe that "the more relevant question today is whether these multinational relationships can be managed in a way that benefits both guests and hosts." Intel's success in this regard started with the awareness of the tight control of the Vietnamese government in all aspects of society and on foreign companies wishing to do business there.

After painstaking and secret negotiations with Vietnamese government officials who were unused to market economics, Intel's general manager, Rick Howath, decided to build its biggest semiconductor manufacturing plant ever along the Hanoi Highway in Vietnam, a nation of 85 million with limited higher education opportunities. This is Intel Corporation's seventh assembly site of its global network. (Other sites include Penang and Kulim, Malaysia; Cavite, Philippines; Chengdu and Shanghai, China; and San Jose, Costa Rica.) The plant has provided thousands of jobs and training for local workers to produce chips for the company's extensive global supply chain. In this way Intel has demonstrated how multinationals which are industry leaders can change the economic and cultural dynamics in a developing country by the decision to locate a plant there. However, this was no light decision. Intel's company strategic decision-makers spent years investigating and evaluating the benefits and constraints of locating in Vietnam and considerable effort in working with the government in Hanoi. The company's investigations were relentless, evaluating school curricula, traffic congestion, the poor infrastructure, and the size of the average adult in order to tailor the factory to them. Their main concern was finding enough qualified engineers.

In the end, the Vietnamese government's desire to attract multinationals, along with the country's proximity to China and its young, low-cost workforce, convinced Intel to invest $1 billion there for its 115-acre construction site in the new Saigon Hi-Tech Park (Saigon is now called Ho Chi Minh City). The company called the project A-9. (Nine is regarded as a lucky number in Vietnam.) However, this was not until the government-owned Saigon Hi-Tech Park signed a pact with Intel to fight against corruption and improper business conduct. This was the first time a state agency had made such a pact and also a first for Intel, which was concerned about Vietnam's reputation as one of the world's most corrupt countries.

Changes resulting from Intel's investment in Vietnam are already evident. The Vietnamese government is giving Intel's managers unprecedented access to high-ranking officials, and other global giants are showing interest in investing there. The plant will create a higher-end manufacturing base beyond garment assembly lines and create desperately needed professional jobs for its youth. Intel is also bringing its culture to Vietnam. Executives work alongside the workers, with no big offices for the bosses—contrary to Vietnam's hierarchical culture. It also sponsors team-building exercises like karaoke Fridays. Intel's company buses shuttle workers to the plant, passing low-slung shacks, which house so many Vietnamese.

In all, the Vietnamese view the new plant in Ho Chi Minh City with patriotic pride and hope for further economic emergence. For its part, Intel's success is largely attributable to cultivating government officials and to understanding the government's goals and working towards them. These include the desire to increase the use of personal computers and the Internet, and also to build a reputation for Vietnam to export high-tech items. Focusing on local traditions and working with the government's Communist youth group, Intel developed a program under the brand Thanh Giong, a Vietnamese hero, with the goal of beating back the enemy of illiteracy.

The Globalization of Human Capital

Firms around the world have been offshoring manufacturing jobs to low-cost countries for decades. An increasing number of firms have been producing or assembling parts of their products in many countries; that is, outsourcing by contracting to a local firm, and then integrating them into their global supply chains. Although, with the recent much higher cost of fuel greatly increasing shipping rates, some firms were fearful that their cost advantage of producing abroad was being lost. Paul Fichter, owner of Taphandles, for example, made a decision in October 2011 to bring back some of its manufacturing to the United States because of the narrowing advantage of producing in China. Taphandles (beer taps for breweries) was employing 33 people in Seattle and 450 in China. His reasons included the increasing labor costs and benefit costs for competing for employees there, the higher shipping costs because of the rise in oil prices, and the increasing appreciation of the renminbi against the dollar.[83] In addition, hundreds of textile manufacturers, for example, have been diversifying their business to countries such as Cambodia, Vietnam, and Indonesia, where wages are lower than those in China, which have risen around 20 percent in the last three years.[84]

But shipping costs do not affect non-manufacturing jobs, and more and more firms are outsourcing white-collar jobs to India, China, Mexico, and the Philippines: customer support, medical analysis, technical work, computer programming, form filling, and claims processing—all these jobs can now move around the globe in the same way that farming and factory jobs could move a century ago.[85] We have all experienced talking to someone in India when we call the airlines or a technology support service; now increasingly sophisticated jobs are being outsourced, leaving many people in developed economies to worry about job retention. For example, General Electric has about 14,500 employees in India, IBM more than 74,000, and Citigroup more than 10,000.[86] MoFirst provides programming services—a part of India's $88.1 billion per year information technology services and outsourcing industry. The company's office in Bangalore houses twenty or so programmers coding on laptops. Most of its clients are in the U.S., Europe, and the Middle East, and MoFirst bills them $15 to $20 an hour—considerably less than the developers in the U.S. charge. India is experiencing considerable demand for its mobile-app development shops, such as for Apple's iPhone and iPad and for devices for running Google's Android software.[87]

In Bangalore, India, MNCs such as Intel, Dell, IBM, Yahoo!, and AOL employ workers in chip design, software, call centers, and tax processing.[88] Dell has four call centers in India, where the bulk of its 10,000 employees work, as well as software development and product testing centers. Overall, the Indian IT-enabled services (ITES) sector has an estimated 700,000 people worldwide and comprises 35 percent of the Business Process Outsourcing (BPO) market.[89] Recently, however, large Indian IT outsourcing companies such as Infosys Limited and the Tata Group were hiring their staff in the United States.

In China—long the world's low-cost manufacturing hub—jobs are on the upswing for back-office support for financial services and for telecom and retail companies in Asia. Such employees communicate with people in Hong Kong and Taiwan in local languages. While backlash from some European and U.S. firms' clients has resulted in them repatriating high-end jobs, white-collar job migration is still on the rise for firms around the world, bringing with it a new phase in economic globalization and competition. For global firms, winning the "war for talent" is one of the most pressing issues, especially as hot labor markets in emerging markets are causing extremely high turnover rates.[90] However, the shift in economic power to the East presents considerable opportunity for companies and economies in the West because of the rising buying power of the 2.5 billion or so people in those developing countries. In addition, firms from China and India, for example, are expanding overseas, bringing their investment and providing jobs, so that. . . .

You might just find, for example, that your biggest customers are in Chengdu, not Chicago, or that your boss sits in New Delhi, not New York City. Your paycheck could come in renminbi or rupees instead of in euro or dollars.

TIME,
MARCH 28, 2011.[91]

The Global Manager's Role

Whatever your level of involvement, it is important to understand the global business environment and its influence on the manager's role. This complex role demands a contingency approach to dynamic environments, each of which has its own unique requirements. Within the larger context of global trends and competition, the rules of the game for the global manager are set by each country (see Exhibit 1-2): its political and economic agenda, its technological status and level of development, its regulatory environment, its comparative and competitive advantages, and its cultural norms. The astute manager will analyze the new environment, anticipate how

EXHIBIT 1-2   An Open Systems Model

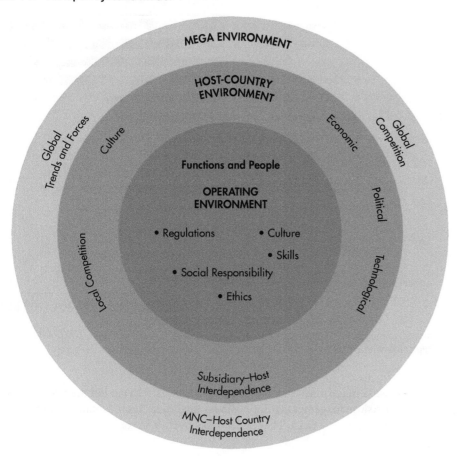

it may affect the future of the company, and then develop appropriate strategies and operating styles. She or he will need to take into account the business practices and expectations of varying sets of suppliers, partners, customers, and local managers. These factors in the manager's role are the subjects of the rest of this book.

THE POLITICAL AND ECONOMIC ENVIRONMENT

Proactive globally-oriented firms maintain an up-to-date profile of the political and economic environment of the countries in which they maintain operations (or have plans for future investment). Surveys of top executives around the world show that **sustainability**—economic, political, social, and environmental—has become a significant worldwide issue. Executives who recognize that fact are leading their companies to develop new policies and to invest in sustainability projects with the purpose of benefiting the environment as well as profitability.[92] The opening profile described the general global risk environment. Among the strategic and operational risks reported by global companies were government regulation, country financial risks and currency risk, and political and social disturbances. These concerns and other risks, as reported by those companies, are shown in Exhibit 1-3.

From a separate survey in 2011 by the Aon Risk Solutions Company, we can see the top ten risks as reported by 960 companies from 58 countries, giving us an overview of how concerns can change over time. The risk of economic slowdown was the number one risk in 17 out of 27 industries surveyed, and across all countries reporting.

Those risks have different relative levels of priority and concern depending on the region. The risk of economic slowdown is the first concern across all regions, while subsequent risks vary across those regions. For example, "failure to attract/retain top talent" is far higher on the list for the Asia Pacific region than for the others. In addition, the Aon report noted that "Senior management's intuition and experience remains the primary method used by survey respondents

EXHIBIT 1-3   **Greatest Risks Affecting FDI Decisions, as Reported by Global Companies**

Risk	Percentage
Government regulation	72%
Country financial risk	67%
Currency risk	63%
Political and social disturbances	62%
Absence of rule of law	34%
Disruption of key supplier, customer, or partner	33%
Corporate governance issues	25%
Security threats to employees or assets	22%
Terrorist attacks	21%
Product quality or safety problems	19%
Theft of intellectual property	17%
IT disruption	17%
Employee fraud or sabotage	8%
Natural disasters	8%
Activist attacks on global or corporate brands	5%

Source: www.atkearney.com, September 12, 2008. Copyright A. T. Kearney, Inc., 2007. All rights reserved.Reprinted with permission.

to identify and assess major risks facing their organizations."[93] That led the researchers to conclude that formal risk management using business analytical tools would be more useful than experience in identifying new risks. The top ten risks overall were:

1. Economic slowdown.
2. Regulatory/legislative changes
3. Increasing competition
4. Damage to reputation/brand
5. Business interruption
6. Failure to innovate/meet customer needs
7. Failure to attract or retain top talent
8. Commodity price risk
9. Technology failure/system failure
10. Cash flow/liquidity risk.[94]

An additional important aspect of the political environment is the phenomenon of ethnicity—a driving force behind political instability around the world. In fact, many uprisings and conflicts that are thought to be political in nature are actually expressions of differences among ethnic groupings. Often, religious disputes lie at the heart of those differences. Uprisings based on religion operate either in conjunction with ethnic differences (as probably was the case in the former Yugoslavia) or as separate from them (as in Northern Ireland). Many terrorist activities are also based on religious differences, as in the Middle East and other parts of the world. Managers must understand the ethnic and religious composition of the host country in order to anticipate problems of general instability, as well as those of an operational nature, such as effects on the workforce, on production and access to raw materials, and on the market.

Political Risk

Clearly, as evidenced by the 2011 "Arab Spring" uprisings in Egypt and elsewhere, major political changes can affect the business environment and risk level almost overnight. As far as political risk is concerned, a 2011 survey—based on 211 countries and territories—by Aon Risk Solutions (the firm discussed earlier), found that the political risk level is rising in more countries than it is declining. That conclusion was based on the level of exposure to factors such as currency inconvertibility and transfer; strikes, riots, and civil commotion; war; sovereign nonpayment; political interference; supply chain interruption; and legal and regulatory risk.[95] It is clear from the past that firms operating in some countries are exposed to political risks that can drastically affect them with little warning, as illustrated by the following example:

After firms from Europe and the United States had moved their factories to China to avoid the taxes and quotas on rare earth exports, China closed the door on them in September 2011:[96]

> *By closing or nationalizing dozens of the producers of rare earth metals . . . China is temporarily shutting down most of the industry and crimping the global supply of the vital resources.*[97]

The managers of a global firm need to investigate the political risks to which they expose their company in certain countries—and the implications of those risks for the economic success of the firm. **Political risks** are any governmental action or politically motivated event that could adversely affect the long-run profitability or value of a firm. The Middle East, as we have seen, has traditionally been an unstable area where political risk heavily influences business decisions.

Nationalization In unstable areas, multinational corporations weigh the risks of nationalization or expropriation. In April 2012, Argentina, under President Cristina Fernandez de Kerchner, announced plans to nationalize Repsol YPF, the Spanish oil company, taking a 51 percent stake in YPF, which accounts for a third of Argentina's oil production.[98] In retaliation, Spain announced that it would restrict imports of biodiesel from Argentina. **Nationalization** refers to the forced sale of an MNC's assets to local buyers, with some compensation to the firm, perhaps leaving a minority ownership with the MNC. As the fallout from the financial meltdown spread around the world in 2009, nationalist impulses gathered storm as government moves to take stakes in ailing industries were verging on partial or full nationalization—though, for the most part, not forcing it. Japan, for example, took a cue from the United States in taking majority stakes in major banks; while in Russia, the Kremlin was exploiting the economic crisis to establish more control over industries that it had long coveted, such as energy.[99]

Expropriation occurs when a local government seizes and provides inadequate compensation for the foreign-owned assets of an MNC; when no compensation is provided, it is confiscation. In countries that have a proven history of stability and consistency, the political risk to a multinational corporation is relatively low. The risk of expropriation is highest in countries that experience continuous political upheaval, violence, and change, as evidenced by actions such as those taken by Hugo Chavez in his continuing drive to place key industries under state control, as shown when he took control of Mexico's Cemex cement plants in Venezuela.

An event that affects all foreign firms doing business in a country or region is called a **macropolitical risk event**. In many regions, **terrorism** poses a severe and random political risk to company personnel and assets and can, obviously, interrupt the conduct of business. According to Micklous, terrorism is "the use, or threat of use, of anxiety-inducing . . . violence for ideological or political purposes."[100] The increasing incidence of terrorism around the world concerns MNCs. In particular, the kidnapping of business executives has become quite common. In addition, the random acts of violence around the world have a downward effect on global expansion, not the least because of the difficulty in attracting and retaining good managers in high-risk areas, as well as the expense of maintaining security to protect people and assets and the cost of insurance to cover them. Companies that go ahead and invest in those high-risk areas do so with the expectation of a higher profit premium to offset risk.

An event that affects one industry or company or only a few companies is called a **micropolitical risk event**. Such events have become more common than macropolitical risk events. Such micro action is often called "creeping expropriation," indicating a government's gradual and subtle action against foreign firms. This is a situation that occurs when you haven't been expropriated, but it takes ten times longer to do anything. Typically, such continuing problems with an investment present more difficulty for foreign firms than do major events that are insurable by political-risk insurers. The following list describes seven typical political risk events common today (and possible in the future):

1. Expropriation of corporate assets without prompt and adequate compensation
2. Forced sale of equity to host-country nationals, usually at or below depreciated book value
3. Discriminatory treatment against foreign firms in the application of regulations or laws
4. Barriers to **repatriation** of funds (profits or equity)

5. Loss of technology or other intellectual property (such as patents, trademarks, or trade names)
6. Interference in managerial decision making
7. Dishonesty by government officials, including canceling or altering contractual agreements, extortion demands, and so forth.[101]

Political Risk Assessment

International companies must conduct some form of political risk assessment to manage their exposure to risk and to minimize financial losses. Typically, local managers in each country assess potentially destabilizing issues and evaluate their future impact on their company, making suggestions for dealing with possible problems. Corporate advisers then establish guidelines for each local manager to follow in handling these problems. Dow Chemical has a program in which it uses line managers trained in political and economic analysis, as well as executives in foreign subsidiaries, to provide risk analyses of each country.

Risk assessment by multinational corporations usually takes two forms. One uses experts or consultants familiar with the country or region under consideration. Such consultants, advisers, and committees usually monitor important trends that may portend political change, such as the development of opposition or destabilizing political parties. They then assess the likelihood of political change and develop several plausible scenarios to describe possible future political conditions. A second and increasingly common means of political risk assessment used by MNCs is the development of internal staff and in-house capabilities. This type of assessment may be accomplished by having staff assigned to foreign subsidiaries, by having affiliates monitor local political activities, or by hiring people with expertise in the political and economic conditions in regions critical to the firm's operations. Frequently, all means are used. The focus must be on monitoring political issues before they become headlines; the ability to minimize the negative effects on the firm—or to be the first to take advantage of opportunities—is greatly reduced once the news spreads through social media or CNN. No matter how sophisticated the methods of political risk assessment become, nothing can replace timely information from people on the front line.

In addition to assessing the political risks facing a firm, alert managers also examine the specific types of impact that such risks may have on the company. For an autonomous international subsidiary, most of the impact from political risks (nationalization, terrorism) will be at the level of the ownership and control of the firm, because its acquisition by the host country would provide the state with a fully operational business. For global firms, the primary risks are likely to be from restrictions (on imports, exports, currency, and so forth), with the impact at the level of the firm's transfers (or exchanges) of money, products, or component parts.

Managing Political Risk

After assessing the potential political risk of investing or maintaining current operations in a specific country, managers face perplexing decisions on how to manage that risk. On one level, they can decide to suspend their firm's dealings with a certain country at a given point—either by the avoidance of investment or by the withdrawal of current investment (by selling or abandoning plants and assets). On another level, if they decide that the risk is relatively low in a particular country or that a high-risk environment is worth the potential returns, they may choose to start (or maintain) operations there and to accommodate that risk through adaptation to the political regulatory environment. That adaptation can take many forms, each designed to respond to the concerns of a particular local area. Some means of adaptation suggested by Taoka and Beeman are as follows:

1. Equity sharing includes the initiation of joint ventures with nationals (individuals or those in firms, labor unions, or government) to reduce political risks.
2. Participative management requires that the firm actively involve nationals, including those in labor organizations or government, in the management of the subsidiary.
3. Localization of the operation includes the modification of the subsidiary's name, management style, and so forth, to suit local tastes. Localization seeks to transform the subsidiary from a foreign firm to a national firm.
4. Development assistance includes the firm's active involvement in infrastructure development (foreign-exchange generation, local sourcing of materials or parts, management training, technology transfer, securing external debt, and so forth).[102]

In addition to avoidance and adaptation, two other means of risk reduction available to managers are dependency and hedging. Some means that managers might use to maintain **dependency**—keeping both the subsidiary and the host nation dependent on the parent corporation—include, for example, maintaining control over key inputs or technology, or control over distribution; other means are through expatriate control in key positions.[103] Firms can also minimize loss through **hedging**, which includes, for example, political risk insurance and local debt financing.

Multinational corporations also manage political risk through their global strategic choices. Many large companies diversify their operations both by investing in many countries and by operating through joint ventures with a local firm or government or through local licensees. By involving local people, companies, and agencies, firms minimize the risk of negative outcomes due to political events. (See Chapters 6 and 7 for further discussion of these and other global strategies.)

Managing Terrorism Risk

No longer is the risk of terrorism for global businesses focused only on certain areas such as South America or the Middle East. That risk now has to be considered in countries such as the United States, which had previously been regarded as safe. Eighty countries lost citizens in the World Trade Center attack on September 11, 2001. Many companies from Asia and Europe had office branches in the towers of the World Trade Center; most of those offices, along with the employees from those countries, were destroyed in the attack. Thousands of lives and billions of dollars were lost, not only by those immediately affected by the attack but also by countless small and large businesses impacted by the ripple effect; global airlines and financial markets were devastated.

As incidents of terrorism accelerate around the world, many companies are increasingly aware of the need to manage the risk of terrorism. In high-risk countries, both IBM and Exxon Mobil try to develop a benevolent image through charitable contributions to the local community. They also try to maintain low profiles and minimize publicity in the host countries by using, for example, discreet corporate signs at company sites.[104]

Some companies have put together teams to monitor the patterns of terrorism around the world. Kidnappings are common in Latin America (as a means of raising money for political activities). In the Middle East, car bombs, airplane hijackings, kidnapping of foreigners, and blackmail (for the release of political prisoners) are common. In Western Europe, terrorists typically aim bombs at U.S.-owned banks and computer companies. Almost all MNCs have stepped up their security measures abroad, hiring consultants in counterterrorism (to train employees to cope with the threat of terrorism) and advising their employees to avoid U.S. airlines when flying overseas. For many firms, however, the opportunities outweigh the threats, even in high-risk areas.

Economic Risk

Closely connected to a country's political stability is its economic environment—and the relative risk that it may pose to foreign companies. A country's level of economic development generally determines its economic stability and, therefore, its relative risk to a foreign firm. Historically, most industrialized nations have posed little risk of economic instability; less-developed nations pose more risk. However, as of 2012, the level of economic risk in Europe, for example, was a great concern around the world, in particular regarding concerns in the eurozone brought about by debt problems in Greece. As in 2008, the interdependence of financial institutions around the world was again threatening a global recession.

In 2011 the Heritage Foundation published its annual Index of Economic Freedom (excerpted in Table 1–2) which covers 183 countries and is based on ten specific freedoms such as trade freedom, business freedom, investment freedom, and property rights—all of which reduce economic risk. Interestingly, the much discussed emerging "BRICs"—Brazil, Russia, India and China—are way down on the list, indicating that there is quite a risk-return trade-off for investment in those markets. (Further details of each country on the index are available at www.heritage.org.)

In economically free societies, governments allow labor, capital, and goods to move freely, and refrain from coercion or constraint of liberty beyond the extent necessary to protect and maintain liberty itself.[105]

TABLE 1–2   Index of Economic Freedom

Rank	Country	Score
1	Hong Kong	89.7
2	Singapore	87.2
3	Australia	82.5
4	New Zealand	82.3
5	Switzerland	81.9
6	Canada	80.8
7	Ireland	78.7
8	Denmark	78.6
9	United States	77.8
10	Bahrain	77.7
113	Brazil	56.3
124	India	54.6
135	China	52.0
143	Russia	50.5

Source: Based on selected data from the Heritage Foundation, 2011. http://www.heritage.org

A country's ability or intention to meet its financial obligations determines its economic risk. The economic risk incurred by a foreign corporation usually falls into one of two main categories. Its subsidiary (or other investment) in a specific country may become unprofitable if (1) the government abruptly changes its domestic monetary or fiscal policies, or (2) the government decides to modify its foreign-investment policies. The latter situation would threaten the company's ability to repatriate its earnings and would create a financial or interest-rate risk. Furthermore, the risk of exchange-rate volatility results in currency translation exposure to the firm when the balance sheet of the entire corporation is consolidated, and may cause a negative cash flow from the foreign subsidiary. Currency translation exposure occurs when the value of one country's currency changes relative to that of another. When exchange-rate changes are radical, repercussions are felt around the world.

Because every MNC operating overseas exposes itself to some level of economic risk, often affecting its everyday operational profitability, managers constantly reassess the level of risk that their companies may face in any specific country or region of the world. Methods of analyzing economic risk or a country's creditworthiness include the quantitative approach, the qualitative approach and the checklist approach.

The **quantitative approach**, says Mathis, "attempts to measure statistically a country's ability to honor its debt obligation"[106] by assigning different weights to economic variables. The **qualitative approach** evaluates a country's economic risk by assessing the competence of its leaders and analyzing the types of policies they are likely to implement. The **checklist approach** relies on a few easily measurable and timely criteria believed to reflect or indicate changes in the creditworthiness of the country. Most corporations recognize that no single approach can provide a comprehensive economic risk profile of a country. Therefore, they try to use a combination of approaches by selecting those variables to follow which they have found to be the most relevant indicators for the company.

THE LEGAL ENVIRONMENT

The prudent global manager consults with legal services, both locally and at headquarters, to comply with host-country regulations and to maintain cooperative long-term relationships in the local area. If the manager waits until a problem arises, little legal recourse may be available outside of local interpretation and enforcement. Indeed, this has been the experience of many foreign managers in China, where financial and legal systems remain limited in spite of attempts to show the world a capitalist face. Managers there often simply ignore their debts to foreign companies as they did under the old socialist system. The lesson for many foreign companies in

China is that they are losing millions because Beijing often does not stand behind the commitments of its state-owned enterprises.

Although no guarantee is possible, the risk of massive losses may be minimized, among other ways, by making sure you get approval from related government offices (national, provincial, and local), by seeing that you are not going to run amok of long-term government goals, and by getting loan guarantees from the headquarters of one of Beijing's main banks. Some of the contributing factors in cases that go against foreign companies are often the personal connections—*guanxi*—involved and the fact that some courts offer their services to the business community for profit. In addition, many judges get their jobs through nepotism rather than by virtue of a law degree.

Although the regulatory environment for international managers consists of the many local laws and the court systems in those countries in which they operate, certain other legal issues are covered by international law, which governs relationships between sovereign countries, the basic units in the world political system. One such agreement, which regulates international business by spelling out the rights and obligations of the seller and the buyer, is the United Nations Convention on Contracts for the International Sale of Goods (CISG). This applies to contracts for the sale of goods between countries that have adopted the convention.

Generally speaking, the manager of the foreign subsidiary or foreign operating division will comply with the host country's legal system. Such systems, derived from common law, civil law, or Islamic law (Sharia Law), are a reflection of the country's culture, religion, and traditions. Under **common law**, used in the United States and 26 other countries of English origin or influence, past court decisions act as precedents to the interpretation of the law and to common custom. **Civil law** is based on a comprehensive set of laws organized into a code. Interpretation of these laws is based on reference to codes and statutes. About 70 countries, predominantly in Europe (e.g., France and Germany), are ruled by civil law, as is Japan. In Islamic countries, such as Saudi Arabia, the dominant legal system is **Islamic law**; based on religious beliefs, it dominates all aspects of life. Islamic law is followed in approximately 27 countries and combines, in varying degrees, civil, common, and indigenous law.

Contract Law

A **contract** is an agreement by the parties concerned to establish a set of rules to govern a business transaction. Contract law plays a major role in international business transactions because of the complexities arising from the differences in the legal systems of participating countries and because the host government in many developing and state-controlled countries is often a third party in the contract. Both common law and civil law countries enforce contracts, although their means of resolving disputes differ. Under civil law, it is assumed that a contract reflects promises that will be enforced without specifying the details in the contract; under common law, the details of promises must be written into the contract to be enforced. Astute international managers recognize that they will have to draft contracts in legal contexts different from their own, and they prepare themselves accordingly by consulting with experts in international law before going overseas. While Western companies want to spell out every detail in a contract, in some countries the contract may be ignored or changed, and in Asia, "there is no shortcut for managing the relationship."[107] In other words, the contract is in the relationship, not on the paper, and the way to ensure the reliability of the agreement is to nurture the relationship.

Neglect regarding contract law may leave a firm burdened with an agent who does not perform the expected functions, or a firm may be faced with laws that prevent management from laying off employees (which, for example, is often the case in some countries in Europe).

Other Regulatory Issues

Differences in laws and regulations from country to country are numerous and complex. These and other issues in the regulatory environment that concern multinational firms are briefly discussed here.

Countries often impose protectionist policies, such as tariffs and non-tariff barriers, quotas, and other import and trade restrictions, to give preference to their own companies and industries. The Japanese have come under much criticism for protectionism, which they use to limit imports of foreign goods while they continue exporting consumer goods (e.g., cars and electronics) on a large scale.

A country's tax system influences the attractiveness of investing in that country and affects the relative level of profitability for an MNC. Foreign tax credits, holidays, exemptions, depreciation allowances, and taxation of corporate profits are additional considerations the foreign investor must examine before acting. Many countries have signed tax treaties (or conventions) that define such terms as "income," "source," and "residency" and spell out what constitutes taxable activities.

The level of government involvement in the economic and regulatory environment varies a great deal among countries and has a varying impact on management practices. In Canada, for example, the government has a significant involvement in the economy. It has a powerful role in many industries, including transportation, petrochemicals, fishing, steel, textiles, and building materials—forming partly owned or wholly owned enterprises. Wholly owned businesses are called Crown Corporations (Petro Canada, Ontario Hydro, Saskatchewan Telecommunications, and so forth), many of which are as large as major private companies. The government's role in the Canadian economy, then, is one of both control and competition. Government policies, subsidies, and regulations directly affect the manager's planning process, as do other major factors in the Canadian legal environment, such as the high proportion of unionized workers (30 percent). In Quebec, the law requiring official bilingualism imposes considerable operating constraints and expenses. For a foreign subsidiary, this regulation forces managers to speak both French and English and to incur the costs of language training for employees, translators, the administration of bilingual paperwork, and so on.

THE TECHNOLOGICAL ENVIRONMENT

The effects of technology around the world are pervasive—both in business and in private lives. In many parts of the world, whole generations of technological development are being skipped over. For example, many people will go straight to a digital phone without ever having had their houses wired under the analog system. In Entasopia, Kenya, its 4,000 inhabitants have no bank, no post office, and scant infrastructure of any kind. Yet it was there that three young engineers, with financial backing from Google, installed a small satellite dish powered by a solar panel, to hook up a handful of computers in the community center to the rest of the world. Google is paying the monthly fees for bandwidth connection. Locals can now send information instantly instead of having to physically travel to deliver it.[108]

Advances in information technology are bringing about increased productivity—for employees, for companies, and for countries. As noted by Thomas Friedman, technology, as well as other factors that are opening up borders—"the opening of the Berlin Wall, Netscape, work flow, outsourcing, offshoring, open-sourcing, insourcing, supply-chaining, in-forming"—have converged to create a more level playing field. The result of this convergence was

> *The creation of a global, Web-enabled playing field that allows for multiple forms of collaboration—the sharing of knowledge and work—in real time, without regard to geography, distance, or, in the near future, even language.*

Now that we are in a global information society, it is clear that corporations must incorporate into their strategic planning and their everyday operations the accelerating macro-environmental phenomenon of *technoglobalism*—in which the rapid developments in information and communication technologies (ICTs) are propelling globalization and vice versa. Investment-led globalization is leading to global production networks, which results in global diffusion of technology to link parts of the value-added chain in different countries. That chain may comprise parts of the same firm, or it may comprise suppliers and customers, or technology-partnering alliances among two or more firms. Either way, technological developments are facilitating, indeed necessitating, the firm network structure that allows flexibility and rapid response to local needs.

Clearly, the effects of technology on global trade and business transactions cannot be ignored; in addition, the Internet is propelling electronic commerce around the world. The ease of use and pervasiveness of the Internet raise difficult questions about ownership of intellectual property, consumer protection, residence location, taxation, and other issues.

New technology specific to a firm's products represents a key competitive advantage to firms and challenges international businesses to manage the transfer and diffusion of proprietary

UNDER THE LENS

Information Technology (IT)

The rapid advancement in IT and its applications around the world has had, and will continue to have, a transformative effect on global business for businesses of all sizes. The speed and accuracy of information transmission are changing the nature of the global manager's job by making geographic barriers less relevant. Indeed, the necessity of being able to access IT is being recognized by managers and families around the world, who are giving priority to that access over other lifestyle accoutrements.

Information can no longer be totally controlled by governments; political, economic, market, and competitive information is available almost instantaneously to anyone around the world, permitting informed and accurate decision making. Even cultural barriers are being lowered gradually by the role of information in educating societies about one another. Indeed, as consumers around the world become more aware, through various media, of how people in other countries live, their tastes and preferences begin to converge, as the "Arab Spring" illustrated.

The explosive growth of information technology is both a cause and an effect of globalism. The information revolution is boosting productivity around the world. Sweden is the most networked economy in the world, followed by Singapore, Finland, Switzerland, and the United States, according to the 2011 edition of the *Global Information Technology Report.* The report assessed 138 economies and ranked their Information Communications Technology (ICT) readiness levels to use and benefit from ICT for increased growth and development. (Table 1–3 shows the top ten as well as the ranks of selected other countries.) The report stresses the key role of ICT as an enabler of a more economically, environmentally, and socially sustainable world. Among the top ten, Finland, Taiwan, and the Republic of Korea posted the most notable improvements.[109]

Indeed, the city of Seoul—where nine of every 10 residents subscribe to a high-speed wireless Internet connection—is already one gigantic hot spot. "By 2015, when 80 percent of the residents are expected to carry smartphones or tablet PCs, wireless connectivity will be almost as free as it is ubiquitous: the municipal authorities are installing free Wi-Fi wireless hot spots in all the city's public spaces, including 360 parks, 3,200 intersections and 2,200 streets around shopping centers."[110] Every subway car, motel room, and street corner has high-speed Internet connectivity.

Making cities such as Seoul "smart" is intended to both improve productivity and attract businesses there. In addition, use of the Internet is propelling electronic commerce around the world (as discussed later in this chapter). Companies around the world are linked electronically to their employees, customers, distributors, suppliers, and alliance partners in many countries, resulting in increased communication and efficiency, as is described in the Procter and Gamble website: "P&G has more than 80 video collaboration studios globally. The immersive environment created by video studios allows employees to

TABLE 1–3   The Network Readiness Index 2011

Top Ten Rank by Country		Selected Other Ranks	
1	Sweden	Germany	13
2	Singapore	United Kingdom	15
3	Finland	Australia	17
4	Switzerland	Japan	19
5	United States	France	20
6	Taiwan, China	China	36
7	Denmark	India	48
8	Canada	Brazil	56
9	Norway	Russia	77
10	Korea, Republic of	Mexico	78

Source: Based on selected data from The Global Information Technology Report 2010–2011, World Economic Forum.

(Continued)

connect face to face from any part of the world—as if they were in the same room. These studios greatly reduce the need for travel—saving money, time, and reducing P&G's carbon footprint."[111]

Technology, in all its forms, gets dispersed around the world by **multinational enterprises (MNEs)** and their alliance partners in many countries. However, some of the information intended for electronic transmission is currently subject to export controls by an EU directive intended to protect private information about its citizens. In addition, some countries, such as China, monitor and limit electronic information flows. So, perhaps IT is not yet "borderless" but rather is subject to the same norms, preferences, and regulations as "human" cross-border interactions.

technology, with its attendant risks. Whether it is a product, a process, or a management technology, an MNC's major concern is the **appropriability of technology**—that is, the ability of the innovating firm to profit from its own technology by protecting it from competitors.

An MNC can enjoy many technological benefits from its global operations. Advances resulting from cooperative research and development (R&D) can be transferred among affiliates around the world, and specialized management knowledge can be integrated and shared. However, the risks of technology transfer and pirating are considerable and costly. Although firms face few restrictions on the creation and dissemination of technology in developed countries, less developed countries often impose restrictions on licensing agreements, royalties, and so forth, as well as on patent protection.

In most countries, governments use their laws to some extent to control the flow of technology. These controls may be in place for reasons of national security. Other countries in earlier stages of development use their investment laws to acquire needed technology (usually labor-intensive technology to create jobs), increase exports, use local technology, and train local people.

The most common methods of protecting proprietary technology are the use of patents, trademarks, trade names, copyrights, and trade secrets. Various international conventions afford some protection in participating countries; more than 80 countries adhere to the International Convention for the Protection of Industrial Property (often referred to as the Paris Union) for the protection of patents. However, restrictions and differences in the rules in some countries not signatory to the Paris Union, as well as industrial espionage, pose continuing problems for firms trying to protect their technology.

One risk to a firm's intellectual property is the inappropriate use of the technology by joint-venture partners, franchisees, licensees, and employees (especially those who move to other companies). Some countries rigorously enforce employee secrecy agreements.

Another major consideration for global managers is the need to evaluate the **appropriateness of technology** for the local environment—especially in less-developed countries. Studying the possible cultural consequences of the transfer of technology, managers must assess whether the local people are ready and willing to change their values, expectations, and behaviors on the job to use new technological methods, whether applied to production, research, marketing, finance, or some other aspect of the business. Often, a decision regarding the level of technology transfer is dominated by the host government's regulations or requirements. In some instances, the host country may require that foreign investors import only their most modern machinery and methods so that the local area may benefit from new technology. In other cases, the host country may insist that foreign companies use only labor-intensive processes, which can help to reduce high unemployment in an area.

When the choice is left to international managers, experts in economic development recommend that managers make informed choices about appropriate technology. The choice of technology may be capital intensive, labor intensive, or intermediate, but the key is that it should suit the level of development in the area and the needs and expectations of the people who will use it.

Global E-Business

Without doubt, the Internet has had a considerable impact on how companies buy and sell goods around the world—mostly raw materials and services going to manufacturers. Internet-based electronic trading and data exchange are changing the way companies do business while breaking down global barriers of time, space, logistics, and culture. However, the Internet is not totally open; governments still make sure that their laws are obeyed in cyberspace. This was evidenced when France forced Yahoo! to stop displaying Nazi trinkets for sale where French people could view them.[112] The reality is that

Different nations, and different peoples, may want a different kind of Internet—one whose language, content, and norms conform more closely to their own.

There is no doubt, however, that the Internet has introduced a new level of global competition by providing efficiencies through reducing the number of suppliers and slashing administration costs throughout the value chain. **E-business** is "the integration of systems, processes, organizations, value chains, and entire markets using Internet-based and related technologies and concepts."[113] **E-commerce** refers directly to the marketing and sales process via the Internet. Firms use e-business to help build new relationships between businesses and customers.[114] The Internet and e-business provide a number of uses and advantages in global business, including the following:

1. Convenience in conducting business worldwide; facilitating communication across borders contributes to the shift toward globalization and a global market.
2. An electronic meeting and trading place, which adds efficiency in conducting business sales.
3. A corporate Intranet service, merging internal and external information for enterprises worldwide.
4. Power to consumers as they gain access to limitless options and price differentials.
5. A link and efficiency in distribution.[115]

Although most early attention was on e-commerce, experts now believe the real opportunities are in business-to-business (**B2B**) transactions. Alibaba (China) for example, is the largest B2B site in the world, with over 60 million subscribers (see the Part 3 comprehensive case on Alibaba). In addition, while the scope, complexity, and sheer speed of the B2B phenomenon, including e-marketplaces, have global executives scrambling to assess the impact and their own competitive roles, estimates for growth in the e-business marketplace may have been overzealous because of the global economic slowdown and its resultant dampening of corporate IT spending. While we hear mostly about large companies embracing B2B, it is noteworthy that a large proportion of current and projected B2B use is by small and medium-sized firms, for three common purposes: supply chain, procurement, and distribution channel.

A successful Internet strategy—especially on a global scale—is, of course, not easy to create. Potential problems abound, as experienced by the European and U.S. companies surveyed by Forrester Research. Such problems include internal obstacles and politics, difficulties in regional coordination and in balancing global versus local e-commerce, languages and cultural differences, and local laws. Such a large-scale change in organizing business clearly calls for absolute commitment from the top, empowered employees with the willingness to experiment, and good internal communications.[116] Barriers to the adoption and progression of e-business around the world include lack of readiness of partners in the value chain, such as suppliers. If companies want to have an effective marketplace, they usually must invest in increasing their trading partners' readiness and their customers' capabilities. Other barriers are cultural. In Europe, for example, "Europe's e-commerce excursion has been hindered by a laundry list of cultural and regulatory obstacles, like widely varying tax systems, language hurdles, and currency issues."[117]

In other areas of the world, barriers to creating global e-businesses include differences in physical, information, and payment infrastructure systems. In such countries, innovation is required to use local systems for implementing a Web strategy. In Japan, for example, very few transactions are conducted using credit cards. Typically, bank transfers and COD are used to pay for purchases. Also, many Japanese use convenience stores, such as 7-Eleven Japan, to pay for their online purchases by choosing that option online.[118]

For these reasons, B2B e-business is likely to expand globally faster than **B2C** (business-to-consumer) transactions, such as Amazon.com. In addition, consumer e-commerce depends on each country's level of access to computers and the Internet, as well as the relative efficiency of home delivery. Clearly, companies who want to go global through e-commerce must localize to globalize, which means much more than just presenting online content in local languages.

Localizing ... also means recognizing and conforming to the nuances, subtleties, and tastes of multiple local cultures, as well as supporting transactions based on each country's currency, local connection speeds, payment preferences, laws, taxes, and tariffs.[119]

In spite of various problems, use of the Internet to facilitate and improve global competitiveness continues to be explored and discovered. In the public sector in Europe, for example, the European Commission advertises tender invitations online in order to transform the way public sector contracts are awarded, using the Internet to build a truly single market.

It is clear that e-business is not only a new Web site on the Internet but also a source of significant strategic advantage. Hoping to capture this strategic advantage, the European Airbus venture—a public and private sector combination—joined a global aerospace B2B exchange for aircraft parts. The exchange illustrates two major trends in global competition: (1) those of cooperative global alliances, even among competitors, to achieve synergies and (2) the use of technology to enable those connections and synergies. Indeed, "leading B2B firms, including Accenture, DuPont, GE, and IBM, spend significant amounts of money and effort building and managing their brands, and those brands account for a significant portion of their market capitalization."[120] In addition, many small businesses exist almost completely online as B2Bs, purchasing, marketing, and selling their products and services in the ether without ever having to build a physical storefront. Their B2B services can even help small businesses look and feel like a large business. Examples of services for small businesses include smallbusiness@yahoo.com, and www.microsoftsmallbusiness.com.[121]

CONCLUSION

A skillful global manager cannot develop a suitable strategic plan or consider an investment abroad without first assessing the environment—political, economic, legal, and technological—in which the company will operate. This assessment should result not so much in a comparison of countries as in a comparison of (1) the relative risk and (2) the projected return on investments among these countries. Similarly, for ongoing operations, both the subsidiary manager and headquarters management must continually monitor the environment for potentially unsettling events or undesirable changes that may require the redirection of certain subsidiaries or the entire company. Some of the critical factors affecting the global manager's environment (and therefore requiring monitoring) are listed in Exhibit 1-4.

Risk in the global environment, as discussed in this chapter, has become the new frontier in global business. The skills of companies and the measures taken to manage their exposure to risk on a world scale will soon largely replace their ability to develop, produce, and market global brands as the key element in global competitive advantage.

EXHIBIT 1-4   **The Environment of the Global Manager**

Political Environment	**Economic Environment**
• Form of government	• Economic system
• Political stability	• State of development
• Foreign policy	• Economic stability
• State companies	• GNP
• Role of military	• International financial standing
• Level of terrorism	• Monetary/fiscal policies
• Restrictions on imports/exports	• Foreign investment
Regulatory Environment	**Technological Environment**
• Legal system	• Level of technology
• Prevailing international laws	• Availability of local technical skills
• Protectionist laws	• Technical requirements of country
• Tax laws	• Appropriability
• Role of contracts	• Transfer of technology
• Protection for proprietary property	• Infrastructure
• Environmental protection	
Cultural Environment (see Part 2)	

The pervasive role of culture in international management will be discussed fully in Part 2, with a focus on how the managerial functions and the daily operations of a firm are also affected by a subtle, but powerful, environmental factor in the host country—that of societal culture.

Chapter 2 presents some increasingly critical, and scrutinized, factors in the global environment—those of sustainability, corporate social responsibility (CSR), and ethical behavior. We will consider a variety of questions: What is the role of the firm in the future of other societies and their people? What stakeholders must managers consider in their strategic and operational decisions in other countries? How do the expectations of firm behavior vary around the world, and should those expectations influence the international manager's decisions? What role does long-term global economic interdependence and sustainability play in the firm's actions in other countries?

Summary of Key Points

1. Competing in the twenty-first century requires firms to invest in the increasingly refined managerial skills needed to perform effectively in a multicultural environment. Managers need a global orientation to meet the challenges of world markets and rapid, fundamental changes in a world of increasing economic interdependence.

2. International management is the process of developing strategies, designing and operating systems, and working with people around the world to ensure sustained competitive advantage.

3. One major direction in world trade is the rise of rapidly developing economies, such as China, India, Brazil, and Russia (often called the BRIC countries). Other emerging markets include Indonesia, Turkey, and South Africa.

4. Drastic worldwide changes present dynamic challenges to global managers. They include the political and economic trend toward the privatization of businesses, uprisings in some countries where people are demanding democracy, rapid advances in information technology, and the management of offshore human capital. Recently, global economic woes have been causing a resurgence of protectionism and nationalism around the world.

5. Global managers must be aware of political risks around the world that can adversely affect the long-run profitability or value of a firm. Managers must evaluate various means to either avoid or minimize the effects of political risk.

6. The risk of terrorist activity represents an increasing risk around the world. Managers have to decide how to incorporate that risk factor in their strategic and operational plans.

7. Economic risk refers to a country's ability to meet its financial obligations. The risk is that the government may change its economic policies, thereby making a foreign company unprofitable or unable to repatriate its foreign earnings.

8. The regulatory environment comprises the many different laws and courts of those nations in which a company operates. Most legal systems derive from the common law, civil law, or Islamic law.

9. Use of the Internet in e-commerce—in particular, in business-to-business (B2B) transactions—and for intracompany efficiencies, has become a critical factor in global competitiveness.

10. The appropriability of technology is the ability of the innovating firm to protect its technology from competitors and to obtain economic benefits from that technology. Risks to the appropriability of technology include technology transfer, pirating, and legal restrictions on the protection of proprietary technology. Intellectual property can be protected through patents, trademarks, trade names, copyrights, and trade secrets.

Discussion Questions

1. Poll your classmates about their attitudes towards "globalization." What are the trends and opinions around the world that underlie those attitudes?

2. Describe the recent effects of financial globalization on the world economy. What actions have governments taken to offset negative effects? Are they working?

3. How has the economic downturn impacted trends in protectionism and nationalization?

4. Discuss examples of recent macropolitical risk events and the effect they have or might have on a foreign subsidiary. What are micropolitical risk events? Give some examples and explain how they affect international business.

5. What means can managers use to assess political risk? What do you think is the relative effectiveness of these different methods? At the time you are reading this, what countries or areas do you feel have political risk sufficient to discourage you from doing business there?

6. Can political risk be "managed"? If so, what methods can be used to manage such risk, and how effective are they? Discuss the lengths to which you would go to manage political risk relative to the kinds of returns you would expect to gain.

7. Explain what is meant by the economic risk of a nation. Use a specific country as an example. Can economic risk in this country be anticipated? How? How does economic instability affect other nations?

8. Discuss the importance of contracts in international management and how contracts are viewed in other countries. What steps must a manager take to ensure a valid and enforceable contract?

9. Discuss the effects of various forms of technology on international business. What role does the Internet play? Where is all this leading? Explain the meaning of the "appropriability of technology."

What role does this play in international competitiveness? How can managers protect the proprietary technology of their firms?

10. Discuss the risk of terrorism. What means can managers use to reduce the risk or the effects of terrorism? Where in the world, and from what likely sources, would you anticipate terrorism?

Application Exercises

1. Do some further research on the technological environment. What are the recent developments affecting businesses and propelling globalization? What problems have arisen regarding use of the Internet for global business transactions, and how are they being resolved?

2. Consider recent events and the prevailing political and economic conditions in the Russian Federation. As a manager who has been considering investment there, how do you assess the political and economic risks at this time? What should be your company's response to this environment?

Experiential Exercise

In groups of three, represent a consulting firm. You have been hired by a diversified multinational corporation to advise on the political and economic environment in different countries. The company wants to open one or two manufacturing facilities in Asia. Choose a specific type of company and two specific countries in Asia and present them to the class, including the types of risks that would be involved and what steps the firm could take to manage those risks.

Internet Resources

Visit the Deresky Companion Website at www.pearsonhighered.com/deresky for this chapter's Internet resources.

CASE STUDY

Apple's iPhones—Not "Made in America"[1]

Source: Alex Segre/Alamy

Apple has become one of the best-known, most admired and most imitated companies on earth, in part through an unrelenting mastery of global operations.[2]

There are risks and rewards for all in a global economy. The globalization of human capital results in a range of winners and losers around the world: companies and their stockholders, consumers, contractors, firms up and down the supply chain, employed people, and unemployed people, as well as their economies. In February 2011, President Obama asked Apple's Steve Jobs why Apple could not bring back all the jobs it used to provide in the United States. The jobs related to most high-tech products made by companies such as Dell, HP, and Apple have now migrated overseas, including those for Apple's 70 million iPhones, 30 million iPads, and 59 million other products sold in 2011. Breaking down the retail price of $500 for Apple's iPhone, for example, *Time* magazine estimates that $61 worth of value comes from Japan, with its high-end technology manufacturing; $30 of value is added from Germany; $23 from South Korea; $7 from Chinese assembly lines; $48 from "unspecified"; and $11 from the U.S. Those inputs total $179 for parts and assembly abroad, leaving Apple, the inventor in the U.S., a profit of $321.[3] For the first quarter of 2012, Apple made $13 billion in profit.

Although Apple directly employs 43,000 in the U.S. and 20,000 overseas, an additional 700,000 people engineer, build, and assemble iPads, iPhones, and Apple's other products in Asia and Europe. Sophisticated component parts outsourced in various countries are assembled in China. Some of those are contracted to the Taiwanese-headquartered company Foxconn's Longhua factory campus in Shenzhen, for example, where over 300,000 employees live in dorms, eat on site, and churn out iPhones, Sony PlayStations, and Dell computers. Foxconn Technology, with 1.2 million employees in plants throughout the country, is China's largest exporter and assembles an estimated 40 percent of the world's consumer electronics, including for customers such as Amazon, Dell, Hewlett-Packard, Nintendo, Nokia, and Samsung. No other factories in the world have the manufacturing scale of Foxconn.

The answer to the President's question is not as simple as the ability to acquire cheaper labor overseas; Apple's executives and those at other high-tech firms claim that "Made in the U.S.A" is not a competitive strategy for them because America does not compare favorably with the industrial skills, hard work, and flexibility that can be found in companies such as Foxconn. Questions as to what corporate America owes to Americans are met with the example of thousands of Chinese workers being roused in the night to accommodate a redesigned iPhone screen, and within a few days being able to produce 10,000 iPhones a day—a feat not possible in U.S. factories. While the cost of labor is a small percentage of an iPhone's cost, the major advantage and cost saving in China is in the management of supply chains and rapid access to component parts and manufacturing supplies from various factories in close proximity. In addition, Apple maintains that the large number of engineers and other skilled workers who could be accessed on short notice in China simply are not readily available in the United States; nor are the factories with the scale, speed, and flexibility that such a high-tech company needs. Apple executives give the example of visiting a factory to consider whether it could do the necessary work to cut the glass for the iPhone's touchscreen. Upon their arrival, a new wing of the plant was already being built "in case you give us the contract."[4] Fareed Zakaria, in *Time,* maintains that this competitive edge is gained largely through Chinese government subsidies and streamlined regulations in order to boost domestic manufacturing. In the end, however, Apple maintains that:

> We don't have an obligation to solve America's problems. Our only obligation is making the best product possible.[5]

However, after a number of suicides at Foxconn in 2010, reportedly attributable to the poor working conditions and excessive hours for very low pay, Apple was under some pressure from negative publicity; subsequently Foxconn raised wages, retained counselors, and literally strung nets from its highest buildings (to catch people). Apple does have a supplier code of conduct. In January 2012, Apple joined the Fair Labor Association (FLA), the first technology company to do so, and asked the group to do an independent assessment of conditions at its major factories. This move followed the company's own report that documented numerous labor violations, including employees doing 60 hour workweeks and not getting paid proper overtime. A few days after the FLA started its investigation, Foxconn said that they would increase salaries for some workers by 16% to 20%—to about $400 a month before overtime—and that they would reduce overtime. While this is encouraging news for workers' rights, it should be noted that Apple and other contractors are known to only allow the slimmest of profits to its suppliers, which results in the suppliers trying anything to reduce their costs, such as using cheaper and more toxic chemicals or making their employees work faster and longer.

> "The only way you make money working for Apple is figuring out how to do things more efficiently or cheaper," said an executive at one company that helped bring the iPad to market. "And then they'll come back the next year, and force a 10 percent price cut."[6]

China is being forced to take notice of such problems and labor is gaining some ground; the issue then is that firms have already started to move jobs to other countries with lower wages.

1. Harding, Robin; Hille, Kathrin; Jung-a, Song; Kwong, Robin, "Apple, HP and Dell Probe Foxconn," *Financial Times,* London (UK), May 27 2010; Charles Duhigg and Keith Bradsher, "How U.S. Lost Out on iPhone Work," www.nytimes.com, January 21, 2012; Jason Dean, "Corporate News: China Worker Suicides Draw Scrutiny," *Wall Street Journal,* May 15, 2010: B.5; Frederik Balfour and Tim Culpan, "The Man Who Makes Your iPhone," *Bloomberg Business Week,* September 9, 2010; Andrew Morse and Nick Wingfield, "Apple Audits Labor Practices—Company Says Suppliers Hired Underage Workers, Violated Other Core Policies," *Wall Street Journal,* March 1, 2010: B.3; Duncan Hewitt, "Labor's Day in China: Still, there's a risk for China: As labor's lot improves, employers may move where wages are lower and workers more pliable," *Newsweek* 155. 25, June 21, 2010; Ton Dokoupil, "The Last Company Town: There was a time when employers provided everything: houses, hospitals, bars. Such a place still exists—but not for long. Welcome to Scotia, Calif.," *Newsweek* 157. 8, February 21, 2011; Charles Duhigg and David Barboza, "In China, Human Costs Are Built Into an iPad," www.nytimes.com, January 25, 2012; Fareed Zakaria, "The Case for Making It in the U.S.A.," *Time,* February 6, 2012; Nick Wingfield, "Apple Announces Independent Factory Inspections," www.nytimes.com, February 13, 2012; David Barboza, "Foxconn Plans to Lift Pay Sharply at Factories in China," *New York Times,* February 18, 2012.
2. Duhigg and Bradsher, 2012.
3. M. Schuman, "Adding Up the iPhone: How an American Invention Makes Money for the World," *Time,* May 16, 2011.
4. Ibid.
5. Duhigg and Bradsher, 2012.
6. Duhigg and Barboza, January 25, 2012.

Case Questions

1. What is meant by the globalization of human capital? Is this inevitable as firms increase their global operations?
2. How does this case illustrate the threats and opportunities facing global companies in developing their strategies?
3. Comment on the Apple executive's assertion that the company's only obligation is making the best product possible. "We don't have an obligation to solve America's problems."
4. Who are the stakeholders in this situation and what, if any, obligations do they have?
5. How much extra are you prepared to pay for an iPhone if assembled in the United States?
6. How much extra are you prepared to pay for an iPhone assembled in China but under better labor conditions or pay? What kind of trade-off would you make?
7. To what extent do you think the negative media coverage has affected Apple's recent decision to ask the FLA to do an independent assessment and the subsequent decision by Foxconn to raise some salaries? What do you think will happen now?

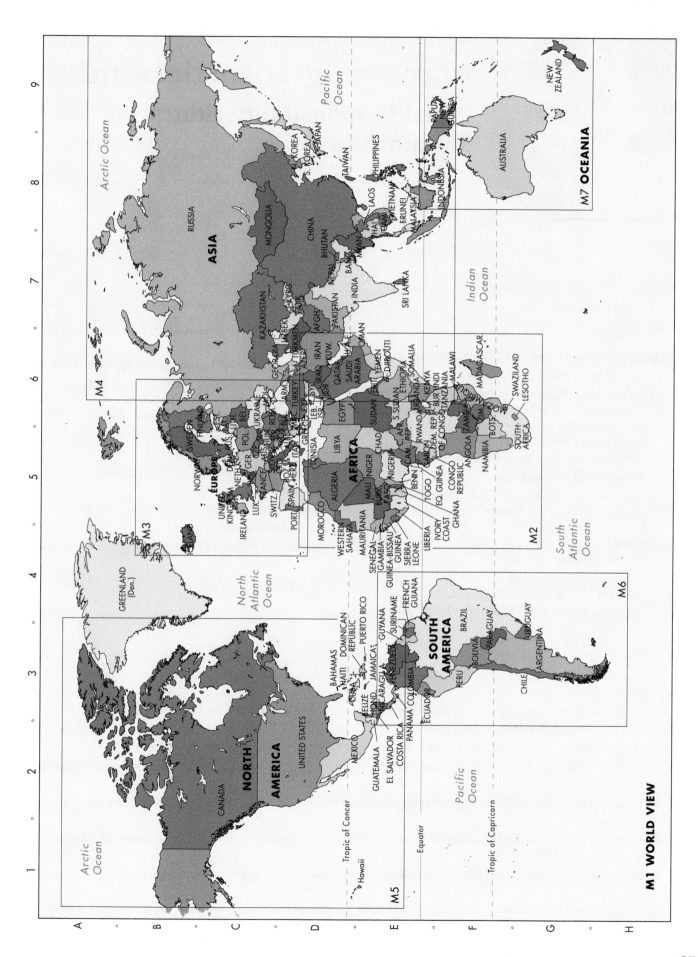

M1 WORLD VIEW

37

2 Managing Interdependence
Social Responsibility, Ethics, Sustainability

OBJECTIVES

1. To appreciate the complexities involved in the corporation's obligations toward its various constituencies around the world.

2. To understand the changing perceptions of and demands on corporations doing business in other countries, in particular their responsibilities toward human rights.

3. To acknowledge the strategic role that CSR and codes of ethics must play in global management.

4. To provide guidance to managers to maintain ethical behavior amid the varying standards and practices around the world.

5. To recognize that companies must provide benefits to the host country in which they operate in order to maintain cooperation.

6. To discuss the need for corporations to consider *sustainability* in their long-term plans in order to manage environmental impacts on host locations.

7. To identify the challenges involved in human rights issues when operating around the world.

OPENING PROFILE: MCDONALD'S CSR EXPERIENCE IN CHINA

CKGSB (Cheung Kong Graduate School of Business) interviews Bob Langert, VP of McDonald's for Corporate Social Responsibility

Q: In the 1990s, McDonald's was seen as promoting waste, unhealthy lifestyles, and a uniform global culture. How did McDonald's address this challenge to its reputation?

A: We learnt not to be defensive, because people will keep on attacking you. During the '90s, we defined our own framework for addressing supply chain issues, health and nutrition issues, people issues, and environmental issues. So when activists come to us now, we can say, "Here's how we're training and developing our people. Here's how we're promoting economic development within McDonald's." We will always be criticized because we're so visible, but today, we invite that criticism. We know we're doing good things and we can back them up with a sound strategy.

Q: McDonald's forged its strategy in response to criticism. Why should Chinese companies create CSR strategies before being attacked?

A: If you wait, usually it's too late to do something that makes sense for your business. If you're strategic, you can find something that will help your business grow. We have found that many of our strategies have helped us become more efficient. When it comes to the environment, if we produce less waste and use less packaging, we will save money. If you're smart about it, CSR could be win-win. If you're not, it could be lose-lose. Producing CSR solutions in a crisis won't be practical and may cost you money.

Q: Chinese companies that develop products for an overseas market often suffer from a credibility gap. How can communication help them overcome this?

A: I identify with that feeling. Every survey I see for multinational companies says that the trust factor for McDonald's is not high. We know we're better off having partnerships with third parties, whether NGOs, academics, or other third-party institutions. So if we're developing an environmental scorecard, we work with a large environmental partner. If we're looking at advancing supply chain practices, we'll work with groups like the World Wildlife Fund. And when they partner with us and they see what we do, they help us gain credibility that is tough to achieve in a very critical marketplace.

Q: But why should Chinese companies marketing their products abroad be interested in involving NGOs and non-profits and in publicizing the reports?

A: At the heart of it, it's about consumers' care. You could debate how much they act upon the information, change their behavior, or buy according to corporate responsibility issues. It varies across the world. But look at the upward trends. The global consumer, in practically every part of the world, is going to act upon this more and more. And even if it's only in their hearts and not in their behavior, that still is a big part of gaining the loyalty of your customer base. So I would encourage it for business reasons. It's a good way to grow, a good way to be more relevant, and a good way to bring more innovation and efficiency into your business.

Q: As you said, consumer attitudes vary greatly across the world. What are you seeing in China? What sort of CSR initiatives is McDonald's doing here, in your largest-growing market?

A: For one, we provide a lot of economic development by bringing business into China. This includes a lot of jobs—I think we employ 60,000 people in China—but also a huge supply chain. When we started in China 20 years ago, very little of what we bought came from China. Today, virtually everything comes from China. So we think that's an important contribution to society. We also started a chapter of philanthropy as well: the Ronald McDonald Charities, which helps kids in need, especially with medical needs, is something we started about four years ago. On the environmental end, I'd say that energy is a big issue. We know that China is a place where there's a lot of booming energy technology and innovation, and we want to tap into that. We use a fair amount of energy in our restaurants, and I'd say that that's our #1 environmental impact that we want to minimize.

Q: And how are you seeing Chinese consumers respond to this? Is there increasing loyalty to McDonald's among Chinese consumers as a result of your CSR activities here?

A: I think it's too soon to tell. But I think the way we would measure that is through our trust scores, and our trust scores in China are on a good trend. But it's very hard to pinpoint things related just to

(Continued)

CSR. Certainly, we think that a big part of our brand and a big part of our reputation involves gaining the trust of customers, including those in China. We want them to trust our business, trust that the food we serve comes from high-quality, safe sources; that we treat our people right; that we treat the environment right. It's going to pay off in the end.

Source: Cheung Kong Graduate School of Business, www.cheungkong-gsb.com, 2011. Used with Permission.

Global interdependence is a compelling factor in the global business environment, creating demands on international managers to take a positive stance on issues of social responsibility and ethical behavior, economic development in host countries, and ecological protection around the world.

Managers today are usually quite sensitive to issues of social responsibility and ethical behavior because of pressures from the public, from interest groups, from legal and governmental concerns, and from media coverage (as illustrated in the opening profile). The United Nations published guidelines for the responsibilities of transnational corporations and called for companies to be subject to monitoring, verification, and censure. Though many companies agree with the guidelines, they resist the notion that corporate responsibility should be regulated and question where to draw the line between socially responsible behavior and the concerns of the corporation's other stakeholders.[1] In the domestic arena, managers are faced with numerous ethical complexities. In the international arena, such concerns are compounded by the larger numbers of stakeholders involved, including customers, communities, allies, and owners in various countries.

This chapter's discussion focuses separately on issues of social responsibility and ethical behavior, though considerable overlap can be observed. The difference between the two is a matter of scope and degree. Whereas ethics deals with decisions and interactions mostly on an individual level, decisions about social responsibility are broader in scope, tend to be made at a higher level, affect more people, and reflect a general stance taken by a company or a number of decision makers. Also discussed separately is the topic of sustainability—although it, too, falls under the umbrella of **corporate social responsibility (CSR)**.

THE SOCIAL RESPONSIBILITY OF MNCs

" … *advocates of corporate social responsibility consider it a wealth-creating opportunity that will attract new consumers, idealistic employees, and the potential for reduced capital cost; … critics claim corporate social responsibility is a form of taxation that reduces the value-creation process of capital.*"[2]

HARVARD BUSINESS REVIEW,
JUNE 2011.

"*Ikea is investing €125 million, or $163 million, in social programs to help women and children in India and elsewhere in South Asia.… We're not on the stock exchange, so we can be very long term.*"

MIKAEL OHLSSON, IKEA CEO, WWW.NYTIMES.COM,
SEPTEMBER 20, 2010[3]

Multinational corporations (MNCs) and multinational enterprises (MNEs) have been, and—to a lesser extent—continue to be, at the center of debate regarding corporate social responsibility (CSR), particularly the benefits versus harm wrought by their operations around the world, especially in developing countries. The criticisms of MNCs have been lessened in recent years by the decreasing economic differences among countries, by the emergence of developing countries' own multinationals, and by the greater emphasis on social responsibility by MNCs.

Issues of social responsibility continue to center on poverty and lack of equal opportunity around the world, the environment, consumer concerns, and employee safety and welfare. Many argue that, since MNCs operate in a global context, they should use their capital, skills, and power to play proactive roles in handling worldwide social and economic problems and that, at the least, they should be concerned with host-country welfare. Others argue that MNCs already

UNDER THE LENS

Shareholders Pressure Walmart for Transparency about How Its Suppliers Treat Workers

Illustrating that shareholders are not always focused only on profits, the New York City Pension Funds, a minority shareholder in Walmart, is pressuring the company to require its suppliers to give annual reports about working conditions in their factories.[4] The fund owns 5.7 million shares in Walmart; however, that is still only less than 0.2 percent of the total.[5] Clearly the public is bringing pressure to bear on companies that source great amounts of supplies from developing countries. Kalpona Akter, a Bangladeshi labor organizer who presented the proposal at the Walmart annual shareholders' meeting on May 27, 2011, complained that many of the Bangladesh factories that produced goods for Walmart mistreated their workers.[6] She said that while many factories have implemented the minimum wage, "we haven't seen any Walmart suppliers giving a living wage to workers; … when the auditor goes to the factory, the worker is coached by the management to tell lies in front of the auditors—that they are being paid living wages, that they are not being harassed."[7]

Labor activists in China, for example, state that Walmart makes suppliers compete for the company's business on the basis of price. "Walmart pressures the factory to cut its price, and the factory responds with longer hours or lower pay," said a Chinese labor official, who declined to be named for fear of punishment. "And the workers have no options."[8]

For its part, Walmart contests these claims, saying that suppliers are required to meet Walmart's standards or lose their contracts; and also that it would be very difficult to get suppliers to give comprehensive annual reports on working conditions. In any event, it is generally known that suppliers often do not enforce the law regarding minimum wages, or enforce standards required by the companies.[9] Walmart is the largest importer of foreign goods in the United States.

have a positive impact on developing economies by providing managerial training, investment capital, and new technology, as well as by creating jobs and improving infrastructure. Certainly, multinational corporations constitute a powerful presence in the world economy and often have a greater capacity than local governments to induce change. The sales, debts, and resources of some of the largest multinationals exceed the gross national product, the public and private debt, and the resources, respectively, of some nations.

The concept of **international social responsibility** includes the expectation that MNCs concern themselves with the social and economic effects of their decisions. The issue is how far that concern should go and what level of planning and control that concern should take, as illustrated by the Walmart example in the accompanying Under the Lens section.

Opinions on the level of social responsibility that a domestic firm should demonstrate range from one extreme—the only responsibility of a business is to make a profit, within the confines of the law, in order to produce goods and services and serve its shareholders' interests[10]—to another extreme—companies should anticipate and try to solve problems in society. Between these extremes are varying positions described as socially reactive, in which companies respond to some degree of currently prevailing social expectations and to the environmental and social costs of their actions, as illustrated in the opening profile on McDonald's.

The stance toward social responsibility that a firm should take in its international operations, however, is much more complex—ranging perhaps from assuming some responsibility for economic development in a subsidiary's host country to taking an active role in identifying and solving world problems. The increased complexity regarding the social responsibility and ethical behavior of firms across borders is brought about by the additional stakeholders in the firm's activities through operating overseas. As illustrated in Exhibit 2-1, managers are faced not only with considering stakeholders in the host country but also with weighing their rights against the rights of their domestic stakeholders. Most managerial decisions will have a trade-off of the rights of these stakeholders—at least in the short term. For example, a decision to discontinue using children in Pakistan to sew soccer balls means the company will pay more for adult employees and will, therefore, reduce the profitability to its owners. That same decision—while taking a stand for human rights according to the social and ethical expectations in the home country and bowing to consumers' demands—may mean that those children and their families go hungry or are forced into worse working situations. Another decision to keep jobs at home to satisfy local

EXHIBIT 2-1   **MNC Stakeholders**

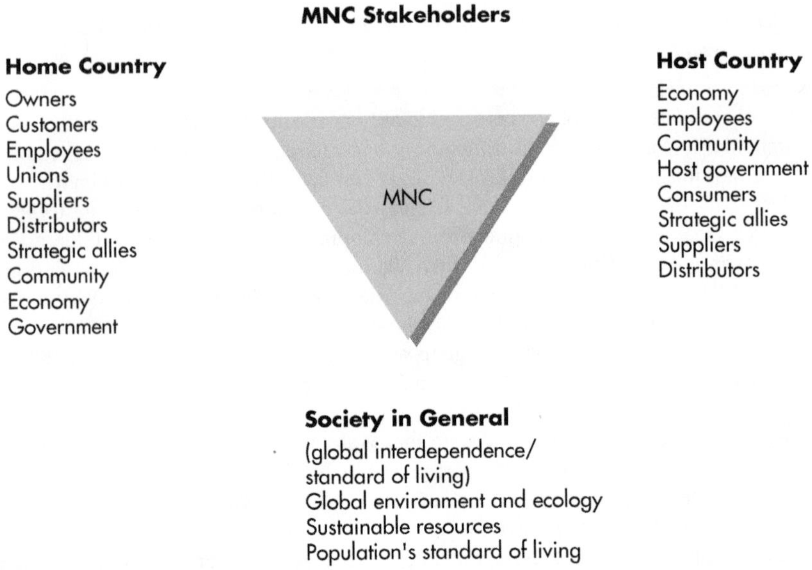

MNC Stakeholders

Home Country
Owners
Customers
Employees
Unions
Suppliers
Distributors
Strategic allies
Community
Economy
Government

MNC

Host Country
Economy
Employees
Community
Host government
Consumers
Strategic allies
Suppliers
Distributors

Society in General
(global interdependence/
standard of living)
Global environment and ecology
Sustainable resources
Population's standard of living

employees and unions will mean higher prices for consumers and less profit for shareholders. In addition, if competitors take their jobs to cheaper overseas factories, a company may go out of business, which will mean no jobs at all for the domestic employees and a loss for the owners.

Paul Krugman contends that opposing industrialization based on low wages "means that you are willing to deny desperately poor people the best chance they have of progress for the sake of what amounts to an aesthetic standard—that is, the fact that you don't like the idea of workers being paid a pittance to supply rich Westerners with fashion items."[11]

Clearly, foreign investment in China, for example, has driven spectacular growth, increased wages, and radically lowered the poverty rate. This compares with Bangladesh, with minimal foreign investment, and a population continuing in abject poverty.[12] Nevertheless, the campaigns of anti-sweatshop activists have resulted in some improvements in workers' lives in other countries, in particular regarding health and safety issues.

In spite of conflicting agendas, there is some consensus about what CSR means at a basic level—that "corporate activity should be motivated in part by a concern for the welfare of some non-owners, and by an underlying commitment to basic principles such as integrity, fairness and respect for persons."[13]

In addition, it is clear that there are long-term competitive benefits deriving from CSR, much of which result from the goodwill, attractiveness, and loyalty of the various stakeholders connected with the company. These may be in the local area, such as government, suppliers, employees, brand reputation, etc., or far-flung, such as consumers. Ikea, quoted previously, is an example of a long-term attitude to CSR. Ikea, the Swedish home retailer with 317 stores worldwide, gave up its plans to open dozens of stores in India after the Indian government would not lift limits on foreign investment in the retail sector. Even so, Ikea plans to double the amount of goods it buys in India, and is investing 125 million euro (about $163 million) in social programs to help women and children in India and elsewhere in South Asia. These investments make Ikea the largest corporate partner in the world to aid agencies including UNICEF and Save the Children.[14] (As an update, as this book goes to press, Ikea announced in June 2012 that the company had been granted permission to open 25 stores in India under a policy change that allows some retailers to own 100 percent of their units there.[15] It would seem, from this development, that the company's benevolence did pay off.)

Manuela Weber suggests that the impact of CSR on business benefits, listed below, can increase the firm's competitiveness and thus economic success.

Business benefits from CSR[16]

- Improved access to capital
- Secured license to operate

- Revenue increases
- Cost decreases
- Risk reduction
- Increase in brand value
- Improved customer attraction and retention
- Improved reputation
- Improved employee recruitment, motivation, and retention.

CSR: Global Consensus or Regional Variation?

With the growing awareness of the world's socioeconomic interdependence, global organizations are beginning to recognize the need to reach a consensus on what should constitute moral and ethical behavior. Some think that such a consensus is emerging because of the development of a **global corporate culture**—an integration of the business environments in which firms currently operate. This integration results from the gradual dissolution of traditional boundaries and from the many intricate interconnections among MNCs, internationally linked securities markets, and communication networks. Nevertheless, there are commonly acknowledged regional variations in how companies respond to CSR:

> The U.S. and Europe adopt strikingly different positions that can be traced largely to history and culture. In the U.S., CSR is weighted more towards "doing business right" by following basic business obligations; ... in Europe, CSR is weighted more towards serving—or at least not conflicting with—broader social aims, such as environmental sustainability.
>
> THE FINANCIAL TIMES[17]

While making good faith efforts to implement CSR, companies operating abroad face confusion about the cross-cultural dilemmas it creates, especially in regard to how to behave in host countries, which have their own differing expectations and agendas. Recommendations about how to deal with such dilemmas include:

- Engaging stakeholders (and sometimes nongovernmental organizations, or NGOs) in a dialogue.

- Establishing principles and procedures for addressing difficult issues such as labor standards for suppliers, environmental reporting, and human rights.

- Adjusting reward systems to reflect the company's commitment to CSR.[18]

Although it is very difficult to implement a generalized code of morality and ethics in individual countries, such guidelines do provide a basis of judgment regarding specific situations. Bowie uses the term **moral universalism** to address the need for a moral standard that is accepted by all cultures.[19] Although, in practice, it seems unlikely that a universal code of ethics will ever be a reality, Bowie says that this approach to doing business across cultures is far preferable to other approaches, such as ethnocentrism or ethical relativism. With an **ethnocentric approach**, a company applies the morality used in its home country—regardless of the host country's system of ethics.

A company subscribing to **ethical relativism**, on the other hand, simply adopts the local moral code of whatever country in which it is operating. With this approach, companies run into value conflicts, such as continuing to do business in China despite home-country objections to China's continued violation of human rights. In addition, public pressure in the home country often forces the MNC to act in accordance with ethnocentric value systems anyway. In one instance, the Food and Drug Administration (FDA) has been pressuring U.S. manufacturers of silicone-filled breast implants (prohibited in the United States for cosmetic surgery because of health hazards) to adopt a voluntary moratorium on exports. While Dow Corning has ceased its foreign sales—citing its responsibility to apply the same standards internationally as it does domestically—other major manufacturers continue to export the implants, often from their factories in other countries. And in 2011, "facing pressure from universities and student groups, Nike announced an agreement on Monday in which it pledged to pay $1.54 million to help 1,800 workers in Honduras who lost their jobs when two subcontractors closed their factories."[20]

The difficulty, even in adopting a stance of moral universalism, is in deciding where to draw the line. Individual managers must at some point decide, based on their own morality, when they feel a situation is simply not right and to withdraw their involvement.

One fact, however, is inescapable: in a globalized market economy, CSR has to be part of modern business.

From CSR to Shared Value?

According to Porter and Kramer, the concept of social responsibility in which societal issues are regarded by corporations as legal or image concerns outside of the main business is a short-sighted approach to value creation and therefore to competitiveness.[21] Creating Shared Value (CSV)—that is, expanding the pool of economic and social value—"leverages the unique resources and expertise of the company to create economic value by creating social value."[22] By viewing the growth, profitability, and sustainability of the corporation as intermeshed with societal and economic progress in the markets in which it operates, companies such as Walmart, Google, and Intel are creating shared value by: "reconceiving products and markets; redefining productivity in the value chain; and enabling local cluster development"[23] (clusters of related business in a local area in which the company operates). Walmart, for example, has reduced its environmental footprint through its revamping of the plastic used in its stores, and by reducing its packaging; it also has cut 100 million miles from its delivery routes, saving $200 million even as it shipped more products.

In spring 2011, Google announced its plan to go all out to establish the company in Europe "as more of a local player that is investing in jobs, in facilities, our physical presence, and all the ancillary things that come with that."[24] Google clearly has developed this new approach in response to challenges on issues including privacy, copyright disputes, antitrust actions, and taxation. "The company is spending hundreds of millions of euro to try to demonstrate that it is a responsible corporate citizen and a valuable contributor to the local economy."[25] In this case, one questions whether this is truly creating shared value or simply practicing CSR in response to Google's negative image and lost opportunities.

MNC Responsibility Toward Human Rights

With almost all tech products now made by contract manufacturers in low-wage nations where sweatshops are common, ... Hewlett Packard, Dell, IBM, Intel, and twelve other tech companies decided to unite to create the Electronic Industry Code of Conduct (EICC)

BUSINESSWEEK[26]

Whereas many situations regarding the morality of the MNC's presence or activities in a country are quite clear, other situations are not, especially when dealing with human rights. So loud has been the cry about products coming from so-called sweatshops around the world that former President Bill Clinton established an Anti-Sweatshop Code of Conduct, which includes a ban on forced labor, abuse, and discrimination, and requires companies to provide a healthy and safe work environment and to pay at least the prevailing local minimum wage, among other requirements. Nike's efforts to address its problems include publishing its entire list of contract manufacturers on the Internet in order to gain transparency. The company admits that it is difficult to keep track of what goes on at its 800-plus contracted factories around the world.[27] (See the case at the end of this chapter for a review of Nike's approach to human rights in its factories.)

What constitutes "human rights" is clouded by the perceptions and priorities of people in different countries. While the United States often takes the lead in the charge against what it considers human rights violations around the world, other countries point to the homelessness and high crime statistics in the United States. Often the discussion of human rights centers around Asia because many of the products sold in the West are imported from Asia by Western companies using manufacturing facilities located there (see, for example, the accompanying "Comparative Management in Focus" section which focuses on China). It is commonly held in the West that the best chance to gain some ground on human rights issues is for large MNCs and governments around the world to take a unified stance; many global players now question the morality of trading for goods that have been produced by forced labor or child labor. Although laws in the United States ban prison imports, shady deals between the manufacturers and companies acting as intermediaries make it difficult to determine the origin of many products—and make it easy for companies wanting access to cheap

COMPARATIVE MANAGEMENT IN FOCUS

Doing Business in China—CSR and the Human Rights Challenge

... the Communist Party's Central Committee called in a report on its annual meeting for an "Internet management system" that would strictly regulate social network and instant-message systems, and punish those who spread "harmful information." The focus of the meeting, held [October 2011], was on culture and ideology.

www.nytimes.com,

October 26, 2011.[28]

A two-year government "action plan" to protect human rights in China has proved to be "largely a series of unfulfilled promises," a leading international human rights watchdog has found.[29]

THE CHRISTIAN SCIENCE MONITOR,

January 11, 2011.

China ranks 78th in the Transparency International 2010 Corruption Perceptions Index— down from 72nd in 2007.[30]

China's growth engine continued to drive the global economy in 2012 (albeit more slowly), propelled by China's $586 billion economic stimulus plan enacted during the global economic downturn. However, although this growth has lifted millions of Chinese out of poverty, many people and their basic rights remain largely behind, and there has been a heavy cost to the environment as energy usage increases and causes pollution. Growth in higher skilled jobs and in services is now well under way. However, there is continuing concern among MNCs about the pitfalls of operating in China—among them the uncertain legal climate; the difficulty of protecting intellectual property there; the repression of free speech; and the difficulty of monitoring, let alone correcting, human rights violations in factories. MNCs such as Walmart face considerable pressure in their home markets to address human rights issues in China and elsewhere. Consumers boycott their products, and trade unions in the United States, for example, complain that repression of workers' rights has enabled Chinese companies to push down labor costs, causing considerable loss of manufacturing jobs at home.[31] In

MAP 2.1 **China**

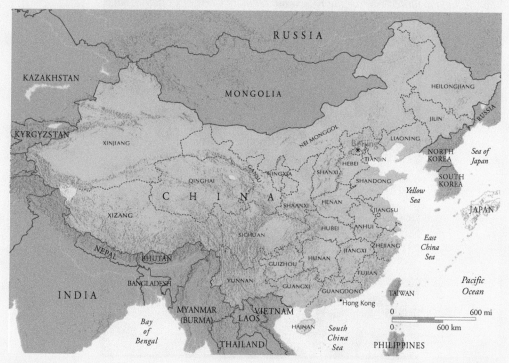

(Continued)

addition, while the culture of profit has resulted in a market economy in much of China, reducing the number of state-owned enterprises while increasing joint ventures and private ownership, that culture seems to have led to shortcuts in manufacturing, leading to problems with products, such as the toxic toys that Mattel had to recall in 2007, and poor treatment of workers.

Freedom of information took a particularly hard hit in October 2011 when the media reported that "Whether spooked by popular uprisings worldwide, a coming leadership transition at home or their own citizens' increasingly provocative tastes, Communist leaders are proposing new limits on media and Internet freedoms that include some of the most restrictive measures in years."[32] This included curbs on "Twitter"–style microblogs that had been critical of the government, and severe limits on television programs.

Previously, as is now well known, Google had agreed to China's demands to apply censors' blacklists to its search engine there. In spite of Google's founding principle, "Don't be evil," their business interests apparently clashed with their principles, leading many to conclude that Google is putting its own freedoms at risk in China; however, that is also occurring with Microsoft and Yahoo! in China.[33]

While Internet and technology executives were called to Capitol Hill in February 2006 to defend their companies' practices in China, it was clear that American corporations and their foreign policy interests would prevail.[34] Rather, the debate continues over how Internet companies can engage more effectively with Beijing on human rights issues. But, in a blow to the industry, in July 2006, Amnesty International accused Yahoo!, Microsoft, and Google of overlooking their human rights obligations in order to tap into China's dynamic online market, stating that "all three companies have in different ways facilitated or participated in the practice of government censorship in China."[35]

The latest censorship moves come as a disappointment because it had seemed that China was becoming more conscious of the need to improve its image regarding CSR as it takes a larger economic

FIGURE 2-1   **Women in Shoe Factory in China**   Shoe factory of an unnamed company in China, where women work very long hours. If they finish their lunch early, they may rest at their posts until the lunch time is over.

Source: © Michael Wolf/Redux Pictures

role on the world stage; indeed, its membership in the WTO obliges the country to act in concert with the policies and values of a free market.[36] Recognition of the UN Social Accountability Code (8000), adopted by over 200 companies worldwide, has helped to establish some norms regarding workers' rights in some provinces and cities in China. Although, as noted by Po Keung Ip, many companies adopted the code because they were forced to do so by their MNC buyers, which were under constant pressure themselves from consumers, investors, NGOs, and government in their home countries. "Major MNCs, like Walmart, Nike, Adidas, Avon, Motorola, Gap, and Carrefour, have been instrumental in transforming the business behaviors of their Chinese contractors through their ethical supply chain management which selects and audits contractors according to ethical codes."[37]

products or materials to ignore the law. However, under pressure from their labor unions (and perhaps their consciences), a number of large image-conscious companies, such as Reebok and Levi Strauss, have established corporate codes of conduct for their buyers, suppliers, and contractors and have instituted strict procedures for auditing their imports. In addition, some companies are uniting with others in their industry to form their own code for responsible action. One of these is the Electronic Industry Code of Conduct (EICC), which comprises Hewlett-Packard, Dell, IBM, Intel, and 12 other tech companies who have agreed on the following policies:

- The EICC bans forced and child labor and excessive overtime.
- The EICC requires contract manufacturers to follow some basic environmental requirements.
- The EICC requires each company to audit its overseas suppliers to ensure compliance, following a common factory inspection system for all members.[38]

A considerable number of organizations have developed their own codes of conduct; some have gone further to group together with others around the world to establish standards to improve the quality of life for workers around the world. Companies such as Avon, Sainsbury Plc., Toys "Я" Us, and Otto Versand have joined with the Council on Economic Priorities (CEP) to establish SA8000 (Social Accountability 8000, on the lines of the manufacturing quality standard ISO9000). Their proposed global labor standards would be monitored by outside organizations to certify whether plants are meeting those standards, among which are the following:

- Do not use child or forced labor.
- Provide a safe working environment.
- Respect workers' rights to unionize.
- Do not regularly require more than 48-hour work weeks.
- Pay wages sufficient to meet workers' basic needs.[39]

In addition, four **international codes of conduct** provide some consistent guidelines for multinational enterprises (MNEs). These codes were developed by the International Chamber of Commerce, the Organization for Economic Cooperation and Development, the International Labor Organization, and the United Nations Commission on Transnational Corporations. Getz has integrated these four codes and organized their common underlying principles, thereby establishing MNE behavior toward governments, publics, and people, as shown in Exhibit 2-2 (the originating institutions are in parentheses). Getz concludes, "As international organizations and institutions (including MNEs themselves) continue to refine the codes, the underlying moral issues will be better identified, and appropriate MNE behavior will be more readily apparent."[40] The examples shown in Exhibit 2-2 are excerpted from the codes and show how companies can provide a cooperative, long-term relationship with the local people and governments where they operate.

ETHICS IN GLOBAL MANAGEMENT

National, as well as corporate, cultures need to be taken into account if multinationals are to enforce their codes across different regions.

FINANCIAL TIMES.[41]

Globalization has multiplied the ethical problems facing organizations. However, business ethics have not yet been globalized. Attitudes toward ethics are rooted in culture and business practices. Swee Hoon Ang found, for example, that while East Asians tended to be less ethical than their expatriate counterparts from the United States and Britain, it was because they considered deception as amoral and acceptable if it has a positive effect on larger issues such as the company, the extended family, or the state.[42] For an MNC, it is difficult to reconcile consistent and acceptable behavior around the world with home-country standards. One question, in fact, is whether it should be reconciled. It seems that, while the United States has been the driving force to legislate moral business conduct overseas, perhaps more scrutiny should have been applied to those

EXHIBIT 2-2 International Codes of Conduct for MNEs

MNE and Host Governments

Economic and Developmental Policies

- MNEs should consult with governmental authorities and national employers' and workers' organizations to ensure that their investments conform to the economic and social development policies of the host country. (ICC; OECD; ILO; UN/CTC)
- MNEs should not adversely disturb the balance-of-payments or currency exchange rates of the countries in which they operate. They should try, in consultation with the government, to resolve balance-of-payments and exchange rate difficulties when possible. (ICC; OECD; UN/CTC)
- MNEs should cooperate with governmental policies regarding local equity participation. (ICC; UN/CTC)
- MNEs should not dominate the capital markets of the countries in which they operate. (ICC; UN/CTC)
- MNEs should provide the information necessary for correctly assessing taxes to be paid to host government authorities. (ICC; OECD)
- MNEs should not engage in transfer pricing policies that modify the tax base on which their entities are assessed. (OECD; UN/CTC)
- MNEs should give preference to local sources for components and raw materials if prices and quality are competitive. (ICC; ILO)
- MNEs should reinvest some profits in the countries in which they operate. (ICC)

Laws and Regulations

- MNEs are subject to the laws, regulations, and jurisdiction of the countries in which they operate. (ICC; OECD; UN/CTC)
- MNEs should respect the right of every country to exercise control over its natural resources, and to regulate the activities of entities operating within its territory. (ICC; OECD; UN/CTC)
- MNEs should use appropriate international dispute settlement mechanisms, including arbitration, to resolve conflicts with the governments of the countries in which they operate. (ICC; OECD)
- MNEs should resolve disputes arising from expropriation by host governments under the domestic law of the host country. (UN/CTC)

Political Involvement

- MNEs should refrain from improper or illegal involvement in local political activities. (OECD; UN/CTC)
- MNEs should not pay bribes or render improper benefits to any public servant. (OECD; UN/CTC)
- MNEs should not interfere in intergovernmental relations. (UN/CTC)

MNEs and the Public

Technology Transfer

- MNEs should cooperate with governmental authorities in assessing the impact of transfers of technology to developing countries and should enhance the technological capacities of developing countries. (OECD; UN/CTC)
- MNEs should develop and adapt technologies to the needs and characteristics of the countries in which they operate. (ICC; OECD; ILO)
- MNEs should conduct research and development activities in developing countries, using local resources and personnel to the greatest extent possible. (ICC; UN/CTC)

Environmental Protection

- MNEs should respect the laws and regulations concerning environmental protection of the countries in which they operate. (OECD; UN/CTC)
- MNEs should cooperate with host governments and with international organizations in the development of national and international environmental protection standards. (ICC; UN/CTC)
- MNEs should supply to appropriate host governmental authorities information concerning the environmental impact of the products and processes of their entities. (ICC; UN/CTC)

MNEs and Persons

Consumer Protection

- MNEs should respect the laws and regulations of the countries in which they operate with regard to consumer protection. (OECD; UN/CTC)
- MNEs should preserve the safety and health of consumers by disclosure of appropriate information, proper labeling, and accurate advertising. (UN/CTC)

(Continued)

EXHIBIT 2-2 *(continued)*

Employment Practices (excerpts)

- MNEs should cooperate with host governments' efforts to create employment opportunities in particular localities. (ICC)
- MNEs should try to increase employment opportunities and standards in the countries in which they operate. (ILO)
- MNEs should give advance notice of plant closures and mitigate the resultant adverse effects. (ICC; OECD; ILO)
- MNEs should provide standards of employment equal to or better than those of comparable employers in the countries in which they operate. (ICC; OECD; ILO)
- MNEs should pay, at minimum, basic living wages. (ILO)
- MNEs should maintain the highest standards of safety and health, and should provide adequate information about work-related health hazards. (ILO)

Human Rights

- MNEs should respect human rights and fundamental freedoms in the countries in which they operate. (UN/CTC)
- MNEs should not discriminate on the basis of race, color, sex, religion, language, social, national and ethnic origin, or political or other opinion. (UN/CTC)
- MNEs should respect the social and cultural objectives, values, and traditions of the countries in which they operate. (UN/CTC)

Sources: OECD: The Organization for Economic Cooperation and Development Guidelines for Multinational Enterprises, ILO: The International Labor Office Tripartite Declarations of Principles Concerning Multinational Enterprises and Social Policy, ICC: The International Chamber of Commerce Guidelines for International Investment, UN/CTC: The United Nations Universal Declaration of Human Rights, The UN Code of Conduct on Transnational Corporations

global MNCs headquartered in the United States, such as Enron and WorldCom, that so greatly defrauded their investors, employees, and all who had business with them.

The term **international business ethics** refers to the business conduct or morals of MNCs in their relationships with individuals and entities. Such behavior is based largely on the cultural value system and the generally accepted ways of doing business in each country or society, as we have discussed throughout this book. Those norms, in turn, are based on broadly accepted guidelines from religion, philosophy, professional organizations, and the legal system. The complexity of the combination of various national and cultural factors in a particular host environment that combine to determine ethical or unethical societal norms is illustrated in Exhibit 2-3. The authors, Robertson and Crittenden, note,

> *Varying legal and cultural constraints across borders have made integrating an ethical component into international strategic decisions quite challenging.*[43]

Should, then, managers of MNC subsidiaries base their ethical standards on those of the host country or those of the home country—or can the two be reconciled? What is the moral responsibility of expatriates regarding ethical behavior, and how do these issues affect business objectives? How do expatriates simultaneously balance their responsibility to various stakeholders—to owners, creditors, consumers, employees, suppliers, governments, and societies? The often conflicting objectives of host and home governments and societies also must be balanced.

The approach to these dilemmas varies among MNCs from different countries. While the American approach is to treat everyone the same by making moral judgments based on general rules, managers in Japan and Europe tend to make such decisions based on shared values, social ties, and their perceptions of their obligations. According to many U.S. executives, there is little difference in ethical practices among the United States, Canada, and Northern Europe. According to Bruce Smart, former U.S. Undersecretary of Commerce for International Trade, the highest ethical standards seem to be practiced by the Canadians, British, Australians, and Germans. As he says, "a kind of noblesse oblige still exists among the business classes in those countries"—compared with the prevailing attitude among many U.S. managers that condones "making it" whatever way one can.[44] Another who experienced few problems with ethical practices in Europe is Donald Petersen, former CEO of Ford Motor Company. However, he warns us about underdeveloped countries, in particular those under a dictatorship where bribery is a generally accepted practice.[45]

Petersen's experience has been borne out by research by Transparency International, a German nongovernmental organization (NGO) that fights corruption. It draws on data from

EXHIBIT 2-3   **A Moral Philosophy of Cross-Cultural Societal Ethics**

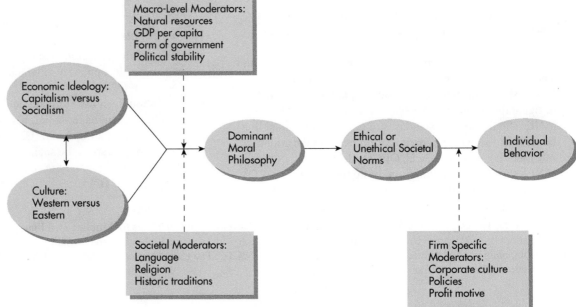

Source: C. J. Robertson and W. F. Crittenden, "Mapping Moral Philosophies: Strategic Implications for Multinational Firms," *Strategic Management Journal* 24: 385–92 (2003). © John Wiley & Sons, Inc. Reproduced with permission.

fourteen different polls and surveys from thirteen independent institutions around the world to rank 180 countries, based on results from 63,199 respondents. The organization's year 2010 Global Corruption Barometer (selections are shown in Exhibit 2-4) shows the results of research into the extent that business and other sectors of their society are affected by corruption, as perceived by businesspeople, academics, and risk analysts in 69 countries. A primary focus of the research was the relative prevalence of bribery in various spheres of people's lives, including political and business practices.

The 2010 Corruption Perceptions Index shows that nearly three-quarters of the 178 countries in the index score below five, on a scale from 10 (highly clean) to 0 (highly corrupt). These results indicate a serious corruption problem.

Overall, the data show that those countries in Western Europe, Singapore, New Zealand, Canada, and Australia, were the least corrupt, closely followed by Hong Kong and Japan; the United Kingdom scored 7.6 (dropping from 8.4 in 2007); and the United States scored 7.1, for example, compared with 9.3 for Denmark. South Korea scored 5.4; South Africa 4.5; Brazil and China 3.5; Mexico scored 3.1; and other countries, such as Vietnam, and African countries scored far lower, with Russia scoring 2.1.[46] Sadly, many scores were lower than previous years:

> *Notable among decliners over the past year are some of the countries most affected by a financial crisis precipitated by transparency and integrity deficits.*[47]

The biggest single problem for MNCs in their attempt to define a corporate-wide ethical posture is the great variation of ethical standards around the world. Many practices that are considered unethical or even illegal in some countries are accepted ways of doing business in others.

Ethics in Uses of Technology

> *"European citizens care deeply about protecting their privacy and data protection rights,"* … *"Any company operating in the E.U. market or any online product that is targeted at E.U. consumers should comply with E.U. rules."*

> VIVIENNE REDING, EUROPEAN JUSTICE COMMISSIONER,
> *MAY 4, 2011.*[48]

EXHIBIT 2-4   **2010 Corruption Perceptions Index—Selected Scores**   Each country's score relates to perceptions of the degree of corruption as seen by business people and country analysts, and ranges between 10 (highly clean) and 0 (highly corrupt).

Rank	Country	Score
1	Denmark	9.3
1	Singapore	9.3
1	New Zealand	9.3
4	Finland	9.2
6	Canada	8.9
8	Australia	8.7
13	Hong Kong	8.4
15	Germany	7.9
17	Japan	7.8
20	UK	7.6
21	Chile	7.2
22	Belgium	7.1
22	USA	7.1
25	France	6.8
33	Taiwan	5.8
39	South Korea	5.4
41	Poland	5.3
56	Greece	4.6
51	South Africa	4.5
56	Turkey	4.4
67	Italy	3.9
72	Brazil	3.5
78	China	3.5
87	India	3.3
98	Mexico	3.1
105	Argentina	2.9
110	Bolivia	2.8
116	Vietnam	2.7
131	Philippines	2.5
143	Indonesia	2.3
154	Russia	2.1

Source: Based on selected data from the TI Corruption Perceptions Index, 2010. www.transparencyinternational.org, accessed June 18, 2011.

The ethical use of technology around the world poses a considerable challenge to have consistent practices because of the varied expectations about the use of technological devices and programs as they intersect with people's private lives. This conflict is illustrated by the electronic data privacy laws in Europe. The EU Directive on Data Protection guarantees European citizens absolute control over data concerning them. A U.S. company wanting personal information must get permission from that person and explain what the information will be used for; the company must also guarantee that the information won't be used for anything else without the person's consent. It appears that the rules are being set by Europe; in May 2011, for example, regulators in France, Germany, and Italy were focusing on whether Apple's iPhone and iPad violated privacy rules by tracking the location of users. Google, for example, had previously started a firestorm in Germany when it was discovered that it had been gathering information for its street mapping service from people's unsecured wireless networks. Later, Sony acknowledged a breach of data of 77 million users of its Play Station Network. As a result of such breaches of privacy, Ms. Redding, the European Justice Commissioner, has proposed extending privacy rules to social media and online banking, shopping, and video games, among others.[49] In the United States there is no agency dedicated to monitoring issues of data privacy as there is in Europe.

Bribery

There are few other areas where a single employee can, with one instance of misjudgment, create huge embarrassment [for the company].

FINANCIAL TIMES[50]

The computer is on the dock, it's raining, and you have to pay $100 [bribe] to get it picked up.
WILLIAM C. NORRIS, CONTROL DATA CORPORATION[51]

MNCs are often caught between being placed at a disadvantage either by refusing to go along with a country's accepted practices, such as bribery, or being subject to criticism at home for using "unethical" tactics to get the job done. Large companies that have refused to participate have led the way in taking a moral stand because of their visibility; their potential impact on the local economy; and, after all, their ability to afford such a stance. Some other large companies, however, have not always taken a moral stand. Such was the case in April 2011 when a Justice Department complaint against a Johnson & Johnson subsidiary found internal company emails that stated that ...

"cash incentives to surgeons is common knowledge in Greece," and that, were the company to stop paying bribes, "we'd lose 95% of our business by the end of the year."

www.nytimes.com,
APRIL 8, 2011.[52]

Whereas the upper limits of ethical standards for international activities are set by the individual standards of certain leading companies—or, more realistically, by the moral values of their top managers—it is more difficult to set the lower limits of those standards; that limit gets set in each specific situation by whether the laws are actually enforced in that location.

The bribery of officials is prohibited by law in all countries, but it still goes on as an accepted practice; often, it is the only way to get anything done. In such cases, the MNC managers have to decide which standard of behavior they will follow. What about the $100 bribe to get the computer off the rainy dock? William Norris says he told his managers to pay the $100 because to refuse would be taking things too far. Generally, Control Data did not yield to such pressure, though it said sales were lost as a result.[53]

A specific ethical issue for managers in the international arena is that of **questionable payments**. These are business payments that raise significant questions of appropriate moral behavior either in the host nation or in other nations. Such questions arise out of differences in laws, customs, and ethics in various countries, and whether the payments in question are political payments, extortion, bribes, sales commissions, or "grease money"—payments to expedite routine transactions. Other common types of payments are made to speed the clearance of goods at ports of entry and to obtain required certifications. They are called different names in different countries: tokens of appreciation, *la mordida* ("the bite," in Mexico), *bastarella* ("little envelope" in Italy), and *pot-de-vin* ("jug of wine" in France). For the sake of simplicity, all these different types of questionable payments are categorized in this text as some form of bribery. In Mexico, for example, companies make monthly payments to the mail carriers or their mail gets "lost."

Most managers perceive bribery as "endemic in business and government in parts of Africa and south and East Asia. Corruption and bribery are considered to be part of the culture and environment of certain markets, and will not simply go away."[54] In some parts of Latin America, for example, customs officers are paid poorly and so are encouraged to take bribes to supplement their incomes. However, developed countries are not immune to bribery—as demonstrated in 2002 when several members of the International Olympic Committee were expelled for accepting bribes during Salt Lake City's campaign to host the 2002 Winter Olympics.

The dilemma for Americans operating abroad is how much to adhere to their own ethical standards in the face of foreign customs or how much to follow local ways to be competitive. Certainly, in some societies, gift giving is common to building social and familial ties, and such gifts incur obligation. Nevertheless, a bribe is different from a gift or other reciprocation, and those involved know that by whether it has a covert nature. In his book on bribes, Noonan takes the following position:

Bribery is universally shameful. There is not a country in the world that does not treat bribery as criminal on its books.... In no country do bribetakers speak publicly of their bribes, nor do bribegivers announce the bribes they pay. No newspaper lists them. No one advertises that he can arrange a bribe. No one is honored precisely because he is a big briber or bribee. No one writes an autobiography in which he recalls the bribes he has taken or paid.... Not merely the criminal law—for the transaction could have happened long ago and prosecution be barred by time—but an innate fear of being considered disgusting restrains briber and bribee from parading their exchange. Significantly, it is often the Westerner with ethnocentric prejudice who supposes that a modern Asian or African society does not regard the act of bribery as shameful in the way Westerners regard it.[55]

However, Americans must be able to distinguish between harmless practices and actual bribery, between genuine relationships and those used as a cover-up. To help them distinguish, the **Foreign Corrupt Practices Act (FCPA)** of 1977 was established, which prohibits U.S. companies from making illegal payments, other gifts, or political contributions to foreign government officials for the purpose of influencing them in business transactions. The goal was to stop MNCs from contributing to corruption in foreign governments and to upgrade the image of the United States and its companies operating overseas. Unfortunately, graft is still pervasive in global business today, and in 2012, the U.S. Justice Department was investigating 78 well-known companies for violation of the FCPA. Those included Walmart, which was being investigated after allegations were made that several executives at Walmart Mexico paid bribes to obtain permits for new stores and that some executives at Walmart headquarters hushed up evidence of the wrongdoing. Subsequently, Mexican government officials began their own investigation into how Walmart gained the permits.[56] The investigations were ongoing as of the completion of this book.

Questions often surface about who in the corporations should be held responsible for infractions under the FCPA. Indeed, on February 23, 2012, Albert Stanley, former CEO of engineering giant KGB, was sentenced to two and a half years for his role in one of the biggest bribery cases in American history. Stanley, who had spent his career in many countries, pleaded guilty to conspiring to bribe officials in Nigeria in return for $6 billion in business contracts.[57] Indeed, the law is not limited to the United States; nine of the ten largest corporate settlements involved companies outside the United States, such as the German giant Siemens, which in 2008 was convicted of bribing officials in several countries. (Amendments in 1998 ruled that the anti-bribery provisions of the FCPA now also apply to foreign firms and their personnel who, directly or indirectly through agents, violate the act within the United States.)[58] While the penalties for violating the FCPA include severe fines and sometimes imprisonment, many managers feel the law has given them a more even playing field, and so they have been more willing to do business in certain countries where it seemed impossible to do business without bribery and kickbacks. For others, the law strikes fear in managers and corporations about criminal liability. In 2012, the Chamber of Commerce was working with authorities to provide more clarity and guidelines for corporations and managers to help them stay within the law.[59]

In 1997 the Organisation for Economic Co-operation and Development's Convention on Bribery was signed by 36 countries in an attempt to combat corruption.[60] The Convention commits signatories to make it a crime to bribe foreign public officials in international business transactions and to set up policies and enforcement procedures. In 2010 there were 38 signatories including non-O.E.C.D. members such as Brazil, South Africa, and Argentina, and there have been 12 prosecutions of individuals and companies under the FCPA. The *New York Times* reported that "148 individuals and 77 entities had been sanctioned under criminal proceedings for foreign bribery in the countries that have been party to the convention from the start, with the greatest number in the United States."[61]

In spite of these efforts, evidential problems continue to hinder prosecutions. Unless there is a complaint or whistle-blowing, there are few avenues for regulators to ferret out incidents of bribery in corporations. Unfortunately, bribery continues, mostly on a small scale, where it often goes undetected. In any event, it is prudent (and hopefully honorable) for companies to set in place processes to minimize the risk of prosecution, including:

• Having a global compliance system that shows that employees have understood, and signed off on, the legal obligations regarding bribery and corruption in the countries where they do business.

- Making employees aware of the penalties and ramifications for lone actions, such as criminal sanctions.
- Having a system in place to investigate any foreign agents and overseas partners who will be negotiating contracts.
- Keeping an effective whistle-blowing system in place.[62]

As far as the actions that individual managers take when doing business overseas, if we agree that accepting or giving a bribe is always wrong, then our decisions as managers, salespersons, and so on are always clear, no matter where we are.

However, many businesspeople believe that it is just part of the cost of doing business in many countries to pay small bribes to simply get people to do their jobs, and they are willing to engage in bribery as an everyday part of meeting their business objectives. Frequently corporate officials, in fact, avoid any moral issue by simply "turning a blind eye" to what goes on in subsidiaries. Some companies avoid these issues by hiring a local agent who takes care of the paperwork and pays all the so-called fees in return for a salary or consultant's fee. The FCPA does allow "grease" payments to facilitate business in a foreign country, if in fact those payments are lawful there. However, other payments prohibited by the FCPA remain subject to prosecution even if the company says it did not know that its agents or subsidiaries were making such payments—the so-called "reason to know" provision.

Critics of the FCPA contend that the law represents an ethnocentric attempt to impose U.S. standards on the rest of the world and puts U.S. firms at a competitive disadvantage. In any event, many feel that business activities that cannot stand scrutiny are clearly unethical, corrupt, and, in the long run, corrupting. Bribery fails three important tests of ethical corporate actions: (1) is it legal? (2) does it work (in the long run)? and (3) can it be talked about?[63]

Many MNCs have decided to confront concerns about ethical behavior and social responsibility by developing worldwide practices that represent the company's posture. Among those policies are the following:

- Develop a worldwide code of ethics.
- Build ethical policies into strategy development.
- Plan regular assessment of the company's ethical posture.
- If ethical problems cannot be resolved, withdraw from that market.

As an example, General Electric (GE) decided to take a hard line on corruption, electing to "level up, not down," and withdrawing from Nigeria and Russia when corruption was especially rife.[64] In fact, according to GE's Mr. Rice:

The firm's hard line on corruption is actually helping it win business in many developing countries. Increasingly they understand that corruption is a barrier to improving the standard of living of the poorest people and they want to do business more and more with an ethical firm.[65]

THE ECONOMIST

Making the Right Decision

How is a manager operating abroad to know what is the "right" decision when faced with questionable or unfamiliar circumstances of doing business? Usually, the manager or salesperson is faced with wanting to make certain decisions which will benefit her company and or her career. That decision, or set of actions, is likely to be profitable for the company and secure new market opportunities. However, there are many other considerations that make it less clear whether to continue to pursue that avenue, in particular in countries or settings that provide less transparency, and often certain pressures, about what to do. If the manager is faced with such a situation, she has a number of steps that can help her clarify the way to proceed.

Steps to an Ethical Decision

1. Consult the laws of both the home and the host countries—such as the FCPA. If any of those laws would be violated, then you, the manager, must look to some other way to complete the business transaction, or withdraw altogether.

FIGURE 2-2   Man Refusing Bribe from a Woman

Source: fuzzbones/Fotolia, LLC

2. Consult the International Codes of Conduct for MNEs (see Exhibit 2-2). These are broad and cover various areas of social responsibility and ethical behavior; even so, many issues are subject to interpretation. If there is no apparent conflict on these legal grounds, then proceed with further consultation.

3. Consult the company's code of ethics (if there is one) and established norms. Note that it is the responsibility of the company to provide guidelines for the actions and decisions made by its employees. What kinds of decisions do your colleagues typically make in these kinds of circumstances? If your intended action runs contrary to the norms or the formal code, discontinue that plan.

4. Consult your superiors if you still need clarification. Unfortunately, often the situation is not that clear-cut, or your boss will tell you to "use your own judgment." Sometimes your superiors in the home office just want you to complete the transaction to the benefit of the company and don't want to be involved in what you have to do to consummate the deal. Failing clear guidance:

5. Weigh stakeholders' rights (see Exhibit 2-1). To whom are you responsible? What are the priorities of responsibilities to those stakeholders? What is the potential benefit versus harm involved in your decision or set of actions? (For example, does the proposed action [rigged contract bid, bribe, etc.] harm anyone? What are the likely consequences of your decision in both the short run and long run? Who would benefit from your contemplated action? Who might be harmed? In the case of a rigged contract bid through bribery, for example, people are put at a disadvantage, especially over the long term, with a pattern of this behavior.)

6. Follow your own conscience and moral code. Ask yourself if you can live with the potential decision and also what would be the next step for you if you continue along that path.

It is important to decide where to draw the line in the sand in order to operate with integrity—otherwise the line moves further and further away with each transgression. In addition, what can start here with a small bribe or cover-up—a matter of personal ethics—can, over time, and in the aggregate of many people covering up, result in a situation of a truly negligent, and perhaps criminal, stance toward social responsibility to society, like that revealed by investigations of the tobacco industry in the United States. Indeed, executives are increasingly being held personally and criminally accountable for their decisions; this is true even for people operating on the board of directors of a company. Criminal charges were brought against 15 executives of WorldCom in 2003, for example; and the noose was thrown around the world after the Enron convictions in 2006 as international banks such as Citigroup and JP Morgan Chase were charged with taking part in sham deals to disguise Enron's financial problems. In 2011 a number of executives of banks and financial institutions were being investigated in the wake of the financial crisis precipitated by the housing mortgage debacle.

MANAGING INTERDEPENDENCE

Because multinational firms (or other organizations, such as the Red Cross) represent global interdependency, their managers at all levels must recognize that what they do, in the aggregate, has long-term implications for the socioeconomic interdependence of nations. Simply to describe ethical issues as part of the general environment does not address the fact that managers must control their activities at all levels—from simple, daily business transactions involving local workers, intermediaries, or consumers, to global concerns of ecological responsibility—for the future benefit of all concerned. Whatever the situation, the powerful long-term effects of MNC and MNE action (or inaction) should be planned for and controlled—and not haphazardly considered as part of the side effects of business. The profitability of individual companies depends on a cooperative and constructive attitude toward global interdependence.

Foreign Subsidiaries in the United States

Much of the preceding discussion has related to U.S. subsidiaries around the world. However, to globally highlight the growing interdependence and changing balance of business power, foreign subsidiaries in the United States should also be considered. Since much criticism about a lack of responsibility has been directed toward MNCs with headquarters in the United States, we must think of these criticisms from an outsider's perspective. The number of foreign subsidiaries in the United States has grown and continues to grow dramatically; FDI in the United States by other countries is, in a number of industries, far more than U.S. investment outward. Americans are thus becoming more sensitive to what they perceive as a lack of control over their own country's business.

Things look very different from the perspective of Americans employed at a subsidiary of an overseas MNC. Interdependence takes on a new meaning when people "over there" are calling the shots regarding strategy, expectations, products, and personnel. Often, Americans' resentment about different ways of doing business by "foreign" companies in the United States inhibits the cooperation that gave rise to the companies' presence in the first place.

Today, managers from all countries must learn new ways, and most MNCs are trying to adapt. In Japan, corporate social responsibility has traditionally meant that companies take care of their employees, whereas in the United States both the public and private sectors are expected to share responsibility for the community. Part of the explanation for this difference is that U.S. corporations get tax deductions for corporate philanthropy, whereas Japanese firms do not; nor are Japanese managers usually familiar with community needs. For these and other reasons, Japanese subsidiaries in the United States have not been active in U.S. philanthropy.

Managing Subsidiary–Host Country Interdependence

> *Nike believes that we are at the beginning of a shift from a service- or knowledge-based economy to a sustainability-based economy, as environmental constraints increasingly influence business choices.*
>
> ORGANIZATIONAL DYNAMICS 39,
> *2010.*[66]

When **managing interdependence**, international managers must go beyond general issues of social responsibility and deal with the specific concerns of the MNC subsidiary–hostcountry relationship. Outdated attitudes that focus only on profitability and autonomy are shortsighted and usually result in only short-term realization of those goals. Managers in those companies must learn to accommodate the needs of other organizations and countries:

> *Interdependence rather than independence, and cooperation rather than confrontation are at the heart of that accommodation ... the journey from independence to interdependence managed badly leads to dependence, and that is an unacceptable destination.*[67]

Most of the past criticism levied at MNCs has focused on their activities in less developed countries (LDCs). Their real or perceived lack of responsibility centers on the transfer in of inappropriate technology, causing unemployment, and the transfer out of scarce financial and other resources, reducing the capital available for internal development. In their defense, those corporations and NGOs help developing countries by contributing new technology and managerial skills, improving the infrastructure, creating jobs, and bringing in investment capital from other countries by exporting products. The infusion of outside capital provides foreign-exchange earnings that can be used for further development. The host government's attitude is often referred to as a love–hate relationship: It wants the economic growth that foreign investment provides, but it does not want the incursions on national sovereignty or the technological dependence that may result. Most criticisms of MNC subsidiary activities, whether in less developed or more developed countries, are along the following lines:

1. MNCs locally raise their needed capital, contributing to a rise in interest rates in host countries.
2. The majority (sometimes even 100 percent) of the stock of most subsidiaries is owned by the parent company. Consequently, host-country people do not have much control over the operations of corporations within their borders.
3. MNCs usually reserve the key managerial and technical positions for expatriates. As a result, they do not contribute to the development of host-country personnel.
4. MNCs do not adapt their technology to the conditions that exist in host countries.
5. MNCs concentrate their research and development activities at home, restricting the transfer of modern technology and know-how to host countries.
6. MNCs give rise to the demand for luxury goods in host countries at the expense of essential consumer goods.
7. MNCs start their foreign operations by purchasing existing firms rather than by developing new productive facilities in host countries.
8. MNCs dominate major industrial sectors, thus contributing to inflation, by stimulating demand for scarce resources and earning excessively high profits and fees.
9. MNCs are not accountable to their host nations but only respond to home-country governments; they are not concerned with host-country plans for development.[68]

Specific MNCs have been charged with tax evasion, union busting, and interference in host-country politics. Of course, corporations have both positive and negative effects on different economies. For every complaint about MNC activities (whether about capital markets, technology transfer, or employment practices), we can identify potential benefits (see Exhibit 2-5).

Numerous conflicts arise between MNC companies or subsidiaries and host countries, including conflicting goals (both economic and noneconomic) and conflicting concerns, such as the security of proprietary technology, patents, or information. Overall, the resulting trade-offs create an interdependent relationship between the subsidiary and the host government, based on relative bargaining power. The power of large corporations is based on their large-scale, worldwide economies, their strategic flexibility, and their control over technology and production location. The bargaining chips of the host governments include their control of raw materials and market access and their ability to set the rules regarding the role of private enterprise, the operation of state-owned firms, and the specific regulations regarding taxes, permissions, and so forth.

MNCs run the risk of their assets becoming hostage to host control, which may take the form of nationalism, protectionism, or governmentalism. Under **nationalism**, for example, public opinion is rallied in favor of national goals and against foreign influences. Under **protectionism**, the host institutes a partial or complete closing of borders to withstand competitive foreign products, using tariff and nontariff barriers, such as those used by Japan. Under **governmentalism**, the government uses its policy-setting role to favor national interests, rather than relying on market forces.[69] This was illustrated by the actions of governments around the world to support their banking systems in 2008 and 2009.

The intricacies of the relationship and the relative power of an MNC subsidiary and a host-country government are situation specific. Clearly, such a relationship should be managed for mutual benefit; a long-term, constructive relationship based on the corporation's socially responsive stance should result in progressive strategic success for the company and economic progress for the host country. The effective management of subsidiary–host country interdependence must have a long-term perspective. Although temporary strategies to reduce interdependence via controls on the transnational flows by firms (for example, transfer-pricing tactics) or by governments (such as new residency requirements for skilled workers) are often successful in the short run, they result in inefficiencies that must be absorbed by one or both parties, with negative long-term results. In setting up and maintaining subsidiaries, managers are wise to consider the long-term

EXHIBIT 2-5 Potential Benefits and Costs to Host Countries of MNC Operations There

Benefits	Costs
Capital Market Effects	
• Broader access to outside capital • Economic growth • Foreign-exchange earnings • Import substitution effects allow governments to save foreign exchange for priority projects	• Risk sharing • Increased competition for local scarce capital • Increased interest rates as supply of local capital decreases • Capital service effects of balance of payments
Technology and Production Effects	
• Access to new technology and R&D developments • Employee training in new technology • Infrastructure development and support • Export diversification • Introduction of new management techniques	• Technology is not always appropriate • Plants are often for assembly only and can be dismantled • Government infrastructure investment is higher than expected benefits • Increased pollution
Employment Effects	
• Direct creation of new jobs • Introduction of more humane employment standards • Opportunities for indigenous management development • Income multiplier effects on local community business	• Limited skill development and creation • Competition for scarce skills • Low percentage of managerial jobs for local people • Employment instability because of ability to move production operations freely to other countries

Source: Based on R. H. Mason and R. S. Spich, *Management: An International Perspective*, p. 202 (Homewood, IL: Irwin, 1987).

trade-offs between strategic plans and operational management. By finding out for themselves the pressing local concerns and understanding the sources of past conflicts, they can learn from mistakes and recognize the consequences of the failure to manage problems. Furthermore, managers should implement policies that reflect corporate social responsibility regarding local economic issues, employee welfare, or natural resources. At the least, the failure to effectively manage interdependence results in constraints on strategy. In the worst case, it results in disastrous consequences for the local area, for the subsidiary, and for the global reputation of the company.

The interdependent nature of developing economies and the foreign companies operating there is of particular concern when discussing social responsibility because of the tentative and fragile nature of the economic progression in those countries. Corporations (and non-governmental organizations [NGOs]) must set a high moral standard and lay the groundwork for future economic development. At the minimum, they should ensure that their actions will do no harm. Some recommendations for MNEs operating in and doing business with developing countries are as follows:

1. Do no intentional harm. This includes respect for the integrity of the ecosystem and consumer safety.
2. Produce more good than harm for the host country.
3. Contribute by their activity to the host country's development.
4. Respect the human rights of their employees.
5. To the extent that local culture does not violate ethical norms, respect the local culture and work with and not against it.
6. Pay their fair share of taxes.
7. Cooperate with the local government in developing and enforcing just background (infrastructure) institutions (i.e., laws, governmental regulations, unions, and consumer groups, which serve as a means of social control).[70]

Managing Environmental Interdependence and Sustainability

Sustainability lies at the intersection of financial, social and environmental health—described sometimes as the "triple bottom line."[71]

International managers can no longer afford to ignore the impact of their activities on the environment and their stakeholders. The demand for corporations to consider **sustainability** in their CSR plans comes from various stakeholders around the world. A generally accepted definition of **sustainable development** for business enterprises is that of. . . .

adopting business strategies and activities that meet the needs of the enterprise and its stakeholders today, while protecting, sustaining and enhancing the human and natural resources that will be needed in the future.[72]

JOURNAL OF SOCIO-ECONOMICS

Existing literature generally agrees on three dimensions of sustainability: (1) economic, (2) social, and (3) environmental. A sustainable business has to take into account "the interests of future generations, biodiversity, animal protection, human rights, life cycle impacts, and principles like equity, accountability, transparency, openness, education and learning, and local action and scale."[73]

A study by Mirvis et al. found that, while most executives agree that sustainability is important to the financial success of their companies, less than half of them are making serious commitments to integrate the necessary steps into their business systems. Reasons include a lack of clear view on what sustainability comprises, and the difficulty in allocating responsibility in the company for the vast and overlapping concerns of environmental, social, and governance issues. As a result sustainability often does not get internalized in the culture or systems of the company, and competing priorities such as short-term profits intervene.[74] However, companies such as General Electric (GE), Nike, and Gap are among the world's prominent sustainable organizations and are providing leadership in their transparent models for other organizations to resolve the complex issues involved in implementing sustainability. Nike, Inc., for example, believes that business success will increasingly depend on contributing to a sustainable world; and GE's chairman and chief executive officer (CEO) Jeff Immelt believes that the next decades will be about technologies and economies to address issues of scarcity.

A more positive report in 2011 from a survey by McKinsey consultants of 3,203 executives representing the full range of industries and geographic regions shows that many companies are actively integrating sustainability principles into their businesses, and they are doing so by pursuing goals that go far beyond earlier concern for reputation management. The McKinsey report noted a more mature attitude toward sustainability and its expected benefits than in prior surveys, saying that "More companies are managing sustainability to improve processes, pursue growth, and add value to their companies rather than focusing on reputation alone."[75] In addition, 57 percent said their companies have integrated sustainability into their strategic planning. Of the 2,956 executives who responded, the areas that the companies were taking action on included: reducing energy use in operations (63 percent), reducing waste from operations (61 percent), and managing corporate reputation for sustainability (51 percent.)[76]

Leaders in the research noted that barriers that prevent further value-capture from sustainability initiatives include the pressure of realizing short-term profitability compared with the long-term value aspects of sustainability initiatives, and the lack of performance incentives tied to sustainability results.[77]

The dilemma for corporations is that they believe they are faced with trying to meet two often contradictory requirements: (1) selling at low prices and (2) being environmentally and socially conscious. However, competitive pressures limit the company's ability to raise prices in order to cover the cost of socially responsible policies. This is obviously contradictory to the well-being of societies.[78] However, a long-term view is that sustainability is good for business, and many companies, such as BP and Nike, have learned this the hard way.

One example of the turnaround in a company's sustainability efforts is The Coca-Cola Company in India. The company is struggling to accommodate the rising concerns and protests from local farmers about the company's depletion of water resources. As reported on the PBS *Newshour*,[79] farmers are particularly angry in Kala Dera, in the drought-stricken state of Rajasthan. The Coca-Cola factory there is one of 49 across India. The company has invested over $1 billion dollars building a market for its products in this country. The plant used about 900,000 liters of water in 2007, about a third of it for the soft drinks, the rest to clean bottles and machinery. It is drawn from wells at the plant but also from aquifers Coca-Cola shares with neighboring farmers. The water is virtually free to all users. The farmers say their problems began after the Coca-Cola factory arrived in 1999. According to the farmers:

> *Before, the water level was descending by about one foot per year. Now it's 10 feet every year. We have a 3.5-horsepower motor. We cannot cope. They (Coca-Cola) have a 50-horsepower pump.*
>
> PBS NEWSHOUR WITH JIM LEHRER,
> *NOVEMBER 17, 2008.*[80]

Coca-Cola agreed to an independent third-party assessment of some of its operations in India, which confirmed that the Rajasthan plant is contributing to a worsening water situation. It recommended that the company bring water in from outside the area or shut the factory down. Coca-Cola rejected that recommendation. For his part, Coca-Cola's India head, Atul Singh, says it would be irresponsible to leave, saying that "walking away is the easiest thing we can do. That's not going to help that community build sustainability."[81] So Coca-Cola, while insisting its impact on the water supply was minimal, said it would stay and help. The company has agreed to subsidize one-third of the cost of water-efficient drip irrigation systems for 15 neighboring farmers. The government pays most of the rest; growers themselves must chip in 10 percent. Coca-Cola has also set up concrete collection systems for rainwater. The farmers remain skeptical. They also are critical of the government locally for attracting Coca-Cola to a water-scarce region and nationally for ignoring water policy in a rush to attract industry and foreign investment.[82]

The Coca-Cola example makes clear to global managers that effectively managing environmental interdependence and sustainability includes considering ecological interdependence as well as the economic and social implications of MNC activities. There is an ever-increasing awareness of, and a mounting concern worldwide about, the effects of global industrialization on the natural environment. Clearly, the disastrous effects of the BP oil spill in the Gulf of Mexico in 2010 has exacerbated that concern—as discussed in the accompanying section *Under the Lens: BP's Sustainability Systems Under Fire.* Government regulations and powerful interest groups are demanding ecological responsibility regarding the use of scarce natural resources and production processes that threaten permanent damage to the planet. MNCs have to deal with each country's different policies and techniques for environmental and health protection. Such variations in approach reflect different levels of industrialization, living standards, government–business relations, philosophies of collective intervention, patterns of industrial competition, and degrees of sophistication in public policy.

In recent years, the export of hazardous wastes from developed countries to less-developed ones has increased considerably. E-waste—from electronic components, computers, and cell phones, for example, all of which are full of hazardous materials—has become a major problem for developing economies, producing sickness and death for its handlers there; this continues in spite of laws against such dumping by U.S. companies and others. Often, companies choose to dispose of hazardous waste in less-developed countries to take advantage of weaker regulations and lower costs. Until we have strict international regulation of trade in hazardous wastes, companies should take it upon themselves to monitor their activities, as Singh and Lakhan demand:

> *To export these wastes to countries which do not benefit from waste-generating industrial processes or whose citizens do not have lifestyles that generate such wastes is unethical. It is especially unjust to send hazardous wastes to lesser-developed countries which lack the technology to minimize the deleterious effects of these substances.*[83]

The exporting of pesticides poses a similar problem, with the United States and Germany being the main culprits. The United States exports about 200 million pounds of pesticides each year that are prohibited, restricted, or not registered for use in the United States. These are only

UNDER THE LENS

BP's Sustainability Systems Under Fire

> *BP had a compelling vision of going "beyond petroleum." What it lacked was the institutional will and managerial acumen to translate its commitments into responsible operations...."*[84]

British Petroleum (BP) has been blamed and extensively criticized for the worst environmental disaster in U.S. history, caused by the explosion of the "Deepwater Horizon" drilling rig in the Gulf of Mexico on April 20, 2010. The explosion killed eleven workers and injured 17, and resulted in a massive oil spill—an estimated five million barrels of oil—that despoiled the southern U.S. coastline, created lasting ecological damage and health concerns, and threatened industries and livelihoods reliant upon the Gulf waters. BP's record and intentions regarding sustainability came under intensive scrutiny as a result of its apparent lack of willingness or preparation to take responsibility and to respond effectively—in particular as it became apparent that the company had inadequate control systems in place to prevent such disasters. As the press then reminded the public of previous BP disasters (such as the Prudhoe Bay oil spill in Alaska in March 2006, resulting in over 212,000 gallons of oil being spilled), the company's environmental record brought into question whether the company was serious in integrating sustainability into its corporate goals, organizational culture, and systems.[85] In fact, many accused BP of negligence and greed after the presidential oil spill commission issued its report in February 2011 laying considerable blame on BP for the disaster in the Gulf of Mexico. The report also highlighted flaws in Halliburton's work and errors by rig owner Transocean. BP was accused of being aware of problems with lab tests of Halliburton's cement for three years, and that "BP decided not to set a lockdown sleeve, an installation deep in the well, during its preparations for temporary abandonment in order to save 5½ days and $2 million in costs.[86]

BP has incurred considerable costs for the cleanup of the beaches and waters in the gulf, for the $20 billion fund to compensate homeowners and workers in the fishing and tourism industries, for penalties for violating the Clean Water Act, and for the loss of value for the shareholders. In addition, BP's image has suffered a terrible blow; the company had long promoted its sunburst logo and its "Be Green" campaigns, but after the oil spill its reputation was based on what the company did, or did not do—not what it said—and as a result, BP lost firm value of over $100 billion.[87] Apart from the moral argument for responsibility to its many stakeholders, and for sustainability of the environment, the consequences to BP clearly make the business case for corporate social responsibility.

The BP disaster has raised deeper concerns about the usefulness of voluntary CSR policies and reports.[88] Clearly, many corporations need to focus carefully on the implementation of their sustainability strategies—a subject discussed later in this chapter.

two of the environmental problems facing countries and large corporations today. According to Graedel and Allenby, the path to truly sustainable development is for corporations to broaden their concept of industrial ecology:

> *The concept [of industrial ecology] requires that an industrial system be viewed not in isolation from its surrounding systems, but in concert with them. It is a systems view in which one seeks to optimize the total materials cycle from virgin material, to finished material, to component, to product, to obsolete product, and to ultimate disposal.*[89]

Essentially, this perspective supports the idea that environmental citizenship is necessary for a firm's survival as well as responsible social performance.

It is clear, then, that MNEs must take the lead in dealing with ecological interdependence by integrating goals of sustainability into strategic planning. Along with an investment appraisal, a project feasibility study, and operational plans, such planning should include an environmental impact assessment. At the least, managers must deal with the increasing scarcity of natural resources in the next few decades by (1) looking for alternative raw materials, (2) developing new methods of recycling or disposing of used materials, and (3) expanding the use of by-products.[90] One company that is doing its part in minimizing waste is TerraCycle, featured in the accompanying Management in Action box.

MANAGEMENT IN ACTION
TerraCycle—Social Entrepreneurship Goes Global[91]

> *In his book 'Revolution in a Bottle,' TerraCycle CEO Tom Szaky boldly claims the company is out to render waste a thing of the past—be it through recycling, downcycling or upcycling. "Our goal over the next ten years is to be operating in every country...."*
>
> BUSINESS WORLD,
> *May 31, 2011.*[92]

TerraCycle—a company that owes its start to worm poop—is the story of Tom Szaky, a Hungarian immigrant and college dropout who became CEO of a company that is now solving global waste problems. Tom Szaky a, 20-year-old Princeton University freshman at the time, founded TerraCycle in 2001 by producing organic fertilizer consisting of liquid worm poop packaged in used soda bottles. Now TerraCycle has 50,000 collecting organizations, including schools, churches, and retail outlets, that run numerous collection programs. Through various alliances, TerraCycle now has 20 million people who collect waste in 20 countries. Some of those recycled goods are then turned into other products. In Mexico, Walmart collects toothbrushes and toothpaste tubes, a program sponsored by Colgate. In Sweden, pen-maker Bic runs an in-store program in Staples. TerraCycle's designers and scientists "manipulate waste streams into new raw materials and products."[93] The TerraCycle logo is on 20 billion packages around the world.

Szaky's idea for a class assignment at Princeton drew upon his high-school experience of trying to grow marijuana, which only did well when he tried the previously mentioned "special" fertilizer. That fertilizer resulted from feeding people's garbage to the worms.

After some hard times approaching businesses and other institutions, the idea of "upcycling"—recycling waste into usable products with added value—took hold with a number of companies such as Walmart and Home Depot; partnerships came next with companies such as Whole Foods, Target, and Kraft, who were happy to get the publicity for being "green." It is clear that "From cost savings to goodwill, being green is a marketable benchmark."[94] Non-profits were happy to be involved with a donation from TerraCycle. Other alliances are with Solo Cups, for example, in which their cups will be recreated into playgrounds. The position of Kim Frankovich, Solo vice president of sustainability, is that "Sustainability is becoming a part of everyday life and making sure our cups can be recycled as part of that ongoing activity is a priority for Solo."[95]

Szaky maintains that people feel good about doing something useful for society. In addition, he says that TerraCycle is fulfilling several needs for society: that corporations have a chance for positive action with the waste created by their processes and that consumers can have a positive feeling about buying eco-friendly products. He maintains that "it is not enough to just offer a green choice at a premium price; the goal is to make green products at a competitive price."[96]

TerraCycle is an example of what Nick et al. call a "social purpose venture." Each exists because of a social, specifically environmental mission, but seeks to achieve profitability and growth.[97] Regardless of the terminology, it is clear that social entrepreneurs such as Skazy provide "the engine of positive, systemic change that will alter what we do, how we do it, and why it matters."[98] In addition, by partnering with companies and institutions around the world, TerraCycle is providing a stimulus and outlet for the CSR of those entities and a direct source of initiatives for environmental sustainability.

Implementing Sustainability Strategies

Effective implementation of sustainability strategies, according to Epstein and Buhovac, requires companies to have both formal and informal systems in place: "Companies need the processes, performance measurement, and reward systems (formal systems) to measure success and to provide internal and external accountability. But they also need the leadership, culture, and people (informal systems) to support sustainability implementation. An alignment among the formal and informal systems along with the organizational structure is critical for success."[99]

Epstein's model (Exhibit 2-6) provides a system for examining, measuring, and managing the drivers of corporate sustainability. Essential to success is the commitment of top leadership and the recognition of sustainability as a process that will benefit the company—i.e., that it is a good

EXHIBIT 2-6   Corporate Sustainability Model[100]

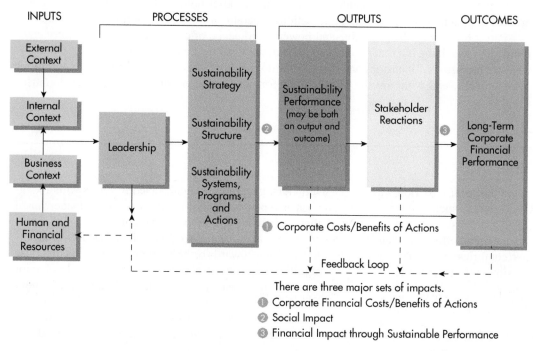

There are three major sets of impacts.
① Corporate Financial Costs/Benefits of Actions
② Social Impact
③ Financial Impact through Sustainable Performance

Source: Marc J. Epstein, "Implementing Corporate Sustainability: Measuring and Managing Social and Environmental Impacts," *Strategic Finance, January 2008.* Copyright 2008 by IMA, Montvale, N.J., www.imanet.org, used with permission.

business idea. Key to understanding the role of corporate sustainability is the relationship between managers' decisions, their impact on the society and its environment, and financial performance. In Epstein's model, the inputs include the external context in which the company operates that are specific to the locations; the internal context of the company's systems and structure; the business context, such as the industry sector, customers, and products; and the human and financial resources available to the corporation for sustainability purposes.[101] Output measures of the success of the corporation's sustainability would include, for example, reduction in energy use or hazardous waste, positive change in human rights complaints, etc. These could result, among other factors, in cost savings and in increased sales from improved reputation (as was the case, for example, when Nike turned around its human rights reputation after a student embargo on its products).

Multinational corporations already have had a tremendous impact on foreign countries, and this impact will continue to grow and bring about long-lasting changes. Because of interdependence at both the local and global level, it is not only moral but also in the best interest of MNCs to establish a single clear posture toward social and ethical responsibilities worldwide and to ensure that it is implemented. In a real sense, foreign firms enter as guests in host countries and must respect the local laws, policies, traditions, and culture as well as those countries' economic and developmental needs.

CONCLUSION

When research findings and corporate actions indicate differential attitudes toward ethical behavior and social responsibility across cultures, MNCs must take certain steps. For example, they must be careful when placing a foreign manager in a country whose values are incongruent with his or her own because this could lead to conflicts with local managers, governmental bodies, customers, and suppliers. As discussed earlier, expatriates, as well as local employees, should be oriented to the legal and ethical ramifications of questionable foreign payments, the differences in environmental regulations, and the local expectations of personal integrity. They should also be supported as they attempt to integrate host-country behaviors with the expectations of the company's headquarters.

Social responsibility, ethical behavior, interdependence, and sustainability are important concerns to be built into management control—not as afterthoughts but as part of the ongoing process of planning and controlling international operations for the long-term benefit of all.

Part 2 focuses on the pervasive and powerful influence of culture in the host-country environment in which the international manager operates. Chapter 3 examines the nature of culture—what are its various dimensions and roots? How does culture affect the behavior and expectations of employees, and what are the implications for how managers operating in other countries should behave?

Summary of Key Points

1. The concept of international social responsibility (known in business circles as CSR—corporate social responsibility) includes the expectation that MNCs should be concerned about the social and economic effects of their decisions on activities in other countries, and that they should build appropriate provisions into their strategic plans to deal with those potential effects.

2. Moral universalism refers to the need for a moral standard that is accepted around the world; however, varying cultural attitudes and business practices make this goal unattainable at this time. A number of groups of corporations within industries have collaborated on sets of policies for CSR both for their companies and those in their supply chains. Such collaborations help to raise the standard in host countries and to level the playing field for managers within those industries.

3. Concerns about MNC social responsibility revolve around issues of human rights in other countries. Many organizations develop codes of conduct that specifically deal with human rights in their operations around the world.

4. International business ethics refers to the conduct of managers in their relationships to all individuals and entities with whom they come into contact. Ethical behavior is judged and based largely on the cultural value system and the generally accepted ways of doing business in each country or society. Managers must decide whether to base their ethical standards on those of the host country or those of the home country and whether these different standards can be reconciled.

5. MNCs must balance their responsibility to various stakeholders, such as owners, creditors, consumers, employees,

suppliers, governments, and societies. Firms with a long-term perspective recognize the need to consider all of their stakeholders in their business plans.

6. Managers operating abroad are often faced with differing attitudes towards bribery or other payments that raise significant questions about appropriate moral behavior in either the host nation or other nations, yet bribery or other payments are frequently demanded to conduct business. The Foreign Corrupt Practices Act prohibits most questionable payments by U.S. companies doing business in other countries.

7. Managers must control their activities relative to interdependent relationships at all levels—from simple, daily business transactions involving local workers, intermediaries, or consumers to global concerns of ecological responsibility. Issues of "sustainability" have come to the forefront as firms consider their long-term relationships with host countries.

8. The failure to effectively manage interdependence will result in constraints on strategy, in the least, or in disastrous consequences for the local area, the subsidiary, and the global reputation of the company.

9. Managing environmental interdependence includes the need to consider ecological interdependence as well as the economic and social implications of MNC activities.

10. Implementation of sustainability strategies requires the company to have both formal and informal systems to support the goals. Essential to success is the commitment of top leadership and the recognition of sustainability as a process that will benefit the company—that it is a good business idea.

Discussion Questions

1. Discuss the concept of CSR. What role does it play in the relationship between a company and its host country?

2. Discuss the criticisms that have been leveled against MNCs in the past regarding their activities in less developed countries. What counterarguments are there to those criticisms?

3. What does moral universalism mean? Discuss your perspective on this concept. Do you think the goal of moral universalism is possible? Is it advisable?

4. What do you think should be the role of MNCs toward human rights issues in other countries? What are the major human rights concerns at this time? What ideas do you have for dealing with these problems? What is the role of corporate codes of conduct in dealing with these concerns?

5. What is meant by international business ethics? Should the local culture affect ethical practices? What are the implications of local norms for ethical decisions by MNC managers?

6. As a manager in a foreign subsidiary, how can you reconcile local expectations of questionable payments with the Foreign Corrupt Practices Act? What is your stance on the problem of "payoffs"? How does the degree of law enforcement in a particular country affect ethical behavior in business?

7. What do you think are the responsibilities of MNCs toward the global environment? Give some examples of MNC activities that run counter to the concepts of ecological interdependence and sustainability.

8. Discuss the ethical issues that have developed regarding the use of IT in cross-border transactions. What new conflicts have developed since the printing of this book? What solutions can you suggest?

Application Exercise

1. Do some research to determine the codes of conduct of two familiar companies. Compare the issues that they cover and share your findings with the class. After several students have presented their findings, prepare a chart showing the commonalities and differences of content in the codes presented. How do you account for the differences?

Experiential Exercise

Consider the ethical dilemmas in the following situation and decide what you would do. Then meet in small groups of students and come to a group consensus. Discuss your decisions with the class.

You are the VP for global sales of a telecommunications equipment company. The accounting manager of your company recently brought to your attention an unusual charge of a 3 percent commission to a purchasing manager in Russia with whom your company had recently started doing business. One state-owned manufacturing company in Russia (for privacy's sake, we will call the company "R") submitted a bid for a large order of your equipment. You remember being surprised to get the contract with "R" because your company had never been able to do business with them since it started there many years ago. As it turned out, your new sales manager for the region had a relative in "R" who promised to supply him with all of your competitors' bids if he paid him a 3 percent commission on all of the sales to his company. The area manager accepted this arrangement. He got the competing bids and secured the deal with your company.

What would you do, given the following: (1) If you refuse to accept the business without any legitimate reasons (presently there are none) your company will be blacklisted in that country—which amounts to about 20 percent of gross yearly profit. (2) If you accept the business and do not pay the 3 percent commission, the purchasing manager will make much trouble when he receives your shipment. No doubt he will not release the 5 percent bank guarantee letter about the quality and quantity of the material. (3) If you accept the business and pay the 3 percent commission, you feel that it would malign your company's reputation and your beliefs.

You have three ethical problems here: First, your company has won a rigged bid. Second, you must pay the person who rigged it or he will make life miserable for you. Third, you have to decide what to do with the area manager who accepted this arrangement.

Source: Based on Delaney and D. Sockell, "Ethics in the Trenches," *Across the Board* (October 1990): 17.

Internet Resources

Visit the Deresky Companion Website at www.pearsonhighered.com/deresky for this chapter's Internet resources.

CASE STUDY

Nike's CSR Challenge

In 2005 Nike returned to reporting on its social and environmental practices after a couple of years of silence due to legal concerns. The sports and clothing company is very important to countries such as Vietnam, where it is the largest private-sector employer with more than 50,000 workers producing shoes through subcontractors.[1] Nike's 2005 report makes sobering reading, as it describes widespread problems in Asian factories. The company said it audited hundreds of factories in 2003 and 2004 and found cases of abusive treatment in more than a quarter of its South Asian plants. For example, between 25% and 50% of the factories in the region restrict access to toilets and drinking water during the workday. The same percentage of factories denies workers at least one day off in seven. In more than half of Nike's factories employees work more than 60 hours per week. In up to 25% of the factories, workers refusing overtime were punished. Wages were below the legal minimum at up to 25% of factories.[2]

For the first time in a major corporate report, the details of all the factories were published. The report was significant for this transparency and being so candid about the problems that workers for Nike faced, and therefore the continuing challenges for the management. The NGOs working on these issues know that such problems are common. Indeed, they realize that the company invested more in improving conditions than many of its competitors. Studies of voluntary corporate attempts at improving labor standards in global supply chains have suggested that while they are delivering widespread improvements, new approaches are needed that engage governments, NGOs, and local businesses.

This realization led to a new strategy from Nike. In May 2005 Nike's vice president of corporate responsibility, Hannah Jones, told delegates at the Ethical Trading Initiative (ETI) conference that, whereas the company had previously been looking into how to solve problems for themselves, now they are exploring how to create systemic change in the industry. She explained that "premium brands are in a lonely leadership position" because "consumers are not rewarding us" for investments in improved social performance in supply chains. Like other companies, they have realized that the responsibility of one is to work towards the accountability of all. Consequently, one of Nike's new corporate citizenship goals is "to effect positive, systemic change in working conditions within the footwear, apparel and equipment industries." This involves the company engaging labor ministries, civil society, and competitors around the world to try to raise the bar so that all companies have to attain better standards of social and environmental performance. One example is Nike's involvement in the Multi-Fibre Agreement (MFA) Forum to help countries, unions, and others plan for the consequences of the end of the MFA. (The agreement and the Forum were set up by the World Trade Organization to help developed countries compete in the textile industry. These have both since ended.)

This new strategy is beyond what many consultants, media commentators, and academics currently understand. By claiming to be an advance in thinking, an article in *The Economist* in May, 2005, by the worldwide managing director of McKinsey & Company, actually illustrated the limits of current consulting advice. It suggested that seeking good societal relations should be seen as both good for society and good for profitability. "Profits should not be seen as an end in themselves," suggested Ian Davis, "but rather as a signal from society that their company is succeeding in its mission of providing something people want.[3] However, those who have experience working in this field for some years, including Nike, realize that, however we may wish to talk about the compatibility of profits with people and planet, the current societal frameworks for business are not making this a reality. The implication is that we have to make this so by changing those frameworks.

The key strategic shift for Nike's management is that they no longer regard the company as a closed system. Instead, they understand its future depends on the way customers, suppliers, investors, regulators, and others relate to it. Their challenge is to reshape the signals being given out by those groups to itself and its competitors, so that the company can operate in a sustainable and just way, which is also financially viable.

Nike's experience is pertinent to other companies, whose voluntary efforts are failing to address the root causes of the problems associated with their industry. Unilever, for example, was criticized by ActionAid for profiting from worsening conditions for workers on plantations.[4] Falling prices have led to plantations laying off workers and wages going unpaid—a trend that has seen a consequent increase in attacks against owners and managers. Applying a systems view to the situation would suggest that Unilever reconsider how it influences the global political economy that is driving down prices for tea.

The challenge is not only one of strategy but also leadership. Traditionally, analysts and educators on corporate leadership have assumed that it involves leading people toward the goal of their employer, the company. In May, 2005 an article on leadership in Conference Board Canada's *Organizational Performance Review* quoted the thoughts of leaders from World War II and the Korean War.[5] This reflects what Mark Gerzon describes as a focus on "leadership within borders," when what the world needs is "leaders beyond borders."[6] This means people are needed who can see across borders created by others, such as the borders of their job, and reach across such borders to engage others in dialogue and action to address systemic problems. We could call this "transcending leadership," which was alluded to by James McGregor Burns in his path-breaking book *Leadership*.[7] It is a form of leadership that transcends the boundaries of one's professional role and the limits of one's own situation to engage people on collective goals. It is a form of leadership that transcends a limited conception of self, as the individual leader identifies with ever-greater wholes. It is a form of leadership that transcends the need for a single leader, by helping people to transcend their limited states of consciousness and concern and inspire them to lead.

Perhaps the best modern example of transcending leadership is Gandhi, who aroused and elevated the hopes and demands of millions of Indians and whose life and personality were enhanced in the process. It is an irony of our times that this anti-imperialist, who chose to spin his own cloth, could be an inspiration for the future direction of executives in large companies sourcing clothes from factories across Asia. Gandhi called on us to understand our connectedness to "all that lives," and identify with ever-greater wholes. There is a lesson here for Nike and others. The apparel sector is an open system, and so the wider issues of trade flows, governance, media, financial markets, and politics impact on the potential of the sector, and thus Nike, to become sustainable and just. Without changes to the financial markets, Nike may find its efforts are in vain.

References

1. www.csr-asia.com/index.php?p=1925
2. www.csr-asia.com/index.php?p=1855
3. Ian Davis, "The Biggest Contract," *The Economist*, May 26, 2005.
4. www.mallenbaker.net/csr/nl/82.html
5. Jeffrey Gandz, "Leadership Character and Competencies," *Organizational Performance Review*, Spring/Summer 2005 (Conference Board Canada).
6. M. Gerzon, *Leaders Beyond Borders* (2004); www.mediatorsfoundation.org.
7. J. M. Burns, *Leadership* (New York: Harper & Row, 1978).

Case Questions

1. Discuss the challenges regarding corporate social responsibility that companies in the apparel industry face in their supply chains around the world.
2. Discuss the meaning and implications of the statement by a Nike representative that "consumers are not rewarding us for investments in improved social performance in supply chains."
3. What does it mean to have an industry open-systems approach to social responsibility? What parties are involved? Who are the stakeholders?
4. What is meant by "leadership beyond borders"?
5. Is it possible to have "a compatibility of profits with people and planet"? Whose responsibility is it to achieve that state?
6. Research Nike's CSR actions since this time frame and why it has earned the reputation as one of the world's foremost organizations in sustainability.

PART I: COMPREHENSIVE CASES

Case 1 *An Ethics Role-Playing Case: Stockholders versus Stakeholders*

–Tim Manuel[1]
University of Montana, USA

Instructions to Students:
Please read the background information (Handout I) and be prepared to discuss it on the assigned class day. Then **read Handout II and write out your Decision 1 and answer the questions.** After these discussions your instructor will provide you with further handouts requiring sequential decisions resulting from your Decision 1.

HANDOUT I. INTRODUCTION AND BACKGROUND[2]

You are a United States citizen employed by HotFeet, a Seattle-based and U.S.-owned shoe company that manufactures many of its shoes overseas. You live in Sri Lanka and work at the wholly-owned subsidiary located there, Asian HotFeet (AHF). You have been employed by HotFeet for twenty years. For fifteen of those years you have lived in Sri Lanka, and for the last five years you have been AHF's Chief Operating Officer. You were hired by George Landon, who is now the president of the company. The two of you continue to have a good relationship, and you play tennis together whenever he visits. Landon's personal loyalty to you has positively affected your career at several critical points, and you know you owe him a lot. You are married to a local who has extensive family, many of whom are directly or indirectly employed by your company. You have three beautiful children. You are quite proud of your family and enjoy your lifestyle very much. A major part of your satisfaction is derived from the knowledge that your company's presence has greatly benefited the local populace. This is, in no small part, because of your efforts to ensure fair treatment of local workers and maintain a high level of reinvestment in the country whenever possible. Because of this, and because of your local connections through your spouse, you are a highly esteemed individual in Sri Lankan society. Although you are still a U.S. citizen, you have begun to notice that you really don't think of yourself as an American anymore. You know that the home office gossip is that you have "gone native," but that's OK with you, because you have no aspirations to move back to the U.S., or live anywhere else for that matter.

[1] This project was funded by a Department of Education Northwest International Business Educators Network grant and by a University of Montana School of Business Summer Research Grant.
[2] All students should receive Handouts I and II. They should receive the appropriate versions of Handouts III, IV, and V depending on their decisions. Detailed instructions appear in the Instructor's Resources.

Asian HotFeet is owned and officially run out of the parent company's Seattle headquarters (USHF), but in reality you have significant leeway in running local operations as long as you meet the company's profit expectations. AHF comprises about 15% of the total operations of USHF, and so this subsidiary is a very important strategic investment for the parent company. The subsidiary is evaluated as a profit center; about 60% of output is sold directly by AHF in the Asian markets, but the remainder is "sold" to the parent at a transfer price set by the parent company. Traditionally, the transfer price has been set fairly high to keep the profits in Sri Lanka, which has a lower tax rate than the United States. USHF then directs how the profits are reinvested around the world and in Sri Lanka, with your consultation on local projects. Long-term financing and foreign exchange management are, however, centralized functions managed directly by USHF. You have little experience with either large scale financing or measuring and managing foreign exchange risk, although you have lobbied many times for more responsibilities in these areas. AHF's profit growth was very high for many years, until the Asian crisis and the continuing weakness in Japan generated several years of losses. More recently, AHF has had acceptable levels of profits, but is now once again having difficulty meeting the profit goals set by USHF. The parent company finance group has asked you to fly to the US and discuss some changes. At that meeting, your bosses indicate that due to a combination of factors, USHF is considering either closing the AHF facility or relocating it to another country. They explain to you that the firm's cost of capital has risen, making AHF's return on investment inadequate to satisfy their goal of maximizing USHF's shareholder wealth. In addition, the firm was surprised by the recent weakening of the dollar, resulting in speculative foreign exchange losses that have exacerbated the parent firm's profit problems. More to the point, newer production technology with higher productivity and automation has recently become available, and the parent is rethinking its strategy about locating in low-cost labor areas that are far from the major markets. In addition, Sri Lankan wage rates are beginning to rise, and the cost advantages of that location are not as great as they once were, particularly considering the added costs and inconveniences of operating in a lesser developed country. Landon tells you that you would most likely be the manager of the new facility, and you would work with the finance and operations groups in determining where the new facility would be located.

You argue that AHF should not be closed or relocated, pointing out the strong, mutually beneficial relationships that have been built between the local populace, the Sri Lankan government, and the AHF—relationships that, though perhaps not measurable in dollars, are very valuable and time consuming to build. These would be forfeited by a move or a closure and would be costly to develop elsewhere. You argue that capital costs and exchange rates are subject to frequent changes and that it is naïve to make long-term operating decisions according to what may be short-lived unfavorable interest rates and exchange rates. You indicate that "your people" can certainly be taught to use any new technology, that they are good at their jobs, and culturally they have a history of taking pride in craftsmanship that would be hard to find elsewhere. That is why AHF has a lower rejection rate and less waste than any other plant owned by USHF. You argue that the rising wage rates in Sri Lanka indicate the success of AHF and other multinationals at improving the quality of life of the local people, and you remind the home office that we are also building potential customers for our product as local incomes rise. Finally, you tell them that they do not understand the differences that businesses like AHF have made in the lives of many of the indigenous people. Education levels are starting to rise, and the use of child labor, a common practice, is dropping. The selling of children by impoverished families with no hope of feeding them has dropped dramatically in the last ten years. But all these gains are precarious, and yes, the Asian economy as a whole is still weak compared to the high-growth years, but you are convinced that better times are ahead as the Japanese and Chinese markets improve. Still, the local economy is very dependent on a few large employers, and if AHF and even one or two others leave the human cost could be high, very high indeed. How do you weigh this potential cost against the shareholder wealth goal?

HANDOUT II. DECISION 1

Landon is impressed by your passion and your arguments. He indicates that they may allow AHF to continue if you can cut costs sufficiently. The finance people are not happy with this, however, and they indicate that allowing AHF to continue at its current profit rate is tantamount to running AHF as a charitable operation, and that USHF's substantial contributions to U.S. charities such as the American Red Cross, United Way, and so forth, will likely have to be eliminated to at least partially offset the drain on profits caused by continuing AHF. Landon is a big supporter of the Red Cross and he does not like that alternative at all.

To wrap it up, Landon lays it on the line for you. He tells you up front that he would prefer to close AHF and start over in another country with the new technology. He explains why: USHF's stockholders are upset at the recent poor stock performance. Shutting down and selling AHF's assets would provide some ready cash and allow the parent firm to pay a bonus dividend to the shareholders, while still providing a sizeable down payment on the capital investment required for the new technology. Given the current economic situation and the skill level of Sri Lankans, it just doesn't make sense to locate the new facilities in Sri Lanka. He obviously thinks this is the best thing for the company, and it would avoid a potentially serious row with the stockholders. Landon indicates, though, that if you can prove that AHF can meet the necessary profit targets, he might reconsider. If you are willing to try, you will have to figure out how to cut costs or otherwise improve profits to keep AHF running. Can you do it? He tells you he will give you six months and then reevaluate if they still want to continue. Landon makes sure you understand that this will mean reducing the work force, cutting wage rates, and trying to find lower-cost supplies without sacrificing quality.

You have looked at the finance group's numbers and profit targets. You also know that, politically, it will be very difficult to fire or lay off people in Sri Lanka, which means that extensive wage cuts of 50% or more will be necessary. This will reduce many families to just enough income to survive. Worse, you will have to act very quickly, and your employees will have no warning of what's coming. Even that may not be enough. Plus, you know that your reputation with Landon and the company is on the line with this decision. If you try and you can't make this go, your career with this company will suffer and you will not only lose your shot at managing the new facility, but will probably lose your job.

Decision 1

Part A: Does this decision involve ethics or is it a business decision? Please explain. Should the shareholder wealth goal be paramount in this situation? Why or why not?

Part B: The decision is up to you. What do you do? Please circle (a) or (b).

(a) Continue operations and try to cut costs within six months.

(b) Decide to shut down now.

Please tell why you made the decision you did.

Case 2 *BlackBerry in International Markets: Balancing Business Interests and Host Nations' Security Concerns*

"Terrorists and criminals have 'thousands of ways' to hide their communications. . . . Eventually we'll get to a point to ban computers. . . . There's always a discussion about things that develop technologically. But we have to live with it."[1]

–SHEIK KHALED BIN AHMED AL KHALIFA,
Bahrain's foreign minister, on BlackBerry Controversy, in 2010

Research in Motion (RIM), a Canadian company, was the maker of the BlackBerry smartphone.[2] Mike Lazaridis, founder and co-CEO of RIM, launched the first BlackBerry smartphone in 2002. Initially Blackberries were sold to business entities and government agencies in the UK, US, and Canada, but later in 2005, as the smartphone market took off all over the world, RIM decided to expand its overseas business. At that time RIM had no clue that its biggest selling point—strong encryption built into the design of the Black-Berry system that guaranteed customer's privacy—would turn out be a major hurdle in its overseas expansion spree, especially in Asia and the Middle East. In 2010, the government of the UAE imposed a ban on BlackBerry and created a furor in countries like India, Saudi Arabia, and Indonesia, among others. Respective governments of these countries considered the phone to be a national security threat due to the strong encryption of the BlackBerry system that guaranteed customer's privacy. Analysts raised questions such as why RIM faced so much controversy in Asian countries, especially in the Middle East and not anywhere else in the world; what were the options available for RIM to avoid a ban in these countries; and would RIM be successful in addressing the security concerns of these nations and its business interests effectively? Some observers felt that the dilemma was hard to solve as the demand of governments (for access to communications) and expectations of customers (privacy) were mutually exclusive.

ABOUT RIM

RIM had operations in 175 countries and partnerships with 550 major carriers[3] across those countries by 2010. (Refer to Box I for a timeline of major BlackBerry events.) Industry observers felt that BlackBerry had come a long way from just 1 million subscribers in 2004 to a whopping 46 million subscribers in June 2010 (refer to Exhibit I).

In the year 2009, RIM's revenue grew at 84%, from around US$6 billion in 2008 to approximately US$11 billion.[4] (Refer to Exhibit II(a) and Exhibit II(b) for RIM's annual revenues). RIM generated revenue from hardware sales of BlackBerry wireless devices to carriers and licensing of software. In

EXHIBIT I   BlackBerry Subscribers: 2002–2010 ('000)

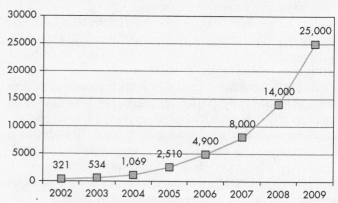

Source: Adapted from various Annual Reports of RIM, http://www.rim.com

This case was written by **Hepsi Swara** and **Saradhi Kumar Gonela**, under the direction of **Debapratim Purkayastha**, IBS Center for Management Research. It was compiled from published sources, and is intended to be used as a basis for class discussion rather than to illustrate either effective or ineffective handling of a management situation.

© 2011, IBS Center for Management Research. All rights reserved.

To order copies, call +91-08417-236667/68 or write to IBS Center for Management Research (ICMR), IFHE Campus, Donthanapally, Sankarapally Road, Hyderabad 501 504, Andhra Pradesh, India or email: info@icmrindia.org www.icmrindia.org

[1] Adam Schreck, "Saudi Arabia Blackberry Ban Lifted," www.huffingtonpost.com, August 10, 2010.

[2] Smartphone is a cellular telephone with built-in applications and Internet access. Smartphones provide digital voice service as well as any combination of text messaging, e-mail, Web browsing, still camera, video camera, MP3 player, video player, television, and organizer. In addition to their built-in functions, smartphones have become application delivery platforms, turning the once single-purpose cell phone into a mobile computer.

[3] Carrier is a term commonly used to refer to a telecom company that provides voice or data services. Carriers can be companies that operate wirelessly or over traditional wired land lines.

EXHIBIT IIA   RIM's Annual Revenue: 2002–2009 (US$ million)

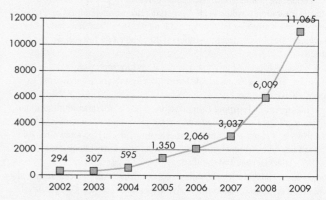

Source: Adapted from various Annual Reports of RIM, http://www.rim.com

[4] "2009 Annual Report," http://www.rim.com

EXHIBIT IIB   Five Year Income Figures of RIM (in thousands of US dollars)

					(in thousands of US dollars)
	Feb 2010	**Feb 2009**	**Feb 2008**	**March 2007**	**March 2006**
Revenue	14,953,224	11,065,186	6,009,395	3,037,103	2,065,845
Gross Profit	6,584,266	5,097,298	3,080,581	1,657,802	1,140,247
Net Income	2,457,144	1,892,616	1,293,857	631,572	374,656

Source: Annual Reports of RIM for 2007 and 2009

Box 1   Timeline of Major BlackBerry Events

- 2002—First Asia-Pacific partnership with Hutchison Telecommunications[5] in Hong Kong and Telstra Corporation Limited[6] in Australia.
- 2004—BlackBerry subscribers pass the one million mark.
- 2005—195 carriers and distribution partners in over 40 countries. BlackBerry devices available in over 50,000 stores globally.
- 2006—An estimated 25% of the BlackBerry subscriber account base is outside North America.
- 2010—550 carriers and distribution partners in 175 countries. 46 million subscribers by mid 2010.

Source: Adapted from, Taylor Paul, "BlackBerry Irritates Spy Masters," www.ft.com, August 6, 2010

addition to this, it earned service revenue through a monthly access fee charged to the carrier depending on the number of end users (using BlackBerry) with an active status. In exchange, RIM provided access to BlackBerry architecture for wireless transmission of data for the end user, via the carrier.[7]

By 2010, BlackBerry was a very popular phone and its popularity, as a trade analyst observed, "can be put down to its main selling point: the fact that it enables users to securely access their email accounts while away from their desks."[8] RIM advertised its strong security as one of its major advantages over its rivals such as Apple Inc.,[9] Google Inc.,[10] and Nokia Corporation.[11] It was reported that RIM used powerful codes to encrypt email messages and calls, which were unmatched by rivals.[12]

And this secure communications offered by RIM helped attract elite users such as President Barack Obama (Obama) in addition to a majority of corporate executives across the globe. When Obama became the US President, he was determined to continue using his BlackBerry amongst legal and security concerns.[13] Obama, who openly displayed his love for BlackBerry, opined, "It's just one tool among a number of tools that I'm trying to use, to break out of the bubble, to make sure that people can still reach me."[14] Obama succeeded in keeping his BlackBerry with enhanced security features. In the UK, BlackBerry is considered so secure that the UK's intelligence community deemed that not using BlackBerry for communication could limit the effectiveness of military operations or compromise law enforcement.[15] BlackBerry's strong security feature became its biggest selling point in the Western countries such as US, Canada, UK, etc.

However, little did RIM know that Blackberry's main selling point would become a major hurdle in its overseas expansion, especially in Asia and the Middle East. (Refer to Exhibit III for RIM's overseas revenue.) A number of countries expressed security concerns over BlackBerry's coding system. (Refer to Exhibit IV for the concerns raised by various countries.) The strong encryption made it difficult for governments of these countries to monitor communications that happened via BlackBerry devices. Most of these countries were demanding that RIM should let them access BlackBerry messages or face a ban as ever-escalating

[5] Hutchison Telecommunications Hong Kong Holdings Limited (HTHKH) is a leading integrated telecommunications provider in Hong Kong. It provides a host of services including mobile and Wi-Fi services, fixed line, and IDD services under the brand name "3ree Broadband."

[6] Telstra Corporation Limited is an Australian telecommunications and media company. Telstra provides both local and long distance fixed line and mobile services, along with dialup, wireless, DSL, and cable Internet access in Australia

[7] "RIM Business Model," http://telecommstrategy.blogspot.com, May 14, 2007

[8] McGinley, "How Big Is the BlackBerry?" www.arabianbusiness.com, August 1, 2010

[9] Apple Inc. (previously Apple Computer, Inc.) is an American multinational corporation engaged in designing and marketing consumer electronics, computer software, and personal computers. The company is best known for its Macintosh line of computers, the iPod, the iPhone (a smartphone competing with RIM's BlackBerry), and the iPad.

[10] Google Inc. is an American multinational company with interests in Internet search, cloud computing, and online advertising technologies. Google develops and provides a number of Internet-based services and products. Its Nexus One (handset) and Android smartphone software compete with BlackBerry.

[11] Nokia Corporation is a Finnish multinational company engaged in designing and manufacturing of mobile devices (including smart phones) along with equipment for Internet and communications industries.

[12] "Endgames for RIM's BlackBerry-India Standoff," *The Economic Times*, August 27, 2010

[13] The U.S. Secret Service prohibits the U.S. President from carrying any sort of cell phone in order to minimize security risks. And by law, all the President's e-mails must be recorded and made available to the public if requested.

[14] "Obama Plans to Keep his Blackberry," www.computerworld.com, January 16, 2009

[15] "Factbox: Where BlackBerry Stands Around the World," www.wired.com, August 13, 2010

EXHIBIT III   RIM's Overseas Revenue Distribution

					(in thousands of US dollars)
Revenue	**Feb 2010**	**Feb 2009**	**Feb 2008**	**March 2007**	**March 2006**
Canada	843,762	887,005	438,302	222,517	178,558
US	8,619,762	6,967,598	3,528,858	1,756,608	1,335,402
UK	1,447,417	711,536	461,592	-	-
Other Countries	4,042,283	2,499,047	1,580,643	1,057,978	551,885
Total	14,953,224	11,065,186	6,009,395	3,037,103	2,065,845

Source: Annual Reports of RIM for 2007 and 2009

EXHIBIT IV   Countries Raising Concerns Regarding BlackBerry

Country	Concerns Raised	BlackBerry Users
India	Indian security agencies were demanding full access to messaging services of RIM and threatened to ban RIM if it fails to oblige.	1,000,000
France	A French protection agency raised security concerns over the usage of BlackBerry by the cabinet.	350,000
UAE	UAE raised objections for exporting data over RIM phones on security grounds.	500,000
Bahrain	Moral and security concerns over the usage of BlackBerry	78,000
Kuwait	Moral and security concerns	NA
Lebanon	Lebanon sought access to encrypted information.	60,000
Saudi Arabia	Saudi Arabia had threatened to ban BlackBerry service as RIM was reluctant to share encryption codes.	700,000
Algeria	Security concerns	NA

Source: Adapted from various sources

global security threats were forcing a tight monitor on all communication channels. The United Nations telecommunications agency urged RIM to allow security agencies to access customer data, and Hamadoun Toure, Secretary-General of the International Telecommunication Union, expressed his support by saying that all governments, fighting terrorism, had the right to access citizens' communication and information.[16] Respective governments warned that if RIM refused these requests, it could face bans. And combined bans (by various countries) would significantly harm RIM's market share.

THE BLACKBERRY CONTROVERSY AND RIM'S REMEDIAL MEASURES

"The company is in a pretty tricky position now. . . . Part of the BlackBerry's appeal is that it offers high levels of security and that same factor is what's getting it blocked."[17]

–MATTHEW REED,
Senior Analyst & Editor, Middle East & Africa Wireless Analyst,[18] _in 2010_

"A company like RIM really needs to think not just about the UAE or Saudi Arabia, but about their customers worldwide. . . . BlackBerry is willing to offer backdoor access (in the Gulf), other countries are going to want that too. And at that point it's really a race to the bottom."[19]

–CINDY COHN,
Legal Director and General Counsel for digital rights group Electronic Frontier Foundation,[20] _in 2010_

"If RIM concedes, they've lost any hope of being distinctive. . . . They will destroy the brand and appear to have a lack of scruples. If they don't 'blink,' they could stand to lose a reasonable amount of volume, but they would also be viewed as courageous."[21]

–GARY SINGER,
founder and CEO of Buyology Inc.,[22] _in 2010_

[16] "RIM should open up user data: UN agency," www.cbc.ca, September 2, 2010

[17] Anthony DiPaola, "RIM Refuses to Give Codes as BlackBerry Faces Bans," www.businessweek.com, August 4, 2010

[18] _Middle East & Africa Wireless Analyst_, a fortnightly, covers key market developments across Africa and the Middle East, including network rollout, new license awards, regulation, mergers and acquisitions, and new service launches.

[19] Adam Schreck, "Saudi Arabia Blackberry Ban Lifted," www.huffingtonpost.com, August 10, 2010

[20] Electronic Frontier Foundation is the leading American civil liberties group defending people's rights and promoting privacy protection in the digital age.

[21] Mangalindan, J. P., "Why the UAE Ban is a Golden Opportunity for Black-Berry," http://tech.fortune.cnn.com, August 6, 2010

[22] Buyology Inc. is a privately held marketing neuroscience firm that measures and manages data regarding non-conscious decision making. By 2010, Buyology had the world's largest brain scan database, with scans collected from five countries—the US, UK, Germany, Japan, and China.

BlackBerry, since its launch, was known for the strong encryption which was so strong that the time taken to crack would be as long, "as it would for the sun to burn out—billions of years,"[23] as claimed by RIM. Scott Totzke, Vice-president of global security at RIM, elaborating it further explained, "Every message that is sent via a BlackBerry is broken up into 2Kb 'packets of information,' each of which is given a 256-bit key by the BlackBerry server... That means to release the contents of a 10Kb e-mail, a person would have to crack 5 separate keys, and each one would take about as long as it would for the sun to burn out—billions of years."[24]

Apart from the strong encryption, when someone used BlackBerry's email or BlackBerry Instant Messenger or sent a message using BlackBerry Personal Index Number (PIN), the data was sent directly in encrypted form to RIM servers in Canada, making it difficult for the local governments to intercept or monitor conversations (regarding illegal or terrorist activities), as the information did not pass through domestic servers. And this inability to access BlackBerry traffic frustrated countries such as India, Saudi Arabia, and the United Arab Emirates (UAE), along many others. Analysts pointed out that among many other web-based mail systems, such as Gmail, which also used encrypted data, only BlackBerry was singled out, because RIM was the only firm that sent users' data to servers in Canada automatically.[25] And many countries were demanding that RIM should set up local servers, apart from seeking access to the data transmitted via BlackBerrys.

Middle East

Citing security concerns, the UAE, which had 500,000 BlackBerry subscribers in mid-2010, announced on August 1, 2010, that it would ban BlackBerry services—e-mail, messaging, and web services—from October 11, 2010 unless RIM offered an acceptable solution to access BlackBerry traffic. The UAE's decision to ban BlackBerry came days after several youths were arrested for organizing a peaceful protest using BlackBerry Messenger. The UAE had raised BlackBerry concerns on national security grounds much earlier, which snowballed into controversies. For instance, in 2009, UAE's state-owned mobile operator Etisalat[26] urged the BlackBerry customers to install software, described as an upgrade for service enhancements. RIM said the tests showed that it turned out to be a spyware, which would have allowed the UAE government to access the private information stored on the BlackBerry phones. RIM criticized UAE, and directed the users on how to remove the software. *Financial Times*[27] reckoned, "The

spyware controversy could be interpreted as the first public signs of the Gulf states' concerns about Canadian-based RIM."[28] Moreover, the assassination of Mahmoud al-Mabhouh, senior leader of Hamas (Palestinian militant group), in a hotel room in Dubai, allegedly by a team of the Israeli intelligence agency in January 2010, made the BlackBerry issue even more sensitive in UAE, as it is believed that the attackers communicated securely on their BlackBerry phones.

UAE's announcement to ban BlackBerry met with a lot of criticism from the western countries. US State Department spokesman P. J. Crowley termed such technological restrictions as a move in the wrong direction.[29] Reporters Without Borders[30] implored the UAE government to lift the ban and reach a compromise to protect the freedom of the population.[31] However, the regulators in UAE argued that some features operated by BlackBerry fell outside the country's laws, therefore causing judicial, social, and national security concerns.[32]

Just a few days before the scheduled ban, UAE and RIM reached an agreement and UAE's Telecommunications Regulatory Authority (TRA) announced that it would not suspend BlackBerry services from October 11, 2010. On October 8, 2010, UAE's TRA stated that "BlackBerry services were now compliant with the UAE's telecommunications regulatory framework"[33] and it also "acknowledged the positive engagement and collaboration of Research in Motion (RIM) in reaching this regulatory compliant outcome."[34] RIM refused to discuss the details of the deal and how it managed to meet UAE's concerns.

Shortly after UAE's action, Saudi Arabia, RIM's biggest Middle East market with 700,000 BlackBerry users, said that it would block BlackBerry Messenger from August 6, 2010, as the service did not meet the regulatory requirements and posed a national security threat. The governments in Middle Eastern countries also drew support from the conservatives to ban smartphones such as BlackBerry, as youth were negatively influenced by it. (Refer to Box II for concerns of Gulf residents.) But later Saudi Arabia delayed the ban, as RIM reached a preliminary agreement with Saudi regulators that would allow the government limited access to BlackBerry instant messages by September 1, 2010. It was reported by the trade journals that the agreement with RIM also included placing a BlackBerry server inside Saudi Arabia.[35]

[23] Jonathan Richards, "RIM to France: BlackBerry Is Safe," http://technology.timesonline.co.uk, June 20, 2007

[24] Jonathan Richards, "RIM to France: BlackBerry Is Safe," http://technology.timesonline.co.uk, June 20, 2007

[25] Jane Wakefield, "Untangling the BlackBerry Ban," www.bbc.co.uk, August 4, 2010

[26] Emirates Telecommunications Corporation, operating under brand name Etisalat, is a UAE-based telecommunications services provider, with operations in 18 countries across Asia, the Middle East, and Africa. As of February 2011, Etisalat is the 13th largest mobile network operator in the world, with a total customer base of more than 135 million.

[27] *Financial Times* is the latest UK and international business, finance, economic and political news daily.

[28] "Concern over Crime behind BlackBerry Plan," *Financial Times*, August 3, 2010, page 4

[29] "UAE: BlackBerry Crackdown Will Affect Visitors Too," www.samoanews.com, August 2, 2010

[30] Reporters Without Borders is an international non-governmental freedom organization, which aims at defending journalists and media assistants imprisoned or persecuted, and it also fights against censorship and laws that undermine press freedom.

[31] Adam Schreck, "UAE: BlackBerry Crackdown Will Affect Visitors Too," http://news.yahoo.com, August 2, 2010

[32] Adam Schreck, "UAE: BlackBerry Crackdown Will Affect Visitors Too," http://news.yahoo.com, August 2, 2010

[33] Andrew England, "UAE Lifts BlackBerry Ban Threat," www.ft.com, October 8, 2010

[34] "United Arab Emirates Will Not Ban Blackberries," www.bbc.co.uk, October 8, 2010

[35] Abdullah Al-Shihri, "BlackBerry, Saudi Arabia Agreement Could Set a Precedent," www.cleveland.com, August 7, 2010

Box II Concerns of BlackBerry's Gulf Customers

- "It's a waste of time and money… I had to buy it for the eldest of my children and since then, the little time he spends at home is punching messages and laughing by himself. It's not normal."

The father of a BlackBerry user

- "My daughter collapsed once. When we took her to the hospital, the doctor said she was suffering from fatigue. After getting her BlackBerry phone she became so attached to it that she even used to be on it while in bed. She reads every SMS she receives and even replies to them late at night."

A mother who confiscated her daughter's BlackBerry

Adapted from "The Flip Side," The Economic Times, *August 7, 2010, page 4*

The other Middle Eastern countries such as Lebanon, Bahrain, and Kuwait also raised security concerns on BlackBerry usage. Lebanon's Telecommunications Regulatory Authority (TRA) said it was assessing the security concerns regarding the smartphones such as BlackBerry. TRA claimed it was not reacting to Saudi Arabia and UAE's stance on Blackberry, but it was worried over the integrity of the telecom network after the arrest of three people suspected of spying for Israel.[36]

Kuwait did not threaten a BlackBerry ban, but it was holding talks with RIM over moral and security concerns. Kuwait asked RIM to block access to pornographic sites, for which RIM asked for four month's time. Most of the Middle Eastern governments considered pornography to be a crime. Using Internet on BlackBerry was different from using Internet on the other smartphones, as Internet was not controlled by the local wireless carrier that BlackBerry was running on. BlackBerry directly connected through the local wireless carrier's network to RIM's servers located in Canada and accessed the Internet. Canada gave freedom to its citizens to watch whatever they wanted to and thus even BlackBerry users in Kuwait were able to access everything that Canadians could.

Bahrain, another Middle Eastern country, also had raised security concerns about BlackBerry messaging services, but later decided not to ban BlackBerry. On August 8, 2010, Sheik Khaled bin Ahmed Al Khalifa, Bahrain's foreign minister, said, "We're not saying there is no security concern . . . But . . . There are many other ways for the criminals or terrorists to communicate, so we decided we might as well live with it."[37]

India

India, the world's second-largest mobile phone market with one million BlackBerry users, threatened to ban BlackBerry if RIM did not let the Indian Government access BlackBerry Enterprise Servers (BES)[38]—which many Indian business and government organizations used—and BlackBerry Messenger. BES was very popular among the enterprise customers, as it offered a higher level of security and RIM claimed neither RIM nor any other third party could access the corporate data on the encrypted BES network.

India had raised concerns over BlackBerry services in 2008 too. RIM's response then was that it did not allow any third party or even its own employees to access the data sent over the network.[39] In the same year the terrorist attacks in Mumbai occurred, in which 173 people were killed and 308 people were injured. This intensified concerns in India over the government's inability to access encrypted communications.[40] Five BlackBerry phones were recovered from the crime scene, and it was suspected that the terrorists would have co-ordinated the entire attack on BlackBerry phones.

India was a very lucrative market for RIM and on September 1, 2010, Informa Telecoms & Media[41] forecasted that BlackBerry sales in India would be more than 600,000 by end of 2010 and that India's smartphone market would have reached approximately 12 million by then—a figure expected to reach 40 million by the end of 2015.[42] RIM, faced with saturated markets in North America and the UK, had no option but to give into the Indian Government demands as "India is an absolute gold mine."[43]

On August 29, 2010, RIM was able to avert a ban by getting a 60-day reprieve from the government to continue its services in India. During this 60-day period the security agencies would be testing the solutions provided by RIM and see if they were able to tap into BlackBerry Messenger and BES. RIM has provided a technical solution to intercept the BBM between two handsets after providing the PIN. The Indian Government on September 6, 2010 asked RIM to provide a technical solution to intercept its BES. But RIM had maintained that it was unable to provide anyone the text of emails sent using its corporate service designed for secure communications.[44] Hence, industry observers could not figure out as to how RIM would fulfill the Indian Government's demand. They stated that RIM would eventually also have to set up a local server in India to

[36] "Nation-by-Nation Look at BlackBerry Controversy," www.msnbc.msn.com, August 13, 2010
[37] Adam Schreck, "Bahrain Says No Plans to Ban BlackBerry Services," http://news.yahoo.com, August 8, 2010
[38] When using the BES, an organisation hosts its own server and encryption key for access to transmitted content, offering a higher level of security.

[39] Dew Alam, "BlackBerry vs World: Should RIM Cave into Government Pressure,?" http://top10.com, August 10, 2010
[40] "BlackBerry's Security Stance Sows Anxiety," http://economictimes.indiatimes.com, August 10, 2010
[41] Informa Telecoms & Media is a leading provider of business intelligence and strategic services to the global telecoms and media markets.
[42] Josh Halliday, "BlackBerry Wins the Battle But Not the War in India," www.guardian.co.uk, September 1, 2010
[43] Douglas Quan, "RIM Reported to Have Made Deal with India," www.montrealgazette.com, August 14, 2010
[44] "RIM Should Open Up User Data: UN Agency," www.cbc.ca, September 2, 2010

continue its services from November 2010 onwards. India had also asked Google Inc.,[45] Skype Technologies,[46] and other Internet service providers to set up local servers to monitor their Internet traffic.

Other Countries

Along with the Middle Eastern countries and India, a number of other countries such as Algeria and Indonesia also opined that BlackBerry phones were a threat to national security. By mid-2010, Algeria was reviewing BlackBerry services, and the government stated that continuing services in the country depended on the degree of threat to the national security, if any. Algerian Telecommunications Minister Moussa Benhamadi said, "We are looking at the issue. If we find out that it is a danger for our economy and our security, we will stop it."[47] Indonesia, with 1.2 million BlackBerry subscribers, also expressed fears on BlackBerry usage for security and moral reasons. In the last week of August, Indonesia was pressuring RIM to block pornographic content or face a ban. Pornography was illegal in Indonesia and the government summoned RIM officials to filter indecent material accessible by roughly one million BlackBerry users in Indonesia.[48] Indonesia had also asked RIM to set up local servers in the country to monitor local communications.

BLACKBERRY CONTROVERSY CENTERED ONLY IN ASIA AND THE MIDDLE EAST?

"The difference between India and Great Britain or between the United Arab Emirates and the United States might be more about their varying abilities to eavesdrop secretly."[49]

–OWEN COTE,
Associate Director, Massachusetts Institute of Technology's Security Studies Program,[50] in 2010

Industry observers noted that the controversy surrounding BlackBerry raised an important question—why did governments of Western countries not have an objection with BlackBerry services? Or, in other words, had their concerns been already secretly addressed by RIM? Some analysts opined, "simply because a government isn't hassling BlackBerry or

Google for access to their customers' conversations doesn't mean their spy agencies aren't listening."[51] Owen Cote elaborated why some countries such as UAE were demanding that RIM provide them access to its data whereas Western countries were not. According to him, all governments did not possess the same capabilities, and that cracking encryption was beyond the reach of governments such as those of Dubai.

As soon as the UAE made an announcement to ban Black-Berry services, Philip J. Crowley, Assistant Secretary in the US State Department Bureau of Public Affairs, stated "We are disappointed at this announcement…It's not about a Canadian company… It's about what we think is an important element of democracy, human rights, and freedom of information and the flow of information in the 21st century."[52] The UAE immediately fired back by saying that the US was maintaining double standards as "UAE is asking for exactly the same regulatory compliance—and with the same principles of judicial and regulatory oversight—that BlackBerry grants the US and other governments and nothing more."[53] According to Dhahi Khalfan Tamim, Lieutenant General and chief of the Dubai Police, "The West has accused us of curbing the liberties of BlackBerry users, while America, Israel, Britain, and other countries are allowed access to all transferred data."[54] Even India's Sachin Pilot, Minister of State for IT and Communications, opined "I don't think the concerns raised by India are out of the ordinary… Most countries in the Western world have raised the issues and to the best of my information—and I am willing to be corrected their concerns have been addressed."[55]

Though RIM claimed that it had not given any country special access to its servers, it was rumored that RIM had struck special deals with countries all over the world. Leslie Harris, chief executive of the Center for Democracy and Technology,[56] Washington, stated that he was aware of rumors that various deals have been struck around the world, including in the US, but he said he was not aware of the details.[57]

RIM is known for its secrecy—as it never revealed the details of its conversations with governments of various countries, nor had it revealed how it had complied with laws of security-conscious countries such as Russia and China, which required the telecom companies to grant the security agencies access to their systems. It was speculated that RIM cracked a deal with

[45] Google, Inc. is a public company focused on Internet search services. Google operates web sites at many international domains, with the most trafficked being www.google.com. Google is widely recognized as the "world's best search engine" because of its speed, accuracy, and ease of use.

[46] Skype's popular Web-based software allows users to make voice and video calls using the Internet. Calls are free when made Skype-to-Skype, and users could make calls to landlines and cell phones at lower rates than traditional phone services. Skype also obtains revenue from voice mail and other services, and offers a platform for business communications geared toward small and midsized firms.

[47] Suzanne Choney, "Amid Talk of Bans, BlackBerry Maker Fights Back," www.msnbc.msn.com, August 6, 2010

[48] Anthony Deutsch, "RIM Faces Battle Over Content in Indonesia," www.ft.com, September 2, 2010

[49] "Global Deals Threaten BlackBerry's Vital Encryption," http://it.tmcnet.com, August 18, 2010

[50] The Security Studies Program at MIT is a graduate-level research and educational program.

[51] "Global Deals Threaten BlackBerry's Vital Encryption," http://it.tmcnet.com, August 18, 2010

[52] Stephen Kurczy, "UAE's BlackBerry Ban: Why Is Canada Silent?" www.csmonitor.com, August 3, 2010

[53] Stephen Kurczy, "UAE's BlackBerry Ban: Why Is Canada Silent?" www.csmonitor.com, August 3, 2010

[54] "U.S., Israel Spying Behind BlackBerry Woe—Dubai Police," http://uk.reuters.com, September 3, 2010

[55] "BlackBerry's Security Stance Sows Anxiety," http://economictimes.indiatimes.com, August 10, 2010

[56] Center for Democracy & Technology (CDT) is a Washington-based, non-profit public-interest group with expertise in law, technology, and policy. CDT works to enhance free expression and privacy in communications technologies by finding practical and innovative solutions to public policy challenges while protecting civil liberties.

[57] "BlackBerry's Security Stance Sows Anxiety," http://economictimes.indiatimes.com, August 10, 2010

Russia in 2008. Carolina Milanesi, Gartner Inc.[58] analyst, said "RIM has, as far as I know, negotiated with Russia. I don't know the specifics because that is something between RIM and the government but Russia did not allow them to sell Black-Berries and from 2008 they were allowed so something must have changed."[59] RIM planned to enter China in 2006, but was delayed for two years due to the security concerns raised by the Chinese authorities. RIM eventually began selling BlackBerry handsets in 2008 in a tie-up with China Mobile Limited,[60] the biggest telecom operator in China, but the response had reportedly been weak.[61] Analysts suspected that RIM, to start operations in China, must have struck a deal that satisfied the strict Chinese laws.

In the US, there were not too many reported issues regarding the BlackBerry encryption. However, it was widely reported that several US law enforcement and security agencies would have had a way to decrypt BlackBerry messages. Legally, the US security agencies could access the BlackBerry or any iPhone data under its Patriot Act—enacted after 9/11 attacks[62]—by obtaining a court order signed by a judge. In the US, post-September 11, 2001 attacks, the National Security Agency convinced several wireless carriers to share records of calls made over more than 200 million phones.[63]

In the UK, public authorities wanting to access past communications data needed to obtain a warrant from the Interior Minister or permission from a senior police, defense, or customs authority.[64] Robert Guerra (Guerra), Director of Freedom House,[65] supporting such privileges in Western countries and discouraging such privileges in Middle Eastern countries, opined that such privileges were allowed in the US and other Western countries due to high standards of human rights, freedom of expression, and due process, but Saudi Arabia and other

Middle Eastern countries lacked the same standards.[66] It was assumed by the analysts that the Middle Eastern countries were trying to gain access to customers' data to restrict the flow of information, in the name of national security. Even though India too wanted to access BlackBerry for security reasons, experts stated only the data of suspected persons should be accessed, given the high levels of corruption in the governance. "What is the protection against a government official sitting in a control room and making use of price-sensitive market information? Or selling intellectual property and confidential information? How about revealing transcripts of embarrassing private conversations among business leaders or celebrities as has happened frequently in Italy?" questioned one skeptical observer.[67]

Human rights organizations worldwide condemned the stance taken on BlackBerry by countries such as the UAE, Saudi Arabia, and India, as such instances undermined the importance of the free flow of information and the right to privacy. Critics of the BlackBerry ban opined, terrorism existed even before the advent of BlackBerry and they argued that terrorists also had other ways to carry their stealthy communications. They pointed out that one could simply save an e-mail as a draft, and share the password for the e-mail to the other to see the draft. This way, communication was completed by no electronic exchange, making it impossible for the security agencies to access the communication.[68] According to Eben Moglen, Chairman of Software Freedom Law Center[69] and Columbia Professor of Law, "No terrorist is going to use an expensive BlackBerry, if they want untapped communication. They can just use free software from the web. When I communicate using software like this (he shows a free email and encryption software on his IBM Thinkpad), no government on earth can overhear."[70]

RIM's nod to provide access to its customer's data to the governments of Saudi Arabia and India, according to some analysts, would compromise customer's privacy and it could damage RIM's strong reputation built on confidentiality. Trade observers said that RIM had chosen commercial gains over customers' privacy, and that it is all about business and protecting market share.[71] The entire BlackBerry controversy highlighted the conflict going on between the technology (and telecom) companies and governments (mostly Asian and Middle-Eastern) over how to balance privacy and national security needs.

ROAD AHEAD

"Companies like RIM need support in determining how to draw principled lines when responding to governmental

[58] Gartner Inc. is a US-based information technology research and advisory company providing technology-related insights to large corporations, government agencies, technology companies, and the investment community.

[59] Jane Wakefield, "Untangling the BlackBerry Ban," www.bbc.co.uk, August 4, 2010

[60] China Mobile Limited, one of the world's largest mobile phone companies with 584 million subscribers (by end of 2010), is a Chinese state-owned telecommunication company that provides mobile voice and multimedia services.

[61] "Factbox: Where BlackBerry Stands Around the World," www.wired.com, August 13, 2010

[62] The September 11 attacks, often referred to as "September 11th" or "9/11," were a series of coordinated suicide attacks by al-Qaeda upon the US on September 11, 2001. On that morning, 19 al-Qaeda terrorists hijacked four commercial passenger jet airliners. The hijackers crashed two of the airliners into the Twin Towers of the World Trade Center in New York City, killing everyone on board and many others working in the buildings. The hijackers crashed a third airliner into the Pentagon in Arlington, Virginia, just outside Washington. The fourth plane crashed into a field near Shanksville in rural Pennsylvania after some of its passengers and flight crew attempted to retake control of the plane, which the hijackers had redirected toward Washington to target either the Capitol Building or the White House. There were no survivors from any of the flights.

[63] "Talk of Banning BlackBerrys over Data Encryption Has Businesses Worried," www.cdt.org, August 17, 2010

[64] "Factbox: Where BlackBerry Stands Around the World," www.wired.com, August 13, 2010

[65] Freedom House is a Washington-based international non-governmental organization engaged in researching and advocating on democracy, political freedom, and human rights.

[66] Stephen Kurczy, "BlackBerry Caved to Saudi Demands: Rights Group," www.csmonitor.com, August 10, 2010

[67] Stephen Mathias, "Rethink Snooping App on BlackBerry," http://economictimes.indiatimes.com, September 2, 2010

[68] Ivor Soans, "Why the Indian Government Is Wrong on BlackBerry," http://biztech2.in.com, August 9, 2010

[69] Software Freedom Law Center (SFLC) is a US-based organization that provides legal representation and related services to not-for-profit developers of free software/open-source software.

[70] Harsimran Julkawhat, "Blackberry Standoff Is About Sovereignty: Moglen," www.economictimes.indiatimes.com, September 7, 2010

[71] Stephen Kurczy, "BlackBerry Caved to Saudi Demands: Rights Group," www.csmonitor.com, August 10, 2010

requests that could compromise the security of their products or increase the human rights risk to their users. One lesson we should draw from RIM's current challenge is that all companies should aggressively advocate for legal standards that respect human rights in all countries in which they operate, democratic and non-democratic alike."[72]

—CENTRE FOR DEMOCRACY AND TECHNOLOGY, IN 2010

"This is the new China and Google story, except now it's happening in the Middle East...Google at least had a fight with China."[73]

—ROBERT GUERRA, *Director of Freedom House,*[74] *in 2010*

The BlackBerry controversy was not the first dispute of its kind between governments and communication companies over information control. The Google-China controversy was very similar to the controversy of RIM. Any company that entered China should abide by the stringent Chinese censorship rules, including the self-censorship rule. On January 12, 2010, Google announced that it was no longer willing to censor the searches and might pull out of the country. On March 22, 2010, Google announced that it would automatically re-route its searches from the Chinese search engine (google.cn) to its Hong Kong–based website, where Google was not required legally to censor searches. This move shifted the responsibility of censoring the searches from Google to China. The official Google Blog read: "attempts over the last year to further limit free speech on the web in China including the persistent blocking of websites such as Facebook, Twitter, YouTube, Google Docs, and Blogger—had led us to conclude that we could no longer continue censoring our results on Google .cn."[75] China responded back by saying Google was violating Chinese censorship rules and threatened Google that it will not renew Google's Internet Content Provider (ICP) license, without which Google's search presence in China would be severely hurt.[76]

Though Google won applauds from human rights organizations worldwide for the tough stance it took against China, Google could not go out of the Chinese market because of the huge potential its Internet market had. China, the world's largest Internet market with 400 million users offered prospects of earning revenues between US$15 billion and US$20 billion annually through the online advertising market. Thus Google, to stay in such a lucrative market, agreed to abide by Chinese law and ensure it was not providing law-breaking content.[77] Google

said that it will stop the automatic redirect of its google.cn users to its uncensored Hong Kong website. On July 9, 2010, it was announced that China agreed to renew Google's license.

RIM had been facing (in various countries) what Google faced in China. All the communication companies in Asia and the Middle East, in order to operate, had to obey the local laws or they could face a ban. In India, in addition to RIM, on September 1, 2010, Google and Skype were also asked to set up servers to enable security agencies to access and monitor the Internet traffic. Nokia,[78] on August 4, 2010, after the BlackBerry controversy, announced that it was not opposing new restrictions on mobile messaging in emerging market countries.[79] Nokia announced that it would host a server in India by November 5, 2010, appeasing the Indian government. Analysts opined that governments always had an upper hand, because at the end, commercial gain and business growth considerations would take first preference and things such as the right to privacy and information took a back seat.[80]

Case Questions

1. Why is the BlackBerry controversy prominent in Asia, particularly in the Middle East, and not anywhere else in the world?

2. Analyze the measures that RIM can take to address security concerns while taking care of its business interests effectively.

3. Discuss the strategic lessons arising from the BlackBerry episode for MNCs operating in the technology arena.

References and Suggested Readings

1. Jonathan Richards, "RIM to France: BlackBerry Is Safe," http://technology.timesonline.co.uk, June 20, 2007

2. Melanie Lee, "Why Is China so Important to Google?" http://www.reuters.com, July 10, 2010

3. Shane McGinley, "How Big Is the BlackBerry?" www .arabianbusiness.com, August 1, 2010

4. Adam Schreck ,"UAE: BlackBerry Crackdown Will Affect Visitors Too," http://news.yahoo.com, August 2, 2010

5. Stephen Kurczy, "UAE's BlackBerry Ban: Why Is Canada Silent?" www.csmonitor.com, August 3, 2010

6. Jane Wakefield, "Untangling the BlackBerry Ban," www .bbc.co.uk, August 4, 2010

7. Anthony DiPaola, "RIM Refuses to Give Codes as BlackBerry Faces Bans," www.businessweek.com, August 4, 2010

8. Anthony DiPaola, "RIM Refuses to Give Codes as BlackBerry Faces Bans," http://www.businessweek.com, August 4, 2010

---

[72] Stephen Kurczy, "BlackBerry Caved to Saudi Demands: Rights Group," www.csmonitor.com, August 10, 2010

[73] Stephen Kurczy, "BlackBerry Caved to Saudi Demands: Rights Group," http://www.csmonitor.com, August 10, 2010

[74] Freedom House is an independent watchdog organization that supports the expansion of freedom around the world. Freedom House supports democratic change, monitors freedom, and advocates for democracy and human rights.

[75] "A new approach to China: An Update," http://googleblog.blogspot.com, March 22, 2010

[76] Melanie Lee, "Why Is China so Important to Google?" http://www.reuters .com, July 10, 2010

[77] "Google vs China," http://www.redherring.com, July 14, 2010

[78] Nokia is the world's leading mobile phone supplier and a leading supplier of mobile and fixed telecom networks, including related customer services.

[79] Anthony DiPaola, "RIM Refuses to Give Codes as BlackBerry Faces Bans," http://www.businessweek.com, August 4, 2010

[80] P. Chacko Joseph, "BlackBerry vs India: Opinions Decrypted," http:// frontierindia.net, August 10, 2010

9. Suzanne Choney, "Amid Talk of Bans, BlackBerry Maker Fights Back," www.msnbc.msn.com, August 6, 2010

10. Mangalindan, J. P., "Why the UAE Ban Is a Golden Opportunity for BlackBerry," http://tech.fortune.cnn.com, August 6, 2010

11. Abdullah Al-Shihri, "BlackBerry, Saudi Arabia Agreement Could Set a Precedent," www.cleveland.com, August 7, 2010

12. Adam Schreck, "Bahrain Says No Plans to Ban Black-Berry Services," http://news.yahoo.com, August 8, 2010

13. Ivor Soans, "Why the Indian Government Is Wrong on BlackBerry," http://biztech2.in.com, August 9, 2010

14. Stephen Kurczy, "BlackBerry Caved to Saudi Demands: Rights Group," www.csmonitor.com, August 10, 2010

15. Adam Schreck, "Saudi Arabia Blackberry Ban Lifted," www.huffingtonpost.com, August 10, 2010

16. P. Chacko Joseph, "BlackBerry vs India: Opinions Decrypted," http://frontierindia.net, August 10, 2010

17. Stephen Kurczy, "BlackBerry Caved to Saudi Demands: Rights Group," www.csmonitor.com, August 10, 2010

18. Dew Alam, "BlackBerry vs World: Should RIM Cave into Government Pressure," http://top10.com, August 10, 2010

19. Douglas Quan, "RIM Reported to Have Made Deal with India," www.montrealgazette.com, August 14, 2010

20. Josh Halliday, "BlackBerry Wins the Battle But Not the War in India," www.guardian.co.uk, September 1, 2010

21. Stephen Mathias, "Rethink Snooping App on Black-Berry," http://economictimes.indiatimes.com, September 2, 2010

22. Anthony Deutsch, "RIM Faces Battle Over Content in Indonesia," www.ft.com, September 2, 2010

23. Harsimran Julkawhat, "Blackberry Standoff Is About Sovereignty: Moglen," www.economictimes.indiatimes.com, September 7, 2010

24. Andrew England, "UAE Lifts BlackBerry Ban Threat," www.ft.com, October 8, 2010

25. "RIM Business Model," http://telecommstrategy.blogspot.com, May 14, 2007

26. "Obama Plans to Keep his Blackberry," www.computerworld.com, January 16, 2009

27. "A New Approach to China: An Update," http://googleblog.blogspot.com, March 22, 2010

28. "Google vs China," http://www.redherring.com, July 14, 2010

29. "UAE: BlackBerry Crackdown Will Affect Visitors Too," www.samoanews.com, August 2, 2010

30. "Concern over Crime behind BlackBerry Plan," *Financial Times*, August 3, 2010, page 4

31. "BlackBerry's Security Stance Sows Anxiety," http://economictimes.indiatimes.com, August 10, 2010

32. "Factbox: Where BlackBerry Stands Around the World," www.wired.com, August 13, 2010

33. "Nation-by-Nation Look at BlackBerry Controversy," www.msnbc.msn.com, August 13, 2010

34. "Talk of Banning BlackBerrys over Data Encryption Has Businesses Worried," www.cdt.org, August 17, 2010

35. "Global Deals Threaten BlackBerry's Vital Encryption," http://it.tmcnet.com, August 18, 2010

36. "Endgames for RIM's BlackBerry-India Standoff," *The Economic Times*, August 27, 2010

37. "RIM Should Open up User Data: UN agency," www.cbc.ca, September 2, 2010

38. "U.S., Israel Spying Behind BlackBerry Woe—Dubai Police," http://uk.reuters.com, September 3, 2010

39. "United Arab Emirates Will Not Ban Blackberries," www.bbc.co.uk, October 8, 2010

40. "2009 Annual Report," http://www.rim.com

41. en.wikipedia.org

42. www.rim.com

2
PART

The Cultural Context of Global Management

3 Understanding the Role of Culture

OBJECTIVES

1. To understand how culture affects all aspects of international management.

2. To be able to distinguish the major dimensions which define cultural differences among societies or groups.

3. To emphasize the need for international managers to have cultural intelligence in order to interact successfully in host countries.

4. To recognize the critical value differences that frequently affect job behaviors.

5. To be able to develop a working "cultural profile" typical of many people within a certain society as an aid to anticipating attitudes toward work, negotiations, etc.

6. To understand the interaction between culture and the use of the Internet.

OPENING PROFILE: ADJUSTING BUSINESS TO SAUDI ARABIAN CULTURE

For most outsiders, Saudi Arabia is a land of contrasts and paradoxes. It has supermodern cities, but its strict Islamic religious convictions and ancient social customs, on which its laws and customs depend, often clash with modern economic and technical realities. Saudi Arabians sometimes employ latitude in legal formation and enforcement to ease these clashes and sometimes accommodate different behaviors from foreigners. Nevertheless, many foreigners misunderstand Saudi laws and customs or find them contrary to their own value systems. Foreign companies have had mixed success in Saudi Arabia, due in large part to how well they understood and adapted imaginatively to Saudi customs.

Companies from countries with strict separation between state and religion or where few people actively engage in religion find Saudi Arabia's pervasiveness of religion daunting. Religious decrees have sometimes made companies rescind activities. For example, an importer halted sales of the children's game Pokémon because the game might encourage the un-Islamic practice of gambling, and a franchisor was forced to remove the face under the crown in Starbucks' logo because Saudi authorities felt the public display of a woman's face was religiously immoral. However, most companies know the requirements in advance. For instance, Coty Beauty omits models' faces on point-of-purchase displays that it depicts in other countries. Companies know that they must remove the heads and hands from mannequins and must not display them scantily clad. Companies, such as McDonald's, dim their lights, close their doors, and stop attending to customers during the five times per day that men are called to pray. Companies also adjust voluntarily to gain the good will of customers—for example, by converting revenue-generating space to prayer areas. (Saudi Arabian Airlines does this in the rear of its planes, and the U.K.'s Harvey Nichols does this in its department store.) During the holy period of Ramadan, people are less active during the day because they fast, so many stores shift some operating hours to the evenings when people prefer to shop.

In 2000, Saudi Arabia ratified an international agreement designed to eliminate the discrimination of women; however, its prescribed behaviors for women appear paradoxical to outsiders. On the one hand, women now outnumber men in Saudi Arabian universities and own about 20 percent of all Saudi businesses. (There are separate male and female universities, and female-owned businesses can sell only to women.) Women also comprise a large portion of Saudi teachers and doctors. On the other hand, women account for only about 7 percent of the workforce. They cannot have private law or architectural firms, nor can they be engineers. They are not permitted to drive, because this may lead to evil behavior. They must wear *abayas* (robes) and cover their hair completely when in public. They cannot work alongside men except in the medical profession, and they cannot sell directly to male customers. If they are employed where men work, they must have separate work entrances and be separated from males by partitions. They must be accompanied by an adult male relative when dealing with male clerks.

The female prescriptions have implications for business operations. For example, the Saudi American Bank established branches for and staffed only by women. Pizza Hut installed two dining rooms—one for single men and one for families. (Women do not eat there without their families.) Both Harvey Nichols and Saks Fifth Avenue have created women-only floors in their department stores. On lower levels, there is mixed shopping, all male salespeople (even for products like cosmetics and bras), and no changing rooms or places to try cosmetics. On upper floors, women can check their *abayas* and shop in jeans, spandex, or whatever. The stores have also created drivers' lounges for their chauffeurs. A downside is that male store managers can visit upper floors only when the stores are closed, which limits their observations of situations that might improve service and performance. Similarly, market research companies cannot rely on discussions with family-focused groups to determine marketing needs. Because men do much more of the household purchasing, companies target them more in their marketing than in other countries.

Why do high-end department stores and famous designers operate in Saudi Arabia, where women cover themselves in *abayas* and men typically wear *thobes* (long robes)? Simply, the many very rich people in Saudi Arabia are said to keep Paris couture alive. Even though Saudi Arabia prohibits fashion magazines and movies, this clientele knows what is in fashion. (The government also prohibits satellite dishes, but some estimates say that two-thirds of Saudi homes have them.) Women buy items from designers' collections, which they wear abroad or in Saudi Arabia only in front of their husbands and other women. Underneath their *abayas*, they often wear very expensive jewelry, makeup, and clothing. Wealthy men also want the latest high-end fashions when traveling abroad.

Another paradox is that about 60 percent of the Saudi private workforce is foreign, even though the unemployment rate is about 30 percent. Changing economic conditions are at least partially responsible

(Continued)

for this situation. In the early 1980s, Saudi oil revenues caused per capita income to jump to about $28,000, but this plummeted to below $7,000 by the early 2000s. When incomes were high, Saudis brought in foreigners to do most of the work. At the same time, the government liberally supported university training, including study abroad. Saudis developed a mentality of expecting foreigners to do all the work—or at least some of the work—for them. The New Zealand head of National Biscuits & Confectionery said that Saudis now want only to be supervisors and complain if they have to work at the same level as people from Nepal, Bangladesh, and India. Although the government has taken steps to replace foreign workers with Saudis, prevailing work attitudes impede this transition. For example, the acceptance by a Saudi of a bellboy job at the Hyatt Regency hotel in Jidda was so unusual that Saudi newspapers put his picture on their front pages.

Saudi Arabian legal sanctions seem harsh to many outsiders. Religious patrols may hit women if they show any hair in public. The government carries out beheadings and hand-severances in public and expects passers-by to observe the punishments, some of which are for crimes that would not be offenses in other countries. For example, the government publicly beheaded three men in early 2002 for being homosexuals. However, there are inconsistencies. For example, religious patrols are more relaxed about women's dress codes in some Red Sea resorts, and they are more lenient toward the visiting female executives of MNEs than toward Saudi women. Whereas they don't allow Saudi women to be flight attendants on Saudi Arabian Airlines because they would have to work alongside men, they permit women from other Arab countries to do so. Further, in foreign investment compounds where almost everyone is a foreigner, these religious patrols make exceptions to most of the strict religious prescriptions.

There are interesting situations concerning the charging of interest and the purchase of accident insurance, both of which are disallowed under strict Islamic interpretations of the Koran. In the case of interest, the Saudi government gives interest-free loans for mortgages. This worked well when Saudi Arabia was awash with oil money, but borrowers must now wait about 10 years for a loan. In the case of accident insurance (by strict Islamic doctrine, there are no accidents, only preordained acts of God), the government eliminated prohibitions because businesses needed the insurance.

Personal interactions between cultures are tricky, and those between Saudis and non-Saudis are no exception. For example, Parris-Rogers International (PRI), a British publishing house, sent two salesmen to Saudi Arabia and paid them on a commission basis. They expected that by moving aggressively, the two men could make the same number of calls as they could in the United Kingdom. They were used to working eight-hour days, to having the undivided attention of potential clients, and to restricting conversation to the business transaction. To them, time was money. However, they found that appointments seldom began at the scheduled time and most often took place at cafés where the Saudis would engage in what the salesmen considered idle chitchat. Whether in a café or in the office, drinking coffee or tea and talking to acquaintances seemed to take precedence over business matters. The salesmen began showing so much irritation at "irrelevant" conversations, delays, and interruptions from friends that they caused irrevocable damage to the company's objectives. The Saudi counterparts considered them rude and impatient.

Whereas businesspersons from many countries invite counterparts to social gatherings at their homes to honor them and use personal relationships to cement business arrangements, Saudis view the home as private and even consider questions about their families as rude and an invasion of privacy. In contrast, Saudi businessmen seldom regard business discussions as private; they thus welcome friends to sit in. The opposite is true in many countries.

In spite of contrasts and paradoxes, foreign companies find ways to be highly successful in Saudi Arabia. In some cases, legal barriers to some products, such as alcoholic beverages and pork products have created boons for other products, such as soft drinks and turkey ham. In addition, some companies have developed specific practices in response to Saudi conditions and have later benefited from them in their home countries. For example, companies such as Fuji and Kodak created technology for while-you-wait photo development for Saudi Arabia because customers wanted to retrieve photos without anyone else seeing them. They transferred this technology to the United States several years later.

This chapter's opening profile describes how an understanding of the local culture and business environment can give managers an advantage in competitive industries. Foreign companies—no matter what their size—can ignore those aspects to their peril. Such differences in culture and the way of life in other countries necessitate that managers develop international expertise to manage on a contingency basis according to the host-country environment. Powerful, interdependent factors in that environment—political, economic, legal, technological, and cultural—influence management strategy, functions, and processes.

> *Cultural Intelligence: an outsider's seemingly natural ability to interpret someone's unfamiliar and ambiguous gestures in just the way that person's compatriots and colleagues would.*
>
> HARVARD BUSINESS REVIEW.[1]

Managing people and processes in other countries requires a working knowledge of the cultural variables affecting management decisions and how to use that knowledge to adapt behaviors and expectations accordingly. This skill has become known as **cultural intelligence**, or **cultural quotient (CQ)**—a measure of how well a person can adapt and manage effectively in culturally diverse settings.[2] There is further discussion of how to adapt to different cultures in Chapter 4. First, we need to gain an understanding of what "culture" is, what are the variables that will enable us to adapt, and how those variables affect the manager's job. Clearly, it is important for anyone wishing to be successful when working with people in other countries to be able to plan ahead as to how to relate to and adapt to people from different cultures.

Managers have often seriously underestimated the significance of cultural factors. According to numerous accounts, many blunders made in international operations can be attributed to a lack of cultural sensitivity.[3] Examples abound. Scott Russell, senior vice president for human resources at Cendant Mobility in Danbury, Connecticut, recounts the following:

> *An American company in Japan charged its Japanese HR manager with reducing the workforce. The Japanese manager studied the issue but couldn't find a solution within cultural Japanese parameters; so when he came back to the Americans, he reduced the workforce by resigning—which was not what they wanted.[4]*

Cultural sensitivity, or **cultural empathy**, is the awareness of and an honest caring about another individual's culture. Such sensitivity requires the ability to understand the perspective of those living in other (and very different) societies and the willingness to put oneself in another's shoes.

International managers can benefit greatly from understanding the nature, dimensions, and variables of a specific culture and how these affect work and organizational processes. This cultural awareness enables them to develop appropriate policies and determine how to plan, organize, lead, and control in a specific international setting. Such a process of adaptation to the environment is necessary to successfully implement strategy. It also leads to effective interaction in a workforce of increasing cultural diversity, in both the United States and other countries.

Company reports and management studies make it clear that a lack of cultural sensitivity costs businesses money and opportunities. One study of U.S. multinational corporations found that poor intercultural communication skills still constitute a major management problem. Managers' knowledge of other cultures lags far behind their understanding of other organizational processes.[5] In a synthesis of the research on cross-cultural training, Black and Mendenhall found that up to 40 percent of expatriate managers leave their assignments early because of poor performance or poor adjustment to the local environment. About half of those who remain are considered only marginally effective. Furthermore, they found that cross-cultural differences are the cause of failed negotiations and interactions, resulting in losses to U.S. firms of over $2 billion a year for failed expatriate assignments alone.[6]

Other evidence indicates, however, that cross-cultural training is effective in developing skills and enhancing adjustment and performance. In spite of such evidence, U.S. firms do little to take advantage of such important research and to incorporate it into their ongoing training programs, whose purpose is ostensibly to prepare managers before sending them overseas. Too often, the importance of such training in developing cultural sensitivity is realized much too late.

This chapter provides a conceptual framework with which companies and managers can assess relevant cultural variables and develop cultural profiles of various countries. This framework is then used to consider the probable effects of cultural differences on an organization and their implications for management. To do this, the powerful environmental factor of cultural context is examined. The nature of culture and its variables and dimensions are first explored, and then specific differences in cultural values and their implications for the on-the-job behavior of individuals and groups are considered. Cultural variables, in general, are discussed in this chapter. The impact of culture on specific management functions and processes is discussed in later chapters as appropriate.

CULTURE AND ITS EFFECTS ON ORGANIZATIONS

We know that cultural values can predict employee outcomes with similar or even more strength than more traditional factors such as demographics, personality traits, and cognitive ability.

V. TARAS ET AL.,
ORGANIZATIONAL DYNAMICS, APRIL 6, 2011.[7]

Societal Culture

As generally understood, the **culture** of a society comprises the shared values, understandings, assumptions, and goals that are learned from earlier generations, imposed by present members of a society, and passed on to succeeding generations. This shared outlook results, in large part, in common attitudes, codes of conduct, and expectations that subconsciously guide and control certain norms of behavior.[8] One is born into, not with, a given culture, and gradually internalizes its subtle effects through the socialization process. Culture results in a basis for living grounded in shared communication, standards, codes of conduct, and expectations.[9] Over time, cultures evolve as societies adapt—by choice or otherwise—to transitions in their external and internal environments and relationships. In 2011, for example, people in Egypt brought about political and cultural changes as a result of economic conditions and oppression and being increasingly exposed through social media to what they perceived to be a better way to live within systems in democratic societies. Globalization, in all its forms of personal and business contacts and information crossing borders, brings about changes that result in **cultural diffusion**. When immigrants adopt some aspects of the local culture while keeping aspects of their culture of origin, this process is called **creolization**. Some countries, such as France, fiercely protect their culture against outside influences and insist that immigrants assimilate into their society and respect their values.[10]

A manager assigned to a foreign subsidiary must expect to find large and small differences in the behavior of individuals and groups within that organization. As depicted in Exhibit 3-1, these differences result from the societal, or sociocultural, variables of the culture, such as religion and language, as well as from prevailing national variables, such as economic, legal, and political factors. National and sociocultural variables, thus, provide the context for the development and perpetuation of cultural variables. These cultural variables, in turn, determine basic attitudes toward work, time, materialism, individualism, and change. Such attitudes affect an

EXHIBIT 3-1   Environmental Variables Affecting Management Functions

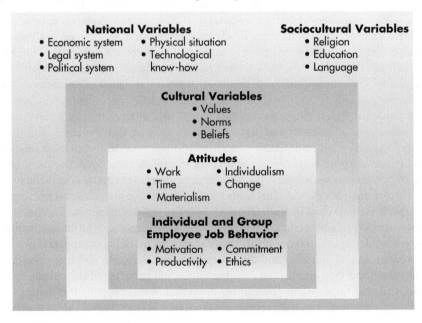

individual's motivation and expectations regarding work and group relations, and they ultimately affect the outcomes that can be expected from that individual.

Organizational Culture

Compared to societal culture, which is often widely held within a region or nation, **organizational culture** varies a great deal from one organization, company, institution, or group to another. Organizational culture represents those expectations, norms, and goals held in common by members of that group. For a business example, consider the oft-quoted comparison between IBM, considered traditionally to be very formal, hierarchical, and rules-bound, with its employees usually in suits, and Apple Computer, whose organizational culture is very organic, or "loose" and informal, with its employees typically wearing casual clothes and interacting informally.

Research shows that societal culture tends to be stronger than organizational culture, so that employees working with or for a "foreign" company may not easily fall into the new organizational culture.[11] Clearly there is a relationship between organizational culture and societal (national) culture, both of which can cause disputes in the workplace at all levels, including the management of cross-border alliances. Such was the case with the DaimlerChrysler AG alliance—largely contributing to the downfall of the alliance in 2007. As observed by Syed Anwar:

> In the auto industry, Daimler-Benz was viewed as a conservative and rigid company regarding its corporate bureaucracy, product development, and quality standards—a corporate culture reflective of Germany's national culture. On the other hand, Chrysler's corporate culture was typical American—informal, outward oriented, and somewhat less rigid in its operations and more risk-taking. Daimler-Benz lacked exposure to the American way of management and business practices. The cultural mismatch eventually created problems in the areas of future planning, supervisory board, research and development, expatriate management, executive salaries, and labor relations.[12]

Culture's Effects on Management

Clearly, societal culture affects organizational culture, and there are often interaction effects, as illustrated by the comments by Kenichi Watanabe, CEO of Japan's Nomura Group, when asked how he would characterize his company's corporate culture:

> The positives: trust, loyalty, teamwork, long-term commitment. The negatives: resistance to change and an overly domestic focus. That's why I tell my people to embrace change and be world class.[13]

FINANCIAL TIMESUK,
SEPTEMBER 23, 2011.

Which organizational processes—technical and otherwise—are most affected by cultural differences, and how they are affected, is the subject of ongoing cross-cultural management research and debate.[14] Oded Shenkar suggests that we should. . . .

> consider cultural differences as having the potential for both synergy and disruption, [and that] this point cannot be overstated as it lies at the intersection of strategic logic and operational challenges that underline the FDI, expatriate adjustment, auditing and other international business issues.[15]

ODED SHENKAR, JOURNAL OF INTERNATIONAL BUSINESS STUDIES,
JANUARY 2012.

Further, Shenkar poses that, rather than focusing on how *different* two cultures are—that is, "cultural distance" (CD)—in reality, it is the *interaction* between them that is the working issue in international management; this is because cultural distance has little effect on management until the two cultures come into contact with each other. He proposes that we focus on the concept of "friction" instead of "distance" by considering how the relevant people and organizational processes would interact and what the effects would be on the relative success of the international business venture.[16]

Some argue that the effects of culture are more evident at the individual level of personal behavior than at the organizational level, as a result of convergence. **Convergence** describes the phenomenon of the shifting of individual management styles to become more similar to one another. The convergence argument is based on the belief that the demands of industrialization, worldwide coordination, and competition tend to factor out differences in organizational-level processes, such as choice of technology and structure. In a study of Japanese and Korean firms, Lee, Roehl, and Choe found that globalization and firm size were sources of convergence of management styles.[17] At the individual level, the research we will discuss in this chapter and throughout the book clearly shows that while an assertive, take-charge management style typically works best in the West, people across Asia typically respond better to a more subtle leadership style where the manager works behind the scenes to accomplish goals; then again, Latino cultures tend to prefer a paternal management style and look up to leaders who command respect by virtue of their position in society.[18] These factors are discussed in more detail later in this chapter.

The effects of culture on specific management functions are particularly noticeable when we attempt to impose our own values and systems on another society. Exhibit 3-2 gives some examples of the values typical of U.S. culture, compares some common perspectives held by people in other countries, and shows which management functions might be affected, clearly implying

EXHIBIT 3-2 U.S. Values and Possible Alternatives

Aspects of U.S. Culture*	Alternative Aspect	Examples of Management Functions Affected
The individual can influence the future (where there is a will there is a way).	Life follows a preordained course, and human action is determined by the will of God.	Planning and scheduling
The individual can change and improve the environment.	People are intended to adjust to the physical environment rather than to alter it.	Organizational environment, morale, and productivity
An individual should be realistic in his or her aspirations.	Ideals are to be pursued regardless of what is "reasonable."	Goal setting and career development
We must work hard to accomplish our objectives (Puritan ethic).	Hard work is not the only prerequisite for success; wisdom, luck, and time are also required.	Motivation and reward system
Commitments should be honored (people will do what they say they will do).	A commitment may be superseded by a conflicting request, or an agreement may only signify intention and have little or no relationship to the capacity for performance.	Negotiating and bargaining
One should effectively use one's time (time is money that can be saved or wasted).	Schedules are important, but only in relation to other priorities.	Long- and short-range planning
A primary obligation of an employee is to the organization.	The individual employee has a primary obligation to his or her family and friends.	Loyalty, commitment, and motivation
The employer or employee can terminate the relationship.	Employment is for a lifetime.	Motivation and commitment to the company
The best-qualified people should be recruited and selected, given the positions available.	Family, friendship, and other considerations should determine employment practices.	Employment, promotions, and reward

*Aspect here refers to a belief, value, attitude, or assumption that is a part of a culture in that it is shared by a large number of people in that culture.

Source: Excerpted from *Managing Cultural Differences* by Philip R. Harris and Robert T. Moran, 5th ed. Copyright © 2000 by Gulf Publishing Company, Houston, TX. Used with permission. All rights reserved.

the need for the differential management of organizational processes. For example, American managers plan activities, schedule them, and judge their timely completion based on the belief that people influence and control the future, rather than assuming that events will occur only at the will of Allah, as managers in an Islamic nation might believe.

Many people in the world understand and relate to others only in terms of their own culture. This unconscious reference point of one's own cultural values is called a **self-reference criterion**. The result of such an attitude is illustrated in the following story:

> Once upon a time there was a great flood, and involved in this flood were two creatures, a monkey and a fish. The monkey, being agile and experienced, was lucky enough to scramble up a tree and escape the raging waters. As he looked down from his safe perch, he saw the poor fish struggling against the swift current. With the very best of intentions, he reached down and lifted the fish from the water. The result was inevitable.[19]

The monkey assumed that its frame of reference applied to the fish and acted accordingly. Thus, international managers from all countries must understand and adjust to unfamiliar social and commercial practices—especially the practices of that mysterious and unique nation, the United States. Japanese workers at a U.S. manufacturing plant learned to put courtesy aside and interrupt conversations with Americans when there were problems. Europeans, however, are often confused by Americans' apparent informality, which then backfires when the Europeans do not get work done as the Americans expect.

As a first step toward cultural sensitivity, international managers should understand their own cultures. This awareness helps to guard against adopting either a parochial or an ethnocentric attitude. **Parochialism** occurs, for example, when a Frenchman expects those from or in another country to automatically fall into patterns of behavior common in France. **Ethnocentrism** describes the attitude of those who operate from the assumption that their ways of doing things are best—no matter where or under what conditions they are applied. Companies both large and small have demonstrated this lack of cultural sensitivity in countless subtle (and not so subtle) ways, with varying disastrous effects.

Procter & Gamble (P&G) was one such company. In an early Japanese television commercial for Camay soap, a Japanese woman is bathing when her husband walks into the bathroom. She starts telling him about her new beauty soap. Her husband, stroking her shoulder, hints that he has more on his mind than suds. The commercial, which had been popular in Europe, was a disaster in Japan. For the man to intrude on his wife "was considered bad manners," says Edwin L. Artzt, P&G's vice chairman and international chief. "And the Japanese didn't think it was very funny." P&G has learned from its mistakes and now generates about half of its revenue from foreign sales.[20]

After studying his or her own culture, the manager's next step toward establishing effective cross-cultural relations is to develop cultural sensitivity. Managers not only must be aware of cultural variables and their effects on behavior in the workplace, but also must appreciate cultural diversity and understand how to build constructive working relationships anywhere in the world. The following sections explore cultural variables and dimensions. Later chapters suggest specific ways in which managers can address these variables and dimensions to help build constructive relationships.

Given the great variety of cultures and subcultures around the world, how can a student of cross-cultural management, or a manager wishing to be culturally savvy, develop an understanding of the specific nature of a certain people? With such an understanding, how can a manager anticipate the probable effects of an unfamiliar culture within an organizational setting, and thereby manage human resources productively and control outcomes?

One approach is to develop a cultural profile for each country or region with which the company does or is considering doing business. Developing a cultural profile requires some familiarity with the cultural variables universal to most cultures. From these universal variables, managers can identify the specific differences found in each country or people—and hence anticipate their implications for the workplace.

Managers should never assume that they can successfully transplant American, or Japanese, or any other country's styles, practices, expectations, and processes. Instead, they should practice a basic tenet of good management—**contingency management**. Contingency management requires managers to adapt to the local environment and people and to manage accordingly. That adaptation can be complex because the manager may confront differences not only in culture, but also in business practices. The need for managers to adapt to local conditions, particularly within a joint venture, was illustrated by Baruch Shimoni in his research of Thai and Israeli managers of two MNCs headquartered in Sweden and the United States. He found that the firms' local management cultures ran into each other and produced new hybrid forms of management cultures.[21] Shimoni found that the managers developed a hybrid management style that was between their own and the corporation's management practices. Whereas the Thai culture focuses on harmonious personal relationships and avoidance of confrontation, in the Israeli offices practices focused on non-formal relationships, performance, work processes, and supervision.[22]

Over time, the Thai managers (Chindakohrn and Hansa) and the Israeli managers (Tamir and Shuki) came to adapt their feelings and management style to create a hybrid style suited to the situation. As Hansa said "I try to compromise. Working together, get your opinion, what you want, what you think, then I make decisions . . . you [I] have to be very quick and execute immediately. . . . I try to change myself, to be adopting to this [the MNCs'] kind of character, culture."[23]

Influences on National Culture

Managers should recognize, of course, that generalizations in cultural profiles will produce only an approximation, or stereotype, of national character. Many countries comprise diverse **subcultures** whose constituents conform only in varying degrees to the national character. In Canada, distinct subcultures include Anglophones and Francophones (English-speaking and French-speaking people) and indigenous Canadians.

Above all, good managers treat people as individuals, and they consciously avoid any form of **stereotyping**. However, a cultural profile is a good starting point to help managers develop some tentative expectations—some cultural context—as a backdrop to managing in a specific international setting. It is useful, then, to look at what cultural variables have been studied and what implications can be drawn from the results.

Before we can understand the culture of a society, we need to recognize that there are subsystems in a society that are a function of where people live; these subsystems influence, and are influenced by, people's cultural values and dimensions and so affect their behaviors, both on and off the job. Harris and Moran identified eight categories that form the subsystems in any society.[24] This systems approach to understanding cultural and national variables—and their effects on work behavior—is consistent with the model shown in Exhibit 3-1 that shows those categories as a broad set of influences on societal culture. Those categories are: the *kinship* system of relationships among families; the *education system*; the *economic* and *political systems*; the *associations* that make up formal and informal groups; the *health system*; attitudes toward *recreation* and leisure; and—perhaps most importantly—*religion* (further discussed in the accompanying Under the Lens feature).

CULTURAL VALUE DIMENSIONS

Cultural variables result from unique sets of shared values among different groups of people. Most of the variations between cultures stem from underlying value systems, which cause people from different cultures to behave differently under similar circumstances. **Values** are a society's ideas about what is good or bad, right or wrong—such as the widespread belief that stealing is immoral and unfair. Values determine how individuals will probably respond in any given circumstance. As a powerful component of a society's culture, values are communicated through the eight subsystems previously described and are passed from generation to generation. Interaction and pressure among these subsystems (or more recently, from foreign cultures) may provide the impetus for slow change. The dissolution of the Soviet Union and the formation of the Commonwealth of Independent States is an example of extreme political change resulting from internal economic pressures and external encouragement to change.

Project GLOBE Cultural Dimensions

Recent research results on cultural dimensions have been made available by the GLOBE (Global Leadership and Organizational Behavior Effectiveness) Project team. The team comprises 170 researchers who have collected data over seven years on cultural values and practices and

UNDER THE LENS

Religion and the Workplace

Since the basis of a religion is the shared beliefs, values, and institutions, then it is closely aligned with the accepted underpinnings of societal culture; thus religion and culture are inextricably linked. As such, religion underlies both moral and economic norms and influences everyday business transactions and on-the-job behaviors. The connections between culture and work behavior for employees and managers in various countries are discussed throughout this book. Here we note specifically that managers in the home country or abroad must recognize both the legal religious rights in the workplace and also the value of such diversity in the workplace. Days off for religious holidays, accommodation for prayers, dietary requirements, etc., are the more obvious considerations. In addition, foreign managers abroad must be particularly sensitive to the local religious context and the expectations and workplace norms of employees and others, because those managers will be immersed within that context in dealing with employees, clients, suppliers, and others. Failure to do so will minimize or negate the goals of the firm in that location.

Most readers of this book are familiar with the major religions of the world, and an in-depth discussion of religions is beyond the focus here. (The four religions with the largest number of followers are: Christianity, with 33.1% of world population; Islam, with 20.4%; Hinduism, with 13.5%; and Buddhism, with 6%. These figures are approximate, since of course they are changing every day.)[25] What we do focus on as we progress through the chapters are the ways in which religion intersects with culture and affects business interactions, expectations, operations, motivations, and leadership, including attitudes toward work, time, ethics, and decision-making.

Hinduism is over 5,000 years old and typically involves worship of many gods. Prayer is usually a private matter in one's own home. The traditional caste system, now illegal, still tends to impact the labor markets. As another example of the effects of religion in the workplace, a Western manager operating in some areas or enterprises in India might note the employees' lack of sensitivity to time. As noted by Agam Nag, that attitude is attributed to the religious belief and the philosophical background. "It has been variously traced to the concept of immortality of soul and reincarnation in Hinduism that gives a sense of infiniteness to life and hence time."[26] Nag explains that the lack of sensitivity to time cuts across all religions in India, including the endless variations of Hinduism as well as many other religions such as Islam, Christianity and Sikhism.[27] Clearly, religious belief is only one dimension of Indian culture to explain the way they view time. However, we can also observe the influence and competitiveness of foreign companies operating in the cities in India, such as the many companies in the information technology industry that are operating there. Their young, educated workforce has adapted to the competitiveness and expectations in those companies, resulting in a meld of their traditional value system and the practical approach typical of western companies. Foreign firms in India and elsewhere are reaping the benefits of this rapidly growing and highly effective workforce.[28]

Christianity originated in the Middle East and is now over 2,000 years old. Christians believe in one God. Christianity is based on the life and death of Jesus Christ, the son of God, and preaches love, the value of human life, self-discipline, and ethics. There are four principal denominations: Orthodox, Pentecostal, Protestant, and Roman Catholic. Roman Catholicism predominates in the Americas and Western Europe. Orthodox Christians mostly live in Eastern Europe. Foreign corporations in Christian locales can assume that most employees and other contacts behave largely according to the Ten Commandments. In Europe, employees typically have a number of days off for religious holidays. In the United States, religious holidays are typically limited to Christmas and Easter; however, there should be respect for people not wanting to work on Sundays. One wonders, also, if the Protestant Ethic of hard work, saving, and efficiency, common in the West and the basis of capitalism, is spreading as a result of global competition and the influence of foreign companies.

Islam was discussed in the opening profile. Muslims believe that there is only one god, Allah, and that the prophet Muhammad was his final messenger. Their lives are based on the Qur'an and Muslim law (Sharia). Businesses can be affected by the Sharia law against receiving or paying interest. As a further example of how religious beliefs impact the workplace, respect for Islam requires that companies operating in Muslim countries make provisions—in time and space allocation—for employees to pray five times a day. This is true, also, in countries and cities such as in the United Kingdom where there is a

(Continued)

MAP 3.1   Major World Religions

MAJOR RELIGIONS

Buddhist

Buddhist/Confucian

Eastern Orthodox

Hindu

Muslim

Mixed Christian
(Catholic, Protestant, and
other Christian groups)

Protestant

Roman Catholic

Other

Source: Data from various sources, including U.S. Census Bureau's International Data Base, U.S. State Department Reports, U.N. Human development report.

large Muslim population. In addition, out of respect for the Ramadan, a month during which Muslims must fast from dawn till dusk, managers must expect and plan for productivity to go down in the event that contractual obligations are scheduled. Businesspeople not familiar with Islam might get frustrated by the lack of precision regarding scheduling and contracts attributable to the perspective that things will happen in good time as Allah wills. However, the Islamic work ethic is a commitment toward fulfillment and the individual's obligation to society, and so there is considerable respect for workers and business motives.[29] In addition, managers operating in Muslim countries must take care to avoid conflict with the prescribed gender roles in their hiring and placement practices, as described in the opening profile. Generally, job opportunities for women are limited in strict Islamic countries such as Saudi Arabia.

Buddhism, founded in India 2,500 years ago, remains the dominant religion of the Far East and is increasingly popular in the West. Buddhism emphasizes compassion and love and the ways in which suffering in the world can be relieved by righteous living and the cycle of rebirth. There is a high regard for others as if they are all part of the family, and an ethical consideration of one's actions upon the well-being of others. Buddhism promotes a strong work ethic, persistence, and hard work, and frowns on laziness. There are likely to be positive outcomes in the work environment by emphasizing teamwork and responsibility. Foreign managers should acknowledge and respect, for example, that employees expect to have a shrine on the wall or floor with a statue of Buddha and cups holding food and drink as offerings.[30]

leadership attributes from 18,000 managers in 62 countries. Those managers were from a wide variety of industries and sizes of organizations from every corner of the globe. The team identified nine cultural dimensions that distinguish one society from another and have important managerial implications: assertiveness, future orientation, performance orientation, humane orientation, gender differentiation, uncertainty avoidance, power distance, institutional collectivism versus individualism, and in-group collectivism. Only the first four are discussed here; this avoids confusion for readers since the other five dimensions are similar to those researched by Hofstede, which are presented in the next section. (Other research results from the GLOBE Project are presented in subsequent chapters where applicable, such as in the Leadership section in Chapter 11.) The descriptions are as follows, along with selected rankings based on the GLOBE results shown in the accompanying bar charts.[31]

ASSERTIVENESS

This dimension refers to how much people in a society are expected to be tough, confrontational, and competitive versus modest and tender. Austria and Germany, for example, are highly assertive societies that value competition and have a "can-do" attitude. This compares with Sweden and Japan, less assertive societies, which tend to prefer warm and cooperative relations and harmony. The GLOBE team concluded that those countries have sympathy for the weak and emphasize loyalty and solidarity.

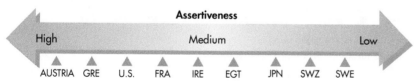

*Not to scale—indicates relative magnitude.

Source: Based on results from the GLOBE project.

FUTURE ORIENTATION

This dimension refers to the level of importance a society attaches to future-oriented behaviors such as planning and investing in the future. Switzerland and Singapore, high on this dimension, are inclined to save for the future and have a longer time horizon for decisions. This perspective compares with societies such as Russia and Argentina, which tend to plan more in the shorter term and place more emphasis on instant gratification.

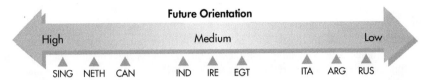

*Not to scale—indicates relative magnitude.

Source: Based on results from the GLOBE project.

PERFORMANCE ORIENTATION

This dimension measures the importance of performance improvement and excellence in society and refers to whether or not people are encouraged to strive for continued improvement. Singapore, Hong Kong, and the United States score high on this dimension; typically, this means that people tend to take initiative and have a sense of urgency and the confidence to get things done. Countries such as Russia and Italy have low scores on this dimension; they hold other priorities ahead of performance, such as tradition, loyalty, family, and background, and they associate competition with defeat.

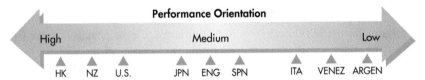

*Not to scale—indicates relative magnitude.

Source: Based on results from the GLOBE project.

HUMANE ORIENTATION

This dimension measures the extent to which a society encourages and rewards people for being fair, altruistic, generous, caring, and kind. Highest on this dimension are the Philippines, Ireland, Malaysia, and Egypt, indicating a focus on sympathy and support for the weak. In those societies paternalism and patronage are important, and people are usually friendly and tolerant and value harmony. This compares with Spain, France, and the former West Germany, which scored low on this dimension; people in these countries give more importance to power and material possessions, as well as self-enhancement.

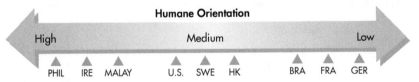

*Not to scale—indicates relative magnitude.

Source: Based on results from the GLOBE project.

Clearly, research results such as these are helpful to managers seeking to be successful in cross-cultural interactions. Anticipating cultural similarities and differences allows managers to develop the behaviors and skills necessary to act and decide in a manner appropriate to the local societal norms and expectations.

Cultural Clusters

Gupta et al., from the GLOBE research team, also analyzed their data on the nine cultural dimensions to determine where similarities cluster geographically. Their results support the existence of ten cultural clusters: South Asia, Anglo, Arab, Germanic Europe, Latin Europe, Eastern

EXHIBIT 3-3   Geographic Culture Clusters

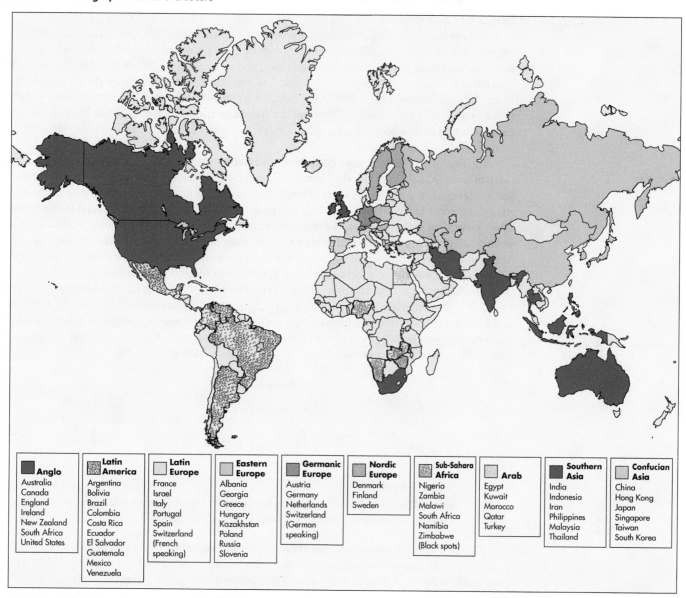

Anglo	Latin America	Latin Europe	Eastern Europe	Germanic Europe	Nordic Europe	Sub-Sahara Africa	Arab	Southern Asia	Confucian Asia
Australia	Argentina	France	Albania	Austria	Denmark	Nigeria	Egypt	India	China
Canada	Bolivia	Israel	Georgia	Germany	Finland	Zambia	Kuwait	Indonesia	Hong Kong
England	Brazil	Italy	Greece	Netherlands	Sweden	Malawi	Morocco	Iran	Japan
Ireland	Colombia	Portugal	Hungary	Switzerland		South Africa	Qatar	Philippines	Singapore
New Zealand	Costa Rica	Spain	Kazakhstan	(German		Namibia	Turkey	Malaysia	Taiwan
South Africa	Ecuador	Switzerland	Poland	speaking)		Zimbabwe		Thailand	South Korea
United States	El Salvador	(French	Russia			(Black spots)			
	Guatemala	speaking)	Slovenia						
	Mexico								
	Venezuela								

Source: Data from V. Gupta, P. J. Hanes, and P. Dorfman, *Journal of World Business* 37, no. 1 (2002): 13.

Europe, Confucian Asia, Latin America, Sub-Sahara Africa, and Nordic Europe. They point out the usefulness to managers of these clusters:

> *Multinational corporations may find it less risky and more profitable to expand into more similar cultures rather than those which are drastically different.*[32]

These clusters are shown in Exhibit 3-3. To compare two of their cluster findings, for example, Gupta et al. describe the Germanic cluster as masculine, assertive, individualistic, and result-oriented. This compares with the Latin American cluster, which they characterize as practicing high power distance, low performance orientation, uncertainty avoidance, and collectivism.

> *Latin American societies tend to enact life as it comes, taking its unpredictability as a fact of life, and not overly worrying about results.*[33]

Most researchers feel that there is a relationship between geographic cultural clusters and their similar economic systems, histories, or environmental characteristics.[34]

Hofstede's Value Dimensions

Earlier research resulted in a groundbreaking framework for understanding how basic values underlie organizational behavior; this framework was developed by Geert Hofstede, based on his research on over 116,000 people in 50 countries. He proposed four value dimensions: power distance, uncertainty avoidance, individualism, and masculinity.[35] We should be cautious when interpreting these results, however, because his research findings are based on a sample drawn from one multinational firm, IBM, and because he does not account for within-country differences in multicultural countries. Although we introduce these value dimensions here to aid in the understanding of different cultures, their relevance and application to management functions will be discussed in later chapters.

The first of Hofstede's value dimensions, **power distance**, is the level of acceptance by a society of the unequal distribution of power in institutions. What are the attitudes toward hierarchy and the level of respect for authority? How reluctant are employees to express disagreement with their managers? In the workplace, inequalities in power are normal, as evidenced in hierarchical boss–subordinate relationships. However, the extent to which subordinates accept unequal power is societally determined. In countries in which people display high power distance (such as Malaysia, the Philippines, and Mexico), employees acknowledge the boss's authority simply by respecting that individual's formal position in the hierarchy, and they seldom bypass the chain of command. This respectful response results, predictably, in a centralized structure and autocratic leadership. In countries where people display low power distance (such as Austria, Denmark, and Israel), superiors and subordinates are apt to regard one another as equal in power, resulting in more harmony, open communication of ideas, and cooperation. Clearly, an autocratic management style is not likely to be well received in low power distance countries.

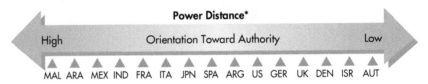

Power Distance*

High — Orientation Toward Authority — Low

MAL ARA MEX IND FRA ITA JPN SPA ARG US GER UK DEN ISR AUT

*Not to scale—indicates relative magnitude.
Note: ARA = Arab Countries
       AUT = Austria

Source: Based on G. Hofstede, "National Cultures in Four Dimensions," International Studies of Management and Organization (Spring-Summer 1983).

The second value dimension, **uncertainty avoidance**, refers to the extent to which people in a society feel threatened by ambiguous situations. Countries with a high level of uncertainty avoidance (such as Japan, Portugal, and Greece) tend to have strict laws and procedures to which their people adhere closely, and a strong sense of nationalism prevails. In a business context, this value results in formal rules and procedures designed to provide more security and greater career stability. Managers have a propensity for low-risk decisions, employees exhibit little aggressiveness, and lifetime employment is common. In countries with lower levels of uncertainty avoidance (such as Denmark, Great Britain, and, to a lesser extent, the United States), nationalism is less pronounced, and protests and other such activities are tolerated. As a consequence, company activities are less structured and less formal, some managers take more risks, and high job mobility is common.

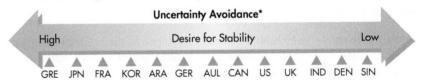

Uncertainty Avoidance*

High — Desire for Stability — Low

GRE JPN FRA KOR ARA GER AUL CAN US UK IND DEN SIN

*Not to scale—indicates relative magnitude.
Note: AUL = Australia

Source: Based on G. Hofstede, 1983.

The third of Hofstede's value dimensions, **individualism**, refers to the tendency of people to look after themselves and their immediate families with less emphasis on the needs of society;

the primary focus is on the individual or the nuclear family. In countries that prize individualism (such as the United States, Great Britain, and Australia) democracy, individual initiative, and achievement are highly valued; the relationship of the individual to organizations is one of independence on an emotional level, if not on an economic level.

In countries such as Pakistan and Panama, where low individualism prevails—that is, where **collectivism** predominates—there is more emphasis on group achievements and harmony, and the importance of the extended family or group. In such societies there are tight social frameworks, emotional dependence on belonging to "the organization," and a strong belief in group decisions. People from a collectivist country, such as Japan, believe in the will of the group rather than that of the individual, and their pervasive collectivism exerts control over individual members through social pressure and the fear of humiliation. The society valorizes harmony and saving face, whereas individualistic cultures generally emphasize self-respect, autonomy, and independence. Hiring and promotion practices in collectivist societies are based on paternalism rather than achievement or personal capabilities, which are valued in individualistic societies. Other management practices (such as the use of quality circles in Japanese factories) reflect the emphasis on group decision-making processes in collectivist societies. The individualism-collectivism dimension, then, relates to the manner in which members of a group relate to one another and work together.[36]

Hofstede's findings indicate that most countries scoring high on individualism have both a higher gross national product and a freer political system than those countries scoring low on individualism—that is, there is a strong relationship among individualism, wealth, and a political system with balanced power. Other studies have found that the output of individuals working in a group setting differs between individualistic and collectivist societies. In the United States, a highly individualistic culture, social loafing is common—that is, people tend to perform less when working as part of a group than when working alone.[37] In a comparative study of the United States and the People's Republic of China (a highly collectivist society), Earley found that the Chinese did not exhibit as much social loafing as the Americans.[38] This result can be attributed to Chinese cultural values, which subordinate personal interests to the greater goal of helping the group succeed.

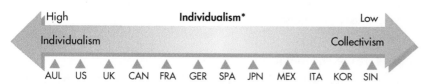

Not to scale—indicates relative magnitude.

Source: Based on G. Hofstede, 1983.

The fourth value dimension, **masculinity**, refers to the degree of traditionally "masculine" values—assertiveness, materialism, and a lack of concern for others—that prevail in a society. In comparison, femininity emphasizes "feminine" values—a concern for others, for relationships, and for the quality of life. In highly masculine societies (Japan and Austria, for example), women are generally expected to stay home and raise a family. In organizations, one finds considerable job stress, and organizational interests generally encroach on employees' private lives. In countries with low masculinity (such as Switzerland and New Zealand), one finds less conflict and job stress, more women in high-level jobs, and a reduced need for assertiveness. The United States lies somewhat in the middle, according to Hofstede's research. American women typically are encouraged to work, and families often are able to get some support for child care (through day-care centers and maternity leaves).

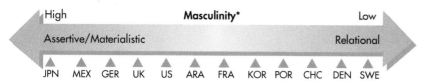

Not to scale—indicates relative magnitude.

Source: Based on G. Hofstede, 1983.

The four cultural value dimensions proposed by Hofstede do not operate in isolation; rather, they are interdependent and interactive—and thus complex—in their effects on work attitudes and behaviors. For example, in a 2000 study of small to medium–sized firms in Australia, Finland, Greece, Indonesia, Mexico, Norway, and Sweden, based on Hofstede's dimensions, Steensma, Marino, and Weaver found that "entrepreneurs from societies that are masculine and individualistic have a lower appreciation for cooperative strategies as compared to entrepreneurs from societies that are feminine and collectivist. Masculine cultures view cooperation in general as a sign of weakness and individualistic societies place a high value on independence and control."[39] In addition, they found that high levels of uncertainty avoidance prompted more cooperation, such as developing alliances to share risk.

LONG-TERM/SHORT-TERM ORIENTATION

Later research in 23 countries, using a survey developed by Bond and colleagues called the Chinese Value Survey, led Hofstede to develop a fifth dimension—called the Confucian work dynamism—which he labeled a long-term/short-term dimension. He defined long-term orientation as "the extent to which a culture programs its members to accept delayed gratification of their material, social, and emotional needs."[40] In other words, managers in most Asian countries are more future-oriented and so strive toward long-term goals; they value investment in the future and are prepared to sacrifice short-term profits. However, managers in countries such as Great Britain, Canada, and the United States place a higher value on short-term results and profitability, and evaluate their employees accordingly.

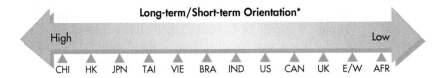

*Not to scale—indicates relative magnitude.

Source: Based on G. Hofstede, 2001.

Trompenaars's Value Dimensions

Fons Trompenaars also researched value dimensions; his work was spread over a ten-year period, with 15,000 managers from 28 countries representing 47 national cultures. Some of those dimensions, such as individualism, people's attitude toward time, and relative inner- versus outer-directedness, are similar to those discussed elsewhere in this chapter and others, and so are not presented here; other selected findings from Trompenaars's research that affect daily business activities are explained next, along with the placement of some of the countries along those dimensions, in approximate relative order.[41] If we view the placement of these countries along a range from personal to societal, based on each dimension, some interesting patterns emerge.[42] One can see that the same countries tend to be at similar positions on all dimensions, with the exception of the emotional orientation.

Looking at Trompenaars's dimension of **universalism versus particularism**, we find that the universalistic approach applies rules and systems objectively, without consideration for individual circumstances, whereas the particularistic approach—more common in Asia and in Spain, for example—puts the first obligation on relationships and is more subjective. Trompenaars found, for example, that people in particularistic societies are more likely to pass on insider information to a friend than those in universalistic societies.

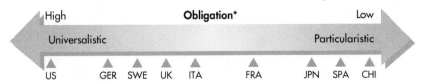

*Not to scale—indicates relative magnitude.

Source: Data based on F. Trompenaars, 1993.

In the **neutral versus affective** dimension, the focus is on the emotional orientation of relationships. The Italians, Mexicans, and Chinese, for example, would openly express emotions, even in a business situation, whereas the British and Japanese would consider such displays unprofessional; they, in turn, would be regarded as "hard to 'read.' "

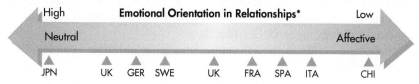

*Not to scale—indicates relative magnitude.

Source: Data based on F. Trompenaars, 1993.

As far as involvement in relationships goes, people tend to be either **specific or diffuse** (or somewhere along that dimension). Managers in specific-oriented cultures—the United States, United Kingdom, France—separate work and personal issues and relationships; they compartmentalize their work and private lives, and they are more open and direct. In diffuse-oriented cultures—Sweden, China—work spills over into personal relationships and vice versa.

*Not to scale—indicates relative magnitude.

Source: Data based on F. Trompenaars, 1993.

In the **achievement versus ascription** dimension, the question that arises is "What is the source of power and status in society?" In an achievement society, the source of status and influence is based on individual achievement—how well one performs the job and what level of education and experience one has to offer. Therefore, women, minorities, and young people usually have equal opportunity to attain position based on their achievements. In an ascription-oriented society, people ascribe status on the basis of class, age, gender, and so on; one is more likely to be born into a position of influence. Hiring in Indonesia, for example, is more likely to be based on who you are than is the case in Germany or Australia.

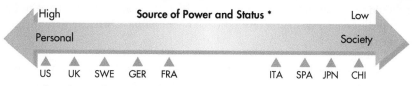

*Not to scale—indicates relative magnitude.

Source: Data based on F. Trompenaars, 1993.

It is clear, then, that a lot of what goes on at work can be explained by differences in people's innate value systems, as described by Hofstede, Trompenaars, and the GLOBE researchers. Awareness of such differences and how they influence work behavior can be very useful to you as a future international manager.

CONSEQUENCE OR CAUSE?

At this point, it is worth considering the results of a study by Steel and Taras, published in 2010, in which they challenge the view held by Hofstede and others of culture as the cause, and not the effect, of variations in cultural values. Steel and Taras argue that the opposite can be true, that "culture is a consequence of certain individual and national-level factors."[43] They conclude that the research results provide a basis for explaining variations in cultural values within and between countries, and that "cultures are determined by a set of individual and country level factors and are likely to change in response to a change in the culture-determining factors."[44] Examples of the factors they considered are macro factors such as wealth and freedom, and micro factors such as age, gender, education, and socio-economic status. Steel and Taras stress, therefore, that we should not rely on national averages to draw conclusions about individuals.[45] Other researchers also hold this broader concept of the origins of cultural behavior; Meuthel and Hoegl, for example, state that "we extend the traditional view of culture as an exclusive country-level determinant to a more comprehensive view that integrates social institutions such as the education system, economic freedom, and civil liberties."[46]

Clearly, the origins, causes, and effects of cultural variables are complex, but the fact remains that culture plays a key role in the workplace and that international managers must be aware of that role and manage accordingly.

Critical Operational Value Differences

After studying various research results about cultural variables, it helps to identify some specific culturally based variables that cause frequent problems for managers around the world. Important variables are those involving conflicting orientations toward time, change, material factors, and individualism. We try to understand these operational value differences because they strongly influence a person's attitudes and probable response to work situations.

TIME

Americans often experience much conflict and frustration because of differences in the concept of time around the world—that is, differences in temporal values. To Americans, time is a valuable and limited resource; it is to be saved, scheduled, and spent with precision, lest we waste it. The clock is always running—time is money. Therefore, deadlines and schedules have to be met. When others are not on time for meetings, Americans may feel insulted; when meetings digress from their purpose, Americans tend to become impatient. Similar attitudes toward time are found in Western Europe and elsewhere.

In many parts of the world, however, people view time from different and longer perspectives, often based on religious beliefs (such as reincarnation, in which time does not end at death), on a belief in destiny, or on pervasive social attitudes. In Latin America, for example, a common attitude toward time is *mañana,* a word that literally means "tomorrow." A Latin American person using this word, however, usually means an indefinite time in the near future. Similarly, the word *bukra* in Arabic can mean "tomorrow" or "some time in the future." While Americans usually regard a deadline as a firm commitment, Arabs often regard a deadline imposed on them as an insult. They feel that important things take a long time and therefore cannot be rushed. To ask an Arab to rush something, then, is to imply that you have not given him an important task or that he would not treat that task with respect. International managers have to be careful not to offend people—or lose contracts or employee cooperation—because they misunderstand the local language of time.

CHANGE

Because they are based largely on long-standing religious beliefs, values regarding the acceptance of change and the pace of change can vary immensely among cultures. Western people generally believe that an individual can exert some control over the future and can manipulate events, particularly in a business context—that is, individuals feel they have some internal control. In many non-Western societies, however, control is considered external; people generally believe in destiny or the will of their God, and therefore adopt a passive attitude or even feel hostility toward those introducing the "evil" of change. In societies that place great importance on tradition (such as Japan), one small area of change may threaten an entire way of life. However, the younger generations are becoming more exposed to change through globalization, technology, and media exposure. International firms are agents of change throughout the world. Some changes are more popular than others.

MATERIAL FACTORS

In large part, Americans consume resources at a far greater rate than most of the rest of the world. Their attitude toward nature—that it is there to be used for their benefit—differs from

EXHIBIT 3-4   Fundamental Differences between Japanese and Mexican Culture That Affect Business Organizations

Dimension	Japanese Culture	Mexican Culture
Hierarchical nature	Rigid in rank and most communication; blurred in authority and responsibility	Rigid in all aspects
Individualism vs. collectivism	Highly collective culture; loyalty to work group dominates; group harmony very important	Collective relative to family group; doesn't transfer loyalty to work group; individualistic outside family
Attitudes toward work	Work is sacred duty; acquiring skills, working hard, thriftiness, patience, and perseverance are virtues	Work is means to support self and family; leisure more important than work
Time orientation	Balanced perspective; future oriented; monochronic in dealings with outside world	Present oriented; time is imprecise; time commitments become desirable objectives
Approach to problem solving	Holistic, reliance on intuition, pragmatic, consensus important	Reliance on intuition and emotion, individual approach
Fatalism	Fatalism leads to preparation	Fatalism makes planning, disciplined routine unnatural
View of human nature	Intrinsically good	Mixture of good and evil

Source: J. J. Lawrence and Ryh-song Yeh, "The Influence of Mexican Culture on the Use of Japanese Manufacturing Techniques in Mexico," *Management International Review* 34, no. 1 (1994): 49–66, used with permission.

the attitudes of Indians and Koreans, for example, whose worship of nature is part of their religious beliefs. Whereas Americans often value physical goods and status symbols, many non-Westerners find these things unimportant; they value the aesthetic and the spiritual realm. Such differences in attitude have implications for management functions such as motivation and reward systems because the proverbial carrot must be appropriate to the employee's value system.

INDIVIDUALISM

In general, Americans tend to work and conduct their private lives independently, valuing individual achievement, accomplishments, promotions, and wealth above any group goals. In many other countries, individualism is not valued (as discussed previously in the context of Hofstede's work). In China, for example, much more of a "we" consciousness prevails, and the group is the basic building block of social life and work. For the Chinese, conformity and cooperation take precedence over individual achievement, and the emphasis is on the strength of the family or community—the predominant attitude being, "We all rise or fall together."

International managers often face conflicts in the workplace as a result of differences in these four basic values of time, change, materialism, and individualism. If these operational value differences and their likely consequences are anticipated, managers can adjust expectations, communications, work organization, schedules, incentive systems, and so forth to provide for more constructive outcomes for the company and its employees. Some of these operational differences are shown in Exhibit 3-4, using Japan and Mexico as examples. Note in particular the factors of time, individualism, change (fatalism), and materialism (attitudes toward work) expressed in the exhibit.

THE INTERNET AND CULTURE

As of January 1, 2012, South Korea had 82.7% of its population who were internet users—compared with 78.3% for the United States for the internet population penetration.

WWW.INTERNETWORLDSTATS.COM.[47]

We would be remiss if we did not acknowledge the contemporary phenomenon of the increasingly pervasive use of the Internet in society, for it seems to be encroaching on many of the social variables discussed earlier—in particular associations, education, and the economy, as well as politics, as evidenced in the 2011 "Arab Spring," discussed in Chapter 1. In South Korea, for example, there is an obsession for anything digital. Over 82 percent of homes are connected to a high-speed Internet service. That compares with an average of 61 percent for the European countries, 78 percent in the United States, and 38 percent for China. Seoul is the most technologically advanced city in the world. This phenomenon seems to be changing the lives of many Koreans. Teenagers, once used to hanging out at the mall, now do so at the country's thousands of personal computer (PC) parlors to watch movies, check email, and surf the Net. Korea's GDP per capita in 2011 was $22,778, compared with $5,414 (estimated) for China.[48] Clearly there is a correlation with the economic development in the country overall, and we would conclude that there is widespread connection between Internet usage and certain cultural effects.

At the same time that the Internet is affecting culture, culture is also affecting how the Internet is used. One of the pervasive ways that culture is determining how the Internet may be used in various countries is through the local attitude to **information privacy**—the right to control information about oneself—as observed in the following quote:

> *You Americans just don't seem to care about privacy, do you?*
>
> SWEDISH EXECUTIVE.[49]

While Americans collect data about consumers' backgrounds and what they buy, often trading that information with other internal or external contacts, the Swedes, for example, are astounded that this is done, especially without governmental oversight.[50] The Swedes are required to register all databases of personal information with the Data Inspection Board (DIB), their federal regulatory agency for privacy, and to get permission from that board before that data can be used. Indeed, the Swedish system is typical of most countries in Europe in their societal approaches to privacy.[51] Generally in Europe, each person must be informed, and given the chance to object, if the information about that person is going to be used for direct marketing purposes or released to another party. That data cannot be used for secondary purposes if the consumer objects.

> *In Italy, data cannot be sent outside—even to other EU countries—without the explicit consent of the data subject. . . .*
>
> *In Spain, all direct mail has to include the name and address of the data owner so that the data subject is able to exercise his rights of access, correction, and removal.[52]*

The manner in which Europe views information privacy has its roots in culture and history, leading to a different value set regarding privacy. The preservation of privacy is considered a human right, perhaps partially as a result of an internalized fear about how personal records were used in war times in Europe. In addition, research by Smith on the relationship between levels of concern about privacy and Hofstede's cultural dimensions revealed that high levels of uncertainty avoidance were associated with the European approach to privacy, whereas higher levels of individualism, masculinity, and power distance were associated with the U.S. approach.[53]

It seems, then, that societal culture and the resultant effects on business models can render the assumptions about the "global" nature of information technology incorrect. U.S. businesspeople, brought up on a strong diet of the market economy, need to realize that they will often need to "localize" their use of IT to different value sets about its use. This advice applies in particular to the many e-commerce companies doing business overseas. With 75 percent of the world's Internet market living outside the United States, multinational e-businesses are learning the hard way that their Web sites must reflect local markets, customs, languages, and currencies to be successful in foreign markets. Different legal systems, financial structures, tastes, and experiences necessitate attention to every detail to achieve global appeal. In other words, e-businesses must localize to globalize, which means much more than translating online content to local languages. Lycos Europe, for example, based its privacy policies upon German law since it is the most stringent.

One problem area often beyond the control of e-business is the costs of connecting to the Internet for people in other countries. Other practical problems in Asia, as well as in Germany, the Netherlands, and Sweden, include the method of payment, which in most of these places still involves cash or letters of credit and written receipts. Dell tackled this problem by offering debit payments from consumers' checking accounts. Some companies have learned the hard way that they need to do their homework before launching sites aimed at overseas consumers. Dell, for example, committed a faux pas when it launched an e-commerce site in Japan with black borders on its Web site; black is considered negative in the Japanese culture, so many consumers took one look and didn't want anything else to do with it. Dell executives learned that the complexity of language translation into Japanese was only one area in which they needed to localize.

As much as cultural and societal factors can affect the use of the internet for business, it is also clear that IT can have dramatic changes on culture and society, as illustrated by the accompanying Management in Action feature about the changes occurring as a result of India's burgeoning IT industry.

MANAGEMENT IN ACTION
India's IT Industry Brings Cultural Changes[54]

Many longtime residents of Bangalore, India, seem to be locked in a cultural struggle with Infosys Technologies (INFY), Wipro Technologies (WIT), and others in the software industry, even though they have made Bangalore famous and increased its wealth. Residents complain that Bangalore used to be one of India's most pleasant cities. But with the addition of 500,000 IT workers living alongside nearly 7 million other residents, the city has become very crowded and expensive. The locals ask,

> *Does the city belong to the IT industry, with all its riches? Or does it belong to those who arrived first, whose children must now work for outsiders who don't speak the local language, Kannada?*[55]

Apart from the early curfew on nightlife, the industry has upended the city's policies. The old-timers contend, in a city where few locals can afford cars, that the government is spending too much of the city's resources on building wider roads to speed tech workers around. In its defense, the software industry claims that it has benefited everyone by improving the city and bringing new wealth and services, such as a new subway system. Although the global credit crunch has slowed its growth, over the past decade the tech sector has created tens of thousands of jobs, not only in the software and back-office support industries, but also for all the people who support those companies. While most of India's IT companies still get at least half of their revenue from the United States alone, now they are finding more business domestically. As a result, the digital divide between urban and rural areas is narrowing, and the IT industry is helping support industries to grow in a domestic economy expanding 9 percent a year—this all thanks to India's IT talent.

It is these kinds of opportunities, amid the benefits of increasing economic openness in India, that have attracted Anand Giridharad, and others whose families had earlier emigrated to the United States, to return to India. The idea of returning to India is spreading virally in émigré homes as the U.S. economy declines and the job market tightens. This phenomenon led Anand to ask:

> *If our parents left India and trudged westward for us, if they manufactured from scratch a new life there for us, if they slogged, saved, sacrificed to make our lives lighter than theirs, then what does it mean when we choose to migrate to the place they forsook?*[56]

He noted that his father, in the 1970s, felt frustrated in companies that awarded roles based on age, not achievement, and that doctors and engineers were revered while others were neglected and mistreated. Since then India has liberalized, privatized, and globalized, with the economy growing rapidly, bringing with it much optimism for its people. At the same time, America has declined and many jobs have moved to India, particularly in IT and back-office services.

In a sign of the times, India offered an Overseas Citizen of India card in 2006, offering foreign citizens of Indian origin visa-free entry for life and making it easier to work in that country. By July 2008, more than 280,000 émigrés had signed up, including 120,000 from the United States.

Those émigrés are now re-learning those many aspects of Indian culture that remain—for example, the formalities and hierarchies left from British rule; that making friends entails befriending the whole family; and the very relaxed attitude toward time. Those second-generation returnees to their motherland are now mixing Western and Indian cultures by starting companies where the employees learn Western management techniques and by using financial instruments involving both local and Wall Street sources for deals. In other ways they are starting companies that offer a mix of Western and Indian products and services.[57]

Much of the traditional cultural underpinnings remain, of course. Narayana Murthy, founder and (until 2011) chairman of the board of Infosys, the Indian IT giant, was asked to comment on what explains the success of great Indian businesses such as Infosys, Wipro, and the Tata group. Mr. Murthy said that there are some culturally specific qualities, but also some universal ones, that lie behind the achievements.

(Continued)

He commented that of course honesty, decency, integrity, and a strong work ethic all matter. But these are not unique to India. Rather, he said:

> It is the concept of the family which perhaps sets India apart. Family bonds are strong and intense in India. People inevitably bring that ethos to work with them.[58]

Of course, much of India has not been directly touched by the IT industry, and so in those areas the Indian culture remains untouched by the IT industry and globalization. Management is often paternalist and autocratic, based on formal authority and charisma (with decision making mostly centralized), an emphasis on rules, and a low propensity for risk. Nepotism prevails in job hiring and placement, and for the most part:

> Relationship orientation seems to be a more important characteristic of effective leaders in India than performance or task orientation.[59]

DEVELOPING CULTURAL PROFILES

Managers can gather considerable information on cultural variables from current research, personal observation, and discussions with people. From these sources, managers can develop cultural profiles of various countries—composite pictures of working environments, people's attitudes, and norms of behavior. As we have previously discussed, these profiles are often highly generalized; many subcultures, of course, may exist within a country. However, managers can use these profiles to anticipate drastic differences in the level of motivation, communication, ethics, loyalty, and individual and group productivity that may be encountered in a given country. More such homework may have helped Wal-Mart's expansion efforts into Germany and South Korea, from which it withdrew in 2006. Wal-Mart's executives simply did not do enough research about the culture and shopping habits of people in those countries; for example:

> In Germany, Wal-Mart stopped requiring sales clerks to smile at customers—a practice that some male shoppers interpreted as flirting—and scrapped the morning Wal-Mart chant by staff members. "People found these things strange; Germans just don't behave that way," said Hans-Martin Poschmann, the secretary of the Verdi union.[60]

It is relatively simple for Americans to pull together a descriptive profile of U.S. culture, even though regional and individual differences exist, because Americans know themselves and because researchers have thoroughly studied U.S. culture. The results of one such study by Harris and Moran are shown in Exhibit 3-5, which provides a basis of comparison with other cultures and, thus, suggests the likely differences in workplace behaviors.

It is not so easy, however, to pull together descriptive cultural profiles of peoples in other countries unless one has lived there and been intricately involved with those people. Still, managers can make a start by using what comparative research and literature are available. The accompanying Comparative Management in Focus feature provides brief, generalized country

EXHIBIT 3-5 **Americans at a Glance**

1. *Goal and achievement oriented*—Americans think they can accomplish anything, given enough time, money, and technology.
2. *Highly organized and institutionally minded*
3. *Freedom-loving and self-reliant*—a belief that all persons are equal; they admire self-made people.
4. *Work-oriented and efficient*—a strong work ethic; conscious of time and efficient in doing things.
5. *Friendly and informal*—informal in greeting and dress; a noncontact culture (avoid embracing in public.)
6. *Competitive and aggressive*—driven to achieve and succeed in play and business.
7. *Values in transition*—traditional family values are undergoing transition.
8. *Generosity*—Americans are a sharing people.

Source: Based on excerpts from *Managing Cultural Differences* by Philip R. Harris and Robert T. Moran, 5th ed. Copyright © 2000 by Gulf Publishing Company, Houston, TX.

profiles based on a synthesis of research, primarily from Hofstede[61] and England,[62] as well as numerous other sources.[63] These profiles illustrate how to synthesize information and gain a sense of the character of a society—from which implications may be drawn about how to manage more effectively in that society. More extensive implications and applications related to managerial functions are drawn in later chapters.

Recent evidence in Japan points to some convergence with Western business culture resulting from Japan's economic contraction and subsequent bankruptcies. Focus on the group, lifetime employment, and a pension has given way to a more competitive business environment with job security no longer guaranteed and an emphasis on performance-based pay. This has led Japan's "salarymen" to recognize the need for personal responsibility on the job and in their lives. Although only a few years ago emphasis was on the group, Japan's long economic slump seems to have caused some cultural restructuring of the individual. Corporate Japan is changing from a culture of consensus and "groupthink" to one touting the need for an "era of personal responsibility" as a solution to revitalize its competitive position in the global marketplace.[64]

To tell you the truth, it's hard to think for yourself, says Mr. Kuzuoka . . . [but, if you don't] . . . in this age of cutthroat competition, you'll just end up drowning.[65]

COMPARATIVE MANAGEMENT IN FOCUS

Profiles in Culture—Japan, Germany, Latin America

JAPAN

The traditional Japanese business characteristics of politeness and deference have left companies without the thrusting culture needed to succeed internationally.[66]

With intense global competition, many Japanese companies are recognizing the need for more assertiveness and clarity in their business culture in order to expand abroad. As a result, Japanese employees are recognizing the need to manage their own careers as companies move away from lifetime employment to be more competitive. Only a handful of large businesses, such as Toyota, Komatsu, and Canon, have managed to become indisputable global leaders by maintaining relationships as a foundation for their operations around the world.[67] For the majority of Japanese, the underlying cultural values still predominate—at least for now.

Japanese culture is strong, formal, and largely homogeneous, and is inculcated to the young through the teachings and expectations conveyed by the extended family. Much of Japanese culture—and the basis of working relationships—can be explained by the principle of *wa*, "peace and harmony." This principle, embedded in the value the Japanese attribute to *amae* ("indulgent love"), probably originated in the Shinto religion, which focuses on spiritual and physical harmony. *Amae* results in *shinyo*, which refers to the mutual confidence, faith, and honor necessary for successful business relationships. Japan ranks high on pragmatism, masculinity, and uncertainty avoidance, and fairly high on power distance. At the same time, much importance is attached to loyalty, empathy, and the guidance of subordinates. The result is a mix of authoritarianism and humanism in the workplace, similar to a family system. These cultural roots are evident in a homogeneous managerial value system, with strong middle management, strong working relationships, strong seniority systems that stress rank, and an emphasis on looking after employees. The principle of *wa* carries forth into the work group—the building block of Japanese business. The Japanese strongly identify with their work groups and seek to cooperate with them. The emphasis is on participative management, consensus problem solving, and decision making with a patient, long-term perspective. Open expression and conflict are discouraged, and it is of paramount importance to avoid the shame of not fulfilling one's duty. These elements of work culture result in a devotion to work, collective responsibility, and a high degree of employee productivity. In meetings, punctuality is essential; the meeting should start with a bow or handshake, then exchanging business cards (*meishi*) using both hands, and then reading the card before you put it in your pocket. Titles and last names should be used and some small talk should take place before business.[68] Do not invade the personal space of the Japanese, and avoid any confrontation, or any non-verbal excess. Also, it is important to avoid singling out any one Japanese person, since it is a group process.

Professor Nonaka, a specialist in how companies tap the collective intelligence of their workers, discusses a similar Japanese concept of *ba*: an interaction among colleagues on the job that leads to knowledge-sharing. He says that

(Continued)

MAP 3.2 Japan/Asia

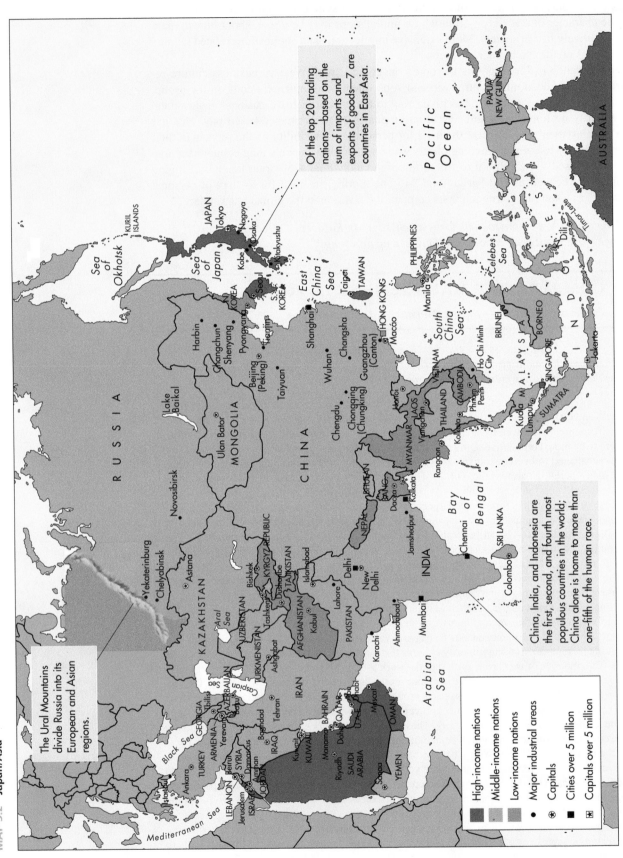

The Ural Mountains divide Russia into its European and Asian regions.

Of the top 20 trading nations—based on the sum of imports and exports of goods—7 are countries in East Asia.

China, India, and Indonesia are the first, second, and fourth most populous countries in the world; China alone is home to more than one-fifth of the human race.

High-income nations
Middle-income nations
Low-income nations
Major industrial areas
Capitals
Cities over 5 million
Capitals over 5 million

Ba can occur in a work group, a project team, an ad hoc meeting, a virtual e-mail list, or at the frontline point of contact with customers. It serves as a petri dish in which shared insights are cultivated and grown.[69]

The message is clear that, in Japan, companies that give their employees freedom to interact informally are likely to benefit from new ideas and collaboration.

If we extend this cultural profile to its implications for specific behaviors in the workplace, we can draw a comparison with common American behaviors. Most of those American behaviors seem to be opposite to those of their Japanese counterparts; it is no wonder that many misunderstandings and conflicts in the workplace arise between Americans and Japanese (See Exhibit 3-6). For example, a majority of the attitudes and behaviors of many Japanese stems from a high level of collectivism, compared with a high level of individualism common to Americans. This contrast is highlighted in the center of Exhibit 3-6—"Maintain the group" compared with "Protect the individual." In addition, the strict social order of the Japanese permeates the workplace in adherence to organizational hierarchy and seniority and in loyalty to the firm. This contrasts markedly with the typical American responses to organizational relationships and duties based on equality. In addition, the often blunt, outspoken American businessperson offends the indirectness and sensitivity of the Japanese, for whom the virtue of patience is paramount, causing the silence and avoidance that so frustrates Americans. As a result, Japanese businesspeople tend to think of American organizations as having no spiritual quality and little loyalty to employees, and they think of Americans as assertive, frank, and egotistic. Their American counterparts, in turn, respond with the impression that Japanese businesspeople have little experience and are secretive, arrogant, and cautious.[70] Westerners doing business in Japan need to be aware

EXHIBIT 3-6   The American-Japanese Cultural Divide

Japanese	American
Man within nature	Man controlling nature
Caution	Risk-taking
Incremental improvement	Bold initiative
Deliberation	Spontaneity
Adherence to form	Improvisation
Silence	Outspokenness
Memorization	Critical thinking
Emotional sensitivity	Logical reasoning
Indirectness	Clarity and frankness
Assuaging	Confronting
Avoiding	Threatening
Consensus building	Decisiveness
Conformity	Individuality
Group convention	Personal principle
Trusted relationships	Legal safeguards
Collective strength	Individual independence
Maintain the group	Protect the individual
Modest resignation	Righteous indignation
Saving face	Being heard
Oppressive unanimity	Chaotic anarchy
Humble cooperation	Proving oneself
Rewarding seniority	Rewarding performance
Loyalty	Track record
Generalists	Specialists
Obligations	Opportunities
Untiring effort	Fair effort
Shame	Guilt
Dependency	Autonomy
Dutiful relationships	Level playing field
Industrial groups	Industrial competition
Strict ranking	Ambiguous/informal ranking
Racial differentiation	Racial equality
Gender differentiation	Gender equality

Left-side groupings: Patience, Harmony, Hierarchy
Right-side groupings: Action, Freedom, Equality

Source: R. G. Linowes, "The Japanese Manager's Traumatic Entry into the United States: Understanding the American–Japanese Cultural Divide," *The Academy of Management Executive* 7, no. 4 (1993): 24.

(Continued)

of the importance of *giri*—the expectations of reciprocity in relationships and how to behave. Managers should inform themselves in particular about the practice of gift-giving and the relationship of the type of gift suitable for the relative status of the parties involved; gift giving is accepted practice, but make sure it is not too big or it will be an embarrassment and also may be considered to be an attempt at a bribe.

Germany The reunited Germany is somewhat culturally diverse, inasmuch as the country borders several nations. Generally, Germans rank quite high on Hofstede's dimension of individualism, although their behaviors seem less individualistic than those of Americans. They score fairly high on uncertainty avoidance and masculinity and have a relatively small need for power distance. These cultural norms show up in the Germans' preference for being around familiar people and situations; they are also reflected in their propensity to do a detailed evaluation of business deals before committing themselves.

Christianity underlies much of German culture—more than 96 percent of Germans are Catholics or Protestants. This may be why Germans tend to like rule and order in their lives, and why there is a clear public expectation of acceptable and the unacceptable ways to act. Public signs everywhere in Germany dictate what is allowed or *verboten* (forbidden). Germans are very strict with their use of time, whether for business or pleasure, frowning on inefficiency or on tardiness.

In business, Germans tend to be assertive, but they downplay aggression. Decisions are typically centralized, although hierarchical processes sometimes give way to consensus decision making. However, strict departmentalization is present in organizations, with centralized and final authority at the departmental manager level. Employees do not question the authority of their managers. German companies typically have a vertical hierarchical structure with detailed planning and standardized rules and procedures; the emphasis is on order and control to avoid risk.

> In the business setting, Germans look for security, well-defined work procedures, rules, established approaches, and clearly defined individual assignments. In short, the German business environment is highly structured. "Ordnung" (order) is the backbone of company life.[71]

What the Germans call *Ordnung* (the usual translation is "order," but it is a much broader concept) is the unwritten road map of how to live one's life. "A group of Germans lined up on an empty street corner, even in the middle of the night, waiting for a light to change before crossing, is one of the favorite first impressions taken away by visiting Americans, who are usually jaywalking past as they observe it."[72] For self-reliant Americans, the German adherence to precise rules and regulations is impressive but often stifling.

Hall and Hall describe the German preference for closed doors and private space as evidence of the affinity for compartmentalization in organizations and in their own lives. They also prefer more physical space around them in conversation than do most other Europeans, and they seek privacy so as not to be overheard. German law prohibits loud noises in public areas on weekend afternoons. Germans are conservative, valuing privacy, politeness, and formality; they usually use last names and titles for all except those close to them. Business interactions are specifically task-focused, and not for relationship-building. Meetings are formal and require written documents in both English and German. Deference is given to people of authority on both sides. There is a strict protocol, including the order of people entering the room and getting seated—according to rank and age, and with men entering before women! It all requires patience with the protocol and formality, and you should wait to sit until it is indicated. The Germans do not respond well to displays of emotions and promises, and any confrontational behavior will backfire. Once a contract is in place it will be strictly followed.[73]

Most Germans prefer to focus on one task or issue at a time, that task taking precedence over other demands; strict schedules are important, as is punctuality, both showing respect for all concerned. Overall, Germany is what Walker et al. call a "doing-oriented" culture—that is, a task and achievement orientation of "work first, pleasure second."[74] Such cultures include Switzerland, Germany, Austria, the Netherlands, and the Scandinavian countries. (This compares with "being-oriented" cultures—such as those of Belgium, France, Greece, Ireland, and most Latin American countries—where the general predisposition is more toward "work to live," rather than "live to work." Priority is given to affiliation and personal qualities in "being-oriented" cultures.)

In negotiations, Germans want detailed information before and during discussions, which can become lengthy. They give factors such as voice and speech control much weight. However, since Germany is a low-context society, communication is explicit, and Americans find negotiations easy to understand.[75] On the other hand, Germans communicating with businesspeople from a high-context culture such as that in Japan will be perceived as abrupt, insensitive, and indifferent. (Low-context refers to a direct communication style, compared with a high-context, indirect style. This variable is further explained in Chapter 4.) Whereas most Asians, for example, will be implicit and indirect, always aware of the need to "save face" for everyone concerned, most Germans are very direct and straightforward; tact and diplomacy takes second place to voicing their opinions.

Latin America Latin America is not one homogenous area, of course; rather, it comprises many diverse, independent nations (most commonly referred to as those territories in the Americas where the Spanish or Portuguese languages prevail: Mexico; most of Central and South America; and Cuba, the Dominican Republic, and Puerto Rico in the Caribbean). Businesspeople are most likely to go to the rapidly developing economies of Chile and Brazil, and, of course, to Mexico. (Portuguese is the language in Brazil.) Christianity—predominantly Roman Catholicism—prevails throughout Latin America. Rapid population growth in the region has brought the population to around 600 million in 2011, and population density is relatively low. Latin America is the second most important emerging area economically, after Southeast Asia, with a GDP about half of China's and three times that of India.[76]

For our purposes here, while we acknowledge some regional cultural differences, we can draw upon the similarities of Latin American culture and business practices as a starting point in developing a helpful profile. Indeed, Latin America is relatively homogeneous culturally. Some of these generalities are discussed in the following paragraphs.

Using Hofstede's dimensions, we can generalize that most people are high on power distance and uncertainty avoidance, fairly high on masculinity, low on individualism, and they tend to have a comparatively short-term orientation toward planning.

Latin Americans are typically "being-oriented"—with a primary focus on relationships and enjoying life in the present—as compared with the "doing-oriented" German (and mostly Western) culture discussed earlier. For Latin Americans, work lives and private lives are much more closely integrated than that of Westerners, and so they emphasize enjoying life and have a more relaxed attitude toward work; because of that, Westerners often stereotype them as "lazy," rather than realizing that it is simply a different attitude to the role of work in life. Connected with that attitude is the tendency to be rather fatalistic—that is, a feeling that events will be determined by God—rather than a feeling of their own control or responsibility for the future.

Most people in those countries have a fluid orientation toward time and tend to be multi-focused, as discussed earlier in this chapter. Planning, negotiations, and scheduling take place in a more relaxed and loose time framework; those processes take second place to building a trusting relationship and reaching a satisfactory agreement.[77] Communication is based on their high-context culture (this concept is discussed further in Chapter 4). This means that communication tends to be indirect and implicit, based largely on non-verbal interactions and the expectation that the listener draws inference from understanding the people and the circumstances, without the need to be blunt or critical. Westerners need to take time, to be subtle and tactful, and to be incremental in discussing business to avoid being viewed as being pushy and so cutting off the relationship. Maintaining harmony and saving face is very important, as is the need to avoid embarrassing the other people involved. Managers must avoid any public criticism of employees and any reprimand should be by way of suggestion.

Communication is also very expressive and demonstrative; courtesy, formality, and good manners are respected and lead to very complimentary and hospitable expressions to guests. Latin Americans tend to stand closer and touch more often than most Westerners, exuding the warmth and hospitality that is typical in the region.

Hierarchy prevails in all areas of life, from family to institutions such as government and the workplace. Each level and relationship is expected to show deference, honor, and respect to the next person or level. Status is conveyed by one's position and title and the formality of dress and etiquette. Traditional managers have the respect of their position and are typically autocratic and paternal. Loyalty is to the superior as a person. Employees expect to be assigned tasks with little participation involved, although younger managers who have been educated in Europe or the United States are starting to delegate. However, while most Latin Americans can show some flexibility in structure, Chile is probably the most order-oriented country; managers there are very high on uncertainty and try hard to minimize risk and strictly adhere to social and business norms.[78]

Relationships have priority whether among family, friends, or business contacts. Loyalty among family and friends leads to obligations, and often nepotism, which can lead to varying levels of quality in the work performance and less initiative than a Western business person might expect. Business is conducted through social contacts and referrals—that is, success does not depend as much on what you know as on who you know. Latin Americans do business with people with whom they develop a trusting relationship, so it behooves businesspeople, here as in much of the world, to take time to develop a friendly, trusting relationship before getting down to business.

Western managers need to develop a warm attitude toward employees and business contacts and cultivate a sense of family at work; they should communicate individually with employees and colleagues and develop a trusting relationship.

Further discussion about the Mexican culture in particular is in the Comparative Management in Focus section in Chapter 11.

CULTURE AND MANAGEMENT STYLES AROUND THE WORLD

As an international manager, once you have researched the culture of a country in which you may be going to work or in which you are going to do business, and after you have developed a cultural profile, it is useful then to apply that information to develop an understanding of the expected management styles and ways of doing business that predominate in that region or in that type of business setting. The nearby feature, *Under the Lens: Doing Business in Brazil—Language, Culture, Customs, and Etiquette*, illustrates the relationship between culture and management. Two further examples then follow: Saudi Arabia and Chinese Small Family Businesses.

 UNDER THE LENS

Doing Business in Brazil—Language, Culture, Customs, and Etiquette

MAP 3.3   **Brazil**

Source: Olinchuk/Shutterstock

FIGURE 3-1   **Brazilian Flag**

Source: © CPJ Photography/Fotolia LLC

FIGURE 3-2   **Rio De Janeiro**

Source: Mark Schwettmann/Shutterstock

FACTS AND STATISTICS

Location: Eastern South America bordering Argentina, 1,224 km; Bolivia, 3,400 km; Colombia, 1,643 km; French Guiana, 673 km; Guyana, 1,119 km; Paraguay, 1,290 km; Peru, 1,560 km; Suriname, 597 km; Uruguay, 985 km; and Venezuela, 2,200 km

Capital: Brazilia

Climate: mostly tropical, but temperate in south

Population: 184,101,109

Ethnic Make-up: white (includes Portuguese, German, Italian, Spanish, and Polish) 55%; mixed white and black, 38%; black, 6%; other (includes Japanese, Arab, Amerindian), 1%

Religions: Roman Catholic (nominal) 80%

Government: federative republic

LANGUAGE IN BRAZIL

Language is one of the strongest elements of Brazil's national unity. Portuguese is spoken by nearly 100 percent of the population. The only exceptions are some members of Amerindian groups and pockets of immigrants, primarily from Japan and South Korea, who have not yet learned Portuguese. The principal families of Indian languages are Tupí, Arawak, Carib, and Gê.

There is about as much difference between the Portuguese spoken in Brazil and that spoken in Portugal as between the English spoken in the United States and that spoken in the United Kingdom. Within Brazil, there are no dialects of Portuguese, but only moderate regional variation in accent, vocabulary, and use of personal nouns, pronouns, and verb conjugations. Variations tend to diminish as a result of mass media, especially national television networks that are viewed by the majority of Brazilians.

BRAZILIAN SOCIETY AND CULTURE

Brazilian Diversity

- Brazil is a mixture of races and ethnicities, resulting in rich diversity.
- Many original Portuguese settlers married native women, which created a new race, called "mestizos."
- "Mulattoes" are descendants of the Portuguese and African slaves.
- Slavery was abolished in 1888, creating over time a further blurring of racial lines.

(Continued)

- Unlike many other Latin American countries where there is a distinct Indian population, Brazilians have intermarried to the point that it sometimes seems that almost everyone has a combination of European, African, and indigenous ancestry.

BRAZILIAN FAMILY VALUES

- The family is the foundation of the social structure and forms the basis of stability for most people.
- Families tend to be large (although family size has been diminishing in recent years) and the extended family is quite close.
- The individual derives a social network and assistance in times of need from the family.
- Nepotism is considered a positive thing, since it implies that employing people one knows and trusts is of primary importance.

THE BRAZILIAN CLASS SYSTEM

- Despite the mixing of ethnicities, there is a class system in Brazil.
- Few Brazilians could be described as racist, although social discrimination on the basis of skin color is a daily occurrence.
- The middle and upper classes often have only brief interaction with the lower classes—usually maids, drivers, etc.
- Class is determined by economic status.
- There is a great disparity in wages—and therefore lifestyle and social aspirations—among the different classes
- Although women make up 40% of the Brazilian workforce, they are typically found in lower-paid jobs such as teaching, administrative support, and nursing.
- The 1988 constitution prohibits discrimination against women, but inequities still exist. The one place where women are achieving equality is in the government.

ETIQUETTE AND CUSTOMS IN BRAZIL

Meeting Etiquette

- Men shake hands when greeting one another, while maintaining steady eye contact.
- Women generally kiss each other, starting with the left and alternating cheeks.
- Hugging and backslapping are common greetings among Brazilian friends.
- If a woman wishes to shake hands with a man, she should extend her hand first.

Gift Giving Etiquette

- If invited to a Brazilian's house, bring the hostess flowers or a small gift.
- Orchids are considered a very nice gift, but avoid purple ones.
- Avoid giving anything purple or black as these are mourning colours.
- Handkerchiefs are also associated with funerals, so they do not make good gifts.
- Gifts are opened when received.

Dining Etiquette

If you are invited to a Brazilian's house:

- Arrive at least 30 minutes late if the invitation is for dinner.
- Arrive up to an hour late for a party or large gathering.
- Brazilians dress with a flair and judge others on their appearance. Casual dress is more formal than in many other countries. Always dress elegantly and err on the side of over-dressing rather than under-dressing.
- If you did not bring a gift to the hostess, flowers the next day are always appreciated.

BUSINESS ETIQUETTE AND PROTOCOL IN BRAZIL

Relationships and Communication

Brazilians need to know who they are doing business with before they can work effectively.

- Brazilians prefer face-to-face meetings to written communication as it allows them to know the person with whom they are doing business.

- The individual they deal with is more important than the company.
- Since this is a group culture, it is important that you do not do anything to embarrass a Brazilian.
- Criticizing an individual causes that person to lose face with the others in the meeting.
- The person making the criticism also loses face, as they have disobeyed the unwritten rule.
- Communication is often informal and does not rely on strict rules of protocol. Anyone who feels they have something to say will generally add their opinion.
- It is considered acceptable to interrupt someone who is speaking.
- Face-to-face, oral communication is preferred over written communication. At the same time, when it comes to business agreements, Brazilians insist on drawing up detailed legal contracts.

BUSINESS NEGOTIATIONS

- Expect questions about your company since Brazilians are more comfortable doing business with people and companies they know.
- Wait for your Brazilian colleagues to raise the business subject. Never rush the relationship-building time.
- Brazilians take time when negotiating. Do not rush them or appear impatient.
- Expect a great deal of time to be spent reviewing details.
- Often the people you negotiate with will not have decision-making authority.
- It is advisable to hire a translator if your Portuguese is not fluent.
- Use local lawyers and accountants for negotiations. Brazilians resent an outside legal presence.
- Brazilian business is hierarchical. Decisions are made by the highest-ranking person.
- Brazilians negotiate with people, not companies. Do not change your negotiating team or you may have to start over from the beginning.

BUSINESS MEETING ETIQUETTE

- Business appointments are required and can often be scheduled on short notice; however, it is best to make them 2 to 3 weeks in advance.
- Confirm the meeting in writing. It is not uncommon for appointments to be cancelled or changed at the last minute.
- In Sao Paulo and Brasilia it is important to arrive on time for meetings. In Rio de Janeiro and other cities it is acceptable to arrive a few minutes late for a meeting.
- Do not appear impatient if you are kept waiting. Brazilians see time as something outside their control and the demands of relationships takes precedence over adhering to a strict schedule.
- Meetings are generally rather informal.
- Expect to be interrupted while you are speaking or making a presentation.
- Avoid confrontations. Do not appear frustrated with your Brazilian colleagues.

DRESS ETIQUETTE

- Brazilians pride themselves on dressing well.
- Men should wear conservative, dark coloured business suits. Three-piece suits typically indicate that someone is an executive.
- Women should wear suits or dresses that are elegant and feminine with good quality accessories. Manicures are expected.

BUSINESS CARDS

- Business cards are exchanged during introductions with everyone at a meeting.
- It is advisable, although not required, to have the other side of your business card translated into Portuguese.
- Present your business card with the Portuguese side facing the recipient.

Source: http://www.kwintessential.co.uk/resources/global-etiquette/brazil-country-profile.html, September 5, 2011. Used with permission of www.kwintessential.co.uk.

Saudi Arabia

Understanding how business is conducted in the modern Middle East requires an understanding of the Arab culture, since the Arab peoples are the majority there and most of them are Muslim. As discussed in the opening profile, the Arab culture is intertwined with the pervasive influence of Islam. Even though not all Middle Easterners are Arab, Arab culture and management style predominate in the Arabian Gulf region. Shared culture, religion, and language underlie behavioral similarities throughout the Arab world. Islam permeates Saudi life—Allah is always present, controls everything, and is frequently referred to in conversation. Employees may spend more than two hours a day in prayer as part of the life pattern that intertwines work with religion, politics, and social life.

Arab history and culture are based on tribalism, with its norms of reciprocity of favors, support, obligation, and identity passed on to the family unit, which is the primary structural model. Family life is based on closer personal ties than in the West. Arabs value personal relationships, honor, and saving face for all concerned; these values take precedence over the work at hand or verbal accuracy. "Outsiders" must realize that establishing a trusting relationship and respect for Arab social norms has to precede any attempts at business discussions. Honor, pride, and dignity are at the core of "shame" societies, such as the Arabs. As such, shame and honor provide the basis for social control and motivation. Circumstances dictate what is right or wrong and what constitutes acceptable behavior.

Arabs avoid open admission of error at all costs because weakness (*muruwwa*) is a failure to be manly. It is sometimes difficult for Westerners to get at the truth, because of the Arab need to avoid showing weakness; instead, Arabs present a desired or idealized situation. Shame is also brought on someone who declines to fulfill a request or a favor; therefore, a business arrangement is left open if something has yet to be completed.

The communication style of Middle Eastern societies is high context (that is, implicit and indirect), and their use of time is polychronic: Many activities can be taking place at the same time, with constant interruptions commonplace. The imposition of deadlines is considered rude, and business schedules take a backseat to the perspective that events will occur "sometime" when Allah wills (*bukra insha Allah*). Arabs give primary importance to hospitality; they are cordial to business associates and lavish in their entertainment, constantly offering strong black coffee (which you should not refuse) and banquets before considering business transactions. Westerners must realize the importance of personal contacts and networking, socializing and building close relationships and trust, practicing patience regarding schedules, and doing business in person. Exhibit 3-7 gives some selected actions and nonverbal behaviors that may offend Arabs. The relationship between cultural values and norms in Saudi Arabia and managerial behaviors is illustrated in Exhibit 3-8.

Chinese Family Small Businesses

The predominance of small businesses in China and the region highlights the need for managers from around the world to gain an understanding of how such businesses operate. Many small businesses—most of which are family or extended-family businesses—become part of the value chain (suppliers, buyers, retailers, etc.) within industries in which "foreign" firms may compete.

EXHIBIT 3-7   **Behavior That Will Likely Cause Offense in Saudi Arabia**

- Introducing business subjects too soon.
- Commenting on a man's wife or female children over 12 years of age.
- Raising colloquial questions that may be considered as an invasion of privacy.
- Using disparaging or swear words and off-color or obscene attempts at humor.
- Talking about religion, politics, or Israel.
- Bringing gifts of alcohol or using alcohol, which is prohibited in Saudi Arabia.
- Requesting favors from those in authority or esteem, for it is considered impolite for Arabs to say no.
- Pointing your finger at someone or showing the soles of your feet when seated.

Source: Based on excerpts from P. R. Harris and R. T. Moran, *Managing Cultural Differences*, 5th ed. (Houston: Gulf Publishing, 2000).

EXHIBIT 3-8 **The Relationship between Culture and Managerial Behaviors in Saudi Arabia**

Cultural Values	Managerial Behaviors
Tribal and family loyalty	Work group loyalty
	Paternal sociability
	Careful selection of employees
	Nepotism
Arabic language	Business as an intellectual activity
	Access to employees and peers
	Management by walking around
	Conversation as recreation
Close and warm friendships	People orientation
	Theory Y management
	Avoidance of judgment
Islam	Sensitivity to Islamic virtues
	Observance of the Qur'an and Sharia
	Work as personal or spiritual growth
	Adherence to norms
Honor and shame	Conflict avoidance
	Positive reinforcement
	Private correction of mistakes
	Avoidance of competition
	Responsibility
Polychronic use of time	Right- and left-brain facility
	Action oriented
	Patience and flexibility
Male domination	Separation of sexes
	Open work life; closed family life

Source: Based on excerpts from P. R. Harris and R. T. Moran, *Managing Cultural Differences,* 5th ed. (Houston: Gulf Publishing, 2000).

Some specifics of Chinese management style and practices in particular are presented here as they apply to small businesses. (Further discussion of the Chinese culture continues in Chapter 5 in the context of negotiation.) It is important to note that no matter the size of a Chinese company, but especially in small businesses, it is the all-pervasive presence and use of *guanxi* that provides the little red engine of business transactions in China. *Guanxi* means "connections"— the network of relationships the Chinese cultivate through friendship and affection; it entails the exchange of favors and gifts to provide an obligation to reciprocate favors. Those who share a *guanxi* network share an unwritten code.[79] The philosophy and structure of Chinese businesses comprise paternalism, mutual obligation, responsibility, hierarchy, familialism, personalism, and connections. Autocratic leadership is the norm, with the owner using his or her power—but with a caring about other people that may predominate over efficiency.

According to Lee, the major differences between Chinese management styles and those of their Western counterparts are human-centeredness, family-centeredness, centralization of power, and small size.[80] Their human-centered management style puts people ahead of a business relationship and focuses on friendship, loyalty, and trustworthiness.[81] The family is extremely important in Chinese culture, and any small business tends to be run like a family.

Globalization has resulted in the ethnic Chinese businesses (in China or other Asian countries) adapting to more competitive management styles. They are moving away from the traditional centralized power structure in Chinese organizations that comprised the boss and a few family members at the top and the employees at the bottom, with no ranking among the workers. In fact, many Chinese businesses are no longer managed by family members. Frequently, the managers are those sons and daughters who have studied and worked overseas before returning to the family company; or even foreign expatriates. Examples of Chinese capitalism responding to change and working to globalize through growth are Eu Yan Sang Holdings Ltd., the Hiap Moh Printing businesses, and the Pacific International Line.[82]

As Chinese firms in many modern regions in the Pacific Rim seek to modernize and compete locally and globally, a tug of war has begun between the old and the new: the traditional Chinese management practices and the increasingly "imported" Western management styles. As discussed by Lee, this struggle is encapsulated in the different management perspectives of the old and young generations. A two-generational study of Chinese managers by Ralston et al. also found generational shifts in work values in China. They concluded that the new generation manager is more individualistic, more independent, and takes more risks in the pursuit of profits. However, they also found the new generation holding on to their Confucian values, concluding that the new generation may be viewed as "crossverging their Eastern and Western influences, while on the road of modernization."[83]

CONCLUSION

This chapter has explored various cultural values and how managers can be prepared to understand them with the help of some general cultural profiles. The following chapters focus on application of this cultural knowledge to management in an international environment (or, alternatively in a domestic multicultural environment)—especially as relevant to cross-cultural communication (Chapter 4), negotiation and decision making (Chapter 5), and motivating and leading (Chapter 11). Culture and communication are essentially synonymous. What happens when people from different cultures communicate, and how can international managers understand the underlying process and adapt their styles and expectations accordingly? For the answers, read the next chapter.

Summary of Key Points

1. The culture of a society comprises the shared values, understandings, assumptions, and goals that are passed down through generations and imposed by members of the society. These unique sets of cultural and national differences strongly influence the attitudes and expectations—and therefore the on-the-job behavior—of individuals and groups.

2. Managers must develop cultural sensitivity to anticipate and accommodate behavioral differences in various societies. As part of that sensitivity, they must avoid parochialism—an attitude that assumes one's own management techniques are best in any situation or location and that other people should follow one's patterns of behavior.

3. From his research in 50 countries, Hofstede proposed four underlying value dimensions that help to identify and describe the cultural profile of a country and affect organizational processes: power distance, uncertainty avoidance, individualism, and masculinity. In his later research, Hofstede explored the concept of long-term versus short-term orientation to explain the cultural variation of the types of decisions people make.

4. Through his research, Fons Trompenaars confirmed some similar dimensions, and also found other unique dimensions: obligation, emotional orientation, privacy, and source of power and status.

5. The GLOBE project team of 170 researchers in 62 countries concluded the presence of a number of other dimensions, and ranked countries on those dimensions, including assertiveness, performance orientation, future orientation, and humane orientation. Gupta et al. from that team found geographical clusters on nine of the GLOBE project cultural dimensions.

6. On-the-job conflicts in international management frequently arise out of conflicting values and orientations regarding time, change, material factors, and individualism.

7. Managers can use research results and personal observations to develop a character sketch, or cultural profile, of a country. This profile can help managers anticipate how to motivate people and coordinate work processes in a particular international context.

Discussion Questions

1. What is meant by the culture of a society, and why is it important that international managers understand it? Do you notice cultural differences among your classmates? How do those differences affect the class environment? How do they affect your group projects?

2. Describe the four dimensions of culture proposed by Hofstede. What are the managerial implications of these dimensions? Compare the findings with those of Trompenaars and the GLOBE project team.

3. Discuss the types of operational conflicts that could occur in an international context because of different attitudes toward time, change, material factors, and individualism. Give examples relative to specific countries.

4. Discuss how the Internet and culture interact. Which most affects the other, and how? Give some examples.

5. Discuss collectivism as it applies to the Japanese workplace. What managerial functions does it affect?

6. Discuss the role of Islam in cross-cultural relations and business operations.

Application Exercises

1. Develop a cultural profile for one of the countries in the following list. Form small groups of students and compare your findings in class with those of another group preparing a profile for another country. Be sure to compare specific findings regarding religion, kinship, recreation, and other subsystems. What are the prevailing attitudes toward time, change, material factors, and individualism?

Any African country
People's Republic of China
Mexico
France
India

2. In small groups of students, research Hofstede's findings regarding the four dimensions of power distance, uncertainty avoidance, masculinity, and individualism for one of the following countries in comparison to the United States. (Your instructor can assign the countries to avoid duplication.) Present your findings to the class. Assume you are a U.S. manager of a subsidiary in the foreign country and explain how differences on these dimensions are likely to affect your management tasks. What suggestions do you have for dealing with these differences in the workplace?

Brazil
Italy
People's Republic of China
Russia

Experiential Exercises

1. A large Baltimore manufacturer of cabinet hardware had been working for months to locate a suitable distributor for its products in Europe. Finally invited to present a demonstration to a reputable distributing company in Frankfurt, it sent one of its most promising young executives, Fred Wagner, to make the presentation. Fred not only spoke fluent German but also felt a special interest in this assignment because his paternal grandparents had immigrated to the United States from the Frankfurt area during the 1920s. When Fred arrived at the conference room where he would be making his presentation, he shook hands firmly, greeted everyone with a friendly *guten tag,* and even remembered to bow the head slightly as is the German custom. Fred, an effective speaker and past president of the Baltimore Toastmasters Club, prefaced his presentation with a few humorous anecdotes to set a relaxed and receptive atmosphere. However, he felt that his presentation was not well received by the company executives. In fact, his instincts were correct, for the German company chose not to distribute Fred's hardware products.

What went wrong?

2. Bill Nugent, an international real estate developer from Dallas, had made a 2:30 P.M. appointment with Mr. Abdullah, a high-ranking government official in Riyadh, Saudi Arabia. From the beginning things did not go well for Bill. First, he was kept waiting until nearly 3:45 P.M. before he was ushered into Mr. Abdullah's office. When he finally did get in, several other men were also in the room. Even though Bill felt that he wanted to get down to business with Mr. Abdullah, he was reluctant to get too specific because he considered much of what they needed to discuss sensitive and private. To add to Bill's sense of frustration, Mr. Abdullah seemed more interested in engaging in meaningless small talk than in dealing with the substantive issues concerning their business.

How might you help Bill deal with his frustration?

3. Tom Forrest, an up-and-coming executive for a U.S. electronics company, was sent to Japan to work out the details of a joint venture with a Japanese electronics firm. During the first several weeks, Tom felt that the negotiations were proceeding better than he had expected. He found that he had very cordial working relationships with the team of Japanese executives, and in fact, they had agreed on the major policies and strategies governing the new joint venture. During the third week of negotiations, Tom was present at a meeting held to review their progress. The meeting was chaired by the president of the Japanese firm, Mr. Hayakawa, a man in his mid-forties, who had recently taken over the presidency from his 82-year-old grandfather. The new president, who had been involved in most of the negotiations during the preceding weeks, seemed to Tom to be one of the strongest advocates of the plan that had been developed to date. Hayakawa's grandfather, the recently retired president, also was present at the meeting. After the plans had been discussed in some detail, the octogenarian past president proceeded to give a long soliloquy about how some of the features of this plan violated the traditional practices on which the company had been founded. Much to Tom's amazement, Mr. Hayakawa did nothing to explain or defend the policies and strategies that they had taken weeks to develop. Feeling extremely frustrated, Tom then gave a fairly strong argued defense of the plan. To Tom's further amazement, no one else in the meeting spoke up in defense of the plan. The tension in the air was quite heavy, and the meeting adjourned shortly thereafter. Within days the Japanese firm completely terminated the negotiations on the joint venture.

How could you help Tom better understand this bewildering situation?

Source: Gary P. Ferraro, *The Cultural Dimensions of International Business,* 2nd ed. (Upper Saddle River, NJ: Prentice Hall, 1994).

Internet Resources

Visit the Deresky Companion Website at www.pearsonhighered.com/deresky for this chapter's Internet resources.

CASE STUDY

Australia and New Zealand: Doing Business with Indonesia

There are thousands of Australians, both individually and as members of organizations, who share trade and education with Indonesia as do New Zealanders. Yet, though geographically part of Asia, citizens of Australia and New Zealand are members of cultures very different from any other in Asia.

As increasingly they seek to trade in Asia, so also do they need to learn to manage such differences; and doing business in Indonesia is a good example. Travelling time by air from Perth, Western Australia, to Indonesia is slightly less than four hours, yet the cultural distance is immeasurable.

In January 2007, the Jakarta Post reported GDP growth had risen to over 5%. Consumer consumption drives the economy but exports are thriving, and therein lay opportunities for Australia and New Zealand.

Indonesia is a country of more than 17,000 islands and the world's largest Muslim nation. In her lecture, Dr. Joan Hardjonoof Monash University discussed the historical and geographic contexts of modern Indonesia. She spoke of the many clusters of islands worldwide that have come together as nation states—for example, the Philippines and some island groups in the Pacific—but described the Indonesian archipelago as in a class of its own.

It is unique in terms of extent and diversity. For example, Java and Bali have fertile volcanic soils, while elsewhere the land is rich in mineral resources such as oil, natural gas, and coal. Climatic conditions vary from island to island. Some regions experience annual heavy rains and floods, while others suffer regularly from droughts that often lead to famines.

With a population of more than 230 million people, Indonesia is the fourth most populous country in the world, but there is a great imbalance in population distribution within the archipelago. Settlement has always been greatest on the island of Java, and today about 60% of the Indonesian population lives there.

National ties are strong, as revealed by the great response from within Indonesia to the recent natural disasters in Aceh and Nias. Unfortunately, there are still very obvious socio-economic disparities in all regions of the country. At the top of the social structure are wealthy elites, below them an increasingly demanding middle class, and at the bottom an impoverished majority.

As Indonesia has become more integrated with ASEAN, North Asian trading partners have become more important: but well-to-do Indonesians now travel the world. Globalization has been the buzzword of international business for many years. International markets have split up into unified trade zones; individual marketplaces, particularly in the developing countries, are exposed to transnational pressures.

Some Asian countries are pulling back from perceived threats of international contagion, but Indonesia continues to open up its markets to world enterprise. However, Australians and New Zealanders cannot expect to do business with Indonesians just because they are neighbors. They have to learn the moves.

Business opportunities in Indonesia include agribusiness; the automotive industry; business and financial services; construction and infrastructure; information and communication technology; e-commerce; education and training; environmental products and services; food and beverages; fresh produce; health and medical provisions; mining and mineral services; oil and petroleum drilling, transport and storage; and science and technology.

Taking advantage of these opportunities requires skillful negotiation. One of the biggest challenges of working in a foreign country is learning how to operate in a different cultural setting. International managers tell endless stories of cross-cultural breakdowns, missed appointments, problems over differences in management style, lost orders or down time on production

MAP 3.4   Australia and New Zealand

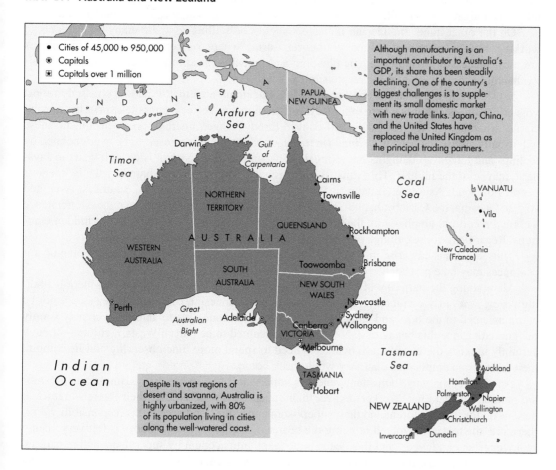

- Cities of 45,000 to 950,000
- Capitals
- Capitals over 1 million

Although manufacturing is an important contributor to Australia's GDP, its share has been steadily declining. One of the country's biggest challenges is to supplement its small domestic market with new trade links. Japan, China, and the United States have replaced the United Kingdom as the principal trading partners.

Despite its vast regions of desert and savanna, Australia is highly urbanized, with 80% of its population living in cities along the well-watered coast.

lines, labor problems between foreign management and local staff, and many other examples of miscommunication. Many could have been avoided or at least mitigated had the expatriate managers and their local counterparts been better prepared for differences in work patterns.

Some cross-cultural behavior, such as patience and courtesy, is no more than good manners. It applies to all interpersonal communication; but in Indonesia, as in the rest of Asia, there is more need to develop a long-term relationship to produce a profit than there is in Australia or New Zealand. Relationships rely on shared expectations—for example, about how first contacts should be made, how appointments should be set and kept, how deals should be closed, how time should be managed (including the Indonesian concept of "jam karet," or "rubber time," that infuriates punctuality-conscious Westerners).

Sensible but inexperienced international managers seek information that more seasoned veterans can provide. They might be colleagues, business associates, friends, or paid consultants, but in any case most people are eager to give advice. On the other hand, even managers with a highly developed global outlook may have too generalist a viewpoint on international business. They may overlook the need for a local perspective in each host country.

Indonesia is one of those countries in which a foreign manager's home office priorities of task over relationship, of corporate rather than human priorities, may not be the most effective ways to achieve productivity and effectiveness. Indonesian managers usually place more value on harmony, understanding, and mutual respect. It may be sometimes that this emphasis outweighs the importance of job performance and productivity.

On the one hand, there are a number of concerns for Indonesian managers working with their Western counterparts. For example, they believe Westerners should make an effort to adjust to the culture, taboos, and language of their Indonesian colleagues. Foreign managers should avoid bad language that might set a bad example for the workers. They should give instructions slowly and clearly in Standard English and should ask for a paraphrase to ensure understanding.

They should be willing to consider individual cases and cultural needs (e.g., prayer times or other religious obligations, time off for cemetery visits before Ramadan, weddings, funerals, etc.).

On the other hand, Indonesian managers should be willing to make many adjustments to working in an international company. Important areas where Western management techniques are most successful include strategic planning and timetable deadlines, efficiency and punctuality, handling conflict, and taking responsibility.

Sensitivity to the needs of employees is a management area that is seldom stressed in most Western business cultures where efficiency, productivity, and effectiveness take priority. For example, when somebody loses their self-control through anger, distress, or confusion, Javanese will usually advise the need to *"eling"* (in translation, not to allow oneself to be overwhelmed by feelings and mixed-up thoughts but to regain self-control). Self-control is of high value to Javanese, maybe of the highest. This value is not unique to Indonesia. It is shared by the indigenous peoples of South Asia, the Himalayan Range and Central Asia, East Asia, Southeast Asia, and Africa; Oceania, the Caribbean, and South America; and Northern America and the Arctic: hence a common cultural emphasis on the art of making and wearing masks to represent hidden emotions. Regardless of the cultures they come from, masks convey the essential emotions.[1]

Thus situations can arise in business contexts where hiding true feelings and keeping up appearances may take precedence over solving a problem.

Maintaining the harmony of the office by giving the outward appearance that there is nothing wrong is a fairly common situation in traditional Indonesian offices. Bad news may not be communicated to the boss and situations that seem insurmountable to an employee may simply be ignored.[2] Since this behavior is not generally accepted to be part of Western culture—though certainly it exists there—Western managers need to spend more time observing and listening to their Indonesian employees than they would back home.

Another reason why such attentiveness is important is that Indonesian business relationships are paternal or maternal. Workers expect their supervisors to look after their interests rather as parents do for their children; and their supervisors understand and accept this responsibility. Furthermore, the tension involved in being the bearer of bad news to one's boss is felt very keenly by Indonesian employees, and this needs to be taken into account by supervisors and managers. The English language injunction is "Don't shoot the messenger," but some Indonesian workers seem to expect a firing squad when they have to report failure. Therefore, Western managers should make clear that they want and expect subordinates to come to them with questions or problems and that the response will be non-judgmental and self-controlled. Faces should be without masks; they should not portray negative emotions of anger, confrontation, or aggression. Managers in Indonesia are expected to always be polite and to keep smiling, no matter how angry they may be inside.

Nevertheless, cross-cultural sensitivity works—or should work—both ways. Foreign managers should understand Indonesian culture and business customs, and Indonesian managers should be given clearly to understand what foreign managers will expect from them.

Case Questions

1. Using this case and the cultural dimensions explored in this chapter, discuss some of the ways in which citizens of Australia and New Zealand are members of cultures very different from any other in Asia.
2. In what respects is the Indonesian archipelago unique in Asia?
3. What characteristics of Indonesian workplaces are referred to in this profile?
4. How does the population appear to be socially stratified?
5. What are some business opportunities in Indonesia for foreign direct investment?

1. *Rupa-Pratirupa, Man & Mask*, February 20–April 12, 1998, Matighar, Indira Gandhi National Centre for the Arts, http://ignca .nic.in/

2. George B. Whitfield, 2006, Executive Orientation Services of Jakarta (EOS).

Sources:

Joan Hardjono, 05/08/2005, Herb Feith Lecture, "Can Indonesia Hold?" Centre of Southeast Asian Studies and Faculty of Arts, Monash University, in association with ABC Radio Australia and the Melbourne Institute of Asian Languages & Societies, University of Melbourne: http://www.abc.net.au/ra/news/infocus/s1429967.htm

Javanese mystical movements, January 2007, http://www.xs4all.nl/~wichm/javmys1.html

Phil King, December 2006, "Facing disaster: The 27 May earthquake shook a kingdom, not just a city," *Inside Indonesia*, http://www.insideindonesia.org/

Rupa-Pratirupa, Man & Mask, February 20–April 12, 1998, Matighar, Indira Gandhi National Centre for the Arts, http://ignca.nic.in/ex_0032.htm.

Stephen Schwartz, January 2007, "Maintain momentum to overcome challenges," *Jakarta Post*, Patrick Underwood, 23/11/2006, "Asia Update," Meat & Livestock Australia Limited (MLA) http://www.mla.com.au/; *Inside Indonesia*, http://www.insideindonesia.org/edit80/p11-12mahony.html

Western Australia Department of Industry and Resources: Export and Trade, http://www.doir.wa.gov.au/exportandtrade/F3130D5AECA54ACF8ABBBBA831766203.asp

George B. Whitfield, 2006, Executive Orientation Services of Jakarta (EOS).

World Bank, http://0-siteresources.worldbank.org.library.vu.edu.au/INTINDONESIA/Resources/htm

Source: Adapted from Helen Deresky and Elizabeth Christopher, "Australia and New Zealand as Part of Asia: Doing Business with Indonesia," *International Management: Managing across Borders and Cultures,* Pearson Education Australia, 2008. Used with permission.

4 Communicating Across Cultures

OBJECTIVES

1. To recognize the cultural variables in the communication process and what factors can cause "noise" in that process.

2. To develop an awareness of differences in non-verbal behaviors, context, and attitudes and how they affect cross-cultural communication.

3. To understand the complexities of Western-Arab communications.

4. To be aware of the impact of IT on cross-border communications.

5. To learn how to successfully manage cross-cultural business communications.

OPENING PROFILE: THE IMPACT OF SOCIAL MEDIA ON GLOBAL BUSINESS

. . . it's becoming more and more evident to enterprises that the social web actually does make sense for businesses.[1]

> K. ANANTH KRISHNAN (TATA CONSULTANCY SERVICES)
> April 27, 2011.

BNP Paribas, the French bank, launched its Facebook and Twitter sites in 2010 and has one of the largest followings, with about 120,000 Facebook "fans."[2]

> FINANCIAL TIMES,
> January 10, 2011.

Managers in international business or non-profit enterprises around the world are grappling with the question of how to benefit from the burgeoning use of social media networks—through the Internet, video, audio, and phone—both external and internal to the organization. The networks, such as Facebook, are directly and indirectly linking people and business around the world. (Facebook, for example, had 1 billion monthly users as of October 2012; 81 percent of users are outside the U.S. and Canada. If Facebook were a country it would be the third most populous country in the world). The power of such linkages for political and social motives was made clear during the "Arab Spring" in 2011, started by one person in Egypt protesting the government through the use of YouTube, iPhones, and other media.

Global business managers are realizing that these social media are potential sources of rich information, outside the normal chain of communication, that their companies could use to find out more about what customers want, how new ideas might be received, what competitors are doing, what problems might be lurking and how to deal with them, and so on. As an example, K. Ananth Krishnan, the chief technology officer (CTO) of Tata Consultancy Services, observed in an interview that "Increasingly, data is coming at businesses in *unstructured ways*. It's coming from outside of companies, in the kinds of networking and SMS messaging habits that customers have. And it's coming from unstructured sources *inside* companies, from in-house blogs to internal knowledge markets."[3] (Tata Consultancy Services, based in India, has 198,000 IT consultants in 42 countries.) Krishnan notes, however, that concerns about privacy of information gathered through such sources must be taken into account.

Another challenge to the effective use of social media is how to measure the effectiveness of each source as a benefit to the company, given the considerable investment their use would require. Firms such as Target, Dell, and Burger King are trying to find what works best for them as social media applications such as Google+, Facebook, LinkedIn, YouTube, blogs, microblogs such as Twitter, etc., have changed the way consumers interact with companies and friends about brands and services—with both positive and negative feedback.[4]

> *39 percent of companies we've surveyed already use social-media services as their primary digital tool to reach customers, and that percentage is expected to rise to 47 percent within the next four years.*
>
> McKINSEY QUARTERLY,
> April 2012.[5]

FIGURE 4-1   Social Media

Source: Anatolii Babii/Alamy

(Continued)

While many companies are trying out social media to market their products or services and to get feedback, others feel that the audience is too general and does not work as well as being able to target their message to specific demographic markets.[6]

Regardless of how companies interact with and use social media networks, it is clear that they are here to stay, that they can have considerable impact on global businesses, and that they are impacting political and social trends as well. In China, for example, over 300 million people use social media, which is very popular because it is less likely to be monitored by the government. Years ahead of the West, with social media such as Renren and Sina Weibo, China's online users spend more than 40 percent of their time online on social media, a figure that continues to rise rapidly, according to McKinsey and Company consultants.[7] There is no Facebook, YouTube, or Twitter. However, in spite of the complexities and challenges, the sheer numbers of users present considerable opportunity for marketing.

Cultural communications are deeper and more complex than spoken or written messages. The essence of effective cross-cultural communication has more to do with releasing the right responses than with sending the "right" messages.

HALL AND HALL[8]

Multi-local online strategy ... is about meeting global business objectives by tuning in to the cultural dynamics of their local markets.

"THINK GLOBALLY, INTERACT LOCALLY," *NEW MEDIA AGE*[9]

As the opening profile suggests, communication is a critical factor in the cross-cultural management issues discussed in this book, particularly those of an interpersonal nature, involving motivation, leadership, group interactions, and negotiation. Culture is conveyed and perpetuated through communication in one form or another. Culture and communication are so intricately intertwined that they are, essentially, synonymous.[10] By understanding this relationship, managers can move toward constructive intercultural management. Nardon et al. point out that while global managers cite multicultural communication as a serious challenge, at the same time it can open up important sources of business opportunity. "It is through communication that relationships are formed, conflicts are resolved, and innovative ideas are created and shared."[11]

Managers doing business around the world invariably complain that cross-cultural communication challenges have led to lost business, unintended offenses, and embarrassment—in particular in countries where it is crucial to develop relationships and trust. Communication, whether in the form of writing, talking, listening, or via the Internet, is an inherent part of a manager's role and takes up the majority of a manager's time on the job. Studies by Mintzberg demonstrate the importance of oral communication; he found that most managers spend between 50 and 90 percent of their time talking to people.[12] The ability of a manager to effectively communicate across cultural boundaries will largely determine the success of international business transactions or the output of a culturally diverse workforce. It is useful, then, to break down the elements involved in the communication process, both to understand the cross-cultural issues at stake and to maximize the opportunities to establish common meaning among the parties communicating.

THE COMMUNICATION PROCESS

The term **communication** describes the process of sharing meaning by transmitting messages through media such as words, behavior, or material artifacts. Managers communicate to coordinate activities, to disseminate information, to motivate people, and to negotiate future plans. It is of vital importance, then, for a receiver to interpret the meaning of a particular communication in the way the sender intended. Unfortunately, the communication process (see Exhibit 4-1) involves stages during which meaning can be distorted. Anything that serves to undermine the communication of the intended meaning is typically referred to as **noise**.

The primary cause of noise stems from the fact that the sender and the receiver each exist in a unique, private world thought of as her or his life space. The context of that private world, largely based on culture, experience, relations, values, and so forth, determines the interpretation of meaning in communication. People filter, or selectively understand, messages consistent with their own expectations and perceptions of reality and their values and norms of behavior.

EXHIBIT 4-1   The Communication Process

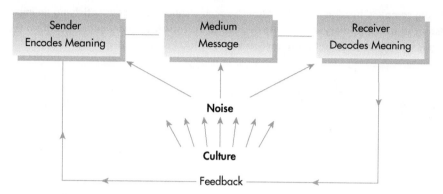

The more dissimilar the cultures of those involved, the more the likelihood of misinterpretation. In this way, as Samovar, Porter, and Jain state in their book, *Understanding Intercultural Communication,* cultural factors pervade the communication process:

> *Culture not only dictates who talks with whom, about what, and how the communication proceeds, it also helps to determine how people encode messages, the meanings they have for messages, and the conditions and circumstances under which various messages may or may not be sent, noticed, or interpreted. In fact, our entire repertory of communicative behaviors is dependent largely on the culture in which we have been raised. Culture, consequently, is the foundation of communication. And, when cultures vary, communication practices also vary.*[13]

Communication, therefore, is a complex process of linking up or sharing the perceptual fields of sender and receiver; the perceptive sender builds a bridge to the life space of the receiver.[14] After the receiver interprets the message and draws a conclusion about what the sender meant, he or she will, in most cases, encode and send back a response, making communication a circular process.

The communication process is rapidly changing, however, as a result of technological developments; therefore it is propelling global business forward at a phenomenal growth rate. These changes are discussed later in this chapter.

Cultural Noise in the Communication Process

> *In Japanese there are several words for "I" and several words for "you" but their use depends on the relationship between the speaker and the other person. In short, there is no "I" by itself; the "I" depends on the relationship.*[15]

Because the focus in this text is on effective cross-cultural communication, it is important to understand what cultural variables cause noise in the communication process. This knowledge of **cultural noise**—the cultural variables that undermine the communication of intended meaning—will enable us to take steps to minimize that noise and so improve communication.

When a member of one culture sends a message to a member of another culture, **intercultural communication** takes place. The message contains the meaning intended by the encoder. When it reaches the receiver, however, it undergoes a transformation in which the influence of the decoder's culture becomes part of the meaning.[16] Exhibit 4-2 provides an example of intercultural communication in which the meaning got all mixed up. Note how the attribution of behavior differs for each participant. **Attribution** is the process in which people look for an explanation of another person's behavior. When they realize that they do not understand another person, they tend, say Hall and Hall, to blame their confusion on the other's "stupidity, deceit, or craziness."[17]

In the situation depicted in Exhibit 4-2, the Indian employee becomes frustrated and resigns after experiencing communication problems with his German boss. How could this outcome have been avoided? We do not have much information about the people or the context of the situation, but we can look at some of the variables that might have been involved and use them as a basis for analysis.

THE CULTURE–COMMUNICATION LINK

The following sections examine underlying elements of culture that affect communication. The degree to which one is able to effectively communicate largely depends on how similar the other person's cultural expectations are to our own. However, cultural gaps can be overcome by prior learning and understanding of those variables and how to adjust to them.

EXHIBIT 4-2   **Cultural Noise in International Communication**[18]

The VP for Operations of a German manufacturing company headquartered in Munich became concerned about satisfying an important client in France with an order that he had outsourced to a subsidiary in India. He decided to visit the local manager and confirm the importance of the order being on time. The following is what transpired in his interaction with the local production manager.

Behavior		Attribution	
German:	"What can be done to make sure this project is completed on time?"	*German:*	I am giving him some responsibility.
		Indian:	Doesn't he know what to do? He is the boss. Why is he asking me?
Indian:	"I don't know. What do you suggest?"	*German:*	Can't he take responsibility?
		Indian:	I asked him for instructions.
German:	"You know the scheduling and staffing situation here better than me."	*German:*	I want to train him to make some decisions.
		Indian:	What kind of manager is he? Well, he expects me to say something.
Indian:	"I'll hire another worker, then we should be ready in two weeks."	*German:*	One more worker is totally insufficient; he doesn't know how to schedule properly. I need a definite deadline commitment—not "should be ready."
German:	"Hire three workers and give them a deadline of three weeks. Are we agreed on that deadline?"	*German:*	I offer a contract.
		Indian:	These are my orders: three weeks.

The German returned to his office in Munich, confident that the project would be completed on time and the order delivered on schedule, which he conveyed to the client. After four weeks, the customer called to complain that he had not received the order. The German VP immediately called the Indian manager:

German:	"Why hasn't the order been sent out as we agreed?"	*German:*	I am holding him responsible for our agreement.
		Indian:	He wants to know why it is not ready.
Indian:	"It will be completed next week."	(Both attribute that it is not ready.)	
German:	"But you told me it would be sent out in three weeks."	*German:*	I must teach him to take responsibility for deadlines.
		Indian:	This person does not know how to manage; it was not possible to complete the project in three weeks. I am going to get another job where the boss knows how to manage!

Trust in Communication

The key ingredient in a successful alliance is trust.

JAMES R. HOUGHTON, *FORMER CHAIRMAN, CORNING, INC.*[19]

Effective communication, and therefore effective collaboration in alliances across national boundaries, depends on the informal understandings among the parties that are based on the trust that has developed between them. However, the meaning of trust, and how it is developed and communicated, varies across societies. In China and Japan, for example, business transactions are based on networks of long-standing relationships based on trust rather than on the formal contracts and arm's-length relationships typical of the United States. When there is trust between parties, implicit understanding arises within communications. This understanding has numerous benefits in business, including encouraging communicators to overlook cultural differences and minimize problems. It allows communicators to adjust to unforeseen circumstances with less conflict than would be the case with formal contracts, and it facilitates open communication in exchanging ideas and information.[20] From his research on trust in global collaboration, John Child suggests the following guidelines for cultivating trust:

- Create a clear and calculated basis for mutual benefit. There must be realistic commitments and good intentions to honor them.
- Improve predictability: Strive to resolve conflicts and keep communication open.
- Develop mutual bonding through regular socializing and friendly contact.[21]

What can managers anticipate with regard to the level of trust in communications with people in other countries? If trust is based on how trustworthy we consider a person to be, then it must vary according to that society's expectations about whether that culture supports the norms and values that predispose people to behave credibly and benevolently. Are there differences across societies in those expectations of trust? Research on 90,000 people in 45 societies by the World Values Study Group provides some insight on cultural values regarding predisposition to trust. When we examine the percentage of respondents in each society who responded that "most people can be trusted," we can see that the Nordic countries and China had the highest predisposition to trust, followed by Canada, the United States, and Britain, while Brazil, Turkey, Romania, Slovenia, and Latvia had the lowest level of trust in people.[22]

The GLOBE Project

Results from the GLOBE research on culture, discussed in Chapter 3, provide some insight into culturally appropriate communication styles and expectations for the manager to use abroad. GLOBE researchers Javidan and House make the following observations:[23] For people in societies that ranked high on performance orientation—for example, the United States—presenting objective information in a direct and explicit way is an important and expected manner of communication; this contrasts with people in Russia or Greece—societies that ranked low on performance orientation—for whom hard facts and figures are not readily available or taken seriously. In those cases, a more indirect approach is preferred. People from countries ranking low on assertiveness, such as Sweden, also recoil from explicitness; their preference is for much two-way discourse and friendly relationships.

People ranking high on the "humane" dimension, such as those from Ireland and the Philippines, make avoiding conflict a priority and tend to communicate with the goal of being supportive of people rather than of achieving objective end results. This contrasts with people from France and Spain, whose agenda is achievement of goals.

The foregoing provides examples of how to draw implications for appropriate communication styles from the research findings on cultural differences across societies. Astute global managers have learned that culture and communication are inextricably linked and that they should prepare themselves accordingly. Most will also suggest that you carefully watch and listen to how your hosts are communicating, and then follow their lead.

Cultural Variables in the Communication Process

On a different level, it is also useful to be aware of cultural variables that can affect the communication process by influencing a person's perceptions; some of these variables have been identified by Samovar and Porter and discussed by Harris and Moran, and others.[24] These variables are as follows: attitudes; social organization; thought patterns; roles; language (spoken or written); nonverbal communication (including kinesic behavior, proxemics, paralanguage, and object language); and time. Although these variables are discussed separately in this text, their effects are interdependent and inseparable—or, as Hecht, Andersen, and Ribeau put it, "Encoders and decoders process nonverbal cues as a conceptual, multichanneled gestalt."[25] As you read the explanations of these variables in the discussion that follows, consider how they apply in the context of communicating and managing in India, as outlined in the nearby feature, *Under the Lens: Communicating in India—Language, Culture, Customs, and Etiquette.*

UNDER THE LENS

Communicating in India—Language, Culture, Customs, and Etiquette

FACTS AND STATISTICS

Location: Southern Asia, bordering Bangladesh, 4,053 km; Bhutan, 605 km; Burma, 1,463 km; China, 3,380 km; Nepal, 1,690 km; and Pakistan, 2,912 km

Capital: New Delhi

Climate: varies from tropical monsoon in south to temperate in north

Population: 1,065,070,607 (July 2004, est.)

Ethnic Make-up: Indo-Aryan, 72%; Dravidian, 25%; Mongoloid and other, 3% (2000)

Religions: Hindu, 81.3%; Muslim, 12%; Christian, 2.3%;

Sikh, 1.9%; other groups including

Buddhist, Jain, and Parsi, 2.5% (2000)

Government: federal republic

FIGURE 4-2   **Map of India**

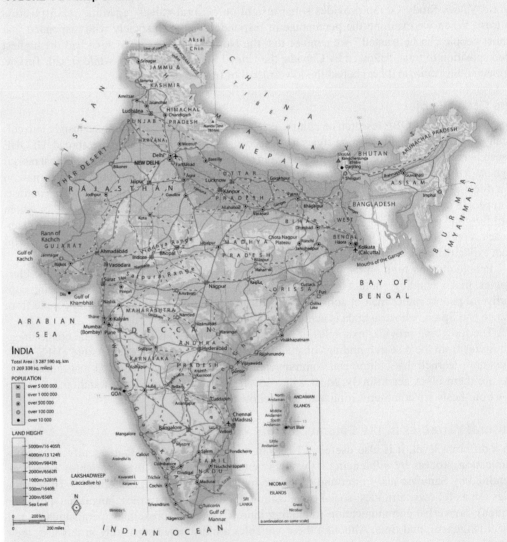

Source: © Dorling Kindersley/Dorling Kindersley Limited

FIGURE 4-3   Indian Flag

Source: Malgorzata Kistryn/Fotolia LLC

LANGUAGES IN INDIA

The different states of India have different official languages, some of them not recognized by the central government. Some states have more than one official language. Bihar in east India has three official languages—Hindi, Urdu and Bengali—that are all recognized by the central government. But Sikkim, also in east India, has four official languages, of which only Nepali is recognized by the central government. Besides the languages officially recognized by central or state governments, there are other languages that don't have this recognition, and their speakers are waging political struggles to obtain this recognition. The central government decided that Hindi was to be the official language of India, and therefore it also has the status of official language in the states.

You can learn some useful Hindi phrases by visiting http://www.kwintessential.co.uk/resources/language/hindi-phrases.html.

INDIAN SOCIETY AND CULTURE

Hierarchy

- The influences of Hinduism and the tradition of the caste system have created a culture that emphasizes established hierarchical relationships.

- Indians are always conscious of social order and their status relative to other people, be they family, friends, or strangers.

- All relationships involve hierarchies. In schools, teachers are called *gurus* and are viewed as the source of all knowledge. The patriarch, usually the father, is considered the leader of the family. The boss is seen as the source of ultimate responsibility in business. Every relationship has a clear-cut hierarchy that must be observed for the social order to be maintained.

The Role of the Family

- People typically define themselves by the groups to which they belong rather than by their status as individuals. Someone is deemed to be affiliated to a specific state, region, city, family, career path, religion, etc.

- This group orientation stems from the close personal ties Indians maintain with their family, including the extended family.

- The extended family creates a myriad of interrelationships, rules, and structures. Along with these mutual obligations comes a deep-rooted trust among relatives.

(Continued)

FIGURE 4-4   The Taj Mahal

Source: olgagomenyuk/Fotolia LLC

Just Can't Say No

- Indians do not like to express "no," be it verbally or non-verbally.
- Rather than disappoint you, for example, by saying something isn't available, Indians will offer you the response that they think you want to hear.
- This behaviour should not be considered dishonest. An Indian would be considered terribly rude if he did not attempt to give a person what had been asked.
- Since they do not like to give negative answers, Indians may give an affirmative answer but be deliberately vague about any specific details. This will require you to look for non-verbal cues, such as a reluctance to commit to an actual time for a meeting or an enthusiastic response.

Etiquette and Customs in India

Meeting Etiquette:

- Religion, education, and social class all influence greetings in India.
- This is a hierarchical culture, so greet the eldest or most senior person first.
- When leaving a group, each person must be bid farewell individually.
- Shaking hands is common, especially in the large cities among the more educated who are accustomed to dealing with Westerners.
- Men may shake hands with other men and women may shake hands with other women; however, there are seldom handshakes between men and women because of religious beliefs. If you are uncertain, wait for them to extend their hand.

Naming Conventions

Indian names vary based upon religion, social class, and region of the country. The following are some basic guidelines to understanding the naming conventions:

Hindus:

- In the north, many people have both a given name and a surname.
- In the south, surnames are less common and a person generally uses the initial of their father's name in front of their own name.
- The man's formal name is their name "s/o" (son of) and the father's name. Women use "d/o" to refer to themselves as the daughter of their father.
- At marriage, women drop their father's name and use their first name with their husband's first name as a sort of surname.

Muslims:

- Many Muslims do not have surnames. Instead, men add the father's name to their own name with the connector "bin." So, "Abdullah bin Ahmed" is "Abdullah, the son of Ahmad."

- Women use the connector "binti."
- The title Hajji (m) or Hajjah (f) before the name indicates the person has made their pilgrimage to Mecca.

Sikhs:

- Sikhs all use the name "Singh." It is either adopted as a surname or as a connector name to the surname.

Gift-Giving Etiquette

- Indians believe that giving gifts eases the transition into the next life.
- Gifts of cash are given to friends and members of the extended family to celebrate life events such as birth, death, and marriage.
- It is not the value of the gift, but the sincerity with which it is given, that is important to the recipient.
- If invited to an Indian's home for a meal, it is not necessary to bring a gift, although one will not be turned down.
- Do not give frangipani or white flowers, because they are used at funerals.
- Yellow, green, and red are lucky colors, so try to use them to wrap gifts.
- A gift from a man should be said to come from both he and his wife, mother, sister, or some other female relative.
- Hindus should not be given gifts made of leather.
- Muslims should not be given gifts made of pigskin or alcoholic products.
- Gifts are not opened when received.

Dining Etiquette

- Indians entertain in their homes, restaurants, private clubs, or other public venues, depending upon the occasion and circumstances.
- Although Indians are not always punctual themselves, they expect foreigners to arrive close to the appointed time.
- Take off your shoes before entering the house.
- Dress modestly and conservatively.
- Politely turn down the first offer of tea, coffee, or snacks. You will be asked again and again. Saying no to the first invitation is part of the protocol.

There are diverse dietary restrictions in India, and these may affect the foods that are served:

- Hindus do not eat beef, and many are vegetarians.
- Muslims do not eat pork or drink alcohol.
- Sikhs do not eat beef.
- Lamb, chicken, and fish are the most commonly served main courses for non-vegetarian meals, because they avoid the meat restrictions of the religious groups.

Table manners are somewhat formal, but this formality is tempered by the religious beliefs of the various groups.

- Much Indian food is eaten with the fingers.
- Wait to be told where to sit.
- If utensils are used, they are generally a tablespoon and a fork.
- Guests are often served in a particular order: the guest of honour is served first, followed by the men, and the children are served last. Women typically serve the men and eat later.
- You may be asked to wash your hands before and after sitting down to a meal.
- Always use your right hand to eat, whether you are using utensils or your fingers.
- In some situations food may be put on your plate for you, while in other situations you may be allowed to serve yourself from a communal bowl.
- Leaving a small amount of food on your plate indicates that you are satisfied. Finishing all your food means that you are still hungry.

(Continued)

Business Etiquette and Protocol in India

Relationships and Communication:

- Indians prefer to do business with those they know.
- Relationships are built upon mutual trust and respect.
- In general, Indians prefer to have long-standing personal relationships prior to doing business.
- It may be a good idea to go through a third-party introduction. This gives you immediate credibility.

Business Meeting Etiquette

- If you will be traveling to India from abroad, it is advisable to make appointments by letter, at least one month and preferably two months in advance.
- It is a good idea to confirm your appointment, because they do get cancelled at short notice.
- The best time for a meeting is late morning or early afternoon. Reconfirm your meeting the week before and call again that morning, since it is common for meetings to be cancelled at the last minute.
- Keep your schedule flexible so that it can be adjusted for last-minute rescheduling of meetings.
- You should arrive at meetings on time, since Indians are impressed with punctuality.
- Meetings will start with a great deal of getting-to-know-you talk. In fact, it is quite possible that no business will be discussed at the first meeting.
- Always send a detailed agenda in advance. Send back-up materials, charts, and other data as well. This allows everyone to review and become comfortable with the material prior to the meeting.
- Follow up a meeting with an overview of what was discussed and the next steps.

Business Negotiating

- Indians are non-confrontational. It is rare for them to overtly disagree, although this is beginning to change in the managerial ranks.
- Decisions are reached by the person with the most authority.
- Decision making is a slow process.
- If you lose your temper, you lose face and prove you are unworthy of respect and trust.
- Delays are to be expected, especially when dealing with the government.
- Most Indians expect concessions in both price and terms. It is acceptable to expect concessions in return for those you grant.
- Never appear overly legalistic during negotiations. In general, Indians do not trust the legal system and someone's word is sufficient to reach an agreement.
- Do not disagree publicly with members of your negotiating team.
- Successful negotiations are often celebrated by a meal.

Dress Etiquette

- Business attire is conservative.
- Men should wear dark-colored conservative business suits.
- Women should dress conservatively in suits or dresses.
- The weather often determines clothing. In the hotter parts of the country, dress is less formal, although dressing as suggested above for the first meeting will indicate respect.

Titles

- Indians revere titles such as Professor, Doctor, and Engineer.
- Status is determined by age, university degree, caste, and profession.
- If someone does not have a professional title, use the honorific title "Sir" or "Madam."
- Titles are used with the person's name or the surname, depending upon the person's name. (See Social Etiquette for more information on Indian naming conventions.)
- Wait to be invited before using someone's first name without the title.

Business Cards

- Business cards are exchanged after the initial handshake and greeting.
- If you have a university degree or any honour, put it on your business card.
- Use the right hand to give and receive business cards.
- Business cards need not be translated into Hindi.
- Always present your business card so the recipient may read the card as it is handed to them.

Source: http://www.kwintessential.co.uk/resources/global-etiquette/India-country-profile.html, September 5, 2011. Used with permission of www.kwintessential.co.uk.

ATTITUDES

We all know that our attitudes underlie the way we behave and communicate and the way we interpret messages from others. Ethnocentric attitudes are a particular source of noise in cross-cultural communication. In the incident described in Exhibit 4-2, both the Indian and the German are clearly attempting to interpret and convey meaning based on their own experiences of that kind of transaction. The German is probably guilty of stereotyping the Indian employee by quickly jumping to the conclusion that he is unwilling to take responsibility for the task and the scheduling.

This problem, **stereotyping**, occurs when a person assumes that every member of a society or subculture has the same characteristics or traits. Stereotyping is a common cause of misunderstanding in intercultural communication. It is an arbitrary, lazy, and often destructive way to find out about people. Astute managers are aware of the dangers of cultural stereotyping and deal with each person as an individual with whom they may form a unique relationship.

SOCIAL ORGANIZATIONS

Our perceptions can be influenced by differences in values, approach, or priorities relative to the kind of social organizations to which we belong. These organizations may be based on one's nation, tribe, or religious sect, or they may consist of the members of a certain profession. Examples of such organizations include the Academy of Management or the United Auto Workers (UAW).[26]

THOUGHT PATTERNS

The logical progression of reasoning varies widely around the world and greatly affects the communication process. Managers cannot assume that others use the same reasoning processes, as illustrated by the experience of a Canadian expatriate in Thailand, related in a book by Harris and Moran:

While in Thailand a Canadian expatriate's car was hit by a Thai motorist who had crossed over the double line while passing another vehicle. After failing to establish that the fault lay with the Thai driver, the Canadian flagged down a policeman. After several minutes of seemingly futile discussion, the Canadian pointed out the double line in the middle of the road and asked the policeman directly, "What do these lines signify?" The policeman replied, "They indicate the center of the road and are there so I can establish just how far the accident is from that point." The Canadian was silent. It had never occurred to him that the double line might not mean "no passing allowed."[27]

In the Exhibit 4-2 scenario, perhaps the German did not realize that the Indian employee had a different rationale for his time estimate for the job. Because the Indian was not used to having to estimate schedules, he just took a guess, which he felt he had been forced to do.

ROLES

Societies differ considerably in their perceptions of a manager's role. Much of the difference is attributable to their perceptions of who should make the decisions and who has responsibility for what. In the Exhibit 4-2 example, the German assumes that his role as manager is to delegate responsibility, to foster autonomy, and to practice participative management. He prescribes the role of the employee without any consideration of whether the employee will understand that role. The Indian's frame of reference leads him to think that the manager is the boss and should give the order about when to have the job completed. He interprets the German's behavior as breaking that frame of reference, and therefore he feels that the boss is "stupid and incompetent" for giving him the wrong order and for not recognizing and appreciating his accomplishments. The manager should have considered what behaviors Indian workers would expect of him and then either should have played that role or discussed the situation carefully, in a training mode.

LANGUAGE

Spoken or written language, of course, is a frequent cause of miscommunication, stemming from a person's inability to speak the local language, a poor or too-literal translation, a speaker's failure to explain idioms, or a person missing the meaning conveyed through body language or certain symbols. Even among countries that share the same language, problems can arise from the subtleties and nuances inherent in the use of the language, as noted by George Bernard Shaw: "Britain and America are two nations separated by a common language." This problem can exist even within the same country among different subcultures or subgroups.[28]

Many international executives tell stories about lost business deals or lost sales because of communication blunders:

> When Pepsi Cola's slogan "Come Alive with Pepsi" was introduced in Germany, the company learned that the literal German translation of "come alive" is "come out of the grave."
> A U.S. airline found a lack of demand for its "rendezvous lounges" on its Boeing 747s. They later learned that "rendezvous" in Portuguese refers to a room that is rented for prostitution.[29]

More than just conveying objective information, language also conveys cultural and social understandings from one generation to the next. Examples of how language reflects what is important in a society include the 6,000 different Arabic words used to describe camels and their parts and the 50 or more classifications of snow used by the Inuit, the Eskimo people of Canada.

Inasmuch as language conveys culture, technology, and priorities, it also serves to separate and perpetuate subcultures. In India, 14 official and many unofficial languages are used, and over 800 languages are spoken on the African continent.

Because of increasing workforce diversity around the world, the international business manager will have to deal with a medley of languages. For example, assembly-line workers at the Ford plant in Cologne, Germany, speak Turkish and Spanish as well as German. In Malaysia, Indonesia, and Thailand, many of the buyers and traders are Chinese. Not all Arabs speak Arabic; in Tunisia and Lebanon, for example, French is the language of commerce.

International managers need either a good command of the local language or competent interpreters. The task of accurate translation to bridge cultural gaps is fraught with difficulties: Joe Romano, a partner of High Ground, an emerging technology-marketing company in Boston, found out on a business trip to Taiwan how close a one-syllable slip of the tongue can come to torpedoing a deal. He noted that one is supposed to say to the chief executive "Au-ban," meaning "Hello, No. 1. Boss." But instead he accidentally said "Lau-ban ya," which means "Hello, wife of the boss." Essentially Mr. Romano called him a woman in front of twenty senior Taiwanese executives, who all laughed; but the boss was very embarrassed, because men in Asia have a very macho attitude.[30]

Even the direct translation of specific words does not guarantee the congruence of their meaning, as with the word "yes" used by Asians, which usually means only that they have heard you, and, often, that they are too polite to disagree. The Chinese, for example, through years of political control, have built into their communication culture a cautionary stance to avoid persecution by professing agreement with whatever opinion was held by the person questioning them.[31]

Sometimes even a direct statement can be misinterpreted instead as an indirect expression, as when a German businessman said to his Algerian counterpart, "My wife would love something like that beautiful necklace your wife was wearing last night. It was beautiful." The next day the Algerian gave him a box with the necklace in it as a gift to his wife. The Algerian had interpreted the compliment as an indirect way of expressing a wish to possess a similar necklace. The German was embarrassed, but had to accept the necklace. He realized he needed to be careful how he expressed such things in the future—such as asking where that kind of jewelry is sold.[32]

In much of the world, politeness and a desire to say only what the listener wants to hear create noise in the communication process. Often, even a clear translation does not help a person to understand what is meant because the encoding process has obscured the true message. With the poetic Arab language—replete with exaggeration, elaboration, and repetition—meaning is attributed more to how something is said rather than to what is actually said.

For the German supervisor and Indian employee cited in Exhibit 4-2, it is highly likely that the German could have picked up some cues from the employee's body language that probably implied problems with the interpretation of meaning. How might body language have created noise in this case?

NONVERBAL COMMUNICATION

Clearly, as explained by Roger Axtel in his book, "Essential Do's and Taboos,"[33] this non-verbal signal (shown in figure 4-5 below) is absolutely not "O.K." in many countries. Axtel gives the example of when Vice President Richard Nixon flew to Brazil in an attempt to improve relations between the two countries. As reported in the newspapers, when Nixon stepped off the plane in Sao Paulo, he gave the "A-O.K." sign—with both hands! The crowd at the airport booed—of course—given the meaning in Brazil (a private part of a woman's body); not surprisingly, photos of this incident were in the paper the next day!

Behavior that communicates without words (although it often is accompanied by words) is called **nonverbal communication**. People will usually believe what they see over what they hear—hence the expression, "A picture is worth a thousand words." Studies show that these subtle messages account for between 65 and 93 percent of interpreted communication.[34] Even minor variations in body language, speech rhythms, and punctuality, for example, often cause mistrust and misperception of the situation among cross-national parties.[35] The media for such nonverbal communication can be categorized into four types: (1) kinesic behavior, (2) proxemics, (3) paralanguage, and (4) object language.

The term **kinesic behavior** refers to communication through body movements—posture, gestures, facial expressions, and eye contact. Although such actions may be universal, often their meaning is not. Because kinesic systems of meaning are culturally specific and learned, they cannot be generalized across cultures. Most people in the West would not correctly interpret many Chinese facial expressions; for example, sticking out the tongue expresses surprise, a widening of the eyes shows anger, and scratching the ears and cheeks indicates happiness.[36] Research has shown for some time, however, that most people worldwide can recognize displays of the basic emotions of anger, disgust, fear, happiness, sadness, surprise, and contempt.[37]

As illustrated previously, visitors to other countries must be careful about their gestures and how they might be interpreted. For example, people in Japan may point with their middle finger, which is considered an obscene gesture to others. To Arabs, showing the soles of one's feet is an insult; recall the reporter who threw his shoe at President Bush in late 2008 during his visit to Iraq. This was, to Arabs, the ultimate insult.

FIGURE 4-5   Cultural Interpretation of Gestures

United States: "A-O.K."
France: "Zero" or "worthless"
Japan: Symbol for money

Many businesspeople and visitors react negatively to what they feel are inappropriate facial expressions, without understanding the cultural meaning behind them. In his studies of cross-cultural negotiations, Graham observed that the Japanese feel uncomfortable when faced with the Americans' eye-to-eye posture. They are taught since childhood to bow their heads out of humility, whereas the automatic response of Americans is "look at me when I'm talking to you!"[38]

Subtle differences in eye behavior (called *oculesics*) can throw off a communication badly if they are not understood. Eye behavior includes differences not only in eye contact but also in the use of eyes to convey other messages, whether or not that involves mutual gaze. For example, during speech, Americans will look straight at you, but the British keep your attention by looking away. The British will look at you when they have finished speaking, which signals that it is your turn to talk. The implicit rationale for this is that you can't interrupt people when they are not looking at you.[39]

It is helpful for U.S. managers to be aware of the many cultural expectations regarding posture and how they may be interpreted. In Europe or Asia, a relaxed posture in business meetings may be taken as bad manners or the result of poor upbringing. In Korea, you are expected to sit upright, with feet squarely on the floor, and to speak slowly, showing a blending of body and spirit.

Proxemics deals with the influence of proximity and space on communication—both personal space and office space or layout. Americans expect office layouts to provide private space for each person, and usually a larger and more private space as one goes up the hierarchy. In much of Asia, the custom is open office space, with people at all levels working and talking in close proximity to one another. Space communicates power in both Germany and the United States, evidenced by the desire for a corner office or one on the top floor. The importance of French officials, however, is made clear by a position in the middle of subordinates, communicating that they have a central position in an information network, where they can stay informed and in control.[40] The following Under the Lens feature illustrates the connections between beliefs about the variables of proxemics and business decisions.

Do you ever feel vaguely uncomfortable and start moving backward slowly when someone is speaking to you? This is because that person is invading your "bubble"—your personal space. Personal space is culturally patterned, and foreign spatial cues are a common source of

UNDER THE LENS
How Feng Shui Affects Business

Feng Shui (pronounced "fung shway") is an ancient Chinese system of aesthetics believed to use the laws of both heaven and earth to help one improve life by receiving positive *qi*. Feng shui translates into English as "wind-water."[41] Qi (pronounced "chee" in English) is "a movable positive or negative life force which plays an essential role in feng shui."[42]

Throughout history, Asian experts have read these energy patterns and how to benefit by facing their buildings and offices in a particular direction, by designing gardens and entrances in a positive way, and by using Qi in rooms to influence aspects in an individual's life. "The quality of Qi is expressed through form, shape, color, direction, time, and the feeling it generates within us.[43] Various methods to establish beneficial settings have included compass directions, dowsing (commonly known as using a rod to move over the earth to try to find underground water or buried metals, etc.), and geomancy (loosely referred to as attempting to interpret meanings from patterns or markings in the soil or sand).

Feng shui is also used by Westerners and is often used in the process of building or decorating offices and homes—though not always following expert advice. When Donald Trump lost some important Asian clients due to his properties' apparently bad feng shui, he hired a feng shui master to analyze the auspiciousness of Trump Towers. In fact, feng shui and other beliefs from Chinese culture can drastically influence business deals. Michael Rudder, a real-estate broker in New York, found this out the hard way and now integrates feng shui in his planning—especially since most of his recent sales of office buildings and condominiums have been to Asians.[44] Also, as found by many others involved in real-estate, certain numbers have specific meanings in different cultures. In Chinese, Japanese, and Korean, for example, the pronunciation of the number four sounds the same as the word for death. No wonder many buildings in Asia do not have a fourth floor. And in Chinese, the number eight is a homophone for the word for getting rich. The eighth floor, and building numbers with eights in them, often sell at a premium.[45]

misinterpretation. When someone seems aloof or pushy, it often means that she or he is operating under subtly different spatial rules.

Hall and Hall suggest that cultural differences affect the programming of the senses and that space, perceived by all the senses, is regarded as a form of territory to be protected.[46] South Americans, Southern and Eastern Europeans, Indonesians, and Arabs are **high-contact cultures**, preferring to stand close, touch a great deal, and experience a "close" sensory involvement. Latin Americans, for example, have a highly physical greeting such as putting their arms around a colleague's back and grabbing him by the arm. On the other hand, North Americans, Asians, and Northern Europeans are **low-contact cultures** and prefer much less sensory involvement, standing farther apart and touching far less. They have a "distant" style of body language. In France, a relationship-oriented culture, good friends greet members of the opposite sex with a peck on each cheek; a handshake is a way to make a personal connection.

Interestingly, high-contact cultures are mostly located in warmer climates, and low-contact cultures in cooler climates. Americans are relatively nontouching, automatically standing at a distance so that an outstretched arm will touch the other person's ear. Standing any closer than that is regarded as invading intimate space. However, Americans and Canadians certainly expect a warm handshake and maybe a pat on the back from closer friends, though not the very warm double handshake of the Spaniards (clasping the forearm with the left hand). The Japanese, considerably less **haptic** (touching), do not shake hands; an initial greeting between a Japanese businessperson and a Spanish businessperson would be uncomfortable for both parties if they were untrained in cultural haptics. The Japanese bow to one another—the depth of the bow revealing their relative social standing.

Imagine the smartphone app that would ask your identity, the identity of the other greeter, where you both are and how many times you have greeted each other. It would then propose a compromise—a namaste followed by a handshake, perhaps, or a bow punctuated by a slap on the back.[47]

When considering high- and low-contact cultures, we can trace a correlation between Hofstede's cultural variables of individualism and collectivism and the types of kinesic and proxemic behaviors people display. Generally, people from individualistic cultures are more remote and distant, whereas those from collectivist cultures are interdependent: They tend to work, play, live, and sleep in close proximity.[48]

The term **paralanguage** refers to how something is said rather than the content—i.e., the rate of speech, the tone and inflection of voice, other noises, laughing, or yawning. The culturally aware manager learns how to interpret subtle differences in paralanguage, including silence. Silence is a powerful communicator. It may be a way of saying "no," of being offended, or of waiting for more information to make a decision. There is considerable variation in the use of silence in meetings. While Americans get uncomfortable after 10 or 15 seconds of silence, Chinese prefer to think the situation over for 30 seconds before speaking. The typical scenario between Americans and Chinese, then, is that the American gets impatient, says something to break the silence, and offends the Chinese by interrupting his or her chain of thought and comfort level with the subject.[49]

The term **object language**, or **material culture**, refers to how we communicate through material artifacts, whether architecture, office design and furniture, clothing, cars, or cosmetics. Material culture communicates what people hold as important. In the United States, for example, someone wishing to convey his important status and wealth would show guests his penthouse office or expensive car. In Japan and China a businessman presents his business card to a new contact and expects the receiver to study it and appreciate his position. The cards are called "name cards" in China and are an essential aspect of doing business—a way to build networks. The exchange of cards occurs as soon as you meet, and visitors should be careful to get an appropriate translation for their cards.[50] In Mexico, a visiting international executive or salesperson is advised to take time out, before negotiating business, to show appreciation for the surrounding architecture, which is prized by Mexicans. The importance of family to people in Spain and much of Latin America would be conveyed by family photographs around the office, and therefore an expectation that the visitor would enquire about the family.

TIME

Another variable that communicates culture is the way people regard and use time (see also Chapter 3). To Brazilians, relative punctuality communicates the level of importance of those involved. To Middle Easterners, time is something controlled by the will of Allah.

To initiate effective cross-cultural business interactions, managers should know the difference between *monochronic time systems* and *polychronic time systems* and how they affect communications. Hall and Hall explain that in **monochronic cultures** (Switzerland, Germany, and the United States), time is experienced in a linear way, with a past, a present, and a future, and time is treated as something to be spent, saved, made up, or wasted. Classified and compartmentalized, time serves to order life. This attitude is a learned part of Western culture, probably starting with the Industrial Revolution. Monochronic people, found in individualistic cultures, generally concentrate on one thing at a time, adhere to time commitments, and are accustomed to short-term relationships.

In contrast, **polychronic cultures** tolerate many things occurring simultaneously and emphasize involvement with people. Two Latin friends, for example, will put an important conversation ahead of being on time for a business meeting, thus communicating the priority of relationships over material systems. Polychronic people—Latin Americans, Arabs, and those from other collectivist cultures—may focus on several things at once, be highly distractible, and change plans often.[51]

The relationship between time and space also affects communication. Polychronic people, for example, are likely to hold open meetings, moving around and conducting transactions with one party and then another, rather than compartmentalizing meeting topics, as do monochronic people.

The nuances and distinctions regarding cultural differences in nonverbal communication are endless. The various forms are listed in Exhibit 4-3; wise intercultural managers will take careful account of the role that such differences might play.

What aspects of nonverbal communication might have created noise in the interactions between the German supervisor and the Indian employee in Exhibit 4-2? Undoubtedly, some cues could have been picked up from the kinesic behavior of each person. It was the responsibility of the manager, in particular, to notice any indications from the Indian that could have prompted him to change his communication pattern or assumptions. Face-to-face communication permits the sender of the message to get immediate feedback, both verbal and nonverbal, and thus to have some idea as to how that message is being received and whether additional information is needed. What aspects of the Indian employee's kinesic behavior or paralanguage might have been evident to a more culturally sensitive manager? Did both parties' sense of time affect the communication process?

Context

East Asians live in relatively complex social networks with prescribed role relations; attention to context is, therefore, important for their effective functioning. In contrast, westerners live in less constraining social worlds that stress independence and allow them to pay less attention to context.

RICHARD E. NISBETT.[52]

EXHIBIT 4-3   **Forms of Nonverbal Communication**

- Facial expressions
- Body posture
- Gestures with hands, arms, head, etc.
- Interpersonal distance (proxemics)
- Touching, body contact
- Eye contact
- Clothing, cosmetics, hairstyles, jewelry
- Paralanguage (voice pitch and inflections, rate of speech, and silence)
- Color symbolism
- Attitude toward time and the use of time in business and social interactions
- Food symbolism and social use of meals

A major differentiating factor that is a primary cause of noise in the communication process is that of context—which actually incorporates many of the variables discussed earlier. The **context** in which the communication takes place affects the meaning and interpretation of the interaction. Cultures are known to be high- or low-context cultures, with a relative range in between.[53] In **high-context cultures** (Asia, the Middle East, Africa, and the Mediterranean), feelings and thoughts are not explicitly expressed; instead, one has to read between the lines and interpret meaning from one's general understanding. Two such high-context cultures are the South Korea and Arab cultures. In such cultures, key information is embedded in the context rather than made explicit. People make assumptions about what the message means through their knowledge of the person or the surroundings. In these cultures, most communication takes place within a context of extensive information networks resulting from close personal relationships. See the following Management Focus for further explanation of the Asian communication style.

In **low-context cultures** (Germany, Switzerland, Scandinavia, and North America), where personal and business relationships are more compartmentalized, communication media have to be more explicit. Feelings and thoughts are expressed in words, and information is more readily available. Westerners focus more on the individual, and therefore tend to view events as the result of specific agents, while Easterners view events in a broader and longer-term context.[54]

In cross-cultural communication between high- and low-context people, a lack of understanding may preclude reaching a solution, and conflict may arise. Germans, for example, will expect considerable detailed information before making a business decision, whereas Arabs will base their decisions more on knowledge of the people involved—the information is present, but it is implicit. People in low-context cultures, such as those in Germany, Switzerland, Austria, and the United States, convey their thoughts and plans in a direct, straightforward communication style, saying something like "we have to make a decision on this today." People in high-context cultures, such as in Asia, and, to a lesser extent, in England, convey their thoughts in a more indirect, implicit manner; this means that someone from Germany needs to have more patience and tact and be willing to listen and watch for clues—verbal and nonverbal—as to their colleagues' wishes.

People in high-context cultures expect others to understand unarticulated moods, subtle gestures, and environmental clues that people from low-context cultures simply do not process. Misinterpretation and misunderstanding often result.[55] People from high-context cultures perceive those from low-context cultures as too talkative, too obvious, and redundant. Those from low-context cultures perceive high-context people as nondisclosing, sneaky, and mysterious. Research indicates, for example, that Americans find talkative people more attractive, whereas the Koreans—a high-context people—perceive less-verbal people as more attractive. (These conflicts are illustrated in the accompanying Management in Action feature. Finding the right balance between low- and high-context communications can be tricky, as Hall and Hall point out: "Too much information leads people to feel they are being talked down to; too little information can mystify them or make them feel left out."[56] Exhibit 4-4 shows the relative level of context in various countries.

EXHIBIT 4-4   Cultural Context and Its Effects on Communication

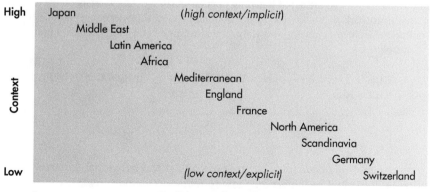

MANAGEMENT IN ACTION
Oriental Poker Face: Eastern Deception or Western Inscrutability?

Among many English expressions that are likely to offend those of us whose ancestry may be traced to the Far East, two stand out quite menacingly for me: "Oriental poker face" and "idiotic Asian smile." The former refers to the supposedly inscrutable nature of a facial expression that apparently reflects no particular state of mind, while the latter pokes fun at a face fixed with a perpetually friendly smile. Westerners' perplexity, when faced with either, arises from the impression that these two diametrically opposed masquerading strategies prevent them from extracting useful information—at least the type of information that at least they could process with a reasonable measure of confidence—about the feelings of the person before them. An Asian face that projects no signs of emotion, then, seems to most Westerners nothing but a facade. It does not matter whether that face wears an unsightly scowl or a shining ray; a facial expression they cannot interpret poses a genuine threat.

Compassionate and sympathetic to their perplexity as I may be, I am also insulted by the Western insensitivity to the significant roles that subtle signs play in Asian cultures. Every culture has its unique modus operandi for communication. Western culture, for example, apparently emphasizes the importance of direct communication. Not only are the communicators taught to look directly at each other when they convey a message, but they also are encouraged to come right to the point of the message. Making bold statements or asking frank questions in a less than diplomatic manner (i.e., "That was really a very stupid thing to do!" or "Are you interested in me?") is rarely construed as rude or indiscreet. Even embarrassingly blunt questions such as "President Clinton, did you have sexual intercourse with Monica Lewinsky?" are tolerated most of the time. Asians, on the other hand, find this direct communicative communication style quite unnerving. In many social interactions, they avoid direct eye contact. They "see" each other without necessarily looking directly at each other, and they gather information about inner states of mind without asking even the most discreet or understated questions. Many times they talk around the main topic, and, yet, they succeed remarkably well in understanding one another's position. (At least they believe they have developed a reasonably clear understanding.)

To a great extent, Asian communication is listening-centered; the ability to listen (and a special talent for detecting various communicative cues) is treated as equally important as, if not more important than, the ability to speak. This contrasts clearly with the American style of communication that puts the utmost emphasis on verbal expression; the speaker carries most of the burden for ensuring that everyone understands his or her message. An Asian listener, however, is prone to blame himself or herself for failing to reach a comprehensive understanding from the few words and gestures performed by the speaker. With this heavier burden placed on the listener, an Asian speaker does not feel obliged to send clearly discernible message cues (at least not nearly so much as he or she is obliged to do in American cultural contexts). Not obligated to express themselves without interruption, Asians use silence as a tool in communication. Silence, by most Western conventions, represents discontinuity of communication and creates a feeling of discomfort and anxiety. In the Orient, however, silence is not only comfortably tolerated but is considered a desirable form of expression. Far from being a sign of displeasure or animosity, it serves as an integral part of the communication process, used for reflecting on messages previously exchanged and for carefully crafting thoughts before uttering them.

It is not outlandish at all, then, for Asians to view Americans as unnecessarily talkative and lacking in the ability to listen. For the Asian, it is the American who projects a mask of confidence by being overly expressive both verbally and nonverbally. Since the American style of communication places less emphasis on the act of listening than on speaking, Asians suspect that their American counterparts fail to pick up subtle and astute communicative signs in conversation. To one with a cultural outlook untrained in reading those signs, an inscrutable face represents no more than a menacing or amusing mask.

Source: Dr. Jin Kim, State University of New York–Plattsburgh. Copyright © 2003 by Dr. Jin Kim. Used with permission of Dr. Kim.

The importance of understanding the role of context and nonverbal language to avoid misinterpretation is illustrated in the accompanying feature, *Comparative Management in Focus: Communicating with Arabs.*

COMPARATIVE MANAGEMENT IN FOCUS
Communicating with Arabs

In the Middle East, the meaning of a communication is implicit and interwoven, and consequently much harder for Americans, accustomed to explicit and specific meanings, to understand.

Arabs are warm, emotional, and quick to explode: "sounding off" is regarded as a safety valve. In fact, the Arabic language aptly communicates the Arabic culture, one of emotional extremes. The language contains the means for overexpression, many adjectives, words that allow for exaggeration, and metaphors to emphasize a position. What is said is often not as important as *how* it is said. Eloquence and flowery speech are admired for their own sake, regardless of the content. Loud speech is used for dramatic effect.

At the core of Middle Eastern culture are friendship, honor, religion, and traditional hospitality. Family, friends, and connections are very important on all levels in the Middle East and will take precedence over business transactions. Arabs do business with people, not companies, and they make commitments to people, not contracts. A phone call to the right person can help to get around seemingly insurmountable obstacles. An Arab expects loyalty from friends, and it is understood that giving and receiving favors is an inherent part of the relationship; no one says "no" to a request for a favor. A lack of follow-through is assumed to be beyond the friend's control.[57]

Because hospitality is a way of life and highly symbolic, a visitor must be careful not to reject it by declining refreshment or rushing into business discussions. Part of that hospitality is the elaborate system of greetings and the long period of getting acquainted, perhaps taking up the entire first meeting. While the handshake may seem limp, the rest of the greeting is not. Kissing on the cheeks is common among men, as is hand-holding between male friends. However, any public display of intimacy between men and women is strictly forbidden by the Arab social code.

Women play little or no role in business or entertainment; the Middle East is a male-dominated society, and it is impolite to inquire about women. Other nonverbal taboos include showing the soles of one's feet and using the left (unclean) hand to eat or pass something. In discussions, slouching in a seat or leaning against a wall communicates a lack of respect.

The Arab society also values honor. Harris and Moran explain: "Honor, social prestige, and a secure place in society are brought about when conformity is achieved. When one fails to conform, this is considered to be damning and leads to a degree of shame."[58] Shame results not just from doing

MAP 4.1 **Saudi Arabia and the Arabian Peninsula**

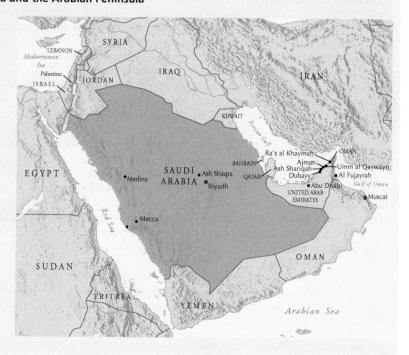

(Continued)

FIGURE 4-6   **Westerner Meeting with Arab Businessman**

Source: Hi Brow Arabia/Alamy

something wrong but from having others find out about that wrongdoing. Establishing a climate of honesty and trust is part of the sense of honor. Therefore, considerable tact is needed to avoid conveying any concern or doubt. Arabs tend to be quite introverted until a mutual trust is built, which takes a long time.[59]

In their nonverbal communication, most Arab countries are high-contact cultures. Arabs stand and sit closer and touch people of the same sex more than Westerners. They do not have the same concept of "public" and "private" space, or as Hall puts it, "Not only is the sheer noise level much higher, but the piercing look of the eyes, the touch of the hands, and the mutual bathing in the warm moist breath during conversation represent stepped-up sensory inputs to a level which many Europeans find unbearably intense. On the other hand, the distance preferred by North Americans may leave an Arab suspicious of intentions because of the lack of olfactory contact."[60]

The Muslim expression *Bukra insha Allah*—"Tomorrow if Allah wills"—explains much about the Arab culture and its approach to business transactions. A cultural clash typically occurs when an American tries to give an Arab a deadline. "'I am going to Damascus tomorrow morning and will have to have my car tonight,' is a sure way to get the mechanic to stop work," explains Hall, "because to give another person a deadline in this part of the world is to be rude, pushy, and demanding."[61] In such instances, the attitude toward time communicates as loudly as words.

In verbal interactions, managers must be aware of different patterns of Arab thought and communication. Compared to the direct, linear fashion of American communication, Arabs tend to meander: They start with social talk, discuss business for a while, loop round to social and general issues, then back to business, and so on.[62] American impatience and insistence on sticking to the subject will "cut off their loops," triggering confusion and dysfunction. Instead, Westerners should accept that there will be considerable time spent on "small talk" and socializing, with frequent interruptions, before getting down to business.

Exhibit 4-5 illustrates some of the sources of noise that are likely to interfere in the communication process between Americans and Arabs, thereby causing miscommunications and misunderstandings.

For people doing business in the Middle East, the following are some useful guidelines for effective communication:

• Be patient. Recognize the Arab attitude toward time and hospitality—take time to develop friendship and trust, for these are prerequisites for any social or business transactions.

EXHIBIT 4-5   **Miscommunication between Americans and Arabs Caused by Cross-Cultural Noise**

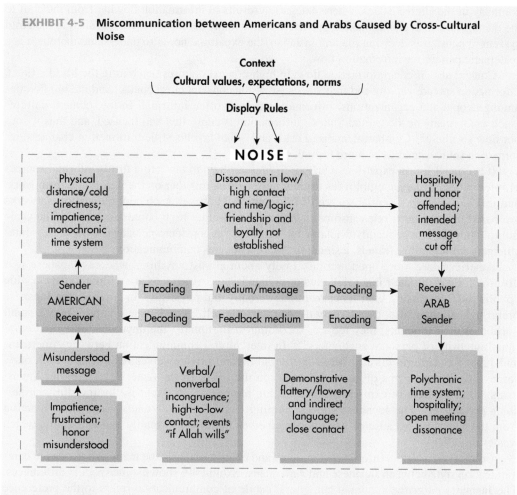

- Recognize that people and relationships matter more to Arabs than the job, company, or contract—conduct business personally, not by correspondence or telephone.

- Avoid expressing doubts or criticism when others are present—recognize the importance of honor and dignity to Arabs.

- Adapt to the norms of body language, flowery speech, and circuitous verbal patterns in the Middle East, and don't be impatient to "get to the point."

- Expect many interruptions in meetings, delays in schedules, and changes in plans.[63]

Communication Channels

In addition to the variables related to the sender and receiver of a message, the variables linked to the channel itself and the context of the message must be taken into consideration. These variables include fast or slow messages and information flows, as well as different types of media.

INFORMATION SYSTEMS

Communication in organizations varies according to where and how it originates, the channels, and the speed at which it flows, whether it is formal or informal, and so forth. The type of organizational structure, the staffing policies, and the leadership style will affect the nature of an organization's information system.

As an international manager, it is useful to know where and how information originates and the speed at which it flows, both internally and externally. In centralized organizational structures, as in South America, most information originates from top managers. Workers take less responsibility for keeping managers informed in a South American company than in a typical company in the United States, where delegation results in information flowing from the staff to the managers. In a decision-making system in which many people are involved, such as the **ringi system** of consensus decision making in Japan, the expatriate needs to understand that there is a systematic pattern for information flow.

Context also affects information flow. In high-context cultures (such as in the Middle East), information spreads rapidly and freely because of the constant close contact and the implicit ties among people and organizations. Information flow is often informal. In low-context cultures (such as Germany or the United States), information is controlled and focused, and thus it does not flow so freely.[64] Compartmentalized roles and office layouts stifle information channels; information sources tend to be more formal.

It is crucial for an expatriate manager to find out how to tap into a firm's informal sources of information. In Japan, employees usually have a drink together on the way home from work, and this becomes an essential source of information. However, such communication networks are based on long-term relationships in Japan (and in other high-context cultures). The same information may not be readily available to "outsiders." A considerable barrier in Japan separates strangers from familiar friends, a situation that discourages communication.

Americans are more open and talk freely about almost anything, whereas Japanese will disclose little about their inner thoughts or private issues. Americans are willing to have a wide "public self," disclosing their inner reactions verbally and physically. In contrast, the Japanese prefer to keep their responses largely to their "private self." The Japanese expose only a small portion of their thoughts; they reduce, according to Barnlund, "the unpredictability and emotional intensity of personal encounters."[65] In intercultural communication between Americans and Japanese, cultural clashes between the public and private selves result when each party forces its cultural norms of communication on the other. In the American style, the American's cultural norms of explicit communication impose on the Japanese by invading the person's private self. The Japanese style of implicit communication causes a negative reaction from the American because of what is perceived as too much formality and ambiguity, which wastes time.[66]

Cultural variables in information systems and context underlie the many differences in communication style between Japanese and Americans. Exhibit 4-6 shows some specific differences. The Japanese *ningensei* ("human beingness") style of communication refers to the preference for humanity, reciprocity, a receiver orientation, and an underlying distrust of words and analytic logic.[67] The Japanese believe that true intentions are not readily revealed in words or contracts but are, in fact, masked by them. In contrast to the typical American's verbal agility and explicitness, Japanese behaviors and communications are directed to defend and give face for everyone concerned; to do so, they avoid public disagreements at all costs. In cross-cultural negotiations, this last point is essential.

The speed with which we try to use information systems is another key variable that needs attention to avoid misinterpretation and conflict. Americans expect to give and receive information very quickly and clearly, moving through details and stages in a linear fashion to the conclusion. They usually use various media for fast messages—IMs, emails, Skype, faxes, social media, and familiar relationships—to give all the facts up front. In contrast, the French use the slower message channels of deep relationships, culture, and sometimes mediators to exchange information. A French written communication will be tentative, with subsequent letters slowly building up to a new proposal. The French preference for written communication, even for informal interactions, echoes the formality of their relationships—and results in a slowing down of message transmission that often seems unnecessary to Americans.[68]

In short, it behooves Americans to realize that, because much of the world exchanges business information through slower message media, it is wise to schedule more time for transactions, develop patience, and learn to get at needed information in more subtle ways—after building rapport and taking time to observe the local system for exchanging information.

We have seen that cross-cultural misinterpretation can result from noise in the actual transmission of the message—the choice or speed of media. Interpreting the meaning of a message can thus be as much a function of examining the transmission channel (or medium) as it is of examining the message itself.

Japanese Ningensei Style of Communication	U.S. Adversarial Style of Communication
1. Indirect verbal and nonverbal communication	1. More direct verbal and nonverbal communication
2. Relationship communication	2. More task communication
3. Discourages confrontational strategies	3. Confrontational strategies more acceptable
4. Strategically ambiguous communication	4. Prefers more to-the-point communication
5. Delayed feedback	5. More immediate feedback
6. Patient, longer-term negotiators	6. Shorter-term negotiators
7. Uses fewer words	7. Favors verbosity
8. Distrustful of skillful verbal communicators	8. Exalts verbal eloquence
9. Group orientation	9. More individualistic orientation
10. Cautious, tentative	10. More assertive, self-assured
11. Complementary communicators	11. More publicly critical communication
12. Softer, heart-like logic	12. Harder, analytic logic preferred
13. Sympathetic, empathetic, complex use of pathos	13. Favors logos, reason
14. Expresses and decodes complex relational strategies and nuances	14. Expresses and decodes complex logos, cognitive nuances
15. Avoids decision making in public	15. Frequent decision making in public
16. Makes decisions in private venues, away from public eye	16. Frequent decision in public at negotiating tables
17. Decisions via *ringi* and *nemawashi* (complete consensus process)	17. Decisions by majority rule and public compromise is more commonplace
18. Uses go-betweens for decision making	18. More extensive use of direct person-to-person, player-to-player interaction for decisions
19. Understatement and hesitation in verbal and nonverbal communication	19. May publicly speak in superlatives, exaggerations, nonverbal projection
20. Uses qualifiers, tentativeness, humility as communicator	20. Favors fewer qualifiers, more ego-centered
21. Receiver/listening–centered	21. More speaker- and message-centered
22. Inferred meanings, looks beyond words to nuances, nonverbal communication	22. More face-value meaning, more denotative
23. Shy, reserved communicators	23. More publicly self-assertive
24. Distaste for purely business transactions	24. Prefers to "get down to business" or "nitty gritty"
25. Mixes business and social communication	25. Tends to keep business negotiating more separated from social communication
26. Utilizes *matomari* or "hints" for achieving group adjustment and saving face in negotiating	26. More directly verbalizes management's preference at negotiating tables
27. Practices *haragei* or "belly logic" and communication	27. Practices more linear, discursive, analytical logic; greater reverence for cognitive than for affective

Source: A. Goldman, "The Centrality of 'Ningensei' to Japanese Negotiating and Interpersonal Relationships: Implications for U.S.-Japanese Communication," *International Journal of Intercultural Relations* 18, no. 1 (1994), with permission from the *International Journal of Intercultural Relations, 2011.*

INFORMATION TECHNOLOGY: GOING GLOBAL AND ACTING LOCAL

Microsoft has struck a deal with the biggest Chinese search engine, Baidu.com, to offer Web search services in English.

WWW.NYTIMES.COM,
JULY 4, 2011.[69]

All information is local; IT systems can connect every corner of the globe, but IT managers are learning they have to pay attention to regional differences.

COMPUTERWORLD.[70]

Using the Internet as a global medium for communication has enabled companies of all sizes to quickly develop a presence in many markets around the world—and, in fact, has enabled them to "go global." However, their global reach cannot alone translate into global business. Those companies are learning that they have to adapt their e-commerce and their enterprise resource planning (ERP) applications to regional idiosyncrasies beyond translation or content management issues; for example, even asking for a name or an email address can incur resistance in many countries where people do not like to give out personal information.[71] (These issues are further discussed in the accompanying Under the Lens feature about Google.) While communication over the Internet is clearly not as personal as face-to-face, cross-cultural communication, those transactions must still be regionalized and personalized to adjust to differences in language, culture, local laws, and business models, as well as differences in the level of development in the local telecommunications infrastructure. Yet, if the Internet is a global medium for communication, why do so many U.S. companies treat the Web as a U.S.-centric phenomenon? Giving preference to some geographic regions, languages, and cultures is "a short-sighted business decision that will result in diminished brand equity, market share, profits and global leadership."[72]

When Baidu.com—China's leading search engine—made a business decision in July 2011 to partner with Microsoft to offer web search services in English, it had clearly realized that it needed to go beyond Chinese because of the 10 million per day searches for English terms on its site.

"More and more people here are searching for English terms," Kaiser Kuo, the company's spokesman, said Monday. *"But Baidu hasn't done a good job. So here's a way for us to do it."*[73]

For its part, Microsoft's expansion of "Bing" in China gave it access to the world's largest Internet population of over 470 million users. Both companies realized that the English-language search results would be censored (as happened to Google, which pulled out of the mainland and went to Hong Kong). Reports in 2012 say that Microsoft is cooperating with China's government on censorship rules regarding the content that can be accessed.[74] Beijing requires those Internet companies operating on the mainland to censor results the government considers threatening, including references to human rights issues and dissidents.[75] Clearly, both going global and acting local can be fraught with difficulties.

It seems essential, then, that a global online strategy must also be multilocal. The impersonal nature of the Web must somehow be adapted to local cultures to establish relationships and create customer loyalty. Effective technological communication requires even more cultural sensitivity than face-to-face communication because of the inability to assess reactions and get feedback or, in many cases, to even retain contact. It is still people, after all, who respond to and interact with other people through the medium of the Internet, and those people interpret and respond according to their own languages and cultures, as well as their local business practices and expectations. In Europe, for example, significant differences in business cultures and e-business technology have slowed e-business progress there. However, some companies are making progress in pan-European integration services, such as *leEurope*, which aims to cross language, currency, and cultural barriers. Specifically, *leEurope* is building a set of services "to help companies tie their back-end e-business systems together across European boundaries through a series of mergers involving regional e-business integrators in more than a dozen countries."[76]

UNDER THE LENS

Google's "Street View" Makes Friends in Japan but Clashes with European Culture[77]

After the 9.0 earthquake in Japan in March 2011, which was followed by a devastating tsunami, Google used its assembly of nine cameras creating 360-degree panoramic digital images of the disaster zone to archive damage. Its Street View mapping service was welcomed after the disaster, as observed by the major of Kesunnuma:

"I'd like them to record Kesennuma's streets now," Mr. Sugawara said. "Then I'd like them to come back, when the city is like new again, and show the world the new Kesennuma."[78]

In addition, Google went live with its online "Person Finder" service less than two hours after the quake. The site helped people find out about the status of family and friends in the aftermath of the disaster. While many did not have Internet access after the disaster and simply posted signs about missing people, others took photos of the signs and uploaded them to Google for use in the Person Finder service. Even the National Police posted information, and soon Person Finder had collected 616,300 records, Japan's largest database of missing people from the disaster. After Google's many blunders in Japan, and privacy concerns about the company's services, it now seems that its technology was able to help the Japanese people and also resulted in raising its brand and social networking identity there.[79]

However, Google has been less well received in Europe. The company has been expanding into European markets for years and now has a headquarters in Dublin, large offices in Zurich and London, and smaller centers in countries such as Denmark, Russia, and Poland. But the company has been caught in a cultural web of privacy laws that threaten its growth and the positive image it has cultivated.

"The framework in Europe is of privacy as a human-dignity right," said Nicole Wong, a lawyer with the [Google] company. "As enforced in the U.S., it's a consumer-protection right."[80]

Google's plan to introduce "Street View," a mapping service that provides a vivid, 360-degree, ground-level photographic panorama from any address, met with considerable resistance. Data protection officials in Switzerland pressured Google to cancel those plans, since "Street View" would violate strict Swiss privacy laws that prohibit the unauthorized use of personal images or property. In Germany, where Street View is also not available, simply taking photographs for the service violates privacy laws. After pressure from a German data protection official, Google had to show what its Street View cars had been collecting: "Snippets of e-mails, photographs, passwords, chat messages, postings on Web sites and social networks—all sorts of private Internet communications."[81] This was a blatant violation of Europe's data protection laws, and European antitrust regulators gave the company an ultimatum to change its search business or face legal consequences. This conflict was continuing to play out in the summer of 2012, and had spread to the United States and other countries, seemingly all having difficulty in holding Google accountable. At the same time, the EU's Article 29 Data Protection Working Group, which is a collaboration among all the information and data protection watchdogs within the European Union, is also contesting Google's practices. The EU Justice Commissioner, Franco Frattini, was backing the investigation. Google, the world's largest search engine, also provoked a debate about Internet privacy in May 2008, when it announced it would institute changes to its policies on holding personal information about its customers. The policy change related to Google's server logs (the information a browser sends back to Google when somebody visits a site). At present, the search engine retains a log of every search indefinitely, including information—such as the unique computer address, browser type, and language—that could be traced back to a particular computer. The policy change was to reduce how long that information was retained to 18–24 months.

Peter Schaar, chair of Article 29 and also Germany's federal commissioner for freedom of information, developed a report on the relationship between search-engine business models and European privacy laws. The draft report concluded that IP addresses are personal information because they can help identify a person. Europeans fiercely protect their privacy and trust that the government enforces it in law. Mr. Schaar has challenged Peter Fleischer of Google's global privacy law team to explain why such a long storage period was chosen and to give a legal justification for the storage of server logs in general. Google's response so far, from founders Sergei Brin and Larry Page, was to identify others as the greater threat to Internet users' privacy. They stated that information posted on social networking sites, such as photographs of young people at drunken parties, are a greater privacy concern. They defended the value of users' information for refining search results, and blamed the way some companies have used that information for privacy problems in the industry. The outcome of this cross-cultural Internet communication clash remains to be seen. One thing that is clear is that the European Union (EU) has fired a warning shot across the bows of the search-engine companies.

MANAGING CROSS-CULTURAL COMMUNICATION

Steps toward effective intercultural communication include the development of cultural sensitivity, careful encoding, selective transmission, careful decoding, and appropriate follow-up actions.

Developing Cultural Sensitivity

When acting as a sender, a manager must make it a point to know the receiver and to encode the message in a form that will most likely be understood as intended. On the manager's part, this requires an awareness of his or her own cultural baggage and how it affects the communication process. In other words, what kinds of behaviors does the message imply, and how will they be perceived by the receiver? The way to anticipate the most likely meaning that the receiver will attach to the message is to internalize honest cultural empathy with that person. What is the cultural background—the societal, economic, and organizational context—in which this communication is taking place? What are this person's expectations regarding the situation, what are the two parties' relative positions, and what might develop from this communication? What kinds of transactions and behaviors is this person used to? Cultural sensitivity (discussed in Chapter 3) is really just a matter of understanding the other person, the context, and how the person will respond to the context. Americans, unfortunately, have a rather negative reputation overseas of not being culturally sensitive. One not-for-profit group, called Business for Diplomatic Action, has the following advice for Americans when doing business abroad, in its attempts to counteract the stereotypical American traits such as boastfulness, loudness, and speed:

- **Read a map:** Familiarize yourself with the local geography to avoid making insulting mistakes.
- **Dress up:** In some countries, casual dress is a sign of disrespect.
- **Talk small:** Talking about wealth, power, or status—corporate or personal—can create resentment.
- **No slang:** Even casual profanity is unacceptable.
- **Slow down:** Americans talk fast, eat fast, move fast, live fast. Many cultures do not.
- **Listen as much as you talk:** Ask people you're visiting about themselves and their way of life.
- **Speak lower and slower:** A loud voice is often perceived as bragging.
- **Religious restraint:** In many countries, religion is not a subject for public discussion.
- **Political restraint:** Steer clear of this subject. If someone is attacking U.S. politicians or policies, agree to disagree.[82]

Careful Encoding

In translating his or her intended meaning into symbols for cross-cultural communication, the sender must use words, pictures, or gestures that are appropriate to the receiver's frame of reference. Of course, language training is invaluable, but senders should also avoid idioms and regional sayings (such as "Go fly a kite" or "Foot the bill") in a translation, or even in English when speaking to a non-American who knows little English.

Literal translation, then, is a limited answer to language differences. Even for people in English-speaking countries, words may have different meanings. Ways to avoid problems are to speak slowly and clearly, avoid long sentences and colloquial expressions, and explain things in several different ways and through several media, if possible. However, even though English is in common use around the world for business transactions, the manager's efforts to speak the local language will greatly improve the climate. Sometimes people from other cultures resent the assumption by English-speaking executives that everyone else will speak English.

Language translation is only part of the encoding process; the message also is expressed in nonverbal language. In the encoding process, the sender must ensure congruence between the nonverbal and the verbal message. In encoding a message, therefore, it is useful to be as objective as possible and not to rely on personal interpretations. To further clarify their messages, managers can hand out written summaries of verbal presentations and use visual aids, such as graphs or pictures. A good general guide is to move slowly, wait, and take cues from the receivers.

Selective Transmission

The type of medium chosen for the message depends on the nature of the message, its level of importance, the context and expectations of the receiver, the timing involved, and the need for personal interaction, among other factors. Typical media include instant messaging (IM), email, letters or memos, reports, meetings, telephone calls, teleconferences, videoconferences, or face-to-face conversations. The secret is to find out how communication is transmitted in the local organization—how much is downward versus upward or vertical versus horizontal, how the grapevine works, and so on. In addition, the cultural variables discussed earlier need to be considered: whether the receiver is from a high- or low-context culture, whether he or she is used to explicit or implicit communication, and what speed and routing of messages will be most effective.

For the most part, it is best to use face-to-face interaction for relationship building or for other important transactions, particularly in intercultural communications, because of the lack of familiarity between parties. Personal interactions give the manager the opportunity to get immediate verbal and visual feedback and to make rapid adjustments in the communication process.

International dealings are often long-distance, of course, limiting the opportunity for face-to-face communication. However, personal rapport can be established or enhanced through telephone calls or videoconferencing and through trusted contacts. Modern electronic media and social networks can be used to break down communication barriers by reducing waiting periods for information, clarifying issues, and allowing instant consultation, such as via Skype, for one-on-one or group video-chat. Ford Europe uses videoconferencing for engineers in Britain and Germany to consult about quality problems. Through the video monitors, they examine one another's engineering diagrams and usually find a solution that gets the factory moving again in a short time.

Careful Decoding of Feedback

Timely and effective feedback channels can also be set up to assess a firm's general communication about the progression of its business and its general management principles. The best means for getting accurate feedback is through face-to-face interaction, because this allows the manager to hear, see, and immediately sense how a message is being interpreted. When visual feedback on important issues is not possible or appropriate, it is a good idea to use several means of attaining feedback, in particular by employing third parties.

Decoding is the process of translating the received symbols into the interpreted message. The main causes of incongruence are (1) the receiver misinterprets the message, (2) the receiver encodes his or her return message incorrectly, or (3) the sender misinterprets the feedback. Two-way communication is thus essential for important issues so that successive efforts can be made until an understanding has been achieved. Asking other colleagues to help interpret what is going on is often a good way to break a cycle of miscommunication.

Perhaps the most important means for avoiding miscommunication is to practice careful decoding by improving one's listening and observation skills. A good listener practices projective listening, or empathetic listening—listening, without interruption or evaluation, to the full message of the speaker; attempting to recognize the feelings behind the words and nonverbal cues; and understanding the speaker's perspective.

At the multinational corporation (MNC) level, avenues of communication and feedback among parent companies and subsidiaries can be kept open through telephone calls, regular meetings and visits, reports, and plans, all of which facilitate cooperation, performance control, and the smooth running of the company. Communication among far-flung operations can be best managed by setting up feedback systems and liaison people. The headquarters people should maintain considerable flexibility in cooperating with local managers and allowing them to deal with the local context as they see fit.

Follow-up Actions

Managers communicate through both action and inaction. Therefore, to keep open the lines of communication, feedback, and trust, managers must follow through with action on what has been discussed and then agreed upon—typically a contract, which is probably the most important formal business communication. Unfortunately, the issue of contract follow-through is a particularly sensitive one across cultures because of the different interpretations regarding what constitutes a contract (perhaps a handshake, perhaps a full legal document) and what actions should result. Trust, future communications, and future business are based on such interpretations, and it is up to managers to understand them and to follow through on them.

The management of cross-cultural communication depends largely on a manager's personal abilities and behavior. Those behaviors that researchers indicate to be most important to intercultural communication effectiveness (ICE) are listed here, as reviewed by Ruben:

1. Respect (conveyed through eye contact, body posture, voice tone, and pitch)
2. Interaction posture (the ability to respond to others in a descriptive, nonevaluative, and nonjudgmental way)
3. Orientation to knowledge (recognizing that one's knowledge, perception, and beliefs are valid only for oneself and not for everyone else)
4. Empathy
5. Interaction management
6. Tolerance for ambiguity
7. Other-oriented role behavior (one's capacity to be flexible and to adopt different roles for the sake of greater group cohesion and group communication)[83]

Researchers have established a relationship between personality traits and behaviors and the ability to adapt to the host-country's cultural environment.[84] What is seldom pointed out, however, is that communication is the mediating factor between those behaviors and the relative level of adaptation the expatriate achieves. The communication process facilitates cross-cultural adaptation, and, through this process, expatriates learn the dominant communication patterns of the host society. Therefore, we can link those personality factors shown by research to ease adaptation with those necessary for effective intercultural communication.

Kim has consolidated the research findings of these characteristics into two categories: (1) **openness**—traits such as open-mindedness, tolerance for ambiguity, and extrovertedness; and (2) **resilience**—traits such as having an internal locus of control, persistence, a tolerance of ambiguity, and resourcefulness.[85] These personality factors, along with the expatriate's cultural and racial identity and the level of preparedness for change, comprise that person's potential for adaptation. The level of preparedness can be improved by the manager before his or her assignment by gathering information about the host country's verbal and nonverbal communication patterns and norms of behavior. However, we must remember the practicalities of situational factors that can affect the communication process—variables such as the physical environment, time constraints, the degree of structure, and feelings of irritability or overwork, among others.

CONCLUSION

Effective intercultural communication is a vital skill for international managers and domestic managers of multicultural workforces. Because miscommunication is much more likely to occur among people from different countries or racial backgrounds than among those from similar backgrounds, it is important to be alert to how culture is reflected in communication—in particular through the development of cultural sensitivity and an awareness of potential sources of cultural noise in the communication process. A successful international manager is thus attuned to these variables and is flexible enough to adjust his or her communication style to best address the intended receivers—that is, to do it "their way."

Cultural variables and the manner in which culture is communicated underlie the processes of negotiation and decision making. How do people around the world negotiate? What are their expectations and their approach to negotiations? What is the importance of understanding negotiation and decision-making processes in other countries? Chapter 5 addresses these questions and makes suggestions for the international manager to handle these important tasks.

Summary of Key Points

1. Communication is an inherent part of a manager's role, taking up the majority of the manager's time on the job. Effective intercultural communication largely determines the success of international transactions or the output of a culturally diverse workforce.

2. Culture is the foundation of communication, and communication transmits culture. Cultural variables that can affect the communication process by influencing a person's perceptions include attitudes, social organizations, thought patterns, roles, language, nonverbal language, and time.

3. Language conveys cultural understandings and social norms from one generation to the next. Body language, or nonverbal communication, is behavior that communicates without words. It accounts for 65 to 93 percent of interpreted communication.

4. Types of nonverbal communication around the world are kinesic behavior, proxemics, paralanguage, and object language.

5. Effective cross-cultural communication must take into account whether the receiver is from a country with a monochronic or a polychronic time system.

6. Variables related to channels of communication include high- and low-context cultures, fast or slow messages and information flows, and various types of media.

7. In high-context cultures, feelings and messages are implicit and must be accessed through an understanding of the person and the system. In low-context cultures, feelings and thoughts are expressed, and information is more readily available.

8. The effective management of intercultural communication necessitates the development of cultural sensitivity, careful encoding, selective transmission, careful decoding, and follow-up actions.

9. Certain personal abilities and behaviors facilitate adaptation to the host country through skilled intercultural communication.

10. Communication via the Internet must still be localized to adjust to differences in language, culture, local laws, and business models.

Discussion Questions

1. How does culture affect the process of attribution in communication? Can you relate this to some experiences you have had with your classmates?
2. What is stereotyping? Give some examples. How might people stereotype you?
3. What is the relationship between language and culture? How is it that people from different countries who speak the same language may still miscommunicate?
4. Give some examples of cultural differences in the interpretation of body language. What is the role of such nonverbal communication in business relationships?
5. Explain the differences between monochronic and polychronic time systems. Use some examples to illustrate their differences and the role of time in intercultural communication.
6. Explain the differences between high- and low-context cultures, giving some examples. What are the differential effects on the communication process?
7. Discuss the role of information systems in a company, how and why they vary from country to country, and the effects of these variations.
8. Discuss the role of social media in global business communication.

Application Exercises

1. Form groups in your class—multicultural groups, if possible. Have each person make notes about his or her perceptions of (1) Mexican-Americans, (2) Native Americans, (3) African Americans, and (4) Americans of European descent. Discuss your notes and draw conclusions about common stereotypes. Discuss any differences and why stereotyping occurs.
2. Invite some students who are from other countries to your class. Ask them to bring photographs, slides, and so forth of people and events in their native countries. Have them explain the meanings of various nonverbal cues, such as gestures, dress, voice inflections, architecture, and events. Discuss with them any differences between their explanations and the attributions you assigned to those cues.
3. Interview a faculty member or a businessperson who has worked abroad. Ask him or her to identify factors that facilitated or inhibited adaptation to the host environment. Ask whether more preparation could have eased the transition and what, if anything, that person would do differently before another trip.

Experiential Exercise

Form two or three pairs to enact skits—separately—in front of the class and then ask your class for feedback and to guess where you are from.

Each person in each pair decides on a different cultural profile to enact—for example, act as if one of you is, say, Japanese or Arab, and the other is, say, German or Mexican. Set up a five-to-ten minute "skit," presumably for an intended business transaction. Research and practice with your partner the typical communication style, both verbal and nonverbal (use English for everyone).

Both you and your class will see how difficult it is to put yourself in the persona of someone from a different cultural background.

Internet Resources

Visit the Deresky Companion Website at www.pearsonhighered.com/deresky for this chapter's Internet resources.

CASE STUDY

Miscommunications with a Brazilian Auto Parts Manufacturer

The Brazilian sun beat down steadily on the tarmac outside as Alessandro Silva and Agosto Ventura stood inside the São Paulo-Guarulhos International Airport. They were awaiting the arrival of two representatives from Lucky Auto Parts Company, a regional wholesaler and retailer based in Ames, Iowa.

Mr. Silva, the president of a mid-sized auto parts manufacturer in São Paulo, and Mr. Ventura, the company's sales manager, were looking forward to a new business relationship with Henry Williams, President of Lucky Auto Parts Company. A few weeks previously, in an initial phone call, President Silva invited President Williams to visit the Brazilian manufacturing facility, a potential source of after-market auto parts for Lucky. This would be the American company's first venture into buying parts directly from a foreign manufacturer. Williams planned to take his new Vice-President of Purchasing, Wally Astor, who also happened to be his son-in-law, on this first trip. Mr. Williams thought this exploratory buying trip would be a good introduction to the auto parts business for Wally; although Wally had experience as a new car salesman, he had no experience in the auto parts field.

Unfortunately, a few days before the trip, Williams had to cancel his trip in order to be available for a deposition on a court case pending against his company. It had taken a long time to get the appointment with Mr. Silva, and Williams did not think it wise to cancel the trip. Since Wally was eager to prove himself in his new role, Williams decided to let him handle this mission without the "old man" looking over his shoulder. In the rush to review the legal documents for the deposition, Williams forgot to notify his Brazilian counterpart that he would not be coming on this visit.

As he was preparing for the trip, Wally Astor realized that it was summer in Brazil and that it was a long flight to Brazil from Ames via Miami. Based on this, he decided to dress as informally and comfortably as possible.

At the airport, both Mr. Silva and Mr. Agosto were dressed as usual when conducting business or in the public eye for social occasions, that is, in suits and ties. As they stood outside the door of the International Arrivals area, Agosto held a neatly printed sign with Wally Astor's name on it. Soon a young man in his late 20's approached them and announced that he was Wally Astor; both Mr. Silva and Mr. Ventura were visibly surprised, especially since the young man was dressed in faded blue jeans, sneakers, and a checked shirt with the sleeves rolled up.

"Hey, thanks for picking me up," Wally said as the three shook hands. "You must be Alexander and Agosto? My father-in-law said you were going to meet us at the airport."

"I am President Alessandro Silva and this is my Marketing Director, Mr. Ventura," Mr. Silva said icily. "We expected to see President Williams. Will he be coming on a later flight?"

"No, he had something important come up, so he sent me to take care of the visit to Brazil," Wally replied. "Oh, here, let me give you my business card so you'll know I really am who I say I am."

President Silva read the card carefully, and turned to Agosto with a frown. The card had the U.S. flag emblazoned on it with an italicized inscription under it: *An American-owned business.*

Agosto turned to Wally and said politely, "I'm certain you are tired from your long journey. Shall we drop you at your hotel and then pick you up for dinner about nine o'clock?"

"Nine o'clock! Isn't that a little late for dinner?" Wally exclaimed. "No, let's just go to your office and get right to it, shall we? I have a contract drawn up by the lawyer-types in my department. I think you'll find it covers all the details and is more than fair."

President Silva spoke up more forcefully than he intended, "Mr. Astor. . . ."

"Please call me Wally."

"No, Mr. Astor. I don't know you or your company well enough to call you by your first name and certainly not well enough to look at an important contract with you today. I was impressed with the phone conversation I had with President Williams, but *he* is not here today, so let's drop you at your hotel and begin our discussion over dinner later this evening."

Wally was surprised and uncomfortable to see Mr. Silva standing very close to him, staring intently into his eyes and gesticulating to emphasize his words. Wally took a step back, but Mr. Silva took a step toward him to close the gap between them.

"OK, Mr. Silva. Maybe I sounded like I was trying to rush things a bit. But you see, I booked my flight out for tomorrow evening so I can spend a couple days in Rio to see what that's about."

There was an uncomfortable silence during which no one spoke. Finally, Wally said, "I guess I would like to go to my hotel and rest up. Then we can have dinner at 9:00. OK?"

Ventura knew that President Silva was not warming to Wally, so he decided to see if he could get the relationship back on track. Since he and Wally were about the same age and held the same status within their respective organizations, he felt comfortable doing this.

"That sounds very good, Wally," Ventura said. "We will pick you up at 9:00. And please, call me Agosto."

Once he was settled in his hotel room, Wally phoned Henry Williams to check in as instructed.

"Yeah, Dad," Wally said. "I met with them at the airport. They drove me to the hotel and we're going to dinner tonight to get acquainted. Can you believe they want to eat at 9 pm?"

"That's good," Williams replied. "Did you see their facility yet?"

"No. The president, Mr. Silva, is kinda stiff. He said he wants to get to know us better before he talks business. I think he's doing the Latin American thing about *mañana*. I tried to get the ball rolling this afternoon, but he wouldn't hear of it."

"Well, he's just being cautious, like I am. I like to know a man personally before I enter into a long-term contract with him, too. Wally, this isn't like selling cars. It's building relationships that have to work day after day. I'm sorry I threw you into this situation alone."

"You know," Wally said, "I think he's upset that you aren't here."

"I hope you conveyed my apology to him," Williams replied, "and explained that this deposition came up at the last minute."

"I sure did."

"OK. Call me tomorrow afternoon to let me know how the dinner conversation went. How long do you think you'll be out there?"

"Well, I made reservations to leave for Rio tomorrow evening for a couple days," Wally said.

"Why are you going to Rio? Who is out there?" Williams asked.

"I promised Mindy I'd check out Rio as a possible vacation spot for later this year."

"Wally, you don't work for Mindy. You work for me. If Mr. Silva wants to talk with you for the next few days, that's exactly what you're going to do. Forget about going to Rio!"

That evening at the restaurant, Mr. Silva insisted that Wally sit across the table from him and Mr. Agosto.

"Mr. Astor, I want to thank you for joining us for a Brazilian business dinner this evening," said Mr. Silva. "We always start with cafezinho, a very strong espresso. We think it helps the conversation to flow."

For the next hour, Wally found himself talking freely about his wife, their relationship, his in-laws, his childhood and parents, and many other topics that would never find their way into a business discussion in the U.S. To encourage Wally, Mr. Silva and Agosto shared humorous stories about themselves, and shared their favorite sports, movies, pastimes, wines, and vacation areas.

Their free exchange about themselves continued throughout the dinner, and as the three men were served cafezinho after the meal, they began to talk business for the first time that evening. President Silva introduced the topic.

"Wally, I think tomorrow morning you should join us to see the plant. I want you to meet with our Purchasing and Quality Assurance Managers. We pride ourselves on using the best materials and maintaining the strictest tolerance standards. After you are more familiar with how we do things, we will meet again for dinner before your flight to Rio and discuss when Mr. Williams can visit us to resume exploring our potential business partnership."

"Sir," Wally began, "I cancelled my trip to Rio so I can learn more about your operation, your products, and where our mutual interests may lie. Perhaps we can have dinner again tomorrow night and decide what our next steps should be for the following few days."

"I'm very happy to hear you say that. And please, call me Alessandro."

Case Questions

1. What are three of the cultural "missteps" that Wally Astor and his father-in-law, Henry Williams, made in this scenario? Why do you think this happened?
2. If you were a native of Brazil and advising American business representatives on what to do when talking with Brazilian business partners, what would you tell the Americans about Brazilian culture?
3. Imagine that the situation in this case study was reversed, that is, the Brazilian businessmen were coming to the U.S. to look for a supplier. What would you tell the Brazilians about American business culture to prepare them for success?

Source:

Linda Catlin. Ms Catlin is an organizational anthropologist and the co-author of *International Business: Cultural Sourcebook and Case Studies*. She consults with clients on projects related to cross-cultural business communications, organizational culture, and organizational change dynamics. Her clients include the Mayo Clinic, the Kellogg Foundation, General Motors, Ascension Health, and BASF.

Linda Catlin, Claymore Associates. Used with permission.

Cross-Cultural Negotiation and Decision Making

OBJECTIVES

1. To learn how to prepare for cross-cultural business negotiations.

2. To recognize the need to build trusting relationships as a prerequisite for successful negotiations and long-term commitments.

3. To be aware of the role of culturally-based behavioral differences, values, and agendas of the negotiating parties.

4. To learn the complexities of negotiating with the Chinese.

5. To appreciate the variables in the decision-making process and understand the influence of culture on decision making.

6. To become familiar with the Japanese decision-making process and how it is influenced by their cultural norms.

OPENING PROFILE: SHISEIDO AND BARE ESCENTUALS—CULTURAL CONFLICTS IN NEGOTIATIONS[1]

"There was an invisible wall between the feelings of the acquirer and the acquired,"
Shiseido's Norio Tadakawa said.

WALL STREET JOURNAL,
December 29, 2011.

Problems in negotiations and decision-making styles between parties from dissimilar cultures are major factors affecting cross-border ventures. Such conflicts evidence themselves both in the negotiations leading up to the settlement of a joint venture or acquisition, and also in the implementation of the companies' goals, policies and practices—often for some time after the venture has been established. Such was the case between Japan's leading cosmetics company, Shiseido, and the American makeup brand Bare Escentuals Inc.

In 2010, Shiseido was dealing with declining demand in its home market in Japan because of a shrinking population, and, as with other Japanese companies, it began to seek out global acquisition targets in order to expand its businesses. At that time, the yen had appreciated considerably against the U.S. dollar, making it attractive to buy American companies. Shiseido's hope was that Bare Escentuals Inc. would give it a lift in the U.S. and China, where the Japanese company was battling American and French giants for leadership. With that hope in mind Shiseido announced on January 15, 2010 that it would acquire Bare Escentuals for $1.7 billion, making it the Japanese company's largest acquisition ever. For Bare Escentuals, which generated about 85% to 90% of its sales from the U.S., the move represented a huge opportunity to expand its brand internationally. Shiseido's goal was for overseas sales to account for half its revenues.

The plan was for CEO Leslie Blodgett to continue to head Bare Escentuals, which was known for its line of "mineral" cosmetics. For her part she admitted "I needed to learn more about the culture," Ms. Blodgett said. "Shiseido was a little mysterious to me, but we have very similar core values."[2] She commented that, while Bare Escentuals is a casual, blue jeans sort of company, appearances are very important at Shiseido's headquarters in Tokyo: Upon entering, three receptionists in matching pink suits stand up and bow ceremoniously, and a small Zen garden with spherical plants sits on the executive floor. Ms. Blodgett said she was planning to spend more time in Tokyo. But only a few months after the acquisition, problems began to emerge, and it wasn't until July 2011 that the general manager of Shiseido's international business division, Norio Tadawa, visited the Bare Escentuals offices in San Francisco.

Confusion over the post-acquisition strategy was driving down the share price and he was concerned about plans for the future. Unfortunately there was a language barrier and general miscommunication between the two companies; Mr. Tadakawa said that "it required sophisticated communication skills to convey his feelings without appearing presumptuous or autocratic."[3] He recognized the challenge in integrating the two companies and the need to develop employees who could bridge the gap between the two cultures, but that had not yet been accomplished. Conflicts remained about the attempt to create a new product line— "bareMinerals Skincare"—and there was a difference of opinion over the launch date. At that point Shiseido's president, Shinzo Maeda, told Mr. Tadakawa to go to San Francisco to repair the relationship.

Subsequently, after a visit by executives on both sides to their counterpart's offices, they were able to come to an understanding and agreed to launch the new line, bareMinerals Skincare, as a Bare product, in March 2012. While it took a long time for the two sides to sufficiently integrate their cultures—both societal and corporate—to put a plan into place to achieve their goals, Shiseido executives maintained that the acquisition represented an extremely important stage in the group's goal of becoming a global force in the cosmetics sector.

As illustrated in the opening profile, global managers negotiate with parties in other countries to make specific plans for strategies (exporting, joint ventures, acquisitions, etc.) as well as for continuing operations. While the complexities of cross-cultural negotiations among firms around the world present challenge enough, managers may also be faced with negotiating with government-owned companies.

Managers must prepare for strategic negotiations. Next the operational details must be negotiated—the staffing of key positions, the sourcing of raw materials or component parts, and the repatriating of profits, to name a few. As globalism burgeons, the ability to conduct successful cross-cultural negotiations cannot be overemphasized. Failure to negotiate productively will result at best in confusion and delays and at worst in lost potential alliances and lost business.

During the process of negotiation—whether before, during, or after negotiating sessions—all kinds of decisions are made, both explicitly and implicitly. A consideration of cross-cultural negotiations must therefore include the various decision-making processes that occur around the world. Negotiations cannot be conducted without decisions being made.

This chapter examines the processes of negotiation and decision making as they apply to international and domestic cross-cultural contexts. The objective is a better understanding of successful management.

NEGOTIATION

Implementing strategy depends on management's ability to negotiate productively—a skill widely considered one of the most important in international business. In the global arena, cultural differences produce great difficulties in the negotiation process. Ignorance of native bargaining rituals, more than any other single factor, accounts for unimpressive sales efforts.[4] Important differences in the negotiation process from country to country include (1) the amount and type of preparation for a negotiation, (2) the relative emphasis on tasks versus interpersonal relationships, (3) the reliance on general principles rather than specific issues, and (4) the number of people present and the extent of their influence.[5] In every instance, managers must familiarize themselves with the cultural background and underlying motivations of the negotiators—and the tactics and procedures they use—to control the process, make progress, and therefore maximize company goals.

The term **negotiation** describes the process of discussion by which two or more parties aim to reach a mutually acceptable agreement. For long-term positive relations, the goal should be to set up a win-win situation—that is, to bring about a settlement beneficial to all parties concerned. This process, difficult enough when it takes place among people of similar backgrounds, is even more complex in international negotiations because of differences in cultural values, lifestyles, expectations, verbal and nonverbal language, approaches to formal procedures, and problem-solving techniques. The complexity is heightened when negotiating across borders because of the greater number of stakeholders involved. These stakeholders are illustrated in Exhibit 5-1. In preparing for negotiations, it is critical to avoid projective cognitive similarity—that is, the assumption that others perceive, judge, think, and reason in the same way when, in fact, they do not because of differential cultural and practical influences. Instead, astute negotiators empathetically enter into the private world or cultural space of their counterparts, while willingly sharing their own view of the situation.[6]

THE NEGOTIATION PROCESS

The negotiation process comprises five stages, the ordering of which may vary according to the cultural norms (in any event, for most people, relationship building is part of a continuous process): (1) preparation, (2) relationship building, (3) the exchange of task-related information, (4) persuasion, and (5) concessions and agreement.[7] Of course, in reality these are seldom distinct stages but rather tend to overlap; negotiators may also temporarily revert to an earlier stage. With that in mind, it is useful to break down the negotiation process into stages to discuss the issues relevant to each

EXHIBIT 5-1   Stakeholders in Cross-Cultural Negotiations

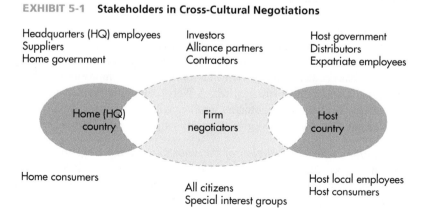

Headquarters (HQ) employees
Suppliers
Home government

Investors
Alliance partners
Contractors

Host government
Distributors
Expatriate employees

Home (HQ) country

Firm negotiators

Host country

Home consumers

All citizens
Special interest groups

Host local employees
Host consumers

EXHIBIT 5-2 **The Negotiation Process**

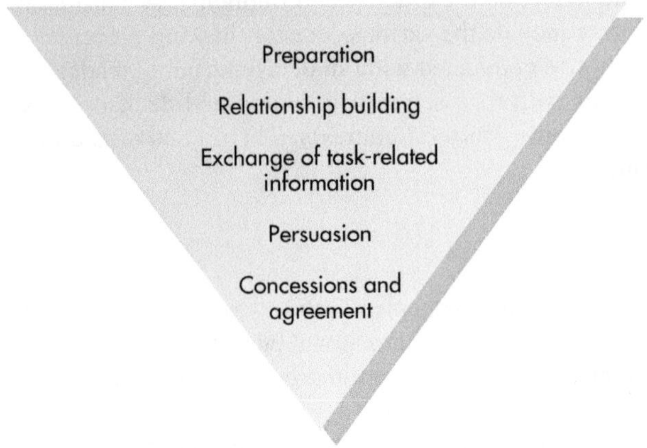

Preparation

Relationship building

Exchange of task-related
information

Persuasion

Concessions and
agreement

stage and what international managers might expect, so that they might more successfully manage this process. These stages are shown in Exhibit 5-2 and discussed in the following sections.

Stage One: Preparation

The importance of careful preparation for cross-cultural negotiations cannot be overstated. To the extent that time permits, a distinct advantage can be gained if negotiators familiarize themselves with the entire context and background of their counterparts (no matter where the meetings will take place) in addition to the specific subjects to be negotiated. Because most negotiation problems are caused by differences in culture, language, and environment, hours or days of tactical preparation for negotiation can be wasted if these factors are not carefully considered.[8]

To understand cultural differences in negotiating styles, managers first must understand their own styles and then determine how they differ from the norm in other countries. They can do this by comparing profiles of those perceived to be successful negotiators in different countries. Such profiles reflect the value system, attitudes, and expected behaviors inherent in a given society. Other sections of this chapter describe and compare negotiating styles around the world.

VARIABLES IN THE NEGOTIATING PROCESS

Adept negotiators conduct research to develop a profile of their counterparts so that they know, in most situations, what to expect, how to prepare, and how to react. Exhibit 5-3 shows some of the variables to consider when preparing to negotiate. These variables can, to a great degree, help managers understand the deep-rooted cultural and national motivations and traditional processes underlying negotiations with people from other countries.

After developing thoughtful profiles of the other party or parties, managers can plan for the actual negotiation meetings, at the same time remaining open to realizing that specific people may not fit the assumed cultural prototype. Prior to the meetings, they should find out as much as possible about (1) the kinds of demands that might be made, (2) the composition of the "opposing" team, and (3) the relative authority that the members possess. After this, the managers can gear their negotiation strategy specifically to the other side's firm, allocate roles to different team members, decide on concessions, and prepare an alternative action plan in case a negotiated solution cannot be found.[9]

Following the preparation and planning stage, which is usually done at the home office, the core of the actual negotiation takes place on-site in the foreign location (or at the manager's home office if the other team has decided to travel there). In some cases, a compromise on the location for negotiations can signal a cooperative strategy, which Weiss calls "Improvise an Approach: Effect Symphony"—a strategy available to negotiators familiar with each other's culture and willing to put negotiation on an equal footing. Weiss gives the following example of this negotiation strategy:

> *For their negotiations over construction of the tunnel under the English Channel, British and French representatives agreed to partition talks and alternate the site between Paris and London. At each site, the negotiators were to use established, local ways, including the language . . . thus punctuating approaches by time and space.*[10]

EXHIBIT 5-3   **Variables in the Negotiation Process**[11]

1. *Approach to negotiation process:* Competitive or problem-solving
2. *Composition of negotiating team:* Number and experience of team members. Relative hierarchy in position. Relationships with counterparts. Decision-making power of team members. Motivated by individual, company, or community goals.
3. *Method of reaching decisions:* By individual determination, by majority opinion, or by group consensus.
4. *Purpose of negotiations:* One-time contract. Joint venture or other alliance. Long-term relationship-building.
5. *Negotiation process:* Behavioral expectations, typical procedures.
6. *Communication context used by teams:* Low context, explicit; high-context, implicit; nature of surroundings.
7. *Nature of persuasive arguments:* Factual presentations and arguments, accepted tradition, or emotion.
8. *Bases of trust:* Relationships, past experience, intuition, or rules.
9. *Risk-taking propensity:* Level and methods of uncertainty avoidance in trading information or making a contract.
10. *Value and uses of time:* Attitude toward time. Use of time in scheduling and proceeding with negotiations; use of time to pressure for agreement.
11. *Form of satisfactory agreement:* Based on trust (perhaps just a handshake), the credibility of the parties, commitment, or a legally binding contract.

In this way, each side was put into the context and the script of the other culture about half the time.

The next stage of negotiation—often given short shrift by Westerners—is that of relationship building. In most parts of the world, this stage usually has already taken place or is concurrent with other preparations.

Stage Two: Relationship Building

Relationship building is the process of getting to know one's contacts in a host country and building mutual trust before embarking on business discussions and transactions. This process is regarded with much more significance in most parts of the world than it is in the United States. U.S. negotiators are, generally speaking, objective about the specific matter at hand and usually want to waste no time in getting down to business and making progress. This approach, well understood in the United States, can be disastrous if the foreign negotiators want to take enough time to build trust and respect as a basis for negotiating contracts. In such cases, American efficiency interferes with the patient development of a mutually trusting relationship—the very cornerstone of an Asian business agreement.[12]

NONTASK SOUNDING

Five minutes of nontask sounding in the United States can translate into five days, weeks, or even months of non-task sounding in Shanghai, Lagos, Rio de Janeiro, or Jeddah. There is no other way because in such countries real business cannot be conducted until a good interpersonal relationship has been established.[13]

In many countries, such as Mexico, Saudi Arabia, and China, personal commitments to individuals, rather than the legal system, form the basis for the enforcement of contracts. Effective negotiators allow plenty of time in their schedules for such relationship building with bargaining partners. This process usually takes the form of social events, tours, and ceremonies, along with much **nontask sounding**—general, polite conversation and informal communication before meetings—while all parties get to know one another. In such cultures, one patiently waits for the other party to start actual business negotiations, aware that relationship building is, in fact, the first phase of negotiations.[14] It is usually recommended that managers new to such scenarios use an intermediary—someone who already has the trust and respect of the foreign managers and who therefore acts as a "relationship bridge." Middle Easterners, in particular, prefer to negotiate through a trusted intermediary, and for them as well, initial meetings are only for the purpose of getting acquainted. Arabs do business with the person, not the company, and therefore mutual trust must be established.

In their best seller on negotiation, *Getting to Yes,* Fisher and Ury point out the dangers of not preparing well for negotiations:

> *In Persian, the word "compromise" does not have the English meaning of a midway solution which both sides can accept, but only the negative meaning of surrendering one's principles. Also, "mediator" means "meddler," someone who is barging in uninvited. In 1980, United Nations Secretary-General Kurt Waldheim flew to Iran to deal with the hostage situation. National Iranian radio and television broadcast in Persian a comment he was said to have made upon his arrival in Tehran: "I have come as a mediator to work out a compromise." Less than an hour later, his car was being stoned by angry Iranians.[15]*

As a bridge to the more formal stages of negotiations, such relationship building is followed by posturing—that is, general discussion that sets the tone for the meetings. This phase should result in a spirit of cooperation. To help ensure this result, negotiators must use words like "respect" and "mutual benefit" rather than language that would suggest arrogance, superiority, or urgency.

Stage Three: Exchanging Task-Related Information

In the next stage—exchanging task-related information—each side typically makes a presentation and states its position; a question-and-answer session usually ensues, and alternatives are discussed. From an American perspective, this represents a straightforward, objective, efficient, and understandable stage. However, negotiators from other countries continue to take a more indirect approach at this stage. Mexican negotiators are usually suspicious and indirect, presenting little substantive material and more lengthy, evasive conversation. French negotiators enjoy debate and conflict and will often interrupt presentations to argue about an issue even if it has little relevance to the topic being presented. The Chinese also ask many questions of their counterparts, and delve specifically and repeatedly into the details at hand; conversely, Chinese presentations contain only vague and ambiguous material. For instance, after about 20 Boeing officials spent six weeks presenting masses of literature and technical demonstrations to the Chinese, the Chinese said, "Thank you for your introduction."[16]

The Russians also enter negotiations well prepared and well versed in the specific details of the matter being presented. To answer their (or any other side's) questions, it is generally a good idea to bring along someone with expertise to answer any grueling technical inquiries. Russians also put a lot of emphasis on protocol and expect to deal only with top executives.

Adler suggests that negotiators should focus not only on presenting their situation and needs but also on showing an understanding of their opponents' viewpoint. Focusing on the entire situation confronting each party encourages the negotiators to assess a wider range of alternatives for resolution, rather than limiting themselves to their preconceived, static positions. She suggests that to be most effective, negotiators should prepare for meetings by practicing role reversal.[17]

Stage Four: Persuasion

In the next phase of negotiations—persuasion—the hard bargaining starts. Typically, both parties try to persuade the other to accept more of their position and to give up some of their own. Often, some persuasion has already taken place beforehand in social settings and through mutual contacts. In the Far East, details are likely to be worked out ahead of time through the "backdoor" approach (*houmani*). For the most part, however, the majority of the persuasion takes place over one or more negotiating sessions. International managers usually find that this process of bargaining and making concessions is fraught with difficulties because of the different uses and interpretations of verbal and nonverbal behaviors. Although variations in such behaviors influence every stage of the negotiation process, they can play a particularly powerful role in persuasion, especially if they are not anticipated.

Studies of negotiating behavior have revealed the use of certain tactics, which skilled negotiators recognize and use, such as promises, threats, and so on. Other, less savory tactics are sometimes used in international negotiations. Often called "dirty tricks," these tactics, according to Fisher and Ury, include efforts to mislead "opponents" deliberately.[18] Some negotiators may give wrong or distorted factual information or use the excuse of ambiguous authority—giving conflicting impressions about who in their party has the power to make a commitment. In the midst of hard bargaining, the prudent international manager will follow up on possibly misleading information before taking action based on trust.

Other rough tactics are designed to put opposing negotiators in a stressful situation physically or psychologically, so that their giving in is made more likely. These include uncomfortable room temperatures, too-bright lighting, rudeness, interruptions, and other irritations. International negotiators must keep in mind, however, that what might seem like dirty tricks to Americans is simply the way other cultures conduct negotiations. In some South American countries, for example, it is common to start negotiations with misleading or false information.

The most subtle behaviors in the negotiation process—and often the most difficult to deal with—are usually the nonverbal messages: the use of voice intonation, facial and body expressions, eye contact, dress, and the timing of the discussions. Nonverbal behaviors, discussed in previous chapters, are ingrained aspects of culture used by people in their daily lives; they are not specifically changed for the purposes of negotiation. Among those behaviors impacting negotiations is the direct communication style, such as with Germans, compared with the indirect style, such as with Japanese. Clearly, also, the individualism-collectivism cultural dimension is one that greatly guides negotiation because of the relative motivation of personal self-interest in individualistic societies, such as the United States; this compares with the group-interest in Asian cultures, so that Asian negotiators will likely give more importance to their social obligations and the needs of the group.[19]

Although persuasion has been discussed as if it were always a distinct stage, it is really the primary purpose underlying all stages of the negotiation process. In particular, persuasion is an integral part of the process of making concessions and arriving at an agreement.

Stage Five: Concessions and Agreement

In the last stage of negotiation—concessions and agreement—tactics vary greatly across cultures. Well-prepared negotiators are aware of various concession strategies and have decided ahead of time what their own concession strategy will be. Familiar with the typical initial positions that various parties are likely to take, they know that Russians and Chinese generally open their bargaining with extreme positions, asking for more than they hope to gain, whereas Swedes usually start with what they are prepared to accept.

Research in the United States indicates that better end results are attained by starting with extreme positions. With this approach, the process of reaching an agreement involves careful timing of the disclosure information and of concessions. Most people who have studied negotiations believe that negotiators should disclose only the information that is necessary at a given point and that they should try to obtain information piece by piece to gradually get the whole picture without giving away their goals or concession strategy. These guidelines will not always work in intercultural negotiations because the American process of addressing issues one at a time, in a linear fashion, is not common in other countries or cultures. Negotiators in the Far East, for example, approach issues in a holistic manner, deciding on the whole deal at the end, rather than making incremental concessions.

Again, at the final stage of agreement and contract, local practices determine how these agreements will be honored. Whereas Americans take contracts very seriously, Russians often renege on their contracts. The Japanese, on the other hand, consider a formal contract to be somewhat of an insult and a waste of time and money in legal costs, since they prefer to operate on the basis of understanding and social trust.[20] More attention to this and all the negotiation phases might have led to better results in the French-Chinese joint venture discussed in the Management in Action section.

MANAGEMENT IN ACTION

Cultural Misunderstanding—The Danone-Wahaha Joint Venture in China Splits after Years of Legal Dispute[21]

Groupe Danone of France resolved a long-running dispute with its Chinese joint venture partner on Wednesday (September 20, 2009), agreeing to exit the venture by selling its 51 percent stake in the Wahaha Group, one of China's largest beverage companies.[22]

What went wrong? Many cross-border joint ventures (JVs) encounter problems because the partners' differences in management styles and corporate control, as well as cross-cultural issues, do not get recognized and resolved during the negotiation phase, and so continue to fester during the operations phase. One such JV is the Sino-French collaboration that was formed by Groupe Danone (hereafter Danone), and Hangzhou Wahaha Group Co. (hereafter WHH). Danone is one of the largest food conglomerates from France. Wahaha, which was started in 1987 and was controlled by the government of Hangzhou's Shangcheng District, is China's largest beverage company. From its inception, Zong Qinghou ran the operations of WHH. When the company converted itself into a private entity, Qinghou took the role of a minority shareholder.

The Danone-WHH joint venture was established in March 1996 and took the trademark name of Wahaha because of its strong brand visibility in the Chinese market. In emerging markets, Danone grew by creating a multitude of profitable JVs in India, Pakistan, Vietnam, Columbia, and other countries. On the other hand, WHH achieved its market expansion and corporate growth in China by turning itself into a national brand and a highly successful food and beverage company. The Danone-Wahaha JV dealt with the areas of food and beverages and grew at a respectable rate. For Danone, this was a good strategy to enter into China. For WHH, the JV helped the company to make a linkage with a well-known global brand.

Negotiations resulted in the following salient features of the JV:

1. Ownership of the JV included foreign partners (51 percent), WHH (39 percent), and employees (10 percent).

2. The JV encompassed five entities: Hangzhou Wahaha Baili Foods, Hangzhou Wahaha Health Foods, Hangzhou Wahaha Foods Co., Hangzhou Wahaha Beverages Co., and Hangzhou Wahaha Quick Frozen Foods. Danone and Peregrine Investment Holdings collectively invested $70 million in the five entities of the JV.

3. As agreed to by Danone, the day-to-day operations of the JV resided with Qinghou.

The JV's business operations expanded in China, eventually growing into a $2 billion beverage behemoth and one of China's best-known brands. However, the activities of Danone and WHH also became intertwined and complex, leading to differences in opinion, corporate control, and management styles. Between 1996 and 2009, the following changes took place in the structure and operations of the Danone-WHH JV:

1. Because of consumer demand and market growth, the JV's operations in China witnessed the emergence of 37 business entities. Danone attempted to buy out Qinghou but the negotiations were unsuccessful.

2. Public rows erupted between the two companies when they kept on blaming each other for breach of contract. Danone blamed Qinghou for going outside of the contract and profiting from 80 unauthorized businesses. This included misusing the Danone brand and its distribution system in China.

3. The dispute between Danone and Qinghou became even more personal when Danone filed a lawsuit against Qinghou's wife and daughter in a Los Angeles court regarding their business interests and unauthorized JV-related dealings outside of China.

4. Danone filed for arbitration proceedings in Stockholm in May 2007.

5. During the dispute, Danone also filed legal claims against ten business entities that were believed to be controlled by WHH in Samoa and the British Virgin Islands.

6. The Danone-WHH case became so much embroiled that Chinese and French governments asked the companies to negotiate an "amicable" resolution.

7. In September 2009, the two companies agreed to drop the protracted legal proceedings and announced that they had agreed to an amicable split: Wahaha would pay cash to acquire Danone's 51 percent, giving the Chinese company control of the venture.

From this highly publicized dispute between Danone and WHH, we learn the following lessons:

1. Cross-cultural misunderstandings and unfamiliarity with the JV partners were at the heart of this dispute. Qinghou's entrepreneurial style and WHH's consistent growth in China could have been one of the causes of this dispute since Danone management was alienated in the process.

2. Both partners used media and public relations campaigns in China and Western markets to justify their arguments, instead of having open negotiations.

3. In any JV, relationship-building and exchange of project-related information is critical in the post-negotiation phase that is based on concessions and agreement.

4. It seems that Danone and WHH lacked open communication in their day-to-day management of the JV. Also important was the area of trust that happened to be missing in the partners' dealings.

5. According to *China Economic Review,* Chinese companies often become an extension of their founders' personal goals regarding day-to-day business operations. Most Chinese businesses do not see a major difference between 51/49 ownership and enforcement of rights. Foreign partners must make sure that their designated managers and staff members are included in the day-to-day management of the JV. In international markets, JV-related contracts can be abused and could lead to cross-cultural misunderstands and operational disruptions.

6. Finally, in JVs, relationship-building takes time and a good amount of interaction is needed between the partners. In the case of the Danone-WHH JV, the partner conflict, face-saving problems, blame-game, and accusations could have been avoided had the two companies communicated openly during the negotiation phase and afterwards. Also it seems that Danone and WHH did not understand their low-context and high-context cultures and management styles that eventually led to this conflict.

Source: Updated by Helen Deresky from a case written exclusively for this book by Syed Tariq Anwar, West Texas A&M University. Used with permission.

UNDERSTANDING NEGOTIATION STYLES

Global managers can benefit from studying differences in negotiating behaviors (and the underlying reasons for them), which can help them recognize what is happening in the negotiating process. Exhibit 5-4 shows some examples of differences among North American, Japanese, and Latin American styles. Brazilians, for example, generally have a spontaneous, passionate, and dynamic style. They are very talkative and particularly use the word "no" extensively—more than 40 times per half-hour, compared with 4.7 times for Americans and only 1.9 times for the Japanese. They also differ markedly from Americans and the Japanese by their use of extensive physical contact.[23]

The Japanese are typically skillful negotiators. They have spent a great deal more time and effort studying U.S. culture and business practices than Americans have spent studying Japanese practices. A typical example of this contrast was apparent when Charlene Barshefsky—a tough American international lawyer who had never visited Japan before—was sent there as a trade negotiator and had little knowledge of her counterparts. But Mr. Okamatsu, like most Japanese negotiators, was very familiar with America. He had lived with his family in New York for three years and had spent many years handling bilateral trade disputes between the two countries. The different styles of the two negotiators were apparent in the negotiations. Ms. Barshefsky wanted specific import goals. Mr. Okamatsu wanted to talk more about the causes of trade problems rather than set specific targets, which he called the "cooperative approach." Ms. Barshefsky snapped that the approach was "nonsense" and "would analyze the past to death, with no link to future change."[24]

Such differences in philosophy and style between the two countries reflect ten years of anger and feelings of betrayal in trade negotiations. John Graham, a California professor who has studied international negotiating styles, says that the differences between United States and Japanese styles are well illustrated by their respective proverbs: the Americans believe that "The squeaking wheel gets the grease," and the Japanese say that "The pheasant would not be shot but for its cry."[25] The Japanese are calm, quiet, patient negotiators; they are accustomed to long, detailed negotiating sessions. Whereas Americans often plunge straight to the matter at hand, the

EXHIBIT 5-4   Comparison of Negotiation Styles—Japanese, North American, and Latin American

Japanese	North American	Latin American
Emotional sensitivity highly valued	Emotional sensitivity not highly valued	Emotional sensitivity valued
Hiding of emotions	Dealing straightforwardly or impersonally	Emotionally passionate
Subtle power plays; conciliation	Litigation not so much as conciliation	Great power plays; use of weakness
Loyalty to employer; employer takes care of employees	Lack of commitment to employer; breaking of ties by either if necessary	Loyalty to employer (who is often family)
Face-saving crucial; decisions often on basis of saving someone from embarrassment	Decisions made on a cost-benefit basis; face-saving does not always matter	Face-saving crucial in decision making to preserve honor, dignity
Decision makers openly influenced by special interests	Decision makers influenced by special interests but often not considered ethical	Execution of special interests on decision expected, condoned
Not argumentative; quiet when right	Argumentative when right or wrong, but impersonal	Argumentative when right or wrong; passionate
What is down in writing must be accurate, valid	Great importance given to documentation as evidential proof	Impatient with documentation as obstacle to understanding general principles
Step-by-step approach to decision making	Methodically organized decision making	Impulsive, spontaneous decision making
Good of group is the ultimate aim	Profit motive or good of individual is the ultimate aim	What is good for group is good for the individual
Cultivate a good emotional social setting for decision making; get to know decision makers	Decision making impersonal; avoid involvements, conflict of interest	Personalism necessary for good decision making

Source: Pierre Casse, *Training for the Multicultural Manager: A Practical and Cross-Cultural Approach to the Management of People* (Washington, D.C.: Society for Intercultural Education, Training, and Research, 1982), used with the permission of the Society for Intercultural Education, Training and Research, 2012.

Japanese instead prefer to develop long-term, personal relationships. The Japanese want to get to know those on the other side and will spend some time in nontask sounding.

In negotiations, the Japanese culture of politeness and hiding of emotions can be disconcerting to Americans when they are unable to make straightforward eye contact or when the Japanese maintain smiling faces in serious situations. It is important that Americans understand what is polite and what is offensive to the Japanese—and vice versa. Americans must avoid anything that resembles boasting because the Japanese value humility, and physical contact or touching of any sort must be avoided.[26] Consistent with the culture-based value of maintaining harmony, the Japanese are likely to be evasive or even leave the room rather than give a direct negative answer.[27] Fundamental to Japanese culture is a concern for the welfare of the group; anything that affects one member or part of society affects the others. Thus, the Japanese view decisions carefully in light of long-term consequences; they use objective, analytic thought patterns; and they take time for reflection.[28]

Further insight into negotiating styles around the world can be gained by comparing the North American, Arab, and Russian styles. Basic cultural values often shed light on the way information is presented, whether and how concessions will be made, and the general nature and duration of the relationship. For North Americans, negotiations are businesslike; their factual appeals are based on what they believe is objective information, presented with the assumption that it is understood by the other side on a logical basis. Arabs use affective appeals based on emotions and subjective feelings. Russians employ axiomatic appeals—that is, their appeals are based on the ideals generally accepted in their society. The Russians are tough negotiators; they stall for time until they unnerve Western negotiators by continuously delaying and haggling. Much of this approach is based on the Russians' different attitude toward time. Because Russians traditionally do not subscribe to the Western belief that "time is money," they are more patient, more determined, and more dogged negotiators. They try to keep smiles and other expressions of emotion to a minimum to present a calm exterior.[29]

In contrast to the Russians, Arabs are more interested in long-term relationships and are, therefore, more likely to make concessions. Compared with Westerners, Arabs have a casual approach to deadlines, and frequently the negotiators lack the authority to finalize a deal.[30]

Successful Negotiators Around the World

Following are selected profiles of what it takes to be a successful negotiator, as perceived by people in their home countries. These are profiles of American, Indian, Arab, Swedish, and Italian negotiators, according to Pierre Casse, and give some insight into what to expect from different negotiators and what they expect from others.[31]

AMERICAN NEGOTIATORS

According to Casse, a successful American negotiator acts as follows:

1. Knows when to compromise
2. Takes a firm stand at the beginning of the negotiation
3. Refuses to make concessions beforehand
4. Keeps his or her cards close to his or her chest
5. Accepts compromises only when the negotiation is deadlocked
6. Sets up the general principles and delegates the detail work to associates
7. Keeps a maximum of options open before negotiation
8. Operates in good faith
9. Respects the "opponents"
10. States his or her position as clearly as possible
11. Knows when he or she wishes a negotiation to move on
12. Is fully briefed about the negotiated issues
13. Has a good sense of timing and is consistent
14. Makes the other party reveal his or her position while keeping his or her own position hidden as long as possible
15. Lets the other negotiator come forward first and looks for the best deal

INDIAN NEGOTIATORS

Indians, says Casse, often follow Gandhi's approach to negotiation, which Gandhi called *satyagraha*, "firmness in a good cause." This approach combines strength with the love of truth. The successful Indian negotiator thus acts as follows:

1. Looks for and says the truth
2. Is not afraid of speaking up and has no fears
3. Exercises self-control ("The weapons of the *satyagraha* are within him.")
4. Seeks solutions that will please all the parties involved ("*Satyagraha* aims to exalt both sides.")
5. Respects the other party ("The opponent must be weaned from error by patience and sympathy. Weaned, not crushed; converted, not annihilated.")
6. Neither uses violence nor insults
7. Is ready to change his or her mind and differ with himself or herself at the risk of being seen as inconsistent and unpredictable
8. Puts things into perspective and switches easily from the small picture to the big one
9. Is humble and trusts the opponent
10. Is able to withdraw, use silence, and learn from within

11. Relies on himself or herself, his or her own resources and strengths
12. Appeals to the other party's spiritual identity ("To communicate, the West moves or talks. The East sits, contemplates, suffers.")
13. Is tenacious, patient, and persistent
14. Learns from the opponent and avoids the use of secrets
15. Goes beyond logical reasoning and trusts his or her instinct as well as faith

ARAB NEGOTIATORS

Many Arab negotiators, following Islamic tradition, use mediators to settle disputes. A successful Arab mediator acts in the following way:

1. Protects all the parties' honor, self-respect, and dignity
2. Avoids direct confrontations between opponents
3. Is respected and trusted by all
4. Does not put the parties involved in a situation where they have to show weakness or admit defeat
5. Has the necessary prestige to be listened to
6. Is creative enough to come up with honorable solutions for all parties
7. Is impartial and can understand the positions of the various parties without leaning toward one or the other
8. Is able to resist any kind of pressure that the opponents could try to exercise on him
9. Uses references to people who are highly respected by the opponents to persuade them to change their minds on some issues ("Do it for the sake of your father.")
10. Can keep secrets and in so doing gains the confidence of the negotiating parties
11. Controls his temper and emotions (or loses it when and where necessary)
12. Can use conferences as mediating devices
13. Knows that the opponents will have problems in carrying out the decisions made during the negotiation
14. Is able to cope with the Arab disregard for time
15. Understands the impact of Islam on the opponents who believe that they possess the truth, follow the Right Path, and are going to "win" because their cause is just

SWEDISH NEGOTIATORS

Swedish negotiators, according to Casse, are:

1. Very quiet and thoughtful
2. Punctual (concerned with time)
3. Extremely polite
4. Straightforward (they get straight down to business)
5. Eager to be productive and efficient
6. Heavy going—serious and contemplative
7. Down to earth and overcautious
8. Rather flexible
9. Able to and quite good at holding emotions and feelings
10. Slow at reacting to new (unexpected) proposals
11. Informal and familiar
12. Conceited
13. Perfectionist
14. Afraid of confrontations
15. Very private

ITALIAN NEGOTIATORS

Italians, says Casse, value a negotiator who acts as follows:

1. Has a sense of drama (acting is a main part of the culture)
2. Does not hide his or her emotions (which are partly sincere and partly feigned)
3. Reads facial expressions and gestures very well

4. Has a feeling for history
5. Does not trust anybody
6. Is concerned about the *bella figura*—the "good impression"—he or she can create among those who watch his or her behavior
7. Believes in the individual's initiatives, not so much in teamwork
8. Is good at being obliging and simpatico at all times
9. Is always on the *qui vive*—the "lookout"
10. Never embraces definite opinions
11. Is able to come up with new ways to immobilize and eventually destroy his or her opponents
12. Handles confrontations of power with subtlety and tact
13. Has a flair for intrigue
14. Knows how to use flattery
15. Can involve other negotiators in complex combinations

COMPARING PROFILES

Comparing such profiles is useful. Indian negotiators, for example, are humble, patient, respectful of the other parties, and very willing to compromise, compared with Americans, who are firmer about taking stands. An important difference between Arab negotiators and those from most other countries is that the negotiators are mediators, not the parties themselves; hence, direct confrontation is made impossible. Successful Swedish negotiators are conservative and careful, dealing with factual and detailed information. This profile contrasts with Italian negotiators, who are expressive and exuberant but less straightforward than their Swedish counterparts.

MANAGING NEGOTIATION

Skillful global managers must assess many factors when managing negotiations. They must understand the position of the other parties in regard to their goals—whether national or corporate—and whether these goals are represented by principles or specific details. They should have the ability to recognize the relative importance attached to completing the task versus developing interpersonal relationships. Managers also must know the composition of the teams involved, the power allotted to the members, and the extent of the teams' preparation. In addition, they must grasp the significance of personal trust in the relationship. As stated earlier, the culture of the parties involved affects their negotiating styles and behavior and thus the overall process of negotiation. However, whatever the culture, research by Tse, Francis, and Walls has found person-related conflicts to "invite negative, more relation-oriented (versus information-oriented) responses," leading them to conclude that "The software of negotiation—that is, the nature and the appearance of the relationship between the people pursuing common goals—needs to be carefully addressed in the negotiation process.[32]

This is particularly true when representatives of individual-focused cultures (such as the Americans) and group-focused cultures (such as the Chinese) are on opposite sides of the table. Many of these culture-based differences in negotiations came to light in Husted's study on Mexican negotiators' perceptions of the reasons for the failure of their negotiations with U.S. teams.[33] The Mexican managers' interpretations were affected by their high-context culture, with the characteristics of an indirect approach, patience in discussing ideas, and maintenance of dignity. Instead, the low-context Americans conveyed an impatient, cold, blunt communicative style. To maintain the outward dignity of their Mexican counterparts, Americans must approach negotiations with Mexicans with patience and tolerance and refrain from attacking ideas because these attacks may be taken personally. The relationships among the factors of cross-cultural negotiation discussed in this chapter are illustrated in Exhibit 5-5.

The successful management of intercultural negotiations requires that a manager go beyond a generalized understanding of the issues and variables involved. She or he must (1) gain specific knowledge of the parties in the upcoming meeting, (2) prepare accordingly to adjust to and control the situation, and (3) be innovative.[34]

Research has shown that a problem-solving approach is essential to successful cross-cultural negotiations, whether abroad or in the home office, although the approach works differently in various countries.[35] This problem-solving approach requires that a negotiator treat everyone with

EXHIBIT 5-5   Cross-Cultural Negotiation Variables

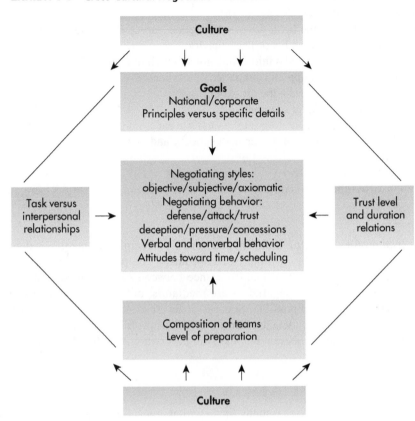

respect, avoid making anyone feel uncomfortable, and not criticize or blame the other parties in a personal way that may make someone feel shame—that is, lose face.

Research by the Huthwaite Research Group reveals how successful negotiators, compared to average negotiators, manage the planning process and their face-to-face behavior. The group found that during the planning process, successful negotiators consider a wider range of options and pay greater attention to areas of common ground. Skillful negotiators also tend to make twice as many comments regarding long-term issues and are more likely to set upper and lower limits regarding specific points. In their face-to-face behavior, skillful negotiators make fewer irritating comments—such as "We're making you a generous offer"—make counterproposals less frequently, and use fewer reasons to back up arguments. In addition, skilled negotiators practice active listening—asking questions, clarifying their understanding of the issues, and summarizing the issues.[36]

Using the Internet to Support Negotiations

Modern technology can provide support for the negotiating process, though it can't take the place of the essential face-to-face ingredient in many instances. A growing component for electronic commerce is the development of applications to support the negotiation of contracts and resolution of disputes. As Web applications develop, they may provide support for various phases and dimensions, such as "Multiple-issue, multiple-party business transactions of a buy–sell nature; international dispute resolution (business disputes, political disputes); and internal company negotiations and communications, among others."[37]

Negotiation support systems (NSS) can provide support for the negotiation process in the following ways:

- Increasing the likelihood that an agreement is reached when a zone of agreement exists (solutions that both parties would accept)
- Decreasing the direct and indirect costs of negotiations, such as costs caused by time delays (strikes, violence), and attorneys' fees, among others
- Maximizing the chances for optimal outcomes[38]

One Web-based support system—called INSPIRE—developed at Carleton University in Ottawa, Canada, provides applications for preparing and conducting negotiations and for renegotiating options after a settlement. Users can specify preferences and assess offers; the site also has graphical displays of the negotiation process.[39]

E-NEGOTIATIONS

The advantages of electronic communications are well known: speed, less travel, and the ability to lay out much objective information to be considered by the other party over time. The disadvantages, however, might kill a deal before it gets off the ground, by not being able to build trust and interpersonal relationships over time before getting down to business. In addition, nonverbal nuances are lost, although videoconferencing is a compromise for that purpose.

Rosette et al. noted that "opening offers may be especially aggressive in e-mail as com pared to face-to-face negotiations because computer-mediated communications, such as e-mail, loosen inhibitions and cause negotiators to become more competitive and more risk seeking. The increase in competitive and risky behavior occurs because e-mail does not communicate social context cues in the same way as does the presence of another person."[40]

Managing Conflict Resolution

Much of the negotiation process is fraught with conflict—explicit or implicit—and such conflict can often lead to a standoff, or a lose–lose situation. This is regrettable, not only because of the situation at hand, but also because it probably will shut off future opportunities for deals between the parties. Much of the cause of such conflict can be found in cultural differences between the parties—in their expectations, in their behaviors, and particularly in their communication styles—as illustrated in *Comparative Management in Focus, Negotiating with the Chinese.*

COMPARATIVE MANAGEMENT IN FOCUS
Negotiating with the Chinese

> *The Chinese way of making decisions begins with socialization and initiation of personal guanxi rather than business discussion. The focus is not market research, statistical analysis, facts, Power-Point presentations, or to-the-point business discussion. My focus must be on fostering guanxi.*
>
> SUNNY ZHOU, *GENERAL MANAGER OF KUNMING LIDA WOOD AND BAMBOO PRODUCTS.*[41]

With the increasing business being conducted in China, or with Chinese allies or other companies, it is clear that firms can greatly benefit from China's rapidly expanding economy and FDI, as well as the improved international relations and government reforms.

When Westerners initiate business negotiations with representatives from the People's Republic of China, cultural barriers confront both sides. However, we should recognize that there are regional cultural differences that may affect negotiation, as well as regional economic differences; some examples of regional differences are noted below as researched by Tung et al. In addition there are considerable generational differences, in particular with those younger people who have been educated in the West and are more familiar with Western ways and languages, in contrast with the older generation, which holds to more traditional culture and negotiation strategies.[42]

Beijing (capital): "Political, bureaucratic, educated, diversified, high relationship orientation, more direct, high 'face.'"[43]

Shanghai (commercial center): "Business savvy, focus on details, bottom line, career-oriented younger people, materialistic, confident."[44]

Guangzhou/Shenzhen (south, near Hong Kong): "Entrepreneurial, hard-working, manufacturing center, outside the norm, more risk-taking, like Hong Kong, more informal."[45]

Western China (Chengdu/Chongqing): "Traditional 'People's' mentality, less experience with international business/negotiations, socializing importance."[46]

For the most part, the negotiation process used by the Chinese is mystifying to most Westerners. For instance, the Chinese put much greater emphasis than Americans and Europeans on respect and

(Continued)

MAP 5.1 **China**

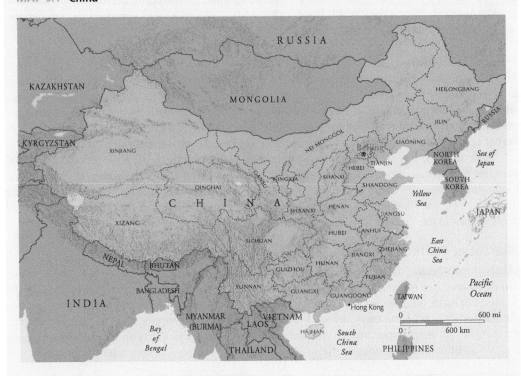

friendship, on saving face, and on group goals. Long-term goals are more important to the Chinese than the specific current objectives typical of Western negotiators. Even though market forces now have more influence in China, political and economic agendas are still expected to be considered in negotiations. Economic conditions, political pervasiveness, and the influence that political and state agencies have on the negotiating parties in China are key practical factors that, added to cultural factors, make up the context affecting Chinese negotiations.

Business people report two major areas of conflict in negotiating with the Chinese: (1) the amount of detail the Chinese want about product characteristics, and (2) their apparent insincerity about reaching an agreement. In addition, Chinese negotiators frequently have little authority, frustrating Americans who do have the authority and are ready to conclude a deal.[47] This situation arises because many Chinese companies report to the government trade corporations, which are involved in the negotiations and often have a representative on the team. Often, the goals of Chinese negotiators remain primarily within the framework of state planning and political ideals. Although China is becoming more profit-oriented, most deals are still negotiated within the confines of the state budget allocation for that project rather than on the basis of a project's profitability or value. It is crucial, then, to find out which officials—national, provincial, or local—have the power to make, and keep, a deal. According to James Broering of Arthur Andersen, who does much business in China, "companies have negotiated with government people for months, only to discover that they were dealing with the wrong people."[48]

Research shows that for the Chinese, the negotiation process is greatly affected by three cultural norms: their ingrained politeness and emotional restraint, their emphasis on social obligations, and their belief in the interconnection of work, family, and friendship. Because of the Chinese preference for emotional restraint and saving face, aggressive or emotional attempts at persuasion in negotiation are likely to fail. Instead, the Chinese tendency to avoid open conflict will more likely result in negative strategies such as discontinuing or withdrawing from negotiation.[49] The concept of "face" is at the heart of this kind of response—it is essential for foreigners to recognize the role that face behavior plays in negotiations. There are two components of face—*lien* and *mien-tzu. Lien* refers to a person's moral character; it is the most important thing defining that person, and without it one cannot function in society. It can only be earned by fulfilling obligations to others. *Mien-tzu* refers to one's reputation or prestige, earned through accomplishments or through bureaucratic or political power.[50] Giving others one's time, gifts, or praise enhances one's own face. In negotiations, it is vital that you do not make it obvious that you have "won," because that means that the other party has "lost" and will lose face. One must, therefore, make token concessions and other attempts to show that respect must be demonstrated, and modesty and control must be maintained; otherwise anyone who feels he or she has "lost face" will not want to deal with you again. The Chinese will later ignore any dealings or incidents that caused them to lose face, maintaining the expected polite behavior out of social consciousness and concern for others. When encountering an embarrassing situation, they will typically smile or laugh in an attempt to save face, responses that are confusing to Western negotiators.[51]

"It is critical that you give face, save face and show face when doing business in China."[52]

Generally, Westerners tend to feel that the Chinese negotiators are not truthful with them and do not give them straight answers. In turn, the Chinese sense that tension and feel a lack of trust in the Westerners.[53]

The emphasis on social obligations underlies the strong orientation of the Chinese toward collective goals. Therefore, appeals to individual members of the Chinese negotiating team, rather than appeals to benefit the group as a whole, will probably backfire. The Confucian emphasis on the kinship system and the hierarchy of work, family, and friends explains the Chinese preference for doing business with familiar, trusted people and trusted companies. "Foreign" negotiators, then, should focus on establishing long-term, trusting relationships, even at the expense of some immediate returns.

Deeply ingrained in the Chinese culture is the importance of harmony for the smooth functioning of society. Harmony is based primarily on personal relationships, trust, and ritual. After the Chinese establish a cordial relationship with foreign negotiators, they use this relationship as a basis for the give-and-take of business discussions. This implicit cultural norm is commonly known as *guanxi*, which refers to the intricate, pervasive network of personal relations that every Chinese carefully cultivates. It is the primary means of getting ahead, in the absence of a proper commercial legal system.[54] In other words, *guanxi* establishes obligations to exchange favors in future business activities.[55] Even within the Chinese bureaucracy, *guanxi* prevails over legal interpretations. Although networking is important anywhere to do business, the difference in China is that "*guanxi* networks are not just commercial, but also social, involving the exchange both of favor and affection."[56] Firms that have special *guanxi* connections and give preferential treatment to one another are known as members of a *guanxihu* network.[57] Sunny Zhou, general manager of Kumming Lida Wood and Bamboo Products, states that when he shops for lumber, "The lumber price varies drastically, depending on whether one has strong *guanxi* with the local administrators."[58] Western managers should thus anticipate extended preliminary visiting (relationship building), in which the Chinese expect to learn more about them and their trustworthiness. The Chinese also use this opportunity to convey their deeply held principles. They attach considerable importance to mutual benefit.[59]

Americans often experience two negotiation stages with the Chinese: the technical and the commercial. During the long technical stage, the Chinese want to hammer out every detail of the proposed product specifications and technology. If there are two teams of negotiators, it may be several days before the commercial team is actually called in to deal with aspects of production, marketing, pricing, and so forth. However, the commercial team should sit in on the first stage to become familiar with the Chinese negotiating style.[60] The Chinese negotiating team is usually about twice as large as the Western team; about a third of the time is spent discussing technical specifications, and another third on price negotiations, with the rest devoted to general negotiations and posturing.[61]

The Chinese are among the toughest negotiators in the world. American managers must anticipate various tactics, such as their delaying techniques and their avoidance of direct, specific answers: Both ploys are used to exploit the known impatience of Americans. The Chinese frequently try to put pressure on Americans by "shaming" them, thereby implying that the Americans are trying to renege on the friendship—the basis of the implicit contract. Whereas Westerners come to negotiations with specific and segmented goals and find it easy to compromise, the Chinese are reluctant to negotiate details. They find it difficult to compromise and trade because they have entered negotiations with a broader vision of achieving development goals for China, and they are offended when Westerners don't internalize those goals.[62] Under these circumstances, the Chinese will adopt a rigid posture, and no agreement or contract is final until the negotiated activities have actually been completed.

Successful negotiations with the Chinese depend on many factors. Research by Fang et al. found the top success factors to be sincerity on behalf of the Western team, their team's preparation, technical expertise, patience, knowledge of PRC (People's Republic of China) business practices, and good personal relationships.[63] Generally speaking, patience, respect, and experience are necessary prerequisites for anyone negotiating in China. For the best outcomes, older, more experienced people are more acceptable to the Chinese in cross-cultural negotiations. The Chinese want to deal with the top executive of an American company, under the assumption that the highest officer has attained that position by establishing close personal relationships and trust with colleagues and others outside the

(Continued)

organization. Western delegation practices are unfamiliar to them, and they are reluctant to come to an agreement without the presence of the Chinese foreign negotiator.[64] From the Western perspective, confusing jurisdictions of government ministries hamper decisions in negotiations. Americans tend to send specific technical personnel with experience in the task at hand; therefore, they have to take care in selecting the most suitable negotiators. In addition, visiting negotiating teams should realize that the Chinese are probably negotiating with other foreign teams, often at the same time, and will use that setup to play one company's offer against the others. On an interpersonal level, Western negotiators must also realize that, while a handshake is polite, physical contact is not acceptable in Chinese social behavior, nor are personal discussion topics such as one's family. However, it is customary to give and take small gifts as tokens of friendship. Keep in mind the following tips:[65]

- Some time before the trip, establish a contact in China who will act as a reference, be your interpreter and navigate you through the bureaucracy, legal system, and local business networks.
- Be very prepared before doing business in China. The Chinese plan meticulously and will know your business and possibly you inside out.
- Send some literature about your company in advance, and convey a set agenda before each meeting. Be punctual, or you will insult them before you start; begin with small, polite social talk, but avoid politics.
- Expect initial meetings to involve long, convoluted discussions that are really intended to get to know one another, establish trust, and find out the actual goals of your team.
- The Chinese are not confrontational and will not say "no." You will need to be observant and recognize that perhaps those items are not negotiable.
- Practice patience. Introducing delays and obstacles is a Chinese negotiating tactic. They will wait until the deadline is passed and demand another concession, knowing that the Westerners are focused on their deadline for departure, so let them know your schedule is open and keep calm.
- Expect prolonged periods of stalemate; hang loose and don't say anything about the point in question. Try to change the momentum by, say, suggesting going for dinner.
- Refrain from exaggerated expectations and discount Chinese rhetoric about future prospects.
- Remember at all times to save "face" for everyone, and keep in mind the importance of trust and "guanxi" in negotiations.

In conclusion, it is evident that China's rapidly changing business environment is evident in more professionalism in the negotiation process. At the same time, research by Fang et al. shows that "one should not underestimate the impact of culture on Chinese business negotiations. Western companies that seek to succeed in China need to demonstrate sincerity and commitment in conducting business in order to gain the Chinese partner's trust as this appears to be the ultimate predictor for success of business relations in China."[66]

Context in Negotiations

As discussed in Chapter 4, much of the difference in communication styles is attributable to whether you belong to a high-context or low-context culture (or somewhere in between, as shown in Exhibit 4-4). In low-context cultures such as that in the United States, conflict is handled directly and explicitly. It is also regarded as separate from the person negotiating—that is, the negotiators draw a distinction between the people involved and the information or opinions they represent. They also tend to negotiate on the basis of factual information and logical analysis. That approach to conflict is called **instrumental-oriented conflict**.[67] In high-context cultures, such as in the Middle East, the approach to conflict is called **expressive-oriented conflict**—that is, the situation is handled indirectly and implicitly, without clear delineation of the situation by the person handling it. Such negotiators do not want to get in a confrontational situation because it is regarded as insulting and would cause a loss of "face," so they tend to use evasion and avoidance if they cannot reach agreement through emotional appeals. Their avoidance and inaction conflict with the expectations of the low-context negotiators who are looking to move ahead with the business at hand and arrive at a solution.

The differences between high- and low-context cultures that often lead to conflict situations are summarized in Exhibit 5-6. Most of these variables were discussed previously in

EXHIBIT 5-6   Negotiation Conflicts Between Low-Context and High-Context Cultures[68]

Low-Context Conflict Area	High-Context Conflict Area
Explicit and direct; verbal; linear presentation of facts, rationale, analysis.	Implicit, indirect discussion and decision-making; non-verbal; may be circular logic.
Individualistic; tend to be short-term-oriented. Task-oriented. Up-front, impatient, sometimes confrontational; action and solution directive.	Collective; group motivations and decisions by consensus Tend to be long-term-oriented "Face" and relationship-oriented; indirect, non-confrontational, patient.

this chapter or in Chapter 4. They overlap because the subjects, culture, and communication are inseparable and because negotiation differences and conflict situations arise from variables in culture and communication.

The point here is, how can a manager from France, Japan, or Brazil, for example, manage conflict situations? The solution, as discussed previously, lies mainly in one's ability to know and understand the people and the situation to be faced. Managers must be prepared by developing an understanding of the cultural contexts in which they will be operating. What are the expectations of the persons with whom they will be negotiating? What kinds of communication styles and negotiating tactics should they expect, and how will they differ from their own? It is important to bear in mind one's own expectations and negotiating style, as well as to be aware of the other parties' expectations. Managers ought to consider in advance what it will take to arrive at a win-win solution. Often it helps to use the services of a host-country adviser or mediator, who may be able to help with early diffusion of a conflict situation.

DECISION MAKING

Negotiation actually represents the outcome of a series of small and large decisions. The decisions include those made by each party before actual negotiations start—for example, in determining the position of the company and what fallback proposals it may suggest or accept. The decisions also include incremental decisions, made during the negotiation process, on how to react and proceed, when to concede, and on what to agree or disagree. Negotiation can thus be seen as a series of explicit and implicit decisions, and the subjects of negotiation and decision making become interdependent.

For instance, sometimes just the way a decision is made during the negotiation process can have a profound influence on the outcome, as this example from a book by Copeland and Griggs shows:

> *In his first loan negotiation, a banker new to Japan met with seven top Japanese bankers who were seeking a substantial amount of money. After hearing their presentation, the American agreed on the spot. The seven Japanese then conferred among themselves and told the American they would get back to him in a couple of days regarding whether they would accept his offer or not. The American banker learned a lesson he never forgot.[69]*

The Japanese bankers expected the American to negotiate, to take time to think it over, and to consult with colleagues before giving the final decision. His immediate decision made them suspicious, so they decided to reconsider the deal.

There is no doubt that the speed and manner of decision making affect the negotiation process. In addition, how well negotiated agreements are implemented is affected by the speed and manner of decision making. In that regard, it is clear that the effective use of technology is playing an important role, especially when dealing with complex cross-border agreements in which the hundreds of decision makers involved are separated by time and space.

The role of decision making in management, however, goes far beyond the finite occasions of negotiations. It is part of the manager's daily routine—from operational-level, programmed decisions requiring minimal time and effort to those nonprogrammed decisions of far broader scope and importance, such as the decision to enter into a joint venture in a foreign country.

The Influence of Culture on Decision Making

It is crucial for international managers to understand the influence of culture on decision-making styles and processes. Culture affects decision making both through the broader context of the nation's institutional culture, which produces collective patterns of decision making, and through culturally based value systems that affect each individual decision maker's perception or interpretation of a situation.[70] The ways in which these factors can come together to affect people's negotiations and decisions is illustrated in the following Under the Lens feature.

UNDER THE LENS
Negotiations and Decisions to Save the Eurozone System[71]

Within each class, attitudes are hardening against the other. "The birth defect of the euro was to put very different cultures of economic activity in the straitjacket of a single currency."[72]

In 2012 a major issue at the intersection of politics, economics, and business was how the Eurozone crisis would get resolved. The outcome of the negotiations and decisions among representatives of the euro countries would have lasting repercussions for businesses around the world, and European businesses in particular. At the heart of the negotiations among the Eurozone countries and the IMF were the potential effects of a massive financial rescue plan for Greece, which was threatened with default. In spite of the passage of radical reforms and austerity cuts in Greece, the European Commission, European Central Bank, and the IMF were demanding further cuts from Greece in order to receive the $170 billion in bailout money that Greece needs in order to avert default.

The Italian economy, the seventh largest in the world, was also in a fragile state with massive debt, and the Prime Minister, Mario Monti, was taking drastic measures to avoid default; there were fears that a default of such a large economy could bring a default of the entire Euro system. At stake in the negotiations was the Eurozone pact, and the continuation of the euro itself.

Italy's problems have become the world's problems, and Monti must fix Italy to prevent another global financial crisis.

And as Italy goes, so goes the euro. Italy looms as the biggest threat to the embattled currency's survival, because Italy is both too big to fail and too big to save.[73]

Mario Monti, then, an unelected official from academia, has almost uncontested control of such weighty decisions which will determine both Italy's fate and that of the euro. His negotiation and decision-making capabilities are vital to so many people. But Monti believes his detachment from the politicians is what is needed to do the job; he has a reputation for being very willful in achieving his objectives.[74]

As negotiations continued, cultural, historical, and lifestyle differences among the major countries involved brought out old prejudices that threatened to derail the negotiations. With Germany as the richest and most stable economy in the Eurozone, its people were resentful and fearful of the prospect of "bailing out" Greece. Angela Merkel, the German prime minister, herself very conservative and consultative, was in the difficult position of making decisions both to protect the German economy and its people, and at the same time needing to play a prominent role in decisions to aid Greece and save the euro system. As such, Ms. Merkel was holding out for Greece and Italy to take on strict reforms. Germany has a much respected manufacturing and export base, and the fear was that the crisis would undermine their businesses. In fact, in February 2012 Angel Gurría, the O.E.C.D.'s secretary general, in a speech in Berlin, congratulated Germany on a well-managed economy, saying that Germany's "growth model has been so successful in navigating through the stormy waters of the crisis."

Interviews by Margaret Warner of PBS in February 2012 revealed the depth of angst of the German people. At the heart of their culture is a strong desire for security and safety, no doubt partly evolving from the German history. Germans are very conservative and cautious, with a focus on frugality and saving. The economy is largely based on cash, not credit; a home mortgage requires a minimum of a 30% down payment, and the banks are very conservative—hence Germany had not had the real estate bubble and subsequent meltdown as in the United States. As such, the German people feel that they should not have to bail out their free-spending southern neighbors. Germany had already taken painful austerity measures a decade ago in absorbing the poorer East Germany. They now have a much respected and robust manufacturing and export base. In addition, their recent sacrifices, such as raising the retirement age to 67, had resulted in lower unemployment and deficits. An additional bone of contention with the German people is that while they pay high taxes, it is commonly understood that a large proportion of Greeks and Italians don't pay taxes.

In all, the negotiations were being undermined by a lack of trust among the EU members. Greeks are very proud of their cultural heritage and felt that negotiations were going to "deprive Greece of the last trace of national sovereignty" according to Georgios Karatzaferis, who heads the right-wing Popular Orthodox Rally; he expressed frustration with German officials, who have taken a hard line in the negotiations. "Greece cannot survive outside the E.U.," he said, "but it can do without a German jackboot."[75]

For their part, Greeks are skilled negotiators and will not be pushed into decisions before they are ready. Business interactions are formal and are based on friendship and trust. This became clear at all levels in the Eurozone negotiations. Within Greece, as the plan for the austerity measures demanded by the Greek creditors went to parliament, it was clear that there would be a lot of debate over then-Prime Minister Papademos's plan:

> *The [Greek] prime minister's comments kicked off what is expected to be a long and chaotic weekend of brinkmanship, with Greek politicians fighting for their survival in the face of unpopular austerity measures and European leaders demanding more concessions in a climate of growing urgency—and mistrust—between Greece and its foreign lenders.*[76]

The Greek people are fearful of a continued downward spiral in their economy under the austerity measures; they blame the tightly knight elite who have run the country for so long. However, they will admit that "The Greek way of life is to spend and then overspend." At the same time, everyone complains that the bureaucracy is a menace. "*Fakelaki* (literally "little envelopes") are a legendary feature of society. If you're starting a business, there are lots of signatures you need, and handing over the cash-stuffed envelopes has traditionally been part of the process."[77] A quarter of all Greek companies have gone out of business since 2009, and half of all small businesses in the country say they are unable to meet payroll.[78]

Meanwhile, businesses in Italy and elsewhere which depended on clients in Greece, Spain, Portugal, and other hurting countries were suffering because their good customers had no cash and no credit. This was relayed in the PBS interview with Roberto Belloli, CEO of Antonio Aspesi Srl in the fashion industry. As a result, he said the company had to retrench. However, Italy's labor laws made it extremely hard to fire anyone, and laying off an employee costs the company 60 months of salary.

The business style in Italy depends on whether you are dealing with someone from the north or the south:

> *In the north, people are direct, see time as money, and get down to business after only a brief period of social talk.*
>
> *In the south, people take a more leisurely approach to life and want to get to know the people with whom they do business.*[79]

Italians prefer to negotiate with high-ranking people; hierarchy is very important to them. In addition, negotiations are likely to be very protracted. Your image is likely to be just as important to your Italian counterparts as the specific business objectives. Networking is important since they like to do business with people they know and trust and also like to conduct face-to-face meetings.[80]

As uncertainty took its toll on all sides it was clear that "*Within each class, attitudes are hardening against the other. 'The birth defect of the euro was to put very different cultures of economic activity in the straitjacket of a single currency.'*"[81] As the situation worsened, national identities hardened, further hampering negotiations.

At the time of you reading this there are likely to have been many developments in the Eurozone crisis. You could discuss what led up to the crisis, what cultural, economic, historical, and lifestyle differences contributed to the situation, and what part those factors played in the negotiations and decisions by all parties.

The extent to which decision making is influenced by culture varies among countries. For example, Hitt, Tyler, and Park have found a "more culturally homogenizing influence on the Korean executives' cognitive models" than on those of U.S. executives, whose individualistic tendencies lead to different decision patterns.[82] The ways that culture influences an executive's decisions can be studied by looking at the variables involved in each stage of the rational decision-making process. These stages are (1) defining the problem, (2) gathering and analyzing relevant data, (3) considering alternative solutions, (4) deciding on the best solution, and (5) implementing the decision.

One of the major cultural variables affecting decision making is whether a people tend to assume an objective approach or a subjective approach. Whereas the Western approach is based on rationality (managers interpret a situation and consider alternative solutions based on objective information), this approach is not common throughout the world. Latin Americans, among others, tend to be more subjective, basing decisions on emotions.

Another cultural variable that greatly influences the decision-making process is the risk tolerance of those making the decision. Research shows that people from Belgium, Germany, and Austria have a considerably lower tolerance for risk than people from Japan or the Netherlands—whereas American managers have the highest tolerance for risk.[83]

In addition, an often-overlooked but important variable in the decision-making process is the manager's perception of the locus of control over outcomes—whether that locus is internal or external. Some managers feel they can plan on certain outcomes because they are in control of events that will direct the future in the desired way. In contrast, other managers believe that such decisions are of no value because they have little control over the future—which lies in the hands of outside forces, such as fate, God, or nature. American managers believe strongly in self-determination and perceive problem situations as something they can control and should change. However, managers in many other countries, Indonesia and Malaysia among them, tend to be resigned to problem situations and do not feel that they can change them. Obviously, these different value systems will result in a great difference in the stages of consideration of alternative actions and choice of a solution, often because certain situations may or may not be viewed as problems in the first place.

Yet another variable that affects the consideration of alternative solutions is how managers feel about staying with familiar solutions or trying new ones. Many managers, particularly those in Europe, value decisions based on past experiences and tend to emphasize quality. Americans, on the other hand, are more future oriented and look toward new ideas to get them there.

Approaches to Decision Making

In addition to affecting different stages of the decision-making process, value systems influence the overall approach of decision makers from various cultures. The relative level of *utilitarianism versus moral idealism* in any society affects its overall approach to problems. Generally speaking, utilitarianism strongly guides behavior in the Western world. Research has shown that Canadian executives are more influenced by a short-term, cost–benefit approach to decision making than their Hong Kong counterparts.

Another important variable in companies' overall approach to decision making is that of *autocratic versus participative leadership*. In other words, who has the authority to make what kinds of decisions? A society's orientation—whether it is individualistic or collectivist (see Chapter 3)—influences the level at which decisions are made. In many countries with hierarchical cultures—Germany, Turkey, and India, among others—authorization for action has to be passed upward through echelons of management before final decisions can be made. Most employees in these countries simply expect the autocrat—the boss—to do most of the decision making and will not be comfortable otherwise. Even in China, which is a highly collectivist society, employees expect autocratic leadership because their value system presupposes the superior to be automatically the most wise. In comparison, decision-making authority in Sweden is very decentralized. Americans talk a lot about the advisability of such participative leadership, but in practice they are probably near the middle between autocratic and participative management styles.

Arab managers have long traditions of consultative decision making, supported by the Qur'an and the sayings of Muhammad. However, such consultation occurs more on a person-to-person basis than during group meetings and thus diffuses potential opposition.[84] Although business in the Middle East tends to be transacted in a highly personalized manner, the final decisions are made by the top leaders, who feel that they must impose their will for the company to be successful. In comparison, in cultures that emphasize collective harmony, such as Japan, participatory or group decision making predominates, and consensus is important. The best-known example is the bottom-up (rather than top-down) decision-making process used in most Japanese companies, described in more detail in the following Comparative Management in Focus section.

EXHIBIT 5-7 Cultural Variables in the Decision-Making Process

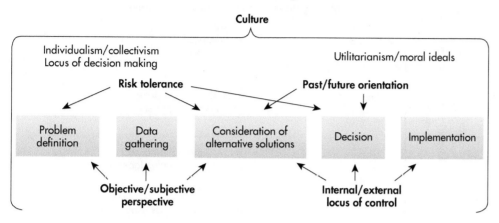

One final area of frequent incongruence concerns the relative speed of decision making. A country's culture affects how fast or slow decisions tend to be made. The relative speed may be closely associated with the level of delegation, as just discussed—but not always. The pace at which decisions are made can be very disconcerting for outsiders. North Americans and Europeans pride themselves on being decisive; managers in the Middle East, with a different sense of temporal urgency, associate the importance of the matter at hand with the length of time needed to make a decision. Without knowing this cultural attitude, a hasty American would insult an Egyptian; a quick decision, to the Egyptian, would reflect a low regard for the relationship and the deal.

Exhibit 5-7 illustrates, in summary form, how all the variables just discussed can affect the steps in the decision-making process.

COMPARATIVE MANAGEMENT IN FOCUS

Decision Making in Japanese Companies

Japanese companies are involved in joint ventures throughout the world, especially with U.S. companies. The GM-Toyota joint venture agreement process, for example, was the result of more than two years of negotiation and decision making; in similar alliances, Americans and Japanese are involved in decision making at all levels on a daily basis. The Japanese decision-making process differs greatly not only from the U.S. process but from that of many other countries—especially at the higher levels of their organizations.

An understanding of the Japanese decision-making process—and indeed of many Japanese management practices—requires an understanding of Japanese national culture. Much of the Japanese culture, and therefore the basis of Japanese working relationships, can be explained by the principle of *wa*, meaning "peace and harmony." This principle is one aspect of the value the Japanese attribute to *amae*, meaning "indulgent love," a concept probably originating in the Shinto religion, which focuses on spiritual and physical harmony. *Amae* results in *shinyo*, which refers to the mutual confidence, faith, and honor required for successful business relationships. The principle of *wa* influences the work group, the basic building block of Japanese work and management. The Japanese strongly identify with their work groups, where the emphasis is on cooperation, participative management, consensus problem solving, and decision making based on a patient, long-term perspective. Open expression of conflict is discouraged, and it is of utmost importance to avoid embarrassment or shame— to lose face—as a result of not fulfilling one's obligations. These elements of work culture generally result in a devotion to work, a collective responsibility for decisions and actions, and a high degree of employee productivity. It is this culture of collectivism and shared responsibility that underlies the Japanese *ringi* system of decision making.

In the *ringi* system, the process works from the bottom up. Americans are used to a centralized system, where major decisions are made by upper-level managers in a top-down approach typical of individualistic societies. The Japanese process, however, is dispersed throughout the organization, relying on group consensus.

(Continued)

EXHIBIT 5-8 Decision-Making Procedure in Japanese Companies

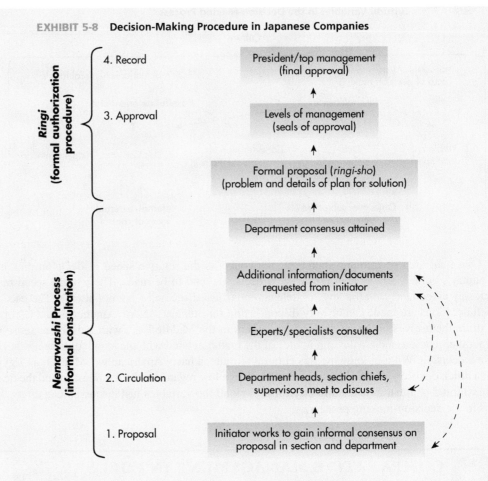

The *ringi* process is one of gaining approval on a proposal by circulating documents to those concerned throughout the company. It usually comprises four steps: proposal, circulation, approval, and record.[85] Usually the person who originates the written proposal, which is called a *ringi-sho*, has already worked for some time to gain informal consensus and support for the proposal within the section and then from the department head.[86] The next step is to attain a general consensus in the company from those who would be involved in implementation. To this end, department meetings are held, and, if necessary, expert opinion is sought. If more information is needed, the proposal goes back to the originator, who finds and adds the required data. In this way, much time and effort—and the input of many people—go into the proposal before it becomes formal.[87]

Up to this point, the process has been an informal one to gain consensus; it is called the *nemawashi* process. Then the more formal authorization procedure begins, called the *ringi* process. The *ringi-sho* is passed up through successive layers of management for approval—the approval made official by seals. In the end, many such seals of approval are gathered, thereby ensuring collective agreement and responsibility and giving the proposal a greater chance of final approval by the president. The whole process is depicted in Exhibit 5-8.

The *ringi* system is cumbersome and very time-consuming prior to the implementation stage, although implementation is facilitated because of the widespread awareness of and support for the proposal already gained throughout the organization. However, its slow progress is problematic when decisions are time-sensitive. This process is the opposite of the Americans' top-down decisions, which are made quite rapidly and without consultation, but which then take time to implement because unforeseen practical or support problems often arise.

Another interesting comparison is often made regarding the planning horizon (aimed at short- or long-term goals) in decision making between the American and Japanese systems. The Japanese spend considerable time in the early stages of the process defining the issue, considering what the issue is all about, and determining whether there is an actual need for a decision. They are more likely than Americans to consider an issue in relation to the overall goals and strategy of the company. In this manner, they prudently look at the "big picture" and consider alternative solutions, instead of rushing into quick decisions for immediate solutions, as Americans tend to do.[88]

Of course, in a rapidly changing environment, quick decisions are often necessary—to respond to competitors' actions, a political uprising, and so forth—and it is in such contexts that the *ringi* system sometimes falls short because of its slow response rate. The system is, in fact, designed to manage continuity and to avoid uncertainty, which is considered a threat to group cohesiveness.[89]

CONCLUSION

It is clear that competitive positioning and long-term successful operations in a global market require a working knowledge of the decision-making and negotiating processes of managers from different countries. These processes are complex and often interdependent. Although managers may make decisions that do not involve negotiating, they cannot negotiate without making decisions, however small, or they would not be negotiating. In addition, managers must understand the behavioral aspects of these processes to work effectively with people in other countries or with a culturally diverse workforce in their own countries.

With an understanding of the environment and cultural context of international management as background, we move next in Part 3 to planning and implementing strategy for international and global operations.

Summary of Key Points

1. The ability to negotiate successfully is one of the most important in international business. Managers must prepare for certain cultural variables that influence negotiations, including the relative emphasis on task versus interpersonal relationships, the use of general principles versus specific details, the number of people present, and the extent of their influence.

2. The negotiation process typically progresses through the stages of preparation, relationship building, exchange of task-related information, persuasion, and concessions and agreement. The process of building trusting relationships is a prerequisite to doing business in many parts of the world.

3. Culturally based differences in verbal and nonverbal negotiation behavior influence the negotiation process at every stage. Such tactics and actions include promises, threats, initial concessions, silent periods, interruptions, facial gazing, and touching; some parties resort to various dirty tricks.

4. The effective management of negotiation requires an understanding of the perspectives, values, and agendas of other parties and the use of a problem-solving approach.

5. Decision making is an important part of the negotiation process, as well as an integral part of a manager's daily routine. Culture affects the decision-making process both through a society's institutions and through individuals' risk tolerance, their objective versus subjective perspectives, their perceptions of the locus of control, and their past versus future orientations.

6. The Internet is used increasingly to support the negotiation of contracts and resolution of disputes. Web sites that provide open auctions take away the personal aspects of negotiations, though those aspects are still essential in many instances.

Discussion Questions

1. Discuss the stages in the negotiation process and how culturally-based value systems influence these stages. Specifically, address the following:
   - Explain the role and relative importance of relationship-building in different countries.
   - Discuss the various styles and tactics that can be involved in exchanging task-related information.
   - Describe differences in culturally-based styles of persuasion.
   - Discuss the kinds of concession strategies a negotiator might anticipate in various countries.

2. Discuss the relative use of nonverbal behaviors, such as silent periods, interruptions, facial gazing, and touching, by people from various cultural backgrounds. How does this behavior affect the negotiation process in a cross-cultural context?

3. Describe what you would expect in negotiations with the Chinese and how you would handle various situations.

4. What are some of the differences in risk tolerance around the world? What is the role of risk propensity in the decision-making process?

5. Explain how objective versus subjective perspectives influence the decision-making process. What role do you think this variable has played in all the negotiations conducted and decisions made by Iraq and the United Nations?

6. Explain differences in culturally-based value systems relative to the amount of control a person feels he or she has over future outcomes. How does this belief influence the decision-making process?

Experiential Exercise

Exercise: Multicultural Negotiations

Goal

To experience, identify, and appreciate the problems associated with negotiating with people of other cultures.

Instructions (Note: Your professor will give out additional instruction sheets)

1. Eight student volunteers will participate in the role play. Four represent a Japanese automobile manufacturer, and four represent a U.S. team that has come to sell microchips and other components to the Japanese company. The remainder of the class will observe the negotiations.

2. The eight volunteers will divide into the two groups and then separate into different rooms, if possible. At that point, they will be given instruction sheets. Neither team can have access to the other's instructions. After dividing the roles, the teams should meet for 10 to 15 minutes to develop their negotiation strategies based on their instructions.

3. While the teams are preparing, the room will be set up using a rectangular table with four seats on each side. The Japanese side will have three chairs at the table with one chair set up behind the three. The American side of the table will have four chairs side by side.

4. Following these preparations, the Japanese team will be brought in, so they may greet the Americans when they arrive. At this point, the Americans will be brought in and the role play begins. Time for the negotiations should be 20 to 30 minutes. The rest of the class will act as observers and will be expected to provide feedback during the discussion phase.

5. When the negotiations are completed, the student participants from both sides and the observers will complete their feedback questionnaires. Class discussion of the feedback questions will follow.

Feedback Questions for the Japanese Team

1. What was your biggest frustration during the negotiations?
2. What would you say the goal of the American team was?
3. What role (e.g., decider, influencer, etc.) did each member of the American team play?

   Mr. Jones
   Mr./Ms. Smith
   Mr./Ms. Nelson
   Mr./Ms. Frost

4. How would you rate the success of each of the American team members in identifying your team's needs and appealing to them?

   Mr./Ms. Jones, Vice President and Team Leader
   Mr./Ms. Smith, Manufacturing Engineer

   Mr./Ms. Nelson, Marketing Analyst
   Mr./Ms. Frost, Account Executive

5. What strategy should the American team have taken?

Feedback Questions for the American Team

1. What was your biggest frustration during the negotiations?
2. What would you say the goal of the Japanese team was?
3. How would you rate the success of each of the American team members?

   Mr. Jones, Vice President and Team Leader
   Mr./Ms. Smith, Manufacturing Engineer
   Mr./Ms. Nelson, Marketing Analyst
   Mr./Ms. Frost, Account Executive

4. What would you say the goal of the American team was?
5. What role (e.g., decider, influencer, etc.) did each member of the Japanese team play?

   Mr. Ozaka
   Mr. Nishimuro
   Mr. Sheno
   Mr. Kawazaka

6. What strategy should the American team have taken?

Feedback Questions for the Observers

1. What was your biggest frustration during the negotiations?
2. What would you say the goal of the Japanese team was?
3. How would you rate the success of each of the American team members?

   Mr./Ms. Jones, Vice President and Team Leader
   Mr./Ms. Smith, Manufacturing Engineer
   Mr./Ms. Nelson, Marketing Analyst
   Mr./Ms. Frost, Account Executive

4. What would you say the goal of the American team was?
5. What role (e.g., decider, influencer, etc.) did each member of the Japanese team play?

   Mr. Ozaka
   Mr. Nishimuro
   Mr. Sheno
   Mr. Kawazaka

6. What strategy should the American team have taken?

Note: Instructions for this exercise will be given by your professor, from the Instructor's Manual.

Source: E. A. Diodati, in C. Harvey and M. J. Allard, *Understanding Diversity* (New York: HarperCollins Publishers, 1995). Used with permission.

Internet Resources

Visit the Deresky Companion Website at www.pearsonhighered.com/deresky for this chapter's Internet resources.

CASE STUDY

Facebook's Continued Negotiations in China[1]

We continue to evaluate entering China. . . . However, this market has substantial legal and regulatory complexities that have prevented our entry into China to date.[2]

As Facebook filed for its IPO (initial public offering—symbol FB) on the stock market in February 2012 (from which the above quote was taken), investors questioned the company's ability to negotiate further expansion overseas to justify its goal of $100 billion market value. As of that time, Facebook had 845 million users—making it the largest institution of all time; if it were a country it would be the world's third most populous country. Of Facebook's users, 80 percent are overseas; however, since six out of ten Internet users in the U.S. and Canada are Facebook's "friends," most of the company's growth must come from other countries. To date, the company's progress overseas has been impressive, although those markets are far less profitable than the home market.

Facebook had 37 million monthly active users in Brazil, a nearly 300 percent increase from the year earlier. In India, the company had 46 million active users, 132 percent more than in 2010. By comparison, Facebook had 161 million active users in the United States, a 16 percent increase from the previous year.[3]

The New York Times, February 1, 2012.

However, negotiations have been thwarted in accessing some important large markets such as China. This has led observers to comment that, as indicated in the company's IPO filing, Facebook's Asia strategy is India, Japan, and South Korea, because Internet censorship in China has left the company with near zero penetration. The Chinese government bars its citizens from direct access to Facebook; instead people are steered toward censored, home-grown social networks like Renren and Sina.

Government agencies in China would probably want not only to censor postings but to have access to personal data posted by Chinese citizens. Much of the population can't afford the products and services needed for Facebook, including broadband Internet access, a personal computer, or a smartphone, Agrawal said.[4]

The Boston Globe, February 6, 2012.

It's clear that Facebook's founder, Mark Zuckerberg, who is learning Mandarin and has made trips to China, is going to continue negotiations to pursue the Chinese market, saying that "We continue to evaluate entering China ... However, this market has substantial legal and regulatory complexities that have prevented our entry into China to date. If we fail to deploy or manage our operations in international markets successfully, our business may suffer."[5] Local competitors in China are Renren Inc. and Sina Corp., which runs a popular Twitter-like microblogging service called Weibo.

While other Internet companies such as Google have tried to negotiate a compromise with the Chinese government, Facebook executives are clearly concerned about the prospect of citizens giving up their personal details to the government authorities, not knowing how that information might be used.

Some progress has been made. In April 2011, after several meetings between Facebook Chief Executive Officer Mark Zuckerberg and Baidu CEO Robin Li, Facebook signed an agreement with Baidu; however, the China website won't be integrated with Facebook's international service, and the start date was not confirmed. Facebook executives have had a number of meetings to negotiate agreements with various partners in China to enter the market, stating that "We are currently studying and learning about China, as part of evaluating any possible approaches that could benefit our users, developers and advertisers."[6]

In 2010 Google withdrew its search engine from China amid protests in the West about allowing content censoring. Websites such as Facebook, Twitter Inc., and Google's YouTube are blocked in China because they don't follow the government's self-censorship rules. China bans anything critical of the government and any pornography or gambling.

Clearly, Zuckerberg is planning to continue negotiations in China, but, as acknowledged in the IPO filing, "We do not know if we will be able to find an approach to managing content and information that will be acceptable to us and to the Chinese government."[7] Meanwhile, Facebook has opened a sales office in Hong Kong to give the company ready access to the 1 billion person–strong market if that ever changes.

Case Questions

1. You are probably a Facebook "friend." What is your opinion about how it is used in your country?
2. Discuss the company's approach to global expansion.
3. Do you think Facebook should operate in China even if it means complying with the restrictions there?

References

1. Hiawatha Bray, "Overseas growth challenges Facebook: Culture, politics make international future uncertain," *Boston Globe*, February 6, 2012: B.8; Jenna Wortham, "Facebook's Filing: The Highlights," *The New York Times*, February 1, 2012; Yun-Hee Kim, "Facebook's Asia Strategy? India, Japan, South Korea," *Bloomberg Businessweek Deal Journal*, February 1, 2012; Shira Ovide, "Facebook IPO: The Company Still Has Hopes for China," *Bloomberg News*, February 2, 2012; Alexandra Stevenson, "Facebook in Hong Kong: Closer to China," www.ft.com, February 9, 2011; Mark Lee, "Facebook Reaches Deal for China Site with Baidu, Sohu Reports," *Bloomberg News,* April 11, 2011.
2. *Deal Journal, 2012*, quoting from Facebook's IPO Filing.
3. www.nytimes.com, 2012.
4. *Boston Globe*, 2012.
5. *Deal Journal*, 2012.
6. Lee, 2011.
7. *Bloomberg News*, February 2, 2012.

PART II: COMPREHENSIVE CASES

Case 3 *Google's Orkut in Brazil: What's So Social about It?*

Nicole Wong, Google Inc.'s Associate General Counsel made it quite clear that Google's position was to balance the interests of users with the request from the authorities in Brazil to cooperate in their criminal investigation.

I lose sleep thinking about the gold mine that Orkut could represent."[1]

–ALEXANDRE HOHAGEN,
Head of Google's Brazil Office.

Orkut, the social networking site of Google, the U.S.-based search engine company, had 51.7 million unique visitors in June 2011. This was greatly because Orkut was immensely popular in Latin America, particularly in Brazil—outranking even Google's own Brazilian search engine version (google.br).

But there was a darker side to this popularity. There were allegations that Orkut was being used for Internet trafficking, pedophilia, and child pornography. In 2007, advertisers had begun to withdraw their ads from Google sites following reports that the ads were appearing alongside illegal content on Orkut. Google's general director in Brazil, Alexandre Hohagen (Hohagen), was facing criminal contempt charges for refusing to turn over Orkut users' data to the police. Google was left grappling with how best to combine the interests of its users, advertisers, and the authorities, while making sure that the revenues kept flowing in.

SOCIAL NETWORKING PHENOMENON

ComScore Media Matrix's survey in July 2007 showed how fast the social networking phenomenon was catching on. All social networking sites had seen an increase in the number of visitors from the previous year. In all the cases, the increase was significant and the number of visitors to some sites had risen manifold (*Exhibit I*).

Social networking sites are web-based services that first ask users to register and then become members. Users do this by filling out online forms about their age, location, hobbies, etc. They can even upload their photos, change the way their profile appears, and add multimedia content. They can then connect with other users and stay in touch.

This case study was written by Shanul Jain, under the direction of R Muthukumar, IBSCDC. It is intended to be used as the basis for class discussion rather than to illustrate either effective or ineffective handling of a management situation. The case was compiled from published sources. © 2011, IBSCDC.

SixDegrees.com, launched in 1997, was the first site recognized as a social network. It initially allowed users to create profiles and list their friends and later allowed surfing of friends' lists. From 1997 to 2001, there were a number of sites that had some features of social networking (*Exhibit II*). The surge in social networking came with the launch of Friendster in 2002. Through word-of-mouth, the number of users on the site soon grew to 300,000. However, the site was ill-equipped to deal with its mounting popularity and it began encountering technical and social difficulties. Its servers proved inadequate to handle the upsurge in the number of users. To add to its woes, its credibility came under attack after a number of people were reported to have created fake profiles. Its popularity began to wane in the U.S., but it skyrocketed in the Philippines, Malaysia, and Indonesia.

Soon after, many social networking sites were launched. Most tried to replicate Friendster's early success or targeted specific demographics. As the social media and user-generated content phenomenon grew, websites focused on media sharing began implementing social networking features and became social networking sites themselves. These included Flickr, a photo-sharing site, and Last.FM, a music site.

MySpace, launched in 2003, sought to attract Friendster users after rumors began making the rounds that Friendster would soon adopt a fee-based system. MySpace grew rapidly, capitalizing on the rumor. It welcomed bands that had been shunned by Friendster. It created a symbiotic relationship between friends and bands. Bands wanted to contact fans, while fans desired attention from their favorite bands. It also differentiated itself by regularly adding features based on user demand and allowing users to personalize their pages. With more teenagers starting to join the site, it changed its policy to allow minors to become members. In 2005, News Corporation, owned by Rupert Murdoch, purchased MySpace.

In 2004, a Harvard student, Mark Zuckerberg, started Facebook as a Harvard-only social networking site. To join, a user had to have a harvard.edu e-mail address. In 2005, however, Facebook was thrown open to anyone above age 13. In May 2007, Facebook launched the Facebook Platform, which provided a framework for developers to create applications that would interact with core Facebook features. At the event called "F8," companies such as Microsoft and the Washington Post Co. were among the 65 participants who launched 85 new

---

[1] Regalado, Antonio and Delaney, Kevin J., "Google Under Fire Over a Controversial Site," *The Wall Street Journal*, October 19, 2007

EXHIBIT I Worldwide Growth of Selected Social Networking Sites (2004–2011)

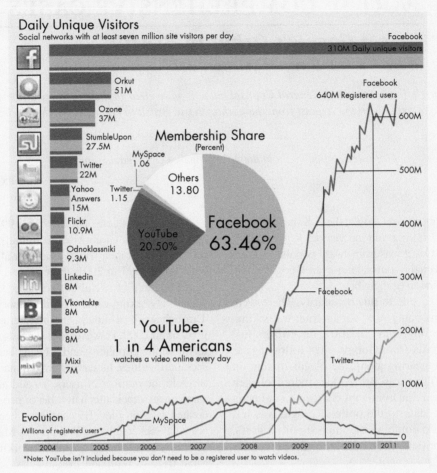

Source: Jenise Uehara Henrikson, "The Growth of Social Media: An Infographic," http://www.searchenginejournal.com/the-growth-of-social-media-an-infographic/32788/, August 30, 2011.

Facebook applications. In October 2007, Microsoft bought a 1.6% stake in the company for $240 million. Microsoft already had an agreement to place banner ads on Facebook in the U.S. through 2011; this deal allowed it to put up ads outside the U.S. as well.

There were a number of social networking sites that sought narrower audiences. There were sites that restricted access to appear niche and selective. There were also activity-centered sites like CouchSurfing, as well as affiliation-focused ones such as MyChurch. They were limited by their target demographic and were smaller.

Start-up social networking sites, including SixDegrees .com, had buckled due to the lack of a sustainable model. However, the growth they had shown prompted many corporations to invest time and money in creating, purchasing, promoting and advertising. The Internet had three proven advertising categories. There were "display" or banner ads in the form of graphical boxes or embedded videos on web pages; classified ads that were postings on certain sites; and search advertising—which was the largest category. Search advertising was popular because it allowed marketers to target consumers who were searching for a product or service. With the popularity of

blogs and social networking sites, the marketers were looking at opportunities in user-generated content, and the idea of targeting caught on. Brands also started profile pages on social networks and accepted friend requests. Warner Bros., a Hollywood studio, for example, had a MySpace page for *300*, its film about Spartan warriors. It signed up some 200,000 friends, who watched trailers, talked the film up before its release, and counted down toward its DVD release.[2] A report by eMarketer, an Internet and emerging technologies research and analysis company, estimated that worldwide, social network advertising would reach nearly $6 billion by 2011 (*Exhibit III*).

However, the nature and popularity of networking sites both enabled and encouraged illegal activities such as child pornography, pedophilia, etc. The social networking companies reacted with remedial measures. In 2006, Facebook, after being accused of being slow to respond to complaints, promised to answer user complaints about pornography or harassment within 24 hours. MySpace, after facing similar complaints, ensured that each of the 8 million pictures uploaded to its site

[2] "Word of Mouse," http://www.economist.com/business/displaystory .cfm?story_id=10102992, November 8, 2007.

EXHIBIT II   **Launch Dates of Major Social Networking Sites**

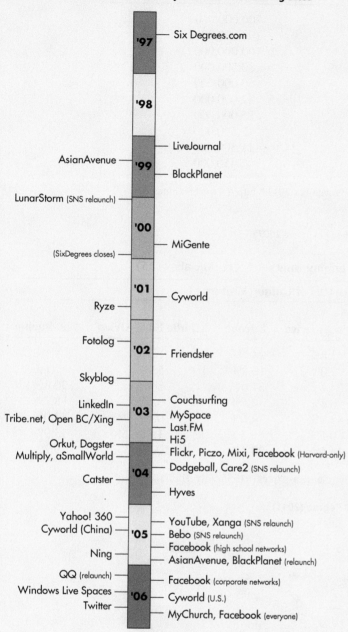

'97 — Six Degrees.com

'98

AsianAvenue — '99 — LiveJournal — BlackPlanet

LunarStorm (SNS relaunch) —

'00 — MiGente

(SixDegrees closes) —

'01 — Cyworld

Ryze —

Fotolog — '02 — Friendster

Skyblog —

LinkedIn — Couchsurfing
Tribe.net, Open BC/Xing — '03 — MySpace — Last.FM — Hi5

Orkut, Dogster — Flickr, Piczo, Mixi, Facebook (Harvard-only)
Multiply, aSmallWorld — Dodgeball, Care2 (SNS relaunch)

Catster — '04 — Hyves

Yahoo! 360 — YouTube, Xanga (SNS relaunch)
Cyworld (China) — '05 — Bebo (SNS relaunch) — Facebook (high school networks) — AsianAvenue, BlackPlanet (relaunch)

Ning —

QQ (relaunch) — Facebook (corporate networks)
Windows Live Spaces — '06 — Cyworld (U.S.)
Twitter — MyChurch, Facebook (everyone)

Source: Boyd M. Danah and Ellison B. Nicole, "Social Network Sites: Definition, History, and Scholarship," http://jcmc.indiana.edu/vol13/issue1/boyd.ellison.html, 2007.

every day was reviewed at least once by someone. The program cost the company millions of dollars a year. MySpace also restricted access to minors and hired many specialists to monitor the site. Microsoft worked with the UK Child Exploitation and Online Protection Center to protect Windows Live Messenger's users who could report directly to authorities about pedophiles in chat rooms.

Google jumped into the social networking arena with the launch of its site Orkut, named after Google engineer and site creator Orkut Büyükkökten, in January 2004. The site was open to users at least 18 years old. Orkut allowed many features, the prime among them being that users could form communities based on shared and common interests.

The site did not find many takers in North America but it became a hit in Brazil, quickly winning millions of users. This big popularity in Brazil made Orkut rank among the top 8 popular websites, alongside heavyweights like MySpace and Facebook (*Exhibit IV*).

ORKUT IN BRAZIL

"Orkut is part of the lives of more than half our Internet users, and an important part of our Internet history."[3]

–DANIEL DUENDE,
A Brazilian tech blogger.

Orkut was such a hit in Brazil that, of the 35 million Brazilian Internet users, nearly 25 million visited the site. Later on, a surge in traffic from Asia-Pacific also fueled growth (*Exhibits V(a)* and *V(b)*). In February 2005, Google made a version of the site available in Portuguese, Brazil's official language. This was the second version to be launched after the English one. The same year in June, Google created a subsidiary in Brazil—Google Brazil Internet Ltd. Orkut's megahit in Brazil had its downside, with many English speakers complaining about Portuguese-language spam and also that English was not the dominant language on the site. So successful was the Orkut model, however, that local Brazilian portals also created their own versions.

[3] Maderazo, Jennifer Woodard, "Orkut, Friendster Get Second Chance Overseas," http://www.pbs.org/mediashift/2007/06/try_try_againorkut_friendster.html, June 15th 2007

EXHIBIT III   **Worldwide Online Social Network Advertising Spending, 2008–2012 (millions)**

	2008	**2009**	**2010**	**2011**	**2012**
U.S.	$1.17	$1.43	$1.99	$3.08	$3.93
Worldwide	$1.995	$2.18	NA	$5.97	NA

Note: Definition includes general social networking sites where social networking is the primary activity; social network offerings from portals such as Google, Yahoo!, and MSN; niche social networks devoted to a specific hobby or interest; and marketer-sponsored social networks that are either stand-alone sites or part of a larger marketer site; in all cases, figures include online advertising spending as well as site or profile page development costs.
Source: Compiled from various sources.

Rank	Site	Estimated Unique Monthly Visitors
1	Facebook.com	700,000,000
2	twitter.com	200,000,000
3	linkedin.com	100,000,000
4	myspace.com	80,500,000
5	Ning.com	60,000,000
6	Google Plus	32,000,000
7	Tagged	25,000,000
8	Orkut	15,500,000
9	Hi5	11,500,000
10	myyearbook	7,450,000

Source: "Top 15 Most Popular Social Networking Sites November 2011," http://www.ebizmba.com/articles/social-networking-websites, November 8, 2011.

EXHIBIT V(A) Visits to Selected Social Networking Sites by Worldwide Region (June 2007)

Social Networking Site	Total Worldwide Home/Work Locations among Internet Users (age above 15)					
	Share (%) of Unique Visitors					
	Worldwide	North America	Latin America	Europe	Middle East-Africa	Asia-Pacific
MySpace	100.0%	62.1%	3.8%	24.7%	1.3%	8.1%
Facebook	100.0%	68.4%	2.0%	16.8%	5.7%	7.1%
Hi5	100.0%	15.3%	24.1%	31.0%	8.7%	20.8%
Friendster	100.0%	7.7%	0.4%	2.5%	0.8%	88.7%
Orkut	100.0%	2.9%	48.9%	4.6%	0.6%	43.0%
Bebo	100.0%	21.8%	0.5%	62.5%	1.3%	13.9%
Tagged	100.0%	22.7%	14.6%	23.4%	10.0%	29.2%

Source: "Social Networking Goes Global," http://www.comscore.com/press/release.asp?press=1555, July 31, 2007.

EXHIBIT V(B) Visits to Selected Social Networking Sites by Worldwide Region (2011)

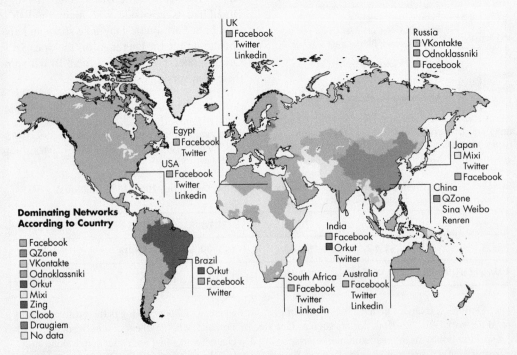

Source: Jenise Uehara Henrikson, "The Growth of Social Media: An Infographic," http://www.searchenginejournal.com/the-growth-of-social-media-an-infographic/32788/, August 30, 2011.

Brazil, the biggest Latin American country, boasts of more than 50% of all Internet users in Latin America. The country, after almost 20 years of military dictatorship, saw the re-establishment of democracy in 1985. Brazil is home to a variety of cultures and ethnicities ranging from the Native Americans, Africans, to Europeans. It also has one of the world's highest levels of socio-economic inequality. More than 80% of Brazilians are concentrated in urban areas, where many live in *favelas* (shantytowns) with inadequate water supply, health facilities, and educational opportunities. These *favelas* are crime-rich, with armed conflicts between the police and different drug gangs being common. Brazil is beset with mayhem including police and prison violence, torture, and extra-judicial killings. Ethnic tensions and a wide gap between the wealthy and the poor have served to escalate crimes. The violence is the criminal underground's challenge to the Brazilian government. Over time, a virtual crime-lush *favela* has come up: the Internet.

Brazil started getting wired in 1988. In May 1995, the Department of Communications and the Department of Science and Technology published a decree creating private-access providers, thus allowing the commercial operation of the Internet. The privatization of telecommunications resulted in a rise in access to the Internet. The use of the Internet surged through Brazilian society and by 1999, it had the third highest number of Internet users in the Americas after the U.S. and Canada.

Brazilians were passionate about the Internet and all the social media applications that it made possible. They were also sensitive to American dominance of the Internet. In 2005, the country joined China in a bid to wrest control from the U.S. of the Internet's domain-name system—the management of suffixes such as ".com" and ".net" that help route Internet traffic. Though there was a surge in Internet activity in the country, there were few laws and limited resources to govern its rapid growth.

Internet laws were not well-defined or developed. With the crackdown in Eastern Europe and the U.S. on illegal activities over the Net, Latin America became a haven for crimes being committed online. The gaps in legislation in Latin American countries only encouraged their proliferation. On the lack of harmonization between the laws of different countries, Thiago Tavares Nunes de Oliveira (Tavares), founder of SaferNet, an NGO tracking Internet crime in Brazil, noted, "There's no co-operation network, policy integration, or strong social movement. No Latin American country has created a plan of action specifically to fight crimes like pedophilia and racism on the Internet."[4]

According to the Brazilian Federal Police, out of every group of 10 hackers worldwide, 8 were probably from Brazil, and almost two-thirds of all pedophilia pages on the Internet originated in Brazil.[5]

A federal appeals court in Brazil ruled that Internet crimes were federal offenses.[6] Finding criminals on the Internet, however, was not easy. Paulo Quintiliano, a criminal expert, commenting on what had caused the burgeoning of the problem, remarked, "Sometimes information can be stored abroad and we have to rely on international cooperation."[7]

Like in Europe, the laws in Latin America permitted prosecution for hate speeches. Brazilian law did not offer Internet companies immunity for defamation-related claims. In 2005, the Brazilian Association of Internet Service Providers (ABRANET), representing 300 companies including Microsoft Brazil, signed an agreement to facilitate investigations into child pornography, racism, and hate mongering. This included willingness on the part of the Internet providers to hand over user information when requested by the police or the judiciary, as well as to store data on clients for a longer period of time.

Orkut came to Brazil at a time when blogs and photologs had proved hugely successful. It served as an answer to the question "What's next on the Internet?" Besides, it came from Google's stable, which had the broad approval of the Brazilians, and was "invite-only" like Gmail, another big hit at that time. Friendster was already there in Brazil, but was not so popular. Brazilians were known to be incredibly community-oriented and tended to associate with groups; they continuously referred to how they were Heavy Metal fans, Evangelical Christians, Sambistas, Macumberos, etc. Analysts put down Orkut's success in Brazil to reasons as wide-ranging as Orkut being easy to pronounce and sounding like *Yakult*, a popular Japanese yogurt drink that all kids in Brazil had, to Orkut's color scheme being the same as that of the Brazilian Football World Cup team. Orkut was so embedded in Brazilian culture that it even inspired a song called *I'm going to delete you from my Orkut*. The song composed by an Orkut user, quickly made its way through the Orkut communities, and soon across Brazil. The fact that Orkut lacked advertising only added to its appeal.

In Brazil, Orkut became a reflection of all the contrasts in Brazilian society. Communities were built around such themes as football, love, and overcoming injustice. It also became a paradise for anti-socials, who formed communities of Neo-Nazis, organized gangs, and pedophiles. Almost 1.3 million Internet users in Brazil were children or adolescents who surfed the Internet from their homes. Out of these, 53% visited social networking and discussion sites.[8] News first started appearing about the violations of human rights on Orkut in September 2004. In 2005, Brazilian police arrested a gang of drug dealers who were using Orkut to sell Ecstasy and marijuana. The criminals had used Orkut to establish a members-only group dedicated to drug dealing, and then traded messages to pitch and purchase the goods. In July 2005, there was news reporting the distribution, in large scale, of pornographic images involving children and adolescents on Orkut.

---

[4] "Latin America: Weak laws create cyber paradise for pedophiles," http://www.safernet.org.br/twiki/bin/view/SaferNet/Noticia20071116141115, November 16, 2007.

[5] "(ISN) 80% of World's Online Hackers and Pedophiles from Brazil," http://www.mail-archive.com/isn@attrition.org/msg03342.html, September 14, 2004.

[6] Brazil is a federal republic in which jurisdiction over safety matters is shared by federal, state, and local authorities.

[7] "(ISN) 80% of World's Online Hackers and Pedophiles from Brazil," op. cit.

[8] "Latin America: Weak laws create cyber paradise for pedophiles," op. cit.

THE BACKLASH

"I don't think a single tribunal would be able to cope with the cultural diversity of the whole of humanity [that is] present on the Internet."[9]

–THIAGO TAVARES,
a Professor and Founder of SaferNet.

The illegal content on Orkut drew the attention of Tavares, a professor at the Catholic University of Salvador. In 2004, he had been given a small grant to track human-rights violations on the Internet. The NGO—SaferNet—that he created in 2005 allowed users to report online crimes via its website. Soon complaints started flooding in and the count of accusations against Orkut kept increasing, reaching 1,582 by December 2005.

This prompted Tavares to request a meeting with Hohagen. Tavares claimed that his requests were repeatedly ignored. This led to his asking for the intervention of the Brazilian Association of Internet Service Providers. Attempts to make contact with Hohagen were again ignored.

As there was no response from Google's Brazil office till February 2006, civil and criminal proceedings were formalized against it. Brazil's Public Attorney's Office filed two lawsuits against Google: a civil one for loss of representativeness and compensation for collective moral damages; and a criminal one for protecting criminals and refusing to comply. Google was asked to give the Internet Protocol (IP) information, access logs, and registration details of users committing crimes of pedophilia and racism on Orkut.

However, the company refused to hand over the data, citing that since the data were stored on servers in the U.S., they were not directly subject to Brazilian law. The U.S. laws included strict protection of users' private data and Google could not reveal private communications without the express consent of the user. It could do so only in limited conditions and when ordered by a U.S. judge. Moreover, some crimes like racist speeches were not recognized as such in the U.S. The U.S. constitution allowed prosecution for hate crimes but not for hate speeches. Tavares claimed that Yahoo! and Microsoft had removed material that had been termed offensive and had even promised to hold copies for authorities. Google, however, resisted. Tavares remarked, "Google's future in Brazil is under threat. If they continue refusing to comply with Brazilian justice then they could be forced to leave the country. We don't want that to happen but we were given no choice. Instead of sitting down and trying to resolve the situation they opted for conflict. They need to start taking responsibility."[10]

Google, by entrusting its Brazilian legal crisis to an outside lawyer, Durval de Noronha Goyos Jr., only added fuel to the fire. The lawyer accused the prosecution of not presenting the demands to Google's California office, and stated that the company would not follow Brazilian but U.S. laws. Company officials were worried that if they handed over the data without demanding proper paperwork, they might face similar demands from less democratic governments elsewhere. Brazilian authorities were told that if they rewrote the summons to Google Inc. rather than Google Brazil, they would take the appropriate action. Google's legal director Nicole Wong at one point threatened to even block the access of Brazilians to Orkut, based on the allegation that they were using the service unduly. However, Sergio Gardenghi Suiama (Suiama), the prosecutor handling the civil lawsuit against Google in Brazil, argued, "We argue that if the crimes were committed by Brazilians, as there is no doubt they were, it is Brazilian law that applies, and Google's subsidiary in Brazil must answer to the authorities here."[11] Human rights activists accused Google of double standards, saying the company had earlier handed over information to avoid paying damages to a São Paulo socialite, who sued Google after someone created a false profile in her name.

Google's stand on releasing data was reminiscent of its approach in China. There, on the grounds that its servers were not on Chinese soil and so it need not follow the censorship requirements, the company had resisted censoring the contents of its site. However, after facing continuing problems of delay in loading and sometimes even a total block, it had finally bowed and started operations in China with a censored version. Yahoo! in China, however, had handed over user information to the authorities; this had subsequently resulted in the jailing of two Chinese Internet dissidents.[12] Even Microsoft, on the demand by Chinese authorities, had deleted the writings of a blogger named Zhao Jing. Similarly, in the U.S., the Department of Justice had demanded that Google turn over a random sampling of 1 million URLs—web addresses—from its index and another 1 million search queries from a 1-week period. The agency hoped to use the data to help it make a case that filtering software was ineffective in fighting online porn. Internet companies like Yahoo!, Microsoft, and AOL had complied. Google, however, dug in its heels and agreed only when the demand was scaled back by authorities.

In 2006 alone, SaferNet passed on more than 100,000 complaints against Orkut to the police. Half of these concerned child pornography and thousands of others concerned hate crimes, violence, or the mistreatment of animals. After waiting two years for Google to comply, a police investigation was requested against Hohagen in August 2006, for disobeying judicial orders. There were also demands for the site to be shut down. Suiama stated, "If they want to do business in Brazil, they must obey the laws here."[13] A court in Brazil gave Google 15 days to hand over the information or face a daily fine of $900,000. The judge in his statement said, "It is peculiar the fact that Google Brazil did not follow the Brazilian Federal Justice orders, under the argument that it is just an office of marketing and sales."[14] He added that Google's posture was

---

[9] "Latin America: Weak laws create cyber paradise for pedophiles," op. cit.

[10] "Google's Brazil Headache," op. cit.

[11] "Latin America: Weak laws create cyber paradise for pedophiles," op. cit.

[12] Yahoo gave information to Chinese authorities that led to the jailing of two journalists, Shi Tao and Wang Xiaoning. In 2007, Yahoo! settled law suits brought on by their families and the company's CEO, Jerry Yang apologized.

[13] "Google under Fire over a Controversial Site," op. cit.

[14] "Crimes on Orkut: understand the chronological evolution of the case that defies the institutions of the Democratic Judicial State in Brazil," http://www.safernet.com.br/twiki/pub/Colaborar/Traduzindo/CrimesOnOrkutEn.txt, September 14, 2006

EXHIBIT VI   Google's Ad System

Google's initial business model was of licensing its search engine services to other websites. In the first quarter of 2000, it introduced its first advertising program—Premium Sponsorships. Through its direct sales force, it allowed advertisers to place text-based ads on its websites targeted at a user's search queries. Advertisers paid based on the number of times their ads were displayed on the user's search-results pages. It launched AdWords in the fourth quarter of 2000, which enabled advertisers to place targeted text-based ads on Google's sites. Here, advertisers paid on a cost-per-click basis—only when a user clicked on the ads. Then in the first quarter of 2002, Google released its AdSense service that distributed relevant ads from advertisers to be displayed alongside search results on the Google Network member's sites. The Google Network was a large group of websites and other products, such as email programs and blogs, that had partnered with Google to display AdWords ads.

Google's AdSense was powered by contextual advertising technology. This meant that the content on a site was first scanned. Based on that, the relevant ad was then displayed. Google used the same technology to target content in its other services such as Gmail, its electronic mail; YouTube, its video-sharing service; Orkut; and others. The technology was powered to understand the changes in content and ruled out the need for human intervention.

Source: Compiled by the author.

"comfortable and complacent" as "to sell services in Brazil, Google is present, but to collaborate with the elucidation of crimes, it is not."[15]

Google did not make any money from Orkut. It had no ads, no subscriptions, and no other revenues. It was felt that if the bad publicity along with the fines continued, then officials could be tempted to cut their losses and shut Orkut down.

However, during the same time, Google changed its strategies. It shared data to help identify users accused of taking part in online communities that encouraged racism, pedophilia, and homophobia; and began expediting the removal of illegal content from the Web. Nicole Wong, Google associate general counsel, on Brazil's demand and Google's decision, said, "What they're asking for is not billions of pages. In most cases, it's relatively discrete—small and narrow."[16]

However, legal experts believed that Google had had no choice but to comply with the court order. Marc Rotenberg, executive director of Washington-based Electronic Privacy Information Center, remarked, "From the law enforcement perspective, if the records are in the possession of the business, the business can be compelled to produce them."[17]

FURTHER CHALLENGES

Internet companies like Google and Yahoo! offered search and other services free. Revenues were generated by allowing advertisers to place highly targeted ads on their web properties. Like most Google services, Orkut on inception was ad free. With the popularity of social networking sites, as well as Orkut's popularity, the company decided to monetize the site. The local subsidiary it had set up to sell online advertising in Brazil included Orkut as part of the strategy. Google, after testing advertising on Orkut in India and the U.S., extended it to Brazil in 2007.

Soon though, critics in Brazil released a report showing ads on Orkut alongside pictures of naked children and abused animals. They stated that Google's ad system could not tell the difference between a site dedicated to pedophilia and one with ordinary content (*Exhibit VI*). So there were ads of a pet-store pitch on a community dedicated to stabbing animals with knives.

Tavares sent an 18-page complaint to Brazil's advertising watchdog, Conar. After an investigation was opened, Google suspended advertising worldwide on Orkut, describing it as part of a test-marketing program involving only 1% of Orkut pages. Google also offered to outfit nonprofits, including SaferNet, with special accounts, so that their complaints about content would receive top priority.

Google's troubles were blamed on the lack of proper control on the subscription process. Though Google specified the minimum age limit as 18, most users of social networks were children below that age.

However, the episode in Brazil had its repercussions. There were concerns that social networks were unreliable advertising vehicles. Advertisers such as liquor maker Diageo PLC of London stopped advertising on all Google properties, after finding out that the ads ran alongside pornographic images on the site. Ads for its brand had appeared on Orkut, where many users were below legal drinking age. Tavares added, "That (advertisers cancelling contracts) was one of the main reasons why Google changed its attitude toward cooperating with Brazilian prosecutors."[18]

On the company's operations in Brazil, Hohagen admitted that Google had not spent enough resources to understand the

[15] Ibid.

[16] Nakashima Ellen, "Google to Give Data to Brazilian Court," http://www.washingtonpost.com/wp-dyn/content/article/2006/09/01/AR2006090100608.html, September 2, 2006

[17] Ibid.

[18] "Latin America: Weak laws create cyber paradise for pedophiles," op. cit.

culture and the country in which it operated and that "we'd do it differently today. The product grew faster than the support. That is a fact."[19]

However, how Google could place ads on its various services was a vexing question. How could the company profit from Orkut and keep increasing revenue from outside the U.S.? How far should the company be willing to compromise with the authorities in handing over user's personal data? How could the company save face from the fallout in Brazil? These were nagging questions that the company needed to answer.

ASSIGNMENT QUESTIONS

1. How do social networking sites work? What has contributed to their immense popularity?

2. Why was Orkut so successful in Brazil? What caused problems later?

3. Why did Google refuse to hand over Orkut user data? How should Internet companies and particularly those with social networking sites decide whether or not to share user information with the legal authorities?

[19] "Google comes under fire in Brazil over its networking site's content," op. cit.

"[. . .] MTV has a penchant for airing controversial material and making a mockery of convention. And of course, it's an American brand. . . . The challenge, therefore, is transforming a notoriously risqué channel into a Middle Eastern-friendly platform for music and creativity without stripping MTV of its edge. It isn't without some irony that a channel known for angering religious, political, and conservative communities is operating in and catering to a region renowned for reacting (and sometimes overreacting) negatively to controversial content."[1]

–DANA EL BALTAJI,
Special Projects Manager, Trends magazine in Dubai, in 2008.

"In many ways (MTV Arabia) is the epitome of our localization strategy. It's a different audience (in the Middle East) but this is what we do—we reflect culture and we respect culture. The programming mix on this one is going to be a little more local than normal."[2]

–WILLIAM H. ROEDY,
Vice Chairman for MTV Networks and President MTVI Network International, in 2007.

A LITMUS TEST FOR MTV'S LOCALIZATION STRATEGY

MTV Networks (MTVN) launched MTV Arabia on November 17, 2007, in partnership with Arabian Television Network[3] (ATN) as part of its global expansion strategy. According to analysts, MTV's presence in the Middle East would provide the region with an international music brand. Until then the Middle East did not have an international music brand though it had clusters of local music channels. On its part, the region promised to offer tremendous growth opportunities to MTVN.

Analysts felt that MTV Arabia was MTVN's most ambitious and challenging venture. The Middle East offered huge growth potential to MTVN given its huge youth populace. However, according to analysts, MTV's success in the Middle East was contingent upon a tactical balancing between delivery of international quality music and the culturally sensitive environment prevalent in the region. Some analysts felt that the channel was well equipped to achieve this considering MTVN's extensive experience in the global market and its ability to provide localized content without diluting what MTV stood for.

Author Information:
This case was written by **Debapratim Purkayastha**, ICMR. It was compiled from published sources, and is intended to be used as a basis for class discussion rather than to illustrate either effective or ineffective handling of a management situation.

To ensure that its programs won over the hearts of the Arabs and adhered to the local taste and culture without diluting MTV's global brand, MTV Arabia designed a much localized Arabic version of its international music and reality shows. In this connection, Patrick Samaha (Samaha), General Manager of MTV Arabia, said, "We've created programs that are an Arabic version of MTV programs. It is the first time that programs like this will really reflect the youth culture here, but we've been mindful all the way about respecting the local culture."[4]

According to the company, the launch of MTV Arabia was also expected to act as a culturally unifying force by propelling Arabic music to the global forefront, and vice versa. While launching MTV Arabia, William H. Roedy, Vice Chairman for MTV Networks and President of MTV International, said, "Tonight's [November 16, 2007] MTV Arabia launch show celebrates one of the most important landmarks in MTV's 25-year history. MTV Arabia will reach the largest potential audience of any MTV channel outside the United States. MTV is proud to celebrate the voice of the Arab youth and through our global network we can showcase what this rich and diverse culture is all about to new audiences around the world."[5]

BACKGROUND NOTE

MTV (short for Music Television), which pioneered the concept of a cable music channel, was launched on August 1, 1981, and marked the commencement of the cable TV revolution. It was promoted by Warner Amex Satellite Entertainment Company, a joint venture between Warner Communications and American Express. In 1984, the company was renamed MTV Networks (MTVN) with its operations confined to the US.

At the time of its launch, the MTV channel primarily catered to those in the 12 to 24 age group, airing heavy-metal and rap music. However, over the years, it also launched many sister channels such as VH-1 (short for Video Hits One) which

[1] Dana El Baltaji, "I Want My MTV," www.arabmediasociety.com, May 11, 2008.

[2] Lynne Roberts, "MTV Set for Middle East Launch," www.arabianbusiness.com, October 17, 2007.

[3] Arabian Television Network (ATN) is a Dubai, United Arab Emirates–based broadcast media company, part of the Arab Media Group's Arabian Broadcasting Network (ABN). ABN is a part of the Arab Media Group (AMG). As of 2007, AMG was the largest media group in the UAE, with approximately 1,500 employees. It was an unit of TECOM Investments that was controlled by Dubai's ruler.

[4] Jolanta Chudy, "MTV's Arab Net Thinking Locally," www.hollywoodreporter.com, November 6, 2007.

[5] "Akon and Ludacris Dazzle the Desert in their Middle East Debuts to Celebrate the Launch of MTV Arabia," www.dubaicityguide.com, November 16, 2007.

was formed in 1985 to play light popular music; Rhythm and Blues (R&B), jazz, country music, and classics targeted at the 18 to 35 age group; and Nickelodeon,[6] which was launched in 1977 keeping children as its target segment. While these sister channels of MTVN continued playing different varieties of music, the core channel MTV began to diversify in 1990. Besides playing music, it also started airing non-music reality shows. *The Real World* and *MTV Fear* were some of the popular reality shows aired. Animated cartoon series were also introduced, the most popular of them being *Beavis and Butthead.*

In 1986, MTVN was acquired by Viacom Inc. (Refer to Exhibit I for a note on Viacom.) Thereafter, in 1987, MTVN launched its first overseas channel in Europe, and this marked the beginning of MTV's global expansion. The international arm of MTVN was known as MTVI. In addition to MTV, MTVI managed a bouquet of channels such as VH-1 and Nickelodeon.

By the mid-1990s MTVI realized that to become a successful brand globally, it had to adapt to local conditions. Hence it adopted a strategy of "Think Globally, Act Locally." Thereafter, MTVI became the first international TV network to offer channels such as MTV Australia, MTV Asia, MTV India, MTV China, MTV Germany, etc. in local languages with localized content.[7] To penetrate any new market, MTVI initially tied up with a local music channel and in the course of time, it acquired the local company in that region. For instance, in the early 2000s, MTVI entered the Australian market by setting up a joint venture between Austereo (a national commercial radio network in the country) and MTVN. Later on, it acquired Austereo to become MTV Australia.

Initially, some analysts were doubtful as to how far MTVN's global expansion would be successful, given the latent and overt anti-American sentiments in various parts of

EXHIBIT I   Note on Viacom Inc.

Viacom was established as a public company in 1971. In 1985, it acquired a 65 percent stake in MTV Networks, which included MTV, VH-1, and Nickelodeon, and purchased the remaining interest in 1986. In 1991, Viacom completed its purchase of MTV Europe by acquiring a 50 percent stake from British Telecommunications and other parties. In 1994, the Viacom Entertainment Group was formed through a merger with Paramount Communications Inc. In 2000, CBS Corporation, a major media network in the U.S., merged with Viacom, as a result of which TNN (re-named as Spike TV in 2003) and CMT (Country Music Television) joined the MTV Networks. The BET (Black Entertainment Television) channel was acquired by Viacom in 2001. In the early 2000s, Viacom launched many channels worldwide under MTV Networks and BET.

In 2005, Viacom Corporation split into Viacom Inc. and CBS Corporation. In 2006, Viacom Inc. was one of the world's leading media companies operating in the Cable and Satellite Television Networks (C&S) and film production divisions.

VIACOM INC. BRANDS*
Cable Networks & Digital Media

• MTV Networks (Comedy Central, CMT, LOGO, MTV, MTV 2, MTV U, MTV Networks Digital Suite, **MTV International**, MTV Networks Online, Nickelodeon, Nick @ Nite, The N, Noggin, Spike, TV Land, VH-1)

• BET Networks presents the best in Black media and entertainment featuring traditional and digital platforms. Brands including BET, BET J, BET Gospel, BET Hip Hop, BET.com, BET Mobile, BET Event Productions, and BET International deliver relevant and insightful content to consumers of Black culture in more than 84 million households.

Entertainment (Film & Music Publishing)
• Paramount Pictures
• Paramount Home Entertainment
• DreamWorks SKG
• Famous Music

*The list is not exhaustive
Source: www.viacom.com

---

[6] Nickelodeon primarily caters to children in age group 7–11, but along with this it also airs weekend programs in TEENick catering to children in age group 12–17 and also weekday morning programs aimed at children in age group 2–6 and a late-night segment known as Nick at Nite aimed at general audiences.

[7] Dirk Smillie, "Tuning in First Global TV Generation," *The Christian Science Monitor,* June 4, 1997.

the world. However, the channel did not face too many difficulties. Commenting on this, Roedy said, "We've had very little resistance once we explain that we're not in the business of exporting American culture."[8] According to some analysts, Roedy was instrumental in taking MTVI across many countries worldwide. To gain an entry into difficult markets such as China, Israel, and Cuba, Roedy even met the political leaders of those countries to explain the network's initiatives to them.

Overall, despite the initial hiccups, the channel's global expansion strategy proved successful. Thus, by following a policy of having a global presence with a local outlook, by mid-2006, MTVI catered to an audience of more than 1 billion and expanded its presence in 179 countries across Europe, Asia, Latin America, and Australia.[9] It operated more than 130 channels in over 25 languages and it comprised MTV Networks Europe (MTVN Europe), MTV Networks Asia-Pacific (MTVN Asia-Pacific), and MTV Networks Latin America (MTVN Latin America). In addition to this, it operated some broadband services and more than 130 websites.[10]

According to analysts, a noteworthy reason behind MTV's global success was that the channel adopted a decentralized structure and gave commercial and creative autonomy to the local staff. This policy of minimal interference in local operations led to innovation and rapid expansion. Commenting on this, Roedy said, "Something we decided early on was to not export just one product for the world but to generate a very different experience for our brands depending on the local cultures."[11]

MTV's impressive growth globally contributed significantly to the revenues of its holding company Viacom over the years and it also became Viacom's core network. As of the end of 2007, MTVI had more than 140 channels around the world catering to a potential 1.5 billion viewers globally.[12] In the U.S. alone, it reached 87.6 million homes.[13] Its Emerging Markets group was the network's fastest growing business segment.[14] For the year ending 2008, Viacom's total revenues (including cable network and entertainment divisions) were US$14,625 million. Out of this, the revenue from Media Network channels (which includes MTVN) was US$8,756 million (Refer to Exhibit II for selected financials of Viacom).

PREPARING FOR THE LAUNCH

With the growing popularity of MTV, there was a mushrooming of many similar channels across the world. Though the Arab media was late in adopting this concept, some European and U.S. channels had started offering such programs in this

EXHIBIT II   Selected Financials of Viacom

(US$, million)	2008	2007	2006
Revenues	14,625	13,423	11,361
Operating Income	2,523	2,936	2,767
Net Earnings	1,251	1,838	1,592
From Media Networks			
Revenue	8,756	8,101	7,241
Operating Income	2,729	3,048	2,904

Source: Adapted from http://www.viacom.com/news/News_Docs/78157ACL.PDF

region, analysts pointed out. In the mid-1990s, some Arab music channels also entered the fray. Some of these channels were influenced by MTV. By the mid-2000s, there were a number of Arab music channels (refer to Exhibit III for a note on major music channels in Saudi Arabia). These channels relied heavily on Arab artists but also aired international numbers by entering into agreements with production houses and other TV networks. MTV was available in the region through a special deal with Showtime Arabia.[15] As part of the deal, Showtime aired Nickelodeon and MTV in English with Arabic subtitles.[16] The channel catered to the middle and upper classes, who had been exposed to the West and had an interest in Western entertainment. Analysts felt that MTV was popular with a section of the audience in the region who were waiting eagerly for its launch there.

The first announcement that MTVI was preparing to launch MTV Arabia came in August 2006. During MTV's 25[17] anniversary of its first US channel, the company said that it was on the lookout for local partners in the Middle East and would provide the audience in the region content that would be very different from that offered by popular Arab music channels. Dean Possenniskie, Vice President and General Manager for Emerging Markets, MTVI, said, "[MTV is] very interested in the [Arab satellite channel] market and realizes how important it is. . . . Hopefully [we] will be in the market in the next 24 months . . . it all depends on finding the right local partners."[18] By the end of the year, it was announced that MTVI would launch the channel in the region in partnership with Arabian Television Network (ATN), which was a part of the Arabian Broadcasting Network (ABN).[19]

MTVI's venturing into the Middle East was a result of the combined efforts of innovative and enthusiastic personalities such as Roedy, Bhavneet Singh,[20] Senior Vice President and

---

[8] Kerry Capell, Catherine Belton, Tom Lowry, Manjeet Kripalani, Brian Bremner, and Dexter Roberts, "MTV's World," *BusinessWeek*, February 18, 2002.

[9] www.viacom.com/cable.jhtml.

[10] MTVI operated more than 130 websites of its international channels while MTVN, totally, operated more than 150 websites, which included online representations of channels broadcast in the US.

[11] Brad Nemer, "How MTV Channels Innovation," *BusinessWeek*, November 6, 2006.

[12] Tamara Walid, "Finally Got My MTV," www.arabianbusiness.com, November 22, 2007.

[13] Ibid.

[14] "Arab Media Group and MTV Networks International to Launch Nickelodeon Arabia in 2008," www.media.ameinfo.com, October 20, 2007.

[15] Showtime Arabia is one of the leading subscription-based television networks in the Middle East. It is partly owned by Viacom.

[16] Zeid Nasser, "Showtime braces for impact of free-to-air MTV Arabia & Arabic Nickelodeon," http://mediame.com, October 16, 2007.

[17] "Arab Satellite TV Channels Rapidly Expanding," www.xrdarabia.org, November 14, 2007.

[18] Faisal Abbas, "MTV Eyes Middle East Market," www.asharq-e.com, August 8, 2006.

[19] "Arabian Television Network Partners with MTV to Launch MTV Arabia," http://mediame.com, December 27, 2006.

[20] On April 23, 2007, Bhavneet Singh was promoted to Senior Vice President and Managing Director of MTVNI's Emerging Markets group.

EXHIBIT III   **Music and Entertainment Channels in Saudi Arabia***

As of early 2008, there are 370 Arabic satellite TV networks broadcasting in the Middle East. This is an increase of 270 percent since 2004.[17] Among these, 56 belong to private companies, 54 are music channels, and 38 are state owned. Most of these are headquartered in United Arab Emirates (22 percent), Saudi Arabia (15 percent), and Egypt (11 percent). In Saudi Arabia alone, there are more than 200 free-to-air satcasters and 50 music channels in the region. Some of the important music and entertainment channels are:

Mazzika, which offers a variety of music and light entertainment programs.

Melody Hits, which is a music channel airing Arabic and international music videos.

MBC, headquartered in Dubai, which is a pan-Arab news and entertainment television channel. MBC 2 is a non-stop premium movie channel. MBC 3 is a children's channel and it broadcasts famous animated kids' shows, including exclusive translated titles and live action and animated feature films. It also airs family shows and family movies for younger audiences as well as the adult audience. MBC 4 broadcasts specifically American programs.

Nojoom, which is a music channel airing Arabic and international music videos.

Rotana TV network, which broadcasts Arabic music and films. It has six channels under its wings—Mousica, Rotana Clip, Rotana Tarab, Rotana Khalijiyya, Rotana Cinema, and Rotana Zaman. The channels are dedicated to Arabic pop music; Arabic classical music; interactive games; Gulf music, cinema, featuring the biggest and latest blockbuster releases; and old classical movies.

Saudi Arabian TV, which features live coverage of Ramadan, Hajj, and Eid prayers. It also shows popular movies and news programs.

Shada channel—a part of the Al Majd Group—which is a channel totally devoted to Islamic songs (Anasheed).

Wanasah TV channel, which broadcasts music videos and some variety programs. All its programs are in Arabic.

Panorama FM, which is a music radio channel in Arabic.

Radio Rotana FM, which broadcasts customized programs and the latest Arabic hits fifteen days ahead of any of its competitors due to an exclusive deal with Rotana Music.

Radio Fann FM, which broadcasts a mix of the latest Arabic, English, and International music hits, along with hourly news broadcasts and various customized programs.

Al-Ikhbariya channel, which broadcasts news and current affairs.

*The list is not exhaustive.
Source: Compiled from various sources.

Managing Director of MTV Networks International MTVNI Emerging Markets group, and Abdullatif Al Sayegh, CEO and Chairman of ABN.

Analysts felt that it would have been very difficult for a Western company like MTVI to venture into the highly regulated and complex business arena of the Middle East on its own. In this regard, Singh said, "A market such as the Middle East, however, also brings a level of complexity in the way business is done and regulatory challenges which mean it takes a western media company a long time to get its head around it."[21] Hence, it entered the Middle East by tying up with a local partner, the Arab Media Group (AMG), an established player in the Arab media industry with eight radio stations and three daily newspapers. The channel MTV Arabia was formed as a result of a licensing arrangement between MTV and AMG. MTV would earn an estimated US$10 million annually in licensing fees from AMG for 10 years.[22]

On the other hand, an alliance with MTV was a winning deal for AMG too as it could access the former's world class resources to enhance its visibility in the Arab media as well as across the globe. "We found it very good to start our TV business with MTV Arabia because it's a great name to start with. Great team, great people; they provided us with a lot of resources. We believe that MTV is the beginning of a new era in television in this part of the world,"[23] said Sayegh.

However, the tie-up with a local partner was not enough to guarantee the success of MTV's launch in the Middle East

[21] Andrew Edgecliffe-Johnson, "MTV Tunes in to a Local Audience," www.us.ft.com, October 26, 2007.

[22] Sarah Raper Larenaudie, "MTV's Arab Prizefight," www.time.com, November 2, 2007.

[23] Tamara Walid, "Finally Got my MTV," www.arabianbusiness.com, November 22, 2007.

given the conflict between the explicit hip-hop music culture portrayed by MTV and the conservative social culture prevalent in the Middle East. Hence, before launching the channel, Samaha conducted an extensive survey of the region to understand what people wanted. The survey team targeted people in the 18–24 age group and travelled around the region to schools and universities canvassing opinions. They also spoke to the elderly and figures of authority to assure them that they were there to entertain people within the limits of Arab traditions and had no intention of showing disrespect to the local culture. On this Samaha commented, "We also spoke to the governments, leaders, and parents and said, 'Don't worry, it will be nice,' so they know what's going on,"[24] said Samaha.

Accordingly, MTV Arabia's programming team decided to air MTVN's globally successful music shows but with a local flavor that would suit the Arab mindset and this laid the foundation for a planned launch of MTV in Arabia. The launch team comprised a mix of Saudis, Palestinians, Emiratis, Iraqis, and Lebanese.[25] "MTV first launched in 1981 when cable television was in its infancy. Since then we've grown into the world's largest TV network by becoming part of the fabric of youth culture, and by respecting audience diversity and different cultures. We're delighted to be launching MTV Arabia and looking forward to working with our partners to provide the best youth programming,"[26] said Singh.

MTV commissioned ad agencies TBWA\Raad and Fortune Promoseven to handle the launch of the channel in the Middle East.[27] "We're targeting normal Arabs. We're not targeting educated, private school people. Those are Arab society's niche. They are not more than 10 percent of the population. We are trying to appeal to the masses,"[28] said Samer Al Marzouqi, channel manager, MTV Arabia.

MTV ENTERS THE MIDDLE EAST

MTV Arabia was considered by experts as the biggest launch in MTVI's history in terms of potential audience at launch.[29] An exclusive, star-studded preview event marked the launch of MTV in the Middle East. The launch featured performances by eminent stars such as Akon, Ludacris, and Karl Wolf along with local hip hop group Desert Heat. The channel was formally launched on November 17, 2007, as a 24-hour, free-to-air television channel, having a target audience in Saudi Arabia, Egypt, United Arab Emirates, Lebanon, Bahrain, Jordan, Kuwait, Oman, Qatar, Yemen, Palestine, and Syria. MTVa.com, an Arabic and English language website, complemented the channel and provided users with a wide range of online community and interactive elements.

In line with its mixed-content strategy, MTV Arabia was to showcase 60 percent international music and 40 percent Arabic music, along with the local version of the channel's popular international non-music shows. About 45 percent of MTV Arabia's content was to be produced locally, with the rest translated. In this regard, Roedy commented, "The key is that the packaging, attitude, and obviously the language, should reflect the country. There is already great music there."[30] The channel's programming was to have a mix of music videos, music-based programming, general lifestyle and animated programs, reality shows, comedy and dramatic series, news specials, interviews, and documentaries. Besides international MTV shows, MTV Arabia was also to design new shows in Arabic to cater to pan-Arab youth audiences.

The company also said that the channel could act as a cultural unifying force in a region known for its political tensions. "The launch of MTV's 60th channel is a chance to correct misconceptions of the region. . . . This part of the world has been associated with stresses and tensions . . . the one thing music can do is act as a unifying cultural force across regions,"[31] Roedy said.

RATIONALE BEHIND THE VENTURE

Favorable demographics had been one of the key rationales behind MTV's commercial launch in the Middle East. About 65 percent of the Arab population consisted of youth under the age of 25, and the launch of MTV Arabia would provide MTV an opportunity to cater to a 190 million audience.[32] Further, though the Arab market was crowded with more than 50 channels, none of them provided a global platform to export the musical talent of the local youth. In this regard, Sayegh said, "Through our network, we now have more platforms to talk to our youth and in ways that have never been done before in the Middle East." Since young people "represent 65% of the population in the Middle East, it's time they were heard. . . . Understanding the next generation is a key priority."[33] MTV being an international brand, it had global reach and this became its key selling proposition for gaining critical mass in the Arab music world. Singh commented, "The fact that there has been no real youth platform, no real brand out there for the kids, makes us [feel] there is an opportunity for us."[34]

Moreover, the Middle East had the potential to offer MTV not only lucrative ad revenues but also numerous media such as mobiles and the Internet to reach its end consumers. Singh said, "There are 37 million mobile subscribers in the wider Middle East, which is phenomenal and the average revenue per user is comparable to Western Europe. We believe that's where the future is—the ability to watch content wherever and however

[24] Matt Pomroy, "The Revolution Will Be Televised," www.arabianbusiness .com, November 15, 2007.

[25] Sarah Raper Larenaudie, "MTV's Arab Prizefight," www.time.com, November 2, 2007.

[26] "Arabian Television Network Partners with MTV to Launch MTV Arabia," www.mediame.com, December 27, 2006.

[27] Iain Akerman, "MTV Hires Two Agencies for Launch of MTV Arabiya," www.brandrepublic.com, May 23, 2007.

[28] Dana El Baltaji, "I Want My MTV," www.arabmediasociety.com, May 2008.

[29] Irene Lew, "MTVNI Ups Singh," www.worldscreen.com, April 30, 2008.

[30] Lynne Roberts, "MTV Set for Middle East Launch," www.arabianbusiness .com, October 17, 2007.

[31] Simeon Kerr and Peter Aspden, "MTV Arabia Beams 'Bling' to Gulf," www.ft.com, November 17, 2007.

[32] "MTV Arabia to launch November 17," www.mediame.com, October 28, 2007.

[33] Ali Jaafar, "MTV Arabia Announces Lineup," www.variety.com, October 28, 2007.

[34] Von Andrew Edgecliffe Johnson, "MTV Tunes in to a Local Audience," www.ftd.de, October 26, 2007.

you want. We want to provide Middle East youth with the opportunity to watch MTV on mobile, on broadband, and on television. We're in discussions with mobile operators in the UAE, Kuwait, and Egypt, to look at how to distribute MTV content. There's been a huge amount of interest in that."[35] Products such as MTV Overdrive, in which the user could download the video at broadband speed, and MTV Flux, in which the online users could create their own TV channel, were expected to help in luring the various Internet service providers in the region to MTV and to become major sources of its revenue.

The existence of various communication media with mass reach was expected to act as a catalyst in augmenting the channel's penetration rate in the Arabic region. In times to come, if the channel validated its success in the Middle East, it would become a major revenue contributor to the MTV group.

KEY CHALLENGES AND SUCCESS STRATEGY

MTV was known for airing sexually explicit and provocative programmes. In other words, it carried with it an image of open Western culture. This explicit Western culture projected by MTV went contrary to the socially conservative culture of the Middle East and could be a key bottleneck to the channel's acceptance in the Arab region, according to analysts. "As a brand, one would think that MTV is the ultimate example of what the religious, conservative cultures of the Middle East would most revile about Western pop culture,"[36] according to leading brand portal Brandchannel.com. Adapting content to suit local tastes too could prove challenging because of many different countries comprising the region. What was acceptable in Dubai may not be acceptable in other parts of Saudi Arabia; what was acceptable in Egypt may not be acceptable in Jeddah (in Saudi Arabia). Analysts felt that the company also had to maintain what it stood for and too much localization could dilute its brand. And to complicate matters, there were strong anti-American sentiments prevalent among a large section of the population. Issues such as the U.S. invasion of Iraq and its support for archenemy Israel had left many Arabs angry.

However, the channel seemed well prepared to overcome such impediments to its growth plans in the Arab market. Though MTV Arabia would air its popular international programs, the network said that music videos and reality shows like "Hip Hop Na" and "Pimp My Ride" would be appropriately edited to ensure their alignment with the cultural ethos prevailing in the Middle East. Commenting on this, Sayegh said, "When we come to people's homes, we want to earn their respect."[37] He explained that there would be "culturally sensitive editors going through content of the programming."[38] In short, the channel expected to respect the local culture without diluting its brand. The channel aimed to prove that despite being a global brand, it would be a channel for the Arabs and made by Arabs—by people just like them.

Analysts said that MTVN's entry into the Middle East, which already had more than 50 local music channels operating, would be marked by stiff competition. In other words, unlike its past forays into India and Europe, MTV would not be entering a virgin music industry when it came to the Middle East. If on the one hand, the existence of a youth population was a business opportunity for MTVN, the same favorable demographic factor had also led to the explosion of dozens of local music channels which had a better understanding of the local audience's taste and could pose a formidable threat to MTVN's growth in the Middle East.

Also channels such as Rotana and Melody, which had already created a niche for themselves in the region, could pose a big competitive threat to MTVN. These channels had been functioning taking into account the tastes of the youth and had been able to attract a huge chunk of their target segment by offering creative concepts like games that allowed viewers to be part of the action from home along with interesting programs, music videos, and various artist albums and concerts. Moreover, some popular Arab music stars had already signed exclusive deals with some local channels. The challenge for MTV would be to not only find the right content but also ways to connect and captivate the Arabian youth, who were habituated to log on to any number of sites and enjoy music channels and videos according to their whims and fancies.

However, MTV Arabia was confident of scoring over its competitors and posting an impressive growth in the years to come. To overcome competition, the channel planned to project itself as unique and different from the existing lot. It proposed to establish itself as a platform wherefrom the Arab youth could voice their local concerns as well as advertise their music talent. For instance, MTV Arabia's flagship show "Hip Hop Na" would audition the best local hip-hop acts in seven different Middle Eastern cities. Thereafter, the winner from each city would get a chance to record a track for a compilation CD produced by FredWreck.[39]

In a nutshell, MTV Arabia would not only provide entertainment but would also leverage on its global reach to advertise the musical talent of Arab youths. In this connection, Samaha said, "We are not only a music channel, we are an entertainment channel where young Arabs will get a voice."[40] He added, "MTV Arabia is a fresh take on MTV the brand, made by Arabs for Arab youth, and is dedicated to their self-expression. We've done extensive research to listen to our audiences, and MTV Arabia will be the first free-to-air channel to celebrate young people and their lives and talents from across this dynamic, vibrant region. We'll also offer audiences a window to the world of global youth culture, bringing top international entertainment to the region and showcasing the Arab region in the context of what's happening around the world. Through MTV's global network, we'll also be able to export Arabic music and culture to the international stage."[41]

[35] "MTV Arabia to Be Launched Soon," www.oceancreep.com, October 8, 2007.

[36] "Will the MTV Brand Change the Middle East?" www.brandchannel.com, December 3, 2007.

[37] "MTV Aims to Win over Middle East," www.cnn.com, November 19, 2007.

[38] "MTV Aims to Win over Middle East," www.cnn.com, November 19, 2007.

[39] FredWreck is a Palestinian-born hip-hop producer who has worked under some of the eminent record labels such as Dogghouse Records, Virgin Records, etc. He has also worked with many distinguished rap stars such as 50 Cent and Snoop Dogg.

[40] "MTV Looks to Conquer Middle East Market," www.aol.in, November 18, 2007.

[41] "MTV Arabia to Launch November 17," www.middleeastevents.com, October 27, 2007.

EXHIBIT IV   Local Productions Aired on MTV Arabia

The flagship local show:

Hip Hop Na, a twelve-episode series which followed auditions to uncover the best local hip hop acts in four different Middle Eastern cities.

Music Related Shows:

Waslati, viewers with webcams become VJs and introduced three of their favorite videos.

Baqbeeq, a music trivia show with a twist, where interesting and hilarious bits of trivia pop up through the most popular videos in the world.

Introducing Block goes behind the scenes in the music industry, with exclusive interviews and performances by the biggest international and Arab stars.

Other Programs:

Al Helm, based on MTV's *MADE* format, follows the journey of aspiring teenagers looking to fulfill their dreams with the help of an MTV Arabia-supplied "coach."

Al Hara tours the Middle East's street scene, and features previously unknown artists displaying innovative talent in skills like beat-boxing, break-dancing, or magic acts. The show is based on MTV's international program format, *Barrio 19*.

In *Akher Takka*, based on MTV's hit format, *Boiling Point*, actors antagonize stressed-out "victims" who can win a cash prize if they manage to keep their cool in extremely annoying situations.

Source: Compiled from various sources.

Also, the programming line-up would feature more local content (refer to Exhibit IV for a note on local production program to be aired on MTV Arabia) in comparison to other localized MTV ventures. There would be a localized version of popular shows such as "MADE" (al Helm) and "Boiling Point" (Akher Takka), which would constitute 40 percent of the content to be aired on MTV Arabia.

The company also said it did not expect anti-American sentiments to affect its chances in the region. MTV said that it expected to win over the target segment with content relevant to them. Moreover, it said that its research before the launch had shown that the majority of respondents thought that MTV was a European or Indian brand.[42]

THE ROAD AHEAD

MTVN catered to a huge market segment of nearly 2 billion people worldwide and was expected to provide a global platform for Arabic music and culture. It had influenced young people all over the world and given them a voice and it would try to do the same in the Middle East. An Arabic category was already added in MTV Europe Music Awards 2007, giving Arabic music the much-needed global platform.

The MTV-AMG combine would not only provide entertainment to the region but would also take up social issues and try to contribute to Arab society, according to the network. In this regard, Sayegh commented, "We are going to encourage education and look for solutions to problems such as unemployment. These are all causes on our agenda."[43]

MTVN, along with AMG, planned to expand its operations in the Middle East. It had already announced the launch of Nickelodeon Arabia in 2008. It would be the first free-to-air channel for children in Arabic. Roedy commented, "Adding the voices of Arab children to our worldwide Nickelodeon family is a significant milestone in our history, and advances our ambitious strategy to build a portfolio of integrated kids businesses across the region. The Middle East is a dynamic, thriving market with vast growth opportunities, and we look forward to launching even more MTVNI brands and businesses through our successful partnership with AMG."[44] Singh added, "The launch of Nickelodeon Arabia is a part of our wider, ongoing multi-platform strategy encompassing consumer products, digital media, hotels and theme parks, which we hope will establish Nickelodeon as the premier destination for kids in the region."[45]

Thus far, MTVN's model of entering a market in partnership with a local partner and following a localization strategy had worked well for the company. Analysts felt that only time would tell whether the company would succeed in the Middle East. But Singh had a rather philosophical take on what success meant. To him, the venture would be a success when people in the smallest cities of the Middle East came up to him and professed their love for MTV. "After all, it's not about how many eyeballs you reach, it's about how many people relate to you," he said.[46]

[42] Adam Sherwin, "MTV Arabia to Feature Regional Talent and Tone Down Network's Risque Content," www.business.timesonline.co.uk, November 16, 2007.

[43] Simeon Kerr and Peter Aspden, "MTV Arabia Beams 'Bling' to Gulf," www.ft.com, November 17, 2007.

[44] "Arab Media Group and MTV Networks International to Launch Nickelodeon Arabia in 2008," www.ameinfo.com, October 20, 2007.

[45] Stuart Kemp, "MTV, Arab Media to Launch Nickelodeon Arabia," www.hollywoodreporter.com, October 17, 2007.

[46] Tamara Walid, "Finally Got My MTV," www.arabianbusiness.com, November 22, 2007.

Case Questions

1. Experts felt that one of the biggest challenges faced by MTV while launching MTV Arabia was the prevalent culture in the Arab world. Discuss the Arab culture. What challenges does the culture pose to MTV?

2. Critically analyze MTV's strategy in the Middle East. Comment on its entry strategy and also its strategy of providing mixed content to the market. Do you think MTV will be able to succeed in this market?

3. Follow up on this case as of the time of your reading it. How successful has MTV been in this market to date? What, if anything, do you think MTV should have done differently? What should the company do now?

References and Suggested Readings

1. Dirk Smillie, "Tuning in First Global TV Generation," *The Christian Science Monitor*, June 4, 1997.

2. Kerry Capell, Catherine Belton, Tom Lowry, Manjeet Kripalani, Brian Bremner, and Dexter Roberts, "MTV's World," *BusinessWeek*, February 18, 2002.

3. "MTV to Launch Music TV Channels in Three Baltic States," www.eubusiness.com, March 6, 2006.

4. Faisal Abbas, "Q&A with Showtime Arabia's CEO Peter Einstein," www.asharq-e.com, June 29, 2006.

5. Faisal Abbas, "MTV Eyes Middle East Market," www.asharq-e.com, August 8, 2006.

6. Brad Nemer, "How MTV Channels Innovation," *BusinessWeek*, November 6, 2006.

7. "Arabian Television Network Partners with MTV to Launch MTV Arabia," www.mediame.com, December 27, 2006.

8. Michael Learmonth, "MTV Maps Mideast Move," www.variety.com, December 27, 2006.

9. Iain Akerman, "MTV Hires Two Agencies for Launch of MTV Arabia," www.brandrepublic.com, May 23, 2007.

10. Salman Dossari, "A Talk with MTV Vice Chairman Bill Roedy," www.asharq-e.com, July 23, 2007.

11. Ali Jaafar, "MTV Arabia Ready to Rock Middle East," www.variety.com, September 25, 2007.

12. "MTV Arabia to Be Launched Soon," www.oceancreep.com, October 8, 2007.

13. Kerry Capell, "The Arab World Wants Its MTV," www.businessweek.com, October 11, 2007.

14. Lynne Roberts, "MTV Set for Middle East launch," www.arabianbusiness.com, October 17, 2007.

15. Stuart Kemp, "MTV, Arab Media to Launch Nickelodeon Arabia," www.hollywoodreporter.com, October 17, 2007.

16. Andrew Edgecliffe Johnson, "MTV Targets Muslim Countries as it Tunes in to Local Audiences," www.theaustralian.news.com, October 18, 2007.

17. "Arab Media Group and MTV Networks International to Launch Nickelodeon Arabia in 2008," www.ameinfo.com, October 20, 2007.

18. Andrew Edgecliffe-Johnson, "MTV Tunes in to a Local Audience," www.ftd.de, October 26, 2007,

19. "MTV Arabia to Launch November 17," www.middle-eastevents.com, October 27, 2007.

20. Ali Jaafar, "MTV Arabia Announces Lineup," www.variety.com, October 28, 2007.

21. "MTV Arabia to Launch November 17," www.mediame.com, October 28, 2007.

22. Irene Lew, "MTV Arabia to Launch in November," www.worldscreen.com, October 29, 2007.

23. Sarah Raper Larenaudie, "MTV's Arab Prizefight," www.time.com, November 2, 2007.

24. Jolanta Chudy, "MTV's Arab Net Thinking Locally," www.hollywoodreporter.com, November 6, 2007.

25. Matt Pomroy, "The Revolution Will Be Televised," www.arabianbusiness.com, November 15, 2007.

26. "Akon and Ludacris Dazzle the Desert in their Middle East Debuts to Celebrate the Launch of MTV Arabia," www.dubaicityguide.com, November 16, 2007.

27. Adam Sherwin, "MTV Arabia to Feature Regional Talent and Tone Down Network's Risque Content," www.timesonline.co.uk, November 16, 2007.

28. Simeon Kerr and Peter Aspden, "MTV Arabia Beams 'Bling' to Gulf," www.ft.com, November 17, 2007.

29. "MTV Launches New Arabic Service," www.news.bbc.co.uk, November 18, 2007.

30. "MTV Looks to Conquer Middle East Market," www.aol.in, November 18, 2007.

31. ""MTV Arabia": Will It Work?" www.scopical.com, November 19, 2007.

32. "MTV Aims to Win over Middle East," www.cnn.com, November 19, 2007.

33. "Muslim Hip-hop Turban Wrote, That's Good," www.reuters.donga.com, November 19, 2007.

34. Barbara Surk, "MTV for Young Arab Is Less Naughty," www.cincinnati.com, November 21, 2007.

35. Barbara Surk, "MTV Launches Arab Music Video Channel," www.theeagle.com, November 22, 2007.

36. Tamara Walid, "Finally Got My MTV," www.arabianbusiness.com, November 22, 2007.

37. "Will the MTV Brand Change the Middle East?" www.brandchannel.com, December 2, 2007.

38. Irene Lew, "MTVNI Ups Singh," www.worldscreen.com, April 30, 2008.

39. Dana El Baltaji, "I Want My MTV," www.arabmediasociety.com, May 11, 2008.

40. www.topfive.com

41. www.en.wikipedia.org

42. www.mtva.com

43. www.viacom.com

3
PART

Formulating and Implementing Strategy for International and Global Operations

PART OUTLINE

Chapter 6
Formulating Strategy

Chapter 7
Implementing Strategy:
Small Businesses, Global Alliances,
Emerging Market Firms

Chapter 8
Organization Structure
and Control Systems

6 Formulating Strategy

OBJECTIVES

1. To understand why companies engage in international business.

2. To learn the steps in global strategic planning and the models available to direct the analysis and decision making involved.

3. To appreciate the techniques of environmental assessment and internal and competitive analysis, and how those results can be used to judge the relative opportunities and threats to be considered in international strategic plans.

4. To become familiar with strategic planning for emerging markets.

5. To profile the types of strategies available to international managers—both on a global level and on the level of specific entry strategies for different markets.

6. To gain insight into the issues managers face when strategic planning for global e-business.

OPENING PROFILE: GLOBAL COMPANIES TAKE ADVANTAGE OF OPPORTUNITIES IN SOUTH AFRICA

Global companies with a presence in South Africa all cite numerous advantages for setting up shop in the country, from low labor costs to excellent infrastructure—and a base to export products internationally. Jim Myers, president of the American Chamber of Commerce in South Africa, says that nearly 50% of the chamber's members are Fortune 500 companies, and that over 90% operate beyond South Africa's borders into southern Africa, sub-Saharan Africa, and across the continent. "The sophisticated business environment of South Africa provides a powerful strategic export and manufacturing platform for achieving global competitive advantage, cost reductions and new market access," says Myers.[1]

Businesses are taking advantage of opportunities because of the legal protection of property, high labor productivity, low tax rates, reasonable regulation, a low level of corruption, and good access to credit, all of which were seen as factors contributing to the country's investment climate. Threats include the low level of skills and education of workers, labor regulation, exchange rate instability, and crime. Nevertheless, the business environment is favorable.

Following are some examples of the many global companies taking advantage of the opportunities and incentives in South Africa.[2] In addition, The 2010 FIFA World Cup generated huge opportunities for businesses, especially emerging entrepreneurs, in South Africa's tourism industry.

ACER AFRICA

In 1995, Acer Africa acquired ownership of a locally based company they had been working with to distribute peripherals and printers since 1980.

MAP 6.1 **South Africa has a population of 50.58 million and consists of 1,221,037 sq. km.**

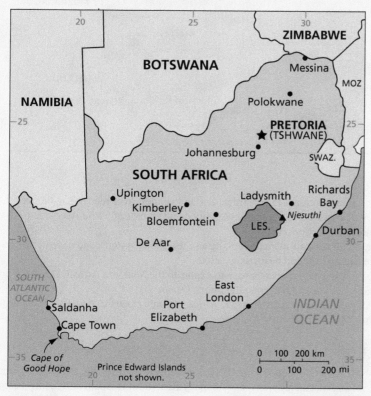

(Continued)

MAP 6.2   **Africa**

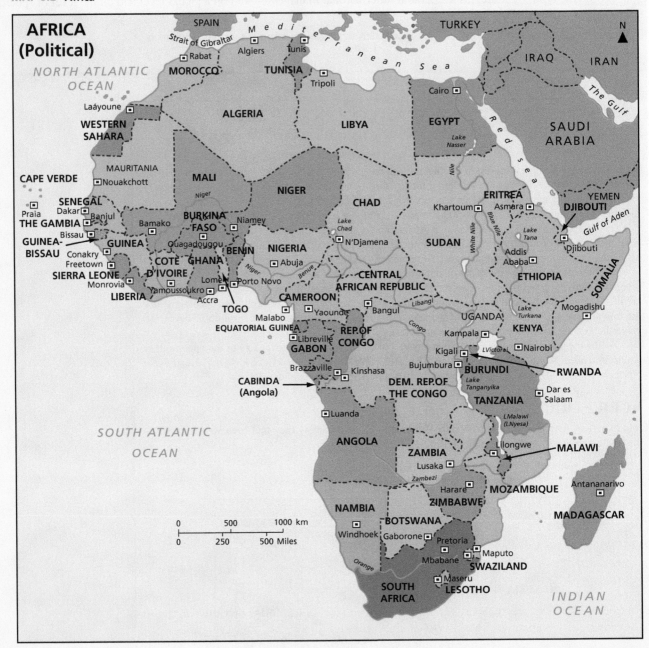

As a leading international PC manufacturer and vendor, Acer recognized the wealth of opportunities in South Africa as local IT companies rapidly came abreast of world standards following the country's first democratic elections in 1994.

For Acer, South Africa's modern banking and telephone systems and exceptional water and power rates made the country a sound business location.

Acer Africa was established as a base to export to the Southern African Development Community (SADC), Angola, and the islands along the Indian Ocean.

"South Africa is the only port of entry to Africa, the only place that one would be able to succeed . . ."
—*Peter Ibbotson (Acer Africa)*

ALCATEL

"Alcatel has built its worldwide reputation on its production. Investing with local partners [electronics group Altech and black empowerment company Rethabile] in South Africa has meant that we have demanded a high standard of technology and capability, and believe that in many respects South Africa compares very favourably with the most advanced countries in the world." —*Bernard Vaslin, executive vice president, Alcatel*

GENERAL ELECTRIC

"The re-entry of General Electric (USA) to the South and southern African market has been exciting and has well exceeded our operating plan expectations.

"South Africa's excellent infrastructure, together with first-class financial, legal and commercial systems, makes this country a natural location to pursue the significant opportunities of South and southern Africa.

"The friendly business environment ensures that we can run our business efficiently, and we look forward to successful and profitable operations in southern Africa that meet our global goals and create wealth for the GE shareholder." —*GE South Africa president Michael C. Hendry*

Source: www.southafrica.info, used with permission.

As the opening profile on South Africa illustrates, companies continue to look for opportunities around the world in search of profitable new markets, outsourcing facilities, acquisitions, and alliances—and this search is increasingly directed at emerging markets.

However, the recent economic slowdown caused many companies to retrench rather than expand in order to conserve cash flow in the economic slowdown. Thus, while much of the focus in this chapter is on "going international" and expansion abroad, we need to keep in mind that retrenchment is also a very real strategy, especially in difficult economic times. However, the long-term trend is clear. After the Boston Consulting Group identified 100 emerging-market companies that they felt have the potential to reach the top rank of global corporations in their industries, *BusinessWeek* challenged that:

> *Multinationals from China, India, Brazil, Russia, and even Egypt are coming on strong. They're hungry—and want your customers. They're changing the global game.*[3]

Management consultant Ram Charan advises that we are now truly in a global game, one that he calls a "seismic change" to the competitive landscape brought about by globalization and the Internet. This first wave of emerging-nation players, he says, are taking advantage of three forces spurred on by the Internet—mobility of talent, mobility of capital, and mobility of knowledge. The strategies of companies such as America Movil of Mexico, China Mobile, Petrobras of Brazil, and Mahindra and Mahindra of India (which is penetrating Deere's market on its own U.S. turf) are to use their bases in their emerging markets—from which they have had to eke out meager profits—as "springboards to build global empires."[4] Add these new challengers to the already hyper-competitive arena of global players, and it is clear that managers need to pay close and constant attention to strategic planning. *BusinessWeek* gives an example of two global companies, challenging us to decide which is more "American":

> *Mumbai-based Tata Consultancy Services (TCS), or Armonk (New York)-based IBM? Evaluate the two based on where they make their sales, and the answer is surprising. TCS, India's largest tech-services company, collected 51 percent of its revenues in North America the first quarter of 2008, while 65 percent of IBM's were overseas.*[5]

As it will be explained in this chapter, however, corporate strategies must change in response to shifting global economic conditions and other environmental and competitive factors. With continuing economic challenges in the U.S. and Europe, TCS must consider how it will respond, but it is strengthened by its geographic diversification. IBM, meanwhile, now making about half its revenues in its services business—in particular in emerging markets—has diversified with a two-track approach. The company is helping clients in the U.S. to cut costs, and in emerging markets, it helps customers develop their technology infrastructure.[6] These are examples of corporate strategies that are being developed to respond to or anticipate current global trends, as noted by Beinhocker et al. of McKinsey & Company and discussed in various chapters throughout this book. They note that:

> Companies' strategic behavior should be tied closely to ten important trends: strains on natural resources, a damper on globalization, the loss of trust in business, the growing role of government, investment in quantitative decision tools, shifting patterns of global consumption, the economic rise of Asia, industry structure upheaval, technological innovation, and price instability.[7]

Because international opportunities are far more complex than those in domestic markets, managers must plan carefully—that is, strategically—to benefit from them. Many experienced managers are wary about expanding into politically risky areas or those countries where they find government practices to be prohibitive.

The process by which a firm's managers evaluate the future prospects of the firm and decide on appropriate strategies to achieve long-term objectives is called **strategic planning**. The basic means by which the company competes—its choice of business or businesses in which to operate and the ways in which it differentiates itself from its competitors—is its **strategy**. Almost all successful companies engage in long-range strategic planning, and those with a global orientation position themselves to take full advantage of worldwide trends and opportunities. Multinational Enterprises (MNEs), in particular, report that strategic planning is essential both to contend with increasing global competition and to coordinate their far-flung operations.

In reality, however, that rational strategic planning is often tempered, or changed at some point, by a more incremental, sometimes messy, process of strategic decision-making by some managers. When a new CEO is hired, for example, she or he will often call for a radical change in strategy. That is why new leaders are carefully chosen, on the basis of what they are expected to do. So, although the rational strategic planning process is presented in this text because it is usually the ideal, inclusive method of determining long-term plans, managers must remember that people are making decisions, and their own personal judgments, experiences, and motivations will shape the ultimate strategic direction.

REASONS FOR GOING INTERNATIONAL

Companies of all sizes "go international" for different reasons—some reactive (or defensive), and some proactive (or aggressive). The threat of their own decreased competitiveness is the overriding reason many large companies adopt an aggressive global strategy. To remain competitive, these companies want to move fast to build strong positions in key world markets with products or services tailored to the needs of increasingly global and diverse sets of customers.

Reactive Reasons

GLOBALIZATION OF COMPETITORS

One of the most common reactive reasons that prompts a company to go overseas is global competition. If left unchallenged, competitors who already have overseas operations or investments may get so entrenched in foreign markets that it becomes difficult for other companies to enter at a later time. In addition, the lower costs and market power available to these competitors operating globally may also give them an advantage domestically. Nor is this global perspective limited to industries with tangible products. Following the global expansion of banking, insurance, credit cards, and other financial services, financial exchanges have been going global by buying or forming partnerships with exchanges in other countries, their strategies facilitated by advances in technology.[8]

Strategic moves by competing global giants prompt countermoves by other firms in the industry in order to solidify and expand their global presence. Such was the case after the Pfizer takeover of Wyeth in January 2009; Pfizer, the world's biggest drug maker, bid $68 billion for Wyeth. Subsequently, Roche, the Swiss pharmaceutical company, paid $46.8 billion to acquire the biotechnology company Genentech, in which it already owned a majority stake. Not to be outdone, Merck, the American pharmaceutical giant, announced in March 2009 that it would pay

$41 billion to acquire its rival Schering-Plough—the combined company to keep the Merck name. Clearly, Merck will benefit from the worldwide reach of Schering-Plough, which generates about 70 percent of its sales outside of the United States, including more than $2 billion per year from emerging markets. Mr. Clark, Merck's CEO, stated that

> We are creating a strong, global health care leader built for sustainable growth and success. The combined company will benefit from a formidable research and development pipeline, a significantly broader portfolio of medicines and an expanded presence in key international markets, particularly in high-growth emerging markets.[9]

TRADE BARRIERS

Although trade barriers have been lessened in recent years as a result of trade agreements that have led to increased exports, some countries' restrictive trade barriers do provide another reactive reason for companies often switching from exporting to overseas manufacturing. Barriers such as tariffs, quotas, buy-local policies, and other restrictive trade practices can make exports to foreign markets too expensive and too impractical to be competitive. Toyota, for example, has manufacturing plants in the United States in order to circumvent import quotas. In May 2011, for example, ZTE—China's second largest telecom equipment maker and a state-controlled company listed in Hong Kong—moved to Brazil; the purpose was to avoid that country's high import tariffs, even though it is cheaper to manufacture in China.[10]

REGULATIONS AND RESTRICTIONS

Similarly, regulations and restrictions by a firm's home government may become so expensive that companies will seek out less restrictive foreign operating environments. Avoiding such regulations prompted U.S. pharmaceutical maker SmithKline and Britain's Beecham to merge. Both thereby guaranteed that they would avoid licensing and regulatory hassles in their largest markets: Western Europe and the United States. The merged company is now an insider in both Europe and America.

CUSTOMER DEMANDS

Operations in foreign countries frequently start as a response to customer demands or as a solution to logistical problems. Certain foreign customers, for example, may demand that their supplying company operate in their local region so that they have better control over their supplies, forcing the supplier to comply or lose the business. McDonald's is one company that asks its domestic suppliers to follow it to foreign ventures. Meat supplier OSI Industries does just that, with joint ventures in 17 countries, such as Germany, so that it can work with local companies making McDonald's hamburgers.

Proactive Reasons

> Many more companies are using their bases in the developing world as springboards to build global empires, such as Mexican cement giant Cemex, Indian drugmaker Ranbaxy, and Russia's Lukoil, which has hundreds of gas stations in New Jersey and Pennsylvania.[11]

ECONOMIES OF SCALE

Careful, long-term strategic planning encourages firms to go international for proactive reasons. One pressing reason for many large firms to expand overseas is to seek economies of scale—that is, to achieve world-scale volume to make the fullest use of modern capital-intensive manufacturing equipment and to amortize staggering research and development costs when facing brief product life cycles.[12] The high costs of research and development, such as in the pharmaceutical industry (for example, Merck and Pfizer), along with the cost of keeping up with new technologies, can often be recouped only through global sales.

GROWTH OPPORTUNITIES

> According to the Small Business Administration (SBA), 96 percent of the world's customers live outside the United States, and two thirds of the world's purchasing power is in foreign countries.[13]

Clearly there are vast opportunities for small businesses—those with fewer than 500 workers—to do business overseas. In fact, as of 2011, small businesses accounted for about 30% of total export revenue, or about $500 billion in annual sales. "Still, only about 1% of the nation's roughly 30 million small businesses sell overseas, according to U.S. Census data. Those that do usually work with no more than one foreign market—typically Canada, Mexico, the United Kingdom, Germany or China, Census data show."[14] As domestic growth declines because of slow-growth economies, opportunities abroad look more attractive, in particular since the Internet now greatly facilitates the ability to quickly link to contacts in other countries. New start-ups in Europe, for example, feeling the weight of the continent's continuing debt crisis, realize that they must go global from the beginning to establish sufficient market size to be viable. Indeed, most European entrepreneurs and managers are well equipped personally to go global because they are accustomed to moving easily among different languages and customers. This is particularly true of Internet-based companies such as audio-sharing Web service SoundCloud, cofounded in Stockholm by Alex Ljung, a multilingual entrepreneur, who observed that:

> *"It was obvious that our business had to be global from the start. We're more like citizens of the Internet than citizens of a country."*
>
> "COMPANIES BORN IN EUROPE, BUT BASED ON THE PLANET," WWW.NYTIMES.COM,
> *JUNE 12, 2012.*[15]

Whatever their size, companies in mature markets in developed countries experience a growth imperative to look for new opportunities in emerging markets. In an effort to continue its long-term strategy to expand into China—with its 1.3 billion consumers—Nestle, the Swiss food giant, announced on July 11, 2011 that it had agreed to pay $1.7 billion for a 60 percent stake in Hsu Fu Chi, a big Chinese confectioner, in one of the biggest deals ever by a foreign company in China. The founding Hsu family eventually retained 40 percent, and Hsu Chen, current CEO, heads the joint venture.[16] And in March 2012, United Parcel Service (UPS) reached an agreement to acquire TNT Express, a Dutch shipping company, for 5.2 billion euro, or $6.8 billion, in order to increase market share in Europe and provide growth opportunities in China. UPS stated that "The additional capabilities and broadened global footprint will support the growth and globalization of our customers' businesses."[17]

Cemex, the Mexican cement giant, has been one company aggressively taking advantage of growth opportunities through acquisitions. After learning his family's business from the bottom up for eighteen years, Lorenzo Zambrano became CEO and started his gutsy expansion into world markets. His strategy has been to acquire foreign companies, allow time to integrate them into Cemex and pay off the debt, and then look for the next acquisition. In 2009, however, environmental factors forced strategic changes, as discussed in the accompanying Management in Action feature, causing Mr. Zambrano to reflect in 2011 on how he has enacted his strategies and to wonder about the future.

RESOURCE ACCESS AND COST SAVINGS

Resource access and cost savings entice many companies to operate from overseas bases. The availability of raw materials and other resources offers both greater control over inputs and lower transportation costs. Lower labor costs (for production, service, and technical personnel)—another major consideration—lead to lower unit costs and have proved a vital ingredient to competitiveness for many companies.

Sometimes just the prospect of shifting production overseas improves competitiveness at home. When the Xerox Corporation started moving copier-rebuilding operations to Mexico, the U.S. union agreed to needed changes in work rules and productivity to keep the jobs at home. Lower operational costs in other areas—power, transportation, and financing—frequently prove attractive.

INCENTIVES

Governments in countries such as Poland seeking new infusions of capital, technology, and know-how willingly provide incentives—including tax exemptions, tax holidays, subsidies, loans, and the use of property. Because they both decrease risk and increase profits, these incentives are attractive to foreign companies. Russia, for example, has a number of special economic zones,

The turnabout underscores a hard lesson of the financial crisis: For all the promise globalization holds for aggressive companies and executives, it carries hidden risks that can slam both operations and reputations.[19]

"I have to admit it: it was an error . . . this time we forgot to ask: 'what is the worst that can happen'."[20]

The Mexican cement giant Cemex is based in Monterrey and operates in more than 50 countries. The company continued its global expansion when it made an unsolicited bid of $12.8 billion for the Rinker Group of Australia, a group with considerable U.S. interests. The Rinker Group accepted a revised $14.25 billion acquisition by Cemex in 2007. The deal created one of the world's largest construction materials companies, and looked sure to strengthen Cemex's leading position in the American housing market, particularly in Sun Belt states like Florida and Arizona. Eighty percent of Rinker's sales come from the United States. However, the deal increased Cemex's gross debt from about $4 billion to $19.1 billion—crucially, by using short-term loans.

Cemex's acquisition of the Rinker Group was the largest ever by a Mexican company. Over the prior 15 years, Cemex's chairman, Lorenzo Zambrano, had transformed his company into a multinational company with operations on five continents and $21 billion in revenue, earning him the reputation as a leader in the push for globalization. He was undoubtedly a role model by creating Mexico's first multinational company with operations on five continents, starting from a small local company.[21]

The global cement and construction materials industry has been slowly consolidating as giants such as Lafarge of France, Holcim of Switzerland, and Cemex have sought to grow through acquisitions.

After taking over 23 years ago at a business co-founded by his grandfather, Mr. Zambrano pushed into country after country with daring acquisitions. Mr. Zambrano, a graduate of Stanford Business School, has been aggressive in expanding Cemex's global presence by taking on billions in debt to expand first in Spain, then in Latin America and the United States. Zambrano's acquisitions in Europe helped the company learn about efficiencies in managing inventory and dealing with clients in other countries.

Cemex became the world's largest producer of ready-mix concrete in 2005 when it bought RMC of Britain for $5.8 billion, giving it a strong presence in Europe. Zambrano also invested heavily in high technology, allowing managers at its Monterrey headquarters in northern Mexico to track global operations.

In 2009, however, the global economic downturn led to declining construction demand, notably in the United States, UK, and Spain. The construction industry stalled for residential and commercial projects, while the prospect for infrastructure projects awaited government spending to prime the economy in those countries.

With rising costs for crucial raw materials such as coal, heavy oil, and gas, the focus for Cemex in 2009 changed from expansion and acquisitions to cost-cutting and retrenchment. The company announced it would cut costs and jobs in its attempt to absorb the effects of the U.S. housing crisis and global market volatility. Added to its reduced sales, the company also suffered because of the weakness of the peso, which had fallen by more than 30 percent against the dollar since July 2008.

Confounding the problems for Cemex—as with many victims of the financial crisis— the company was not able to refinance a significant portion of its debt (estimated at between $16 billion to $20 billion). Emerging market companies across the board were falling prey to the perception of a higher risk in refinancing debt. In a rapid reversal of fortune, the company known for relentless expansion was forced into selling assets, negotiating with creditors, and cutting its work force and spending. However, the tightened credit market also reduced the price Cemex could get for selling its assets in Spain, Hungary, and Austria.

It is unfortunate that the ill-timed takeover of the Rinker group, along with the global financial crisis, has so negatively affected not only the Cemex company, but also the reputation of Mr. Zambrano. He had become corporate Mexico's informal ambassador to the world. Cemex gave other Latin American businesspeople the confidence to expand abroad. Mr. Zambrano was a philanthropist and arts patron, and he raised millions of dollars for a prominent university, El Instituto Tecnologico de Monterrey, from which he received an engineering degree. However, strategists may challenge whether Mr. Zambrano had sufficiently considered potential global threats that could cause such a rapid downturn in the company.

What is your opinion? Was the situation a result of a rare confluence of negative events, or was Mr. Zambrano insufficiently apprised and cautious about the risks in continuing expansion and debt burdens?

Update As of August 2011, Cemex had secured a $15 billion restructuring deal, had cut 11 percent of its workforce worldwide, and halved it in Spain, and Mr. Zambrano was becoming more optimistic. Reflecting on all that had happened, he said "I had to hide my true feelings, you have to be brave and appear brave . . . It was a terrible time."[22] Although this admission is contrary to Mexican culture for a leader, it did signal a change of direction within the company.

both for industrial production and for technical research, offering various tax concessions such as exemption from property and land taxes for the first five years, as well as customs privileges.[23]

In February 2009, for example, companies were rushing to conclude M&A deals in Brazil while a tax break that allows companies to deduct 34 percent of the premium paid in an acquisition is still guaranteed, amid fears that it would be rescinded. This kind of tax incentive is rare, so it attracts considerable interest from foreign investors. Coupled with the recent devaluation of the Brazilian real—which made acquisitions cheaper for foreign bidders—tax deductions are currently one of the great attractions for acquisition deals in Brazil.[24] Nor are those incentives limited to emerging economies. The state of Alabama in the United States has spent hundreds of millions of dollars in incentives to attract the Honda, Hyundai, and Toyota plants.[25]

STRATEGIC FORMULATION PROCESS

Typically, the strategic formulation process is necessary both at the headquarters of the corporation and at each of the subsidiaries. Most organizations operate on planning cycles of five or more years, with intermediate reviews. However, adjustments are frequently necessary to respond to changes in a dynamic global environment, in particular in rapidly changing industries such as those driven by technological developments.

The global strategic formulation process, as part of overall corporate strategic management, parallels the process followed in domestic companies. However, the variables, and therefore the process itself, are far more complex because of the greater difficulty in gaining accurate and timely information; the diversity of geographic locations; and the differences in political, legal, cultural, market, and financial processes. These factors introduce a greater level of risk in strategic decisions. However, for firms that have not yet engaged in international operations (as well as for those that do), an ongoing strategic planning process with a global orientation identifies potential opportunities for (1) appropriate market expansion, (2) increased profitability, and (3) new ventures by which the firm can exploit its strategic advantages. Even in the absence of immediate opportunities, monitoring the global environment for trends and competition is important for domestic planning.

The strategic formulation process is part of the strategic management process in which most firms engage, either formally or informally. The planning modes range from a proactive, long-range format to a reactive, more seat-of-the-pants method, whereby the day-by-day decisions of key managers, in particular owner-managers, accumulate to what can be discerned retroactively as the new strategic direction.[26] The stages in the strategic management process are shown in Exhibit 6-1. In reality, these stages seldom follow such a linear format. Rather, the process is continuous and intertwined, with data and results from earlier stages providing information for the next stage.

The first phase of the strategic management process—the *planning phase*—starts with the company establishing (or clarifying) its mission and its overall objectives. The next two steps comprise an assessment of the external environment that the firm faces in the future and an analysis of the firm's relative capabilities to deal successfully with that environment. Strategic alternatives are then considered, and plans are made based on the strategic choice. These five steps constitute the planning phase, which will be further explained in this chapter.

The second part of the strategic management process is the *implementation phase*. Successful implementation requires the establishment of the structure, systems, and processes suitable to make the strategy work. These variables, as well as functional-level strategies, are explored in detail in the remaining chapters on strategic implementation, organizing, leading, and staffing. At this point, however, it is important to note that the strategic planning process by itself does not change the posture of the firm until the plans are implemented. In addition, feedback from the interim and long-term results of such implementation, along with continuous environmental monitoring, flows directly back into the planning process.

STEPS IN DEVELOPING INTERNATIONAL AND GLOBAL STRATEGIES

In the planning phase of strategic management—strategic formulation—managers need to carefully evaluate dynamic factors, as described in the stages that follow. However, as discussed earlier, managers seldom consecutively move through these phases; rather, changing events and variables prompt them to combine and reconsider their evaluations on an ongoing basis.

EXHIBIT 6-1   The Strategic Management Process

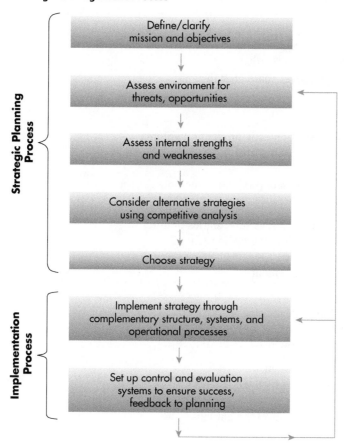

Step 1. Establish Mission and Objectives

The *mission* of an organization is its overall *raison d'être* or the function it performs in society. This mission charts the direction of the company and provides a basis for strategic decision making. It also conveys the cultural values that are important to the company, as contrasted in the following two mission statements:

SANYO (A Japanese Company)

Corporate philosophy: to make products and services indispensable for people all over the world, offering a more enjoyable life. Digital technology and core competence (the source of our competitiveness) generate joy, excitement, and impact, a more comfortable life in harmony with the global environment.[27]

SIEMENS (A German Company)

Success depends on success of our customers. We provide experience and solutions so they can achieve their objectives fast and effectively. We turn our people's imagination and best practices in successful technologies and products. This makes us a premium investment for our shareholders. Our ideas, technologies and activities help create a better world.[28]

While both mission statements indicate a focus on customers, Sanyo offers them a more enjoyable life, is more relationship-oriented, and emphasizes harmony and the environment, indicating a long-term focus, factors typical of Japanese culture. Siemens offers efficiency to its customers and a premium return to its shareholders; this mission statement is explicit and decisive, typical of German communication; this compares with the more descriptive and implicit statement given by Sanyo.[29]

A company's overall *objectives* flow from its mission, and both guide the formulation of international corporate strategy. Because we are focusing on issues of international strategy, we

EXHIBIT 6-2   **Global Corporate Objectives**

Marketing
Total company market share—worldwide, regional, national
Annual percentage sales growth
Annual percentage market share growth
Coordination of regional markets for economies of scale

Production
Relative foreign versus domestic production volume
Economies of scale through global production integration
Quality and cost control
Introduction of cost-efficient production methods

Finance
Effective financing of overseas subsidiaries or allies
Taxation—globally minimizing tax burden
Optimum capital structure
Foreign-exchange management

Profitability
Long-term profit growth
Return on investment, equity, and assets
Annual rate of profit growth

Research and Development
Develop new products with global patents
Develop proprietary production technologies
Worldwide research and development labs

will assume that one of the overall objectives of the corporation is some form of international operation (or expansion). The objectives of the firm's international affiliates should also be part of the global corporate objectives. A firm's global objectives usually fall into the areas of marketing, profitability, finance, production, and research and development, among others, as shown in Exhibit 6-2. Goals for market volume and for profitability are usually set higher for international than for domestic operations because of the greater risk involved. In addition, financial objectives on the global level must take into account differing tax regulations in various countries and how to minimize overall losses from exchange rate fluctuations.

Step 2. Assess External Environment

After clarifying the corporate mission and objectives, the first major step in weighing international strategic options is the **environmental assessment**. This assessment includes environmental scanning and continuous monitoring to keep abreast of variables around the world that are pertinent to the firm and that have the potential to shape its future by posing new opportunities (or threats). Firms must adapt to their environment to survive. The focus of strategic planning is how to adapt.

The process of gathering information and forecasting relevant trends, competitive actions, and circumstances that will affect operations in geographic areas of potential interest is called **environmental scanning**. This activity should be conducted on three levels—global, regional, and national (discussed in detail later in this chapter). Scanning should focus on the future interests of the firm and should cover the major variables such as political and economic risk; major technological, legal, and physical constraints; and the global competitive arena, as well as the opportunities available in different countries. Some generalized areas of risk to consider are shown in Exhibit 6-3. As an example of nationalism, Wal-Mart and other retailers were given an unexpected set-back in December 2011, as discussed in the nearby Under the Lens section.

The firm can also choose varying levels of environmental scanning. To reduce risk in investments, many firms take on the role of the "follower," meaning that they limit their own investigations. Instead, they simply watch their competitors' moves and go where they go, assuming that

EXHIBIT 6-3 **Levels of Risk for Strategic Entry Scanning**

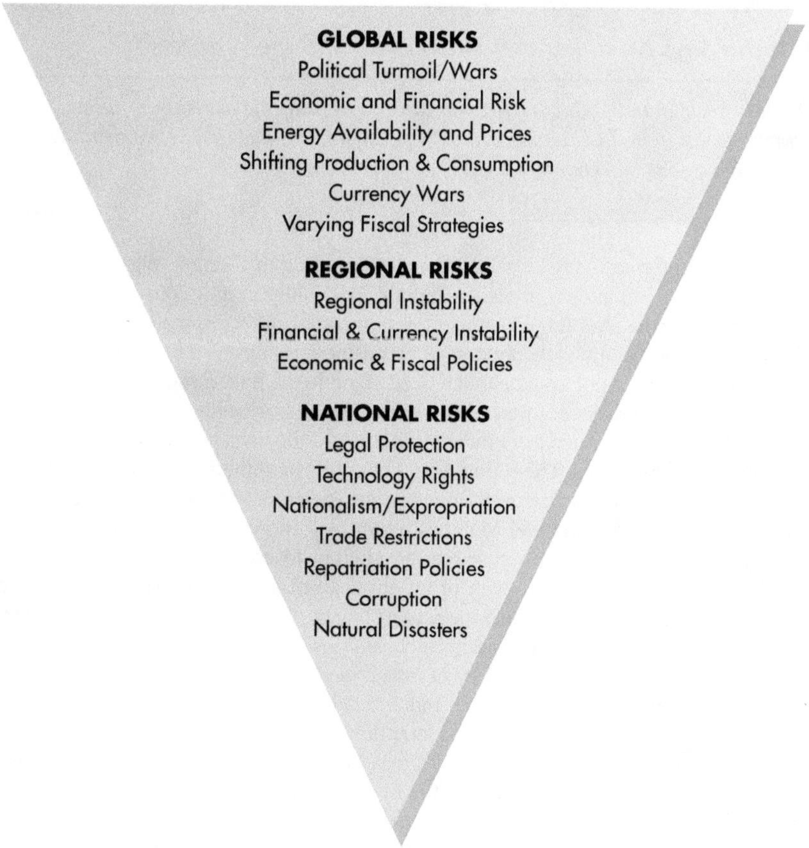

GLOBAL RISKS
Political Turmoil/Wars
Economic and Financial Risk
Energy Availability and Prices
Shifting Production & Consumption
Currency Wars
Varying Fiscal Strategies

REGIONAL RISKS
Regional Instability
Financial & Currency Instability
Economic & Fiscal Policies

NATIONAL RISKS
Legal Protection
Technology Rights
Nationalism/Expropriation
Trade Restrictions
Repatriation Policies
Corruption
Natural Disasters

the competitors have done their homework. Other firms go to considerable lengths to carefully gather data and examine options in the global arena.

Ideally, the firm should conduct global environmental analysis on three different levels: multinational, regional, and national. Analysis on the multinational level provides a broad assessment of significant worldwide trends—through identification, forecasting, and monitoring activities. These trends would include the political and economic developments of nations around the world, as well as global technological progress. From this information, managers can choose certain appropriate regions of the world to consider further.

Next, at the regional level, the analysis focuses in more detail on critical environmental factors to identify opportunities (and risks) for marketing the company's products, services, or technology. For example, one such regional location ripe for investigation by a firm seeking new markets is Asia.

Having zeroed in on one or more regions, the firm must, as its next step, analyze at the national level. Such an analysis explores in depth specific countries within the desired region for economic, legal, political, and cultural factors significant to the company. For example, the analysis could focus on the size and nature of the market, along with any possible operational problems, to consider how best to enter the market. In many volatile countries, continuous monitoring of such environmental factors is a vital part of ongoing strategic planning. Another important factor that must be considered in the environmental assessment at all levels is that of how institutions might affect potential opportunities to compete.

INSTITUTIONAL EFFECTS ON INTERNATIONAL COMPETITION[30]

Various institutions can create opportunities or constraints for firms considering entry into specific global markets. Recently, researchers such as Peng have argued that " . . . firm strategies and performance are, to a large degree, determined by institutions popularly known as the 'rules of the game' in a society."[31] Institutions include both those formal institutions that promulgate laws,

UNDER THE LENS
India Says No to Foreign Ownership of Supermarkets[32]

> *On Wednesday, Finance Minister Pranab Mukherjee said the decision to allow 51% foreign direct investment in multi-brand retail, as it's called here, was suspended pending "consultations among various stakeholders."*
>
> Mumbai (MarketWatch), December 7, 2011.

The decision followed fierce opposition to a proposal granting to foreign "big-box" supermarkets such as Wal-Mart Stores, Inc. unfettered access to India's $450 billion retail consumer market. The reversal was ruled only a short time after the November 24 approval of the foreign retail measure by Mr. Singh's cabinet; the measure had been widely welcomed by business groups as a bold reform that would benefit consumers and farmers while providing a much-needed jolt to the Indian economy. Opposition parties had condemned the proposal as a direct threat to millions of small businesses across India. This was just one more instance of political resistance from Indian traders and shop owners that had blocked previous efforts to push through similar measures. The ruling would have allowed multi-brand stores such as Wal-Mart to open stores with a minority Indian partner. However, the Indian government already allows foreign companies to own wholesale stores, and Wal-Mart has set up 14 of those in a joint venture with an Indian firm.

The retail measure had been proposed as an attempt to create jobs by improving supply-chain infrastructure, therefore reducing the strain of inflation. But India's many small shop owners saw it as certain death for their own businesses and the protest began. The government has not, however, stopped a policy that will allow single-brand retailers such as Nike and Ikea to own 100% of their businesses, whereas before they were only allowed 51%. In fact, Ikea announced in June 2012 that the company had been granted permission to open 25 stores in India under a policy change that allows some retailers to own 100 percent of their units there.[33] Reforms later in 2012 eased the restrictions on Wal-Mart and other firms, producing uncertainty as to what reversals may occur next.

The fear among foreign retailers is that it is becoming harder for outside companies to enter into India, one of the most promising emerging consumer markets in the world. Starbucks and Dunkin Brands are forming alliances in order to open outlets in the populous country. "It was easier to operate in the country a year ago than it is today," the CEO of General Electric's Indian unit told Bloomberg. "It is frustrating to look at unresolved issues and know that they're resolvable if you can get some leadership and orientation around them." In addition, in early 2012 investors were postponing new plans for business in India while they awaited the budgetary decisions regarding a number of proposed new taxes on foreign investment.[34]

regulations, and rules, as well as informal ones that exert influence through norms, cultures, and ethics (discussed elsewhere in this book.)[35]

Specific ways in which formal institutions affect international competition are (1) the attractiveness of overseas markets, (2) entry barriers and industry attractiveness, and (3) antidumping laws.[36]

ATTRACTIVENESS OF OVERSEAS MARKETS The extent to which countries have institutions to promote the rule of law affects the attractiveness of those economies to outside investors. Specifically, institutions provide a broad framework of liberty and democracy, as well as human rights protections. In addition, institutions contribute to a stable environment for firms by creating specific laws such as those protecting property rights. Countries with more developed institutions are seen as more stable and attractive to foreign firms.[37]

ENTRY BARRIERS AND INDUSTRY ATTRACTIVENESS Institutions create barriers to entry in certain industries and hence make those industries more attractive (profitable) for incumbent firms. For example, in the U.S. pharmaceutical industry, barriers are created by the U.S. Food and Drug Administration in the form of stringent drug approval requirements. Since new entrants (with potentially cheaper drugs) are restricted, Americans pay double what Canadians and Europeans pay for the same drugs produced in the United States. Americans spend about $240 billion a year on drugs, more than Britain, Canada, France, Germany, Italy, and Japan combined. In turn, U.S. firms in this industry earn above-average profits as the institutional barriers restrict entrants and reduce rivalry.[38]

ANTIDUMPING LAWS AS AN ENTRY BARRIER A second example of an entry barrier is illustrated by current U.S. antidumping laws, which place a foreign entrant at a disadvantage if accused of "dumping" (defined as selling a product below the cost of producing that product with the intent to later raise prices), because of the extensive legal forms and evidence that the U.S. requires.[39]

Clearly, there are many formal institutions that affect international strategy. But, what explains successes of companies despite the failure or absence of these formal institutions? China is a common illustration of where domestic firms have built competitive advantages despite poorly developed formal institutions. The answer lies in the extensive use of informal institutions or networks of interpersonal connections known in Chinese as *guanxi*. These networks function as substitutes for the weaknesses of the formal institutions. Research has shown that these informal networks are common in a variety of emerging markets with different cultural traditions and are a response to transitions in many emerging markets where formal institutions are evolving.[40]

SOURCES OF ENVIRONMENTAL INFORMATION

The success of environmental scanning depends on the ability of managers to take a global perspective and to ensure that their sources of information and business intelligence are global. A variety of public resources are available to provide information. In the United States alone, more than 2,000 business information services are available on computer databases tailored to specific industries and regions. Other resources include corporate "clipping" services and information packages. However, internal sources of information are usually preferable—especially alert field personnel who, with firsthand observations, can provide up-to-date and relevant information for the firm. Extensively using its own internal resources, Mitsubishi Trading Company employs worldwide more than 50,000 people in 50 countries, many of whom are market analysts, whose job it is to gather, analyze, and feed market information to the parent company.[41] Internal sources of information help to eliminate unreliable information from secondary sources, particularly in developing countries, where even the "official" data from such countries can either be misleading or tampered with for propaganda purposes or it may be restricted.[42]

In summary, this process of environmental scanning, from the broad global level down to the local specifics of entry planning, is illustrated in Exhibit 6-4. The first broad scan of all potential world markets results in the firm being able to eliminate from its list those markets that are closed or insignificant or do not have reasonable entry conditions. The second scan of remaining regions, and then countries, is done in greater detail—perhaps eliminating some countries based on, for example, political instability. Remaining countries are then assessed for competitor strengths, suitability of products, and so on. This analysis leads to serious entry planning in selected countries; managers start to work on operational plans, such as negotiations and legal arrangements.

Step 3. Analyze Internal Factors

After the environmental assessment, the second major step in weighing international strategic options is the **internal analysis**. This analysis determines which areas of the firm's operations represent strengths or weaknesses (currently or potentially) compared to competitors, so that the firm may use that information to its strategic advantage.

The internal analysis focuses on the company's resources and operations and on global synergies. The strengths and weaknesses of the firm's financial and managerial expertise and functional capabilities are evaluated to determine what key success factors (KSFs) the company has and how well they can help the firm exploit foreign opportunities. Those factors increasingly involve superior technological capability (as with Apple and Huawei Technologies) as well as other strategic advantages such as effective distribution channels (Carrefour and Wal-Mart), superior promotion capabilities (Nike and Disney), a low-cost production and sourcing position (Toyota), a superior patent and new product pipeline (Merck), and so on.

All companies have strengths and weaknesses. Management's challenge is to identify both and then take appropriate action. Many diagnostic tools are available for conducting an internal resource audit. Financial ratios, for example, may reveal an inefficient use of assets that is restricting profitability; a sales-force analysis may reveal that the sales force is an area of distinctive competence for the firm. If a company is conducting this audit to determine whether to start

EXHIBIT 6-4 **Global Environmental Scanning and Strategic Decision-Making Process**

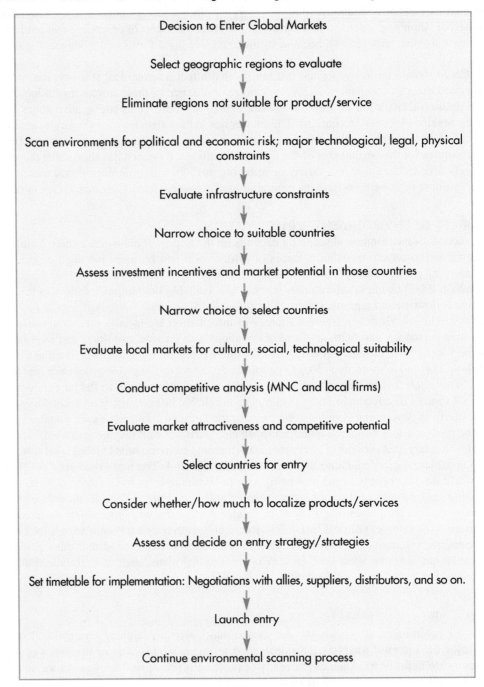

Decision to Enter Global Markets

Select geographic regions to evaluate

Eliminate regions not suitable for product/service

Scan environments for political and economic risk; major technological, legal, physical constraints

Evaluate infrastructure constraints

Narrow choice to suitable countries

Assess investment incentives and market potential in those countries

Narrow choice to select countries

Evaluate local markets for cultural, social, technological suitability

Conduct competitive analysis (MNC and local firms)

Evaluate market attractiveness and competitive potential

Select countries for entry

Consider whether/how much to localize products/services

Assess and decide on entry strategy/strategies

Set timetable for implementation: Negotiations with allies, suppliers, distributors, and so on.

Launch entry

Continue environmental scanning process

international ventures or to improve its ongoing operations abroad, certain operational issues must be taken into account. These issues include (1) the difficulty of obtaining marketing information in many countries, (2) the often poorly developed financial markets, (3) the complexities of exchange rates and government controls, (4) institutional voids in target countries, and (5) poor infrastructure.

Competitive Analysis

At this point, the firm's managers perform a *competitive analysis* to assess the firm's capabilities and key success factors compared to those of its competitors. They must judge the relative current and potential competitive position of firms in that market and location—whether that is a global position or that for a specific country or region. Managers must also specifically assess their current competitors—global and local—for the proposed market. They must ask

EXHIBIT 6-5   **Global Competitor Analysis**

A. U.S. Firm Compared with Its International Competitors in Malaysian Market

Comparison Criteria	A (U.S. MNC)	B (Korean MNC)	C (Local Malaysian Firm)	D (Japanese MNC)	E (Local Malaysian Firm)
Marketing capability	0	0	0	0	–
Manufacturing capability	0	+	0	0	0
R&D capability	0	0	0	–	0
HRM capability	0	0	0	0	0
Financial capability	+	–	0	0	–
Future growth of resources	+	0	–	0	–
Quickness	–	0	+	–	0
Flexibility/adaptability	0	+	+	0	0
Sustainability	+	0	0	0	–

Key:
+ = Firm is better relative to competition.
0 = Firm is same as competition.
– = Firm is poorer relative to competition.
Source: Diane J. Garsombke, "International Competitor Analysis," *Planning Review* 17, no. 3 (1989): 42–47, used with permission of Emerald Insight.

some important questions: What are our competitors' positions, their goals and strategies, their resources, and their strengths and weaknesses, relative to those of our firm? What are the likely competitor reactions to our strategic moves? Like a chess game, the firm's managers also need to consider the strategic intent of competing firms and what might be their future moves (strategies). This process enables the strategic planners to determine where the firm has distinctive competencies that will give it strategic advantage as well as what direction might lead the firm into a sustainable competitive advantage—that is, one that will not be immediately eroded by emulation. The result of this process will also help to identify potential problems that can be corrected or that may be significant enough to eliminate further consideration of certain strategies.

This stage of strategic formulation is often called a **SWOT analysis** (Strengths, Weaknesses, Opportunities, and Threats), in which a firm's capabilities relative to those of its competitors are assessed as pertinent to the opportunities and threats in the environment for those firms. In comparing their company with potential international competitors in host markets, it is useful for managers to draw up a competitive position matrix for each potential location. For example, Exhibit 6-5 analyzes a U.S. specialty seafood firm's competitive profile in Malaysia. The U.S. firm has advantages in financial capability, future growth of resources, and sustainability, but a disadvantage in quickness. It also is at a disadvantage compared to the Korean MNC in important factors such as manufacturing capability and flexibility and adaptability. Because the other firms seem to have little **comparative advantage**, the major competitor is likely to be the Korean firm. At this point, then, the U.S. firm can focus in more detail on assessing the Korean firm's relative strengths and weaknesses.

Most companies develop their strategies around key strengths, or **distinctive competencies**. Distinctive—or "core"—competencies represent important corporate resources because, as Prahalad and Hamel explain, they are the "collective learning in the organization, especially how to coordinate diverse production skills and integrate multiple streams of technologies."[43] Core competencies are usually difficult for competitors to imitate and represent a major focus for strategic development at the corporate level.[44] Apple, for example, has used its capacity to constantly innovate and apply its technology to new products and services.

Managers must also assess their firm's weaknesses. A company already on shaky ground financially, for example, will not be able to consider an acquisition strategy, or perhaps any growth strategy. Of course, the subjective perceptions, motivations, capabilities, and goals of the managers involved in such diagnoses frequently cloud the decision-making process. The result is that because of poor judgment by key players, sometimes firms embark on strategies that are contraindicated by objective information.

EXHIBIT 6-6   A Hierarchical Model of Strategic Decision Making

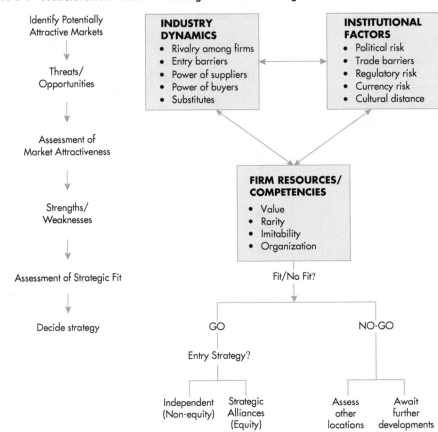

STRATEGIC DECISION-MAKING MODELS

We can further explain and summarize the hierarchy of the strategic decision-making process described here by means of three leading strategic models. Their roles and interactions are conceptualized in Exhibit 6-6. At the broadest level are those global, regional, and country factors and risks discussed above and in Chapter 1 that are part of those considerations in an **institution-based theory** of existing and potential risks and influences in the host area.[45] For example, firms considering operating in Russia are realizing the potential vulnerability to a changing political attitude to the market reforms and openness from recent progress since President Putin's actions to exert control over key industries. Secondly, or concurrently, the firm's potential competitive position in its industry can be reviewed using Michael Porter's **industry-based model** of five forces that examines the dynamics within an industry, discussed below:

Porter's Five Forces Industry-Based Model

1. The relative level of global and local competition already in the industry; for example, in computers, social networking sites, and auto manufacturing. A high level of competition presents barriers to entry; firms may then decide on a different entry strategy or be deterred from that market altogether.

2. The relative ease with which new competitors may or may not enter the field, which determines the level of threat of new entrants. In other words, if your firm is already competing in that industry, what level of protection, or barriers to new entrants, do you have? Toyota, for example, presents huge barriers to entry for new car manufacturers—worldwide scale, volume, alliance partners and suppliers, and reputation.

3. How much power the buyers have within the industry; that is, what is the level of bargaining power that buyers have to influence competition? Wal-Mart, for example, has a lot of buying power because of the volume of its business, and therefore has a downward pressure on prices. Potential entrants would therefore have to provide some

differentiation or innovation in order to combat that pressure on prices and thus the profitability of the firm.

4. The level of bargaining power of suppliers in the industry. High bargaining power would exert pressure and vulnerability to a potential entrant as well as squeeze profits. Suppliers of raw materials or component parts could disrupt production if alternate sources are not available.

5. The level of threat of substitute products or services, including the likelihood of new innovations.[46] Kodak, for example, declared bankruptcy in 2012—put out of business by digital photography, in spite of the fact that the company originally invented it. And, as everyone is aware, the Internet is threatening the survival of print newspapers, movie rental stores, the U.S. Post Office, and so on.

These strategic models can provide the decision makers with a picture of the kinds of opportunities and threats that the firm would face in a particular region or country within its industry. This assumes, of course, that the locations that are under consideration have already been pinpointed as attractive and growing markets for the industry. However, that picture would be true for any firm within the particular industry. In other words, all firms within an industry face the same environmental and industrial factors; the difference among firms' performance is as a result of each firm's own resources, capabilities, and strategic decisions. The factors that determine a firm's unique niche or competitive advantage within that arena are a function of its own capabilities (strengths and weaknesses) as relative to those opportunities and threats which are perceived for that location; this is the **resource-based** view of the firm—when considering the unique value of the firm's competencies and that of its products or services.[47]

While these models may indicate varying choices, this strategic decision-making process should enable the managers to give an overall assessment of the strategic fit between the firm and the opportunities in that location and so result in a "go/no go" decision for that point in time. Those managers may want to start the process again relative to a different location in order to compare the relative levels of strategic fit. If it is determined that there is a good strategic fit and a decision is made to enter that market/location, the next step, as indicated in Exhibit 6-6, is to consider alternative entry strategies. A discussion of these entry strategies follows after we first examine the broader picture of the overall strategic approach that a firm might take toward world markets.

Step 4. Evaluate Global and International Strategic Alternatives

The strategic planning process involves considering the advantages (and disadvantages) of various strategic alternatives in light of the competitive analysis. While weighing alternatives, managers must take into account the goals of their firms and the competitive status of other firms in the industry. Depending on the size of the firm, managers must consider two levels of strategic alternatives. The first level, *global strategic alternatives* (applicable primarily to MNCs), determines what overall approach to the global marketplace a firm wishes to take. The second level, *entry strategy alternatives,* applies to firms of any size; these alternatives determine what specific entry strategy is appropriate for each country in which the firm plans to operate. Entry strategy alternatives are discussed in a later section. The two main global strategic approaches to world markets—global strategy and regional, or local, strategy—are presented in the following subsections.

Approaches to World Markets

GLOBAL STRATEGY

In the last decade, increasing competitive pressures have forced businesses to consider global strategies—to treat the world as an undifferentiated worldwide marketplace. Such strategies are now loosely referred to as **globalization**—a term that refers to the establishment of worldwide operations and the development of standardized products and marketing. Many analysts, such as Porter, have argued that globalization is a competitive imperative for firms in global industries: "In a global industry, a firm must, in some way, integrate its activities on a worldwide basis to capture the linkages among countries. This includes, but requires more than, transferring intangible assets among countries."[48] The rationale behind globalization is to compete by establishing worldwide economies of scale, offshore manufacturing, and international cash flows. The term *globalization,* therefore, is as applicable to organizational structure as it is to strategy. (Organizational structure is discussed further in Chapter 8.)

The pressures to globalize include (1) increasing competitive clout resulting from regional trading blocs; (2) declining tariffs, which encourage trading across borders and open up new markets; and (3) the information technology explosion, which makes the coordination of far-flung operations easier and also increases the commonality of consumer tastes.[49] Use of Web sites has allowed entrepreneurs, as well as established companies, to go global almost instantaneously through e-commerce—either B2B or B2C.[50] Examples are eBay, Yahoo!, and Lands' End. In addition, the success of Japanese companies with global strategies has set the competitive standard in many industries—most visibly in the automobile industry. Other companies, such as Caterpillar, ICI, and Sony, have fared well with global strategies. Another company bent on a global strategy is Lenovo, a Chinese computer-maker that became a global brand when it bought IBM's PC business in 2005 for $1.75 billion. Says Mr. Yang, Lenovo's Chairman:

We are proud of our Chinese roots, but we no longer want to be positioned as a Chinese company. We want to be a truly global company."[51]

As a result, Lenovo has no headquarters and its senior managers rotate meetings around the world. The company's global marketing department is in Bangalore, and its development teams comprise people in several centers around the world, often meeting virtually. Mr. Yang himself moved his family to North Carolina in order to immerse himself in the culture and language of global business.[52]

One of the quickest and cheapest ways to develop a global strategy is through strategic alliances. Many firms are trying to go global faster by forming alliances with rivals, suppliers, and customers. The rapidly developing information technologies are spawning cross-national business alliances from short-term virtual corporations to long-term strategic partnerships. (Strategic alliances are discussed further in Chapter 7.)

A global strategy is inherently more vulnerable to environmental risk, however, than a regionalization (or "multi-local") strategy. Global organizations are difficult to manage because doing so requires the coordination of broadly divergent national cultures. It also means that firms must lose some of their original identity—they must "denationalize operations and replace home-country loyalties with a system of common corporate values and loyalties."[53] In other words, the global strategy necessarily treats all countries similarly, regardless of their differences in cultures and systems. Problems often result, such as a lack of local flexibility and responsiveness and a neglect of the need for differentiated products. Many companies, such as Google, now feel that regionalization/localization is a more manageable and less risky approach, one that allows them to capitalize on local competencies as long as the parent organization and each subsidiary retain a flexible approach to each other. Wal-Mart is one global company that has learned the hard way that it should have acted more "local" in some regions of the world, including Germany and South Korea, where it has had to abandon operations.

REGIONALIZATION/LOCALIZATION

Nokia, Nestle, Google, and Wal-Mart have failed to adjust to the tastes of South Korean consumers.[54]

For those firms in multidomestic industries—those industries in which competitiveness is determined on a country-by-country basis rather than a global basis—regional strategies are more appropriate than globalization. The **regionalization strategy [multidomestic (or multi-local) strategy]** is one in which local markets are linked together within a region, allowing more local responsiveness and specialization. Top managers within each region decide on their own investment locations, product mixes, and competitive positioning; in other words, they run their subsidiaries as quasi-independent organizations.

While there are pressures to globalize—such as the need for economies of scale to compete on cost—there are opposing pressures to regionalize, especially for newly developed economies (NDEs) and developing, or emerging, economies. These localization pressures include unique consumer preferences resulting from cultural or national differences (perhaps something as simple as right-hand-drive cars for Japan), domestic subsidies, and new production technologies that facilitate product variation for less cost than before.[55] By "acting local," firms can focus individually in each country or region on the local market needs for product or service characteristics, distribution, customer support, and so on. The British retailer Tesco has enjoyed considerable success with its localizing strategy; in South Korea, for example, Samsung Tesco, which is 89 percent owned by Tesco Ltd., owes much of its acceptance to hiring local managers from Samsung. Their success compares well with those from other well-known companies which did not localize to the South Korean market, including Wal-Mart and Google.[56]

Ghemawat argues that strategy cannot be decided either on a country-by-country basis or on a one-size-fits-all-countries basis, but rather that both the differences and the similarities between countries must be taken into account. He bases his perspectives on the cultural administrative, geographic, and economic (CAGE) distances between countries, for example:

Cultural distance: differences in values, languages, religion, trust.

Administrative Distance: Lack of common trading bloc or currency, political hostility, nonmarket or closed economy.

Geographical Distance: Remoteness, different time zones, weak transportation or communication links.

Economic Distance: Differences in level of development, natural or human resources, infrastructure, information or knowledge.

He concludes:

A semiglobalized perspective helps companies resist a variety of delusions derived from visions of the globalization apocalypse: growth fever, the norm of enormity, statelessness, ubiquity, and one-size-fits-all.

Semi-globalization is what offers room for cross-border strategy to have content distinct from single-country strategy.[57]

As with any management function, the strategic choice as to where a company should position itself along the globalization-regionalization continuum is contingent on the nature of the industry, the type of company, the company's goals and strengths (or weaknesses), and the nature of its subsidiaries, among many factors. In addition, each company's strategic approach should be unique in adapting to its own environment. Many firms may try to "Go Global, Act Local" to trade off the best advantages of each strategy. Matsushita, which grew to be Japan's largest electronics firm and renamed itself as the Panasonic Corporation in October 2008, is one firm with considerable expertise at being a "GLOCAL" firm (GLObal, LoCAL). Panasonic has operations in 60 countries and employs over 300,000 people in its 634 domain companies; those companies follow policies to develop local R&D to tailor products to markets, to let plants set their own rules, and to be a good corporate citizen in every country.[58] Google is another company that has had to step back from its ideal of being just "Global" to instead adapting to local markets. Ghemawat explains why the company had problems with a "one-size-fits-all-countries" strategy by using his CAGE distance framework, as follows:

Cultural distance: Google's biggest problem in Russia seems to have been associated with a relatively difficult language.

Administrative distance: Google's difficulties in dealing with Chinese censorship reflect the difference between Chinese administrative and policy frameworks and those in its home country, the United States.

Geographic distance: Although Google's products can be digitized, it had trouble adapting to Russia from afar and has had to set up offices there.

Economic distance: The underdevelopment of the payment infrastructure in Russia has been another handicap for Google relative to local rivals.[59]

Global Integrative Strategies

Many MNCs have developed their global operations to the point of being fully integrated—often both vertically and horizontally, including suppliers, productive facilities, marketing and distribution outlets, and contractors around the world. Dell, for example, is a globally integrated company, with worldwide sourcing and a fully integrated production and marketing system. It has factories in Ireland, Brazil, China, Malaysia, Tennessee, and Texas, and it has an assembly and delivery system from 47 locations around the world. At the same time, it has extreme flexibility. Since Dell builds each computer to order, it carries very little inventory and, therefore, can change its operations at a moment's notice. Thomas Friedman described the process that his notebook computer went through when he ordered it from Dell:

> *The notebook was co-designed in Austin, Texas, and in Taiwan. . . . The total supply chain for my computer, including suppliers of suppliers, involved about four hundred companies in North America, Europe, and primarily Asia, but with thirty key players. (It was delivered by UPS 17 days after ordering.)*[60]

Although some companies move very quickly to the stage of global integration—often through mergers or acquisitions—many companies evolve into multinational corporations by going through the entry strategies in stages, taking varying lengths of time between stages. Typically, a company starts with simple exporting, moves to large-scale exporting with sales branches abroad (or perhaps begins licensing), then—for a manufacturing company—proceeds to assembly abroad (either by itself or through contract manufacturing), and eventually evolves to full production abroad with its own subsidiaries. Finally, the company will undertake the global integration of its foreign subsidiaries, setting up cooperative activities among them to achieve economies of scale. By this point, the MNC has usually adopted a geocentric orientation, viewing opportunities and entry strategies in the context of an interrelated global market instead of regional or national markets. In this way, alternative entry strategies are viewed on an overall portfolio basis to take maximum advantage of potential synergies and leverage arising from operations in multi-country markets.[61] While Procter & Gamble, for example, took around 100 years to fully go global, more recently many companies are "**born global**"—that is, they start out with a global reach, typically by using their Internet capabilities and also through hiring people with international experience and contacts around the world.

> *Born globals globalize some aspects of their business—manufacturing, service delivery, capital sourcing, or talent acquisition, for instance—the moment they start up.*
>
> *. . . Standing conventional theory on its head, start-ups now do business in many countries before dominating their home markets.*[62]

Isenberg notes that successful entrepreneurs are able to establish multinational organizations from the outset by setting up and managing global supply chains and striking alliances from positions of weaknesses. The major challenges of born globals are those of accessing resources, and physical and cultural distances in their markets and operations.[63]

Using E-Business for Global Expansion

Companies of all sizes are increasingly looking to the Internet as a means of expanding their global operations. Clearly the Internet is available to anyone and serves to level the playing field for small businesses.

> *"Just think," said Ms. Sinha, "my little six-person operation is now a global business."*
>
> WWW.NYTIMES,
> *September 10, 2011.*[64]

Ms. Sinha, a Silicon Valley entrepreneur, has six employees in her software company—two in the United States and four in New Delhi. There are many micro-multinationals such as hers and, just as with large companies, they run their businesses using e-mail, Web pages, voice-over-Internet phone services, and other Internet technology to coordinate their far-flung operations.

The globalization of the Web is evident, as shown in Table 6–1. Out of a total number of Internet users of 2,267,233.742 as of January 1, 2012, Asia already had 44.8 percent of world usage, with those numbers growing rapidly, as is so around the word. The telling statistic is the penetration rate of users for Asia of only 26.2 percent, which indicates a far greater growth capacity than, for example, the U.S. penetration of 78.3 percent. In China alone there are over 513 million Internet users, including over 150 million online shoppers. However, there, as in other countries, the logistics to providing customer service is often a barrier to efficient e-commerce. The growth of

TABLE 6–1   World Internet Usage as of January 1, 2012

Regions	Usage % of World	Penetration Rates (%)
Africa	6.2	13.5
Asia	44.8	26.2
Europe	22.1	61.3
Middle East	3.4	35.6
North America	12.0	78.6
Latin America/Caribbean	10.4	39.5
Oceana/Australia	1.1	67.5

Source: Selected data from www.internetworldstats.com, accessed October 5, 2012.

express delivery over a broad geographic base has lagged behind the growth of the e-commerce market there.[65] Three strategies are recommended to deal with the logistics problems in China and elsewhere:

- Build your own internal logistics network.
- Outsource delivery services to third-party providers.
- Form partnerships with or acquire existing logistics companies.[66]

Many developing nations, in particular, are realizing the opportunities for e-commerce and are improving their infrastructure to take advantage of those opportunities. Governments and business are experiencing pressure to "go online," especially those companies that export goods to countries where a significant amount of business is conducted through the Internet, such as the United States. For example, Everest S.A., a family-run business in San Salvador, sold a 69-kilogram lot (152 pounds) of coffee beans from one of its five farms in an Internet auction for a record price of $14.06 a pound.[67]

As a result, American technology giants are devoting great amounts of money and time to build and develop foreign-language Web sites and services. "Gone are the days in which you can launch a Web site in English and assume that readers from around the globe are going to look to you simply because of the content you're providing."[68]

There are many benefits of e-business, including rapid entrance into new geographic markets and lower operational costs, as indicated by respondents to the IDC Internet Executive Advisory Council surveys (see Exhibit 6-7). Less touted, however, are the many challenges inherent in a global B2B (Business-to-Business) or B2C (Business-to-Consumer) strategy. These include cultural differences and varying business models as well as governmental wrangling and border conflicts—in particular the question over which country has jurisdiction and responsibility over disputes regarding cross-border electronic transactions.[69] Potential problem areas that managers must assess in their global environmental analysis include conflicting consumer protection, intellectual property, and tax laws; increasing isolationism, even among democracies; language barriers; and a lack of tech-savvy legislators worldwide.[70]

Savvy global managers will realize that e-business cannot be regarded as just an extension of current businesses. It is a whole new industry in itself, complete with a different pool of competitors and entirely new sets of environmental issues. A reassessment of the environmental forces in the newly configured industry, using Michael Porter's five forces analytical model, should take account of shifts in the relative bargaining power of buyers and suppliers, the level of threat of new competitors, existing and potential substitutes, as well as a present and anticipated competitor analysis.[71] The level of e-competition will be determined by how transparent and imitable the company's business model is for its product or service as observed on its Web site. In addition, competitors may also be other brick-and-mortar stores as well as their own—such as for Staples or J.C. Penney.

There is no doubt that the global e-business competitive arena is a challenging one, both strategically and technologically. But many companies around the world are plunging in, fearing that they will be left behind in this fast-developing global e-marketplace.

EXHIBIT 6-7   **Benefits of B2B**

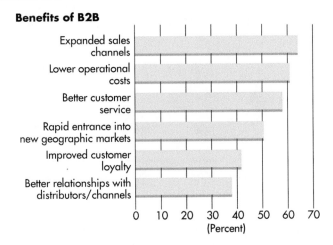

Source: Data from IDC Internet executive Advisory Council Surveys, 2001

For companies like eBay, e-business is their business—services are provided over the Internet for end users and for businesses. With a unique business model, eBay embarked on a global e-strategy. The company has positioned itself to be global and giant: part international swap meet, and part clearinghouse for the world's manufacturers and retailers.

E-Global or E-Local?

Alibaba has more than 8 million small and midsize companies using its business-to-business online marketplace. . . . The company has launched local versions of its B2B service in Japan, South Korea, and India.[72]

Although the Internet is a global medium, a company is still faced with the same set of decisions regarding how much its products or services can be "globalized" or how much they must be "localized" to national or regional markets. Local cultural expectations, differences in privacy laws, government regulations, taxes, and payment infrastructure are just a few of the complexities encountered in trying to "globalize" e-commerce. Further complications arise because the local physical infrastructure must support e-businesses that require the transportation of actual goods for distribution to other businesses in the supply chain, or to end users. In those instances, adding e-commerce to an existing "old-economy" business in those international markets is likely to be more successful than starting an e-business from scratch without the supply and distribution channels already in place. However, many technology consulting firms, such as NextLinx, provide software solutions and tools to penetrate global markets, extend their supply chains, and enable new buyer and seller relationships around the globe.

Going global with e-business, as Yahoo! has done, necessitates a coordinated effort in a number of regions around the world at the same time to gain a foothold and to grab new markets before competitors do. Certain conditions dictate the advisability of going e-global:

The global beachhead strategy makes sense when trade is global in scope; when the business does not involve delivering orders; and when the business model can be hijacked relatively easily by local competitors.[73]

This strategy would work well for global B2B markets in steel, plastics, and electronic components.

The e-local, or regional strategic, approach is suited to consumer retailing and financial services, for example. Amazon and eBay have started their regional approach in Western Europe. Again, certain conditions would make this strategy more advisable:

[The e-local/regional approach] is preferable under three conditions: when production and consumption are regional rather than global in scope; when customer behavior and market

structures differ across regions but are relatively similar within a region; and when supply-chain management is very important to success.[74]

The selection of which region or regions to target depends on the same factors of local market dynamics and industry variables as previously discussed in this chapter. However, for e-businesses, additional variables must also be considered, such as the rate of Internet penetration and the level of development of the local telecommunications infrastructure.

One company which learned the hard way how to localize its e-business is Handango, Inc., of Hurst, Texas—a maker of smartphone and wireless-network software. As Clint Patterson, the company's vice president of marketing, said while reflecting on their move into Asian markets several years ago: "We didn't understand what purchasing methods would be popular or even what kinds of content. We didn't have a local taste. We realized we needed someone on the street to hold our hand."[75] For example, Handango found it needed a local bank account to do business in Japan, because Japanese consumers use a method called *konbini* to make online payments. This means that when they place their order online, instead of paying with a credit card, they go to a local convenience store and pay cash to a clerk, who then transfers the payment into the online vendor's account. In order to adapt to this system, Handango formed an alliance with @irBitway, a local consumer-electronics Web portal, which now acts as Handango's agent in the konbini system and also has taken over Handango's local marketing and translation.[76] Handango ran into a similar problem in Germany, finding out that Germans do not like debt and prefer to pay for their online purchases with wire transfers from their bank accounts. To get around this, the company found a local partner to interface with local banks, and then adapted its Web site to the new payment method.[77]

Step 5. Evaluate Entry Strategy Alternatives

For a multinational corporation (or a company considering entry into the international arena), a more specific set of strategic alternatives, often varying by targeted country, focuses on different ways to enter a foreign market. Managers need to consider how potential new markets may best be served by their company in light of the risks and the critical environmental factors associated with their entry strategies. The following sections examine the various entry and ownership strategies available to firms, including exporting, licensing, franchising, contract manufacturing, offshoring, service-sector outsourcing, turnkey operations, management contracts, joint ventures, fully owned subsidiaries set up by the firm, and e-business. These alternatives are not mutually exclusive; several may be employed at the same time. They are addressed in order of ascending risk (typically), although e-business is usually low-risk.

EXPORTING

Exporting is a relatively low-risk way to begin international expansion or to test out an overseas market. Little investment is involved, and fast withdrawal is relatively easy. Small firms seldom go beyond this stage, and large firms use this avenue for many of their products. Because of their comparative lack of capital resources and marketing clout, exporting is the primary entry strategy used by small businesses to compete on an international level. Jordan Toothbrush, for example, a small company with one plant in Norway and with limited resources, is dependent on good distributors. Since Jordan exports around the world, the company recognizes the importance of maintaining good distributor relations. Many firms from emerging or developing markets use exporting extensively to compete overseas in a narrow product category; an example is the Hong Kong-based Johnson Electric (Johnson), which exports most of the 3 million tiny electric motors it produces per day.

An experienced firm may want to handle its exporting functions by appointing a manager or establishing an export department. Alternatively, an export management company (EMC) may be retained to take over some or all exporting functions, including dealing with host-country regulations, tariffs, duties, documentation, letters of credit, currency conversion, and so forth. Frequently, it pays to hire a specialist for a given host country.

Certain decisions need special care when managers are setting up an exporting system, particularly the choice of distributor. Many countries have regulations that make it very hard to remove a distributor who proves inefficient. Other critical environmental factors include export-import tariffs and quotas, freight costs, and distance from supplier countries.

LICENSING

An international licensing agreement grants the rights to a firm in the host country to either produce or sell a product, or both. This agreement involves the transfer of rights to patents, trademarks, or technology for a specified period of time in return for a fee paid by the licensee. Anheuser-Busch, for instance, has granted licenses to produce and market Budweiser beer in England, Japan, Australia, and Israel, among other countries. Many food-manufacturing MNCs license their products overseas, often under the names of local firms, and products like those of Nike and Disney can be seen around the world under various licensing agreements. Like exporting, licensing is also a relatively low-risk strategy because it requires little investment, and it can be a useful option in countries where market entry by other means is constrained by regulations or profit-repatriation restrictions.

Licensing is especially suitable for the mature phase of a product's life cycle, when competition is intense, margins decline, and production is relatively standardized. It is also useful for firms with rapidly changing technologies, for those with many diverse product lines, and for small firms with few financial and managerial resources for direct investment abroad. A clear advantage of licensing is that it avoids the tariffs and quotas usually imposed on exports. The most common disadvantage is the licensor's lack of control over the licensee's activities and performance.

Critical environmental factors to consider in licensing are whether sufficient patent and trademark protection is available in the host country, the track record and quality of the licensee, the risk that the licensee may develop its competence to become a direct competitor, the licensee's market territory, and legal limits on the royalty rate structure in the host country.

FRANCHISING

Similar to licensing, **franchising** involves relatively little risk. The franchisor licenses its trademark, products and services, and operating principles to the franchisee for an initial fee and ongoing royalties. Franchises are well known in the domestic fast-food industry; Pizza Hut, for example, operates primarily on this basis. For a large up-front fee and considerable royalty payments, the franchisee gets the benefit of the firm's reputation, existing clientele, marketing clout, and management expertise. Pizza Hut is well recognized internationally, as are many other fast-food and hotel franchises, such as Hampton Hotels, along with, for example, MyGym of Mexico, Nike's and Disney's products as well as other services such as Supercuts and H & R Block. A critical consideration for the franchisor's management is quality control, which becomes more difficult with greater geographic dispersion.

Franchising can be an ideal strategy for small businesses because outlets require little investment in capital or human resources. Through franchising, an entrepreneur can use the resources of franchisees to expand; most of today's large franchises started out with this strategy. An entrepreneur can also use franchisees to enter a new business. Higher costs in entry fees and royalties are offset by the lower risk of an established product, trademark, and customer base, as well as the benefit of the franchisor's experience and techniques.

Franchising in some countries can be complicated. In China, for example, franchising is a rather new concept. Almost all firms that franchise in China "either manage the operations themselves with Chinese partners (typically establishing a different partner in each major city or region), or sell to a master franchisee, which then leases out and oversees several franchise areas within a territory."[78] There are considerable problems, including finding suitable franchisees, and collecting royalty payments.

CONTRACT MANUFACTURING

A common means of outsourcing cheaper labor overseas is contract manufacturing (also commonly called outsourcing), which involves contracting for the production of finished goods or component parts. These goods or components are then imported to the home country, or to other countries, for assembly or sale. Alternatively, they may be sold in the host country. If managers can ensure the reliability and quality of the local contractor and work out adequate means of capital repatriation, this strategy can be a desirable means of quick entry into a country with a low capital investment and none of the problems of local ownership. Firms such as Nike use contract manufacturing around the world. However, in 2011, the Boston Consulting Group warned about assuming that this strategy would continue to deliver big cost reductions by itself and that it should be considered as just one part of a global sourcing strategy, saying:

> *But suddenly, the case for outsourcing isn't so clear. Recent headlines trumpet the skyrocketing wages at Foxconn and Honda factories in China. These and other factors like quality concerns, the weakening U.S. dollar, rising fuel costs, and the risks inherent in longer supply chains have many companies rethinking their sourcing strategies.*

> WWW.BCGPERSPECTIVES.COM,
> *JANUARY 12, 2011*[79]

OFFSHORING

Offshoring is when a company moves one or all of its factories from the "home" country to another country, as is the case with some of Nissan's factories in the U.S. In fact, over 40 percent of cars built in the United States are made by Japanese and other foreign companies.[80] Offshoring provides the company with access to foreign markets while avoiding trade barriers, as well as, frequently, an overall lower cost of production. According to the U.S. Commerce Department, approximately 90 percent of the output from U.S.-owned offshore factories is sold to foreign consumers.[81]

However, some companies attribute their global success to their local connections for part or all of their manufacturing. An example is the BAG shoe company in Italy. Just over half the upper shoe parts are made in low-cost countries such as Serbia and Tunisia. The rest of the uppers and the soles are made locally. Having such a large part of its shoes made by local suppliers enables BAG's CEO, Mr. Bracalente, to emphasize the "Made in Italy" label as a big marketing advantage. And having suppliers close by means production problems are quickly solved. "Our technicians can go and visit the suppliers, often in just half an hour," says Mr. Bracalente. He feels that splitting the assembly functions between BAG and many outside companies is a strength, not a weakness.[82] He argues that this mix of production locations gives the company a vital source of flexibility and the capacity to make rapid changes in shoe style.[83]

One means of gaining increased efficiencies and therefore lower costs is through **clustering**— used when contract manufacturing, offshoring, or service-sector outsourcing (explained below). Sirkin et al. note that many companies from emerging market economies—companies that they call "challengers"—have gained rapid success by clustering:

> *Challengers are particularly expert at keeping their costs low by clustering—operating in concentrations of related, interdependent companies within an industry that use the same suppliers, specialized labor, and distribution channels.*[84]

Examples of industry clusters are an appliance cluster in Monterey, Mexico, serving the North American market and firms both global and local, and including around two hundred local suppliers; the many manufacturing clusters in China; and service center clusters in India, as discussed elsewhere in this chapter.

SERVICE SECTOR OUTSOURCING

According to the 2011 A. T. Kearney Global Services Location Index, the service sector outsourcing industry has grown significantly and

> *The part of the value chain that can be performed offshore has increased in value-add and complexity as we continue to see new types of services being handled remotely and across borders.*[85]

Clearly an increasing number of firms are outsourcing "white-collar" jobs overseas in an attempt to reduce their overall costs. Indeed, the practice is not limited to large firms. Research by Gregorio et al. found that "Offshore outsourcing enhances international competitiveness by enabling SMEs to reduce costs, expand relational ties, serve customers more effectively, free up scarce resources, and leverage capabilities of foreign partners."[86]

Firms that outsource services usually enter overseas markets by setting up local offices, research laboratories, call centers, and so on in order to utilize the highly skilled but lower-wage "**human capital**" that is available in countries such as India, the Philippines, and China, as well as the ability to offer global, round-the-clock service from different time zones.

Overall, it seems that India has benefited in IT jobs; as noted by Bill Gates of Microsoft, "India is the absolute leader in IT services offered on the world market."[87] However, as Indians get more sophisticated at taking over high-skilled jobs outsourced from European and U.S. multinationals, they are starting to turn away call-center work, saying that it doesn't pay well any longer. In addition, companies are finding that salaries in India are increasing with the demand for jobs from MNCs, and with the Indian technology companies themselves growing in global clout. Outsourcing of low-end office jobs may then migrate to other countries such as the Philippines or South Africa. In turn, both Indian and American IT service providers are opening offices in Hungary, Poland, and the Czech Republic to take advantage of the German and English-speaking workforce for European clients. Indeed, as found by the A. T. Kearney survey, *the geography of offshore delivery has expanded to include a large number of countries specializing in different parts of the service-production ecosystem*."[88]

Exhibit 6-8 shows the results of the A. T. Kearney survey of the global outsourcing landscape in 50 countries and those countries' potential across three major categories: financial attractiveness, people skills and availability, and business environment. The survey results identify the top countries for delivering information technology (IT), business-process outsourcing (BPO), and voice services. While India and China remain the leaders—in particular as far as people skills and availability are concerned—there are many countries that are attractive, depending on the types of services required. Picking the right location depends on many factors specific to the firm's industry and tasks required for IT, BPO, or voice services. The survey found that India is by far the leader in all fields of offshore services—in large part due to its highly educated and English-language staff availability. China is gaining strength in the IT area, but remains problematic regarding the use of other languages.[89]

Whether firms outsource (or "offshore") white-collar or blue-collar jobs, they must consider the strategic aspects of that decision beyond immediate cost savings.

In addition to the lack of consideration for factors other than production costs, sending jobs to a particular country is typically a short-term cost-reduction strategy, because at some point competitive pressures will increase costs there, necessitating moving those jobs again to still lower-cost countries (a transition known as "the race to the bottom.")

Managers are in fact broadening their strategic view of sending skilled work abroad, now using the term "transformational outsourcing" to refer to the growth opportunities provided by making better use of skilled staff in the home office that are brought about by the gains in efficiency and productivity through leveraging global talent.[90] The risk of backlash from customers, community, and current employees necessitates careful consideration of the reasons for a company to go offshore. Managers also must consider the risk of losing control of proprietary technology and processes and must decide whether to set up the company's own subsidiary offshore (a "captive" operation) instead of contracting with outside specialists. Bank of America, for example, split its strategy by opening its own subsidiary in India, but also allied with Infosys Technologies and Tata Consultancy Services for 30 percent of its IT resources to be outsourced.[91]

TURNKEY OPERATIONS

In a so-called **turnkey operation**, a company designs and constructs a facility abroad (such as a dam or chemical plant), trains local personnel, and then turns the key over to local management—for a fee, of course. The Italian company Fiat, for example, constructed an automobile plant in the former Soviet Union under a turnkey agreement. Critical factors for success are the availability of local supplies and labor, reliable infrastructure, and an acceptable means of repatriating profits. There may also be a critical risk exposure if the turnkey contract is with the host government, which is often the case. This situation exposes the company to risks such as contract revocation and the rescission of bank guarantees.

MANAGEMENT CONTRACTS

A management contract gives a foreign company the rights to manage the daily operations of a business but not to make decisions regarding ownership, financing, or strategic and policy changes. Usually, management contracts are enacted in combination with other agreements, such

EXHIBIT 6-8 The A. T. Kearney Global Services Location Index, 2011

Rank	Country	Financial Attractiveness	People Skills and Availability	Business Environment	Total Score
1	India	3.11	2.76	1.14	7.01
2	China	2.62	2.55	1.31	6.49
3	Malaysia	2.78	1.38	1.83	5.99
4	Egypt	3.10	1.36	1.35	5.81
5	Indonesia	3.24	1.53	1.01	5.78
6	Mexico	2.68	1.60	1.44	5.72
7	Thailand	3.05	1.38	1.29	5.72
8	Vietnam	3.27	1.19	1.24	5.69
9	Philippines	3.18	1.31	1.16	5.65
10	Chile	2.44	1.27	1.82	5.52
11	Estonia	2.31	0.95	2.24	5.51
12	Brazil	2.02	2.07	1.38	5.48
13	Latvia	2.56	0.93	1.96	5.46
14	Lithuania	2.48	0.93	2.02	5.43
15	United Arab Emirates	2.41	0.94	2.05	5.41
16	United Kingdom	0.91	2.26	2.23	5.41
17	Bulgaria	2.82	0.88	1.67	5.37
18	United States	0.45	2.88	2.01	5.35
19	Costa Rica	2.84	0.94	1.56	5.34
20	Russia	2.48	1.79	1.07	5.34
21	Sri Lanka	3.20	0.95	1.11	5.26
22	Jordan	2.97	0.77	1.49	5.23
23	Tunisia	3.05	0.81	1.37	5.23
24	Poland	2.14	1.27	1.81	5.23
25	Romania	2.54	1.03	1.65	5.21
26	Germany	0.76	2.17	2.27	5.20
27	Ghana	3.21	0.69	1.28	5.18
28	Pakistan	3.23	1.16	0.76	5.15
29	Senegal	3.23	0.78	1.11	5.12
30	Argentina	2.45	1.58	1.09	5.12
31	Hungary	2.05	1.24	1.82	5.11
32	Singapore	1.00	1.66	2.40	5.06
33	Jamaica	2.81	0.86	1.34	5.01
34	Panama	2.71	0.72	1.49	4.98
35	Czech Republic	1.81	1.14	2.03	4.98
36	Mauritius	2.41	0.87	1.70	4.98
37	Morocco	2.83	0.87	1.26	4.96
38	Ukraine	2.86	1.07	1.02	4.95
39	Canada	0.56	2.14	2.25	4.95
40	Slovakia	2.33	0.93	1.65	4.91
41	Uruguay	2.42	0.91	1.42	4.75
42	Spain	0.81	2.06	1.88	4.75
43	Colombia	2.34	1.20	1.18	4.72
44	France	0.38	2.12	2.11	4.61
45	South Africa	2.27	0.93	1.37	4.57
46	Australia	0.51	1.80	2.13	4.44
47	Israel	1.45	1.35	1.64	4.44
48	Turkey	1.87	1.29	1.17	4.33
49	Ireland	0.42	1.74	2.08	4.24
50	Portugal	1.21	1.09	1.85	4.15

Note: The weight distribution for the three categories is 40:30:30. Financial attractiveness is rated on a scale of 0 to 4, and the categories for people skills and availability, and business environment are on a scale of 0 to 3.

Source: The A.T. Kearney Global Services Location Index™, 2011, Copyright A.T. Kearney, 2011. All rights reserved. Reprinted with permission.

as joint ventures. By itself, a management contract is a relatively low-risk entry strategy, but it is likely to be short term and provide limited income unless it leads to another more permanent position in the market.

INTERNATIONAL JOINT VENTURES

At a much higher level of investment and risk (though usually less risky than a wholly owned plant), joint ventures present considerable opportunities unattainable through other strategies. A joint venture involves an agreement by two or more companies to produce a product or service together. In an **international joint venture (IJV)** ownership is shared, typically by an MNC and a local partner, through agreed-upon proportions of equity. This strategy facilitates an MNC's rapid entry into new markets by means of an already established partner who has local contacts and familiarity with local operations. IJVs are a common strategy for corporate growth around the world. They also are a means to overcome trade barriers, to achieve significant economies of scale for development of a strong competitive position, to secure access to additional raw materials, to acquire managerial and technological skills, and to spread the risk associated with operating in a foreign environment.[92] Not surprisingly, larger companies are more inclined to take a high-equity stake in an IJV in order to engage in global industries and to be less vulnerable to the risk conditions in the host country.[93] The joint venture reduces the risks of expropriation and harassment by the host country. Indeed, it may be the only means of entry into certain countries, such as Mexico and Japan, that stipulate proportions of local ownership and local participation.

In recent years, IJVs have made up about 20 percent of direct investments by MNCs in other countries, including such deals as the one between Mittal Steel of India and Arcelor of France in 2006—creating the world's biggest steel company.[94] Many companies have set up joint ventures with European companies to gain the status of an "insider" in the European Common Market. IJVs are quite common in India because the government encourages foreign collaborations to facilitate capital investments, import of capital goods, and transfer of technology.[95] Most of these alliances are not just tools of convenience but are important—perhaps critical—means to compete in the global arena. To compete globally, firms have to incur, and defray, immense fixed costs—and they need partners to help them in this effort.[96]

In a joint venture, the level of relative ownership and specific contributions must be worked out by the partners. The partners must share management and decision making for a successful alliance. The company seeking such a venture must maintain sufficient control, however, because without adequate control, the company's managers may be unable to implement their desired strategies. Initial partner selection and the development of a mutually beneficial working agreement are, therefore, critical to the success of a joint venture. In addition, managers must ascertain that there will be enough of a "fit" between the partners' objectives, strategies, and resources—financial, human, and technological—to make the venture work. Unfortunately, too often the need for preparation and cooperation is given insufficient attention, resulting in many such marriages ending in divorce. About 60 percent of IJVs fail, usually because of ineffective managerial decisions regarding the type of IJV, its scope, duration, and administration, as well as careless partner selection.[97] In 1998, the chief executive of Daimler-Benz, Jürgen Schrempp, said that its joint venture with Chrysler would be a "marriage made in heaven." But it ended in a messy divorce in 2007 because of cross-cultural conflicts and because the German company's luxury-car lineup had little in common with Chrysler's portfolio of vehicles.[98] IJVs, as well as the many forms of strategic global alliances, are further discussed in Chapter 7.

For companies in emerging markets or developing economies, joint ventures, mergers, and acquisition strategies provide opportunities to internationalize by gaining access to customers, supply networks, technology, local brand image and knowledge, and natural resources. The local alliances also typically provide to the new management a learning curve for manufacturing and management skills and technologies.

FULLY OWNED SUBSIDIARIES

In countries where a **fully owned subsidiary** is permitted, an MNC wishing total control of its operations can start its own product or service business from scratch, or it may acquire an existing firm in the host country. In September 2011, the South African company SABMiller announced it would buy Australia's Foster's—which commands 50 percent of the Australian beer market—for $10.15 billion, rounding out its global beer portfolio. South African Breweries bought Miller in 2002; since then, it has expanded into Latin America, Asia, and Africa.[99] Another deal that closed in 2011 was the purchase of Sara Lee by Grupo Bimbo, the Mexican-based bakery company, for $959 million; the deal allows Grupo Bimbo the right to sell Sara Lee baked goods everywhere except Western Europe, Australia, and New Zealand.[100]

Often the decision to acquire foreign companies will turn on opportunities presented by financial and economic situations at the time, as with companies who, for tax reasons, keep cash overseas. In 2011, for example, money sheltered from U.S. taxes resulted in cheaper acquisitions for a number of companies, including Apple, Cisco, and Pfizer, amounting to $174 billion in foreign asset purchases. Microsoft said it used $8.5 billion of offshore cash to acquire Luxembourg-based Internet–phone service Skype Technologies in May 2011.

> *U.S. companies such as General Electric and Microsoft are using cash parked overseas to snap up foreign companies at more than double last year's pace. Through the first seven months of 2011, there have been about $174 billion in deals in which U.S. companies bought foreign assets."*[101]
>
> BLOOMBERG-BUSINESSWEEK,
> *AUGUST 15–28, 2011.*

The Tata Group, an Indian conglomerate for cars, steel, software, and tea, continues to make acquisitions around the world including Corus, a European steel company, and Ford's Jaguar and Land Rover.[102] Such acquisitions by MNCs allow rapid entry into a market with established products and distribution networks and provide a level of acceptability not likely to be given to a "foreign" firm. These advantages somewhat offset the greater level of risk stemming from larger capital investments, compared with other entry strategies. Other examples of acquisitions to gain further growth and entry into global markets include the Procter and Gamble acquisition of Gillette, which paved the way for the creation of the world's largest consumer goods company.[103]

At the highest level of risk is the strategy of starting a business from scratch in the host country—that is, establishing a new wholly owned foreign manufacturing or service company or subsidiary with products aimed at the local market or targeted for export. This strategy exposes the company to the full range of risk, to the extent of its investment in the host country. As evidenced by events in the Middle East, political instability can be devastating to a wholly owned foreign subsidiary. Add to this risk a number of other critical environmental factors—local attitudes toward foreign ownership, currency stability and repatriation, the threat of expropriation and nationalism—and you have a high-risk entry strategy that must be carefully evaluated and monitored. There are advantages to this strategy, however, such as full control over decision making and efficiency, as well as the ability to integrate operations with overall company-wide strategy.

E-BUSINESS

Discussed earlier as a global strategy, e-business is an entry strategy at the local level. As such, the failure risk of entry depends greatly on the country or region, even though it is relatively low globally. Yahoo!, for example, bought the largest Arabic-language web portal in August 2009. Although fewer than 50 million of the world's 320 million Arabic-language speakers are online, then-CEO Carol Bartz said that "emerging markets and new languages are a key part of the strategy. Acquisition costs are modest, and while advertising spending is too low for immediate payback, the medium-term prospects for significant growth are surer than in more mature markets."[104]

Exhibit 6-9 summarizes the advantages and critical success factors of these entry strategies that must be taken into account when selecting one or a combination of strategies, depending on the location, the environmental factors and competitive analysis, and the overall strategy with which the company approaches world markets.

Complex situational factors face the international manager as she or he considers strategic approaches to world markets along with which entry strategies might be appropriate, as illustrated in *Comparative Management in Focus: Strategic Planning for Emerging Markets.*

Step 6. Decide on Strategy

The strategic choice of one or more of the entry strategies will depend on (1) a careful evaluation of the advantages (and disadvantages) of each in relation to the firm's capabilities and resources,

EXHIBIT 6-9 International Entry Strategies: Advantages and Critical Success Factors

Strategy	Advantages	Critical Success Factors
Exporting	Low risk No long-term assets Easy market access and exit	Choice of distributor Transportation costs Tariffs and quotas
Licensing	No asset ownership risk Fast market access Avoids regulations and tariffs	Quality and trustworthiness of licensee Appropriability of intellectual property Host-country royalty limits
Franchising	Little investment or risk Fast market access Small business expansion	Quality control of franchisee and franchise operations
Contract manufacturing/Offshoring	Limited cost and risk Short-term commitment	Reliability and quality of local contractor Operational control and human rights issues
Service-sector outsourcing	Lower employment costs	Quality control
Turnkey operations	Access to high skills and markets Revenue from skills and technology where FDI restricted	Domestic client acceptance Reliable infrastructure Sufficient local supplies and labor Repatriability of profits Reliability of any government partner
Management contracts	Low-risk access to further strategies	Opportunity to gain longer-term position
Joint ventures	Insider access to markets Share costs and risk Leverage partner's skill base, technology, local contacts	Strategic fit and complementarity of partner, markets, products Ability to protect technology Competitive advantage Ability to share control Cultural adaptability of partners
Wholly owned subsidiaries	Realize all revenues and control Global economies of scale Strategic coordination Protect technology and skill base	Ability to assess and control economic, political, and currency risk Ability to get local acceptance Repatriability of profits
E-Business	Rapid entry into (or exit from) new markets (often through alliance or purchase of local websites); relatively low-risk	Differences in business models, culture, language, and laws regarding intellectual property, consumer protection, and taxes.

(2) the critical environmental factors, and (3) the contribution that each choice would make to the overall mission and objectives of the company. Exhibit 6-9 summarized the advantages and the critical success factors for each entry strategy discussed. However, when it comes down to a choice of entry strategy or strategies for a particular company, more specific factors relating to that firm's situation must be taken into account. These include factors relating to the firm itself, the industry in which it operates, location factors, and venture-specific factors, as summarized in Exhibit 6-15.

After consideration of those factors for the firm as well as considering what is available and legal in the desired location, some entry strategies will no doubt fall out of the feasibility zone. With those options remaining, then, strategic planners need to decide which factors are more important to the firm than others. One method is to develop a weighted assessment to compare the overall impact of factors such as those in Exhibit 6-15 relative to the industry, the location, and the specific venture—on each entry strategy. Specific evaluation ratings, of course, would depend on the country conditions at a given point in time, the nature of the industry, and the local company.

COMPARATIVE MANAGEMENT IN FOCUS
Strategic Planning for Emerging Markets

Davos, Switzerland, 29 January 2011 – The global economy is rebounding, led by developing economies including China and India, with developed countries growing much more slowly.[105]

WORLD ECONOMIC FORUM ANNUAL MEETING, 2011.

The 2011 GRDI ranking mirrors the dramatic changes that have taken place in global markets, and the varying impacts they have had on different emerging economies. South American countries have fared well during the recession, posting an impressive 6 percent GDP growth in 2010.[106]

The 2011 Global Retail Development Index, www.atkearney.com

As we can see from the quotes above, there continue to be many indicators of the increasing business opportunities available for companies wanting to set up operations in or export to the emerging markets, in particular in light of the slowdown in growth in many developed economies brought about by economic problems.

In planning for global opportunities for retail businesses, for example, one can consider the A. T. Kearney Global Retail Development Index, which ranks 30 emerging countries on the urgency for retailers to enter the country. The scores are based on 25 variables across four primary categories: economic and political risk, market attractiveness, market saturation, and time pressure (whether retail growth is keeping up with gross domestic product (GDP)). Table 6–2 shows the top ten ranks and Russia (14th place). Interestingly, South American countries rated as the top three positions, China slipped to 6th place, and India dropped to 4th place.

Table 6–2 Emerging Market Attractiveness for Retail Strategies

Country	2011 Rank	2010 Rank
Brazil	1	5
Uruguay	2	8
Chile	3	6
India	4	3
Kuwait	5	2
China	6	1
Saudi Arabia	7	4
Peru	8	9
U.A.E.	9	7
Turkey	10	18
Russia	14	10

Source: Based on selected data from the A. T. Kearney Global Retail Development Index 2011, www.atkearney.com.

While the study highlights those countries heading the list, Hana Ben-Shabat, A. T. Kearney partner and co-leader of the study, cautions that, since they started the annual study ten years ago, it has become clear that "there is no 'one size fits all' formula for global expansion. Different countries are at different levels of development and have different risk/return profiles, which require retailers to tailor their approaches accordingly and assemble a portfolio of markets to balance short-term risk with long-term growth aspirations."[107] The World Economic Forum report also cautions that emerging markets are not a single homogenous group: "They develop differently, have different infrastructural,

(Continued)

socio-economic and regulatory challenges, face different environmental and geographical constraints, and, to a certain extent, afford different opportunities for business. We argue that the lack of adequate development in the areas of trade facilitation and trade logistics can curtail the growth for these markets and the world."[108]

In jumping on the bandwagon, firms of all sizes, in particular small businesses, must realize that investing in developing economies usually entails considerably higher levels of risk than they are familiar with—in particular those risks of political turmoil, corruption, and contract enforcement. However, avoiding emerging markets will, over time, make firms less competitive than those who invest there in some form. The question is then how to minimize the risks without losing out to the competition and losing growth opportunities. After going through the steps of the strategic decision-making process as outlined in this chapter, including those operational factors in the institutional context such as infrastructure, availability of suppliers, labor markets, and capital markets (such as the effectiveness of banking and financial institutions), CEOs must then decide whether to enter that market and, if so, decide what needs to be changed. As *Harvard Business Review* authors Khanna, Palepu, and Sinha recommend: "decide whether to work around the country's institutional weaknesses, create new market infrastructures, or stay away because adapting your business model would be impractical and uneconomical."[109] McDonald's, for example, worked around infrastructure problems in Russia by setting up their own food supply farms and chains. Dell also chose to adapt its business model in China when the company realized that consumers there did not order computers over the Internet, and so it had to use Chinese ordering and supply chains rather than the company's usual model of just-in-time inventory. Financial MNCs have helped to improve the financial systems in Brazil and therefore their own firm's prospects. For its part, Home Depot has declined to enter markets with poor transportation and banking infrastructures, because its model and its success depend on competitive inventory systems and employee stock ownership.[110]

However, as noted by Washburn and Hunsaker:

> *"Too many companies in mature markets assume that the only reason to enter emerging countries is to pursue new customers. They fail to perceive the potential for innovation in those countries or to notice that a few visionary multinationals are successfully tapping that potential for much needed products and services."*

> *Source: Harvard Business Review, September 2011.*[111]

In their research, Washburn and Hunsaker have found that forward-thinking global managers (they call them "bridgers") have identified and developed innovations in emerging markets (often with the insight of the local managers) and been able to integrate those ideas and improvements into their companies' product lines. Innovations percolating from emerging market companies already indicate the potential, such as Tata's $2,500 Nano car in India.[112]

In addition, when considering opportunities for firms within emerging markets, we can see that, for example, firms such as Tata and Infosys of India, BYD and Tencent Holdings of China, and Samsung Electronics of Korea have become prominent players in a number of technology-intensive industries that have traditionally been the domain of firms from the U.S., Europe, and Japan.[113]

Entry Strategies

The following section discusses the findings of a study by Deloitte of 247 executives regarding the choices companies make among entry strategies for emerging markets, along with a comparison of strategic objectives and operating strategies.

Strategic Expansion in Emerging Markets

[A study by Deloitte] involving interviews with several executives and a survey of 247 executives from consumer and industrial product companies with presence in emerging markets revealed that companies are increasingly making emerging geographic markets a centerpiece of their global business model. Over the next three years, upwards of 88 percent of companies plan to expand their presence in emerging markets. In fact, nearly half of these organizations expect 20 percent or more of their global revenues to have their origins in emerging markets. Furthermore, a third of these companies plan to place more than 20 percent of their investments in these regions. None of these figures suggest an imminent end to offshoring as we know it, but rather a renewed interest in its pursuit.

That's not to say manufacturers would call their endeavors business-as-usual in emerging markets. Forward-thinking companies have not been content to simply increase their presence in low-cost centers. They have become more strategic in their operations by establishing core functions of their

FIGURE 6-1

Source: Deloitte Services LP

value chains in these regions. While cost savings is still a key motivator for nearly three-quarters of manufacturing companies, it's no longer the sole reason to set up shop abroad. Almost seventy percent of the manufacturers in our study consider market expansion an important factor (see Exhibit 6-10).

In fact, more than two-thirds of companies think it's equally important to cost savings. Similarly, 55 percent of manufacturing companies reported that they establish operations in emerging markets to improve their speed to market. Nokia has been in India since 1995, an early investment that earned it 50 percent of a mobile phone market – one that adds 8–10 million new users every month. D. Shivakumar, managing director of Nokia India, attributes this success to the company's completely localized value chain. Indian operations for everything from R&D to manufacturing, marketing, and sales give Nokia the power to launch new phones in a matter of weeks, rather than months, with designs that cater directly to the needs of its local customers.

Increasingly, organizations are broadening the scope of their pursuits in emerging economies. Nearly 40 percent of the companies in our study have established commercial operations in addition to their manufacturing endeavors that cater to global as well as local markets. After-sales service, material sourcing, and sales and marketing—relative newcomers to low-cost centers—are becoming increasingly prevalent. Forward-thinking companies are beginning to realize that future returns will

EXHIBIT 6-10   **Top Three Strategic Objectives for Establishing Functions in Emerging Markets**

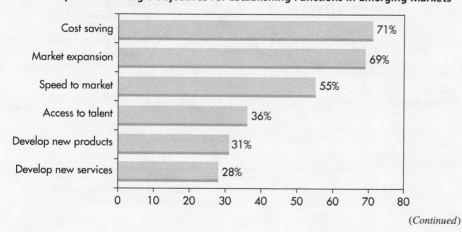

(Continued)

EXHIBIT 6-11 Number of Functions in Emerging Markets vs. Percentage of Global Profits from Emerging Markets

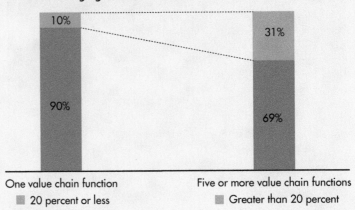

One value chain function

Five or more value chain functions

- 20 percent or less
- Greater than 20 percent

depend on emulating global business models in emerging markets. Intuitively, a strong correlation exists between the number of functions a company establishes in emerging markets and the percentage of global profits that come from these regions. A third of the organizations in our study with five or more functions in emerging markets earn 20 percent or more of their global profits from these operations (see Exhibit 6-11). By comparison, the majority of manufacturers with only a single operation in these low-cost centers reported that they derive 10 percent or less of their global profits from their endeavors.

But these numbers don't paint a complete picture, either. Many manufacturers reported that they are increasing their expectations along with their investments in emerging markets. As a result, operational and financial performance goals can become as elusive as they are lofty. In fact, raw materials and manufacturing have become more expensive over the last three years for over 40 percent of the companies who cited cost savings as a key objective in their emerging market strategies. Likewise, only 13 percent of the companies that cited market expansion as their key objective have realized a significant increase in their global market share. The problem is a fundamental one: companies' endeavors in developing countries haven't kept pace with the evolving capacity and capabilities of these regions, and they're not part of a global business model. As a result, performance in these countries pale by comparison to other parts of their global business.

When companies were content merely to outsource low-complexity work to low-cost centers, strategies were narrow and straightforward. This simplicity has evaporated as companies begin to strategically shift specific functions of their value chains to account for new objectives pertaining to growth, innovation, and sustainability. From a strategy standpoint, three factors determine the emerging market business model: capacity, capability, and risk (see Exhibit 6-12).

EXHIBIT 6-12 New Strategies for Emerging Markets

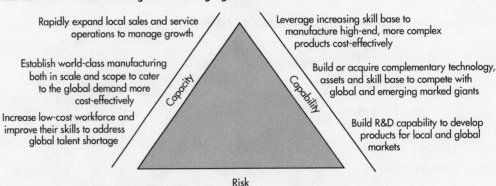

Rapidly expand local sales and service operations to manage growth

Leverage increasing skill base to manufacture high-end, more complex products cost-effectively

Establish world-class manufacturing both in scale and scope to cater to the global demand more cost-effectively

Build or acquire complementary technology, assets and skill base to compete with global and emerging marked giants

Increase low-cost workforce and improve their skills to address global talent shortage

Build R&D capability to develop products for local and global markets

Capacity

Capability

Risk

Diversify capabilities and capacity across multiple locations aligned with the strategic goals to manage cross-border business risks—exchange rate volatility, geopolitical uncertainty, demand and supply chain risk

Getting the Operating Model Right

In recent years, the rate of IJV (international joint venture) formation has continued to increase steadily, especially among emerging markets in Asia, Eastern Europe, and Latin America. These emerging markets account for about 70 percent of all IJV entries by multinational corporations. As companies deepen their business activities in low-cost centers and incorporate these endeavors into global value chains, their existing operating models may not be effective in emerging markets. According to our survey, 35 percent of companies used joint ventures to enter emerging markets, but only 21 percent still use them.

The type of business activities, market opportunities, country regulations, tax advantages, and experience in emerging markets are the key determinants of operating model (see Exhibit 6-13). Thirty-eight percent of manufacturing companies in our study reported that they currently use wholly owned subsidiaries in emerging markets. As they build complete product lines and develop new products, companies require a significant level of control over strategic business activities. For example, Sweden's Volvo group, the world's second largest truck manufacturer, owns a subsidiary in India that builds trucks to sell in India, Myanmar, Indonesia, Vietnam, and China. Volvo India has also established a product development center in Bangalore, India that employs over 200 people. The wholly owned subsidiary model allows companies to take advantage of global brands and existing business processes and protects intellectual property by keeping development effectively in-house.

Similarly, companies expanding sales activities in emerging markets need access to deeper knowledge of local customers, support networks, distribution, and advertising. In many cases, companies choose joint ventures with experienced players in a local market, as noted earlier with Volvo's recently formed joint venture with Eicher Motors in India to sell heavy vehicles and leverage its network of over 200 service centers across the country.

In many cases, market opportunities also drive the choice of operating models in emerging markets. Multinational companies that struggle to stay competitive and innovative sometimes find emerging market companies with a new line of products that has potential to add significant cash flow. In such cases, the choice of operating model depends on size of investment, risk appetite, competition and expected return on the investment. Companies should choose between joint ventures and acquisitions only after thorough due diligence, depending on how these factors play out.

Country regulations and experience in specific countries also drive decisions about operating models. The types of operating model vary significantly by country. For example, in new and comparatively smaller emerging markets like Brazil, Czech Republic, and Mexico, more companies prefer wholly owned subsidiaries compared to China and India. Many countries have strict regulations on operating models for foreign direct investment to support protectionism and growth of domestic industries. However, as many countries are committed to becoming open market economies, these regulations are

EXHIBIT 6-13   **Operating Model for Emerging Markets**

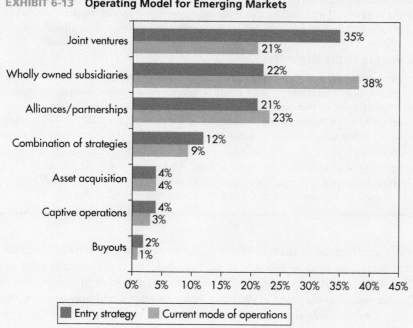

(Continued)

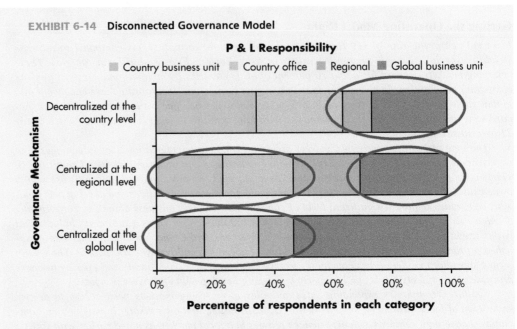

EXHIBIT 6-14   Disconnected Governance Model

loosening. For instance, just a few years ago, China required all automotive companies to enter Chinese markets via joint venture. Over the years, as countries become economically stronger, they tend to ease such regulations on the operating model. However, to stay competitive over the long run, wholly owned subsidiaries might not be the best model for building an understanding of local markets.

Based on our study, companies with more experience in emerging markets tend to choose wholly owned subsidiaries to expand their presence. With the spotlight on emerging markets, thousands of studies have been commissioned by governments, private companies, and academia that now provide deep know-how of these markets. Based on our survey, more than half the companies that have been in the emerging markets for more than ten years choose "wholly owned subsidiary."

In addition to choosing the right operating model, alignment to the global governance model is also a critical success factor. Global governance models and P&L responsibilities are misaligned in over a third of manufacturing companies in our study (see Exhibit 6-14). For instance, almost 50 percent of the companies that have a governance model centrally managed by their global headquarters reported that they hold their local or regional businesses responsible for managing profit and loss. As a consequence, local or regional businesses do not have much flexibility to change policies that will favorable to their region. Organizations that have misaligned governance models lose out on operational efficiencies and the chance to take advantage of emerging markets on a global scale.

From Off-shoring to the Right One

For manufacturers, maybe the term "emerging market" is misleading. Emergence, after all, suggests a singular, upward path, but many companies are quick to call their operations a two-way street. If companies are to evolve along with host countries that are already becoming highly developed in their own right, they must take a closer look at how to adapt their operating models and global value chains and how to offset the risks and challenges associated with these locations, mindful of the fact that the competition is doing the same thing.

Source: Excerpted section from Deloitte Review, Issue 4 (January 2009) article titled "Rethinking Emerging Market Strategies: From offshoring to strategic expansion," by Vikram Mahidhar, Craig Giffi, and Ajit Kambil with Ryan Alvanos. Used with permission of the Deloitte Review.

Based on a study of more than 10,000 foreign entry activities into China, Pan and Tse concluded that managers tend to follow a hierarchy-of-decision sequence in choosing an entry mode. They found that the location choice—specifically the level of country risk—was the primary influence factor at the level of deciding between equity and non-equity modes. Host-country government incentives also encouraged the choice of equity mode. Managers first decide between non–equity based for high-risk locations, and equity based where it is perceived there is lower risk. Then, non-equity modes are divided into contractual agreements such as franchising,

EXHIBIT 6-15   Factors Affecting Choice of International Entry Mode[114]

Factor Category	Examples
Internal factors	Global experience of firm and managers
	Distinctive competencies, patents, technology
	Corporate culture and structure
	Global objectives
	Long-term strategy
	Financial assets
External factors	Industry globalization
	Industry growth rate
	Barriers to entry
	Level of global competition
	Opportunities and incentives
	Extent of scale and location economies
	Country risk—political, economic, legal
	Cultural distance
	Knowledge of local market
	Potential of local market
	Competition in local market
Venture-specific factors	Value of firm—assets risked in foreign location
	Ability to protect proprietary technology
	Costs of making or enforcing contracts with local partners
	Size of planned foreign venture
	Intent to conduct research and development with local partners

licensing, outsourcing, e-business, and exporting; equity modes are split into wholly owned operations, acquisitions, offshoring, and equity joint ventures (EJVs) with varying levels of equity investment. [115]

Gupta and Govindarajan also propose a hierarchy-of-decision factors sequence but consider two initial choice levels. The first is the extent to which the firm will export or produce locally; the second is the extent of ownership control over activities that will be performed locally in the target market.[116] There is an array of choice combinations within those two dimensions. Gupta and Govindarajan point out that, among the many factors to take into account, alliance-based entry modes are more suitable under the following conditions:

- Physical, linguistic, and cultural distance between the home and host countries is high.
- The subsidiary would have low operational integration with the rest of the multinational operations.
- The risk of asymmetric learning by the partner is low.
- The company is short of capital.
- Government regulations require local equity participation.[117]

The choice of entry strategy for McDonald's, for example, varies around the world according to the prevailing conditions in each country. As of August 2011, McDonalds had 33,000 restaurants in 118 countries, employing 1.7 million people worldwide.[118] In Europe, the company prefers wholly owned subsidiaries, since European markets are similar to those in the United States and can be run similarly. Those subsidiaries in the United States both operate company-owned stores and license out franchises. Approximately 80 percent of McDonald's stores around the world are franchised. In Asia, joint ventures are preferred so as to take advantage of partners' contacts and local expertise, and their ability to negotiate with bureaucracies such as the Chinese government. McDonald's has more than 1,000 stores in Japan and it continues its expansion in China, in spite of conflicts with the Chinese government, such as when it made McDonald's move from its leased Tiananmen Square restaurant. In other markets, such as in Saudi Arabia, McDonald's prefers to limit its equity risk by licensing the name—adding strict quality standards—and keeping an option to buy later.

Timing Entry and Scheduling Expansions

As with McDonald's, international strategic formulation requires a long-term perspective. Entry strategies, therefore, need to be conceived as part of a well-designed, overall plan. In the past, many companies have decided on a particular means of entry that seemed appropriate at the time, only to find later that it was shortsighted. For instance, if a company initially chooses to license a host-country company to produce a product, then later decides that the market is large enough to warrant its own production facility, this new strategy will no longer be feasible because the local host-country company already owns the rights.

The Influence of Culture on Strategic Choices

> *Certain cultures are considered attractive to other cultures. A foreign culture's perceived attributes may be a major reason for the preferences expressed by potential partners and host countries.*[119]

> JOURNAL OF INTERNATIONAL BUSINESS,
> *JANUARY 2012.*

It is clear that cultural distance (CD), or at least the perception of it, affects strategic choice. Potential partners and their host counterparts tend to feel more confident about their international allies when they seem "culturally attractive," in particular when new to international business. The more similar the culture, the more likely managers are to select that region for investment—for example, between the United States and England. However, often that assumption of similarity leads to problems because preparation and allowance is not made for existing subtle differences. Shenkar gives the examples that the "friction" between dissimilar cultures is more likely in a merger or acquisition than in an IJV—because there is more interaction among parties in the former—whereas an IJV is set up as a separate entity with less interaction from the parent firms.[120] Managers armed with such insight might then chose an IJV over other strategic options which necessitate more cross-cultural interaction.

In addition, strategic choices at various levels often are influenced by specific cultural factors, such as a long-term versus a short-term perspective. Hofstede found that most people in such countries as China and Japan generally had a longer-term horizon than those in Canada and the United States.[121] Whereas Americans, then, might make strategic choices with a heavy emphasis on short-term profits, the Japanese are known to be more patient in sacrificing short-term results in order to build for the future with investment, research and development, and market share.

Risk orientation was also found to explain the choice between equity and non-equity modes.[122] Risk orientation relates to Hofstede's uncertainty avoidance dimension.[123] Firms from countries where, generally speaking, people tend to avoid uncertainty (for example, Latin American and African countries) tend to prefer non-equity entry modes to minimize exposure to risk. Managers from firms from low-uncertainty avoidance countries are more willing to take risks and are, therefore, more likely to adopt equity entry modes.[124]

The choice of the equity versus non-equity mode has also been found to be related to level of power distance. According to Hofstede, a high power-distance country (such as Arab countries and Japan) is one where people observe interpersonal inequality and hierarchy.[125] Pan and Tse found that firms from countries tending toward high power distance are more likely to use equity modes of entry abroad.[126]

These are but a few of the examples of the relationships between culture and the choices that are made in the strategic planning and implementation phase. They serve to remind us that it is people who make those decisions and that the ways people think, feel, and act are based on their ingrained societal culture. People bring that context to work, and it influences their propensity toward or against certain types of decisions.

CONCLUSION

The process of strategic formulation for global competitiveness is a daunting task in the volatile global arena and is further complicated by the difficulties involved in acquiring timely and credible information. However, early insight into global developments provides a critical advantage in positioning a firm for future success.

When an entry strategy is selected, the international manager focuses on translating strategic plans into actual operations. Often this involves strategic alliances; always it involves functional-level activities for strategic implementation. These subjects are covered in Chapter 7.

Summary of Key Points

1. Companies "go international" for many reasons, both proactive and reactive. Those companies that are proactive from their outset in establishing a presence in many countries are referred to as "Born Globals." The Internet is facilitating companies of all sizes to expand around the world within a short time frame—thus leveling the field for small businesses relative to companies with greater resources.

2. International expansion and the resulting realization of a firm's strategy are the products of both rational planning and responding to emergent opportunities. For example, those opportunities may develop as a result of economic, competitive, demographic, or political changes in other countries. Firms are increasingly taking advantage of opportunities for expansion into emerging markets such as the "BRICs."

3. The steps in the rational planning process for developing an international corporate strategy comprise defining the mission and objectives of the firm, scanning the environment for threats and opportunities, assessing the internal strengths and weaknesses of the firm, considering alternative international entry strategies, and deciding on strategy. The strategic management process is completed by putting into place the operational plans necessary to implement the strategy and then setting up control and evaluation procedures.

4. Competitive analysis is an assessment of how a firm's strengths and weaknesses vis-à-vis those of its competitors affect the opportunities and threats in the international environment. Such assessment allows the firm to determine where the company has distinctive competencies that will give it strategic advantage or where problem areas exist.

5. Corporate-level strategic approaches to international competitiveness include globalization and regionalization. Many MNCs have developed to the point of using an integrative global strategy. Entry and ownership strategies are exporting, licensing, franchising, contract manufacturing, offshoring, outsourcing services, turn-key operations, management contracts, joint ventures, and fully owned subsidiaries, as well as the local level of e-business. Critical environmental and operational factors for implementation must be taken into account.

6. Companies of all sizes are increasingly looking to the Internet as a means of expanding their global operations, but localizing Internet operations is complex, involving various logistical and cultural challenges.

Discussion Questions

1. Discuss why companies "go international," giving specific reactive and proactive reasons.
2. What effects on company strategy have you observed as a result of the global economic downturn?
3. Give examples of the impact of the Internet on small businesses.
4. Discuss the ways in which managers arrive at new strategic directions—formal and informal. Which is the best?
5. Explain the process of environmental assessment. What are the major international variables to consider in the scanning process? Discuss the levels of environmental monitoring that should be conducted. How well do you think managers conduct environmental assessment?
6. Discuss the impact of the rise of emerging market countries on the strategic planning of firms around the world.
7. How can managers assess the potential relative competitive position of their firm in order to decide on new strategic directions?
8. Discuss the relative advantages of globalization versus regionalization/localization.
9. Compare the merits of the entry strategies discussed in this chapter. What is their role in an integrative global strategy?
10. Discuss the considerations in strategic choice, including the typical stages of the MNC and the need for a long-term global perspective.

Application Exercises

1. Choose a company in the social media industry or a chain in the fast-food industry. In small groups, conduct a multilevel environmental analysis, describing the major variables involved, the relative impact of specific threats and opportunities, and the critical environmental factors to be considered. The group findings can then be presented to the class, allowing a specific time period for each group so that comparison and debate of different group perspectives can follow. Be prepared to state what regions or specific countries you are interested in and give your rationale.

2. In small groups, discuss among yourselves and then debate with the other groups the relative merits of the alternative entry strategies for the company and countries you chose in Exercise 1. You should be able to make a specific choice and defend that decision.

3. For this exercise, research (individually or in small groups) a company with international operations and find out the kinds of entry strategies the firm has used. Present the information you find, in writing or verbally to the class, describing the nature of the company's international operations, its motivations, its entry strategies, the kinds of implementation problems the firm has run into, and how those problems have been dealt with.

Experiential Exercise

In groups of four, develop a strategic analysis for a type of company that is considering entry into an emerging market country.

Which entry strategies seem most appropriate? Share your results with the class.

Internet Resources

Visit the Deresky Companion Website at www.pearsonhighered.com/deresky for this chapter's Internet resources.

CASE STUDY

Search Engines in Global Business

A search engine is designed in such a way to actually find useful information on the World Wide Web (WWW) and file transfer protocol (FTP) servers. In technical terms, the search queries and their results show up in the forms of search engine results pages (SERPS) and related information. This information may encompass Web images and other types of useful files. Data mining is also part of this process.[1] In today's fast-changing global business and MNCs' diverse operations in domestic and global markets, search engines are highly useful and have been introduced in a multitude of languages. Local cultures and environments matter a lot when designing country-specific search engines.

In global business, data is an important part of search engines. As of 2012, the need for large-scale data is everywhere (consumers and businesses) in global business. The *Economist* in its annual *World in 2012* wrote: "*Many more firms will start to analyze huge piles of data to optimize everything from their supply chains to their customer relationships.*"[2] Search engines come in different forms and types and may include: general search engines, P2P search engines, meta-search engines, information-specific search engines, geographically based search engines, business search engines, enterprise search engines, and others.[3]

Figure 6-2 provides information on the main search engines in global business. Interestingly, most of the search engines are available worldwide but are based in the U.S. This shows the power of information-related companies that own these search engines. As of 2012, Google is the most popular and powerful search engine in the world, followed by Yahoo, Baidu (China), Bing, and Ask. Of course Google is highly diversified in its products and maintains sites in various languages. This is a perfect reflection of today's global business with diverse markets and consumers. Google also maintains Google Docs, Google Calendar, Google Site Search, Google Maps, etc.[4] In 2012, Google sales surpassed $37 billion with a market capitalization of $200 billion. This shows the immense power and coverage of this search engine.

Search engines in global business are mostly impacted by local cultures, country-specific data, and national identities. For example, as of 2012, "Baidu" is the largest search engine in China with sales of $2.5 billion, and it carries a market capitalization of $48 billion.[5] "Yandex" is a major search engine in Russia. In addition, South Korea maintains "Naver," Czech Republic has "Seznam"; "Sohu" is distinctly available in the Chinese market and continues to be a dominant player. Regardless of their types and forms, search engines in global business are highly differentiated on the basis of their functions, country image, and usage. Search engines' transaction data and search results can reveal an interesting array of data. The search engines and their commercial identity are highly country- and region-specific. No wonder we witness a few search engines that continue to dominate global business. This is also the result of complex value chains where information is commoditized and content specific. In short, search engines such as Google, Yahoo, Baidu, Yandex, Naver, and others will play a major role in their country-specific

FIGURE 6-2   Search Engine Market Share in Global Markets (2012)

A. Top five search engines by market share (%)

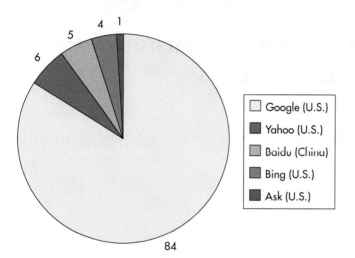

B. Other popular search engines and related sites in global markets:

- All the Web.com (U.S.)
- AOL Search (U.S.)
- HotBot (U.S.)
- Alta Vista (U.S.)
- Live Search (U.S.)
- Lycos (U.S.)
- Netscape (U.S.)
- Sohu (China)
- Yandex (Russia)
- Naver (South Korea)
- Seznam (Czech Republic)

Sources: Marketshare.hitslink.com (2012); Pinnaclepixel.com (2012); *Search Engine Colossus* (2012); *Wikipedia* (2012).

environments because of business efficiencies and productivity issues. The area is still in its infancy and growth stage and will have massive repercussions for MNCs, domestic companies, governments, and consumers worldwide.[6] Above all, consumers' privacy and national policies are major variables in the growth of global search engines.

Case Questions

1. Compare and contrast the top five search engines in global business.
2. Within today's changing global business, what do you see happening in the next five years regarding search engines' growth and country-specific issues?
3. Search engines carry national identities and cultures. Compare major search engines from each continent on the basis of their local characteristics and national identities.

Source:

Written exclusively for this book by Syed Tariq Anwar, West Texas A&M University. Copyright © 2012 by Syed Tariq Anwar. Used with permission.

References

1. *Wikipedia.* (2012). Web search engine, http://en.wikipedia.org/wiki/Web_search_engine.
2. The Economist. (2012). Welcome to the yotta world, *The World in 2012*, London, UK: 126.
3. *Wikipedia.* (2012). List of search engines, http://en.wikipedia.org/wiki/List_of_search_engin.
4. See: Google. (2012). *Google search*, http://www.google.com/intl/en/about/index.html.
5. *Value Line* (2012). Various companies, Value Line LLC, New York.
6. For more information, see: Chang et al., Y. "Multimedia search capabilities of Chinese language search engines," *Information Processing and Management* 46 (2010): 308–319; Jansen, B. J., and Spink, A. "How are we searching the World Wide Web? A comparison of nine search engine transaction logs," *Information Processing & Management* 42(1), (2006): 248–263; Kim, K., and Tse, E. T. S. "Dynamic search engine competition with a knowledge-sharing service." *Decision Support Systems*, 52 (2012). 427–437; Tjondronegoro, D., Spink, A., and Jansen, B. J. "A study and comparison of multimedia Web searching: 1997–2006," *Journal of the American Society for Information Science & Technology* 60(9), (2009): 1756–1768.

CHAPTER 7

Implementing Strategy
Strategic Alliances; Small Businesses; Emerging Economy Firms

OUTLINE

OBJECTIVES

1. To realize that much of international business is conducted through strategic alliances.

2. To understand the reasons that firms seek international business allies and the benefits they bring.

3. To become familiar with the ways that SMEs can expand through alliances with MNCs.

4. To understand the complexities involved in managing international joint ventures.

5. To focus on how emerging economy firms can implement their expansion strategies.

6. To appreciate the governmental and cultural factors that influence strategic implementation, as well as the impact of e-commerce.

7. To recognize the changing factors, opportunities, and threats involved in joint ventures in the Russian Federation.

OPENING PROFILE: FROM BP TO EXXON: BEWARE THE ALLIANCE WITH THE BEAR.[1]

"Memo to Exxon: Business with Russia Might Involve Guns and Balaclavas."[2]

A smiling Vladimir Putin, then–Prime Minister of Russia (now President again), looked on as Exxon Mobil and OAO Rosneft, Russia's largest oil producer, signed on for a partnership involving as much as $500 billion of investments. The deal involves a $3.2 billion exploration project in Russia's Arctic waters and in the Black Sea. For its part, Rosneft, which is 75 percent owned by the Kremlin, will also get shares in at least six Exxon Mobil projects in the United States. The deal also provides $450 million for a joint Arctic research center in St. Petersburg. Rosneft does not have the technology for deep-sea drilling.

The alliance is a blow for Britain's BP, with which Rosneft had struck an accord in January to jointly develop the Arctic fields—but the deal fell through after BP's Russian shareholders managed to block it. The Exxon-Rosneft alliance marks the end of long and combative negotiations between Russian oligarchs and the joint venture TNK-BP. In addition, the day after the Exxon-Rosneft deal was announced, BP's Moscow offices were raided.

BP's spokeswoman Sheila Williams declined to comment on the Exxon-Rosneft deal, but said BP is still "committed both to Russia and to the continuing success of TNK-BP," its Russian venture.[3] Indeed, as reported by the *Financial Times*, "BP defended itself against a raid by bailiffs and armed special forces troopers on its Moscow office on Wednesday (August 31, 2011), describing it as 'part of a pressure campaign against BP's business in Russia.' "[4] In fact, in a scene reminiscent of bad movies, the *New York Times* reported that "*commandos* armed with assault rifles raided the offices of the British oil company BP on Wednesday, in one of the ritual armed searches of white-collar premises that are common enough here to have a nickname: masky shows (so-called because of the balaclavas the agents often wear.)"[5]

Run-ins with the Russian police have been frequent for BP, including the revocation of visas of BP's executives, such as the current BP chief executive Robert Dudley, then director of TNK-BP, who was forced to leave Russia. Considering recent events has prompted a leading risk-analysis organization, the Eurasia Group, to put out a warning to its clients about partnering in Russia and what can happen to companies that get into a bad relationship with the government there. Other companies in Moscow have also been targeted. Deutsche Bank's office in Moscow was raided in February by masked and armed law enforcement agents apparently looking for documents related to a commercial mortgage.[6]

Events such as these clarify why investors are reluctant to invest in Russia, given the political and economic climate that leads to such harassment; in addition, there has been considerable flight of capital out of the country. Ironically, the Exxon-Rosneft deal is connected to the arrest of former Russian oil tycoon Mikhail Khodorkovsky and his re-conviction at the beginning of 2011. Putin had Khodorkovsky—then head of the Yukos Oil Company—arrested in 2003, charged with negotiating a joint venture with Exxon without getting permission from the Kremlin. Putin has now used Rosneft, which acquired the Yukos assets stripped from Khodorkovsky, to make the deal with Exxon himself.[7]

STRATEGIC ALLIANCES

As discussed in the opening profile, strategic alliances present great opportunities but sometimes great peril for the uninformed, especially when dealing with the lesser-known risks in emerging markets.

Strategic alliances are partnerships between two or more firms that decide they can better pursue their mutual goals by combining their resources—financial, managerial, and technological—as well as their existing distinctive competitive advantages. Alliances—often called *cooperative strategies*—are transition mechanisms that propel the partners' strategies forward in a turbulent environment faster than would be possible for each company alone.[8] The explosion of international strategic alliances (ISAs) over the last decade has been caused by the need for organizations to respond to the globalization of markets and the opportunities presented by technological advances. However, the rush to take advantage of those opportunities has resulted in an estimated half of ISAs having poor results or failing.[9] (These problems will be discussed later in this chapter.)

Alliances typically fall under one of three categories: joint ventures, equity strategic alliances, and non-equity strategic alliances, and they can be for various purposes such as sharing technology, marketing, or production joint ventures. Cross-border alliances frequently necessitate a local partner in order to counteract political risk factors and to take advantage of local knowledge and contacts.

Indeed, the goals of technology sharing and the move towards green technology led BMW and Toyota to announce an alliance in December 2011. Toyota had been through a tough year of natural disasters and a strong yen. The chief executive of Toyota Motor Europe, Didier Leroy, said that an alliance would let both sides bolster efficiency, improve economies of scale, reduce development costs, and achieve quicker speeds to market.[10] Alliances with electronics makers Sanyo Electric and Panasonic have also been precipitated by the search for better batteries. Still, "alliances have been one way that Toyota has hedged its bets: It has forged partnerships with Aston Martin and Ford, and last year, it announced a tie-up with Tesla Motors, the Silicon Valley-based maker of high-end electric cars."[11]

It should be noted, however, that, while the last decade brought a surge in companies seeking growth through mergers and acquisitions (M&As), joint ventures, and other alliances, the global economic downturn caused many companies to postpone or cancel out on such plans, often instead retrenching or "de-merging." Examples were General Motors and Citigroup having to spin off partners as well as retrench operations in order to maintain sufficient cash flow. The rate of deals collapsing increased amid the credit crisis and global equity market volatility. An example was the C$34.8 billion (US$28.2 billion) leveraged buy-out of BCE, the Canadian telecommunications giant, which was under threat after auditor KPMG said BCE might not meet solvency tests if it absorbed the C$32 billion of debt required to finance the transaction.[12] Other proposed deals were going ahead, but with revised terms: For example, Dow Chemical, the largest U.S. chemical group, entered into a deal to inject its low-growth plastics business into a joint venture with Kuwait's state oil company—but at a reduced price.

Still other deals, made under duress, involved government alliances in an attempt to save companies and industries from default, as with a number of banks that become subject to partial nationalization. As one example, the British Government struck a deal in March 2009 to increase its stake in Lloyds' Banking Group (LBG) to 65 percent from 43 percent. The Government guaranteed some $575 billion worth of toxic assets as part of the deal, which was brokered between bank and Treasury officials. Lloyds Banking Group was created early 2009 when Lloyds TSB bought rival lender HBOS, which faced collapse because it was struggling to raise funds due to the credit crunch.[13]

Joint Ventures

MUMBAI, India—After years of studying the Indian market, Starbucks Coffee said Monday that it would open its first store here by September (2012) through a 50-50 joint venture with Tata Global Beverages, a unit of the largest business group in India.

THE NEW YORK TIMES,
JANUARY 20, 2012.[14]

As discussed in Chapter 6, a **joint venture (JV)** is a new independent entity jointly created and owned by two or more parent companies. The JV agreement for a firm may comprise a majority JV (where the firm has more than 50 percent equity), a minority JV (less than 50 percent equity), or a 50-50 JV (where two firms have equal equity). An international joint venture (IJV) is a joint venture among companies in different countries. In that case, the firm shares the profits, costs, and risks with a local partner (or a global partner) and benefits from the local partner's local contacts and markets. (Advantages and disadvantages of IJVs were discussed in Chapter 6). The Starbucks agreement with Tata Global Beverages is an example of a 50-50 equity IJV. "The announcement came a year after the company said it was going to enter the market and nearly two months after the Indian government fumbled an effort to attract more foreign investment in its retailing industry."[15] Although India is a nation of tea-drinkers, Starbucks decided it was time to look for market growth in such a fast-growing economy. Tata's motivation is to create a national cafe chain. It earlier had a minority stake in a chain called Barista, but that venture fell apart when the partners were having a lot of disagreements.

Another example of a 50-50 equity IJV is that between France's PSA Peugeot-Citroen Group and Japan's Toyota at Kolin in the Czech Republic. As noted by Fujio Cho, president of Toyota Motors, the world's richest carmaker:

> *Each company has brought its own style, culture and way of thinking to this partnership—but our different approaches have benefited our joint venture enormously.*[16]

Among the benefits noted by the two companies are that Toyota "gains an insight into the mindset of one of Europe's biggest indigenous carmakers and knowledge of its suppliers and their capabilities."[17] And Peugeot-Citroen can gain experience from Toyota's lean manufacturing system. The companies acknowledge that the IJV has resulted in faster development and increased production capacity, and that costs are shared without either company renouncing its independence.[18]

Equity Strategic Alliances

> *Abu Dhabi's state-owned Advanced Technology Investment Company, the latest entrant in the $20bn contract chipmaking industry, is proving it has the capital to back its ambition of making Abu Dhabi a chip industry heavyweight through yesterday's $1.8bn deal to buy a majority stake in Singapore's Chartered Semiconductor.*
>
> FINANCIAL TIMES,
> *SEPTEMBER 9, 2009.*[19]

Two or more partners have different relative ownership shares (equity percentages) in the new venture in an equity strategic alliance. Most global manufacturers have equity alliances with suppliers, sub-assemblers, and distributors—forming a network of internal family and financial links. Risk-sharing is often the motive behind equity alliances, as when Daiichi Sankyo, a Japanese pharmaceutical giant, bought a 51 percent equity share in India's Ranbaxy Laboratories in June 2008. The goal for Daiichi was to add value to its research and development expertise, and to use Ranbaxy's low-cost manufacturing base; in turn Ranbaxy would gain access to Japan's markets.[20]

Sometimes an international, or global, joint venture is part of a desperate strategy. This was the case in January 2009 when Chrysler reached for another lifeline in its equity deal to join forces with Italy's Fiat. The plan was for Fiat to get a 35 percent ownership stake in Chrysler with the goal of bringing its Fiat and Alfa Romeo brands back to the United States through Chrysler's dealership network. In return Chrysler would get the opportunity to stay alive by presenting a strategic partnership as part of its plan to the U.S. government in its quest for an additional $3 billion loan to allow it to stay in business.[21] However, further developments led to a change in plans when some creditors did not make concessions, and President Obama announced on April 30, 2009:

> *Chrysler, the third-largest American auto company, will seek bankruptcy protection and enter an alliance with the Italian automaker Fiat, the White House announced Thursday.*[22]

However, the deal with Fiat would be intact after bankruptcy, with Fiat to take part in running Chrysler, provide technical operations, and build at least one vehicle in a Chrysler plant. Fiat did not put up any financing as part of the agreement. Considerable additional financing from the U.S. government was planned after Chrysler's restructuring, with the Canadian government also offering some financing.[23]

Non-Equity Strategic Alliances

Agreements are carried out through contract rather than ownership sharing in a non-equity strategic alliance. Such contracts are often with a firm's suppliers, distributors, or manufacturers, or they may be for purposes of marketing and information sharing, such as with many airline partnerships. UPS, for example, is a global supply-chain manager for many companies around the world, such as Nike, that essentially do not touch their own products but contract with UPS to arrange the entire delivery process from factory to warehouse to customer to repair, even collecting the money.[24]

Global Strategic Alliances

Working partnerships between companies (often more than two) across national boundaries and increasingly across industries are referred to as global strategic alliances. A glance at the global airline industry, for example, tells us that global alliances have become a mainstay of competitive strategy. Not one airline is competing alone; each major U.S. carrier has established strategic links with non-U.S. companies. The Star Alliance, for example, has code sharing among 26 member airlines around the world.

Alliances are also sometimes formed between a company and a foreign government, or among companies and governments. In addition, changing regulations and policies by governments and institutions lead to new opportunities for alliances with national industries abroad. As an example, when the Nuclear Suppliers Group, a global consortium that regulates the sale of the items, voted to lift the ban on deals with India, that freed up any country to sign nuclear plant deals there. The company Areva, which is owned mostly by the French government, joined with the state-run Nuclear Power Corporation of India to build at least two and possibly as many as six nuclear power plants in the energy-starved country. Their two-reactor project could be worth about $10 billion.[25]

Alliances may comprise full global partnerships, which are often joint ventures in which two or more companies, while retaining their national identities, develop a common, long-term strategy aimed at world leadership. The European Airbus Industrie consortium, for example, comprises France's Aerospatiale and Germany's Daimler-Benz Aerospace, each with 37.9 percent of the business; British Aerospace with 20 percent; and Spain's Construcciones Aeronauticas with 4.2 percent.

Whereas such alliances have a broad agenda, others are formed for a narrow and specific function, such as production, marketing, research and development, or financing. More recently these have included electronic alliances, such as Covisint, which is redefining the entire system of car production and distribution through a common electronic marketplace. Covisint is an e-business exchange developed by Ford, General Motors, Nissan, Renault, and (then) Daimler Chrysler AG to meet the needs of the automotive industry, and is focused on procurement, supply chain, and product development solutions.[26]

Global and Cross-Border Alliances: Motivations and Benefits

Some of the typical reasons behind cross-border alliances are as follows:

1. *To avoid import barriers, licensing requirements, and other protectionist legislation:* Japanese automotive manufacturers, for example, use alliances such as the GM–Toyota venture, or subsidiaries, to produce cars in the United States so as to avoid import quotas.

2. *To share the costs and risks of the research and development of new products and processes:* In the semiconductor industry, for example, where each new generation of memory chips is estimated to cost more than $1 billion to develop, those costs and the rapid technological evolution typically require the resources of more than one (or even two) firms. Intel, for example, has alliances with Samsung and NMB Semiconductor for technology (DRAM) development; Sun Microsystems has partners for its technology (RISC), including N. V. Philips, Fujitsu, and Texas Instruments. Toshiba, Japan's third-largest electronics company, has more than two dozen major joint ventures and strategic alliances around the world, including partners such as Olivetti, Rhone-Poulenc, GEC Alstholm in Europe, LSI Logic in Canada, and Samsung in Korea. Fumio Sato, Toshiba's CEO, recognized long ago that a global strategy for a high-tech electronics company such as his necessitated joint ventures and strategic alliances.

3. *To gain access to specific markets, such as China and Russia, where regulations favor domestic companies:* Firms often find that the only way—or, at least, the best way—to enter markets such as China and Russia is through alliances, as discussed elsewhere. In addition, in spite of the severe economic problems in the EU, firms around the world are still investing there and forming strategic alliances with European companies to bolster their chances of competing in the European Union (EU) and to gain access to markets in Eastern European countries as they further develop their businesses. Chun Joo Bum, chief executive of the Daewoo Electronics unit, acknowledged his desire for local partners in Europe for two reasons: (1) to provide sorely needed capital, and (2) to help Daewoo navigate Europe's still disparate markets, saying "I need to localize our management. It is not one market."[27]

4. *To reduce political risk while making inroads into a new market:*

Carefully orchestrated partnerships with governments and other business groups are crucial to the [Disney] entertainment group's thrust into China and the rest of south-east Asia.

Bob Iger, President and COO, Walt Disney[28]

Hong Kong Disneyland is jointly owned by the Chinese government, which owns a 57 percent stake. Beijing is especially interested in promoting tourism through the venture and in employment for the 5,000 workers Disney employs directly, as well as the estimated 18,000 workers in related services.[29] Maytag Corporation, also determined to stay on the right side of the restrictive Chinese government while gaining market access, formed a joint venture with RSD, the Chinese appliance maker, to manufacture and market washing machines and refrigerators. Maytag also invested large amounts in jointly owned refrigeration products facilities to help RSD get into that market. Coca-Cola—a global player with large-scale alliances—is not beyond using some very small-scale alliances to be "political" in China. The company uses senior citizens in the Chinese Communist Party's neighborhood committees to sell Coke locally.

5. *To gain rapid entry into a new or consolidating industry and to take advantage of synergies:* Technology is rapidly providing the means and products—such as the iPad—for the overlapping and merging of traditional industries such as entertainment, computers, and telecommunications in new digital-based systems. Disney's business model of cellular partnerships and content sales, for example, created Disney mobile operations in Hong Kong, Taiwan, South Korea, Singapore, and the Philippines.[30] The company uses joint venture partners such as the Hong Kong government, or licensees and distributors such as Oriental Land and NTT DoCoMo.[31]

In many cases, technological developments are necessitating strategic alliances across industries in order for companies to gain rapid entry into areas in which they have no expertise or manufacturing capabilities. Competition is so fierce that they cannot wait to develop those resources alone. Many of these objectives, such as access to new technology and to new markets, are evident in AT&T's network of alliances around the world. Agreements with Japan's NEC, for example, gave AT&T access to new semiconductor and chip-making technologies, helping it learn how to better integrate computers with communications.

Challenges in Implementing Global Alliances

G.E. to Share Jet Technology with China in New Joint Venture

New York Times,
January 17, 2011[32]

Effective global alliances are usually tediously slow in the making but can be among the best mechanisms to implement strategies in global markets. In a highly competitive environment, alliances present a faster and less risky route to globalization. It is extremely complex to fashion such linkages, however, especially where many interconnecting systems are involved, forming intricate networks. Many alliances fail for complex reasons. Many also end up in a takeover in which one partner swallows the other. McKinsey & Company, a consulting firm, surveyed 150 companies that had been in alliances and found that 75 percent of them had been taken over by Japanese partners. Problems with shared ownership, differences in national cultures, the integration of vastly different structures and systems, the distribution of power between the companies involved, and conflicts in their relative locus of decision making and control are but a few of the organizational issues that must be worked out. When the joint venture between France Telecom and Deutsche Telekom was announced in September 2009, Tim Hottges, France Telecom finance director, said that the two sides had already agreed on a "solution mechanism" for potential problems in the United Kingdom. Noting that "This is a sign that even those who embark on such partnerships with optimism recognize that conflict about who is in charge is a constant risk," the *Financial Times* observed that "joint ventures start with smiles, but often end in tears."[33]

Often, the form of governance chosen for multinational firm alliances greatly influences their success, particularly in technologically intense fields such as pharmaceuticals, computers, and semiconductors. Thus, joint ventures are often the chosen form for such alliances because they provide greater control of proprietary technology as well as providing increased coordination in high-technology industries.

Cross-border partnerships, in particular, often become a "race to learn"—with the faster learner later dominating the alliance and rewriting its terms. In a real sense, an alliance becomes a new form of competition. In fact, according to researcher David Lei,

> *Perhaps the single greatest impediment managers face when seeking to learn or renew sources of competitive advantage is to realize that co-operation can represent another form of unintended competition, particularly to shape and apply new skills to future products and businesses.*[34]

All too often, cross-border allies have difficulty collaborating effectively, especially in competitively sensitive areas; this creates mistrust and secrecy, which then undermine the purpose of the alliance. The difficulty that they are dealing with is the dual nature of strategic alliances—the benefits of cooperation versus the dangers of introducing new competition through sharing their knowledge and technological skills about their mutual product or the manufacturing process. Managers may fear that they will lose the competitive advantage of the firm's proprietary technology or the specific skills that their personnel possess.

The cumulative learning that a partner attains through the alliance could potentially be applied to other products or even other industries that are beyond the scope of the alliance, and therefore would hold no benefit to the partner holding the original knowledge.[35] Some of the trade-offs of the duality of cross-border ventures are shown in Exhibit 7-1 and are illustrated by the 2011 joint venture between General Electric (GE) and Avic, a state-owned Chinese company. The alliance shows the tricky risk-and-reward calculations American corporations must increasingly make in their pursuit of the lucrative markets in China. This is a 50-50 venture with Avic

EXHIBIT 7-1   **The Dual Role of Strategic Alliances**

Cooperative	Competitive
Economies of scale in tangible assets (e.g., plant and equipment).	Opportunity to learn new intangible skills from partner, often tacit or organization-embedded.
Upstream–downstream division of labor among partners.	Accelerate diffusion of industry standards and new technologies to erect barriers to entry.
Fill out product line with components or end products provided by supplier.	Deny technological and learning initiative to partner via outsourcing and long-term supply arrangements.
Limit investment risk when entering new markets or uncertain technological fields via shared resources.	Encircle existing competitors and preempt the rise of new competitors with alliance partners in "proxy wars" to control market access, distribution, and access to new technologies.
Create a "critical mass" to learn and develop new technologies to protect domestic, strategic industries.	Form clusters of learning among suppliers and related firms to avoid or reduce foreign dependence for critical inputs and skills.
Assist short-term corporate restructurings by lowering exit barriers in mature or declining industries.	Alliances serve as experiential platforms to "demature" and transform existing mature industries via new components, technologies, or skills to enhance the value of future growth options.

Source: David Lei, "Offensive and Defensive Uses of Alliances," in Heidi Vernon-Wortzel and L. H. Wortzel, *Strategic Management in Global Economy*, 3rd ed. (New York: John Wiley & Sons, 1997), used with permission.

planned for a 50-year duration. Additional risks are that such technology-sharing could advance the Chinese military-aviation status.

> *But doing business in China often requires Western multinationals like G.E. to share technology and trade secrets that might eventually enable Chinese companies to beat them at their own game—by making the same products cheaper, if not better.*[36]

The enticing benefits of cross-border alliances often mask the many pitfalls involved. In addition to potential loss of a company's technology and knowledge or skills base, other areas of incompatibility often arise, such as conflicting strategic goals and objectives, cultural clashes, and disputes over management and control systems. Sometimes it takes a while for such problems to evidence themselves, particularly if insufficient homework has been done in meetings between the two sides to work out the implementation details. The alliance between KLM Royal Dutch Airlines and Northwest Airlines linking their hubs in Detroit and Amsterdam, for example, resulted in a bitter feud among the top officials of both companies over methods of running an airline business—the European way or the American way—and over cultural differences between the companies, as well as a power struggle at the top over who should call the shots.[37]

Implementing Alliances Between SMEs and MNCs

All countries have a large proportion of business enterprises, as well as NGOs, that are small or medium-sized enterprises (SMEs). But, increasingly, MNCs are dominating the markets in which SMEs operate, often crowding them out of business altogether. However, astute managers of SMEs can often find opportunities for alliances with those multinationals, providing "complementary resources and capabilities that can lead to, for instance, an innovative product offering being rolled out on a global scale, or a worldwide licensing agreement."[38] For example, MNCs often partner with local small enterprises to capture new ideas and innovations. Sun Microsystems, for instance, engaged with a number of small enterprises in Scotland on RFID projects in order to bolster its competitiveness in this emerging area.[39] SMEs should seek out those opportunities to offer MNCs complementary technologies as well as local market networks, as discussed in the nearby Under the Lens feature.

UNDER THE LENS

Dancing with Gorillas: How SMEs Can Internationalize through Relationships with Foreign Multinationals[40]

SHAMEEN PRASHANTHAM

International expansion is no longer the exclusive domain of large multinational corporations (MNCs). Internationalizing small and medium enterprises (SMEs) feature prominently in today's economic landscape especially, but not exclusively, in knowledge-intensive sectors such as software and biotech. How do these SMEs overcome their resource constraints and accelerate their internationalization process? In part, by leveraging their network relationships with other companies—such as key clients or strategic partners.

In this article I focus on one potentially valuable network relationship that is seemingly overlooked by many SMEs: a local relationship with a foreign MNC. That is, a relationship with a local MNC subsidiary (e.g., IBM India). While SMEs often collaborate with other SMEs, they may also forge links with larger firms that can provide them with both resources and opportunities that would ordinarily be beyond their reach. Also, associating with larger firms can provide legitimacy to SMEs, especially for new ventures, where an unproven track record may deprive them of credibility in the marketplace. A relationship with an MNC could potentially help in all these ways. Although possibly advantageous for SMEs, interaction between SMEs and MNCs is unlikely to take place easily or naturally. Indeed, the mismatch between a small firm and a large global player can be so intimidating that one might ask: Why should SMEs bother about forging relationships with local MNC subsidiaries? I once posed this very question to management guru C. K. Prahalad at a conference. His response was: "SMEs cannot [avoid] large companies. If you want a global reach you have to put up with it. . . .

(Continued)

It is not a choice. The question is: How do you learn to dance with the big gorilla?" My research in India and the UK suggests that it is not easy for SMEs to dance with gorillas—but it can be done by adopting the following strategies:

(i) *Forming MNC relationships* Most MNCs wishing to engage with a partner of similar size will take a direct frontal approach to that relationship, perhaps through a dedicated alliance department or through key individuals who have direct counterparts in the prospective partner company. In direct contrast, for an SME seeking to partner with an MNC, the lack of access and attention coupled with the asymmetry in resources means that a direct frontal approach is likely to fail. Instead, the SME would be better off using an indirect means of access. That is, it may be necessary to form a bridge between the two disparate organizations. So, for example, some MNCs such as Microsoft run active partner programs through which SMEs can receive technical and sales support. Additionally, some public policy initiatives provide even greater "hand-holding" for SMEs that may include, for example, legal advice while formulating agreements concerning intellectual property. Such initiatives will of course only make a positive difference if both SMEs and MNCs have access to them. SMEs would do well to identify and leverage these opportunities, where available. In particular, using local allies to forge MNC relationships can help the SME gain commitment from its larger partner. Commitment—in the form of a memorandum of understanding, for example—strengthens the commitment to a joint project from all the parties. Even if pressures from MNC headquarters begin to impede progress, subsidiaries—particularly entrepreneurial ones—are likely to push on with a view to achieving the agreed outcome. Apart from the actual benefits of the collaborative activity, a major motivation for persisting with a joint project when there is a written understanding is to avoid losing face in the local community. As one interviewee suggested, when there is mutual commitment to a collaborative project, an MNC subsidiary is likely to be "shamed into carrying out its end of the bargain."

(ii) *Consolidating MNC relationships* Having formed a relationship with an MNC, an SME must establish its credentials by being clear about, and focusing on, the greatest value that it can add to the relationship. The SME can then proactively leverage the MNC's complementary capabilities. For instance, if the SME's main contribution pertains to specialized technology, then in order to enhance its prospects of internationalization it can draw upon complementary technical expertise from the MNC as well as its marketing base to achieve greater international visibility. Here, the development of a meaningful SME-MNC relationship must be underpinned by the SME's solid innovation base. Integral to the process of consolidating the relationship from there on is the process of building trust incrementally. This calls for investing time and energy in regular interaction with the MNC partner. However, the SME should also be aware of the inherent instability in such relationships. One way to deal with this vulnerability is by "modularizing" knowledge transfer from the MNC partner. This is because when collaborative projects have discrete knowledge transfers, it is possible to achieve partial success even if the project gets shelved at some point down the road. Joint projects can be broken down into specific knowledge transfer milestones. This was certainly the case with one software SME that I studied. Decisions beyond its control led to the termination of a collaborative partnership with an MNC subsidiary after about six months of activity. A modular approach to knowledge transfer, however, meant that this SME ended up with a perfectly functioning prototype using the MNC's hardware platform, which required no further additional technological development going forward.

(iii) *Extending MNC Relationships* Given the asymmetry of resources and differences in long-term objectives, SME-MNC relationships are bound to unfold in an unpredictable pattern. Yet SMEs ideally would want to extend a successful relationship with an MNC. The SMEs most successful at collaborating effectively with MNC subsidiaries over a long period of time were those that built links with individuals who spanned boundaries and who could, in turn, tap into resources and knowledge elsewhere in the MNC network. The virtues of boundary-spanning networking can be seen in cases where the SME's visibility with, for example, Microsoft in Bangalore is extended to the global HQ in Seattle. Another SME that I studied dealt with an MNC technology specialist who was well connected with European and North American subsidiaries, and therefore could obtain useful information from the wider MNC network. Apart from extending the relationship in geographic terms, SMEs should also seek to broaden the value chain activities they undertake jointly with MNCs. One attraction of dealing with MNCs is the prospect of receiving support in both upstream activities, such as R&D, as well as downstream activities, like sales. Joint product development efforts provide an example of an upstream benefit, while joint promotion activities (e.g., being featured on the MNC's global website) illustrate downstream benefits. SMEs would do well to adopt a holistic perspective seeking to derive,

EXHIBIT 7-2   Strategies for Overcoming Asymmetry

Relationship Stage	Forming	Consolidating	Extending
Strategic focus	Partner selection	Strategic renewal (including innovation)	International expansion
Examples of relational strategies	Leveraging allies and network entry-points (e.g., partner programs)	Modularizing knowledge transfer (i.e., discrete milestones)	Cultivating boundary-spanning champions

where feasible, both upstream and downstream benefits, thus achieving economies of scope—getting more bang for their buck—from network relationships with MNC subsidiaries. (These strategies are summarized in Exhibit 7-2).

Given the considerable challenges involved, it is conceivable that some SMEs will wonder whether collaborative SME-MNC relationships are really worth the trouble. Indeed for some SMEs, specifically those that are content to focus on relatively less knowledge-intensive offerings and pick the low-lying fruit, engaging with MNCs may not be truly beneficial. However for those SMEs that do have cutting-edge technologies to offer, spurning the prospect of engaging with MNCs is likely to result in missed opportunities. And, as noted at the outset, there may really be little option for innovative SMEs with global ambitions but to learn to dance with the gorillas.

Source: Dr. Shameen Prashantham is Associate Professor in International Business and Strategy at Nottingham University Business School China. His research focuses on social capital and the internationalization of young firms, particularly in the Bangalore software industry. He has published in *British Journal of Management, California Management Review, Entrepreneurship Theory & Practice, Journal of International Business Studies, Journal of Management Studies*, and *Organization Studies*, among other journals. He is also the author of *The Internationalization of Small Firms: A Strategic Entrepreneurship Perspective* (London: Routledge, 2008). Used with the permission of Dr. Shameen Prashantham.

Guidelines for Successful Alliances

As discussed earlier, many global companies, such as IBM, the Tata Group, and Toyota, build extensive alliance portfolios that involve multiple concurrent alliances. Oracle's Partner Network, for example, includes 19,500 partners. Alliance partners can provide synergies and value to corporate performance by providing access to new resources and markets, generating economies of scale and scope, reducing costs, sharing risks, and enhancing flexibility.[41] Unfortunately, the complexities involved in managing many alliances often means that many—around half by most estimates—are unsuccessful, often because of poor partner selections initially, and then also because of poor management to ensure that the expected competencies and synergies are realized. Research by Dovev Lavie of 20,000 alliances involving about 8,800 unique partners provides some insight into how managers can manage their alliances in ways that will increase the likelihood of success. The results enabled the identification of "value-creation and value-capture strategies that can guide partner selection decisions, and developed alliance portfolio management practices to help managers extract more value from their alliance portfolios."[42] Value creation strategies include, for example, the importance of assimilating network resources so as to acquire new skills and capabilities. Value capture strategies caution that it is important to "avoid partners that compete in your industry if they enjoy superior bargaining power."[43] One key factor in managing alliance portfolios is to consider not only what each alliance partner will bring to the company, but also how that partner will affect other partners in the portfolio.

It is clear that many difficulties arise in cross-border alliances in melding the national and corporate cultures of the parties, in overcoming language and communication barriers, and in building trust between the parties over how to share proprietary assets and management processes. Some basic guidelines, as follow, will help to minimize potential problems. However, nothing is as important as having a long "courtship" with a potential partner to establish compatibility strategically and interpersonally and set up a plan with the prospective partner. Even setting up some pilot programs on a short-term basis for some of the planned combined activities can highlight areas that may become problematic.

1. Choose a partner with compatible strategic goals and objectives and with whom the alliance will result in synergies through the combined markets, technologies, and management cadre.
2. Seek alliances where complementary skills, products, and markets will result. If each partner brings distinctive skills and assets to the venture, there will be reduced potential for direct competition in end products and markets. In addition, each partner will begin the alliance in a balanced relationship.[44]
3. Work out with the partner how you will each deal with proprietary technology or competitively sensitive information—what will be shared, and what will not, and how shared technology will be handled. Trust is an essential ingredient of an alliance, particularly in these areas; but this must be backed up by contractual agreements.
4. Recognize that most alliances last only a few years and will probably break up once a partner feels it has incorporated the skills and information it needs to go it alone. With this in mind, managers need to "learn thoroughly and rapidly about a partner technology and management: transfer valuable ideas and practices promptly into one's own operations."[45]

Some of the opportunities and complexities in cross-border alliances are illustrated in the following Comparative Management in Focus on joint ventures in the Russian Federation. Such alliances are further complicated by the different history of the two parties' economic systems and the resulting business practices.

COMPARATIVE MANAGEMENT IN FOCUS

Joint Ventures in the Russian Federation

Russia ranks 67th out of 139 countries covered by the 2012–2013 Global Competitiveness Index.

World Economic Forum.[46]

The new deal (a Disney television channel) comes as regulators take a softer look at foreign takeovers, a change evident in the number of recent transactions. Two weeks ago Unilever acquired Kalina, a Russian make-up producer, for euro 500m ($693m), while last year PepsiCo spent $5.4bn to acquire Wimm-Bill-Dann.

www.ft.com, October 27, 2011.[47]

Judging by the above quotes, it seems that Russia poses a number of contradictions to would-be investors. In 2011, as Disney pushed into Russia with a new Disney television channel, its CEO Bob Iger said "we really believe in Russia as a growth market."[48] On the other hand, investors get concerned when they hear about incidents such as the raid on the offices of BP in Moscow in August 2011 (described in the Opening Profile), and the seizure of the Norwegian cell phone company Telenor in 2009—just two in a series of events shaking faith in the Russian market. It's clear that foreign companies have started to think twice about investing in international joint ventures (IJVs) in Russia since (then) President Putin's moves to take control of key industries, including banks, newspapers, and oil assets. In May 2008, President Putin signed the Strategic Industries Bill, which regulates foreign investment. The new law identifies 42 strategic sectors (compared to 16 in 2005) in which foreign investors have to seek special permission before investing. Indeed, "*since the financial exodus from Russia in the wake of the world credit crisis and Moscow's heavy-handed military incursion into Georgia, the country's capacity to tap the tens of billions of dollars in foreign investment it needs to overhaul its creaking infrastructure has been thrown into doubt.*"[49]

MAP 7.1 Russia

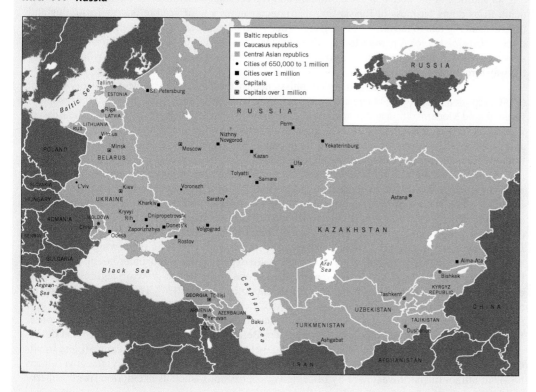

In spite of those caveats, Russia—the world's largest country, spanning eleven time zones, clearly offers substantial opportunity for companies willing to go for the risk-return trade-off. However, its significant growth over the last decade has slowed considerably since the global economic downturn, making it less competitive than the other "BRIC" countries, although, at 4.2 percent in 2011, third highest among the leading economies. According to the 2011 World Economic Forum Russia report, the most important single element explaining a country's medium-term growth performance is productivity; labor productivity in Russia is less than half the value achieved by workers in the OECD member states. The decline in manufacturing competitiveness in Russia "is due to the combination of an increase in real wages and shortcomings of the business climate, which puts Russia at a disadvantage in international comparison."[50] Russia ranks 67th out of 139 countries covered by the 2012–2013 Global Competitiveness Index. In addition, there is concern that the long-term business climate will remain for some time as an unbalanced, corruption-ridden, natural resource-based economy because of the persistent lack of formal institutions:

> *Russian managers have relied excessively on informal institutions, including personal networks, to conduct business due to the void created by the weak legitimacy of the country's formal institutions.*[51]

All in all, investors are confused, though many are determined to take advantage of a more stable ruble; the vast, underexploited natural resource potential; a skilled, educated population of 145 million; and a huge market. Indeed the abundance of technically skilled Russians has attracted a number of companies such as Intel, Cisco, Sun Microsystems, and Microsoft. Many MNCs claim that they must have a presence in Russia to be globally competitive. But a survey of 158 corporate investors and non-investors in Russia indicated that respondents thought that doing business in Russia was more risky and less profitable than China, India, or Southeast Asia. Their main concerns were corruption and bribe-taking at all levels of the state bureaucracy and weak legislative and enforcement regimes.[52] Russia was ranked 147th out of 180 countries by Transparency International, based on clean government and business.[53] Indeed, Ikea, the Swedish retailer, has found that Russian graft on several levels has so far won out against the company's efforts to thwart extortion efforts by power companies; even the courts found in favor of the power companies.[54]

(Continued)

In addition to the potential for corruption and the constant uncertainty in the business environment, firms doing business in Russia find that implementing a joint venture is very frustrating and time-consuming due to the all-consuming regulations and bureaucracy there. For these reasons, many foreign firms pick a local partner to help them navigate the myriad of negotiations to obtain permissions, get visas, acquire property, and so on. Other firms hire a security firm (Krisha) which smooths the way through the bureaucracy, often with payments.[55]

Nevertheless, the results of a study commissioned by the Foreign Investment Advisory Council (FIAC) reported in 2010 that "there are many reasons to be positive and optimistic about the prospects for increased Modernization and Innovation (in technology) and higher levels of FDI into the Russian Federation."[56] The recommendations are to put Russia on a path to improve its competitive position among other BRIC countries by boosting its internal market demand for high-tech innovation, and through infrastructure development, among other plans.

At the same time, those 50 executives representing large companies around the world who were surveyed by the FIAC expressed concern about political interference in business, arbitrariness in the application of laws, complexity of the tax system, and the lack of skilled staff. They also expressed concern that small companies would have difficulties in registering and start up, thus limiting economic growth.[57] Nevertheless, investment continues from companies such as Dutch brewer Heineken, and Citibank, which says its business in Russia is growing at an annual rate of 70 percent. Moscow and other major cities are experiencing a consumer boom, spurred on by rising incomes in the middle class, making Russia one of the fastest growing regions for global consumer giants such as Coca-Cola, Procter & Gamble, and Nestlé.[58] They join those already taking advantage of those opportunities such as Caterpillar, IBM, GE, Ford, Hewlett-Packard, PepsiCo, Eastman Kodak, and AT&T, as well as thousands of smaller IJVs—primarily in software, hotels, and heavy industrial production. Many, like Bell Labs, are involved in research and development, taking advantage of the Russians' high-level education and technical capabilities. In addition, Russia is promoting its several special economic zones around the country; the government hopes to attract further investment by offering tax concessions, such as exemption from property and land tax for the first five years.[59]

In addition Western managers need to recognize that there are cultural factors affecting cross-border business, in particular that Russians are distrustful of outsiders; managers attempting to develop joint ventures will therefore need to be aware that they will need to spend considerable time communicating and developing a trusting relationship. Reliance on their own networks and the use of favors (*blat*) present obstacles to business relations between Russians and "outsiders."[60]

Overall, managers of foreign companies planning to set up business in Russia should carefully consider the following:

- Investigate whether a joint venture is the best strategy. If a lot of real estate is needed, it may be better to acquire a Russian business, because of the difficulties involved in acquiring land.
- Set up meetings with the appropriate ministry and regional authorities well in advance. Have good communication about your business needs and build local relationships.
- Be sure to be totally above board in paying all relevant taxes to avoid crossing the Russian authorities.
- Set up stricter controls and accountability systems than usual for the company.
- Communicate clearly up front that your firm does not pay bribes.
- Assign the firm's best available managers and delegate to them enough authority to act locally.
- Take advantage of local knowledge by hiring appropriate Russian managers for the venture.
- Designate considerable funds for local promotion and advertising so as to establish the corporate image with authorities and consumers.[61]

Foreign managers' alliance strategy must also take into account the goals of potential Russian partners. An awareness and acceptance of the motivations of Russian firms for alliances with foreign companies will aid in finding and achieving a cooperative joint venture.

Researchers for the *Wall Street Journal* reported their findings about what local Russian firms want from an alliance with a foreign firm; they made it clear that they expect assistance with market entry through forming an alliance, and that they need assistance in solving bribes, kickbacks, and other under-the-table transactions.[62]

IMPLEMENTING STRATEGY

Implementing Strategy McDonald's Style

- *Form paradigm-busting arrangements with suppliers.*
- *Know a country's culture before you hit the beach.*
- *Hire locals whenever possible.*
- *Maximize autonomy.*
- *Tweak the standard menu only slightly from place to place.*
- *Keep pricing low to build market share. Profits will follow when economies of scale kick in.*[63]

Decisions regarding global alliances and entry strategies must now be put into motion with the next stage of planning: strategic implementation—also known as functional level strategies. Implementation plans are detailed and pervade the entire organization because they entail setting up overall policies, administrative responsibilities, and schedules throughout the organization to enact the selected strategy and to make sure it works. In the case of a merger or IJV, this process requires compromising and blending procedures among two or more companies and is extremely complex. The importance of the implementation phase of the strategic management process cannot be overemphasized. Until they are put into operation, strategic plans remain abstract ideas: verbal or printed proposals that have no effect on the organization.

Successful implementation requires the orchestration of many variables into a cohesive system that complements the desired strategy—that is, a *system of fits* that will facilitate the actual working of the strategic plan. In this way, the structure, systems, and processes of the firm are coordinated and set into motion by a system of management by objectives (MBO), with the primary objective being the fulfillment of strategy. Managers must review the organizational structure and, if necessary, change it to facilitate the administration of the strategy and to coordinate activities in a particular location with headquarters (as discussed further in Chapter 8). In addition to ensuring the strategy-structure fit, managers must allocate resources to make the strategy work, budgeting money, facilities, equipment, people, and other support. Increasingly, that support necessitates a unified technology infrastructure in order to coordinate diverse businesses around the world and to satisfy the need for current and reliable information. An efficient technology infrastructure can provide a strategic advantage in a globally competitive environment. Jack Welch, while CEO of General Electric (he retired in late 2001), was prescient when he referred to his e-commerce initiative, saying, "It will change relationships with suppliers. Within 18 months, all our suppliers will supply us on the Internet, or they won't do business with us."[64]

An overarching factor affecting all the other variables necessary for successful implementation is that of leadership; it is people, after all, who make things happen. The firm's leaders must skillfully guide employees and processes in the desired direction. Managers with different combinations of experience, education, abilities, and personality tend to be more suited to implementing certain strategies. In an equity-sharing alliance, sorting out which top managers in each company will be in which position is a sensitive matter. Who in which company will be CEO is usually worked out as part of the initial deal in alliance agreements. This problem seems to be frequently settled these days by setting up joint CEOs, one from each company. Setting monitoring systems into place to control activities and ensure success completes, but does not end, the strategic management process. Rather, it is a continuous process, using feedback to reevaluate strategy for needed modifications and for updating and recycling plans.

Of particular note here we should consider what is involved in implementing strategies for SMEs and the issues involved in the effective management of the global sourcing strategy. Then we will review what is involved in managing performance in international joint ventures, since they are such a common form of global alliance, and yet they are fraught with implementation challenges.

Implementing Strategies for SMEs

For small businesses venturing abroad, however, the first step is often that of exporting. This can be a daunting task; however, there are many sources available to help the small business managers embark on exporting, as discussed in the nearby feature *Under the Lens: Breaking Down Barriers for Small Business Exports.* Of particular note, China offers substantial opportunities for exports for SMEs (businesses with fewer than 500 employees), which have accounted for an estimated third of exports to China in recent years. All exports to China were expected to be around $115 billion for 2011, with agricultural products leading the way, followed by computers and electronics, chemicals, non-electrical machinery, and waste and scrap.[65] China is the third largest export market for U.S. companies, after Canada and Mexico, and followed by Japan and the United Kingdom.

> *But there is still room for growth. Though China is the third-largest market for SME exports, only 10.2 percent of American SME exporters shipped goods to China in 2009.*
>
> CHINA BUSINESS REVIEW,
> *2011.*[66]

UNDER THE LENS
Breaking Down Barriers for Small Business Exports

Small businesses made up 97 percent of all U.S. companies that exported goods and services abroad in 2009, but they only generated roughly one-third of all export revenue, according to the U.S. Census Bureau. The U.S. government is looking to boost small business exports with the National Export Initiative (NEI)—an initiative started in January 2010 by U.S. President Barack Obama—which aims to double U.S. exports and create millions of jobs in the United States by the end of 2014.

"To double exports we need to increase the number of small business exporters," said Richard Ginsburg, an international trade specialist with the U.S. Small Business Administration (SBA). Fifty-eight percent of roughly 250,000 U.S. small and medium-sized enterprise (SME) exporters ship to just one market. Ginsburg says one of the key goals of NEI is to help those firms ship to multiple markets.

China has been a growing market for American SMEs—companies with fewer than 500 employees. According to the U.S. International Trade Administration, the number of American SMEs exporting to China increased by 776 percent from 1992 to 2009. But there is still room for growth. Though China is the third-largest market for SME exports, only 10.2 percent of American SME exporters shipped goods to China in 2009.

U.S. EXPORT ASSISTANCE CENTERS

Of the 20 U.S. government agencies involved in export assistance, SBA specifically aims to increase the number of small business exporters through programs delivered through U.S. Export Assistance Centers. Senior SBA trade and finance specialists—along with employees from the U.S. Commercial Service and the U.S. Export-Import (Ex-Im) Bank—staff 20 of more than 100 U.S. Export Assistance Centers in metropolitan areas around the country. The centers help "export-ready" companies begin to export or expand to new markets abroad by providing counseling, training, export insurance, and loans to these businesses; conducting market research; and facilitating contracts between U.S. exporters and foreign buyers.

Ginsburg says small business owners usually approach an Export Assistance Center when they want to make a deal with a foreign buyer or when they receive an order from a foreign buyer and have never exported before. The centers can help companies understand payment terms and conditions, help them handle logistics such as shipping, and refer them to translators. These transactions are often simple when doing business in the United States, but they can be complicated when crossing international borders.

Counseling, outreach, and loan programs help break down what Ginsburg calls the "psychological trade barriers" that prevent small businesses from exporting. "There are people who feel they can lose their business if they export," Ginsburg says. "The risks are so much more than shipping across town or across the state or across the country." For example, small business owners sometimes fear that they will not be able to collect payments from overseas buyers.

Companies that want to export face barriers such as language and lack of knowledge of the foreign regulatory environment, and—specifically for businesses exporting to China—fear of intellectual property rights infringement, Ginsburg says.

EXPORT LOANS FOR SMALL BUSINESSES

In addition to counseling and training, SBA guarantees loans of up to $5 million, while the Ex-Im Bank provides export financing for amounts over $5 million. "It's a success story for SBA when we're working with a small business exporter and they outgrow the small loan amount and need more than the $5 million SBA threshold," Ginsburg says.

SBA runs four loan programs for small business exporters: the Export Express Program, the Export Working Capital Program, International Trade Loan Program, and SBA and Ex-Im Bank Co-Guarantee Program. The Export Express Program, formerly a pilot program, was made permanent in 2010 with the passage of the Small Business Jobs Act of 2010 to support the NEI goal of increasing small business exports. The program aims to streamline the export loan process for small businesses. SMEs that have been operating for at least 12 months can receive up to $500,000 to finance export activities, such as participating in foreign trade shows, purchasing equipment, and translating product literature. The law also permanently increased loan limits on export working capital and international trade loans.

Companies can obtain more information on export loans from the nearest Export Assistance Center and apply directly for loans through SBA lenders. Visit www.export.gov/eac to contact the nearest center or www.sba.gov/content/us-export-assistance-centers for a list of centers with SBA representatives.

Christina Nelson

Christina Nelson (cmnelson@uschina.org) is associate editor of the *CBR*.

Source: "U.S. Exports in China Rebound in 2010." This article first appeared in the July-September 2011 *China Business Review*. Used with the permission of the *China Business Review*.

Implementing a Global Sourcing Strategy

Multinational corporations and their manufacturing partners in emerging markets need to rethink how they manage their relationships with each other in light of the global downturn.

Harvard Business Review,
Jul/Aug 2009.[67]

The entry strategy of global sourcing was discussed in Chapter 6. Outsourcing abroad—alliances with firms in other countries to perform specific functions for the firm (offshoring)—is often in the news because of the politically charged issue of domestic jobs apparently being "lost" to others overseas. Beyond finding lower paid workers, however, the strategic view of global sourcing is developing into "transformational outsourcing"—that is, the view that, properly implemented, global sourcing can produce gains in efficiency, productivity, quality, and profitability by fully leveraging talent around the world.[68] Procter & Gamble, for example, having outsourced everything from IT infrastructure and the functions of Human Resources around the world, announced that CEO Alan G. Lafley wanted 50 percent of all new P&G products to come from other countries.[69] However, implementing such a strategy is more difficult than it is made to seem in the press, as many companies have encountered unexpected problems when outsourcing. Advice on implementation from experiences by companies such as Dell, IBM, and Reuters Group PLC lead us to the following guidelines:

1. *Examine your reasons for outsourcing:* Make sure that the advantages of efficiency and competitiveness will outweigh the disadvantages from your employees, customers, and community; don't outsource just because your competitors are doing it.
2. *Evaluate the best outsourcing model:* Opening your own subsidiary in the host country (a "captive" operation) may be better than contracting with an outside firm if it is crucial for you to keep control of proprietary technology and processes.
3. *Gain the cooperation of your management and staff:* Open communication and training is essential to get your domestic managers on board; uncertainty, fear, and disagreement from them can jeopardize your plans.
4. *Consult your alliance partners:* Consult with your partners and treat them with the respect that made you decide to do business with them.
5. *Invest in the alliance:* Plan to invest time and money in training in the firm's business practices, in particular those to deal with quality control and customer relations.[70]

Further advice comes from Josh Green, CEO of Panjiva, which is an information resource for companies doing business across borders. Green asks "How healthy is your global partner?" as he noted that an increasing number of firms in developed economies were finding that their suppliers in Asia had gone out of business following the protracted global economic downturn that caused firms to reduce their demand from their suppliers. He notes that both buyers and suppliers have learned the hard way that in future they need to carefully investigate and evaluate their potential partners. He suggests, for example, that both sides should do a background check on the financial health and future viability of the company; get references from other partners of the firm; be prepared to give those assurances and data about their own companies; and be prepared for problems by having alternate partners ready to fill in.[71] The need to be prepared for the unexpected was suddenly brought home on March 11, 2011 when the Japanese earthquake and tsunami struck—a disaster for the Japanese people, and a problem for supply chains of companies around the world (see *Under the Lens: Global Supply Chain Risks—The Japanese Disaster*). The quake and tsunami left nearly 28,000 people dead or missing, thousands homeless, and Japan's northeast coast devastated. Clearly the first responsibility for Japan was to their people, but also this disaster threatened the country economically—not the least because 15 percent of its GDP was in its supply chain business to global firms ranging from semiconductor makers to shipbuilding.[72]

UNDER THE LENS

Global Supply Chain Risks—The Japanese Disaster[73]

With different component parts for everything from cell phones to cars being sourced from various countries, supply chains have become longer and far more complex to manage than in the past. It is not surprising, then, that companies around the world, from Lenovo to General Motors, had to scramble to find alternate supply sources after the Japanese earthquake and tsunami on March 11, 2011 disrupted supplies. As well as being a disaster for the Japanese people, major problems arose due to the nuclear alert, power shortages, damaged infrastructure, and loss of port access. At Hewlett Packard, for example, Tony Prophet, senior VP for Operations, gathered his team in the wee hours of the morning to brainstorm back-up plans for its $65 billion a year global supply chain, saying

> *"It's like being in an emergency room, doing triage."*[74]

The auto industry in particular was hard hit. Japan exports 2.5 million engines and 8.5 million transmissions annually to assembly plants around the world, and 2,200 separate parts are used in the typical vehicle. Ironically, it was the Japanese automakers with plants in the U.S. and Europe who were the most disrupted, not expecting to be able to get up to full production again for several months. Toyota, for example, which sources about 15 per cent of its parts from Japan for its U.S. plants, was reduced to about 30 percent of its normal production capacity.

General Motors set up its disaster response teams in three "crisis rooms" at its Vehicle Engineering Center in Warren, Michigan. Problems included being able to identify tiers of sub-suppliers and what parts were affected. Shortages led to temporary plant shut-downs. Lack of information due to communication outages was a problem and so GM sent forty employees to Japan to visit suppliers; determine what parts were being held up and the reasons why, such as the supplier's inability to get the steel they needed to make the parts or to acquire enough electricity to run their factories; and also to offer help.

These days, sourcing risk is somewhat reduced because sourcing is done globally, and technological developments have enabled the ability to manage these complex networks through Internet communications, RFID tags, and sensors attached to valued parts. In addition sophisticated software can now be used for tracking and orchestrating the flow of goods worldwide. However, as supply chains become longer—that is suppliers of suppliers of suppliers—control is more difficult and therefore the risk is greater. A further difficulty is the lack of alternative sources for the thousands of tiny specialized parts for those ubiquitous electronics - like connectors, speakers, microphones, batteries and sensors. If any of these parts cannot be sourced, the entire plant may be put on hold. Five parts in the new Apple iPad, for example, come from Japanese suppliers.

Clearly, executives around the world have learned that there are unforeseen risks in implementing a global sourcing strategy—in particular combined with the just-in-time inventory practice. As a result, they realize that they need to have back-up sourcing plans to manage the risk of supply chain disruption.

Implementing Strategies for Emerging Economy Firms

Firms from emerging economies have, out of necessity, expanded globally through different paths and strategies than those traditional paths followed by firms in the developed world. Their motives for expansion into developed countries often include the need to acquire specific resources, such as technological know-how, R&D capability, managerial skills, and global brands so as to make them competitive with established firms. It is interesting to observe how those firms are coping with strategic implementation. Rather than the gradual, staged internationalization process typical of traditional firms from the "developed" world, the emerging firms—of all sizes—are finding that they have to move quickly or skip various stages in order to expand into both developed as well as developing markets.[75] As a result, firms such as Brazil's Natura Cosmeticos, China's Lenovo, and Argentina's Tenaris—now significant global players—have tended to expand globally through acquisitions and alliances and have had to be more flexible organizationally. Mauro F. Guillén and Estaban García-Canal point out from their research that firms from emerging and developing countries "face a significant dilemma when it comes to international expansion because they need to balance the desire for global reach with the need to upgrade their capabilities. They can readily use their home-grown competitive advantages in other emerging or developing countries, but they must also enter more advanced countries in order to expose themselves to sophisticated, cutting-edge demand and develop their capabilities."[76] As Guillén and García-Canal demonstrate in Exhibit 7-3, those firms must decide how to balance their geographic expansion with their ability to upgrade their capabilities in the market because they lack the resources and capabilities of established MNEs; they must realize that "prioritizing global reach without improving firm competencies jeopardizes the capability upgrading process."[77] (This puts them in the "unsustainable region" in the exhibit). Huei-Ting Tsai and Eisingerich also note "the dual challenge faced by emerging market firms, namely, market creation and/or R&D knowledge creation."[78] They note that firms with less technological and selling capabilities tend to enter new markets one at a time. In addition, firms with strong technological capabilities often expand to overseas markets shortly after the firm is established. They found from the firms in their sample that those that were stronger technologically and had more financial resources would compete in the developed markets, whereas those with a lesser stable of competitive resources pursued less-competitive markets during the early stages of their internationalization.

EXHIBIT 7-3   **Expansion Paths for Emerging Economy Firms**

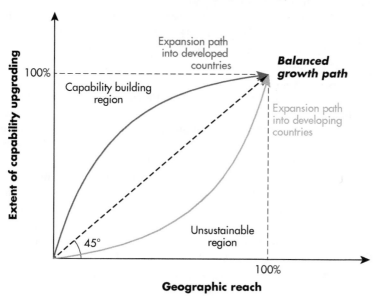

Source: Based on Mauro F. Guillén and Estaban García-Canal, "The American Model of the Multinational Firm and the 'New' Multinationals from Emerging Economies," *Academy of Management Perspectives*, May, 2009: 23–35.

Challenges in Implementing Strategies in Emerging Markets

Firms expanding into emerging market countries are often unaware of the considerable differences from their home markets and the challenges they face in getting started. Because of their lack of familiarity and preparation for those challenges, "foreign" firms are often surprised that they are not able to compete successfully with local firms. They may be operating under assumptions that firms from more developed countries have better experience, management knowledge, technology, and other resources than those in the target regions. Unfortunately, it is that mindset that may lead foreign firms to enter those new markets without sufficient research and preparation for the differences and difficulties they may face.

The initial challenge is likely to be how to navigate poor infrastructures, supply chains, and distribution networks—problems that local firms know how to navigate through experience and contacts. The same edge is enjoyed by local firms when dealing with the myriad regulations and bureaucracies prevalent in some developing economies.

Expansion into emerging markets also brings personnel challenges, especially at management levels. Here too, often the domestic companies have the advantage of knowing how to source, attract, and train local talent; those employees also tend to prefer to work for local companies that are perceived to be more invested in their future.[79] On the other hand, those employees often do not have the experience or familiarity with cross-border business compared with the "foreign" firms that may bring in their own talent.

Clearly, firms going into developing markets need to thoroughly explore how to navigate the infrastructure and institutions, evaluate the area for their personnel needs, and make local contacts in order to assess the feasibility of operating there and competing with local firms.

Managing Performance in International Joint Ventures

Much of the world's international business activity involves international joint ventures (IJVs), in which at least one parent is headquartered outside the venture's country of operation. IJVs require unique controls. Ignoring these specific control requisites can limit the parent company's ability to efficiently use its resources, coordinate its activities, and implement its strategy.

The term **IJV control** refers to the processes that management puts in place so as to direct the success of the firm's goals. Most of a firm's objectives can be achieved by careful attention to control features at the outset of the joint venture, such as the choice of a partner, the establishment of a strategic fit, and the design of the IJV organization.

The most important single factor determining IJV success or failure is the choice of a partner. Most problems with IJVs involve the local partner, especially in less-developed countries. In spite of this fact, many firms rush the process of partner selection because they are anxious to "get on the bandwagon" in an attractive market. In this process, it is vital to establish whether the partners' strategic goals are compatible (see Chapter 6). The strategic context and the competitive environment of the proposed IJV and the parent firm will determine the relative importance of the criteria used to select a partner.[80] IJV performance is also a function of the general fit between the international strategies of the parents, the IJV strategy, and the specific performance goals that the parents adopt.[81] Research has shown that, to facilitate this fit, the partner selection process must determine the specific task-related skills and resources needed from a partner, as well as the relative priority of those needs.[82] To do this, managers must analyze their own firms and pinpoint any areas of weakness in task-related skills and resources that can be overcome with the help of the IJV partner.

Partnerships with companies in India present both positive and negative examples of IJV performance, although, overall, IJVs there run into considerable problems. Although India still insists on joint ventures in sectors such as telecommunications, agriculture, and insurance, it has lifted restrictions for other industries, allowing wholly-owned operations in them. However, a number of recent IJVs have done poorly, especially for the Indian partner. TVS Motor Company, for example, which is the third-largest motorbike manufacturer in India (a market with around 8 million bikes per year), recently bought out its Japanese partner Suzuki. From Suzuki's perspective, the only entry strategy available to the company under government regulations at the time was a joint venture. However, after a while TVS complained that it was not able to develop the company's own capabilities because "Suzuki wanted to keep its technology for itself. It was a frustrating episode."[83] On the other hand, an IJV between Indian engineering group Kirloskar and Japan's Toyota, for vehicle production, has had more positive results, with

Mr. Kirloskar acknowledging that Toyota has been open in sharing ideas and improving the productivity of his firm.[84]

Organizational design is another major mechanism for factoring in a means of control when an IJV is started. Beamish et al. discuss the important issue of the strategic freedom of an IJV. This refers to the relative amount of decision-making power that a joint venture will have, compared with the parents, in choosing suppliers, product lines, customers, and so on.[85] It is also crucial to consider beforehand the relative management roles each parent will play in the IJV because such decisions result in varying levels of control for different parties. An IJV is usually easier to manage if one parent plays a dominant role and has more decision-making responsibility than the other in daily operations. Alternatively, it is easier to manage an IJV if the local general manager has considerable management control, keeping both parents out of most of the daily operations.

International joint ventures are like a marriage: the more issues that can be settled before the merger, the less likely it will be to break up. Control over the stability and success of the IJV can be largely built into the initial agreement between the partners. The contract can specify who has what responsibilities and rights in a variety of circumstances, such as the contractual links of the IJV with the parents, the capitalization, and the rights and obligations regarding intellectual property. Of course, we cannot assume equal ownership of the IJV partners; where ownership is unequal, the partners will claim control and staffing choices proportionate to the ownership share. The choice of the IJV general manager, in particular, will influence the relative allocation of control because that person is responsible for running the IJV and for coordinating relationships with each of the parents.[86]

Where ownership is divided among several partners, the parents are more likely to delegate the daily operations of the IJV to the local IJV management—a move that resolves many potential disputes. In addition, the increased autonomy of the IJV tends to reduce many common human resource problems: staffing friction, blocked communication, and blurred organizational culture, to name a few, which all result from the conflicting goals and working practices of the parent companies.[87] Regardless of the number of parents, one way to avoid such potential problem situations is to provide special training to managers about the unique nature and problems of IJVs. The extent of control exercised over an IJV by its parent companies seems to be primarily determined by the decision-making autonomy that the parents delegate to the IJV management—which is largely dependent on staffing choices for the top IJV positions and thus on how much confidence the partners have in these managers. In addition, if top managers of the IJV are from the headquarters of each party, the compatibility of the managers will depend on how similar their national cultures are. This is because there are many areas of control decisions where agreement will be more likely between those of similar cultural backgrounds.[88]

Knowledge Management in IJVs

The most effective strategic leadership practices in the 21st century will be ones through which strategic leaders find ways for knowledge to breed still more knowledge.[89]

Managing the performance of an IJV for the long term, as well as adding value to the parent companies, necessitates managing the knowledge flows within the IJV network. When managed correctly, "alliances serve as a source of new knowledge for the firm."[90] Sirmon et al. contend that if firms can access and "absorb" this new knowledge, it can be used to alter existing capabilities or create new ones.[91] Yet, as found by Hitt et al., "cultural differences and institutional deficits can serve as barriers to the transfer of knowledge in alliance partnerships"[92] Clearly, then, managers need to recognize that it is critical to overcome cultural and system differences in managing knowledge flows to the advantage of the alliance.

Knowledge management, then, is "the conscious and active management of creating, disseminating, evolving, and applying knowledge to strategic ends."[93] Research on eight IJVs by Berdrow and Lane led them to define these processes as follows:

1. *Transfer:* managing the flow of existing knowledge between parents and from the parents to the IJV.
2. *Transformation:* managing the transformation and creation of knowledge within the IJV through its independent activities.
3. *Harvest:* managing the flow of transformed and newly created knowledge from the IJV back to the parents.[94]

In particular, the sharing and development of technology among IJV partners provides the opportunity for knowledge transfer among those individuals who have internalized that information, beyond any tangible assets; the challenge is to develop and harvest that information to benefit the parents through complementary synergies. Those IJVs that were successful in meeting that challenge were found to have personal involvement by the principals of the parent company in shared goals, in the activities and decisions being made, and in encouraging joint learning and coaching.[95]

The many operational activities and issues involved in strategic implementation—such as negotiating, organizing, staffing, leading, communicating, and controlling—are the subjects of other chapters in this book. Elsewhere we include discussion of the many variables involved in strategic implementation that are specific to a particular country or region, such as goals, infrastructure, laws, technology, ways of doing business, people, and culture. In the following sections, the focus is on three pervasive influences on strategy implementation: government policy, societal culture, and the Internet.

Government Influences on Strategic Implementation

Host governments influence, in many areas, the strategic choices and implementations of foreign firms. The family-run Vermeer Company, for example, with its equipment-manufacturing factory in Pella, Iowa, earns about a third of its revenues from exports. However, the company realized its share of the market was falling rapidly due to competition from China, and so it decided to open a plant in Beijing, taking a Chinese partner and drawing help for the venture from the Chinese. The chief executive, Ms. Mary Vermeer Andringa, noted that:

> If we wanted to stay in the Chinese market, we needed to be there. That was the reality.[96]

The profitability of those firms which set up operations abroad is greatly influenced, for example, by the level of taxation in the host country and by any restrictions on profit repatriation. Other important influences are government policies on ownership by foreign firms, on labor union rules, on hiring and remuneration practices, on patent and copyright protection, and so on. For the most part, however, if the corporation's managers have done their groundwork, all these factors are known beforehand and are part of the location and entry strategy decisions. However, what hurts managers is to set up shop in a host country and then have major economic or governmental policy changes after they have made a considerable investment. Vodafone, for example, the British mobile phone giant, bought an Indian wireless company in 2007 for $11 billion. However, they soon found the market was full of hazards—including a surprise tax bill of $2.5 billion, and a corruption scandal over awarding contracts for additional wireless capacity.

> In emerging markets "there are new hurdles every day, and they can change the rules of the market as you are playing it," Marten Pieters, the chief executive of Vodafone's India business, said.
> The lesson from India? "If you don't have the stomach for that," Mr. Pieters said, "please don't come."
>
> WWW.NYTIMES.COM,
> *MARCH 27, 2011.*[97]

Unpredictable changes in governmental regulations can be a death knell to businesses operating abroad. Recent changes in Russia causing uncertainty for foreign investors were already discussed. Another country that is often the subject of concern for foreign firms is China. Already one of the toughest countries for mergers and acquisitions, China recently added new restrictions on foreign investors, thus prolonging the time that a number of firms have to continue to wait to find out if their deals will go through: "*Acquisitions that will require the ministry's approval include companies with a well-known brand or those that could have an impact on 'China's economic security.'*"[98] While China contends it is more committed to a market economy since it joined the World Trade Organization (WTO) in November 2001, history shows that foreign firms need to be cautious about entering China.

Cultural Influences on Strategic Implementation

When managers are responsible for implementing alliances among partners from diverse institutional environments, such as transition- and established-market economies, they are faced with the critical challenge of reconciling conflicting values, practices, and systems. Research by Danis shows how those important differences among Hungarian managers and Western expatriates can affect implementation. When considering key differences in practices, for example, Danis found that the Western expatriates evidenced a team orientation, a consensual management style, and a future planning mentality. This compared with the findings for the Hungarian managers, who showed an individual orientation, an autocratic management style, and a survival mentality.[99] Such advance knowledge can provide expatriate managers with valuable information to help them in successful local operations.

In other situations, the culture variable is often overlooked when deciding on and implementing entry strategies and alliances, particularly when we perceive the target country to be familiar to us and similar to our own. However, cultural differences can have a subtle and often negative effect. In fact, in a study of 129 U.K. cross-border acquisitions in continental Europe, Schoenberg found that 54 percent of the acquiring firms cited poor performance resulting from the implementation of their acquisitions, compared to their domestic mergers.[100] The researchers' study of those firms revealed six dimensions of national and corporate cultural differences between the management styles of the U.K. firms and the continental European firms:

Cultural Differences in U.K.-European Alliances

- Organizational formality
- The extent of participation in decision making
- Attitude toward risk
- Systemization of decision-making
- Managerial self-reliance
- Attitudes toward funding and gearing (financial leveraging).[101]

Among these dimensions, risk-orientation was the key factor that impacted the performance of the combined firm, because risk-taking propensity impacts managers' approach toward strategic options. Overall, risk-taking firms are likely to pursue aggressive strategies and deal well with change, whereas risk-averse companies are likely to tread more carefully and employ incremental strategies. Clearly, for companies entering into an IJV, successful implementation will depend largely on careful planning to take account of such differences, in particular that of risk-orientation, to improve organizational compatibility. The greater the cultural distance between the allied firms, the more likely problems will emerge such as conflict regarding the level of innovation and the kinds of investments each firm is willing to pursue.

Since many of Europe's largest MNCs—including Nestlé, Electrolux, Grand Metropolitan, and Rhone-Poulenc—experience increasing proportions of their revenues from their positions in the United States, and employ more than 2.9 million Americans; they have decided to shift the headquarters of some product lines to the United States. As they have done so, however, there is growing evidence that managing in the United States is not as easy as they anticipated it would be because of their perceived familiarity with the culture. Rosenzweig documents some reflections of European managers on their experiences of managing U.S. affiliates. Generally, he has found that European managers appreciate that Americans are pragmatic, open, forthright, and innovative. However, they also say that the tendency of Americans to be informal and individualistic means that their need for independence and autonomy on the job causes problems in their relationship with the head office Europeans. Americans simply do not take well to directives from a foreign-based headquarters.[102] Rosenzweig presents some comments from French managers on their activities in the United States:

French Managers Comment on Their Activities in the United States:

- Americans see themselves as the world's leading country, and it's not easy for them to accept having a European in charge.
- It is difficult for Americans to develop a world perspective. It's hard for them to see that what may optimize the worldwide position may not optimize the U.S. activities.

- The horizon of Americans often goes only as far as the U.S. border. As a result, Americans often don't give equal importance to a foreign customer. If a foreign customer has a special need, the response is sometimes: It works here, why do they need it to be different?

- It might be said that Americans are the least international of all people, because their home market is so big.[103]

Other European firms have had more successful strategic implementation in their U.S. plants by adapting to U.S. culture and management styles. When Mercedes-Benz of Germany launched its plant in Tuscaloosa, Alabama, U.S. workers and German "trainers" had doubts. Lynn Snow, who works on the car-door line of the Alabama plant, was skeptical whether the Germans and the Americans would mesh well. Now, she proudly asserts that they work together, determined to build a quality vehicle. As Jürgen Schrempp, then CEO of Mercedes's parent, Daimler-Benz, observed, "'Made in Germany'—we have to change that to 'Made by Mercedes,' and never mind where they are assembled."[104]

The German trainers recognized that the whole concept of building a Mercedes quality car had to be taught to the U.S. workers in a way that would appeal to them. They abandoned the typically German strict hierarchy and instead designed a plant in which any worker could stop the assembly line to correct manufacturing problems. In addition, taking their cue from Japanese rivals, they formed the workers into teams that met every day with the trainers to problem solve. Out the window went formal offices and uniforms, replaced by casual shirts with personal names on the pocket. To add to the collegiality, get-togethers for a beer after work became common. "The most important thing is to bring together the two cultures," says Andreas Renschler, who has guided the M-Class since it began in 1993. "You have to generate a kind of ownership of the plant."[105] The local community has also embraced the mutual goals, often having beer fests and including German-language stations on local cable TV.

The impact of cultural differences in management style and expectations is perhaps most noticeable and important when implementing international joint ventures, mergers, or acquisitions. The complexity of such alliances requires that managers from each party learn to compromise to create a compatible and productive working environment, particularly when operations

MANAGEMENT IN ACTION
Mittal's Marriage to Arcelor Breaks the Marwari Rules

The biggest steel merger in history was consummated in June 2006 during a 20-minute meeting at a hotel near the Brussels Airport after a five-month takeover battle. The combination of India's Mittal Steel and Luxembourg steelmaker Arcelor creates the world's biggest steel company. The Arcelor acquisition brings Mittal's production to over 100 million tons, creating a company with 333,000 employees on four continents.[106]

The deal did not come about easily, but Lakshmi Mittal, Mittal Steel's founder and 90 percent owner, skillfully managed opposition on two fronts—strategically and culturally.

Strategically, Mr. Mittal worked hard to overcome overwhelming hostility by Arcelor to his initial proposal. Arcelor had planned a deal with Russian steelmaker Severstal in a bid to block the Mittal acquisition.[107] But after two rejected bids from Mittal Steel, Mr. Mittal reached an agreement to acquire Arcelor in a deal valued at $33.7 billion. Mittal, his son Aditya, and a team of negotiators gained agreement to a business plan and provided a comparison of their deal to the one from Severstal. Mittal also provided a plan for corporate governance rules to promote Arcelor's business model and a commitment that his family would vote its share to support the board's recommendations.[108] It was clear to Mr. Mittal that the Arcelor executives had an outdated view of Mittal Steel, but he spent a lot of time explaining and showing Arcelor executives how Mittal Steel operates. The Arcelor chairman, Joseph Kinsch, spent some time talking to the members of Mittal family and discussing the potential alliance. Finally a better relationship was acknowledged by both sides and the deal was sealed, with Kinsch saying "I hope it can become a love marriage between our teams."[109]

Apart from the strategic negotiations of the deal, which finally turned from hostile to friendly, there was opposition for other reasons. There was a battle from France, seemingly over a perception of losing control of a company that was already a European multinational, though there was no objection to Arcelor's effort to bring in the Russian company Severstal as a white knight.[110] In addition, critics in the French and Luxembourg governments seemed to view the takeover by a family-run company as "a betrayal of old continental European traditions to a new cost-cutting imperative of globalization."[111] A similar objection came from India, showing how growth can bring Indians into conflict with cultural traditions. The objection was that Lakshmi Mittal, Indian-born head of Mittal Steel, was breaking the Marwari rules. Mittal belongs to an ethnic group called Marwari that "traditionally believes it is critical for companies to maintain family ownership."[112] Three of the five major steel companies in India, as well as companies in a number of other industries, are controlled and run by Marwari families. Various family members run the operations of those companies, managing separate factories and strategic deals with other firms. The Marwaris, often India's most affluent families, whose businesses thrived under the old protective government policies, had considerable business networks among the families, favoring doing business with them over others. As an ethnic group, they developed their own business practices:

> *Marwaris started business days with Hindu prayer and ended with an accounting of that day's cash flow. This practice, called partha, allowed them to respond quickly to market changes. Another, called modi, was a secret language that other Indians couldn't decipher and was used for trading data and business records.*[113]

When Lakshmi Mittal, billionaire steel tycoon—a global strategist based in London running a Dutch-registered company—launched a dramatic bid to take over Mittal Steel's chief rival, the reaction in India was one of shock. But Mittal said, "We have to put behind our family interest for the interest of the industry and the shareholders at large."[114] In giving up half of his 90 percent share of his company, to hold less than 45 percent of the combined company, he stated that he did not think his cultural traditions should deter the company from growth. In addition, Arcelor-Mittal will be based in Luxembourg, not in London where Mr. Mittal lives. He will share the chairmanship and be able to appoint only one-third of the board's 18 seats. Mittal recognizes that to be globally competitive, Marwari family businesses will have to change their governance policies.[115]

are integrated. Sometimes a cross-border alliance deal may in itself contradict cultural traditions, as explained in the nearby Management in Action feature.

In China, too, strategic implementation necessitates an understanding of the pervasive cultural practice of *guanxi* in business dealings. Discussed in previous chapters, *guanxi* refers to the relationship networks that "bind millions of Chinese firms into social and business webs, largely dictating their success."[116] Tapping into this system of reciprocal social obligation is essential to get permits, information, assistance to access material and financial resources, and tax considerations. Nothing gets done without these direct or indirect connections. In fact, a new term has arisen—*guanxihu*—which refers to a bond between specially connected firms that generates preferential treatment for members of the network. Without *guanxi*, even implementing a strategy of withdrawal is difficult. Joint ventures can become hard to dissolve and as bitter as an acrimonious divorce. Problems include the forfeiture of assets and the inability to gain market access through future joint venture partners—all experienced by Audi, Chrysler, and Daimler-Benz. For example:

> *Audi's decision to terminate its joint venture prompted its Chinese partner, First Automobile Works, to expropriate its car design and manufacturing processes. The result was an enormously successful, unauthorized Audi clone, with a Chrysler engine and a First Automobile Works nameplate.*[117]

E-commerce Impact on Strategy Implementation

With subsidiaries, suppliers, distributors, manufacturing facilities, carriers, brokers, and customers all over the globe, global trade is complicated and fragmented. Shipments cross borders multiple times a day. Are they compliant with all the latest trade regulations? Are they consistently classified for each country? Can you give your buyers, customers, and service providers the latest information, on demand?[118]

As indicated in this quote, global trade is extremely complicated. Deciding on a global strategy is one thing; implementing it through all the necessary parties and intermediaries around the world presents a whole new level of complexity. Because of that complexity, many firms decide to implement their global e-commerce strategy by outsourcing the necessary tasks to **e-commerce enablers**, companies that specialize in providing the technology to organize transactions and follow through with the regulatory requirements. These specialists can help companies sort through the maze of different taxes, duties, language translations, and so on specific to each country. Such services allow small and medium-sized companies to go global without the internal capabilities to carry out global e-commerce functions. One of these specialist e-commerce enablers is NextLinx, which applies technology to the wide range of services it provides for strategic implementation, allowing all trading partners to collaborate in a single online location, using the same information and processes. These kinds of Web-based services allow a company to manage an entire global trade operation, including automation of imports and exports by screening orders and generating the appropriate documentation, paying customs charges, complying with trade agreements, etc.[119]

CONCLUSION

Cross-border strategic alliances are becoming increasingly common as innovative companies seek rapid entry into foreign markets and as they try to reduce the risks of going it alone in complex environments. Those companies that do well are those that do their groundwork and pick complementary strategic partners. Too many, however, get "divorced" because "the devil is in the details"—which is what happens when "a marriage made in heaven" runs into unanticipated problems, such as cultural clashes and government restrictions, during actual strategic implementation. Alliances in various forms are particularly important for emerging market firms to be able to expand to developed economies. For SMEs, they too can work to ally with MNCs in the target locations so as to act fast to internationalize.

Summary of Key Points

1. Strategic alliances are partnerships with other companies for specific reasons. Cross-border, or global, strategic alliances are working partnerships between companies (often more than two) across national boundaries, and increasingly across industries.

2. Cross-border alliances are formed for many reasons, including market expansion, cost- and technology-sharing, avoiding protectionist legislation, and taking advantage of synergies.

3. SMEs can overcome their resource constraints and accelerate their internationalization process by leveraging their network relationships with other companies—such as key clients or strategic partners. Strategies include forming MNC relationships, consolidating those relationships with MNCs, and then extending the relationships to other endeavors.

4. Alliances may be short or long term; they may be full global partnerships, or they may be for more narrow and specific functions such as research and development sharing.

5. Alliances often run into trouble in the strategic implementation phase. Problems include loss of technology and knowledge skill-base to the other partner, conflicting strategic goals and objectives, cultural clashes, and disputes over management and control systems.

6. Emerging economy firms are finding that they have to move quickly or skip various stages in order to expand into both developed as well as developing markets. They tend to expand globally through acquisitions and alliances and have had to be more flexible organizationally. Their motives in developing alliances often include the need to access specific resources such as technology or management skills in order to compete globally.

7. Successful alliances require compatible partners with complementary skills, products, and markets. Extensive preparation is necessary to work out how to share management control and technology and to understand each other's culture.

8. Strategic implementation—also called *functional level strategies*—is the process of setting up overall policies, administrative responsibilities, and schedules throughout the organization. Successful implementation results from setting up the structure, systems, and processes of the firm, as well as the functional activities that create a *system of fits* with the desired strategy.

9. Differences in national culture and changes in the political arena or in government regulations often have unanticipated effects on strategic implementation.

10. Strategic implementation of global trade is increasingly being facilitated by *e-commerce enablers*—companies that specialize in providing the software and Internet technology for complying with the specific regulations, taxes, shipping logistics, translations, and so on for each country with which their clients do business.

Discussion Questions

1. Discuss the reasons that companies embark on cross-border strategic alliances. What other motivations may prompt such alliances? What are the driving forces for firms in emerging economies to embark on strategic alliances? How can SMEs expand abroad through relationships with MNCs?

2. Why are there an increasing number of mergers with companies in different industries? Give some examples. What industry do you think will be the next for global consolidation?

3. Discuss the problems inherent in developing a cooperative alliance to enhance competitive advantage, which also incurs the risk of developing a new competitor.

4. What are the common sources of incompatibility in cross-border alliances? What can be done to minimize them?

5. Explain what is necessary for companies to successfully implement a global sourcing strategy.

6. Discuss the political and economic situation in the Russian Federation with your class. What has changed since this writing? What are the implications for foreign companies to start a joint venture there now?

7. What is involved in strategic implementation? What is meant by creating a "*system of fits*" with the strategic plan?

8. Explain how the host government may affect strategic implementation—in an alliance or another form of entry strategy.

9. How might the variable of national culture affect strategic implementation? Use the Mittal Steel example to highlight some of these factors.

10. Discuss the importance of knowledge management in IJVs and what can be done to enhance the effectiveness of that process.

Application Exercise

Research some recent joint ventures with foreign companies situated in Russia or China. How are they doing? Bring your information to class for discussion. What is the climate for foreign investors in Russia/China at the time of your reading this chapter?

Internet Resources

Visit the Deresky Companion Website at www.pearsonhighered.com/deresky for this chapter's Internet resources.

CASE STUDY

The Nokia-Microsoft Alliance in the Global Smartphone Industry (circa 2011)

The Nokia-Microsoft strategic alliance was announced in early 2011 to cooperate in the development of smartphones. *The Wall Street Journal* wrote: "*Nokia calls Microsoft for help.*"[1] The *Financial Times* observed: "*Elop jumps into the arms of former boss.*"[2] The alliance was specifically initiated by Stephen Elop, an ex-Microsoft executive who had worked with Steve Ballmer, CEO of Microsoft. No wonder Nokia hired Elop to become its CEO in 2010. This was a calculated move by Nokia to grow in an industry that carried good prospects for the future. In addition, Elop's expertise was in the software sector, where Nokia wanted to venture into the future. Both companies needed a partner to expand in an industry that was in a growth mode. Besides this, Nokia was particularly vulnerable because of its losing market share and because Apple's iPhone was growing in the U.S. and global markets. Microsoft was interested in Nokia because of its long-term interest regarding introducing Windows phone technology/software. Since Nokia continued to be a global player in the cell phone industry, it made sense to create a corporate tie-up that aimed at global expansion for both companies. Success of Apple's iPhone was another factor in seeking a long-term alliance in a market that has grown multifold in the global mobile phone market.

In 2012, Nokia was the largest manufacturer of mobile phones and other telecom gear in the world with revenues of $55 billion and a market capitalization of $19 billion. Microsoft, on the other hand, was the largest software maker in the world and generated revenues of $69 billion. The company carried a healthy market capitalization in 2011 that stood at $266 billion.[3] By being a cash-rich company, Microsoft was able to inject a sizable amount of money in the alliance. As of February 2012, a closer look at the alliance reveals that both companies' plans worked well. Nokia has released a new series of mobile devices, called Lumina, with Microsoft's Windows technology. At the same time, Nokia continues to lose market share in the global mobile industry because of its aging technology ("Symbian"). Google's Android is a clear winner because of high demand, followed by Apple's iPhone. Google has done well since its acquisition of Motorola's Mobility.[4] Value Line in 2012 wrote: "*Nokia's operating results continue to deteriorate; the transition of the smartphone is under way; over time, Windows Phone will be the software driving Nokia's upscale handsets.*"[5] Although Nokia was always the market leader in mobile technology, its anemic strategies in the global market indicate that the company is losing steam in the mobile phone industry. The situation is the same with Research in Motion's Blackberry, which continues to lose market share in global markets. Just a few years ago, Blackberry was the main player in the global mobile industry with its well know technology and brand name.[6]

Regarding the issues of technology diffusion and changing consumer trends, the smartphone industry has gone through major structural changes that demand large-scale investment, new technologies, and resources. Companies such as Apple and Google that invested billions in the industry with competitive technologies are the main winners. No wonder Apple's market capitalization in early 2012 surpassed $490 billion. Value Line commented: *"The remarkable growth story at Apple appears far from over; the company maintains a deep talent pool. . . . But we still expect the company to reach further heights as it leverages its hardware and software platforms. . . . "*[7] The situation is the same with Google, which maintained a market value of $200 billion during the same period. By 2014, global mobile subscribers are expected to grow beyond nine billion, with the industry's expenditures surpassing $1.7 trillion. This clearly shows the level of competition and capital investment needed in the industry.[8] In many regions of the world, there is a strong demand for mobile technologies, where product life cycles are becoming shorter.[9]

The above discussion about the changing mobile phone industry reveals the following issues in global business: (1) Technologies do not remain static and are always on the move because of changing demand and consumer needs; (2) Product life cycles are always short because of competition and new entrants; and (3) To survive in the market, companies need to seek alliances and collaborations regarding sharing technologies and markets.

Regarding the Nokia-Microsoft alliance, the initiative makes sense in global markets because of the companies' organic growth and expansion. Of course competition will be heightened in those segments where new technologies are being introduced by Google and Apple. At the same time, Nokia maintains a good competitive advantage in Asia and Latin America because of its established operations and clientele. The company has been exceptionally efficient regarding introducing those technologies and product lines that are competitive and adaptable. Nokia also carries an advantage in global markets because of its first-mover advantage in the mobile phone industry and its stable networks. Of course, markets are changing in favor of firms such as Apple and Google that aim at introducing new technologies and know how to compete efficiently and effectively.

Case Questions

1. Do a SWOT analysis of the Nokia-Microsoft strategic alliance in the global mobile phone industry.
2. Compare and contrast Nokia and Microsoft regarding their global operations and competitive advantages.
3. Within today's changing global software and mobile phone industries, evaluate and assess Nokia's and Microsoft's product lines and market shares.
4. What did you learn from the Nokia-Microsoft case when applying the main theories and topics from this chapter?

Source:

Copyright © 2012 by Syed Tariq Anwar, West Texas A&M University. Written exclusively for this book and used with permission.

References

1. "Nokia calls Microsoft for help," *The Wall Street Journal*, (February 12–13, 2011), B18.
2. "Elop jumps into the arms of former boss," *Financial* Times (February 12–13, 2011), 9.
3. Microsoft and Nokia pages, *Value Line* (2012). New York, Value Line LLC.
4. See: "One year later, Nokia and Microsoft deliver," *New York Times* (2012). (http://www.nytimes.com/2012/02/28/technology/one-year-later-nokia-and-microsoft-start-to-deliver.html?partner=yahoofinance). Accessed on February 28, 2012.
5. Nokia, *Value Line* (2012). New York, Value Line LLC.
6. "Glory days an old memory in RIM's new world," *Financial Times* (January 24, 2012), 18.
7. Apple page, *Value Line* (2012). New York, Value Line LLC.
8. "Smartphone proliferation sparks calls for new investment," *Financial Times* (February 24, 2012), 17.
9. Anwar, S. T., "Internationalization, investment opportunities, expansion strategies, and the changing telecom industry in the MENA region," *The Journal of World Investment & Trade*, 12(6), (2011): 891–917.

Organization Structure and Control Systems

OUTLINE

OBJECTIVES

1. To understand the importance of appropriate organizational structures to effective strategy implementation.

2. To become familiar with the types of organizational designs suitable for the level and scope of internationalization of the firm.

3. To be able to recognize why and when organizational restructuring is needed.

4. To understand the role of technology in the evolution of the networked structure; and to appreciate the role of "human networks" in achieving business goals.

5. To realize how organizational design affects the manager's job; for example, on the level and location of decision making.

6. To emphasize the role of control and monitoring systems suitable for specific situations and locations in the firm's international operations.

OPENING PROFILE: KRAFT'S POST-MERGER INTEGRATION AND REORGANIZATION

Organizational structures are major pillars on which firms build their foundations. Also important are interorganizational alliances, and control and monitoring systems that help to maintain efficient operations. Firms normally seek short-term/long-term changes when dealing with new markets, corporate expansion, and competition. This has been the case with Kraft Foods Inc. (hereafter "Kraft"), which is the largest food and beverage firm from the U.S. In 2012, the company's high-profile and billion-dollar brands included Oreo cookies, Milka and Cadbury chocolates, Trident gum, Tang (powdered beverage), etc. Kraft also sold other brands such as Nabisco, LU, Jacobs and Maxwell House coffees, Philadelphia cream cheeses, and Oscar Mayer meats.[1]

In 2011, the company's sales stood at $55.30 billion versus 2010's $49.20 billion, and its net profit surpassed $4 billion. To capitalize on the BRICs (Brazil, Russia, India, and China) and other emerging markets, Kraft sought two major acquisitions. In 2007, the company bought LU, a biscuit firm that was owned by Groupe Danone of France for $7.6 billion. In 2009, Kraft acquired the UK's Cadbury Plc for $19 billion that turned into a hostile takeover on the part of Kraft. Both acquisitions were the results of cost pressures, global consolidation, and long-term brand building.[2] Interestingly, in December 2011, Kraft announced its plan of splitting the whole company into two corporate entities: "snack business" ($32 billion) and "grocery business" ($16 billion).[3] This high-profile reorganization and these corporate spinoffs were the result of Kraft's post-merger integration that aimed at creating business efficiencies and productivity. Of course, Kraft's post-merger spinoffs and cost-cutting plans attracted analysts' criticism and media attention. Scott Moeller in the *Financial Times* observed: "*Little did Cadbury's management know that Kraft's plan was to split in two to eliminate its conglomerate nature and become two more focused businesses, thereby creating more value for its shareholders.*"[4] In the business world, this was a normal process to cut cost and make changes in the post-merger period. Of course, investors and stakeholders were equally involved behind the scene when dealing with "*trophy assets*" and future plans of the company.[5] The British Parliament's Commons Select Committee also commented on the post-takeover developments in May 2011 and stated:

"*Our overall conclusion, therefore, is that, while there remain some significant concerns about Kraft's takeover of Cadbury, a number of positive signs may be beginning to emerge. Those positive messages would have been considerably more convincing if conveyed directly to bodies such as ourselves from the top of the organization*".[6]

Source: Syed Tariq Anwar, West Texas A&M University. Written exclusively for this book. Copyright © 2012 by Syed Tariq Anwar; used with permission.

Strategic plans are abstract sets of decisions that cannot affect a company's competitive position or bottom line until they are implemented. Having decided on the strategic direction for the company, international managers must then consider two of the key variables for implementing strategy: the organizational structure and the control and coordinating mechanisms. The necessity of adapting organizational structures to facilitate changes in strategy, competitive moves, and changes in the environment is illustrated in the opening profile describing Kraft Food Inc.'s reorganization to accommodate new strategic directions. The failure to adapt to changing market conditions both strategically and structurally is evidenced by the short life-span of even large companies. As one example of studies highlighting corporate mortality, only 160 out of 1008 large corporations studied by Foster and Kaplan survived between 1962 and 1998.[7] This is particularly apparent in times of radical change such as new technologies and the economic relapse that started in 2008 and resulted in many firms, such as Eastman Kodak Inc. and Borders Bookstores, going out of business or filing for Chapter 11 bankruptcy. Even General Motors, one of the largest global companies, was tipped over the edge into bankruptcy after decades of poor management, surviving only with radical downsizing and government aid. Comparatively, IBM has adapted in various ways. After realizing that the company had missed opportunities for growth initiatives, the company developed its EBO (emerging business opportunities) model into three horizons—current core businesses, growth businesses, and future growth businesses.[8]

ORGANIZATIONAL STRUCTURE

There is no permanent organization chart for the world. . . . It is of supreme importance to be ready at all times to take advantage of new opportunities.

ROBERT C. GOIZUETA,
(FORMER) CHAIRMAN AND CEO, COCA-COLA COMPANY[9]

Organizational structures must change to accommodate a firm's evolving internationalization in response to worldwide competition. Considerable research has shown that a firm's structure must be conducive to the implementation of its strategy.[10] In other words, the structure must "fit" the strategy, or it will not work. Managers are faced with how best to attain that fit in organizing the company's systems and tasks.

The design of an organization, as with any other management function, should be contingency based, taking into account the variables of that particular system at that specific point in time. Major variables include the firm's strategy, size, and appropriate technology, as well as the environment in those parts of the world in which the firm operates. Given the increased complexity of the variables involved in the international context, it is no easy task to design the most suitable organizational structure and subsystems. In fact, research shows that most international managers find it easier to determine what to do to compete globally (strategy) than to decide how to develop the organizational capability (structure) to do it.[11] Additional variables affecting structural choices—geographic dispersion as well as differences in time, language, cultural attitudes, and business practices—introduce further layers of complication. We will show how organizational structures need to, and typically do, change to accommodate strategies of increasing internationalization.

EVOLUTION AND CHANGE IN MNC ORGANIZATIONAL STRUCTURES

Historically, a firm reorganizes as it internationalizes to accommodate new strategies. The structure typically continues to change over time with growth and with increasing levels of investment or diversity and as a result of the types of entry strategy chosen. Internationalization is the process by which a firm gradually changes in response to international competition, domestic market saturation, and the desire for expansion, new markets, and diversification. As discussed in Chapter 6, a firm's managers weigh alternatives and decide on appropriate entry strategies. Perhaps the firm starts by exporting or by acting as a licensor or licensee, and then over time continues to internationalize by engaging in joint ventures or by establishing service, production, or assembly facilities or alliances abroad, moving into a global strategy. At each stage, the firm's managers redesign the organizational structure to optimize the strategy's chances to work, making changes in the firm's tasks and relationships and designating authority, responsibility, lines of communication, geographic dispersal of units, and so forth. This model of **structural evolution** has become known as the **stages model**, resulting from Stopford's research on 187 U.S. multinational corporations (MNCs).[12] Of course, many firms do not follow the stages model because they may start their internationalization at a higher level of involvement—perhaps a full-blown global joint venture without ever having exported, for example, or a "born global" e-company.

Even a mature MNC must make structural changes from time to time to facilitate changes in strategy—perhaps a change in strategy from globalization to regionalization (see Chapter 6), or an effort to improve efficiency or effectiveness. The reorganization of Aluminum Company of America (Alcoa), for example, split the company into smaller, more autonomous units, thereby giving more focus to growing businesses, such as automotive products, where the market for aluminum is strong. It also enabled Alcoa to link businesses with similar functions that are geographically divided—that is, to improve previously insufficient communication between Alcoa's aluminum operations in Brazil and its Australian counterparts. Alcoa, as with most MNCs, has found the need to continuously adapt its structure to accommodate global expansion and new ventures. As of February 2012, Alcoa had a presence in 31 countries, employing 61,000 people worldwide. In other situations, firms find the need to consolidate and restructure to respond to negative environmental conditions; such was the case for Samsung Electronics, as described in the nearby Under the Lens feature.

UNDER THE LENS
Samsung Electronics Reorganizes to Fight Downturn[13]

Companies change their structures not only to align with new strategic directions and competition, but also to respond to developments in their operating environment. Such was the case early in 2009 when Samsung Electronics of Seoul, South Korea, implemented a radical reorganization in order to become more efficient to deal with worsening economic conditions.

Samsung Electronics is the world's leading manufacturer of memory chips, liquid crystal displays, and flat screen televisions, and is second in mobile phones after Finland's Nokia Corp. (Samsung Electronics is part of the Samsung Group, which includes dozens of companies, with interests in shipbuilding, construction, life insurance and leisure. Samsung, which began as a small noodle business in 1938, was, in 2012, a network of 83 companies that account for a staggering 13% of South Korea's exports.[14]) But Samsung had been badly hit by the global economic downturn that resulted in falling prices for semiconductors and flat screens, and such a radically declining profitability could "threaten its existence," according to a Samsung spokeswoman Hwang Eun-ju. She stated that the changes were needed to "effectively respond to the current global recession."[15]

As a result, Samsung Electronics Co. announced a major restructuring, consolidating business operations into two operating divisions: one focused on consumer products such as televisions and cellphones, and the other on components such as memory chips and displays. Thus the company integrated four business units—semiconductors, LCDs, mobile phones, and consumer electronics—into two divisions, regarded as "parts" and "sets." This necessitated reassigning two-thirds of its executives and relocating 1,200 staff members, cutting executives' pay by 20 percent, and reducing other benefits. The company also replaced the heads of five of its eight overseas operations—North America, Europe, the CIS (Commonwealth of International States), and the Middle East and Africa.

Clearly, the company strategy has had to change from high-tech competition to controlling cash flow and profitability. The reorganization was expected to eliminate bureaucracy and speed decision making. Another goal of the restructuring was to help resolve conflicts in that Samsung's components businesses serve customers who are competitive with its own consumer-products businesses. Samsung's CEO Lee Yoon-woo was selected to directly oversee the components division, and Mr. Choi Gee-sung was to head the consumer products division.

The typical ways in which firms organize their international activities are shown in the following list. (Larger companies often use several of these structures in different regions or parts of their organization.) After the presentation of some of these structural forms, the focus will turn to transitional organizational arrangements.

- Domestic structure plus export department
- Domestic structure plus foreign subsidiary
- International division
- Global functional structure
- Global product structure
- Matrix structure

As previously stated, many firms—especially smaller ones—start their international involvement by exporting. They may simply use the services of an export management company for this, or they may reorganize into a simple *domestic structure plus export department.*

To facilitate access to and development of specific foreign markets, the firm can take a further step toward worldwide operations by reorganizing into a *domestic structure plus foreign subsidiary* in one or more countries (see Exhibit 8-1). To be effective, subsidiary managers should have a great deal of autonomy and be able to adapt and respond quickly to serve local markets. This structure works well for companies with one or a few subsidiaries located relatively close to headquarters.

With further market expansion, the firm may then decide to specialize by creating an *international division* organized along functional, product, or geographic lines. With this structure, the various foreign subsidiaries are organized under the international division, and the subsidiary managers report to its head, who is typically given the title "Vice President, International

EXHIBIT 8-1   Domestic Structure Plus Foreign Subsidiary

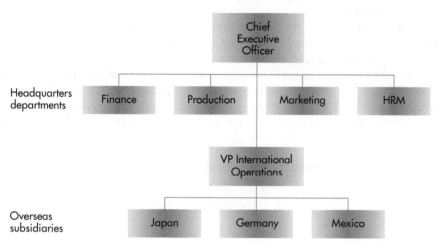

Division." This vice president, in turn, reports directly to the CEO of the corporation. The creation of an international division facilitates the beginning of a global strategy. It permits managers to allocate and coordinate resources for foreign activities under one roof, and thus enhances the firm's ability to respond, both reactively and proactively, to market opportunities. Some conflicts may arise among the divisions of the firm because more resources and management attention tend to get channeled toward the international division than toward the domestic divisions and because of the different orientations of various division managers. Companies such as IBM and PepsiCo have international divisions called, respectively, IBM World Trade and Pepsi-Cola International.

Integrated Global Structures

To respond to increased product diversification and to maximize benefits from both domestic and foreign operations, a firm may choose to replace its international division with an integrated global structure. This structure can be organized along functional, product, geographic, or matrix lines.

The **global functional structure** is designed on the basis of the company's functions—production, marketing, finance, and so forth. Foreign operations are integrated into the activities and responsibilities of each department to gain functional specialization and economies of scale. This form of organization is primarily used by small firms with highly centralized systems. It is particularly appropriate for product lines using similar technology and for businesses with a narrow spectrum of customers. This structure results in plants that are highly integrated across products and that serve single or similar markets.

Much of the advantage resulting from economies of scale and functional specialization may be lost if the managers and the work systems become too narrowly defined to have the necessary flexibility to respond to local environments. An alternative structure can be based on product lines.

For firms with diversified product lines (or services) that have different technological bases and that are aimed at dissimilar or dispersed markets, a **global product (divisional) structure** may be more strategically advantageous than a functional structure. In this structure, a single product (or product line) is represented by a separate division. Each division is headed by its own general manager, and each is responsible for its own production and sales functions. Usually, each division is a **strategic business unit** (SBU)—a self-contained business with its own functional departments and accounting systems. The advantages of this organizational form are market concentration, innovation, and responsiveness to new opportunities in a particular environment. It also facilitates diversification and rapid growth, sometimes at the expense of scale economies and functional specialization. H. J. Heinz Company CEO William R. Johnson came on board in April 1998 and decided that the company should restructure to implement a global strategy. He changed the focus of the company from a multidomestic international strategy using the global geographic area structure to a global strategy using the global product divisional structure. His goal was further growth overseas by building international operations; this structure also readily incorporated Heinz's Specialty Pet Food Division for marketing those products around the world.[16] As of 2012, Heinz was a $10.7 billion global company with 35,000 employees around the world.

Particularly appropriate in a dynamic and diverse environment, the global product structure is illustrated in Exhibit 8-2.

With the global product (divisional) grouping, however, ongoing difficulties in the coordination of widely dispersed operations may result. One answer to this problem, particularly for large MNCs, is to reorganize into a global geographic structure.

In the **global geographic (area) structure**—the most common form of organizing foreign operations—divisions are created to cover geographic regions (see Exhibit 8-3). Each regional manager is responsible for the operations and performance of the countries within a given region. In this way, country and regional needs and relative market knowledge take precedence

EXHIBIT 8-2 Global Product (Divisional) Structure

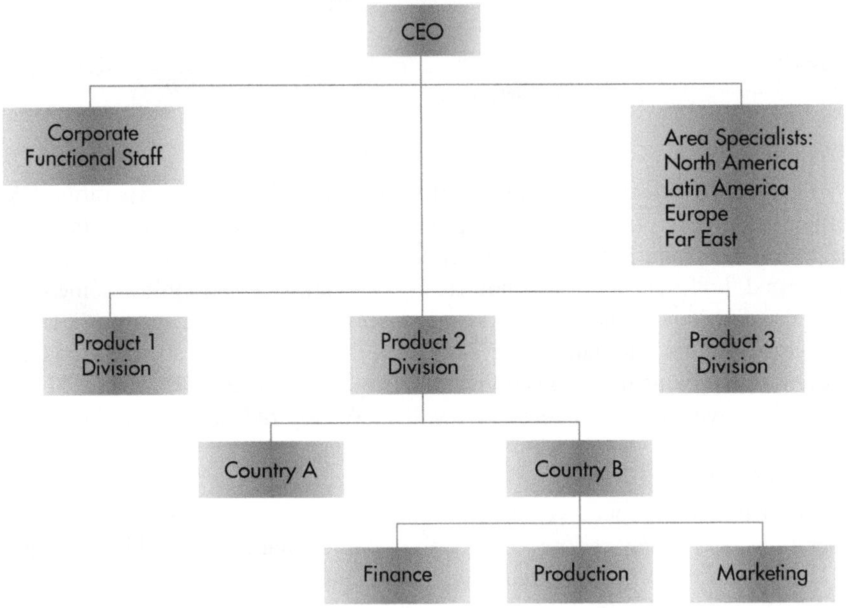

EXHIBIT 8-3 Global Geographic Structure

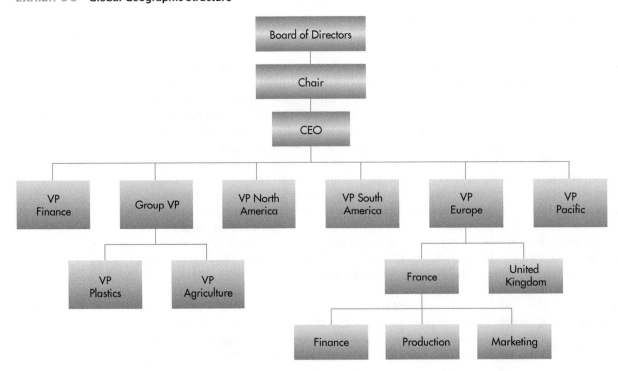

over product expertise. Local managers are familiar with the cultural environment, government regulations, and business transactions. In addition, their language skills and local contacts facilitate daily transactions and responsiveness to the market and the customer. While this is a good structure for consolidating regional expertise, problems of coordination across regions may arise.

With the geographic structure, the focus is on marketing, since products can be adapted to local requirements. Therefore, marketing-oriented companies, such as Nestlé and Unilever, which produce a range of products that can be marketed through similar (or common) channels of distribution to similar customers, will usually opt for this structure. Nestlé SA, for example, uses this decentralized structure, which is more typical of European companies, because it is Nestlé's policy to generate most of its sales outside of Switzerland. The company strives to be an insider in every country in which it operates.[17] In 2005, Nestlé reinforced its global business strategy of emphasizing its brands by making its head of marketing responsible for Nestlé's seven strategic business units (SBUs)—dairy, confectionery, beverages, ice cream, food, pet care, and food services. Those SBUs help determine the company's regional business strategy, which then shapes the local market business strategies.[18] Still Peter Brabeck-Letmathe, who was Nestlé's marketing manager, and in 2012 is the Chairman, insisted that . . .

> *There is no such thing as a global consumer, especially in a sector as psychologically and culturally loaded as food. . . . This means having a local character.*[19]

As of 2012, Nestle had a presence in almost every country in the world, including emerging markets; and it had various partnerships around the world—most recently with the Chinese confectionery company Hsu Fu Chi. The Nestlé company website describes the organization of the food and beverage business, with some product exceptions, as being managed by geographies in three zones—Europe, the Americas, and Asia/Oceania/Africa. The other products, such as Nestlé Purina Petcare, Nestlé Nutrition, and Nestlé Waters, are managed on a global basis; the company calls this group the Globally Managed Businesses.[20]

A **matrix structure** is a hybrid organization of overlapping responsibilities. The structure is developed to combine geographic support for both global integration and local responsiveness; also it can be used to take advantage of personnel skills and experience shared across both functional and divisional structures. In the matrix structure the lines of responsibility are drawn both vertically and horizontally as illustrated in Exhibit 8-4. While this method of management and organization maximizes the focus of skills and experience in the company brought to bear on a particular product as well as a particular region, it often brings confusion, communication problems, and conflict over having more than one boss to whom to report as well as stress over prioritizing time among overlapping and conflicting responsibilities. Indeed, in their research of 36 Dutch organizations, including subsidiaries of global firms, Strikwerda and Stoelhorst concluded from the majority of interviewees that:

> *executives associate the matrix organization with unclear responsibilities, a lack of accountability, and political battles over resources, resulting in risk-averse behavior and loss of market share.*[21]

EXHIBIT 8-4 **Matrix Geographic Structure**

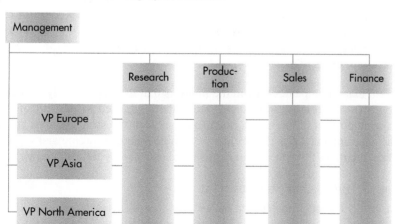

ORGANIZING FOR GLOBALIZATION

No matter what the stage of internationalization, a firm's structural choices always involve two opposing forces: the need for **differentiation** (focusing on and specializing in specific markets) and the need for **integration** (coordinating those same markets). The way the firm is organized along the differentiation–integration continuum determines how well strategies—along a localization–globalization continuum—are implemented. This is why the structural imperatives of various strategies such as globalization must be understood to organize appropriate worldwide systems and connections.

As previously presented, global trends and competitive forces have put increasing pressure on multinational corporations to adopt a strategy of **globalization**, a specific strategy that treats the world as one market by using a standardized approach to products and markets. The following are two examples of companies reorganizing to achieve globalization:

- **IBM.** Big Blue decided to move away from its traditional geographic structure to a global structure based on its 14 worldwide industry groups, such as banking, retail, and insurance, shifting power from country managers to centralized industry expert teams.
- **Asea-Brown Boveri (ABB).** A global leader in the power and the oil and gas industries, ABB is legendary in its record of changing its organizational structure to fit its new strategic directions and its competitive environment, such as the losses it incurred resulting from the East Asian currency crisis. Exhibit 8-5 illustrates two phases of the company's strategic direction and organization structure.

Organizing to facilitate a globalization strategy typically involves rationalization and the development of strategic alliances. To achieve rationalization, managers choose the manufacturing location for each product based on where the best combination of cost, quality, and technology can be attained. It often involves producing different products or component parts in different countries. Typically, it also means that the product design and marketing programs are essentially the same for all end markets around the world—to achieve optimal economies of scale. The downside of this strategy is a lack of differentiation and specialization for local markets.

Organizing for global product standardization necessitates close coordination among the various countries involved. It also requires centralized global product responsibility (one manager at headquarters responsible for a specific product around the world), an especially difficult task for multiproduct companies. Henzler and Rall suggest that structural solutions to this problem can be found if companies rethink the roles of their headquarters and their national subsidiaries. Managers should center the overall control of the business at headquarters, while treating national subsidiaries as partners in managing the business—perhaps as holding companies responsible for the administration and coordination of cross-divisional activities.[22]

Governments as well as firms may structure their holdings in order to attract and integrate strategic allies. Such was the case for Brazil's federal energy company Petrobas (NYSE: PBR) when it announced in February 2009 that it had created six wholly owned companies, along product lines, for the Rio de Janeiro Comperj petrochemical complex, commenting that:

> *Petrobras will hold a 100% stake in the companies and voting capital at the initial stage while it integrates and defines the relationship between Comperj's component parts. By establishing these companies Petrobras is laying the foundations for the potential involvement of partners. Planned investments in Comperj are expected to total US$8.4bn and operations are scheduled to begin in 2012.*[23]

A problem many companies face in the future is that their structurally sophisticated global networks, built to secure cost advantages, leave them exposed to the risk of environmental volatility from all corners of the world. Such companies must restructure their global operations to reduce the environmental risk that results from multicountry sourcing and supply networks.[24] In other words, the more links in the chain, the more chances for things to go wrong.

Organizing to "Be Global, Act Local"

In their rush to get on the globalization bandwagon, too many firms have sacrificed the ability to respond to local market structures and consumer preferences. Managers are now realizing

EXHIBIT 8-5 ABB's Old Versus New Corporate Strategy and Organizational Models During the Tenures of CEOs Percy Barnevik and Jürgen Dormann (1988–2004) and Fred Kindle (2005–2008) (Joseph Hogan took over in 2008)

Old Corporate Strategy/Organizational Model

(Percy Barnevik, 1988–2001)

- Create a powerful global corporation
- Seek aggressive global expansion
- Design and implant matrix management structure
- Encourage entrepreneurship, decentralization, and multiculturalism in overseas subsidiaries
- Seek internal benchmarking and corporate parenting
- Keep local corporate identities while seeking globalization
- Seek cosmopolitan conglomerates
- Seek pan-European and global strategies
- Concentrate on Asian markets

Net Output
- Global corporation
- Matrix structure

- Networking

- Horizontal structure

New Corporate Strategy/Organizational Model

(Jürgen Dormann, 2002–2004) and Fred Kindle to 2008

- Revise core competencies
- Sell off non-core businesses
- Seek corporate restructuring
- Improve financial health of company
- Seek more regional strategies
- Resolve old disputes such as asbestos liabilities
- Simplify ABB's global structure; create two divisions (power technology and automation)
- Seek cost cutting; seek downsizing
- Unload unproductive units
- Improve credit rating

Net Output
- Rationalization
- Simplicity
- Avoid non-core businesses
- Downsizing
- Save money
- Redesign the company

Sources: Based on *BusinessWeek, The Economist,* the *Financial Times,* and the *Wall Street Journal.* Updated by Helen Deresky, originally compiled by Syed Tariq Anwar, case study "ABB, Sweden: What Went Wrong?" in the 6th edition of this book.

that—depending on the type of products, markets, and so forth—a compromise must be made along the globalization–regionalization continuum, and they are experimenting with various structural configurations to "be global and act local."

Levi Strauss is another example of a company attempting to maximize the advantages of different structural configurations. The company employs a staff of approximately 10,000 people worldwide, including approximately 1,010 people at its San Francisco, California, headquarters. Approximately half of the company's revenues comes from outside the United States. The company is organized into three geographic divisions:

Levi Strauss Americas (LSA), based in the San Francisco headquarters.

Levi Strauss Europe, Middle East, and North Africa (LSEMA), based in Brussels.

Asia Pacific Division (APD), based in Singapore.

In the LSEMA division there is a network of nine sales offices, six distribution centers, and three production facilities, employing a total of approximately 4,600 people. The headquarters are located in Brussels, Belgium. The company's European franchise partners bring the products to consumers throughout the region.[25]

Levi Strauss & Co.'s Asia Pacific Division is comprised of subsidiary businesses, licensees, and distributors throughout the Asia Pacific region, the Middle East, and Africa.

Thus, through these various structural global–local formats, the company has ensured its ability to respond to local needs by allowing its managers to act independently: Levi's success turns on its ability to fashion a global strategy that doesn't snuff out local initiative. It's a delicate balancing act, one that often means giving foreign managers the freedom needed to adjust their tactics to meet the changing tastes of their home markets. The company's website in 2012 states that "our goal is to expand the Levi Strauss & Co. brands in India, China, Russia, Brazil and other emerging markets."[26]

One well-known global consumer products company, Procter & Gamble, is succeeding with its global–local "Four Pillars" structure, as described in the accompanying Management in Action feature.

MANAGEMENT IN ACTION

Procter & Gamble's "Think Globally-Act Locally" Structure—
10 Years of Success

In 2012, Procter & Gamble (P&G) attributes much of its success to its global/local "Four Pillars" organization structure. The well-known $83 billion company melds its global scale efficiencies with a local focus in the 180 countries in which it operates. The company lauds its growth and competitive advantage in adopting new business models and in more than doubling of its capacity to innovate.

P&G touches the lives of people around the world three billion times a day with its broad portfolio of leading brands, including Pampers®, Tide®, Charmin®, Downy®, Crest®, Gillette®, and Braun®.[27]

P&G's organizational structure is broadly divided into three heads: GBU (Global Business Unit), MDO (Market Development Organization), and GBS (Global Business Services). Upon the acquisition of Gillette, it was decided that the structure would change from business units based on geographic regions to GBUs based on product lines. "MDOs will develop market strategies to build business based on local knowledge and GBS will bring together business activities such as accounting, human resource systems, order management, and information technology, thus making it cost-effective."[28]

Since 2001, P&G has acquired three leading companies with leading brands in Clairol, Wella, and Gillette. The acquisition of Gillette in 2006 added five brands with annual sales in excess of $1 billion. CEO A. G. Lafley had expressed confidence that the company could deliver on a full decade of growth because of P&G's strategies and strengths, and the company's unique organizational structure. P&G's structure makes it the only consumer-products company with global business unit profit centers, global market development organizations, and global shared services, all supported by innovative corporate functions. P&G's organization structure as of 2012 is described below, as provided in the company's corporate information description on their Web site.[29]

P&G'S GLOBAL/LOCAL STRUCTURE—2012

Four pillars—Global Business Units, Market Development Organizations, Global Business Services, and Corporate Functions—form the heart of P&G's organizational structure.

- Global Business Units (GBUs) build major global brands with robust business strategies.
- Market Development Organizations (MDOs) build local understanding as a foundation for marketing campaigns.
- Global Business Services (GBS) provide business technology and services that drive business success.
- Corporate Functions (CFs) work to maintain our place as a leader of our industries.

P&G approaches business knowing that we need to Think Globally (GBUs) and Act Locally (MDOs). This approach is supported by our commitment to operate efficiently (GBS) and our constant striving to be the best at what we do (CFs). This streamlined structure allows us to get to market faster.

Global Business Units

Philosophy: Think Globally

General Role: Create strong brand equities, robust strategies, and ongoing innovation in products and marketing to build major global brands.

GBUs:

- Baby Care/Family Care
- Beauty Care/Feminine Care

- Fabric & Home Care
- Snacks & Beverage
- Health Care

Market Development Organizations (MDO)

Philosophy: Act Locally

General Role: Interface with customers to ensure marketing plans fully capitalize on local understanding, to seek synergy across programs to leverage corporate scale, and to develop strong programs that change the game in our favor at point of purchase.

MDO Regions:

- North America
- Asia/India/Australia
- Northeast Asia
- Greater China
- Central-Eastern Europe/Middle East/Africa
- Western Europe
- Latin America

Global Business Services (GBS)

Philosophy: Enabling P&G to win with customers and consumers

General Role: Provide services and solutions that enable the Company to operate efficiently around the world, collaborate effectively with business partners, and help employees become more productive.

GBS Centers:

- GBS Americas located in Costa Rica
- GBS Asia located in Manila
- GBS Europe, Middle East, & Africa located in Newcastle

Corporate Functions (CF)

Philosophy: Be the Smartest/Best

General Role: Ensure that the functional capability integrated into the rest of the company remains on the cutting edge of the industry. We want to be the thought leader within each CF.

Corporate Functions:

- Customer Business Development
- External Relations
- Finance & Accounting
- Human Resources
- Information Technology
- Legal
- Marketing
- Consumer & Market Knowledge
- Product Supply
- Research & Development
- Workplace Services

Although strategy may be the primary means to a company's competitive advantage, the burden of realizing that advantage rests on the organizational structure and design; that structure, in turn, establishes the responsibilities and guides the decisions, actions, and communications of its employees. Because of the difficulties experienced by companies trying to be "glocal" companies (global and local), researchers are suggesting new, more flexible organizational designs involving interorganizational networks and transnational design.

EMERGENT STRUCTURAL FORMS

Companies are increasingly abandoning rigid structures in an attempt to be more flexible and responsive to the dynamic global environment. Some of the ways they are adapting are by transitioning to formats known as interorganizational networks, global e-corporation network structures, and transnational corporation network structures, described below. An increasing number of companies, like Cisco Systems and IBM, create customized structures according to the client needs. By selectively moving their skilled employees into cross-company teams they are able to move rapidly and flexibly to take advantage of their portfolios of opportunities. To do this,

> *They assemble and disassemble teams of hundreds of people from across the company who move from opportunity to opportunity. Their reconfigurable organizations consist of a stable part and a variable part. The stable structure is usually the functional and/or geographical home for nurturing talent.*
>
> J. R. GALBRAITH,
> 2010.[30]

Other new structural formats are evolving as emerging market companies make their rapid entré onto the global scene, as discussed in the following Comparative Management in Focus section.

 ## COMPARATIVE MANAGEMENT IN FOCUS

Changing Organizational Structures of Emerging Market Companies

---

Rapidly changing competition and global business activities demand that companies run their worldwide operations efficiently and effectively, based on the right business models and organizational structures. Stable organizational structures and control systems are necessary to seek timely internationalization. The major variables involved in choosing the right organizational structure depend on a company's global involvement and degree of localization. Fast-growing companies from emerging markets (EMs), BRIC countries (Brazil, Russia, India, and China), and rapidly developing economies (RDEs) continue to internationalize their operations. Examples are: CNOOC (China), Dr. Reddy's Laboratories (India), Embraer (Brazil), Gazprom (Russia), Haier Company (China), Infosys Technologies (India), Koc Holdings (Turkey), Lenovo Group (China), Tata Motors (India), and Wipro (India).[31] These emerging market companies are the first wave of highly successful firms benefiting from the globalization phenomenon.[32]

Interestingly, the expansion models sought by these new emerging-market companies from Asia, Latin America, and Eastern Europe are unique and may not fit with today's mainstream multinational corporation (MNC) model because of the following three reasons: First, many emerging market companies are avoiding the traditional roadmap to internationalization and are instead capitalizing on the "born-global phenomenon," which means running their operations and opening subsidiaries worldwide from the beginning. Second, they are finding niche businesses where competition is limited. Third, they are thriving in those old-economy industries that have been abandoned by established MNCs from developed countries.

A new breed of companies is emerging in those geographic areas that have excelled in global business because of their unique organizational structures and design. Like Korean chaebols (industrial conglomerates), most emerging market companies were started as family businesses and entrepreneurial entities where ownership and control of the firms resided with the families. Therefore, the control mechanism is somewhat bureaucratic and headquarters-centered. Currently, a multitude of changes are in the pipeline that will force emerging market companies to redefine their family-based governance structures and rigid control systems.

Major structural changes include simplifying hierarchies, reducing family ownerships, providing more powers to subsidiaries, and seeking organizational structures based on either the traditional MNC model or company-specific hybrid structures. Interestingly, many emerging market companies have been following the model of "be global, act local" in becoming responsible citizens and also adapting their products and services. Embraer, Haier Group, Lenovo, Mittal Steel, Orsacom, and others fit in this category. In addition, overseas Chinese business networks (OCBNs) are also changing to become part of the globalization phenomenon. Increasingly, emerging market companies from Asia, Latin America, and Eastern Europe will seek internationalization in their own unique ways, leading to hybrid structures and fast-growth entities. Of course, these newly emerging MNCs will become globally integrated, utilizing multidomestic synergies, and international/global/transnational strategies. Their future goals and scope of operations will determine organizational structures and global initiatives.

Source: Written exclusively for this text by Syed Tariq Anwar, Professor, West Texas A&M University.

Interorganizational Networks

Whether the ever-expanding transnational linkages of an MNC consist of different companies, subsidiaries, suppliers, or individuals, they result in relational networks. These networks may adopt very different structures of their own because they operate in different local contexts within their own national environments. Similarly, the "I-form" is described by Miles et al. as a collaborative, multi-firm network along with community-based structures, used by innovative firms such as Taiwan's Acer.[33] By regarding the MNC's overall structure as a network of interconnected relations, we can more realistically consider its organizational design imperatives at both global and local levels. Royal Philips Electronics of the Netherlands, one of the world's biggest electronics companies, has operating units in 100 countries as of 2012, using a network structure. These units range from large subsidiaries, which might be among the largest companies in a country, to very small single-function operations, such as research and development or marketing divisions for one of Philips's businesses. Some have centralized control at Philips's headquarters; others are quite autonomous. For some time, Philips had fallen far behind its Japanese competitors in productivity because of missteps and seemingly endless restructurings. However, when Philips' then chief executive Gerard J. Kleisterlee—a 30-year Philips veteran—took over in 2001, he again reorganized the company. He divested $850 million in less important or unprofitable businesses and shuttered a dozen factories, and outsourced manufacturing for much of the electronics and appliance manufacturing as well as chip production.[34]

In yet another structural variation, Intel, in adapting to changes in the semiconductor industry, announced in early 2005 a wholesale reorganization of its businesses. Intel's executives decided that they wanted the company to focus more on what was going on outside the business, and developed a structural focus they call "Platformisation"—that is, customizing a range of chips in a combination suitable for a particular target market, as a response for the increasing need for speedy adaptation to the market.[35] As the world's biggest semiconductor maker, with 82,500 employees worldwide, the company's general description of its approach to organizing, in response to an inquiry by this author, is as follows:

> *Intel is not a very hierarchical company so a formalized organizational structure is not a particularly good representation of how the company works. At the highest level, Intel is organized into largely autonomous divisions. Intel uses matrix management and cross-functional teams including IT, knowledge management, human resources, finance, legal, change control, data warehousing, common directory information management, and cost reduction teams (to name a few) to rapidly adapt to changing conditions.*

www.intel.com.[36]

The network framework makes clear that the company's operating units link vastly different environmental and operational contexts based on varied economic, social, and cultural milieus. This complex linkage highlights the intricate task of a giant MNC to rationalize and coordinate its activities globally to achieve an advantageous cost position while simultaneously tailoring itself to local market conditions (to achieve benefits from differentiation).[37]

The Global E-Corporation Network Structure

The organizational structure for global e-businesses, in particular for physical products, typically involves a network of virtual e-exchanges and "bricks and mortar" services, whether those services are in-house or outsourced. This structure of functions and alliances makes up a combination of electronic and physical stages of the supply chain network, as illustrated in Exhibit 8-6.

As such, the network comprises some global and some local functions. The centralized e-exchanges for logistics, supplies, and customers could be housed anywhere; suppliers, manufacturers, and distributors may be in various countries, separately or together, wherever efficiencies of scale and cost may be realized. The final distribution system and the customer interaction must be tailored to the customer-location physical infrastructure and payment infrastructure, as well as local regulations and languages.[38]

The result is a global e-network of suppliers, subcontractors, manufacturers, distributors, buyers, and sellers, communicating in real time through cyberspace. This spreads efficiency throughout the chain, providing cost-effectiveness for all parties.[39] Dell Computer is an example of a company that uses the Internet to streamline its global supply systems. It has a number of factories around the world that supply custom-built PCs to customers in that region. Customers'

EXHIBIT 8-6 A Global E-Corporation Network Structure

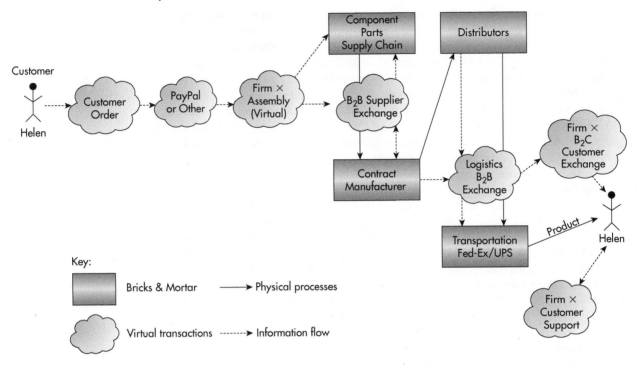

orders are received through call centers or Dell's own Web site. The order for components then goes to its suppliers, which have to be within a 15-minute drive of its factory. The component parts are delivered to the factory, and the completed customers' orders are collected within a few hours. Dell maintains Internet connections with its suppliers and connects them with its customer database so that they have direct and real-time information about orders. Customers also can use Dell's Internet system to track their orders as they go through the chain.[40]

Dell's organizational structure to implement its business model has evolved to what is known as a virtual company, or value web. Dell's strategy is to conduct critical activities in-house, while outsourcing non-strategic activities.

The Transnational Corporation (TNC) Network Structure

To address the globalization–localization dilemma, firms that have evolved through the multinational form and the global company seek the advantages of horizontal organization in the pursuit of transnational capability—that is, the ability to manage across national boundaries, retaining local flexibility while achieving global integration.[41] This capability involves linking foreign operations to each other and to headquarters in a flexible way, thereby leveraging local and central capabilities. ABB (discussed earlier) is an example of such a decentralized horizontal organization. In 2012, ABB operates in 100 countries with 145,000 employees and eight geographic region managers. with only one management level separating the business units from top management. ABB prides itself on being a truly global company, with 11 board members representing seven nationalities. Thus, this structure is less a matter of boxes on an organizational chart and more a matter of a network of the company's units and their system of horizontal communication. This involves lateral communication across networks of units and alliances rather than in a hierarchy. The system requires the dispersal of responsibility and decision making to local subsidiaries and alliances. The effectiveness of that localized decision-making depends a great deal on the ability and willingness to share current and new learning and technology across the network of units. The matrix structure typical of the transnational company creates a complex coordination and control system as it attempts to combine:

- The capabilities and resources of a multinational corporation
- The economies of scale of a global corporation
- The local responsiveness of a domestic company
- The ability to transfer technology efficiently typical of the international structure[42]

Whatever the names given to the organizational forms emerging to deal with global competition and logistics, the MNC organizational structure as we know it, with its hierarchical pyramid, subsidiaries, and world headquarters, is gradually evolving into a more fluid form to adapt to strategic and competitive imperatives. As is now well known, these more flexible forms are facilitated by the ever-developing technologies that enable various forms of electronic instant communication to connect elaborate networks of people and information around the world, regardless of their locations. In this new global web, the location of a firm's headquarters is unimportant. Various alliances tie together units and subunits in the web. Corning Glass, for instance, changed from its national pyramid-like organization to a global web, giving it the capability of making optical cable through its European partner, Siemens AG, and medical equipment with Ciba-Geigy.

CHOICE OF ORGANIZATIONAL FORM

Two major variables in choosing the structure and design of an organization are the opportunities and need for (1) globalization and (2) localization. Exhibit 8-7 depicts alternative structural forms appropriate to each of these variables and to the strategic choices regarding the level and type of international involvement desired by the firm.

This figure thereby updates the evolutionary stages model to reflect alternative organizational responses to more recent environments and to the anticipated competitive environments ahead. The updated model shows that, as the firm progresses from a domestic to an international company—and perhaps later to a multinational and then a global company—its managers adapt the organizational structure to accommodate their relative strategic focus on globalization versus localization, choosing a global product structure, a geographic area structure, or perhaps a matrix form. The model proposes that, as the company becomes larger, more complex, and more sophisticated in its approach to world markets (no matter which structural route it has taken), it may evolve into a transnational corporation (TNC). The TNC strategy is to maximize opportunities for both efficiency and local responsiveness by adopting a transnational structure that uses alliances, networks, and horizontal design formats. The relationships between choice of global strategy and the appropriate structural variations necessary to implement each strategic choice are further illustrated in Exhibit 8-8.

Organizational Change and Design Variables

When a company makes drastic changes in its goals, strategy, or scope of operations, it will usually also need a change in organizational structure. However, other, less obvious indications of organizational inefficiency also signal a need for structural changes: conflicts among divisions and subsidiaries over territories or customers, conflicts between overseas units and headquarters staff,

EXHIBIT 8-7   **Organizational Alternatives and Development for Global Companies**

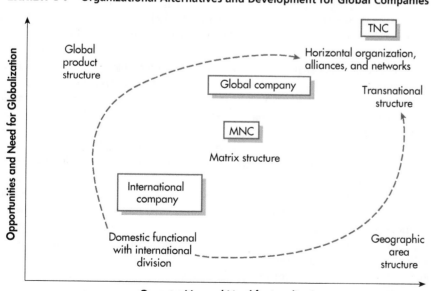

EXHIBIT 8-8 **Structural Variables to Implement Global Strategies**

Strategy	Organizational Structure	Delegation	Need to Coordinate	Organizational Culture
Multidomestic	Global area	To national unit	Low	Low impact
International	Intl. Division	Centralize core; rest to units	Medium	Medium
Global	Product Group	Locate where globally optimum	High	Important
Transnational	Global Matrix	Centralized and decentralized	Very High	Crucial

Source: Based on C. W. L. Hill and E. R. Jones, *Strategic Management: An Integrated Approach,* 3rd ed., 390. 1995, Houghton Mifflin Company.

EXHIBIT 8-9 **Changes That May Necessitate New Structural Designs**[43]

- New management with different goals and strategies
- Downturn in profitability or finances
- Lack of competitiveness; failure to meet goals or capitalize on opportunities
- Poor management, leadership, communication, delegation, or morale
- New strategic directions: growth, alliances, retrenchment; expanding globally from directing export activities to controlling overseas manufacturing and marketing units; a change in the size of operations on a country, regional, or worldwide basis; or failure of foreign operations to grow in accordance with plans and expectations
- Clashes among divisions, subsidiaries, or individuals over territories or customers in the field
- Divisive conflicts between overseas units and domestic division staff or corporate staff
- Underutilization of overseas manufacturing or distribution facilities
- Duplication of sales offices or geographic operational units within an area
- An increase in overseas customer service complaints
- Breakdowns in communications within and among organizations
- Bottlenecks, too many reporting layers, and ill-defined executive responsibilities
- Lack of innovation

complaints regarding overseas customer service, and overlapping responsibilities are some of these warning signals. Exhibit 8-9 lists some indications of the need for change in organizational design.

At persistent signs of ineffective work, a company should analyze its organizational design, systems, and work flow for the possible causes of those problems. The nature and extent of any design changes must reflect the magnitude of the problem. In choosing a new organizational design or modifying an existing structure, managers must establish a system of communication and control that will provide for effective decision making. At such times, managers need to localize decision making and integrate widely dispersed and disparate global operations.

Besides determining the behavior of the organization on a macro level (in terms of what the different divisions, subsidiaries, departments, and units are responsible for), the organizational design must determine behavior on a micro level. For example, the organizational design affects the level at which certain types of decisions will be made. Determining how many and what types of decisions can be made and by whom can have drastic consequences; both the locus and the scope of authority must be carefully considered. This centralization–decentralization variable actually represents a continuum. In the real world, companies are neither totally centralized nor totally decentralized: The level of centralization imposed is a matter of degree. Exhibit 8-10 illustrates this centralization–decentralization continuum and the different ways that decision making can be shared between headquarters and local units or subsidiaries. In general, centralized decision making is common for some functions (finance, research and development) that are organized for the entire corporation, whereas other functions (production, marketing, sales) are more appropriately decentralized. Two key issues are the speed with which the decisions have to be made and whether they primarily affect only a certain subsidiary or other parts of the company as well.

As noted, culture is another factor that complicates decisions on how much to decentralize and how to organize the work flow and the various relationships of authority and responsibility.

EXHIBIT 8-10   Locus of Decision Making in an International Organization

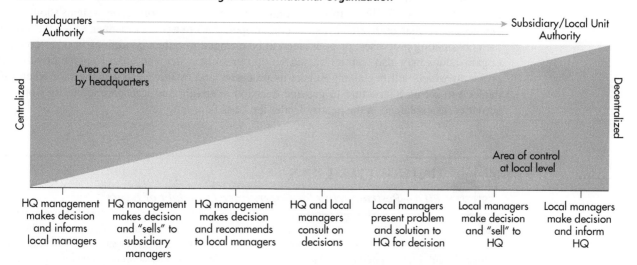

Part 4 of this book more fully presents how cultural variables affect people's attitudes about working relationships and about who should have authority over whom. At this point, it is important merely to note that cultural variables must be taken into account when designing an organization. Delegating a high level of authority to employees in a country where workers usually regard "the boss" as the rightful person to make all the decisions is not likely to work well. Clearly, managers must think through the interactions of organizational, staffing, and cultural issues before making final decisions.

In summary, no one way to organize is best. Contingency theory applies to organizational design as much as to any other aspect of management. The best organizational structure is the one that facilitates the firm's goals and is appropriate to its industry, size, technology, and competitive environment. Structure should be fluid and dynamic, and highly adaptable to the changing needs of the company. The structure should not be allowed to get bogged down in the administrative heritage of the organization (that is, "the way we do things around here" or "what we've always done") to the point that it undermines the very processes that will enable the firm to take advantage of new opportunities.

Most likely, however, the future for the MNC structure, as well as for small businesses and "born globals," lies in a global web of networked companies. Ideally, a company tries to organize in a way that will allow it to carry out its strategic goals; the staffing is then done to mesh with those strategic goals and the way the organizational structure has been set up. In reality, however, the existing structural factors often affect strategic decisions, so the end result may be a trade-off of desired strategy with existing constraints. So, too, with staffing: "ideal" staffing plans have to be adjusted to reflect the realities of assigning managers from various sources and the local regulations or cultural variables that make some organizing and staffing decisions more workable than others.

What may at first seem a linear management process of deciding on strategy, then on structure, and finally on staffing is actually an interdependent set of factors that must be taken into consideration and worked out as a set of decisions. Chapter 9 explores how staffing decisions are—or should be—intricately intertwined with other decisions regarding strategy, structure, and so forth. A unique set of management cadre and skills in a particular location can be a competitive advantage in itself, and so it may be a smart move to build strategic and organizational decisions around that resource rather than risk losing that advantage. The following sections present some other processes that are involved in implementing strategy and are interconnected with coordinating functions through organizational structure.

CONTROL SYSTEMS FOR GLOBAL OPERATIONS

To complement the organizational structure, the international manager must design efficient coordinating and reporting systems to ensure that actual performance conforms to expected organizational standards and goals. The challenge is to coordinate far-flung operations in vastly different environments with various work processes; rules; and economic, political, legal, and cultural norms. The feedback from the control process and the information systems should signal any necessary change in strategy, structure, or operations in a timely manner. Often the strategy, the coordinating processes, or both, need to be changed to reflect conditions in other countries. Organizations may also restructure and set up reporting systems in order to preemptively avoid problems which will negatively impact its processes and image. Such was the case when FIFA decided to set up a structure to provide decision oversight and transparency to its worldwide activities, as explained in the nearby Under the Lens feature.

UNDER THE LENS
FIFA—Restructuring for Governance Oversight of Ethics[44]

Most sports organizations developed on a small scale but have now grown in size and complexity to organizations similar to multinational corporations. As such, those sports organizations should have a structure and a set of policies in place to oversee anti-corruption and conflict-of-interest compliance; this awareness has grown in particular in the wake of the scandal surrounding the International Olympic Committee (IOC) and the Salt Lake City Olympics. However, the governance structure of FIFA for example, had not previously encompassed the responsibility for ethical behavior in the organization. In October 2011, however, FIFA restructured and took the steps as outlined below and as described in www.FIFA.com.

The Fédération Internationale de Football Association (FIFA), located in Zurich, Switzerland, is the international governing body of association football. The association, which has 208 national associations within six regional areas, oversees the governance and organization of the FIFA World Cup; the next one will be held in Brazil in 2014. The administrative organization chart is shown in Exhibit 8-11.

EXHIBIT 8-11 **FIFA Administrative Organization Chart**

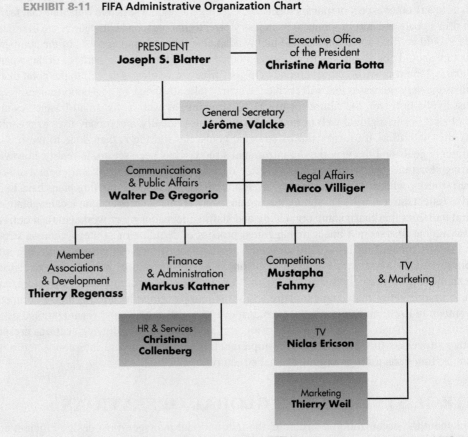

Source: Administrative Organization Chart, www.FIFA.com, accessed February 1, 2012.

EXHIBIT 8-12 **Independent Governance Committee**

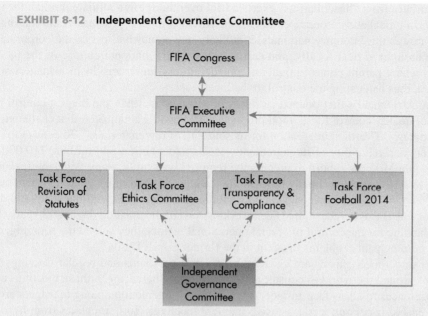

Source: www.FIFA.com, accessed February 1, 2012, used with permission.

Following the proposals made by the FIFA President, Joseph S. Blatter, at the FIFA Congress on June 1, 2011 in terms of good governance, transparency, and zero tolerance toward wrongdoing on and also off the pitch (during games or at any time), the FIFA Executive Committee, meeting on October 20–21, 2011 at the home offices of FIFA in Zurich, agreed on the following measures:

- The creation of four task forces, mandated to propose reforms: *Task Force Revision of Statutes*, chaired by Dr. Theo Zwanziger (Germany); *Task Force FIFA Ethics Committee*, chaired by the Chairman of the Ethics Committee, Claudio Sulser (Switzerland); *Task Force Transparency and Compliance*, chaired by Juan Ángel Napout (President of the Paraguayan FA) and Frank Van Hattum (President of the New Zealand FA); and *Task Force Football 2014* (operating since May 2011), chaired by Franz Beckenbauer (Germany).

- The creation of an Independent Governance Committee (see Exhibit 8-12) which, among other tasks, will oversee reforms undertaken by FIFA. It comprises of representatives not only from the international football family but also from other spheres.

- The establishment of a "FIFA Good Governance" road map between October 2011 and the 2013 FIFA Congress.

The design and application of coordinating and reporting systems for foreign subsidiaries and activities can take any form that management wishes. MNCs usually employ a variety of direct and indirect coordinating and control mechanisms suitable for their organization structure. For example, in the transnational network structure, decision-making control is centralized to key network nodes, greatly reducing emphasis on bureaucratic control. Other specific mechanisms are summarized in the next sections.[45]

Direct Coordinating Mechanisms

Direct mechanisms that provide the basis for the overall guidance and management of foreign operations include the design of appropriate structures (discussed previously in this chapter) and the use of effective staffing practices (discussed in Chapters 9 and 10). Such decisions proactively set the stage for operations to meet goals, rather than troubleshooting deviations or problems after they have occurred.

Staffing is not only a means of control, but also a venue through which groups and individuals bring their cultural properties into a system.[46]

ODED SHENKAR, JOURNAL OF INTERNATIONAL BUSINESS,
JANUARY 2012.

Expatriates from "headquarters" exert control over the foreign affiliate through the expectations of the national and corporate culture of the parent company; whereas, if the staffing assignment is through third country nationals, it is likely that somewhat less of the corporate culture might be brought to bear locally, and certainly less of the national culture of the parent.[47] In situations where parent control might be considered less important, local managers would be considered, thus delegating the control to the local level.

When McDonald's first opened its doors in Moscow in 1990, the biggest control problem was that of quality control for its food products. McDonald's anticipated that challenge and adopted a strategy of vertical integration for its sourcing of raw materials.[48] To control the quality, distribution, and reliability of its ingredients, McDonald's built a $40 million, 110,000-square-foot plant in a Moscow suburb to process the required beef, milk, buns, vegetables, sauces, and potatoes. In addition, the company brought the managers to Toronto, Canada, for five months of training.[49] Top management at McDonald's anticipated difficulties with the setup and daily operations of this IJV and, indeed, had been working toward the opening day for 13 years. Through careful planning for the control of crucial operational factors, they solved the sourcing, distribution, and employment problems inherent in the former Soviet Union.[50]

Other direct mechanisms are visits by head-office personnel and regular meetings to allow employees around the world to consult and troubleshoot. Increasingly, those meetings comprise videoconferences to allow face-to-face, if not physical, interaction among managers around the world to enable faster and less-expensive frequent meetings. Top executives from headquarters may use periodic visits to subsidiaries to check performance and help to anticipate future problems. The meetings allow each general manager to keep in touch with her or his associates, with the overall mission and strategy of the organization, and with comparative performance data and new problem-solving techniques. Increasingly, the tools of technology are being applied as direct mechanisms to ensure up front that operations will be carried out as planned, in particular in countries where processes such as efficient infrastructure and goods forwarding cannot be taken for granted. An example of this is the logistics monitoring system set up by Air Express International in Latin America to minimize its many problems there.[51]

Indirect Coordinating Mechanisms

Indirect coordinating mechanisms typically include sales quotas, budgets, and other financial tools, as well as feedback reports, which give information about the sales and financial performance of the subsidiary for the last quarter or year.

Domestic companies invariably rely on budgets and financial statement analyses, but for foreign subsidiaries, financial statements and performance evaluations are complicated by *financial variables in MNC reports,* such as exchange rates, inflation levels, transfer prices, and accounting standards.

To reconcile accounting statements, MNCs usually require three different sets of financial statements from subsidiaries. One set must meet the national accounting standards and procedures prescribed by law in the host country. This set also aids management in comparing subsidiaries in the same country. A second set must be prepared according to the accounting principles and standards required by the home country. This set allows some comparison with other MNC subsidiaries. The third set of statements translates the second set of statements (with certain adjustments) into the currency of the home country for consolidation purposes, in accordance with FASB Ruling Number 52 of 1982. A foreign subsidiary's financial statements must be consolidated line by line with those of the parent company, according to International Accounting Standard Number 3, adopted in the United States.

Researchers have noted comparative differences between the use of direct versus **indirect controls** among companies headquartered in different countries. One study by Egelhoff examined the practices of 50 U.S., U.K., and European MNCs over their foreign subsidiaries. It compared the use of two mechanisms—the assignment of parent-company managers to foreign subsidiaries and the use of performance reporting systems (that is, comparing behavior mechanisms with output reporting systems).[52] The results of this study show that considerable differences exist in practices across MNC nationalities. For example, U.S. MNCs monitor subsidiary outputs and rely more on frequently reported performance data than do European MNCs. The latter tend to assign more parent-company nationals to key positions in foreign subsidiaries and can count on a higher level of behavior control than their U.S. counterparts.[53]

These findings imply that the U.S. system, which measures more quantifiable aspects of a foreign subsidiary, provides the means to compare performance among subsidiaries. The European system, on the other hand, measures more qualitative aspects of a subsidiary and its environment, which vary among subsidiaries—allowing a focus on the unique situation of the subsidiary but making it difficult to compare its performance to other subsidiaries.[54]

MANAGING EFFECTIVE MONITORING SYSTEMS

Management practices, local constraints, and expectations regarding authority, time, and communication are but a few of the variables likely to affect the **appropriateness of monitoring (or control) systems**. The degree to which headquarters' practices and goals are transferable probably depends on whether top managers are from the head office, the host country, or a third country. In addition, information systems and evaluation variables must all be considered when deciding on appropriate systems.

The Appropriateness of Monitoring and Reporting Systems

One example of differences in the expectations regarding monitoring practices, and therefore in the need for coordination systems, is indicated by a study of Japanese and U.S. firms. Ueno and Sekaran state that their research shows that "the U.S. companies, compared to the Japanese companies, tend to use communication and coordination more extensively, build budget slack to a greater extent, and use long-term performance evaluations to a lesser extent."[55] Furthermore, Ueno and Sekaran conclude that those differences in reporting systems are attributable to the cultural variable of individualism in U.S. society, compared to collectivism in Japanese society. For example, U.S. managers are more likely to use formal communication and coordination processes, whereas Japanese managers use informal and implicit processes. In addition, U.S. managers, who are evaluated on individual performance, are more likely to build slack into budget calculations for a safety net than their Japanese counterparts, who are evaluated on group performance. The implications of this study are that managers around the world who understand the cultural bases for differences in control practices will be more flexible in working with those systems in other countries.

The Role of Information Systems

Reporting systems, such as those described in this chapter, require sophisticated information systems to enable them to work properly—not only for competitive purposes but also for purposes of performance evaluation. Top management must receive accurate and timely information regarding sales, production, and financial results to be able to compare actual performance with goals and to take corrective action where necessary. Most international reporting systems require information feedback at one level or another for financial, personnel, production, and marketing variables.

The specific types of functional reports, their frequency, and the amount of detail required from subsidiaries by headquarters will vary. Neghandi and Welge surveyed the types of functional reports submitted by 117 MNCs in Germany, Japan, and the United States.[56] They found that U.S. MNCs typically submit about double the number of reports than do German and Japanese MNCs, with the exception of performance reviews. German MNCs submit a few more reports than do Japanese MNCs. Thus U.S. MNCs seem to monitor much more via specific functional reports than do German and Japanese MNCs. The Japanese MNCs put far less emphasis on personnel performance reviews than do the U.S. and German MNCs—a finding consistent with the Japanese culture of group decision making, consensus, and responsibility.

Unfortunately, the accuracy and timeliness of information systems are often less than perfect, especially in less-developed countries, where managers typically operate under conditions of extreme uncertainty. Government information, for example, is often filtered or fabricated; other sources of data for decision making are usually limited. Employees are not used to the kinds of sophisticated information generation, analysis, and reporting systems common in developed countries. Their work norms and sense of necessity and urgency may also confound the problem. In addition, their available technology, and the ability to manipulate and transmit data are usually limited. The **MIS adequacy** in foreign affiliates is a sticky problem for headquarters managers in their attempt to maintain efficient coordination of activities and consolidation of results. Another problem is the **noncomparability of performance data across countries**—the control problem caused by the difficulty of comparing performance data across various countries because of the variables that make that information appear different—which hinders the evaluation process.

The Internet has, of course, made the availability and use of information attainable instantaneously. Many companies are starting to supply Internet MIS systems for supply-chain management. European partners Nestlé S.A. and the Danone Group, world leaders in the food industry, set up Europe's first Internet marketplace for e-procurement in the consumer goods sector, called CPGmarket.com:

> *CPGmarket.com will enhance the efficiency of logistics while at the same time reducing procurement costs for businesses producing, distributing and selling consumer goods. CPG (based on mySAP.com e-business platform) allows companies not only to buy and sell, but also to access industry information.*[57]

Evaluation Variables Across Countries

A major problem that arises when evaluating the performance of foreign affiliates is the tendency by headquarters managers to judge subsidiary managers as if all of the evaluation data were comparable across countries. Unfortunately, many variables can make the evaluation information from one country look very different from that of another country, owing to circumstances beyond the control of a subsidiary manager. For example, one country may experience considerable inflation, significant fluctuations in the price of raw materials, political uprisings, or governmental actions. These factors are beyond the manager's control and are likely to have a downward effect on profitability—and yet, that manager may, in fact, have maximized the opportunity for long-term stability and profitability compared with a manager of another subsidiary who was not faced with such adverse conditions. Other variables influencing profitability patterns include transfer pricing, currency devaluation, exchange-rate fluctuations, taxes, and expectations of contributions to local economies.

One way to ensure more meaningful performance measures is to adjust the financial statements to reflect the uncontrollable variables peculiar to each country where a subsidiary is located. This provides a basis for the true evaluation of the comparative return on investment (ROI), which is an overall control measure. Another way to provide meaningful, long-term performance standards is to take into account other nonfinancial measures. These measures include market share, productivity, sales, relations with the host-country government, public image, employee morale, union relations, and community involvement.[58]

CONCLUSION

The structure, control, and coordination *processes* are the same whether they take place in a domestic company, a multinational company with a network of foreign affiliates, or a specific IJV. It is the extent, the focus, and the mechanisms used to organize those activities that differ. More coordination is needed in global companies because of uncertain working environments and information systems and because of the variable loci of decision making. Headquarters managers must design appropriate systems to take into account those variables and to evaluate performance.

Summary of Key Points

1. An organization must be designed to facilitate the implementation of strategic goals. Other variables to consider when designing an organization's structure include environmental conditions, the size of the organization, and the appropriate technology. The geographic dispersion of operations as well as differences in time, language, and culture affect structure in the international context.

2. The design of a firm's structure reflects its international entry strategy and tends to change over time with growth and increasing levels of investment, diversity, or both.

3. Global trends are exerting increasing pressure on MNCs to achieve economies of scale through globalization. This involves rationalization and the coordination of strategic alliances.

4. MNCs can be regarded as interorganizational networks of their own dispersed operations and other strategic alliances. Such relational networks may adopt unique structures for their particular environment, while also requiring centralized coordination.

5. The transnational structure allows a company to "be global and act local" by using networks of decentralized units with horizontal communication. This permits local flexibility while achieving global integration.

6. Indications of the need for structural changes include inefficiency, conflicts among units, poor communication, and overlapping responsibilities.

7. Coordinating and monitoring systems are necessary to regulate organizational activities so that actual performance conforms to expected organizational standards and goals. MNCs use a variety of direct and indirect controls.

8. Financial monitoring and evaluation of foreign affiliates are complicated by variables such as exchange rates, levels of inflation, transfer prices, and accounting standards.

9. The design of appropriate monitoring systems must take into account local constraints, management practices and expectations, uncertain information systems, and variables in the evaluation process.

10. Two major problems in reporting for subsidiaries must be considered: (1) inadequate management information systems and (2) the noncomparability across countries of the performance data needed for evaluation purposes.

Discussion Questions

1. What variables have to be considered in designing the organizational structure for international operations? How do these variables interact, and which do you think are most important?

2. Explain the need for an MNC to "be global and act local." How can a firm design its organization to enable this?

3. What is a transnational organization? Since many large MNCs are moving toward this format, it is likely that you could at some point be working within this structure. How do you feel about that?

4. Discuss the implications of the relative centralization of authority and decision making at headquarters versus local units or subsidiaries. How would you feel about this variable if you were a subsidiary manager?

5. As an international manager, what would make you suggest restructuring your firm? What other means of direct and indirect monitoring systems do you suggest?

6. What is the role of information systems in the reporting process? Discuss the statement "Inadequate MIS systems in some foreign affiliates are a control problem for MNCs."

Application Exercises

1. If you have personal access to a company with international operations, try to conduct some interviews and find out about the personal interactions involved in working with the organization's counterparts abroad. In particular, ask questions about the nature and level of authority and decision making in overseas units compared with headquarters. What kinds of conflicts are experienced? What changes would your interviewees recommend?

2. Do some research on monitoring and reporting issues facing an MNC with subsidiaries in (1) a country in Asia, and (2) a country in South America. Discuss problem areas and your recommendations to the MNC management as to how to control potential problems.

3. Find out about a foreign company with an IJV in the United States. Google some articles, email the company for information, and if possible visit the company and ask questions. Present your findings on the company's major control issues to the class—both at the beginning of the venture and now. What is the company doing differently in its control process compared to a typical domestic operation? Are the control procedures having the desired results? What recommendations do you have?

Experiential Exercise

- In groups of four, consider a fast-food chain going into Russia. Decide on your initial level of desired involvement in Russia and your entry strategy. Draw up an appropriate organizational design, taking into account strategic goals, relevant variables in Russia, technology used, size of the firm, and so on. At the next class, present power points of your organization chart and describe the operations and rationale. What are some of the major control issues to be considered?

Internet Resources

Visit the Deresky Companion Website at
www.pearsonhighered.com/deresky for this chapter's Internet
resources.

CASE STUDY

HSBC's Global Reorganization and Corporate Performance in 2012

HSBC Holdings owns subsidiaries throughout Europe, Hong Kong and the rest of the Asia/ Pacific region, the Middle East and Africa, and the Americas."[1]

The above statements truly reflect HSBC Holdings' (hereafter HSBC) massive and distinct operations in 2012 that maintained 89 million customers worldwide. Originally known as Hong Kong Shanghai Banking Corp., the bank was founded in Hong Kong and Shanghai in 1865. Currently based in London, UK, HSBC is a well-known global entity (with two nationalities), has 7,200 offices in 80 countries, and employs 295,000 workers worldwide. In emerging markets, HSBC continues to be a visible player and has expanded because of tangible consumer demand and growth opportunities.

In 2011, HSBC had revenues of $105.80 billion and made a pretax profit of $21.95 billion. The bank's total assets stood at $2.55 trillion. As of 2012, HSBC's operations are in most major parts of the world.[2] The bank's main revenues come from commercial banking, global banking, retail banking and wealth management, and private banking. HSBC did lose money during the 2008 global financial crisis. At the same time, the bank did not seek any bailout in Europe and Asia and continues to be a visible brand in the global banking industry. No wonder HSBC's distinct slogan ("*The world's local bank*") reflects its strong corporate identity and global networks.

The global banking industry is a major strategic industry in world business, impacting countries, industries, and firms alike. Historically the industry's growth has been based on region- and country-specific strategies because of national developmental agendas and ideologies. Banks may be global in their operations but mostly thrive because of national identities, networks, and financial resources.

In July 2011, HSBC was rated the third largest bank in its tier one capital ($163 billion).[3] Other top banks in the list included Bank of America, JPMorgan, CitiGroup, Mitsubishi UFJ Financial Group, Industrial Commercial Bank (China), and Wells Fargo. The top 25 banks originated from the U.S., the UK, Japan, China, Japan, France, Italy, and the Netherlands. The pace of change and competition in the global banking industry is highly dynamic and fierce. The 2008 global financial crisis created havoc in the banking industry. During the crisis, banks' and financial institutions' "*systematic distress*" and "*spillover effects*" created major problems for the industry.[4] HSBC was also impacted by the crisis and ended up losing money and customers. Unlike American banks, HSBC's operations were somewhat spared but growth remained stagnant during this period. The bank closed its money-losing operations and sold a few assets. This was a major disruption in HSBC's history and weakened the bank's well established business model.

To deal with the 2008 financial crisis, HSBC embarked on a major reorganization that changed its strategy and growth patterns. In 2011, HSBC trimmed its North American operations because of losses in the area of subprime lending.[5] At the same time, HSBC started expanding in emerging markets of Asia. China was selected to be the bank's major market for future growth. Other reorganization took place that aimed at mostly downsizing and trimming operations. These changes did impact the bank's massive operations in global markets.

In February 2012, HSBC announced its financial results where the bank increased its net by 27 percent. This was clearly the result of HSBC's 2010 restructuring plan, which was designed in the post-financial crisis period. While HSBC trimmed its operations in North America, the bank's Asian markets witnessed a good increase in revenues because of growth in emerging markets.[6] *Financial Times* called HSBC "*the world's Asian bank*."[7] No wonder HSBC plans on having a major presence in China and has announced increasing its share in China's Bank of Communications. HSBC also plans on expanding its branches in China from 110 locations to 800.[8] This is a major part of the bank's reorganization that was initiated by Stuart Gulliver (CEO) and his team in 2009–2010.[9]

Although competition in emerging markets has been heightened because of the arrival of local and multinational banks,[10] markets are available to those financial institutions that carry efficient business models and operations. HSBC has major plans in the Asia markets. Because of its long history and brand identity, the bank's future plans and restructuring initiatives can bear fruit if implemented accurately. In a special research report ("The World in 2050: Quantifying the shift in the global economy"), Karen Ward, HSBC's chief economist, observed with convincing data and logical arguments:

> "19 of the 30 largest economies will be emerging economies; the emerging economies will collectively be bigger than the developed economies; global growth will accelerate thanks to the contribution from the emerging economies. . . . Asia will continue demonstrating extremely strong growth rates and those with large population will overtake Western powerhouses."[11]

This clearly shows HSBC's long-term ambitions in the emerging markets of Asia, where growth is significantly available to those banks that carry prudent policies and networks. At the same time, the areas of technology and financial services have become more efficient because of the availability of online banking, the accessibility of large-scale and real time data, useful analytics, and other technologies on hand. This has helped multinational and local banks to be more competitive, efficient, and effective in their markets.

In conclusion, firms' organizational structures, interorganizational networks and alliances, and control and monitoring systems are important when seeking expansion in the global banking industry, which thrives on strategic locations, networks, and customer service. The same areas apply to other industries and firms as well. Above all, firms must change on a continuous basis when dealing with growth opportunities, corporate expansion, and unexpected events in global markets.

Case Questions

1. How do you evaluate HSBC's global reorganization and expansion in the post–financial crisis period?
2. Compare and contrast HSBC's global operations with its main competitors.
3. What did you learn from the HSBC's case when applying concepts and theories from Chapter 8?

Sources:

Written exclusively for this book by Syed Anwar Tariq. Copyright © 2012 by Syed Tariq Anwar, West Texas A & M University. Used with Permission.

References

1. "HSBC Holding Plc," Hoovers.com. (2012), http://www.hoovers.com/company/HSBC_Holdings_plc/crksif-1-1njht4-1njfaq.html. Accessed on March 3, 2012.
2. "HSBC" (2012). http://www.hsbc.com/1/PA_esf-ca-app-content/content/assets/investor_relations/hsbc2011arn.pdf. Accessed on March 4, 2012.
3. For details, see: "Top 1000 world banks," *The Banker* (July, 2011): 182.
4. For more discussion on these topics, see: Giesecke, K. and Kim, B., "Systemic risk: What defaults are telling us," *Management Science*, 57(8) (2011): 1387–1405.
5. See: Menon, J., "HSBC rues household deal, halts U.S. subprime lending (Update 1)." *Bloomberg*, (March 2, 2009), http://www.bloomberg.com/apps/news?pid=newsarchive&sid=ajBfkUKrgsZY. Accessed on March 5, 2012.
6. See: Jenkins, P. and Goff, S., "HSBC progress fails to rally investors," *Financial Times* (February 28, 2012), 17; Munoz, S. S., and Colchester, M., "HSBC profit climbs, so do costs," *Wall Street Journal*, February 28, 2012, C3.
7. "The World's Asian Bank," *Financial Times*, February 28, 2012, 14.
8. Sender, H., "HSBC to build China presence by seeking to raise stake in BoCom," *Financial Times*, February 15, 2012, 13.
9. "Gulliver's travels," *The Economist*, April 16, 2011, 75.
10. Alloway, T. and Wigglesworth, R., "New lenders move to fill the gap left by ailing banks." *Financial Times*, October 6, 2011, 22.
11. Ward, K., *The World in 2050: Quantifying the shift in the global economy* (London, UK: HSBC Plc, 2011): 1, 21.

"Alibaba has a first-mover advantage that makes it very hard for competitors to chip away at their lead in the market."[i]

–DICK WEI,
Analyst, J.P. Morgan Securities Inc.,[1] *in 2007.*

"For us, the goal has been to build a company that lasts 102 years and a company that changes China. We're only six years old, so while other people may call us a success, we still do not consider ourselves successful yet. We have a long way to go and the intense competition is what keeps us sharp. The success we've had so far has not made us lose our edge."[ii]

–JACK MA,
Founder and CEO of Alibaba.com, in 2006.

"If there's a company outside of America that can introduce a new business model to the world, it's Alibaba."[iiii]

–MASAYOSHI SON,
Founder and CEO, Softbank Corporation,[2] *Japan, in 2005.*

INTRODUCTION

On November 11, 2011, Bloomberg[3] reported that China's leading e-commerce company, Alibaba Group (Alibaba), in association with Softbank Corporation (Softbank), The Blackstone Group[4] (Blackstone), and Bain Capital[5] (Bain), was considering making a bid for Yahoo! Inc.[6] (Yahoo!). While Jack Ma (Ma), founder and CEO of Alibaba, expressed an interest in buying back Yahoo!'s 40 percent stake in Alibaba, Softbank wanted to buy Yahoo!'s 35 percent stake in Yahoo! Japan. Blackstone and Bain were reported to be participating in the bid to buy Yahoo!'s remaining operations in the US.[iv]

This case was written by **Hadiya Faheem,** under the direction of **Debapratim Purkayastha,** IBS Hyderabad. It was compiled from published sources, and is intended to be used as a basis for class discussion rather than to illustrate either effective or ineffective handling of a management situation.

[1] J.P. Morgan Securities Inc., New York City, New York, USA is the non-banking subsidiary of JPMorgan Chase. It focuses on activities related to investment banking.

[2] Softbank Corporation, headquartered in Tokyo, Japan, is a leading Japanese telecommunications and media company. It has investments in e-commerce, financial services, Internet infrastructure, IT-related distribution services, publishing and marketing, and technology services.

[3] Bloomberg is a U.S.-based financial news reporting company.

[4] The Blackstone Group is an asset management and financial services company.

[5] Bain Capital is a Boston-based private-equity firm.

[6] Yahoo! Inc., headquartered in Sunnyvale, California, USA, is an online portal with a network of websites—news, search engine, entertainment, e-commerce, etc. Its primary source of revenues is through online advertising, but it also offers commercial services such as online marketing, etc.

[7] B2B or Business-to-Business e-commerce is trading between two businesses using the Internet.

[8] C2C or Consumer-to-Consumer e-commerce is trading between two consumers through the Internet.

Alibaba had several Internet businesses focused on various e-commerce business models such as Business-to-Business[7] (B2B), Consumer-to-Consumer[8] (C2C), and Business-to-Consumer[9] (B2C). It also had a presence in the intensely competitive web search market. In 2010, the company had also launched a transaction-based wholesale platform, AliExpress, for Chinese merchants to sell goods to foreign buyers. Being one of the first companies to enter the Chinese Internet industry, Alibaba played a major role in bringing about an Internet revolution in the country (refer to *Exhibit I* for a brief note on the Internet market in China). Alibaba was launched with the vision of serving the small and medium enterprises (SMEs) in China and across the world. As of 2011, it had 69 million registered users spread across more than 240 countries.[v]

According to the Hangzhou-based, e-commerce–information provider China e-Business Research Center, Alibaba had been the clear market leader in the Chinese e-commerce market with a market share of 63.5 percent for the FY 2010.[vi] However, the company lagged behind in the Chinese online search engine market despite having acquired Yahoo! China's operations in 2005. The Chinese search engine market was dominated by players such as Baidu.com, Inc.[10] (Baidu) and Google Inc.[11] (Google) with market shares of 77.7 percent and 18.3 percent, respectively, in Q3 of 2011, according to iResearch Consulting Group[12] (iResearch).[vii] In August 2010, Alibaba had acquired Sogou, a search engine of Chinese portal Sohu.com, in a bid to increase its dominance in the Chinese web search market. It also had ambitious plans of investing US$ 157 million in its shopping search engine eTao

[9] B2C or Business-to-Consumer e-commerce relates to business transactions between a company and a customer using the Internet.

[10] Baidu.com, headquartered in Beijing, China, is a leading Chinese search engine.

[11] Google Inc., headquartered in Mountain View, California, USA, is one of the leading Internet companies in the world.

[12] iResearch Consulting Group is a market research company based in China. It offers companies market research services related to e-commerce, the Internet, online games, etc.

EXHIBIT I   **Internet Market in China**

According to a China Internet Network Information Center[13] (CNNIC) report in June 2010, China had 363.8 million broadband users.[viii] As of mid-2011, China was the world's largest Internet market in the world. According to DCCI, the number of Internet users in China had reached 508 million by the end of 2011.[ix] The Internet users in China comprised only a meager portion of the country's population of 1.3 billion, which meant that there was a huge potential for future growth. China was important for Internet companies not only because of its large market size but also for its vast talent pool.

Apart from the main business activities of Internet companies such as online search, online auctions, online communications, and online advertising, special features like blogging and SMS (Short Messaging Service) were also gaining popularity in China. Blogging was a popular feature, especially among Chinese youth. They were attracted to blogs[14] and the Bulletin Board System[15] (BBS) because of the freedom they offered to them to express their opinions and get to know those of others. These blogs were posted on a variety of topics, like what clothes to buy, what music to listen to, and what movies to watch, product reviews, comparison of products and advertisements, etc. Analysts opined that people expressed their likes and dislikes more strongly in blogs than they would otherwise. Blogs also generated a huge amount of information about customer choices and customer feedback throughout the country, which could be of great use for companies and the government. SMS was another popular practice in China, generating heavy revenue for Internet portals. According to Gartner Inc.[16] (Gartner), messaging via cell phones and hand-held devices was a common practice in China and local Internet companies like Sina Corporation, Sohu.com Inc., and NetEase.com, Inc. received a good amount of revenue from the SMSs delivered through their portals.[x]

Despite the huge opportunities it offered, the Chinese Internet market was not without its challenges. The political environment in China had a bearing on the existence and performance of Internet companies in China. The Chinese Internet market was strictly regulated by the government. The government imposed a censorship on pornographic content and content related to controversial topics like Tiananmen Square[17], Taiwan independence[18], the Dalai Lama[19], etc. According to media reports, the Chinese government employed around 30,000 people to ensure that such restricted content did not spread in the Chinese Internet space.

In addition to complying with the government rules, it was important for Internet companies in China to know how to successfully launch a Chinese language website or design a search engine that would suit the complex Chinese language. The Chinese language makes extensive use of pictograms[20] and ideograms[21]. The characters are written without spaces between them, which made it hard to distinguish one word or phrase from the next. Due to all these political, cultural, and linguistic factors, many international Internet companies had to seek local help to understand the Chinese consumers and deal with the local nuances. Industry experts felt that many domestic Internet companies had managed to gain popularity and market share because of their familiarity with the local environment and customers. Because of their intimate knowledge of the local language, culture, and dealings with the government, the local players had an edge over their foreign counterparts in the Chinese Internet market.

Source: Compiled from various sources.

[13] The China Internet Network Information Center (CNNIC) is the state network information center of China, founded as a non-profit organization in June 1997. The Computer Network Information Center of the Chinese Academy of Sciences runs CNNIC. CNNIC looks after everything related to the Internet in China like domain names registration, IP addresses, relevant researches, surveys and information services, and international liaison and policy research.

[14] A blog is a user-generated website where entries are made in journal style and displayed in chronological order.

[15] A Bulletin Board System allows users to dial into the system over a phone and using a terminal program, perform functions such as downloading software and data, uploading data, reading news, and exchanging messages with other users.

[16] Gartner Inc. is a U.S.-based business consulting firm established in 1979. It delivers technology-related insights to around 10,000 clients around the world.

[17] Between April 15, 1989, and June 4, 1989, there were protests in China against the Communist Party of China government. The protests, which were centered at Tiananmen Square in Beijing, were led by students, intellectuals, and labor activists. On June 4, 1989, the Chinese government dispersed the mobs at Tiananmen Square using military force, which led to the deaths of hundreds of protesters. The incident came to be known as the "Tiananmen Square massacre."

[18] For years, the Taiwan independence movement was opposed by China, which described it as a separatist movement that would divide the nation and people. The pro-independence groups described it as a nationalist movement.

[19] The literal meaning of "Dalai Lama" is "spiritual leader." The Dalai Lama is considered the supreme head of Tibetan Buddhism. The 14th Dalai Lama demanded greater autonomy for Tibet, which is under Chinese control.

[20] A pictogram is a character that represents an object, a concept, or an activity through a picture.

[21] An ideogram is a character that represents an idea.

in order to gain a strong foothold in the online shopping market in China.[xi]

The company was also making efforts to increase its global footprint. In June 2010, Alibaba acquired Vendio Services Inc.[22] (Vendio). The site was linked to Alibaba's network of suppliers and buyers. To fuel its global growth, in August 2010, Alibaba acquired Auctiva[23] to reach U.S. businesses and connect with buyers and suppliers outside China.

In December 2011, Alibaba announced that it was testing a social-networking product. This was part of its efforts to expand outside its e-commerce platforms to seek different streams of revenues. Industry experts felt Alibaba was devising strategies to fuel its growth and, with the acquisition of Yahoo!'s stake, it would gain a stronger foothold in China since Internet penetration and e-commerce were rapidly growing in China.

BACKGROUND NOTE

Jack Ma (Ma), founder of Alibaba, was born in Hangzhou, a city in China's Zhejiang province, in 1964. At the age of twelve, Ma developed a fascination for the English language. He began learning English by listening to the Voice of America[24] and acting as a free guide to foreigners who visited Hangzhou. Another event that changed Ma was when he traveled to Australia to visit a friend in 1985. He had grown up believing that the world outside China was a terrible place to live in. He was taught that China was the richest country in the world and that the Chinese were the most contented people in the world. According to Ma, "Everything I'd learned in China was that China was the richest country in the world. When I arrived in Australia, I realized it's totally different. I started to think you have to use your own mind to judge, to think."[xii]

In 1988, Ma earned a degree in English from the Hangzhou Teacher's Institute and began teaching English and international trade at the Hangzhou Electronic and Engineering Institute. In 1992, he founded an English translation agency in Hangzhou and soon built up a good reputation for his language skills.

In 1995, Ma was sent to Malibu, near Los Angeles, by a Chinese businessman. Ma was to mediate in a dispute between the businessman and his American counterpart who had not put in the money he had promised into the man's firm. Ma approached the American ready to mediate but to his shock, he was locked up for a couple of days in the American's house. Ma was released only after he promised the American that he would start an Internet company in China in association with him. Though this joint venture never actually happened, Ma was able to leave. The same year, Ma went to Seattle with a trade delegation as an interpreter. This was to become a turning point in his life. During the visit, a friend introduced him to the Internet. Ma typed in "beer" in the search engine. It yielded results like German beer, Japanese beer, and American beer. Nothing called Chinese beer came up. He then typed in "China" and "beer" but this gave no results. This made Ma decide to start a company to bring

information regarding Chinese companies to the Internet. After returning to Hangzhou, Ma resigned from his teaching job, borrowed US$ 2,000 from his relatives, and launched China Pages, China's first commercial website, in 1995. About launching this website, Ma said, "At 9:30 we launched the home page, and by 12:30 I had six e-mails. I said, 'Whoa! Interesting!' If I could help Chinese companies list on the Internet and help foreigners find their websites, that might be a good thing."[xiii] The website contained a list of companies operating in China. The Hong Kong media called Ma the "father of the Chinese Internet" and credited him with bringing about an Internet revolution in China.

In 1998, Ma moved to Beijing to work for the Chinese Ministry of Foreign Trade and Economic Cooperation (MOFTEC) as the Head of the Information Department of the China International Electronic Commerce Center[25] (CIECC). He designed a website for MOFTEC. This became the first government website in China.

ALIBABA IN ITS INITIAL YEARS

In 1998, Ma left MOFTEC and returned to Hangzhou to fulfill his dream of establishing his own e-commerce company. He said, "I realized that you can never expect a government company to grow. So I left to set up my own."[xiv] Ma gathered 18 people in his apartment to explain his vision to them. He warned his colleagues who wanted to join him that his venture was a risky one and that they would be paid only Renminbi[26] (RMB) 500 every month. He gave them three days to think it over. He was touched when, finally, all 18 of them decided to follow him to Hangzhou. Ma and his colleagues put in some money. This money, which came up to US$ 60,000, was used to start Alibaba from Ma's apartment in Hangzhou in March 1999. Asked why Alibaba had been chosen as the name, Ma said, "The name [Alibaba], taken from the Arabian Nights, was chosen because it's universally well known and is easy to spell."[xv]

In August 1999, the Chinese Bureau of Industrial and Commercial Administration registered Alibaba as a computer company since the company's business could not be classified under any other category. Because of the strict IPO regulations in Beijing, Alibaba was registered in Hong Kong. At the same time, Ma started looking out for potential investors for the venture. But since the business model was new, the investors initially did not believe in the venture.

However, by September 1999, a few venture capitalists approached Ma, attracted by the novel concept of the business. Ma told them frankly that launching Alibaba was a risky proposition and that he expected it to make hardly any profits during the initial years. Some of the prospective investors were still eager to lend. Ma said, "I told them at the very first meeting, 'Don't push us. We know what we are doing.'"[xvi] Initially, Ma rejected offers from 38 venture capitalists. Later, he accepted an offer from a group of investors including The Goldman Sachs

---

[22] Vendio Services Inc. is a U.S.-based e-commerce site. As of June 2010, it hosted services for 80,000 small businesses in the U.S.

[23] Auctiva offered listing and marketing tools to vendors on e-commerce sites.

[24] Started in 1942, Voice of America is an international radio and television broadcasting service of the U.S. government.

[25] China International Electronic Commerce Center (CIECC) was founded in 1996 to build and operate a secure network for government communications and commerce. It provided services related to e-commerce and e-government that are used by government agencies in China.

[26] Renminbi is the currency of the mainland of the People's Republic of China. Its principal unit is called the Yuan. As of December 4, 2011, US$ 1 was approximately equal to RMB 6.32.

Group Inc.[27] (Goldman Sachs), Fidelity Investments,[28] Investor AB,[29] Templeton Dragon Fund Inc.,[30] and Transpac Industrial Holdings Limited[31] and was able to raise US$ 5 million from them in October 1999.[xvii] In January 2000, Ma successfully persuaded Softbank to invest US$ 20 million in his venture.[xviii] Softbank was, at that time, the largest global investor in Internet businesses, owning stakes in hundreds of Internet companies such as Yahoo!, Chinadotcom Corporation[32] (CDC), etc. In return, Peter Sutherland, Chairman of Goldman Sachs, and Masayoshi Son (Son), CEO of Softbank, were made members of Alibaba's board of advisors. In 2000, Ma moved the company's headquarters from Hangzhou to a new building in Shanghai.

Alibaba concentrated on small and medium-sized Chinese firms that aspired to go global but found it very expensive to do so. Ma aimed at connecting these Chinese manufacturers with small and medium-sized buyers from across the world. Ma said, "We want to help SMEs from all over the world grow their business and benefit from cross-border trade. Alibaba.com is like the World Trade Organization for SMEs."[xix] Alibaba's mission was "to help small and medium enterprises (SMEs) grow." Commenting on its focus on SMEs, Ma said, "SMEs are the future of Asia, and the future of China. Many people believe in big companies, saying we should get more money from big companies, we should do transactions with them, et cetera. But I disagree. Asia is Asia. China is China. Unfortunately, in Asia, the market is too fragmented that we have no standard. There is no standard for e-commerce, SMEs, or B2B. Our job is to establish the standard. We cannot create beautiful PowerPoints, but we know how to listen to our customers."[xx]

During the late 1990s and early 2000s, the Internet had not yet become too popular in China and banks were not networked. Credit card usage was limited and providing logistics service in the country was difficult, to say the least. In this scenario, Alibaba thought it wisest to limit its business model to connecting buyers and suppliers. Suppliers were allowed to list their products on the website while buyers could post their requests on the bulletin boards. Deals were struck through e-mails or offline messages. The services were offered for free and no other value-added services were offered. Ma believed that Alibaba was still in its infancy stage and had to build a loyal customer base before it started charging for its services.

Initially, Alibaba had two websites—www.alibaba.com, an English website for international B2B trade, and www.china.alibaba.com for B2B trade in China. However, the company soon noticed that despite Japan being China's biggest trading associate, the online business carried out from that country was less compared to enterprises from the U.S., South Korea, India, and Europe. Alibaba therefore launched www.alibaba.co.jp, a Japanese site for Japanese traders, in 2002. According to Ma, "Chinese and Japanese entrepreneurs have a digital ditch on the Internet. We want to help them stride this ditch with Alibaba Japan Website."[xxi] Also, the Japanese preferred to use the site in Japanese. David Wei (Wei), CEO, Alibaba, said, "They prefer to use the Japanese language as their commercial language, and with China and Japan as each other's second-largest trading partner, there was a big demand."[xxii]

Ma found that SMEs were hesitant about using the Internet, as they assumed that it would require some expertise in computer use. Ma ensured that Alibaba's websites were simple and easy to browse through. He considered himself a non-technical person, and this, he believed, helped him keep the websites more user-friendly. According to Ma, "I use my computer for two things, e-mail and surfing the Web. Most of our customers are not high-tech people, so we have always tried to make the technology invisible. When a member goes on Alibaba.com to find a supplier, we want the website to be very simple and user-friendly. We have a great engineering team, but their job is to make sure everything passes the 'Jack test.' If I can understand our website, then I am sure our customers can too."[xxiii] In May 2000, Ma brought in John Wu (Wu), the creator of the Yahoo! search engine, and appointed him as the Chief Technology Officer of Alibaba.

Another major concern for Ma was that many SMEs distrusted the idea of online payments. Ma managed to convince them about the safety of the practice by stressing the fact that Alibaba's system for online transactions was managed in partnership with a leading bank in China.

By the end of the first year in business, Alibaba had become the largest online global trading website in Asia, with about 200,000 members from 194 countries (70 percent of the members were Chinese), and approximately 1,000 new members joining every day.[xxiv] On the whole, the websites were receiving about 1,500 new subscribers every day.[xxv] Nearly half the requests were from companies based in the U.S., Europe, and India, while the remaining were from Greater China. In March 2000, Alibaba started catering to the European market and also planned to expand its operations in North and South America, Japan, etc. Buyers from any country could locate and strike deals with sellers in any country or countries across the world.

Alibaba aimed to have a global presence and expand in the U.S. and hence the company's R&D was mainly done at Silicon Valley. It did not spend any money on marketing its website—its membership was the result of the exceptional services that it offered to its customers.

During the early 2000s, the huge manufacturing potential of Asia, especially of China, and the rising popularity of Alibaba attracted a number of other companies to start e-commerce ventures in China. In the early 2000s, Hutchison Whampoa Limited[33] launched a web portal called "www.tom.com." A group of businessmen from Hong Kong partnered with America's B2B major

---

[27] The Goldman Sachs Group Inc., headquartered in New York City, New York, USA, is a leading investment banking, securities, and investment management firm.

[28] Fidelity Investments, headquartered in Boston, Massachusetts, USA is an investment products and services company.

[29] Investor AB, headquartered in Stockholm, Sweden, is an investment company whose key products include core equity, private equity, operating and financial investments.

[30] Templeton Dragon Fund Inc., headquartered in Fort Lauderdale, Florida, USA, is a non-diversified, closed-ended investment company.

[31] Transpac Industrial Holdings Limited, headquartered in Singapore, is an investment holding company providing venture capital to private companies.

[32] Chinadotcom Corporation, headquartered in Hong Kong, China, is a leading provider of business solutions, enterprise software solutions, and mobile and Internet applications.

[33] Hutchison Whampoa Limited, headquartered in Hong Kong, China, is a diversified conglomerate with business interests in ports and related services; telecommunications; property and hotels; retail and energy; etc.

Commerce One.[34] Hong Kong–based Global Sources Limited[35] (Global Sources) and San Francisco–based MeetChina.com (MeetChina) also announced their plans to enter the Chinese e-commerce market. MeetChina planned an aggressive expansion in Asia. While some of these firms concentrated on particular industries, others such as Commerce One and Ariba[36] concentrated on big businesses in Europe and the U.S.

Ma refused to worry about the rising competition. Instead, he set to work to make plans to provide various products targeting the SMEs in various countries. He made several efforts to differentiate Alibaba from others by providing innovative features like wireless access to its services in partnership with Motorola Inc.[37] (Motorola). To attract more users, Alibaba also started offering additional services for registered members (registration was free) such as e-mail, etc.

In March 2000, when the dotcom bubble[38] burst, a number of dotcom and e-commerce companies filed for bankruptcy. A vast majority of dotcom companies could not withstand the sharp fall in revenues from Internet advertising. Web-based retailers failed to gauge the infrastructure they required to carry on with their retailing activities on the Internet and so many companies were forced to shut down their businesses. Commerce One was also affected and it filed for bankruptcy in October 2004.[39] A few companies such as Ariba merged with FreeMarkets Inc.,[40] a leading B2B in June 2004.[41] Alibaba, however, was able to withstand the dotcom crash since its business was not dependent on advertising revenues.

To deal with the dotcom crash, Alibaba reformulated its strategies. By September 2000, Ma was left with hardly any revenues and so had no choice but to curb his expansion plans. He told his employees that Alibaba would be in trouble if it did not adopt the right strategies. He announced three B2C strategies. These were:

- "Back to China," under which Alibaba would concentrate mainly on improving its business in China rather than focusing on global markets.

[34] Commerce One, headquartered in Westbury, New York, USA, was an e-commerce solutions provider and a leading marketplace for B2B transactions.

[35] Global Sources Limited, headquartered in Hong Kong, China, is a leading B2B media company.

[36] Ariba, headquartered in Sunnyvale, California, USA, is a provider of Intranet and e-commerce solutions. The Ariba B2B Commerce Platform allows online transactions between buyers and suppliers.

[37] Motorola Inc., headquartered in Schaumburg, Illinois, USA, is an electronics and telecom goods company.

[38] The increase in popularity of the Internet fueled the growth of dotcom companies—firms that provided products and services related to or by using the Internet. They grew rapidly in number between 1995 and 2000 as many individuals started their own companies. Most of these companies offered similar products and services. The uncontrolled proliferation of such companies ended with the bubble busting in March 2000, leading to the closure of many of these companies.

[39] Commerce One was later acquired by Perfect Commerce in February 2006. Perfect Commerce is one of the largest providers of On-Demand Supplier Relationship Management (SRM) solutions.

[40] FreeMarkets Inc., headquartered in Pittsburgh, Pennsylvania, USA, is a leading e-commerce company.

[41] The merged entity was called Ariba Inc. and since then has been a leading provider of Spend Management solutions to help companies analyze, understand, and manage their corporate spending.

- "Back to Central," under which the headquarters was moved back from Shanghai to Hangzhou.
- "Back to the Coast," under which Alibaba would concentrate on improving its presence in the coastal areas, the richest region of China.

In July 2000, Alibaba started selling its advertising space. However, the revenues generated were very limited. Alibaba also began selling reports and statistics on various sellers. For the year 2000, Alibaba's revenues were just US$ 1 million and the company had not made any profits.[xxvi] According to Ma, "The year 2000 was a difficult year. Our team was young—only a year old. We saw things were still going up, but knew it would surely go down. We didn't know how deep the fall would be, how bad it would be. Besides which, we had virtually no revenue."[xxvii]

In early 2001, Alibaba started offering a customized online marketplace for its members called "Alibabies" for a premium. However, this generated only a small amount of revenue—US$ 0.3 million a year.[xxviii] Several analysts were quick to write off Alibaba. They expressed doubts about its survival in the long run in light of the dotcom crash. The increasing competition from other B2B companies targeting the Chinese B2B markets was also building up tremendous pressure on Alibaba to merge or to fall. In the same year, Ma brought in Savio Kwan (Kwan), general manager of GE's China equipment division, as Chief Operating Officer of Alibaba with the aim of turning around the company. Kwan said, "We need to ground [Alibaba] in reality and make it into a business."[xxix]

In late 2001, Alibaba began charging its members for its services. The fee was US$ 3,000 per year for a membership in "China Supplier"— an online community for qualified Chinese exporters who were verified by third-party credit agencies. In mid-2002, the membership fee was increased to US$ 8,000.

By March 2002, Alibaba's members had touched the one million mark (refer to *Exhibit II* for different types of membership). In 2002, Ma set a target of US$ 1 profit for Alibaba. Commenting on this, Ma said, "We said, 'Let's make one dollar in profits for the whole year. We spend five million US dollars, we should make at least one back. If we spend 10 million, we should still earn one dollar.' So, we spent the whole year trying to make one dollar. When we set the target, everyone said I was stupid. But the whole company had a clear target throughout the year. The young people in the company had never had experience making money. Even if we say we are going to make 10 million dollars, how are we going to make it? But the one dollar target is something we could make if we just saved electricity, for example."[xxx]

In March 2002, Alibaba set a TrustPass membership fee of US$ 299 for companies wanting to join Alibaba, after which they were verified and authenticated. However, this fee did not deter companies from joining; about 200 Chinese companies were registering themselves every day.

BUSINESS PORTFOLIO

Despite its struggles, by the year 2000, the Alibaba Group had emerged as the largest e-commerce company in China and was

EXHIBIT II   **Types of Membership at Alibaba.com**

- **Free Membership:** Free members were offered basic services, free of cost. Sellers registered under this category could post products they wanted to sell, search for buyers, and contact them. Buyers were allowed to post buying leads and send inquiries to the suppliers. However, Chinese companies had to join as "Gold Supplier" members in order to become a seller.

- **TrustPass Membership:** It consisted of supplier members from outside Hong Kong, Macau, and Mainland China. TrustPass Membership was a paid service where the member had to pay US$ 299. The member would be authenticated and verified by a third-party credit reporting agency.[xxxi] The supplier would then be able to display a TrustPass icon symbolizing credibility to online buyers. However, this facility was available to Chinese companies only if they were "Gold Suppliers." TrustPass members were allowed to have their own websites that contained information about the company, its products, etc.

- **Gold Supplier:** This membership was primarily for export-oriented suppliers. It consisted of premium suppliers from Hong Kong, Macau, and Mainland China. The process of authentication and verification was more rigorous for such membership. The suppliers were classified into 27 industries which enabled buyers to locate the companies conveniently. The member would display the TrustPass icon and a Gold Supplier icon to symbolize the highest level of seller qualification. Some of the advantages that such members enjoyed were listing of products on Alibaba's home page and unrestricted access to buyers' trade leads.

Source: www.alibaba.com

one of the leading players in the international e-commerce market. Alibaba was the flagship company of the Alibaba Group with marketing and sales offices across Beijing, Seoul, Silicon Valley, London, Japan, and Latin America. Alibaba's business portfolio included the following:

Alibaba China: Launched in 1999, Alibaba China (www.china.alibaba.com) was a website in the Chinese language serving domestic B2B trade in China. As of November 2011, it had a registered user base of 50 million paying an annual subscription fee for posting their products on the website.[xxxii] The authenticity of the members was verified by a third-party credit-reporting agency.

Alibaba International: Launched in 1999, Alibaba International (www.alibaba.com) was an English website which connected a number of Chinese SMEs with a number of businesses worldwide. It had 18 million registered users from around 200 countries as of April 2011.[xxxiii]

Taobao: Taobao (www.taobao.com) was launched in May 2003. It was China's most popular C2C trading site. As of June 2011, Taobao had more than 800 million product listings with 370 million registered users and more than 60 million page views per day.[xxxiv] According to Ma, Taobao had garnered a market share of 80 percent for the FY 2010.[xxxv] In 2011, Alibaba Group reorganized Taobao into three separate companies—Taobao Marketplace, Taobao Mall, and eTao—in a bid to capture Chinese e-commerce consumer opportunities. Taobao Mall was Alibaba's B2C platform. For the Q2 of 2011, the site recorded a 48.5 percent market share in China's B2B online retail market, according to iResearch.[xxxvi] In November 2010, Taobao Mall launched Tmall.com as an independent web domain.

AliPay: Launched in 2004, AliPay was an online payment solution that enabled the users to carry out online money transactions easily, quickly, and safely. As of September 2011, AliPay had over 600 million registered accounts with around 11 million daily transactions.[xxxvii]

Yahoo! China: Yahoo! China (www.yahoo.com.cn) was China's third most popular search engine after Baidu and Google. It was started in October 2005 after Yahoo! merged its China operations with Alibaba in August 2005. Alibaba had the exclusive rights to use the Yahoo! brand and technologies in China.

Alisoft: In January 2007, Alibaba launched Alisoft, a software services company that catered to the needs of several SMEs in China. Alisoft allowed customers to use various services such as customer relationship management (CRM), marketing information management, sales force management, inventory management, and financial tools. Other services provided were e-mail, information management, inquiries, bookkeeping, and invoicing. Alisoft also provided an instant communication tool called "Aliwangwang," which was offered to users as Trade-Manager[42] on Taobao. As of January 2007, Alisoft had operations in Shanghai and Hangzhou. In July 2009, Alisoft was merged with Alibaba Group R&D Institute.

Alimama: In November 20, 2007, Alibaba launched Alimama, an online advertising exchange company. The company allowed advertisers and publishers on the web to trade advertising inventory online. It was intended to serve the more than one million SMEs in China that accounted for 80 percent of web traffic in China.[xxxviii] In 2008, Alimama was integrated with Taobao.

---

[42] TradeManager is an instant communication tool that is offered to buyers and sellers for interaction.

THE COMPETITION

B2B Market

Alibaba was launched at a time when the Chinese Internet industry was in its infancy. Considering the growth potential of the budding e-commerce market, other players like Global Sources and MeetChina were launched in 1999. These players were expected to intensify competition in the emerging B2B market. Global Sources had an advantage over Alibaba because of its search technology and detailed information about the products listed on its site. Moreover, in 1999 the company had an employee strength of 1,600 people with several salespeople across the world to build its supplier community. There was also the threat of many new players entering this space. In order to gain a strong foothold in the B2B market, Ma announced that Alibaba would not charge any transaction fees. Commenting on Ma's strategy, Craig Pepples, CEO, Global Sources, said, "Some players are focusing on building as much 'community' as possible in a short period of time, usually by giving things away. The problem with this approach is . . . the free sites have very little depth. What customers need is detailed [information] and the tools to slice, dice, and compare."[xxxix] Unfazed by the competition, Ma said that he was unaware of his competitors' existence. Ma said, "The world is changing so fast, you don't know what each other is thinking about, you don't even know what you are thinking yourselves. How do you know who are your competitors?"[xl]

Despite several attempts made by Alibaba's competitors to carve out a place for themselves in the rapidly growing B2B market, they failed to make a mark, largely because of Alibaba's dominance in that market. Alibaba, on the other hand, continued to enjoy phenomenal growth. According to Q3 2011 China B2B Market data released by iResearch in 2011, the size of the B2B market in China had reached RMB 3.48 billion in the third quarter of 2011. Alibaba was the market leader in the Chinese B2B market with a market share of 53.8 percent (refer to Table I for market shares of B2B players in China).

C2C and B2C Market

Alibaba's increasing popularity and the burgeoning Chinese e-commerce market attracted several foreign competitors to China (refer to *Exhibit III* for a discussion of the e-commerce market in China). In 2002, U.S.-based eBay Inc.[43] (eBay) entered China by acquiring a 33 percent equity stake in the Shanghai-based e-commerce website EachNet.com[44] (Each-Net), at an investment of US$ 30 million. eBay launched its Chinese site based on its business model in the U.S. By 2002, it had emerged as one of the leading online auction sites in China with 3.5 million registered users.[xli] By 2003, eBay had cornered a 79 percent market share in the Chinese online auction market.[xlii]

TABLE I   Market Shares of B2B Players in China (Q3 2011)

Players	Market Share (in %)
Alibaba	53.8
Global Sources	11.6
Made-in-China.com	3.8
HC360	4.3
Dhgate	3.2
Mysteel	1.7
Global Market	1.6
Toocle.com	1.2
Others	18.7

Source: Adapted from "Market Scale of China B2B Ecommerce Increases to 3.48 Billion Yuan in Q3 2011," www.iresearchchina.com, November 11, 2011.

eBay's success in China and the good prospects offered by the budding e-commerce market, spurred Ma on to team up again with Son to start a rival website to compete with eBay. Ma raised funds of up to US$ 56 million from Softbank. His decision to team up with Son was due to Son's experience in defeating eBay in Japan by collaborating with Yahoo! Japan. Subsequently, eBay had to move out of Japan in 2002. Ma, in association with his experienced employees, drafted a plan for launching a consumer auction website in his apartment in Hangzhou. Finally, they came up with the idea of launching Taobao, which means "digging for treasure."

In May 2003, Ma launched Taobao as a wholly-owned subsidiary of Alibaba. Taobao aimed to create an online trading platform for both B2C and C2C models. Taobao differentiated itself from rival eBay by allowing free listings on its website. eBay, on the other hand, charged for listings on its website so as to ensure quality. According to Ma, Taobao would have to build up a loyal customer base before it could start charging for its services.

Analysts were uncertain about Taobao's success since the C2C market was still in its infancy in China. On the other hand, Ma was confident and cited the fact that EachNet had only five million users among the 82 million-odd Internet users in China (refer to *Exhibit IV* for the growing Internet usage in China). Ma said, "We launched Taobao not to make money, but because in the U.S., eBay gets a lot of its revenue from small businesses. We knew that some day, eBay would come in our direction."[xliii]

To gain a strong foothold in the Chinese e-commerce market and combat competition from Taobao, eBay bought the remaining equity stake in EachNet for US$ 150 million in July 2003. The website was called eBay EachNet.[45] Yibo Shao, one of the founders of EachNet who remained with eBay, believed that there could only be one big consumer auction site in China and predicted that eBay would win the race against Taobao. Soon after, Ma announced his plans to invest another US$ 12 million in Taobao. He said that it would be unwise to wait until the market

---

[43] eBay Inc., headquartered in San Jose, California, USA, is the world's largest online auction company. In addition to providing online auction markets, eBay also has an online payment service called PayPal and a communications business under Skype, which offers Voice-over-Internet Protocol (VoIP) services.

[44] Founded in August 1999 by Chinese entrepreneurs Bo Shao and Haiyin Tan, EachNet was a major electronic commerce company based in China. It was later acquired by eBay in July 2003.

[45] eBay EachNet is a subsidiary of eBay Inc. in China.

EXHIBIT III   e-Commerce Market in China

Though the concept of e-commerce was introduced in China in 1993, it took some time for it to catch on. But once it did, e-commerce in China began to grow at a frantic pace. For instance, the market scale for e-commerce in China grew from RMB 120 billion in 2001 to RMB 680 billion in 2005.[46] In comparison to the overall e-commerce market, the C2C market was smaller but had kept pace with the growth in the overall market.

The e-commerce market was a surging market in China. According to iResearch, the online shopping market had reached RMB 197.5 billion for the third quarter of 2011. Despite huge opportunities, the Chinese e-commerce market was not without its challenges. It was influenced by government regulations, logistics, and payment systems. The Chinese government enforced regulations related to Internet access, content regulation, encryption, and domain name.

The government also set certain provisions related to Internet access. There was a four-tier system for accessing the Internet. The first tier consisted of the Ministry of Information Industry[47] (MII) that acted as the main gateway for transmission of information to and from the World Wide Web. The MII operated an international gateway at the top of this system. The second tier comprised four government-owned Internet Service Providers (ISPs), which were called the interconnected networks. The third tier comprised privately owned ISPs that were linked through the interconnected networks to the Internet. The final tier included the Internet users. The users could gain access to the Internet either through the government or privately owned ISPs. Internet users were instructed to register themselves with local public security authorities as part of Internet security regulations.

The regulations related to security involved censoring the content and preventing dissemination of sensitive information relating to the Chinese economy. Under this regulation, all Internet companies were obliged to censor sensitive content.

Domain regulations required e-commerce companies to register their domain names with the CNNIC. The encryption regulation forced e-commerce companies to obtain approval from the National Commission on Encryption Code Regulations (NCECR), an encryption regulation agency, for using Chinese products and encrypted imported products.

Payment systems were another problem as Chinese consumers were used to paying cash rather than using credit cards. The consumers raised doubts over the security of the payment systems, the quality of the purchased products, and after-sales service.

An inefficient logistics system was considered as another major constraint in the development of e-commerce. This was due to the underdeveloped transportation systems, inadequate use of technology, and inconsistent distribution systems, which resulted in an unreliable logistics system.

Source: Compiled from various sources.

matured and hinted at using the money on building infrastructure, recruitment, and an online credit system for the customers.

Analysts observed that the growth in the Chinese e-commerce market was hampered due to the absence of the trust factor between buyers and sellers while trading online. Buyers refused to send money to sellers before they had received the goods while sellers were unwilling to ship the goods until they had received payment. To counter this problem, Alibaba launched an online payment platform called "AliPay" based on the lines of eBay's payment system, Paypal, in 2004. AliPay was an escrow[48]-based payment solution that allowed customers to safely and quickly send and receive money online. Once a deal had been finalized, the buyer paid the money through AliPay. The money was held in an AliPay account and was sent to the seller only after the buyer informed AliPay about the receipt of the product. Alibaba partnered with a number of Chinese banks such as China Merchants Bank, Agricultural Bank of China, etc. to provide AliPay services.

[46] "China E-commerce Profit Model Report, 2006–2007," www.researchinchina .com, January 2007.

[47] MII has the authority to regulate the software and communications industry and is accountable for the manufacture of electronic and information products. It is also responsible for information dissemination related to the Chinese economy.

[48] Escrow is a financial instrument held by a third party on behalf of the other two parties in a transaction. The funds are held by the escrow service until it receives the appropriate written or oral instructions or until obligations have been fulfilled (source: www.dictionary.com).

EXHIBIT IV Growing Internet Usage in China

Year	Users	% of Population Using the Internet
2000	22,500,000	1.7
2001	33,700,000	2.6
2002	59,100,000	4.6
2003	69,000,000	5.4
2004	94,000,000	7.3
2005	103,000,000	7.9
2006	137,000,000	10.4
2007	162,000,000	12.3
2008	253,000,000	19
2009	384,000,000	28.7
2010	420,000,000	31.6

Source: Adapted from "China Internet Usage Stats and Telecommunications Market Report," www.internetworldstats.com, March 30, 2011.

Alibaba devised an aggressive promotional strategy for Taobao in order to compete with eBay EachNet. Taobao advertised itself online by placing ads on the websites and through billboards at major city centers. All these promotional strategies were ignored by eBay EachNet. In the first quarter of 2004, eBay EachNet garnered a 90 percent market share in the Chinese online C2C market against Taobao's 9 percent. By the fourth quarter of 2004, Taobao's market share had jumped to 41 percent while eBay EachNet's had declined to 53 percent.[xliv] While eBay EachNet had about 10 million users,[xlv] Taobao quickly gained four million users[xlvi] in 2004. Further, Taobao's easy-to-use features on the website attracted a number of users and resulted in users shifting to it. Taobao provided additional features like e-mail and chat facilities to users on its site. It also allowed the buyers to call the sellers before buying a product while eBay EachNet concealed the seller's identity until the end of the auction and allowed communication only through offline messages that could be left on the site. Another reason cited for users shifting to Taobao was the difficulty they faced while using the new eBay website that was created after it fully acquired EachNet. The number of product listings decreased from 780,000 to 250,000 after the website was changed.[xlvii] Further, the lack of a secure online payment system like AliPay hindered eBay EachNet's growth.

In 2005, eBay EachNet's market share slipped further to 29.1 percent compared to Taobao's 67.3 percent.[xlviii] Taobao was ahead of eBay EachNet on various counts. Some of the parameters included the number of page views per user, which was 10.7 for Taobao and 7.4 for eBay EachNet in August 2005. At the same time, Taobao's listings generated a Gross Merchandise Volume[49] (GMV) of US$ 120 million compared to eBay EachNet's GMV of US$ 90 million.[xlix] Porter Erisman, Vice President, International Marketing, Alibaba,

said in 2006, "The real source of eBay's woes in Asia is its inability to understand local market conditions in this part of the world."[l]

According to Ma, eBay's business model might work well in other countries of the world but it would face difficulties in China because the Chinese consumers and their preferences were very different from those in other countries. Commenting on the rivalry with eBay, Ma said, "Taobao didn't win the first battle, but eBay lost it. eBay may be a shark in the ocean, but I am a crocodile in the Yangtze River. If we fight in the ocean, we lose—but if we fight in the river, we win."[li]

In October 2005, Ma announced a new strategy to phase out eBay EachNet from China—the services at Taobao would be offered free of charge for three consecutive years. Challenging eBay EachNet to follow its strategy, Ma said, "We call on eBay to do what's right for this phase of China's e-commerce development and make your services free for buyers and sellers in China. Cutting prices is not enough—it's time to make your services free and affordable for all of China's entrepreneurs and consumers."[lii] In response, eBay issued a statement saying that free was not a business model and the fact that Taobao was providing its services for free was proof of eBay EachNet's success in China.

In May 2006, Ma announced the launch of B2C services on Taobao. By then, Taobao had already begun to outshine eBay EachNet by gaining more than 20 million users. According to Ma, the B2C services were launched with the aim of removing the middleman concept by directly connecting large sellers with consumers. For this, Taobao had already tied up with companies such as Motorola, the Haier Group, Nokia Corporation, Adidas Group, etc., and was aggressively planning to expand its product offerings. Taobao expected a large number of Alibaba's members to join its program along with leading global companies.

Sensing the need for the support of a local company to control its declining market share, eBay EachNet entered into

---

[49] Gross Merchandise Volume refers to the total value derived from closed listings in the online trading market.

a joint venture (JV) with TOM Online Inc.[50] (TOM Online) to form TOM eBay in December 2006. Subsequently, the company also stopped charging its sellers listing fees and decided that free was indeed a business model. Despite all these efforts, TOM eBay continued to lose market share. According to Analysys International,[51] TOM eBay's market share plummeted from 16 percent in the first quarter of 2007 to 7.2 percent in the second quarter of 2007.[liii] In sharp contrast, Taobao reported a market share of 82.95 percent in the second quarter of 2007 compared to its 74 percent market share in the first quarter of 2007.[liv]

Industry observers opined that foreign companies failed to make a mark in China because of their lack of understanding of the language and culture. Shaun Rein, Managing Director, China Market Research Group (CMR),[52] said, "Alibaba and Taobao have been much more successful in China than their competitors because they were able to cater their services specifically for the China market. eBay, on the other hand, tried to bring what worked in the United States. But many other global-brand companies, like eBay or Google, run into this problem when they enter China: They simply do not adjust to local realities enough."[lv]

By the end of 2008, Taobao had 98 million registered users, according to Alibaba.[lvi] In comparison, eBay recorded 86.3 million users for the same period, according to iResearch.[lvii] According to industry analysts, Taobao had successfully captured the C2C market in China with a 90.5 percent market share for the Q3 of 2011 (refer to Table II for market shares of C2C players in China).

Alibaba's B2C platform, Taobao Mall, was also ahead of all competitors in the Chinese B2C market. According to iResearch, Taobao Mall recorded a market share of 50.9 percent for the Q3 of 2011 (refer to Table III for market shares of B2C players for the Q3 of 2011).

Web Search Market

After having conquered the lucrative e-commerce market, Alibaba aimed to enter the lucrative Chinese online search market, considered the most popular Internet business. The Chinese web search market was dominated by the strong local company, Baidu, which had mastered the Internet search market in the local language. Even the international leader in the search market, Google, could not crack the Chinese web search market. According to certain estimates by iResearch, around 49 percent of the C2C users visited a search engine before visiting C2C sites.[lviii]

In August 2005, Alibaba struck a deal to acquire the operations of Yahoo! in China. Alibaba acquired Yahoo! China's main website www.cn.yahoo.com and search engines

---

[50] TOM Online Inc., headquartered in Beijing, China was a leading internet company in China.

[51] Analysys International, headquartered in Beijing, China, is a leading advisor of technology, media, and telecom industries in China.

[52] China Market Research Group is a market research company based in Shanghai. It provides companies with data, strategic recommendations, and analyses that help companies understand consumer behavior and evaluate opportunities for long-term growth (Source: www.researchcmr.com).

TABLE II   Market Shares of C2C Players in China (Q3 2011)

Players	Market Share (in %)
Taobao	90.5
Paipai	8.9
Eachnet.com	0.6

Source: Adapted from "Market Scale of Q3 2011 China Online Shopping Market Surges to 200 Billion Yuan," www.iresearchchina.com, November 1, 2011.

TABLE III   Market Shares of B2C Players in China (Q3 2011)

Players	Market Share (in %)
Taobao Mall	50.9
360 buy	18.6
Suning	3.4
Amazon	2.9
Vancl	2.3
Dangdang	2.2
Icson	1.4
Newegg	1.4
Coo8	1.3
M18	0.8
Redbaby	0.4
Others	14.4

Source: Adapted from "Market Scale of Q3 2011 China Online Shopping Market Surges to 200 Billion Yuan," www.iresearchchina.com, November 1, 2011.

including www.yisou.com and www.3721.com. Yahoo! invested US$ 1 billion on acquiring an equity stake of 40 percent in Alibaba. This was the largest investment by a foreign company in an e-commerce business in China. With this deal, Alibaba expected to gain a strong foothold in the web search market while having its presence in the B2B, B2C, and C2C e-commerce segments, as well as the online payments segments through its online payment solution, AliPay. Ma said, "With the addition of Yahoo! China to Alibaba.com's business, we're expanding our services to provide a leading search offering to China's Internet users."[lix] According to analysts, by defeating its arch-rival eBay and with Yahoo! China's acquisition, Alibaba had become the dominant player in the Chinese Internet market.

In addition to having a presence in the web search market, Alibaba's announcement that it would acquire Yahoo! China came after Baidu had launched an IPO in the U.S. According to Ma, the addition of Yahoo!'s Chinese operations would allow Alibaba to expand in the rapidly growing Chinese search engine market. Further, Ma aimed to use Yahoo!'s search engine to direct customers to its online commerce sites that linked foreign buyers with Chinese wholesalers. Alibaba aimed to expand its search engine by leveraging on its huge customer base coming from its B2B, B2C, and C2C sites.

In August 2005, Ma stopped the operations of Yisou, a search engine built by Zhou Hongyi (Zhou), former President,

Yahoo! China. The search engine offered search facilities to users in addition to the Yahoo! China portal. In the same year, Ma also stopped using 3721, a search engine bought by Zhou in 2003. With all these changes, Ma developed a simple search page that was quite in contrast to the portal-like features offered by Yahoo! China, in order to make Yahoo! China the number one search engine in China. However, this looked an uphill task as Yahoo! China continued to lose market share. Contrary to Ma's beliefs, Yahoo! China's acquisition did not help Alibaba gain a larger portion of the pie in the web search market since it was already dominated by strong players such as Baidu and Google. According to an internal research study by Yahoo! China, Baidu was the most favored choice among college students, and Google and Yahoo! China were preferred by affluent and business-oriented customers.

According to estimates by iResearch in 2006, Baidu and Google were the two most popular search engines with market shares of 46.5 percent and 26.9 percent, respectively, while Yahoo! China had a share of just about 15.6 percent.[lx] However, Ma dismissed competition from Google and said, "For the search engine, I think Google is very powerful. But it is not that powerful in China now."[lxi] Commenting on his strategy to defeat Google, Ma said, "We win eBay, buy Yahoo! and stop Google. That is for fun. Competition is for fun."[lxii]

In September 2006, Ma adopted a new homepage strategy by promoting Yahoo! China's home page as a separate search engine page. Commenting on Ma's strategy, Zhou said, "Now he [Ma] has completely flipped back and wants to rebuild Yahoo! China into a portal. As a result, there's no search strategy. He continues to lose market share. There's brand ambiguity. No one's sure whether it's a search engine or a portal."[lxiii]

Ma opined that Yahoo! China would have to leverage on its understanding of the Chinese consumers and chart its own path in the online search market. Describing Yahoo! China's future course of action, Ma said, "If you follow Google's way, you will always be a follower … We have to make the Yahoo! search engine more human, more interactive ... something for the 1.3 billion people in China who aren't technology-oriented, who don't know how to ask the right questions to a search engine—for people who are like me."[lxiv]

In January 2007, Ma announced his new strategy to reorganize the Yahoo! China portal into a business-oriented search engine. As part of its new strategy, Yahoo! China's search results were to be directed more toward corporate or business-oriented websites. Describing the new strategy, Ma said, "We don't want those not interested in business or making money. They can go to Baidu. Our main focus is the high-end. We don't need to compare ourselves with Baidu in market share."[lxv] Ma was confident that the new strategy would help Yahoo! China gain leadership and succeed in the highly competitive Chinese Internet market. Industry experts felt that by positioning itself in the high-end segment, Yahoo! China would be on a different platform when compared to Baidu. But it would have to compete with Google, a dominant player in that segment. Baidu too was reported to have initiated efforts to woo the high-end customers.

However, Yahoo! China continued to lose market share to Baidu and Google. But Ma had no plans to give up since the

TABLE IV   **Market Shares of Players in Online Search Market in China (Q3 2011)**

Players	Market Shares (in %)
Baidu	77.7
Google	18.3
Sougou	2.1
Soso	1.4
Others	0.49

Source: Adapted from "China's Search Engine Market Update for Q3 2011," www.chinainternetwatch.com, November 21, 2011.

Chinese web search market had reached RMB 811.7 million in the third quarter of 2007.[lxvi] Yahoo! China's market share fell from 1 percent in 2008 to 0.3 percent in 2009 while Baidu recorded a 76 percent market share and Google garnered a market share of 19 percent.[lxvii]

In order to gain a strong foothold in the rapidly growing Chinese web search market, Alibaba bought a 16 percent stake in Sogou.com in August 2010. With the acquisition of the stake in Sohou, Ma aimed to tap the potential in US$ 1 billion worth of online search market in China.[lxviii] However, Baidu continued with its dominance in the Chinese web search market with a market share of 77.7 percent for the Q3 of 2011 (refer to Table IV for market shares of players in online search market in China).

In October 2011, Alibaba launched an online shopping search engine called eTao. This was a bid to combat competition from Baidu and also to maintain Alibaba's control in the lucrative B2C market in China.

ANOTHER IPO AT ALIBABA?

In June 2011, Ma expressed his desire to raise an IPO for the Alibaba Group. In a letter to his employees, Ma said, "We won't rule out the possibility of taking Alibaba Group public in the future, as a way to reward our employees and shareholders who support and continue to believe in us."[lxix] Earlier in October 2007, Alibaba went public on the Hong Kong stock exchange by launching an IPO (refer to *Exhibit V* for Alibaba's IPO in 2007).

In September 2011, Alibaba also announced its plans to spin off and raise an IPO for its Internet application service provider, HiChina Group Ltd. (HiChina). The *International Financing Review*[53] reported that Alibaba expected to raise between US$ 200 million and US$ 300 million from HiChina's IPO.[lxx]

OUTLOOK

For the year ended December 31, 2010, Alibaba's revenues grew by 43.4 percent to RMB 5.55 billion as compared with revenues of RMB 3.87 billion for the FY ended December 31, 2009 (refer to *Exhibit VI* for Alibaba.com's three-year financials).[lxxi] The revenue growth was attributed to

---

[53] The *International Financing Review* is the world's leading source of information related to capital markets for the investment banking community.

EXHIBIT V   Alibaba's IPO in 2007

In October 2007, Alibaba Group's Chinese website, Alibaba.com, went public on the Hong Kong stock exchange by launching an IPO. The IPO was arranged (underwritten) by Deutsche Bank AG[54] (Deutsche Bank), Goldman Sachs, and Morgan Stanley[55] (Morgan Stanley).[56] Over 85 percent of the shares in the IPO were marked for institutional investors. The IPO received a very good response from both individual and institutional investors and the individual portion was oversubscribed by 257 times. The response prompted a reallocation of the individual-investor portion to 25 percent, up from the initial 15 percent. The company raised US$ 1.5 billion from the IPO, the second largest IPO after Google, which had raised US$ 1.7 billion in 2004.[57] Alibaba sold a 17 percent stake consisting of 858.9 million shares at US$ 1.75 per share. Alibaba's shares opened at HK$ 30 on the first day of trading, almost double the price of their IPO of HK$ 13.5, and reached HK$ 39.55, a raise of nearly 200 percent at close. The share closing at HK$ 39.55 gave Alibaba a market value of US$ 25.7 billion. The IPO was the most expensive trading stock at the Hong Kong stock exchange, where shares were valued at HK$ 17.5 billion.[58] The shares of Alibaba traded almost 155 times the estimated earnings of the company for the next year. In comparison, the shares of Google were trading at 36 times of the estimated profits for the next year during the same period.[59]

With this IPO, Ma aimed to position Alibaba's business model on a global scale. According to Ma, "This is a golden opportunity, one we probably won't see again for another 20 years. Sure we could just be like an easy guy and enjoy life. But by going public now, we have a chance to be a focus of attention—not just from China but from the rest of the world—to say, 'Hey, ecommerce in China can make money; it can help China get to the next stage.' When the time comes, you have to grab it."[60] Ma had announced that around 60 percent of the earnings raised through the IPO would be spent on acquisitions and enhancing its technologies, another 20 percent on the development of its Chinese and international sites. The remaining was expected to be used as working capital. Ma announced that using the IPO proceeds, the company would expand in Europe considering the growth potential in the European market. According to Wei, "With more than 20 million SMEs, Europe is a very important market for us."[61]

Even though the Alibaba IPO was hugely successful, analysts and industry observers criticized it, saying it had been valued too high. Some others opined that Alibaba could justify the high valuation if it could increase its revenues by making its customers pay for its services. Commenting on the high valuation, Rafe Xu, an analyst at Sinopac Securities Asia Ltd., a financial services company, said, "It's a high valuation but if Alibaba can use its leadership position in the e-commerce market to get more Chinese businesses to pay for its services, it will justify it. They have a lot of work to do."[62] However, the investors justified the price considering the huge growth outlook for the company. Ma also justified the pricing by showing the post-IPO performance of its shares on the stock market. The other senior executives of the company defended the higher valuation in view of the huge future growth potential of the company. Some analysts even attributed the spectacular success of the Alibaba IPO to the rise in the demand for the Chinese companies' shares.

According to certain estimates by Goldman Sachs, the IPO was expected to boost Alibaba's earnings to US$ 166 million with profits estimated at RMB 1.02 billion in 2008.[63] However, they were also of the view that Alibaba had to tap a huge customer base since only a percent of the 24.6 million registered users it had were paying members. The rest were using the services free of charge. With this IPO, Alibaba aimed to focus on increasing its community of users while providing enhanced services to customers who were paying a premium in the range of RMB 2,800 to 60,000. The company had announced its ambitious plans to tap the Asian markets like India and Japan.

Source: Compiled from various sources.

the increasing number of paying members at Alibaba's online trading platform.

With the growth in revenues and paying members, Alibaba was touted to be one of the biggest Internet companies in China in 2011. However, its image took a beating when the company reported a series of frauds that took place through its e-commerce site, in February 2011. It was reported that some of the vendors had offered small electronic items to buyers at attractive prices. The payments were settled using less reliable methods. According to John Spelich (Spelich), the company's Hong Kong–based spokesman, the employees at Alibaba either intentionally or negligently evaded verification and authentication measures. Industry analysts felt that the fraud cases could hurt the reputation of Alibaba and hamper its ability to attract

[54] Deutsche Bank AG, headquartered in Frankfurt, Germany, is an international financial institution whose main products include banking and insurance.

[55] Morgan Stanley, headquartered in New York City, New York, USA, is a leading investment banking and financial services corporation in the world.

[56] "Alibaba IPO Approved in Hong Kong," www.tagedge.com, October 6, 2007.

[57] "Alibaba IPO Boosts Yahoo!" www.seekingalpha.com, November 7, 2007.

[58] Amy Or, Lorraine Luk, and Sky Canaves, "China IPO Frenzy Rolls on with Alibaba.com Debut—Shares of B2B Site Skyrocket as Investors Buy its Growth Story," www.resources.alibaba.com, November 7, 2007.

[59] Mark Lee and John Liu, "Alibaba Shares Triple in Hong Kong Trading Debut (Update8)," www.bloomberg.com, November 6, 2007.

[60] Clay Chandler, "China's Web King," *Fortune*, December 10, 2007.

[61] "China's Alibaba.com Aims to Expand in Europe through Acquisitions—CEO," www.forbes.com, December 28, 2007.

[62] Mark Lee and John Liu, "Alibaba Shares Triple in Hong Kong Trading Debut (Update8)," www.bloomberg.com, November 6, 2007.

[63] Mark Lee and John Liu, "Alibaba Shares Triple in Hong Kong Trading Debut (Update8)," www.bloomberg.com, November 6, 2007.

EXHIBIT VI Alibaba.com's Three Year Financials (RMB in Thousands)

For the Year Ended December 31,	2008	2009	2010
Revenue			
International marketplace	1,883,966	2,406,804	3,238,243
China marketplace	1,094,059	1,414,897	1,893,899
Others	26,102	53,027	425,444
Total revenue	3,004,127	3,874,728	5,557,586
Cost of revenue	(400,651)	(534,438)	(931,016)
Gross profit	2,603,476	3,340,290	4,626,570
Sales and marketing expenses	(1,108,129)	(1,623,845)	(2,050,561)
Product development expenses	(214,038)	(384,333)	(580,173)
General and administrative expenses	(322,246)	(409,708)	(568,324)
Other operating income, net	182,637	150,566	109,026
Profit from operations	1,141,700	1,072,970	1,536,538
Finance income, net	239,207	140,941	176,398
Share of losses of associated companies and a jointly controlled entity, net of tax:	(16,087)	(37,492)	(6,479)
Profit before income taxes	1,364,820	1,176,419	1,706,457
Income tax charges	(210,317)	(163,393)	(236,445)
Profit for the year	1,154,503	1,013,026	1,470,012
Other comprehensive income/(expense)			
Net fair value gains/(losses) on available-for-sale investments	—	222	5,640
Currency translation differences	(24,650)	247	(21,533)
Total comprehensive income	1,129,853	1,013,495	1,454,119
Profit/(loss) for the year attributable to			
Equity owners of our Company	1,154,503	1,013,026	1,469,464
Non-controlling interests	—	—	548
Profit for the year	1,154,503	1,013,026	1,470,012
Total comprehensive income/(expense) attributable to			
Equity owners of our Company	1,129,853	1,013,495	1,453,571
Non-controlling interests	—	—	548
Total comprehensive income	1,129,853	1,013,495	1,454,119
Dividend per share Special cash dividend (HK$)	—	20 cents	22 cents
Earnings per share, basic and diluted (RMB)	22.85 cents	22 cents	29 cents
Earnings per share, basic and diluted (HK$) (Note 1)	26 cents	23 cents	33 cents

Note 1: The translation of Renminbi amounts into Hong Kong dollars has been made at the rate of RMB0.8714 to HK$1.0000 (2009: RMB0.8812 to HK$1.0000). No representation is made that the Renminbi amounts have been, could have been or could be converted into Hong Kong dollars or vice versa, at that rate, or at any rates or at all.

Source: "Alibaba Annual Report 2010," http://img.alibaba.com/ir/download/201104/2010_AnnualReport_ENG.pdf and "Alibaba Annual Report 2009," http://img.alibaba.com/ir/download/201102/e1688_AR.pdf.

global players. It was also reported that the fraud had led to a loss of US$ 1 billion in market value.[lxxii] Some experts opined that the fraudulent listings on Alibaba's online trading platform had led to a decrease in the number of members at the company.

On the other hand, the company remained positive about its prospects. According to Spelich, "We are the same company today that our customers have known for the last 11 years, and the whole point of the announcement earlier this week was to demonstrate our sacrosanct commitment to integrity. We believe, over time, our customers will understand that."[lxxiii] The company said that it was taking measures to boost the quality of services, check its sellers on-site, and offer an escrow service to protect its buyers and sellers through AliExpress, an online trading platform for small-quantity orders.

By the end of June 2011, the number of Internet users in China had reached 508 million, according to Data Center for China Internet[64] (DCCI). It was reported that the Internet users in China would reach 551 million by 2012.[lxxiv] Given the attractiveness of the Chinese Internet market, analysts opined that Internet companies that could crack the market would be rewarded handsomely. The growth outlook remained positive for Alibaba considering the potential of Internet market in China, experts felt.

While experts remained positive about Alibaba's future, it posted a 12 percent increase in net profit and recorded revenues of RMB 1.602 million or US$ 250.4 million for the third quarter ended September 30, 2011.[lxxv] Analysts attributed these results to a weak macroeconomic climate that resulted in slower customer additions. Alibaba reported that "The third quarter of 2011 presented a picture filled with challenges arising from the weaknesses in the U.S. economy and the debt troubles in the euro zone, which have threatened to spin out of control."[lxxvi]

[64] Data Center for China Internet offers data on the Chinese Internet, advertising, search engine, e-commerce, digital entertainment, and web services market.

Alibaba's chief executive, Jonathan Lu, vouched for the fact that despite the troubles in the external environment, the company would continue with its focus on upgrading its business model and building trustworthy and quality e-commerce platforms.

As of November 2011, the company was also making efforts to increase the revenue per user by planning to offer value-added services such as extra ways to advertise on the site. Industry experts felt that with the acquisition of 40 percent of Yahoo!'s stake in Alibaba, Ma would take the company forward.

Suggested Questions for Discussion

1. Critically analyze the factors that led to Alibaba sustaining its leadership position in the Chinese e-commerce market.

2. Discuss the rationale behind Ma establishing Taobao.com. What are the factors that led to Taobao's success as compared to eBay in the Chinese online auctions market?

3. Though Alibaba was the market leader in the Chinese e-commerce market, it failed to make a mark in the lucrative Chinese web search market. Do you think Alibaba's strategy of launching eTao, an online shopping search engine, would help it combat competition with Baidu? Why (not)? Do you think Alibaba's decision to acquire its 40 percent stake in Yahoo! China would help it gain some momentum in the Chinese web search market? Why (not)?

4. Critically examine Alibaba's business model. Do you think it is sustainable? After having captured the Chinese e-commerce market, what steps should Alibaba take to expand globally?

Endnotes

i. Bei Hu and John Liu, "Alibaba.com Offers $1.3 Billion Share Sale," www.iht.com, October 15, 2007.

ii. Chua Chin Hon, "Yahoo! Jack Wants it to Be No.1 in China," www.asiamedia.ucla.edu, April 28, 2006.

iii. "Meet Jack Ma, Who Will Guide Yahoo in China," www.bdachina.com, August 12, 2005.

iv. Antoine Gara, "Alibaba Consortium Looks to Buy Yahoo: Report," www.thestreet.com, November 30, 2011.

v. "Company Overview," http://news.alibaba.com, 2011.

vi. "Alibaba Develops Logistics Platform," www.china.org.cn, May 30, 2011.

vii. "Baidu 78%, Google 18% in China's Search Engine Market as of Q3," http://news.ichinastock.com, October 27, 2011.

viii. Michael Kan, "China's Alibaba Invests $157M in Own Search Engine," www.pcworld.com, November 2, 2011.

ix. Sonia Kolesnikov-Jessop, "Spotlight: Jack Ma, Co-founder of Alibaba.com," www.iht.com, January 5, 2007.

x. Clay Chandler, "China's Web King," *Fortune*, December 10, 2007.

xi. Sumie Kawakami, "China's Visionary B2B: Who Says the Dot-com Era Is Over? Alibaba.com Thrives as Chinese Imports and Exports Boom. CEO Jack Ma Has a Vision: Helping SMEs Buy and Sell Goods through his Sites—Upfront—Company Profile," www.encyclopedia.com, May 2003.

xii. "Open Sesame to the Net Highway," www.crienglish.com, April 17, 2005.

xiii. Sumie Kawakami, "China's Visionary B2B: Who Says the Dot-com Era Is Over? Alibaba.com Thrives as Chinese Imports and Exports Boom. CEO Jack Ma Has a Vision: Helping SMEs Buy and Sell Goods through His Sites—Upfront—Company Profile," www.encyclopedia.com, May 2003.

xiv. "Fast as a Rabbit, Patient as a Turtle," www.resources.alibaba.com, July 3, 2000.

xv. Ibid.

xvi. "Alibaba.com Opens its First European Office in Geneva," www.alibaba.com, October 2, 2007.

xvii. Sumie Kawakami, "China's Visionary B2B: Who Says the Dot-com Era Is Over? Alibaba.com Thrives as Chinese Imports and Exports Boom. CEO Jack Ma Has a Vision: Helping SMEs Buy and Sell Goods through His Sites—Upfront—Company Profile," www.encyclopedia.com, May 2003.

xviii. "Alibaba Is to Land at Japan, as Planned," www.resources .alibaba.com, October 17, 2002.

xix. Fara Warner, "Alibaba.com's Helm," www.forbes.com, November 26, 2007.

xx. Chua Chin Hon, "Yahoo! Jack Wants it to Be No.1 in China," www.asiamedia.ucla.edu, April 28, 2006.

xxi. Justin Deobele, "B2B for the Little Guys," www.forbes.com, July 24, 2000.

xxii. "Alibaba.com," www.lupaworld.com, 2001.

xxiii. "Alibaba's Magic Carpet Is Losing Altitude," www.businessweek .com, April 9, 2001.

xxiv. Sumie Kawakami, "China's Visionary B2B: Who Says the Dot-com Era Is Over? Alibaba.com Thrives as Chinese Imports and Exports Boom. CEO Jack Ma Has a Vision: Helping SMEs Buy and Sell Goods through His Sites—Upfront—Company Profile," www.encyclopedia.com, May 2003.

xxv. "Alibaba's Magic Carpet Is Losing Altitude," www.businessweek .com, April 9, 2001.

xxvi. Ibid.

xxvii. Sumie Kawakami, "China's Visionary B2B: Who Says the Dot-com Era Is Over? Alibaba.com Thrives as Chinese Imports and Exports Boom. CEO Jack Ma Has a Vision: Helping SMEs Buy and Sell Goods through His Sites—Upfront—Company Profile," www.encyclopedia.com, May 2003.

xxviii. "Alibaba's China B2B Site Reaches 50 Million Registered Users," www.penn-olson.com, November 30, 2011.

xxix. Gady Epstein, "Alibaba's Jack Ma Fights to Win Back Trust," www.forbes.com, April 11, 2011.

xxx. Jin Zang, "Alibaba Restructures Taobao into 3 Units," http:// en.21cbh.com, June 16, 2011.

xxxi. Eric Jackson, "Pulling Back the Curtain on Taobao—and Yahoo!'s Hidden Value," http://www.forbes.com, March 5, 2011.

xxxii. "Company Overview," http://news.alibaba.com, 2011.

xxxiii. "Company Overview," http://news.alibaba.com, 2011.

xxxiv. "Corporate Overview," www.alibaba.com, 2008.

xxxv. "Alibaba.com," www.lupaworld.com, May 29, 2007.

xxxvi. Ibid.

xxxvii. "eBay and EachNet Team up in China," www.investing.ebay .com, March 17, 2002.

xxxviii. "eBay's Exit from China Opens the Door for News Corp.," www.seekingalpha.com, December 21, 2006.

xxxix. Susan Kuchinskas, "Jack Ma, CEO, Alibaba," www .venturetdf.com, October 22, 2004.

xl. "China's Online Auction Market," www.bbb.typepad.com, March 2005.

xli. "eBay Outlines Global Business Strategy at 2005 Analyst Conference," www.investor.ebay.com, February 10, 2005.

xlii. "China's Online Auction Market," www.bbb.typepad.com, March 2005.

xliii. "Ebay Oversold Recently Standing up to a Giant," www .marketmillionaires.com, April 2005.

xliv. "China Online Shopping Market Survey Report," www .cnnic.cn, May 2006.

xlv. Bill Powell and Jeffrey Resner, "Why Ebay Must Win in China," www.time.com, August 22, 2005.

xlvi. Ina Steiner, "Competitor Comments on eBay China Rumors," www.auctionbytes.com, November 8, 2006.

xlvii. Justin Doebele, "Standing up to eBay," www.forbes.com, March 18, 2005.

xlviii. Ina Steiner, "Alibaba Calls on eBay to Make China Site Free, eBay Responds," www.auctionbytes.com, October 20, 2005.

xlix. Simon Burns, "Going Local No Help for eBay in China," www.vnunet.com, August 23, 2007.

l. Simon Burns, "Going Local No Help for eBay in China," www.vnunet.com, August 23, 2007.

li. Sonia Kolesnikov-Jessop, "Spotlight: Jack Ma, Co-founder of Alibaba.com," www.iht.com, January 5, 2007.

lii. "Taobao.com Announces 2008 Full-Year Key Metrics," www.alibaba.com, February 10, 2009.

liii. "How Taobao beats eBay in China," www.thomascrampton .com, January 11, 2010.

liv. "Baidu to Enter Chinese E-Commerce Market," www.baidu .com, October 17, 2007.

lv. "Yahoo! and Alibaba.com Form Strategic Partnership in China," http://docs.yahoo.com, August 11, 2005.

lvi. www.baiduyahoogoogle.com.cn

lvii. "Alibaba's Chief Vows to Beat Google in China," www.blog .searchenginewatch.com, November 17, 2005.

lviii. "Watch Jack Ma," www.battellemedia.com, November 19, 2005.

lix. Matt Marshall, "China Wars: Zhou Fights Back, Says Alibaba's Ma Is Desperate," www.venturebeat.com, November 5, 2006.

lx. John Heilemann, "Jack Ma Aims to Unlock the Middle Kingdom," www.money.cnn.com, October 2, 2006.

lxi. Christopher Bodeen, "Yahoo China Portal to Be Reorganized," www.washingtonpost.com, January 8, 2007.

lxii. Elmer W. Cagape, "Baidu Corners 61.5% Market Share in China Search Engine Market in Q3," www.seo-hongkong .com, 2007.

lxiii. Juan Carlos Perez, "Google Stops Censoring in China," www.macworld.com, March 23, 2010.

lxiv. "Sohu Sells Shares of its Sogou Search Engine," www.them .pro, 2010.

lxv. David Barboza, "Alibaba Group to Split up E-Commerce Site," http://dealbook.nytimes.com, June 16, 2011.

lxvi. "Alibaba Plans to Spin off HiChina Group, List Stock in U.S.," www.businessweek.com, September 25, 2011.

lxvii. "Alibaba Annual Report 2010," http://img.alibaba.com/ir/ download/201104/2010_AnnualReport_ENG.pdf.

lxviii. "Alibaba Fraud Scandal May Help Google, Global Sources," www.businessweek.com, February 28, 2011.

lxix. Ibid.

lxx. "Total Chinese Internet Users to Reach 551MM by 2012," www.bloodyamazing.com, August 27, 2011.

lxxi. "Alibaba.com Reports 12 Percent Year-on-Year Profit Growth in Q3," http://img.alibaba.com, November 2011.

lxxii. "Alibaba.com Posts Slowest Quarterly Growth in Almost 2 Years," http://techcircle.vccircle.com, November 25, 2011.

lxxiii. "China Internet Usage Stats and Population Report," www .internetworldstats.com, March 30, 2011.

lxxiv. "Total Chinese Internet Users to Reach 551MM by 2012," www.bloodyamazing.com, August 27, 2011.

lxxv. Elizabeth Millard, "The Mushrooming Chinese Internet Market," www.ecommercetimes.com, January 11, 2007.

lxxvi. Sumie Kawakami, "China's Visionary B2B: Who Says the Dot-com Era Is Over? Alibaba.com Thrives as Chinese Imports and Exports Boom. CEO Jack Ma Has a Vision: Helping SMEs Buy and Sell Goods through His Sites— Upfront—Company Profile," www.encyclopedia.com, May 2003.

Case 6 *Carrefour's Misadventure in Russia*

"In the space of just four months, Russia has gone from a "strategic priority" to an afterthought at Carrefour, the giant French retailer."[1]

—*New York Times, in October 2009.*

"Carrefour's pending exit underlines the fact that Russia remains a highly challenging market despite its fundamental draw. Although MGR (Mass Grocery Retail) sales are forecast to strengthen by a dynamic 66.4% to RUB 1,423bn (US$ 48.53bn) through to 2014, the country's business environment is among the least forthcoming in emerging Europe. Despite topping our Q110 food and drink regional business environment ratings, Russia's market risks score (encompassing regulatory environment and barriers to entry) is the region's second lowest behind Ukraine."[2]

—*Business Monitor International*[3], *in October 2009.*

CARREFOUR EXITS RUSSIA

On October 15, 2009, just four months after opening its first store in Russia, France-based Carrefour SA (Carrefour), the second largest retailer in the world, announced that it planned to exit the Russian market. The company announced, "Carrefour has decided to sell its activities in Russia and pull out of the market, given the absence of sufficient organic-growth prospects and acquisition opportunities in the short- and medium-term that would have allowed Carrefour to attain a position of leadership. This decision is consistent with the Group's strategy which aims at building leadership positions that will ensure strong and lasting profitable growth."[4]

Carrefour started the groundwork to enter the Russian market in 2007, looking out for suitable locations for opening its stores. It opened its first store in the country, a hypermarket, in June 2009. Its second store was opened soon after. It also procured a location for its third store, which was to open by the end of the year. However, in a move that took industry analysts and observers alike by surprise, Carrefour announced its exit from the country in October 2009.

Analysts opined that Carrefour's failure to acquire Russia-based grocery chain Sedmoi Kontinent[5] (Seventh Continent) and shareholders' pressure on the company to focus on its core business were the main reasons for the exit decision. They were of the view that the bureaucracy, complicated legislative

framework, corruption, and red tape that existed in the country were factors that could have influenced Carrefour's decision to quit Russia. Some of them opined that Carrefour had not given enough time for its operations to stabilize in the market. Viktoria Sokolova, Senior Analyst at Troika Dialog,[6] said the company's strategy was flawed and had come too late. She said, "Carrefour simply failed with its strategy to enter Russia. There are plenty of growth opportunities out there. Its nearest competitor, Auchan, has opened its 34th hypermarket in Russia, and continued its opening program, even during the crisis times. Carrefour came to Russia a little bit too late, and was talking, perhaps, not to the best operator in the market, without the distribution reach, to acquire them, as a means of an entry point."[7]

Industry analysts, who had observed the Russian market closely, said that Carrefour's exit could affect the entry of other international retailers such as Wal-Mart and Tesco, which had plans to enter the country. According to *New York Times*, "It also indicates that a good deal of the shine has come off the Russian retail market, in recent years one of the fastest growing in the world because of trickle-down oil wealth that helped lead a consumer boom built on decades of pent-up demand from the bleak Soviet era."[8]

BACKGROUND NOTE

Carrefour was founded in 1960 by two entrepreneurs—Marcel Fournier, a textile retailer, and Louis Defforey, a wine and food wholesaler from Annecy in Eastern France. The first two stores that they opened were highly successful. In 1963, a 2,500 square meter store was opened in Sainte-Genevieve des Bois, a Paris suburb. It occupied an area of 2,500 square meters and had enough space to park more than 400 cars. The store provided a wide

This case was written by **P. Indu,** under the direction of **Vivek Gupta,** IBS Center for Management Research. It was compiled from published sources, and is intended to be used as a basis for class discussion rather than to illustrate either effective or ineffective handling of a management situation.

[1] Matthew Saltmarsh, Andrew E. Kramer, "French Retailer to Close Its Russia Stores," www.nytimes.com, October 16, 2009.

[2] "Carrefour to Quit Russia," store.businessmonitor.com, October 16, 2009.

[3] London-based Business Monitor International is an independent information provider in the areas of country risk and information research.

[4] "French Hypermarket Chain Carrefour Leaves Russian Market," http://en.rian.ru, October 15, 2009.

[5] Sedmoi Kontinent or Seventh Continent is a Russia-based grocery chain. As of December 2009, it operated through nine hypermarkets and 130 supermarkets in Russia. Its revenues for the year ending 2008 were 43.8 billion Rubles.

[6] Troika Dialog is one of the largest private investment banks in CIS. Its main lines of businesses include capital markets, investment banking, asset management, personal investments, and finance. About 33% of the equity stake in the company is owned by the Standard Bank Group and the rest is owned by 109 employee partners.

[7] "Retail Market Fight Too Tough for Carrefour," http://rt.com, October 17, 2009.

[8] Matthew Saltmarsh, Andrew E. Kramer, French Retailer to Close Its Russia Stores, www.nytimes.com, October 16, 2009.

range of items, including self-service grocery at discount prices, and clothing, sporting equipment, electronic goods, and auto accessories. The store was inaugurated in June 1963 and its huge size earned it the name "hypermarket" in the media. Carrefour offered products at the lowest prices as compared to its competitors by negotiating with wholesalers and suppliers. The concept of a hypermarket found instant acceptance among the younger people, suburban dwellers, and price-conscious consumers.

In 1966, a 10,000 sq. meter hypermarket was opened in Lyon and a 20,000 sq. meter hypermarket was opened in Vitrolles. In 1967, Carrefour opened an office in Paris to coordinate the activities of its various stores in the country. The company began to enter international markets after a law was passed in France in 1963 to restrict the development of large stores. Its first international venture was in Belgium, where it opened an outlet in association with Delhaize Fréres-Le-Lion,[9] in 1969.

In 1970, Carrefour's shares were listed on the Paris stock exchange. By 1971, Carrefour was directly operating 16-wholly owned stores, with an equity interest in five more stores. It also operated through franchises. In its first venture outside Europe, Carrefour opened a hypermarket in Brazil in 1975.

In 1978, Carrefour developed a hard discount store[10] format under the banner "Ed" in France. The stores offered a limited range of products at very low prices. By 1985, Carrefour was operating in ten countries and had introduced private-label products that were priced 10–20% lower than branded products and were said to be of superior quality. In 1988, Carrefour entered the U.S. market by opening a 330,000 sq. ft. hypermarket in Philadelphia. Another hypermarket was set up in 1991.[11] In 1991, Carrefour acquired the French hypermarket chains Euromarche and Montiaur. In 1992, Carrefour reported sales of € 17.86 billion and a net income of € 271 million.

In the early 1990s, Carrefour concentrated on establishing larger stores (with an area of more than 2,500 square meters) in France and sold off its smaller stores. By the mid-1990s, Carrefour's European operations were spread across Italy, Spain, Turkey, Greece, and Portugal. In 1996, Carrefour opened 30 hypermarkets across the world, of which 15 were in South America. By 1997, the number of stores in South America had increased to 60. (Refer to *Exhibit I* for the timeline of Carrefour's entry into international markets.)

Carrefour operated through franchises in the UAE, Saudi Arabia, Oman, Qatar, Egypt, Tunisia, Algeria, and the Dominican Republic. In 1998, it acquired Comptoirs Modernes SA, which brought 790 supermarkets into its fold. In 1999, it acquired Promodès SA,[12] which owned several hypermarkets,

---

[9] Delhaize Fréres-Le-Lion is a part of The Delhaize Group, a food retailer headquartered in Belgium. The group was founded in 1867 and operates food supermarkets in North America, Europe, and Southeast Asia. In 2008, its revenues were € 19.02 billion and profit was € 467 million.

[10] Hard discount stores sell products at prices that are even lower than those in traditional discount stores like Wal-Mart. They are small in area and sell a limited assortment of products.

[11] Subsequently, Carrefour suspended the U.S. operations in 1993, as the stores were not profitable.

[12] Promodès SA was established in 1950, and played a major role in promoting supermarkets in France. During the 1960s and 1970s, the group expanded rapidly in other countries in Europe and South America. In 1999, Carrefour purchased Promodès SA to become the second largest retailer in the world.

EXHIBIT I   **Carrefour—International Expansion**

Year	Country
1969	Belgium
1973	Spain
1975	Brazil
1982	Argentina
1989	Taiwan
1991	Greece, Cyprus
1992	Portugal
1993	Italy, Turkey
1994	Mexico,* Malaysia
1995	China
1996	South Korea,* Thailand, Hong Kong*
1997	Singapore, Poland
1998	Chile,* Colombia, Indonesia
1999	Czech Republic,* Slovakia
2000	Japan,* Dominican Republic
2001	Romania, Switzerland**
2002	Egypt
2004	Saudi Arabia
2005	Algeria
2006	Cyprus
2007	Jordan, Kuwait
2008	Bahrain
2009	Iran, Syria, Morocco, Bulgaria, Russia

*By 2006, Carrefour had exited from these countries.
**By 2007, Carrefour exited Switzerland
Source: Compiled from Carrefour's Annual Reports and other sources.

---

supermarkets, convenience stores, and discount stores. The acquisitions helped Carrefour become the top retailer in Europe by the late 1990s.

As of 2008, Carrefour was the second largest retailer in the world and the largest retailer in Europe. (Refer to *Exhibit II* for the list of global powers of retailing.)

By the end of 2008, it was operating 15,430 stores globally. It operated through different store formats such as hypermarkets, supermarkets, convenience stores, hard discount stores, and "cash & carry" outlets. (Refer to *Exhibit III* for Carrefour's store formats.)

Carrefour's revenues were at € 108.629 billion for the year ending December 2008. (Refer to *Exhibit IV* for Carrefour's country-wise sales.)

CARREFOUR'S PLANS FOR RUSSIA

In every international market in which Carrefour operated, it essentially focused on becoming one of the top three players in

EXHIBIT II   Top Global Retailers (2009*)

Rank	Company	Country	Retail Sales (US$ Million)
1	Wal-Mart Stores Inc.	USA	374,526
2	Carrefour SA	France	112,604
3	Tesco Plc	UK	94,740
4	Metro AG	Germany	88,189
5	The Home Depot Inc.	USA	77,349
6	The Kroger Co.	USA	70,235
7	Schwarz Unternehmens Treuhand KG	Germany	69,346
8	Target Corp.	USA	63,367
9	Costco Wholesale Corp.	USA	63,088
10	Aldi GmbH & Co OHG	Germany	54,847

*For the fiscal year ended June 2008.
Source: Deloitte, Global Powers of Retailing, 2009.

EXHIBIT III   Carrefour—Store Formats

Format	Description
Hypermarkets	Offers a wide range of food and non-food products
	Offers about 80,000 items.
	Floor area of 5,000 square meters to 20,000 meters.
	Services like Carrefour travel, Carrefour insurance, Carrefour bookings
	Banner: Carrefour, Atacado
Supermarkets	Offers a wide selection of mostly food products
	Offers about 10,000 items
	Floor area of 1,000 to 2,000 square meters
	Banner: GS, GB, Carrefour Express, Carrefour Market, Carrefour Bairro
Hard Discount Stores	Offers products at low prices
	About 800 retail branded food products
	Floor areas of 300 to 800 square meters
	Banner: Dia, Ed, Minipreco
Convenience Stores	District or village shops
	Products covering all the food requirements
	Offers a wide range of services like home delivery and ATMs
	Banner: Shopi, Marche Plus, 8 à Huit, DiperDi, Proxi, Carrefour City, Carrefour Express, Carrefour 5 Minut
Cash-and-Carry and Food Service	Wholesale and retail self-service
	Food products for businesses
	Banner: Promocash, Docks, Super Gross

Source: www.carrefour.com.

terms of market share. Commenting on the criteria for entering new markets, the Chairman of the Management Board of Carrefour, José Luis Duran, said, "We'll look toward new markets. That means local acquisitions in countries where we currently operate, but it also includes the possibility of establishing a presence in new countries, such as Russia and India. However, any such store openings will have to satisfy three criteria: we must be able to capture a leading market position within the

EXHIBIT IV   Carrefour—Sales Country Wise (2008)

Country	Sales (In € Million)	No. of Stores
France	47,119	5,517
Spain	15,527	3,073
Italy	7,806	1,608
Belgium	5,269	627
Greece and Cyprus	2,944	888
Portugal	989	498
Poland	2,424	330
Turkey	1,641	760
Romania	1,190	41
Brazil	8,218	536
Argentina	2,647	589
Colombia	1,228	59
Taiwan	1,361	59
China	3,464	456
Thailand	584	31
Malaysia	326	16
Indonesia	893	73
Singapore	94	2
Partners Franchisees	4,905	267
Total Group	**108,629**	**15,430**

Source: Annual Report, Carrefour, 2008.

medium term, establish our brand quickly, and secure a return on investment. It is only under these conditions that we will expand our scope of operations."[13]

Carrefour initially showed an interest in operating in Russia during the mid-1990s and opened a representative office in Moscow. It also finalized two prime locations, one in the center of the city and the other on the outskirts. However, during the 1998 financial crisis,[14] it exited from the country.

In June 2006, Carrefour again started contemplating an entry into the Russian retail market. A delegation from Carrefour toured across Russia looking for locations, met local officials, and interacted with other retailers. After spending considerable time studying the markets, Carrefour announced its intention of entering the Russian market in June 2007. The retailer planned to open only hypermarkets initially. It would then follow this up with other store formats. At that time, it intended to open its chain in 20 cities. A group of managers from France were stationed in Russia to prepare for the launch of a new store by early 2008.

Analysts were of the view that Carrefour had delayed its entry into Russia. (Refer to *Exhibit V* for a note on the retail industry in Russia.)

According to Maria Sulima, a retail analyst with Metropol,[15] "They are rather late in coming. At this point, it would be more effective to purchase a chain with already developed logistics and distribution networks."[16] By the time Carrefour entered the market, Auchan SA[17] (Auchan) and Metro AG[18] (Metro) had established a significant presence in the country. Auchan had a presence in eight Russian cities, while in Moscow alone it had 20 stores. Metro had 74 stores across the country. Other competitors included local players like X5 Retail Group NV[19] (X5) and Mosmart CJSC[20] (Mosmart). On Carrefour's delayed entry

[13] "Interview with the Chairman of the Management Board," Annual Report 2006.

[14] The Russian financial crisis of 1998 was triggered by the Asian financial crisis of 1997 and resulted in high inflation. The food prices went up by 100% and with people stocking up essential items, shortages were witnessed. By 1999, the country recovered from the crisis.

[15] IFC Metropol is a Russia-based investment and financial company. Its activities include corporate finance, debt instruments, equities, research, depository services, and legal services.

[16] "Carrefour Opens First Russian Store," www.russianamericanchamber.com, June 19, 2009.

[17] Auchan is a France-based multinational retail group. The group is controlled by the Mulliez family of France. In 2008, its revenue was € 39.284 billion and net income was € 744 million.

[18] Metro is a Germany-based retail group. It was the fifth largest retailer in the world as of 2009. In 2008, its revenue was € 67.96 billion and profit was € 403 million.

[19] X5 was the largest retail group in Russia as of 2009. It operates through three formats—hypermarkets, supermarkets, and soft discount stores. In 2008, its sales were US$ 8892 million and EBITDA was US$ 803 million.

[20] Mosmart is a Russia-based multi-format retail chain.

EXHIBIT V **A Note on Retailing Industry in Russia (2008–09)**

As of 2008, the retailing industry in Russia was valued at US$ 480 billion, witnessing a growth of 27.5% over the previous year. The growth was attributed to high oil prices and strong economic growth in the market. Food retailing accounted for 45.3% of total retail sales.

As of 2009, Russia was Europe's fastest growing consumer economy and by 2012, it was expected to overtake the UK and Germany in terms of retail sales, making it Europe's second largest retail market after France. According to the Economist Intelligence Unit, the retail market in Russia was expected to grow to US$ 745 billion by 2011. Moscow and St. Petersburg were the two largest cities in Russia. About 14 of its cities had a population of over 1 million and were expected to account for 60% of the retail growth in the country by 2012.

The country's retail industry began to grow after 2004 and the growth was mainly in areas like supermarkets, electrical stores, fashion retailers, etc. (Refer to Table A for the major retailers in Russia and their turnover for 2008.)

Table A Major Retailers in Russia and their Turnover (2008)

Retailer	Turnover (In US$ Billion)
X5 Retail Group	9.0
Magnit	5.0
M.Video	2.7
Kopieka	2.0
Lenta	2.0
Dixy Group	1.5
Seventh Continent	1.4

The growth in the retailing industry in Russia was fueled by high disposable incomes as most of the Russians, unlike U.S. citizens were free of mortgages and lived in their family homes. As many Russians saw their savings being wiped out during the crisis during the late 1990s, they preferred to spend money rather than save it. In 2002, people in Moscow spent 94% of their monthly earnings. By 2007, per capita income in Russia, which was at US$ 1185 in 2001, had increased to US$ 4803.

However, non-Russian companies found it very difficult to do business in the country, due to the high degree of bureaucracy existing there. Every activity, from obtaining permission for land, finalizing property deals, clearing goods through customs, or obtaining visas, consumed a lot of time and effort. According to Chris Skirrow, Head of PricewaterhouseCoopers' retail and consumer practice in Moscow, "It is the day-to-day bureaucracy that can grind people down. It sometimes seems that if a comma is in the wrong place on an invoice you can lose the tax deduction. One of the biggest problems is unpredictability and unreliability – including tax authorities and the judiciary. There is not only potential for corruption but also uncertainty, which makes the operating environment a lot more difficult."[21]

In several cases, companies opted to bribe the authorities in order to obtain the necessary permissions. Some of the businesses hired a Krisha (security firm), which handled payments, etc. that enabled businesses to operate smoothly. Many foreign companies opted to partner with a local company to lead highly complex negotiations or operate through a franchisee. At the same time, there were retailers like Ikea, which from the beginning emphasized that it would work only with those local governments that would agree to its no-bribery policy. Several local governments wanted Ikea to open stores in their region to show that they were against bribery, to attract other investors.

Much of the retail activity in Russia was concentrated around Moscow, where the salaries were double that in other regions. But the market was highly saturated with several retailers, both international and local, having a presence in these cities.

Another problem that investors faced in Russia was the crumbling infrastructure. Finding the right people to fit into retail roles was also a major challenge. Though the country's education system was highly sophisticated, it churned out more scientists than management graduates.

(continued)

EXHIBIT V   A Note on Retailing Industry in Russia (2008-09) *(continued)*

In mid-2008, UBS predicted that Russia's retail sales would grow by 22% per year till 2010. But by early 2009, the global economic crisis had started showing its impact on Russia and the retail sales slowed down after several years of growth. The retail sales in August 2009 were down 9.8% as compared to retail sales in August 2008. The crisis showed that Russia lacked good quality retail assets. In 2008, the top ten players accounted for only a 10% market share. The spending patterns of the Russian consumers also underwent a change with consumers exercising caution on spending due to the economic crisis. The growing unemployment rate also had an adverse impact on the retail sector in Russia. The Russian retail sector was estimated to grow by 3% in 2010.

In the third quarter ending September 2009, the Russian economy witnessed a net capital outflow of US$ 31.5 billion. By October 2009, with oil prices going up, the Russian economy showed signs of revival. In spite of all the problems, Russia, with a population of 143 million, remained an attractive destination for retailing.

According to the analysts, the top five retailers had a share of 12% in the Russian food market, and this was expected to increase to 14% by the end of the year. Consumers still preferred to shop at outdoor markets, street stands, and unbranded shops but a gradual shift toward larger outlets was being seen.

Source: Compiled from various sources.

into the country, Thierry Garnier (Garnier), Group Executive Director, Carrefour, said, "We were waiting for the best moment to enter the market. We are in Russia for the long term."[22]

In order to step up its presence, Carrefour wanted to have an association with a local partner, and intended to acquire local grocery chain Seventh Continent, which operated through 140 stores.

In February 2009, Carrefour made a non-binding offer to Seventh Continent valuing it at US$ 1.25 billion. On Carrefour's interest in Seventh Continent, Marie Lhome, analyst with Aurel BGC[23] in Paris, said, "It is more expensive and difficult to set up operations in Russia. Some retailers, like Ikea, have run into legal issues there. The interest in Seventh Continent comes from the company's stores prime locations in the center of Moscow."[24] Analysts also expressed doubts about the fit of Seventh Continent with Carrefour's overall strategy, as Seventh Continent was a luxury store. However, the offer was rejected by the shareholders of Seventh Continent.

Carrefour persisted with its acquisition effort and in May 2009, the company signed a preliminary letter of intent to acquire a 75% equity stake in Seventh Continent. Reports suggested that both the companies were under the exclusivity period[25] due to which Seventh Continent could not enter into agreements or talks with any other potential buyers. Analysts were of the view that after the acquisition, the Russian retail market would account for 1% of Carrefour's total sales.

But before Carrefour could conclude the deal, the owner of Seventh Continent ran into financial problems. The company defaulted on bond payments in June 2009 and went in for debt restructuring. Ultimately, Valdimir Gruzdev, who controlled a 10% equity in Seventh Continent, decided not to sell the company, citing that the time was not right to sell well-performing assets.

OPENING STORES

In June 2009, Carrefour opened its first store in Moscow. Commenting on this occasion, Jacobo Caller, General Director of Carrefour in Russia, said, "We are very happy to start our business operations in Russia where we will follow our client-oriented principles: offering quality products at low price, great value, and high level of services to Muscovites. We believe that the opening of the first Carrefour store in Moscow is an important step for Carrefour's development in Russia and will have a positive impact on the economic development of the city."[26]

At that time, Carrefour announced that it believed in the long-term potential of the country and considered the Russian market to be strategically important for the development of Carrefour. According to Garnier, "As the second world and most internationalized retailer, the Carrefour Group is now developing its activities in a new country. Starting our operations in Russia is an important milestone for our company. The Carrefour Group believes that the Russian retail market has outstanding long-term potential and considers it to be one of the strategic priorities for the company's international development."[27] However, analysts cautioned that it would be difficult for Carrefour to expand in the country without acquiring an established player. According to Mikhail Terentiev, analyst with Nomura International[28] in Moscow, "It is not very easy to establish a footprint in Russia. If you want to expand in Russia rapidly it would be a good idea to buy somebody else with a very developed market."[29]

---

[22] "Carrefour Opens First Russian Store," www.russianamericanchamber.com, June 19, 2009.

[23] Aurel BGC is the result of a merger between ETC Pollak, Aurel, and BGC. The services provided by Aurel BGC include fixed income and equity derivatives. It also conducts economic and financial research and provides forecasts.

[24] Javier Espinoza, "Carrefour Flirts with Seventh Continent," www.forbes.com, April 20, 2009.

[25] During the exclusivity period, both Carrefour and Seventh Continent was banned from negotiating with any other potential buyers. This, according to analysts, showed that the deal was imminent.

[26] "Carrefour Starts Business Operations in Russia and Moves Forward with its International Expansion," Press Release, Groupe Carrefour, June 18, 2009.

[27] "Carrefour Starts Business Operations in Russia and Moves Forward with its International Expansion," Press Release, Groupe Carrefour, June 18, 2009.

[28] Nomura International is a part of Japan-based Nomura Group, which is an industrial and financial conglomerate. The group has interests in oil and gas, construction, chemicals, foodstuff, and finance.

[29] Javier Espionoza, "Carrefour May be Stumbling with Russian Dreams," www.forbes.com, June 18, 2009.

Carrefour's first store was located in Filion Shopping Mall, and occupied two floors with a sales area of 8,000 square meters, 58 checkout counters, and 450 staff. It sold 15,000 food items and 30,000 non-food items. Of the total 45,000 SKUs on offer, over 5,000 were private-label products. Filion Shopping mall occupied an area of 87,000 sq. meters and included a 10-screen multiplex cinema and a theme park. The shopping mall had facilities to park 3,000 cars. Carrefour had reportedly invested € 8.8 million on its first store and its opening was a grand event with the guests being entertained by mime artists, musicians, dancing troupes, etc.

However, industry experts were not impressed with the location of Filion Shopping Mall, pointing out that though it was located close to the city center, it was not easily accessible, not prominently visible, and was located among low-income group families.

Carrefour instantly attracted customers who mostly shopped there for food products. One item that proved to be highly attractive was the different varieties of bread that Carrefour sold. As most of the customers were used to the French retailer Auchan, they found shopping at Carrefour convenient due to the high service standards, availability, and wide choice of products.

Just after the first store was opened, newspapers reported that negotiations between Carrefour and Seventh Continent had been stopped. Thus, Carrefour was not able to acquire Seventh Continent on which it was banking for its expansion in Russia.

The second store was opened on September 10, 2009, at Krasnodar in South Russia. For this store, Carrefour entered into a Memorandum of Understanding (MoU) with the local government to implement an investment project. As per the MoU, the company planned to invest up to US$ 100 million in the region, over five years. Carrefour was to be provided with support in terms of business development, finding suitable plots, infrastructure, etc. by the regional authorities.

On this store, Carrefour invested € 8 million. The store had a sales area of 8,500 meters, and employed 350 people. The company invested € 7.8 million on developing the store. At that time, it announced that though Russia was under a recession, for the first time in a decade, the crisis would not change Carrefour's plans for the market and it would open its third store as planned. According to Jacobo Caller, Carrefour Russia's Director, "For Carrefour, (the) Russian retail market has outstanding long-term potential. Despite the crisis, we are not going to change our long-term vision of this country. With Brazil, India, and China, Russia is one of the priorities in the long-term expansion of Carrefour."[30] At that time, he also announced that in a few months' time, Carrefour would come out with its elaborate expansion strategy for Russia.

By the time the second store was opened, Carrefour had already announced its plans to open a third store in Lipetsk and had also entered into a lease agreement to open its fourth store at River Mall in Moscow. According to the analysts, Carrefour chose these locations because the major locations such as Moscow and St. Petersburg were stagnating and Krasnodar and Lipetsk were some of the regions that were experiencing rapid growth.

.... AND PULLS OUT

In September 2009, a report in *Le Monde*[31] mentioned that Carrefour was under pressure from top shareholders to pull out of emerging markets. Carrefour, on its part, denied the report. According to a Reuters report, "French retailer Carrefour is seriously considering exiting Latin America, one of its most lucrative markets, under pressure from top shareholders, *Le Monde* newspaper reported.... But the board of the world's second-biggest retailer has rejected the idea of abandoning all emerging markets including Asia as this would give the impression the company was being broken up, the newspaper said."[32]

However, on October 15, 2009, Carrefour announced that it had decided to close down its Russian operations. The company cited inadequate growth and acquisition opportunities as the reasons for its exit. It did not reveal details of total investments in Russia and said that the losses due to the exit were not significant. Carrefour also said that there were no prospects of its being among the top three retailers in the country, as it had planned.

Carrefour also announced that the stores in Russia would continue to remain open till the company found a buyer for them, and that it would also open the third one as planned. This was done in order to cut the costs of exit and also to reduce the penalties that it could attract for severing the contracts with suppliers and landlords. Carrefour also looked around for a franchising partner to operate the stores and to develop the brand in the country.

Industry experts opined that it took retailers several years to establish themselves in new markets, especially emerging markets like Russia that had high growth potential. They were surprised that Carrefour did not stay long enough to test the market. According to them, four months was too short a time to gauge the potential of the market. They said that Carrefour's justification about lack of acquisition and poor sales targets appeared more like excuses. The exit also made analysts question Carrefour's commitment to countries with high potential but short-term difficulties and problems. According to Jaime Vazquez, an analyst at JPMorgan Chase & Co. in London, "Turning around the hypermarkets in a deflationary environment and with a weak price image is not going to be easy. Stores in emerging markets are the only ones doing well and offering good growth prospects," so selling them makes no sense other than making short-term financial gain.[33]

Analysts also said that Carrefour had spent more than three years studying and understanding the market and this time was sufficient to understand the difficulties associated with the retailing industry in Russia and also about the potential acquisition targets. As it knew the market well, it was not right for Carrefour to expect positive results within such a short span of time, that too when Russia was in the midst of recession, they said. The analysts said Carrefour could have halted expansion

[30] "Carrefour Says Looking at Acquisitions in Russia," www.ibtimes.com, September 10, 2009.

[31] *Le Monde* is a French newspaper.

[32] "Carrefour Mulls Exit from Latin America—Le Monde," http://uk.reuters.com, October 07, 2009.

[33] Ladka Bauerova, "Carrefour Replaces Head of French Superstores, Exits Russia," www.bloomberg.com, October 15, 2009.

and waited in the market for a few more years before taking a final decision on its operations in the country.

According to industry observers, Carrefour's failure to acquire Seventh Continent was the main reason for its exit. They said that without Seventh Continent, Carrefour did not find enough scope to grow in the country, though the market was highly lucrative. The retail industry in Russia was concentrated mainly around Moscow and St Petersburg, and in these locations, retailers like X5 and Auchan were firmly established and the markets were also oversaturated. With the retail space in limited supply, it was not possible to establish a significant presence in these markets without acquisitions.

(Refer to *Exhibit VI* for major retailers in Moscow and St Petersburg.)

In spite of its high growth potential, there were several obstacles which international retail companies had to face in the Russian retailing industry. A complicated legislative framework, bureaucracy, along with corruption hampered the operations of several companies in Russia. Analysts said red tape, poor economic conditions, etc. could have influenced Carrefour's decision to exit the market.

Carrefour was also caught up in bureaucratic hassles as its first store in Moscow could not get a license to sell alcohol, which cost it almost 15% of the stores' revenues. Legislation in

EXHIBIT VI   Major Retailers in Moscow and St. Petersburg (October 2009)

St. Petersburg			
Retailer	**Brand**	**Format**	**No. of Outlets**
X5 Retail Group	Perekriostok	Supermarket	21
	Pisterochka	Discounter	278
	Karusel	Hypermarket	16
Okay	Okay	Hypermarket	14
	Okay	Supermarket	13
Lenta	Lenta	Hypermarket	14
Dixy	Dixy	Discounter	84
Auchan	Auchan City	Hypermarket	2
Metro	Metro CC	Cash & Carry	3
Moscow			
Retailer	**Brand**	**Format**	**No. of Outlets**
X5 Retail Group	Perekriostok	Supermarket	76
	Pisterochka	Discounter	181
	Karusel	Hypermarket	10
Auchan	Auchan City	Hypermarket	9
Metro	Metro CC	Cash & Carry	11
Real	Real	Hypermarket	3
Alye Parusa	Alye Parusa	Supermarket	16
ABC of Taste	ABC of Taste	Supermarket	25
Sellgross	Sellgross	Cash & Carry	1
Spar	Spar	Supermarket	1
Seventh Continent	Nash Hypermarket	Hypermarket	4
	Seventh Continent	Corner Shop	30
	Seventh Continent	Supermarket	54
	Seventh Continent 5 Stars	Supermarket	31
Mosmart	Mosmart	Hypermarket	4
Stokmann	Stokmann	Hypermarket	4
Billa	Super	Supermarket	3
Paterson	Paterson	Supermarket	20

Source: www.bordbia.ie.

Russia that aimed at increasing the competition in the country[34] was also cited as one of the main reasons for Carrefour's plan to exit.

Due to volatile economic conditions in the Russian market, acquiring a Russian retailing company also proved to be a tough task for Carrefour. Although due to the global financial crisis[35] the share prices of Russian retailers were down—making them an ideal target for acquisition—the lack of credit to the retailers for carrying out the acquisitions and the high debt burden of the local retailers proved to be unattractive for Carrefour. The acquisitions were also priced high. For example, X5 with a share of 4% in the food retail market in Russia was valued at US$ 7 billion. According to Datamonitor, "Facing these challenges, Carrefour has probably made the right call in making an early withdrawal from the market. A dire macroeconomic environment and the strength of domestic discounters in the current climate make breaking into Russia organically a significant challenge. Furthermore, the difficulties in acquiring a local player and other market hindrances would have made Carrefour's quest to gain scale and leadership in the country a costly uphill struggle."[36]

There were also reports that the company was under pressure from key shareholders such as Colony Capital LLC[37] and Bernard Arnault,[38] a French investor and Chairman of LVMH, who insisted that Carrefour concentrate on its French operations and exit from the emerging markets including China and Latin America after its global sales dropped by 2.9% in the third quarter ending September 2009 to € 24 billion. Reports in *Le Monde* suggested that the top investors were insisting on Carrefour exiting China and Brazil too, in order to regain their investment, after Carrefour lost 30% of its market value between March 2007 and September 2009.

However, at the same time, other retailers in Russia were performing well. The X5 Retail Group reported that its profits had grown by 38% between January and September 2009, as compared to the corresponding period the previous year. The store count in 2009 was expected to increase by 25%. The net revenues of another leading retailer Magnit increased by 31% in the first nine months of 2009. As of September 2009, it had 2,981 stores in operation.

Many analysts opined that the withdrawal from Russia meant that Carrefour remained committed to its goal of attaining a leadership position in the markets in which it operated and exiting the countries where it did not find the opportunity to be among the top retailers in a span of few years.

Earlier, in 2005, Carrefour had exited from four countries, namely Japan, Mexico, the Czech Republic, and Slovakia, where it failed to make a mark, and decided to focus on Eastern Europe and Latin America. Analysts pointed out that as far as the Russian market was concerned, it had realized soon that there were not enough opportunities for it to become the top player in the country. According to Pierre Bouchut, Chief Financial Officer, Carrefour Group, "It is precisely because we are adopting a long-term stance that we are exiting from Russia."[39] Carrefour, however, maintained that it would remain committed to its expansion plans in other emerging markets where it already had a significant presence.

Case Questions

1. According to Thierry Garnier, member of the Carrefour Group Executive Committee, "We are confident that retail business in Russia has considerable long-term potential, and the market is strategically important for the development of our company." In light of this statement, what were the factors that led to Carrefour's sudden exit from the Russian retail market?

2. According to Jamie-Vazquez, analyst at JPMorgan Chase & Company in London, "Stores in emerging markets are the only ones doing well and offering good growth prospects, so selling them makes no sense other than making short-term financial gain." Do you agree with this statement? Take a stand and justify it.

3. Critically analyze the Russian retail market in light of Porter's five forces model. Do you think the market is lucrative enough to attract more foreign players? Explain.

Suggested Readings and References

1. "Carrefour to Approach from Regions," www.kommersant.com, November 09, 2006.

2. "Carrefour or Perekrestok—What will Russians Prefer?" www.freshplaza.com, January 11, 2007.

3. "Russia's Retail Revolution," www.managementtoday.co.uk, June 01, 2008.

4. "Carrefour Starts the Investment Programme in Krasnodar Region (South Russia)," www.carrefour.com, September 22, 2008.

5. Jess Halliday, "Russian Regions Present New Possibilities for Food Firms," www.foodnavigator.com, October 21, 2008.

6. "Carrefour to Open at Least Three Russian Stores in 2009," www.reuters.com, April 15, 2009.

7. Javier Espinoza, "Carrefour Flirts with Seventh Continent," www.forbes.com, April 20, 2009.

---

[34] The new retail trade law in Russia was passed in December 2009. According to the law, the government can impose price ceilings on specific products (whose prices have grown by 30% in a span of 30 days) for a specific time frame (not more than 90 days). Limitations were set on bonuses suppliers could pay to the retailers to stock their products, payment time frames within which retailer had to pay suppliers, etc. The Russian government aimed to increase the competition in the retail sector by passing the law.

[35] The global financial crisis refers to the credit, banking, trade, and currency crisis that emerged in 2007–2008. This was the result of the failure of several U.S.-based investment companies, mortgage companies, and insurance companies due to the sub-prime crisis in the country. The sub-prime crisis was the result of mortgage delinquencies and foreclosures, which had an impact on banks and markets around the world.

[36] "Carrefour: Abandoning Russia," Datamonitor, October 19, 2009.

[37] Colony Capital LLC is an investment firm based in the U.S.

[38] Bernard Arnault is the founder, Chairman and CEO of LVMH Moët Hennessy Louis Vuitton SA (LVMH), which consists of over fifty luxury brands such as Louis Vuitton, Mercier, TAG Heuer, Donna Karan, Dior, and Fendi. He was the 15th richest person in the world as of 2009 according to *Forbes*.

[39] "Carrefour to Exit Russia, Hit by Challenging Markets," www.reuters.com, October 15, 2009.

8. "Carrefour Looks East to Russia," *Checkout*, April 2009.

9. Javier Espinoza, "Carrefour Wants a Piece of Russia," www.forbes.com, May 05, 2009.

10. Javier Espinoza, "Carrefour May Be Moving to Russia Soon," www.forbes.com, May 05, 2009.

11. Lionel Laurent, "Carrefour's Mission to Moscow," May 29, 2009.

12. "Carrefour Starts Business Operations in Russia and Moves Forward with its International Expansion," Press Release, Groupe Carrefour, June 18, 2009.

13. Javier Espionoza, "Carrefour May Be Stumbling with Russian Dreams," www.forbes.com, June 18, 2009.

14. "Carrefour Opens First Russian Store," www .russianamericanchamber.com, June 19, 2009.

15. "Carrefour Opens up in Moscow for the Longer Term," http://rt.com, June 19, 2009.

16. Maria Antonova, "Carrefour Opens First Russian Store," www.straightstocks.com, June 19 2009.

17. "Carrefour Says Looking at Acquisitions in Russia," www.ibtimes.com, September 10, 2009.

18. "Carrefour Mulls Exit from Latin America—Le Monde," http://uk.reuters.com, October 07, 2009.

19. "Carrefour Says Looking at Acquisitions in Russia," www.reuters.com, October 09, 2009.

20. "French Hypermarket Chain Carrefour Leaves Russian Market," http://en.rian.ru, October 15, 2009.

21. Ladka Bauerova, "Carrefour Replaces Head of French Superstores, Exits Russia," www.bloomberg.com, October 15, 2009.

22. "Carrefour to Exit Russia, Hit by Challenging Markets," www.reuters.com, October 15, 2009.

23. Scheherazade Daneshkhu, Jonathan Birchill, "Carrefour Beats Hasty Russian Retreat," www.ft.com, October 15, 2009.

24. "French Hypermarket Chain Carrefour Leaves Russian Market," http://en.rian.ru, October 15, 2009.

25. Lionel Laurent, Robin Paxton, "Carrefour to Exit Russia, Hit by Challenging Markets," www.reuters.com, October 15, 2009.

26. Ladka Bauerova, "Carrefour Replaces Head of French Superstores, Exits Russia," www.bloomberg.com, October 15, 2009.

27. Matthew Saltmarsh, Andrew E. Kramer, "French Retailer to Close Its Russia Stores," www.nytimes.com, October 16, 2009.

28. "Carrefour to Quit Russia," http://store.businessmonitor .com, October 16, 2009.

29. "Carrefour Reports Challenging Q3, Exits Russia," www .igd.com, October 16, 2009.

30. "Carrefour Abandons Russia," www.fis.com, October 16, 2009.

31. "Carrefour to Quit Russia," ehttp://store.businessmonitor .com, October 16, 2009.

32. "Retail Market Fight too Tough for Carrefour," http:// rt.com, October 16, 2009.

33. "Carrefour to Exit Russia, Hit by Challenging Markets," www.reuters.com, October 16, 2009.

34. Jennifer Creevy, "Carrefour to Pull out of Russia," www .retail-week.com, October 16, 2009.

35. "Retail Market Fight too Tough for Carrefour," http:// rt.com, October 17, 2009.

36. "Carrefour: Abandoning Russia," Datamonitor, October 19, 2009.

37. "Carrefour Turns its Back on Russia's Promise—Fast," www.worldfinance.com, October 19, 2009.

38. "Carrefour to Keep Operating in Russia Until Selloff Complete, http://en.rian.ru, October 19, 2009.

39. Maria Antonova, Carrefour to Leave Russia 4 Months af- ter Opening," *The St. Petersburg Times*, October 20, 2009.

40. Jason Bush, "Russia's Foreign Investment Revival?" www.forbes.com, October 20, 2009.

41. Greg Hodge, "Carrefour's Retreat from Russia a Mysterious Move," www.retail-week.com, October 23, 2009.

42. "Carrefour Abandons Russian Food Retail Market," www .stat-usa.gov, November 03, 2009.

43. Tim Gosling, "Russian Supermarket Chains—Seats Reserved at the Top Table," http://businessneweurope.eu, November 3, 2009.

44. *Deloitte Global Powers of Retailing*, 2009.

45. Carrefour Annual Reports, 2005–2009.

46. www.carrefour.com.

Case 7 *Walmart's Expansion in Africa: A New Exploration Strategy*

–Prof. S. Bhaskaran

Walmart, a leading U.S. retail giant, had gained international experience through joint ventures and subsidiaries in many countries like Mexico, Canada, Argentina, and China. It had been successful in attracting the consumers on a large scale through its policy of "Every Day Low Price" (EDLP), customer centric approach, and an encouragement given to customers to return the purchased items in case of any defect in the products. The customers were also enticed to purchase large quantities because of the low pricing when compared with the competitors. Walmart also offered a wide range of products and groceries that was another attraction to the customers to shop under a single roof. Through their international operations in Japan and Germany, Walmart had also learnt lessons on different consumer behavior. While Japanese consumers felt that a low price was indicative of low quality and did not patronise Walmart stores much, in Germany governmental restrictions on low price strategies favoured the local retailers leading to a disfavor of Walmart by the consumers. The South American experience and Chinese experience for Walmart had boosted the international revenue to a comfortable level due to the policy of EDLP and also adapting to local cultures, employing local people, and procuring major stocks locally. In spite of failures in some of the countries, Walmart had a large-scale presence in 15 countries and projected revenue of $405 billion for 2010. In the backdrop of this successful journey, Walmart had planned to enter the African continent, where many of the countries had shown reasonably good economic growth and increased levels of consumption, through acquisition of Massmart, a retail giant in South Africa having 288 stores. This joint venture would provide opportunities to Walmart to expand its footprint in African countries, which were expected to register a growth of over 5% in their GDP. The case study analyses the opportunities and challenges that await Walmart in its African venture.

Pedagogical Objectives

The case study helps to understand and analyse:

- Walmart's global growth strategies
- Massmart growth in African countries
- Walmart acquisition strategy of Massmart
- Opportunities and challenges for Walmart in African continent.

CASE STUDY

"The more we learn about South Africa and the surrounding countries the more we are convinced that this is an important region with attractive growth characteristics."[1]

–Doug McMillon,
Wal-Mart International President and CEO

Walmart, which initially started its retail operation in the U.S. in 1962,[2] grew phenomenally as a giant retailer in the U.S. offering consumers products and services on the "Every Day Low Price" theme. The customer-centric approach of Walmart had kept the consumer patronage growing over the years. This had encouraged Walmart to enter into the neighbouring countries like Mexico, Argentina, and Canada through joint ventures and subsidiaries. The American style of retail management replicated in these countries had proved to be successful. Encouraged by this trend Walmart entered into Germany, UK, and Japan. The Japan and German markets proved to be tough due to consumers' different behaviour on low price strategy and also the governmental regulation on Every Day Low Price. Against this background Walmart entered into a joint venture in China that was fast growing, and the strategy of local management and local sourcing had proved to be successful. More than 25% of the Walmart's revenue was contributed through its international operations.[3] While the U.S. market was nearing saturation, Walmart had decided to venture into the African continent with the acquisition of South African retail giant Massmart,[4] which had over 20 years of experience. The African economy is poised for a growth rate of over 5% and many of the countries are rich with agricultural and mineral resources.[5] The entry of Walmart through a joint venture in Africa will enable greater opportunities for its growth in the African continent. The case study analyses the opportunities and challenges that Walmart may have to face to establish their footprint in Africa.

[1] Bryson Donna and Chapman Michelle, "Wal-Mart to buy 51 percent of South Africa company," http://news.yahoo.com/s/ap/20101129/ap_on_bi_ge/af_wal_mart_massmart/print, November 29, 2010.

[2] "Our Mission," http://bus.cba.utulsa.edu/sif/annualreports/2001SIFAnnualReport.doc, January 23, 2001.

[3] "Walmart's Next Continent: Africa", http://news.findtarget.com/business/wal-marts_next_continent_africa/, December 1, 2010.

[4] Is a South African–based globally competitive regional management group, invested in a portfolio of differentiated, complementary, focused wholesale and retail formats, each reliant on high volumes and operational excellence as the foundation of price leadership, in the distribution of mainly branded consumer goods for cash.

[5] "African Economic Outlook 2010 forecasts uneven economic growth for Africa for the next two years," http://www.pnowb.org/admindb/docs/African%20Economic%20Outlook%202010%20(2).pdf, May 27, 2010.

EXHIBIT I Walmart's Retail Store Formats (2010)

Discount Stores

Offers quality and value-priced general merchandise including apparels, electronics, toys, sporting goods, hardware, house wares, and pet supplies. Around 700 discount stores were operated across U.S. and each store employed 225 people.

Supercenters

One-stop family shop with grocery and general merchandise. Each store had more than 350 employees and there were more than 2,890 shops in the U.S.

Neighborhood Markets

Goods such as groceries, pharmaceuticals, and general merchandise were offered. Around 150 stores were set up and each had 95 employees.

Marketside

Small community pilot grocery stores specializing in fresh ingredients and delicious meals at great prices.

Source: Compiled from "Walmart," http://walmartstores.com/AboutUs/7606.aspx

WALMART'S GROWTH IN THE INTERNATIONAL MARKET

Walmart, the retail giant, had started its operations in 1962 with a view to change the retail business profile. Sam Walton (Walton), the founder of Walmart, decided to capitalise on the retail business as there were only a few discount shops located in the urban areas. Walmart opened its first discount store in Rogers, Arkansas, U.S. Walmart's business was successful and in a span of five years (1967) Walmart operated 24 stores and had net sales of $12.6 million.[6] Walton's unique strategies drove Walmart to success. Walmart's key focus was customer satisfaction and relied on three principles—respect for the individual, service to customers, and to strive for excellence.[7] As employees had a major role in customer satisfaction, Walton devised strategies to create a healthy working environment and satisfy the workers. Walton referred to employees as associates and had introduced a profit sharing plan, stock options, and store discounts to motivate the workers. In addition, he had also conducted weekly meetings where the employees could share their innovative ideas and grievances, if any.[8] Walton educated his associates about the importance of customer satisfaction and practiced customer-centric culture. To facilitate the customers and provide a better shopping experience at Walmart stores, unique strategies such as the Sundown rule[9] and the 10 Foot rule[10] were implemented. As a result of such strategies customer requests and complaints were attended in a day.

As a part of its customer centric initiatives, Walmart had devised a unique pricing strategy with an aim to offer customers their daily needs at the lowest price possible. "The Every Day Low Price" (EDLP) strategy provided the customers the lowest price for all products on all days. In addition Walmart had also implemented "Special Buy" and "Roll Back" policies. Through the Special Buy policy, customers were offered a quantity discount and the Roll Back policy offered the lowest price whenever Walmart was able to reduce the cost of purchase. Walmart had procured the goods directly from the manufacturers, eliminating middlemen and thereby reduced the costs. Walmart believed in low profit margin and high sales volume.[11] Over the years, Walmart streamlined their logistics and distribution system through technologies such as Electronic Data Interchange[12] and Satellite Communication System during the 1980s. The company could track the movement of stocks and the major suppliers were connected and provided with inventory and sales data. This facilitated replenishment of stock whenever needed and also reduced the operational costs.[13]

Walmart had operated different retail store formats—Discount Stores, Supercenters, Neighborhood Markets, and Marketside to meet the varied needs of its customers[14] (*Exhibit I.*) Sam's club was another kind of store operated by Walmart. This was a member-only warehouse club that sold groceries and general merchandise in large quantities to registered members.[15] To enhance customer service further, Walmart

---

[6] "Our Mission," op.cit.

[7] "Case Study: Wal-Mart's Competitive Advantage," http://www.mbaknol.com/management-case-studies/case-study-wal-mart%E2%80%99s-competitive-advantage/

[8] Galiano Amanda, "Sam Walton & Wal-Mart," http://littlerock.about.com/cs/homeliving/a/aasamwalton.htm

[9] Answer requests by the close of business on the day it was received by them.

[10] Sam Walton encouraged associates (employees) to take the pledge that when they see a customer within 10 feet, they would look into their eye, greet them, and ask them what they want.

[11] John, D., et al., "Wal-Mart's 'Think Global, Act Local': Can 'Americanisation' Have Its Way?," *IBS Research Center,* 2008 (Ref. No: 308-215-1).

[12] Is the structured transmission of data between organisations by electronic means. It is used to transfer electronic documents or business data from one computer system to another computer system, i.e., from one trading partner to another trading partner without human intervention.

[13] "Wal-Mart's 'Think Global, Act Local': Can 'Americanisation' Have Its Way?" op.cit.

[14] "Walmart," http://walmartstores.com/AboutUs/7606.aspx

[15] "Sam's Club," http://walmartstores.com/AboutUs/7605.aspx

had set up information kiosks to provide the details and location of various products in the stores. With the increased use of the Internet during the 90s, Walmart launched their website, which provided customers information about the products available in the stores.[16]

Subsequent to the economic recession in the U.S. during the early 90s and with an aim to expand their business, Walmart had ventured into international markets. As an initial step, Walmart concentrated on neighbouring countries like Mexico, Canada, Brazil, and Argentina during the 90s. Based on the market conditions, Walmart entered the international markets through joint venture, acquisition, or as a subsidiary company.[17] Mexico was the first international market for Walmart. It entered the market in 1991 through a joint venture with Grupo Cifra SA de CV (Cifra)[18] and was called Wal-Mart de Mexico SAB de CS (Walmex). After a span of six years with a clear understanding of Mexico's retail market, Walmart acquired a majority stake in Cifra and consolidated its position. Walmex soon promoted its retail activities in Mexico. Initially it had concentrated in the urban areas. Realising the opportunities in suburban areas, Walmex expanded its business in the interior. Subsequently, by the end of the decade (90s), Walmart implemented its low price model in Mexico. Though it faced initial hurdles from the local purchasers, Walmex was successful to attract and retain its customers through its daily discount strategy. Similar to the U.S., Walmex had also operated in different retail formats catering to different class of customers and varied needs. Over the years, Walmex stores were into retailing of apparel, accessories, footwear, pharmaceuticals, groceries, and food products. Walmex offered all kinds of products that had a demand in Mexico. For example, it had also dealt with imported products other than regular goods to meet the needs of elite customers. In addition Walmex was into the restaurant and the banking business (was started in 2007) in Mexico. Though the banking business was not successful for Walmart in the U.S., it turned out to be successful in Mexico as their banking industry was dominated by international banks, which charged high rates of interest and demanded high minimum balances.[19] In October 2010, Walmex had operated 1,578 units across Mexico.[20]

Similar to the Mexico venture, Walmart had expanded its business in Canada. It entered into the Canadian market by acquiring the popular retail chain Woolco[21] in 1994. Woolco stores were in financial crunches and had high operating costs. Walmart with its expertise restructured the retail stores in Canada and also implemented its popular EDLP strategy targeting low-income groups. As the Mexico, U.S., and Canadian markets were similar, Walmart's business expansion in Canada turned to be successful. Over the years it had also set up warehouse clubs similar to the U.S. Walmart further expanded its business horizon to Brazil and Argentina in 1995. Whereas Walmart entered Brazil through a joint venture with local retailer Lojas Americana,[22] in Argentina it had operated as a wholly owned subsidiary. The business model practiced in the U.S. proved to be successful in other American countries for Walmart.[23]

With the emerging opportunities in the Asian countries, Walmart ventured into this region in 1996. China was the first Asian market tapped by the retail giant. It had partnered with a Chinese retailer to set up shops in the Chinese market. Walmart had faced several hurdles before it could implement its U.S.-style business strategies. Prior to 1999, the Chinese government restricted the number of stores to be operated by foreign retailers. Apart from this change in culture, language was another problem for Walmart to attract customers. Majority of the people in China were in low-income groups who preferred to shop in the neighborhood areas. Walmart had to study the Chinese market and consumer behavior and tune their business strategies accordingly. Local players were tough competitors for Walmart in China. To attract consumers, Walmart had to resort to changes in leadership (from American to Chinese), extend their time frame for returning goods, and also had to sell fresh foods and a few live animals like snake and frog. Though localised strategies were implemented, Walmart faced stiff competition from the "Du Sha," a Chinese retailer, Metro[24] from Germany, and Carrefour[25] from France. Hence Walmart acquired a 35% stake in Bounteous Company Ltd (BCL), a retailer who operated hypermarket chains in China, to gain a strong foothold in China.[26]

While Walmart had been experimenting with new strategies to gain a substantial share in the overseas market, it continued with new business expansions. During the late 90s Walmart had moved to UK, Germany and Korea to set up operations and gain market. Though Walmart's low price model was well received by UK, it was a major failure in Korea and Germany. Worldwide, Walmart had tried to build its business upon its low pricing strategy and setting up shops in the outskirts. Misfortune struck Walmart in Germany as the government restricted retailers

[16] "Wal-Mart's 'Think Global, Act Local': Can 'Americanisation' Have Its Way?" op.cit.

[17] John Rajakumari Doris, "Bharti Wal-Mart Tie-up: Opportunities and Challenges," http://www.ibscdc.org/Case_Studies/Strategy/Market%20Entry%20Strategies/MES0069C.htm, 2007.

[18] Is a holding company that, through its subsidiaries, constitutes one of the largest retailers in Mexico. The company's Tiendas Gigante, Bodegas Gigante, and Super G chain stores sell both groceries—including Gigante's own line of private-label goods—and general merchandise.

[19] "Wal-Mart's 'Think Global, Act Local': Can 'Americanisation' Have Its Way?," op.cit.

[20] "Mexico," http://walmartstores.com/AboutUs/277.aspx

[21] Was an American-based discount retail chain. It was founded in 1962 and was a full-line discount department store. At its peak, Woolco had hundreds of stores in the U.S., as well as in Canada and the United Kingdom. While the American stores were closed in 1982, the chain remained active in Canada until it was sold in 1994 to rival Wal-Mart.

[22] Is a Brazilian company's retail segment founded in 1929 in the city of Niterói, Rio de Janeiro, by Americans John Lee, Glen Matson, James Marshall, and Batson Borger.

[23] "Wal-Mart's 'Think Global, Act Local': Can 'Americanisation' Have Its Way?," op.cit.

[24] Is a diversified retail and wholesale/cash and carry group based in Düsseldorf, Germany. It has the largest market share in its home market, and is one of the most globalised retail and wholesale corporations.

[25] Is a French international hypermarket chain. Headquartered in Levallois-Perret, France, Carrefour is the largest hypermarket chain in the world in terms of size, the second largest retail group in the world in terms of revenue, and third largest in profit after Wal-Mart and Tesco.

[26] "Wal-Mart's 'Think Global, Act Local': Can 'Americanisation' Have Its Way?," op.cit.

selling products below cost on permanent basis. The Korean and German markets were filled with discounters and the people were not ready to encourage the American style of business. Customers felt it inconvenient to travel far and shop at Walmart stores. Moreover, the Western style of customer service was also not encouraged. As Walmart failed to understand the consumer behaviour and market trends, it had to withdraw from these markets due to huge losses in 2006. Walmart had also faced survival problems in Japan since its entry in 2002. The low-price strategy was not very attractive to the consumers and they linked it with low quality. In addition, Walmart faced problems in procuring goods at low cost due to local restrictions. The suppliers in Japan depended on the traditional distribution system 'keiretsu', where foreign players were not allowed to become members. Goods were sold at high prices for the nonmembers. Store format was another issue for Walmart. The Japanese wished to shop in luxurious stores with ample parking lots. Walmart's warehouse stores were not attractive for the customers.[27]

With varied experiences in the overseas markets, Walmart had planned to enter the Indian market and had joint ventured with Bharti Group in 2007. However, due to the restriction on foreign investment in multi-brand retailing, Walmart had opened up cash and carry stores in 2009. Growth in India was slow as Walmart was not able to sell directly to the consumers. In spite of failure and slow progress in some markets, Walmart's international operations were expected to generate profit of around $14 billion with a sales revenue of $405 billion in 2010. It had more than 8,500 outlets under 55 different names in 15 countries.[28]

MASSMART SOUTH AFRICAN OPERATIONS

Massmart, a leading retailer of general merchandise, was started in 1990 to carry on wholesale and retail distribution of branded consumer goods in South Africa for cash. The group had successfully carried on their business for a decade and in 2000 was listed in the Johannesburg Stock Exchange[29] (JSE).[30] Over the years, with its well defined business model and strategies, the group operated nine wholesale and retail chains in 14 countries in the African continent.[31] The four core operating groups of Massmart were Massdiscounters, Masswarehouse, Massbuild, and Masscash. Massdiscounter operated as a general merchandise discounter, Masswarehouse dealt with warehouse clubs, Massbuild was concerned with home improvement equipment and building material supplies, and the Masscash segment operated as a food wholesaler.[32] The group's business

model revolved around high volume, low margin, low-cost distribution of branded consumer goods and successfully held the third position in the distribution of consumer goods in Africa[33]. Through its business model, Massmart had empowered its divisions to make trading decisions based on their operating needs. However, it was ensured that those decisions were within the framework set by the group. Decentralised decision-making had contributed for business growth, and in the meantime, the group's core policy was also implemented throughout their network.[34]

To extend its top class customer service, Massmart had constantly focused on improving their service through enhanced technology. The company had operated around 288 stores across Africa and garnered net sales of R[35] 47451 million in 2010[36] (*Exhibit II*). Key drivers of sales were increased disposable income, consumer confidence, opening up of new stores, and increased product availability. The South African operations accounted for 92% of the total sales. Massmart believed strongly that its low-price strategy was crucial for its business. Hence it focused on lowering its operating costs. In a span of three years (2013), the company had planned to improve their supply chain and launch several private brands. It had also planned to add format stores and expand their product range in pharmacy, clothing, and furniture. Massmart strongly believed that continued investment would enhance their business growth over the years.[37]

WALMART ACQUISITION OF MASSMART

The world's largest corporation, Walmart had been gaining ground in the overseas market in the early 21st century. Walmart had experienced slow sales in the U.S. in 2009. Walmart's U.S. sales in 2010 were $258 billion, just 1.1% higher than the previous year.[38] To keep its overall sales up and have fresh growth, Walmart had turned its focus to international business expansion. In the recent years, Walmart's investment in the BRIC nations, a few countries in Latin America, and Mexico had started to generate reasonable profit though at a slow pace. But Walmart had failed in Germany and Korea due to governmental policies and different consumer behavior. It had gained a foothold in China and Brazil. Walmart's spokesman Kevin Gardner had said that Walmart's international operations had accounted for 25% of their total revenue.[39] Developing

[27] "Wal-Mart's 'Think Global, Act Local': Can 'Americanisation' Have Its Way?" op.cit.

[28] "The Beast goes on Safari," http://www.economist.com/node/17150234?story_id=17150234, September 30, 2010.

[29] Is the largest stock exchange in Africa. It is situated at the corner of Maude Street and Gwen Lane in Sandton, Johannesburg, South Africa.

[30] "Massmart," http://www.tradeintelligence.co.za/TradeProfiles/Massmart.aspx

[31] "Massmart At a Glance," http://www.massmart.co.za/invest_profile/financial_results/2010/massmart_ar2010/downloads/massmart_at_a_glance.pdf, 2010.

[32] "Massmart Holdings Ltd," http://www.corporateinformation.com/Company-Snapshot.aspx?cusip=C710BW150

[33] "Overview," http://www.massmart.co.za/corp_profile/corp_overview.asp

[34] "Massmart At a Glance," op.cit.

[35] The rand (sign: R; code: ZAR) is the currency of South Africa. It takes its name from the Witwatersrand (*White-watersridge* in English), the ridge upon which Johannesburg is built and where most of South Africa's gold deposits were found. The rand has the symbol "R" and is subdivided into 100 *cents*, symbol "c."

[36] "Massmart At a Glance," op.cit.

[37] "Dedicated to Value Massmart Reviewed Results for the 52 weeks to 27 June 2010: Presentation to Investors, Analysts and Media," http://www.massmart.co.za/invest_profile/presentations/aug10_audited/pdf/massmart_aug2010_audited.pdf, August 2010.

[38] "Walmart 2010 Annual Report," http://cdn.walmartstores.com/sites/AnnualReport/2010/PDF/WMT_2010AR_FINAL.pdf, January 2010.

[39] "Walmart's Next Continent: Africa," op.cit.

EXHIBIT II   **Massmart Geographical Presence**

Chain	South Africa	International	Total
Game	79	12	91
DionWired	11	—	11
Makro	13	—	13
Builders Warehouse	24	—	24
Builders Trade Depot	31	—	31
Builders Express	21	—	21
CBW	78	13	91
Jumbo	6	—	6
Total	**263**	**25**	**288**

Source: "Massmart At a Glance," http://www.massmart.co.za/invest_profile/financial_results/2010/ massmart_ar2010/downloads/massmart_at_a_glance.pdf, 2010.

economies like China proved to be a right option for Walmart's business model. Hence the retailer had decided to capitalise on China's strategy and had planned for the African venture.[40]

Africa had gained attraction of the leading businesses with its strong economic growth in the recent years. McKinsey & Co[41] had revealed in a report that the African population had exceeded 1 billion in 2009 and had an average growth of 4.8% during 2000–08.[42] The middle income group was also expanding, which in turn increased the purchasing power there by spurring the demand for food and other consumer products.[43] In addition, China had been investing heavily upon African minerals and infrastructure projects, facilitating further economic growth.[44] While all nations worldwide suffered from the economic crisis in 2009, Africa had survived and progressed during the crisis. It was also expected to report 4.3% economic growth in 2010.[45] Walmart, the retail behemoth, who was keen on further overseas expansion, had corned the African continent to utilise the emerging opportunities there.

Walmart had chosen Massmart, another retail giant in Africa, as a route to enter the African continent. Initially there was a speculation that Walmart would fix a deal with Shoprite,[46] another African retailer, for their African venture. However, in 2010 Walmart had revealed its decision about taking up

Massmart for a consideration of around $4 billion. Massmart had 263 stores in South Africa and 25 stores in other African countries[47] and reported net sales of $6.7 billion in 2010.[48] Hence acquisition of Massmart will provide Walmart access to sub-Saharan countries where there was lot of scope for business expansion. Craig Johnson, the President of a retail consultancy called Customer Growth Partners[49] opined that, "If any retailer knows how to market products en masse to a lower income international consumer (Africa), Walmart is suited to that".[50] While Walmart's deal with Massmart was a road towards expansion, labour unions in Africa feared the loss of rights and job. They feared that the American retailer would not respect the African labour unions. Walmart had said that it would give due respect to the labour unions and existing contracts. Shareholders were also concerned about the listing of Massmart in the JSE.[51] Finally, Massmart and Walmart had finalised the deal for $2.32 billion for a 51% stake in Massmart. Such a deal had not impacted the shareholders and the labour unions. However, Walmart could also gain access to the African retail market through this deal as planned. Hence this decision had pleased all the parties concerned—Massmart shareholders, Walmart, African government, and labour unions.[52] Paul Ausick had specified in his article titled "Wal-Mart Takes Its Chances in South Africa" that, "The company's success in China may, in fact, be the impetus for Wal-Mart's move into

[40] Duff Mike, "Walmart Moves into South Africa, but It Won't Be Easy," http://www.bnet.com/blog/retail-business/walmartmoves-into-south-africa-but-it-won-8217t-be-easy/11047, September 28, 2010.

[41] Is a global management consulting firm that focuses on solving issues of concern to senior management. McKinsey serves as an adviser to the world's leading businesses, governments, and institutions.

[42] Wild Franz, "Africa's 1 Billion Consumers Draw Giant Walmart," http:// www.bloomberg.com/news/2010-10-20/africa-s-1-billion-consumers-getting-richer-can-t-be-ignored-by-wal-mart.html, October 21, 2010.

[43] "Walmart Moves into South Africa, but It Won't Be Easy," op.cit.

[44] "Africa's 1 Billion Consumers Draw Giant Walmart," op.cit.

[45] "The Beast goes on Safari," op.cit.

[46] Is one of the leaders in South African food retailing and is, according to independent market research, the brand of choice of the highest percentage of South Africans consumers. Since starting out as a small chain of supermarkets in 1979, the Shoprite brand gained valuable experience from selling to the emerging market.

[47] "Walmart's Next Continent: Africa," op.cit.

[48] Struck Heather, "Wal-Mart Eyes Growth In Africa," http://www.forbes.com/ fdc/welcome_mjx.shtml, September 27, 2010.

[49] Offers actionable research and strategy to Fortune 500 consumer and service companies in accelerating topline growth, building customer loyalty, and increasing marketing productivity. It provides strategic counsel to investors and developers looking to maximise returns in the Retail and other Consumer service sectors.

[50] "Walmart's Next Continent: Africa," op. cit.

[51] Bryson Donna, et al., "Wal-Mart to buy 51 percent of South Africa company," http://news.yahoo.com/s/ap/20101129/ap_on_bi_ge/af_wal_mart_massmart, November 29, 2010.

[52] "Wal-Mart Takes Its Chances in South Africa (WMT)," http://247wallst .com/2010/11/29/wal-mart-takes-its-chances-in-south-africa-wmt/#ixzz171G8fgWL, November 29, 2010.

Africa. China and the African nations have a lot in common in terms of the experience consumers in these countries have with retail stores".[53]

OPPORTUNITIES AND CHALLENGES

An African analyst of Rand Merchant Bank[54], Celeste Fauconnier had opined that, "It will be to their own detriment if companies ignore Africa. We are seeing massive growth in the population, an increasing middle class and people having more access to money".[55] Mckinsey had reported that, due to economic and population growth, consumer spending increased at 16% during 2005–08, International Monetary Fund[56] had estimated sub-Saharan Africa's economy would expand at 5.5% in 2011. Massive economic growth provided wide opportunities to the retailers as a result of which African retailers have planned for expansion. While Shoprite had been expanding internationally since 1995, other retailers such as Pick n Pay[57] and Woolworths Holdings Ltd.[58] have announced plans for expansion in 2010. People in Africa also welcomed the opening up of big retail stores in their neighbourhood. Anita Guambe, a 45-year-old housewife in Mozambique[59] had said that, "The entry of big chains is welcome because most of their products are of high quality and they are well packaged"[60]. In such a scenario, Walmart's entry into the African market would enhance their business and revenue.

Walmart's success would depend upon the lessons learned from its overseas business. Massmart had focused upon low price and efficient operations. This would be well-suited for Walmart's business model. Massmart technical expertise would favour Walmart to gain a sustainable market in the African continent. In Mexico, Walmart succeeded better than in other markets as it had utilised local managers for their operations, which facilitated in managing the customers and the staff in the retail chain. Hence a similar strategy in Africa would be successful for Walmart because the African continent comprises different countries that have varied rules and issues. Massmart had spread across the African countries and such experience would facilitate retail chain management in Africa.[61] Nigeria, an African country, was an oil-based economy where the purchasing power of the people had increased to $20 billion in 2007

($1000 – $5000 in 2000). Massmart had planned to increase its outlets to 20 from 1 in a span of two years (2012). Such expansion plans would now (after acquisition) help Walmart's revenue growth.[62]

Though the African venture would provide a lot of opportunities for Walmart's growth in terms of sourcing and maintaining continuous supply chain management, it would not be very easy from the management perspective. In the world's poorest region, the retail giant would face cultural and infrastructural barriers. The countries have very poor legal systems and weak security. As the continent was filled with different cultures, rules, and regulations, Walmart expansion might not be too fast. Jeanine van Zyl, retail analyst for Old Mutual Investment Group[63] had opined that, "Perhaps they will fail if they try and do it too fast. You have to step away from markets that are not ready to be entered. The process can't be rushed".[64] Many analysts doubt whether Walmart would benefit from this deal as expected. However, they had also expressed that if Walmart could succeed in Africa, then it would have a bright future ahead.[65] According to Joel Makower, Executive Editor of GreenBiz.com,[66] "What makes Walmart interesting is its influence, both upstream with its 60,000-plus suppliers, and downstream to its 300 million or so consumers. They can make a big difference. If they can succeed as a business along the way, that's terrific, but they're a long way from that".[67] It needs to be seen whether Walmart could cash upon its low-price business model in a business environment filled with opportunities and challenges.

Analysis Questions

1. Detail the growth of Walmart and its international experience.

2. Describe the growth strategies of Massmart in the African continent.

3. Detail Walmart's acquisition of Massmart and the expected strategic advantages.

4. Analyse the challenges Walmart will have to face in the African continent.

5. What happened to Walmart's operations after taking a 51% share in Massmart in 2011?

[53] Ibid.

[54] Is a diversified financial services brand encompassing investment banking, fund management, private wealth management, and advisory services.

[55] "Africa's 1 Billion Consumers Draw Giant Walmart," op.cit.

[56] Is the intergovernmental organization that oversees the global financial system by following the macroeconomic policies of its member countries, in particular those with an impact on the exchange rate and the balance of payments.

[57] Is one of Africa's largest and most consistently successful retailers of food, general merchandise, and clothing.

[58] Is one of the top 100 companies listed on the JSE and, as a leading South African company, is committed to growth through responsible retail.

[59] Is a country in southeastern Africa bordered by the Indian Ocean to the east, Tanzania to the north, Malawi and Zambia to the northwest, Zimbabwe to the west, and Swaziland and South Africa to the southwest.

[60] "Africa's 1 Billion Consumers Draw Giant Walmart," op.cit.

[61] Lal Rajiv, "Why Wal-Mart Went Shopping in Africa," http://www.hbs.edu/news/item.html?id=2010-10-04, September 28, 2010.

[62] "Africa's 1 Billion Consumers Draw Giant Walmart," op.cit.

[63] Is the largest investment manager in South Africa based on size of assets.

[64] "Africa's 1 Billion Consumers Draw Giant Walmart," op.cit.

[65] Bradley Luanne, "Walmart to Invade Africa," http://ecosalon.com/massmart-to-invade-africa/, October 1, 2010.

[66] Is the leading source for news, opinion, best practices, and other resources on the greening of mainstream business. Launched in 2000, its mission is to provide clear, concise, accurate, and balanced information, resources, and learning opportunities to help companies of all sizes and sectors integrate environmental responsibility into their operations in a manner that supports profitable business practices.

[67] "Walmart to Invade Africa," op.cit.

Case 8 *Evaluating the Chrysler-Fiat Auto Alliance in 2012*

Syed Tariq Anwar, DBA

"The country that gave us Sophia Loren and Leonardo da Vinci also gave us the century-old Fiat. The group's cars range from models like the popular Fiat Nuova 500 to the Alfa Romeo, Ferrari (85% owned), and Maserati brands. Fiat holds a 53% stake in Chrysler, and has management control of the US carmaker."

Hoovers.com (2012).[1]

"Chrysler hopes its crisis remains in its rearview mirror. The company has engineered an automotive resurrection by choosing a back-to-basics alliance with Fiat; the collaboration gives Fiat a 53% stake in the US car company. Chrysler continues to manufacture its Chrysler brands, as well as Dodge, Jeep, and Ram vehicles; it will also produce smaller Chrysler-brand cars based on Fiat design and technology."

Hoovers.com (2012).[2]

THE CHRYSLER-FIAT TIE-UP

In today's global business, the majority of corporate marriages (alliances, mergers and acquisitions, JVs, etc.) encounter problems that emerge from operational and post-alliance integration hurdles and end up in failure. Unlike other corporate tie-ups, the Chrysler-Fiat alliance has survived since its 2009 inception and continues to enjoy a solid growth in its post-alliance integration. The above statements also testify to the alliance's synergies and stability that have taken place in the Chrysler Group (hereafter Chrysler) and Fiat Group Automobiles S.p.A. (hereafter Fiat). Chrysler manufactures the Chrysler brand, Jeep, Dodge, Ram, and SRT and other products and is headquartered in Auburn Hills, Michigan. Chrysler was founded as Chrysler Corporation in 1925. Fiat, on the other hand, sells a diverse range of brands that include Fiat, Alfa Romeo, Lancia, Fiat Professional, and the Maserati and Ferrari sport cars. Fiat first started manufacturing cars in Turin, Italy in 1899. As of 2012, the two auto companies have survived their financial exigencies and market-share problems. Of course the whole process forced the companies to go through tough restructuring measures and corporate changes that took place on both sides

of the Atlantic (see Table 1). Chrysler's alliance with Fiat initially provided the company a tangible lifeline when Fiat took 20 percent ownership in Chrysler.

In 2009, on the recommendation of the U.S. Treasury Department and under the leadership of Sergio Marchionne, CEO of Fiat, Chrysler filed for Chapter 11 in a New York court to initiate the bankruptcy proceedings. Business history reveals that Chrysler's financial problems and other business-related difficulties were the result of its de-merger with Germany's Daimler and massive losses. Chrysler's financial problems were also the result of weakened global markets and the 2008

TABLE 1 Selected Financial and Corporate Data of Chrysler and Fiat (2011)

	Chrysler	Fiat
Revenue	$55 billion	€35.88 billion*
Net income	$183 million	€179 million
Operating profit	$2 billion	€992 million
Total Assets	$35.44 billion	€73.44 billion
Stockholder equity	$ − 4.48 billion	€12.46 billion
U.S. market share	10.5 %	NA
Vehicles manufactured	2 million	2.09 million
Year founded	1925	1899
Founder	Walter Chrysler	Giovanni Agnelli
CEO	Sergio Marchionne	Sergio Marchionne
Owner	Fiat (58.5%)	NA
Type	Limited liability co.	Societá per azioni
Headquarters	Auburn, Michigan	Turin, Italy
Total Employees	51,623	137,800

Source: Value Line (various issues); *Wikipedia* (2012). Various sites, (http://en.wikipedia.org/wiki/Main_Page).
* Conversion into US dollars: $47.97 billion.

Written exclusively for this text by Professor Syed Tariq Anwar, West Texas A&M University. Used with permission. Copyright Syed Tariq Anwar 2012

*The material in this case is intended to be used as a basis for classroom/academic discussion rather than to illustrate either effective or ineffective handling of a managerial situation or business practices.

[1] Hoovers. (2012). *Fiat*, (http://www.hoovers.com/company/Fiat_SpA/crkkki-1-1njht4-1njfaq.html). Accessed on February 24, 2012.

[2] Hoovers. (2012). *Chrysler Group LLC*. (http://www.hoovers.com/company/Chrysler_Group_LLC/rfyyci-1-1njht4-1njfaq.html). Accessed on February 24, 2012.

FIGURE 1   Brand Platforms of Chrysler and Fiat (2012)

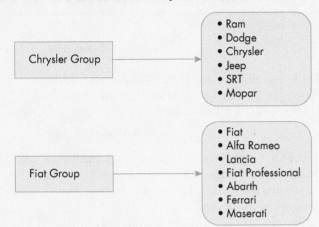

Source: Chrysler and Fiat Websites.

global financial crisis. Since 1998, Chrysler's ownership had gone through two hands. First the company was acquired by Daimler until 2007. Later Chrysler was bought by Cerberus Capital Management, a New York–based private equity firm. Cerberus could not reap tangible benefits from the deal because of the 2008 global financial crisis and cost problems in the industry. High oil prices and a recession in the U.S. were the last blows leading to Chrysler's demise.

In 2007, Chrysler again became homeless when Daimler sold its 80 percent stake in the company to Cerberus for $7.4 billion.[3] Interestingly, Daimler paid $36 billion to acquire Chrysler in 1998 and ended up losing $29 billion in the deal. DaimlerChrysler's de-merger was a major financial setback and a public relations blunder for the German Group. In the auto industry, the DaimlerChrysler breakup was called "Chrysler's private bailout." Although the DaimlerChrysler merger was hailed as a *"merger of equals,"* both companies encountered problems in the areas of post-merger integration and corporate cultures. Kirk Kerkorian, a billionaire from Las Vegas, was equally interested in buying Chrysler for $4.5 billion but Daimler sold Chrysler to Cerberus for a good price.[4]

CHANGING HISTORY AND CHRYSLER'S SURVIVAL IN NORTH AMERICA

Business history tells us that Chrysler was always the number three automaker in North America because of its quality problems and low market share. The company often remained behind GM and Ford in its quality rankings and visibility. In the area of consumer satisfaction, Chrysler had problems making satisfactory scores. Right from its inception, Chrysler

concentrated on those segments that required inexpensive autos by middle-income consumers. The company was further left behind in the auto industry with the arrival of Japanese competitors such as Toyota, Honda, and Nissan. No wonder Chrysler remained synonymous with its low-quality image that often brought problems. At the same time, because of its minivans and the Jeep brand, the company was a competitive player and witnessed a solid growth in North America.

Chrysler was founded in 1925 by Walter P. Chrysler, who had worked for Buick Motor Company. As stated earlier, Chrysler manufactured cars for the masses and particularly targeted the mainstream American consumer. Between 1941 and 1960, Chrysler introduced a variety of newer models and took credit for technological innovations in North America. As the third largest auto manufacturer, Chrysler always rated as one of the late movers in the industry. In the early eighties, the company was on the verge of bankruptcy but was rescued by the U.S. government. In the nineties, Chrysler vehicles started to get good ratings from analysts but continued to remain behind other manufacturers in quality and consumer satisfaction. When Daimler-Benz proposed the merger in January 1998, Chrysler's Board saw a major opportunity for future survival and access to new markets. In the next four months, both companies negotiated extensively and closed the deal in May 1998.

The next eight years witnessed many ups and downs for Chrysler because of the issues of post-merger problems, losses, and lay-offs. In 2007, DaimlerChrysler announced that Cerberus would acquire 80 percent of Chrysler for $7.4 billion. As Chrysler dealt with the 2008–2009 global recession and high oil prices, Cerberus kept on exploring the possibilities of either selling Chrysler or creating an alliance with GM, Nissan, Fiat, or Volkswagen. Early in 2009, Fiat turned out to be the key contender for Chrysler. In April 2009, Chrysler and Fiat announced their strategic alliance and agreed on a new ownership structure. In May 2009, Chrysler filed for Chapter 11 bankruptcy in a New York court and started the process of a company-wide restructuring. As of 2012 the company has recovered because of its alliance with Fiat and continues to expand in North America and beyond. The company Website observed about its leadership and innovation as follows:

> *"All automobile manufacturers build vehicles, but Chrysler Group creates entirely new automotive categories. Our leadership and innovation earned us the label of Detroit's engineering company."*[5]

FIAT'S CORPORATE ENDURANCE IN THE EUROPEAN MARKETS

Fiat is an interesting company from Italy and carries a long history in global business regarding its corporate initiatives, restructuring, and growth. The company has survived corporate disruptions, labor crises, and many technology shifts. Most

---

[3] For more information on Cerberus, see: www.cerberus.com; Thornton, E. (2005). What's bigger than CISCO, Coke, or McDonald's? *BusinessWeek*, (October 3): 101–110.

[4] For detail, see: Anwar, S. T. (2011). The 2009 Chrysler-Fiat strategic alliance, in Deresky, H., *International Management: Managing Across Borders and Cultures*, (7th edition), Upper Saddle River, New Jersey: Pearson/Prentice Hall: 288–297.

[5] Chrysler Group. (2012). *Innovation Overview*, (http://www.chryslergroupllc .com/Innovation/Pages/default.aspx). Accessed on February 24, 2012.

of Fiat's problems arose from Italian labor laws, weakened business environments, and cost issues. From business history perspectives, Fiat has come a long way in the European market regarding dealing with quality areas and reputation.[6] The company has reinvented itself by fixing its brand portfolio and quality areas. This is clearly evident from the company's current and long-term plans and strategic initiatives. Fiat's Website stated:

"Following the demerger of the capital goods businesses to Fiat Industrial (January 2011) and the increase in its stake in Chrysler to 58.5%, Fiat S.p.A. is accelerating and consolidating the industrial integration of the two groups to create a global automaker determined to position itself as a leader in the industry. Fiat and Chrysler already share a philosophy based on integrity, dedication, delivering on commitments, transparency, reliability—and passion. The Group's objective is to write the new chapters of the story upon which it has just embarked through leveraging synergies to reduce costs, sharing know-how, expanding the global product offering and improving market penetration worldwide."[7]

Like Chrysler, Fiat's evolutionary growth and survival had encountered problems in the areas of technology and quality standards. The company history has been unique and reflects Italy's industry-specific problems and rigid labor laws. Fiat was founded in 1899 and employed 35 workers in 1900. Gianni Agnelli, a former cavalry officer, became the company's chairman in 1966. In 2009, the Agnelli family controlled 35 percent of Fiat.[8] During the sixties and the seventies, Fiat witnessed massive labor strikes and assembly-line disruptions that resulted in 15 million lost worker hours. Between 1980 and 1985, the company reduced its labor force by cutting 100,000 jobs. In 1986, Fiat acquired Alfa Romeo from the Italian government and became the largest automaker in Europe. In 1996, Agnelli resigned as chairman and was given the position of an honorary chairman.

In 2000, GM acquired 20 percent of Fiat for $2.4 billion. In 2002, Fiat encountered financial problems and laid off thousands of workers. In 2003, Agnelli died and his brother Umberto took over the company.[9] In 2004, Fiat recruited a well-known turnaround executive, Sergio Marchionne, to become its CEO. In 2005, Fiat and GM dissolved their five-year partnership when GM paid Fiat $2 billion in cash to get out of the partnership.[10] In 2007, Fiat introduced its iconic Cinquecento 500 model after being out of production for 32 years. In early 2009, Fiat announced a deal to acquire 20 percent of Chrysler in exchange for a technology-sharing pact and distribution networks in Europe and North America. During the same period, Marchionne also showed interest in acquiring GM's Opel and Vauxhall brands in Germany and the UK.

THE GLOBAL AUTO INDUSTRY IN 2012 AND BEYOND

"The most important trends in the automotive industry generally involve two related developments: competition and globalization. As the global market for vehicles expands and as more producers enter new markets around the globe, competition escalates worldwide and companies seek to achieve economies of scale for their vehicle manufacturing."[11]

The above quote accurately reflects what is taking place in the global auto industry, which continues to witness structural changes because of competition and growth (see Figure 2 and Table 2).

As of 2012, the global auto industry is a major industry impacting countries, regions, technologies, and consumers at every level of the society. The industry is always on the move because of changing technologies, demographics, and consumption. The industry originated in a haphazard way and continues to expand in emerging markets because of tangible demand and growth prospects.[12] Industry-specific clusters and value chain networks are common in the industry because of changing technologies and cost issues.[13] No wonder collaborations and alliances are common in the industry.[14]

The global auto industry has been one of the largest industries in the world that impacts countries as well as their sociopolitical environments. In the U.S., Japan, and Europe, auto companies often became part of their country-specific policies and national prides. Today's auto industry is totally different since it does not excite national emotions, although worker

---

[6] For more discussion on Fiat's history and its evolutionary growth and company-related issues, see: Fauri, F. (1996). The role of Fiat in the development of the Italian car industry in the 1950s, *Business History Review*, 70(1): 167–206; Garibaldo, F. (2008). A company in transition: Fiat Mirafiori of Turin, *International Journal of Technology and Management*, 8(2): 185–193; Maielli, G. (2005). The machine that never changed: Intangible specialization and output-mix optimization at Fiat, 1960s–1990s, *Competition & Change*, 9(3): 249–276; Whitford, J., & Enrietti, A. (2005). Surviving the fall of a king: The regional institutional implications of crisis at Fiat Auto, *International Journal of Urban and Regional Research*, 29(4): 771–795.

[7] Fiat Group. (2012). *Mission*, (http://www.fiatspa.com/en-US/group/mission/Pages/default.aspx). Accessed on February 24, 2012.

[8] Meichtry, S., & Toll, J. (2009). Fiat nears stake in Chrysler that could lead to takeover, *The Wall Street Journal*, (January 20): A1&A13.

[9] Galloni, A. (2003). Death of Fiat's Agnelli's marks the end of an era, *The Wall Street Journal*, (January 27): A3.

[10] Galloni, A., & White, G. L. (2002). Fiat head sees GM write-off as tuneup to bid, *The Wall Street Journal*, (October 11): A2.

[11] S&P Net Advantage. (2011). *Auto & Auto Parts*, (http://www.netadvantage .standardandpoors.com/NASApp/NetAdvantage/showIndustrySurvey .do?code=aup). Accessed on February 24, 2012.

[12] *The Economist*. (2012). The world in figures: Industries. *The world in 2012*, London, UK: *The Economist*, 119.

[13] For more discussion, see: Rothenberg, S., & Ettlie, J. E. (2011). Strategies to cope with regulatory uncertainty in the auto industry. *California Management Review*, 54(1), 126–144; Sturgeon, T., Biesebroeck, J., & Gereffi, G. (2008). Value chains, networks and clusters: Reframing the global automobile industry. *Journal of Economic Geography*, 8(3), 297–322; Türkcan, K., & Ates, A. (2011). Vertical intra-industry trade and fragmentation: An empirical examination of the US auto-parts industry. *World Economy*, 34(1), 154–172.

[14] See: Lin, L. (2009). Mergers and acquisitions, alliances and technology development: An empirical study of the global auto industry. *International Journal of Technology Management*, 48(3), 295–307.

FIGURE 2 Auto Market and Company-Specific Market Share in the U.S. (2011)

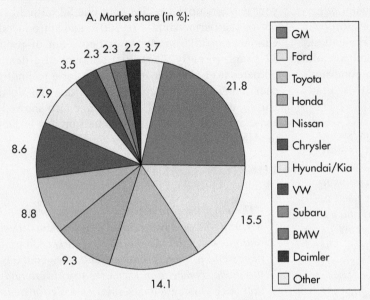

A. Market share (in %):

GM, Ford, Toyota, Honda, Nissan, Chrysler, Hyundai/Kia, VW, Subaru, BMW, Daimler, Other

21.8, 15.5, 14.1, 9.3, 8.8, 8.6, 7.9, 3.5, 2.3, 2.3, 2.2, 3.7

B. Auto sales (top seven manufacturers):

1. GM: 2,503,797 (+13%)
2. Ford: 2,143,101 (+11%)
3. Toyota: 1,644,161 (−7%)
4. Chrysler: 1,369,114 (+26%)
5. Honda: 1,147,285 (−7%)
6. Nissan: 1,042,534 (+15%)
7. Hyundai: 645,691 (+20%)

Source: Auto Nation; Good Car Bad Car; Value Line; The Wall Street Journal (various issues).

TABLE 2 Auto Sales in Selected Global Markets and Countries (Millions of Units, 2009–2012)

Region	2009	2010	2011	2012*
North America	**12.61**	**13.96**	**15.22**	**16.10**
Canada	1.46	1.56	1.59	1.61
U.S.	10.40	11.55	12.73	13.50
Mexico	0.75	0.85	0.90	0.99
Western Europe	**13.62**	**12.98**	**12.80**	**12.16**
Germany	3.81	2.92	3.176	3.24
Eastern Europe	**2.58**	**3.14**	**3.90**	**4.25**
Russia	1.47	1.91	2.65	2.95
Asia	**17.68**	**22.47**	**22.50**	**24.23**
China	7.32	9.41	10.04	10.94
India	1.43	1.87	1.95	2.09
South America	**3.93**	**4.27**	**4.47**	**4.65**
Brazil	2.53	2.69	2.64	2.74
Total Global Sales	**50.42**	**56.82**	**58.89**	**61.39**

Source: Gomes, C. (2012). *Global Auto Report*, Toronto, Canada, Scotia Bank, p. 2.
* 2012 forecast.

unions continue to exert pressure on their governments.[15] As of 2012, the global auto industry is a mixture of complex and modular technologies and assembly line operations that contains suppliers and parts manufacturers, raw material providers, and outsourcing firms. At the global level, these entities are highly diverse, intertwined, and dynamic. Small disruptions in the industry can cause major delays in the industry's

value chains and established platforms.[16] In the last 15 years, the auto industry has witnessed cross-border alliances, joint ventures, and other corporate tie-ups that mostly aimed at economies of scale and value chain efficiencies.[17] In 2012, only three American auto manufacturers prevailed in North America (General Motors, Ford, and Chrysler) while Japan had three major firms: Toyota, Honda, and Nissan. Interestingly, Europe has been left with four large auto companies (Daimler, Volkswagen, Fiat, and Renault-Nissan). In 2011, revenues of the top auto firms were as follows: Toyota, $235 billion; Volkswagen, $168 billion; GM, $149 billion; Ford, $136 billion; and Honda, $117 billion. During the same period, Chrysler-Fiat's revenue surpassed $102 billion.[18] The auto industry has witnessed many structural changes in the forms of strategic alliances and collaborative activities in R&D, distribution agreements, joint

[15] For more discussion on this topic, see: Dowd, M. (2009). No more Hummer nation, *The New York Times*, (April 1): 25; Ingrassia, P. (2009). The UAW in the driver's seat, *The Wall Street Journal*, (April 30): A15; Ingrassia, P. (2009). How Ford restructured without federal help, *The Wall Street Journal*, (May 11): A19.

[16] For detail, see: *The New York Times*. (2005). Japan makes more cars elsewhere, (August 1): C1&C9; *Financial Times*. (2002). Fitting together a modular approach, (August 15): 6; *Financial Times*. (2006). FT – Motor industry, (September 28): 1–4; Symonds, M. (2008). A global love affair: A special report on cars in emerging markets, *The Economist*, (November 15): 1–20.

[17] For more discussion on cross-border alliances, joint ventures, and mergers and acquisition, see the following recent studies: Brannen, M. Y., & Paterson, M. F. (2009). Merging without alienating: Interventions promoting cross-cultural organizational integration and their limitations, *Journal of International Business Studies*, 40, 468–489; Haeussler, C., Patzelt, H., & Zahra, S. A. (2012). Strategic alliances and product development in high technology new firms: The moderating effect of technological capabilities. *Journal of Business Venturing*, 27(2), 217–233; Jiang, X, Li, Y., & Gao, S. (2008). The stability of strategic alliances: Characteristics, factors and stages, *Journal of International Management*, 14, 173–189; Keil, T., & Laamanen, T. (2011). When rivals merge, think before you follow suit. *Harvard Business Review*, (December), 25–27; Kumar, S., & Park, J. (2012). Partner characteristics, information asymmetry, and the signaling effects of joint ventures. *Managerial & Decision Economics*, 33(2), 127–145; Tjemkes et al., B. (2012). Response strategies in an international strategic alliance experimental context: Cross-country differences. *Journal of International Management*, 18(1), 66–84.

[18] See: Company Websites; Value Line (2012). (various issues). New York: Value Line Publishing, LLC.

ventures, and equity stakes. The reasons behind these changes are the industry's evolutionary processes, economies of scale in manufacturing, and consolidations (see Figure 2).

Changing demographics and rising costs have compelled large-scale auto manufacturers to move assembly plants to low-cost economies. In addition, consumer demand in emerging markets (EMs) has forced large auto manufacturers to move facilities abroad to take advantage of cheaper labor and market opportunities. Auto analysts believe that in the coming years, only a small number of auto manufacturers will be left at the global level because of consolidations and mergers. As of 2012, companies maintaining strong brand identities with competitive technologies and quality are able to compete effectively. Restructuring by GM, Ford, Chrysler, and other auto manufacturers have brought cost efficiencies and flexible manufacturing. At the same time, the global auto industry is a complex industry and will take time to recover and restructure. Reed in the *Financial Times* convincingly predicts:[19]

"All the European carmakers are running against the treadmill, in some cases with increasing speed.... Analysts are describing Europe as the sector's 'sick man', a status held until recently by Detroit's three carmakers, which restructured deeply during the Crisis."

PROFILE AND STATUS OF THE CHRYSLER-FIAT ALLIANCE IN 2012

Table 3 and Figure 3 provide Chrysler-Fiat's post-integration progress and related areas that help us evaluate the alliance. As of 2012, both companies have made major structural changes to meet their integration goals. Academic and practitioner studies authenticate that strategic alliances link two or more companies' operations by combining manufacturing resources and knowledge.[20] These tie-ups combine R&D, produce development, distribution networks, and other areas in knowledge sharing. Strategic alliances mostly aim at seeking economies of scale and raising productivity.[21] Interorganizational cooperation is a unique competitive weapon that helps companies to expand their managerial and financial resources.[22] Such is the case with the Chrysler-Fiat strategic alliance in 2012 that continues to bring changes to the companies. The alliance has allowed Chrysler and Fiat not only to survive in the auto industry but expand in global markets. In its initial phase in 2009, Fiat owned

20 percent of Chrysler and later raised its stake to 58.6 percent in 2011. Fiat has already delivered what it planned in 2009.

The Chrysler-Fiat strategic alliance is heavily influenced by today's global competition in the auto industry that continues to seek consolidations. The industry has witnessed downsizing, massive losses, and weak consumer demand. The auto manufacturers from North America have been heavily burdened with debt and expensive labor union contracts. Chrysler was in a more dire situation and saw Fiat as the only available partner for survival. Other factors that helped form this alliance are R&D opportunities, access to markets, and long-term rationalization in manufacturing. In the context of the global auto industry, the companies' growth, and the companies' strategy, we now discuss the status of the alliance as follows:

1. *What went well in the alliance?* After the tie-up, the top managers of Chrysler and Fiat planned and operationalized major synergies that aimed at a common R&D platform, restructuring, streamlining global operations, and image building in both companies (see Table 3 and Figure 3). Both Chrysler and Fiat raised their quality ratings and established dealer networks in Europe and the U.S. Although downsizing was pursued to cut cost and operations, this did not cause the companies to lose sales. Both firms developed common assembly platforms in those sectors where technologies were similar. As of 2012, the alliance has brought major savings in the areas of joint product development, supplier networks, and dealer networks (see Table 3 and Figure 3).

2. *Problems that surfaced in the post-alliance integration:* In the post-alliance integration, Fiat's sales declined in the European markets in 2011 because of the economic downturn. Dealing with labor unions in Italy and their work ethic–related issues also hampered corporate efficiencies in the alliance. Chrysler's U.S. operations mostly went well because of stable financial resources and sales (see Table 3 and Figure 3).

3. *Globalization and the changing global auto industry:* Globalization is a major force impacting countries and their industries.[23] The same applies to the global auto industry, which continues to be dynamic yet highly competitive in sales and market shares (see Figure 2 and Table 2). Regardless of the auto industry's consolidations and mergers and acquisitions, there are opportunities available to those companies that introduce new technologies and auto models. Chrysler and Fiat may have a good opportunity to target the small car and hybrid segments. If planned accurately, both companies have the potential to target the middle classes in North America, Europe, and emerging markets.

4. *Evaluating Marchionne's leadership:* As of 2012, Marchionne enjoys a great reputation in Italy and

19 Reed, J. (2012). In the slow lane. *Financial Times*, (February 2): 7.

20 For more information on alliances and collaboration, see: Anwar, S. T. (2012). Strategic Alliances, JVs/IJVs, M&As, Interorganizational Cooperation & Related Links. (http://wtfaculty.wtamu.edu/~sanwar.bus/otherlinks .htm#StrAlliances_JV_MAs). Accessed on February 22, 2012.

21 For more discussion on the concepts, theories and problems of strategic alliances, see: Doz, Y. L., & Hamel, G. (1998). *Alliance advantage: The art of creating value through partnering*, Boston, Massachusetts: Harvard Business School Press; Dyer, J. H., & Hatch, N. W. (2006). Relation-specific capabilities and barriers to knowledge transfers: Creating advantage through network relationships, *Strategic Management Journal*, 27, 701–719; Kuglin, F. A. (2002). *Building, leading and managing strategic alliances*, New York: AMACOM.

22 Lynch, R. P. (1993). *Business alliances guide: The hidden competitive weapon*, New York: John Wiley & Sons.

23 See: Anwar, S. T. (2007). Global business and globalization. *Journal of International Management*, 13(1), 78–89; Anwar, S. T. (2011). Internationalization, investment opportunities, expansion strategies, and the changing telecom industry in the MENA region, *The Journal of World Investment & Trade*, 12(6), 891–917.

TABLE 3   Chrysler-Fiat Alliance: Selected Coverage and Reporting by the Print Media (2009–2012)

"*Alliance with Fiat gives Chrysler another partner and lifeline*" (NYT, January 21, 2009, p. B1).

"*Chrysler's new ally takes a pragmatic approach*" (NYT, February 3, 2009, p. B1).

"*After its turnaround, Fiat finds an opportunity with Chrysler*" (NYT, April 1, 2009, p. B4).

"*Possible Chrysler savior Fiat has low reliability scores*" (USAT, April 1, 2009, p. 2B).

"*Chrysler ax falls across U.S.*" (WSJ, May 15, 2009, p. A1).

"*Fiat CEO sets new tone at Chrysler*" (WSJ, June 19, 2009, p. B1).

"*Fiat goes full throttle in restructuring plan*" (FT, June 19, 2009, p. 15).

"*Chrysler to make Fiat in Mexico*" (WSJ, August 17, 2009, p. B2).

"*Italians get to work at Chrysler*" (FT, September 4, 2009, p. 14).

"*Fiat plans to spend $11 billion on growth*" (WSJ, December 23, 2009, p. B1).

"*A long haul for Detroit's prince*" (FT, January 14, 2010, p. 11).

"*Dual control*" (FT, February 20–21, 2010, p. L and A17).

"*Fiat to spin off non-car divisions*" (FT, April 22, 2010, p. 15).

"*Chrysler ads aim to rebuild image*" (WSJ, June 9, 2010, p. B1).

"*Chrysler to set up 200 Fiat dealerships*" (NYT, July 7, 2010, p. B2).

"*Fiat pushes work ethic at an Italian plant*" (FT, July 23, 2010, p. B1).

"*To counter slump, Chrysler plans new-model barrage*" (WSJ, September 15, 2010, p. B3).

"*Marchionne's gamble*" (FT, September 20, 2010, p. 7).

"*Chief says Fiat may try to add to stake in Chrysler before a public offering*" (NYT, January 4, 2011, p. B4).

"*Marchionne upends Chrysler's ways*" (WSJ, January 12, 2011, p. B1).

"*Fiat's CEO presses Italy for changes*" (WSJ, February 16, 2011, p. B4).

"*Fiat plans a 'product offensive'*" (FT, March 3, 2011, p. 16).

"*Chrysler bail-out is a working model*" (FT, April 27, 2011, p. 8).

"*Resurrecting Chrysler*" (WSJ, July 3, 2010, p. A9).

"*Alfa Romeo readies a stirring stateside return*" (WSJ, April 16–17, 2011, p. D12).

"*Fiat takes Alfa Romeo for a U.S. test drive*" (BBW, April 18–24, 2011, p. 19).

"*Payback time at Chrysler*" (WSJ, April 29, 2011, p. B1).

"*Marchionne settles $7 billion bill with taxpayers early*" (FT, May 28–29, 2011, p. 9).

"*Fiat has U.S. share deal*" (WSJ, June 3, 2011, p. B3).

"*Fiat weighs majority in Chrysler*" (WSJ, July 21, 2011, p. B3).

"*Fiat management team takes reins at Chrysler*" (WSJ, July 21, 2011, p. B3).

"*Fiat acquires majority share of Chrysler*" (WSJ, July 22, 2011, p. B4).

"*Fiat and Chrysler closer to full tie-up*" (FT, July 25, 2011, p. 17).

"*Joint structure for Chrysler and Fiat*" (FT, July 29, 2011, p. 14).

"*Chrysler's turnaround gets wheels*" (WSJ, October 26, 2011, p. B4).

"*Fiat's chief faces hard fight on the home front*" (FT, October 26, 2011, p. 13).

"*Chrysler gains momentum*" (WSJ, December 14, 2011, p. B3).

"*Fiat jumper-clad revolutionary*" (FT, December 17–18, 2011, p. 13).

"*The Fiat 500C can't fail – not for lack of trying*" (WSJ, December 17–18, 2011, p. D16).

"*Power steering: How Chrysler's Italian boss drives an American auto revival*" (TM, December 19, 2011, p. 36).

"*Chrysler hits profit stride*" (WSJ, February 2, 2012, p. B2).

"*A merger once scoffed at bears fruit in Detroit*" (NYT, January 10, 2012, p. B1).

Note: BBW—*Bloomberg Businessweek*; FT—*Financial Times*; NYT— *New York Times*; TM—*Time*; USAT—*USA Today*; WSJ—*Wall Street Journal*.

FIGURE 3   Major Developments and Achievements of the Chrysler-Fiat Alliance (2010–2012)

2010

- Fiat utilizes its alliance with Chrysler to seek a high-profile entry into the U.S. market.
- John Elkann (grandson of Gianni Agnelli) becomes the chairman of Fiat Group.
- Fiat puts major emphasis on quality control and work ethic; major changes are in place.
- Chrysler announces setting up 200 Fiat dealerships in the U.S. to sell the "Fiat 500" brand.
- Fiat maintains its Chrysler share at 20 percent.
- Fiat shareholders approve the Group to spin off/demerge automotive operations and Fiat Industrial.

↓

2011

- Fiat raises its Chrysler share to 25 percent.
- Chrysler-Fiat repays $7.6 billion of its bailout loans to the U.S. and Canadian governments, six years before the required date.
- Analysts and the media praise the Chrysler-Fiat alliance for cost cutting, synergies, and good integration.
- Fiat plans on fixing its brand portfolio by 2013.
- Fiat S.p.A. (automotive unit) and Fiat Industrial S.p.A. are officially separated.
- Fiat has a team of 22 top international managers in global markets; the alliance's management structure is fully operational.
- Fiat has a good control over its labor relations in Italy; labor contracts have been negotiated.
- "Fiat 500" model is available in the U.S. after 26 years; Fiat runs a major publicity campaign to unveil this car.
- The Chrysler-Fiat alliance sells 4.2 million vehicles (cars and trucks) worldwide.

↓

2012

- Fiat owns 58.5 percent of Chrysler, a major achievement in the alliance history.
- The top leadership in the alliance is well entrenched on both sides of the Atlantic.
- Integration and tie-up of Chrysler-Fiat is almost achieved.
- The alliance can be a good benchmark for business-related "Trans-Atlantic alliances" and cooperation.
- Chrysler-Fiat management team is fully in place to make short-term and long-term decisions.
- "Maserati Kubang" is planned to be assembled in Jeep's Detroit plant.
- Fiat's core segments (small cars) in the European markets are somewhat flat.
- The alliance is based on an "equal partnership" although there is no plan in place for the joint headquarters; Chrysler witnesses 18 percent sales increase.
- Battery operated Fiat 500 is expected to be available in the U.S.
- The Chrysler-Fiat alliance has a plan to sell six million automobiles worldwide by 2014.

Source: Automotive News; The Economist; Financial Times; Fortune; The New York Times; The Wall Street Journal (various issues).

North America (see Table 3). Under his leadership, the alliance has worked well and continues to seek additional synergies (see Figure 3). Originally trained as a chartered accountant and solicitor, Marchionne joined Fiat in 2004. He received a master's degree in business administration from the University of Windsor and worked for SGS S.A., a Swiss company that dealt with trade goods.[24] Under his

tenure at Fiat, Marchionne was able to convince the board to seek major changes in difficult times.[25] Marchionne sought a planned and systematic restructuring of Fiat by concentrating on new technologies and consumer issues. Fiat successfully realigned its management structure and was able to show a profit.

5. *Brand portfolios and branding issues:* As of 2012, Chrysler and Fiat's brand portfolios seem compatible and are competitive in global markets (see Figure 1). Both

---

[24] For more information on Sergio Marchionne, see: *The Economist.* (2009). Pedal to the metal, (April 25): 72; Meichtry, S. (2009). Fiat CEO builds record of bold strategic moves, *The Wall Street Journal*, (January 20): A13; Reed, J., & Vincent B. (2009). Fiat's front-seat driver, *Financial Times*, (January 24–25): 7; Wayne, L. (2009). New leaders hold Detroit's prospects in their hands, *The New York Times*, (March 31), B4.

[25] Marchionne, S. (2008). Fiat's extreme makeover, *Harvard Business Review*, (December): 45–48.

manufacture small cars that are in demand because of high gasoline prices and cost issues. In their alliance, the companies have successfully pooled their resources together to consolidate brand portfolios that aim at significant cost savings in R&D and technology platforms. The companies' joint dealer networks have brought required savings and efficiencies.

6. *Company-specific issues:* History books reveal that Fiat left the North American market in the eighties because of its weakened market share, quality problems, and mismanagement. To re-enter into the North American market, Fiat needed a well-established auto manufacturer that knew the market and had the technology available. In 2008, Chrysler was the only choice available for this tie-up. As we evaluate the Chrysler-Fiat alliance in 2012, it is clear that the tie-up was a logical choice on the part of Fiat, which desperately wanted to come back to North America for future expansion and growth.

7. *Dealing with government loans in North America:* In May 2011, Chrysler-Fiat repaid $7.6 billion of its loans to U.S. and Canadian governments, six years ahead of their due date.[26] This was a major achievement of the Chrysler-Fiat alliance and its credibility in the auto industry. Initially in 2009, the Obama Administration initiated the auto bailout by specifically targeting GM and Chrysler. This step was taken by the U.S. government because of Chrysler's losses that amounted to $8 billion. Under the auto bailout plan, Chrysler was given $4 billion with strings attached.

8. *Availability of Fiat's technology platforms:* One of the major clauses of the Chrysler-Fiat alliance was it technology-sharing agreement. Fiat supplied four technology platforms and two types of engines to Chrysler. This helped Chrysler to get involved in small cars technology.[27] In Europe, Fiat was always known for its *"small car production model"* that particularly helped the company to seek recovery since 2004.[28]

SYNERGIES AND CHALLENGES AHEAD

At the time of Chrysler-Fiat's alliance, analysts and industry watchers were not sure of the success of the tie-up. As we evaluate the alliance in 2012, the companies' tie-up carries a long-term synergy and has benefitted immensely in cost savings, corporate integration, common technology platforms, and distribution networks. The alliance has brought synergies in those areas of production where the companies were similar (see Figure 3). The alliance did face challenges and some obstacles in the areas of brand portfolios, labor unions, management structures, and integration. Fiat had been successful in Europe but lacked visibility in North America. Chrysler, on the

other hand, had a brand name in North America but was short of dealer networks in the European markets. Both companies' brand portfolios were reinvigorated in the alliance structure to reap benefits from economies of scale. This did cause a few delays and disruptions. In 2012, both Chrysler and Fiat carry acceptable brands and deliver consumer benefits.

Although the alliance's major objectives have been achieved in the areas of cost, technology sharing, global integration, and R&D platforms, some work remain incomplete in global integration and common assembly platforms. Chrysler is no longer the laughing stock in the auto industry. Marchionne and his top global managers' initiatives have been praised by the media and industry analysts because of their well thought-out plans and unique tie-up of the two companies. Both companies have been credited with crafting a successful "transatlantic auto alliance" that continues to remain at the helm of the ship. Just a few years back, a long-term alliance between two auto companies from two different cultures was unthinkable. In academic and practitioner research, alliances, mergers, and corporate tie-ups always attract researchers because of their known and unknown outcomes and synergies. At the same time, these activities can also bring tangible benefits if managed properly. As of 2012, Chrysler and Fiat seem to be in a good position regarding capitalizing on the alliance. Above all, Marchionne and his top managers and advisors are firmly in control of the ship that was in troubled waters just a few years ago. We finish this case with Colman and Lunnan's insightful and thought provoking comments from the *Journal of Management* that apply to the Chrysler-Fiat alliance:

> *"The objective of an acquisition is to create value. Value can be created through the integration of the target and acquiring firms' organization and activities.... Expected value motivates the deal, whereas serendipitous value arises primarily from the sharing of knowledge between the target and acquirer during the integration process, which can result in new, superior but unexpected procedures and processes."[29]*

Case Questions

1. What are your views of the Chrysler-Fiat auto alliance and its status in 2012?

2. Analyze and evaluate Chrysler and Fiat's strengths and weaknesses before and after the alliance.

3. Compare and contrast Chrysler and Fiat with other auto manufacturers.

4. Analyze Chrysler and Fiat's 2012 brand portfolio in the world auto industry. How do you see both companies making changes to compete with their competitors?

5. What did you learn from the Chrysler-Fiat Alliance and its integration strategies?

[26] See: Reed, J. (2011). Marchionne settles $7 billion bill with taxpayer early. *Financial Times*, (May 28–29): 9.

[27] Simon, B. (2009). Time is tight for Chrysler in drive for reinvention, *Financial Times*, (May 4), 15.

[28] Boland, V. (2009). Rome throws weight behind Fiat pact, *Financial Times*, (May 2/3), 9.

[29] Colman, H. L., & Lunnan, R. (2011). Organizational identification and serendipitous value creation in post-acquisition integration. *Journal of Management*, 37(3), 839.

4

Global Human Resources Management

CHAPTER

9

Staffing, Training, and Compensation for Global Operations

OBJECTIVES

1. To understand the strategic importance to the firm of the IHRM function and its various responsibilities.

2. To learn about the major staffing options for global operations and the factors involved in those choices.

3. To appreciate the challenges involved in staffing operations in emerging market countries.

4. To emphasize the need for managing the performance of expatriates through careful selection, training, and compensation.

5. To discuss the role of host country managers and the need for their training and appropriate compensation packages.

6. To distinguish among various IHRM practices around the world.

OPENING PROFILE: STAFFING COMPANY OPERATIONS IN EMERGING MARKETS[1]

In the 2012 Brookfield Global Relocation Trends Survey (GRTS), firms' HR Staff were asked to identify the top three countries that represented new assignment locations for them. They were: China (5 percent), India (4 percent), and Columbia, Russia and South Africa (3 percent). Those that were considered the most challenging for assigning people, as well as for the assignees, were China, India, Brazil and Russia.[2] However, distinction was made between relatively developed cities and less-developed locations in other areas of those countries.

In addition to the challenge of assigning and maintaining expatriates in emerging market economies, the ability to staff subsidiaries in emerging market economies with local managers has become a major challenge in the race for recruiting and retaining local talent. Emerging economies such as Brazil, Russia, India, and China have been developing so rapidly and have so attracted increasing overseas investment that they have outpaced the supply of suitable mid- and upper-level managers in their own markets. Foreign firms wishing to expand their investments in such economies are competing for what talent is available with both local companies and other global companies; however, they are falling behind the curve in not recognizing that they need different approaches than those they use domestically.

The problem is so acute that many companies have had to reconsider how fast they can expand in developing economies. A study by the McKinsey Global Institute predicts that 75,000 business leaders will be needed in China in the next ten years. It estimates the current availability at just 3,000 to 5,000, and that many of those are simply not at the skill level required by foreign companies.[3] According to *The Economist*:

> *In a recent survey, 600 chief executives of multinational companies with businesses across Asia said a shortage of qualified staff ranked as their biggest concern in China and South-East Asia. It was their second-biggest headache in Japan (after cultural differences) and the fourth-biggest in India (after problems with infrastructure, bureaucracy and wage inflation).*[4]

Reasons for the shortage of upper-level managers vary by country. Research by Ready, et al. shows that while Brazil has an influx of new graduates available to staff at the low- to mid-management level, there is a deficit at the upper levels. In India there is also a surplus at the lower level, but a deficit starting at the middle levels; one additional explanation is the "brain drain," in particular in the technology industry. In Russia, there is a deficit at all management levels as a result of decades of operating under a planned economy, together with the great increase in demand by foreign companies. In China, there is a sizable surplus at the entry level—though of varying quality—but a considerable deficit at all levels up from there.[5]

Clearly the competition for talent has become global, as has the competition for jobs. The brain drain from emerging economies has contributed to the dearth of local talent available. Over a million Chinese went to the United States to study between 1978 and 2006, and 70 percent of them did not go back. Exacerbating the problem is the high turnover of those highly-sought managers, and, as a result of that, the escalating salary requirements.[6] For these reasons, the challenge to companies operating around the world is not only to recruit capable local managers, but also to be able to retain them. Advice from professionals includes "growing your own"—that is, to provide sufficient training and career mentoring to elicit loyalty with managers; and, in particular, to balance local human resource needs with global standards. This may require tailoring employment packages to local markets to attract and keep top talent, rather than applying global policies for the sake of global consistency.[7]

Ready et al. suggest a framework for attracting and retaining talent that recognizes that managers in developing markets are motivated by factors that are a function of their culture, business practices, and personal goals, and which are usually dissimilar to what is expected in the home office. They conclude that successful companies offer more than a good salary and that they comprise four distinguishing characteristics that provide meaning for potential recruits in emerging markets:[8]

1. *Brand:* that is, a global "name brand" known for its excellence and with a distinctive competence in a particular area, for example technology, in which new recruits would have confidence in their future.

2. *Purpose:* that is, a company that is breaking into new markets with new models and strategy, giving new employees a chance to be part of something meaningful.

3. *Opportunity:* that is, a company that provides a fast-track training and career path for new recruits.

4. *Culture:* that is, a company that has an organizational culture of openness and transparency for employees, with support for their work and career development.[9]

We believe the war for talent will continue to be the major human resource issue to 2020, when the people pipeline looks to be the most crucial variable separating winners and losers in the marketplace. . . . Global mobility will play a key role in solving the labor availability conundrum.

THE 2011 PRICEWATERHOUSECOOPERS' 14TH
ANNUAL CEO SURVEY.[10]

This chapter's opening profile describes the challenges involved in assigning, recruiting and retaining suitable managers to staff operations in emerging markets, where the burgeoning demand by both foreign and local companies is outstripping the supply. Other challenges for companies around the world include growing workforce mobility and the increasing trend of outsourcing employees because service and professional jobs have now joined manufacturing jobs in the category of "boundaryless" human capital (discussed in previous chapters).

The need to outsource employees is just one of the complex issues for international human resource (IHR) managers as they seek to support strategic mandates (see Chapter 6). Global firms are finding that their practices of outsourcing skilled and professional jobs have implications for their human resource practices at home and around the world. Consequently, a firm such as Infosys, one of India's top outsourcing companies, also experiences complex human resource challenges involved in recruiting, training, and compensating increasingly sophisticated employees in its attempt to meet the escalating demand for its services; in addition, Infosys has the same challenges with its operations abroad.

It is clear, then, that a vital component of implementing global strategy is *international human resource management* (IHRM). Executives questioned about the major challenges the HR function faces in the global arena cited: "1) Enhancing global business strategy; 2) aligning HR issues with business strategy; 3) designing and leading change; 4) building global corporate cultures; and 5) staffing organizations with global leaders."[11] IHRM is therefore increasingly being recognized as a major determinant of success or failure in international business. In a highly competitive global economy, where the other factors of production—capital, technology, raw materials, and information—are increasingly able to be duplicated, "the caliber of the people in an organization will be the only source of sustainable competitive advantage available to U.S. companies."[12] Corporations operating overseas need to pay careful attention to this most critical resource—one that also provides control over other resources. In fact, increasing recognition is being given to the role of *Strategic Human Resource Management (SHRM)*—that is, the two-way role of HRM in both helping to determine strategy as well as to implement it. That role in helping the organization to develop the necessary capabilities to be able to enact the desired strategy includes the reality that strategic plans are developed in large part based on the resources possessed by the firm, including the human resources capabilities.[13] IBM is one company that clearly uses its global workforce to convey and implement its strategy of a globally integrated company—doing business with clients in whatever location is appropriate, rather than in its previous structure of 160 subsidiaries.[14] As of 2011, IBM had 426,751 employees worldwide; the majority of those are in countries such as India, Japan, Britain, and Brazil. The company uses various staffing modes and considers international assignments important to its goal of global integration.

The IHRM function comprises varied responsibilities involved in managing human resources in global corporations, including recruiting and selecting employees, providing preparation and training, and setting up appropriate compensation and performance management programs. While firms would like to be able to harmonize their IHRM practices around the world, there are considerable and powerful variables that confound that goal, making it either impractical or undesirable for many localities. Among these are the complexities of local government laws and regulations, varying cultural norms and practices, as well as the long-entrenched and accepted business practices in the local area. Some examples are shown in Exhibit 9-1. These factors, in turn, are influenced by national variables in the political, economic, legal, and institutional arena as well as by competitive factors.

Of particular importance to the IHRM function is the management of **expatriates**—employees assigned to a country other than their own. An overview of those functions is provided here, while further IHRM challenges in developing a global management cadre and working within host-country practices and laws are discussed in the following chapter.

EXHIBIT 9-1   Influences on Local HRM Practices

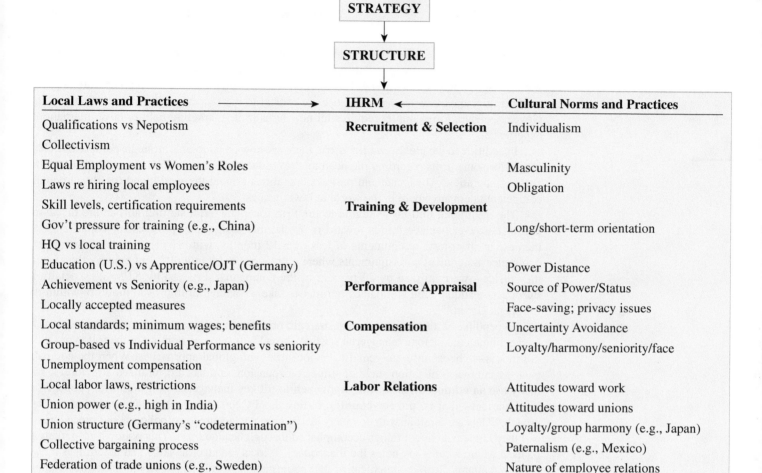

Local Laws and Practices	IHRM	Cultural Norms and Practices
Qualifications vs Nepotism	Recruitment & Selection	Individualism
Collectivism		
Equal Employment vs Women's Roles		Masculinity
Laws re hiring local employees		Obligation
Skill levels, certification requirements	Training & Development	
Gov't pressure for training (e.g., China)		Long/short-term orientation
HQ vs local training		
Education (U.S.) vs Apprentice/OJT (Germany)		Power Distance
Achievement vs Seniority (e.g., Japan)	Performance Appraisal	Source of Power/Status
Locally accepted measures		Face-saving; privacy issues
Local standards; minimum wages; benefits	Compensation	Uncertainty Avoidance
Group-based vs Individual Performance vs seniority		Loyalty/harmony/seniority/face
Unemployment compensation		
Local labor laws, restrictions	Labor Relations	Attitudes toward work
Union power (e.g., high in India)		Attitudes toward unions
Union structure (Germany's "codetermination")		Loyalty/group harmony (e.g., Japan)
Collective bargaining process		Paternalism (e.g., Mexico)
Federation of trade unions (e.g., Sweden)		Nature of employee relations
Joint Venture union regulations (e.g., China)		

At the first level of planning, decisions are required on the staffing policy suitable for a particular kind of business, its global strategy, and its geographic locations. Key issues involve the difficulty of control in geographically dispersed operations, the need for local decision-making independent of the home office, and the suitability of managers from alternate sources.

The interdependence of strategy, structure, and staffing is particularly worth noting. Ideally, the desired strategy of the firm should dictate the organizational structure and staffing modes considered most effective for implementing that strategy. In reality, however, there is usually considerable interdependence among those functions. Existing structural constraints often affect strategic decisions; similarly, staffing constraints or unique sets of competences in management come into play in organizational and sometimes strategic decisions. It is thus important to achieve a system of fits among those variables that facilitates strategic implementation.

STAFFING FOR GLOBAL OPERATIONS

Over half of CEOs were planning to send more staff on international assignments in 2011. The number of international assignments among multinationals increased 25% over the past decade; we forecast a further 50% growth over the next one.[15]

THE 2011 PRICEWATERHOUSECOOPERS' 14TH
ANNUAL CEO SURVEY

Globalization in the 21st century has resulted in an even higher demand for businesses to send the right talent to the right place at the right time.

KPMG 2012 GLOBAL ASSIGNMENT SURVEY[16]

WWW.KPMG.COM.

Despite concerns over the weaker global economy and the costs of international assignment programs, international assignments remain on the upswing, according to the results of the Price-waterhouseCoopers' CEO Survey. Those executives made it clear that when competing in global markets, global experience and expertise are critical to the success of the organization and employee. Colgate, for example, requires all new hires in its marketing field to have international experience.

In addition to the global war for talent, there are now considerable strategic competitive challenges for some firms regarding the need to: "(a) reduce and remove talent in order to lower the costs of operations; (b) locate and relocate operations around the world; and (c) obtain equally competent talent anywhere in the world at lower wages."[17]

The traditional options available to the firm for managerial staffing abroad are discussed below. However, we see trends toward more flexible assignment policies for expatriates: an increase in short-term assignments of less than 12 months, with 81 percent using this option; commuter assignments—assignments where employees work in a different country than where they reside—were utilized by 22 percent of the companies surveyed by KPMG, especially in European-headquartered companies in order to take advantage of improved mobility within the European Union.[18]

Depending on the firm's primary strategic orientation and stage of internationalization, as well as situational factors, managerial staffing abroad falls into one or more of the following staffing modes—ethnocentric, polycentric, regiocentric, and global approaches. When the company is at the internationalization stage of strategic expansion, and has a centralized structure, it will likely use an **ethnocentric staffing approach** to fill key managerial positions with people from headquarters—that is, **parent-country nationals (PCNs)**. Among the advantages of this approach, PCNs are familiar with company goals, products, technology, policies, and procedures—and they know how to get things accomplished through headquarters. This policy is also likely to be used where a company notes the inadequacy of local managerial skills and determines a high need to maintain close communication and coordination with headquarters. For German companies, the most important reason for assigning expatriates was "to develop international management skills." For companies in Japan and the United Kingdom, it was "to set up a new operation," and in the United States it was "to fill a skill gap."[19]

Frequently, companies use PCNs for the top management positions in the foreign subsidiary—in particular, the chief executive officer (CEO) and the chief financial officer (CFO)—to maintain close control. PCNs are usually preferable when a high level of technical capability is required. They are also chosen for new international ventures requiring managerial experience in the parent company and where there is a concern for loyalty to the company rather than to the host country—in cases, for example, where proprietary technology is used extensively.

In addition, the strategic goal of understanding the needs and opportunities in emerging markets has led an increasing number of top-level executives, including board members and CEOs, to assign themselves to Asia. As an example, in 2011, John Rice, vice chairman of G.E. and president and chief executive of global growth and operations, relocated to Hong Kong with his wife. Saying his motives were part substance and part symbolism, Mr. Rice conceded that "Being outside the United States makes you smarter about global issues. It lets you see the world through a different lens." [20] He noted that he had learned more about China since moving there 18 months ago than he had in the 100 or so times he had visited before. According to a survey by the Economist Corporate Network, 45.3 percent of respondents expected to have board members in Asia by 2016.[21] Others in the survey noted that their continuing presence gave them more access to key leaders who regarded them as more committed to the region.

Generally speaking, however, there can be important disadvantages to the ethnocentric approach including (1) the lack of opportunities or development for local managers, thereby decreasing their morale and their loyalty to the subsidiary; and (2) the poor adaptation and lack of effectiveness of expatriates in foreign countries. Procter & Gamble, for example, routinely appointed managers from its headquarters for foreign assignments for many years. After several unfortunate experiences in Japan, the firm realized that such a practice was insensitive to local cultures and also underutilized its pool of high-potential non-American managers.[22] Furthermore, an ethnocentric recruiting approach does not enable the company to take advantage of its worldwide pool of management skill. This approach also serves to perpetuate particular personnel selections and other decision-making processes because the same types of people are making the same types of decisions.

With a **polycentric staffing approach**, local managers—**host-country nationals (HCNs)**—are hired to fill key positions in their own country. This approach is more likely to be effective when implementing a multinational strategy. If a company wants to "act local," staffing with HCNs has obvious advantages. These managers are naturally familiar with the local culture, language, and ways of doing business, and they already have many contacts in place. In addition, HCNs are more likely to be accepted by people both inside and outside the subsidiary, and they provide role models for other upwardly mobile personnel. For these and other reasons, this staffing policy is followed by Tata Consultancy Services (TCS) for some of its subsidiaries, as detailed in the accompanying Under the Lens section.

With regard to cost, it is usually less expensive for a company to hire a local manager than to transfer one from headquarters, frequently with a family, and often at a higher rate of pay. Transferring from headquarters is a particularly expensive policy when the manager and her or his family do not adjust and have to be prematurely transferred home. Rather than opening their own facilities, some companies acquire foreign firms as a means of obtaining qualified local personnel. Local managers also tend to be instrumental in staving off or more effectively dealing with problems in sensitive political situations. Some countries, in fact, have legal requirements that a specific proportion of the firm's top managers must be citizens of that country.

One disadvantage of a polycentric staffing policy is the difficulty of coordinating activities and goals between the subsidiary and the parent company, including the potentially conflicting loyalties of the local manager. Poor coordination among subsidiaries of a multinational firm could constrain strategic options. An additional drawback of this policy is that the headquarters managers of multinational firms will not gain the overseas experience necessary for any higher positions in the firm that require the understanding and coordination of subsidiary operations.

UNDER THE LENS

Tata's Staffing Challenges in the United States[23]

Tata Consultancy Services (TCS) provides IT services, business solutions, and outsourcing around the world. The Indian company, which sends thousands of employees abroad to work in client locations, is part of the Tata Group—one of India's largest industrial conglomerates—and operates in 43 countries. For the fiscal year ending March 31, 2011, TCS had revenue of $8.2 billion. In 2008, TCS decided to buy a facility in Milford, Ohio, to be closer to a number of Fortune 500 clients in the area, and also to hire American graduates from the several nearby universities. TCS's strategy is to compete with consultancy giants such as IBM and Accenture on their home turf. Over half of TCS's revenue is from North America, with about 16,000 employees. TCS was anxious to compete for the estimated $52 billion in U.S. federal contracts. In 2011, TCS had 450 employees in Ohio, nearly all American, partly because of the difficulty of getting visas for Indians, and the company had plans to hire a further 500-plus, adding to its 215,000-strong global workforce.[24]

Factors affecting TCS's staffing practices in the United States include the Ohio government's ban in September 2010 of the outsourcing of government contracts to overseas operations, a protectionist move that sent a chill through the Indian outsourcing industry. This raised fears about continued access to outsourcing services in the U.S. because of concerns about unemployment among U.S. workers. The company had been suspended by the U.S. Embassy in 2010 for alleged irregularities in visa applications but was later reinstated to allow temporary U.S. work visas for employees. This issue no doubt triggered the tougher immigration regulations for foreign software engineers on short-term contracts who are being targeted as taking American jobs, as well as the difficulty in finding sufficient numbers of qualified engineers in the U.S. Even so, TCS faces a cost increase of around seven times for a U.S. worker compared with one hired to do similar work in India.

Clearly, the staffing challenges TCS faces in its U.S. subsidiary are just the tip of the iceberg for an IT company needing highly qualified employees around the world.

In the **global staffing approach**, the best managers are recruited from within or outside of the company, regardless of nationality. This practice—recruiting **third country nationals (TCNs)**—has been used for some time by many European multinationals. Now, HRM professionals everywhere are realizing that . . .

> . . . the emergence of a global talent pool following China and India's decade of growth will increasingly influence talent development and acquisition.
>
> ORGANIZATIONAL DYNAMICS (2011) 40, 246–254[25]

A global staffing approach has several important advantages. First, this policy provides a greater pool of qualified and willing applicants from which to choose, which, in time, results in further development of a global executive cadre. As discussed further in Chapter 10, the skills and experiences that those managers use and transfer throughout the company result in a pool of shared learning that is necessary for the company to compete globally.

Second, where third country nationals are used to manage subsidiaries, they usually bring more cultural flexibility and adaptability to a situation, as well as bilingual or multilingual skills, than parent-country nationals, especially if they are from a similar cultural background as the host-country coworkers and are accustomed to moving around. In addition, when TCNs are placed in key positions, they are perceived by employees as acceptable compromises between headquarters and local managers, and thus appointing them works to reduce resentment.

Third, it can be more cost-effective to transfer and pay managers from some countries than from others because their pay scale and benefits packages are lower. Indeed, those firms with a truly global staffing orientation are phasing out the entire ethnocentric concept of a home or host country. In fact, as globalization increases, terms such as *TCNs*, *HCNs*, and *expatriates* are becoming less common, because of the kind of situation where a manager may leave her native Ireland to take a job in England, then be assigned to Switzerland, then to China, and so on, without returning to Ireland. As part of that focus, the term **transpatriate** is increasingly replacing the term *expatriate*. Firms such as Philips, Heinz, Unilever, IBM, and ABB have a global staffing approach, which makes them highly visible and seems to indicate a trend.

Overall, firms still tend to use expatriates in key positions in host countries that have a less familiar culture and also in less-developed economies. Clearly, this situation arises out of concern about uncertainty and the ability to control implementation of the corporation's goals. However, given the generally accepted consensus that staffing, along with structure and systems,

EXHIBIT 9-2   Maintaining a Globalization Momentum

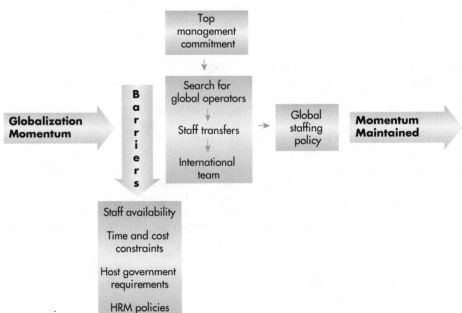

Source: Based on and adapted from D. Welch, "HRM Implications of Globalization," *Journal of General Management* 19, no. 4 (Summer 1994): 52–69, used with permission of Braybrooke Press 2011.

must "fit" the desired strategy, firms desiring a truly global posture should adopt a global staffing approach. That is easier said than done. As shown in Exhibit 9-2, such an approach requires the firm to overcome barriers such as the availability and willingness of high-quality managers to transfer frequently around the world, dual-career constraints, time and cost constraints, conflicting requirements of host governments, and ineffective human resource management policies.

In a **regiocentric staffing approach**, recruiting is done on a regional basis—say, within Latin America for a position in Chile. This staffing approach can produce a specific mix of PCNs, HCNs, and TCNs, according to the needs of the company or the product strategy.

More recently a staffing option known as **inpatriates** has been utilized to provide a linking pin between the company's headquarters and local host subsidiaries. Inpatriates are managers with global experience who are transferred to the organization's headquarters country so that their overseas business and cultural experience and contacts can facilitate interactions among the country's far-flung operations.[26]

> *Because power will always reside at world headquarters, you have to "inpatriate" foreign executives if you want to ensure that those in leadership positions know and trust them.*
>
> HARVARD BUSINESS REVIEW,
> SEPTEMBER 2010.[27]

Inpatriate managers can provide communication of strategic goals and change processes and provide continuity among revolving expatriates and host nationals; in addition, they can facilitate multicultural management teams in global organizations.[28] Nestlé, for example, brings in managers at all levels from around the world to its Swiss headquarters to ensure that its executives get acquainted with the firm's best talent. The inpatriates are also happy to do this since they gain relationships all around and are able to network with one another, in addition to gaining the knowledge and familiarity with the firm's headquarters people and processes.[29] Other companies that have brought inpatriate managers into their headquarters operations are Quaker Chemical Company (Guus Lobsen, Holland); Coca-Cola Co. (John Hunter, Australia); and Sara Lee Corporation (Cornelis Boonstra, Holland).

A critical success factor in the use of an inpatriate is the ability of that person to develop acceptance and trust among the people in the various locations, making it imperative for the firm to retain him or her on a long-term basis.[30] For her part, there is considerable challenge in that . . .

> *"The inpatriate is expected to become a parent country manager in language and lifestyle, yet play a double role as a host country national when returning to her or his home country."*
>
> ORGANIZATIONAL DYNAMICS, 2010.[31]

Some of the pros and cons of the different staffing practices are shown in Exhibit 9-3.

> *Foreign parent expatriates bring with them both the national and corporate culture of the parent, while third country nationals recruited by the foreign parent will likely bring the parent firm's culture into the venture, but less of its national culture.[32]*
>
> ODED SHENKAR, JOURNAL OF INTERNATIONAL BUSINESS,
> JANUARY 2012.

What factors influence the choice of staffing policy? Among them are the strategy and organizational structure of the firm, as well as the factors related to the particular subsidiary (such as the duration of the particular foreign operation, the types of technology used, and the production and marketing techniques necessary). Factors related to the host country also play a part (such as the level of economic and technological development, political stability, regulations regarding ownership and staffing, and the sociocultural setting).[33] Clearly, there are many complex factors and interactions to consider, as illustrated by the quote above. As a practical matter, however, the choice often depends on the availability of qualified managers in the host country. Most MNCs use a greater proportion of PCNs (also called expatriates) in top management positions, staffing middle and lower management positions with increasing proportions of HCNs (locals) as one moves down the organizational hierarchy. The choice of staffing policy has a considerable influence on organizational variables in the subsidiary, such as the locus of decision-making authority, the methods of communication, and the perpetuation of human resource management

EXHIBIT 9-3   **Key Advantages and Drawbacks of Global Staffing Practices**

	Advantages	**Drawbacks**
PCNs	• Transfer and control firm strategy	• Costly to relocate family
	• Assignments abroad develop managers	• Little development of HCNs
	• Integrate knowledge firm-wide	• Lack local familiarity/contacts
	• Suitable managers not available locally	• PCN/family adaptation problems
	• Protect proprietary technology	• Limits use of global skills/ideas
HCNs	• Firm "acts local"; develops HCNs	• May have short-term loyalty
	• Familiarity with culture, procedures, politics, language, contacts, laws	
	• Fulfill government hiring requirements	
	• Can hit the ground running vs PCNs	
	• Likely to be less costly	• Less firm-wide coordination
	• Local role model; employee morale	• Possible conflict of interests
	• Business may be more accepted	
TCNs	• Broad global experience	• Little development of HCNs
	• Pool of shared learning	• May lack local contacts
	• Cultural flexibility and adaptability	• Complex to manage and harmonize
	• Language skills	
	• Often more acceptable than PCNs	• Less acceptable than HCNs
	• Often less-costly transferees	• Costly compared to HCNs
	• Liaison between HQ and local firm	
Inpatriates	• Linking pin between firm HQ and local host subsidiaries	• Does not replace need for PCNs or HCNs
	• Utilizes overseas experience and contacts to coordinate global operations	• Probably still perceived as an HQ manager
	• Provide continuity among revolving PCNs and HCNs.	• Difficulty in gaining trust
	• Facilitate global multicultural teams	

practices. These variables are illustrated in Exhibit 9-4. The ethnocentric staffing approach, for example, usually results in a higher level of authority and decision making in headquarters compared to the polycentric approach.[34]

Without exception, all phases of IHRM should support the desired strategy of the firm. In the staffing phase, having the right people in the right places at the right times is a key ingredient to success in international operations. An effective managerial cadre can be a distinct competitive advantage for a firm.

The initial phase of setting up criteria for global selection, then, is to consider which overall staffing approach or approaches would most likely support the company's strategy, as previously discussed—such as HCNs for localization, the (multilocal) strategic approach, and transpatriates and inpatriates for a global strategy. These are typically just starting points using idealized criteria, however. In reality, other factors creep into the process, such as host-country regulations, stage of internationalization, and—most often—who is both suitable and available for the position. It is also vital to integrate long-term strategic goals into the selection and development process, especially when rapid global expansion is intended. Insufficient projection of staffing needs for global assignments will likely result in constrained strategic opportunities because of a shortage of experienced managers suitable to place in those positions.

A more flexible approach to maximizing managerial talent, regardless of the source, would certainly consider more closely whether the position could be suitably filled by a host-country

EXHIBIT 9-4 Relationships Among Strategic Mode, Organizational Variables, and Staffing Orientation[35]

Aspects of the Enterprise	Orientation			
	Ethnocentric	**Polycentric**	**Regiocentric**	**Global**
Primary strategic orientation/stage	International	Multidomestic	Regional	Transnational
Perpetuation (recruiting, staffing, development)	People of home country developed for key positions everywhere in the world	People of local nationality developed for key positions in their own country	Regional people developed for key positions anywhere in the region	Best people everywhere in the world developed for key positions everywhere in the world
Complexity of organization	Complex in home country; simple in subsidiaries	Varied and independent	Highly interdependent on a regional basis	"Global Web": complex, worldwide alliances/network
Authority; decision	High in headquarters	Relatively low in headquarters	High in regional headquarters and/or high collaboration among subsidiaries	Collaboration of headquarters and subsidiaries around the world
Evaluation and control	Home standards applied to people and performance	Determined locally	Determined regionally	Globally integrated
Rewards	High in headquarters; low in subsidiaries	Wide variation; can be high or low rewards for subsidiary performance	Rewards for contribution to regional objectives	Rewards to international and local executives for reaching local and worldwide objectives based on global company goals
Communication; information flow	High volume of orders, commands, advice to subsidiaries	Little to and from headquarters; little among subsidiaries	Little to and from corporate headquarters, but may be high to and from regional headquarters and among countries	Horizontal; network relations; "virtual" teams
Geographic identification	Nationality of owner	Nationality of host country	Regional company	Truly global company, but identifying with national interests ("glocal")

national, as put forth by Tung, based on her research.[36] This contingency model of selection and training depends on the variables of the particular assignment, such as length of stay, similarity to the candidate's own culture, and level of interaction with local managers in that job. Tung concludes that the more rigorous the selection and training process, the lower the failure rate.

The selection process is set up as a decision tree in which the progression to the next stage of selection or the type of orientation training depends on the assessment of critical factors regarding the job or the candidate at each decision point. The simplest selection process involves choosing a local national because minimal training is necessary regarding the culture or ways of doing business locally. However, to be successful, local managers often require additional training in the MNC company-wide processes, technology, and corporate culture. If the position cannot be filled by a local national, yet the job requires a high level of interaction with the local community, careful screening of candidates from other countries and a vigorous training program are necessary.

Most MNCs tend to start their operations in a particular region by selecting primarily from their own pool of managers. Over time, and with increasing internationalization, they tend to move to a predominantly polycentric or regiocentric policy because of (1) increasing pressure (explicit or implicit) from local governments to hire locals (or sometimes legal restraints on the use of expatriates) and (2) the greater costs of expatriate staffing, particularly when the company has to pay taxes for the parent-company employee in both countries.[37] In addition, in recent years, MNCs have noted an improvement in the level of managerial and technical competence in many countries, negating the chief reason for using a primarily ethnocentric policy in the past. One researcher's comment represents a growing attitude: "All things being equal, a local national who speaks the language, understands the culture and the political system, and is often a member of the local elite should be more effective than an expatriate alien."[38] However, concerns about the need to maintain strategic control over subsidiaries and to develop managers with a global perspective remain a source of debate about staffing policies among human resource management professionals. A globally oriented company such as ABB (Asea Brown Boveri), for example, has 500 roving transpatriates who are moved every two to three years, thus developing a considerable management cadre with global experience.[39]

For MNCs based in Europe and Asia, human resource policies at all levels of the organization are greatly influenced by the home-country culture and policies. For Japanese subsidiaries in Singapore, Malaysia, and India, for example, promotion from within and expectations of long-term loyalty to and by the firm are culture-based practices transferable to subsidiaries. At Matsushita, however, selection criteria for staffing seem to be similar to those of Western companies. Its candidates are selected on the basis of a set of characteristics the firm calls SMILE: specialty (required skill, knowledge); management ability (particularly motivational ability); international flexibility (adaptability); language facility; and endeavor (perseverance in the face of difficulty).[40]

MANAGING EXPATRIATES

The survey identified three significant challenges facing corporations: finding suitable candidates for assignments, helping employees—and their families—complete their assignments, and retaining these employees once their assignments end.[41]

An important responsibility of IHR managers is that of managing expatriates—those employees who they assign to positions in other countries—whether from the headquarters country or third countries. Most multinationals underestimate the importance of the human resource function in the selection, training, acculturation, and evaluation of expatriates. The 2011 PricewaterhouseCoopers Survey found that CEOs anticipate a 50 percent increase in overseas assignments in the next decade. However, while the number of employers sending staff abroad is on the rise, only half actually have policies in place to govern these assignments, research shows.

Expatriate Selection

The selection of personnel for overseas assignments is a complex process. The criteria for selection are based on the same success factors as in the domestic setting, but additional criteria must be considered, relative to the specific circumstances of each international position. Unfortunately, many personnel directors have a long-standing, ingrained practice of selecting potential expatriates simply on the basis of their domestic track records and their technical expertise.[42] The need to ascertain whether potential expatriates have the necessary cross-cultural awareness and interpersonal skills for the position is too often overlooked. In their research of 136 large MNCs based in four countries—Germany, Japan, the United Kingdom, and the United States—Tungli and Peirperl examined the differences in frequency of using various selection criteria for expatriates, though of course they are not mutually exclusive criteria. While MNCs from all four countries highly rated "Technical/professional skills," the highest score for the German companies was the expatriate's willingness to go (let's assume that's a relative term, since presumably all those being considered must be willing to go); for the Japanese sample, it was "experience in the company," reflecting their traditional long-term employment contract. It is interesting to note, also, that "personality factors," which seems the closest "cultural adaptability" test, was given a far lower rating in the United States companies than those in Japan.[43]

Research by Mansour Javidan points to three major global mind-set attributes that successful expatriates possess:

- Intellectual capital, or knowledge, skills, understanding, and cognitive complexity.
- Psychological capital, or the ability to function successfully in the host country through internal acceptance of different cultures and a strong desire to learn from new experiences.
- Social capital, or the ability to build trusting relationships with local stakeholders, whether they are employees, supply chain partners, or customers.[44]

It is also important to assess whether the candidate's personal and family situation is such that everyone is likely to adapt to the local culture. Studies have shown there are five categories of success for expatriate managers: job factors, relational dimensions such as cultural empathy and flexibility, motivational state, family situation, and language skills. However, deciding before the expatriate goes on assignment whether he or she will be successful in those dimensions poses considerable problems for recruitment and selection purposes. Whereas language skills, for example, may be easy to ascertain, characteristics such as flexibility and cultural adjustment—widely acknowledged as most vital for expatriates—are difficult to judge beforehand. Human Resource managers wish for ways to prejudge such capabilities of candidates for assignments in order to avoid the many problems and considerable expense that can lead to expatriate failure (discussed further in this chapter and the next).

In order to address the problem of predicting how well an expatriate will perform on an overseas assignment, Tye and Chen studied factors that HR managers used as predictors of expatriate success. They found that the greatest predictive value was in the expatriate characteristics of stress tolerance and extraversion, and less on domestic work experience, gender, or even international experience. The results indicate that a manager who is extraverted (sociable, talkative) and who has a high tolerance for stress (typically experienced in new, different contexts such as in a "foreign" country) is more likely to be able to adjust to the new environment, the new job, and interacting with diverse people than those without those characteristics. HR selection procedures, then, often include seeking out managers with those characteristics because they know there will be a greater chance for successful job performance, and a lesser turnover likelihood.[45]

These expatriate success factors are based on studies of American expatriates. One could argue that the requisite skills are the same for managers from any country—and particularly so for third-country nationals. A study of expatriates in China, for example, found that expatriate success factors included performance management, training, organizational support, willingness to relocate, and strength of the relationship between the expatriate and the firm.[46]

Expatriate Performance Management

While 89 percent of companies formally assess a candidate's job skills prior to a foreign posting, less than half go through the same process for cultural suitability. Even fewer gauge whether the family will cope.[47]

Deciding on a staffing policy and selecting suitable managers are logical first steps, but they do not alone ensure success. When staffing overseas assignments with expatriates, for example, many other reasons, besides poor selection, contribute to *expatriate failure* among U.S. multinationals. A large percentage of these failures can be attributed to poor preparation and planning for the entry and reentry transitions of the manager and his or her family. One important variable, for example, often given insufficient attention in the selection, preparation, and support phases, is the suitability and adjustment of the spouse. The inability of the spouse to adjust to the new environment has been found to be a major—in fact, the most frequently cited—reason for expatriate failure in U.S. and European companies.[48] A Global Relocation Trends Survey found that 67 percent of respondents cited family concerns as the main cause for assignment failure. They cited spouse dissatisfaction as the primary reason, which they attributed to cultural adjustment problems and lack of career opportunities in the host country.[49] Yet only about half of those companies studied had included the spouse in the interviewing process. In addition, although research shows that human relational skills are critical for overseas work, most of the U.S. firms surveyed failed to include this factor in their assessment of candidates.[50] The following is a synthesis of the factors frequently mentioned by researchers and firms as the major causes of expatriate failure:

- Selection based on headquarters criteria rather than assignment needs
- Inadequate preparation, training, and orientation prior to assignment
- Alienation or lack of support from headquarters
- Inability to adapt to local culture and working environment
- Problems with spouse and children—poor adaptation, family unhappiness
- Insufficient compensation and financial support
- Poor programs for career support and repatriation

After careful selection based on the specific assignment and the long-term plans of both the organization and the candidates, plans must be made for the preparation, training, and development of expatriate managers. In the following sections we discuss training and development and then compensation. However, it is useful to note that these should be components of an integrated performance management program, specific to expatriates, which includes goal setting, training, performance appraisal, and performance-related compensation.

Hsi-An Shih et al. conducted a study in which they interviewed expatriates and human resource professionals in global information technology companies headquartered in five different countries. These were Applied Materials (American) with 16,000 employees in 13 countries, Hitachi High Technologies (Japanese) with 470,000 employees in 23 countries, Philips Electronics (Dutch) with 192,000 employees in 60 countries, Samsung (Korean) with 173,000 employees in 20 countries, and Winbond Electronics (Taiwanese) with 47,000 employees in six countries. Shih et al. found that those companies used standardized forms from headquarters, rather than tailoring them to the host environment; as such they reflected the company culture but not the local culture in which those expatriates were operating. There also was lack of on-the-job training from those companies.[51] The differences in procedures for goal setting, performance appraisal, training, and performance-related pay among those five companies are detailed in Exhibit 9-5.

EXPATRIATE TRAINING AND DEVELOPMENT

It is clear that preparation and training for cross-cultural interactions are critical. A Global Relocation Trends Survey revealed that attrition rates for expatriates were more than double the rate of non-expatriates. They found that 21 percent of expatriates left their companies during the assignments, and another 23 percent left within a year of returning from the assignment.[52] Moreover, about half of those who remain longer in their overseas assignment function at a low level of effectiveness. The direct cost alone of a failed expatriate assignment is estimated to be from $200,000 to $1.2 million. The indirect costs may be far greater, depending on the expatriate's position. Relations with the host-country government and customers may be damaged, resulting in a loss of market share and a poor reception for future PCNs.

Both cross-cultural adjustment problems and practical differences in everyday living present challenges for expatriates and their families. Examples are evident from a survey of expatriates in which they ranked the countries that presented the most challenging assignments to them, along with some pet peeves from their experiences:

China: a continuing problem for expatriates; one complained that at his welcome banquet he was served duck tongue and pigeon head.

Brazil: Expatriates stress that cell phones are essential because home phones don't work.

India: Returning executives complain that the pervasiveness of poverty and street children is overwhelming.

Indonesia: Here you need to plan ahead financially because landlords typically demand rent two to three years in advance.

Japan: Expatriates and their families remain concerned that, although there is excellent medical care, the Japanese doctors reveal little to their patients.[53]

EXHIBIT 9-5   **Expatriate Performance Management from MNEs of Five National Origins**

Company	Goal Setting	Performance Appraisal	Training and Development	Performance-related Pay
AMT (American)	Short-term: sending unit's general manager Long term: host country's general manager	Annual performance appraisal Open feedback Interview	Applied global university Seldom take training programs while on assignment No clear connection between performance result and career development	Clear link between performance and compensation Cash bonuses and stock options
Hitachi (Japanese)	Self-setting, then finalized by host-country manager	Annually for managerial purposes, biannually for development purposes; One-way feedback discussion Seldom take training programs while on assignment	Orientation Language training Can apply to host location supervisor No clear connection between performance result and career development	Link between performance and compensation not clear Seniority-based pay system Cash bonuses
Philips (Dutch)	Self-setting, then finalized by host-country manager	Biannual performance appraisal; Open feedback in interview	Orientation Seldom take training programs while on assignment No clear connection between performance result and career development	Clear link between performance and compensation Cash bonuses and stock options
Samsung (Korean)	Self-setting, then finalized by host-country manager	Biannually for managerial purposes, annually for development purposes; Open feedback in interview	Orientation Language training Can apply to host location supervisor No clear connection between performance result and career development	Clear link between performance and compensation Senior managers: cash bonuses and stock options Ordinary expatriates: cash bonuses
Windbond (Taiwanese)	Self-setting, then finalized by host-country manager	Biannual performance appraisal; Feedback depends on manager	Orientation Seldom take training programs while on assignment Can apply to host location supervisor No clear connection between performance result and career development	Clear link between performance and compensation Cash bonuses and stock options

Source: Adapted from His-An Shih, Yun-Hwa Chiang, and In-Sook Kim, "Expatriate Performance Management from MNEs of Different National Origins," *International Journal of Manpower* 26, no. 2 (2005): 161–62. Reprinted with permission of Emerald Group Publishing Ltd, 2011.

Even though cross-cultural training has proved to be of high value in making the assignment a success, only 20 percent of companies surveyed had formal cross-cultural training for expatriates.[54] Much of the rationale for this lack of training is an assumption that managerial skills and processes are universal. In a simplistic way, a manager's domestic track record is used as the major selection criterion for an overseas assignment.

In most countries, however, the success of the expatriate is not left so much to chance. Foreign companies provide considerably more training and preparation for expatriates than U.S. companies. Therefore, it is not hard to understand why Japanese expatriates experience significantly fewer incidences of failure than their U.S. counterparts, although this may be partially because fewer families accompany Japanese assignees. Japanese multinationals typically have recall rates of below 5 percent, signifying that they send abroad managers who are far better prepared and more adept at working and flourishing in a foreign environment.[55] While this success is largely attributable to training programs, it is also a result of intelligent planning by the human resource management staff in most Japanese organizations, as reported by Tung.[56] This planning begins with a careful selection process for overseas assignments, based on the long-term knowledge of executives and their families. An effective selection process, of course, will eliminate many potential "failures" from the start. Another factor is the longer duration of overseas assignments, averaging almost five years, which allows the Japanese expatriate more time to adjust initially and then to function at full capacity. In addition, Japanese expatriates receive considerable support from headquarters and sometimes even from local divisions set up for that purpose. At NEC Corporation, for example, part of the Japanese giant's globalization strategy is its permanent boot camp, with its elaborate training exercises to prepare NEC managers and their families for overseas battle.[57]

The demands on expatriate managers have always been as much a result of the multiple relationships that they have to maintain as they are of the differences in the host-country environment. Those relations include family relations; internal relations with people in the corporation, both locally and globally, especially with headquarters; external relations (suppliers, distributors, allies, customers, local community, etc.); and relations with the host government. It is important to pinpoint any potential problems that an expatriate may experience with those relationships so that these problems may be addressed during predeparture training. Problem recognition is the first stage in a comprehensive plan for developing expatriates. The three areas critical to preparation are cultural training, language instruction, and familiarity with everyday matters.[58] In the model shown in Exhibit 9-6, various development methods are used to address these areas during predeparture training, postarrival training, and reentry training. These methods continue to be valid and used by many organizations. Two-way feedback between the executive and the trainers at each stage helps to tailor the level and kinds of training to the individual manager. The desired goal is the increased effectiveness of the expatriate as a result of familiarity with local conditions, cultural awareness, and an appreciation of his or her family's needs in the host country.

Cross-cultural Training

Training in language and practical affairs is quite straightforward, but cross-cultural training is not; it is complex and deals with deep-rooted behaviors. The actual process of cross-cultural training should result in the expatriate learning both content and skills that will improve interactions with host-country individuals by reducing misunderstandings and inappropriate behaviors.

CULTURE SHOCK

The goal of training is to ease the adjustment to the new environment by reducing **culture shock**—a state of disorientation and anxiety about not knowing how to behave in an unfamiliar culture. The cause of culture shock is the trauma people experience in new and different cultures, where they lose the familiar signs and cues that they had used to interact in daily life and where they must learn to cope with a vast array of new cultural cues and expectations.[59] The symptoms of culture shock range from mild irritation to deep-seated psychological panic or crisis. The inability to work effectively, stress within the family, and hostility toward host nationals are the common dysfunctional results of culture shock—often leading to the manager giving up and going home.

It is helpful to recognize the stages of culture shock to understand what is happening. Culture shock usually progresses through four stages, as described by Oberg: (1) *honeymoon*, when positive attitudes and expectations, excitement, and a tourist feeling prevail (which may last up to several weeks); (2) *irritation and hostility*, the crisis stage when cultural differences result in problems at work, at home, and in daily living—expatriates and family members feel homesick

EXHIBIT 9-6   IHRM Process to Maximize Effectiveness of Expatriate Assignments

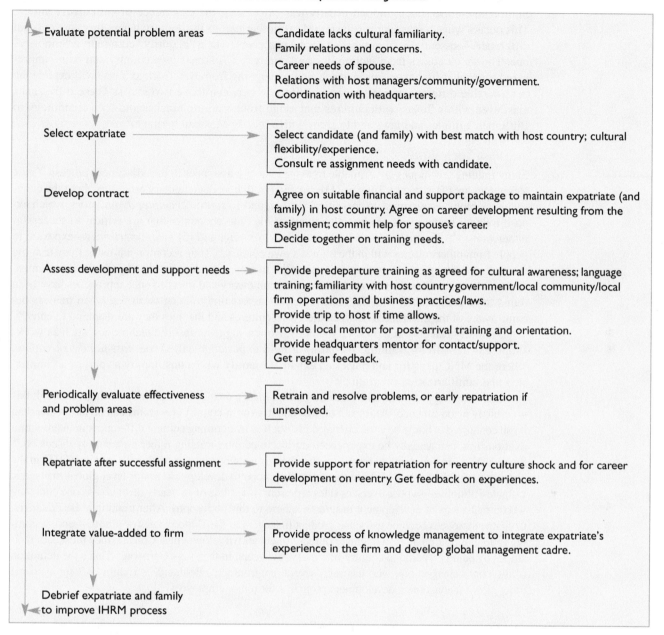

and disoriented, lashing out at everyone (many never get past this stage); (3) *gradual adjustment*, a period of recovery in which the "patient" gradually becomes able to understand and predict patterns of behavior, use the language, and deal with daily activities, and the family starts to accept their new life; and (4) *biculturalism*, the stage in which the manager and family members grow to accept and appreciate local people and practices and are able to function effectively in two cultures.[60] Many never get to the fourth stage—operating acceptably at the third stage—but those who do report that their assignment is positive and growth oriented. In recognition of the importance of helping expatriates adapt to the local environment, companies such as PepsiCo provide a number of localized programs to aid the transition. Pepsico's 600 expats and their families are encouraged to join the company's health and wellness programs and various local sports programs such as soccer in Dubai, ping-pong in China, and Zumba in Latin countries. The company believes such activities help their people to adjust to the new culture and get involved in the local community. In addition, the company provides families language lessons and help with child tuition.[61]

SUBCULTURE SHOCK

Similar to culture shock, though usually less extreme, is the experience of **subculture shock**. This occurs when a manager is transferred to another part of the country where there are cultural differences—essentially from what she or he perceives to be a "majority" culture to a "minority" one. The shock comes from feeling like an "immigrant" in one's own country and being unprepared for such differences. For instance, someone going from New York to Texas will experience considerable differences in attitudes and lifestyle between those two states. These differences exist even within Texas, with cultures that range from roaming ranches and high technology to Bible-belt attitudes and laws and to areas with a mostly Mexican heritage.[62]

Training Techniques

Many training techniques are available to assist overseas assignees in the adjustment process. These techniques are classified by Tung as (1) *area studies*, that is, documentary programs about the country's geography, economics, sociopolitical history, and so forth; (2) *culture assimilators*, which expose trainees to the kinds of situations they are likely to encounter that are critical to successful interactions; (3) *language training*; (4) *sensitivity training*; and (5) *field experiences*—exposure to people from other cultures within the trainee's own country.[63] Tung recommends using these training methods in a complementary fashion, giving the trainee increasing levels of personal involvement as she or he progresses through each method. Documentary and interpersonal approaches have been found to be comparable, with the most effective intercultural training occurring when trainees become aware of the differences between their own cultures and the ones they are planning to enter.[64]

Similarly categorizing training methods, Ronen suggests specific techniques, such as workshops and sensitivity training, including a field experience called the *host-family surrogate*, where the MNC pays for and places an expatriate family with a host family as part of an immersion and familiarization program.[65]

Most training programs take place in the expatriate's own country prior to leaving. Although this is certainly a convenience, the impact of host-country (or in-country) programs can be far greater than those conducted at home because crucial skills, such as overcoming cultural differences in intercultural relationships, can actually be experienced during in-country training rather than simply discussed.[66] Some MNCs are beginning to recognize that there is no substitute for on-the-job training (OJT) in the early stages of the careers of those managers they hope to develop into senior-level global managers. Colgate-Palmolive—whose overseas sales represent two-thirds of its yearly revenue—is one company whose management development programs adhere to this philosophy. After training at headquarters, Colgate employees become associate product managers in the United States or abroad—and, according to John R. Garrison, then manager of recruitment and development at Colgate, they must earn their stripes by being prepared to country-hop every few years. In fact, says Garrison, "That's the definition of a global manager: one who has seen several environments firsthand."[67] Exhibit 9-7 shows some other global management development programs for junior employees.

EXHIBIT 9-7   **Corporate Programs to Develop Global Managers**

- ABB (Asea Brown Boveri) rotates about 500 managers around the world to different countries every two to three years in order to develop a management cadre of transpatriates to support their global strategy.
- PepsiCo has an orientation program for its foreign managers, which brings them to the United States for one-year assignments in bottling division plants.
- British Telecom uses informal mentoring techniques to induct employees into the ways of their assigned country; existing expatriate workers talk to prospective assignees about the cultural factors to expect (www.FT.com).
- Honda of America Manufacturing gives its U.S. supervisors and managers extensive preparation in Japanese language, culture, and lifestyle and then sends them to the parent company in Tokyo for up to three years.
- General Electric likes its engineers and managers to have a global perspective whether or not they are slated to go abroad. The company gives regular language and cross-cultural training for them so that they are equipped to conduct business with people around the world (www.GE.com).

EXHIBIT 9-8 Stage of Globalization and Training Design Issues[68]

Export Stage	MNC Stage
Training Need: Low to moderate	*Training Need:* High moderate to high
Content: Emphasis should be on interpersonal skills, local culture, customer values, and business behavior.	*Content:* Emphasis should be on interpersonal skills, two-way technology transfer, corporate value transfer, international strategy, stress management, local culture, and business practices.
Host-Country Nationals: Train to understand parent-country products and policies.	*Host-Country Nationals:* Train in technical areas, product and service systems, and corporate culture.
MDC Stage	**Global Stage**
Training Need: Moderate to high	*Training Need:* High
Content: Emphasis should be on interpersonal skills, local culture, technology transfer, stress management, and business practices and laws.	*Content:* Emphasis should be on global corporate operations and systems, corporate culture transfer, customers, global competitors, and international strategy.
Host-Country Nationals: Train to familiarize with production and service procedures.	*Host-Country Nationals:* Train for proficiency in global organization production and efficiency systems, corporate culture, business systems, and global conduct policies.

INTEGRATING TRAINING WITH GLOBAL ORIENTATION

In continuing our discussion of "strategic fit," it is important to remember that training programs, like staffing approaches, should be designed with the company's strategy in mind. Although it is probably impractical to break down those programs into a lot of variations, it is feasible to at least consider the relative level or stage of globalization that the firm has reached, because obvious major differences would be appropriate—for example, from the initial export stage to the full global stage. Exhibit 9-8 suggests levels of rigor and types of training content appropriate for the firm's managers, as well as those for host-country nationals, for four globalization stages—export, multidomestic, multinational, and global. It is noteworthy, for example, that the training of host-country nationals for a global firm has a considerably higher level of scope and rigor than that for the other stages, and borders on the standards for the firm's expatriates.

As a further area for managerial preparation for global orientation—in addition to training plans for expatriates and for HCNs separately—there is a particular need to anticipate potential problems with the interaction of expatriates and local staff. In a study of expatriates and local staff (inpatriates) in Central and Eastern European joint ventures and subsidiaries, Peterson found that managers reported a number of behaviors by expatriates that helped them to integrate with local staff, but also some that were hindrances (see Exhibit 9-9).[69] Clearly, this kind of feedback from MNC managers in the field can provide the basis for expatriate training and also help HCNs to anticipate and work with the expatriates in order to meet joint strategic objectives.

Compensating Expatriates

If you're an expatriate working alongside another expatriate and you're being treated differently, it creates a lot of dissension.

CHRISTOPHER TICE, MANAGER,
GLOBAL EXPATRIATE OPERATIONS, DUPONT INC.[70]

The significance of an appropriate compensation and benefits package to attract, retain, and motivate international employees cannot be overemphasized. Compensation is a crucial link between strategy and its successful implementation: There must be a fit between compensation and the

EXHIBIT 9-9   Factors That Facilitate or Hinder the Integration of Expatriate Staff with Local Staff

Facilitates Integration	Hinders Integration
Relationship-building	Not using team concept
Speaking the local language	Not learning local language
Knowledge sharing	Withholding useful information
Cultural adaptability/flexibility	Spouse and family problems in adjusting
Respect	Superior and autocratic behavior
Overseas experience	Limited time in assignment
Develop local value-added from venture	Headquarters mentality
Encourage local innovation	Dominate from head office

Source: Based on R. B. Peterson, *Journal of World Business* 38 (2003): 55–69. "The Use of Expatriates and Inpatriates in Central and Eastern Europe Since the Wall Came Down."

goals for which the firm wants managers to aim. So that they will not feel exploited, employees need to perceive equity and goodwill in their compensation and benefits, whether they are PCNs, HCNs, or TCNs. The premature return of expatriates or the unwillingness of managers to take overseas assignments can often be traced to their knowledge that the assignment is detrimental to them financially and usually to their career progression. One company that recognizes the need for a reasonable degree of standardization in its treatment of expatriates is DuPont. The company has centralized programs in its Global Transfer Center of Expertise for its approximately 400 annual international relocations, so its expatriates know that everyone is getting the same package. The company seems to be on the cutting edge; however, a recent study by Mercer Human Resource Consulting found that "25 percent of multinational corporations do not have a benefits policy for globally mobile employees, 30 percent have no formal governance procedures and 11 percent have never reviewed their policies."[71]

From the firm's perspective, the high cost of maintaining appropriate compensation packages for expatriates has led many companies—Colgate-Palmolive, Chase Manhattan Bank, Digital Equipment, General Motors, and General Electric among them—to find ways to cut the cost of PCN assignments as much as possible. "Transfer a $100,000-a-year American executive to London—and suddenly he [or she] costs the employer $300,000," explains the *Wall Street Journal*. "Move him to Stockholm or Tokyo, and he [or she] easily becomes a million-dollar [manager]."[72]

Firms try to cut overall costs of assignments by either extending the expatriate's tour, since turnover is expensive—especially when there is an accompanying family to move—or to assign expatriates to a much shorter tour as an unaccompanied assignment.[73]

Designing and maintaining an appropriate compensation package is more complex than it would seem because of the need to consider and reconcile parent- and host-country financial, legal, and customary practices. The problem is that although little variation in typical executive salaries at the level of base compensation exists around the world, a wide variation in net spendable income is often present. U.S. executives may receive more in cash and stock, but they have to spend more for what foreign companies provide, such as cars, vacations, and entertainment allowances. In addition, the manager's purchasing power with that net income is affected by the relative cost of living. The cost of living is considerably higher in most of Europe than in the United States. In designing compensation and benefit packages for PCNs, then, the challenge to IHRM professionals is to maintain a standard of living for expatriates equivalent to their colleagues at home, plus compensating them for any additional costs incurred. This policy is referred to as "keeping the expatriate whole."[74]

To ensure that expatriates do not lose out through their overseas assignment, the **balance sheet approach**, or **home-based method**, (see Exhibit 9-10 for an example) is often used to equalize the standard of living between the host country and the home country and to add some compensation for inconvenience or qualitative loss.[75] However, recently some companies have begun to base their compensation package on a goal of achieving a standard of living comparable to that of host-country managers, which does help resolve some of the problems of pay differentials.

EXHIBIT 9-10   The Balance Sheet Approach to Expatriate Compensation Package—Hypothetical Examples (Estimates in U.S. Dollars)

Sample Components for Expat	Chicago	Tokyo	Mexico City
Base Salary + COLA	$100,000	$150,000	$75,000
Relocation Allowance (20%)		30,000	15,000
Housing Allowance (20%)		30,000	15,000
Private Education for two children		30,000	20,000
Two trips per year home for four		12,000	10,000
	$100,000	252,000	135,000

Additional costs not estimated here include any local tax differential, health insurance, placement services for spouse, moving expenses and home sale, predeparture training and preparation, etc., as well as other negotiated items. In some "dangerous" locales, there will be additional costs pertaining to the safety of personnel, such as insurance, security guards, etc.

In fairness, the MNC is obliged to make up additional costs that the expatriate would incur for taxes, housing, and goods and services. The tax differential is complex and expensive for the company, and MNCs generally use a policy of tax equalization. This means that the company pays any taxes due on any type of additional compensation that the expatriate receives for the assignment; the expatriate pays in taxes only what she or he would pay at home. The burden of foreign taxes can be lessened, however, by efficient tax planning—a fact often overlooked by small firms. The timing and methods of paying people determine what foreign taxes are incurred. For example, a company can save on taxes by renting an apartment for the employee instead of providing a cash housing allowance. All in all, MNCs have to weigh the many aspects of a complete compensation package, especially at high management levels, to effect a tax equalization policy. The total cost to the company can vary greatly by location; for example:

> *Expatriates in Germany may incur twice the income tax they would in the U.S., and they are taxed on their housing and cost-of-living allowances as well. This financial snowball effect is a great incentive to make sure we really need to fill the position with an expatriate.*[76]

Managing expatriate compensation is a complex challenge for companies with overseas operations. All components of the compensation package must be considered in light of both home- and host-country legalities and practices. Those components include:

Salary: Local salary buying power and currency translation, as compared with home salary; bonuses or incentives for dislocation

Taxes: Equalize any differential effects of taxes as a result of expatriate's assignment

Allowances: Relocation expenses; cost-of-living adjustments (COLA); housing allowance for assignment and allowance to maintain house at home; trips home for expatriate and family; private education for children

Benefits: Health insurance; stock options.

The **localization**, or **going-rate, approach** pays the expatriate the going rate for similar positions in the host country, plus whatever allowances and benefits for the assignment that the manager negotiates. With the basic pay similar to other managers in the host country, no matter where they come from, there is less resentment and more opportunity for open cooperation. However, when the going rate in a location is less than that in the home country—which is likely the case for a U.S.-based expatriate—she or he is likely to be reluctant to accept that assignment unless there are considerable perks in addition to the salary.

With the increasing number of companies that operate around the world and assign and move personnel (whether one calls them expatriates, transpatriates, or inpatriates) from one country to another, the design of equitable pay scales has become exceedingly complex. In a 2011 International

Assignments Policies and Practices Survey by KPMG, companies noted the need to "review mobility policies to focus on harmonization of the treatment of globally mobile employees."[77] Should those managers in similar positions who come from different countries to a host country be paid according to the MNE headquarters location, or the host location, or that manager's home location? Or should they all be paid the same according to a globally-determined rate for that job? Further complications arise from any legal or cultural restrictions on compensation in a particular location.

Most important, to be strategically competitive, the compensation package must be comparatively attractive to the kinds of managers the company wishes to hire or relocate. Some of those managers will, of course, be local managers in the host country. This, too, is a complex situation requiring competitive compensation policies that can attract, motivate, and retain the best local managerial talent. In many countries, however, it is a considerable challenge to develop compensation packages appropriate to the local situation and culture, while also recognizing the differences between local salaries and those expected by expatriates or transpatriates (that difference itself often being a source of competitive advantage).

TRAINING AND COMPENSATING HOST-COUNTRY NATIONALS

Training HCNs

We found that the key human resource role of the MNC [in Central and Eastern Europe] was to expose the local staff to a market economy; to instill world standards of performance; and provide training and functional expertise.[78]

The continuous training and development of HCNs and TCNs for management positions is also important to the long-term success of multinational corporations. As part of a long-term staffing policy for a subsidiary, the ongoing development of HCNs will facilitate the transition to an indigenization policy. Furthermore, multinational companies like to have well-trained managers with broad international experience available to take charge in many intercultural settings, whether at home or abroad, and, increasingly, in developing countries. Kimberly-Clark, for example, with over 60,000 employees around the world, has steadily increased its talent development and training programs in all countries, but more recently has focused on developing markets. "In Latin America, the average employee has gone from receiving practically no training time to about 38 hours each year. By contrast, workers in Europe now receive 40 hours per year—eight hours more than in 1996."[79]

Training for HCNs by foreign companies operating in the United States can be quite surprising for managers operating in their own country when they have to learn new ways. Toyota is an example of how employees at all levels must be trained in "the Toyota Way." As recounted by Ms. Newton, a 38-year-old Indiana native who joined Toyota after college 15 years ago and now works at the North American headquarters in Erlanger, Kentucky:

For Americans and anyone, it can be a shock to the system to be actually expected to make problems visible. Other corporate environments tend to hide problems from bosses.[80]

What Ms. Newton is referring to are the colored bar charts against a white bulletin board, which represent the work targets of individual workers, visibly charting their successes or failures to meet those targets. This is part of the Toyota Way. The idea is not to humiliate, but to alert co-workers and enlist their help in finding solutions. Ms. Newton, now a general manager in charge of employee training and development at Toyota's North American manufacturing subsidiary, said it took a while to fully accept that but now she is a firm believer.[81]

Certainly, there is no arguing with success—in 2009 Toyota became the largest global automaker in sales. The training institute in Mikkabi has trained over 700 foreign executives, including cultural orientation with the same intensity as its training in the production processes. Core concepts such as ownership of problems and visibility are impressed upon new employees. A shared sense of shared purpose is conveyed with open offices—often without even cubicle partitions between desks.[82]

Many multinationals, in particular "chains," wish to train their local managers and workers to bridge the divide between, on the one hand, the firm's successful corporate culture and practices, and on the other, the local culture and work practices. One example of how to do this in China is the Starbucks firm, featured in *Management In Action: Success! Starbucks' Java Style Helps to Recruit, Train, and Retain Local Managers in Beijing.*

Many HCNs are, of course, receiving excellent training in global business and Internet technology within their home corporations. For example, Kim In Kyung, twenty-four, has a job involving world travel and high technology with Samsung Electronics Company of Seoul, South Korea. Part of Samsung's strategy is to promote its new Internet focus, reflecting Seoul's sizzling tech boom.[83]

Whether in home corporations, MNC subsidiaries, or joint ventures in any country, managerial training to facilitate e-business adoption is taking on increasing competitive importance in order to take advantage of new strategic opportunities. While large companies are well ahead on the curve for information and communication technologies (ICT), there is considerable need for small and medium-sized enterprises (SMEs) to adopt such knowledge-creating capabilities.

Managerial training in ICT is particularly critical for firms in new economy and emerging markets, and, in the aggregate, can provide leverage for rapid economic growth in regions such as Eastern Europe. Research by Damaskopoulos and Evgeniou addressed these needs by surveying more than 900 SME managers in Slovenia, Poland, Romania, Bulgaria, and Cyprus. While most managers recognized the opportunities in implementing e-business strategies, they also noted the urgent need for training in order to take advantage of those opportunities. Some of the training needs and issues as perceived by those SME managers are shown below. Some of these factors are at the firm level, while other issues relate to the market and regulatory levels, such as the need to increase security for commercial activity on the Internet.[84] Such findings highlight the need to recognize the strategy-staffing-training link and its importance to the overall growth of emerging economies.

Training Priorities for E-Business Development[85]

- How to develop a business plan and an e-business strategy
- How to develop the partnerships and in-house expertise for e-business
- How to finance e-business initiatives
- Addressing security and privacy concerns
- How to set up electronic payments
- How to develop good customer relations on the Internet
- Training in technology management
- How to collect marketing intelligence online

 MANAGEMENT IN ACTION

Success! Starbucks' Java Style Helps to Recruit, Train, and Retain Local Managers in Beijing

When we first started, people didn't know who we were and it was rough finding sites. Now landlords are coming to us.

DAVID SUN,

President of Beijing Mei Da Coffee Company (former Starbucks' partner for Northern China), *The Economist*, October 6, 2001.

As we see from the above quote, Starbucks has achieved a remarkable penetration rate in China, given that it is a country of devoted tea drinkers who do not take readily to the taste of coffee.

Starbucks is no stranger to training leaders from around the world into the Starbucks style. As of October 2011, Starbucks has both store-owned and licensed locations in 54 countries, as detailed below:

Starbucks' Global Presence as of 2011

UNITED STATES STORES

50 states, plus the District of Columbia.

7,087 Company-operated stores.

4,081 Licensed stores.

FIGURE 9-1   A Starbucks Coffee Shop in Old Beijing-Style Building
in Beijing, China

Source: © Jack Young-Places/Alamy

INTERNATIONAL STORES

43 countries outside the United States.

Company-operated: 1,796 stores, in Australia, Canada, Chile, China (Northern China, Southern China), Germany, Ireland, Puerto Rico, Singapore, Thailand, and the United Kingdom.

Joint Venture and Licensed Stores: 2,792 stores, in Austria, the Bahamas, Bahrain, Brazil, Canada, China (Shanghai/Eastern China), Cyprus, Czech Republic, Denmark, Egypt, France, Greece, Hong Kong, Indonesia, Ireland, Japan, Jordan, Kuwait, Lebanon, Macau S.A.R., Malaysia, Mexico, the Netherlands, New Zealand, Oman, Peru, the Philippines, Qatar, Romania, Russia, Saudi Arabia, South Korea, Spain, Switzerland, Taiwan, Turkey, the United Arab Emirates, and the United Kingdom.[86]

Company managers nevertheless have had quite a challenge in recruiting, motivating, and retaining managers for its Beijing outlets (and, more recently, in its Qunguang Square outlet in Central China). Starbucks' primary challenge has been to recruit good managers in a country where the demand for local managers by foreign companies expanding there is far greater than the supply of managers with any experience in capitalist-style companies. Chinese recruits have stressed that they are looking for opportunity to get training and to advance in global companies rather than for money. They know that managers with experience in Western organizations can always get a job. The brand's pop-culture reputation is also an attraction to young Beijingers.

In order to expose the recruits to java-style culture as well as to train them for management, Starbucks brings them to Seattle, Washington, for three months to give them a taste of the West Coast lifestyle and the company's informal culture, such as Western-style backyard barbecues.

Then they are exposed to the art of cappuccino-making at a real store before dawn and concocting dozens of fancy coffees. They get the same intensive training as anyone else anywhere in the world. One recruit, Mr. Wang, who worked in a large Beijing hotel before finding out how to make a triple grande latte, said that he enjoys the casual atmosphere and respect. The training and culture are very different from what one would expect at a traditional state-owned company in China, where the work is strictly defined and has no challenge for employees.

Starbucks has found that motivating their managers in Beijing is multifaceted. They know that people won't switch jobs for money alone. They want to work for a company that gives them an opportunity to learn. They also want to have a good working environment and a company with a strong reputation. The recruits have expressed their need for trust and participation in an environment where local nationals are traditionally not expected to exercise initiative or authority. In all, what seems to motivate them more than anything else is their dignity.

Source: www.Starbucks.com, *Corporate Information: October 2011 and March 5, 2009; Associated Press, "Starbucks Reorganizes for Growth,"* www.nytimes.com; *J. Adamy, "Starbucks Raises New-Stores Goal, Enters iTunes Deal," Wall Street Journal, October 6, 2006; "China: Starbucks Opens New Outlet in Beijing," Info-Prod (Middle East) Ltd., July 20, 2003; "Coffee with Your Tea? Starbucks in China," The Economist, October 6, 2001.*

In another common scenario also requiring the management of a mixture of executives and employees, American and European MNCs presently employ Asians as well as Arab locals in their plants and offices in Saudi Arabia, bringing together three cultures: well-educated Asian managers living in a Middle Eastern, highly traditional society who are employed by a firm reflecting Western technology and culture. This kind of situation requires training to help all parties effectively integrate multiple sets of culturally based values, expectations, and work habits.

Compensating HCNs

How do firms deal with the question of what is appropriate compensation for host-country nationals, given local norms and the competitive needs of the firm? According to a survey of 90 MNCs by Mercer Human Resource Consulting, 85 percent of MNCs have a global pay strategy in place. Those firms adjust pay according to market conditions and design methods for job grading and incentive plans.[87]

Of course, no one set of solutions can be applicable in any country. Many variables apply—including local market factors and pay scales, government involvement in benefits, the role of unions, the cost of living, and so on. In Eastern Europe, for example, Hungarians, Poles, and Czechs spend 35 to 40 percent of their disposable income on food and utilities, which may run as high as 75 percent in the Russian Federation.[88] Therefore, East European managers must have cash for about 65 to 80 percent of their base pay, compared to about 40 percent for U.S. managers (the rest being long-term incentives, benefits, and perks). In addition, they still expect the many social benefits provided by the "old government." To be competitive, MNCs can focus on providing goods and services that are either not available at all or are extremely expensive in Eastern Europe. Such upscale perks can be used to attract high-skilled workers.

Nestlé Bulgaria offers a company car and a cellular phone to new recruits.[89]

In Japan, in response to a decade-long economic slump, companies are revamping their HRM policies to compete in a global economy. The traditional lifetime employment and guaranteed tidy pension are giving way to the more Western practices of competing for jobs, of basing pay on performance rather than seniority, and of making people responsible for their own retirement fund decisions.[90]

"Finding the appropriate talent to take advantage of the growth prospects of emerging markets is one of the biggest challenges we face," said Louis Camilleri, chairman and CEO of Philip Morris International.

THE 2011 PRICEWATERHOUSECOOPERS' 14TH
ANNUAL CEO SURVEY

According to the PricewaterhouseCoopers' survey, 40 percent of CEOs report difficulty forecasting talent availability in the Asia Pacific Region, in particular China and India. A key concern of Western managers in China, and India, as well as the firms that outsource there, are the rapidly rising pay rates in those countries, as well as a shortage of top talent. This shortage of talent is especially problematic in India. With the considerable growth in emerging markets, foreign firms trying to get on the bandwagon there are finding themselves in a "war for talent." With that kind of supply-demand ratio for local skilled managers, salaries are being pushed up; that situation then lowers the rationale for hiring local managers instead of sending expatriates.

According to Citigroup, it is also imperative to make clear what benefits, as well as salary, come with a position because of the way compensation is perceived and regulated around the world.[91] In Latin America, for example, an employee's pay and title are associated with what type of car they can receive.

In a 2011 study by the Society for Human Resource Management and the employee-engagement consulting firm Globoforce found that 80 percent of 745 organizations surveyed have some kind of incentive and reward program. However, the respondents cited the tremendous challenge of aligning their programs within a diversity of cultural values and local systems.[92]

COMPARATIVE MANAGEMENT IN FOCUS

IHRM Practices in Australia, Canada, China, Indonesia, Japan, Latin America, Mexico, South Korea, Taiwan, and the United States

In a comparative long-term study of how the major IHRM functions are performed around the world, a team of 37 researchers in ten locations, led by Mary Ann von Glinow, studied how and in what environments various organizations conducted those functions. Exhibit 9-11 is a summary of the findings from their "Best International Human Resource Management Practices Project." For the practice of compensation, for example, the first column shows those practices the researchers found to be universal within the cultures studied. The second column shows countries or regions where those practices are similar. The third column shows where those practices were specific to certain countries. For the practice of selection, for example, a major tool in Korea is the employment test, whereas in Taiwan the job interview is considered the most important criterion. Korea and Taiwan also "cluster" in de-emphasizing proven work experience; whereas the Anglo cluster showed the job interview, technical skill, and work experience to be the most important selection criteria. Those "universals" found for the selection function were "getting along with others" and "fit with the corporate values."[93]

EXHIBIT 9-11 Trends in International Human Resource Management Practices Across Selected Countries and Regions

Practice	Universal Derived ETICS "Best Practices"	Regional or Country Clusters	Country Specific
Compensation	Pay incentives should not comprise too much of an employee's compensation package. Compensation should be based on individual job performance. There should be a reduced emphasis on seniority. Benefits should comprise an important part of a compensation package.	Seniority-based pay, pay based on group/team or organizational goals, and pay based on future goals—all are used to a larger extent in the Asian and Latin countries now.	U.S. and Canada has less use of pay incentives than expected. China and Taiwan had above-average use of pay incentives, and wanted more based on individual contributions.
Selection	"Getting along with others," and "Fit with the Corporate Values" signals a shift in selection from "West meets East."	Selection practices were remarkably similar among the Anglo countries. Specifically, job interview, technical skill, and work experience are the most important selection criteria. How well the person fits the company's values replace work experience as one of the top selection criteria for future selection practices. Selection practices are quite similar in Korea, Japan, and Taiwan. Specifically, proven work experience is de-emphasized as a selection practice in these countries. In the Anglo and Latin American countries, allowing subordinates to express themselves is perceived as an important future appraisal practice.	In Japan, a heavy emphasis is placed on a person's potential (thus hiring new graduates) and his/her ability to get along with others. A relatively low weight was given to job-related skills and experience as a selection criterion. In Korea, employment tests are considered crucial and are used to a large extent as a selection tool, as well as hiring new graduates. Koreans de-emphasize experience. In Taiwan, the job interview is considered the most important criterion in the selection process.

EXHIBIT 9-11 **Trends in International Human Resource Management Practices Across Selected Countries and Regions** *(Continued)*

Performance appraisal	In all countries, "should-be" scores were higher on every purpose, suggesting that the purposes of PA have fallen short in every country. All countries indicated that a greater emphasis be placed on development and documentation in future PA practices. In particular, recognizing subordinates, evaluating their goal achievement, planning their development activities, and (ways to) improving their performance are considered the most important appraisal practices for the future.	In contrast, in the Asian countries expression is used to a low extent, particularly in Korea. In the Latin American countries, the administrative purposes of performance appraisal are considered important in future practice.	In Taiwan, the administrative purposes of performance appraisal are considered important in future practice.
T&D	In most countries, T&D practices are used to improve employees' technical skills. There is a growing trend toward using T&D for team building and "soft management practices."	In the Anglo countries, the softer T&D practices such as team building, understanding business practices and corporate culture, and the pro-active T&D practices such as preparation for future assignment and cross-training are used moderately; however, a significant increase in these practices is desired. In the Latin countries, an increase in the extent to which all T&D practices are used is desired.	In Mexico, T&D as a reward to employees is considered a highly desirable practice. In the U.S. and Korea, preparing employees for future job assignments is used to a lesser extent. U.S. is using outsourcing more. In the Asian countries, most T&D practices are used moderately and are consistently considered satisfactory. In Japan, remedying past performance is used to a small extent, however, a significant increase in this practice is desired. In Korea, team building is used extensively and emphasized in all T&D practices.
Relation to business strategy	Across most countries, the HRM practices most closely linked to organizational capability are training and development and performance appraisal.	In the Asian countries, linkages were indicated between both low cost and differentiation strategies and HRM practices.	In Mexico, no linkages were indicated between organizational capability and HRM practices.
Status of HRM function			In Japan and Taiwan few linkages were indicated between organizational capability and HRM practices. Status of HRM was highest in Australia and lowest in Indonesia.

Source: Mary Ann Von Glinow, Ellen A. Drost, and Mary B. Teagarden, "Converging on IHRM Best Practices: Lessons Learned from a Globally Distributed Consortium on Theory and Practice," *Human Resource Management* 41, no. 1 (2002): 133–35.
Reprinted with permission of John Wiley and Sons, Inc., 2011.

CONCLUSION

The IHRM function is a vital component of implementing the global strategy of a firm. In particular, managing the IHRM functions for and in emerging markets presents complex challenges at all employee levels; these include the war for talent for managerial and professional people, and the issues of outsourcing employees in those markets. Careful decisions regarding the appropriate staffing policy for foreign locations are crucial to the success of the firm's operations, particularly because of the lack of proximity to and control by headquarters executives. In particular, the ability of expatriates to initiate and maintain cooperative relationships with local people and agencies will determine the long-term success, even the viability, of the operation. In a real sense, a company's global cadre represents its most valuable resource. Proactive management of that resource by headquarters will result in having the right people in the right place at the right time, appropriately trained, prepared, and supported. MNCs using these IHRM practices can anticipate the effective management of the foreign operation, the fostering of expatriates' careers, and, ultimately, the enhanced success of the corporation.

Summary of Key Points

1. Global human resource management is a vital component of implementing global strategy and is increasingly being recognized as a major determinant of success or failure in international business.

2. The main staffing alternatives for global operations are the ethnocentric, polycentric, regiocentric, and global approaches; the use of inpatriates supplements those choices. Each approach has its appropriate uses, according to its advantages and disadvantages, and, in particular, the firm's strategy.

3. The causes of expatriate failure include the following: poor selection based on inappropriate criteria, inadequate preparation before assignment, alienation from headquarters, inability of manager or family to adapt to local environment, inadequate compensation package, and poor programs for career support and repatriation.

4. The three major areas critical to expatriate preparation are cultural training, language instruction, and familiarity with everyday matters.

5. Common training techniques for potential expatriates include area studies, culture assimilators, language training, sensitivity training, and field experiences.

6. Appropriate and attractive compensation packages must be designed by IHRM staffs to sustain a competitive global expatriate staff. Compensation packages for host-country managers must be designed to fit the local culture and situation, as well as the firm's objectives.

Discussion Questions

1. What are the major alternative staffing approaches for international operations? Explain the relative advantages of each and the conditions under which you would choose one approach over another.

2. Why is the HRM role so much more complex, and important, in the international context?

3. Discuss the challenges involved in staffing operations in emerging markets.

4. Explain the common causes of expatriate failure. What are the major success factors for expatriates? Explain the role and importance of each.

5. What are the common training techniques for managers going overseas? How should these vary as appropriate to the level of globalization of the firm?

6. Explain the balance sheet approach to international compensation packages. Why is this approach so important? Discuss the pros and cons of aligning the expatriate compensation package with the host-country colleagues compared to the home-country colleagues.

7. Discuss the importance of a complete program for expatriate performance management. What are the typical components for such a program?

Application Exercises

1. Make a list of the reasons you would want to accept a foreign assignment and a list of reasons you would want to reject it. Do they depend on the location? Compare your list with a classmate and discuss your reasons.

2. Research a company with operations in several countries and ascertain the staffing policy used for those countries. Find out what kinds of training and preparation are provided for expatriates and what kinds of results the company is experiencing with expatriate training.

Experiential Exercise

This can be done in groups or individually. After the exercise, discuss your proposals with the rest of the class.

You are the expatriate general manager of a British company's subsidiary in Brazil, an automobile component parts manufacturer. You and your family have been in Brazil for seven years, and now you are being reassigned and replaced with another expatriate—Ian Fleming. Ian is bringing his family—Helen, an instructor in computer science, who hopes to find a position; a son, age twelve; and a daughter, age fourteen. None of them has lived abroad before. Ian has asked you what he and his family should expect in the new assignment. Remembering all the problems you and your family experienced in the first couple of years of your assignment in Brazil, you want to facilitate their adjustment and have decided to do two things:

1. Write a letter to Ian, telling him what to expect, both on the job and in the community. Tell him about some of the cross-cultural conflicts he may run into with his coworkers and employees, and how he should handle them.

2. Set up some arrangements and support systems for the family and design a support package for them, with a letter to each family member telling them what to expect.

Internet Resources

Visit the Deresky Companion Website at www.pearsonhighered.com/deresky for this chapter's Internet resources.

CASE STUDY

Kelly's Assignment in Japan

Well, it's my job that brought us here in the first place … I am going to have to make a decision to stick with this assignment and hope I can work things out, or to return to the United States and probably lose my promised promotion after this assignment—maybe even my job.

As she surveyed the teeming traffic of downtown Tokyo from her office window, Kelly tried to assess the situation her family was in, how her job was going, and what could have been done to lead to a better situation four months ago when she was offered the job.

As a program manager for a startup Internet services company, she had been given the opportunity to head up the sales and marketing department in Tokyo. Her boss said that "the sky's the limit" as far as her being able to climb the corporate ladder if she was successful in Tokyo. She explained that she did not speak Japanese and that she knew nothing about Japan. But he said he had confidence in her since she had done such a great job in Boston and in recent short assignments to London and Munich. Moreover, the company offered her a very attractive compensation package that included a higher salary, bonuses, a relocation allowance, a rent-free apartment in Tokyo, and an education allowance for their two children, Lisa and Sam, to attend private schools. She was told she had two days to decide, and that they wanted her in Tokyo in three weeks because they wanted her to prepare and present a proposal for a new account opportunity there as soon as possible. Her boss said they would hire a relocation company to handle the move for her.

That night Kelly excitedly discussed the opportunity with her husband, Joe. He was glad for her and thought it would be an exciting experience for the whole family. However, he was concerned about his own job and what the move would do to his career. She told him that her boss had said that Joe would probably find something or get transferred there, but that her boss did seem unconcerned about that. In the end, Joe felt that Kelly should have this opportunity, and he agreed to the move. He talked to his boss about a transfer and was told that they would look into that and get back to him. However, he knew that his company was having layoffs because of the economic decline that was taking its toll on profits. The problem was that Kelly had to make a decision before he could fully explore his options, so Kelly and Joe decided to go ahead with the plans. To sweeten the deal, Kelly's company had offered to buy her house in Boston since the housing market decline had her concerned about whether she could sell without taking a loss.

After the long trip, they arrived at their apartment in Tokyo; they were tired but excited, but did not anticipate that the apartment would be so tiny, given the very high rent that the company was paying for it. Kelly realized at once that they had included way too much in their move of personal belongings to be able to fit into this apartment. Undaunted, they planned to spend the weekend sightseeing and looked forward to some travel. Japan was beautiful in the spring and they were anxious to see the area.

On Monday, Kelly took a cab to the office. She had emailed requesting a staff meeting at 9 a.m. She knew that her immediate staff would include seven Japanese, two Americans, and two Germans—all men. Her assistant, Peter, to whom she had not yet spoken, was an American who had also just arrived, coming from an assignment in London. He greeted her at the elevator, looking surprised, and they proceeded to the conference room, where everyone was awaiting "the new boss." Kelly exchanged the usual handshake greetings with the Westerners, and then bowed to the Japanese; an awkward silence and exchange took place, with the Japanese looking embarrassed. While she attempted a greeting in her limited Japanese that she had studied on the plane, she was relieved to find that the Japanese spoke English, but they seemed very quiet and hesitant. Peter then told her that they all thought that "Kelly" was a man, and they all attempted a laugh.

After that, Kelly decided that she would just meet with Peter, and postpone the general meeting until the next day. She asked them to each prepare a short presentation for her on their ideas for the new account. While the Americans and Germans said they would have it ready, the Japanese seemed reluctant to commit themselves.

Meanwhile, at home Joe was looking into the schools for the children and also trying to make some contacts to look for a job. Travelling, getting information, and shopping for groceries proved bewildering, but they decided that they would soon get acquainted with local customs.

At the office the next day, Kelly received a short presentation from the Westerners on the staff, but when it came to the Japanese they indicated that they had not yet had a chance to meet with their groups and other contacts in order to come to their decisions. Kelly asked them why they had not told her the day before that they needed more time, and when could they be ready. They seemed unwilling to give a direct answer and kept their eyes lowered. In an attempt to lighten the atmosphere and get to know her staff, Kelly then began chatting casually and asked several of them about their families. The Americans chatted on about their children's achievements, the Germans talked about their family positions, and the Japanese went silent, seemingly very confused and offended.

Still attempting to get everyone's ideas for an initial proposal to the potential new client, Kelly later asked one of the Americans who had been there for some time what he thought was the problem and delay in getting presentations from the Japanese. He told her that they did not like to do individual presentations, but rather wanted to gain consensus among themselves and their contacts and present a group presentation. Having learned her lesson, but feeling irritated, she asked him to intervene and have the presentations ready for the next week. When that time came, the rest of the presentations were made by the Japanese, but, oddly, they seemed to be addressed primarily to Peter. Later, Kelly decided to finalize her own presentation to put forth a proposal for the client, which she set up for the following week.

At home, Joe said that he had not heard anything from his company in Boston and asked Kelly to again contact her company to request some networking in Tokyo that might lead to job opportunities for him. Kelly said she would do that, but that there didn't seem to be any one person "back home" who was keeping up with her situation or giving any support about that or about her job.

The children, meanwhile, complained that, although their schools were meant to be bilingual English-Japanese, a majority of the children were Japanese and did not speak English; Lisa and Sam felt confused and left out. They were disoriented by the different customs, classes, and foods for lunch. At home they complained that there was no back yard to go out to play, and that they could not get their programs on the television, or understand the Japanese programs.

Back at the office, Kelly worked with her staff to finalize the proposal, but noticed a strained atmosphere. Peter told her that some of them would drop by a local bar for a drink after work, which helped the whole group to relax together. However, she felt that she could not do that, nor that she would be accepted as a female.

The next week, as arranged, Kelly and Peter went to the offices of the client; she knew that a lot was riding on getting this big new contract. She had asked Peter to let them know ahead of time that she is a woman, yet the introductions still seemed strained. She planned to get straight down to business, so when the client company's CEO handed her his business card, she put it in her pocket without a glance, and did not give him her card. Again she noticed some shock and embarrassment all around. (She found out much later that a business card is very important to a Japanese businessman because it conveys all his accomplishments and position without having to say it himself.) Flustered, she tried to make light of the situation, patted him on the back, and asked him what his first name was, saying, rather loudly, that hers' was Kelly. He went quiet again, backed away from her, and, with his head bowed, whispered "Michio." He glanced around at his Japanese colleagues rather nervously.

After a period of silence, Michio pointed to the table of refreshments, and indicated that they sit and eat; however, Kelly was anxious to present her power-point slides and went to the end of the table where the equipment was and asked Peter to set up the slides. As she proceeded to go through the proposal, telling them what her company could do for them, she paused and asked for questions. However, when Michio and his two colleagues asked questions, they directed them to Peter, not to her. In fact, they made little eye contact with her at all. She tried to remain cool, but insisted on answering the questions herself. In the end, she sat down and asked Michio what he thought of the proposal. He bowed politely and said "very good" and that he would discuss it with his colleagues and get back to her. However, Kelly did not hear from them, and after a couple of weeks she asked Peter to follow up with them. He did that, but reported that they were not going to pursue the contract. Frustrated, she said, "Well, why did Michio say that it looked very good, then?" She knew that it was a very competitive proposal and felt that something other than the proposed contract was to blame for the loss of the contract.

Disillusioned, but determined not to give up without success in the assignment, Kelly took a cab to go home and think about it, but the driver misunderstood her and went the wrong way and got stuck in traffic. She felt discouraged and wished that she had some female American friends to whom she could confide her problems.

When Kelly got home, Peter was angrily trying to fix dinner, complaining about the small appliances and not being able to understand the food packages or how to prepare the food. He said he needed something else to do, but that there did not seem to be a job on the horizon for him. He was also concerned about continuing to live in such a high-cost city on only one salary.

Kelly went to the other room to see the children; they were fighting and complaining that they had nothing to do and wanted to go home. Kelly felt that the three months that they had been there was not a fair trial, and was wondering what to do. She wished she had had more time to prepare for this assignment, and whenever she contacted the home office no one seemed able to advise her.

Case Questions

1. Explain the clashes in culture, customs, and expectations that occurred in this situation.
2. What stage of culture shock is Kelly's family experiencing?
3. Turn back the clock to when Kelly was offered the position in Tokyo. What, if anything, should have been done differently, and by whom?
4. You are Kelly. What should you do now?

OUTLINE

OBJECTIVES

1. To emphasize the critical role of expatriates in managing in host subsidiaries and in transferring knowledge to and from host operations.

2. To appreciate the importance of international assignments in developing top managers with global experience and perspectives.

3. To recognize the need to design programs for the careful preparation, adaptation, and repatriation of the expatriate and any accompanying family, as well as programs for career management and retention.

4. To become familiar with the use of Global Management Teams to coordinate cross-border business.

5. To recognize the varying roles of women around the world in international management.

6. To understand the variations in host-country labor relations systems and the impact on the manager's job and effectiveness.

OPENING PROFILE: THE EXPAT LIFE[1]

What is it like to take an assignment abroad? Would you like to be an "expat" (expatriate)? Is it an adventure or a hardship? Experiences of those who have done a stint abroad are mixed. But it is clear that it is very likely an opportunity that will present itself at some point during your career. Most companies with global business transactions want their top employees to have overseas experience. At Procter and Gamble, for example, 39 of the company's top 44 global officers have had an international assignment and 22 were born outside the United States. Most multinational companies are moving from 0.5 to 1 percent of their employees abroad, and about 68 percent expect that to increase, according to the Global Relocation Trends Survey.

Experiences vary by job type, and especially by location. Adjustment is easier for those who go to places where the culture and business practices are similar to their own. Those transitioning between Western Europe and the United States or Canada, for example, typically adapt easier than those going to China or Yemen, as related below. Some expatriates enjoy perks that they do not get at home, and others find they fare worse financially, either while overseas or when they return home. In addition, with more firms expanding operations in emerging economies, expats often face considerable challenges such as inefficient infrastructure, limited housing, medical, or education facilities, security risks, political instability. Such conditions often mean that the assignment is turned down, or that the manager will decide to go without his or her family. In most places, assignees expect the assignment to be career-broadening and hope it will leverage them to a promotion. Some expat experiences are described below.

As an example of how quickly the changing global environment can affect expats, we can look at the typical expat life for Wall Street executives as described in the *New York Times in 2008*: "When Wall Streeters pack their bags for Dubai or Shanghai, for example, they get much more than a plane ticket and coverage of per-diem expenses. These days, moving abroad can mean scoring a nanny, a driver, or even a bodyguard."[2] In Shanghai, there are 70,000 expatriates from around the world, in various capacities. For those in the finance industry the expat package typically includes round trips home a year; fees for a real estate agency; moving expenses; at least one month of temporary accommodation; and language classes, if required. For an accompanying family, fees for private schools, for example, are usually included, as well as help for the spouse to find a job. A cost of living adjustment is typically included, as well as an adjustment for tax equalization. A very nice assignment—however, in spring 2009, the *New York Times* was then reporting about the number of expats in the banking and finance industry who were getting laid off:

> "Losing your job anywhere is disorienting, but imagine being laid off when you work in
> a foreign country. Not only is your source of income, and perhaps a good part of your
> identity, suddenly yanked away, but often you lose your right to remain in the country."[3]

That, however, was an unusual development; for most expats the overseas assignment has been very rewarding in terms of both personal and job experience.

In many circumstances the adventure that started out with many concerns turns out to be one that the expats and their families do not want to end. According to the Global Relocation Trends Survey, 26% of expats opt to continue their overseas assignment when the original term ends. Those people have settled in to their position and life in the host country and enjoy their situations.

One reporter assigned to Beijing commented, "That's why we recently decided to extend our stay for a fourth year. For me, it was an easy decision. The three years that seemed so ominous turned out to be not nearly enough time to settle into a new life." The family wanted to do more travelling, as well as really understanding and enjoying the culture of Beijing.[4]

Assignments in some locations can turn out to be more challenging. One example is that of Mr. Deffontaines, who moved to Yemen in 2008 as the local manager for Total, the French oil giant, along with his family. Since then, Mr. Deffontaines has seen his main export pipeline damaged by terrorists, endured devastating flash floods, and sent expatriate families back home because of security concerns.

Recounting some of the interesting challenges he had faced there, Mr. Deffontaines, a 43-year-old Parisian, described "negotiating with tribal leaders and sending actors to remote villages to stage a play about the hazards of gas pipelines. In meetings with government officials to thrash out problems, participants typically chew khat, a mildly narcotic plant that is widely consumed in Yemen but banned in many places around the world."[5]

A particularly difficult decision, in response to growing security concerns, was to send the families of his workers back to France. His own wife, son, and twin daughters were among those forced to depart.

Robert Kneupfer, a lawyer, reflects that, in spite of inconveniences like the 17-year wait for a telephone line and the absence of any McDonald's, the five years he spent in Budapest with his family on behalf of the international law firm Baker & McKenzie were a "defining moment both personally and professionally." The 56-year-old partner, now based in Chicago, didn't speak the language, and his children had been reluctant to leave family and friends. His advice: "Don't sweat the small stuff. You need to appreciate the bigger-picture experience."[6] His advice follows that of many others:

- Learn the customs of a new country before arriving, be flexible, and maintain a lifeline to your home office. You don't want to become out of sight, out of mind.
- Learn the language, or at least practice a few key phrases.
- Prepare for the cultural differences as a family.
- Develop a support network with the local expatriate community.
- Set up a routine for the whole family as soon as possible.[7]
- Be aware of the potential negative effects on the whole family. The initial excitement can turn to culture shock, loneliness, identity loss, and depression, and it is often the employee's spouse and children—without the familiar routine of work—who are most affected.

Further advice from a well-travelled expat comes from Philip Shearer, Group President, Clinique, Estee Lauder. His mother was French, his father British, and he was born in Morocco. After going to college in France and then business school in the United States, he worked at a pharmaceutical company in Minneapolis. Then he worked in France, Mexico, Britain, Japan, and again in the United States for companies such as L'Oréal and the Elizabeth Arden division of Eli Lilly.

Shearer's advice melds with that of other successful expats who seem to be able to distill their experiences and travels to arrive at common themes. They recommend that, above all, you should be yourself and gain a reputation for being trustworthy. In that way people will trust you and relate to you no matter where you are from. Shearer warns, however, that Americans generally show off too much. "But in the end, you have to deliver. And that's the same all over the world."[8]

A crucial factor in global competitiveness is the ability of the firm to maximize its global human resources in the long term. In the globalized economy, the knowledge and management resources, as well as the skilled and non-skilled employee resources, required for the firm to succeed are no longer concentrated in a single region but are distributed around the world. There are various categories of those resources—both people and processes—which IHR managers and others must develop and maintain; in particular it is essential for them to:

1. Maximize long-term retention and use of international cadre through career management so that the company can develop a top management team with global experience.
2. Develop effective global management teams.
3. Understand, value, and promote the role of women in international management in order to maximize those underutilized resources.
4. Work with the host-country labor relations system to effect strategic implementation and employee productivity.

EXPATRIATE CAREER MANAGEMENT

Martin Walker, senior director of the Global Business Policy Council at A. T. Kearney, a consultancy, maintains that the dearth of talent is mainly evident at the very top: "Shortages do exist—most notably, of people with the internationalized business skills to thrive at senior management level in global companies."

THE GLOBAL TALENT INDEX REPORT: THE OUTLOOK TO 2015,
HEIDRICK & STRUGGLES.[9]

It is clear from the above quote that the road to the top necessitates that managers have overseas experience. For the firm, the ability to develop a top management team, globally experienced, depends largely on the success of expatriates' assignments—and that depends on the ability to well manage the transitions for the expatriate and any accompanying family members. The importance of this was determined by the 2011 Global Relocation Trends survey that found that "only 22% of respondents had formal career-management processes for international assignees and 18% of respondents had a formal candidate pool for international assignments."[10]

Preparation, Adaptation, and Repatriation

The top family challenges identified as very critical to companies were partner resistance (47%), family adjustment (32%), children's education (29%), and location difficulties (25%).[11]

THE 2011 GMAC GLOBAL RELOCATIONS TRENDS SURVEY

Effective human resource management of a company's global cadre does not end with the overseas assignment. It ends with the successful repatriation of the executive into company headquarters. A study by Heidrick & Struggles, the international headhunting firm, revealed that international experience has become much more important to get to the top of FTSE (London Stock Exchange) 100 companies than a decade ago. "Chief executives such as Mark Tucker at Prudential, who has experience in the United States and Asia, and Unilever's Patrick Cescau, who has worked in Europe, Asia and the United States, are becoming the norm in top companies."[12] Clearly, those executives and their companies have paid careful attention to what is necessary for successful assignments, career management, and repatriation of their experiences and skills. Such firms realize that long-term, proactive management of such critical resources should begin with the end of the current assignment in mind—that is, it should begin with plans for the repatriation of the executive as part of his or her career path. The management of the reentry phase of the career cycle is as vital as the management of the cross-cultural entry and training. Otherwise, the long-term benefits of that executive's international experience may be negated. Shortsightedly, many companies do little to minimize the potential effects of **reverse culture shock** (return shock). The KPMG Global Assignment Policies and Practices Survey found that just four percent of the 430 HRM executives surveyed agreed that they handle the repatriation process well and only 12 percent offer a formal mentoring/career coaching plan for their assignees. In fact, the survey results concluded that "25 percent of organizations surveyed do not know if assignees have left the organization within 12 months of returning from international assignment. For repatriated assignees that are tracked as leaving the organization soon after returning from assignment, the overriding reason cited is the lack of an appropriate job after repatriation."[13] For smaller companies, little, if any pre- or post-assignment counseling was provided.

A study by Lazarova and Caligiuri with 58 expatriates from four North American companies found that repatriates who received supportive practices from their firms felt that their companies had an interest in their careers and well-being and so were more likely to stay with the firm upon reentry. The expatriates were asked their opinions about the importance of various factors to them, using the HRM practices most frequently associated with successful repatriation. The first five in importance ranking were as follows:

- Visible signs that the company values international experience
- Career planning sessions
- Communications with home office of details of the repatriation process
- Continuous communications with the home office
- Agreement about position upon repatriation[14]

However, the extent to which each practice was available, or perceived to be available, within the participating companies did not meet the level of importance. "Career Planning Sessions," for example, was rated very important (3.57 out of 4), yet was offered only 36.2 percent of the time; and "signs that the company values international experience" received only a 28 percent rating.[15] The long-term implications of ineffective repatriation practices for any particular company are clear—few good managers will be willing to take international assignments because they will see what happened to their colleagues. If a certain manager lost out on promotion opportunities while overseas and is now, in fact, worse off than before he or she left, the only people willing to take on foreign assignments in the future will be those who have not been able to succeed on the home front or those who think that a stint abroad will be like a vacation. Research has shown that employees commonly see overseas assignments as negative career moves in some U.S. multinational companies.[16] In contrast, such moves are seen as positive in most European, Japanese, and Australian companies because they consider international experience necessary for advancement to top management. In a study of dual-career couples, "the perceived impact of the international assignment upon returning to the U.S." was one of the most important issues stated by managers regarding their willingness to relocate overseas.[17]

Reverse culture shock occurs primarily because of the difficulty of reintegrating into the organization but also because, generally speaking, the longer a person is away, the more difficult it is to get back into the swing of things. Not only might the manager have been overlooked and lost in the shuffle of reorganization, but her or his whole family might have lost social contacts or jobs and feel out of step with their contemporaries. These feelings of alienation from what has always been perceived as "home"—because of the loss of contact with family, friends, and daily life—delay the resocialization process. Such a reaction is particularly serious if the family's overall financial situation has been hurt by the assignment and if the spouse's career has also been kept "on hold" while he or she was abroad.

For companies to maximize the long-term use of their global cadre, they need to make sure that the foreign assignment and the reintegration process are positive experiences. This means careful career planning, support while overseas, and use of the increased experience and skills of returned managers to benefit the home office. Research into the practices of successful U.S., European, Japanese, and Australian multinational corporations (MNCs) indicates the use of one or more of the following support systems, as recommended by Tung, for a successful repatriation program:

- A mentor program to monitor the expatriate's career path while abroad and upon repatriation.

- As an alternative to the mentor program, the establishment of a special organizational unit for the purposes of career planning and continuing guidance for the expatriate.

- A system of supplying information and maintaining contacts with the expatriate so that he or she may continue to feel a part of the home organization.[18]

The Role of the Expatriate Spouse

We began to realize that the entire effectiveness of the assignment could be compromised by ignoring the spouse.

STEVE FORD,
CORPORATION RELOCATIONS, HEWLETT-PACKARD[19]

Many companies are beginning to recognize the importance of providing support for spouses and children—in particular because both spouses are often corporate fast-trackers and demand that both sets of needs be included on the bargaining table. Research shows that 83 percent of married expatriates were accompanied by their spouses. However, while 54 percent of the spouses were employed before the assignment, only 12 percent were employed during the assignment.[20] "That's underscored by the fact that 61 percent of respondents noted that the impact of family issues on early returns from assignment was very critical or of high importance."[21]

Firms often use informal means, such as intercompany networking, to help find the trailing spouse a position in the same location. They know that with the increasing number of dual-career couples, if the spouse does not find a position, the manager will very likely turn down the assignment. They decline because they cannot afford to lose the income or because the spouse's career may be delayed entirely if he or she is out of the workforce for a few years. As women continue to move up the corporate ladder, the accompanying ("trailing") spouse is often male—estimated at more than 25 percent.[22] Companies such as Hewlett-Packard, Shell, Medtronic, and Monsanto offer a variety of options to address the dual-career dilemma.

Clearly, then, the selection process must include spouses, partners, and entire families. Global assignments must take account of the expatriate's personal concerns and future career; otherwise the company will they face the possibility of early return and a possible doubling of the chances for employee attrition. The GMAC survey revealed that the annual turnover rate is 13 percent for all employees, compared to 25 percent for expatriate employees during assignments, and 27 percent within one year of completing assignments. Those assignees indicated that they felt their firms did not appreciate the difficulties of their overseas stints; nor did they fully utilize the expatriates' skills on return to the home country.[23]

At Procter & Gamble, employees and spouses destined for China are sent to Beijing for two months of language training and cultural familiarization. Nissho Iwai, a Japanese trading company, gets together managers and spouses who are leaving Japan with foreign managers and spouses who are on their way there. In addition, the firm provides a year of language training and information and services for Japanese children to attend schools abroad. Research on

321 American expatriate spouses around the world shows that effective cross-cultural adjustment by spouses is more likely (1) when firms seek the spouse's opinion about the international assignment and the expected standard of living and (2) when the spouse initiates his or her own predeparture training (thereby supplementing the minimal training given by most firms).[24]

Expatriate Retention

Managers returning from expatriate assignments are two to three times more likely to leave the company within a year because attention has not been paid to their careers and the way they fit back into the corporate structure back home.[25]

Firms must design support services to provide timely help for the manager and, therefore, are part of the effective management of an overseas assignment. The overall transition process experienced by the company's international management cadre over time comprises three phases of transition and adjustment that must be managed for successful socialization to a new culture and resocialization back to the old culture. These phases are (1) the exit transition from the home country, the success of which will be determined largely by the quality of preparation the expatriate has received; (2) the entry transition to the host country, in which successful acculturation (or early exit) will depend largely on monitoring and support; and (3) the entry transition back to the home country or to a new host country, in which the level of reverse culture shock and the ease of re-acculturation will depend on previous stages of preparation and support.[26]

A company may derive many potential benefits from carefully managing the careers of its expatriates. By helping managers make the right moves for their careers, the company will be able to retain people with increasing global experience and skills.

But from the individual manager's perspective, most people understand that no one can better look out for one's interests than oneself. With that in mind, managers must ask themselves, and their superiors, what role each overseas stint will play in career advancement and what proactive role each will play in one's own career. Retaining the returning expatriate within the company (assuming he or she has been effective) is vitally important in order to gain the knowledge and benefit from the assignment. Yet, as discussed earlier, the attrition rate for expatriates is about double that of non-expatriates for the following reasons:

- Expatriates are more marketable and receive more attractive offers from other employers.
- Expatriates find that their compensation packages on overseas assignments are more generous than at home and go from one company to another to take advantage of that.
- Expatriates feel unappreciated and dissatisfied both during and after the assignment and leave the company.[27]

It is essential, therefore, that the company pays careful attention to maintaining and retaining the expatriate by managing both the assignment and the repatriation of the expatriate and the family.

THE ROLE OF REPATRIATION IN DEVELOPING A GLOBAL MANAGEMENT CADRE

In the international assignment, both the manager and the company can benefit from the enhanced skills and experience gained by the expatriate. Many returning executives report an improvement in their managerial skills and self-confidence. Some of these acquired skills, as reported by Adler, include the following:

- **Managerial skills, not technical skills:** learning how to deal with a wide range of people, to adapt to their cultures through compromise, and not to be a dictator.
- **Tolerance for ambiguity:** making decisions with less information and more uncertainty about the process and the outcome.
- **Multiple perspectives:** learning to understand situations from the perspective of local employees and businesspeople.
- **Ability to work with and manage others:** learning patience and tolerance—realizing that managers abroad are in the minority among local people; learning to communicate more with others and empathize with them.[28]

Knowledge Transfer

In addition to the managerial and cross-cultural skills acquired by expatriates, the company benefits from the knowledge and experience those managers gain about how to do business overseas, and about new technology, local marketing, and competitive information. Expatriates have long served as facilitators of intra-firm knowledge transfer and application. Traditionally, it has been assumed that the role of expatriates is partly to bring knowledge from the corporate headquarters to subsidiaries; however, it is clear that there is a potential strategic advantage when expatriates acquiring knowledge while on international assignment bring it back to the center of the organization or disseminate it across other subsidiaries.[29] Consider, for example, Claire Molyneux, Associate Marketing Director for P&G West Africa. Claire, who was born and raised in England, started her P&G career there in 1998 as an assistant brand manager. Over the years, she worked for P&G in Geneva and Israel. In 2008 Claire was assigned to Nigeria as marketing director for Ariel detergent, Duracell batteries and Gillette razors, and to lead research into West Africa's consumers. Claire has taken up the challenge, saying "Africa has this huge diversity. Our job is to find the similarities."[30] Consider the wealth of knowledge and information she has gathered in those ten years—cultural, consumer- and product-related, and technical, as well as her contacts around the world—that she is transferring across subsidiaries and benefiting the organization. Claire's situation is an example of the five types of knowledge gained abroad discussed by Berthoin:

- Knowledge about **what** (such as differences in customer preferences)
- Knowledge about **why** (e.g., understanding how culture differences affect cross-cultural understanding)
- Knowledge about **how** (e.g., management skills, such as delegating responsibilities)
- Knowledge about **when** (e.g., knowledge about the effect of timing)
- Knowledge about **who** (e.g., relationships created over the life of an assignment).[31]

Berthoin also points out that expatriate experience not only brings about knowledge about culture differences but also creates insights about HQ–subsidiary relations, from which ideas about improving business could be derived.[32] However, as found by Lazarova and Tarique, "repatriates' motivation to contribute to collective organizational learning is primarily driven by the fit between their individual career objectives and the career development opportunities offered by the organization upon return."[33] They found that several conditions have to be met in order to successfully transfer knowledge: first, that the repatriates have to (a) have valuable knowledge to transfer and (b) be motivated to transfer that knowledge; secondly, that organizations need to (a) have the right tools to capture knowledge, and (b) create the right incentives for repatriates to share their knowledge. Knowledge transfer is optimized when the type of knowledge gained by repatriates is matched by the right knowledge transfer mechanisms—for example, by assigning repatriates to strategic teams—and when career opportunities provided by the organization are congruent with repatriate career goals and aspirations.[34] Exhibit 10-1 illustrates the conditions and process by which knowledge may be successfully integrated into the organization.

The company should therefore position itself to benefit from that enhanced management knowledge if it wants to develop a globally experienced management cadre—an essential ingredient for global competitiveness—in particular where there is a high degree of shared learning among the organization's global managers. If the company cannot retain good returning managers, then their potential shared knowledge is not only lost but also conveyed to another organization that hires that person. This can be very detrimental to the company's competitive stance. Some companies are becoming quite savvy about how to use technology to utilize shared knowledge to develop their global management cadre, to better service their customers, and—as a side benefit—to store the knowledge and expertise of their managers around the world in case they leave the company. That knowledge, it can be argued, is an asset in which the company has invested large amounts of resources. One such savvy company is Booz-Allen & Hamilton, which instituted a Knowledge On-Line (KOL) intranet as a means to enhance knowledge sharing among its employees worldwide and to improve client service. By using its intranet to link islands of information separated by geography and platform-specific applications, the renowned consulting firm has enabled its 2,000 private sector consultants to collect and share firm-wide their best thoughts and expertise.[35]

EXHIBIT 10-1   **Variables Influencing Success of Knowledge Transfer from Repatriated Manager**

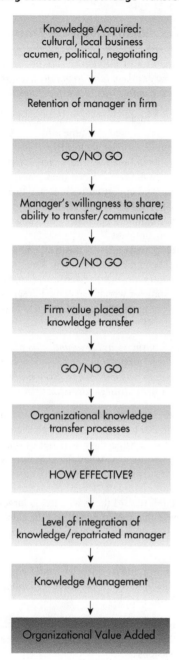

Black and Gregersen's research of 750 U.S., European, and Japanese companies concluded that those companies that reported a high degree of job satisfaction and strong performance, and that experienced limited turnover, used the following practices when making international assignments:

- They focus on knowledge creation and global leadership development.
- They assign overseas posts to people whose technical skills are matched or exceeded by their cross-cultural abilities.
- They end expatriate assignments with a deliberate repatriation process.[36]

A successful repatriation program, then, starts before the assignment. The company's top management must set up a culture that conveys the message that the organization regards international assignments as an integral part of continuing career development and advancement, and that it values the skills of the returnees. The company's objectives should be reflected in its long-range plans, commitment, and

UNDER THE LENS

Expatriates' Careers Add to Knowledge Transfer [37]

> *Brazil's distinctive culture, the lack of English spoken at street level and the country's labyrinthine politics and bureaucracy make it hard to import foreign talent. Meanwhile, the global financial crisis is also prompting more Brazilian expatriates to consider going back.* [38]

Developments around the world and in an expatriate's "original" country can redirect an expatriate's career choices in unexpected ways, and at the same time affect the firms involved. Such was the case for Casio Calil. As reported in the *Financial Times*, he left Brazil in 1987, in very poor economic times, to seek his fortune elsewhere. After stints in Japan, Australia, and Ireland, he went to New York and in 2005 took a job with J. P. Morgan's investment bank. Since then, through his business contacts in Brazil, he realized that the expanding economy and opportunities in Brazil made a move back home very attractive. So, in 2011, he found himself head of J. P. Morgan Asset Management in Sao Paulo. He is now one of many Brazilians bringing their international experience and knowledge back to help a rapidly growing country with a shortage of management talent. [39]

Sometimes those world developments are less positive, causing unwanted upheaval to the lives of expats and their families. Such has been the case in Libya. After booming with international businesses taking advantage of the oil-rich country, the war to overthrow Col. Gaddafi drove out foreign businesses and their expatriates and families, some of whom had come to regard it as home. In 2012, after a year of disrupted lives, those expatriates were gradually going back, and hoping that the business climate would improve after elections in June 2012. If not . . .

> *The challenges for conducting business in Libya under its old rules are daunting. Regulators required companies to hire large proportions of Libyan workers and managers even if they were unqualified. Land ownership was impossible. Even majority ownership in joint ventures did not translate into authority over strategic decisions.* [40]

Similar upheavals were experienced by expatriates in Japan, and, of course, the Japanese themselves, during their triple disaster in 2011 comprised of the earthquake, tsunami, and nuclear meltdown. Foreign companies naturally wanted to bring their staff out of danger, and, of course, the expatriates wanted to get their families out of harm's way, when the U.S. embassy sent in planes to ferry them out. However, the Japanese felt betrayed by the expatriates leaving while they worked through the crisis. In their anger they were calling those who left "flyjin" as a take-off from their term "gaijin," meaning foreigner. The anger the Japanese felt toward those who left is largely based on the difference between the cultural attitude of the Japanese that the company and the family are almost one entity, compared with that in the West, where family comes before the company. One expat who clearly recognized this was Gerry Dorizas, who said . . .

> *"If I had left as the president, my role as a leader would have been diminished," said Gerry Dorizas, the president of Volkswagen AG's operations in Japan, who has been in that role four years. "We've been very transparent."* [41]

There is no doubt that the events in Japan and Libya, rare as they are, have proven to add valuable experience and knowledge transfer for those expatriates and their companies about how to prepare for and deal with such events and their repercussions.

compensation on behalf of the expatriate. GE sets a model for effective expatriate career management. With its 500 expatriates worldwide, it takes care to select only the best managers for overseas jobs and then commits to placing them in specific positions upon reentry. The following Under the Lens section illustrates some expatriates' experiences that contribute to their firms' store of knowledge.

GLOBAL MANAGEMENT TEAMS

MNCs realize it is essential to maximize their human assets in the form of global management teams so they can share resources and manage the transnational transfer of knowledge. The term **global management team** describes a collection of managers in or from several countries who must rely on group collaboration if each member is to experience optimum success and goal achievement. Whirlpool International, for example, is a U.S.-Dutch joint venture, with administrative headquarters in Comerio, Italy, where it is managed by a Swede and a six-person management team from Sweden, Italy, Holland, the United States, Belgium, and Germany. To achieve the individual and collective goals of the team members, international teams must "provide the means to communicate corporate culture, develop a global perspective, coordinate and integrate the global enterprise, and be responsive to local market needs."[42] The role and importance of international teams increase as the firm progresses in its scope of international activity. Similarly, the manner in which multicultural interaction affects the firm's operations depends on its level of international involvement, its environment, and its strategy.

The team's ability to work effectively together is crucial to the company's success. In addition, technology facilitates effective and efficient teamwork around the world. This was found by the Timberland U.K. sales conference planning team. In the past, the company's large sales conferences were cumbersome to organize because their offices were in France, Germany, Spain, Italy, and the United Kingdom. Then the team started using the British Telecom (BT) Conference Call system for the arrangements, which saved them much travel and expense. The company subsequently adopted the BT Conference Call system for the executive team's country meetings.[43] Teleconferencing and videoconferencing are now much of the way of life for global businesses. However, research indicates that face-to-face meetings are the best way to kick off a virtual team project so that the members can agree on goals and schedules and who is responsible for what. IBM project teams start with all members in a personal meeting to help to build an understanding of the other members' cultures and set up a trusting relationship.[44]

For global organizations and alliances, the same cross-cultural interactions hold as in MNCs, and, in addition, considerably more interaction takes place with the external environment at all levels of the organization. Therefore, global teamwork is vital, as are the pockets of cross-cultural teamwork and interactions that occur at many boundaries.[45] For the global company, worldwide competition and markets necessitate global teams for strategy development, both for the organization as a whole and for the local units to respond to their markets.

When a firm responds to its global environment with a global strategy and then organizes with a networked "glocal" structure (see Chapter 8), various types of cross-border teams are necessary for global integration and local differentiation. These include teams between and among headquarters and subsidiaries; transnational project teams, often operating on a "virtual" basis; and teams coordinating alliances outside the organization.[46] In joint ventures, in particular, multicultural teams work at all levels of strategic planning and implementation, as well as on the production and assembly floor. Clearly, the team's success is highly dependent on the members' ability to understand the culture and communication style of members in other countries. The United Kingdom is one example where considerable differences in behavior, expectations of business protocol, and communication are often dismissed by other Westerners because of the assumption of similarity between English-speaking countries. This brings to mind a quote often attributed to Winston Churchill, "Britain and America are two nations divided by a common language."

"Virtual" Transnational Teams

Virtual groups, whose members interact through computer-mediated communication systems (such as desktop video conferencing systems, e-mail, group support systems, internets, and intranets), are linked together across time, space, and organizational boundaries.[47]

As illustrated in the diagram, advances in communication now facilitate **virtual global teams**, a horizontal networked structure, with people around the world conducting meetings and exchanging information via the Internet, enabling the organization to capitalize on 24-hour productivity. In this way, too, knowledge is shared across business units and across cultures.[48] The advantages and cost savings of virtual global teams are frequently offset by their challenges—including cultural misunderstandings and the logistics of differences in time and space, as shown in Exhibit 10-2. Group members must build their teams while bearing in mind the group diversity and the need for careful communication.[49]

Many of these challenges have been noted by virtual team leaders from Alcoa Company's operations in 20 diverse countries. (Alcoa is the world leader in the production of aluminum and has 63,000 employees in 31 countries.) The teams are called parallel Global Virtual Teams (pGVTs)—teams that operate outside the formal structure, focusing on innovation and improvement. All their meetings are conducted electronically through videoconferencing, teleconferencing, discussion boards, e-mail, instant messaging, knowledge repositories, and planning and scheduling tools.

Virtual Transnational Teams

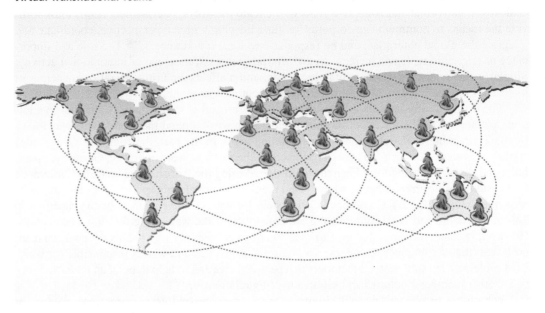

Source: Janos Levente/Shutterstock

EXHIBIT 10-2   Operational Challenges for Global Virtual Teams[51]

Geographic Dispersal:	The complexity of scheduling communications such as teleconferences and video conferences across multiple time zones, holidays, and so on. Lack of face-to-face meetings to establish trust or for cross-interaction processes such as brainstorming.
Cultural Differences:	Variations in attitudes and expectations toward time, planning, scheduling, risk taking, money, relationship building, and so on. Differences in goal sets and work styles arising out of such variables as individualism/collectivism; the relative value of work compared with other life factors; and variable sets of assumptions, norms, patterns of behavior.
Language and Communications:	Translation difficulties, or at least variations in accents, semantics, terminology, or local jargon. Lack of personal and physical contact, which greatly inhibits trust and relationship building in many countries; the social dynamics change. Lack of visibility of nonverbal cues makes interpretation difficult and creates two-way noise in the communication process.
Technology:	Variations in availability, speed, acceptability, and cost of equipment necessary for meetings and communications through computer-aided systems. Variable skill levels and willingness to interact through virtual media.

There is clearly a cross-cultural issue here—one that is particularly important to the success of pGVTs as, more than other forms of team, their success vitally depends on all members contributing and debating ideas.

"LESSONS FROM ALCOA,"
ORGANIZATIONAL DYNAMICS.[50]

In Cordery et al.'s studies of Alcoa's teams, leadership problems were highlighted. One GVT leader described the problems in not being able to always interpret or understand the subtleties of language being expressed and to respond accordingly when sharing ideas, because of not being able to observe the body language of members. She observed, "People from some cultures will say, 'yes' even if they have not understood. They do not feel comfortable asking you to repeat what they have not understood, being in such a large group. Others will commit to do almost anything (quite willingly) in the meeting, but it doesn't get done."[52]

A survey of 200 of Alcoa's virtual team members by Cordery et al. revealed that they view successful team leaders as having the following skills: *Interpersonal facilitation*—the ability to build teams and resolve conflicts; *task facilitation*—the ability to convey goals and train team members to effectively use the collaborative technology; *resource acquisition;* and *external alignment/vision*—that is, being able to mesh the team's activities with the organization's goals.[53]

In a separate survey of 440 training and development professionals across a variety of industries conducted by Rosen, Furst, and Blackburn, the respondents indicated which training techniques for virtual teams were more effective than others, and reported which of those programs were most needed in the future. The relative priority of the training modules is shown in Exhibit 10-3. On the top of the list and considered very valuable, for example, was "Training on how to lead a virtual team meeting" and "Leader training on how to coach and mentor team members virtually," as well as "how to monitor team progress, diagnose problems and take corrective action."[54]

Managing Transnational Teams

The ability to develop and lead effective transnational teams (whether they interact "virtually," physically, or, as is most often the case, a mixture of both) is essential in light of the increasing proliferation of foreign subsidiaries, joint ventures, and other transnational alliances. The

EXHIBIT 10-3 Virtual Team Training

**Importance of Virtual Team
Training Modules
(in order of value and effectiveness)**

Training on how to lead a virtual team meeting

Leader training on how to coach and mentor team members virtually

Training on how to monitor team progress, diagnose team problems, and take corrective actions

Training to use communications technologies

Leader training on how to manage team boundaries, negotiate member time commitments with local managers, and stay in touch with team sponsors

Training on how to establish trust and resolve conflicts in virtual teams

Communications skills training—cultural sensitivity, etc.

Team-building training for new virtual teams

Training to select the appropriate technologies to fit team tasks

Leader training on how to evaluate and reward individual contributions on the virtual team

Training on how to select virtual team members, establish a virtual team charter, and assign virtual team roles

Realistic preview of virtual team challenges

Training on what qualities to look for in prospective virtual team members and leaders

Source: Based on B. Rosen, S. Furst, and R. Blackburn, "Training for Virtual Teams: An Investigation of Current Practices and Future Needs," *Human Resources Management* 45, no. 2 (2006): 229–247.

primary corporate question is how to integrate a diverse pool of cultural values, traditions, and norms in order to be competitive. These challenges were experienced when Nomura, Japan's largest investment bank, acquired most of Lehman Brothers' operations in Asia, Europe, and the Middle East in October 2008, after Lehman's collapse. Nomura had to absorb hundreds of Lehman employees immediately. Although Nomura is the acquirer, it is trying to transform its own culture to be more globally competitive. As observed by one manager:

> Nomura has "a completely domestic culture" . . . one based on Japanese customs of employment, and where company loyalty is strong, decision-making is slow and tolerance for risk is low.[55]

The cultural divide was being felt by both the Japanese and the Americans trying to work together. In particular, the Japanese were shocked when Nomura's management introduced American-style pay and career structures.[56]

Teams comprising people located in far-flung operations are faced with often-conflicting goals of achieving greater efficiency across those operations, responding to local differences, and facilitating organizational learning across boundaries; conflicts arise based on cultural differences, local work norms and environments, and varied time zones. A study by Joshi et al. of a 30-member team of human resource (HR) managers in six countries in the Asia-Pacific region showed that network analysis of the various interactions among team members can reveal when and where negative cross-cultural conflicts occur, and thus provide top management with information for conflict resolution so that a higher level of synergy may be attained among the group members. The advantages of synergy include a greater opportunity for global competition (by being able to share experiences, technology, and a pool of international managers) and a greater opportunity for cross-cultural understanding and exposure to different viewpoints. The disadvantages include problems resulting from differences in language, communication, and varying managerial styles; complex decision-making processes; fewer promotional opportunities; personality conflicts, often resulting from stereotyping and prejudice; and greater complexity in the workplace.[57] In the Joshi study, the greatest conflict, and therefore lack of synergy, was not, as one would expect, resulting from the headquarters-subsidiary power divide. Rather, the critical conflicts were between the Country A subsidiary and Country B subsidiary, given the required communication and workflow patterns between them. (Names were kept confidential so that individuals in the study would not be identified.)

What are other ways that management can ascertain how well its international teams are performing and what areas need to be improved?

In recognizing the areas needing better team management, executives in a study by Govindarajan and Gupta ranked five key tasks based on their level of importance, as show below:

Tasks for Global Business Teams[58]
- Cultivating trust among members
- Overcoming communication barriers
- Aligning goals of individual team members
- Obtaining clarity regarding team objectives
- Ensuring that the team possesses necessary knowledge and skills

The managers also rated the level of difficulty to accomplish that task. The researchers concluded from their study that the ability to cultivate trust among team members is critical to the success of global business teams if they want to minimize conflict and encourage cooperation.[59]

Following are some general recommendations the researchers make for improving global teamwork:

- Cultivating a culture of trust: one way to do this is by scheduling face-to-face meetings early on, even if later meetings will be "virtual."
- Rotating meeting locations: this develops global exposure for all team members and also legitimizes each person's position.
- Rotating and diffusing team leadership.

- Linking rewards to team performance.
- Building social networks among managers from different countries.[60]

What other techniques do managers actually use to deal with the challenge of achieving cross-cultural collaboration in multinational horizontal projects? A comparative study of European project groups in several countries by Sylvie Chevrie revealed three main strategies:[61]

- **Drawing upon individual tolerance and self-control:** In this R&D consortium, the Swiss manager treated all team members the same, ignoring cultural differences, and the team members coexisted with patience and compromise. Many of the members said they were used to multinational projects and just tried to focus on technical issues.

- **Trial-and-error processes coupled with personal relationships:** This is a specific strategy in which the project manager sets up social events to facilitate the team members getting acquainted with one another. Then, they discover, through trial and error, what procedures will be acceptable to the group.

- **Setting up transnational cultures:** Here the managers used the common professional, or occupational, culture, such as the engineering profession, to bring the disparate members together within a common understanding and process.

The managers in the study admitted their solutions were not perfect, but met their needs as best they could in the situation. Chevrie suggests that, where possible, a "cultural mediator" should be used who helps team members interpret and understand one another and come to an agreement about processes to achieve organizational goals.[62]

Whether in global management teams, as expatriates, or as host-country nationals, the importance of women as a valuable, and often-underutilized, resource, should not be overlooked in IHRM efforts to maximize the company's global management cadre. Their role is explored in the following Management in Action feature.

MANAGEMENT IN ACTION
The Role of Women in International Management

The world's expatriate workforce is becoming increasingly female.[63]

While it is clear that women are increasingly making their way into the international management cadre, their numbers and clout vary greatly around the world.

The 2011 ranking by *Fortune* magazine of the most powerful women in business in the United States lists Irene Rosenfeld, Kraft Chairman and CEO, as number one, followed by Indra Nooyi, Pepsi's CEO, the Indian-born strategist and former CFO and president. The article also includes a separate list called "International Power 50" (the first twenty of those are listed in Exhibit 10-4). The *Fortune* surveyors conclude that "power knows no bounds for this diverse group."[64] The list includes the woman who built Australia's biggest bank (No. 2) and the Siemens executive (No. 4), the first woman to sit on the Siemens board in its 160-year history. GM Brazil Chief Grace Lieblein is No. 22. There are also many newcomers on the list from India and China. Chanda Kochhar (No. 5), for example, was responsible for the turnaround of ICICI Bank, India; in addition, she is serving as co-chair of the 2011 World Economic Forum annual meeting in Davos, Switzerland. She joined the bank in 1984 as a management trainee. "Her diligence and operational prowess caught the eye of K. V. Kamath, ICICI's longtime CEO, who became her mentor and advocate." [65]

Other women around the world in powerful positions include those in the Arab world, two of whom were described in a *Financial Times* article in June 2008:

Soha Nashaat, 41, in Dubai, who was appointed head of Barclays Private Bank, Middle East in 2006, was tasked with building the business from the ground up. Half-Egyptian, half-Syrian, she was raised in Kuwait and educated in the U.S., and her career, beginning in New York as an intern with Merrill Lynch in 1991, has echoed the international flavor of her upbringing.

(Continued)

EXHIBIT 10-4   Women in Top Business Positions Around the Globe

Cynthia Carroll, CEO, Anglo American, Britain

Gail Kelly, Managing Director and CEO, Westpac, Australia

Marjorie Scardino, CEO, Pearson, Britain

Barbara Kux, Member of Managing Board, Siemens AG, Germany

Chanda Kochhar, Managing Director and CEO, ICICI Bank, India

Guler Sabanci, Chairman and Managing Director, Sabanci Holding, Turkey

Maria Ramos, Group CEO, ABSA, South Africa

Sock Chua Koong, CEO, Singapore Telecommunications, Singapore

Ornella Barra, Chief Executive, Pharmaceutical Wholesale Division, Alliance Boots, Britain

Annika Falkengren, President and CEO, SEB, Sweden

Ho Ching, Executive Director and CEO, Temasek, Singapore

Marina Berlusconi, Executive Chairman, Fininvest, Italy

Nancy McKinstry, Chairman and CEO, Wolters Kluwer, Netherlands

Ana Patricia Botin, Chief Executive, Santander UK, Britain

Dominique Reiniche, President, Europe Group, Coca-Cola, France

Dominique Senequier, Chairman and CEO, AXA Private Equity, France

Yafang Sun, Chairman, Huawei Technologies, China

Patricia Barbizet, CEO, Artemis Holding, Vice Chair, PPR, France

Deborah Henretta, Group President, Asia and Global Specialty Channel, P&G Singapore

Cher Wang, Chairman, HTC, Taiwan

Source: Based on the selections of "The International Power 50," *Fortune International (Europe),* October 17, 2011, and the Web sites of the listed companies.

Sheikha al-Bahar, in Kuwait, described as "the billion dollar banker," has reached the summit of the Gulf's financial community. She started as a trainee at NBK and now, as group general manager, corporate banking, oversees more than $12 billion of assets and almost 150 employees.[66]

However, while women's advancement in some global companies is impressive, it is still true that there are limitations on managerial opportunities for many women in their own country—some more than others—and there are even more limitations on their opportunities for expatriate assignments. Research on expatriate assignments continues to show that females are disproportionately underrepresented in expatriate assignments.[67]

Overall, more managerial opportunities are available for American women than for women in most other countries. However, even for American women, who now fill more than 46 percent of the managerial positions at home, commensurate opportunities abroad are still limited for them.[68]

A report by the 2010 World Economic Forum stated that companies in the United States, Spain, Canada, and Finland lead the world in employing the largest numbers of women from entry level to senior management. Yet the report also found that, "despite increasing awareness of gender disparities in the workplace, women at many of the world's top companies continued to lag behind their male peers in many areas, including pay and opportunities for professional advancement."[69] In addition, the study found that overall only 5 percent of the chief executives of the 600 companies surveyed were women. Finnish companies were at the top with 13 percent, Norway and Turkey with 12 percent, and Italy and Brazil with 11 percent.[70]

The reasons for the different opportunities for women among various countries can often be traced to the cultural expectations of the host countries—the same cultural values that keep women in these countries from the managerial ranks. Cultural expectations may also contribute to different opportunities for women at the top levels between northern and southern Europe.

> *The North-South Divide in Europe, Inc. . . . Women are far more likely to serve on the boards of Scandinavia's biggest companies than Italy's or Spain's, and attitudes to their promotion remain deeply split.*
>
> *Financial Times*[71]

While, in 2010, top boardrooms were only 5 percent female in Italy, and 10 percent in Spain, women occupied 32 percent of board seats in the largest companies in Norway and 27 percent in Sweden. But overall, over half of major European companies have no female representation on their executive committees.[72] The female composition on executive committees in 2010 was similarly divided, although overall lower than the female board composition:

Females on Executive Committees—2010 Sample:[73]

- Sweden   17%
- U.S.   14%
- Britain   14%
- Norway   12%
- Russia   11%
- China   8%
- France   7%
- Spain   6%
- Brazil   6%
- Germany   2%
- India   2%

Given the powerful figure at the top in Germany—Chancellor Angela Merkel—it seems surprising to see the low female participation at the top levels, "but a decade of earnest vows from the corporate sector has not dented male-dominated Deutschland AG . . . all 30 DAX companies are run by men."[74] Clearly, traditional cultural values about gender roles in Germany, as well as lifestyle and laws, can account for much of the disparity in Germany. For example, most children attend school only in the mornings, which restricts the ability for both parents to work. But, in spite of considerable recent government encouragement in its attempts to capitalize on females as an economic resource, only about 14 percent of German mothers with one child resume full-time work, and only 6 percent of those with two children. Even though the German birthrate—at 1.39—is the lowest in Europe, and even though there is a generous 14-month shared parental leave after childbirth, conservative family values that expect mothers to stay home with their children still predominate.

Opportunities for indigenous female employees to move up the managerial ladder in a given culture depend on the values and expectations regarding the role of women in that society. In Japan, for example, the workplace has traditionally been a male domain as far as managerial careers are concerned (although rapid changes are now taking place). To the older generation, a working married woman represented a loss of face to the husband because it implied that he was not able to support her. Women were usually only allowed clerical positions, under the assumption that they would leave to raise a family and perhaps later return to part-time work. Employers, thus, made little effort to train them for upper-level positions.[75] As a result, very few women workers have been in supervisory or managerial posts—thus limiting the short-term upward mobility of women through the managerial ranks.[76]

The younger generation and increased global competitiveness have brought some changes to traditional values regarding women's roles in Japan. More than 60 percent of Japanese women are now employed, including half of Japanese mothers. But how and when these cultural changes will affect the number of Japanese women in managerial positions remains to be seen. Currently, only about 9 percent are in managerial positions, compared with about 45 percent in the United States and 30 percent in Sweden, for example. One can understand the problems Japanese women face when trying to enter and progress in managerial careers when we review the experiences of Yuko Suzuki, who went into business for herself after the advertising company she worked for went bankrupt. However, she could not gain respect or even attention from customers, who often asked her who her boss was after she finished a presentation. She eventually hired a man to accompany her, which increased her sales. But, to her dismay, customers would only establish eye contact with him, even though she was doing the talking and he had nothing to do with the company.[77] Japanese labor economists observe that "Japan has gone as far as it can go with a social model that consists of men filling all of the economic, management and political roles."[78]

(Continued)

While the variation in women's roles around the world can be attributed to complex social and cultural issues, firms ought to be aware of the effects on their bottom line. Research by Catalyst showed that—of the 353 Fortune 500 companies they surveyed—the quartile with the largest proportion of women in top management had a return on equity of 35.1 percent higher than the quartile with the lowest female representation.[79]

The lack of expatriates who are female or represent other minority groups does not reflect their lack of desire to take overseas assignments. Indeed, studies indicate women's strong willingness to work abroad and their considerable success on their assignments. For example, Adler's major study of North American women working as expatriate managers in countries around the world showed that they are, for the most part, successful.[80]

The most difficult job seems to be getting the assignment in the first place. North American executives are reluctant to send women and minorities abroad because they assume they will be subject to the same culturally based biases as at home, or they assume a lack of understanding and acceptance, particularly in certain countries. Research on 52 female expatriate managers, for example, shows this assumption to be highly questionable. Adler showed, first and foremost, that foreigners are seen as foreigners; furthermore, a woman who is a foreigner (a *gaijin* in Japan) is not expected to act like a local woman. According to Adler and Izraeli, "Asians see female expatriates as foreigners who happen to be women, not as women who happen to be foreigners." The other women in the study echoed this view. One woman based in Hong Kong noted, "'It doesn't make any difference if you are blue, green, purple, or a frog. If you have the best product at the best price, they'll buy."[81]

Women and minorities represent a significant resource for overseas assignments—whether as expatriates or as host-country nationals—a resource that is underutilized by U.S. companies. Adler studied this phenomenon regarding women and recommends that businesses (1) avoid assuming that a female executive will fail because of the way she will be received or because of problems experienced by female spouses; (2) avoid assuming that a woman will not want to go overseas; and (3) give female managers every chance to succeed by giving them the titles, status, and recognition appropriate to the position—as well as sufficient time to be effective.[82]

WORKING WITHIN LOCAL LABOR RELATIONS SYSTEMS

If you have to close a plant in Italy, in France, in Spain or in Germany, you have to discuss the possibility with the state, the local communities, the trade unions; everybody feels entitled to intervene . . . even the Church.

JACOB VITTORELLI,
FORMER DEPUTY CHAIRMAN OF PIRELLI [83]

An important variable in implementing strategy and maximizing host-country human resources for productivity is that of the labor relations environment and system within which the managers of a multinational enterprise (MNE) will operate in a foreign country. Differences in economic, political, and legal systems result in considerable variation in labor relations systems across countries. It is the responsibility of the IHRM function to monitor the labor relations systems in host countries and advise local managers accordingly. In fact, that information should be considered as one input to the strategic decision of whether to operate in a particular country or region.

The Impact of Unions on Businesses

European businesses, for example, continue to be undermined by their poor labor relations and by inflexible regulations. As a result, businesses have to move jobs overseas to cut labor costs, resulting from a refusal of unions to grant any reduction in employment protection or benefits in order to keep the jobs at home. In addition, non-European firms wishing to operate in Europe have to carefully weigh the labor relations systems and their potential effect on strategic and operational decisions. However, some change may be on the horizon to provide relief to businesses in Europe as some unions grant concessions to firms in order to keep their jobs. Recently, unions in Germany, France, and Italy have been losing their battle to derail labor-market reforms by the governments in those countries, who are increasingly concerned that excess regulation and benefits to workers are smothering growth opportunities. Firms such as the Swedish furniture company Ikea, for example, have set up plants abroad. Ikea opened its non-unionized plant in Danville, southern Virginia, where the unemployment rate is very high, and received incentive grants for $12 million. However, in July 2011, employees at the plant voted 221 to 69 to allow the International Association of Machinists and Aerospace Workers union to negotiate salary and benefits with the retailer's manufacturing subsidiary, Swedwood. The union organizers claimed that Ikea's high corporate standards for employees stopped at the U.S. border and that employees were "grossly underpaid compared to their Swedish counterparts, suffer high injury rates, are forced to work overtime, and demoted or fired for expressing union sympathies."[84]

The term **labor relations** refers to the process through which managers and workers determine their workplace relationships. This process may be through verbal agreement and job descriptions, or through a union's written labor contract, which has been reached through negotiation in **collective bargaining** between workers and managers. The labor contract determines rights regarding workers' pay, benefits, job duties, firing procedures, retirement, layoffs, and so on.

The prevailing labor relations system in a country is important to the international manager because it can constrain the strategic choices and operational activities of a firm operating there. The three main dimensions of the labor-management relationship that the manager will consider are (1) the participation of labor in the affairs of the firm, especially as this affects performance and well-being; (2) the role and impact of unions in the relationship; and (3) specific human resource policies in terms of recruitment, training, and compensation.[85] Constraints take the form of (1) wage levels that are set by union contracts and leave the foreign firm little flexibility to be globally competitive, (2) limits on the ability of the foreign firm to vary employment levels when necessary, and (3) limitations on the global integration of operations of the foreign firm because of incompatibility and the potential for industrial conflict.[86]

Organized Labor Around the World

The percentage of the workforce in trade unions in industrialized countries has declined in the last decade, most notably in Europe. In the U.S., union membership fell from a third in 1950 to about 11.9 percent in 2010.[87] This global trend is attributable to various factors, including an increase in the proportion of white-collar and service workers as proportionate to manufacturing workers, a rising proportion of temporary and part-time workers, offshoring of jobs to gain lower wage costs, and a reduced belief in unions in the younger generations.[88] In addition, the global economic decline and loss of jobs has put downward pressure on union demands and power when the focus changed to job retention rather than increased benefits.

The numbers do not show the nature of the system in each country. In most countries, a single dominant industrial relations system applies to almost all workers. Both Canada and the United States have two systems—one for the organized and one for the unorganized. Each, according to Adams, has "different rights and duties of the parties, terms and conditions of employment, and structures and processes of decision making." Basically, in North America, an agent represents unionized employees, whereas unorganized employees can only bargain individually, usually with little capability to affect major strategic decisions or policies or conditions of employment.[89]

The traditional trade union structures in Western industrialized societies have been in *industrial unions*, representing all grades of employees in a specific industry, and *craft unions*, based on certain occupational skills. More recently, the structure has been conglomerate unions, representing members in several industries—for example, the metal workers unions in Europe, which cut across industries, and general unions, which are open to most employees within a country.[90] The system of union representation varies among countries. In the United States, most unions are national and represent specific groups of workers—for example, truck drivers or airline pilots—so a company may have to deal with several different national unions. A single U.S. firm—rather than an association of firms representing a worker classification—engages in its own negotiations. In Japan, on the other hand, it is common for a union to represent all workers in a company. In recent years, company unions in Japan have increasingly coordinated their activities, leading to some lengthy strikes.

Industrial labor relations systems across countries can only be understood in the context of the variables in their environment and the sources of origins of unions. These include government regulation of unions, economic and unemployment factors, technological issues, and the influence of religious organizations. Any of the basic processes or concepts of labor unions, therefore, may vary across countries, depending on where and how the parties have their power and achieve their objectives, such as through parliamentary action in Sweden. For example, collective bargaining in the United States and Canada refers to negotiations between a labor union local and management. However, in Europe collective bargaining takes place between the employer's organization and a trade union at the industry level.[91] This difference means that North America's decentralized, plant-level, collective agreements are more detailed than Europe's industry-wide agreements because of the complexity of negotiating myriad details in multi-employer bargaining. In Germany and Austria, for example, such details are delegated to works councils by legal mandate.[92]

The resulting agreements from bargaining also vary around the world. A written, legally binding agreement for a specific period, common in Northern Europe and North America, is less prevalent in Southern Europe and Britain. In Britain, France, and Italy, bargaining is frequently informal and results in a verbal agreement valid only until one party wishes to renegotiate.[93]

Other variables of the collective bargaining process are the objectives of the bargaining and the enforceability of collective agreements. Because of these differences, managers in MNEs overseas realize that they must adapt their labor relations policies to local conditions and regulations. They also need to bear in mind that, while U.S. union membership has declined by about 50 percent in the last 20 years, in Europe, overall, membership is still quite high, particularly in Italy and the United Kingdom—though it, too, has been falling, but from much higher levels.

Most Europeans are covered by collective agreements, whereas most Americans are not. Unions in Europe are part of a national cooperative culture between government, unions, and management, and they hold more power than in the United States. Increasing privatization will make governments less vulnerable to this kind of pressure. It is also interesting to note that some labor courts in Europe deal separately with employment matters from unions and works councils.

In Japan, labor militancy has long been dead, since labor and management agreed 40 years ago on a deal for industrial peace in exchange for job security. Unions in Japan have little official clout, especially in the midst of the Japanese recession. In addition, not much can be negotiated, because wage rates, working hours, job security, health benefits, overtime work, insurance, and the like have traditionally been legislated. However, global competition is putting pressure on companies to move away from guaranteed job security and pay. Often, however, the managers and labor union representatives are the same people, a fact that serves to limit confrontation, as well as does the cultural norm of maintaining harmonious relationships.

In the industrialized world, tumbling trade barriers are also reducing the power of trade unions because competitive multinational companies have more freedom to choose alternative production and sourcing locations. Most new union workers—about 75 percent—will be in emerging nations, like China and Mexico, where wages are low and unions are scarce. However, in some countries, such as India, outmoded labor laws are very restrictive for MNEs, making it difficult to lay off employees under any circumstances and forcing foreign companies to be very careful in their selection of new employees.

In China, for example, in a surprising move, the government passed a new law that will grant power to labor unions, in spite of protests by foreign companies with factories there. The order was in response to a sharp rise in labor tension and protests about poor working conditions and industrial accidents.[94] The All-China Federation of Trade Unions claimed that foreign employers often force workers to work overtime, pay no heed to labor-safety regulations, and deliberately find fault with the workers as an excuse to cut their wages or fine them. The move, which underscores the government's growing concern about the widening income gap and threats of social unrest, is setting off a battle with American and other foreign corporations that have lobbied against it by hinting that they may build fewer factories in China.[95]

Protests arose after Wal-Mart Stores, the world's biggest retailer, was forced to accept unions in its Chinese outlets; other MNCs then joined the effort to get the Chinese government to reverse its decision. State-controlled unions in China have traditionally not wielded much power; however, after years of reports of worker abuse, the government seems determined to give its union new powers to negotiate worker contracts, safety protection, and workplace ground rules.[96] However, in spite of such well-publicized incidences, the union situation in China is generally regarded as *The Economist* states in the following:

> *In name, the All-China Federation of Trade Unions (ACFTU) is a vast union bureaucracy running from the national level to small enterprises. In practice it is controlled by the Communist Party at the national level and, in companies, is mostly a tool of the management.*
>
> THE ECONOMIST.[97]

Workers' basic rights for reasonable working conditions, safety, and even the right to get paid are often ignored by Chinese managers.

> *Less than two years after the worker suicides at electronics giant Foxconn and a strike at Honda suppliers in Guangdong province, labor troubles are again roiling China.*[98]
>
> BUSINESS WEEK,
> DECEMBER 19, 2011.

At Foxconn Technology, for example, which is a major supplier to several electronics giants such as Hewlett Packard, Apple, and Microsoft, there were large protests in January 2012 by workers at its Wuhan plant that involved threats from some workers to commit suicide. The employees were protesting that they had been forced to work long hours under poor conditions with little pay. Foxconn resolved the dispute and, under pressure from Apple and other companies, pledged to improve working conditions in China.[99] Increasing protests and strikes across China are partly attributed to more awareness of labor laws, as well as inflationary pressures. The next day Apple, following the lead of companies such as Intel and Nike, released a list of its major suppliers, including a list of troubling practices at some of its suppliers.[100]

> *Apple said in the report that it recently became the first technology company to join the Fair Labor Association, a nonprofit group that aims to improve conditions in factories around the world.*
>
> INTERNATIONAL HERALD TRIBUNE,
> JANUARY 14, 2012.

However, because problems occur in factories that are outsourced by Apple's suppliers, or which supply parts to the suppliers, retaining control and oversight is very difficult. Hopefully, as discussed in Chapter 2, the improved social responsibility of foreign firms operating in China might exert pressure for better working conditions for Chinese employees. "Meanwhile, the government is expanding the Party-controlled official union. Policymakers want 80% of all companies to have collective bargaining agreements by 2013."[101]

Historically, the existence of unions in the West has been linked closely to improved social responsibility toward workers, and countries around the world are beginning to catch up as far as improved conditions for workers. This happens when unions are permitted and have some power, or when governments put some pressure to improve life for workers so that unions will not take hold. However, strict adherence to union regulations is often traded-off by all parties in order for the local factory to remain competitive and viable and thus provide jobs and a reasonable level of living conditions compared to those experienced previously. This connection is illustrated in the following feature, *Under the Lens: Vietnam—The Union Role in Achieving Manufacturing Sustainability and Global Competitiveness.*

Convergence Versus Divergence in Labor Systems

> *The world trade union movement is poised to follow the lead of transnational companies, by extending its reach and throwing off the shackles of national boundaries. Unions are about to go global.*[102]

In October 2006 the International Trade Union Confederation (ITUC) was formed in Vienna, comprising the affiliated organizations of the former ICFTU (International Confederation of Free Trade Unions) and WCL (World Confederation of Labor), plus eight other national trade union organizations, to form a global body.[103] The ITUC is the world's largest trade union and, as of

UNDER THE LENS

Vietnam—The Union Role in Achieving Manufacturing Sustainability and Global Competitiveness

In most aspects, Vietnam has been gone from the attention of Americans for an entire generation. The country is, however, open for business—and business is booming. Capital is flowing in large amounts from Asia Pacific interests based in Singapore, Japan, Australia, Taiwan, and South Korea. The U.S. is Vietnam's seventh-largest foreign direct investment country, primarily through apparel and footwear manufacturing.

FAST DEVELOPMENT SINCE 2000

Vietnam's appearance as a global competitor is comparatively recent. After the North and South were united in 1975, the country languished for ten years. Finally in 1986, the Vietnamese government woke up and initiated an overall economic renewal policy, known as *doi moi*. Business privatization was encouraged, commerce restrictions came down, and relations with other countries were normalized. It has only been since 2000 that their stock market has been established. Moving rapidly from there, they have been admitted to the Association of Southeast Asian Nations (ASEAN) Free Trade Area (AFTA) and to the World Trade Organization (WTO). Trade relations with the U.S. were normalized in 2006. The results are that Vietnam has gone from triple-digit annual inflation and the inability to grow enough food even for its own use, to single-digit inflation and becoming a mass exporter of both agricultural and manufactured goods.

Major components of their manufacturing for export are footwear and apparel. Unfortunately, most of what the West sees of these types of manufacturing operations comes through non-governmental organizations (NGOs), whose agendas are often far from being unbiased. The purpose of this author's visit in June, 2011 was to see if low labor costs are synonymous with exploitation of workers.

It is important to note that footwear and apparel manufacturing sites in Vietnam are frequently offshored operations owned by outsourced contractors from Taiwan and South Korea. This puts the actual production and labor management considerably removed from the oversight and control of the companies whose brands are being manufactured. Images of sweatshops and exploitation are generally associated with offshored apparel manufacturing.

FIGURE 10-1   **Not the Comfort Inn, But Even the Bosses Don't Live this Well Back on the Rice Farm**

Source: Photo by Dr. Robert Buchanan, used with permission.

MODERN INDUSTRIAL PARKS

In visiting Ho Chi Minh City in 2011, the industrial developments look quite modern. Closest to the city is the Saigon High Tech Park, which is in the early stages of developing a world-class industrial park. Intel is in the process of a $1 billion investment on those grounds. A few kilometers further out are the Linh Trung Processing Zone, Vietnam Singapore Industrial Park, and Song Than Park. Along with Western firms, such as Siemens and Kimberly Clark, are various apparel and footwear manufacturers owned by Asian outsourcers. The industrial parks are very similar to Western-style developments in terms of the grounds, infrastructure, cleanliness, and the spaciousness of the layouts. The main difference is the size of the buildings, some of which are enormous four-level structures containing as many as 10,000 workers at any given time. At 6:00 a.m. a sea of humanity floods the roadways, mostly on foot but many on motorbikes carrying up to three passengers. Workers clock in for 12-hour shifts, and factories operate on a 24-hour basis when orders and deadlines are high. Employment turnover is very high, but jobs are plentiful. Interestingly, the high turnover and high need for workers has not led to fast wage growth. Employers are finding an adequate supply of workers to keep their lines running.

WAGES AND HOUSING

The typical factory worker comes from farming provinces in order to earn higher wages. Workers start at $80–85 per month, with more for experience and productivity. This is often double the potential in their home towns. Many workers will take the option to work 7-day weeks and beyond their 12-hour shifts when factory orders are high. They send as much of their wages home as possible. Workers like to take a yearly 20-day holiday to return home, often on a very long bus ride to the north of the country. Research by Dr. Rhys Jenkins found the migrant textile workers to be appreciative of their job situation, as it had raised their standard of living.[104]

In a tour and interview with a Vietnamese housing owner, as well as several current tenants, the workers were observed to have satisfactory living accommodations, although understandably modest. Workers' rooms rent for $30 per month, and are usually shared by four workers, making their housing cost about 25 cents per day or $8 per month. This is just 10% of base wages. The rooms are clean, austere, and approximately the size of a budget hotel room, with an upper deck for sleeping. Residents cook and have running water downstairs, with a communal bathroom down the hall. The rooms are in single-story buildings, situated along covered, secure corridors. Out on the street, a multitude of vendors serve the food and service needs of this demographic. We observed nothing about these living arrangements that would be characterized as inhumane or even depressing. The housing owners are typically hard-working locals who bought the properties from their own savings, live on-site, and have a congenial, patriarchal relationship with their tenants.

GOVERNMENT OVERSIGHT AND CSR

The general consensus is that the Vietnam government is providing effective levels of oversight and threats to keep factories from being exploitative. Better Work Vietnam is an NGO sponsored by the World Bank and the International Labor Organization (ILO). It has been vocal and credible in its reporting. Their most recent report indicates widespread noncompliance with government overtime standards, as well as health and safety standards. They did not find child labor in any of the large factories. While labor unions are commonplace and protected by law, the reality is that the union officers in many factories are managerial staff. This fails the non-interference test.

Corporate Social Responsibility (CSR) is a luxury that only the largest manufacturers can afford. Nonetheless, the emergence of CSR to benefit Vietnamese workers can be quite similar to those of developed nations. An April, 2011 "Fun Run" in Ho Chi Minh City to raise safety awareness was sponsored by the ILO along with such companies as Abercrombie & Fitch, Levi's, Nike, and The Walt Disney Company. Entertainment, education, and an appearance by a Vietnam Idol winner were sponsored.

CONCLUSIONS

The upshot of these observations is that Vietnam appears to be a successful model for sustainable low-cost labor manufacturing. While it is debatable whether large apparel manufacturers really contribute much to the country overall, there is no question that the jobs they provide are beneficial to that category of worker. Hopefully unions can improve the conditions further for the workers while those plants can remain competitive and retain the jobs locally.

Source: Dr. F. Robert Buchanan, University of Central Oklahoma, used with permission.

2012, represents 175 million workers through its 308 affiliated organizations in 153 countries and territories.[105] Its objective is to provide "a countervailing force in a society that has changed enormously, with workers' rights being flouted under the pressure created by the current trajectory of 'race to the bottom' globalization."[106]

Political changes, external competitive forces, increased open trade, and frequent moves of MNCs around the world are forces working toward convergence in labor systems. **Convergence** occurs as the migration of management and workplace practices around the world reduce workplace disparities from one country to another. This occurs primarily as MNCs seek consistency and coordination among their foreign subsidiaries and as they act as catalysts for change by "exporting" new forms of work organization and industrial relations practices.[107] It also occurs as harmonization is sought, such as for the EC countries, and as competitive pressures in free-trade zones, such as the NAFTA countries, eventually bring about demands for some equalization of benefits for workers.[108] It would appear that economic globalization is leading to labor transnationalism and will bring about changes in labor rights and democracy around the world.[109]

Other pressures toward convergence of labor relations practices around the world come from the activities and monitoring of labor conditions worldwide by various organizations. One of these organizations is the International Labor Organization (ILO)—comprising union, employer, and government representation—whose mission is to ensure that humane conditions of labor are maintained. Other associations of unions in different countries include various international trade secretariats representing workers in specific industries. The activities and communication channels of these associations provide unions and firms with information about differences in labor conditions around the world.[110]

However, there are considerable forces for continued divergence of unions. These include government attitudes toward unions; union competition to attract foreign investment and provide jobs locally; different approaches to structuring unions and how to organize collective bargaining and deal with workers' rights. Exhibit 10-5 shows the major forces for and against convergence in labor relations systems.

ADAPTING TO LOCAL INDUSTRIAL RELATIONS SYSTEMS

Although forces for convergence are found in labor relations systems around the world (as discussed previously), for the most part, MNCs still adapt their practices largely to the traditions of national industrial relations systems, with considerable pressure to do so. Those companies, in fact, act more like local employers, subject to local and country regulations and practices.

EXHIBIT 10-5   Trends in Global Labor Relations Systems

Forces for Global Convergence →	Dynamic Forces Acting on Current System ←	Forces to Maintain or Establish Divergent Systems
Global competitiveness		National labor relations systems and traditions
MNC presence or consolidation initiatives		Social systems
Political change		Local regulations and practices
New market economies		Political ideology
Free-trade zones: harmonization		Cultural norms
(EU), competitive forces (NAFTA)		Competition for jobs
Technological standardization, IT		Collective bargaining methods
Declining role of unions		
Agencies monitoring world labor practices		

Although the reasons for continued divergence in systems seem fewer, they are very strong: Not the least of these reasons are political ideology and the overall social structure and history of industrial practices. In the European Union (EU), where states are required to maintain parity in wage rates and benefits under the Social Charter of the Maastricht Treaty, a powerful defense of cultural identity and social systems still exists, with considerable resistance by unions to comply with those requirements. Managers in those MNCs also recognize that a considerable gap often exists between the labor laws and the enforcement of those laws—in particular in less-developed countries.

THE NAFTA AND LABOR RELATIONS IN MEXICO

About 40 percent of the total workforce in Mexico is unionized, with about 80 percent of the workers unionized in industrial organizations that employ more than 25 workers. However, government control over union activities is very strong, and although some strikes occur, union control over members remains rather weak.[111] Most labor unions are affiliated with the Institutional Revolutionary Party (PRI) through the Confederation of Mexican Workers (Confederación de Trabajadores Mexicanos—CTM). In April 2011, the Teamsters Union charged that Mexico's oligarchs, led by President Felipe Calderon, were trying to take away workers' collective bargaining rights through various labor law reforms. The union charged that

> In reality, the growing power of corporations (enabled by NAFTA) has undermined those rights, especially in the maquiladora district in northern Mexico. Half of all Mexicans live in poverty, and even those with a formal job don't make much money.[112]
>
> TEAMSTER NATION,
> APRIL 21, 2012.

MNCs are required by government regulation to hire Mexican nationals for at least 90 percent of their workforce; preference must be given to Mexicans and to union personnel. In reality, however, the government permits hiring exceptions. The HSBC Bank, for example, found the following:

In all Mexican companies the owner must employ a minimum of 90% Mexican workers in accordance with Mexican Federal Labor Law (MFLL). In the case of technicians and professional workers, they must be Mexican; in the event that Mexican technicians or professional workers are not available, the business may temporarily hire a foreign worker, but both will then have the obligation of training a Mexican technician or professional worker in order to comply with the MFLL. For management or director levels, the rule does not apply.[113]

Many foreign firms set up production in Mexico—utilizing the advantages of the NAFTA—at least in part for the lower wages and lower overall cost of operating there, and the Mexican government wants to continue to attract that investment, as it has for many years before NAFTA. Mexican workers claim that some of the large U.S. companies in Mexico violate basic labor rights and cooperate with pro-government labor leaders in Mexico to break up independent unions. Workers there believe that MNCs routinely use blacklists, physical intimidation, and economic pressure against union organization and independent labor groups that oppose Mexican government policies or the pro-government Confederation of Mexican Workers (CTM).

This example illustrates the complexities of labor relations when a firm operates in other countries—particularly when there are linkages and interdependence among those countries, such as through the NAFTA or the EU. Of interest are the differences among NAFTA nations in labor law in the private sector. For example, while the minimum wage in Mexico is far less than that in Canada or the United States, a number of costly benefits for Mexican workers are required, such as 15 days of pay for a Christmas bonus and 90 days of severance pay. For comparison, the following Comparative Management in Focus feature examines labor relations in Germany.

COMPARATIVE MANAGEMENT IN FOCUS

Labor Relations in Germany

IG Metall union and German government reaffirm their collaboration

DIETMAR HENNING, WWW.WSWS.ORG,

October 21, 2011.

Given the continuing EU crisis, and the deepest global economic crisis since the 1930s, there was considerable commitment to Germany's largest union, IG Metall, at its 2011 annual congress in Karlsruhe. "The union's executive used the occasion to confirm and celebrate its policy of class collaboration. Federal President Christian Wulff and Chancellor Angela Merkel (both from the Christian Democratic Union—CDU) came to the gathering to pay their respects."[114]

It is noteworthy that the German economy has done very well over the last couple of years—while the rest of Europe staggered—leading Angel Gurría, the O.E.C.D.'s secretary general, to say in a speech in Berlin in February 2012 that Germany's "growth model has been so successful in navigating through the stormy waters of the crisis."[115] The German unemployment level fell to the lowest level in decades, while in the rest of Europe it went up. Part of that result is due to the fact that, in the labor system in Germany, companies tend to move employees to part-time status and give them continued training the rest of the time rather than laying them off. Also, the overtime pay of employees is often "banked" by the company to use when times are difficult and they have to reduce employees' hours. Unfortunately, many of the younger generation workers do not have permanent jobs; rather they have "contract," (temporary) jobs, which makes it easier for companies to let them go when the term of the contract ends.[116]

In spite of the commitment to IG Metall, Germany's **codetermination** law (*mitbestimmung*) is coming under pressure from German companies dealing with global competition, and as a result of global trends of outsourcing, industrial restructuring, and the expansion of the service sector.[117] That pressure is increasingly taking the form of concession bargaining to keep jobs at home. Still, some companies—tired of restrictions on their strategic decisions and necessary job cuts—are sidestepping those restrictions by registering as public limited companies in the United Kingdom.[118]

Mitbestimmung refers to the participation of labor in the management of a firm. The law mandates representation for unions and salaried employees on the supervisory boards of all companies with more than 2,000 employees and "works councils" of employees at every work site. Those companies with 2,000 or more staff have to give employees half the votes; those with 500 employees or more have to give a third of supervisory board seats to union representatives.[119] Unions are well integrated into managerial decision-making and can make a positive contribution to corporate competitiveness and restructuring; this seems different from the traditional adversarial relationship of unions and management in the United States. However, the fact is that German firms, in the form of affiliated organizations of companies, have to contend with negotiating with powerful industry-wide unions. Employment conditions that would be negotiated privately in the United States, for example, are subject to federal mandates in Germany—a model unique in Europe. The average metalworker, for example, earns around $2,500 a month, works a 35-hour week, and has six weeks of annual vacation. Germans on average work fewer hours than those in any other country than the Netherlands.[120] Under pressure from global competition, German unions have incurred huge membership losses in the last decade—In 2010 there were 7.9 million members - 40 percent fewer than in 1990 - but that includes about 20 percent of retired union members.[121] In fact, only 20 percent of employees in Germany are union members, compared to 28 percent in the United Kingdom and 67 percent in Denmark.[122] As a result, the unions are now more willing to make concessions and trade flexibility for increased job security. This was the case in 2005 when the German engineering group Linde decided to build a factory in Eastern Europe to take advantage of lower wages there. However, Linde reversed the decision after the IG Metall trade union local decided to match the savings by working longer hours and taking less pay.[123]

Union membership in Germany is voluntary, usually with one union for each major industry, and union power traditionally has been quite strong. Negotiated contracts with firms by the employers' federation stand to be accepted by firms that are members of the federation, or used as a guide for other firms. These contracts, therefore, result in setting the pay scale for about 90 percent of the country's workers.[124]

The union works councils play an active role in hiring, firing, training, and reassignment during times of reorganization and change.[125] Because of the depth of works council penetration into personnel and work organization matters, as required by law, their role has been described by some

MAP 10-1 Germany and Western Europe

EU members using the euro
EU members using own national currency
Countries not members of the EU
■ Cities over 1 million
⊞ Capitals over 1 million

as "co-manager of the internal labor market."[126] This situation has considerable implications for how managers of MNCs plan to operate in Germany. IG Metall (*Industriegewerkschaft Metall*—Industrial Union of Metalworkers) has nearly 2.4 million members. After losing about 400,000 members over the past two decades, the union experienced a slight growth this year of 4,000. IG Metall has traditionally negotiated guidelines regarding pay, hours, and working conditions on a regional basis. Then, works councils use those guidelines to make local agreements. In 2006 the bargaining role started to devolve to the local unit. IG Metall's proactive role on change illustrates the evolving role of unions by leading management thinking instead of reacting to it. In addition, management and workers tend to work together because of the unions' structure. Indeed, such institutional accord is a powerful factor in changing deeply ingrained cultural traits. However, as of 2009, with an increasingly competitive

(*Continued*)

business environment, IG Metall's traditional and inflexible views on labor relations, has led to a decline in membership and bargaining power.

Codetermination has clearly helped to modify German managerial style from authoritarian to something more akin to humanitarian, without, it should be noted, altering its capacity for efficiency and effectiveness.[127] This system compares to the lack of integration and active roles for unions in the U.S. auto industry—for example, conditions that limit opportunities for change.

Pay for German production workers has been among the highest in the world, about 150 percent of that in the United States and about ten times that in Mexico. German workers also have the highest number of paid vacation days in the world and prefer short workdays. However, in July 2004, Jürgen Peters, chairman of Germany's powerful IG Metall engineering trade union, announced the agreement with what was then DaimlerChrysler to accept smaller raises and increased working hours after the company threatened to move 6,000 jobs elsewhere.[128] The agreement followed one by 4,000 Siemens employees in June 2004 to extend their work week.

Foreign companies operating in Germany also have to be aware that termination costs—including severance pay, retraining costs, time to find another job, and so on—are very high, and that is assuming the company is successful in terminating the employee in the first place, which is very difficult to do in Europe. This was brought home to Colgate-Palmolive when it tried to close its factory in Hamburg. The company offered the 500 employees an average severance of $40,000 each, but the union would not accept, and eventually Colgate had to pay a much higher (undisclosed) amount.

The German model, according to Rudiger Soltwedel of the Institute for the World Economy at Kiel, holds that competition should be based on factors other than cost.[129] Thus, the higher wage level in Germany should be offset by higher-value goods like luxury cars and machine tools, which have been the hallmark of Germany's products. To the extent that the West German unions have established the high-wage, high-skill, and high-value-added production pattern, they have also become dependent on the continued presence of that pattern.[130]

Conflicting opinions over the value of codetermination are increasingly evident, as business practices become increasingly subject to EU policies. A major concern was that firms from other countries that were considering cross-border mergers would be discouraged by the EU statute that would oblige them to incorporate codetermination if the new company includes significant German interests.

CONCLUSION

The role of the IHRM department has expanded to meet the strategic needs of the company to develop a competitive global management cadre. Maximizing human resources around the world requires attention to the many categories and combinations of those people, including expatriates, inpatriates, host-country managers, third country nationals, global teams, and local employees. Competitive global companies need top managers with global experience and understanding. To that end, attention must be paid to the needs of expatriates before, during, and after their assignments in order to maximize their long-term contributions to the company.

Summary of Key Points

1. Expatriate career management necessitates plans for retention of expatriates during and after their assignments. Through retention, the firm can benefit from the knowledge and experiences attained on assignments; otherwise the next firm that hires the returnee will benefit from that knowledge. Support programs for expatriates should include information from and contact with the home organization, as well as career guidance and support after the overseas assignment.

2. The expatriate's spouse plays a crucial role in the potential retention and effectiveness of the manager in host locations. Companies should ensure the spouse's interest in the assignment, include him or her in the predeparture training, and provide career and family support during the assignment and upon return.

3. Global management teams offer greater opportunities for competition—by sharing experiences, technology, and international managers—and greater opportunities for cross-cultural understanding and exposure to different viewpoints. Disadvantages can result from communication and cross-cultural conflicts and greater complexity in the workplace.

4. Virtual global teams enable cost effective, rapid knowledge sharing and collaboration, but are fraught with cross-cultural and logistical challenges.

5. Women represent an underutilized resource in international management. A major reason for this situation is the assumption that culturally based biases may limit the opportunities and success of female managers and employees.
6. The labor relations environment, system, and processes vary around the world and affect how the international manager must plan strategy and maximize the productivity of local human resources.
7. Labor unions around the world are becoming increasingly interdependent because of the operations of MNCs worldwide, the outsourcing of jobs around the world, and the "leveling of the playing field" for jobs.

Discussion Questions

1. What steps can the company's IHRM department take to maximize the effectiveness of the expatriate's assignment and the long-term benefit to the company?
2. Discuss the role of reverse culture shock in the repatriation process. What can companies do to avoid this problem? What kinds of skills do managers learn from a foreign assignment, and how can the company benefit from them? What is the role of repatriation in the company's global competitive situation?
3. What are the reasons for the small numbers of female expatriates? What more can companies do to use women as a resource for international management?
4. What is a virtual global management team? How do the members interact? Discuss the advantages and the challenges faced by these teams. Give some suggestions as to how to maximize the effectiveness of virtual teams across borders.
5. Discuss the reasons behind the growing convergence and interdependence of labor unions around the world.

Application Exercise

Interview one or more managers who have held positions overseas. Try to find a man and a woman. Ask them about their experiences both in the working environment and in the foreign country generally. How did they and their families adapt? How did they find the stage of reentry to headquarters, and what were the effects of the assignment on their career progression? What differences do you notice, if any, between the experiences of the male and the female expatriates?

Experiential Exercise

Form groups of six students, divided into two teams, one representing union members from a German company and the other representing union members from a Mexican company. These companies have recently merged in a joint venture, with the subsidiary to be located in Mexico. These union workers, all line supervisors, will be working together in Mexico. You are to negotiate six major points of agreement regarding union representation, bargaining rights, and worker participation in management, as discussed in this chapter. Present your findings to the other groups in the class and discuss. (It may help to read the *Comparative Management in Focus: Motivation in Mexico* feature in Chapter 11.)

Internet Resources

Visit the Deresky Companion Website at www.pearsonhighered.com/deresky for this chapter's Internet resources.

CASE STUDY

Expatriate Management at AstraZeneca

Over the years, AstraZeneca Plc (AstraZeneca) has developed a strong reputation for its expatriate management practices. Expatriate management at AstraZeneca went beyond tackling issues such as compensation, housing, issues related to the spouse's career abroad, etc. It also took care to ensure that employees on international assignment were able to adapt well to the new environment and achieve a work/life balance. With the global economic situation continuing to be grim, AstraZeneca also began placing emphasis on a "more thoughtful planning and selection process" of candidates for international assignments.[1]

Source: Deloitte Services LP.

AstraZeneca is the world's fifth-largest pharmaceutical company by global sales.[2] It is headquartered in London, UK and Södertälje, Sweden. For the year 2008, AstraZeneca's revenues were US$31.6 billion and it employed around 66,000 employees. As of 2009, AstraZeneca had around 350 employees working on international assignments in 140 countries worldwide. These were employees who were on short-term, long-term, or commuter assignments.[3] According to Ashley Daly (Daly), senior manager of international assignments for AstraZeneca in the U.S., the company's employees were mainly concentrated in Belgium, the U.S., and the UK, but they "also have a significant presence in the Asia-Pacific and Latin America regions."[4] AstraZeneca's policy stipulates that for any international assignment, there had to be a business rationale. The company saw to it that the costs involved were acceptable, and that the career management of the employee during the assignment was consistent with personal development goals as well as business needs. The contractual arrangements for the assignment were also centrally managed.[5] "From the outset, if there is not a clear sense of how the international assignment experience can be applied at the end of the assignment term—at least in broad terms—the business should strongly consider whether an international assignment should even move forward,"[6] said Daly.

Once an assignment offer was made to a potential expat, AstraZeneca paired them up with an international assignment manager ("IA manager"), who briefed them on company policy and opportunities for cultural and language training. Before leaving for their international assignment, employees were provided training in a workshop that focused on relevant issues (such as leaving the destination location and returning back to the home country). The expats were given information about the culture of the destination country—particularly differences with the home country—as well as social considerations and do's and don'ts. If necessary, the employee and his/her spouse were given training in the local language. Tessi Romell (Romell), research and development projects and HR effectiveness leader at AstraZeneca, said that the company also helped connect new expats with those who had already served in that location.

Sometimes, follow-up workshops were held in the host country. Once on assignment, expats stayed in touch with their IA manager in addition to the manager they reported back to in the home country. AstraZeneca saw to it that expats were given the necessary flexibility required for them to achieve a work/life balance. "AstraZeneca is really good at allowing people to manage their own time and being aware that we are working across different time zones. It's always something that we try to take into consideration so we don't have people [taking care of work matters] in the middle of the night,"[7] said Romell.

With AstraZeneca taking various initiatives on this front, there were few complaints about work/life balance among the company's expat population. Romell attributed this to the mechanisms the company had put in place to prepare the employees for life in a different country. "It's a combination of things that the company is doing and having a culture that is supportive of work/life balance, as well as encouraging individuals themselves to think about their own work/life balance,"[8] she said. Experts too felt that the practices followed by AstraZeneca, such as preparing the employees for international assignments, providing them with support, and assigning IA managers, were effective. They lauded AstraZeneca's practices, which were in contrast to those of many companies that rushed employees to foreign assignments without adequate support. Chris Buckley, manager of international operations for St. Louis-based Impact Group Inc., pointed out that the expats knew that the organization was spending a lot of money on them and they might be wary about coming up with any complaints regarding their new assignment with their boss. In such a scenario, contact with the IA manager was useful, as it could encourage them to open up.

With the economic situation around the globe continuing to be grim, experts felt that organizations would be forced to take a second look at the costs associated with international staffing. Some felt that organizations would send fewer people on international assignments, or allot them to shorter terms abroad. They even predicted that the high compensation and benefits generally associated with foreign assignments could also see cuts. While AstraZeneca had also taken measures to cut costs (specifically tax costs) by sending employees on short-term assignments, Daly noted that this was not always possible. When the expat had a family and was being posted for a longer term, Daly pointed out that some of the elements of AstraZeneca's expat packages, such as comprehensive destination support and educational counseling for expatriate children, played a critical role in ensuring the employee's productivity. These supports ensured that the expatriate family was able to settle down in the host country. Not providing them could result in employees not being able to focus on their new job, putting the company's investment at risk. So, the company was not looking at this issue in terms of expenditures alone. The company also did not have any plans to decrease the number of its staff deployed internationally. According to Daly, "Our recent focus has been less on reducing numbers of international assignees and more on making the right decisions about who goes on assignment; why they go; and perhaps most important, how the skills and experience gained abroad will be leveraged in their next role, post assignment."[9]

Case Questions

1. Critically analyze AstraZeneca's expatriate management practices.
2. According to the *2007 Expatriate Work/Life Balance Survey*, 65 percent of expats report feeling the strain of managing the demands of work and home, leading to more anxieties at home and at the workplace. What steps can an organization take to mitigate this?
3. What decisions related to expatriates can organizations take to maximize the benefits to the company despite the ongoing economic recession? Do you think a company that paid more careful attention to selection could further boost their chances of success?

References

1. Tanya Mohn, "When U.S. Home Isn't Home Anymore," www.mydigitalfc.com, March 10, 2009.
2. "The Pharm Exec 50," www.pharmexec.com, May 2009.
3. www.ideas.astrazeneca.com.
4. Susan Ainsworth, "Expatriate Programs," http://pubs.acs.org, April 6, 2009.
5. "AstraZeneca Global Policy: People," www.astrazeneca.com.
6. Susan Ainsworth, "Expatriate Programs," http://pubs.acs.org, April 6, 2009.
7. Julie Cook Ramirez, "Finding Balance Abroad," www.hreonline.com, August 1, 2009.
8. Julie Cook Ramirez, "Finding Balance Abroad," www.hreonline.com, August 1, 2009.
9. Susan Ainsworth, "Expatriate Programs," http://pubs.acs.org, April 6, 2009.

Suggested Readings

1. Julie Cook Ramirez, "Finding Balance Abroad," www.hreonline.com, August 1, 2009.
2. "The Pharm Exec 50," www.pharmexec.com, May 2009.
3. Susan Ainsworth, "Expatriate Programs," http://pubs.acs.org, April 6, 2009.
4. Tanya Mohn, "When U.S. Home Isn't Home Anymore," www.mydigitalfc.com, March 10, 2009.
5. *2007 Expatriate Work/Life Balance Survey*
6. "AstraZeneca Global Policy: People," www.astrazeneca.com.
7. www.ideas.astrazeneca.com.
8. www.astrazeneca.com.

CHAPTER **11** Motivating and Leading

OBJECTIVES

1. To understand the complexity and the variables involved in cross-cultural motivation and leadership.
2. To learn how to use the research on cultural dimensions as tools to understand how to motivate people in different cultural contexts.
3. To become familiar with some common features of Mexican culture and context and how to motivate employees.
4. To understand how leadership styles and practices vary around the world, with focus on Russia, India, the EU.
5. To emphasize what makes a successful "global leader."
6. To gain familiarity with the variables of context, people, and situations affecting the leadership role.

OPENING PROFILE: THE EU BUSINESS LEADER—MYTH OR REALITY?

The eurozone crisis means *"the already shaky European identity will weaken further . . . [causing] reemergence of hard-edged national identities."*

INTERNATIONAL HERALD TRIBUNE, AUGUST 27, 2012.[1]

Is "the EU business leader" a myth or reality? The European Union now comprises a 27-nation unified market of over 400 million people. Can a businessperson have an effective leadership style across such diverse contexts and people? Not according to a survey of 200 chief executives in France, Germany, and the United Kingdom. Steve Newhall, of DDI Europe, an international human resources consultancy, notes that "the danger for any leader is only being able to operate within one of these styles. If you take an autocratic style into a culture that expects a more democratic or meritocratic style, the chances are that you will trip up."[2] In 2012, in particular, conflicts brought about by the euro crisis heightened ethnic differences in attitudes.

Perhaps some people can lead well in firms that stretch across countries in the EU. But, consider the complexity in its many forms: different histories and languages, government systems, business practices, educational systems, religions, organizations, and, not the least, national cultures. We have already examined, in this book, the many dimensions of culture along which societies differ and which determine how people behave on the job—their attitudes toward work and their superiors, their perspectives on time and scheduling, their level of motivation, and so on. In addition, countries in the EU are fiercely defensive of any incursions on national culture and identity. Given those factors, the prospect of convergence of leadership styles across the EU countries seems dim. On the other hand, argue Kets de Vries and Korotov:

> *Can European organizations afford not to have some form of European leadership? Can an organization remain Belgian, or Polish, or Italian and not include a "toolset" of European capabilities?*[3]

The strategic argument for convergence of leadership styles for EU business executives is that, while the Japanese or Americans, for example, can succeed domestically with their predominantly "local" leadership style, it is not a good option for executives in most EU companies. For them, retaining "national styles and processes" will not lead to those companies being competitive in the EU and global markets because of the blending of labor, goods, services, and processes across the EU countries. Rather, EU leaders need an "EU style" which will work across their markets.[4]

With that lofty goal in sight—whether one considers that goal desirable or undesirable—research shows that differences in leadership style still dominate. The DDI survey on leadership asked 200 executives what they liked or disliked about being a leader. It was found that, for example, the French are three times more likely than the British and eight times more likely than the Germans to regard being in a position of power as important.[5] In other words, there are differences in attitude toward being a leader and making decisions. Whereas French leaders liked to make decisions unilaterally, German executives indicated their concern about the responsibility of their decisions; leaders in the United Kingdom, however, seemed less troubled about their decisions.[6]

Research on the German culture, for example, tells us that German leaders most likely will evidence high assertiveness and high individualism, but low humane orientation.[7] Their primary focus is on structured tasks and performance, and less on relationships. While very organized, based on technical expertise, they have been criticized for lack of innovation as leaders.[8]

The status of leaders in France is known to be based on position and the educational institutions that they attended—known as the "grand écoles." Title and position are attained through this elite status and thus are paramount over advancement through skills or training. French leadership style is very hierarchical and autocratic. French managers do not typically use a participative leadership style.[9] These conclusions about French leaders are supported by Javidan et al., who found that:

> *To French managers, people in positions of leadership should not be expected to be sensitive or empathetic, or to worry about another's status because such attributes would weaken a leader's resolve and impede decision making. Leaders should make decisions without being distracted by other considerations.*

JAVIDAN, DORFMAN, DE LUQUE, AND HOUSE.[10]

We also see a predominantly autocratic style in the United Kingdom. Top positions of leadership are usually attained through the "old boy network" as a function of the tripartite class system that still

(Continued)

permeates British society (upper-, middle-, and "working"-class). In this respect, leadership is based on traits, not skills, and there tends to be a highly cynical attitude throughout this style.[11]

These brief glimpses of leadership style in three of the EU countries indicate the difficulty, at least for now, of being an EU leader. Clearly, however, any leaders in positions where they deal with people and processes in several EU countries need to consider the context and cultures where they are operating and try to be flexible with their leadership style.

As the opening profile illustrates, leadership—at any level and in any location—is complicated by the norms and expectations of the people involved and by the local business practices. A successful leader must be an effective motivator, a process that is also culturally-contingent. We review the processes of motivating and leading in this chapter, bearing in mind the fact that they are intricately intertwined.

Motivating

The Westerners can't understand that we need the fork on our neck, not all these nice words and baby techniques. The Technique is the fork.

RUSSIAN MIDDLE MANAGER[12]

After managers set up a firm's operations by planning strategy, organizing the work and responsibilities, and staffing those operations, they turn their attention to everyday activities. This ongoing behavior of individual people carrying out various daily tasks enables the firm to accomplish its objectives. Getting those people to perform their jobs efficiently and effectively is at the heart of the manager's challenge.

Motivation—and therefore appropriate leadership style—is affected by many powerful variables (societal, cultural, and political). When considering the Japanese culture, for example, as discussed throughout this book, it is not surprising to find that Fujitsu uses some motivational techniques very different from those used in the West, such as when it cut the salaries of around 14,000 managers to motivate them and their subordinates to work harder. Fujitsu management said that if the company met their profit goal for the year the managers might have their full salaries restored. The logic was to build a sense of urgency and team spirit. Japanese workers typically feel a strong kinship to their employers and will work harder if they see their managers making similar sacrifices for the group goals.[13] Clearly Fujitsu's decision to cut pay is based on the Japanese tradition of "sink or swim," co-workers and employer together, and its collectivist culture.

Our objective in this chapter is to consider motivation and leadership in the context of diverse cultural milieus. We need to know what, if any, differences exist in the societal factors that elicit and maintain behaviors leading to high employee productivity and job satisfaction. Are effective motivational and leadership techniques universal or culture based?

CROSS-CULTURAL RESEARCH ON MOTIVATION

Motivation is very much a function of the context of a person's work and personal life. That context is greatly influenced by cultural variables, which affect the attitudes and behaviors of individuals (and groups) on the job. The framework of this context was described in Chapter 3 and illustrated in Exhibit 3-1. In applying Hofstede's research on the cultural dimensions of individualism—uncertainty avoidance, masculinity, and power distance, for example—we can make some generalized assumptions about motivation, such as the following:

- High uncertainty avoidance suggests the need for job security, whereas people with low uncertainty avoidance would probably be motivated by more risky opportunities for variety and fast-track advancement.

- High power distance suggests motivators in the relationship between subordinates and a boss, whereas low power distance implies that people would be more motivated by teamwork and relations with peers.

- High individualism suggests people would be motivated by opportunities for individual advancement and autonomy; collectivism (low individualism) suggests that motivation will more likely work through appeals to group goals and support.

- High masculinity suggests that most people would be more comfortable with the traditional division of work and roles; in a more feminine culture, the boundaries could be looser, motivating people through more flexible roles and work networks.

More recent research, based on Hofstede's dimensions of individualism and masculinity, was conducted by Gelade, Dobson, and Auer. They compared what 50,000 workers in a global pharmaceutical company in 29 nations valued most in their jobs and how that positively impacted their company. The results, based on Hofstede's individualism dimension, showed that the higher the level of national individualism (such as is typical in the United States), the more employees valued their autonomy, opportunities for personal achievements, and a work–life balance. This compared with employees in the more collectivistic countries (such as in China and Singapore), who apparently are more motivated when they felt that their jobs fully utilized their skills, and when they felt that the company was providing them with good working conditions, fringe benefits, and training.[14] The findings based on the masculinity dimension were that the higher the level of "masculinity" (such as in Japan and Mexico), the more motivated employees were by being given opportunities for high pay, personal accomplishment, and job advancement. This compared with those from more "feminine" cultures (such as in Denmark and Sweden), who claimed that factors related to their relationships with their managers and co-workers provided more commitment to the organization. The authors conclude that:

> *These findings show that the sources of organizational commitment are culturally conditioned and that their effects are predictable from Hofstede's value dimensions*
>
> JOURNAL OF CROSS-CULTURAL PSYCHOLOGY 39.[15]

Misjudging the importance of these cultural variables in the workplace may result not only in a failure to motivate but also in demotivation. Rieger and Wong-Rieger present the following example:

> *In Thailand, the introduction of an individual merit bonus plan, which runs counter to the societal norm of group cooperation, may result in a decline rather than an increase in productivity from employees who refuse to openly compete with each other.[16]*

In considering what motivates people, we have to understand their needs, goals, value systems, and expectations. No matter what their nationality or cultural background, people are driven to fulfill needs and to achieve goals. But what are those needs, what goals do they want to achieve, and what can motivate that drive to satisfy their goals?

The Meaning of Work

Because the focus in this text is on the needs that affect the working environment, it is important to understand first what work means to people from different backgrounds. For most people, the basic meaning of work is tied to economic necessity (money for food, housing, and so forth) for the individual and for society. However, the additional connotations of work are more subjective, especially about what work provides other than money—achievement, honor, social contacts, and so on.

Another way to view work, however, is through its relationship to the rest of a person's life. The Thais call work *ngan,* which is the same as the Thai word for "play," and they tend to introduce periods of play in their workdays. On the other hand, most people in China, Germany, and the United States have a more serious attitude toward work. Especially in work-oriented China, seven-day work weeks with long hours and few days off are common. A study of average work hours in various countries conducted by Steers found that Koreans worked longer hours and took fewer vacation days than workers in Thailand, Hong Kong, Taiwan, Singapore, India, Japan, and Indonesia.[17] The study concluded that the Koreans' hard work was attributable to loyalty to the company, group-oriented achievement, and emphasis on group harmony and business relationships.

Studies on the meaning of work in eight countries were carried out by George England and a group of researchers who are called the Meaning of Work (MOW) International Research Team.[18] Their research sought to determine a person's idea of the relative importance of work compared to that of leisure, community, religion, and family. They called this concept of work **work centrality**, defined as "the degree of general importance that working has in the life of an individual at any given point in time." The results showed, for example, that the Japanese hold work to be very important in their lives; the Brits, on the other hand (in this author's birth country) seem to like their leisure time more than those in the other countries surveyed. However, given the complexity of cultural and economic variables involved in people's attitude toward work, the results are difficult to generalize, in particular as concerns the implications of on-the-job work motivation. More relevant to managers (as an aid to understanding culture-based differences in motivation) are the specific reasons for valuing work. What kinds of needs does the working environment satisfy, and how does that psychological contract differ among populations?

The MOW research team provided some excellent insights into this question when it asked people in the eight countries what they valued about work and what needs are satisfied by their jobs. Their research results showed the relative order of importance overall as follows:

1. A needed income
2. Interest and satisfaction
3. Contacts with others
4. A way to serve society
5. A means of keeping occupied
6. Status and prestige.[19]

Note the similarities of some of these functions with Maslow's need categories[20] and Herzberg's categories of motivators and maintenance factors. (Frederick Herzberg's research focused on how some people are motivated by internal aspirations and life goals, whereas others are primarily motivated by the job conditions.[21]) Clearly, these studies can help international managers to anticipate what attitudes people have toward their work, what aspects of work in their life context are meaningful to them, and therefore what approach the manager should take in setting up motivation and incentive plans.

In addition to the differences among countries within each category—such as the higher level of interest and satisfaction derived from work by the Israelis as compared with the Germans—it is interesting to note the within-country differences. Although income was the most important factor for all countries, it apparently has a far greater importance than any other factor in Japan. In other countries, such as the Netherlands, the relative importance of different factors was more evenly distributed.

The broader implications of such comparisons about what work means to people are derived from considering the total cultural context. The low rating given by the Japanese to the status and prestige found in work, for instance, suggests that those needs are more fully satisfied elsewhere in their lives, such as within the family and community. In the Middle East, religion plays a major role in all aspects of life, including work. The Islamic work ethic is a commitment toward fulfillment, and so business motives are held in the highest regard.[22] The origin of the Islamic work ethic is in the Muslim holy book, the Qur'an, and the words of the Prophet Mohammed:

On the day of judgment, the honest Muslim merchant will stand side by side with the martyrs.

MOHAMMED

Muslims feel that work is a virtue and an obligation to establish equilibrium in one's individual and social life. The Arab worker is defined by his or her level of commitment to family, and work is perceived as the determining factor in the ability to enjoy social and family life.[23] A study of 117 managers in Saudi Arabia by Ali found that Arab managers are highly committed to the Islamic work ethic and that there is a moderate tendency toward individualism.[24]

Exhibit 11-1 shows the results of the study and gives more insight into the Islamic work ethic. Another study by Kuroda and Suzuki found that Arabs are serious about their work and that favoritism, give-and-take, and paternalism have no place in the Arab workplace. They contrasted this attitude to that of the Japanese and Americans, who consider friendship to be an integral part of the workplace.[25]

EXHIBIT 11-1 The Islamic Work Ethic: Responses by Saudi Arabian Managers

Item*	Mean*
Islamic Work Ethic	
1. Laziness is a vice.	4.66
2. Dedication to work is a virtue.	4.62
3. Good work benefits both one's self and others.	4.57
4. Justice and generosity in the workplace are necessary conditions for society's welfare.	4.59
5. Producing more than enough to meet one's personal needs contributes to the prosperity of society as a whole.	3.71
6. One should carry work out to the best of one's ability.	4.70
7. Work is not an end in itself but a means to foster personal growth and social relations.	3.97
8. Life has no meaning without work.	4.47
9. More leisure time is good for society.	3.08
10. Human relations in organizations should be emphasized and encouraged.	3.89
11. Work enables man to control nature.	4.06
12. Creative work is a source of happiness and accomplishment.	4.60
13. Any man who works is more likely to get ahead in life.	3.92
14. Work gives one the chance to be independent.	4.35
15. A successful man is the one who meets deadlines at work.	4.17
16. One should constantly work hard to meet responsibilities.	4.25
17. The value of work is derived from the accompanying intention rather than its results.	3.16

* On a scale of 1–5 (5 = highest)
Source: Based on Abbas J. Ali, *Journal of Psychology* 126, no. 5 (1992): 507–19.

Other variables affect the perceived meaning of work and how it satisfies various needs, such as the relative wealth of a country. When people have a high standard of living, work can take on a meaning different from simply providing the basic economic necessities of life. Economic differences among countries were found to explain variations in attitudes toward work in a study by Furnham et al. of over 12,000 young people from 41 countries on all five continents. Specifically, the researchers found that young people in Far East and Middle Eastern countries reported the highest competitiveness and acquisitiveness for money, while those from North America and South America scored highest on work ethics and "mastery" (that is, continuing to struggle to master something).[26] Such studies show the complexity of the underlying reasons for differences in attitudes toward work—cultural, economic, and so on—which must be taken into account when considering what needs and motivations people bring to the workplace. All in all, research shows a considerable cultural variability affecting how work meets employees' needs.

The Needs Hierarchy in the International Context

How can a manager know what motivates people in a specific country? Certainly, by drawing on the experiences of others who have worked there and also by inferring the likely type of motivational structure present by studying what is known about the culture in that region.

People's opinions of how best to satisfy their needs vary across cultures also. One clear conclusion is that managers around the world have similar needs but show differing levels of satisfaction of those needs derived from their jobs. Variables other than culture may be at play, however. One of these variables may be the country's stage of economic development. With regard to the transitioning economy in Russia, for example, a study by Elenkov found that Russian managers stress security and belongingness needs as opposed to higher-order needs, such as self-actualization.[27] Whatever the reason, many companies that have started operations in other countries have experienced differences in the apparent needs of the local employees and how they expect work to be recognized. Mazda, of Japan, experienced this problem in its Michigan plant.

Japanese firms tend to confer recognition in the form of plaques, attention, and applause, and Japanese workers are likely to be insulted by material incentives because such rewards imply that they would work harder to achieve them than they otherwise would. Instead, Japanese firms focus on group-wide or company-wide goals, compared with the American emphasis on individual goals, achievement, and reward.

When considering the cross-cultural applicability of Maslow's hierarchy of needs theory, then, it is not the needs that are in question as much as the ordering of those needs in the hierarchy. The hierarchy reflects the Western culture where Maslow conducted his study; he concluded that people progress from satisfying basic needs on to satisfying belongingness and esteem needs, and then to self-actualization needs.[28] However, different hierarchies might better reflect other cultures. For example, Eastern cultures focus on the needs of society rather than on the needs of individuals. It is difficult to observe or measure the individual needs of a Chinese person because, from childhood, these are intermeshed with the needs of society. Clearly, however, along with culture, the political beliefs at work in China dominate many facets of motivation. As the backbone of the industrial system, cadres (managers and technicians) and workers are given exact and detailed prescriptions of what is expected of them as members of a factory, workshop, or work unit. This results in conformity at the expense of creativity. Workers are accountable to their group, which is a powerful motivator. Because being "unemployed" has not been an option in China traditionally, it is important for employees to maintain themselves as cooperating members of the work group.[29] Money is also a motivator, stemming from the historical political insecurity and economic disasters that have perpetuated the need for a high level of savings.[30]

Although more cross-cultural research on motivation is needed, one can draw the tentative conclusion that managers around the world are motivated more by intrinsic than by extrinsic factors. Considerable doubt remains, however, about the universality of "Western" theories because it is not possible to take into account all of the relevant cultural variables when researching motivation. Different factors have different meanings within the entire cultural context and must be considered on a situation-by-situation basis. The need to consider the entire national and cultural context is shown in the *Comparative Management in Focus: Motivation in Mexico* feature, which highlights motivational issues for Mexican workers and indicates the meaning of work to them.

COMPARATIVE MANAGEMENT IN FOCUS

Motivation in Mexico

In Mexico, everything is a personal matter; but a lot of managers don't get it. To get anything done here, the manager has to be more of an instructor, teacher, or father figure than a boss.

ROBERT HOSKINS,

Manager, Leviton Manufacturing, Juarez

To understand the cultural milieu in Mexico, we can draw on research that concludes that Latin American societies, including Mexico, rank high on both power distance (the acknowledgment of hierarchical authority) and on uncertainty avoidance (a preference for security and formality over risk). In addition, they rank low on individualism, preferring collectivism, which values the good of the group, family, or country over individual achievement.[31] It is important for managers to recognize that Mexican society is very hierarchical, with a clear power structure for family, religion, business, politics, and other areas of life. People are accorded respect according to their age, sex, and rank or position.[32]

The Mexican culture, generally, is "being-oriented," compared to the "doing-oriented" culture that prevails in the rest of North America; business takes a back seat to socializing.[33] Integral to the being-orientation is the high-context and implicit communication style of most Mexicans; much takes place on the level of non-verbal cues, and the assumption of unspoken communication is based on the personal relationships and trust developed with colleagues. Implicit communication is also based on the importance attached to respect, whereas any conflict would lose face for all concerned.[34] On the other hand, they maintain a small personal space with others and are a "touching" society. They are also frequently very expressive and passionate communicators. In addition, that being-orientation leads to a rather fluid attitude towards time, whereas relationships and commitment to individuals frequently take precedence over scheduled time commitments.[35]

MAP 11-1 Mexico–North America

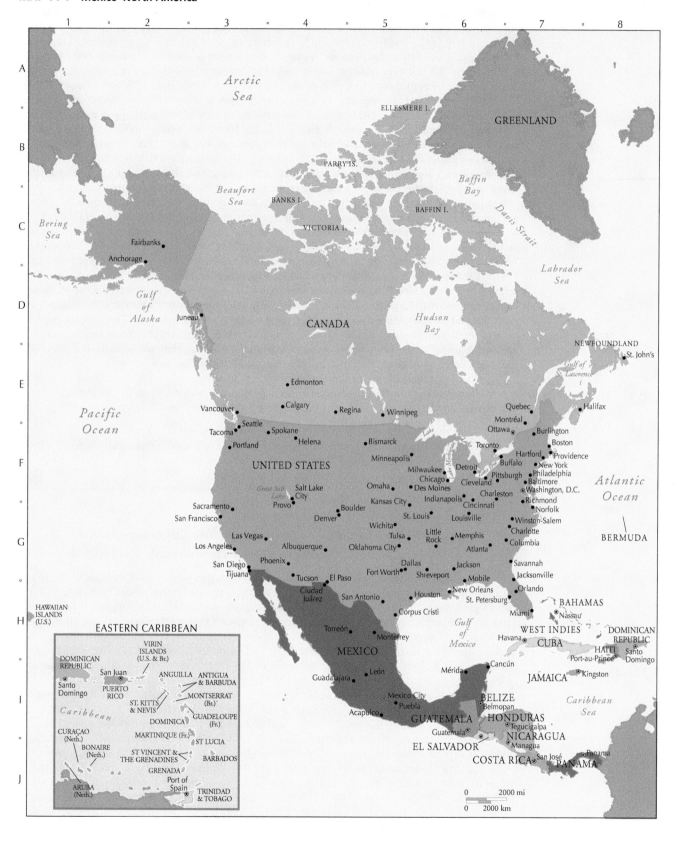

It is said that Mexicans "work to live" compared to those in the United States, for example, who "live to work." One reason for that is that in Mexico the family is of central importance; loyalty and commitment to family and friends frequently determine employment, promotion, or special treatment for contracts. Decisions and actions are usually based on what is good for the family and the group. Unfortunately, it is this admirable cultural norm that often results in motivation and productivity problems on the job by contributing to very high absenteeism and turnover, especially in the *maquiladoras*. This high turnover and absenteeism are costly to employers, thereby offsetting the advantage of the relatively low labor cost per hour. "Family reasons" (taking care of sick relatives or elderly parents) are the most common reasons given for absenteeism and for failing to return to work.[36] Workers often simply do not come back to work after vacations or holidays. For many Mexican males, the value of work lies primarily in its ability to fulfill their culturally imposed responsibilities as head of household and breadwinner rather than to seek individual achievement. Machismo (sharp role differentiation based on gender) and prestige are important characteristics of the Mexican culture.

As a people, speaking very generally, Mexicans are very proud and patriotic; *respeto* (respect) is important to them, and a slight against personal dignity is regarded as a grave provocation.[37] Mexican workers expect to be treated in the same respectful manner that they use toward one another. As noted by one U.S. expatriate, foreign managers must adapt to Mexico's "softer culture;" Mexican workers "need more communication, more relationship-building, and more reassurance than employees in the U.S."[38] The Mexican people are very warm and have a leisurely attitude toward time; face-to-face interaction is best for any kind of business, with time allowed for socializing and appreciating the Mexicans' cultural artifacts, buildings, and so forth. Taking time to celebrate a worker's birthday, for instance, will show that you are a *simpático* boss and will increase workers' loyalty and effort. The workers' expectations of small considerations that seem inconsequential to U.S. managers should not be discounted. In one *maquiladora*, when the company stopped providing the annual Halloween candy, the employees filed a grievance to the state arbitration board—the Junta de Conciliación y Arbitraje.

Personal relationships are of utmost importance to the Mexican people, usually taking priority over work goals. Trust in friends and family takes precedence over purely business relationships, so that networking through personal contacts is the best way to do business. Following are some general guidelines on the Mexican culture to guide "foreign" managers in Mexico:

- Family and friends are first priority; maintaining those relationships and trust takes precedence over "outsiders" and so are important for business success.
- Works to live; scheduling and time management is secondary.
- Fatalistic, based on strong religious influence.
- Nationalistic; importance of history and tradition.
- Work harmony is important; sensitive to conflict situations; need to maintain "face."
- Very proud; status is evidenced by title, position, and formality in dress and etiquette.

Most managers in Mexico find that the management style that works best there is authoritative and paternal. Paternalism is expected; the manager is regarded as *el patrón* (pronounced "pah-trone"), or the father figure, whose role it is to take care of the workers as an extended family.[39] Employees expect managers to be the authority; they are the "elite"—power rests with the owner or manager and other prominent community leaders. Frequently, if not told to do something, the workers will not do it, nor will they question the boss or make any decisions for the boss.[40] Nevertheless, employees perceive the manager as a person, not as a concept or a function, and success often depends on the ability of a foreign manager to adopt a personalized management style, such as by greeting all workers as they arrive for their shifts.

Generally speaking, many Mexican factory workers doubt their ability to personally influence the outcome of their lives. They are apt to attribute events to the will of God, or to luck, timing, or relationships with higher authority figures. For many, decisions are made on the basis of ideals, emotions, and intuition rather than objective information. However, individualism and materialism are increasingly evident, particularly among the upwardly mobile high-tech and professional Mexican employees.

Corrective discipline and motivation must occur through training examples, cooperation, and, if necessary, subtle shaming. As a disciplinary measure, it is a mistake to directly insult a Mexican; an outright insult implies an insult to the whole family. As a motivation, one must appeal to the pride of the Mexican employees and avoid causing them to feel humiliated. Given that, "getting ahead" is often associated more with outside forces than with one's own actions; the motivation and reward system becomes difficult to structure in the usual ways.

Past experiences have indicated that, for the most part, motivation through participative decision-making is not as effective as motivation through the more traditional and expected autocratic methods.

With careful implementation, however, the mutual respect and caring that the Mexican people have for one another can lead to the positive team spirit needed for the team structure to be used successfully by companies. One example is GM's highest-quality plant in the world in Ramos Arizpe, near Saltillo, Mexico.[41] Although a study by Nicholls, Lane, and Brechu concluded cultural constraints are considerable when it comes to using self-managing teams in Mexico, the Mexican executives surveyed suggested that the relative success depends on the implementation. The conflicts are between the norms of behavior in self-managed teams typical of U.S. and Canadian culture (such as initiative and self-leadership and bottom-up decision making), and typical values in Mexican business culture (such as resistance to change, adherence to status roles, and top-down hierarchical structure). These differences in work-role norms seem to create a behavioral impasse, at least initially, when it comes to the potential for setting up self-managed teams.[42]

Although self-managed teams require individual leaders to take risks by spearheading team initiatives, those behaviors, according to the survey of Mexican executives, "are in sharp contrast to the behavioral norms of the paternalistic and hierarchical tradition of managers and workers in the Mexican work place." The workers expect the managers to give instructions and make decisions.[43] The business culture in Mexico is also attributable to prevailing economic conditions in Mexico, which include low levels of education, training, and technical skills. The Mexican executives surveyed gave some suggestions for implementing work teams and cautioned that the process of implementation will take a long time. They suggested the following:

- Foster a culture of individual responsibility among team members.
- Anticipate the impact of changes in power distribution.
- Provide leadership from the top throughout the implementation process.
- Provide adequate training to prepare workers for teamwork.
- Develop motivation and harmony through clear expectations.
- Encourage an environment of shared responsibility.[44]

For the most part, Mexican workers expect that authority will not be abused but rather that it will follow the family model in which everyone works together in a dignified manner according to their designated roles.[45] Any event that may break this harmony, or seems to confront authority, will likely be covered up. This may result in a supervisor hiding defective work, for example, or, as in the case of a steel conveyor plant in Puebla, a total worker walkout rather than using the grievance process.[46] Contributing to these kinds of problems is the need to save face for oneself and to respect others' place and honor. Public criticism is regarded as humiliating. Employees like an atmosphere of formality and respect. They typically use flattery and call people by their titles rather than their names to maintain an atmosphere of regard for status and respect.

A context of continuing economic problems and a relatively low standard of living for most workers help explain why Maslow's higher-order needs (self-actualization, achievement, status) are generally not very high on most Mexican workers' lists of needs. In discussing compensation, Mariah de Forest, who consults for American firms in Mexico, suggests the following:

> *Rather than an impersonal wage scale, Mexican workers tend to think in terms of payment now for services rendered now. A daily incentive system with automatic payouts for production exceeding quotas, as well as daily/monthly attendance bonuses, works well.*[47]

Global economic problems and cutbacks in auto manufacturing in 2009 have also affected Mexico, making money a pressing motivational factor for most employees. Benefits that most workers cannot afford are prized. For example, since workers highly value the enjoyment of life, many companies in Mexico provide recreation facilities—a picnic area, a soccer field, and so forth. Bonuses are expected regardless of productivity. In fact, it is the law to give Christmas bonuses of 15 days of pay to each worker. Fringe benefits are also important to Mexicans; because most Mexican workers are poor, the company provides the only source of such benefits for them. In particular, benefits that help to manage family-related issues are positive motivators for employees to at least show up for work. To this end, companies often provide on-site health care facilities for workers and their families, nurseries, free meals, and even small loans in crisis situations.[48] In addition, those companies that understand the local infrastructure problems often provide a company bus to minimize the pervasive problems of absenteeism and tardiness.

The foregoing statements are broad generalizations about Mexican factory workers. Increasing numbers of American managers are in Mexico because the NAFTA has encouraged more U.S. businesses to move operations there. For firms on U.S. soil, managers may employ many Mexican-Americans in an intercultural setting. As the second-largest and fastest-growing ethnic group in the United States, Mexican-Americans represent an important subculture requiring management attention as they take an increasing proportion of the jobs there.

Research shows that little conclusive information is available to answer a manager's direct question of exactly how to motivate in any particular culture. The reason is that we cannot assume the universal applicability of the motivational theories, or even concepts, that have been used to research differences among cultures. Furthermore, the entire motivational context must be taken into account. For example, Western firms entering markets in both Russia and Eastern Europe invariably run into difficulties in motivating their local staffs. Most workers have been accustomed to working under entirely different circumstances and usually do not trust foreign managers. Typically, then, the work systems and responsibilities must be highly structured because workers in Eastern Europe and Russia are less likely to use their own judgment in making decisions and because managerial skills are less developed.[49] Russia for example, while rapidly becoming "Westernized" in the big cities, still presents foreign managers challenges regarding motivation and leadership styles, as discussed in the accompanying Under the Lens feature.

UNDER THE LENS

Managing in Russia—Motivation and Leadership Challenges

> *A principal rule in the [Russian] workplace is "Superiors know better."*
>
> SNEJINA MICHAILOVA[50]

Russia has enjoyed considerable GDP growth in recent years. In spite of its political unpredictability and instability, Russia is thriving with opportunities for foreign investors because of its vast natural resources, its educated workforce, and a growing middle class of consumers. However, for foreign managers, there are considerable differences and challenges in how to adapt their styles to best motivate and lead employees, as well as leading the company.

A study by Michailova concluded that most Russian employees are still used to the management style that prevailed in a centrally planned economic system. This context resulted in vertically managed hierarchies, one-man authority, and anti-individualism. The continued prevalence of the authoritative, paternalistic leadership style restricts innovation and teamwork. The employees in the study experienced conflict when faced with different managerial styles from their Russian and Western managers in joint venture situations. Those employees were in traditional industries, were on average 45 years old, and were more motivated by the authoritarianism of their Russian managers than the attempts at empowerment by their Western managers. More importantly, the conflicting motivational techniques left them in a "double bind," as shown in Exhibit 11-2.[51]

From his studies of Russian managers, Carl Fey found that typically they "simply want employees to carry out designated tasks set by top management rather than to think creatively about those tasks."[52] The employees themselves would say:

> *You don't understand. Workers work and managers make decisions.*[53]

The report notes that Per Kaufman, the general director of IKEA in Russia, is trying to create a flat and open organization with employee involvement. Kaufman notes that since most Russians feel more comfortable with strong leaders and little empowerment, then that is the easiest way to lead in Russia; however, he realizes that that approach will not develop employees or make them customer-focused.

From his interviews and research, Fey makes a number of suggestions for leaders. For example: employees must be given training and information about the company's challenges and goals and the

EXHIBIT 11-2　**Conflicting Motivational Techniques in Western–Russian Joint Ventures**

Western Managers to Russian Employees	Russian Managers to Russian Employees
Be independent; have initiative	Stick to the rules and procedures
Learn from mistakes and move on	Mistakes are not allowed and should be punished
Take the long-term perspective	Focus on the present
Be a team member	Stick to your own job and business

Source: Based on S. Michailova, "When Common Sense Becomes Uncommon: Participation and Empowerment in Russian Companies with Western Participation," *Journal of World Business 37* (2002): 180–87.

reasons for them. Employees then must be encouraged to share ideas and concerns by providing multiple channels for them to do so without fear of reprisals, and there must be involvement by the managers. Constructive feedback must be given in a timely manner, and a reward system should be set up.[54]

Additional insight can be gleaned from Fey and Stanislav Shekshnia, who have worked and consulted in Russia for 15 years, and recently interviewed 36 executives from foreign firms operating in Russia (examples are Ikea, Microsoft, SAP, Huawei, Cisco, and Ericsson). Their 2011 paper, based on those interviews, gave a number of recommendations, as discussed in the following paragraph.

Foreign managers can provide meaning for employees by practicing authoritative, not authoritarian, leadership. The researchers conclude that Russians are motivated by powerful, charismatic leaders who reflect leaders in their history, and so they respect managers who they perceive to have the authority of proven competence. The employees expect foreign managers to be more competent than local managers, and if that expectation is met, they are then more motivated.[55] In addition, because of Russia's tradition of limited empowerment of employees and severe punishment for mistakes, Fey and Shekshnia concluded that considerable motivation and success can be achieved by gradually creating an empowered organization. This means that managers should encourage employees to make decisions and to allow them to make mistakes without criticism; in this way employees will gradually understand and accept the value of empowerment.[56] Recall that the GLOBE study found that Russian culture was among the least "Performance Oriented" and the least "Future Oriented."[57] Hopefully, since that time, Russia's transitioning society and the influence of more proactive management processes and leadership will have more positive outcomes for business there. In the past, the owner and manager were usually the same, and little value was placed on management techniques such as motivating. Further, as noted in an interview with Russian entrepreneur Ruben Vardanian, Russian companies have traditionally not considered employees very important—to the extent that there have been no HR people on boards, and no real HR systems in place.[58] Because of the continuing level of uncertainty in Russian society, the main motivation for employees and managers is still often just to work for a large company—and thus to feel secure.

In another study by Puffer and McCarthy in 2011, the authors determined that Russian leaders rely on informal personal networks to conduct business due to the weak legitimacy of the country's formal institutions. Therefore, it is important for Western leaders in Russia to realize that it is informal networks and institutions that drive business and decision-making in Russia. Through those networks people are hired as board members, and contacts with officials are made to speed up the bureaucratic permissions process for business. "Foreign" leaders are likely to experience a lack of trust by Russians toward them, creating a barrier to communication and therefore to motivation and leadership; they will need to take time to develop relationships and build trust with employees and others in their business and personal interactions while there.[59] In particular, it is essential to develop a network of contacts with people in government agencies at all levels. The Russian word "svyasi" means "connections" and refers to having friends in high places, which is often required to cut through red tape.[60]

In sum, motivation is situational, and savvy managers use all they know about the relevant culture or subculture—consulting frequently with local people—to infer the best means of motivating in that context. Furthermore, tactful managers consciously avoid an ethnocentric attitude in which they make assumptions about a person's goals, motivations, or work habits based on their own frames of reference, and they do not make negative value judgments about a person's level of motivation because it differs from their own.

Many cultural variables affect people's sense of what is attainable, and thus affect motivation. One example is how much control people believe they have over their environment and their destiny—whether they believe that they can control certain events, and not just be at the mercy of external forces. Although people in the United States typically feel a strong internal locus of control, others attribute results to, for example, the will of God (in the case of Muslims) or to the good fortune of being born in the right social class or family (in the case of many Latin Americans). For example, whereas most Westerners feel that hard work will get the job done, many Hong Kong Chinese believe that outcomes are determined by *joss,* or luck. Clearly, then, managers must use persuasive strategies to motivate employees when they do not readily connect their personal work behaviors with outcomes or productivity.

The role of culture in the motivational process is shown in Exhibit 11-3. An employee's needs are determined largely by the cultural context of values and attitudes—along with the national variables—in which he or she lives and works. Those needs then determine the meaning

EXHIBIT 11-3 **The Role of Culture in Job Motivation**

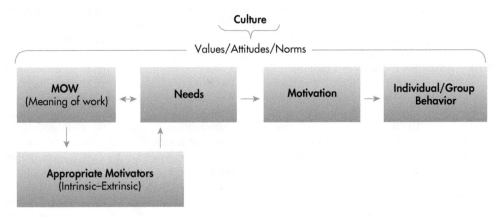

of work for that employee. The manager's understanding of what work means in that employee's life can then lead to the design of a culturally appropriate job context and reward system to guide individual and group employee job behavior to meet mutual goals.

Reward Systems

"The rewards must be 100 percent street-level local," says Derek Irvine, Globoforce's vice president, client strategy and consulting. "Our motto is: 'Think global, thank local.'"

WORKFORCE MANAGEMENT,
SEPTEMBER 2011.[61]

Incentives and rewards are an integral part of motivation in a corporation. Recognizing and understanding different motivational patterns across cultures leads to the design of appropriate reward systems. In the United States, there are common patterns of rewards, varying among levels of the company and types of occupations and based on experience and research with Americans. Rewards usually fall into five categories: financial, social status, job content, career, and professional. The relative emphasis on one or more of these five categories varies from country to country. In Japan, for example, reward systems are based primarily on seniority, and much emphasis is put on the bonus system. In addition, a distinction is made there between the regular workforce and the temporary workforce, which usually traditionally comprises women expected to leave when they start a family. As is usually the case, the regular workforce receives considerably more rewards than the temporary workforce in pay and benefits and the allocation of interesting jobs.[62] For the regular workforce, the emphasis is on the employee's long-term effectiveness in terms of behavior, personality, and group output. Rewarding the individual is frowned on in Japan because it encourages competition rather than the desired group cooperation. Therefore, specific cash incentives are usually limited. In Taiwan, recognition and affection are important; company departments compete for praise from top management at their annual celebration. O. C. Tanner, a consultant firm on such matters, found in their research, for example, that:

clocks or watches, popular gifts in the U.S. for employees celebrating a workplace anniversary, are taboo in Asian countries because timepieces are reminders of mortality. In France, O. C. Tanner learned that workers tend to scoff at effusive gratitude and view thank you notes with skepticism.

WORKFORCE MANAGEMENT,
SEPTEMBER 2011[63]

In contrast, the entire reward system in China is very different from that of most countries. The low wage rates are compensated for by free housing, schools, and medical care. While egalitarianism still seems to prevail, the recent free-enterprise reform movements have encouraged *duo lao, duo de* ("more work, more pay"). One important incentive is training, which gives workers more power. One approach used in the past—and one that seems quite negative to Americans—is best illustrated by the example of a plaque award labeled "Ms. Wong— Employee of the Month." While Westerners would assume that Ms. Wong had excelled as an employee, actually this award given in a Chinese retail store was for the worst employee; the plaque was designed to shame and embarrass her.[64] Younger Chinese in areas changing to a more market-based economy have seen a shift toward equity-based rewards, most likely resulting from a gradual shift in work values.[65]

No doubt culture plays a significant role in determining the appropriate incentive and reward systems around the world. Employees in collectivist cultures such as Japan, Korea, and Taiwan would not respond well to the typical U.S. merit-based reward system to motivate employees, because that would go against the traditional value system and would disrupt the harmony and corporate culture.

Leading

Research results label French captains of industry as "autocrats," Germans as "democrats," and British as "meritocrats."

DDI, LEADERS ON LEADERSHIP SURVEY.[66]

This section on leadership (and the above quote) prompts consideration of the following questions: To what extent, and how, do leadership styles and practices around the world vary? What are the forces perpetuating that divergence? Where, and why, will that divergence continue to be the strongest? Is there any evidence for convergence of leadership styles and practices around the world? What are the forces leading to that convergence, and how and where will this convergence occur in the future? What implications do these questions have for cross-cultural leaders?

The task of helping employees realize their highest potential in the workplace is the essence of leadership. The goal of every leader is to achieve the organization's objectives while achieving those of each employee. Today's global managers realize that increased competition requires them to be open to change and to rethink their old culturally conditioned modes of leadership.

THE GLOBAL LEADER'S ROLE AND ENVIRONMENT

"I don't want to change Sony's culture to the point that it's unrecognizable from the founder's vision," he observed. "That's the balancing act." He thought for a moment and then concluded, "You can't go through a Japanese company with a sledgehammer."

HOWARD STRINGER,
CEO SONY CORPORATION,
QUOTED IN ORGANIZATIONAL DYNAMICS, 2011.[67]

The greatest competitive advantage global companies in the twenty-first century can have is effective global leaders. Yet this competitive challenge is not easy to meet, as observed by the astute British-born leader Howard Stringer when asked to take over as CEO of Tokyo-based Sony Corporation and revitalize its competitive position. People tend to rise to leadership positions by proving themselves able to lead in their home-country corporate culture and meeting the generally accepted behaviors of that national culture. However, global leaders must broaden their horizons, both strategically and cross-culturally, and develop a more flexible model of leadership that can be applied anywhere—one that is adaptable to locational situations around the world.[68]

The critical factors necessary for successful leadership abroad have come to be known as the "Global Mindset." Typically that mindset compares with the traditional mindset in the areas of general perspective, organizational life, work style, view of change, and learning.[69] Harvard Business School authors Javidan et al. describe a leader with a global mindset as having three major qualities:

- "Intellectual capital: the general knowledge and capacity to learn, including global business savvy

- Psychological capital: the openness to differences and capacity to change, such as a thirst for adventure

- Social capital: the ability to build trusting relationships with and among people who are different from you, including intercultural empathy and diplomacy."[70]

EXHIBIT 11-4   The Global Mindset of Successful Leaders[71]

Personal work style	High "cultural quotient" (CQ)
	Open-minded and flexible
	Effective cross-cultural communicator and collaborator
	Team player in a global matrix
	Supports global objectives and balances global with local goals and practices
General perspective	Broad, systems perspective
	Personal autonomy and emotional resilience
	Change is welcomed and facilitated
	Enables boundaryless organizations
	Operates easily in cross-cultural and cross-functional environments
	Global learning is sought and used for career development

Other researchers describe the attributes in terms of the manager's personal work style and general perspective; they articulate some of the typical actions and attitudes of a leader with a global mindset as shown in Exhibit 11-4.

One successful leader with a "global mindset" is Carlos Ghosn, a French businessman and CEO of Nissan and Renault, as well as the chairman and CEO of the Nissan-Renault alliance. He was born in Brazil of Lebanese parents and educated in France. While at Renault, he was sent to Japan to turn around the ailing auto company, Nissan, which he did very successfully, surprising everyone that he could work so well within the intricate culture of Japanese business. Ghosn was voted man of the Year 2003 by *Fortune* magazine's Asian edition; he also sits on the boards of Alcoa, Sony, and IBM. This global leader and multicultural manager conveyed his high CQ when interviewed by *Newsweek:*

> *Companies are going global, but the teams are divided and scattered all over the planet. . . . You have to know how to motivate people who think very differently than you, who have different kinds of sensitivities, so I think the most important message is to get prepared to deal with teams who are multicultural.*[72]

Further information regarding leadership effectiveness abroad was found by Morrison, Gregersen, and Black; their research involved 125 global leaders in 50 companies. They concluded that effective leaders must have global business and organizational savvy. They explain global business savvy as the ability to recognize global market opportunities for a company and having a vision of doing business worldwide. Global organizational savvy requires an intimate knowledge of a company's resources and capabilities in order to capture global markets, as well as an understanding of each subsidiary's product lines and how the people and business operate on the local level. Morrison, Gregersen, and Black outline four personal development strategies through which companies and managers can meet these requirements of effective global leadership: travel, teamwork, training, and transfers (the four "T's").[73]

Travel, of course, exposes managers to various cultures, economies, political systems, and markets. Working on global teams teaches managers to operate on an interpersonal level while dealing with business decision-making processes that are embraced by differences in cultural norms and business models. Although formal training seminars also play an important role, most of the global leaders interviewed said that the most influential developmental experience in their lives was the international assignment. Increasingly, global companies are requiring that their managers who will progress to top management positions must have overseas assignment experience. The benefits accruing to the organization depend on how effectively the assignment and repatriation are handled, as discussed in Chapter 10. There are many top leaders in the world, for example, who have had their start with both a homegrown training and an "international assignment" in India, which provided them with considerable skills to operate in the global marketplace, as illustrated in the accompanying box *Under the Lens: Global Leaders from India.*

UNDER THE LENS
Global Leaders from India[74]

India's globalized business elite seem to owe much of their multiculturalism to the conditions in which they grew up. It is notable that there are more Indian CEOs in the S&P 500 companies than any other nationality except American. Well known are PepsiCo's Indra Nooyi, Citigroup's Vikram Pandit, Motorola's Sanjay Jha, and ArcelorMittal's Lakshmi Mittal. But among the numerous articles about homegrown successful global business executives, two stand out because they are brothers—Ajay and Vindi Banga. Vindi attended IIT, the elite engineering school in India; Ajay graduated in economics from Delhi's prestigious St. Stephen's College. They both went on to get an M.B.A. in marketing from the Indian Institute of Management in Ahmedabad, five years apart. Vindi became a top executive at the global giant Unilever, and then became a partner at a private equity firm. Ajay, the younger brother, went from heading up Citigroup's Asian operations to CEO of MasterCard . . . "all without a degree from a Western business school and without abandoning his Sikh turban."[75] The *Times of India* named Ajay one of the top ten CEOs of 2011. He is known for his extensive network of contacts around the world, and he spent his first months at MasterCard travelling around the world to meet with clients, employees, and regulators. His experience was considered invaluable since the company directors considered Asia and Latin America as prime growth prospects.

If one wonders what kind of environment and upbringing produces so much success, one only has to look at the Banga brothers. They were raised in a Sikh family with a very demanding father, who is a retired lieutenant general in the Indian army, and they were constantly moving to a new post. But, more than that . . .

It could be because today's generation of Indian managers grew up in a country that provided them with the experience so critical for today's global boss. Multiculturalism? Check. Complex competitive environment? Check. Resource-constrained developing economy? You got that right. And they grew up speaking English, the global business language.

Time, August 2, 2011.[76]

Indian managers learn to work around the bureaucratic culture of myriad local, state, and national permits, often having to go to 80 different agencies for permission. This, together with being raised in a multiethnic, multifaith, multilingual society, makes them naturals for the diverse global business environment. India is ranked 134th by the World Bank for ease of doing business, resulting in the necessity to develop and draw upon considerable transnational networks. In addition, those getting accepted to the extremely selective universities such as IIT have already shown their mettle for hard work and competition. Adding to that, their adaptability—so crucial to global business—has become natural as a result of working around a resource-constrained and bureaucratic system.

For other Indian globalists, such as Gautam Adani, the power mogul, the answer was simple: "the easiest and most profitable way to meet India's rising demand for electricity is to avoid the obstacles, divisive political confrontations and practical inefficiencies of India. In the spirit of the workaround ethos typical of India's private sector, Mr. Adani is working around the subcontinent itself."[77] Mr. Adani's plan is to be sufficiently vertically integrated so as not to have to rely on the creaking infrastructure of the Indian state. Among other assets, he owns coal mines in Indonesia and Australia, an Indian power plant, and the private Mundra port. He is yet another example of one of India's most successful exports—global, multicultural managers—produced by the oft-dysfunctionality of the Indian state.

Effective global leadership involves the ability to inspire and influence the thinking, attitudes, and behavior of people anywhere in the world. The importance of the leadership role cannot be overemphasized, because the leader's interactions strongly influence the motivation and behavior of employees, and ultimately, the entire climate of the organization. The cumulative effects of one or more weak managers can have a significant negative impact on the ability of the organization to meet its objectives.

Managers on international assignments try to maximize leadership effectiveness by juggling several important, and sometimes conflicting, roles as (1) a representative of the parent firm, (2) the manager of the local firm, (3) a resident of the local community, (4) a citizen of either the host country or of another country, (5) a member of a profession, and (6) a member of a family.[78]

The leader's role comprises the interaction of two sets of variables—the content and the context of leadership. The content of leadership comprises the attributes of the leader and the decisions to be made; the context of leadership comprises all those variables related to the particular situation.[79] The increased number of variables (political, economic, and cultural) in the context of the managerial job abroad requires astute leadership. Some examples of the variables in the content and context of the leader's role in foreign settings are given below.[80] The multicultural leader's role thus blends leadership, communication, motivational, and other managerial skills within unique and ever-changing environments. We will examine the contingent nature of such leadership throughout this section.

The Leader and the Job:[81]

- Leadership experience and technical knowledge
- Cultural adaptability
- Clarity of information available in host area
- Level of authority and autonomy
- Level of cooperation among partners, government, and employees.

The Job Context:

- Level of authority granted to leader
- Physical location and local resource availability
- Host professional contacts, and community relations
- Organizational structure, scope of internationalization, technology, etc.
- Business environment: social-cultural, political-economic, level of risk
- Systems of staffing, coordination, reward system and decision making, locally and in home office.

The E-Business Effect on Leadership

An additional factor—technology—is becoming increasingly pervasive in its ability to influence the global leader's role and environment and will, perhaps, contribute to a lessening of the differences in motivation and leadership around the world. More and more often, companies like Italtel S.p.A. are using technology such as the Intranet to share knowledge and product information throughout their global operations. In the case of Italtel, this required wide delegation and empowerment of their employees so that they could decentralize.

Individual managers are realizing that the Internet is changing their leadership styles and interactions with employees, as well as their strategic leadership of their organizations. They have to adapt to the hyperspeed environment of e-business, as well as to the need for visionary leadership in a whole new set of competitive industry dynamics. Some of these new-age leadership issues are discussed in the feature *Management in Action: Leadership in a Digital World*.

MANAGEMENT IN ACTION
Leadership in a Digital World

What does leadership mean in a digital world in which organizations are flexible and fluid and the pace of change is extremely rapid? What's it like to lead in an e-business organization? Jomei Chang of Vitria Technology describes it as follows: "There's no place to hide. [The Internet] forces you to be on your toes every minute, every second." Is leadership in e-businesses really all that different from traditional organizations? Managers who've worked in both think it is. How? Three differences seem to be most evident: the speed at which decisions must be made, the importance of being flexible, and the need to create a vision of the future.

Making decisions fast Managers in all organizations never have all the data they want when making decisions, but the problem is multiplied in e-business. The situation is changing rapidly and the competition is intense. For example, Meg Whitman, then-president and CEO of eBay, said, "We're growing at

40 percent to 50 percent per quarter. That pace absolutely changes the leadership challenge. Every three months we become a different company. In one year, we went from 30 employees to 140, and from 100,000 registered users to 2.2 million. At Hasbro [where she was previously an executive], we would set a yearlong strategy, and then we would simply execute against it. At eBay, we constantly revisit the strategy—and revise the tactics."

Leaders in e-businesses see themselves as sprinters and their contemporaries in traditional businesses as long-distance runners. They frequently use the term "Internet time," which is a reference to a rapidly speeded-up working environment. "Every [e-business] leader today has to unlearn one lesson that was drilled into each one of them: You gather data so that you can make considered decisions. You can't do that on Internet time."

Maintaining flexibility In addition to speed, leaders in e-businesses need to be highly flexible. They have to be able to roll with the ups and downs. They need to be able to redirect their group or organization when they find that something doesn't work. They have to encourage experimentation. This is what Mark Cuban, president and co-founder of Broadcast.com, had to say about the importance of being flexible. "When we started, we thought advertising would be the core of our business. We were wrong. We thought that the way to define our network was to distribute servers all over the country. We were wrong. We've had to recalibrate again and again—and we'll have to keep doing it in the future."

Focusing on the vision Although visionary leadership is important in every organization, in a hyper-speed environment, people require more from their leaders. The rules, policies, and regulations that characterize more traditional organizations provide direction and reduce uncertainty for employees. Such formalized guidelines typically don't exist in e-businesses, and it becomes the responsibility of the leaders to provide direction through their vision. For instance, David Pottruck, co-CEO of Charles Schwab, gathered nearly 100 of the company's senior managers at the southern end of the Golden Gate Bridge. He handed each a jacket inscribed with the phrase "Crossing the Chasm" and led them across the bridge in a symbolic march to kick off his plan to turn Schwab into a full-fledged Internet brokerage. Getting people to buy into the vision may require even more radical actions. For instance, when Isao Okawa, chairman of Sega Enterprises, decided to remake his company into an e-business, his management team resisted—that is, until he defied Japan's consensus-charged, lifetime-employment culture by announcing that those who resisted the change would be fired, risking shame. Not so amazingly, resistance to the change vanished overnight.

Source: S. P. Robbins and M. Coulter, Management, 7th ed. (Upper Saddle River, NJ: Prentice Hall, 2001), used with permission.

CROSS-CULTURAL RESEARCH ON LEADERSHIP

Numerous leadership theories focus in various ways on individual traits, leader behavior, interaction patterns, role relationships, follower perceptions, influence over followers, influence on task goals, and influence on organizational culture.[82] Here it is important to understand how the variable of societal culture fits into these theories and what implications can be drawn for international managers as they seek to provide leadership around the world. Although leadership is a universal phenomenon, what makes effective leadership varies across cultures.

In addition to research studies that indicate variations in leadership profiles, the generally accepted image that people in different countries have about what they expect and admire in their leaders tends to become a norm over time, forming an idealized role for these leaders. Industry leaders in France and Italy, for example, are highly regarded for their social prominence and political power. In Latin American countries, leaders are respected as total persons and leaders in society, with appreciation for the arts being important. In Germany, polish, decisiveness, and a wide general knowledge are respected, with their leaders granted a lot of formality by everyone. Foreigners are often surprised at the informal off-the-job lifestyles of executives in the United States and would be surprised to see them pushing a lawn mower, for example.

Most research on U.S. leadership styles describes managerial behaviors on, essentially, the same dimensions, variously termed *autocratic* versus *democratic, participative* versus *directive, relations-oriented* versus *task-oriented,* or *initiating structure* versus *consideration continuum.*[83] These studies were developed in the West, and conclusions regarding employee responses largely reflect the opinions of U.S. workers. The democratic, or participative, leadership style has been recommended as the one more likely to have positive results with most U.S. employees.

CONTINGENCY LEADERSHIP: THE CULTURE VARIABLE

Modern leadership theory recognizes that no single leadership style works well in all situations.[84] A considerable amount of research, directly or indirectly, supports the notion of cultural contingency in leadership. This means that, as a result of culture-based norms and beliefs about how people in various roles should behave, what is expected of leaders, what influence they have, and what kind of status they are given vary from nation to nation. Clearly, this has implications for what kind of leadership style a manager should expect to adopt when going abroad.

The GLOBE Project

Research by the Global Leadership and Organizational Behavior Effectiveness (GLOBE) research program comprised a network of 170 social scientists and management scholars from 62 countries for the purpose of understanding the impact of cultural variables on leadership and organizational processes. Using both quantitative and qualitative methodologies to collect data from 18,000 managers in those countries, representing the majority of the world's population, the researchers wanted to find out which leadership behaviors are universally accepted and which are culturally contingent. Not unexpectedly, they found that the positive leadership behaviors generally accepted anywhere are behaviors such as being trustworthy, encouraging, an effective bargainer, a skilled administrator and communicator, and a team builder; the negatively regarded traits included being uncooperative, egocentric, ruthless, and dictatorial.[85] Those leadership styles and behaviors found to be culturally contingent are charismatic, team-oriented, self-protective, participative, humane, and autonomous.

The results for some of those countries researched are shown in Exhibit 11-5. The first column *(N)* is the sample size within that country. The scores for each country on those leadership dimensions are based on a scale from 1 (the opinion that those leadership behaviors would not be regarded favorably) to 7 (that those behaviors would substantially facilitate effective leadership). Note that reading from top to bottom on a single dimension allows comparison among those countries on that dimension. For example, being a participative leader is regarded as more important in Canada, Brazil, and Austria than it is in Egypt, Hong Kong, Indonesia, and Mexico. In addition, reading from left to right for a particular country on all dimensions allows development of an effective leadership style profile for that country. In Brazil, for example, one can conclude that an effective leader is expected to be very charismatic, team-oriented and participative, and relatively humane but not autonomous.

The charismatic leader shown in this research is someone who is, for example, a visionary, an inspiration to subordinates, and performance-oriented. A team-oriented leader is someone who exhibits diplomatic, integrative, and collaborative behaviors toward the team. The self-protective dimension describes a leader who is self-centered, conflictual, and status conscious. The participative leader is one who delegates decision making and encourages subordinates to take responsibility. Humane leaders are those who are compassionate to their employees. An autonomous leader is, as expected, an individualist, so countries that ranked participation as important tended to rank autonomy in leadership as relatively unimportant. In Egypt, participation and autonomy were ranked about equally.[86]

This broad, path-breaking research by the GLOBE researchers can be very helpful to managers going abroad, enabling them to exercise culturally appropriate leadership styles. In another stage of this ongoing research project, interviews with managers from various countries led the researchers, headed by Robert House, to conclude that the status and influence of leaders vary a great deal across countries or regions according to the prevailing cultural forces. Whereas Americans, Arabs, Asians, the English, Eastern Europeans, the French, Germans, Latin Americans, and Russians tend to glorify leaders in both the political and organizational arenas, those in the Netherlands, Scandinavia, and Germanic Switzerland have

EXHIBIT 11-5   Culturally Contingent Beliefs Regarding Effective Leadership Styles

Country	N	Charisma	Team	Self-Protective	Participative	Humane	Autonomous
Australia	345	6.09	5.81	3.05	5.71	5.09	3.95
Brazil	264	6.01	6.17	3.50	6.06	4.84	2.27
Canada (English-speaking)	257	6.16	5.84	2.96	6.09	5.20	3.65
China	160	5.57	5.57	3.80	5.05	5.18	4.07
Denmark	327	6.01	5.70	2.82	5.80	4.23	3.79
Egypt	201	5.57	5.55	4.21	4.69	5.14	4.49
England	168	6.01	5.71	3.04	5.57	4.90	3.92
Greece	234	6.02	6.12	3.49	5.81	5.16	3.98
India	231	5.85	5.72	3.78	4.99	5.26	3.85
Ireland	157	6.08	5.82	3.01	5.64	5.06	3.95
Israel	543	6.23	5.91	3.64	4.96	4.68	4.26
Japan	197	5.49	5.56	3.61	5.08	4.68	3.67
Mexico	327	5.66	5.75	3.86	4.64	4.71	3.86
Nigeria	419	5.77	5.65	3.90	5.19	5.48	3.62
Philippines	287	6.33	6.06	3.33	5.40	5.53	3.75
Poland	283	5.67	5.98	3.53	5.05	4.56	4.34
Russia	301	5.66	5.63	3.69	4.67	4.08	4.63
Singapore	224	5.95	5.77	3.32	5.30	5.24	3.87
South Korea	233	5.53	5.53	3.68	4.93	4.87	4.21
Spain	370	5.90	5.93	3.39	5.11	4.66	3.54
Sweden	1,790	5.84	5.75	2.82	5.54	4.73	3.97
Thailand	449	5.78	5.76	3.91	5.30	5.09	4.28
Turkey	301	5.96	6.01	3.58	5.09	4.90	3.83
USA	399	6.12	5.80	3.16	5.93	5.21	3.75

Note: Scale 1 to 7 in order of how important those behaviors are considered for effective leadership (7 = highest).
Source: Based on selected data from Den Hartog, R. House et al. (GLOBE Project) *Leadership Quarterly* 10, no. 2 (1999).

very different views of leadership.[87] Following are some sample comments made by managers from various countries:

- Americans appreciate two kinds of leaders. They seek empowerment from leaders who grant autonomy and delegate authority to subordinates. They also respect the bold, forceful, confident, and risk-taking leader, as personified by John Wayne in his movies.
- The Dutch place emphasis on egalitarianism and are skeptical about the value of leadership. Terms like *leader* and *manager* carry a stigma. If a father is employed as a manager, Dutch children will not admit it to their schoolmates.
- Arabs worship their leaders—as long as they are in power!
- Iranians seek power and strength in their leaders.
- Malaysians expect their leaders to behave in a manner that is humble, modest, and dignified.
- The French expect leaders to be "cultivated"—highly educated in the arts and in mathematics.[88]

Subsequently, further conclusions were drawn from the GLOBE results by Javidan et al. as to which leadership variables are found to be universally effective, which are found to be universal impediments to effectiveness, and which are considered to be culturally contingent attributes. Their findings are listed in Exhibit 11-6, with the corresponding GLOBE dimension in parentheses.

Earlier Leadership Research

Other research also provides insight on the relative level of preference for autocratic versus participative leadership styles. For example, Hofstede's four cultural dimensions (discussed in

EXHIBIT 11-6   **Cultural Views of Leadership Effectiveness**

Behaviors and Traits Universally Considered Facilitators of Leadership Effectiveness

• Trustworthiness (integrity)
• Visionary (charismatic-visionary)
• Inspirational and motivating (charismatic-inspirational)
• Communicative (team builder)

Behaviors and Traits Universally Considered Impediments to Leadership Effectiveness

• Being a loner and asocial (self-protective)
• Non-cooperative (malevolent)
• Dictatorial (autocratic)

Culturally Contingent Endorsement of Leader Attributes

• Individualistic (autonomous)
• Status-conscious (status-conscious)
• Risk-taking (charismatic: self-sacrificial)

Source: Based on Mansour Javidan, Peter W. Dorfman, Mary Sully de Luque, and Robert J. House, "In the Eye of the Beholder: Cross Cultural Lessons in Leadership from Project GLOBE," *The Academy of Management Perspectives* 20, no. 1 (2006): 75.

Chapter 3) provide a good starting point to study leader–subordinate expectations and relationships. We can assume, for example, that employees in countries that rank high on power distance (i.e., India, Mexico, the Philippines) are more likely to prefer an autocratic leadership style and some paternalism because they are more comfortable with a clear distinction between managers and subordinates rather than with a blurring of decision-making responsibility.

Employees in countries that rank low on power distance (Sweden and Israel) are more likely to prefer a consultative, participative leadership style, and they expect superiors to adhere to that style. Hofstede, in fact, concludes that participative management approaches recommended by many American researchers can be counterproductive in certain cultures.[89] The crucial fact to grasp about leadership in any culture, he points out, is that it is a complement to "subordinate-ship" (employee attitudes toward leaders). In other words, perhaps we concentrate too much on leaders and their unlikely ability to change styles at will. Much depends on subordinates and their cultural conditioning, and it is that subordinateship to which the leader must respond.[90] Hofstede points out that his research reflects the values of subordinates, not the values of superiors.

In another part of his research, Hofstede ranked the relative presence of autocratic norms in the following countries, from lowest to highest: Germany, France, Belgium, Japan, Italy, the United States, the Netherlands, Britain, and India. India ranked much higher than the others on autocracy.[91]

Expectations about managerial authority versus participation were also among the managerial behaviors and philosophies studied by Laurent, a French researcher. In a study conducted in nine Western European countries, the United States, Indonesia, and Japan, he concluded that national origin significantly affects the perception of what is effective management.[92] For example, Americans and Germans subscribe more to participation than do Italians and Japanese; Indonesians are more comfortable with a strict autocratic structure. Managers in Sweden, the Netherlands, the United States, Denmark, and Great Britain believe that employees should participate in problem solving rather than simply be "fed" all the answers by managers, compared with managers in those countries on the higher end of this scale, such as Italy, Indonesia, and Japan. Laurent's findings about Japan, however, seem to contradict common knowledge about Japan's very participative decision-making culture. In fact, research by Hampden-Turner and Trompenaars places Japan as second highest, after Sweden, in the extent to which leaders delegate authority.[93] Findings regarding the other countries are similar, as shown in Exhibit 11-7. However, participative leadership should not mean a lack of initiative or responsibility.

Other classic studies indicate cross-cultural differences in the expectations of leadership behavior. Haire, Ghiselli, and Porter surveyed more than 3,000 managers in 14 countries. They found that, although managers around the world consistently favored delegation and participation,

EXHIBIT 11-7 **Comparative Leadership Dimensions: Participation and Initiative**

Managerial Initiative, Managers' Sense of Drive and Responsibility		Extent to Which Leaders Delegate Authority	
0 = low; 100 = high		0 = low; 100 = high	
USA	73.67	Sweden	75.51
Sweden	72.29	Japan	69.27
Japan	72.20	Norway	68.50
Korea	67.86	Singapore	65.37
France	64.64	Australia	61.22
Austria	62.56	Germany	60.85
New Zealand	59.46	France	53.62
Greece	58.50	Italy	46.80
UK	58.25	Spain	44.31
Norway	54.50	Portugal	42.56
Portugal	49.74	Greece	37.95

Source: Based on selected data from C. Hampden-Turner and A. Trompenaars, *The Seven Cultures of Capitalism* (New York: Doubleday, 1993).

those managers also had a low appreciation of the capacity and willingness of subordinates to take an active role in the management process.[94]

In addition, several studies of individual countries or areas conclude that a participative leadership style is frequently inappropriate. Managers in Malaysia, Indonesia, Thailand, and the Philippines were found to prefer autocratic leadership, whereas those in Singapore and Hong Kong are less autocratic.[95] Similarly, the Turks have been found to prefer authoritarian leadership, as do the Thais.[96]

In the Middle East, in particular, little delegation occurs. A successful company there must have strong managers who make all the decisions and who go unquestioned. Much emphasis is placed on the use of power through social contacts and family influence, and the chain of command must be rigidly followed.[97]

The effects of participative leadership can vary even in one location when the employees are from different cultural backgrounds—from which we can conclude that a subordinate's culture is usually a more powerful variable than other factors in the environment. Research that supports this conclusion includes a study conducted in Saudi Arabia that found participative leadership to be more effective with U.S. workers than with Asian and African employees, and a study in a U.S. plant that found that participative leadership resulted in greater satisfaction and communication among U.S. employees than among Mexican employees.[98]

Exhibit 11-8 depicts an integrative model of the leadership process that pulls together the variables described in this book and in the research on culture, leadership, and motivation—and shows the powerful contingency of culture as it affects the leadership role. Reading from left to right, Exhibit 11-8 presents contingencies from the broad environmental factors to the outcomes affected by the entire leadership situation. As shown, the broad context in which the manager operates necessitates adjustments in leadership style to all those variables relating to the work and task environment and the people involved. Cultural variables (values, work norms, the locus of control, and so forth), as they affect everyone involved—leader, subordinates, and work groups—then shape the content of the immediate leadership situation.

The leader-follower interaction is then further shaped by the leader's choice of behaviors (autocratic, participative, and so on) and by the employees' attitudes toward the leader and the incentives. Motivation effects—various levels of effort, performance, and satisfaction—result from these interactions, on an individual and a group level. These effects determine the outcomes for the company (productivity, quality) and for the employees (satisfaction, positive climate). The results and rewards from those outcomes then act as feedback (positive or negative) into the cycle of the motivation and leadership process.

Clearly, then, international managers should take seriously the culture contingency in their application of the contingency theory of leadership: They must adjust their leadership behaviors

EXHIBIT 11-8 The Culture Contingency in the Leadership Process: An Integrative Model

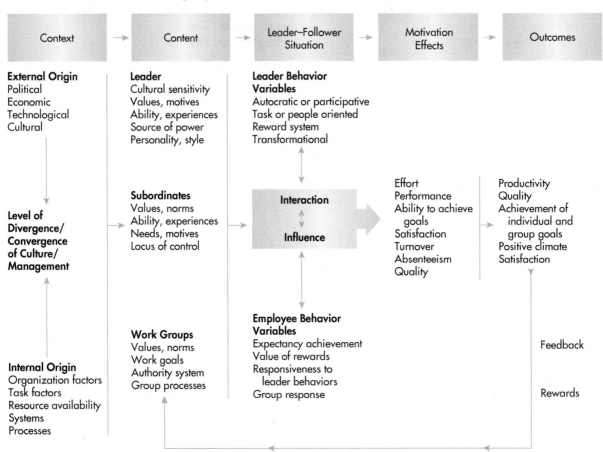

according to the context, norms, attitudes, and other variables in that society. One example of the complexity of the leadership situation involving obvious contextual as well as cultural factors can be seen in the results of a study of how Russian employees responded to the participative management practices of North American managers. It was found that the performance of the Russian workers decreased, which the researchers attributed to a history of employee ideas being ignored by Russian managers, as well as cultural value differences.[99]

As noted, leadership refers not just to the manager-subordinate relationship, but also to the important task of running the whole company, division, or unit for which a manager is responsible. When that is a global responsibility, it is vital to be able to adapt one's leadership style to the local context on many levels. Nancy McKinstry, an American leader in Europe, is very sensitive to that imperative. Since she moved to Europe, charged with the task of turning around the troubled Wolters Kluwer, the Dutch publishing group, she "has had plenty of experience of the way national and cultural differences can both bedevil and enliven business."[100] One immediate difference she noticed is that she is one of few women in senior management in Holland. That fact, added to the focus of the Dutch media on the executive as a person and the views of the employees, rather than the focus on the company, as in the United States, was surprising to her. As she continues her restructuring plan, Ms. McKinstry (whose physician husband commutes every two weeks between his hospital job in New York and his family in Amsterdam) has found that there is a misconception that she is going to apply an American, bottom-line leadership style. However, she says:

> There isn't that one-size-fits-all approach, not even within Europe. . . . If you have a product or a customer problem in France, there might be an approach that works extremely well. But if you took that same approach and tried to solve the exact same problem in Holland, you might fail.[101]

NANCY MCKINSTRY,
CHAIRMAN AND CEO, WOLTERS KLUWER PUBLISHING GROUP, HOLLAND.[102]

Ms. McKinstry explains that in southern Europe, there is far more nuance to what people are saying compared to northern Europe, and in particular compared to the direct, optimistic style of the U.S. She finds that they often don't want to say "No" to her, even though they may not be able to achieve what she is asking them. Her leadership approach is to listen hard and say "How are you going to go about meeting this goal?"[103]

CONCLUSION

Because leadership and motivation entail constant interactions with others (employees, peers, superiors, outside contacts), cultural influences on these critical management functions are very strong. Certainly, other powerful variables are intricately involved in the international management context, particularly those of economics and politics. Effective leaders carefully examine the entire context and develop sensitivity to others' values and expectations regarding personal and group interactions, performance, and outcomes—and then act accordingly.

Summary of Key Points

1. Motivation and leadership are factors in the successful implementation of desired strategy. However, while many of the basic principles are universal, much of the actual content and process are culture-contingent—a function of an individual's needs, value systems, and environmental context.

2. One problem in using content theories for cross-cultural research, such as that created by Maslow, is the assumption of their universal application. Because they were developed in the United States, even the concepts, such as achievement or esteem, may have different meanings in other societies, resulting in a noncomparable basis of research.

3. Implicit in motivating an employee is an understanding of which of the employee's needs are satisfied by work. Studies on the "meaning of work" indicate considerable cross-cultural differences.

4. A reexamination of motivation relative to Hofstede's dimensions of power distance, uncertainty avoidance, individualism, and masculinity provides another perspective on the cultural contexts that can influence motivational structures.

5. Incentives and reward systems must be designed to reflect the motivational structure and relative cultural emphasis on five categories of rewards: financial, social status, job content, career, and professional.

6. Effective leadership is crucial to the ability of a company to achieve its goals. The challenge is to decide what is effective leadership in different international or mixed-culture situations.

7. The perception of what makes a good leader—both traits and behaviors—varies a great deal from one society to another. The GLOBE leadership study across 62 countries provides considerable insight into culturally appropriate leadership behaviors.

8. Contingency theory is applicable to cross-cultural leadership situations because of the vast number of cultural and national variables that can affect the dynamics of the leadership context. These include both leader–subordinate and group relations, which are affected by cultural expectations, values, needs, attitudes, perceptions of risk, and loci of control.

9. Joint ventures with other countries present a common but complex situation in which leaders must work together to anticipate and address cross-cultural problems.

Discussion Questions

1. What have you learned from the research on work centrality and the relative importance of work dimensions to people around the world?

2. What are the implications for motivation of Hofstede's research findings on the dimensions of power distance, uncertainty avoidance, individualism, and masculinity?

3. Explain what is meant by the need to design culturally appropriate reward systems. Give some examples.

4. Develop a cultural profile for workers in Mexico and discuss the management style you would use.

5. Describe the variables of content and context in the leadership situation. What additional variables are involved in cross-cultural leadership? What are the major elements of a "Global Mindset?"

6. Explain the theory of contingency leadership and discuss the role of culture in that theory.

7. How can we use Hofstede's four dimensions—power distance, uncertainty avoidance, individualism, and masculinity—to gain insight into leader–subordinate relationships around the world? Give some specific examples.

8. Describe the autocratic versus democratic leadership dimension. Discuss the cultural contingency in this dimension and give some examples of research findings indicating differences among countries.

9. Discuss how you would develop a profile of an effective leader from the research results from the GLOBE project. Give an example.

10. Can there be an effective "EU Leader"? Is this a realistic prospect? Discuss the factors involved with this concept. What role has the financial crisis in the Eurozone played in this concept?

Application Exercises

1. Using the material on motivation in this chapter, design a suitable organizational reward system for the workers in your company's plant in Mexico.

2. Choose a country and do some research (and conduct interviews, if possible) to create a cultural profile. Focus on factors affecting behavior in the workplace. Integrate any findings regarding motivation or work attitudes and behaviors. Decide on the type of approach to motivation you would take and the kinds of incentive and reward systems you would set up as manager of a subsidiary in that country. Use the theories on motivation discussed in this chapter to infer motivational structures relative to that society. Then decide what type of leadership style and process you would use. What major contingencies did you take into account?

3. Try to interview several people from a specific ethnic subculture in a company or in your college regarding values, needs, expectations in the workplace, and so on. Sketch a motivational profile of this subculture and present it to your class for discussion.

Experiential Exercise

Meet with another student, preferably one whom you know well. Talk with that person and draw up a list of leadership skills you perceive him or her to possess. Then consider your research and readings regarding cross-cultural leadership. Name two countries where you think the student would be an effective leader and two where you think there would be conflict. Discuss those areas of conflict. Then reverse the procedure to find out more about yourself. Share with the class, if you wish.

Internet Resources

Visit the Deresky Companion Website at
www.pearsonhighered.com/deresky for this chapter's Internet
resources.

CASE STUDY

The Olympus Debacle—Western Leader Clashes with Japan's Corporate Leadership Style[1]

In a public ousting rare in staid corporate Japan, Olympus on Friday demoted its British chief executive, Michael C. Woodford, after only six months in the job, citing a management culture clash with the company's mainly Japanese executive team.[2]

The success of Japan's Olympus was based largely on the corporate leadership system—consensus driven, government supported, and rife with cronyism—that was successful when Japan was one of the fast-growing economies in the world. The camera maker and medical-imaging company was largely protected in the folds of the keiretsu system in which Japanese corporations had cross-shareholdings and close cooperative ties. But the new CEO, Michael Woodford, a Briton with over 30 years at the company, was determined to expose some problems when he demanded an investigation into the $687 million in advisory fees that Olympus paid to an unknown group of people for the $1.9 billion purchase of the Gyrus Group of Britain. The advisory fee, which was 30 percent of the purchase price of Gyrus, has not since been traced. Woodford had demanded that chairman Tsuyoshi Kikukawa resign over a shameful situation involving $1.3 billion in acquisition writedowns and fees to mysterious advisers. Shortly after his demands, Woodford was ousted as the company's president on October 14, 2011, after barely six months in the job.

Tsuyoshi Kikukawa, the 71-year-old chairman, blasted him for failing to hew to Japanese cultural practices. The board voted unanimously at a ten-minute meeting where Mr. Woodford was not allowed to speak. Take a bus to the airport, he was told.[3]

The outcome was predictable in light of the typical interweaving of boards and companies in Japan. Twelve of the 15 board members are Olympus executives who owe loyalty to Mr. Kikukawa and 60 percent of its shares are held either by Japanese institutions or by other

Japanese companies, none of which is likely to make waves. In fact, most Japanese companies tend to rely on personal intermediaries and relationships in business, thereby avoiding independent boards willing to raise tough questions.

Of course, Mr. Woodford's Western style of attacking the problem head on no doubt clashed with the typical Japanese implicit leadership style of discreet enquiries rather than exposing particular people. To the Japanese, management consensus means one does not question the big boss. Directors rise through the seniority-based advancement system, thereby ensuring everyone is in the old boys' club—which still rules. Although Chairman Kikukawa initially introduced Mr. Woodford with glowing reports, crediting him with the successful restructuring of European operations, and saying he represented the new global face of the company, Chairman Kikukawa later said that Woodford did not understand the Japanese corporate structure, frequently going around the hierarchy by going straight to employees with directives. Chairman Kikukawa said of Woodford that he did not understand the Japanese art of "nemawashi" consensus building, and that . . .

> *he was unable to understand that we need to reflect a management style we have built up in our 92 years as a company, as well as Japanese culture.*[4]

For his part, Woodford later reported that Japan is one of the most impenetrable cultures. He admitted that he has a blunt style, but also said that his proposed restructuring included avoiding forced redundancies for cultural reasons. As of March 2011, Olympus's profit had declined 41 percent from the previous year, a situation that had prompted the hiring of Woodford to turn around the company. After his dismissal, Olympus stock dropped 18 percent, the largest drop since 1974, with shareholders concerned that the financial reforms that Woodford had promised would now not happen. Two weeks later Mr. Kikukawa resigned as company chairman after about fifty years with the company, without assuming any responsibility, but using the ritualised apologies that Japanese firms tend to use in order to attempt to close off a subject. Subsequently, in October 2011, the F.B.I. in the United States was investigating the exorbitant advisory fees that the Japanese company Olympus paid to a firm with links to the Cayman Islands, as well as other questionable deals that the audits had revealed regarding the syphoning off of Olympus money into other companies.

The boardroom conflict with Woodford is a rare one in Japan, where only few of the top major corporations, such as Sony Corp. and Nissan Motor Co., are run by expatriates.

> *And so began a boardroom battle that has now cost both men their jobs, wiped out over half the company's stock-market value—and once again cast a harsh spotlight on seemingly grave lapses of corporate governance at a top-tier Japanese company.*[5]

The Olympus conflict and subsequent scandal were precipitated by a clash of cultural expectations from both parties. The situation highlights the problem of conflict between old-school business practices in Japan—where personal relationships sometimes take precedence over accepted accounting practices—and the modern management practices of due diligence expected by Westerners. Subsequently, in February 2012, Tsuyoshi Kikukawa, former chairman and president of the company, was among seven who were arrested and charged with falsifying financial statements.[6] As a result of this scandal involving the cover-up of massive losses, the entire board resigned and Yasuyuki Kimoto, former executive at Sumitomo Mitsui bank, took over as chairman.[7] In September 2012, three of those charged pled guilty to the $1.7 billion accounting fraud and received up to 10 years in jail.[8]

Case Questions

1. How does the Japanese culture affect their corporate management style?
2. Discuss the differences between the leadership styles of the British and the Japanese.
3. What effect did the corporate governance composition at Olympus have on the company's problems?
4. Discuss how both Woodford and Kikukawa could have acted differently to resolve the problems that Woodford had uncovered.
5. Research what has happened with Olympus since this case was written in late 2012.

References

1. "Olympus Redux," www.ft.com, October 22, 2011; Hiroko Tabuchi, "In 2 Resignations, a Culture Clash at Olympus," www.nytimes.com, October 26, 2011; Hiroko Tabuchi, "Acquisitions at Olympus Scrutinized," www.nytimes.com, October 24, 2011; John Gapper, "Olympus shows Japan's negative side," www.ft.com, October 23, 2011; "Olympus fires British CEO, a self-confessed loud-mouth," Reuters, www.IBNLive.in.com, October 14, 2011; "Olympus sacks British CEO," Reuters, *The Times of India,* October 14, 2011; Mariko Yasu, "Olympus Dismisses First Non-Japanese President, Shares Tumble," *Bloomberg Businessweek,* October 14, 2011; Hiroko Tabuchi, "In a Culture Clash, Olympus Ousts Its British Chief," www.nytimes.com, October 14, 2011; Robert Boxwell, "The old boys run Japanese business: Good luck changing it," *Financial Times*, London (UK), October 28, 2011; "Business: Olympian depths; Corporate governance in Japan," *The Economist* 401. 8756, October 22, 2011; Steven M. Davidoff, "Olympus Scandal Reveals How Little Japan Has Changed," www.nytimes.com, DealBook, November 1, 2011; Hiroko Tabuchi, "7 Arrested in Olympus Accounting Cover-Up," www.nytimes.com, February 16, 2012.

2. www.nytimes.com, October 14, 2011.

3. *The Economist,* 2011.

4. www.nytimes, November 1, 2011.

5. www.nytimes.com, October 26, 2011.

6. Hiroko Tabuchi, "7 Arrested in Olympus Accounting Cover-Up," www.nytimes.com, February 16, 2012.

7. Associated Press, "Olympus Board Resigns, Taps Chairman from Bank," *New York Times*, February 27, 2011.

8. www.nytimes.com, September 25, 2012.

PART IV: COMPREHENSIVE CASES

Case 9 *Foreign Investment in Chinese Banking Sector: HR Challenges*

China seemed to view foreign participation as compatible with the state's overall control over its banks and as a potentially valuable source of assistance in: (i) promoting bank restructuring, (ii) enhancing banking skills through business cooperation, (iii) supplementing equity capital, without recourse to the fiscal budget, and (iv) boosting the status of Chinese financial institutions in domestic and foreign capital markets. The Chinese government had been quite successful in attracting foreign investment, despite having extremely conservative FDI (foreign direct investment) guidelines. But the real challenge remained in the successful implementation of Human Resource (HR) policies in such international strategic alliances. The partnership not only needed to be a strategic fit and complementary in nature, but also had to be in line with the Chinese culture and value system.

BANKING INDUSTRY IN CHINA

China's banking sector was regulated by the central bank, People's Bank of China (PBC), and the China Banking and Regulatory Commission (CBRC), and both of them were ultimately overseen by the State Council (the cabinet). PBC was in charge of the monetary policy and the liquidity of the financial system, while CBRC looked over the regulatory and supervisory functions. The banking system included four State-Owned Commercial Banks (SOCBs), three policy lending banks, and a large number of other commercial banks, credit cooperatives, and financial institutions. Among the commercial banks, there were 13 joint-stock commercial banks (JSCBs), which were initially created to provide specialized product niches, but later offered a full range of financial services. At the local level, there were 115 city commercial banks (CCBs), 1,000 urban credit cooperatives (UCCs), and 35,000 rural credit cooperatives (RCCs).[1] The 225 foreign bank branches and subsidiaries played a very limited role, accounting for only 2% of the retail banking and foreign-exchange market (*Exhibit I*).

The total assets of the Chinese banks, which stood at $2.4 trillion at the end of 2000, rose sharply to $4.9 trillion in 2006. The four SOCBs, namely Industrial and Commercial Bank of China, Bank of China, China Construction Bank, and Agricultural Bank of China were among the largest banks in the world, with total assets of $2,710 billion[2] and an extensive network of 120,000 branches[3] and over 1,400,000 employees.[4] Joint-stock commercial banks (JSCBs), which were owned partly by local governments and partly by private parties, were used to finance small state-owned enterprises (SOEs) and private small- and medium-sized enterprises (SMEs), and maintained much smaller branch networks than the SOCBs. These banks were typically confined to the region of origin or to the fast-growing coastal area, although they were generally allowed to operate at the

EXHIBIT I **Structure of the Chinese Financial System**

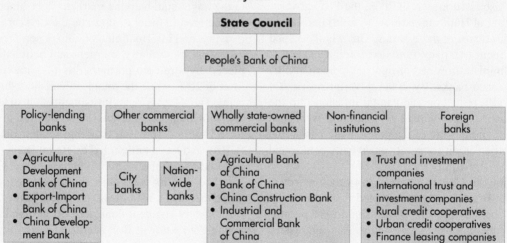

Source: Sayuri Shirai, "Banking Sector Reforms in the People's Republic of China—Progress and Constraints," www.unescap.org/drpad/publication/fin_2206/part3.pdf

This case was written by Chaudhuri S, IBS Research Center. It is intended to be used as the basis for class discussion rather than to illustrate either effective or ineffective handling of a management situation. The case was compiled from published sources.

[1] García Herrero and Daniel Santabárbara, "Where Is the Chinese Banking System Going with the Ongoing Reform?" www.ideas.repec.org/p/wpa/wuwpma/0408001.html

[2] CBRC Statistics; Total Assets & Total Liabilities in the First Half of 2006 (2006-08-22); Total Assets was 21,571.48 billion. Yuan Renminbi converted to USD with the prevailing exchange rate on August 22, 2006.

[3] Douglas Clement, "China's Rich but Troubled Banking Sector," http://www.minneapolisfed.org/pubs/region/03-12/banking.cfm, December 2003

[4] http://sec.edgar-online.com/2005/12/27/0001104659-05-062761/Section12.asp

EXHIBIT II   **Distribution of Assets in China's Financial System**

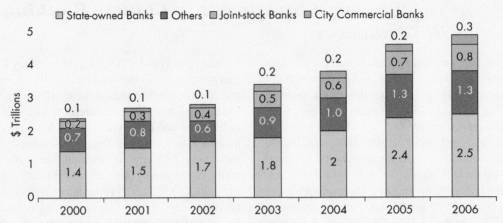

Source: Compiled by the author, IBS Research Centre, Kolkata.

national level. Their relative market-oriented corporate culture had allowed the JSCBs to gain market share over the years at the expense of the SOCBs. Joint-stock banks, which held a 12% share in the Chinese banking industry at the end of Q3-2002, raised their share to 21% at the end of Q3-2006 (*Exhibit II*).

After China's entry into the WTO in 2001, more emphasis was given to the management of "Non Performing Loans" (NPL), which included the recapitalization of the SOCBs and the disposal of the NPLs. As a result of directive lending, PRC banks were burdened with high levels of NPLs. In 1999, the government set up four Asset Management Companies (AMCs), Huarong, Great Wall, Orient, and Cinda, to reduce the NPL level of SOCBs. Initially, these AMCs together took on NPLs worth RMB 400 billion ($169 billion) and slowly sold or auctioned off some of those distressed assets. In 2003, the PRC government established Central Huijin Investment (Huijin) in order to increase the capital reserves of those banks. This wholly owned government investment company funneled foreign exchange from the State Administration of Foreign Exchange (SAFE) to the large state-owned banks. By 2006, government capital spending on both NPL reduction and capital infusion into the Big Four banks reached roughly $283 billion. Steps were also taken for the merger and closure of the problematic banks, the transformation of urban credit cooperatives into city banks, and the promotion of the debt-equity swaps.

Further, revisions to China's banking laws took effect in February 2004. The Big Four were exempted from providing loans to the State Council-approved projects and were permitted to carry out commercial banking activities.[5] The aggressive banking reform decreased the NPL level to a great extent, but the NPL ratio still stood high at 9% for the SOCBs, as compared to 0.3% to 3% in the developed economies.[6] In 2005, the Paris-based Organization for Economic Cooperation and Development calculated that China would have to inject another $203 billion (the government figure was $137 billion) to clear the bad loans of its SOCBs.

Foreign Investment in Chinese Banks

Worldwide, the banking industry had undergone a process of restructuring and reorientation, both at the structural and organizational levels. Phenomena of mergers and acquisitions, globalization and internationalization of products and services, and changes in organizational structures became a global trend in the developing countries. Although the Chinese banking industry was not an exception to this, there was a basic difference in their reform process from that of other developing economies. While most of the developing nations had to adopt the trend set up by the global banking giants, China had made its own norms and forced those banking giants to comply with them. The global banks developed customized lending policies, bank cards, and asset management products so as to cater to the huge retail banking market. The Chinese banks had been restructured in order to upgrade their risk management, global treasury, and information technology services.

Most importantly, mergers and acquisitions had been replaced by strategic partnerships to a maximum permissible limit of 20%, while the total foreign ownership in any bank was capped at 25%.[7] Foreign investments flew in large volume, starting with Bank of America (BoA) holding a 9% stake of CCB for $3 billion. Temasek Holding, United Bank of Switzerland (UBS), and a consortium led by Royal Bank of Scotland (RBS) invested a total of $5.1 billion in the Bank of China (*Exhibit III*).

The SOCBs were attractive investment opportunities, because they had a nationwide presence. Thus, the investors could significantly augment their position in mainland China through a single investment. But, acquiring a significant stake in those banks was very costly and, at the same time it would be very difficult to have any influence over the management due their large state ownership. Moreover, these banks were strategically well suited for those global players who intend to increase their business in the areas of credit cards, consumer finance, treasury management, etc. But, there was another category of foreign investors, who intended to spread their commercial banking business in mainland China through their strategic investments and thus wanted a higher ownership control as well as better asset

[5] Activities included trading on government bonds, dealing in foreign exchange, and offering credit card services.

[6] Vittaldas Leeladhar, "Recent banking developments in India," http://www .bis.org/publ/bppdf/bispap28n.pdf

[7] "IBM plans to join bid for Guangdong bank," http://www.iht.com/articles/2006/ 11/13/business/bank.php?page=1, November 13, 2006.

EXHIBIT III **Strategic Partnerships with State-Owned Commercial Banks**

Bank	Assets RMB bn	Employees	Branch Network	Deal Date	Foreign Partner	Stake	Deal Amount
China Construction Bank	4,586	260,000	14,250	Jun-05	Bank of America	9%	$3 billion
				Jul-05	Temasek Holdings	5%	$1.5 billion
Bank of China	4,743	209,265	12,157	Aug-05	RBS	8%	$3 billion
					UBS AG	1%	$0.6 billion
					Temasek Holdings	5%	$1.5 billion
Industrial and Commercial Bank of China	6,454	361,623	18,870	Jan-06	Goldman Sachs	10%	$2.6 billion
					Allianz AG subsidiary		€0.8 billion
					Dresdner Bank		$0.2 billion
					American Express		
Agricultural Bank of China	4,771	300,000	31,000				

Source: Compiled by the author, IBS Research Centre, Kolkata.

EXHIBIT IV **Strategic Partnerships with Joint Stock Commercial Banks**

Bank	Rating (S&P)	Deal Date	Foreign Partner	Stake	Deal Amount
Bank of Communications	BBB	Aug-04	HSBC Holdings Plc	19.90%	$1.75 billion
China CITIC Bank	N.R.	Dec-06	Banco Bilbao Vizcaya Argentaria (BBVA)	5% (With option to increase to 9.9%)	€501million
China Everbright Bank	Bpi	Jan-07	ADB	3%	US$20 million
China Minsheng Bank	Bpi	Oct-04	Hang Seng Bank	8%	NA
			IFC	1.20%	$23.5 million
			Temasek Holdings	4.55%	$106 million
Guangdong Development Bank	Bpi	Jan-07	Citigroup, IBM	85.6% (Citigroup 20%, China Life 20%, State Grid 20%, Puhua 8%, CITIC Trust 12.85%, IBM 4.74%)	RMB 24.267 bn/ US$3.06 billion
Hua Xia Bank	Bpi	Oct-05	Deutsche Bank	14.00%	$325 million
Industrial Bank (Fujian)	N.R.	Dec-03	Hang Seng Bank	16%	$208 million
Shanghai Pudong Development Bank	BBpi	Dec-02	Citigroup	19.9%	$72 million for 4.62% (in 2003)
			PING An Insurance	4.94%	$238 million for 3.04%
Shenzhen Development Bank	Bpi	Oct-05	Newbridge Capital	17.89%	$149 million
		May-04	(Texas Pacific Group) GE Consumer Finance	7.00%	$100 million
Evergrowing Bank	N.R.	Jun-08	United Overseas Bank	15.38%	US$114 million
China Bohai Bank	N.R.	Sep-05	Standard Chartered	19.90%	US$123 million

Source: Compiled by the author, IBS Research Centre, Kolkata.

quality. Joint Stock commercial banks (JSCBs) were best suited for that purpose, because these banks were strong enough compared to the city commercial and other co-operative banks. There was also scope for forming consortiums in order to get rid of the ownership restrictions. Citigroup formed such a consortium with China Life, State Grid, CITIC trust, Puhua, and IBM to acquire an 85% stake in Guangdong Development Bank[8] (*Exhibit IV*).

[8] "Citigroup Completes Guangdong Development Bank Transaction," http://www.citigroup.com/citigroup/press/2006/061219a.htm, December 19, 2006.

EXHIBIT V   Strategic Partnerships with City Commercial Banks

Bank	Deal Date	Foreign Partner	Stake	Deal Amount
Ningbo Commercial Bank	Jan-06	OCBC	12%	$71 million
Tianjin City Commercial Bank	Nov-05	ANZ Banking Group	19.90%	$120 million
Nanjing City Commercial Bank	Oct-05	BNP Paribas	19.20%	$87 million
	2002	IFC	15.00%	$27 million
Hangzhou City Commercial Bank	Apr-05	Commonwealth Bank of Australia	19.90%	$76 million
Bank of Beijing	Mar-05	ING	19.90%	$215 million
Ji'Nan City Commercial Bank	Dec-04	Commonwealth Bank of Australia	11.00%	$17 million
Xi'an City Commercial Bank	Nov-04	Bank of Nova Scotia	5%	$7 million
	Dec-04	IFC	19.90%	$12.5 million
Bank of Shanghai	Dec-01	HSBC	8%	$62.6 million
		IFC	7%	$50.3 million

Source: Compiled by the author, IBS Research Centre, Kolkata.

As the coastal regions of China were financially most developed and there was also a surplus of capital, the city banks in those regions were also considered to be good targets for foreign strategic alliances. By 2006, city banks in Shanghai, Tianjin, Beijing, Hangzhou, Ningbo, and Ji'Nan got foreign strategic investors, though the deal amounts were comparatively small in nature. On an aggregate, the total foreign investments in the city banks amounted to around $1 billion (*Exhibit V*).

The PRC government had initiated the "Socialist New Countryside" campaign in a bid to promote the development of its vast rural areas, where 53% of its population lived. The Agricultural Bank of China had planned to inject $58 billion in the next five years and the campaign was estimated to gobble up around $2.5 trillion by 2020.[9] Sooner or later, foreign banks would also start investing in the rural credit cooperatives.

Strategic Foreign Partnership: HRM Issues

Foreign banks had been aiming to tap the growing credit card and asset management business in China, either individually or through potential synergies with the domestic banks. But for a considerable period the Chinese government had imposed various restrictions on the entry of the foreign banks. After China's entry into the WTO in 2001, the Chinese government had permitted entry to the foreign investors on a provincial basis and guaranteed that from December 2006, the foreign banks could compete with the domestic banks under identical conditions. The government apparently decided that the foreign participation in the domestic banks via equity investment would to be an effective way to enhance their competitiveness. But the PRC government had been very conservative with respect to allowing foreign investments in the banking sector. Chinese banks, specially the JSCBs and CCBs, typically used a range

of criteria to judge the potentiality of the foreign banks as a strategic investor (*Exhibit VI*).

In international joint ventures with Chinese firms, strategic fit was considered to be the foundation for exploring and reaping the benefits. The foreign banks needed to clearly understand the Chinese management style and have at least a minimum level of commitment towards the Chinese society. The Chinese management style was based on relationship building and development of trust. Thus, there was a strong overlap between the private life and business life. Still, the Chinese had a fast and task-oriented approach and they were meticulous time planners. They could juggle demands and were extremely flexible. International businesses differed hugely from their Chinese counterparts in terms of women employees. Chinese women were usually the first to be laid off from the businesses, economically losing their competitive edge, and very few businesses have women leaders. Chinese society also had a strong preference toward entrepreneurship. Running one's own business was appreciated more than working in a large multinational firm. Chinese businesses also had a relatively long-term view than foreign investors regarding employment. Thus, for an international partner, it was extremely important that it incorporated the values, objectives, and methods of the Chinese partners (*Exhibit VII*), and gradually modify those in order to fit strategically in the international joint ventures.

Chinese culture holds the Confucian values, which include loyalty to family and building interpersonal relationships. Chinese people were very sensitive in "maintaining face" in everything they did. Saying or doing anything that caused someone to lose face could instantly destroy a relationship and any business that might result from it. Openly criticizing someone was unappreciated in Chinese society. Chinese people were highly focused on acquisition of skills rather than on getting formal higher education. Thus, there were few highly educated managers and employees, who had the liberty to demand premium salaries. Managers with

---

[9] "Chinese bank sees chances in 'New Countryside' initiative," http://en.ce.cn/ Industries/Financial-services/200608/04/t20060804_8008896.shtml, August 4, 2006.

EXHIBIT VI Criteria Commonly Used by Chinese Banks in Selecting Potential Investors

Categories	Criteria	Relevancy/Benefits
Profile	Asset size Market cap Financial strength/credit ratings	Strong world-class profile and powerful endorsement of Chinese banks Financial strength provides long-term stability
Strategic Fit	China strategy and presence International revenues/profits as % of total revenues/profits Expansion strategy (organic vs. mergers and acquisitions)	Level of interest in Chinese banks Only a subset of investors have an international mindset and knowledge of Asia Strategic fit as foundation for exploring and reaping benefits
Management/ Cultural Fit	Vision and capabilities Cohesive management culture and disciplined management system Interest in working with partners	Willingness and ability to help Chinese bank to reinvent itself by committing management resources
Core Competency	Business mix: retail banking, corporate banking, risk control, wealth management Infrastructure, Cross-selling capabilities Distribution: IT, MIS, back office, operating and financial results	Tangible benefits to Chinese banks in its execution of strategy Availability of international best practices
Acquisition Appetite	Mergers and acquisitions experience in financial services Experience in minority stake investments	Interest in committing to an investment in Chinese banks Willingness to negotiate reasonable terms
Ability to Pay	Market cap Impacts of potential investment on capital adequacy and earnings Accounting treatment	Indication of ability to pay for an investment Impact on transaction structure (composition of investors)

Source: http://ideas.repec.org/p/wpa/wuwpma/0408001.html

EXHIBIT VII Values, Objectives, and Methods of Chinese and Foreign Partners in International Joint Ventures

Objective of JV	Chinese Partners	Foreign Partners
Financial Outcomes	To increase foreign exchange reserves To invest for future development	To repatriate profits over the long term To maximize long-term returns
Investment	To minimize initial investment	To provide an acceptable minimum investment
Process of Negotiation	Holistic	Sequentially, step-by-step
Nature of the Contract	Adaptable Short term Ambiguous	Enforceable Long term Precise and unambiguous
Planning	To obtain congruence between state plan and aims of joint venture	To obtain maximum flexibility
Inputs	To focus on domestic suppliers	To minimize poor quality To minimize unpredictability
Outputs	To generate foreign exchange To increase exports	To access Chinese domestic markets To develop Chinese domestic markets
Strategic Intent	Short to medium term Domestic and international	Short to long term Domestic and international
Operations Emphasis	Stress on quality	Stress on quality
Personal Requirements	Maximum number of local employees	Fewest people possible for acceptable output Maximum productivity
Management Style	Traditional	Modern

Source: Jackson Terence, "International HRM: A cross-cultural approach," page 172.

EXHIBIT VIII   Human Resource Management Practices in the U.S. and China

HRM Practices	U.S.	China
Selection	Job interview is an essential step for filling major positions.	Most jobs are still allocated by the government or the university based on credentials. Interviews are not yet common.
Reward System	A wide variety of rewards are used in the incentive system.	The range of wages and salary is narrow. Bonus is not based on individual performance. Pay is more motivating than in U.S.
Performance Appraisal	Two-way communication and counseling are widely used in the performance appraisal system.	Superiors have absolute authority to evaluate subordinates. Standards of performance are vague and generic.
Participative Management	Participative management is welcome and encouraged, but is not particularly prevalent yet.	Collective leadership is widely used. Participation of workers in major decisions is superficial and symbolic.

Source: Jackson Terence, "International HRM: A cross-cultural approach," page 179.

degrees from international universities or with experience in foreign companies were in much demand. On the other side, there was high unemployment among the uneducated workforce and there was an extensive movement of population into the industrialized cities. Chinese firms had a traditional hierarchical structure, where superiors had the absolute authority over their subordinates. Workers' participation in decision making was very superficial. The universities and government followed the practice of allocating jobs to the students and the individual firms had a very limited role to play in the selection of trainees. Thus, the human resource management (HRM) practices in China were significantly different from those in the U.S. (*Exhibit VIII*).

The strategic partnerships with the banks were not limited to only their investments; they also extented to building their core competencies. As part of its agreement with BoA, CCB brought in 50 BoA experts to help upgrade CCB operations in risk management, global treasury services, and information technology areas, where BoA had strong expertise. The BoA experts also developed new products and services, such as wealth management and credit cards.[10] In another deal, CCB acquired the Asian subsidiary of Bank of America, under which CCB retained all its senior management and BoA Asia's 750 staff members, including chief executive Samuel Tsien.[11] The deal supplemented the core competencies of both the banks in numerous ways. To start with, BoA (Asia) had a strong orientation on retail and SME (Small and Medium Enterprises) banking, while CCB focused on the wholesale banking market. BoA was one of the best global brand names and the Asian business had a valuable high net worth customer base. CCB had five branches in Hong Kong, but none in Macau. For CCB, this

was a rarely available target, which offered 100% control. BoA (Asia) was also lucrative for its impressive earnings growth and asset quality (*Exhibit IX*).

The investment cap of 20% also helped in the PRC government's objective of skill development and share of know-how. In order to get rid of the ownership restrictions, Citigroup formed a consortium with China Life, State Grid, CITIC Trust, Puhua, and, IBM to acquire an 85% stake in Guangdong Development Bank (GDB). Citigroup would be able to bring international management expertise and corporate governance standards, instill operational and lending best practices, improve risk management and internal controls, and further develop its customer service and product offerings.[12] IBM had brought business value and technology expertise to the clients to help them strengthen their infrastructure and viewed GDB as a similar opportunity. China Life was the largest insurer in China, with over 70 million individual and group life and health insurance policies.[13] State Grid was a state-owned backbone enterprise, and the construction and operation of the national power grid was its core business. China Life and State Grid together had around one million employees.[14] The consortium would enable the Chinese firms to be acquainted with world-class technology, management expertise, and banking products. On the other hand, Citigroup would be able to conceptualize the Chinese values, culture and practices, and, most importantly, employee relations.

---

[10] Stephen Thomas and Chen Ji, "Banking on Reform," *China Business Review*, May–June 2006; www.chinabusinessreview.com/public/0605/thomas.html

[11] "CCB announces acquisition of Bank of America (Asia)," *People's Daily Online*, August 25, 2006; http://english.people.com.cn/200608/25/eng20060825_296588.html

[12] "Citigroup-Led Consortium Sign a Strategic Investment and Cooperation Agreement with GDB," http://www.citigroup.com/citigroup/press/2006/061116a.htm, November 16, 2006.

[13] "China Life Insurance Co Ltd: Company Overview," http://www.investor.reuters.com/business/BusCompanyOverview.aspx?sortby=0&sortorder=asc&ticker=LFC&symbol=LFC&target=%2fbusiness%2fbuscompany%2fbuscompfake%2fbuscompoverview, December 31, 2005

[14] "Fortune Global 500: State Grid," http://money.cnn.com/magazines/fortune/global500/2006/snapshots/1271.html and "Fortune Global 500: China Life Insurance," http://money.cnn.com/magazines/fortune/global500/2006/snapshots/2490.html

EXHIBIT IX   **A Comparative Analysis of Core Competencies of Chinese (CCB) and Foreign Banks (BOA Asia)**

Source: "Acquisition of Bank of America (Asia) Limited," www.ccb.cn/portal/html/tz/2006/CCB's%20Acquisition%20 of%20Bank%20of%20America%20Asia.pdf, August 24, 2006.

Citibank's consortium was viewed as one of the most successful achievements of the Chinese policymakers. But most of the strategic alliances failed to achieve the similar cross-cultural synergy. In spite of having strategic partners in the ranks of United Bank of Switzerland (UBS), Royal Bank of Scotland (RBS), Bank of America (BoA), Goldman Sachs, American Express, etc., the corporate culture of the SOCBs and some JSCBs still lacked a developed profit motive. Some old lending practices still persisted, such as focusing on market share, rather than profitability, and providing loans based on direct orders from the government, rather than the ability to repay. Shareholder accountability was also lacking and the senior management's loyalty was divided between the government and the stockholders. Successful implementation of the international joint venture was thus a huge challenge for all the banks. The foreign partner not only needed to be strategically fit and complementary to the Chinese bank but also had to adopt the Chinese culture and value system and had to gradually modify the system to make it more beneficial. In order to succeed, the foreign partner must design its HR policies on the lines of the prevalent practices in China. The biggest challenge of such international alliances remained in the alignment of the critical HRM functions such as HR planning, staffing, appraisal, training and development, employee retention, etc., with the Chinese culture (*Exhibit X*).

The main task of successfully building an appropriate HR system within such an international strategic alliance was to develop an understanding of stakeholder interests, aspirations, and needs. While the Chinese bank would expect to achieve international benchmarking and compete in the international markets, the foreign partner might be interested in accessing the huge market potential in the world's largest emerging economy. The challenge of such alliances was to bring in community stakeholders, first by a rigorous stakeholder analysis and then by involving the different stakeholders in the process of developing relevance and by effective interaction among the stakeholders. This might lead the international strategic alliances to move from a convergence form of management toward a more hybrid process of cross vergence. While convergence was a movement toward a single approach for universalization of principles, policies, and practices, cross-vergence involved a number of different movements toward the development of the new forms of managing.[15] The process of cross vergence was more adaptable in Chinese culture, in which the focus was on transfer of know-how and development of human skill, rather than increasing profitability and market share. It thus remains to be seen how much of a larger role the foreign strategic partners could play in the improvement of the banking expertise and technological development as well as in achieving rapid professional development and overhaul of their staff.

[15] Jackson Terence, "International HRM: A cross-cultural approach," page 224.

EXHIBIT X   HR Challenges in International Strategic Alliances in China

HR Function	Key Obstacles
HR Planning	• Short-term and static planning horizon • Lack of involvement by HR function and low priority of learning activities
Staffing	• Compulsory labor contract system in both private and public sectors at all levels • Insufficient lead-time for staffing decisions and low quality of staffing • Decentralization of employment practices, staffing dependent on the partners • Nepotism and over-hiring: Chinese partner influences HR policies • Transferring employees from state enterprises to joint ventures becomes problematic
Appraisal & Reward	• Appraisal focused on short term goals and the rewards are not tied to global strategy • No encouragement of learning and limited incentives for transfer of know-how • Difficult to dismiss people in case of unsatisfactory performance
Compensation	• Diversified wage packages with emphasis on enterprise profitability and performance • Position-and-skills wage system based on four factors: skills required, responsibility assumed, work involved, and working conditions
Training & Development	• Lack of cross-functional competence and unidirectional transfer of know-how • Career structure not conducive to learning, poor climate for transfer of learning
Labor Relations	• Right to form Trade Unions to protect employee rights and negotiate terms • Trade Union Labor Law contains no provision such as "worker's right to strike" • No social security laws like ESI, provident fund, gratuity, etc. • Laborers work 7 days a week and get only 2 days off in a month • Though normal shift is of 8 hours, they have to submit in writing that they would work 10–12 hours when required at no extra cost and overtime
Employee Retention	• Difficult to retain good employees due to poaching • Lack of high compensation as a major deterrent for retention
Expatriate Relations	• Lack of cross-cultural training provided to the expatriates • Lack of career prospects and undervaluation of international experience • Lack of management succession planning (balancing of local and international staff)
Organizational Design & Control	• Responsibility for learning not clear, fragmentation of the learning process • Control over the HR function given away, no insight into partner's HR strategy

Source: Compiled from the author, IBS Research center, Kolkata.

Assignment Questions

1. "China's banking sector was regulated by the central bank, the People's Bank of China (PBC), and the China Banking and Regulatory Commission (CBRC), and both of them were ultimately overseen by the State Council (the cabinet)." (Section: "Banking Industry in China," paragraph 1 of the case study.) Analyze the banking industry in China.

2. "The Chinese government had been quite successful in attracting foreign investment, despite having extremely conservative FDI (foreign direct investment) guidelines." (Section: "Introduction," paragraph 1 of the case study.) According to you, what factors attract foreign investors into China? Identify the pros and cons for a foreign player.

3. "This might lead the international strategic alliances to move from a convergence form of management toward a more hybrid process of crossvergence." (Section: "Strategic Foreign Partnership: HRM Issues", the last paragraph of the case study.) In light of the HRM challenges that foreign banks face in China, do you think crossvergence is a solution? If yes, why? If no, suggest other ways in which it can manage strategic alliances.

Case 10 *Indra Nooyi: A Transcultural Leader*

"If all you want is to screw this company down tight and get double-digit earnings growth and nothing else, then I'm the wrong person . . . companies today are bigger than many economies. We are little republics. We are engines of efficiency. If companies don't do [responsible] things, who is going to? Why not start making change now?"[i]

– INDRA NOOYI,
Chairman and CEO, PepsiCo, Inc.

"If you look at the job entirely from the American perspective, then it becomes impossible to run a global business . . . you have to relate your interests to the interests of other parts of the world—to be relevant in their societies. Indra seems to understand this instinctively."[ii]

– HENRY KISSINGER,
Former Secretary of State, United States of America

Indra Krishnamurthy Nooyi (Nooyi), chairman and CEO of PepsiCo, Inc. (PEP) and considered one of the most highly influential CEOs in the world, was for five consecutive years from 2006 at the very top of the list of the 50 most powerful women prepared by *Fortune*[1] magazine.[iii] PEP—one of the 500 biggest companies in the world—manufactured, distributed, and marketed a range of food and beverage items, with revenues from 200 countries in excess of US\$57 billion for the fiscal year ended December 25, 2010.[iv] Nooyi rose through the ranks after joining PEP in 1994 as its chief strategic officer.[v] She went on to shatter the glass ceiling when she was appointed its CEO in 2006. During her tenure, the firm took a serious look at the health issues involved with its products and redefined its links with business and society.[vi] She was regarded as the creator of PEP's growth strategy, "Performance with Purpose," that strove to balance strong financial returns with giving back to communities all over the world. As part of the strategy, PEP offered a range of choices that were healthy, convenient, and fun while reducing their impact on the environment and promoting an inclusive culture at the workplace. In line with this strategy, PEP was listed both on the Dow Jones North America Sustainability Index and Dow Jones World Sustainability Indexes.[2] [vii] "I have been particularly impressed by her willingness to do the right thing for her employees and consumers . . . I believe that all socially responsible companies could learn from Indra Nooyi's style of leadership,"[viii] said Howard Schultz, chairman, president

and CEO of Starbucks Coffee Co. Rosabeth Moss Kanter[3] described Nooyi as a visionary who was cross-cultural, female, and values-driven whose approach would be required in this era of globalization, where an individual's problems belong to everyone else.[ix]

HER EARLY YEARS

Nooyi was born on October 28, 1955 in Chennai, India. She was heavily influenced by her stay-at-home mother, Shantha Krishnamoorthy (Shantha), whom she considered the first management teacher in her life.[x] Though she had a conservative South Indian upbringing, there were many contrasting influences in her life. Observers noted that though she belonged to a Hindu home, she went to a Roman Catholic School. Nooyi admitted that Shantha "encouraged us but held us back, told us we could rule the country as long as we kept the home fires burning."[xi] Observers described how Shantha would remind a young Nooyi that she would get her married at the age of eighteen, while also giving her daughter the freedom to dream about rising high in life.[xii, xiii] Nooyi noted that she was made to compete with her sister for a piece of chocolate after meals, with questions like "What will you do if you were to become a prime minister?" or, "How would you change the world?"[xiv] Nooyi believed that this process encouraged her to think, and made her come up with different ideas in order to get the reward.[xv] Another influence was her grandfather, who kept a tab on her scholastic progress while ensuring that she was always prepared in advance with her lessons.[xvi] Nooyi recalled that while she was taught Indian classical music, she also had the permission to be part of a rock band in which she played the guitar.[xvii]

Nooyi went on to graduate from Madras Christian College in Chemistry, Physics, and Mathematics.[xviii] This was immediately followed by an MBA from the Indian Institute of Management, Calcutta. Then she went on to work with ABB[4] and

This case was written by *Amrit Chaudhari* and *Debapratim Purkayastha,* IBS Center for Management Research. It was compiled from published sources, and is intended to be used as a basis for class discussion rather than to illustrate either effective or ineffective handling of a management situation.

---

[1] *Fortune* is a global business magazine published by Time Inc.
[2] The Dow Jones Sustainability Indexes were launched in 1999 and were the first global indexes for tracking financial performance of the leading sustainability-driven companies all over the world.

---

[3] Rosabeth Moss Kanter is a professor at the Harvard Business School.
[4] ABB is a multinational headquartered in Zurich, with operations in power and automation technology.
[5] Johnson and Johnson is a global American pharmaceutical, medical devices, and consumer packaged-goods manufacturer.

Johnson and Johnson,[5] where she successfully launched various products.[xix] However, Nooyi's heart was set on other things. She said, "I always had this urge, this desire, this passion . . . to settle in the United States."[xx] Nooyi said her parents were apprehensive about letting her go to the U.S., and derived comfort from their belief that she would not get admission. However, she proved them wrong and got an excellent scholarship at Yale,[6] where she pursued her Master's in Public and Private Management.[xxi] For Nooyi, the experience led to a profound shift in thinking, and she observed: "You come from India off the boat, you go to business school, and you realize that you come from a fairly sheltered life . . . I learnt everything over again."[xxii] While studying, she worked as a dorm receptionist on night shifts to support herself and saved some money to buy herself a Western suit for her first job interview out of Yale.[xxiii] Nooyi had opted for the night shift as it paid an extra 50 cents an hour.[xxiv]

Nooyi learned to be herself the hard way. She recalled that the Western suit that she bought for US$ 50 from the local budget store was ill fitting and that she wore orange snow boots to the interview, leading to gasps from the interview board.[xxv] She was rejected. When she sought the advice of a professor, the professor advised her to wear a sari for the next interview, and told her that "if they can't accept you in a sari, it's their loss, not yours."[xxvi] Nooyi wore a sari for the next interview at the leading global management consulting firm, Boston Consulting Group (BCG), and got the job.[xxvii] Nooyi averred, "Never hide what makes you."[xxviii] She added, "I am so secure in myself, I don't have to be American to play in the corporate life."[xxix] She followed the same philosophy ever since—of being herself and not changing her basic beliefs and drawing strength from her traditions.

Describing her experience at the BCG, Nooyi said that each of her six and a half years there equaled three years in the corporate world, given the number of challenges thrown at a person in consulting (Refer to *Exhibit I* on the positions held by Nooyi).

After a stint in strategy with telecom major Motorola Inc. and with ABB, Nooyi made a move to PEP as its chief strategist in 1994, attracted by the chance of making a difference to a company that was then struggling.[xxx] She began working under then-CEO Roger Enrico (Enrico).

RISE AT PEPSICO

PEP was going through a difficult time—its restaurant business was not doing well in the saturated fast-food market and its revenues from the international markets were lagging far behind archrival Coca-Cola Company[7] (Coca-Cola). Nooyi was instrumental in the spinning off of the restaurant chains—KFC, Pizza Hut, and Taco Bell—in 1997, a difficult move that shrank the company by a third.[xxxi] However, as a part of the strategic view, the company acquired Tropicana in 1998 for US$ 3.3 billion and Quaker Oats in 2001 for US$ 14 billion.[xxxii] Nooyi went on to prove her mettle with a presentation to the board in 1998. Enrico remarked, "At that moment the PEP board understood Coke's business model better than Coke's board did"! They also realized that Coca-Cola's growth was not sustainable. Nooyi was vindicated when the share price of Coca-Cola began sliding after four months.[xxxiii] The moves pushed up earnings and grew Nooyi's stature in the company.[xxxiv] Enrico admitted that Nooyi was "the best negotiator I've ever seen in my entire life."[xxxv] During the subsequent tenure of Steven Reinemund (Reinemund), Nooyi was elevated to president because he was impressed by her acquisition of Quaker.

Nooyi progressed fast in her career and was eventually declared as one of the two finalists—along with colleague Mike White (White)—to succeed Reinemund as CEO in 2006. After being appointed to the post, Nooyi personally flew down to retain her former colleague, with whom she had worked for

---

EXHIBIT I Positions Held by Indra Nooyi

Academics:

Bachelors in Mathematics, Physics, and Chemistry from Madras Christian College, Chennai, India, 1976.
MBA from Indian Institute of Management, Kolkata, 1978.
Masters in Public and Private Management, Yale University, 1980.

Before PepsiCo:

Manager positions at Mettur Beardsell Ltd. and Johnson and Johnson Ltd.
Senior Vice-President of Strategy and Strategic Marketing for Asea Brown Boveri.
International Corporate Strategy Projects at Boston Consulting Group.
Motorola—Vice-President and Director of Corporate Strategy and Planning.

At PepsiCo:

Senior Vice-President of Strategic Planning and Development.
Chief Financial Officer, 2001.

Source: www.mba.yale.edu/alumni/alumni_profiles/nooyii.shtml

---

[6] Yale is a private Ivy League university in Connecticut, U.S.

[7] The Coca-Cola Company is a beverage retailer, manufacturer, and marketer of non-alcoholic beverages, concentrates, and syrups.

EXHIBIT II   **Food Portfolio of PepsiCo Inc.***

Fun for You	These products are a part of PepsiCo's core food and beverages business. They include Pepsi Cola, Mirinda, Doritos, Lays, Cheetos, Mountain Dew, 7Up, and Red Rock Deli Potato Chips.
Better for You	These products are foods and beverages that have levels of total fat, saturated fat, sodium, and sugar that are in line with global dietary intake recommendations. They include Lay's Baked Potato Crisps, Pepsi Max, Diet Mug Root Beer, Diet Sierra Mist, H2Oh!, Diet Pepsi, and Propel Zero water.
Good for You	These products offer positive nutrition through inclusion of whole grain fruits, vegetables, low-fat dairy, nuts and seeds or significant amounts of important nutrients, while moderating total fat, saturated fat, sodium, and added sugar. They also address the performance needs of athletes. They include Quaker Instant Oatmeal, G series, Tropicana, Nut Harvest, and Naked juice.

* Data as of 2011.

Source: www.PEP.com/Download/PEP_Annual_Report_2010_Full_Annual_Report.pdf

several years. Nooyi offered him a compensation that nearly matched hers, creating in the process her right-hand man.[xxvi] The following week, while addressing PEP employees, White remarked "I play the piano and Indra sings." Nooyi emphasized, "I treat Mike as my partner. He could easily have been CEO." She ensured that he was always next to her during key meetings.[xxxvii]

Nooyi was candid enough to admit that she had had a difficult journey to reach the top from her humble middle-class background in South India. She said, "Immigrant, person of color, and woman, three strikes against you. . . . So I would work extra hard at it. More hours, yes. More sacrifices and trade-offs, yes. That has been the journey." [xxxviii] Some observers said Nooyi was true to her name Indra, the Hindu "God of War."[xxxix] According to Nooyi, it was essential to focus on establishing an ethical corporate culture and long-term planning to avoid any corporate scandals.[xl]

A NEW CORPORATE VISION

Nooyi continued to be a major change agent at PEP after taking over as CEO. Observers said that the earlier acquisitions of Tropicana, Quaker Oats, and Gatorade pointed to the direction that PEP would take in the future—toward "better-for-you" products, and away from junk foods.[xli] (Refer to *Exhibit II* on the Food Portfolio of PEP.)

At the World Economic Forum in Davos in 2008, Nooyi remarked that it was essential that "we use corporations as a productive player in addressing some of the big issues facing the world."[xlii] She said that an important way of achieving this was to inspire people to have a vision that everyone could relate to.[xliii] Critics noted that as a child growing up in a developing India, she had seen the success of the Green Revolution[8] in transforming society; they felt that this had made her sensitive to the role of the corporate sector in sharing their expertise in the developing world.[xliv] Going forward, Nooyi wanted to leverage

[8] Green Revolution refers to the introduction of high-yielding varieties of seeds after 1965, along with the increased use of fertilizers and irrigation, to increase production and make India self-sufficient in food grains.

on PEP's formidable distribution system to tackle the under-nutrition issues facing the world.[xlv]

Observers appreciated the unusual and tremendously ambitious vision that Nooyi had of reinventing PEP.[xlvi] This came under her leadership banner and corporate mission of "Performance with Purpose," which ensured that PEP achieved financial success and social responsibility along with it.[xlvii] The initiative was composed of three important elements: human sustainability, environmental sustainability, and talent. (Refer to Table I.)

The company began to focus on getting an increased amount of earnings from health products, such as oatmeal. There was a push away from snack food, caffeine colas, and shareholder value toward health foods, fruit juices, and sustainable enterprise.[xlviii] For Nooyi, the most important issue was the linkage of performance *with* a sense of purpose in the sense of "a very closely linked ecosystem" and not performance *and* purpose or performance *or* purpose. She emphasized that unless one focused on purpose, there could not be performance; unless there was performance there could be no purpose in the

TABLE I   **Food Portfolio of PepsiCo Inc. ***

Components of "Performance with Purpose" Initiative

Human Sustainability	Ensuring that products ranging from treats to health foods allow customers to make balanced, sensible choices.
Environmental Sustainability	Ensuring that the company replenishes the planet and leaves the world a much better place than it was before.
Talent Sustainability	Ensuring that the employees of PEP also have a life while they earn their living with the company.

Source: www.leadership.bcg.com/americas/nooyi.aspx

actions.[xlix] She clarified further, "It doesn't mean subtracting from the bottom line . . . (but rather) that we bring together what is good for business with what is good for the world. . . . People these days are bringing their principles to their purchasing . . . we, in return, are bringing a purpose to our performance."[l]

Nooyi emphasized that the economic downturn since 2008 had made the idea of performance with purpose even more important. For instance, it required that PEP's portfolio be transformed in such a way as to ensure performance. PEP's green initiatives ensured that costs were controlled, while talented and young people were attracted to work with the firm.[li] Observers appreciated the fact that the vision had enabled the firm to be adaptable in order to continue growth at a time where there was increasing public awareness about the environment, customer concern about health, and a difficult economic climate.[lii]

Her philosophy made her back "Pepsi Refresh" and other social-responsibility positioning.[liii] The "Pepsi Refresh" project worked under Nooyi's vision of "Performance with Purpose" and allowed tapping into the Millennials,[9] who would be more likely to choose brands that would contribute to the society at large. Observers termed the project a phenomenal success in terms of participation as it allowed people to put their ideas into action in the form of grants that were voted on by the public.[liv]

Critics noted that Nooyi was able to understand the culture of Pepsi, and to go on to challenge its accepted beliefs and practices in ways that were quite non-confrontational. For many critics, this was the result of Nooyi's Indian cultural background that had various regional and lingual influences.[lv] Nooyi was named the CEO of the year 2009 by the Global Supply Chain Leaders Group[10] (GSCLG) for her continued contribution to responsible corporate citizenship even at a time when there was a global economic slowdown. They acknowledged Nooyi's long-term vision and execution capabilities and her efforts to provide a wider portfolio of healthier foods and beverages.[lvi] Some experts said that if Nooyi could actually deliver on both wholesome food and healthy profits, the future of PEP would be very bright.[lvii]

LEADERSHIP AND MANAGEMENT STYLE

Nooyi had the good fortune of being guided by three former PEP CEOs—Reinemund, Enrico, and Don Kendall. Observers noted that her mix of South Asian heritage and mentoring at PEP had given her a strategic view of world markets. Though critics held that Nooyi might not treat everybody the same way as she did White, they agreed that she was ready to take help from others in whatever areas she felt there was a need.[lviii] Nooyi admitted that even after retirement, Reinemund continued to reply to her emails within seconds and was ready to be at her side if she needed advice.

Experts felt that her experiences early in her career with organizations such as the BCG had taught her the inductive

thinking that had shaped her leadership style. "I don't think I could have gotten here without a strategy consultant background because it taught me inductive thinking. It taught me how to think of the problem in micro terms but also to zoom out and put the problem in the context of its broader environment and then zoom back in to solve the problem,"[lix] she said. Experts noted that she could successfully predict the slowdown in the aerated soft drinks market and lead the foray of PEP into the sports drink market with Gatorade.[lx] Her deep knowledge of the products and financial affairs of the company was widely appreciated.[lxi]

Nooyi felt that no matter what the previous experience of a person, nothing could really prepare him/her for the top job at an organization. She believed that leaders should have the ability to draw on their previous experiences while having an enduring commitment to the learning process. According to her, "If you want to improve the organization, you have to improve yourself and the organization gets pulled up with you. That is a big lesson. I cannot just expect the organization to improve if I don't improve myself and lift the organization."[lxii] According to some experts, Nooyi also had the traits of being a Level 5 leader that lead the company's transition from good to great.[lxiii]

Nooyi saw five things that would change the workings of a CEO. First, she believed that there had to be an emphasis on the long-term outcomes rather than a focus on short-term earnings emphasized by shareholders. Second, for working effectively in a world that was becoming increasingly complex, there would have to be an emphasis on strong public-private partnerships. Nooyi felt that governments had become intrusive and had begun to challenge corporate governance since the trust in companies had touched an all-time low; that the parties saw themselves as adversaries. Third, there had to exist a strong ability to think local while acting globally, especially in the context of newer markets in the developing world. Nooyi said that in developed countries there were large stores that allowed the development of hundreds of new products. However, for the developing world, which typically had small, tiny stores, the need was to give choices in a completely different way. Fourth, Nooyi wanted CEOs to be more open minded, so that they not only understood better leadership principles but also the needs of the newer technologies and the younger generations. She wanted greater openness toward cultures. To get this, she believed in having great people to run the company so that the CEO got a chance to travel. Nooyi herself spent nearly two weeks in China, where she went to customers' homes and interacted with people to understand how they lived, what they thought about the products, and what the company should do differently in order to succeed. Fifth, she felt that there would be increased requirements of emotional intelligence for leaders, so that they could create a bond between the company and the employee, through the business model and the values the company stood for.[lxiv]

Nooyi was known to be highly charismatic, with a clear voice.[lxv] She retained her Indian accent and went on to use Americanisms in her interactions.[lxvi] Experts noted that Nooyi could inspire employees to take on monotonous and difficult tasks.[lxvii] According to Nooyi, a great leader was one who could get people to follow her to the ends of the earth. She remained

---

[9] The Millennials are Generation Y with birth-dates between the mid '70s to the late '90s. Given the stronger reach of the media during the formative years of this generation, many of these members have a neo-liberal approach.

[10] The GSLG award is given to individuals who get the highest aggregate ratings in leading, developing, and maintaining sustainable, responsible business practices on a global scale.

tough on herself and set high standards for everyone. Experts pointed out that since she had been held to high standards in her childhood, she applied the same to everybody else. They pointed to her practice of using green, red, and purple pens to highlight issues on documents. Nooyi admitted that her scribbles were legendary, and she would write statements like "I have never seen such gross incompetence," or "this is unacceptable" and would underline "unacceptable" three times. Employees remembered the time when they were asked to find an alternative to the use of palm oil. Nooyi pushed them hard until they came up with a solution. One employee recalled, "Don't try to delegate up, because she will bounce it right back in your face."[lxviii]

However, she nurtured the employees at the same time so that her followers aspired to be like her in the future.[lxix] Reinemund considered Nooyi a "deeply caring person . . . who can relate to people from the boardroom to the front line."[lxx] Nooyi always seemed comfortable with her leadership presence, as she often moved around in the office barefoot, singing in the halls.[lxxi] She was said to have gifted former CEO Enrico a karaoke machine and was herself known to sing out during management conferences.[lxxii] Known to be a style apostle, she preferred wearing saris topped with a simple shawl and pearls. Nooyi's attire showed her deep connection with India.[lxxiii] She attended board meetings in a sari, as she believed that the corporate world preferred people who were genuine.[lxxiv]

She became a mother figure at PEP, looking after the company as if it were her family. Observers noted that she made time for regular staff who needed to interact with her—be it even the security guards at the Purchase, New York, headquarters. Every quarter, she sent a hand-written letter to the spouses of all 27 of her top executives, thanking them for their support despite the long hours of work and travel that the executives had to undergo.[lxxv] As she was very demanding at the workplace, she made up by throwing dinner parties for the members of her team and their spouses. At these dinners she interacted with her team members' spouses and fielded questions from them. Nooyi also took the personal initiative to thank the parents of the senior executives at PEP for the great job they had done in bringing up capable children, and this unleashed strong emotions that created a bond between the executives, their parents, and her.[lxxvi] She also insisted on celebrating everyone's birthdays with a cake. Her extracurricular activities were not limited to playing the electric guitar at office parties, but also included reading a book every day from 11 p.m. to 2 a.m. to keeping herself up-to-date on innovation.[ixxvii]

Nooyi strongly believed that globalization and the spread of information technology had turned organizations inside out and upside down. The decision-making ability had shifted to lower levels that tended to operate through self-organizing networks.[ixxviii] PEP saw a broadening of the power structure when the executive team was nearly doubled to reach 29 members. High-profile additions included Mehmood Khan, who became PEP's first chief scientific officer for looking into food research.[lxxix] Nooyi used her leadership banner of "Performance with Purpose" to ensure that PEP's leaders had an opportunity to work for achieving an integrated life.[lxxx] While focusing on the talent sustainability pillar, Nooyi rolled out her "cherish" principles for valuing employees, encouraging people to bring their

values to work, and to use them every day. Observers pointed to the increased levels of pride at PEP, an integration of work and life values, and the satisfaction of contributing to consumers, communities, and countries. They noted that the initiatives had enabled employees to hit their career "sweet spot" and to make talent sustainability a strategic advantage at PEP.[11] Nooyi launched the "Leading with Purpose" program at Yale University for all the divisions at PEP, which enabled leaders to move in the direction of "Performance with Purpose."[lxxxi] She treated the employees at PEP as leaders and built a culture that recognized hard work and encouraged initiatives from employees. She defined her leadership philosophy into the "Five C's":[lxxxii]

- *Competency:* Being an expert in your field, stand out from the crowd and be a lifelong learner.
- *Courage and Confidence:* Having the courage and confidence to do and say what you believe is right. Establish the knowledge base and be confident.
- *Communication skills:* Good communication skills are critical for progress.
- *Consistency:* Being steady, reliable, and determined so that one is credible and has a baseline to measure successes and failures.
- *Coaching:* Being surrounded by mentors that enable change.
- *Having a Moral Compass:* Having the desired strength and courage to do what is right and not what may be expedient.[lxxxiii]

At PEP, Nooyi ensured that employees balanced life and work and had an extended family at the workspace to achieve that balance.

STRIKING A BALANCE

Nooyi sums up the trade offs and sacrifices she has made in her life "Any woman who reaches the kinds of positions we do, and I'll speak for myself here, there are so many tradeoffs, compromises, heartbreaks, regrets that we've had to make along the way. It has not been easy. You know, I have two daughters. I have a husband, been married for 28 years. I have a mother still alive, and my family is very close."[lxxxiv] She candidly admitted that between the roles of being a mother and a CEO, it was the role of the mother that came first. She said that she would take a call from her daughters any time, even during work hours. She held on to her value system that gave emphasis on being there for her children.[lxxxv] During long trips, Nooyi called up her family to keep in touch; if she was on a domestic trip, she tried her best to be there with her daughters for breakfast. She also acknowledged the support she got from her husband in her progress. According to her, she faced enormous pressures in meeting the expectations of being a wife, a daughter, and a daughter-in-law while being responsible for the affairs of PEP. She admitted that it was late in life that she stopped being consumed by the guilt of not being good at everything and did

---

[11] A career "sweet spot" enables employees to work harder with higher impact and yet feel less stressed.

the best that she could.[lxxvi] She also made it a point to call her mother in India twice a day.[lxxxvii]

Nooyi was a tireless worker who would sleep not more than four to five hours every night. Observers remarked that despite her highly successful career, Nooyi held on to her Indian roots and balanced her high octane job with the calm, collected behavior required for a wife and mother at home. Visitors to her house were required to take off their shoes before entering. The house had a worship room where the *diya* (traditional lamp) was kept burning. Carnatic music was played at her house almost all day, creating the aura of a temple at home. Nooyi believed that her belief in religion enabled her to do a better job. She quipped, "I don't know about a better job, but it certainly makes me calm . . . there are times when the stress is so incredible between office and home . . . then you close your eyes and think about a temple like Tirupati, and suddenly you feel 'Hey—I can take on the world.'"[lxxxviii] She also kept a *Ganesha* (a Hindu deity) in her office. According to Nooyi, when things got difficult, it was her family and her belief in God that kept her going. "At the end of the day . . . don't forget that you're a person, don't forget you're a mother, don't forget you're a wife, don't forget you're a daughter . . . what you're left is family, friends, and faith."[lxxix]

HANDLING THE DOWNTURN

According to Nooyi, setting the agenda in a downturn was of prime importance. She ensured that she was visible in order to convey a strong message that things were all right and the organization would come out of the problems. To tide over the downturn, the company made substantial reductions in spending, but not at the cost of long-term investments.[xc] Nooyi emphasized the realistic optimism considering the fact that they were a consumer staple company, which would not be affected much.

PEP launched a restructuring program in October 2008 with the focus clearly on prioritization. The company set priority points which were repeated at each and every interaction the company had with its employees. The line managers were given agendas—but also the freedom to achieve their goals. Nooyi gave substantial freedom of action, and intervened only when businesses were in dire need of a turnaround. While employees traditionally could be motivated by the high growth being enjoyed in developed markets, the thrust in the future would only come from developing markets. Nooyi felt that people should have the inclination to work in international environments.[xci]

However, Nooyi was also criticized for laying off almost 3,300 employees—nearly 1.8% of PEP's global workforce in 2008—and closing factories to survive the downturn, moves that would enable it to save almost US$ 1.2 billion.[xcii] Nooyi's response then had been, "This will enable our competitiveness and give us breathing room to respond . . . it is no news to you the economy is turbulent and there are uncertainties and volatility in every part of the environment."[xciii]

RISING STAKES?

While some industry observers and experts described her as a New Age hybrid leader (refer to *Exhibit III* on Characteristics of a Hybrid Leader) and praised her leadership style, Nooyi also came in for some strong criticism. Critics termed Nooyi's

EXHIBIT III   **Characteristics of Hybrid Leaders**

1. Are deep enough to deliver
2. Have genuine concern for people
3. Drive collaboration through the organization
4. Celebrate diversity
5. Are excellent communicators
6. Emphasize work/life balance
7. Admit their constraints

Source: www.lesaffaires.com/uploads/references/1266_creatingthehybridleader.pdf; www.jumpassociates.com/a-hybrid-leader-for-a-hybrid-school.html

slogan of "Performance with Purpose" as a marketing ploy that happened to be in vogue. They pointed out that the company was still best known for making soda and potato chips.[xciv] She was also criticized for the way she handled issues such as the pesticide controversy in India in 2006, and health issues related to the company's products. They argued that despite being an Indian she did not take the initiative to reassure the Indian public that the company's product was safe.[xcv] At a Fox Business show, Nooyi had also infamously quipped, "Doritos is not bad for you . . . Doritos is nothing but corn mashed up, fried a little bit with just very little oil, and then flavored in the most delectable way."[xcvi] The statement led to a flurry of criticism against Nooyi.[xcvii] Her image took a beating when, at the last moment, she pulled out of a major soft-drink industry conference at which she was to give the keynote speech. The participants felt that her excuse for not attending was quite lame and were not satisfied with the fact that she sent a subordinate in her place. Nooyi's explanation, that she wanted to give the spotlight to the CEO-designate of Coca Cola, Mukhtar Kent, did not find many takers. Critics were convinced that Nooyi could be quite temperamental.[xcviii]

Nooyi's strategy was also criticized as there were reports that developing markets were not seeing a change in dietary habits. For instance, PEP was banking on a successful launch of Pepsi Max in the summer of 2010 to extend its market share in India. However, the launch was not successful. Experts believed that many people in the developing world were not buying into the healthy food habits concept being propagated by Nooyi. Sales of 100% juices continued to lag behind sugary ones by a wide margin, while pizza chains like Dominos continued to beat sales targets.[xcix] Moreover, some of PEP's new forays were not doing too well: its Flat Earth chips[12] had disappointed at the market and had to be discontinued because of slow sales.[c] Critics accused the products of having a taste-barrier and even went to the extent of saying that some of them had a really awful taste.[ci] Meanwhile, Quaker Oats had had little success in attracting attention to its oatmeal, which was tagged as a "best-for-you" food by PEP. The company was criticized for diverting funds from expensive Super Bowl[13] commercials to the "Pepsi Refresh"

---

[12] Flat Earth Chips were snacks that had half a serving of fruits or vegetables per ounce.

[13] The Super Bowl is the annual championship for the National Football League in the U.S.

EXHIBIT IV   **Total Net Revenue and Operating Profit of PepsiCo Inc.**

	2010	2009	2008	2007	2006	2005
Total Net Revenue	US$ 57,838	US$ 43,232	US$ 43,251	US$ 39,474	US$ 35,137	US$ 32,562
Operating Profit						
FLNA	US $3,549	US $3,258	US $2,959	US$ 2,845	US $2,615	US $2,529
QFNA	568	628	582	568	554	537
LAF	1,004	904	897	714	2,016	1,661
PAB	2,776	2,172	2,026	2487	—	—
PepsiCo Europe	1,020	932	910	855	—	—
AMEA	742	716	592	466	—	—
Corporate Unallocated						
Market-to-market (net)	91	274	346	19	—	—
Merger and Integration Charges	(191)	(49)	—	—	—	—
Restructuring and Impairment Charges	—	—	(10)	—	—	—
Venezuela currency devaluation	(129)	—	—	—	—	—
Asset Write Off	(145)	—	—	—	—	—
Foundation contribution	(100)	—	—	—	—	—
Other	(853)	(791)	(651)	(772)	(738)	(780)
Total Operating Profit	US $ 8,332	US $ 8,044	US $ 6,959	US $ 7,182	US $ 6,502	US $ 5,984
Total Operating Profit Margin	14.4%	18.6%	16.1%	18.2%	18.5%	18.4%

Note: PepsiCo is organized into four business units. These are PepsiCo Americas Foods (PAF), which is comprised of FLNA, QFNA and LAF; the PepsiCo Americas Beverages (PAB); PepsiCo Europe; and AMEA.
FLNA: Frito Lay North America
QFNA: Quaker Foods North America
LAF: Latin American Food
PAB: PepsiCo Americas Beverages
AMEA: PepsiCo Asia, Middle East and Africa
Figures in US$, (millions)
Source: www.pepsico.com/Investors/Annual-Reports.html

challenge.[14] Critics pointed out that PEP had returned to TV advertising in June 2011 after three years of focus on social media and crowdsourcing through corporate philanthropy-based programs such as Pepsi Refresh. Nooyi was accused of ignoring marketing and product positioning while giving too much emphasis on "Performance with Purpose." However, Nooyi termed as "rubbish" claims that she had not paid attention to the leading brands of PEP and argued that emphasis on corporate citizenship and healthy foods did not come at the cost of driving sales.[cii]

Critics said that Coca-Cola had emerged stronger during Nooyi's tenure as the CEO at PEP, with increasing sales and a much lower cost structure. According to a report in 2011, Coke had held on to the #1 slot in sales and unseated Pepsi from the #2 spot as well with Diet Coke in the U.S. Globally, while PEP was being affected by increased commodity costs and the uncertain economic conditions and had to cut its earnings growth to single digit levels in 2011, Coca-Cola had reported increasing sales volumes. Though both Coke and Pepsi had agreed to pass on some of the higher costs of drinks to customers, PEP was in a difficult position given its substantial food business where it could not turn away customers given the high prices.[ciii] Critics argued that though PEP had created a desirable association with itself, the association remained vague and the firm was paying through loss of market share. But Nooyi countered, saying, "From my perspective, we are a different company . . . different

[14] The Pepsi Refresh Challenge aimed at finding innovative not-for-profit organizations.

from a business makeup, different culturally, in the way we think, the way we act. We are different every which way . . . we are in businesses that give you more good-for-you products, and that means closer to crops. When you're closer to crops, you're going to have some inflation."[civ] However, there was considerable pressure on her from shareholders to improve the market share of PEP's flagship brands.[cv] A shareholder remarked, "I think it is hard to give Indra much better than a C-plus as a CEO," given the fact that PEP shares had fallen by 7% by 2009, compared to a 28% surge for Coke during the same period, from the time she took over."[cvi] (Refer to *Exhibit IV* on the Total Net Revenue and Operating Profit of PepsiCo.)

However, Nooyi was confident of the vision she had for PEP, even as industry observers were closely watching her next moves. "We are confident that we will reinvent the cola business the right way,"[15] she quipped. She was willing to stretch herself while taking the firm forward. According to her, "Just

because you are CEO, don't think you have landed . . . You must continually increase your learning, the way you think, and the way you approach the organization. I've never forgotten that."[16]

Assignment Questions

1. What were the factors that shaped Indra Nooyi as a leader?

2. What are the factors that could make Nooyi change her decision about corporate sustainability?

3. Do you think Nooyi has a life outside of PepsiCo?

4. Which leadership style is being used by Nooyi at PepsiCo? Highlight the mix of various leadership styles found in Nooyi, such as that of servant leadership, ethical leadership, socialized charismatic leadership, and authentic leadership.

---

[15] Dale Buss, "Stakes Rising for PEP's Nooyi," www.brandchannel.com, June 29, 2011.

[16] Gary Burnison, "How Pepsi's Indra Nooyi Learned to be a CEO," www.fastcompany.com, April 29, 2011

Endnotes

i. Betsy Morris, "The Pepsi Challenge," www.money.cnn.com, February 19, 2008.

ii. Ibid.

iii. Jessica Shambora and Beth Kowitt, "50 Most Powerful Women," www.money.cnn.com, September 30, 2010.

iv. www.sec.gov/Archives/edgar/ata/77476/000119312511040427/d10k.htm

v. Ding Qingfen, "Introducing a Woman's Touch," www.chinadaily.com.cn, June 21, 2010.

vi. "Adding Values to Valuations: Indra Nooyi and Others as Institution-Builders," www.blogs.hbr.org, May 3, 2010.

vii. "Indra Nooyi," www.huffingtonpost.com/indra-nooyi

viii. Howard Schultz, "The 2008 TIME 100: Indra Nooyi," www.time.com, April 30, 2009.

ix. "Adding Values to Valuations: Indra Nooyi and Others as Institution-Builders," www.blogs.hbr.org, May 3, 2010.

x. Aravind Patrudu, "Indra Nooyi: PEP CEO," www.bharatentrepreneurs.com, March 11, 2008.

xi. Betsy Morris, "The Pepsi Challenge," www.money.cnn.com, February 19, 2008.

xii. Simon Hobbs, "Indra Nooyi," www.cnbcmagazine.com, June 2008.

xiii. Michael Useem, "America's Best Leaders: Indra Nooyi, PEP CEO," www.usnews.com, November 19, 2008.

xiv. Aravind Patrudu, "Indra Nooyi: PEP CEO," www.bharatentrepreneurs.com, March 11, 2008.

xv. "Life Stories to Inspire: Indra Nooyi – CEO PEP," www.changeminds.wordpress.com, August 25, 2008.

xvi. Betsy Morris, "The Pepsi Challenge," www.money.cnn.com, February 19, 2008.

xvii. "Indra Nooyi's Mantras for Success," www.specials.rediff.com, September 12, 2008.

xviii. Simon Hobbs, "Indra Nooyi," www.cnbcmagazine.com, June 2008.

xix. "Indra Nooyi Profile," www.iloveindia.com/indian-heroes/indra-nooyi.html

xx. "Indra Nooyi," www.brainsandcareers.com/phpBB3/viewtopic.php?f=9&t=1545&start=0

xxi. Simon Hobbs, "Indra Nooyi," www.cnbcmagazine.com, June 2008.

xxii. "FT Top 50 Women in World Business," www.ft.com, September 25, 2009.

xxiii. "Life Stories to Inspire: Indra Nooyi – CEO, PEP," www.changeminds.wordpress.com, August 25, 2008.

xxiv. Michael Useem, "America's Best Leaders: Indra Nooyi, PEP CEO," www.usnews.com, November 19, 2008.

xxv. "Life Stories to Inspire: Indra Nooyi – CEO, PEP," www.changeminds.wordpress.com, August 25, 2008.

xxvi. "Indra Nooyi's Mantra for Success," www.changeminds.wordpress.com, January 7, 2009.

xxvii. "Indra Nooyi: Keeping Cool in Hot Water," www.businessweek.com, June 11, 2007.

xxviii. "Indra Nooyi's Mantra for Success," www.changeminds.wordpress.com, January 7, 2009.

xxix. "Life Stories to Inspire: Indra Nooyi – CEO, PEP" www.changeminds.wordpress.com, August 25, 2008.

xxx. "Indra Nooyi: Keeping Cool in Hot Water," www.businessweek.com, June 11, 2007.

xxxi. Betsy Morris, "The Pepsi Challenge," www.money.cnn.com, February 19, 2008.

xxxii. Kim S. Nash and Mel Duvall, "No Deposit, No Return; A Salty-Snack Maker in Texas Pioneered the Use of Wireless Communications on Delivery Routes," www.allbusiness.com, May 1, 2003.

xxxiii. Betsy Morris, "The Pepsi Challenge," www.money.cnn.com, February 19, 2008.

xxxiv. Michael Useem, "America's Best Leaders: Indra Nooyi, PEP CEO," www.usnews.com, November 19, 2008.

xxxv. Betsy Morris, "The Pepsi Challenge," www.money.cnn.com, February 19, 2008.

xxxvi. Michael Useem, "America's Best Leaders: Indra Nooyi, PEP CEO," www.usnews.com, November 19, 2008.

xxxvii. Betsy Morris, "The Pepsi Challenge," www.money.cnn.com, February 19, 2008.

xxxviii. Homa Khaleeli, "Indra Nooyi," www.guardian.co.uk, March 8, 2011.

xxxix. "FT Top 50 Women in World Business," www.ft.com, September 25, 2009

xl. Kathryn A. Marrone, "Weinberg Center marks 10th" www.udel.edu, April 12, 2011.

xli. Dale Buss, "Stakes Rising for PEP's Nooyi," www.brandchannel.com, June 29, 2011.

xlii. Betsy Morris, "The Pepsi Challenge," www.money.cnn.com, February 19, 2008.

xliii. Tony Bingham, "Doing Well While Doing Good," *T'D*, June 2008.

xliv. "2009 Borlaung Dialogue by Indra Nooyi," www.208.109.245.191/assets/Symposium/2009/transcripts/2009-Borlaug-Dialogue-Nooyi.pdf

xlv. "Food Frontiers," www.foodfrontiers.PEPblogs.com/author/indranooyi/

xlvi. Harry K. Jones, "Little-known Facts about Well-known Leaders – Indra Nooyi," www.achievemax.com, January 21, 2009.

xlvii. Michael Useem, "America's Best Leaders: Indra Nooyi, PEP CEO," www.usnews.com, November 19, 2008.

xlviii. Harry K. Jones, "Little-known Facts about Well-known Leaders – Indra Nooyi," www.achievemax.com, January 21, 2009.

xlix. "Indra K. Nooyi," leadership.bcg.com/americas/nooyi.aspx

l. Michael Useem, "America's Best Leaders: Indra Nooyi, PEP CEO," www.usnews.com, November 19, 2008.

li. "Indra K. Nooyi," www.leadership.bcg.com/americas/nooyi.aspx

lii. Tony Bingham, "Doing Well While Doing Good," *T&D*, June 2008.

liii. Dale Buss, "Stakes Rising for PEP's Nooyi," www.brandchannel.com, June 29, 2011.

liv. Christie Garton, "Pepsi Exec Dishes on Pepsi Refresh, Future Plans for Cause Marketing," www.yourlife.usatoday.com, November 2010.

lv. William J. Holstein, "Indian CEOs in Demand – Indra Nooyi of Pepsi," February 27, 2008.

lvi. "Indra Nooyi Hits it Once Again; Named CEO of the Year by GSCLG," www.fnbnews.com, July 17, 2009.

lvii. Michael Useem, "America's Best Leaders: Indra Nooyi, PEP CEO," www.usnews.com, November 19, 2008.

lviii. Betsy Morris, "The Pepsi Challenge," www.money.cnn.com, February 19, 2008.

lix. Gary Burnison, "How Pepsi's Indra Nooyi Learned to Be a CEO," www.fastcompany.com, April 29, 2011.

lx. "Pride of India—Indra Nooyi," www.goiit.com, October 21, 2010.

lxi. Michael Useem, "America's Best Leaders: Indra Nooyi, PEP CEO," www.usnews.com, November 19, 2008.

lxii. Gary Burnison, "How Pepsi's Indra Nooyi Learned to Be a CEO," www.fastcompany.com, April 29, 2011.

lxiii. Biswanath Bhattacharya, "Steve Jobs: An Enigmatic Leader," www.tripurainfo.in, March 25, 2010.

lxiv. "Indra K. Nooyi," www.leadership.bcg.com/americas/nooyi.aspx

lxv. Aravind Patrudu, "Indra Nooyi: PEP CEO," www.bharatentrepreneurs.com, March 11, 2008.

lxvi. Anand Giridharadas, "New Leaders Find Strength in Diversity," www.nytimes.com, May 6, 2010.

lxvii. Betsy Morris, "The Pepsi Challenge," www.money.cnn.com, February 19, 2008.

lxviii. Ibid.

lxix. "Indra Nooyi," www.cnbcmagazine.com/story/indra-nooyi/452/1/June 2008

lxx. Michael Useem, "America's Best Leaders: Indra Nooyi, PEP CEO," www.usnews.com, November 19, 2008.

lxxi. "Indra Nooyi: Keeping Cool in Hot Water," www.businessweek.com, June 11, 2007

lxxii. Ibid.

lxxiii. "Pride of India-Indira Nooyi," www.goiit.com, October 21, 2010.

lxxiv. "Life Stories to Inspire: Indra Nooyi – CEO, PEP," www.changeminds.wordpress.com, August 25, 2008

lxxv. Heidi Brown, "Management Advice from Mom," www.forbes.com, April 15, 2009.

lxxvi. "Indra K. Nooyi," www.leadership.bcg.com/americas/nooyi.aspx

lxxvii. "Indra Nooyi," www.brainsandcareers.com, April 3, 2011.

lxxviii. "Adding Values to Valuations: Indra Nooyi and Others as Institution-Builders," www.blogs.hbr.org, May 2010.

lxxix. Betsy Morris, "The Pepsi Challenge," www.money.cnn.com, February 19, 2008.

lxxx. "Elevating Aspirations at PEP," www.store.astd.org/Default.aspx?tabid=167&ProductId=19225

lxxxi. Ibid.

lxxxii. "PepsiCo CEO Indra Nooyi: The 5 Leadership Principles that Guide Me," www.sbomag.org, September 5, 2011.

lxxxiii. www.leadershipnow.com/leadingblog/2008/06/PEP_ceo_indra_nooyi_on_dev.html

lxxxiv. "The Condi Rice and Indra Nooyi Show" www.rediff.com, October 24, 2008.

lxxxv. Sue Shellenbarger, "PEP's Indra Nooyi on Tough Calls," www.blogs.wsj.com, April 10, 2011.

lxxxvi. "Indra Nooyi," www.cnbcmagazine.com, June 2008.

lxxxvii. Michael Useem, "America's Best Leaders: Indra Nooyi, PEP CEO," www.usnews.com, November 19, 2008.

lxxxviii. "Life Stories to Inspire: Indra Nooyi – CEO, PEP," www.changeminds.wordpress.com, August 25, 2008

lxxxix. Michael Useem, "America's Best Leaders: Indra Nooyi, PEP CEO," www.usnews.com, November 19, 2008.

xc. "Indra K. Nooyi," www.leadership.bcg.com/americas/nooyi.aspx

xci. Ibid.

xcii. "PEP to Lay Off 3,300, Says 3Q Profit Fell 9.5%," www.articles.baltimoresun.com, October 15, 2008.

xciii. Susan Thompson, "PEP Cuts 3,300 Jobs to Save $1.2bn," www.business.timesonline.co.uk, October 14, 2008.

xciv. "Indra Nooyi: Keeping Cool in Hot Water," www.businessweek.com, June 11, 2007.

xcv. Betsy Morris, "The Pepsi Challenge," www.money.cnn.com, February 19, 2008.

xcvi. "Quotes in the News," www.newsweek.com/2011/02/08/quotes-in-the-news.html

xcvii. Melanie Warner, "Inside Frito-Lay's All-Natural, Kinda Healthy Junk-Food Adventure," www.bnet.comFebruary 11, 2011.

xcviii. Betsy Morris, "The Pepsi Challenge," www.money.cnn.com, February 19, 2008.

xcix. Gus Lubin, "Pepsi Learns the Hard Way that Indians Don't Like Diet Soda," www.wikinvest.com, July 11, 2011.

c. "Feedin Mama," www.feedinmama.blogspot.com/2008/11/sad-sad-news.html

ci. "Flat Earth Baked Veggie Crisps Wild Berry Patch," www
.taquitos.net/chips/FlatEarthVeggieCrispsWildBerry

cii. Dale Buss, "Stakes Rising for PEP's Nooyi," www.brand-
channel.com, June 29, 2011.

ciii. "PEP, Citing Rising Commodity Costs, Posts a Drop in
Profit," www.nytimes.com, February 10, 2011.

civ. Betsy Morris, "The Pepsi Challenge," www.money.cnn
.com, February 19, 2008.

cv. Dale Buss, "Stakes Rising for PEP's Nooyi," www
.brandchannel.com, June 29, 2011.

cvi. "Indra Nooyi Faces Flak for Falling PEP Shares," www
.zeenews.india.com, December 30, 2009.

PART 5 INTEGRATIVE SECTION

Integrative Term Project
Case 11 Mahindra and Mahindra (B): An Emerging Global Giant? (India/Global)
Case 12 After the Breakup: The Troubled Alliance Between Volkswagen and Suzuki (Germany/Japan)

Integrative Term Project

This project requires research, imagination, and logic in applying the content of this course and book.

In groups of three to five students, create an imaginary company that you have been operating in the domestic arena for some time. Your group represents top management, and you have decided it is time to go international.

- Describe your company and its operations, relative size, and so forth. Give reasons for your decision to go international.

- Decide on an appropriate country in which to operate, and give your rationale for this choice.

- State your planned entry strategy, and give your reasons for this strategy.

- Describe the environment in which you will operate and the critical operational factors that you must consider and how they will affect your company.

- Give a cultural profile of the local area in which you will be operating. What are the workers going to be like? What kind of reception do you anticipate from local governments, suppliers, distributors, and so on?

- Draw up an organization chart showing the company and its overseas operations, and describe why you have chosen this structure.

- Decide on the staffing policy you will use for top-level managers, and give your rationale for this policy.

- Describe the kinds of leadership and motivational systems you think would be most effective in this environment. Give your rationale.

- Discuss the kinds of communication problems your managers might face in the host-country working environment. How should they prepare for and deal with these problems?

- Explain any special control issues for this overseas operation that concern you. How do you plan to deal with them?

- Identify the concerns of the host country and the local community regarding your operations there. What plans do you have to deal with their concerns and to ensure a long-term cooperative relationship?

Case 11 *Mahindra & Mahindra (B): An Emerging Global Giant?*

"I have been on record to say that my philosophy of going global is because if you don't succeed abroad or don't have the capacity to succeed abroad and to carve out some turf abroad you are not going to be safe at home [. . .]. If you want to compete with multinationals you have to be a multinational. So that is the logical rationale for going abroad."[1]

–ANAND G. MAHINDRA,
*Vice Chairman and Managing Director,
Mahindra & Mahindra Ltd., in 2010.*

In 2011, India-based automotive giant Mahindra & Mahindra Ltd. (M&M) was featured on the Forbes Global 2000 list,[2] a ranking of the biggest and most powerful companies in the world. Besides M&M, some of the other Indian companies that figured on the list were Reliance Industries, State Bank of India, Oil & Natural Gas Corp., ICICI Bank, NTPC, Bharti Airtel, Larsen & Toubro, and Tata Motors. Emerging markets such as China and India, with 113 and 56 members respectively on the list, were growing steadily and gaining prominence at the global level, industry analysts said.

Based in Mumbai, India, M&M was one of the leading players in the Indian Multi Utility Vehicles (MUV) and tractor segments of the automotive industry as of 2011. Besides the automotive industry, the company has a presence in agribusiness, aerospace, components, consulting services, defense, energy, financial services, industrial equipment, logistics, real estate, retail, steel, and two-wheelers. The Group's automotive sector, which manufactures and markets utility vehicles and light commercial vehicles, was the fourth-largest automaker in India as of 2010. As of 2011, M&M's model range included more than 20 vehicles, including the Scorpio and the Xylo utility vehicles. After establishing its leadership in the Indian automotive market, M&M began to seek opportunities in global markets. The company stormed into the global limelight with the formidable success of its Sports Utility Vehicle (SUV)—the "Scorpio."[3] Going forward, M&M planned to expand its global reach by launching its vehicles in the international markets including North America, Europe, Africa, and Asia. However, analysts said it

was debatable whether M&M would be able to sustain a diverse product portfolio at the global level. They questioned whether M&M could be successful in the overseas markets, particularly the U.S., given that it was an emerging-market company.

"EMERGING-MARKET" COMPANIES— CHANGING GLOBAL BUSINESS SCENARIO

Based on their economies, the countries of the world have been categorized as developed and developing. While the developed economies include various countries in Western Europe, the U.S., Canada, and Japan, the developing economies include Argentina, Brazil, Chile, China, Egypt, Hungary, India, Indonesia, Malaysia, Mexico, Poland, Russia, Thailand, and Turkey. The group of Brazil, Russia, India, China, Mexico, and South Korea are commonly referred to as the Big Six ("B6") by global management consulting firm Accenture, as they are the leading developing economies.

Earlier, owing to their low-cost structures, the developing economies served as mere outsourcing locations for the Multi-National Companies (MNCs) of the West. However, the changing global economic scenario had brought down trade and investment barriers and integrated global supply chains, thereby paving the way for the development of emerging markets. Some of the developing countries were witnessing rapid growth and thus the nomenclature Rapidly Developing Economies (RDEs) was assigned to them. The term "Rapidly Developing Economies" was used to denote emerging markets such as China, India, Mexico, Brazil, Russia, South Africa, Poland, Indonesia, Turkey, and South Korea. Moreover, the importance of the emerging markets to the global economy came into sharp focus as the world came out of the global economic recession. Experts said that the importance of emerging economies to world trade had been steadily increasing. Between 1990 and 2010, the annual growth rate of exports and imports from emerging and developing economies averaged around 7.5% compared to the figure of around 5% for developed economies.[4]

It was reported that the share of the RDEs in global trade was growing significantly. Notably, RDEs were receiving high Foreign Direct Investments (FDI). Between 2001 and 2006, the growth rate of outward FDI (OFDI) from the B6 countries in the form of Mergers & Acquisitions (M&A) was more than 50% annually.[5] By 2006, the FDI outflows from the developing economies stood at US$174 billion, equivalent to 14% of the

This case study was written by **Syeda Maseeha Qumer** and **Vandana Jayakumar,** under the direction of **Vara Vasanthi,** IBS Hyderabad. It is intended to be used as the basis for class discussion rather than to illustrate either effective or ineffective handling of a management situation. The case was compiled from published sources.

[1] Shamindra Kulamannage, "Going Global to Be Competitive in India: Anand Mahindra," www.lbr.lk, August 25, 2010.
[2] The Forbes Global 2000 is an annual ranking by Forbes magazine of the top 2000 public companies in the world. The ranking is based on sales, profit, assets, and market value.
[3] Until M&M launched the Scorpio in 2002, it was associated with rural vehicles. The transformation of the company from an aging family business into a formidable model business player occurred under the able leadership of Anand G. Mahindra. For further information, refer to the case study by Vasanthi Vara and Jayakumar Vandana, "Mahindra & Mahindra (A): Transformation of an Indian Family Business into a Globally Competitive Firm," www.ibscdc.org.

[4] http://www.internationalbusinessreport.com/files/gti_ibr_emarkets_2010final .pdf.
[5] Crennan Karen, et al., "Trends: Back to the Future," www.accenture.com, September 2008.

TABLE I   Some of the Emerging Giants*

Country	Company
China	Baosteel, Galanz Group, Anshan Iron and Steel Group, Lenovo Group, Huawei Technologies, Haier, Hisense, Chery Automobile, Wahaha Group, China Communications Construction
India	Bharti Airtel, Dr. Reddy's Laboratories, Infosys Technologies, Ranbaxy Laboratories, Tata Group, Wipro Technologies, Mahindra & Mahindra Ltd., Bajaj Auto
Brazil	Embraer, Sadia and Perdigão S.A., Votorantim Group, JBS, Odebrecht Group
Chile	Falabella, LAN Airlines
South Africa	Bidvest Group, SABMiller Plc., Nando's, Sappi, Sasol
Indonesia	Bumi Resources
Mexico	Grupo Alfa, Group Bimbo
Turkey	Koc Holding, Sabanci Holding
Philippines	Jollibee Foods Corporation, Ayala Corporation
Taiwan	Inventec Corporation
UAE	DP World, Emirates Airline
Russia	United Company Rusal, Gazprom

* This list is not exhaustive.
Source: Compiled from various sources.

world's total. Thereby, the developing economies shared 13% of the total global FDI stock, equivalent to US$1.6 trillion.[6] It was reported that the BRIC countries (Brazil, the Russian Federation, India, and China) were the driving forces behind the rise of emerging market OFDI flows in 2008. With OFDI flows of about US$141.7 billion in 2008, this group accounted for approximately 40% of total OFDI flows from emerging markets. In 2010, developing and transition economies accounted for more than half of global FDI inflows. According to a World Bank report in 2010, the FDI flows into developing countries, including India, were projected to increase by 17% to US$416 billion, up from its 2009 level of US$354 billion.[7]

Another interesting trend in the RDEs was the high growth rate of the domestic markets. According to the Global Challengers Report published in 2011 by global management consulting firm Boston Consulting Group (BCG), despite the economic slowdown, between 2000 and 2010, the share of global GDP generated by the RDEs increased from 18% to 31% and their share of world trade jumped almost as much, from 18% to 28%. The RDEs were expected to capture about 45% of global GDP by 2020.[8]

Earlier, companies from the RDEs could not compete with those from the developed economies. The MNCs of the West had certain advantages over the RDE companies. For instance, Western brands were well established, their management practices and innovation systems were quite efficient, and good talent and finance were also readily available to them. This was due to their well-established financial markets. Also, their labor markets worked efficiently and they could boast of sophisticated technologies. Incidentally, the strengths of the companies

from developed economies were the weaknesses of the companies from developing economies. However, with the changing economic scenario, various companies from the RDEs were emerging on the global scene. (Refer to Table I for some of the emerging giants.) For example, the Lenovo Group from China bought the PC business of IBM, and Tata Motors (car-maker from India) acquired Jaguar and Land Rover from Ford Motor Co.[9] Notably, companies from the RDEs had large businesses, were active on a global scale, and demonstrated the potential for globalization. They had their own brands and products. They began to compete with the established MNCs of the West for supplies, capital, talent, innovation, acquisition, and a share of domestic as well as foreign markets.

Moreover, the RDEs could fit into any of the following categories compared to the MNCs of the West—competitors, customers, probable partners, or acquirers. In effect, they were proving themselves to be formidable competitors by challenging the MNCs. The companies from the emerging markets were hectically pursuing globalization. Also, when the emerging markets adopted liberal economic policies, the domestic companies were subjected to competition from foreign companies. The domestic companies lost some of their domestic market share to the foreign players. As a result, the RDE companies started exploring the global markets to make up for the loss. At the same time, the rationale behind globalization stemmed from their desire for growth. Being confined to the domestic markets would not make these firms sustainable in the long-term. With globalization, their scale of business improved and they were able to compete with the MNCs.

Apart from these reasons, the RDE companies went global for various other reasons. For instance, by pursuing

[6] "Emerging-Market Multinationals," www.economist.com, January 10, 2008.
[7] "FDI into Developing Countries to Rise 17% in 2010: WB," www.business-standard.com, December 10, 2010.
[8] "Companies on the Move," www.bcg.com.cn, January 2011.

[9] In 2008, Tata Motors acquired the Jaguar and Land Rover business from Ford Motor Company in a US$2.3 billion deal, thereby entering the international luxury car market.

globalization, these companies could develop supportive activities such as R&D and acquire abstract assets such as established brands. Moreover, by going global, they could experiment with new business models as well. Globalization of the RDE companies was evident from their presence in BCG's list of global challengers for 2011[10], in which there were as many as 33 companies from China, 20 companies from India, seven from Mexico, and six from Russia.

Global challengers were companies based in the RDEs. These companies employed new ways of doing business and modeled their businesses in compliance with their domestic conditions. The global challengers developed innovative business models and tapped emerging markets, which served as the growth engines of the global economy. The revenues of the global challengers rose by 18% annually from 2000 through 2009. By 2020, the global challengers were expected to grow at an average rate of 5.5% and to generate US$ 8 trillion in revenue.[11]

EMERGING-MARKET COMPANIES: REDEFINING BUSINESS

The companies from emerging markets strategically exploited their domestic conditions to be successful. To begin with, RDE companies had good knowledge about local customers, domestic manufacturing capacity, local brands and products, and key supply sources, and they had control over various channels. They also shared a good relationship with government officials and regulators. As a result, the emerging-market companies had an edge in identifying the needs of the market and fulfilling its demands in a cost-effective manner. For example, Inventec Corporation (Inventec), a Taiwanese company, was one of the largest manufacturers of notebook computers, PCs, and servers. Exploiting the knowledge of local supply chains, Inventec manufactured most of its products in China and supplied them to Toshiba Corporation and Hewlett-Packard Co. Inventec benefitted from the talented hardware and software professionals and low manufacturing costs of China.

Emerging market companies employed strategies that were similar to each other's but were in a way unique to them. In pursuing globalization, the RDEs adopted different brand strategies. One of their strategies was to take the brand to a global level after establishing themselves domestically. A case in point was Hisense, a consumer-electronics group from China. The company started shifting its focus to the global market after having achieved a significant market share for TV sets domestically. It took advantage of its domestic Chinese market, which provided a cheap manufacturing base. The strategies adopted by RDE companies could be broadly interpreted as strategies of low-optimizer, low-cost partner, global consolidator, global first-mover,[12] and M&A. (Refer to *Exhibit I* for strategies of emerging market companies.)

The RDE companies converted their domestic expertise in engineering into innovative expertise at the global level. They focused on innovation as it supported their companies' growth. They fostered innovation as they were experienced in working with a low-income customer base, low-cost business model, and risk management. For example, after privatization, Embraer of Brazil, which had initially been supported by the Brazilian government, took over Bombardier Inc., of Canada and became the leading manufacturer of regional jets worldwide. Its strengths were mainly low-cost manufacturing and high-class R&D. It also entered into a joint venture with China Aviation Industry Corporation II and even challenged the Boeing Company and Airbus. Embraer focused on high-growth markets and on innovation aimed at creating aircraft that featured low price tags and operating costs and as well as higher reliability, comfort, and safety.

At the same time, the RDE companies were strategically exploiting the natural resources to fuel their growth. They used them to their full potential through effective marketing and distribution. Perdigão, Brazil's largest food company, and Sadiaa, a large poultry exporter also based in Brazil, effectively employed this strategy. They exploited Brazil's abundant resources to produce pork, poultry, and grain, which were supported by low labor costs and congenial growth conditions for the industry. From January 2006 through August 2010, challengers in the resources and commodities industry announced 154 cross-border mergers and acquisitions, far more than any other sector. Some of the RDE companies also used new business models for diverse markets. Using this strategy, CEMEX (Mexican cement manufacturer), became the largest supplier of ready-mixed concrete in the world. It acquired companies and by using standardized procedures and a well-developed IT system, effectively managed the acquisitions in its own style.

The local governments also played a significant role in the development of RDE companies. By being active investors, they made the environment conducive for business for the RDE companies and provided the required infrastructure. Further, they helped in boosting exports and offered low-cost finance. They also supported RDE companies by providing technology and R&D. For example, the "State-Owned Assets Supervision and Administration Commission" (SASAC)[13] controlled many emerging giants of China. Similarly, the Brazilian Development Bank (BNDES) supported programs such as infrastructure projects and exports financing for the development of Brazil.

As the RDE companies strategically exploited the domestic conditions to be successful, they were often in an advantageous position as compared to companies from the developed world. For instance, the RDE companies benefitted from the market structures of the developing economies. Though the foreign MNCs and RDE companies competed with each other in the global tier, the MNCs were able to serve only the global tier of the market due to the drawbacks present in the developing economies. At the same time, RDE companies exploited the similarities of geographies and grew across borders. They also

[10] The global challengers included Argentina, Brazil, Chile, China, Egypt, Hungary, India, Indonesia, Malaysia, Mexico, Russia, Saudi Arabia, South Africa, Thailand, Turkey and The United Arab Emir

[11] "Companies on the Move," www.bcg.com.cn, January 2011.

[12] "No Longer a One-Way Street: The Growing Impact of India's Emerging Multinationals," http://knowledge.wharton.upenn.edu, June 28, 2007.

[13] SASAC is a Chinese government holding company, which manages the state-owned enterprises.

EXHIBIT I **Strategies of Emerging Market Companies**

Low-optimizer Strategy

- The companies from the emerging markets focus on the products and processes specifically for the emerging markets.
- They develop niches in the developed countries—for example, automotive divisions of Tata Motors and Mahindra & Mahindra Ltd.
- They try to achieve global leadership in a narrow product category—Hong Kong-based Johnson Electric (Johnson) makes more than 3 million tiny electric motors per day, most of which are exported.
- They focus on such products that cannot be common to countries with varied characteristics such as income levels, tastes, etc.

Low-cost Partner Strategy

- This strategy is applicable to those businesses where the processes have been already optimized and the RDE companies do not have to upgrade an outdated system. For example, Business Process Outsourcing (BPO) operations of Infosys Technologies and Wipro Technologies. India has an advantageous position as it has a good resource of well educated, English speaking, and reasonably priced workforce.

Global Consolidator Strategy

- This strategy is used by those RDE companies which are in the business of products that can be standardized across countries. Further, these companies belong to the industries that have already matured in the developed economies and are flourishing in the developing economies.
- Benefitting from the experience as domestic consolidators, they consolidate at a global level. For example, Tata Steel took over the Anglo-Dutch steel giant Corus, thereby becoming the fifth-largest steel company of the world. Similarly, CEMEX became the largest supplier of building materials in the world after it bought a majority stake in Rinker Group of Australia.

Global First Mover Strategy

- While the market for wind turbines and wind-generated electricity is rapidly growing across the globe, India's Suzlon has benefitted from its dominance in the domestic market.
- Suzlon dominates the home market as well as Asia and is the fifth largest wind power company in the world.
- It has achieved efficiencies of scale, a vast knowledge base and a strong financial support, which is aiding in expansion.

Merger & Acquisition Strategy

- Provides opportunities for growth—for example, by acquiring Novelis Inc., Hindalco Industries Ltd., became the number one aluminum rolling company of the world and one of top five aluminum companies of the world.
- Helps the company to acquire tangible and intangible assets such as—brands, image in the market, control over natural resources, technological know how, customer base, distribution networks, and knowledge about the market. On acquiring Inco Ltd. (Inco), Companhia Vale Do Rio Roce (CVRD) gained access to the largest reserves of nickel in the world. Further, with Inco came a good resource of present and future products, technological know-how about the nickel industry, a competent workforce, and a well-established brand name.
- Helps in bringing home the superior manufacturing capabilities of the developed nations, which supplements low-cost production domestically.

Source: Compiled by the author from "No Longer a One-Way Street: The Growing Impact of India's Emerging Multinationals", http://knowledge.wharton.upenn.edu/india/article.cfm?articleid=4206, June 28th 2007 and Aguiar Marcos, et al., "The 2008 BCG 100 New Global Challengers", http://www.bcg.com/impact_expertise/publications/files/New_Global_Challengers_Feb_2008.pdf, December 2007

served their home community spread across countries. For instance, the cooked chicken of Pollo Campero of Guatemala was sold to the Latino people of Central America and South America as well. It was successful despite competition from fast food chains such as KFC Corporation and McDonald's Corporation.

Further, the RDE companies also derived competitive advantages from their low-cost model due to the ready availability of low-cost resources. The low cost of labor significantly contributed to their business model. The low-cost approach helped these companies achieve a cost advantage and economies of scale. They also benefitted from the large and rapidly growing domestic markets. For example, in the BPO and IT sectors, Indian companies such as Infosys Technologies (Infosys), Tata Consultancy Services (TCS), and Wipro Technologies benefitted from the low-cost strategy. They gave tough competition to the companies from developed economies.

Further, the RDE companies were in an advantageous position compared to companies from the developed nations due to the availability of an abundant workforce in the RDEs. The companies from developed nations, on the other hand, had to source their workforce globally due to the aging baby boomer[14] generation in the U.S. and Europe. In the U.S., 75 million baby boomers were on the verge of retirement as of 2011. A similar situation prevailed in the European Union (EU) nations. For the EU nations, it was predicted that the working population would fall by 16% or 48 million by 2050.[15] On the contrary, in China, it was estimated that around 375 million students would enroll for higher studies between 2007 and 2015, making available enough talent even for the future. Moreover, the companies of the West also found it difficult to compete with the domestic companies in scouting good local talent. Also, in sourcing workforce in the emerging markets, the companies of the West found it difficult to compete with the domestic companies. Significantly, the local companies were better positioned in attracting talented workforce and selecting the right candidates.

However, the RDE companies faced several other challenges. For example, while RDEs had an abundant entry-level workforce, there was a dearth of talent in the senior positions. The RDE companies tackled this challenge by imparting in-house training to the employees, as seen in the case of Tenaris (manufacturer of specialty steel pipes) from Argentina. The company developed programs for its global workforce because it recognized the value of training. Its "Tenaris University" not only imparted training to existing Tenaris employees but also recruited new employees for the company. Further, the RDE companies tried to be the best employers as their global growth plans gave employees an opportunity to have a global career path. As a result, talented young professionals of the RDEs preferred to work in the domestic companies as against the local subsidiaries of MNCs.

However, while many RDE companies had succeeded in the midst of global competition because their businesses were modeled on low-cost structures, the demand patterns of the domestic consumers had become sophisticated. As such, analysts felt that the RDE companies might not find it possible to make the products as per customer requirements by sticking to the low-cost models. Moreover, the costs of doing business were higher in going global, which affected the cost-focused positioning of the RDE companies. Therefore, experts said it was practical for the RDE companies to explore other factors such as offering superior services.

Another challenge that the RDE companies faced was the presence of institutional voids in the developing economies. Institutional voids were the weaknesses inherent in their domestic business environments. This referred to the situation wherein the regulatory systems and the mechanisms that enforced contracts were not well developed. These voids had some direct implications for companies from developing economies. For example, resources such as capital for doing business were not available. Therefore, these companies were unable to spend much on effective R&D. As a result, such companies were not able to build global brands. However, while operating in the emerging markets, the domestic companies were better equipped to handle these institutional voids as compared to their foreign counterparts, as they were experienced in working without proper facilities. They sought opportunities in the institutional voids and tackled this challenge through innovation. The case of Suzlon Energy Ltd. (Suzlon)—a wind-energy company from India—serves as a good example in this context.

Suzlon's founder, Tulsi Tanti (Tanti), was in the textiles business before venturing into wind energy. However, his business was not doing well due to high costs as well as irregular availability of electricity. To address this problem, Tanti set up two windmills to generate power for his textile mills. Soon, Tanti realized that wind-energy generation had better prospects than textiles. Having initiated the business in the wind power industry, Tanti became one of the wealthiest men in India and Suzlon became a well-established global player. Its production plants, R&D facilities, and sales and support offices were located at many prominent places across the globe. Like Suzlon, many other RDE companies had converted their weaknesses into opportunities. They had their own typical mechanisms for conducting business. For example, the Philippines' Ayala Group was able to raise capital from the local stock market as it enjoyed a very good reputation there. Another mechanism that such companies employed was making their managers work across businesses. This helped them in performing under diverse circumstances.

MNCs, on the other hand, found it difficult to cope with the institutional voids. They were accustomed to working within well-developed infrastructures. Therefore, they were hesitant about doing business in the emerging markets. For instance, in the absence of proper market research mechanisms, the MNCs were unable to understand the needs of the customers. Similarly, due to the lack of a system of supply-chain partners, the MNCs were unable to make their products available to

---

[14] Post–World War II, there was a spurt in the birth rate, especially in the U.S. People born between 1946 and 1964 are generally referred to as the baby boomer generation.

[15] Friedman, Daniel, et al., "Aligning Talent for Global Advantage," www.bcg.com, September 2007.

the interior regions of the developing countries. In short, their business models did not work in such economies.

According to industry experts, emerging market companies became successful by employing unique strategies and by deriving competitive advantages from their domestic conditions. This was evident from the presence of many companies from the emerging markets in BCG's 2011 Value Creators Report.[16] Companies from emerging markets were well represented among the global top ten. These included Chinese companies Shandong Weigao and Baidu; Hong Kong-based Tencent and Xinyi Glass; India-based Jindal Steel and Power; Mexico-based Industrias Penoles; and the Philippines-based Aboitiz Equity Ventures. Notably, in BCG's report, M&M occupied the fifth position in the Automotive Original Equipment Manufacturer (OEM) top ten. The list also included other Indian automobile companies like Hero Honda Motors and Maruti Suzuki India. The top four positions were occupied by companies from China (Dongfeng Motors), Hong Kong (Brilliance China Automotive), Germany (Volkswagen) and Turkey (Tofaş). M&M's key to success had been "frugal engineering," i.e., developing products that were lower in cost as compared to similar products developed in the West. M&M positioned itself as a global player despite hurdles such as poor infrastructure, tax burdens, and bureaucratic complexities.

M&M: AN EMERGING GLOBAL GIANT?

The origins of M&M can be traced back to 1945 when brothers J. C. Mahindra and K. C. Mahindra joined hands with Ghulam Mohammad, an entrepreneur, and started Mahindra & Mohammad, a steel company in Mumbai. Two years later, when India attained independence, Ghulam Mohammad left the company to become Pakistan's first finance minister. The Mahindra brothers took over and entered into a collaboration with Willys-Overland Corporation[17] to import and assemble the Willys Jeep for the Indian market. Over the years, the group's automotive sector emerged as one of the leading arms of the Mahindra Group. It manufactured and marketed utility vehicles and light commercial vehicles, including three-wheelers.

From the beginning, M&M nurtured ambitions of becoming a global player in the auto industry. Globalization was an inextricable part of its business strategy. Having established itself in the domestic utility vehicle market, M&M went on a global expansion spree to enhance its presence in the international markets. As part of its globalization strategy, it collaborated with many international companies. During the 1950s and 1960s, M&M tied up with many foreign companies such as Chrysler Corp., Dr. Beck, International Harvester Company, and Willys-Overland Motors. It worked in collaboration with several MNCs, which included France's Peugeot and Japan's Nissan Motor Company (Nissan) for engine technology, Ford Motor

Company (Ford)[18] in the passenger car segment, and British Telecom Plc., in the field of telecommunications and software.

As part of its globalization strategy, M&M launched its products in the global markets including Africa, Europe, the Middle East, the U.S., Latin America, China, and Malaysia. It set up dealerships and assembly plants in several countries. M&M's automotive division exported its products to several countries in Africa, Asia, Europe, and Latin America. The company had established its presence across all the continents except Antarctica as of 2011. Further, it was also forging alliances with companies at home and abroad. It entered into strategic partnerships in Eurasia, Africa, and South America and set up assembly plants in Brazil and Egypt. Notably, M&M was also in the fray to buy Jaguar and Land Rover from Ford Motor Co. when this business was up for sale. Though M&M could not clinch the deal, it indicated its ambitious global plans.

In pursuing its globalization plans, M&M followed a strategy common among companies from the emerging markets. Generally, after attaining dominance in the domestic markets, the RDE companies went global by entering those markets that were similar to their domestic markets. By doing this, the RDE companies gained confidence as well as expertise. Thereafter, they took up the challenging and sophisticated markets of the developed nations. Likewise, M&M ventured into emerging markets such as Malaysia, Indonesia, and Thailand before going on to explore the developed markets. Its global ventures were strategically thought out and well planned for. The company focused on improving the quality of its products, which was critical to gaining acceptance in key global markets. M&M also developed capabilities to develop new products that could meet global standards. One of the emerging trends in the global auto industry was outsourcing of business processes to low-cost countries like China and India. This was primarily driven by the increasing competitiveness of the advanced markets and the need to cut costs in order to remain profitable. This created a number of opportunities for Indian players. M&M acquired the expertise to capitalize on these opportunities and offered global OEM and Tier 1 suppliers, products, and services across the chain. It focused on achieving cost leadership through focused cost optimization, value engineering, improved efficiency measures such as supply chain management and countrywide connectivity of all its suppliers and dealers, and by exploiting synergies between its divisions.

M&M entered the U.S. as Mahindra USA (MUSA) in 1994 with compact utility tractors, a segment that was underserved. The company began by importing tractors from India and later set up assembly plants in the U.S. where it assembled complete knock down (CKD)[19] kits imported from low-cost manufacturing centers such as India and other Asian countries. In January 2009, the company entered the SUV market in the U.S. by launching its SUVs there. The strategy was to sell the SUVs as fuel-efficient vehicles.

[16] The 2011 Value Creators Report of BCG was based on corporate strategy wherein it was suggested that the Total Shareholder Return (TSR) should be pivotal in any corporate strategy process.
[17] Willys-Overland Corporation was an American automobile company known for its design and production of military Jeeps and civilian versions during the 20th century.

[18] Ford had entered the Indian market in the 1990s through a joint venture with M&M. The two companies had at that time launched the Ford Escort.
[19] CKD is a complete kit needed to assemble a vehicle.

In the U.S., the company followed a "low-optimizer strategy" commonly employed by emerging market companies. As per this strategy, the companies first focused on those products and processes which were useful for the emerging markets. While focusing on such products, they tried to create a niche for themselves in the developed markets. Likewise, operating in various business segments domestically, M&M focused on products demanded by the consumers in the emerging markets. At the same time, it tried to carve a niche for itself in the market for SUVs in the developed markets, particularly the U.S. It consciously worked on the fuel-efficiency and environmental safety aspects of its vehicles in the U.S. M&M's Unique Selling Proposition (USP) in the U.S. was its highly fuel-efficient diesel engines. It launched its vehicles in the U.S. with T2B5 emission norms, considered to be the most stringent of all emission norms. M&M also focused on keeping the number of defects in its vehicles to the minimum.

The company emphasized innovation and the customer-centric approach of doing business, i.e., developing new products by anticipating customer demands. Concepts such as innovation were generally unheard of in companies from emerging markets because they focused on cost-related advantages. As Anand Mahindra (Mahindra), vice chairman and managing director of M&M, noted, "Once a company has paid the fees, in a manner of speaking, to enter a sector, it becomes even harder to stay afloat."[20] Moreover, Mahindra observed, "If M&M is going to compete with the world's best companies, it has to become an innovation factory. . ."[21] In compliance with its emphasis on innovation, the company plans to launch many new products in the future.

Besides in the U.S., the company established a presence in South America, Europe, the Middle East, Africa, Asia, and Australia. In South America, the company's products included Mahindra Reva electric cars and a range of diesel Mahindra vehicles. The company also sold Rakshak armored vehicles to the government of Guyana and Nepal through its defense products company, Defence Land Systems. The company sold many Mahindra vehicles across Europe, including the electric cars under the Mahindra Reva brand. It set up plants across Germany, the UK, and Italy. The company exported tractors to Iran, Syria, and the United Arab Emirates in the Middle East and Nigeria, Mali, Chad, Gambia, Angola, Sudan, Ghana, and Morocco in Africa. It entered the markets of South Africa, Uruguay, and Malaysia for the first time in 2004. The company sold a wide range of Mahindra vehicles in South Africa. In Malaysia, the Mahindra Reva electric car enjoyed a significant market share. With the launch of a tractor assembly and customer support center in 2005, M&M launched its operations in Australia. The company served a loyal and growing customer base through a network of 40 dealerships across Australia, and expanded

distribution to New Zealand and Fiji. It launched its Chinese operations in July 2005, through Mahindra (China) Tractor Co. Ltd., an 80-20 joint venture with Jiangling Motor Co. Group[22] (JMCG). M&M also planned to utilize its partnership with JMCG to source components from China and to sell tractors in China through JMCG's network. Strategically, this venture gave M&M a quick entry into China as well as other export markets.

In 2002, with the goal of achieving revenues from outside India, M&M decided to enter the UV segment at the global level, through the Scorpio and the Bolero (M&M's utility vehicles). As Pawan Goenka (Goenka), President (Automotive & Farm Equipment Sectors), M&M, observed, ". . . Between 2002 and 2004, we had taken a clear call that we will aspire to be a global UV company, spanning pickup trucks, Sports Utility Vehicles (SUVs), and Multi-purpose Utility Vehicles (MUVs)."[23] In 2004, M&M began exporting Scorpios to countries such as Sri Lanka, Nepal, and Bangladesh, and countries of the Middle East. It entered the Latin American market by launching the Bolero in Uruguay under the name "Mahindra Cimarron," because Uruguay was a favorable market for M&M vehicles. Further, it launched the Scorpio as the "Mahindra Goa" in Europe. At the same time, in 2004, M&M entered South Africa through a local joint venture.

According to experts, the Scorpio exemplified how M&M had exploited the domestic manufacturing conditions in being successful. For instance, when M&M was developing the Scorpio, there were large foreign production facilities available in India. These facilities, however, were not able to utilize their capacity fully, as the automobile business in India at that time was not a volume-based business. Exploiting this condition, various parts of the Scorpio were produced in India at low cost with foreign technology. Goenka spoke about referring to the German Behr Group, which had a facility for the manufacture of heating, ventilating, and air-conditioning systems for cars, in India, "They had huge capacity and were looking for business. (In return) we had German engineering at Indian cost."[24] Further, M&M also benefited from the low-cost model. It was able to achieve cost competitiveness by emphasizing cost-cutting and efficiency. For instance, the entire Scorpio project maintained quite low costs compared to those which any global automaker would have incurred. While the cost of investment for the Scorpio plant was US$120million, the same for global automakers would have been US$289 million.

To access products, technology, and new markets, M&M entered into strategic partnerships with other international automakers. In 2005, it entered into a joint venture with Renault S.A.[25] (Renault) of France to manufacture and sell the mid-sized sedan, the Renault Logan in India. The partnership also helped M&M sell SUVs in Europe through the French auto major's

[20] Stewart A. Thomas and Raman P. Anand, "Finding a Higher Gear," Harvard Business Review, July–August 2008.
[21] Stewart A. Thomas and Raman P. Anand, "Finding a Higher Gear," Harvard Business Review, July–August 2008.
[22] Jiangling Motor Co. Group is one of the leading commercial vehicles manufacturers in China.
[23] Layak Suman, "Mahindra's New Growth Engines," http://businesstoday.digitaltoday.in, October 2, 2008.
[24] Khanna Tarun, et al., "Mahindra and Mahindra: Creating Scorpio," Harvard Business School, February 22, 2005.
[25] Renault SA is a French automaker producing passenger cars and light commercial vehicles. The Company produces the Twingo, Clio, Kangoo, Megane, Scenic, Laguna, Espace, Avantime and Vel Satis automobiles, and vans.

distribution channel. Analysts said that by partnering with Renault, M&M tried to undermine the edge which Maruti Suzuki and Tata Motors enjoyed in the domestic passenger car market. However, in April 2010, M&M and Renault parted ways as the car failed to meet expectations. M&M had agreed to buy out Renault's 49% stake in the JV for an undisclosed sum. The company renamed Mahindra Renault as Mahindra Verito.

In June 2005, M&M also launched a joint venture with International Truck & Engine Corporation, one of the leading commercial vehicle producers in the U.S., to manufacture and market LCVs, MCVs, and HCVs for both the domestic and export markets in Asia, the Middle East, Africa, Russia, and Central Europe. That same year, the company also entered into an agreement with USF-HICOM (Malaysia) Sdn Bhd[26] to market the Scorpio in Malaysia. In 2008, M&M entered the two-wheeler segment by acquiring an 80% stake in Kinetic Motor Company Ltd.[27] In January 2008, it announced the launch of the Mahindra Scorpio SUV in Egypt in partnership with the Bavarian Auto Group.[28] Industry observers said that M&M also gained from the economic downturn as the demand for smaller pickups increased in the U.S. Domestically, M&M has managed the downturn well, they said. (Refer to Table II for the details of M&M Vehicles sold in 2006, 2007 and 2008).

TABLE II M&M Vehicles Sold

(Year ending March 31)	2008	2007	2006
Vehicles	161,001	135,961	125,772
3 Wheelers	34,076	33,718	22,419
MUV (domestic)	148,761	127,856	114,694
Exports	12,359	8,021	5,534
LCVs	10,373	8,652	6,777
Tractors	99,042	102,531	85,029

Compiled from the Annual Reports of Mahindra & Mahindra

In January 2009, to strengthen its position in the UV market, M&M launched the "Xylo"—a luxury MUV. By entering the two-wheeler segment and with the launch of the Xylo, M&M established its presence in almost all the segments of the automobile industry. The rationale behind M&M venturing into all the segments was clear from Goenka's statement, "The idea is to have such products (trucks, scooters, cars) under our umbrella offering, without losing our focus (on UVs). . ."[29]

To strengthen its position in the electric vehicles domain, M&M acquired a majority stake in REVA Electric Car Co Ltd.,[30] Bangalore, in May 2010. REVA was renamed Mahindra REVA Electric Vehicle Co. Ltd. Under the agreement, M&M owned 55.2% equity in Mahindra REVA. According to industry experts, the buyout would make the Mahindra group a strong global player in the electric vehicle space. Mahindra REVA would have access to Mahindra's vehicle development technology and distribution network, significantly enhancing its ability to launch a state-of-the-art electric vehicle for global markets. According to Goenka, "This is a key strategic acquisition for Mahindra in its march towards sustainable mobility. Mahindra and REVA bring together complementary strengths. With Mahindra's vehicle engineering expertise, global distribution network, sourcing clout, and financing support, REVA's vehicles have the potential to significantly gain in market penetration. Mahindra will also benefit from REVA's EV technology for its own products."[31]

In March 2011, to become a dominant player in the global SUV arena, M&M acquired a 70% controlling stake in the ailing South Korean auto maker, SsangYong Motor Company (SsangYong),[32] for US$463 million. The acquisition helped M&M utilize the strong R & D capabilities of SsangYong. M&M could benefit from the strong dealer network of SsangYong in 98 countries, said analysts. As SsangYong had a strong presence in premium-segment vehicles, this could help the Indian automaker expand its profile into this particular segment. Talking about the acquisition, Goenka said, "The coming together of Mahindra and SsangYong will result in a competitive global UV (utility vehicle) player. Together with its financial capability, M&M offers competence in sourcing and marketing strategy, while SsangYong has strong capabilities in technology. We are committed to leverage the combined synergies by investing in a new SsangYong product portfolio, to gain momentum in global markets."[33]

In September 2011, M&M announced the roll-out of the Mahindra series of pick-ups, the Genio, in the global markets. The Genio was targeted at the small and medium entrepreneurs (SMEs). This was followed by the launch of the company's first global SUV, the XUV_{500}, in October 2011. The XUV_{500}, launched simultaneously in India and South Africa, was designed and developed entirely in-house at the company's world-class R&D facility—the Mahindra Research Valley in Chennai, India. Experts said that the vehicle would be a litmus

[26] Based in Kuala Lumpur, Malaysia, USF-HICOM operates as an importer, assembler, and distributor of multi-purpose vehicles, commercial vehicles, double-cabs, and buses.

[27] Kinetic Motor Company Limited was one of the leading two-wheeler manufacturers in India.

[28] The Bavarian Group is the importer and assembler of the BMW Group with exclusive rights for the assembly, import, and distribution of BMW vehicles in Egypt.

[29] Layak Suman, "Mahindra's New Growth Engines," http://businesstoday .digitaltoday.in, October 2, 2008.

[30] REVA was established in Bangalore in 1994 as a joint venture between the Maini Group of Bangalore, India, and AEV LLC of California, U.S. REVA is one of the leading electric car brands in the global market, available in 24 countries across Europe, Asia, and Central and South America.

[31] "Mahindra Acquires Majority Stake in REVA," http://theindiacar.com, May 26, 2010.

[32] SsangYong is a premier manufacturer of sports utility vehicles (SUVs) and recreational vehicles (RVs) in Korea. Founded in 1954, it has been manufacturing automobiles for more than five decades. The group's product portfolio comprises of a luxury sedan, four sport utility vehicles, and a multipurpose vehicle.

[33] "Mahindra Buys 70% in SsangYong," www.business-standard.com, November 24, 2010.

test of Mahindra's ability to make it in the auto business overseas. "The XUV$_{500}$ represents Mahindra's global ambitions as it seamlessly integrates world-class technology with the very best in Indian innovation. Its distinctive value proposition—bolstered by a New Age digital strategy—has resulted in the XUV$_{500}$ becoming an overnight sensation in its home country, India, and I am sure this success will be replicated across the globe,"[34] said Mahindra.

In November 2011, M&M debuted in the Ecuador market with the launch of the Scorpio and the Mahindra Pik-Up series. "Mahindra has carved a distinct niche for itself in markets across the globe with its unique combination of rugged utility and style. We are now delighted to launch the Mahindra product range in Ecuador, a market which has strategic importance for Mahindra in the Andean region. Our partner, Eljuri, is one of Ecuador's oldest and most respected groups and their sound knowledge of the local market coupled with professional expertise will ensure our success. With this launch, we have further expanded our extensive footprint in the South American market where we are present in Brazil, Chile, Paraguay, Peru, and Uruguay,"[35] said Pravin Shah (Shah), Chief Executive of the Automotive Division at M&M.

Taking its tractor business to the global level, M&M started exporting its tractors to Africa, Australia, China, and the nations of the South Asian Association for Regional Cooperation (SAARC), which includes Bangladesh, Bhutan, the Maldives, Nepal, Pakistan, and Sri Lanka. In January 2012, M&M overtook John Deere,[36] the Chicago-based market leader in the field, in terms of the number of tractors sold between 2010 and 2012. The company attributed this milestone to a concentrated push into emerging markets such as China, Turkey, Indonesia, and Australia. Between April and December 2011, M&M sold 183,274 tractors worldwide, an increase of nearly 20% compared to the previous year. As of February 2012, M&M occupied the fifth and sixth positions in the tractor market in China and in the U.S., respectively, in terms of volume. Commenting on the company's plans, Goenka said, "Our next focus is on China and USA, where my company will try to become number one in the next few years."[37]

Though the company registered an increase in sales, some auto analysts were concerned about its plans for the international markets, particularly the U.S. They felt that as the U.S. auto market was stagnating, and that M&M would have to have an advantage over existing rivals to attract customers and increase sales. There might even be quality issues due to the demanding regulatory standards in the U.S. Further, they felt

the name "Mahindra" sounded too ethnic for U.S. consumers and that they would not be ready to switch to a foreign brand, especially from a developing country like India. Commenting on the rationality of selling the Indian brand to American consumers, Goenka said, "In early days when Japanese or Koreans launched their products for the first time into U.S., they had similar problems . . . Launching a new brand is never easy. However we have aspirations to become a global SUV and pickup brand, and we cannot lay our claim to be global without success in the U.S. market."[38]

According to analysts, another challenge that M&M was likely to face was that the company's vehicles ran on diesel, which was expensive compared to gasoline in the U.S. While the average price of diesel was US$4.06 a gallon, the average price of gasoline was US$3.69 per gallon as of May 2011.[39] The U.S. customers might therefore not be willing to invest in diesel vehicles, which would affect sales of M&M vehicles, said experts. Moreover, the market for SUVs in the U.S. was highly competitive and M&M had to compete with some big players such as General Motors, Ford, Dodge, Nissan, and Toyota. Though there were challenges galore, M&M clearly identified its targeted market segments of prospective buyers in the U.S. through an extensive consumer survey. These groups included customers who believed in green technologies, people who had bought M&M tractors, and the Indian expatriate households in the U.S. Besides the U.S., M&M planned to enhance its presence in China, one of the largest auto markets in the world. It planned to launch the Scorpio, the Bolero, the Xylo, and pickup trucks in China. However, experts said that M&M could face some tough challenges in the Chinese passenger car segment, too, because the Chinese market was a restrictive market due to the strict rules and regulations of the Chinese government. It would be practical for M&M to enter the Chinese market through collaboration with a local company, they said.

Apart from the challenges that the individual overseas markets posed to M&M, there were various other challenges that M&M had to tackle in pursuing globalization and operating in various business segments, said analysts. As globalization involved many risks, M&M should be selective about the businesses that would go global first, they added. Moreover, as M&M adopted the strategy of acquisition in pursuing globalization, it would have to effectively manage its cross-border acquisitions and integrate new supply chains and distribution networks with its domestic supply chains and distribution networks. The differences arising out of processes, technologies, and languages would also have to be addressed, they said. On the talent front, M&M would have to source talent globally to ensure the presence of quality personnel in all the locations, opined some experts. Lastly, M&M would have to ensure harmony between all the group companies, they added.

[34] "Indian Company Mahindra's first global SUV – XUV500 Set to Take on the Global Stage," www.mahindra.com, October 18, 2011.

[35] "Mahindra Enters Ecuador Market with Launch of Mahindra Vehicles," www.mahindraautoworld.com, November 29, 2011.

[36] John Deere was founded in 1837 in Moline, Illinois, in the U.S. It was present in four main businesses—agricultural equipment, commercial and consumer equipment, construction and forestry equipment, and credit. As of 2011, it was the world's leading farm equipment manufacturer.

[37] Bagish K Jha, "M&M Sets Sights on Tractor Market in US, China," http://timesofindia.indiatimes.com, February 20, 2012.

[38] Kiley David, "Mahindra's Bold US Plans," www.businessweek.com, October 25, 2008,

[39] "Gasoline Price Falls First Time in 8 Weeks: Energy Department," www.reuters.com, May 16, 2011.

Though M&M was prepared to tackle the challenges in the overseas markets, it would take a long time for the company to build its markets abroad, opined experts. Therefore, M&M could experiment in the domestic market and bring about the requisite improvisations to satisfy the expectations of the overseas customers, they said. While on the one hand, M&M could learn from the domestic market, on the other, it could benefit from the booming Indian automobile industry, opined analysts. Notably, by 2014, India was expected to become a global hub for small cars. According to a report by global consultancy IHS Global Insight, the production of small cars in India would reach about 2.2 million by 2014 and, with this, India would account for a 29% share of the world's small car manufacturers.[40]

While M&M was ready to tackle challenges in India and abroad, there were some other issues. For instance, M&M was venturing into all the segments of the automobile industry and the sustainability of this diverse product portfolio was debatable. This diversification was reminiscent of the diversification that happened at M&M post-liberalization. M&M was at that time unable to sustain all the businesses and many of them were subsequently closed down. However, the company believed that in emerging markets, it made sense for companies to function as group companies because it gave them an edge over competitors.

Similarly, as M&M operated in various business segments, the heads of various M&M group companies had a lot of power in their hands. This delegation of authority was justified, as managing so many business units simultaneously was a complicated task. Given this situation, analysts wondered whether M&M could successfully sustain itself as a consolidated company. Though freedom might foster the growth of group companies, they wondered whether going forward, M&M would become vulnerable to splits. However, Mahindra said the company had review mechanisms such as the annual planning cycle, whereby the activities of all the group companies could be overseen. He said, "These mechanisms help me compose the music so that my soloists can play in my orchestra."[41] However, analysts said that it remained to be seen if the strategies adopted by Mahindra would hold all the M&M group companies together and ensure their success in diverse markets.

THE ROAD AHEAD

In January 2012, M&M reported a 26% rise in its auto sales numbers, which stood at 42,761 units during December 2011 as against 34,062 units during December 2010. In the following month, M&M's automotive sector registered a 29% rise in its auto sales numbers to 43,087 units as against 33,378 units during February 2011. The Passenger Vehicles segment (which includes the UVs and Verito) registered a growth of 33%, having sold 20,573 units in February 2012, as against 15,439 units during February 2011. In March 2012, M&M registered the highest-ever monthly sales number in the history of the company. The company registered a 25% rise in its auto sales numbers, which stood at 47,001 units during March 2012 as against 37,522 units during March 2011.[42] The company's domestic sales stood at 44,342 units during March 2012, compared to 35,488 units during March 2011, an increase of 25%. Commenting on the company's performance, Shah said, "We are happy to have achieved a growth of 28% in 2011–12 given the pressures the auto industry is facing. All our brands have done well this year and we hope to create excitement in the market during FY 2013 with the addition of new products in our portfolio. We thank our customers for the continued trust which they have reposed in us."[43]

In January 2012, at the Delhi Auto Expo, M&M announced that it would be launching a range of its mobility products during the financial year 2012–13. These would include products in the personal as well as the commercial vehicles segments. One of the most anticipated launches from Mahindra was its SUV, the SsangYong Rexton. The Maxximo Passenger Van was to be launched in the first quarter of 2012 while the Verito was scheduled for launch in the last quarter of 2012–13. "I see growth across all the sectors we're in. For autos, I think the biggest growth will be in Latin America. For tractors, Africa. South Asia is a very hot market for us too,"[43] said Mahindra.

Going forward, M&M plans to set up assembly plants in emerging markets of the world such as Russia, Brazil, and China. The company said it was planning to set up a vehicle production facility in Russia in 2014, in collaboration with its Korean subsidiary SsangYong. Experts said that if the plan materialized, M&M would be the first Indian automaker to set up an assembly operation in Russia. However, some analysts were concerned whether an emerging market company like M&M would be able to overcome its challenges and make a mark in the global automobile market. With liberalization in India, huge competition around the world, a threatened Western world, and MNCs making strong efforts to target India, they wondered whether M&M could survive and gain a top spot in the highly competitive global auto industry.

Assignment Questions

1. What are the unique strategies that the emerging-market companies employ in pursuing globalization?

2. What strategies will M&M have to employ in the U.S. to be able to sell its SUVs?

3. What are the various alternatives in front of M&M in building its brand at the global level?

[40] "India to be the Small Car Hub," www.cardekho.com, July 27, 2011.
[41] Stewart A. Thomas and Raman P. Anand, "Finding a Higher Gear," Harvard Business Review, July–August 2008.
[42] http://www.mahindra.com/News/Press-Releases/1333272096.
[43] "Mahindra's Auto Sector Registers Highest Ever Sales Volume at 47001 Units & a 25% Growth in March 2012," www.mahindra.com, April 1, 2012.
[44] "Anand Mahindra Sets Sight on Global Footprint," www.indianexpress.com, October 14, 2011.

Case 12 *After the Breakup: The Troubled Alliance between Volkswagen and Suzuki*

"VW and Suzuki wanted access to each other's crown jewels, so it was always a little doomed from the start."[i]

–TIM URQUHART,
IHS Global Insight[1] auto analyst, September 2011.

"Clearly there are cultural differences between European or US-based (carmakers) and Japanese manufacturers and, with the exception of Renault/Nissan, alliances between Western and Japanese (carmakers) have often ended without tangible results,"[ii]

–CHRISTIAN AUST,
analyst, UniCredit,[2] in September 2011.

On November 18, 2011, the relationship between Suzuki Motor Corporation (Suzuki) and Volkswagen AG (VW) came to an end, with Suzuki terminating the framework agreement between them. Suzuki also demanded that VW return its 19.9% shareholding in the company.

In December 2009, VW and Suzuki made headlines when the German company purchased a 19.9% stake in the Japanese manufacturer. Both agreed to share their technologies and cooperate with each other. VW agreed to provide its larger-vehicle technologies to Suzuki; Suzuki, in turn, agreed to provide VW access to its small-displacement motors and Indian presence. While the proposed partnership goals spurred interest among industry observers, both the auto manufacturers failed to arrive at an agreement on any of their proposed goals. Since the second quarter of 2011, there were indications in the media that the partnership was failing. Suzuki claimed that VW did not give it access to the hybrid technology that it had promised to share when forming the alliance. Similarly, VW accused Suzuki of violating the agreement by procuring diesel engines from Fiat S.p.A[3] (Fiat). The partnership further soured because of their cultural differences and failed joint business proposals. Apprehensive that the issue might adversely affect their cooperation with other companies, the two parties finally terminated their partnership in November 2011.

After the break-up, Suzuki wanted to buy back its 19.9% stake from VW and sell the 1.5% stake of VW back to the German company. However, VW made it clear that it would not forego its stake in Suzuki and that it was not legally bound to do so. As a result, Suzuki filed for arbitration with the International Chamber of Commerce's[4] (ICC) International Court of Arbitration[5] in London. VW, on the other hand, was prepared to go through the arbitration process. While the partnership did no good to either party, both the parties stuck to their respective stands. Some industry observers opined that while Suzuki had lost huge financial and technological support, VW had lost the opportunity to leverage on Suzuki's small car platform and its entry ticket into the fast-growing Indian market. They opined that both the companies needed to clear off the rubble and start afresh—which, while not impossible, would be a difficult task for both.

ABOUT SUZUKI

Headquartered in Hamamatsu, Shizuoka, Japan, Suzuki Motor Corporation specialized in manufacturing compact automobiles, motorcycles, all-terrain vehicles (ATVs), outboard marine engines, wheelchairs, and a variety of other small internal combustion engines. As of 2011, the company was the 9th largest automobile manufacturer in the world and the 4th largest in Japan after Toyota Motor Corporation,[6] Nissan Motor Company Ltd.,[7] and Honda Motor Company Ltd.[8] The company produced 2,878,000 automobiles and 2,735,000 motorcycles during 2010–2011, earning revenue of ¥[9] 2.6 trillion and making a profit of ¥45.17 billion during FY2011.[iii] (Refer to *Exhibit I* for Suzuki's key financials.)

Michio Suzuki founded Suzuki Motor Corporation (Suzuki) in 1909 as Suzuki Loom Works in the village of Hamamatsu, Japan. The company built weaving looms for Japan's textile industry for 30 years and then diversified into manufacturing small cars. However, with the onset of the Second World War, the government declared civilian passenger cars

This case was written by **Syed Abdul Samad,** under the direction of **Debapratim Purkayastha,** IBS Hyderabad. It was compiled from published sources, and is intended to be used as a basis for class discussion rather than to illustrate either effective or ineffective handling of a management situation.

[1] IHS Global Insight provides economic, financial, and political coverage of countries, regions, and industries and is recognized as one of the most consistently accurate forecasting companies in the world.
[2] UniCredit S.p.A is an Italy-based, pan-European banking organization.
[3] Fiat S.p.A. is the largest automobile and engine manufacturer in Italy, with a production output of more than 2 million units, revenue of €35.88 billion, and a profit of €179 million in 2010.

[4] The International Chamber of Commerce (ICC), the largest, most representative business organization in the world, was founded in 1919 to serve world business by promoting trade and investment, open markets for goods and services, and the free flow of capital. The organization's international secretariat was established in Paris.
[5] The International Court of Arbitration is an institution for the resolution of international commercial disputes. The International Court of Arbitration is a part of the International Chamber of Commerce that was created in 1923.
[6] Toyota Motor Corporation (TMC) is a multinational automaker headquartered in Toyota, Aichi, Japan. In 2010, it was the world's largest automobile manufacturer by production.
[7] Nissan Motor Company Ltd. is a multinational automaker headquartered in Yokohama, Japan.
[8] Honda Motor Company, Ltd. is a Japanese manufacturer of automobiles and motorcycles. Honda has been the world's largest motorcycle manufacturer since 1959 and is the sixth-largest automobile manufacturer in the world.
[9] ¥ is the symbol for the Japanese currency Yen. As on March 15, 2012, $1 = 83.57 ¥ and 1€ = 109.15¥.

EXHIBIT I   Suzuki Financials (2007–2011)

Years Ended March 31	Millions of Yen (¥) (except per share amounts)					Thousands of US $ (except per share amounts)
	2011	2010	2009	2008	2007	2011
Net sales	2,608,217	2,469,063	3,004,888	3,502,419	3,163,669	31,367,622
Net income	45,174	28,913	27,429	80,254	75,008	543,283
Net income per share:						
- Primary	80.65	62.76	61.68	177.96	169.41	0.969
- Fully diluted	74.11	55.26	53.97	155.89	151.41	0.891
Cash dividends per share	13.00	12.00	16.00	16.00	14.00	0.156
Net assets	1,106,999	1,089,757	742,915	902,894	855,973	13,313,285
Total current assets	1,372,885	1,479,336	1,267,790	1,483,038	1,435,405	16,510,954
Total assets	2,224,344	2,381,314	2,157,849	2,409,165	2,321,441	26,750,988
Depreciation and amortization	138,368	141,846	141,203	161,600	149,910	1,664,088

Automobile Production (in thousand units)

Year Ended March 31	Overseas	Japan	Total
2007	1,199	1,212	2,412
2008	1,418	1,219	2,637
2009	1,355	1,139	2,494
2010	1,586	959	2,545
2011	1,884	994	2,878

Motorcycle Production (in thousand units)

Year Ended March 31	Overseas	Japan	Total
2007	2,562	621	3,183
2008	2,841	549	3,391
2009	2,993	312	3,305
2010	2,743	162	2,904
2011	2,550	185	2,735

Source: Adapted from "Annual Report 2011 – Suzuki Motor Corporation," www.globalsuzuki.com

as a "non-essential commodity" and Suzuki stopped producing cars. After the war, Suzuki was back to producing looms. However, the cotton market collapsed in 1951 and Suzuki again took up the production of motor vehicles. During those times, the Japanese had a great need for affordable and reliable personal transportation. Banking on this need, many firms were producing "clip-on" gas-powered engines that could be attached to a common bicycle, which could then be used as a motor vehicle.

Recognizing the need for motorcycles, Suzuki created its first two-wheeled motorized bicycle called the "Power Free" in 1952. This innovation was considered ingenious and the patent office of the new democratic government of Japan granted Suzuki a financial subsidy to continue research in motorcycle engineering. In

1954, the company officially changed its name to Suzuki Motor Co., Ltd. and was producing 6,000 motorcycles per month.

Over the years, many more innovations followed at the company. By 2011, the company had expanded its reach to all over the world, with 35 production facilities across 23 countries and 133 distributors in 192 countries. The company had three subsidiaries. Maruti Suzuki India Limited, formed in 1982, had a 54.2% stake owned by Suzuki, and the rest was owned by various Indian public and financial institutions. The other two subsidiaries of Suzuki were Pak Suzuki Motor Co. Ltd. in Karachi, Pakistan, and Magyar Suzuki in Esztergom, Hungary, which were established in 1982 and 1991, respectively. The company had also formed technological and sales

EXHIBIT II   Volkswagen Financials (2007–2011)

Volume Data	2011	2010	2009	2008	2007
Vehicle Sales (units)	8,361,294	7,278,440	6,309,743	6,271,724	6,191,618
Production (units)	8,494,280	7,357,505	6,054,829	6,346,515	6,213,332
Employees as of December 31	501,956	399,381	368,500	369,928	329,305
Financial Data (IFRSs), € million					
Sales revenue	159,337	126,857	105,187	113,808	108,897
Operating profit	11,271	7,141	1,855	6,333	6,151
Profit before tax	18,926	8,994	1,261	6,608	6,543
Profit after tax	15,799	7,226	911	4,688	4,122
Profit attributable to shareholders of Volkswagen AG	15,409	6,835	960	4,753	4,120
Cash flows from operating activities	8,500	11,455	12,741	10,799	15,662
Cash flows from investing activities attributable to operating activities	16,002	9,278	10,428	19,710	13,474
Automotive Division					
EBITDA	17,815	13,940	8,005	12,108	
Cash flows from operating activities	17,109	13,930	12,815	8,771	13,675
Cash flows from investing activities attributable to operating activities	15,995	9,095	10,252	11,450	6,550
Of which: investments in property, plant and equipment	7,929	5,656	5,783	6,762	4,555
As a percentage of sales revenue	5.6	5.0	6.2	6.6	4.6
Capitalized development costs	1,666	1,667	1,948	2,216	1,446
As a percentage of sales revenue	1.2	1.5	2.1	2.2	1.5
Net cash flow	1,112	4,835	2,563	-2,679	7,125
Net liquidity at Dec 31	16,951	18,639	10,636	8,039	13,478
Return Ratios in %					
Return on sales before tax	11.9	7.1	1.2	5.8	6.0
Return on investment after tax (automotive division)	17.7	13.5	3.8	10.9	9.5
Return on equity before tax (financial services division)	14.0	12.9	7.9	12.1	16.1

Source: Adapted from Volkswagen AG Annual Reports 2011, 2009, and 2008, www.volkswagenag.com

tie-ups with many global automobile companies such as General Motors Corporation,[10] Fiat, Nissan, etc. It also entered into a tie-up with VW for technological and sales cooperation in 2009.

ABOUT VOLKSWAGEN

Volkswagen AG, headquartered in Wolfsburg, Germany, was ranked as Europe's largest and the world's third-largest

motor vehicle manufacturer in 2011. The company had sales of 8,361,294 vehicles, garnering revenues of €159.33 billion and a profit after tax amounting to €15.8 billion during 2011.[iv] (Refer to *Exhibit II* for VW's key financials.)

Volkswagen, meaning "People's Car" in German, was established on May 28, 1937, as the *Gesellschaft zur Vorbereitung des Deutschen Volkswagens mbH* (Society for the preparation of the German People's Car) by the Nazi *Deutsche Arbeitsfront* (German Labor Front). The company was established to manufacture the Porsche Type 60, with the basic air-cooled, rear-engine, rear-drive platform, which later came to be

---

[10] General Motors Corporation is a U.S. multinational company headquartered in Detroit. It is the world's largest automaker and owns brands such as Buick, Cadillac, Chevrolet, GMC, Opel, Vauxhall, and Holden.

known as the Volkswagen Beetle. On September 16, 1938, the company was renamed *Volkswagenwerk GmbH* (Volkswagen Factory Limited Liability Company).

However, during the Second World War, Volkswagen primarily manufactured military vehicles, and the production of the Beetle was reduced to only a small number. After the war, the production of the Beetle started slowly, but, with the introduction of new models, the pace picked up in the 1950s and 1960s. In 1960, the German federal government acquired a stake in the company.

In addition to product development, the company was also actively expanding itself through mergers and acquisitions. In January 1965, Volkswagenwerk acquired Auto Union GmbH[11] from Daimler-Benz to produce Audi. In August 1969, NSU Motorenwerke AG was acquired and merged with Auto Union to form Audi NSU Auto Union AG (later renamed Audi AG in 1985). In September 1982, Volkswagenwerk expanded out of Germany by signing a co-operation agreement with the Spanish car manufacturer SEAT, S.A.[12] By 1990, Volkswagenwerk acquired SEAT's entire equity. In the meanwhile, the company again changed its name to *Volkswagen Aktiengesellschaft* (*Volkswagen AG*) on July 4, 1985. In March 1991, the company signed a joint venture with Škoda automobilová a.s.[13] of Czechoslovakia, but gradually raised its stake in the company, making Skoda its wholly-owned subsidiary by May 2000.

As of September 2011, Volkswagen AG consisted of 342 Group companies, which were involved in either vehicle production or other related automotive services. The VW Group comprised eleven active automotive companies, and their corresponding marques—Volkswagen Passenger Cars, Volkswagen Commercial Vehicles, Audi, Bentley, Bugatti, Lamborghini, Porsche, SEAT, Scania AB, MAN SE, and Škoda—each with its own unique identity and operating independently. It also owned five inactive marques—Auto Union, Dampf-Kraft-Wagen (DKW), Horch, NSU Motorenwerke AG, and Wanderer. The VW Group operated worldwide with 62 production plants in 15 European countries and 7 other countries in the continents of the Americas, Asia, and Africa. The company had its reach in 153 countries, with China being its largest single country market followed by Germany, with sales of 1,924,649 units and 1,038,596 units, respectively, in 2010.[v] The company's recent acquisitions included Wilhelm Karmann GmbH in November 2009, Italdesign Giugiaro S.p.A. in May 2010, and a 19.9% stake in Suzuki Motor Corporation in December 2009.

ABOUT THE INDUSTRY

Since 2009, there had been a decline in auto sales worldwide due to the economic crisis. This had prompted global carmakers

to form partnerships and alliances to save billions and develop state-of-the-art powertrains. For instance, Europe's second-biggest carmaker, PSA Peugeot Citroen, and Japan's Mitsubishi Motors Corp. formed a strategic partnership involving an equity investment. Industry experts saw this pair-up as a union of the weak, to strengthen their positions in the global automobile industry. Carmakers were also shifting their investments to emerging markets that had withstood the economic slump.

Another tie-up was formed when Italy's Fiat S.p.A. acquired a 20% stake in Chrysler Group LLC in June 2009. General Motors and China's Shanghai Automotive Industry Corporation too announced that they would make small cars in India. Another alliance that tasted success during these tough times was that of Renault from France and Nissan Motor of Japan, which had developed low-emissions vehicles. Similarly, many manufacturers were keen to raise their presence in China and India to tap the soaring demand in the Asian countries.

While major Western markets suffered a setback, the emerging markets of China and India, with their booming sales, had become a lifeline for many automobile companies. However, the interesting aspect that had arisen amidst the crisis was that Asian automakers, too, were looking to buy into brands on sale from global automobile behemoths such as GM and Ford Motor Co. to strengthen their technological capacities and increase their global presence.

The emerging markets had a high demand for fuel-efficient cars. Even in the developed markets, particularly in Europe, there was a move toward more eco-friendly cars. With the introduction of stricter emission regulations and the introduction of incentives for manufacturers doing research in green technologies, the demand for green vehicles had increased. Vehicle manufacturers all over the world were trying to fit in with the EU's emission norms (Euro 5 and Euro 6[14] standards). Automobile manufacturers were trying to acquire or indigenously develop such green technologies to tap the soaring demand.

THE SUZUKI-VW PARTNERSHIP

In its annual report of FY2009–2010, VW said that it intended to position itself as a global economic and environmental leader among automobile manufacturers and termed this plan "Strategy 2018." Through this strategy it aimed to be the most successful and fascinating automaker in the world by 2018, using intelligent innovations and technologies to deliver customer satisfaction and quality, increase unit sales to more than 10 million vehicles a year, and capture major growth markets.

In line with the global trend of alliances and its own goals of becoming the world's biggest automaker, VW joined the flurry of realignments and alliances and discussed a partnership with Suzuki in June 2009. Battered by the falling demand in the U.S. and Europe and the stricter environmental standards, it hoped that the alliance would create a formidable new force in the global car industry. "This comes right after the Mitsubishi deal and shows that foreign carmakers are coming to take stakes in Japanese firms, raising expectations of a reorganization in the

---

[11] Auto Union was an amalgamation of four German automobile manufacturers—Audi, DKW, Horch, and Wanderer—in 1932. The company has evolved into the present day Audi, as a subsidiary of Volkswagen Group.

[12] SEAT, S.A. was a Spanish state-owned automobile manufacturer founded on May 9, 1950. It is currently a wholly owned subsidiary of the Volkswagen Group.

[13] Škoda Auto (founded as an arms manufacturer in 1859) is an automobile manufacturer based in the Czech Republic. Škoda became a wholly owned subsidiary of the Volkswagen Group in 2000.

[14] Euro 5 are emission limits set by the EU for diesel vehicles. Euro 6 are emission limits set by the EU for vehicles using petrol, natural gas, or LPG.

autos sector,"[vi] said Noritsugu Hirakawa, a strategist at Okasan Securities.[vii] VW had performed better than its rivals during the recession and had taken a bold step to strengthen itself. However, analysts opined that the move had been made too early (the second in a week) after VW's €3.9 billion (US$5.8 billion) purchase of a 49.9%[vii] stake in sports car–maker Porsche AG.

On December 9, 2009, VW and Suzuki officially announced that they had reached a common understanding to establish a "close long-term strategic partnership." Both the companies opined that they would complement each other's strengths and make a perfect fit in exploiting their advantages and rise to the challenges of the global automobile industry. According to the deal, VW would purchase 19.9% of Suzuki's issued shares for €1.7 billion (¥222.5 billion or US$2.5 billion) and Suzuki would invest up to half of the amount received from VW (about ¥100 billion or US$1.13 billion) to purchase a 1.5% voting stake in VW. Owing to these developments, Suzuki's shares rose 3.5% in Tokyo and VW's rose 2.3% in Germany.[viii]

VW's chief executive, Martin Winterkorn (Winterkorn), had a 10-year goal of increasing VW-brand sales by 80% (6.6 million vehicles) by 2018 and with this purchase, VW became a top shareholder in Suzuki. Analysts, too, opined that the VW-Suzuki deal would be game-changing and would help them in competing head-to-head with Toyota. It was also expected to open for VW the doors to one of the world's fastest-growing carmakers and give more visibility to Suzuki globally. Earlier, GM had owned a 20% stake in Suzuki (invested in 1981). However, since 2006, Suzuki had been cutting its ties with GM and had completed the purchase of its shares back from GM in 2008. After the deal with VW was finalized, the company planned to use ¥100 billion of the proceeds from VW to repay its debt and ¥122.5 billion on its research and development.[ix]

THE RATIONALE FOR THE ALLIANCE

VW entered into this partnership to tap Suzuki's strengths in small cars and its dominance in the fast-growing Indian market, as well as to allow the automakers to pool management resources, share auto parts to cut down production costs, and jointly develop the next generation of fuel-efficient cars. However, the companies were not in favor of the idea of sharing dealership or service center space. Industry analysts expected that the VW-Suzuki combined vehicle sales (3.265 million and 1.15 million in the first half of 2009) would easily take the numbers above Toyota's (4.415 million).[x] "Together, we can maximize our opportunities for growth. In partnership with Suzuki, the Volkswagen group can take a big step forward in the compact car segment, particularly in the emerging markets in Asia. In turn, Suzuki can benefit from our experience with efficient and environmentally friendly vehicles. In 8 to 10 years from now, we want to become No. 1 in the world. I believe we will be able to accelerate that with the cooperation with Suzuki,"[xi] said Winterkorn.

VW was struggling to make its presence felt in the Indian market because it did not have small cars to offer and its only mini vehicle, UP, was still under development. It hoped to crack the Indian and Southeast Asian markets through Suzuki's Indian subsidiary Maruti Suzuki India Limited—a powerful player in India. (Refer to *Exhibit III* for some key statistics related to the Indian market.)

Suzuki was known for its minicar models, such as WagonR, the Swift hatchback, and Jimny, a small sport-utility vehicle that was sold mainly in Japan, India, and Southeast Asia. Suzuki was considered a world leader in the mini-car segment. It also had close to a 50% share of the fast-growing Indian market and a huge network of dealerships across the subcontinent. However, it lagged behind in gas-electric hybrids, electric vehicles, and other fuel-efficient cars.[xii]

Suzuki's chairman and chief executive, Osamu Suzuki, also highlighted the need for better economies of scale to keep up with the cut-throat competition, as mass production (by having common parts and components) and mass sales played a key role in controlling costs. However, he made it clear that his company would be an equal partner and would not become a subsidiary of VW. He also bristled at the idea of having a German CEO at his company and said, "I don't want other folks telling me how to do things."[xiii]

Industry experts were of the opinion that the cross-border deal would have a positive effect on Maruti Suzuki, catapulting it into a global small-car hub for supplying these cars through VW's strong network. "Volkswagen has looked at Suzuki obviously from a small car angle. India could become an original equipment manufacturer and supplier of small cars for Volkswagen. It is too early to speculate on its (deal's) implications on India (Maruti). The deal means Volkswagen and Suzuki see much value in the arrangement in terms of technology sharing,"[xiv] said Maruti Suzuki India chairman, R. C. Bhargava. The deal (sale of shares) was finally completed on January 15, 2010.

JOINT PROJECTS

A few days after the two companies announced their tie-up, VW sought to leverage on its partner's R&D facility to jointly work on hybrid[16] and electric car projects. Jochem Heizmann, VW board member responsible for production, said, "It's too early to give out concrete details of our plans, but what is definite are common projects on hybrids and electro mobile cars. VW can offer hybrids and electric technology. Suzuki also has a fuel cell technology program going on at its end."[xv] They planned to develop cars together under both brand names and expected their first car—using parts from both manufacturers—to be introduced by the end of 2010. VW also intended to supply diesel engines to Suzuki in the future. The partnership also spurred some interesting thoughts of a VW motorcycle coming to fruition.

After the tie-up, Suzuki announced that it did not intend to sell more shares to VW, but was open to buying more stakes in VW. However, on the production front, it planned to increase the production capacity of its Indian subsidiary by 50% and

---

[15] Okasan Securities Group Inc. is a securities company group established in 1923 and is committed to a wide spectrum of securities-investment and asset-management businesses.

[16] A hybrid electric vehicle combines a conventional internal combustion engine propulsion system with an electric propulsion system, and is, therefore, more fuel-efficient.

EXHIBIT III   Some Key Statistics Related to the Indian Automobile Market

Gross Turnover of the Automobile Industry in India (In US$ Million)

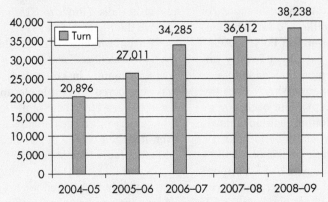

Sales of Automobiles in India

Category	2004–05	2005–06	2006–07	2007–08	2008–09	2009–10	2010–11
Passenger Vehicles	1,061,572	1,143,076	1,379,979	1,549,882	1,552,703	1,951,333	2,520,421
Commercial Vehicles	318,430	351,041	467,765	490,494	384,194	532,721	676,408
Three-Wheelers	307,862	359,920	403,910	364,781	349,727	440,392	526,022
Two-Wheelers	6,209,765	7,052,391	7,872,334	7,249,278	7,437,619	9,370,951	11,790,305
Grand Total	**7,897,629**	**8,906,428**	**10,123,988**	**9,654,435**	**9,724,243**	**12,295,397**	**15,513,156**

Change in Market Shares of Different Automobile Manufacturers in India

	2011–2012	2010–2011
Maruti Suzuki	40.4%	44.9%
Hyundai	14.9%	14.3%
Tata Motors	12.3%	14%
M&M	9.2%	6.8%
Toyota	5.6%	3.3%
GMI	4.6%	4.2%
Ford	3.7%	3.9%
Volkswagen	3.2%	2.1%
Honda	2.0%	2.4%
Others	4.2%	4.1%

Source: SIAM

to boost its annual production to 1.5 million vehicles by 2015. VW, on the other hand, was optimistic about the positive influence of Suzuki's partnership on its future products—such as the concept car VW New Compact Coupe (NCC), the New Beetle Final Edition, the subcompact car Polo, the Phaeton Luxury sedan, the UP! Lite, the VW Jetta TDI, etc.—all with a clean diesel technology powertrain, which it intended to introduce in the U.S. market.

On January 20, 2010, Osamu Suzuki announced that a co-developed car would be released in 2013. He furthered clarified

that the companies were working on all models of common components like air conditioning, power steering, etc. The Japanese automaker was also interested in procuring VW's power plants (probably diesel and V6 gasoline engines) for its midsized Kizashi sedan, but was of the opinion that it might take some time to discover the synergies and then collaborate.

By April 2010, the two companies were planning to develop an eco-car in Thailand. These plans were developed as a result of Nissan's eco-car launch in Thailand followed by announcements from other Japanese companies like Toyota and

Honda. While it was not clear whether the eco-cars would be developed jointly or separately, cooperation between the two partners was expected in terms of supply chain, parts procurement, shared production facilities, and distribution. Suzuki's eco-car investment involved building the facilities for pressing, welding, painting, assembly, and engine production with production starting from early 2012 at 10,000 units per annum.

In August 2010, both the partners explored the possible synergies. While VW was keen on controlling costs by harnessing Suzuki's production practices and generating volumes in the small car segment, Suzuki decided that it would not share its car platforms in India with VW. "There is no possibility of platform sharing (with Volkswagen) as the German company's production and product development costs are very high and that could make our business unviable. There is a possibility of an original equipment manufacturing deal with Volkswagen, like the way we have with Nissan which sells hatchback A-Star as the Pixo in Europe. Volkswagen's cost of products is high whereas Maruti's product management costs are very low; so they can learn from us,"[xvi] said Shinzo Nakanishi, MD and CEO of Maruti Suzuki India. Moreover, he made it clear that Maruti Suzuki did not want to use VW India's facilities to overcome its capacity crunch as they were too expensive. Later in November 2010, both companies were expected to design a mutually beneficial global business model and unveil joint projects by December or January 2011. However, by mid-2011, there were clear indications that the companies were not able to cooperate with each other and had not made any progress in terms of co-development of cars, technology sharing, platform sharing, etc.

THE PROBLEMS

In March 2011, VW, in its annual report, termed Suzuki as its "associate" and stated that VW could "significantly influence financial and operating policy decisions" of the company. This angered Suzuki executives, as the two companies were intended to cooperate as equals in the partnership. After that, the disagreements between the two partners only escalated.

CULTURAL MISMATCH

In addition to policy differences, the partnership faced a cultural mismatch in their working approach. (Refer to *Exhibit IV* for the differences in the work cultures of Japanese and German companies.)

While VW bemoaned what they considered to be the slow decision-making of the Japanese company, Suzuki criticized VW's high-handed approach to the alliance and the level of technological access being offered by the Germans. Winterkorn said that VW's managers were trying to build mutual trust but this was difficult as there were significant cultural differences in the working approach of the two companies. "Volkswagen and Suzuki had a different approach in taking decisions. Working with a Japanese partner is not easy. . . . European companies were fast in making decisions. In the West sometimes, we make decisions more quickly. In the Japanese culture, sometimes things are a little different."[xvii] But analysts opined that issues such as decision-making structures, cultural differences, and

building of mutual trust should have been addressed before the alliance was formed rather than being discussed a year after.

DISAGREEMENTS IN TECHNOLOGY SHARING

There were disagreements in terms of technology sharing and cooperation as well. Since the framing of the partnership, the collaboration between the two companies was not progressing as expected. In almost two years of their alliance, there was nothing fruitful that emerged from it. During June–July 2011, Hans Dieter Poetsch, chief manager for finance at VW, announced that the company might have to rethink its agreement. In response to VW's announcement, Suzuki vice-president, Yasuhito Harayama, blamed the lack of progress in the collaboration on the fact that VW was hoping to influence Suzuki as a company. In addition to this, Osamu Suzuki also indicated that VW had nothing on the shelves in terms of technology that Suzuki immediately wanted.

The relationship further deteriorated when Winterkorn stated, "Suzuki wants as much modern technology as possible from Volkswagen, but is not willing to reciprocate. The Japanese still need some training in proper cooperation."[xviii] Osamu Suzuki fired back through his blog stating, "Since the companies differ in size, people of Volkswagen may develop a mistaken impression that Suzuki is placed under their umbrella. The initial basic agreement seems to falter. We learnt about Volkswagen's technologies, but we did not find any one of them interesting enough to adopt immediately. If we are short of any technology, we have an option to ask other companies with which we benefit from technological exchanges."[xix]

Earlier, in 2005, Suzuki had formed an alliance with Fiat to make diesel engines in Asia. In January 2011, the company entered into an agreement with Fiat to supply diesel engines for its Indian subsidiary, Maruti Suzuki. It further extended its partnership with Fiat in June 2011 to buy Multijet engines from the company in Hungary. This led to speculation in the industry that a new global alliance could be in the offing. "The general impression was that VW would be Suzuki's first choice for diesel engines and opting for Fiat instead sure set tongues wagging,"[xx] said an automobile executive. VW accused Suzuki of a breach in the agreement for taking technology from Fiat. VW's reaction to this supply arrangement between Suzuki and Fiat—which pre-dated the VW alliance by several years—was the final straw for Suzuki and hastened the decision to part.

PROBLEMS IN POLICY AND COOPERATION

The media war between the companies got wilder by the day. While VW felt that it was not getting enough cooperation from its Japanese counterpart, Suzuki opined that VW was not giving it the respect due to it as an independent company. However, the industry experts opined that the partners were lacking in the areas of control and planning regarding the alliance and needed to do a reconfiguration of the stake-holding arrangement. By August 2011, rumors about the possible breakup surfaced but were quickly laid to rest by VW. "VW and Suzuki still are, and will continue to be, two independent companies with different business models from different cultural

EXHIBIT IV   Comparison of Japanese and German Business Etiquette

Japanese Business Etiquette:

- The "unhurried" Japanese concept is gone; decisions are made swiftly and efficiently.
- Making a personal call for a business appointment is more effective than sending a letter.
- Punctuality is essential; arriving 5 minutes early is good practice.
- Strong hierarchical structure in negotiation process; begins from executive and goes to middle level management; but decisions are made by the group.
- In business meetings, the Japanese will line up in the order of seniority with the most senior person in the front and least senior person closest to the door.
- It is important to show greater respect to the eldest members; age and rank are strongly connected; however, even a low-ranking individual can become a manager if he performs well.
- Personal space is highly valued; being silent at meetings is acceptable; it is considered to be a thought process.
- Business cannot start until the exchange of business cards or "meishi"; use both hands to present or take the card and examine it carefully before placing it away.
- Gift-giving is accepted with gratitude; but too big a gift is considered a bribe.
- Engaging in small talk about education and family and social life before business negotiations is a good practice.
- Business protocols are not necessarily final agreements; after-care and long-term relationships are positively encouraged.
- Greet your counterparts with a bow or handshake, use apologies and express gratitude frequently.
- Avoid confrontation and showing negative emotions during business negotiations.
- Don't praise a single Japanese colleague; the group is more important than the individual.
- Don't use first names unless invited to do so; use titles and their family names.
- Don't use large hand gestures, unusual facial expressions, or dramatic movements.

German Business Etiquette:

- A personal relationship is not needed to do business; your academic credentials and experience in business will do.
- Germans work with their office doors closed, so knock and wait till invited in.
- Communication is formal and following the established protocol is important to maintaining a business relationship. Maintain direct eye contact while speaking.
- Germans are suspicious of hyperbole, promises, and displays of emotions.
- Germans require a great deal of written communication, both in English and German.
- They display great deference to people in authority, so it is imperative that they understand your level relative to their own.
- Appointments are mandatory and are to be made 1–2 weeks in advance; punctuality is taken extremely seriously.
- Meetings are generally formal. Initial meetings are used to get to know each other. They allow your German colleagues to determine if you are trustworthy.
- Meetings adhere to strict agendas, including starting and ending times.
- The eldest or highest ranking person enters the room first. Men enter before women, if their age and status are roughly equivalent.
- Do not sit until invited and told where to sit. There is a rigid protocol to be followed.
- Germany is heavily regulated and extremely bureaucratic. They prefer to get down to business and only engage in the briefest of small talk.
- Contracts are strictly followed. Once a decision is made, it will not be changed.
- You must be patient and not appear ruffled by the strict adherence to protocol. Germans are detail oriented and want to understand every innuendo before coming to an agreement.
- Business is hierarchical. Decision making is held at the top of the company. Final decisions are translated into rigorous, comprehensive action steps that you can expect will be carried out to the letter.
- Avoid confrontational behavior or high-pressure tactics. It can be counterproductive.
- Men should wear dark colored, formal, and conservative business suits and women should wear either business suits or conservative dresses without ostentatious jewelry or accessories.

Source: Adapted from "Doing Business in Japan- Japanese Social and Business Culture," www.communicaid.com; and "Germany—Language, Culture, Customs and Business Etiquette," www.kwintessential.co.uk

environments. The cooperation is marked by highest respect and acceptance,"[xxi] said Hans Demant, VW's coordinator for international projects.

According to analysts, a tiff that started over VW's statement had turned into a public feud and escalated into a spat threatening the alliance. Since the initial agreement, both companies had tried to move the partnership forward but had failed due to cultural differences and the ethoses of the companies. Suzuki regarded its operational independence as sacrosanct and also opined that VW had acted in an arrogant and high-handed manner. Suzuki in its statement said, "Suzuki thinks that it is crucial to secure 'independence' in its operating policy decision for maintaining its competitiveness in the domestic Kei-car market and Asian markets including India. However, Volkswagen AG publicly reported that Suzuki was a company over which Volkswagen AG had significant influence where financial and operating policy decisions were concerned. Taking these facts into account, Suzuki concluded that it was difficult to attain its primary aim for of entering into the partnership. Also there was concern that the partnership would have a negative impact on Suzuki's autonomous decision-making in its operating policy."[xxii]

SERVING NOTICE: BREACH OF CONTRACT

In September 2011, VW served a notice of breach of contract on Suzuki stating that Suzuki had gone to Fiat for its engines instead of approaching VW. This upset Suzuki further and it demanded that VW withdraw the claim. However, according to Suzuki, "the matter of buying Fiat engines had been discussed with Volkswagen back in January and both sides accepted the terms. The reason behind the deal is Suzuki's need of an engine that would meet specified parameters for their SX4 compact. Fiat had such a 1.6 liter diesel engine available while Volkswagen did not."[xxiii] Osamu Suzuki also stressed that the deal with Fiat did not violate any contractual agreements with VW and decided to dissolve the partnership and cross-shareholding deal as it would disrupt and disparage its honor.

Following these incidents, on October 13, 2011, Suzuki, too, served VW with a "notice of breach" of the Framework Agreement that was drawn up in 2009. The notice required VW to remedy the breach. Osamu Suzuki, said, "This capital alliance was intended to facilitate Suzuki's access to VW's core technologies. I remain disappointed that we have not received what we were promised. If Volkswagen will not allow access it must return Suzuki's shares. We are very encouraged by Suzuki's consistently solid performance. We remain on track for profitability and are excited about the potential for future growth."[xxiv]

In response to the notice, Ulrich Hackenberg, Executive Vice President and Member of the Board of Management, VW Brand, explained, "The association with Suzuki Motor is purely financial and not technical. There has been some misinterpretation of the issue. The collaboration with Suzuki is financial only. The investment in the company has been positive so far. Stocks have gone up because of the collaboration. The collaboration was possible because they approached Volkswagen. Actually, we do not have the same interpretation of the partnership."[xxv] The company also insisted that a clause existed in the agreement that barred VW from getting more shares of Suzuki, but once the agreement was cancelled it was no longer bound to that clause and could start buying shares from the open market. Citing the development of the UP!, he opined that the small car had been conceptualized and developed without the help of Suzuki's small car platform and much before the partnership had been entered into.

THE BREAKUP

Finally, on November 18, 2011, Suzuki terminated its partnership with VW and demanded the return of its shares. In his statement on the termination, Osamu Suzuki said, "Today Suzuki terminated the partnership with VW. Suzuki will be seeking the return of its shares from VW in arbitration. I am disappointed that we have to take this action but VW's actions have left us no choice. They have continued to refuse our attempts on numerous occasions to resolve these issues through negotiation. I am more disappointed that having shaken the hand of Dr. Winterkorn in agreeing to this partnership, he has not honored his commitment to grant Suzuki access to what was originally agreed. In the absence of VW's cooperation and given its failure to do what was agreed, there is no basis for the partnership to continue. With the cessation of the partnership there is also no basis for VW to hold on to Suzuki's shares. We will now work to restore the relationship between Suzuki and VW to its original state as independent parties who do not restrict each other's business. I call on Dr. Winterkorn to honor this."[xxvi]

The move had left VW baffled, opined an industry observer. "It's clear VW hoped to learn more about Suzuki's almost miraculous ability to engineer profitable low-cost cars, something VW struggles with. If the partnership is over, they're going to have to figure it out themselves. It's also going to cost them more to get into the Indian market that it would have done with Suzuki. But neither are insurmountable challenges for a company with VW's money, ambition, and, I would assume, patience,"[xxvii] said Max Warburton at Bernstein Research.[17]

Industry analysts opined that finding another partner for VW to build small cars or entering the fast-growing Indian market on its own would be a costly affair for the German carmaker. They also described Suzuki's diesel engine deal with Fiat as a "snub" to VW, because Suzuki, in partnership with VW, would have gotten global scale and access and superior hybrid technologies. (Refer to *Exhibit V* for a diagram summarizing the VW-Suzuki Breakup.)

THE AFTERMATH

After termination of the partnership, Suzuki wanted VW to sell back its 19.9% stake. However, VW refused to acknowledge Suzuki's request, saying that it was not legally bound to do so. As a result, Suzuki filed for arbitration with the International Chamber of Commerce's (ICC) International Court of Arbitration in London. But VW braced up to fight all the way.

---

[17] Bernstein Research, founded in 1967, is widely recognized as Wall Street's premier sell-side research firm.

EXHIBIT V   Suzuki-VW Breakup

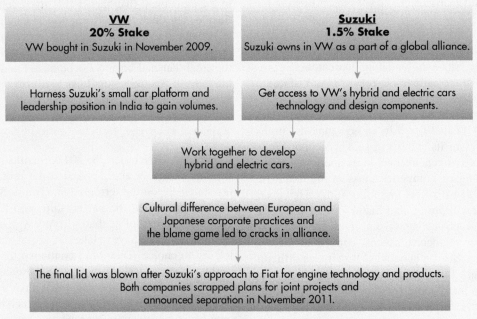

Source: Adapted from: Chanchal Pal Chauhan, "Volkswagen May Bring Special UP!" The Economic Times, Page 7, September 13, 2011.

"We won't sell our Suzuki stake. If the current management at Suzuki doesn't want to work together with us, then maybe the next generation will,"[xxviii] said Winterkorn.

Frank Schwope, a NordLB[18] analyst, opined that there was no urgent financial need for VW to return Suzuki's shares unless the arbitration court forced it to do so. Instead it could keep them as an investment and wait for Suzuki to weaken to a point where it would need a partner again. Other analysts argued that VW would retain the shares to ensure that no other competitor, such as Fiat, took a stake in Suzuki. "They will just keep the stake as a financial investment and see what they do with it. . . even if it's only to annoy them. They won't take a loss selling down their stake,"[xxix] said a London-based equity analyst.

Industry observers debated on the possibilities of the outcome of the feud. They opined that the chances of VW selling its stake were slim, because the German carmaker had no immediate need for further liquidity. But Suzuki might be willing to pay a premium to put the partnership behind it, they felt. However, some analysts felt that the stalemate could be broken if both companies built up mutual trust. For instance, they opined that Suzuki could buy some diesel engines while VW could grant access to its alternative technology. However, if both the companies were adamant about their decisions, then analysts opined that the relationship between the two would be bitter even after Osamu Suzuki's regime. Observers did not rule out the possibility of a hostile takeover of Suzuki, but opined that it would be a tough battle for VW. Commerzbank[19] analyst Daniel Schwarz said, "First of all, (Suzuki chairman and CEO) Osamu Suzuki would not want to sell. VW simply won't be able to take over all of Suzuki against his will."[xxx]

THE ROAD AHEAD

Both the companies were pegged back due to the breakup of the alliance. According to Aleksej Wunrau, a Frankfurt-based BHF Bank AG[20] analyst, "Suzuki really needs a big manufacturer behind it, so the effect of a withdrawal would be far worse for them. Volkswagen could very well step back from Suzuki and either seek another partner or start afresh on their own in Japan and India, which would of course be a lot more expensive."[xxxi] As the Indian market was central to VW's plans of becoming the world's number one automaker by 2018, analysts and top industry executives felt that the company needed a revamped strategy and a new alliance partner to compete in India's small-car market or it needed to develop a strong small-car product line-up on its own. In 2010–2011, VW India offered seven models across price points that included the Polo hatchback and the Vento sedan. VW planned to introduce a special variant of its UP! and more compact cars for India in 2012 to consolidate its position in the fast-growing small-car market, which constituted more than 70% of the total cars sold in the country.[xxxii] The company expected that the UP! would take on Maruti's A-star and WagonR and help increase its market share in India. In 2010, VW had sold 53,300 cars in India and aimed to double that figure in 2011. It further aimed to raise its market share to 11% by 2015–2016. "The tie-up would have offered Volkswagen an automatic advantage as they would have got a strong local partner in Maruti Suzuki. The Indian market is skewed toward low-cost cars while Volkswagen's expertise lies in the premium cars. The (market share) target looks ambitious,"[xxxiii] said Colin Couchman, a European automotive analyst at IHS Automotive.

---

[18] The Norddeutsche Landesbank (abbreviated Nord/LB) is a German landesbank and is one of the largest commercial banks in Germany.

[19] Founded in 1870, Commerzbank AG is the second-largest bank in Germany, after Deutsche Bank, and is headquartered in Frankfurt am Main.

[20] BHF-Bank is a leading German investment bank currently owned by Deutsche Bank.

After distancing itself from VW, Suzuki sought help from the Mitsubishi Group of Companies[21] to power its hybrid cars. Meanwhile, Fiat CEO, Sergio Marchionne said, "Suzuki would be an interesting partner for Fiat in Asia. This doesn't shock us because we have already speculated that Fiat was right partner for Suzuki and not VW." He also said that Suzuki and Fiat had been working together for a very long time and were familiar with each other's business methods and thus could leverage on the strengths of each other. Suzuki had made a deal with Fiat to supply the SX4 crossover in mid-2011. Later, the Maruti Suzuki SX4 was launched with a Fiat Multijet engine and it planned to deploy the same engine for the 2011 Swift and Swift Dzire. The VW TDi engines had proved to be too expensive to procure and had higher maintenance costs for Suzuki. Suzuki further offered to build the next generation Sedici (a rebadged SX4crossover) for Fiat in Italy and a small SUV for Chrysler (now owned by Fiat). With all these improvements in the Suzuki-Fiat relationship when compared to the Suzuki-VW alliance, analysts opined that Fiat would have been the right partner for Suzuki rather than VW.

While some industry analysts expected a full takeover of Suzuki by VW, there were others who trashed the idea and felt that both the companies should move on. Tim Urquhart, IHS Global Insight auto analyst, stated, "I don't see what good it will do either company getting into a silly litigation either about what the terms of the alliance were supposed to be, or from Suzuki's point of view a defamation case."[xxxiv]

---

[21] The Mitsubishi Group of Companies, or Mitsubishi Companies, founded in 1870, is a Japanese multinational conglomerate comprising a range of autonomous businesses including mining, shipbuilding, telecom, financial services, insurance, electronics, automotive, construction, heavy industries, oil and gas, real estate, foods and beverages, chemicals, steel, aviation, and others. The revenue and profit of the group for the FY 2010 were US$ 248.6 billion and US$ 7.2 billion, respectively.

Endnotes

i. Chris Bryant and John Reed, "VW Tie-up with Suzuki Hits Slippery Patch," www.ft.com, September 12, 2011.

ii. "Volkswagen Suzuki Divorce Raises Doubts Over Auto Alliances," http://economictimes.indiatimes.com, September 13, 2011.

iii. "Annual Report 2011 – Suzuki Motor Corporation," www.globalsuzuki.com, 2011.

iv. "Volkswagen AG – Annual Report 2011," www.volkswagenag.com

v. Ibid.

vi. Chang-Ran Kim and Christiaan Hetzner, "VW Buys $2.5 Billion Suzuki Stake," www.reuters.com, December 9, 2009.

vii. Ibid.

viii. Makiko Kitamura and Andreas Cremer, "Eyeing India Market, VW Buys 20% of Suzuki," www.businessweek.com, December 2009.

ix. Ibid.

x. "Volkswagen AG Buys $2.5 Billion Stake in Suzuki Motor Corp, Eyes World #1 Automaker Spot," http://articles.nydailynews.com, December 9, 2009.

xi. Hiroko Tabuchi and Bettina Wassener, "Volkswagen to Buy 20 Percent Stake in Suzuki," www.nytimes.com, December 9, 2009.

xii. Ibid.

xiii. Chang-Ran Kim and Christiaan Hetzner, "VW Buys $2.5 Billion Suzuki Stake," www.reuters.com, December 9, 2009.

xiv. "VW Buys $2.5 bn Stake in Suzuki, a Foothold in India," www.indianexpress.com, December 10, 2009.

xv. "VW-Suzuki Plans to Carry out Hybrid Car R&D in India," http://suzukifan.com, December 14, 2009.

xvi. "Suzuki and Volkswagen May Make Some Solid Global Announcements in the Next Six to Eight Months," http://suzukifan.com, August 5, 2010.

xvii. "Volkswagen CEO Admits to Differences with Suzuki on JV," http://suzukifan.com, March 13, 2011.

xviii. Bertel Schmitt, "Osamu Suzuki Blog Bombs Volkswagen," www.thetruthaboutcars.com, July 7, 2011.

xix. Ibid.

xx. Murali Gopalan, "VW, Suzuki Go Nowhere Despite Two-year Drive," www.thehindubusinessline.com, August 8, 2011.

xxi. Makiko Kitamura, Yuki Hagiwara, and Andreas Cremer, "Volkswagen-Suzuki Alliance Unraveling Over Control of Driver's Seat: Cars," www.bloomberg.com, September 6, 2011.

xxii. "Suzuki Made a Timely Disclosure Regarding the Partnership with Volkswagen AG," www.globalsuzuki.com, September 12, 2011.

xxiii. Danny Choy, "Suzuki Demands Volkswagen Withdraw Claim of Breached Contract," www.autoguide.com, September 23, 2011.

xxiv. "Suzuki Motor Corporation Serves Volkswagen AG a Notice of Breach Regarding Partnership," www.theautochannel.com, October 14, 2011.

xxv. V. Rishi Kumar, "Volkswagen-Suzuki Tie Up Is Financial, Not Technical, Says VW Official," www.thehindubusinessline.com, September 14, 2011.

xxvi. "Termination of the Framework Agreement Regarding the Business Alliance and Cross-holding of Shares with Volkswagen AG," www.globalsuzuki.com, November 18, 2011.

xxvii. Chris Bryant and John Reed, "VW Tie-up with Suzuki Hits Slippery Patch," www.ft.com, September 12, 2011.

xxviii. Chikafumi Hodo and Christiaan Hetzner, "Suzuki Files for Arbitration in VW Dispute," www.reuters.com, November 24, 2011.

xxix. "Volkswagen and Suzuki's Crumbling Partnership," http://business-standard.com, October 3, 2011.

xxx. "Full Takeover of Suzuki by Volkswagen Unlikely," http://economictimes.indiatimes.com, September 20, 2011.

xxxi. Makiko Kitamura, Yuki Hagiwara, and Andreas Cremer, "Volkswagen-Suzuki Alliance Unraveling over Control of Driver's Seat: Cars," www.bloomberg.com, September 6, 2011.

xxxii. Chanchal Pal Chauhan, "Volkswagen May Bring Special UP!" *The Economic Times*, Page 7, September 13, 2011.

xxxiii. Shally Seth Mohile, "Volkswagen to Bring More Small Cars to India to Raise Market Share," www.livemint.com, November 2011.

xxxiv. "Volkswagen and Suzuki's Crumbling Partnership," http://business-standard.com, October 3, 2011.

Glossary

achievement versus ascription The source of power and status in society—one's achievement versus personal factors such as class, age, gender.

administrative distance Lack of common trading bloc or currency, political hostility, non-market or closed economy.

affective appeals Negotiation appeals based on emotions and subjective feelings.

appropriability of technology The ability of an innovating firm to protect its technology from competitors and to obtain economic benefits from that technology.

appropriateness of monitoring (or control) systems Those systems that will not run counter to local practices, culture, and expectations.

appropriateness of technology The use of technology in production or processes that is in line with local skills and level of development.

attribution The process in which a person looks for an explanation of another person's behavior.

axiomatic appeals Negotiation appeals based on the ideals generally accepted in a society.

B2B Business-to-business electronic transactions.

B2C Business-to-consumer electronic transactions.

balance-sheet approach An approach to the compensation of expatriates that equalizes the standard of living between the host and home countries, plus compensation for inconvenience.

born global companies that start out with a global reach, typically by using their Internet capabilities.

CAFTA The U.S.-Central America Free Trade Agreement

chaebol South Korea's large industrial conglomerates of financially linked, and often family-linked, companies that do business among themselves whenever possible—for example, Daewoo.

checklist approach Measurement criteria to indicate changes in the creditworthiness of a country; ability to withstand economic volatility.

civil law The comprehensive set of laws organized into a code; laws are interpreted based on codes and statutes; used in Europe and Japan.

clustering Geographic concentrations of related, interdependent companies within an industry that use the same suppliers, labor, and distribution channels.

codetermination (mitbestimmung) The participation of labor in the management of a firm.

collective bargaining In the United States, for example, negotiations between a labor union local and management; in Sweden and Germany, for example, negotiations between the employer's organization and a trade union at the industry level.

collectivism The tendency of a society toward tight social frameworks, emotional dependence on belonging to an organization, and a strong belief in group decisions.

common law Law based on past court decisions and common custom (precedents); used in the United States and other countries of English origin.

communication The process of sharing meaning by transmitting messages through media such as words, behavior, or material artifacts.

comparative advantage A mutual benefit in the exchange of goods between countries, where each country exports those products in which it is relatively more efficient in production than other countries.

competitive advantage of nations The existence of conditions that give a country an advantage in a specific industry or in producing a particular good or service.

context in cultures (low to high) Low-context cultures, such as Germany, tend to use explicit means of communication in words and readily available information; high-context cultures, such as those in the Middle East, use more implicit means of communication, in which information is embedded in the non-verbal context and understanding of the people.

contract An agreement by the parties concerned to establish a set of rules to govern a business transaction.

control system appropriateness The use of control systems that are individually tailored to the practices and expectations of the host-country personnel.

convergence (of management styles, techniques, and so forth) The phenomenon of increasing similarity of leadership styles resulting from a blending of cultures and business practices through international institutions, as opposed to the **divergence** of leadership styles necessary for different cultures and practices.

core competencies Important corporate resources or skills that bring competitive advantages.

corporate social responsibility (CSR) The belief that corporate activities should take into consideration the welfare of the various stakeholders affected by those activities.

creeping expropriation A government's gradual and subtle action against foreign firms.

creeping incrementalism A process of increasing commitment of resources to one or more geographic regions.

creolization When countries fiercely protect their culture against outside influences and insist that immigrants assimilate into their society and respect their values.

cultural distance differences in values, languages, religion, trust.

cultural diffusion When immigrants adopt some aspects of the local culture while keeping aspects of their culture of origin.

cultural noise Cultural variables that undermine the communications of intended meaning.

cultural savvy A working knowledge of the cultural variables affecting management decisions.

cultural sensitivity (cultural empathy) A sense of awareness and caring about the culture of other people.

culture The shared values, understandings, assumptions, and goals that over time are passed on and imposed by members of a group or society.

culture shock A state of disorientation and anxiety that results from not knowing how to behave in an unfamiliar culture.

culture-specific reward systems Motivational and compensation approaches that reflect different motivational patterns across cultures.

degree of enforcement The relative degree of enforcement, in a particular country, of the law regarding business behavior, which therefore determines the lower limit of permissible behavior.

dependency (in managing political risk) Keeping the subsidiary and the host nation dependent on the parent corporation.

differentiation Focusing on and specializing in specific markets.

direct control The control of foreign subsidiaries and operations through the use of appropriate international staffing and structure policies and meetings with home-country executives (as compared with **indirect control**).

distinctive competencies Strengths that allow companies to outperform rivals.

divergence *See* **convergence**.

domestic multiculturalism The diverse makeup of the workforce comprising people from several different cultures in the home (domestic) company.

e-business The integration of systems, processes, organizations, value chains, and entire markets using Internet-based and related technologies and concepts.

e-commerce The selling of goods or services over the Internet.

e-commerce enablers Fulfillment specialists who provide other companies with services such as Web site translation.

economic distance Differences in level of development, natural or human resources, infrastructure, information, or knowledge.

economic risk The level of uncertainty about the ability of a country to meet its financial obligations.

environmental assessment The continuous process of gathering and evaluating information about variables and events around the world that may pose threats or opportunities to the firm.

environmental scanning The process of gathering information and forecasting relevant trends, competitive actions, and circumstances that will affect operations in geographic areas of potential interest.

ethical relativism An approach to social responsibility in which a country adopts the moral code of its host country.

ethnocentric approach An approach in which a company applies the morality used in its home country—regardless of the host country's system of ethics.

ethnocentric staffing approach An approach that fills key managerial positions abroad with persons from headquarters—that is, with parent-country nationals (PCNs).

ethnocentrism The belief that the management techniques used in one's own country are best no matter where or with whom they are applied.

expatriate One who works and lives in a foreign country but remains a citizen of the country where the employing organization is headquartered.

expressive-oriented conflict Conflict that is handled indirectly and implicitly, without clear delineation of the situation by the person handling it.

expropriation The seizure, with inadequate or no compensation, by a local government of the foreign-owned assets of an MNC.

Foreign Corrupt Practices Act A 1977 law that prohibits most questionable payments by U.S. companies to officials of foreign governments to gain business advantages.

foreign direct investment (FDI) Multinational firm's ownership, in part or in whole, of an operation in another country.

franchising An international entry strategy by which a firm (the franchiser) licenses its trademark, products, or services and operating principles to the franchisee in a host country for an initial fee and ongoing royalties.

fully owned subsidiary An overseas operation started or bought by a firm that has total ownership and control; starting or buying such an operation is often used as an entry strategy.

generalizability of leadership styles The ability (or lack of ability) to generalize leadership theory, research results, and effective leadership practices from one country to another.

geocentric staffing approach A staffing approach in which the best managers are recruited throughout the company or outside the company, regardless of nationality—often, third-country nationals (TCNs) are recruited.

geographical distance Remoteness, different time zones, weak transportation, or communication links.

global corporate culture An integration of the business environments in which firms currently operate, resulting from a dissolution of traditional boundaries and from increasing links among MNCs.

global functional structure Operations are integrated into the activities and responsibilities of each department to gain functional specialization and economies of scale.

globalism Global competition characterized by networks of international linkages that bind countries, institutions, and people in an interdependent global economy and a one-world market.

global geographic (area) structure Divisions are created to cover geographic regions; each regional manager is responsible for operations and performance of the countries within a given region.

globalization The global strategy of the integration of worldwide operations and the development of standardized products and marketing approaches.

global management The process of developing strategies, designing and operating systems, and working with people around the world to ensure sustained competitive advantage.

global management team Collection of managers in or from several countries who must rely on group collaboration if each member is to experience optimum success and goal achievement.

global product (divisional) structure A single product (or product line) is represented by a separate division; each division is headed by its own general manager; each is responsible for its own production and sales functions.

global staffing approach Staff recruited from within or outside of the company, regardless of nationality.

global strategic alliances Working partnerships that are formed around MNCs across national boundaries and often across industries.

governmentalism The tendency of a government to use its policy-setting role to favor national interests rather than relying on market forces.

guanxi The intricate, pervasive network of personal relations that every Chinese person carefully cultivates.

guanxihu A bond between specially connected firms, which generates preferential treatment to members of the network.

haptic Characterized by a predilection for the sense of touch.

hedging Companies may hedge their bets to reduce asset loss due to political risk by taking out insurance or using local debt financing, for example.

high-contact culture One in which people prefer to stand close, touch a great deal, and experience a "close" sensory involvement.

high-context communication One in which people convey messages indirectly and implicitly.

high-context cultures Those cultures where feelings and thoughts are not explicitly expressed; communication is implicit and as a function of the context and understanding of the person.

horizontal organization (dynamic network) A structural approach that enables the flexibility to be global and act local through horizontal coordination, shared power, and shared decision-making across international units and teams.

host-country national (HCN) A worker who is indigenous to the local country where the plant is located.

human capital Those direct or subcontracted employees whose labor becomes part of the value-added of the firm's product or service. MNCs are increasingly offshoring (outsourcing) that asset around the world in order to lower the cost of human capital

IJV control How a parent company ensures that the way a joint venture is managed conforms to its own interest.

indirect control The control of foreign operations through the use of reports, budgets, financial controls, and so forth. *See also* **direct control**.

individualism The tendency of people to look after themselves and their immediate families only and to value democracy, individual initiative, and personal achievement.

information privacy The right to control information about oneself.

information technology (IT) Electronic systems to convey information.

inpatriates Managers with global experience who are transferred to the organization's headquarters country.

instrumental-oriented conflict An approach to conflict in which parties tend to negotiate on the basis of factual information and logical analysis.

integration Coordination of markets.

intercultural communication Type of communication that occurs when a member of one culture sends a message to a receiver who is a member of another culture.

internal analysis Determines which areas of a firm's operations represent strengths or weaknesses (currently or potentially) compared to competitors.

internal versus external locus of control Beliefs regarding whether a person controls his own fate and events or they are controlled by external forces.

international business The profit-related activities conducted across national boundaries.

international business ethics The business conduct or morals of MNCs in their relationships to all individuals and entities with whom they come in contact when conducting business overseas.

international codes of conduct The codes of conduct of four major international institutions that provide some consistent guidelines for multinational enterprises relative to their moral approach to business behavior around the world.

international competitor analysis The process of assessing the competitive positions, goals, strategies, strengths, and weaknesses of competitors relative to one's own firm.

internationalization The process by which a firm gradually changes in response to the imperatives of international competition, domestic market saturation, desire for expansion, new markets, and diversification.

international joint venture (IJV) An overseas business owned and controlled by two or more partners; starting such a venture is often used as an entry strategy.

international management The process of planning, organizing, leading, and controlling in a multicultural or cross-cultural environment.

international management teams Collections of managers from several countries who must rely on group collaboration if each member is to achieve success.

international social responsibility The expectation that MNCs should be concerned about the social and economic effects of their decisions regarding activities in other countries.

Islamic law The dominant legal system in Islamic countries; based on religious beliefs, and followed in approximately 27 countries.

joint venture A new independent entity jointly created and owned by two or more parent companies.

keiretsu Large Japanese conglomerates of financially linked, and often family-linked, groups of companies, such as Mitsubishi, that do business among themselves whenever possible.

kibun Feelings and attitudes (Korean word).

kinesics Communication through body movements.

kinesic behavior Communication through posture, gestures, facial expressions, and eye contact.

knowledge management The process by which the firm integrates and benefits from the experiences and skills learned by its employees, for example when repatriating managers from the host country.

labor relations The process through which managers and workers determine their workplace relationships.

licensing An international entry strategy by which a firm grants the rights to a firm in the host country to produce or sell a product.

localization approach When firms focus on the local market needs for product or service characteristics, distribution, customer support, and so on.

low-context cultures Those societies where people convey their thoughts and plans in a direct, straightforward communication style; communication and information is explicit.

locus of decision making The relative level of decentralization in an organization—that is, the level at which decisions of varying importance can be made—ranging from all decisions made at headquarters to all made at the local subsidiary.

love–hate relationship An expression describing a common attitude of host governments toward MNC investment in their country—they love the economic growth that the MNC brings but hate the incursions on their independence and sovereignty.

low-contact culture Cultures that prefer much less sensory involvement, standing farther apart and touching far less; a "distant" style of body language.

low-context communication One in which people convey messages directly and explicitly.

macropolitical risk event An event that affects all foreign firms doing business in a country or region.

managing environmental interdependence The process by which international managers accept and enact their role in the preservation of ecological balance on the earth.

managing interdependence The effective management of a long-term MNC subsidiary–host-country relationship through cooperation and consideration for host concerns.

maquiladoras U.S. manufacturing or assembly facilities operating just south of the U.S.–Mexico border under special tax considerations.

masculinity The degree to which traditionally "masculine" values—assertiveness, materialism, and the like—prevail in a society.

material culture *See* **object language**.

matrix structure A hybrid organization of overlapping responsibilities.

micropolitical risk event An event that affects one industry or company or only a few companies.

MIS adequacy The ability to gather timely and accurate information necessary for international management, especially in less-developed countries.

monochronic cultures Those cultures in which time is experienced and used in a linear way; there is a past, present, and future, and time is treated as something to be spent, saved, wasted, and so on. *See also* **polychronic cultures**.

moral idealism The relative emphasis on long-term, ethical, and moral criteria for decisions versus short-term, cost-benefit criteria. *See also* **utilitarianism**.

moral universalism A moral standard toward social responsibility accepted by all cultures.

multicultural leader A person who is effective in inspiring and influencing the thinking, attitudes, and behavior of people from various cultural backgrounds.

multidomestic (or multi-local) strategy Emphasizing local markets, allowing more local responsiveness and specialization.

multinational corporation (MNC) A corporation that engages in production or service activities through its own affiliates in several countries, maintains control over the policies of those affiliates, and manages from a global perspective.

nationalism The practice by a country of rallying public opinion in favor of national goals and against foreign influences.

nationalization The forced sale of an MNC's assets to local buyers with some compensation to the firm, perhaps leaving a minority ownership with the MNC; often involves the takeover of an entire industry, such as the oil industry.

negotiation The process by which two or more parties meet to try to reach agreement regarding conflicting interests.

neutral versus affective Level of emotional orientation in relationships.

noise Anything that serves to undermine the communication of the intended meaning.

noncomparability of performance data across countries The control problem caused by the difficulty of comparing performance data across various countries because of the variables that make that information appear different.

nontask sounding (*nemawashi*) General, polite conversation and informal communication before meetings.

nonverbal communication (body language) The transfer of meaning through the use of body language, time, and space.

object language (material culture) How we communicate through material artifacts, whether architecture, office design and furniture, clothing, cars, or cosmetics.

objective–subjective decision-making approach The relative level of rationality and objectivity used in making decisions versus the level of subjective factors, such as emotions and ideals.

open systems model The view that all factors inside and outside a firm—environment, organization, and management—work together as a dynamic, interdependent system.

openness Traits such as open-mindeness, tolerance for ambiguity, and extrovertedness.

organizational culture (as different from societal culture) The norms and generally accepted ways of doing things within an organization.

outsourcing or offshoring The use of professional, skilled, or low-skilled workers located in countries other than that in which the firm is domiciled.

paralanguage How something is said rather than the content—the rate of speech, the tone and inflection of voice, other noises, laughing, or yawning.

parent-country national (PCN) An employee from the firm's home country sent to work in the firm's operations in another country (*see also* **expatriate**).

parochialism The expectation that "foreigners" should automatically fall into host-country patterns of behavior.

political risk The potential for governmental actions or politically motivated events to occur in a country that will adversely affect the long-run profitability or value of a firm.

polycentric staffing approach An MNC policy of using local host-country nationals (HCNs) to fill key positions in the host country.

polychronic cultures Those cultures that welcome the simultaneous occurrence of many things and emphasize involvement with people over specific time commitments or compartmentalized activities. *See also* **monochronic cultures**.

posturing General discussion that sets the tone for negotiation meetings.

power distance The extent to which subordinates accept unequal power and a hierarchical system in a company.

privatization The sale of government-owned operations to private investors.

projective cognitive similarity The assumption that others perceive, judge, think, and reason in the same way.

proxemics The distance between people (personal space) with which a person feels comfortable.

protectionism A country's use of tariff and nontariff barriers to partially or completely close its borders to various imported products that would compete with domestic products.

quantitative approach A means to develop a composite index used to monitor a country's creditworthiness and compare with other countries.

questionable payments Business payments that raise significant ethical issues about appropriate moral behavior in either a host nation or other nations.

regiocentric staffing approach An approach in which recruiting for international managers is done on a regional basis and may comprise a specific mix of PCNs, HCNs, and TCNs.

regionalization strategy The global corporate strategy that links markets within regions and allows managers in each region to formulate their own regional strategy and cooperate as quasi-independent subsidiaries.

regulatory environment The many laws and courts of the nation in which an international manager works.

relationship building The process of getting to know one's contacts in a host country and building mutual trust before embarking on business discussions and transactions.

repatriation The process of the reintegration of expatriates into the headquarters organization and career ladder as well as into the social environment.

resilience Traits such as having an internal locus of control, persistence, a tolerance of ambiguity, and resourcefulness.

reverse culture shock A state of disorientation and anxiety that results from returning to one's own culture.

ringi system "Bottom-up" decision-making process used in Japanese organizations.

self-reference criterion An unconscious reference to one's own cultural values; understanding and relating to others only from one's own cultural frame of reference.

separation The retention of distinct identities by minority groups unwilling or unable to adapt to the dominant culture.

specific or diffuse Relative level of privacy in relationships.

stages model *See* **structural evolution**.

stereotyping The assumption that every member of a society or subculture has the same characteristics or traits, without regard to individual differences.

strategic alliances Partnerships between two or more firms that decide they can better pursue their mutual goals by combining their resources and competitive advantages.

strategic alliances (global) Working partnerships between MNCs across national boundaries and often across industries.

strategic business unit (SBU) A self-contained business within a company with its own functional departments and accounting systems.

strategic freedom of an IJV The relative amount of control that an international joint venture will have, compared with the parents, in choosing suppliers, product lines, customers, and so on.

strategic implementation The process by which strategic plans are realized through the establishment of a *system of fits* throughout an organization with the desired strategy—for example, in organizational structure, staffing, and operations.

strategic planning The process by which a firm's managers consider the future prospects for their company and evaluate and decide on strategy to achieve long-term objectives.

strategy The basic means by which a company competes: the choice of business or businesses in which it operates and how it differentiates itself from its competitors in those businesses.

structural evolution (stages model) The stages of change in an organizational structure that follow the evolution of the internationalization process.

subcultures Groups within a societal culture that differ in some degree from one another.

subculture shock A state of disorientation and anxiety that results from the unfamiliar circumstances and behaviors encountered when exposed to a different cultural group in a country than one the person is familiar with.

SWOT analysis An assessment of a firm's capabilities (strengths and weaknesses) relative to those of its competitors as pertinent to the opportunities and threats in the environment for those firms.

subsidiary A business incorporated in a foreign country in which the parent corporation holds an ownership position.

sustainability The ability for firms to operate on the principles of sustainable development.

sustainable development Business activities that meet the needs of the stakeholders in the present while also protecting and sustaining future needs for human and natural resources.

synergy The greater level of effectiveness that can result from combined group effort than from the total of each individual's efforts alone.

technoglobalism A phenomenon in which the rapid developments in information and communication technologies (ICTs) are propelling globalization and vice versa.

terrorism The use of, or threat to use, violence for ideological or political purposes.

third-country nationals (TCNs) Employees hired from a country other than the headquarters or the host country of a firm's activities.

transnational corporations (TNCs) Multinational corporations that are truly globalizing by viewing the world as one market and crossing boundaries for whatever functions or resources are most efficiently available; structural coordination reflects the ability to integrate globally while retaining local flexibility; typically owned and managed by nationals from different countries.

transpatriate A term similar to expatriates but referring to managers who may be from any country other than that in which the firm is domiciled, and who tend to work in several countries over time—that is, a manager who has no true corporate "home."

turnkey operation When a company designs and constructs a facility abroad, trains local personnel, and turns the key over to local management, for a fee.

uncertainty avoidance The extent to which people feel threatened by ambiguous situations; in a company, this results in formal rules and processes to provide more security.

universalism versus particularism The relative obligation towards an objective application of rules, versus a more personal and individual application.

utilitarianism The relative emphasis on short-term cost-benefit (utilitarian) criteria for decisions versus those of long-term, ethical, and moral concerns. *See also* **moral idealism**.

values A person or group's ideas and convictions about what is important, good or bad, right or wrong.

virtual global teams Employees in various locations around the world who coordinate their work and decisions through teleconferencing, e-mail, and so on.

work centrality The degree of general importance that working has in the life of an individual at any given time.

workforce diversity The phenomenon of increasing ethnic diversity in the workforce in the United States and many other countries because of diverse populations and joint ventures; this results in intercultural working environments in domestic companies.

works council In Germany, an employee group that shares plant-level responsibility with managers.

World Trade Organization (WTO) A formal structure for continued negotiations to reduce trade barriers and settling trade disputes.

Notes

Chapter 1

1. World Economic Forum, http://reports.weforum.org/global-risks-2012/; Eric Pfanner, "Divining the Business and Political Risks of 2012," *The International Herald Tribune*, January 11, 2012; Financial Times reporters, "Across the Zone: Member States Finances Dissected," *Financial Times*, September 22, 2011.
2. Peter Gumbel, "Behind the Global Markets' Meltdown," *Time*, October 8, 2008.
3. Bill Powell, "When Supply Chains Break," *Fortune*, 164, no. 10 (December 26, 2011): 29–32.
4. Carlos Ghosn, quoted in *Fortune, December 26, 2011*.
5. "Half of the global growth now comes from emerging markets," Robert Zoellick, President World Bank, September 19, 2011, interviewed on *PBS Newshour*.
6. R. Atkins, A. Beattie, "Global trade growth slows sharply," *Financial Times*, London (UK), September 23, 2011, 3.
7. Thomas L. Friedman, *The World is Flat* (New York: Farrar, Strauss and Giroux, 2005): 5.
8. Ramamurti, R., Singh, J., 2009. *Emerging Multinationals in* Emerging Markets. Cambridge: Cambridge University Press.
9. H. L. Sirkin, J. W. Hemerling, and A. K. Bhattacharya, *Globality*, Boston Consulting Group, 2008. New York: Hachette Book Group.
10. Pankaj Ghemawat, *Redefining Global Strategy*, Harvard Business School Publishing Corporation, 2007.
11. Pankaj Ghemawat, "Remapping Your Strategic Mindset," *McKinsey Quarterly*, August, 2011.
12. Rana Foroohar, "Why the World Isn't Getting Smaller," *Time*, June 27, 2011, 20.
13. Peter Bisson, Elizabeth Stephenson, and S. Patrick Viguerie, "Global Forces: An Introduction," *McKinsey Quarterly*, June, 2010.
14. Ibid.
15. Bettinna Wassener, "Nestle to Buy Control of China's Biggest Confectioner," *The New York Times Online Dealbook*, July 11, 2011.
16. Paul Sullivan, "Latin America, the Land of Opportunity and Caution," www.nytimes.com, December 2, 2011.
17. Stephen Wagstyl, "Globalization Cuts Both Ways," www.FT.com, September 15, 2011.
18. *www.atkearney.com*, accessed June 27, 2012.
19. Fareed Zakaria, *The Post-American World*. New York: Norton, 2008.
20. "The World's Largest Corporations," *Fortune International (Europe)*, 07385587, July 25, 2011, Vol. 164, Issue 2.
21. "A Bigger World," *The Economist*, September 20, 2008.
22. P. Stephens, "A Perilous Collision Between Nationalism and Globalisation," *Financial Times*, March 3, 2006.
23. Joseph E. Stiglitz, *Making Globalization Work*, New York: Norton, 2006.
24. Daniel Gross, "Is America Losing at Globalization?" *Newsweek*, September 8, 2008, 66.
25. Peter Coy, *BusinessWeek*, July 31, 2008.
26. Section contributed by Charles M. Byles, Virginia Commonwealth University, April 3, 2009.
27. Europa: European Union institutions and other bodies, "The European Commission," Retrieved March 30, 2009, http://europa.eu/institutions/inst/comm/index_en.htm
28. Matthew de Paula, "Do You Really Drive an American Car?" *MSN Autos*, January 5, 2011.
29. J. Sapsford and Norihiko Shirouzu, "Mom, Apple Pie and . . . Toyota?" *The Wall Street Journal*, May 11, 2006.
30. David E. Sanger, Jeff Zeleny, and Bill Vlasic, "GM to Seek Bankruptcy and a New Start," www.nytimes.com, May 31, 2009.
31. Charlie Rose talks to Cisco's John Chambers. By: Rose, Charlie, *Bloomberg Businessweek*, 00077135, April 23, 2012, Issue 4276.
32. Rana Foroohar, "Companies Are the New Countries," *Time*, February 13, 2012.
33. *The Economist*, September 20, 2008.
34. J. L. Levere, "A Small Company, a Global Approach," www.nytimes.com, January 1, 2004.
35. www.groupon.com; Evelyn Rusli, "As Investors Flee, Outlook for IPOs Darkens," www.nytimes.com, January 16, 2012; *"60 Minutes,"* CBS Interview.
36. Financial Times reporters, "Across the Zone: Member States Finances Dissected," *Financial Times,* September 22, 2011.
37. Ibid.
38. Excerpts from interviews on the PBS *Newshour*, February 8, 2012.
39. *Global Competitiveness Report 2011–12*, www.worldeconomicforum.org, September 16, 2011.
40. George Parker and Quentin Peel, "A Fractured Europe," *Financial Times*, September 17, 2003, 15.
41. U.S. Department of Commerce, www.export.gov, accessed September 16, 2011.
42. Eric Beinhocker, Ian Davis, and Lenny Mendonca, "The Ten Trends You Have to Watch," *Harvard Business Review* 87, no. 7/8 (2009): 55–60.
43. *James C. Cooper*, "A Resurgent Asia Will Lead the Global Recovery," *BusinessWeek,* 4140, (2009): 16.
44. FT Summer School, "China: Rough But Ready for Outsiders," *Financial Times,* August 26, 2003.
45. Zachary Karabell, "Staying on Track," www.time.com, Monday, July 18, 2011.
46. Charlie Rose talks to Cisco's John Chambers. By: Rose, Charlie, *Bloomberg Businessweek*, 00077135, April 23, 2012, Issue 4276.
47. Heather Dale, "Renminbi pauses for breather as GDP growth slows: China," *Financial Times*. London (UK), April 2, 2012, 7.
48. Vicki Needham, "Report: US exports to China surpass $100 billion," http://thehill.com/blogs/on-the-money/1005-trade/218513-report-us-exports-to-china-surpass-100-billion, March 27, 2012.
49. Sources for this section include: Karabell, 2011; U.S. Department of Commerce: *Doing Business in China—2011 Country Commercial Guide for U.S. Companies,* www.export.gov, accessed September 20, 2011; Keith Bradsher, "China Plans to Bolster its Slowing Economy," www.nytimes.com, October 21, 2008; Jim Yardley and Keith Bradsher, "China, an Engine of Growth, Faces a Global Slump," www.nytimes.com, October 23, 2008; CEQ on FT.com: "Large and in charge," by Arthur Kroeber and Rosealea Yao, July 14 2008; Fareed Zakaria, *The Post American World* (New York: Norton, 2008); www.worldeconomicforum.gov, accessed October 20, 2008; Thomas Friedman, *The World Is Flat* (New York: Farrar, Straus and Giroux, 2005); Tony Fang, Verner Worm, Rosalie L. Tung, "Changing success and failure factors in business negotiations with the PRC," *International Business Review* 17, no. 2 (2008).
50. Keith Bradsher, "China-U.S. Trade Dispute Has Broad Implications," www.nytimes.com, September 15, 2009.
51. Scott Cendrowski, "China Takes the Lead," *Fortune* 160, no. 5 (2009): 24.
52. Anon, "China at 7.5%." *Wall Street Journal,* March 10, 2012, A.12.
53. U.S. Department of Commerce: *Doing Business in China—2011 Country Commercial Guide for U.S. Companies*, www.export.gov, accessed September 20, 2011.
54. Simon Rabinovitch in Beijing, "Chinese foreign exchange reserves shrink," www.ft.com/asia, January 13, 2012.
55. Hookway, J. et al., "China's Wage Hikes Ripple Across Asia," *Wall Street Journal,* (March 14, 2012), pp. A1–A10.
56. Press Release, www.bcg.com, April 20, 2012.
57. Xu, C. (2011). The fundamental institutions of China's reforms and development. *Journal of Economic Literature,* Vol. 49, No. 4, pp. 1076–1151.
58. U.S. Department of Commerce, September 20, 2011.
59. U.S. Department of Commerce: "Doing Business with India," www.export.gov, September 21, 2011.
60. Vikas Bajaj, "India's Tax Plan Troubles Foreign Investors," www.nytimes.com, April 6, 2012.
61. "Family firms: The Bollygarchs' magic mix," *The Economist*, 401. 8756, (October 22, 2011).
62. "State-controlled firms: The power and the glory," *The Economist*, 401. 8756. (October. 22, 2011): 17.
63. "A Second-best Choice," *The Economist*, September 6, 2008.
64. U.S. Department of Commerce: "Doing Business in Mexico," www.export.gov, accessed September 26, 2011.

65. "World Briefing," *Time,* July 2, 2012.

66. A.T. Kearney 2012 FDI Confidence Index.

67. www.wikipedia.org, May 27, 2006.

68. Geri Smith, "Look Who's Pumping out Engineers," *Business Week* (May 22, 2006): 42–43.

69. John Paul Rathbone, "South America's Giant comes of Age," www.FT.com, June 28, 2010.

70. www.wola.org/economic/cafta/htm, May 13, 2006.

71. B. Appelbaum and J. Steinhauer, "Congress Ends 5-year Standoff on Trade Deals in Rare Accord," www.nytimes, October 12, 2011.

72. Associated Press, "Coca-Cola, Bottler Plan to Invest $3B in Russia," *New York Times,* September 26, 2011.

73. Camilla Hall, "Signs of recovery in M&A," *Financial Times,* London (UK), September 22, 2011, 11.

74. Ibid.

75. Khalid Abdulla-Janahi, Chairman of Ithmaar Bank and Co-Chair of the World Economic Forum on the Middle East.

76. Dambisa Moyo, *"Beijing, a Boon for Africa,"* www.nytimes.com, June 27, 2012.

77. Roger Cohen, "The Age of Possibility," *International Herald Tribune,* January 6, 2011.

78. www.statisticssa.gov.za, accessed February 1, 2009.

79. U.S. Department of Commerce, "Doing Business in South Africa," www.export.gov, accessed September 30, 2011.

80. N. Itano, "South African Companies Fill a Void," www.nytimes.com, November 4, 2003.

81. Sources for this section include: www.intel.com; John Boudreau, *San Jose Mercury News,* April 17, 2008; Daniel Altman, "Peeking under the surface of globalization," *International Herald Tribune,* May 4, 2007; Intel Plant Put Vietnam on High-Tech Map, *Bloomberg News*—October 29, 2010.

82. *Bloomberg News*—*October 29, 2010.*

83. Adriana Gardella, "A Company Grows, and Builds a Plant Back in the U.S.A.," *The New York Times,* October 12, 2011.

84. Dexter Roberts, "Where Made-in-China Textiles Are Emigrating," www.bloombergbusinessweek.com, January 12, 2012.

85. Friedman, 6.

86. Heather Timmons, "Obama's Plan on Corporate Taxes Unnerves the Indian Outsourcing Industry," www.nytimes.com, May 6, 2009.

87. "Technology," *Bloomberg BusinessWeek,* September 5–11, 2011.

88. J. Fox, "Where Your Job Is Going," *Fortune,* November 24, 2003, 84–87.

89. Sol E. Solomon, "India's IT Services Sector Reassesses Itself," *BusinessWeek ZD Net Asia,* September 19, 2008.

90. *The Economist,* September 20, 2008.

91. M. Schuman, "Your New Job: Made in India or China," *Time,* March 28, 2011.

92. www.A.T.Kearney, accessed September 12, 2008.

93. 2011 *Aon Global Risk Management Survey,* www.aon.com, accessed October 4, 2011.

94. Ibid.

95. Aon Risk Solutions, 2011.

96. Keith Bradsher, "China Consolidates Grip on Rare Earths," www.nytimes.com, September 15, 2011.

97. Ibid.

98. Raphael Minder and Simon Romero, "Spain Weighs Response to Nationalization of YPF," www.nytimes.com, April 17, 2012.

99. Clifford J. Levy, "In Hard Times, Russia Tries to Reclaim Industries," www.nytimes.com, December 8, 2008.

100. E. F. Micklous, "Tracking the Growth and Prevalence of International Terrorism," in *Managing Terrorism: Strategies for the Corporate Executive,* eds. P. J. Montana and G. S. Roukis (Westport, CT: Quorum Books, 1983), 3.

101. W. Shreeve, "Be Prepared for Political Changes Abroad," *Harvard Business Review,* (July–August 1984): 111–118.

102. G. M. Taoka and D. R. Beeman, *International Business* (New York: HarperCollins, 1991) p. 112.

103. Ibid.

104. B. O'Reilly, "Business Copes with Terrorism," *Fortune,* January 6, 2004, 48.

105. Heritage Foundation, http//www.heritage.org, accessed August 8, 2011.

106. F. John Mathis, "International Risk Analysis," in *Global Business Management in the 1990s,* ed. R. T. Moran (Washington, DC: Beacham, 1990), 33–44.

107. Rahul Jacob, "Asian Infrastructure: The Biggest Bet on Earth," *Fortune,* October 31, 1994, 139–46.

108. Chris Nicholson, "Bringing the Internet to Remote African Villages," February 1, 2009.

109. World Economic Forum: *2011 Global Information Technology Report.*

110. Choe Sang Hun, "I. H. T. Special Report: Smart Cities—No Rest for the Wired," *http://global.nytimes.com/?iht,* October 1, 2011.

111. Press Release, www.pg.com, accessed October 21, 2011.

112. Jack Goldsmith and Tim Wu, *Who Controls the Internet? Illusions of a Borderless World* (London: Oxford UP, 2006).

113. Hans Dieter Zimmerman, "E-Business," www.businessmedia.org, June 13, 2000.

114. J. Rajesh, "Five E-Business Trends," Net.Columns, www.indialine.com, February 18, 1999.

115. "Europe's Borderless Market: The Net," www.businessweek.com, May 17, 2003.

116. "E-Management," *The Economist,* November 11, 2000, 32–34.

117. "E-commerce Report, *New York Times,* March 26, 2001, 7–8.

118. S. Mohanbir and M. Sumant, "Go Global," *Business 2.0,* May 2000, 178–213.

119. A. Chen and M. Hicks, "Going Global? Avoid Culture Clashes," *PC Week,* April 3, 2000, 9–10.

120. Steve Muylle, Niraj Dawar, Deva Rangarajan, "B2B Brand Architecture," *California Management Review,* Vol. 54, No. 2, Winter 2012.

121. B2B Directory, www.Forbes.com, accessed March 29, 2012.

Chapter 2

1. A. Maitland, "No Hiding Place for the Irresponsible Business," *Financial Times Special Report,* September 29, 2003, 4.

2. Theo Vermaelen, "An Innovative Approach to Funding CSR Projects," *Harvard Business Review,* June 2011, Vol. 89, Issue 6, 28–29.

3. Heather Timmons, "For Now, Ikea Gives More than it Gets from India," www.nytimes.com, September 10, 2010.

4. T. A. Frank, "Whipping Wal-Mart Into Shape: There's new pressure on the chain to clean up its record with foreign suppliers," *The New Republic,* June 7, 2012.

5. http://gothamist.com/2011/05/31/wal-mart_faces_tough_labor_question.php, accessed April 18, 2012.

6. http://www.ufcw.org/makingchange/shareholder.cfm, accessed April 18, 2012.

7. S. Clifford, "Walmart Is Being Pressured to Disclose How Suppliers Treat Workers," www.nytimes.com, May 30, 2011.

8. P. S. Goodman, "Chinese Workers Pay for Wal-Mart's Low Prices," www.washingtonpost.com, February 23, 2004.

9. Clifford.

10. Milton Friedman, *Capitalism and Freedom* (Chicago: University of Chicago Press, 1962).

11. Eduardo Porter, "Dividends Emerge in Pressing Apple Over Working Conditions in China," www.nytimes.com, March 6, 2012.

12. Ibid.

13. T. Donaldson, "Defining the Value of Doing Good Business," *Financial Times,* June 3, 2005.

14. Heather Timmons, "Ikea Expects to Double Buying of Goods from India," www.nytimes.com, September 21, 2010.

15. Amol Sharma and Jens Hansegard, "Ikea Says It Is Ready to Give India a Try," *The Wall Street Journal,* June 25, 2012, p. B.1.

16. Based on Manuela Weber, "The Business Case for Corporate Social Responsibility: A Company-Level Measurement Approach for CSR," *European Management Journal* 26, no. 4. (2008): 247–261.

17. *Financial Times,* June 3, 2005.

18. Weber, 2008.

19. N. Bowie, "The Moral Obligations of Multinational Corporations," in *Problems of International Justice,* ed. Steven Luper-Foy (New York: Westview Press: 1987), 97–113.

20. Steven Greenhouse, "Nike Agrees to Help Laid-Off Workers in Honduras," www.nytimes.com, July 26, 2011.

21. Michael E. Porter and Mark R. Kramer, "Creating Shared Value," *Harvard Business Review,* 00178012, (January-February 2011), 89, no. 1/2.

22. Ibid.

23. Ibid.

24. Eric Pfanner, "Google Turns on Charms to Win over Europeans," www.nytimes.com, May 15, 2011.

25. Ibid.

26. Peter Burrows, "Stalking High-Tech Sweatshops," *BusinessWeek,* June 19, 2006, p. 63.

27. Jem Bendell, "Nike Says Time to Team Up," *The Journal of Corporate Citizenship,* Autumn 2005 i19, p. 10(3).

28. Sharon Lafraniere, Michael Wines, and Edward Wong, "China Reins in Liberalization of Culture," www.nytimes.com, October 26, 2011.

29. Ford, Peter, China's human rights 'action plan' short on any action, say rights groups, *The Christian Science Monitor* (Boston, Mass.), January 11, 2011.

30. www.transparencyinternational.org, accessed June 22, 2011.

31. Steven Greenhouse, "A.F.L.-C.I.O. Files a Trade Complaint against China's Labor Practices," *New York Times,* June 9, 2006.

32. LaFraniere et al., October 26, 2011.

33. John Gapper, "Google Is Putting its Own Freedoms at Risk in China," *Financial Times,* January 20, 2006.

34. R. Waters, M. Dickie, and S. Kirchgaessner, "Evildoers? How the West's Net Vanguard Toils Behind the Great Firewall of China," *Financial Times,* February 15, 2006.

35. M. Dickie, "Amnesty Accuses Web Groups over Human Rights in China," *Financial Times,* July 20, 2006.

36. Po Keung Ip, "The Challenge of Developing a Business Ethics in China," *Journal of Business Ethics* (2009) 88:211–224.

37. Ibid.

38. *BusinessWeek,* June 19, 2006, 63.

39. "Sweatshop Police," *BusinessWeek,* October 20, 1997, 30–32.

40. Kathleen A. Getz, "International Codes of Conduct: An Analysis of Ethical Reasoning," *Journal of Business Ethics* 9 (1990): 567–77.

41. Alison Maitland, "How Ethics Codes Can Be Made to Work," *Financial Times,* March 7, 2005.

42. Swee Hoon Ang, "The Power of Money: A Cross-Cultural Analysis of Business-Related Beliefs," *Journal of World Business* 35, no. 1 (2000): 43.

43. C. J. Robertson and W. F. Crittenden, "Mapping Moral Philosophies: Strategic Implications for Multinational Firms," *Strategic Management Journal* 24 (2003): 385–392.

44. A. Singer, "Ethics—Are Standards Lower Overseas?" *Across the Board* (September 1991): 31–34.

45. Ibid.

46. www.transparencyinternational.org, accessed June 17, 2011.

47. Ibid.

48. James Kanter, "Europe Leads in Pushing for Privacy of User Data," *New York Times,* May 3, 2011.

49. Ibid.

50. Reena SenGupta, "Trouble at Home for Overseas Bribes," *Financial Times,* February 2, 2006.

51. Ibid.

52. Gardiner Harris, "Johnson and Johnson Settles Bribery Complaint," www.nytimes.com, April 8, 2011.

53. G. R. Laczniak and J. Naor, "Global Ethics: Wrestling with the Corporate Conscience," *Business,* July–August–September 1985, 152.

54. "How to Respond When Only Bribe Money Talks," *Financial Times,* July 11, 2005.

55. J. T. Noonan, Jr., *Bribes* (New York: Macmillan, 1984), ii.

56. Barney Jopson, "Mexico opens investigation into Walmart store permits," *Financial Times.* London (UK), April 26, 2012: 14.

57. Leslie Wayne, "Hits, and Misses, in the War on Bribery," *The New York Times,* March 10, 2012.

58. The United States Department of Justice, http://www.justice.gov/criminal/fraud/fcpa/, accessed July 20, 2012.

59. Ibid.

60. SenGupta.

61. M. Saltmarsh, "U.S. Sees Improved Cooperation on Fighting Bribery," www.nytimes, October 14, 2010.

62. SenGupta.

63. M. E. Shannon, "Coping with Extortion and Bribery," in *Multinational Managers and Host Government Interactions,* ed. Lee A. Tavis (South Bend, IN: University of Notre Dame Press, 1988).

64. "Oil, politics and corruption," *The Economist,* September 20, 2008, 20.

65. Ibid.

66. Marc J. Epstein, A. R. Buhovac, and K. Yuthas, "Why Nike Kicks Butt in Sustainability," *Organizational Dynamics* 39, 353–356.

67. P. W. Beamish et al., *International Management* (Homewood, IL: Irwin, 1991).

68. Based on Asheghian and Ebrahimi, *International Business* (NY: Harper and Row, 1990).

69. R. H. Mason and R. S. Spich, *Management: An International Perspective* (Homewood, IL: Irwin, 1987).

70. R. T. De George, *Competing with Integrity in International Business* (New York: Oxford University Press, 1993), 3–4.

71. Hilary Bradbury-Huang, "Sustainability by Collaboration: The SEER Case," *Organizational Dynamics* 39, Issue 4, October-December 2010, 335–344.

72. György Málovics, Noémi Nagypál Csigéné, and Sascha Kraus, "The Role of Corporate Social Responsibility in Strong Sustainability," *Journal of Socio-Economics* 37, no. 3, (2008): 907–918.

73. J. A. G. van Kleef and N. J. Roome, "Developing Capabilities and Competence for Sustainable Business Management as Innovation: a Research Agenda," *Journal of Cleaner Production* 15 (2007): 38–51.

74. Philip Mirvis, Bradley Googins, and Sylvia Kinnicutt, "Vision, mission, values: Guideposts to Sustainability," *Organizational Dynamics* 39, issue 4, October–December 2010, 316–324.

75. "The business of sustainability: McKinsey Global Survey results," *McKinsey Quarterly,* October 2011.

76. Ibid.

77. Ibid.

78. B. Atkins, "Corporate Social Responsibility: Is it 'Irresponsibility'?" *Corporate Governance Advisor* 14 (2006): 28–29.

79. *Newshour with Jim Lehrer,* PBS news report, November 17, 2008.

80. Ibid.

81. Ibid.

82. Ibid.

83. Jang B. Singh and V. C. Lakhan, "Business Ethics and the International Trade in Hazardous Wastes," *Journal of Business Ethics* 8 (1989): 889–899.

84. Philip Mirvis, Bradley Googins, and Sylvia Kinnicutt, "Vision, mission, values; Guideposts to Sustainability," *Organizational Dynamics* 39, issue 4, October–December 2010, 316–324.

85. Ibid.

86. Steven Mufson, "Federal report lays bulk of fault for gulf oil spill on BP," *The Washington Post* (Washington, D.C.) February 18, 2011: 18.

87. D. Minor, J. Morgan, "CSR as Reputation Insurance: Primum Non Nocere," *California Management Review,* 53, 3, Spring 2011.

88. Jem Bendell, "World Review: July–September 2010," *The Journal of Corporate Citizenship,* Winter 2010; 40.

89. T. E. Graedel and B. R. Allenby, *Industrial Ecology* (Upper Saddle River, NJ: Prentice Hall, 1995).

90. P. Asheghian and B. Ebrahimi, *International Business* (New York: Harper and Row, 1990), 640–641.

91. Linda M. Castellito, "TerraCycle founder's journey started with worm poop: Even the book about the company is green," *USA Today,* July 27, 2009: 5; Blair Koch, "The business of being green," *McClatchy-Tribune Business News* (Washington), April 22, 2011; Victoria Vizcarra, *BusinessWorld* (Philippines): "SPECIAL FEATURE: LEED-Certified Properties," May 31, 2011; "Terra-Cycle Inc., Garbage In, Products Out," *Retail-Merchandiser.com,* November–December, 2011; Heidi Neck, Candida Brush, and Elaine Allen, "The landscape of social entrepreneurship," *Business Horizons,* 2009, 52: 13.9.

92. *Business World,* 2011.

93. *Retail-Merchandiser.com,* 2011.

94. *Tribune Business News,* 2011.

95. Ibid.

96. *Business World,* 2011.

97. *Business Horizons.*

98. *Business Horizons.*

99. Marc J. Epstein and Adriana Rejc Buhovac, "Solving the Sustainability Implementation Challenge," *Organizational Dynamics* 39, (2010), 306–315.

100. Marc J. Epstein, "Implementing Corporate Sustainability: Measuring and Managing Social and Environmental Impacts," *Strategic Finance,* January 2008.

Chapter 3

1. P. Christopher Earley and Elaine Mosakowski, "Cultural Intelligence," *Harvard Business Review,* 82 (10), October 2004, 139–146.

2. Earley, P. C., & Ang, S. *Cultural intelligence: Individual interactions across cultures.* (Palo Alto, CA: Stanford University, 2003). Press.

3. David A. Ricks, *Big Business Blunders: Mistakes in Multinational Marketing* (Homewood, IL: Dow Jones–Irwin, 1983).

4. Carla Joinson, "Why HR Managers Need to Think Globally," *HR Magazine* (April, 1998): 2–7.

5.

6. J. Stewart Black and Mark Mendenhall, "Cross-Cultural Training Effectiveness: A Review and a Theoretical Framework for Future Research," *Academy of Management Review* 15, no. 1 (1990): 113–136.

7. V. Taras, et al., Three decades of research on national culture in the workplace, *Organizational Dynamics* (2011), doi:10.1016/j.orgdyn.2011.04.006.

8. Geert Hofstede, *Culture's Consequences: International Differences in Work-Related Values* (Beverly Hills, CA: Sage Publications, 1980), 25; E. T. Hall, *The Silent Language* (Greenwich, CT: Fawcett, 1959). For a more detailed definition of the culture of a society, see A. L. Kroeber and C. Kluckholhn, "A Critical Review of Concepts and Definitions," in *Peabody Museum Papers* 47, no. 1 (Cambridge, MA: Harvard University Press, 1952), 181.

9. David Dressler and Donald Carns, *Sociology, The Study of Human Interaction* (New York: Knopf, 1969), 56–57.

10. Maia de la Baume and Steven Erlanger, "Social and economic ills feed rise of a far-right party in France," www.nytimes.com, March 27, 2011.

11. Hofstede.

12. Syed Anwar, "DaimlerChrysler AG: A Decade of Global Strategic Challenges Leads to Divorce in 2007," Case Study, in Helen Deresky, *Managing Across Borders and Cultures,* 6th ed., Upper Saddle River, NJ: Prentice Hall, 325–337.

13. Emma Jacobs, "20 questions: Kenichi Watanabe, Nomura: 'I don't like to analyse myself,'" *Financial Times*, London (UK), September 23, 2011: 12.

14. Lane Kelley, Arthur Whatley, and Reginald Worthley, "Assessing the Effects of Culture on Managerial Attitudes: A Three-Culture Test," *Journal of International Business Studies* (Summer 1987): 17–31.

15. Oded Shenkar, "Cultural Distance Revisited: Towards a More Rigorous Conceptualization and Measurement of Cultural Differences," *Journal of International Business,* (43), 1, January 2012, pp. 1–11.

16. Ibid.

17. Jangho Lee, T. W. Roehl, and Soonkyoo Choe, "What Makes Management Style Similar and Distinct Across Borders? Growth Experience and Culture in Korean and Japanese Firms," *Journal of International Business Studies* 31, no. 4 (2000): 631–52.

18. C. Sanchez-Runde, et al., "Looking beyond Western leadership models," *Organizational Dynamics* (2011), doi:10.1016/ j.orgdyn.2011.04.008, in press.

19. E. T. Hall, "The Silent Language in Overseas Business," *Harvard Business Review* (May–June 1960).

20. "One Big Market," *Wall Street Journal*, February 6, 1989, 16.

21. Baruch Shimoni, "The representation of cultures in international and cross cultural management: Hybridizations of management cultures in Thailand and Israel," *Journal of International Management* 17 (2011), 30–41.

22. Ibid.

23. Ibid.

24. Philip R. Harris and Robert T. Moran, *Managing Cultural Differences* (Houston: Gulf Publishing, 1987).

25. Data from various sources, including U.S. Census Bureau's International Data Base, U.S. State Department Reports, U.N. Human Development Report.

26. Agam Nag, "Cross Cultural Management: An Indian Perspective," *The Business Review, Cambridge* 17.2 (Summer 2011): 255–260.

27. Ibid.

28. Ibid.

29. A. Ali, "The Islamic Work Ethic in Arabia," *Journal of Psychology* 126 (1992): 507–19.

30. "Buddhism in the Thai Workplace," www.businesstrendsasia.com, accessed February 10, 2012.

31. Mansour Javidan and Robert J. House, "Cultural Acumen for the Global Manager: Lessons from Project GLOBE," *Organizational Dynamics* (Spring 2001): 289–305.

32. V. Gupta, P. J. Hanges, and P. Dorfman, "Cultural Clusters: Methodology and Findings," *Journal of World Business* 37 (2002): 11–15.

33. Ibid.

34. Taras et al., 2011.

35. Geert Hofstede, *Cultures and Organizations: Software of the Mind* (New York: McGraw-Hill, 1997), 79–108.

36. K. Roth, T. Kostova, M. Dakhli, "Exploring cultural misfit: Causes and consequences," *International Business Review,* 20 (2011), 15–26.

37. Elizabeth Weldon and Elisa L. Mustari, "Felt Dispensability in Groups of Coactors: The Effects of Shared Responsibility on Cognitive Effort" (unpublished manuscript, Kellogg Graduate School of Management, Northwestern University).

38. P. Christopher Earley, "Social Loafing and Collectivism: A Comparison of the United States and the People's Republic of China," *Administrative Science Quarterly* 34 (1989): 565–81.

39. H. K. Steensma, L. Marino, and K. M. Weaver, "Attitudes towards Cooperative Strategies: A Cross-Cultural Analysis of Entrepreneurs," *Journal of International Business Studies* 31, no. 4 (2000): 591–609.

40. G. Hofstede, *Culture's Consequences: Comparing Values, Behaviors, Institutions, and Organizations Across Nations,* 2nd ed (Thousand Oaks, CA: Sage, 2001), 500–502.

41. F. Trompenaars, *Riding the Waves of Culture* (London: Nicholas Brealey, 1993).

42. L. Hoeklin, *Managing Cultural Differences: Strategies for Competitive Advantage* (New York: The Economist Intelligence Unit/Addison-Wesley, 1995).

43. P. Steel and V. Taras, "Culture as a consequence: A multi-level multivariate meta-analysis of the effects of individual and country characteristics on work-related cultural values," *Journal of International Management,* 16 (2010) 211–233.

44. Ibid.

45. Ibid.

46. M. Muethel and M. Hoegl, "Cultural and societal influences on shared leadership in globally dispersed teams," *Journal of International Management* 16 (2010), 234–246.

47. www.internetworldstats.com, accessed April 18, 2012.

48. www.imf.org, accessed October 1, 2012.

49. H. Jeff Smith, "Information Privacy and Marketing: What the U.S. Should (and Shouldn't) Learn from Europe," *California Management Review* 43, no. 2 (2001): 30–34.

50. Ibid.

51. Ibid.

52. R. Howells, "Update on Safe Harbor for International Data Transfer," *Direct Marketing* 63, no. 4 (2000): 40.

53. Smith, 30–34.

54. Sources include: "The Indian advantage," November 21, 2008, by Stefan Stern, www.FT.com; Mehul Srivastava, "A Backlash Grows in Bangalore Over Tech Revolution: Old-timers and anti-poverty groups are fighting a culture war over the cultural and economic costs of the high-tech boom," www.businessweek.com, November 6, 2008; Anand Giridharadas, "India Calling," www.nytimes.com, November 23, 2008; Chhokar, Jagdeep S. (2007). India: Diversity and complexity in action. In J. S. Chhokar, F. C. Brodbeck, and R. J. House (Eds.), Culture and Leadership across the World: The GLOBE Book of In-Depth Studies of 25 Societies. Mahwah, N.J.: Lawrence Erlbaum Associates (now Routledge/Psychology Press), pp. 971–1020; "Emerging Markets: India's Role in the Globalization of IT," by Alok Aggarwal, *Association for Computing Machinery: Communications of the ACM*. New York: July, 2008. Vol. 51, Iss. 7: 17; "India's IT Looks Inward," Anonymous, *InformationWeek*. Manhasset: March 10, 2008, Iss. 1176: 34.

55. Mehul Srivastava, "A Backlash Grows in Bangalore Over Tech Revolution: Old-timers and anti-poverty groups are fighting a culture war over the cultural and economic costs of the high-tech boom" www.businessweek.com, November 6, 2008.

56. Anand Giridharadas, "India Calling," www.nytimes.com, November 23, 2008.

57. Ibid.

58. Stefan Stern, "The Indian advantage," November 21, 2008, www.FT.com.

59. Jagdeep S. Chhoker, 2007.

60. Mark Landler and Michael Barbaro, "Wal-Mart Finds That Its Formula Doesn't Fit Every Culture," *New York Times,* August 2, 2006.

61. Geert Hofstede, *Culture's Consequences: International Differences in Work-Related Values* (Beverly Hills, CA: Sage, 1980).

62. George W. England, "Managers and Their Value Systems: A Five-Country Comparative Study," *Columbia Journal of World Business* (Summer 1978): 35–44.

63. Philip R. Harris and Robert T. Moran, *Managing Cultural Differences* (Houston: Gulf Publishing, 2004); Lennie Copeland and Lewis Griggs, *Going International* (New York: Random House, 1985); Boye De Mente, *Japanese Etiquette and Ethics in Business* (Lincolnwood, IL: NTC Business Books, 1989); R. L. Tung, *Business Negotiations with the Japanese* (Lexington, MA: Lexington Books, 1984); W. G. Ouchi and A. M. Jaeger, "Theory Z Organization: Stability in the Midst of Mobility," *Academy of Management Review* 3, no. 2 (1978): 305–314; Fernando Quezada and James E. Boyce, "Latin America," in *Comparative Management*, ed. Raghu Nath (Cambridge, MA: Ballinger Publishing, 1988), pp. 245–70; Simcha Ronen, *Comparative and Multinational Management* (New York: John Wiley and Sons, 1986); and V. Terpstra and K. David, *The Cultural Environment of International Business,* 3rd ed. (Cincinnati, OH: South-Western, 1991).

64. Akio Kuzuoka, a forty-year employee at a Japanese company, quoted in *The Wall Street Journal,* December 29, 2000.

65. Ibid.

66. FT Business School, "Go West for a New Mind-Set," *Financial Times,* October 10, 2004.

67. Ibid.

68. "Doing Business in Japan—Japanese Social and Business Culture," www.communicaid.com, accessed April 20, 2012.

69. www.ft.com, November 26, 2008.

70. Yumiko Ono and William Spindle, "Japan's Long Decline Makes One Thing Rise—Individualism," *Wall Street Journal*, December 29, 2000, 5.

71. D. Walker, T. Walker, and J. Schmitz, *Doing Business Internationally,* 2ed. (New York: McGraw-Hill, 2003), 188–189.

72. Nicholas Kulish, "The lines a German won't cross," www.nytimes.com, April 4, 2009.

73. "Germany – Language, Culture, Customs and Business Etiquette," www.kwintessential.co.uk, accessed April 21, 2012.

74. Walker et al., 2003.

75. E. T. Hall and M. R. Hall, *Understanding Cultural Differences* (Yarmouth, ME: Intercultural Press, 1990), 4.

76. Roberto S. Vassolo, Julio O. De Castro, and Luis R. Gomez-Mejia, "Managing in Latin America: Common Issues and a Research Agenda," *Academy of Management Perspectives,* November 2011.

77. Walker et al., 2003, 188.

78. Ibid., 195.

79. John A. Pearce II and Richard B. Robinson, Jr., "Cultivating *Guanxi* as a Foreign Investor Strategy," *Business Horizons* 43, no. 1 (2000): 31.

80. J. Lee, "Culture and Management—A Study of Small Chinese Family Business in Singapore," *Journal of Small Business Management* (July 1996): 17–24.

81. R. Sheng, "Outsiders' Perception of the Chinese," *Columbia Journal of World Business* 14, no. 2 (Summer 2000): 16–22.

82. Henry Yeung Wai-chung, "Debunking the Myths of Chinese Capitalism," May 11, 2005, www.nus.edu.sg/cororate/research/gallery/research30.htm.

83. D. A. Ralston, Yu-Kai-Ceng, Xun Wang, R. H. Terpstra, and He Wei, "An Analysis of Managerial Work Values Across the Six Regions of China," paper presented at the Academy of International Business, Boston, November 1994.

Chapter 4

1. K. Ananth Krishnan (Tata Consultancy Services), interviewed by Michael S. Hopkins, "The 'Unstructured Information' Most Businesses Miss Out On," *MIT Sloan Management Review: The Magazine,* April 27, 2011.

2. Goff, Sharlene, "Lenders eye social media angles," *Financial Times,* London (UK), January 10, 2011: 18.

3. Krishnan.

4. Donna L. Hoffman and Marek Fodor, "Can You Measure the ROI of Your Social Media Marketing?" *MIT Sloan Management Review,* Fall 2010, 52: 1.

5. Roxane Divol, David Edelman, and Hugo Sarrazin, "Demystifying Social Media," *McKinsey Quarterly,* April 2012; "What marketers say about working online: McKinsey Global Survey results," *mckinseyquarterly.com,* November 2011.

6. "Facebook Takes a Dive: Why Social Networks Are Bad Businesses," http://www.time.com/time/business/article/0,8599,1888796,00.html#ixzz1RosHjXUq, accessed July 10, 2011.

7. Cindy Chiu, Chris Ip, and Ari Silverman, "Understanding Social Media in China," *McKinsey Quarterly,* April 2012.

8. E. T. Hall and M. R. Hall, *Understanding Cultural Differences* (Yarmouth, ME: Intercultural Press, 1990), 4.

9. E. Wilmott, "New Media Vision," *New Media Age,* September 9, 1999, 8.

10. Hall and Hall; K. Wolfson and W. B. Pearce, "A Cross-cultural Comparison of the Implications of Self-discovery on Conversation Logics," *Communication Quarterly* 31 (1983): 249–56.

11. L. Nardon, R. M. Steers, and C. J. Sanchez-Runde, "Seeking common ground: Strategies for enhancing multicultural communication," *Organizational Dynamics,* 2011, in press. http://dx.doi.org/10.1016/j.orgdyn.2011.01.002

12. H. Mintzberg, *The Nature of Managerial Work* (New York: Harper and Row, 1973).

13. L. A. Samovar, R. E. Porter, and N. C. Jain, *Understanding Intercultural Communication* (Belmont, CA: Wadsworth Publishing, 1981).

14. P. R. Harris and R. T. Moran, *Managing Cultural Differences,* 3rd ed. (Houston: Gulf Publishing, 1991).

15. H. C. Triandis, quoted in *The Blackwell Handbook of Cross-cultural Management,* eds. M. Gannon and K. Newman (Oxford, UK: Blackwell Publishers, 2002).

16. Samovar, Porter, and Jain.

17. Hall and Hall, 15.

18. Based on H. C. Triandis, *Interpersonal Behavior* (Monterey, CA: Brooks/Cole, 1997), 248.

19. James R. Houghton, Former Chairman of Corning, Inc., quoted in *Organizational Dynamics* 29, no. 4 (2001).

20. J. Child, "Trust: The Fundamental Bond in Global Collaboration," *Organizational Dynamics* 29, no. 4 (2001): 274–88.

21. Ibid.

22. World Values Study Group (1994), *World Values Survey, ICPSR Version* (Ann Arbor, MI: Institute for Social Research); R. Inglehart, M. Basanez, and A. Moreno, *Human Values and Beliefs: A Cross-cultural Sourcebook* (Ann Arbor: University of Michigan Press, 1998).

23. Mansour Javidan and Robert J. House, "Cultural Acumen for the Global Manager," *Organizational Dynamics* 29, no. 4 (2001), 289–305.

24. Samovar and Porter; Harris and Moran.

25. M. L. Hecht, P. A. Andersen, and S. A. Ribeau, "The Cultural Dimensions of Nonverbal Communication, in *Handbook of International and Intercultural Communication,* eds. M. K. Asante and W. B. Gudykunst (Newbury Park, CA: Sage Publications, 1989), 163–85.

26. H. C. Triandis, *Interpersonal Behavior* (Monterey, CA: Brooks/Cole, 1977).

27. Harris and Moran.

28. Adapted from N. Adler, *International Dimensions of Organizational Behavior,* 2nd ed. (Boston: PWS-Kent, 1991).

29. D. A. Ricks, *Big Business Blunders: Mistakes in Multinational Marketing* (Homewood, IL: Dow Jones–Irwin, 1983).

30. P. Garfinkel, "On Keeping Your Foot Safely Out of Your Mouth," www.nytimes.com, July 13, 2004.

31. Jiatao Li, Katherine R. Xin, Anne Tsui, and Donald C. Hambrick, "Building Effective International Joint Venture Leadership Teams in China," *Journal of World Business* 34, no. 1 (1999): 52–68.

32. D. Walker, T. Walker, and J. Schmitz, *Doing Business Internationally* (New York: McGraw-Hill, 2003).

33. Roger E. Axtell, *Essential Do's and Taboos,"* (Hoboken, New Jersey: John Wiley and Sons, Inc., 2007).

34. R. L. Daft, *Organizational Theory and Design,* 3rd ed. (St. Paul, MN: West Publishing, 1989).

35. Li et al., 1999.

36. O. Klineberg, "Emotional Expression in Chinese Literature," *Journal of Abnormal and Social Psychology* 33 (1983): 517–30.

37. P. Ekman and W. V. Friesen, "Constants Across Cultures in the Face and Emotion," *Journal of Personality and Social Psychology* 17 (1971): 124–29.

38. J. Pfeiffer, "How Not to Lose the Trade Wars by Cultural Gaffes," *Smithsonian* 18, no. 10 (January 1988).

39. E. T. Hall, *The Silent Language* (New York: Doubleday, 1959).

40. Hall and Hall.

41. *Random House, American Heritage, Merriam Webster, "feng-shui," Oxford English Dictionary, 2nd ed. (Oxford University Press, 1989);* Tina Marie, "Feng Shui Diaries," *Esoteric Feng Shui* (2007–2009); "Baidu Baike," *Huai Nan Zi;* Field, Stephen L., "The Zangshu, or Book of Burial."

42. http://www.instituteoffengshui.com/fengshui.html, accessed June 24, 2011.

43. Ibid.

44. Jonathan Vatner, "When Feng Shui Helps Determine a Deal's Fate," www.nytimes.com, August 24, 2010.

45. Ibid.

46. Hall and Hall.

47. Anand Giridharada, "How to Greet in a Global Microcosm," *New York Times Online,* October 15, 2010.

48. Hecht, Andersen, and Ribeau.

49. Li et al., 1999.

50. "The Name Game: Business Cards an Essential Part of Operating in China," *The International Herald Tribune,* January 10, 2011.

51. Hall and Hall.

52. Robert Matthews, "Where East Can Never Meet West," *Financial Times,* October 21, 2005.

53. Hall and Hall.

54. Matthews, 2005.

55. Hecht, Andersen, and Ribeau.

56. Hall and Hall.

57. M. K. Nydell, *Understanding Arabs* (Yarmouth, ME: Intercultural Press, 1987).

58. Harris and Moran.

59. E. T. Hall, *The Hidden Dimension* (New York: Doubleday, 1966): 15.

60. Hall and Hall.

61. Ibid.

62. Based largely on the work of Nydell; and R. T. Moran and P. R. Harris, *Managing Cultural Synergy* (Houston: Gulf Publishing, 1982): 81–82.

63. Ibid.

64. Hall and Hall.

65. D. C. Barnlund, "Public and Private Self in Communicating with Japan," *Business Horizons* (March–April 1989): 32–40.

66. Hall and Hall.

67. A. Goldman, "The Centrality of 'Ningensei' to Japanese Negotiating and Interpersonal Relationships: Implications for U.S.–Japanese Communication," *International Journal of Intercultural Relations* 18, no. 1 (1994).

68. Jean-Louis Barsoux and Peter Lawrence, "The Making of a French Manager," *Harvard Business Review* (July–August 1991): 58–67.

69. D. Barboza, "Microsoft Forms Partnership with China's Leading Search Engine," www.nytimes.com, July 4, 2011.

70. D. Shand, "All Information Is Local: IT Systems Can Connect Every Corner of the Globe, But IT Managers Are Learning They Have to Pay Attention to Regional Differences," *Computerworld* 88 no. 1 (2000).

71. Shand.

72. Wilmott.

73. Barboza, July 4, 2011.

74. Doug Tsuruoka, "Hudong to Help Microsoft's Bing in Chinese Search," *Investor's Business Daily,"* June 6, 2012.

75. Barboza, July 4, 2011.

76. T. Wilson, "B2B Links, European Style: Integrator Helps Applications Cross Language, Currency and Cultural Barriers," *InternetWeek,* October 9, 2000, 27.

77. Hiroko Tabuchi, "Quick Action Helps Google Win Friends in Japan," *New York Times Online*, July 10, 2011; Kevin J. O'Brien, "Privacy Laws Trip Up Google's Expansion in Parts of Europe," www.nytimes.com, November 18, 2008; Scott Bradner, "Telling Google and Others to do Less Evil," *Network World*, 25, no. 16 (2008): 25; "EU Panel Queries Google on Privacy Concerns," *Wall Street Journal*, May 26, 2007; Laura Smith, "Spotlight on the spy in the surf," *Information World Review*, Oxford, U.K., November 2007, i.240; Andrew Edgecliffe-Johnson, "Google founders in web privacy warning," www.ft.com, May 19, 2008.

78. Hiroko Tabuchi, "Quick Action Helps Google Win Friends in Japan," *New York Times Online*, July 10, 2011.

79. Ibid.

80. Adam Liptak, "When American and European Ideas of Privacy Collide," www.nytimes.com, February 26, 2010.

81. www.nytimes.com, May 22, 2012.

82. Based on www.Businessfordiplomaticaction.org, retrieved August 19, 2006.

83. R. B. Ruben, "Human Communication and Cross-cultural Effectiveness," in *Intercultural Communication: A Reader*, eds. L. Samovar and R. Porter (Belmont, CA: Wadsworth, 1985), 339.

84. D. Ruben and B. D. Ruben, "Cross-cultural Personnel Selection Criteria, Issues and Methods," in *Handbook of Intercultural Training*, Vol. 1, *Issues in Theory and Design*, ed. D. Landis and R. W. Brislin (New York: Pergamon, 1983), 155–75.

85. Young Yun Kim, *Communication and Cross-cultural Adaptation: An Integrative Theory* (Clevedon, UK; Multilingual Matters, 1988).

Chapter 5

1. Sources include: Mariko Sanchanta, Ayai Tomisawa, Anjali Cordeiro, "Japan's Shiseido Agrees to Acquire Bare Escentuals," *Wall Street Journal*, January 21, 2010: B.1; Anonymous, "Japan's Shiseido Completes Acquisition of U.S. Rival," *Jiji Press English News Service*, March 15, 2010; Kana Inagaki, "Shiseido, U.S. Unit Begin to See Eye to Eye," *Wall Street Journal*, December 29, 2011; Mariko Sanchanta, Ayai Tomisawa, "Corporate News: Shiseido Focuses on China, U.S.—Purchase of Bare Escentuals Is Viewed as Vital to Revenue Growth as Japan Sales Shrink," *Wall Street Journal*, January 21, 2010: B.4.

2. Mariko Sanchanta, January 21, 2012.

3. *Wall Street Journal*, December 29, 2011.

4. John Pfeiffer, "How Not to Lose the Trade Wars by Cultural Gaffes," *Smithsonian* 18, no. 10 (1988): 145–56.

5. Nancy J. Adler, *International Dimensions of Organizational Behavior*, 4th ed. (Boston: PWS-Kent, 2002), 208–32.

6. Philip R. Harris and Robert T. Moran, *Managing Cultural Differences*, 3rd ed. (Houston: Gulf Publishing, 1991).

7. John L. Graham and Roy A. Herberger, Jr., "Negotiators Abroad—Don't Shoot from the Hip," *Harvard Business Review* (July–August 1983): 160–68; Adler; John L. Graham, "A Hidden Cause of America's Trade Deficit with Japan," *Columbia Journal of World Business* (Fall 1981): 5–15.

8. Phillip D. Grub, "Cultural Keys to Successful Negotiating," in *Global Business Management in the 1990s*, eds. F. Ghader et al. (Washington, DC: Beacham, 1990): 24–32.

9. R. Fisher and W. Ury, *Getting to Yes* (Boston: Houghton Mifflin, 1981).

10. S. Weiss, "Negotiating with 'Romans,'" *Sloan Management Review* (Winter 1994): 51–61.

11. Based on excerpts from S. E. Weiss and W. Stripp, *Negotiation with Foreign Business Persons: An Introduction for Americans with Propositions on Six Cultures* (New York University Faculty of Business Administration, February 1985).

12. John A. Reeder, "When West Meets East: Cultural Aspects of Doing Business in Asia," *Business Horizons* (January–February 1987): 72.

13. John L. Graham, William Hernandez Requejo, "Managing Face-to-Face International Negotiations," *Organizational Dynamics*, Vol. 38, No. 2, 2009, pp. 167–177.

14. Adler, 197.

15. Fisher and Ury.

16. Lennie Copeland and Lewis Griggs, *Going International* (New York: Random House, 1985), 85.

17. Adler, 197–98.

18. Fisher and Ury.

19. Jeanne M. Brett, *Negotiating Globally* (San Francisco, CA: John Wiley and Sons, 2001).

20. G. Fisher, *International Negotiation: A Cross-cultural Perspective* (Chicago: Intercultural Press, 1980).

21. David Barboza, "Danone Exits China Venture After Years of Legal Dispute," *New York Times*, September 30, 2009; *China Economic Review*. (2007). Danone vs. Wahaha, (September 2007). The *Economist* (various issues); *Financial Times* (various issues); Tao, Jingzhou, and Hillier, Edward. (2008). A tale of two companies, Chinabusinessreview.com, (May–June 2008): 44–47; *Wall Street Journal* (various issues); *Wikipedia*. (2009). Groupe Danone, http://en.wikipedia.org/wiki/Groupe_Danone; *Wikipedia*. (2009). Wahaha, http://en.wikipedia.org/wiki/Wahaha.

22. David Barboza, "Danone Exits China Venture After Years of Legal Dispute," *New York Times*, September 30, 2009.

23. Pfeiffer.

24. *Wall Street Journal*, February 2, 1994.

25. John L. Graham, "Brazilian, Japanese, and American Business Negotiations," *Journal of International Business Studies* (Spring–Summer 1983): 47–61.

26. T. Flannigan, "Successful Negotiating with the Japanese," *Small Business Reports* 15, no. 6 (1990): 47–52.

27. Graham, 1983; Boye De Mente, *Japanese Etiquette and Ethics in Business* (Lincolnwood, IL: NTC Business Books, 1989).

28. Robert H. Doktor, "Asian and American CEOs: A Comparative Study," *Organizational Dynamics* (Winter 1990): 49.

29. Harris and Moran, 461.

30. Adler, 181.

31. These profiles are based on and adapted from Pierre Casse, *Managing Intercultural Negotiations: Guidelines for Trainers and Negotiators* (Washington, DC: Society for Intercultural Education, Training, and Research, 1985).

32. D. K. Tse, J. Francis, and J. Walls, "Cultural Differences in Conducting Intra- and Inter-Cultural Negotiations: A Sino-Canadian Comparison," *Journal of International Business Studies* (3rd Quarter 1994): 537–55.

33. B. W. Husted, "Bargaining with the Gringos: An Exploratory Study of Negotiations Between Mexican and U.S. Firms," *International Executive* 36, no. 5 (1994): 625–44.

34. Pierre Casse, *Training for the Cross-cultural Mind*, 2nd ed. (Washington, DC: Society for Intercultural Education, Training, and Research, 1981).

35. Nigel Campbell, John L. Graham, Alain Jolibert, and Hans Meissner, "Marketing Negotiations in France, Germany, the United Kingdom, and the United States," *Journal of Marketing* 52 (1988): 49–63.

36. Neil Rackham, "The Behavior of Successful Negotiators" (Reston, VA: Huthwaite Research Group, 1982).

37. J. Teich, H. Wallenius, and J. Wallenius, "World-Wide-Web Technology in Support of Negotiation and Communication," *International Journal of Technology Management* 17, nos. 1/2 (1999): 223–39.

38. Ibid.

39. Ibid.

40. A. Rosette, Jeanne Brette, Zoe Barsness, Anne Lytle, "When Cultures Clash Electronically: The Impact of E-mail and Culture on Negotiation Behavior," The Dispute Resolution Research Center, Northwestern University, accessed February 9, 2009.

41. J. A. Pearce II and R. B. Robinson, Jr., "Cultivating *Guanxi* as a Foreign Investor Strategy," *Business Horizons* 43, no. 1 (January 2000): 31.

42. Rosalie L. Tung, Verner Worm, and Tony Fang, "Sino-Western Business Negotiations Revisited—30 Years after China's Open Door Policy," *Organizational Dynamics* 37, no. 1 (2008): 60–74.

43. Tung, 2008.

44. Ibid.

45. Ibid.

46. Ibid.

47. Joan H. Coll, "Sino–American Cultural Differences: The Key to Closing a Business Venture with the Chinese," *Mid-Atlantic Journal of Business* 25, no. 2–3 (December 1988/January 1989): 15–19.

48. M. Loeb, "China: A Time for Caution," *Fortune*, February 20, 1995, 129–30.

49. O. Shenkar and S. Ronen, "The Cultural Context of Negotiations: The Implications of Chinese Interpersonal Norms," *Journal of Applied Behavioral Science* 23, no. 2 (1987): 263–75.

50. Tse et al.

51. J. Brunner, teaching notes, the University of Toledo.

52. http://www.kwintessential.co.uk/etiquette/doing-business-china.html, accessed September 15, 2011.

53. Kam-hon Lee, Guang Yang, and John L. Graham, "Tension and Trust in International Business Negotiations: American Executives Negotiating with Chinese Executives," *Journal of International Business Studies* 37, no. 5 (2006): 623.

54. J. M. Banthin and L. Stelzer, "'Opening' China: Negotiation Strategies When East Meets West," *Mid-Atlantic Journal of Business* 25, no. 2–3 (December 1988/January 1989).

55. Brunner.

56. Pearce and Robinson.

57. Ibid.

58. Ibid.

59. C. Blackman, "An Inside Guide to Negotiating," *China Business Review*, 27, no. 3 (May 2000): 44–45.

60. Boye De Mente, *Chinese Etiquette and Ethics in Business* (Lincolnwood, IL: NTC Business Books, 1989), 115–23.

61. S. Stewart and C. F. Keown, "Talking with the Dragon: Negotiating in the People's Republic of China," *Columbia Journal of World Business* 24, no. 3 (Fall 1989): 68–72.

62. Banthin and Stelzer, "'Opening' China."

63. Tony Fang, Verner Worm, and Rosalie L. Tung, "Changing Success and Failure Factors in Business Negotiations with the PRC," International Business Review, 17, 2008.

64. Blackman.

65. "Doing Business in China," www.kwintessential.com, accessed October 2, 2011; "Avoiding Pitfalls, and Forging Success, in East-West Contract Negotiations," *International Herald Tribune*, January 24, 2011; Lucian Pye, *Chinese Commercial Negotiating Style* (Cambridge, MA: Oelgeschlager, Gunn, and Hain, 1982).

66. Fang et al., 2008.

67. W. B. Gudykunst and S. Ting Tomey, *Culture and Interpersonal Communication* (Newbury Park, CA: Sage Publications, 1988).

68. Based on W. Gudykunst, L. Stewart, and S. Ting-Toomey, *Communication, Culture, and Organizational Processes* (Sage Publications, 1985).

69. L. Copeland and L. Griggs, *Going International* (New York: Random House, 1985), 80.

70. M. A. Hitt, B. B. Tyler, and Daewoo Park, "A Cross-cultural Examination of Strategic Decision Models: Comparison of Korean and U.S. Executives," in *Best Papers Proceedings of the 50th Annual Meeting of the Academy of Management* (San Francisco, CA, August 12–15, 1990), 111–15; G. Fisher, *International Negotiation: A Cross-cultural Perspective* (Chicago: Intercultural Press, 1980); G. W. England, "Managers and Their Value Systems: A Five-Country Comparative Study," *Columbia Journal of World Business* 13, no. 2 (1978); W. Whitely and G. W. England, "Variability in Common Dimensions of Managerial Values Due to Value Orientation and Country Differences," *Personnel Psychology* 33 (1980): 77–89.

71. Program: *PBS NewsHour* Episode: "Italian Prime Minister on 'Prejudices' in Europe," February 9, 2012; *PBS NewsHour* Episode: "Italy: 'Going the Greece Way' Would Be Disastrous," February 10, 2012; Niki Kitsantonis and Rachel Donadio, "As Europe Seeks More, Divisions Rise in Greece Over New Austerity Plan," *New York Times,* February 10, 2012; Mohamed El-Erian, "Sadly this Greek deal faces the sorry fate of its forebears," *Financial Times*, London (UK), February 10, 2012: 9; Russell Shorto, "The Way Greeks Live Now," www.nytimes.com, February 16, 2012; http://www.kwintessential.co.uk/resources/global-etiquette/italy-country-profile.html, accessed February 15, 2012; Michael Schuman, "The Most Important man in Europe," *Time*, February 20, 2012; Floyd Norris, "Germany vs. the Rest of Europe," *New York Times*, February 16, 2012.

72. Floyd Norris, February 16, 2012.

73. *Time,* February 20, 2012.

74. Ibid.

75. *New York Times,* February 10, 2012.

76. Ibid.

77. Russell Shorto, "The Way Greeks Live Now," www.nytimes.com, February 16, 2012.

78. Ibid.

79. www.kwintessential.co.uk.

80. Ibid.

81. Floyd Norris, "Germany vs. the Rest of Europe," *New York Times,* February 16, 2012.

82. Hitt, Tyler, and Park, 114.

83. B. M. Bass and P. C. Burger, *Assessment of Managers: An International Comparison* (New York: Free Press, 1979), 91.

84. Copeland and Griggs; M. K. Badawy, "Styles of Mideastern Managers," *California Management Review* 22 (1980): 51–58.

85. N. Namiki and S. P. Sethi, "Japan," in *Comparative Management—A Regional View,* ed. R. Nath (Cambridge, MA: Ballinger Publishing, 1988), 74–76.

86. De Mente, *Japanese Etiquette,* 80.

87. S. Naoto, *Management and Industrial Structure in Japan* (New York: Pergamon Press, 1981); Namiki and Sethi.

88. Harris and Moran, 397.

89. S. P. Sethi and N. Namiki, "Japanese-Style Consensus Decision-Making in Matrix Management: Problems and Prospects of Adaptation," in *Matrix Management Systems Handbook,* ed. D. I. Cleland (New York: Van Nostrand, 1984), 431–56.

Chapter 6

1. www.southafrica.info, accessed September 20, 2011.

2. Ibid.

3. Pete Engardio, "Emerging Giants," *BusinessWeek*, July 31, 2006, 41–49.

4. Ibid.

5. Steve Hamm, "IBM vs. Tata: Who's More American?" *BusinessWeek*, April 23, 2008.

6. Ibid.

7. Eric Beinhocker, Ian Davis, and Lenny Mendonca, *Harvard Business Review* 87, no. 7/8 (2009): 55–60.

8. A. MacDonald, A. Lucchetti, and E. Taylor, "Long City-Centric, Financial Exchanges Are Going Global," *Wall Street Journal*, May 27, 2006.

9. David Jolly, "Merck to Buy Schering-Plough for $41.1 Billion," *New York Times*, March 10, 2009.

10. Kathrin Hille, "ZTE: Telecoms manufacturer makes move to Latin America," www.FT.com/Reports, May 20, 2011.

11. Engardio.

12. A. K. Gupta and V. Govindarajan, "Managing Global Expansion: A Conceptual Framework," *Business Horizons* (March/April 2000).

13. Rob Ciccone, Vice President, American Express, "What Businesses Need to Know About Expanding Internationally," *Industrial Maintenance and Plant Operation*, June 1, 2011.

14. Angus Loten, "Firms Face Hurdles Overseas: Small Companies Seek Growth Abroad, but Lack Resources of Bigger Rivals," www.wsj.com, August 25, 2011.

15. Mark Scott, "Companies Born in Europe, but Based on the Planet," www.nytimes.com, June 12, 2012.

16. Bettina Wassener, "Nestle to Buy Control of China's Biggest Confectioner," www.nytimes.com, DealBook, July 11, 2011.

17. Michael J. De La Merced and Mark Scott, "U.P.S. to Buy TNT Express for $6.8 Billion," www.nytimes.com, March 18, 2012.

18. Haig Simonian, "Cement Industry suffers amid global downturn," www.FT.com, November 13, 2008; E. Malkin, "Mexican Cement Company Bids for Australian Concern," www.nytimes.com October 28, 2006; David Oakley and Adam Thomson, "Cemex tumbles as it fails to refinance debt," www.FT.com, December 11, 2008; Joel Millman, "The Fallen: Lorenzo Zambrano: Hard Times for Cement Man," *Wall Street Journal*, December 11, 2008.

19. Joel Millman, "The Fallen: Lorenzo Zambrano: Hard Times for Cement Man," *Wall Street Journal*, December 11, 2008.

20. Adam Thomson, "Indebted Cemex Turns Corner, www.FT.com, April 26, 2010.

21. Ibid.

22. Ibid.

23. "Special Zones Offer Oasis for Investment," *Washington Post Supplement*, April 29, 2009.

24. Priscilla Murphy, "Companies rush to complete M&A deals in Brazil ahead of uncertainty about tax break after 2009," www.mergermarket.com, February 19, 2009.

25. M. Maynard, "Foreign Makers, Settled in South, Pace Car Industry," *New York Times*, June 17, 2006.

26. Henry Mintzberg, "Strategy Making in Three Modes," *California Management Review* (Winter 1973): 44–53.

27. www.sanyo.com, accessed March 24, 2009.

28. www.siemens.com, accessed March 24, 2009.

29. Helen Deresky and Elizabeth Christopher, *International Management* (Pearson Education Australia, 2008.)

30. This section contributed by Charles M. Byles, Professor, Virginia Commonwealth University, March 11, 2009.

31. Mike W. Peng, *Global Strategy*, 2nd, Southwestern, Cengage Learning, 2009.

32. Kim Peterson, "India Backs Away from Wal-Mart," www.money.msn.com, Dec 7, 2011; Nick Godt, "India says no to foreign ownership of supermarkets," *MarketWatch, Mumbai*, December 7, 2011; Jim Yardley, "India Suspends Plan to Let in Foreign Retailers," www.nytimes.com, December 7, 2011; Neva Happel, "India Superstores like Walmart Plans on Hold," *Z6Mag*, December 7, 2011.

33. Amol Sharma and Jens Hansegard, "Ikea Says It Is Ready to Give India a Try," *The Wall Street Journal*, June 25, 2012, p. B.1.

34. Vikas Bajaj, "India's Tax Plan Troubles Foreign Investors," www.nytimes.com, April 6, 2012.

35. Douglass C. North, *Institutions, Institutional Change, and Economics Performance,* New York: Cambridge University Press, 1990; W. Richard Scott, *Institutions and Organizations*, Thousand Oaks, CA, Sage Publications, 1995.

36. Peng, 2009; Mike W. Peng, Denis YL Yang, and Yi Jiang, "An institution-based view of international business strategy: A focus on emerging economies," *Journal of International Business Studies*, 39, no. 5, July–August 2008; *The Economist*, "Order in the Jungle," March 13, 2008.

37. *The Economist*, 2008.

38. Peng, 2009.

39. Ibid.

40. Ibid.

41. www.Mitsubishi.com, January 20, 2009.

42. Diane J. Garsombke, "International Competitor Analysis," *Planning Review* 17, no. 3 (1989): 42–47.

43. C. K. Prahalad and Gary Hamel, "The Core Competence of the Corporation," *Harvard Business Review* (May–June 1990): 79–91.

44. Ibid.

45. P. Ghemawat, "Distance Still Matters," *Harvard Business Review* 79, no. 8 (2001): 137–47.

46. M. E. Porter, "Changing Patterns of International Competition," in *The Competitive Challenge*, ed. D. J. Teece (Boston: Ballinger, 1987), 29–30.

47. T. Chen, "Network Resources for Internationalization," *Journal of Management Studies* 40: 1107–30.

48. Porter, 1987.

49. P. W. Beamish et al., *International Management* (Homewood, IL: Irwin, 1991).

50. A. Palazzo, "B2B Markets—Industry Basics," www.FT.com, January 28, 2001.

51. "A Bigger World," *The Economist*, September 20, 2008.

52. Ibid.

53. A. J. Morrison, D. A. Ricks, and K. Roth, "Globalization versus Regionalization: Which Way for the Multinational?" *Organizational Dynamics* 19 (Winter 1991).

54. "Wal-Mart Selling Stores and Leaving South Korea," www.nytimes.com, March 23, 2006.

55. Beamish et al.

56. www.nytimes.com, March 23, 2006.

57. Pankaj Ghemawat, *Redefining Global Strategy*, Harvard Business School Publishing, 2007.

58. www.panasonic.net, accessed October 6, 2012.

59. Ghemawat, 2007.

60. Thomas Friedman, *The World Is Flat* (New York: Farrar, Straus, and Giroux, 2005).

61. Yoram Wind and Susan Douglas, "International Portfolio Analysis and Strategy: The Challenge of the 1980s," *Journal of International Business Studies* (Fall 1991): 69–82.

62. Daniel J. Isenberg, "The Global Entrepreneur," *Harvard Business Review*, December 2008.

63. Ibid.

64. "Technology Levels the Business Playing Field," www.nytimes.com, accessed September 10, 2011.

65. "China's E-commerce Market: The Logistics Challenges," research report, www.atkearney.com, accessed August 12, 2011.

66. Ibid.

67. Bob Tedeschi, "E-Commerce Report; Sensing economic opportunities, many developing nations are laying the groundwork for online commerce," www.nytimes, November 20, 2008.

68. Sorid, 2008.

69. P. Greenberg, "It's Not a Small eCommerce World, After All," www.ecommercetimes.com, February 23, 2001.

70. Ibid.

71. M. Porter, *The Competitive Advantage of Nations* (New York: Free Press, 1990).

72. Bruce Einhorn, "How China's Alibaba Is Surviving and Thriving," *BusinessWeek*, April 9, 2009.

73. M. Sawhney and S. Mandal, "Go Global," *Business 2.0*, May 2000.

74. Ibid.

75. B. Bright, "E-Commerce: How Do You Say 'Web?' Planning to Take Your Online Business International? Beware: E-Commerce Can Get Lost in Translation," *Wall Street Journal*, May 23, 2005.

76. Ibid.

77. Ibid.

78. U.S. Department of Commerce, "2011 Country Commercial Guide for U.S. Companies: Doing Business in China," www.export.gov, accessed September 20, 2011.

79. J. Mangier and P. Mercier, "What Happens When Offshoring Isn't so Cheap," www.bcgperspectives.com, January 12, 2011.

80. Bill Vlasic, Hiroko Tabuchi and Charles Duhigg, "In Pursuit of Nissan, a Jobs Lesson for the U.S. Tech Industry," www.nytimes.com, August 5, 2012.

81. U.S. Department of Commerce, 2005.

82. Peter Marsh, "Play the Home Advantage," *Financial Times*, November 26, 2008.

83. Ibid.

84. Harold L. Sirkin, James W. Hemerling, and Arindam K. Bhattacharya, *Globality: Competing with Everyone from Everywhere for Everything* (New York: Hachette Publishing Company, 2008.)

85. The A. T. Kearney Global Services Location Index 2011, www.ATKearney.org, August 9, 2011.

86. Dante Di Gregorio, Martina Musteen, and Douglas E. Thomas, "Offshore outsourcing as a source of international competitiveness for SMEs," *Journal of International Business Studies*. Vol. 40, Iss. 6, August 2009: p. 969.

87. J. Johnson, "India at Center of Microsoft's World," *Financial Times*, December 8, 2005.

88. A. T. Kearney, 2011.

89. Ibid.

90. Manjeet Kripalani, "Call Center? That's so 2004," *BusinessWeek*, August 7, 2006, 40–42.

91. Manjeet Kripalani, "Five Offshore Practices that Pay Off," *BusinessWeek*, January 30, 2006, 60.

92. S. Zahra and G. Elhagrasey, "Strategic Management of IJVs," *European Management Journal* 12, no. 1 (1994): 83–93.

93. Yigang Pan and Xiaolia Li, "Joint Venture Formation of Very Large Multinational Firms," *Journal of International Business Studies* 31, no. 1 (2000): 179–81.

94. R. Bream and Arkady Ostrovsky, "Merger Leaves Rivals Lagging Behind," *Financial Times*, June 27, 2006.

95. U.S. Department of Commerce: "Doing Business in India," www.export.gov, accessed September 21, 2011.

96. Kenichi Ohmae, "The Global Logic of Strategic Alliances," *Harvard Business Review* (March–April 1989): 143–54.

97. Zahra and Elhagrasey.

98. Bill Vlasic and Nick Bunkley, "Alliance with Fiat Gives Chrysler Another Partner and Lifeline," www.nytimes.com, January 21, 2009.

99. Julia Werdigier, "SABMiller to Buy Foster's for $10.15 Billion," www.nytimes.com, September 21, 2011.

100. Adam Thomson, "Bimbo advances in US," www.ft.com, October 25, 2011.

101. "Overseas Cash Fuels a Shopping Spree," *Bloomberg Businessweek*, August 15–28, 2011.

102. "A Bigger World," *The Economist*, September 20, 2008.

103. P. Meller, "Procter and Gamble Gets European Approval to Buy Gillette," *New York Times*, July 16, 2005.

104. Simeon Kerr, Joseph Menn, "Yahoo buys Arabic internet portal," *Financial Times*. London (UK): August 26, 2009. pg. 18

105. *World Economic Forum Annual Meeting, 2011.*

106. *2011 Global Retail Development Index*, www.atkearney.com

107. www.atkearney.com, accessed August 28, 2011.

108. World Economic Forum: http://www3.weforum.org/docs/WEF_GAC_LogisticsSupplyChain_Report_2010-11.

109. Tarun Khanna, K. Palepu, J. Sinha, "Strategies That Fit Emerging Markets," *Harvard Business Review*, June 2005.

110. Ibid.

111. N. T. Washburn and B. T. Hunsaker, "Finding Great Ideas in Emerging Markets," *Harvard Business Review*, September 2011.

112. Ibid.

113. J. Li and R. K. Kozhikode, "Organizational learning of emerging economy firms," *Organizational Dynamics* (2011), doi:10.1016/ j.orgdyn.2011.04.009.

114. Based on *International Management—Concepts and Cases* by A. V. Phatak, 270–75, Cincinnati, OH: South-Western College Publishing, 1997.

115. Yigang Pan and David K. Tse, "The Hierarchical Model of Market Entry Modes," *Journal of International Business Studies* 31, no. 4 (2000): 535–54.

116. Gupta and Govindarajan.

117. Ibid.

118. www.McDonalds.com, accessed August 14, 2011.

119. Oded Shenkar, "Cultural Distance Revisited: Towards a More Rigorous Conceptualization and Measurement of Cultural Differences," *Journal of International Business* 43, January 2012: 1–11.

120. Ibid.

121. G. Hofstede, *Cultures and Organizations: Software of the Mind* (London: McGraw-Hill, 1991).

122. Pan and Tse.

123. Hofstede.

124. Pan and Tse.

125. Hofstede.

126. Pan and Tse.

Chapter 7

1. The Associated Press, "Exxon in Multibillion-Dollar Russian Arctic Deal," www.npr.org, August 31, 2011; "Russia: Exxon's Land of Opportunity," wsj.com August 30, 2011; Bill Sweet, "Significance of Exxon-Russia Deal," http://spectrum.ieee.org, August 31, 2011; Andrew E. Kramer, "Memo to Exxon: Business with Russia Might Involve Guns and Balaclavas," www.nytimes.com, August 31, 2011; http://blogs.ft.com/beyond-brics/2011/09/01/london-headlines-330/#ixzz1Wjp9DO1g, September 1, 2011.

2. Andrew E. Kramer, "Memo to Exxon: Business with Russia Might Involve Guns and Balaclavas," www.nytimes.com, August 31, 2011.

3. www.npr.org.

4. www.ft.com.

5. A. Kramer.

6. Ibid.

7. http://spectrum.ieee.org.

8. D. Lei and J. W. Slocum, Jr., "Global Strategic Alliances: Payoffs and Pitfalls," *Organizational Dynamics* (Winter 1991).

9. Jung-Ho Lai, Shao-Chi Chang, and Sheng-Syan Chen, "Is experience valuable in international strategic alliances?" *Journal of International Management 16 (2010), 247–261*; Walter, J., Lechner, C., Kellermanns, F. W., 2008, "Disentangling alliance management processes: Decision making, politicality, and alliance performance," *The Journal of Management Studies 45 (3), 530.*

10. Ibid.

11. Ibid.

12. Julie MacIntosh and Francesco Guerrera, "Cancelled M&As Close to Eclipsing Takeovers," www.ft.com, December 1, 2008.

13. Dana Cimilluca and Sara Schaefer Munoz, "Lloyds Reaches Deal with U.K. on Bailout," *Wall Street Journal*, March 7, 2009.

14. Vikas Bajaj, "After a Year of Delays, the First Starbucks Is to Open in Tea-Loving India This Fall," *New York Times*, January 20, 2012.

15. Ibid.

16. J. Griffiths, "A Marriage of Two Mindsets," *Financial Times*, March 16, 2005.

17. Ibid.

18. Ibid.

19. Robin Harding and Robin Kwong, "Abu Dhabi to take on Taiwan in chipmaking big league," *Financial Times*, London (UK): September 8, 2009. pg. 16.

20. "The Empire Strikes Back," Anonymous, *The Economist*, September 20, 2008.

21. Bill Vlasic and Nick Bunkley, "Alliance with Fiat Gives Chrysler another Partner and Lifeline," www.nytimes.com, January 21, 2009.

22. Micheline Maynard, "Chrysler Bankruptcy Plan Is Announced." www.nytimes.com, April 30, 2009.

23. Ibid.

24. Thomas Friedman, *The World Is Flat* (New York: Farrar, Straus and Giroux, 2005), 144.

25. Heather Timmons, "French Company Joins Indian Utility in a Deal for Nuclear Plants," www.nytimes.com, February 5, 2009.

26. www.covisint.com.

27. www.e4engineering.com, January 4, 2001.

28. Tim Burt, "Disney's Asian Adventure," *Financial Times*, October 30, 2003.

29. Ibid.

30. Ibid.

31. Ibid.

32. D. Barboza, C. Drew, and S. Lohr, "G.E. to Share Jet Technology with China in New Joint Venture," *New York Times*, January 17, 2011.

33. Andres Parker and Gerrit Wiesmann, "Cross-border Sensitivities Give Grounds for Pessimism," *Financial Times*, Sep 9, 2009.

34. David Lei, "Offensive and Defensive Uses of Alliances," in Heidi Vernon-Wortzel and L. H. Wortzel, *Strategic Management in Global Economy*, 3rd ed. (New York: John Wiley & Sons, 1997).

35. Lei, 1997.

36. New York Times, January 17, 2011.

37. T. L. Wheelen and J. D. Hunger, *Strategic Management and Business Policy,* 6th ed. (Reading, MA: Addison-Wesley, 1998).

38. Shameen Prashantham and Julian Birkinshaw, "Dancing with Gorillas: How Small Companies Can Partner Effectively with MNCs," *California Management Review* 51, no. 1 (2008), 6–23.

39. Ibid.

40. In this article I draw upon Prashantham, S. (2007), *Dancing with Gorillas: How SMEs Can Go Global by Forging Links with MNCs*, London: Advanced Institute of Management; and Prashantham, S. and Birkinshaw, J. (2008), "Dancing with Gorillas: How Small Companies Can Partner Effectively with Large MNCs," *California Management Review*, 51(1): 6–23.

41. Dovev Lavie, "Capturing Value from Alliance Portfolios," *Organizational Dynamics* 38, no. 1 (2009): 26–36.

42. Ibid.

43. Ibid.

44. Lei, 1997.

45. Wheelen and Hunger.

46. http://www3.weforum.org/docs/WEF_GCR_Russia_Report_2011.

47. M. Garrahan and Courtney Weaver, "Disney Expands New TV Channel to Russia," www.ft.com, October 27, 2011.

48. Ibid.

49. Catherine Belton in Moscow, "Foreign investment: Future unclear as perceived risk grows," www.ft.com, September 30, 2008.

50. http://www3.weforum.org/docs/WEF_GCR_Russia_Report_2011.

51. Sheila M. Puffer and Daniel J. McCarthy, "Two Decades of Russian Business and Management Research: An Institutional Theory Perspective," *Academy of Management Perspectives*, May 2011, 21–36.

52. N. Buckley, "Huge Gains but Also a Lot of Pain," *Financial Times*, October 11, 2005.

53. www.transparencyinternational.org

54. Andrew E. Kramer, "Ikea Tries to Build a Case Against Russian Graft," www.nytimes.com, September 12, 2009.

55. "Russia's Retail Revolution," www.managementtoday.co.uk, June 1, 2008.

56. Foreign Investment Advisory Council Report October 2010, http://www.fiac.ru/.

57. Ibid.

58. N. Buckley, "An Unmissable Opportunity," *Financial Times*, April 5, 2005.

59. "Special Zones Offer Oasis for Investment," *Washington Post Supplement*, April 29, 2009.

60. Puffer and McCarthy, May 2011.

61. N. Buckley, "Huge Gains but Also a Lot of Pain," *Financial Times*, October 11, 2005.

62. Garry Bruton, David Ahistrom, Michael Young, and Yuri Rubanik, "In Emerging Markets, Know What Your Partners Expect." *Wall Street Journal*, December 15, 2008.

63. A. E. Serwer, "McDonald's Conquers the World," *Fortune*, October 17, 1994.

64. Jack Welch (then CEO of GE) interviewed in *Fortune*, March 8, 1999.

65. "U.S. Exports to China Rebound in 2010," *China Business Review*, July–September, 2011.

66. Ibid.

67. Josh Green, "Just How Healthy Is Your Global Partner?" *Harvard Business Review*, 87 no. 7/8 (2009): 19.

68. P. Engardio, "The Future of Outsourcing," *BusinessWeek*, January 30, 2006, 50.

69. Ibid.

70. Based on M. Kripalani, D. Foust, S. Holmes, and P. Enga, "Five Offshore Practices that Pay Off," *BusinessWeek*, January 30, 2006, 60.

71. Josh Green, *Harvard Business Review* 87 no. 7/8 (2009): 19.

72. "Japan seeks Russian help to end nuclear crisis," *Financial Post* (Karachi), April 6, 2011.

73. Steve Lohr, "Stress Test for the Global Supply Chain," www.nytimes.com, March 19, 2011; Nick Bunkley, "G.M. Pieces Together a Japanese Supply Chain," www.nytimes.com, May 12, 2011; Anonymous, "Japan Earthquake: Global Supply Chains to Suffer Extensive Disruption," *Business Wire* (New York), March 17, 2011; Nigel Davis, "Japan's Crisis Affects Global Supply Chains," *ICIS Chemical Business*, March 28 – April 3, 2011.

74. Steve Lohr.

75. Huei-Ting Tsai and Andreas B. Eisingerich, "Internationalization Strategies of Emerging Market Firms," *California Management Review*, Vol. 53, No. 1, Fall 2010.

76. Mauro F. Guillén and Esteban García-Canal, "The American Model of the Multinational Firm and the 'New' Multinationals from Emerging Economies," *Academy of Management Perspectives*, May, 2009: 23–35.

77. Ibid.

78. Huei-Ting Tsai, 2010.

79. "Mahindra and Mahindra (B): An Emerging Global Giant?" Case study from IBSCDC India.

80. J. M. Geringer, "Strategic Determinants of Partner Selection Criteria in International Joint Ventures," *Journal of International Business Studies* (First Quarter 1991): 41–62.

81. J. M. Geringer and L. Hebert, "Control and Performance of International Joint Ventures," *Journal of International Business Studies* 20, no. 2 (1989).

82. Geringer, 1991.

83. P. Marsh, "Partnerships Feel the Indian Heat," *Financial Times*, June 22, 2006.

84. Ibid.

85. P. W. Beamish et al., *International Management* (Homewood, IL: Irwin, 1991).

86. J. L. Schaan and P. W. Beamish, "Joint Venture General Managers in Less Developed Countries," in *Cooperative Strategies in International Business*, eds. F. Contractor and P. Lorange (Toronto: Lexington Books, 1988), 279–99.

87. Oded Shenkar and Yoram Zeira, "International Joint Ventures: A Tough Test for HR," *Personnel* (January 1990): 26–31.

88. R. Mead, *International Management* (Cambridge, MA: Blackwell Publishers, 1994).

89. R. Duane Ireland and M. A. Hitt, "Achieving and Maintaining Strategic Competitiveness in the 21st Century: The Role of Strategic Leadership," *Academy of Management Executive* 19, no. 4 (2005): 63.

90. R. S. Bhagat, B. L. Kedia, P. D. Harveston, and H. C. Triandis, "Cultural Variations in the Cross-Border Transfer of Organizational knowledge: An Integrative Framework," *Academy of Management Review* 27, no. 2 (2002): 204–21.

91. D. G. Sirmon, M. A. Hitt, R. D. Ireland, in press. "Managing Firm Resources in Dynamic Environments to Create Value: Looking Inside the Black Box," *Academy of Management Review*, January 2007, Vol. 32. Issue 1, 273–292.

92. M. H. Hitt, V. Franklin, and Hong Zhu, "Culture, Institutions and International Strategy," *Journal of International Management* 12, no. 2 (2002): 222–34.

93. I. Berdrow and H. W. Lane, "International Joint Ventures: Creating Value through Successful Knowledge Management," *Journal of World Business* 38, no. 1 (2003): 15–30.

94. Ibid.

95. Ibid.

96. Louis Uchitelle, "Is Manufacturing Falling off the Radar?" *New York Times,* September 10, 2011.

97. Heather Timmons, "For Vodafone in India, a Swift but Bumpy Rise," www .nytimes.com, March 27, 2011.

98. "China's New Restrictions on Deals," *Financial Times,* August 10, 2006.

99. W. M. Danis, "Differences in Values, Practices, and Systems Among Hungarian Managers and Western Expatriates: An Organizing Framework and Typology," *Journal of World Business* (August 2003): 224–44.

100. R. Schoenberg, "Dealing with a Culture Clash," *Financial Times,* September 23, 2006.

101. Ibid.

102. P. Rosenzweig, "Why Is Managing in the United States so Difficult for European Firms?" *European Management Journal* 12, no. 1 (1994): 31–38.

103. Ibid.

104. "In Alabama, the Soul of a New Mercedes?" *BusinessWeek*, March 31, 1997.

105. Ibid.

106. M. Craze and J. Simmons, "Road from Acrimony to Giant Steel Merger: How Mittal and Arcelor Came to Terms," *International Herald Tribune*, July 6, 2006.

107. P. Marsh, "Deal Finalised in a Palace, but Sealed in an Airport," *Financial Times*, June 27, 2006.

108. Craze and Simmons, 2006.

109. Ibid.

110. P. Betts, "Steel Deals France a Hard Lesson in Reality," *Financial Times*, June 27, 2006.

111. H. James, "Europe Rediscovers the Tradition of Family Capitalism," *Financial Times*, July 4, 2006.

112. P. Glader and E. Bellman, "Breaking the Marwari Rules," *The Wall Street Journal*, July 10, 2006.

113. Ibid.

114. Ibid.

115. Ibid.

116. J. A. Pearce, II, and R. B. Robinson, Jr., "Cultivating *Guanxi* as a Foreign Investor Strategy," *Business Horizons* 43, no. 1 (2000): 31.

117. Ibid.

118. www.NextLinx.com, September 10, 2001.

119. Ibid.

Chapter 8

1. "Kraft Foods, Inc.," *YahooFinance* (2012), http://finance.yahoo.com/q/pr?s=KFT+Profile. Accessed on March 6, 2012.

2. Hellman, J., "Kraft Foods, Inc.," *Value Line*, January 27, 2012, New York, Value Line Publishing LLC.

3. See: Jargon, J., and Ziobro, P., "Kraft picks leaders for split," *Wall Street Journal*, December 6, 2011, B3; "Kraft to split into two companies," *BBC News Business* (2011), http://www.bbc.co.uk/news/business-14403616. Accessed on March 6, 2012.

4. Moeller, S., "Focus on the real decision makers," *Financial Times*, January 10, 2012, 10.

5. Lucas, L., and Rappeport, A., "A bitter taste," *Financial Times*, May 24, 2011, 9.

6. Commons Select Committee, *Business, Innovation and Skills Committee—Sixth Report: Is Kraft working for Cadbury*? http://www.publications.parliament.uk/pa/cm201012/cmselect/cmbis/871/87109.htm. (London, UK: Publications, Parliament, 2011). Accessed on March 6, 2012.

7. R. Foster and S. Kaplan, Creative Destruction: Why Companies That Are Built to Last Underperform the Market—And How to Successfully Transform Them (New York, NY: Currency, 2001).

8. Charles A. O'Reilly, III, J. Bruce Harreld, and Michael L. Tushman, "Organizational Ambidexterity: IBM and Emerging Business Opportunities," *California Management Review* 51, no. 4 (2009): 75–99.

9. Roberto C. Goizueta, (Former) Chairman and CEO, Coca-Cola Company.

10. A. D. Chandler, *Strategy and Structure: Chapters in the History of the American Industrial Enterprise* (Cambridge, MA: MIT Press, 1962); R. E. Miles et al., "Organizational Strategy, Structure, and Process," *Academy of Management Review* 3, no. 3 (1978): 546–62; and J. Woodward, *Industrial Organization: Theory and Practice* (Oxford University Press, 1965).

11. C. A. Bartlett and S. Ghoshal, *Managing Across Borders* (Boston: Harvard Business School Press, 1989).

12. J. M. Stopford and L. T. Wells, Jr., *Managing the Multinational Enterprise* (New York: Basic Books, 1972).

13. Greg Tarr, "Samsung Restructures, Combines Biz Units," *TWICE: This Week in Consumer Electronics* 24, no. 3 (2009): 4–8; Kelly Olsen, "Samsung Electronics Reorganizes to Fight Slump," www.nytimes, January 16, 2009. Evan Ramstad, "Corporate News: Samsung Overhaul Will Form 2 Divisions," *Wall Street Journal* (Eastern edition), January 16, 2009.

14. Leaders: "Asia's new model company"; "Samsung and its attractions," *The Economist*, October 1, 2011: 14.

15. Kelly Olsen, "Samsung Electronics Reorganizes to Fight Slump," www .nytimes, January 16, 2009.

16. "Heinz's Johnson to Divest Operations, Scrap Management of Firm by Regions," *The Wall Street Journal*, December 8, 1997.

17. www.Nestle.com, December 7, 2000.

18. *Financial Times*, February 22, 2005.

19. Ibid.

20. www.Nestle.com, April 15, 2012.

21. J. Strikwerda and J. W. Stoelhorst, "The Emergence and Evolution of the Multidimensional Organization," *California Management Review* 51, no. 4 (2009): 11–31.

22. H. Henzler and W. Rall, "Facing Up to the Globalization Challenge," *McKinsey Quarterly* (Fall 1986): 52–68.

23. "Petrobras creates 6 companies for Comperj project—Brazil." *Business News Americas*, February 5, 2009.

24. T. Levitt, "The Globalization of Markets," *Harvard Business Review* (May–June 1983): 92–102; and S. P. Douglas and Yoram Wind, "The Myth of Globalization," *Columbia Journal of World Business* (Winter 1987): 19–29.

25. www.levistrauss.com, accessed April 18, 2009.

26. http://www.levistrauss.com/about/global-workplaces, accessed August 7, 2012.

27. www.pg.com, News Releases, November 22, 2006.

28. "P&G Corporate Information: How the Structure Works," www.pg.com, November 22, 2006.

29. "P&G Corporate Information: How the Structure Works," www.pg.com, March 4, 2012.

30. J. R. Galbraith, "The Multidimensional and Reconfigurable Organization," *Organizational Dynamics*, Vol. 39, No. 2 (2010): 115–125.

31. For more detail, see *The New Global Challengers: How 100 Top Companies from Rapidly Developing Economies Are Changing the World* (Boston, MA: The Boston Consulting Group, 2006); *Organizing for Global Advantage in China, India, and Other Rapidly Developing Economies* (Boston, MA: The Boston Consulting Group, 2006); Khanna, Tarun and Krishna Palepu, "Emerging Giants: Building World-Class Companies in Developing Countries," *Harvard Business Review* (October 2006): 60–69.

32. See Syed T. Anwar, "Global Business and Globalization," *Journal of International Management* 71 (2007); "Emerging Giants," *BusinessWeek*, July 31, 2006, 40–49.

33. Raymond E. Miles, Miles Grant, Charles C. Snow, Kirsimarja Blomqvist, and Hector Rocha, "The I-form Organization," *California Management Review* 51, no. 4 (2009): 61–76.

34. Andy Reinhardt, "Philips: Back on the Beam," www.businessweek.com, May 3, 2004.

35. *Financial Times*, February 9, 2005.

36. www.Intel.com, August 18, 2005.

37. S. Ghoshal and C. A. Bartlett, "The Multinational Corporation as an Inter-organizational Network," *Academy of Management Review* 15, no. 4 (1990): 603–25.

38. Mohanbir Sawhney and Sumant Mandal, "Go Global," *Business 2.0* (May 5, 2001): 178–213.

39. J. D. Daniels, L. H. Radebaugh, and D. P. Sullivan, *Globalization and Business* (Upper Saddle River, NJ: Prentice Hall, 2002).

40. "Energizing the Supply Chain," *The Review*, Deloitte & Touche, January 17, 2000, 1.

41. C. A. Bartlett and S. Ghoshal, "Organizing for Worldwide Effectiveness: The Transnational Solution," *California Management Review* (Fall 1988): 54–74.

42. Ibid.

43. Based on Business International Corporation, *New Directions in Multinational Corporate Organization* (New York: Business International Corporation, 1981).

44. Sources include: Mark Pieth, "Fifa must finally show a red card to corruption in football," *Financial Times*, January 20, 2012: 13; Grant Wahl, "Rotten All Around: FIFA's Year of Corruption shows that real change will only come when the man at the top leaves," http://sportsillustrated.cnn.com/vault/article/magazine/MAG1193195/index.htm, December 26, 2011; http://en.wikipedia.org/wiki/FIFA, accessed February 1, 2012; www.FIFA.com, accessed February 1, 2012.

45. John B. Cullen and K. Praveen Parboteeah, *Multinational Management: A Strategic Approach*, 3rd ed. (Cincinnati: South-Western, 2005), 281.

46. Oded Shenkar, "Cultural Distance Revisited: Towards a More Rigorous Conceptualization and Measurement of Cultural Differences," *Journal of International Business*, 43 (1), January 2012.

47. Ibid.

48. www.McDonalds.com, February 20, 2001.

49. Andrew Jack, "Russians Wake up to Consumer Capitalism," www.FT.com, January 30, 2001.

50. Ibid.

51. G. Rohrmann, CEO, AEI Corp., press release.

52. W. G. Egelhoff, "Patterns of Control in U.S., U.K., and European Multinational Corporations," *Journal of International Business Studies* (Fall 1984): 73–83.

53. Ibid.

54. Ibid.

55. S. Ueno and U. Sekaran, "The Influence of Culture on Budget Control Practices in the U.S.A. and Japan: An Empirical Study," *Journal of International Business Studies* 23 (Winter 1992): 659–74.

56. A. R. Neghandi and M. Welge, *Beyond Theory Z* (Greenwich, CT: J.A.I. Publishers, 1984), 18.

57. www.Nestle.com, press release, March 21, 2000.

58. A. V. Phatak, *International Dimensions of Management*, 2nd ed (Boston: PWS-Kent, 1989).

Chapter 9

1. 2012 Brookfield Global Relocation Trends Survey, www.brookfieldgrs.com, accessed August 12, 2012; www.McKinsey.com/mgi/; "Capturing Talent," *The Economist*, August 18, 2007, 59–61; Douglas A. Ready, Linda A. Hill, and Jay A. Conger, "Winning the Race for Talent in Emerging Markets," *Harvard Business Review* (November 2008); Harold L. Sirkin, "Need Global Talent? Grow Your Own," *BusinessWeek* Online, September 17, 2008; "Talent Retention: Ongoing Problem for Asia-Pacific Region," *T+D* 61 no. 3 (2007): 12.

2. 2012 Brookfield Global Relocation Trends Survey, www.brookfieldgrs.com, accessed August 12, 2012.

3. www.McKinsey.com/mgi/; "Capturing Talent," *The Economist*, August 18, 2007, 59–61.

4. *The Economist*, 2007.

5. Douglas A. Ready, Linda A. Hill, and Jay A. Conger, "Winning the Race for Talent in Emerging Markets," *Harvard Business Review* (November 2008).

6. Sirkin, 2008.

7. Sirkin, 2008.

8. Ready et al., 2008.

9. Ibid.

10. www.pricewaterhousecoopers.com, accessed November 19, 2011.

11. Mendenhall, J. E., Jensen, R. J., Black, J. S., and Gregerson, H. B. (2003) "Seeing the Elephant: Human Resource Management Challenges in the Age of Globalization," *Organizational Dynamics* 32 (3), 261–274.

12. J. L. Laabs, "HR Pioneers Explore the Road Less Traveled," *Personnel Journal* (February 1996): 70–72, 74, 77–78.

13. Friso Den Hertog, Ad Van Iterson, and Christian Mari, "Does HRM Really Matter in Bringing about Strategic Change? Comparative Action Research in Ten European Steel Firms," *European Management Journal* 28(1), 2010: 14–24.

14. www.ibm.com, accessed December 1, 2011; S. Hamm, "International Isn't Just IBM's First Name," www.businessweek.com, January 28, 2008, 36–40.

15. *The 2011 PricewaterhouseCoopers' 14th Annual CEO Survey.*

16. KPMG 2012 Global Assignment Survey, www.kpmg.com, accessed August 9, 2012.

17. J. Stewart Black and Allen J. Morrison, "A Cautionary Tale for Emerging Market Giants," *Harvard Business Review*, September 2010.

18. Ibid.; "International Assignments Remain on the Upswing Despite Economic Concerns, Says KPMG," Anonymous, *PR Newswire*, Dec 3, 2008.

19. Ibid.

20. Bettina Wassener, "Living in Asia Appeals to More Company Leaders," *New York Times* [New York, N.Y.] 21 June 2012: B.3.

21. Ibid.

22. C. A. Bartlett and S. Ghoshal, "Matrix Management: Not a Structure, a Frame of Mind," *Harvard Business Review* (July–August 1990).

23. www.tcs.com, accessed November 21, 2011; Stefan Wagstyl, "Indian outsourcers in US hiring push," FT.com, September 21, 2010; R. Jai Krishna and R. Guha, "U.S. Visa rejections Hit TCS," July 18, 2011, *The Wall Street Journal*, July 18, 2011; Bruce Einhorn, "Demand Grows Despite H-1B Fight, TCS Exec Says," www.bloombergbusinessweek.com, August 18, 2010; Charlie Adith, "TCS, IBM back in US' fast-track visa facility," *The Hindu Business Line*, June 13, 2010; "Business: From Mumbai to the Midwest; TCS in America," *The Economist* 401. 8758 (November 5, 2011): 74.

24. "Business: From Mumbai to the Midwest; TCS in America," *The Economist* 401. 8758 (November 5, 2011): 74.

25. Lynda Gratton, "Workplace 2025—What Will It Look Like?" *Organizational Dynamics* (2011) 40, 246–254.

26. M. Harvey et al., "Developing Effective Global Relationships Through Staffing with Inpatriate Managers: The Role of Interpersonal Trust," *Journal of International Management*, 2011, doi:10.1016/j.intman 2011.01.02.

27. J. Stewart Black and Allen J. Morrison, "A Cautionary Tale for Emerging Market Giants," *Harvard Business Review*, September 2010.

28. M. Harvey, Novivenic, M. M., Speier, C., "Strategic Global Human Resource Management: The Role of Inpatriate Managers," *Human Resource Management Review*, 10 (2), (2000):153–175.

29. Ibid.

30. M. Harvey, 2011.

31. Michael Harvey, Helene Mayerhofer, Linley Hartmann, and Miriam Moeller, "Corralling the 'Horses' to Staff the Global Organization of the 21st Century," *Organizational Dynamics*, Vol. 39, No. 3, (2010): 258–268.

32. Oded Shenkar, "Cultural Distance Revisited: Towards a More Rigorous Conceptualization and Measurement of Cultural Differences," *Journal of International Business*, 43 (1), January 2012.

33. S. B. Prasad and Y. K. Krishna Shetty, *An Introduction to Multinational Management* (Upper Saddle River, NJ: Prentice Hall, 1979).

34. Rochelle Kopp, "International Human Resource Policies and Practices in Japanese, European, and United States Multinationals," *Human Resource Management* 33, no. 4 (1994): 581–99.

35. Based on, updated, and adapted by H. Deresky in 2007, from original work by D. A. Heenan and H. V. Perlmutter. *Multinational Organization Development* (Reading, MA: Addison-Wesley, 1979), 18–19.

36. R. L. Tung, "Selection and Training of Personnel for Overseas Assignments," *Columbia Journal of World Business*, (Spring 1981): 68–78.

37. P. Dowling and R. S. Schuler, *International Dimensions of Human Resource Management (Boston: PWS-Kent, 1990)*.

38. S. J. Kobrin, "Expatriate Reduction and Strategic Control in American Multinational Corporations," *Human Resource Management* 27, no. 1 (1988): 63–75.

39. Company information, www.ABB.com, accessed July 26, 2004.

40. Hem C. Jain, "Human Resource Management in Selected Japanese Firms, the Foreign Subsidiaries and Locally Owned Counterparts," *International Labour Review* 129, no. 1 (1990): 73–84; Bartlett and Ghoshal.

41. www.GMACGlobalrelocation.com, accessed March 1, 2009.

42. M. Mendenhall and G. Oddou, "The Dimensions of Expatriate Acculturation: A Review," *Academy of Management Review* 10, no. 1 (1985): 39–47.

43. Zsuzsanna Tungli and Mauri Peiperl, "Expatriate Practices in German, Japanese, U.K., and U.S. Multinational Companies: A Comparative Survey of Changes," Human Resource Management, January–February 2009, Vol. 48, No. 1, pp. 153–171 © 2009 Wiley Periodicals, Inc.

44. Theresa Minton-Eversole, "Best Expatriate Assignments Require Much Thought, Even More Planning," SHRM's 2009 Global Trend Book, *HRMagazine (2009)*: 74–75.

45. M. G. Tye and P. Y. Chen (2005). "Selection of expatriates: Decision-making models used by HR professionals," *Human Resource Planning* 28(4): 15–20.

46. D. Erbacher, B. D'Netto, and J. Espana, "Expatriate Success in China: Impact of Personal and Situational Factors," *Journal of American Academy of Business* 9, no. 2 (2006): 183.

47. www.FT.com, March 5, 2001.

48. Rosalie Tung, "American Expatriates Abroad: From Neophytes to Cosmopolitans," *Journal of World Business* 33 (1998): 125–44.

49. Business Editors, "International Job Assignment: Boon or Bust for an Employee's Career?" *Business Wire, Inc.*, March 13, 2006.

50. R. D. Hays, "Expatriate Selection: Insuring Success and Avoiding Failure," *Journal of International Business Studies* 5, no. 1 (1974): 25–37; Tung, 1998.

51. His-An Shih, Yun-Hwa Chiang, and In-Sook Kim, "Expatriate Performance Management from MNEs of Different National Origins," *International Journal of Manpower* 26, no. 2 (2005): 161–62.

52. *Business Wire*, 2006.

53. Ibid.

54. Ibid.

55. Tung, 1998.

56. Ibid.

57. B. Wysocki, Jr., "Prior Adjustment: Japanese Executives Going Overseas Take Anti-Shock Courses," *The Wall Street Journal*, December 4, 1987.

58. Mendenhall and Oddou.

59. K. Oberg, "Culture Shock: Adjustments to New Cultural Environments," *Practical Anthropology* (July–August 1960): 177–82.

60. Ibid.

61. Lynette Clemetson, "The Pepsi Challenge: Helping Expats Feel At Home," *Workforce Management* 89, no. 12 (December 2010): 36.

62. Ibid.

63. P. R. Harris and R. T. Moran, *Managing Cultural Differences*, 4th ed. (Houston, TX: Gulf Publishing, 1996), 139.

64. Tung, "Selection and Training of Personnel for Overseas Assignments."

65. S. Ronen, "Training the International Assignee," In Irwin L. Goldstein (Ed.) *Training and Development in Organizations*, San Francisco, Ca. Jossey-Bass, 1989, pp. 417–453.

66. Ibid.

67. D. J. Kealey, (1989). A study of cross-cultural effectiveness: Theoretical issues, practical applications. *International Journal of Intercultural Relations, 13*, 387–427.

68. Based on J. S. Black, Mark. E. Mendenhall, Hal B. Gregersen, and Linda K. Stroh, *Globalizing People Through International Assignments* (Reading, MA: Addison Wesley Longman, 1999).

69. R. Peterson, "The Use of Expatriates and Inpatriates in Central and Eastern Europe Since the Wall Came Down," *Journal of World Business* 38 (2003): 55–69.

70. Christopher Tice, Manager, Global Expatriate Operations, DuPont Inc., quoted in Mark Schoeff, "International Assignments Best Served by Unified Policy," *Workforce Management* 85, no. 3 (2006): 36.

71. Ibid.

72. "Living Expenses," www.economist.com, July 22, 2000; "Runzheimer International Compensation Worksheet," www.runzheimer.com, 2000.

73. *Business Wire*, 2006.

74. B. W. Teague, *Compensating Key Personnel Overseas* (New York: Conference Board, 1992).

75. C. Reynolds, "Compensation of Overseas Personnel," in J. Famularo, *Handbook of Human Resource Administration*, 2nd ed. New York: McGraw-Hill, 1989.

76. S. F. Gale, "Taxing Situations for Expatriates," *Workforce* 82, no. 6 (2003): 100.

77. International Assignment Policies and Practices Survey, 2011, www.kpmg.com, accessed November 11, 2011.

78. R. B. Peterson, "The Use of Expatriates and Inpatriates in Central and Eastern Europe Since the Wall Came Down," *Journal of World Business* (2003): 55–69.

79. Gina Ruiz, "Kimberly-Clark: Developing Talent in Developing World Markets," *Workforce Management* 85, no. 7 (2006): 34.

80. Martin Fackler, "The 'Toyota Way' Is Translated for a New Generation of Foreign Managers," www.nytimes.com, February 17, 2007.

81. Ibid.

82. Ibid.

83. "Seoul Is Supporting a Sizzling Tech Boom," www.businessweek.com, September 25, 2000.

84. P. Damaskopoulos and T. Evgeniou, "Adoption of New Economy Practices by SMEs in Eastern Europe," *European Management Journal* 21, no. 2 (2003): 133–45.

85. Based on Damaskopoulos and Evgeniou, 2003.

86. Company website, www.starbucks.com, accessed March 5, 2012.

87. Fay Hansen, "The Great Global Talent Race: One World, One Workforce: Part 1 of 2," *Workforce Management* 85, no. 7 (2006): 1.

88. D. Kiriazov, S. E. Sullivan, and H. S. Tu, "Business Success in Eastern Europe: Understanding and Customizing HRM," *Business Horizons* (January/February 2000): 39–43.

89. Ibid.

90. Y. Ono and W. Spindle, "Japan's Long Decline Makes One Thing Rise: Individualism," *The Wall Street Journal*, January 3, 2001.

91. "Personnel Demands Attention Overseas," *Mutual Fund Market News*, March 19, 2001, 1.

92. Rita Pyrillis, "Just a Token of Your Appreciation? Avoid Cultural Faux Pas When Rewarding International Employees," *Workforce Management* 90, no. 9, September 2011: 3–6.

93. Mary Ann Von Glinow, Ellen A. Drost, and Mary B. Teagarden, "Converging on IHRM Best Practices: Lessons Learned from a Globally Distributed Consortium on Theory and Practice," *Human Resource Management* 41, no. 1 (2002): 133–35.

Chapter 10

1. Julia Werdigier, "Paychecks and Passports," *New York Times*, April 2, 2008; Doreen Carvajal, "Paid in Dollars, Some Americans Are Struggling in Europe," *New York Times*, December 15, 2007; Alan Paul, "The Expat Life: Clock Counts Down as Decision Weighs: Should I Stay or Go?" www.wallstreetjournal, February 28, 2008; Monica Ginsburg, "Getting Ahead by Going Abroad," *Crain's Chicago Business* 31, no. 50 (2008): 20; Philip Shearer and Abby Ellin, "Foreign from the Start," www.nytimes.com, September 21, 2003; Jad Mouawad, "Total, the French Oil Company, Places It Bets Globally," www.nytimes.com, February 22, 2009; www.Global Relocation Trends

Survey, www.brookfieldgrs.com, accessed March 1, 2009; Keith Bradsher and Julia Werdigier, "Abruptly Expatriate Bankers Are Cut Loose," www.nytimes.com March 4, 2009.

2. Werdigier.

3. Bradsher and Werdigier.

4. *Wall Street Journal*, February 28, 2008.

5. www.nytimes.com, February 22, 2000.

6. Ginsburg.

7. Ibid.

8. Shearer and Ellin.

9. The *Global Talent Index Report: The Outlook to 2015* was written by the Economist Intelligence Unit and published by Heidrick & Struggles.

10. 2011 Global Relocation Trends Survey, www.brookfieldgrs.com, accessed February 26, 2011.

11. Ibid.

12. A. Maitland, "Top Companies Value Overseas Experience," www.Financial Times, July 3, 2006.

13. "International Assignments Remain On the Upswing Despite Economic Concerns, Says KPMG," *PR Newswire*, December 3, 2008; www.kpmglink.com.

14. M. Lazarova and P. Caligiuri, "Retaining Repatriates: The Role of Organizational Support Practices," *Journal of World Business* 36 no. 4 (2001): 389–401.

15. Ibid.

16. Rosalie Tung, "Career Issues in International Assignments," *Academy of Management Executive* 2, no. 3 (1988): 241–44.

17. M. Harvey, "Dual-Career Expatriates: Expectations, Adjustments and Satisfaction with International Relocation," *Journal of International Business Studies* 28, no. 3 (1997): 627.

18. Tung.

19. Charlene M. Solomon, "One Assignment, Two Lives," *Personnel Journal* (May 1996): 36–44.

20. 2011 Global Relocation Trends Survey, www.brookfieldgrs.com, accessed March 1, 2009.

21. Ibid.

22. Solomon.

23. 2011 Global Relocation Trends Survey, 2009.

24. R. Pascoe, "Employers Ignore Expatriate Wives at Their Own Peril," *Wall Street Journal*, March 29, 1992.

25. www.FT.com, March 5, 2001.

26. P. Asheghian and B. Ebrahimi, *International Business* (New York: HarperCollins, 1990), 470.

27. Global Relocation Trends Survey, 2009.

28. N. J. Adler, *International Dimensions of Organizational Behavior*, 4th ed. (Boston: PWS-Kent, 2002).

29. J. Bonache and C. Brewster, "Knowledge Transfer and the Management of Expatriation," *Thunderbird International Business Review* 43, no. 1 (2001): 145–68.

30. David Holthaus, "P&G At Work: Key Managers in Africa," *Cincinnati Enquirer*, April 16, 2011; www.pg.com, accessed December 9, 2011.

31. Berthoin-Antal, "Expatriates' Contributions to Organizational Learning," *Journal of General Management* 26, no. 4 (2001): 62–84.

32. Ibid.

33. Mila Lazarova and Ibraiz Tarique, "Knowledge Transfer upon Repatriation," *Journal of World Business* 40, no. 4 (2005): 361–73.

34. Ibid.

35. Excerpted from www.Netscape.com case studies.

36. J. S. Black and H. B. Gregersen, "The Other Half of the Picture: Antecedents of Spouse Cross-cultural Adjustment," *Journal of International Business Studies* (1992): 461–77.

37. Joe Leahy, "Brazil hosts a homecoming," *Financial Times*, 23 August, 2011: 8; Guy Chazan, "Middle East: Oil Firms Suspend Libyan Operations," *Wall Street Journal*, 22 Feb 2011: A.11.; Borzou Daragahi, "Expats trickle back to Libya but business remains slow," *Financial Times*, London (UK), February 11, 2012: 2; Mariko Sanchanta, "Disaster in Japan: Expatriates Tiptoe Back to the Office," *Wall Street Journal*, March 23, 2011: A.7.

38. *Financial Times*, August 23, 2011.

39. Ibid.

40. *Financial Times*, February 11, 2012.

41. *Wall Street Journal*, March 23, 2011.

42. T. Gross, E. Turner, and L. Cederholm, "Building Teams for Global Operations," *Management Review* (June 1987): 32–36.

43. www.BritishTelecom.com/cases, February 19, 2001.

44. J. Conger and E. Lawler, "People Skills Still Rule in the Virtual Company," *Financial Times*, August 26, 2005.

45. Based largely on Adler, 2002.

46. T. Gross, E. Turner, and L. Cederholm, "Building Teams for Global Operations," *Management Review* (June 1987), 34.

47. T. R. Kayworth and D. E. Leidner, "Leadership Effectiveness in Global Virtual Teams," *Journal of Management Information Systems* 18, no. 3 (2001–02): 7–40.

48. C. Solomon, "Building Teams Across Borders," *Global Workforce* (November 1998): 12–17.

49. Ibid.

50. J. Cordery, C. Soo, B. Kirkman, B. Benson, and J. Mathieu, "Leading Parallel Virtual Teams: Lessons from Alcoa," *Organizational Dynamics* 38, no. 3 (2009): 204–16.

51. Some of this content is based on Kenneth W. Kerber and Anthony F. Buono, "Leadership Challenges in Global Virtual Teams: Lessons from the Field," *SAM Advanced Management Journal* 69, no. 4 (2004): 4–10.

52. Ibid.

53. Ibid.

54. B. Rosen, S. Furst, and R. Blackburn, "Training for Virtual Teams: An Investigation of Current Practices and Future Needs," *Human Resources Management* 45, no. 2 (2006): 229–47.

55. Michiyo Nakamoto, "Cultural Revolution in Tokyo," www.ft.com, September 17, 2009.

56. Ibid.

57. A. Joshi, G. Labianca, and P. M. Caligiuri, "Getting Along Long Distance: Understanding Conflict in a Multinational Team through Network Analysis," *Journal of World Business* 37 (2002): 277–84.

58. V. Govindarajan and A. K. Gupta, "Building an Effective Global Business Team," *MIT Sloan Management Review* 42, no. 4 (2001): 63.

59. Ibid.

60. Ibid.

61. S. Chevrier, "Cross-cultural Management in Multinational Project Groups," *Journal of World Business* 38, no. 2 (2003): 141–49.

62. Ibid.

63. Business Editors, "International Job Assignment: Boon or Bust for an Employee's Career?" *Business Wire Inc.*, March 13, 2006.

64. Rupali Arora, "International Power 50," *Fortune International (Europe)* (October 17, 2011), vol. 164, Issue 6.

65. Ibid.

66. Shyamantha Asokan and David Patrikarakos, "Leading Businesswomen in the Arab World: Who's Who: Extended Version of Our List of Personalities," www.ft.com, June 23, 2008.

67. R. L. Tung, "Female Expatriates: The Model Global Manager?" *Organizational Dynamics* 33, no. 3 (2004): 243–53.

68. G. K. Stahl, E. L. Miller, and R. L. Tung, "Toward the Boundaryless Career: A Closer Look at the Expatriate Career Concept and the Perceived Implications of an International Assignment," *Journal of World Business* 37 (2002): 216–27.

69. Nicola Clark, "Awareness Rises, but Women Still Lag in Pay," www.nytimes.com, March 8, 2010.

70. Ibid.

71. Alison Maitland, "The North-South Divide in Europe, Inc.," *Financial Times*, June 14, 2004.

72. Katrin Bennhold, "Women Nudged Out of German Workforce," www.nytimes.com, June 28, 2011.

73. Based on selected data from Bennhold, June 28, 2011, and McKinsey's 2010 "Women Matter" Report.

74. Bennhold.

75. M. Kaminski and J. Paiz, "Japanese Women in Management: Where Are They?" *Human Resource Management* 23, no. 2 (1984): 277–92.

76. P. Lansing and K. Ready, "Hiring Women Managers in Japan: An Alternative for Foreign Employers," *California Management Review* 26, no. 4 (1988): 112–27.

77. Japan's Neglected Resource—Female Workers," www.nytimes.com, July 24, 2003.

78. Ibid.

79. Maitland, 2004.

80. M. Jelinek and N. Adler, "Women: World Class Managers for Global Competition," *Academy of Management Executive* 11, no. 1 (February 1988): 11–19.

81. N. J. Adler and D. N. Izraeli, *Women in Management Worldwide* (Armonk, NY: M. E. Sharpe, 1988).

82. Ibid.

83. Jacob Vittorelli, Former Deputy Chairman of Pirelli.

84. Stuart Pfeifer, "Workers at Ikea's first U.S. factory O.K. Union," *Los Angeles Times,* July 29, 2011.

85. "A New Deal in Europe?" www.businessweek.com, July 14, 2003.

86. M. R. Czinkota, I. A. Ronkainen, and M. H. Moffett, *International Business*, 3rd ed. (New York: Dryden Press, 1994).

87. *Bureau of Labor Statistics News Release*, January 21, 2011.

88. C. K. Prahalad and Y. L. Doz, *The Multinational Mission: Balancing Local Demands and Global Vision* (New York: Free Press, 1987).

89. R. J. Adams, *Industrial Relations Under Liberal Democracy* (University of South Carolina Press, 1995).

90. J. S. Daniels and L. H. Radebaugh, *International Business*, 10th ed. (Reading, MA: Addison-Wesley, 2004).

91. P. J. Dowling, R. S. Schuler, and D. E. Welch, *International Dimensions of Human Resource Management,* 2nd ed. (Belmont CA: Wadsworth, 1994).

92. Adams.

93. Ibid.

94. D. Barboza, "China Passed Law to Empower Unions and End Labor Abuse," *New York Times*, October 12, 2006.

95. David Barboza, www.nytimes.com, October 12, 2006.

96. Ibid.

97. Anonymous. "Asia: Arbitration needed: China's Labour Laws," *The Economist*. London: August 1, 2009, 392, no. 8642 (2009): 37.

98. Dexter Roberts, "Using Propaganda to Stop China's Strikes," *BusinessWeek,* (Dec 19, 2011): 1.

99. David Barboza, "Foxconn Resolves a Dispute with Some Workers in China," *International Herald Tribune,* January 12, 2012.

100. Nick Wingfield and Charles Duhigg, "Apple Lists its Suppliers for the First Time," *International Herald Tribune,* January 14, 2012.

101. *BusinessWeek, 2011.*

102. Jenkins, R., "Globalisation of Production, Employment and Poverty: Three Macro-Meso-Micro Studies," *The European Journal of Development Research,* 17(4), (2005): 601–625.

103. B. Barber, "Workers of the World Are Uniting," *Financial Times*, December 7, 2004.

104. www.ituc-csi.org, accessed April 19, 2012.

105. International Confederation of Free Trade Unions, www.icftu.org, October 31, 2006.

106. Ibid.

107. M. M. Lucio and S. Weston, "New Management Practices in a Multinational Corporation: The Restructuring of Worker Representation and Rights?" *Industrial Relations Journal* 25, no. 2 (2004): 110–21.

108. D. B. Cornfield, "Labor Transnationalism?" *Work and Occupations* 24, no. 3 (August 1997): 278.

109. R. Martin, A. Vidinova, and S. Hill, "Industrial Relations in Transition Economies: Emergent Industrial Relations Institutions in Bulgaria," *British Journal of Industrial Relations* 34, no. 1 (1996): 3.

110. Daniels and Radebaugh.

111. A. M. Rugman and R. M. Hodgetts, *International Business* (New York: McGraw-Hill, 1995).

112. "Mexico prez trying to crush labor unions legally," *Teamster Nation,* April 21, 2011.

113. "Maximum number of permitted foreign employees," (*HSBC Bank,* www.hsbc.com, accessed October 3, 2011).

114. Dietmar Henning, "IG Metall union and German government reaffirm their collaboration," www.wsws.org, October 21, 2011.

115. Floyd Norris, "Germany vs. the Rest of Europe," *New York Times,* February 16, 2012.

116. Ibid.

117. R. Milne and H. Williamson, "Selective Bargaining: German Companies Are Driving a Hidden Revolution in Labour Flexibility," *Financial Times,* January 6, 2006.

118. Gerrit Wiesmann, "Germans Eye U.K. Listings as a Way Out of Worker Law," *Financial Times*, May 24, 2006.

119. Ibid.

120. "A New Deal in Europe?" www.businessweek.com; *BW Online,* July 14, 2003.

121. http://www.worker-participation.eu/National-Industrial-Relations/Countries/Germany/Trade-Unions, accessed August 22, 2012.

122. http://www.worker-participation.eu, accessed August 22, 2012.

123. Milne and Williamson.

124. J. Hoerr, "What Should Unions Do?" *Harvard Business Review* (May–June 1991): 30–45.

125. H. C. Katz, "The Decentralization of Collective Bargaining: A Literature Review and Comparative Analysis," *Industrial and Labor Relations Review* 47, no. 1 (1993): 3–22.

126. Williamson, *Financial Times,* July 22, 2004.

127. www.nytimes.com, July 24, 2004.

128. Adams.

129. "The Perils of Cozy Corporatism," *The Economist*, May 21, 1994.

130. Wofgang Streeck, "More Uncertainties: German Unions Facing 1992," *Industrial Relations* (Fall 1991): 30–33.

Chapter 11

1. Nicholas Sambanis, "The Euro Crisis as Ethnic Conflict," *International Herald Tribune*, August 27, 2012.
2. A. Maitland, "Le patron, der Chef and the Boss," *Financial Times*, January 9, 2006.
3. M. Kets de Vries and K. Korotov, "The Future of an Illusion: In Search of the New European Business Leader," *Organizational Dynamics* 34, no. 3 (2005): 218–30.
4. Ibid.
5. Maitland.
6. Ibid.
7. R. J. House, *Culture, Leadership and Organizations: The GLOBE Study of 62 Societies* (Thousand Oaks, CA: Sage, 2004).
8. F. C. Brodbeck, M. Frese, and M. Javidan, "Leadership Made in Germany: Low on Compassion, High on Performance," *Academy of Management Executive* 16, no. 1 (2002).
9. R. House and M. Javidan, "Cultural Acumen for the Global Manager: Lessons from Project GLOBE," *Organizational Dynamics* (2001).
10. Mansour Javidan, Peter W. Dorfman, Mary Sully de Luque, Robert J. House, "In the Eye of the Beholder: Cross Cultural Lessons in Leadership from Project GLOBE," *The Academy of Management Perspectives* 20, no. 1 (2006).
11. N. Payton, "Leaderships Skills Hold Britain Back," *The Guardian*, February 22, 2003.
12. S. Michailova, "When Common Sense Becomes Uncommon: Participation and Empowerment in Russian Companies with Western Participation," *Journal of World Business* 37 (2002): 180–87.
13. "Fujitsu Uses Pay Cuts as a Motivational Tool," www.nytimes.com, January 27, 2004.
14. Garry A. Gelade, Paul Dobson, and Katharina Auer, "Individualism, Masculinity, and the Sources of Organizational Commitment," *Journal of Cross-Cultural Psychology* 39 (2008): 599.
15. Ibid.
16. F. Rieger and D. Wong-Rieger, "A Configuration Model of National Influence Applied to Southeast Asian Organizations," *Proceedings of the Research Conference on Business in Southeast Asia*, May 12–13, 1990, University of Michigan.
17. R. M. Steers, *Made in Korea: Chung Ju Yung and the Rise of Hyundai* (New York: Routledge, 1999).
18. Meaning of Work International Research Team, *The Meaning of Working: An International Perspective* (New York: Academic Press, 1985).
19. Ibid.
20. A. H. Maslow, *Motivation and Personality* (New York: Harper and Row, 1954).
21. F. Herzberg, *Work and the Nature of Man* (Cleveland: Cleveland World Press, 1966).
22. D. Siddiqui and A. Alkhafaji, *The Gulf War: Implications for Global Businesses and Media* (Apollo, PA: Closson Press, 1992): 133–35.
23. Ibid.
24. A. Ali, "The Islamic Work Ethic in Arabia," *Journal of Psychology* 126 (1992): 507–19.
25. Yasamusa Kuroda and Tatsuzo Suzuki, "A Comparative Analysis of the Arab Culture: Arabic, English and Japanese Language and Values," paper presented at the 5th Congress of the International Association of Middle Eastern Studies, Tunis (September 20–24, 1991), quoted in Siddiqui and Alkhafaji.
26. A. Furnham, B. D. Kirkcaldy, and R. Lynn, "National Attitudes to Competitiveness, Money, and Work among Young People: First, Second, and Third World Differences," *Human Relations* 47, no. 1 (1994): 119–32.
27. D. S. Elenkov, "Can American Management Concepts Work in Russia? A Cross-cultural Comparative Study," *California Management Review* 40, no. 4 (1998): 133–57.
28. Abraham Maslow, *Motivation and Personality* (New York: Harper & Row, 1954).
29. R. L. Tung, "Patterns of Motivation in Chinese Industrial Enterprises," *Academy of Management Review* 6, no. 3 (1981): 481–89.
30. Swee Hoon Ang, "The Power of Money: A Cross-cultural Analysis of Business-Related Beliefs," *Journal of World Business* 35, no. 1 (2000): 43.
31. Geert Hofstede, "National Cultures in Four Dimensions," *International Studies of Management and Organization* (Spring–Summer 1983).
32. D. Walker, T. Walker, and J. Schmitz, *Doing Business Internationally*, 2nd ed. (New York: McGraw-Hill, 2003).
33. Ibid.
34. Ibid.
35. Ibid.
36. M. B. Teagarden, M. C. Butler, and M. Von Glinow, "Mexico's Maquiladora Industry: Where Strategic Human Resource Management Makes a Difference," *Organizational Dynamics* (Winter 1992): 34–47.
37. John Condon, *Good Neighbors: Communication with the Mexicans* (Yarmouth, ME: Intercultural Press, 1985).
38. G. K. Stephens and C. R. Greer, "Doing Business in Mexico: Understanding Cultural Differences," *Organizational Dynamics* (Summer 1995): 39–55.
39. Teagarden, Butler, and Von Glinow.
40. Stephens and Greer.
41. Ibid.
42. C. E. Nicholls, H. W. Lane, and M. B. Brechu, "Taking Self-Managed Teams to Mexico," *Academy of Management Executive* 13, no. 3 (1999): 15–25.
43. Ibid.
44. Ibid.
45. Mariah E. de Forest, "Thinking of a Plant in Mexico?" *Academy of Management Executive* 8, no. 1 (1994): 33–40.
46. Ibid.
47. Ibid.
48. Teagarden, Butler, and Von Glinow.
49. Malgorzata Tarczynska, "Eastern Europe: How Valid Is Western Reward/Performance Management?" *Benefits and Compensation International* 29, no. 8 (2000): 9–16.
50. Snejina Michailova, "When Common Sense Becomes Uncommon: Participation and Empowerment in Russian Companies with Western Participation," *Journal of World Business* 37 (2002), 180–87.
51. S. Michailova, "When Common Sense Becomes Uncommon: Participation and Empowerment in Russian Companies with Western Participation," *Journal of World Business* 37 (2002): 180–187.
52. Carl Fey, "Overcoming a Leader's Greatest Challenge: Involving Employees in Firms in Russia," *Organizational Dynamics* 37, No. 3 (2008): 254–265.
53. Ibid.
54. Ibid.
55. Carl F. Fey, Stanislav Shekshnia, "The Key Commandments for Doing Business in Russia," *Organizational Dynamics* 40 (2011): 57–66.
56. Ibid.
57. M. Javidan and R. J. House, "Cultural Acumen for the Global Manager: Lessons from Project GLOBE," *Organizational Dynamics* (Spring 2001): 289–305.
58. Stanislav Shekshnia, Manfred Kets de Vries, "Interview with a Russian Entrepreneur: Ruben Vardanian," *Organizational Dynamics* 37, No. 3 (2008): 288–299.
59. Sheila M. Puffer and Daniel J. McCarthy, "Two Decades of Russian Business and Management Research: An Institutional Theory Perspective," *Academy of Management Perspectives*, May, 2011.
60. "Doing Business in Russia," www.kwintessential.co.uk, accessed May 1, 2012.
61. Rita Pyrillis, "Just a Token of Your Appreciation? Avoid Cultural Faux Pas When Rewarding International Employees," *Workforce Management* 90, No. 9, September 2011: 3–6.
62. M. A. Von Glinow and Byung Jae Chung, "Comparative HRM Practices in the U.S., Japan, Korea and the PRC," in *Research in Personnel and HRM—A Research Annual: International HRM*, ed. A. Nedd, G. R. Ferris, and K. M. Rowland (London: JAI Press, 1989).
63. Pyrillis, 2011.
64. A. Ignatius, "Now if Ms. Wong Insults a Customer, She Gets an Award," *The Wall Street Journal*, January 24, 1989.
65. T. Saywell, "Motive Power: China's State Firms Bank on Incentives to Keep Bosses Operating at Their Peak," *Far Eastern Economic Review* (July 8, 2000): 67–68.
66. A. Maitland, "Le patron, der Chef and the Boss," *Financial Times*, January 9, 2006.
67. Carlos Sanchez-Runde, Luciara Nardon, Richard M. Steers, "Looking beyond Western leadership models: Implications for global managers," *Organizational Dynamics* 40, No. 4 (2011): 207–213.
68. A. Morrison, H. Gregersen, and S. Black, "What Makes Savvy Global Leaders?" *Ivey Business Journal* 64, no. 2 (1999): 44–51; and *Monash Mt. Eliza Business Review* 1, no. 2 (1998).
69. D. Walker, T. Walker, and J. Schmitz, *Doing Business Internationally* (New York: McGraw-Hill, 2003).
70. Mansour Javidan, Mary Teagarden, "Making it Overseas," *Harvard Business Review,* April 2010.
71. Based on Walker et al., 2003; and Gary P. Ferraro, *The Cultural Dimension of International Business,* 5th ed. (Upper Saddle River, NJ: Prentice Hall, 2006).
72. "In the Driver's Seat," *Newsweek*, June 30, 2008.
73. A. Morrison, H. Gregersen, and S. Black, "What Makes Savvy Global Leaders?" *Ivey Business Journal* 64, no. 2 (1999): 44–51; and *Monash Mt. Eliza Business Review* 1, no. 2 (1998).
74. Nazneem Karmali, "India's Banga Brothers," *Forbes Asia Magazine,* August 9, 2010; "My Top 10 CEOs of 2011," *Times of India,* December 28, 2011; Carla Power, "India's Leading Export: CEOs," *Time Magazine,* August 1,

2011; Andrew Martin and Eric Dash, "Naming a New Chairman, MasterCard Signals It Is Open to Changes," *The New York Times,* April 12, 2010; topics .npr.org, accessed January 5, 2011; Jim Yardley and Vikas Bajaj, "Billionaires' Rise Aids India, and the Favor Is Returned," www.nytimes.com, July 26, 2011.

75. Carla Power, August 1, 2011.

76. Time, 2011.

77. Jim Yardley and Vikas Bajaj, "Billionaires' Rise Aids India, and the Favor Is Returned," www.nytimes.com, July 26, 2011.

78. R. H. Mason and R. S. Spich, *Management: An International Perspective* (Homewood: IL: Irwin, 1987).

79. Ibid., p. 184.

80. Ibid., p. 186.

81. Based on and excerpted from Mason and Spich.

82. B. M. Bass, *Bass & Stogdill's Handbook of Leadership* (New York: Free Press, 1990).

83. D. McGregor, *The Human Side of Enterprise* (New York: McGraw-Hill, 1960). See, for example, R. M. Stogdill, *Manual for the Leader Behavior Description Questionnaire—Form XII* (Columbus: Ohio State University, Bureau of Business Research, 1963); R. R. Blake and J. S. Mouton, *The New Managerial Grid* (Houston: Gulf Publishing, 1978).

84. F. E. Fiedler, "Engineering the Job to Fit the Manager," *Harvard Business Review* 43, no. 5 (1965): 115–22.

85. Den Hartog, N. Deanne, R. J. House, Paul J. Hanges, P. W. Dorfman, S. Antonio Ruiz-Quintanna, et al., "Culture Specific and Cross-culturally Generalizable Implicit Leadership Theories: Are Attributes of Charismatic/Transformational Leadership Universally Endorsed?" *Leadership Quarterly* 10, no. 2 (1999): 219–56.

86. Ibid.

87. R. House et al., "Cultural Influences on Leadership and Organizations: Project GLOBE," *Advances in Global Leadership*, vol. 1 (JAI Press, 1999).

88. Ibid.

89. Geert Hofstede, "Motivation, Leadership and Organization: Do American Theories Apply Abroad?" *Organizational Dynamics* (Summer 1980): 42–63.

90. Ibid.

91. Geert Hofstede, "Value Systems in Forty Countries," *Proceedings of the 4th International Congress of the International Association for Cross-Cultural Psychology* (1978).

92. Andre Laurent, "The Cultural Diversity of Western Conceptions of Management," *International Studies of Management and Organization* 13, no. 1–2 (1983): 75–96.

93. C. Hampden-Turner and A. Trompenaars, *The Seven Cultures of Capitalism* (New York: Doubleday, 1993).

94. M. Harie, E. E. Ghiselli, and L. W. Porter, *Managerial Thinking: An International Study* (New York: John Wiley and Sons, 1966).

95. S. G. Redding and T. W. Case, "Managerial Beliefs Among Asian Managers," *Proceedings of the Academy of Management* (1975).

96. I. Kenis, "A Cross-cultural Study of Personality and Leadership," *Group and Organization Studies* 2 (1977): 49–60; F. C. Deyo, "The Cultural Patterning of Organizational Development: A Comparative Case Study of Thailand and Chinese Industrial Enterprises," *Human Organization* 37 (1978): 68–72.

97. M. K. Badawy, "Styles of Mid-Eastern Managers," *California Management Review* (Spring 1980): 57; various newscasts, 2001.

98. A. A. Algattan, "Test of the Path-Goal Theory of Leadership in the Multinational Domain," paper presented at the Academy of Management Conference, 1985, San Diego, CA; J. P. Howell and P. W. Dorfman, "A Comparative Study of Leadership and Its Substitutes in a Mixed Cultural Work Setting," unpublished manuscript, 1988.

99. D. H. Welsh, F. Luthans, and S. M. Sommer, "Managing Russian Factory Workers: The Impact of U.S.-Based Behavioral and Participative Techniques," *Academy of Management Journal* 36 (1993): 58–79.

100. Alison Maitland, "An American Leader in Europe," leadership interview with Nancy McKinstry, Wolters Kluwer, *Financial Times*, July 15, 2004.

101. Ibid.

102. Ibid.

103. Ibid.

Index

Note: The locators followed by 'b', 'ex', 'n' and 't' refer to box, exhibits, notes and tables cited in the text.